The University of Chicago Spanish–English Dictionary

Diccionario Universidad de Chicago Inglés-Español

The University of Chicago Spanish–English Dictionary

Diccionario Universidad de Chicago Inglés–Español

Originally Compiled by Carlos Castillo and Otto F. Bond
Compilación original de Carlos Castillo y Otto F. Bond

SIXTH EDITION · *SEXTA EDICIÓN*

David A. Pharies
Editor in Chief · *Director*

María Irene Moyna
Editor · *Editora*

Gary K. Baker
Assistant Editor · *Redactor*

Meagan M. Day
Editorial Assistant · *Redactora*

The University of Chicago Press
Chicago & London

DAVID A. PHARIES is associate dean for humanities in the College of Liberal Arts and Sciences and professor of Spanish at the University of Florida. He is the author of *A Brief History of the Spanish Language* and *Breve historia de la lengua española*, both published by the University of Chicago Press.

The University of Chicago Press, Chicago 60637
The University of Chicago Press, Ltd., London
© 2012 by The University of Chicago
All rights reserved. Published 2012.
First Edition published 1948
Printed in the United States of America

21 20 19 18 17 16 15 14 13 12   1 2 3 4 5

ISBN-13: 978-0-226-66695-2 (cloth)
ISBN-13: 978-0-226-66696-9 (paper)
ISBN-10: 0-226-66695-6 (cloth)
ISBN-10: 0-226-66696-4 (paper)

Library of Congress Cataloging-in-Publication Data

The University of Chicago Spanish-English dictionary / originally compiled by Carlos Castillo and Otto F. Bond ; David A. Pharies, editor in chief ; María Irene Moyna, editor ; Gary K. Baker, assistant editor ; Meagan M. Day, editorial assistant. — Sixth edition.
        pages ; cm
        Added t.p. title: Diccionario Universidad de Chicago inglés-español.
        Includes bibliographical references.
        ISBN 978-0-226-66695-2 (cloth : alkaline paper) — ISBN 0-226-66695-6 (cloth : alkaline paper) — ISBN 978-0-226-66696-9 (paperback : alkaline paper) — ISBN 0-226-66696-4 (paperback : alkaline paper)   1. Spanish language—Dictionaries—English.   2. English language—Dictionaries—Spanish.   I. Castillo, Carlos, 1890–, compiler.   II. Bond, Otto Ferdinand, 1885–, compiler.   III. Pharies, David A., editor.   IV. Moyna, María Irene, editor.   V. Title: Diccionario Universidad de Chicago inglés-español.
        PC4640.U5 2012
        463'.21—dc23
                                                        2012005113

♾ This paper meets the requirements of the ANSI/NISO Z39.48-1992 (Permanence of Paper).

Contents

Preface to the Sixth Edition   vii

Preámbulo a la sexta edición   ix

How to Use *The University of Chicago Spanish-English Dictionary*   xi

Cómo usar el *Diccionario Universidad de Chicago Inglés-Español*   xvi

Spanish-English · Español-Inglés

List of Abbreviations   1

Spanish Pronunciation   2

Notes on Spanish Grammar   6

Common Spanish Suffixes   8

Spanish Regular Verbs   10

Spanish Irregular and Orthographic Changing Verbs   12

Spanish–English Dictionary, A–Z   31

Inglés-Español · English-Spanish

Lista de abreviaturas   293

Pronunciación inglesa   294

Notas sobre gramática inglesa   296

Sufijos comunes del inglés   298

Verbos irregulares de la lengua inglesa   300

Diccionario inglés–español, A–Z   307

Preface to the Sixth Edition

The *University of Chicago Spanish–English Dictionary* has been compiled for the general use of Spanish-speaking learners of American English and American English-speaking learners of Spanish. In step with the rapid pace of cultural and linguistic change at the beginning of the twenty-first century, we have thoroughly revised the *Dictionary* for its sixth edition to reflect the most current vocabulary and usage in both languages.

Since our goal is to ensure that users will always find the words and phrases they seek, the greatest change for this new edition is the addition of some six thousand words and meanings. In choosing among possible additions, we have paid particular attention to frequency of use in written and spoken contexts, since a user is more likely to seek a word that appears frequently (e.g., *libertad* 'liberty', number 540 in frequency according to the extensive list available at www.wordfrequency.info) than one that appears infrequently (e.g., *verdolaga* 'purslane', number 19,705).

Frequency of use cannot serve as the sole criterion for new material, however, for three reasons. First, some words become current so quickly that no frequency list can possibly capture them. Digital terminology offers good examples of this trend, such as the word *app*, which has risen from obscurity to universal acceptance in very little time. Second, some of the changes that a dictionary should reflect occur at a semantic or phrasal level not captured by frequencies. Current expressions such as *to go off on* 'to scold' and *to be down with* 'to be in agreement with' consist of extremely frequent words used in novel ways. Finally, a word can be essential without being frequent. Medical terms, for example, can be vitally important to anyone negotiating another nation's health system, even if they are used infrequently outside of medical contexts.

Medicine is in fact one of four cultural and technical areas of increasing global importance for which we have specially enhanced our coverage for this edition. Along with the 600 new words and meanings that have been added in this field, the sixth edition incorporates 750 new items from the field of business, 500 relating to digital technology, and over 400 relating to the terminology of several globally popular sports, including basketball, baseball, soccer, tennis, and golf.

In many cases, the additions in these four areas warranted completely new entries, as in the case of *allergen* (Sp. *alérgeno*), *auditing* (*auditoría*), *adapter* (*adaptador*), and *unplayable* (*injugable*). In many others, we added a meaning or an equivalent to an existing entry, as in the case of *pinza* (to whose entry was added Eng. [*medical*] *clamp*), *fraudulento* (adding *bogus*), *descifrar* (*to decrypt*), and *abanicar* (*to swing and miss*). On the English side, many additions take the form of compounds attached to existing entries—for example, *clubfoot* (*pie zambo*), added to the *club* entry; *business agreement* (*con-*

venio comercial), added to the *business* entry; *copy protection* (*protección contra copias*) added to *copy*; and *corner kick* (*córner*) added to *corner*.

To further increase the utility of the *Dictionary* for beginning learners of both Spanish and English, we have added "blind" or reference entries for irregular verb forms that differ markedly from their citation forms. These entries take the following form: *quepa, quepo*: ver *caber* (Spanish–English) and *frozen*: see *freeze* (English–Spanish).

Finally, we have invested considerable effort in expanding and perfecting the already well-developed set of semantic delimiters or disambiguators whose purpose is to help users differentiate among meanings in polysemic words. The English word *easy*, for example, has different Spanish equivalents according to whether it means 'simple' (*fácil, sencillo*), 'compliant' (*fácil*), 'comfortable' (*cómodo*), 'informal' (*desenvuelto*), or 'unworried' (*tranquilo*). Similarly, the Spanish word *gusto* has different equivalents for its several meanings: 'sentido', 'sabor', 'sentido estético' (*taste*), 'agrado' (*pleasure*), and 'preferencia personal' (*like*).

Preámbulo a la sexta edición

El *Diccionario Universidad de Chicago Inglés-Español* se ha compilado para el uso general de estudiantes hispanoparlantes que aprenden el inglés de los Estados Unidos y para estudiantes angloparlantes de los Estados Unidos que estudian español. Para acompasarse a los rápidos cambios culturales y lingüísticos que se vienen sucediendo desde comienzos del siglo XXI, se ha hecho una revisión profunda del *Diccionario* con el fin de reflejar el vocabulario y los usos más actualizados en ambas lenguas.

Ya que nuestro propósito es asegurar que los usuarios siempre encuentren los términos y expresiones que buscan, el cambio más sustancial de esta nueva edición es la inclusión de unos seis mil términos y significados nuevos. Para elegir entre las muchas posibles adiciones, se le prestó mucha atención a la frecuencia de uso en el medio escrito y oral, ya que es más probable que un usuario se encuentre con una palabra que aparece con frecuencia (v.g., *libertad*, que ocupa el puesto 540 en frecuencia según la exhaustiva lista de frecuencias disponible en www.wordfrequency.info) que con otra palabra que aparece con baja frecuencia (v.g., *verdolaga*, que ocupa el puesto 19.705 en la misma lista).

Sin embargo, la frecuencia de uso no puede ser el único criterio empleado para incluir material nuevo, por tres razones. En primer lugar, algunas palabras se generalizan tan rápidamente que no alcanzan a ser incluidas en listas de frecuencia. Un buen ejemplo de esta tendencia lo constituye la terminología digital; considérese la palabra inglesa *app* 'aplicación informática', que en muy poco tiempo ha pasado de ser casi desconocida a tener aceptación general. En segundo lugar, algunos de los cambios que debe reflejar un diccionario suceden al nivel de la frase, y estos cambios no se pueden registrar meramente a partir de las frecuencias de los términos. Algunas expresiones actuales tales como *to go off on* 'regañar' y *to be down with* 'estar de acuerdo con' están constituidas por palabras de alta frecuencia empleadas en combinaciones novedosas. Por último, una palabra puede ser esencial sin por ello ser muy frecuente. Por ejemplo, la terminología médica puede ser de importancia vital para alguien que está tratando de resolver un problema de salud mientras se encuentra en un país extranjero. Por lo tanto, esas palabras deben figurar en el *Diccionario* aunque sean de poca frecuencia fuera de los contextos médicos.

De hecho, la medicina es una de las cuatro áreas culturales y técnicas cuya cobertura se ha aumentado en esta edición, debido a su importancia cada vez mayor en el contexto internacional. Además de 600 nuevos términos y significados del área médica, la presente edición incorpora 750 nuevos términos del campo de los negocios, 500 relacionados con el mundo de la informática y la tecnología digital y más de 400 relacionados con varios deportes de popularidad mundial, incluyendo el baloncesto, el béisbol, el fútbol, el tenis y el golf.

En muchos casos, las incorporaciones a estos cuatro campos nos llevaron a crear entradas completamente nuevas, como es el caso de *alérgeno* (ing. *allergen*), *auditoría* (*auditing*), *adaptador* (*adapter*) e *injugable* (*unplayable*). En muchos otros casos, se agregó un significado o un equivalente nuevo a una entrada preexistente. Tal es el caso de *pinza* (a cuya entrada se le agregó el significado inglés de [*medical*] *clamp*), *fraudulento* (*bogus*), *descifrar* (*decrypt*) y *abanicar* (con el significado en béisbol de *to swing and miss*). En el lado inglés, se incorporaron muchos términos compuestos a entradas ya existentes, tales como *clubfoot* (*pie zambo*), que fue agregado a la entrada de *club*; *business agreement* (*convenio comercial*), que fue agregado a la entrada de *business*; *copy protection* (*protección contra copias*) agregado a *copy*; y *corner kick* (*córner*) agregado a *corner*.

Para hacer todavía más útil el *Diccionario* para los estudiantes principiantes tanto de español como de inglés, se han agregado entradas "ciegas" o de referencia, para las formas verbales irregulares que son muy diferentes de sus formas infinitivas. Estas entradas tienen la siguiente estructura: *quepa, quepo*: ver *caber* (español–inglés) y *frozen*: see *freeze* (inglés–español).

Por último, se ha hecho un esfuerzo considerable para expandir y perfeccionar todavía más los delimitadores semánticos o desambiguadores, que tienen como propósito asistir a los usuarios a distinguir entre los diversos significados de palabras polisémicas. Por ejemplo, la palabra inglesa *easy* tiene diferentes equivalentes en español según signifique 'simple' (*fácil* o *sencillo*), 'compliant' (*fácil*), 'comfortable' (*cómodo*), 'informal' (*desenvuelto*) o 'unworried' (*tranquilo*). Del mismo modo, la palabra española *gusto* tiene diferentes equivalentes ingleses para sus múltiples significados: *taste* para 'sentido', 'sabor', 'sentido estético', *pleasure* para 'agrado' y *like* para 'preferencia personal'.

How to Use *The University of Chicago Spanish-English Dictionary*

Order of Entries

Alphabetical order is observed irrespective of hyphens or spaces, such that *air conditioner* precedes *aircraft* and *middle school* precedes *middle-sized*. Homographs are placed under a single entry (*lie* 'to prevaricate', *lie* 'to recline', both pronounced [laɪ]), unless they are pronounced differently (e.g., *bow* [baʊ] 'forward end of a vessel', *bow* [bo] 'bend, curve'). Regarding Spanish, according to the current policy of the Spanish Royal Academy,[1] *ch* and *ll* are no longer recognized as separate letters, such that *ch* now follows *ce* and precedes *ci*, and *ll* follows *li* and precedes *lo* in alphabetization.

Compounds listed within entries are also alphabetized. However, the need to list compounds under their first element sometimes interferes with alphabetization, as when *slumlord*, a compound listed under *slum*, comes before the next headword, *slumber*, even though strict alphabetization would require the reverse.

Spelling

Spelling of English words reflects common American usage, variants being noted where applicable (*ax, axe*; *sulfur, sulphur*; *stymie, stymy*). The spelling of Spanish words, where possible, follows the conventions of the Spanish Royal Academy. For the orthography of problematic Spanish words such as recent borrowings (*escáner, scooter*), country names (*Malí, Irak*) and adjectives of nationality (*zimbabuo*), a variety of authorities were consulted, including the *Diccionario del español actual*, the *Diccionario de dudas*, the *Libro de estilo* published by the Madrid newspaper *El País*, and various Internet sources.[2] It should be noted that there is vacillation in some cases, such as *Bahrain*, which is listed as *Bahrein* in the *Libro de estilo* and as *Bahráin* or *Bahréin* in the *Diccionario de dudas*. In these cases, we either opt for the form that appears to be most generally accepted or provide multiple equivalents.

1. Real Academia Española, *Ortografía de la lengua española* (Madrid: Espasa-Calpe, 1999), 2.

2. Manuel Seco, Olimpia Andrés, and Gabino Ramos, *Diccionario del español actual* (Madrid: Aguilar, 1999); Manuel Seco, *Diccionario de dudas y dificultades de la lengua española*, 10th ed. (Madrid: Espasa-Calpe, 1998); *El País: Libro de estilo*, 9th ed. (Madrid: Ediciones El País, 1990).

Omissions

Some categories of words are systematically omitted from the vocabulary entries. Adverbial forms ending in -*ly* (English) and -*mente* (Spanish) are included only when their usage and meaning are not transparently derivable from their adjectival bases. Thus, *clearly* is omitted, as its usage is predictable from its adjectival base ('in a clear way'), while *surely* is included, since in addition to 'in a sure way', it means 'undoubtedly' or 'without fail'. Similarly, *claramente* 'clearly' is omitted, while *atentamente* is retained, since the latter, in addition to meaning 'in an attentive manner', is used as a farewell, equivalent to 'yours truly'. Also, English nouns ending in -*ing* and adjectives in -*ed*, which may appear as glosses of Spanish words, are not always accorded separate entries on the English–Spanish side, due to their derivational regularity and to considerations of space.

Structure of Entries

1. HEADWORD. Spelling variants, if any, follow the most frequent form, which appears first. In Spanish, occupational designations, titles, and kinship terms are shown in both masculine and feminine forms, as in *abogado -da*.

2. PRONUNCIATION. Pronunciation of English words is indicated through a modified version of the International Phonetic Alphabet, whose conventions are explained on pp. 294–95. No individual transcription of Spanish words is required, given the simplicity and consistency of the Spanish orthographic system. See "The Spanish Spelling System and the Sounds Represented" (p. 2) for an explanation.

3. GRAMMATICAL CATEGORY. Meanings are marked according to whether they reflect usage as a noun (N), adjective (ADJ), adverb (ADV), conjunction (CONJ), preposition (PREP), pronoun (PRON), interjection (INTERJ), transitive verb (VT), or intransitive verb (VI). The exception to this rule is that nouns on the Spanish–English side are marked only by gender, M (masculine noun) or F (feminine noun).

    Order of meanings within an entry reflects frequency of usage. Where more than one grammatical category can be rendered by the same gloss, the two are listed together, cf. Eng. *red*, which can be glossed as Sp. *rojo* in both its adjective and noun meanings.

    Traditionally, Spanish adjectives are listed in their masculine form only. However, where the adjective normally functions as a noun as well, it is shown with both masculine and feminine forms if both are possible, cf. the case of *africano -na*, which can mean *African* in the adjectival sense as well as *African (man)* and *African (woman)*.

    Special mention must be made of the combination "VI/VT." Occasionally, a single verb form may function both transitively and intransitively, e.g., both *to eat* and its Spanish equivalent *comer*. Not infrequently, however, Spanish glosses of English intransitives require the addition of the pronominal particle -*se*. Thus, in cases such as *to bathe*, marked "VI/VT" and glossed *bañar(se)*, it should be understood that the bare form is transitive and the -*se* form intransitive. Finally, where transitivity differs between a headword and its equivalent in the second language, particles must be added to reflect this, as in the case of the transitive English verb *to regret*, which is glossed in Spanish as *arrepentirse de*, since *arrepentirse* alone is intransitive. Where an English verb can be used both transitively and intransitively and its Spanish equivalent is only intransitive, the latter may sometimes be made transitive through the addition of a preposition, which appears in brackets. Thus, English *fight* is glossed as *pelear [con]* to show that its intransitive equivalent is *pelear*, whereas its transitive equivalent is *pelear con*.

Again for reasons of economy, pronominal forms of Spanish verbs are omitted in two cases: first, when the particle -*se* functions as a direct object, either reflexive or reciprocal, cf. *mirarse*, which can mean both *to look at oneself* and *to look at each other*, and second, when the addition of -*se* does not affect the English translation, cf. *bañar(se)*, glossed in both meanings as *to bathe*. In contrast, pronominal forms of verbs are included when they differ substantially in meaning from the bare forms, cf. *ir*, glossed as *to go*, vs. *irse*, which means *to leave*.

4. DELIMITERS. Whenever a word, within a grammatical category, is considered to have two or more meanings, these are differentiated by means of delimiters, that is, explanatory markers. Most commonly, synonyms are used, cf. *retort*, which in the meaning 'reply' is glossed as *réplica* and in the meaning 'vessel' as *retorta*. On occasion, however, other strategies may be adopted. Thus, transitive verbs are sometimes best differentiated according to the objects they take, cf. *to negotiate* (a contract), which is glossed *negociar*, while *to negotiate* (an obstacle) is glossed *salvar*. Similarly, adjectives may be most easily distinguished by showing the referents to which they regularly apply, cf. *refreshing*, which applied to drink is *refrescante*, to sleep is *reparador*, and to honesty is *amable*. Not infrequently, a single equivalent covers almost all meanings of a headword in a single grammatical category. In such cases, only the "exceptional" meaning, placed second, is delimited. For example, the equivalent of Eng. *net* in almost all its meanings is Sp. *red*, but when it refers specifically to a hairnet it is *redecilla*. Although delimiters typically precede the gloss they are meant to distinguish, occasionally they are placed afterward. In these cases they are meant to erase doubts about the applicability of a given gloss in a specific secondary context, cf. *site*, whose gloss *sitio* is followed by the delimiter "also Internet."

5. GLOSSES. Insofar as is possible, glosses are intended to match the headword in terms of meaning, register, and frequency. Thus, *cop* is glossed as *poli* rather than the more formal *policía*. Similarly, *orinar* is glossed as *to urinate* rather than the informal and vulgar *to piss*. Glosses separated by a comma are to be considered interchangeable, if not perfectly synonymous. Semicolons, on the other hand, indicate separate meanings.

6. REGIONAL USAGE. No systematic attempt has been made to reflect regional usage in either English or Spanish, since in the great majority of cases a word of more general currency is available as a gloss. Thus, among the many Spanish equivalents of Eng. *peasant*, Sp. *campesino* is understood everywhere, even where a local term also exists, such as Puerto Rican *jíbaro*, Cuban *guajiro*, and Chilean

guaso. However, Spanish regional usage is marked where any of the following conditions are met: (1) there is no term of international currency, or it might not be understood in a given location (cf. the various regional Spanish equivalents of Eng. *bean*), (2) the use of a given term in a given region could cause embarrassment or misunderstanding, as in the case of *coger*, which means 'to catch' or 'to get' in Spain and Cuba, but is a vulgar term meaning 'to have sexual relations with' in large parts of Spanish America, or (3) a specific regionalism is known throughout the Spanish-speaking world to be typical of a given dialect, cf. River Plate *che* 'hey!', Mexican *ándale* 'come on!', *cuate* 'pal'.

7. STYLISTIC MARKERS. Because, as mentioned earlier, equivalents are chosen in order to match headwords in all aspects of their meaning, including register and frequency, stylistic markers are only infrequently employed. They are included, redundantly, in the case of taboo or offensive words, in order to provide a second level of warning to potential users. Thus, whereas there is no need to mark the Spanish gloss *tonto* as familiar, since it is meant to be equivalent to the equally familiar Eng. *fool*, the gloss of Eng. *whore*, viz., *puta*, is marked "offensive," on the chance that a given user might not realize that this is also true of *whore*. Only five register markers are employed: literary (*lit*), which also includes poetic and formal language; familiar (*fam*), which designates words used among family and friends; vulgar (*vulg*), for words whose use is socially censured; pejorative (*pej*), which implies a negative evaluation; and *offensive* (not abbreviated), for words meant to insult people.

Taboo and offensive words are included in this dictionary because of its purely descriptive rather than prescriptive nature; that is, this dictionary is intended to reflect how the vocabularies of English and Spanish are actually used by their speakers, rather than how we or other people may feel that they should be used. The inclusion of vulgar and offensive words here should not be construed as an indication that we condone or encourage their use.

8. COMPOUNDS. Ease of usage would dictate that each lexical item receive its own entry, but for reasons of economy this is not possible in a concise dictionary. This explains why compound words, which are composed of two or more preexisting words, are listed in almost all cases under the entry of their initial constituent, at the end of the corresponding grammatical category. Thus, *doghouse* is listed as —*house*, under *dog*. There are certain exceptions to this convention, however. First, compounds are listed under the headword of their second constituent when the first is extremely frequent, as are the so-called empty verbs such as Eng. *keep*, *take*, *turn*, Sp. *hacer*, *tener*, *tomar*. Thus, *to have a good time*, glossed *divertirse*, is listed under *time* rather than *have*, and *tener paciencia*, glossed *to be patient*, is under *paciencia* rather than *tener*. Second, English compounds whose first element is a preposition (*offsides*, *outcast*, *overcome*) are listed as separate headwords, chiefly because of their frequent grammatical complexity, cf. *overhead*, which can be an adverb (*it flew overhead*), an adjective (*overhead projector*), or a noun (*overhead from grant money*). Conversely, derived words, that is, words that contain one or more affixes (e.g., *antiabortion*, composed of the prefix *anti-* plus *abortion*, and *kingdom*, composed of *king* plus the suffix -*dom*), are listed as separate headwords.

9. ILLUSTRATIVE PHRASES. Appearing together with the compound words pertinent to any given grammatical category are illustrative phrases, a category defined so as to include idioms, collocations, proverbs, and, especially, sentences required to clarify usage in some way, as when the usage of *gustarle a uno* as a gloss of *to like* is illustrated by the phrase *he likes dogs*, with the translation *le gustan los perros*.

Cómo usar el *Diccionario Universidad de Chicago Inglés-Español*

Orden de las entradas

Se respeta el orden alfabético, independientemente de la presencia de guiones o espacios, de tal manera que *air conditioning* precede a *aircraft* y *middle school* precede a *middle-sized*. Los homógrafos se ubican en una sola entrada (*lie* 'mentir' y *lie* 'yacer', ambos con la pronunciación [laɪ]), a no ser que se pronuncien de forma diferente (e.g., *bow* [baʊ] 'proa' y *bow* [bo] 'curva'). En cuanto al español y siguiendo la política oficial de la Real Academia Española,[1] *ch* y *ll* ya no se reconocen como letras independientes, de tal manera que *ch* ahora sigue a *ce* y precede a *ci*, y *ll* sigue a *li* y precede a *lo* en el orden alfabético.

Asimismo, los compuestos incluidos dentro de una entrada determinada aparecen en orden alfabético a continuación de su primer elemento, lo cual a veces interfiere con el orden alfabético general. Así, por ejemplo, *rompeolas* aparece a continuación de *romper*, porque se trata de un compuesto de dicho verbo, si bien el orden alfabético requeriría lo contrario.

Ortografía

La ortografía de los vocablos ingleses refleja el uso general en inglés americano, y las variantes se incluyen en los casos pertinentes (*ax, axe; sulfur, sulphur; stymie, stymy*). La ortografía española sigue las convenciones de la Real Academia Española. Para la grafía española de palabras problemáticas, tales como préstamos recientes (*escáner, scooter*), nombres de países (*Malí, Irak*) y gentilicios (*zimbabuo*), se consultaron fuentes tales como el *Diccionario del español actual*, el *Diccionario de dudas*, el *Libro de estilo* de *El País* de Madrid y varios sitios en el internet.[2] Corresponde hacer notar que la grafía de algunos términos vacila entre varias posibles, cf. la versión española de *Bahrain*, que aparece como *Bahrein* en el *Libro de estilo* y como *Bahráin* o *Bahréin* en el *Diccionario de dudas*, en cuyo caso damos la forma que parece más generalmente aceptada u ofrecemos varias.

1. Real Academia Española, *Ortografía de la lengua española* (Madrid: Espasa-Calpe, 1999), 2.

2. Manuel Seco, Olimpia Andrés y Gabino Ramos, *Diccionario del español actual* (Madrid: Aguilar, 1999); Manuel Seco, *Diccionario de dudas y dificultades de la lengua española*, 10ª ed. (Madrid: Espasa-Calpe, 1998); *El País: Libro de estilo*, 9ª ed. (Madrid: Ediciones El País, 1990).

Omisiones

Algunas categorías de palabras se omiten sistemáticamente de las entradas del diccionario. Las formas adverbiales que terminan en -*mente* (español) y en -*ly* (inglés) se incluyen solamente cuando su uso y significado no pueden deducirse claramente de sus bases adjetivas. De esta forma, *claramente* se omite, ya que su significado es predecible a partir de su base adjetiva ('de manera clara'), mientras que *atentamente* se incluye, ya que además de significar 'de manera atenta', también se usa como fórmula de despedida epistolar. Del mismo modo, se omite *clearly*, porque su equivalente, 'de manera clara', se deduce de su base adjetiva, mientras que se incluye *surely* porque además de significar 'de forma segura' también quiere decir 'sin duda'. Debe notarse también que los sustantivos ingleses terminados en -*ing* y los adjetivos en -*ed*, que pueden aparecer como traducción de palabras españolas en la parte español–inglés, no figuran siempre como cabezas de artículo en la parte inglés–español debido a la total regularidad de su formación y a consideraciones de espacio.

Estructura de las entradas

1. PALABRAS CABEZA DE ARTÍCULO. Las variantes ortográficas, si las hay, siguen a la forma más frecuente, que aparece en primer término. En español, las designaciones de profesiones y oficios, los títulos y las relaciones de parentesco aparecen tanto en la forma masculina como en la femenina, como por ejemplo, *abogado -da*.

2. PRONUNCIACIÓN. La pronunciación de las palabras inglesas se indica mediante una versión modificada del Alfabético Fonético Internacional, cuyas convenciones se explican en las pgs. 294–95. No se requiere transcripción individual de las palabras españolas, gracias a la simplicidad y sistematicidad de la ortografía española. Para detalles, ver la sección titulada "The Spanish Spelling System" en la p. 2.

3. CATEGORÍA GRAMATICAL. Los significados se marcan según reflejen el uso de la palabra como sustantivo masculino (*m*), sustantivo femenino (*f*), adjetivo (*adj*), adverbio (*adv*), conjunción (*conj*), preposición (*prep*), pronombre (*pron*), interjección (*interj*), verbo transitivo (*vt*) o verbo intransitivo (*vi*). En inglés, en cambio, los sustantivos se marcan con *n*, abreviación de *noun*.

   Los significados dentro de una entrada aparecen ordenados de manera que el más frecuente figure primero. Cuando la misma traducción cubre el significado de dos categorías gramaticales, ambas aparecen juntas, cf. el inglés *red*, que puede traducirse como *rojo* tanto en su significado sustantivo como en el adjetivo.

   Siguiendo la tradición, los adjetivos españoles aparecen exclusivamente en su forma masculina. Sin embargo, cuando el adjetivo frecuentemente funciona además como sustantivo, se muestra tanto en la forma masculina como en la femenina si ambas son posibles, cf. el caso de *africano -na*, traducido al inglés como *African*, forma adecuada para todos sus usos.

   La combinación *vi/vt* merece mención especial. En ocasiones, una única forma verbal funciona tanto transitiva como intransitivamente, v.g., tanto *comer* como su equivalente inglés *to eat*. Sin embargo, es también frecuente que las traducciones españolas de verbos intransitivos ingleses requieran el agregado de una partícula pronominal *-se*. Así, en casos tales como *to bathe*, que se marca "vi/vt" y se traduce como *bañar(se)*, debe entenderse que la forma no pronominalizada es transitiva y la forma con *-se* es intransitiva. En aquellos casos cuando la palabra cabeza de artículo y su equivalente en la otra lengua difieren en transitividad, se deben agregar partículas para reflejar esta diferencia. Tal es el caso del verbo *aprobar*, que se traduce al inglés como *to approve of* en algunos de sus significados, ya que *to approve* es intransitivo si no va acompañado de preposición. Finalmente, en los casos en los que un verbo español puede usarse tanto intransitiva como transitivamente y su equivalente inglés es exclusivamente intransitivo, este último puede a veces volverse transitivo mediante el agregado de una preposición entre corchetes. Así, el esp. *chivar* se traduce como *to snitch [on]* para mostrar que su forma intransitiva en inglés es *to snitch* mientras que el equivalente transitivo es *to snitch on*.

Por razones de espacio se omiten las formas pronominales de los verbos españoles en dos casos. En primer lugar, se omiten si la partícula pronominal hace las veces de complemento directo reflexivo o recíproco, cf. *mirarse* (a sí mismo o el uno al otro). En segundo lugar no se incluyen tampoco si la partícula pronominal no afecta la traducción al inglés, como en el caso de *bañar* y *bañarse*, ambos *to bathe*. Sí se incluyen aquellas formas pronominales que difieren semánticamente de sus verbos de base, cf. *ir* vs. *irse*.

4. INDICADORES SEMÁNTICOS. En aquellos casos en los que una palabra, dentro de una misma categoría gramatical, tiene dos o más acepciones, estas se distinguen por medio de indicadores semánticos, o sea, explicaciones parentéticas. Lo más frecuente es que se empleen sinónimos, cf. *arco*, que se traduce *arc* cuando se trata de una curva, como *arch* cuando se refiere a una estructura arquitectónica, y como *bow* cuando se trata de un arma, aunque en otras ocasiones se adoptan otras estrategias. Así, los verbos transitivos a veces se distinguen con mayor facilidad mediante los tipos de complementos directos que los acompañan, cf. *acordonar* (un zapato) *to lace*, (un lugar) *to rope off*, (una moneda) *to mill*, mientras que la forma más sencilla de distinguir adjetivos es mostrar los tipos de referentes a los cuales se aplican con mayor frecuencia, cf. *inseguro*, que aplicado a una personalidad se traduce por *insecure*, a un vehículo por *unsafe*, y al andar por *unsteady*. Es frecuente que un único equivalente abarque casi todas las acepciones de una palabra cabeza de artículo dentro de una categoría gramatical determinada. En esos casos, solamente el significado "excepcional", que aparece en segundo lugar, se acompaña de un indicador semántico. Por ejemplo, el equivalente de *acceso* en casi todas sus acepciones es *access*, excepto cuando se refiere a un ataque de tos o rabia, en cuyo caso se traduce como *fit*. Aunque los indicadores semánticos normalmente preceden a la traducción que les corresponde, en ocasiones se ubican después. En estos casos tienen como objetivo eliminar dudas acerca del empleo de una traducción determinada en un contexto secundario específico, cf. *acompañar*, cuya traducción *to accompany* va seguida de un indicador semántico "también en música" para confirmar al lector su aplicación a ese contexto.

5. TRADUCCIONES. En la medida de lo posible, se ha tratado de que las traducciones sean equivalentes a la palabra cabeza de artículo en cuanto a su significado, registro y frecuencia. Así, *poli* se traduce como *cop* y no como *policeman*, palabra más formal. De la misma forma, *to urinate* se traduce como *orinar* y no como *mear*, palabra más familiar. Las traducciones separadas por una coma deben considerarse equivalentes, aunque no sean exactamente sinónimas. El uso del punto y coma indica acepciones distintas.

6. USO REGIONAL. No se ha hecho ningún esfuerzo sistemático por reflejar usos regionales, ni en inglés ni en español, ya que en la gran mayoría de los casos existe una palabra de uso general. Así, entre los muchos equivalentes españoles de la palabra inglesa *peasant*, su equivalente español *campesino* se entiende en todo el mundo de habla hispana, aun cuando existan términos locales, tales como *jíbaro* en Puerto Rico, *guajiro* en Cuba y *guaso* en Chile. Sin embargo, el uso regional se indica para el español en tres casos específicos. En primer lugar se encuentran los casos en los que una palabra determinada podría resultar desconocida en una región dada, como los varios equivalentes españoles del ingl. *bean*. En segundo lugar, hay casos en que el empleo de una palabra podría dar lugar a situaciones bochornosas o equívocas. Tal es el caso de *coger*, que significa 'tomar' u 'obtener' en España y Cuba, pero es un vulgarismo para 'tener relaciones sexuales con' en gran parte de Hispanoamérica. En tercer término, se han incluido regionalismos que se reconocen en todo el mundo de habla hispana como típicos de un dialecto determinado, cf. español rioplatense *che*, mexicano *ándale*, *cuate*.

7. INDICADORES DE ESTILO. Ya que, como se mencionó anteriormente, los equivalentes se eligen para que correspondan a las palabras cabeza de artículo en todos los aspectos de su significado, incluyendo nivel de lengua y frecuencia, los indicadores de estilo se usan poco. Aunque son redundantes, se incluyen en los casos de palabras tabú o términos ofensivos para reforzar la advertencia a los usuarios potenciales del término. Así, aunque no hay necesidad de indicar que la palabra inglesa *fool* es familiar, ya que figura como equivalente del español *tonto*, la traducción de *puta* como *whore* va acompañada del indicador *ofensivo* por si el usuario ignora las connotaciones de la palabra española. Se han empleado cinco indicadores de estilo: literario (*lit*), que incluye lenguaje poético y formal, familiar (*fam*), que designa palabras que se usan en situaciones de intimidad, vulgar (*vulg*), que designa términos cuyo uso está censurado socialmente, peyorativo (*pey*), que designa palabras que tienen una carga connotativa negativa hacia el referente, y *ofensivo* (sin abreviar), que designa insultos. Las palabras tabú y los términos ofensivos se incluyen en el diccionario debido a la naturaleza descriptiva y no prescriptiva del mismo. Es decir, el diccionario tiene como objetivo reflejar el uso que los hablantes nativos dan a los términos y no las opiniones nuestras o ajenas de cómo deberían usarse, de manera que la inclusión de estas palabras no debe interpretarse como una indicación de que preconizamos su empleo.

8. COMPUESTOS. El criterio de facilidad de uso requeriría que cada palabra recibiera su propia entrada, pero por razones de economía de espacio esto no es posible en un diccionario conciso. Por lo tanto, las palabras compuestas, formadas por dos o más vocablos preexistentes, aparecen en casi todos los casos en la entrada de su

primer constituyente, al final de la categoría gramatical correspondiente. De tal forma, *hombre rana* aparece como — *rana*, en la entrada de *hombre*. Hay ciertas excepciones a esta regla, sin embargo. En primer lugar, los compuestos aparecen bajo la cabeza de artículo de su segundo constituyente cuando el primero es extremadamente frecuente, tal como lo son los verbos semánticamente "vacíos" como el español *hacer, tener, tomar* y el inglés *to keep, to take, to turn*. De este modo, *tener paciencia* aparece en la entrada de *paciencia* y no en la de *tener*, y *to have a good time* figura bajo *time* y no bajo *to have*. En segundo lugar, los compuestos ingleses cuyo primer elemento es una preposición (*offsides, overcome, outcast*) aparecen como cabezas de artículo independientes, sobre todo debido a su complejidad gramatical, cf. *overhead*, que puede ser adverbio (*it flew overhead*, que equivale a *voló en lo alto*), adjetivo (*overhead projector*, es decir, *retroproyector*) y sustantivo (*overhead from grant money*, o sea, *gastos generales de una subvención*). No obstante, las palabras derivadas, i.e., aquellas que contienen uno o más afijos (e.g., *anticuerpo*, compuesta del prefijo *anti-* y *cuerpo*, y *cabezón*, compuesta por *cabeza* y el sufijo *-ón*), figuran como cabezas de artículo independientes.

9. FRASES ILUSTRATIVAS. Junto con las palabras compuestas de una determinada categoría gramatical figuran las frases ilustrativas, una categoría que incluye expresiones idiomáticas, colocaciones típicas, refranes y, especialmente, oraciones necesarias para aclarar el uso de alguna palabra, como cuando el uso de *like* como traducción de *gustar* se ilustra con la frase *he likes dogs*, que se traduce *le gustan los perros*.

Spanish–English · Español–Inglés

List of Abbreviations / Lista de abreviaturas

adj	adjective	adjetivo
adv	adverb, adverbial	adverbio, adverbial
Am	America	América
art	article	artículo
Carib	Caribbean	Caribe
conj	conjunction	conjunción
def	definite	definido
dem	demonstrative	demostrativo
Esp	Spain, Spanish	España, español
f	feminine	femenino
fam	familiar	familiar
indef	indefinite	indefinido
interj	interjection	interjección
interr	interrogative	interrogativo
inv	invariable	invariable
lit	literary	literario
loc	locution	locución
m	masculine	masculino
Méx	Mexico	México
num	numeral	numeral
pej, pey	pejorative	peyorativo
pers	personal	personal
pl	plural	plural
pos	possessive	posesivo
prep	preposition, prepositional	preposición, preposicional
pron	pronoun	pronombre
rel	relative	relativo
RP	River Plate	Río de la Plata
sg	singular	singular
Sp	Spain, Spanish	España, español
v aux	auxiliary verb	verbo auxiliar
vi	intransitive verb	verbo intransitivo
vt	transitive verb	verbo transitivo
vulg	vulgar	vulgar

Spanish Pronunciation

Spanish orthography very closely mirrors Spanish pronunciation, much more so than is the case in English. This explains why, in bilingual dictionaries such as this, each English entry must be accompanied by a phonetic representation, while Spanish pronunciation may be presented in synoptic form.

This synopsis is meant only as an introduction, however. In spite of the clarity of the orthographical system of Spanish, the individual sounds of the language are difficult for adult native speakers of English to pronounce, and this difficulty is compounded by the syllabic structure of the language. For these reasons, readers who wish to perfect their pronunciation of Spanish are strongly advised to seek the help of a competent teacher.

To say that orthography mirrors pronunciation means that there is a close correlation between letters and sounds. Thus, most Spanish letters correspond to a single sound, or to a single family of closely related sounds, as is the case for all vowels and the consonants *f, l, m, n, p, t*, and *s*. In a few cases a single letter represents two very different sounds, as *c*, which is pronounced as *k* before *a, o,* and *u,* but *th* (as in *thin*, in parts of Spain, or as *s* in America) before *e* or *i*. Rarely, two letters represent a single sound, as in the case of *ch*.

The overarching differences between Spanish and English pronunciation are tenseness of articulation and syllabification within the breath group. Due to the tenseness of their articulation, for example, all Spanish vowels have a clear nondiphthongal character, unlike English long vowels, which tend to be bipartite (e.g., *late*, pronounced [le^{i}t]). Syllabification is a problem for English speakers because in Spanish, syllables are formed without respect to word boundaries, such that *el hado* 'fate' and *helado* 'ice cream' are both pronounced as e-la-do, and the phrase *tus otras hermanas* 'your other sisters' is syllabified as tu-so-tra-ser-ma-nas. In fast speech, vowels may combine, as in *lo ofendiste* 'you offended him', pronounced lo-fen-dis-te. Finally, when Spanish consonants occur in clusters, very often the articulation of the second influences that of the first, as when *un peso* 'one peso' is pronounced um-pe-so, and *en que* 'in which' is pronounced eŋ ke, where ŋ represents the sound of the letters *ng* in English.

The Spanish Spelling System and the Sounds Represented

I. VOWELS

i as a single vowel always represents a sound similar to the second vowel of *police*. Examples: **hilo, camino, piso.** As a part of a diphthong, it sounds like the *y* of English *yes, year.* Examples: **bien, baile, reina.**

e is similar to the vowel of *late* ([le^{i}t]), but without the diphthong. Examples: **mesa, hablé, tres.**

a is similar to the vowel of *pod*. Examples: **casa, mala, América.** Notably, **a** is always pronounced this way, even when not stressed. This contrasts with the English tendency to reduce unstressed vowels to schwa ([ə]), as in *America*, pronounced in English as [ə-mɛ́-rɪ-kə].

o has a value similar to that of the vowel in Eng. *coat* [koʷt], but without the diphthong. Examples: **no, modo, amó.**

u has a value similar to that of English *oo*, as in *boot* [buʷt], but without the diphthong. Examples: **cura, agudo, uno.** Note that the letter **u** is not pronounced in the syllables **qui, que, gui,** and **gue** (unless spelled with dieresis, as in *bilingüe*). When **u** occurs in diphthongs such as those of **cuida, cuento, deuda,** it has the sound of *w* (as in *way*).

II. CONSONANTS

b and **v** represent the same sounds in Spanish. At the beginning of a breath group or when preceded by the *m* sound (which may be spelled *n*), they are both pronounced like English *b*. Examples: **bomba, en vez de, vine, invierno.** In other environments, especially between vowels, both letters are pronounced as a very relaxed *b*, in which the lips do not completely touch and the air is not completely stopped. This sound has no equivalent in English. Examples: **haba, uva, la vaca, la banda.**

c represents a *k* sound before **a, o, u, l,** and **r.** However, this sound is not accompanied by a puff of air as it is in Eng. *can* and *coat* (compare the *c* in *scan*, which is more similar to the Spanish sound). Examples: **casa, cosa, cuna, crudo, aclamar.** In contrast, when appearing before the vowels **e** and **i, c** is pronounced as *s* in Spanish America and the southwest of Spain, and as *th* (as in *thin*) in other parts of Spain (see **s** for more information).

ch is no longer considered to be a separate letter in the Spanish alphabet. However, it represents a single sound, which is similar to the English *ch* in *church* and *cheek*. Examples: **chato, chaleco, mucho.**

d is phonetically complex in Spanish. In terms of articulation, it is pronounced by the tongue touching the teeth rather than the alveolar ridge as in English. Second, it is represented by two variants. The first of these, which is similar to that of English *dame* and *did*, occurs at the beginning of breath groups or after **n** and **l.** Examples: **donde, falda, conde.** In all other situations the letter represents a sound similar to the *th* of English *then*. Examples: **hado, cuerda, cuadro, usted.** This sound tends to be very relaxed, to the point of disappearing in certain environments, such as word-final and intervocalic.

f is very similar to the English *f* sound. Examples: **faro, elefante, alfalfa.**

g is phonetically complex. Before the vowels **e** and **i,** it is pronounced as *h* in many American dialects, while in northern Spain it is realized like the *ch* in the German word *Bach.* Examples: **gente, giro.** At the beginning of breath groups and after nasals before the vowels **a, o, u,** and the consonants **l** and **r,** it is pronounced like the **g** of English *go.* Examples: **ganga, globo, grada.** In all other environments it is pronounced as a very relaxed *g.* Examples: **lago, la goma, agrado.**

h is silent. Examples: **hoja, humo, harto.**

j is realized in most American dialects as *h,* while in northern Spain it is pronounced like the *ch* in the German word *Bach.* Examples: **jamás, jugo, jota.**

k sounds like Eng. *k,* but without the accompanying puff of air. Examples: **kilo, keroseno.**

l is pronounced forward in the mouth, as the *l* in *leaf, leak,* never in the back, as in *bell, full.* Examples: **lado, ala, sol.**

ll is no longer considered to be a separate letter in the Spanish alphabet. However, it does represent a single sound, which differs widely in pronunciation throughout the Spanish-speaking world. In most areas, it is pronounced like the *y* of Eng. *yes,* though with greater tension. In extreme northern Spain and in parts of the Andes, it sounds like the *lli* in Eng. *million.* In the River Plate area it is pronounced like the *g* in *beige* or the *sh* in *ship.* Examples: **calle, llano, olla.**

m is essentially the same as in English. Examples: **madre, mano, cama.** However, in final position, as in **álbum** 'album', it is pronounced as [ŋ], the final sound of Eng. *sing.*

n is normally pronounced like Eng. *n.* Examples: **no, mano, hablan.** There are exceptions, however. For example, before **b, v, p,** and **m,** it is pronounced *m,* as in **en Barcelona, en vez de, un peso,** while before **k, g, j, ge-,** and **gi-,** it is realized as [ŋ], the final sound of Eng. *sing,* as in **anca, tengo, naranja, engendrar.**

ñ is similar to but more tense than the *ny* of Eng. *canyon.* Examples: **cañón, año, ñato.**

p is like English *p* except that it is not accompanied by a puff of air, as it is in Eng. *pill* and *papa* (compare the *p* in *spot,* which is more similar to the Spanish sound). Examples: **padre, capa, apuro.**

q combined with **u** has the sound of *k.* Examples: **queso, aquí, quien.**

r usually represents a sound similar to that of the *tt* in Eng. *kitty* and the *dd* in *ladder*. Examples: **caro, tren, comer.** In contrast, at the beginning of words and after **n, l, s,** the letter **r** is realized as a trill, as in **rosa, Enrique, alrededor, Israel.** The double letter **rr** always represents a trill, as in **carro, correr, guerrero.**

s is pronounced the same as in standard American English in most parts of Spanish America and in parts of southern Spain. In most of Spain, in contrast, it is realized with the tip of the tongue against the alveolar ridge, producing a whistling sound that is sometimes heard in southern dialects of American English. Examples: **solo, casa, es.** In the Caribbean and in coastal Spanish generally, there is a strong tendency to pronounce **s** in certain environments (usually preconsonantal) as *h*, or to eliminate it entirely. In these dialects, *esta* may be pronounced as *ehta* or *eta*.

t differs from English *t* in two respects: first, it is articulated by the tongue touching the teeth rather than the alveolar ridge, and second, it is not accompanied by a puff of air, as it is in English *too* and *titillate* (compare the *t* in *stop*, which is more similar to the Spanish sound). Examples: **tela, tino, tinta.**

x has a wide range of phonetic realizations. Between vowels, it is usually pronounced *ks* or *gs* (but never *gz*), as in **examen, próximo,** though in a few words it is pronounced as *s*, e.g., *exacto, auxilio*. Before a consonant, **x** is almost always pronounced *s*, as in **extranjero, experiencia.** In many Mexican and Central American words of indigenous origin, **x** represents *h*, as in **México.**

y varies regionally in its pronunciation. In most areas it is pronounced like the *y* of Eng. *yes*, though with greater tension. In the River Plate area it is pronounced like the *g* in *beige* or the *sh* in *ship*. Examples: **yo, ayer.**

z is subject to dialectal variation as well. In most parts of Spain, except the southwest, it is pronounced as the *th* in Eng. *thin, cloth*. In southwestern Spain and all of Spanish America, in contrast, it is pronounced *s*. Examples: **zagal, hallazgo, luz.**

Stress Assignment in Spanish and the Use of the Written Accent

Spanish words are normally stressed on the next-to-last syllable when they end in a vowel or the consonants **n** or **s.** Examples: **mesa, zapato, acontecimiento, hablan, mujeres.** Words whose pronunciation does not conform to this rule are considered exceptions, and their stressed syllable is indicated with an accent mark. Examples: **lámpara, estómago, género, acá, varón, además.**

Conversely, Spanish words are normally stressed on the final syllable when they end in a consonant other than **n** or **s.** Examples: **mujer, actualidad, pedal, voraz.** Words whose pronunciation does not conform to this rule are considered exceptions, and their stressed syllable is indicated with an accent mark. Examples: n<u>á</u>car, vol<u>á</u>til, l<u>á</u>piz.

For the purposes of stress assignment, diphthongs are considered the same as simple vowels. Thus, **arduo** and **industria** are considered to have two and three syllables respectively, with regular stress on the penultimate syllable. However, some sequences of vowels are not considered diphthongs. For example, **alegría** and **continúo** are both considered to have four syllables, with the stress mark indicating the absence of a diphthong.

Until recently certain words received written accents in order to differentiate functions, even though they are pronounced identically (this is still true in certain cases, such as **de** 'of', **dé** 'give'). Thus, the orthography **esta** was assigned to the demonstrative adjective ('this', fem.), while the demonstrative pronoun ('this one', fem.) was written **ésta.** This convention is no longer observed by most writers.

Notes on Spanish Grammar

The Noun

Gender. All Spanish nouns, not just those that denote male or female beings, are assigned either masculine or feminine gender. As a general rule, male beings (**muchacho** 'boy', **toro** 'bull') and all nouns ending in -o (**lodo** 'mud') are assigned masculine gender (exceptions: **mano** 'hand', **foto** 'photo', both feminine). Similarly, female beings (**mujer** 'woman', **vaca** 'cow') and nouns ending in -a (**envidia** 'envy') tend to be assigned feminine gender (exceptions: **mapa** 'map', **drama** 'drama', **día** 'day', all masculine). In addition, nouns ending in -**ción, -tad, -dad, -tud,** and -**umbre** are always feminine: **canción** 'song', **facultad** 'college', **ciudad** 'city', **virtud** 'virtue', and **muchedumbre** 'crowd'. Otherwise, nouns ending in consonants and vowels other than -**o** and -**a** are of unpredictable gender. Some are feminine (**barbarie** 'savagery', **clase** 'class', **nariz** 'nose', **tribu** 'tribe'), while others are masculine (**antílope** 'antelope', **corte** 'cut', **mesón** 'lodge', **nácar** 'mother of pearl').

Nouns in -**o** that denote human beings (and to some extent, animals) form the feminine by replacing -**o** with -**a,** as in **tío** 'uncle' / **tía** 'aunt', **niño** 'boy' / **niña** 'girl', **oso** 'bear' / **osa** 'she-bear'. Where the masculine noun does not end in -**o,** the rules of formation are more complex. For example, nouns ending in -**ón, -or,** and -**án** require the addition of -**a,** as in the pairs **patrón / patrona** 'patron', **pastor / pastora** 'shepherd', **holgazán / holgazana** 'lazy person'. In other cases the difference is more unpredictable: **emperador** 'emperor' / **emperatriz** 'empress', **abad** 'abbot' / **abadesa** 'abbess'.

Some nouns have different genders according to their meanings: **corte** (m) 'cut', (f) 'court', **capital** (m) 'money capital', (f) 'capital city', while others have invariable endings which are used for both the masculine and the feminine: **artista** 'artist' (and all nouns ending in -**ista**), **amante** 'lover', **aristócrata** 'aristocrat', **homicida** 'murderer', **cliente** 'customer'. Finally, some words vacillate as to gender, e.g., **mar** 'sea', which is normally masculine but is feminine in certain expressions (**en alta mar** 'on the high seas') and in poetic contexts, and **arte,** which is masculine in the singular but feminine in the plural. Some words, such as **armazón** and **esperma,** can be both masculine and feminine.

Pluralization. Nouns ending in an unaccented vowel and **-é** add **-s** to form the plural: **libro / libros, casa / casas, café / cafés.** Nouns ending in a consonant, in **-y,** or in an accented vowel other than **-é** add **-es: papel / papeles, canción / canciones, ley / leyes, rubí / rubíes.** Exceptions to this rule include the words **papá / papás** and **mamá / mamás,** as well as the small group of nouns ending in unaccented **-es** or **-is,** which do not change in the plural: **lunes** 'Monday', 'Mondays', **tesis** 'thesis', 'theses'.

Articles

Definite Article. The equivalent of English **the** is as follows: masculine singular, **el;** feminine singular, **la;** masculine plural, **los;** feminine plural, **las.** Feminine words beginning with stressed **a** or **ha** take **el** in the singular and **las** in the plural: **el alma** 'the soul' / **las almas** 'the souls', **el hacha** 'the hatchet' / **las hachas** 'the hatchets'. In spite of this, these nouns remain feminine in the singular, as shown by adjective agreement: **el alma bendita** 'the blessed soul'. When preceded by the prepositions **a** and **de,** the masculine singular article **el** forms the contractions **al** and **del.**

Indefinite Article. The equivalent of English **a, an** is as follows: masculine singular, **un;** feminine singular, **una.** In the plural, masculine **unos** and feminine **unas** are equivalent to English **some.** Feminine words beginning with stressed **a** or **ha** take **un** in the singular and **unas** in the plural: **un alma** 'a soul' / **unas almas** 'some souls', **un hacha** 'a hatchet' / **unas hachas** 'some hatchets'.

Adjectives

Agreement. The adjective in Spanish agrees in gender and number with the noun it modifies: **el lápiz rojo** 'the red pencil', **la casa blanca** 'the white house', **los libros interesantes** 'the interesting books', **las flores hermosas** 'the beautiful flowers'.

Formation of the Plural. Adjectives follow the same rules as nouns for the formation of the plural: **pálido, pálidos** 'pale', **fácil, fáciles** 'easy', **cortés, corteses** 'courteous', **capaz, capaces** 'capable'.

Formation of the Feminine. Adjectives ending in **-o** change to **-a: blanco, blanca** 'white'. Adjectives ending in other vowels are invariable: **verde** 'green', **fuerte** 'strong', **indígena** 'indigenous, native', **pesimista** 'pessimistic', **baladí** 'trivial', as are adjectives ending in a consonant: **fácil** 'easy', **cortés** 'courteous', **mayor** 'older', 'larger'. Some cases are more complex: (a) adjectives ending in **-ón, -án, -or** (except comparatives like **mayor**) add **-a** to form the feminine: **holgazán, holgazana** 'lazy', **preguntón, preguntona** 'inquisitive', **hablador, habladora** 'talkative'; (b) adjectives of nationality ending in a consonant add **-a** to form the feminine: **francés, francesa** 'French', **español, española** 'Spanish', **alemán, alemana** 'German'.

Adverbs

Most adverbs are formed by adding **-mente** to the feminine form of the adjective: **clara** 'clear' / **claramente** 'clearly', **fácil** 'easy' / **fácilmente** 'easily'.

Comparison of Inequality in Adjectives and Adverbs

The comparative of inequality is formed by placing **más** or **menos** before the positive form of the adjective or adverb: **más rico que** 'richer than', **menos rico que** 'less rich than', **más tarde** 'later', **menos tarde** 'less late'. The superlative is formed by placing the definite article **el** before the comparative: **el más rico** 'the richest', **el menos rico** 'the least rich'.

The following adjectives and adverbs have irregular forms of comparison:

Positive	Comparative	Superlative
bueno	mejor	el (la) mejor
malo	peor	el (la) peor
grande	mayor	el (la) mayor
pequeño	menor	el (la) menor

Common Spanish Suffixes

-aco   is a pejorative suffix: **pajarraco** 'ugly bird' (from **pájaro** 'bird'), **libraco** 'large, bulky book' (**libro** 'book')

-ada *a.* attaches to verbal stems to indicate an action: **mirada** 'look' (**mirar** 'to look'), **empujada** 'push' (**empujar** 'to push')

  b. attaches to noun stems to indicate a blow: **cachetada** 'blow on the cheek' (**cachete** 'cheek'), **puñalada** 'stab with a dagger' (**puñal** 'dagger')

  c. attaches to nominal stems to indicate an action characteristic of a person or group: **bobada** 'foolish act' (**bobo** 'fool'), **niñada** 'childish act' (**niño** 'child')

-al, -ar   attach to nouns indicating trees to form nouns that denote a grove: **naranjal** 'orange grove' (from **naranjo** 'orange tree'), **pinar** 'pine grove' (**pino** 'pine tree')

-azo   attaches to noun stems, forming nouns that indicate

  a. augmentation: **hombrazo** 'big man' (**hombre** 'man'), **marranazo** 'large hog' (**marrano** 'hog')

b.	a blow or explosion: **porrazo** 'blow with a club' (**porra** 'club'), **cañonazo** 'cannon shot' (**cañón** 'cannon')

-cito is a diminutive suffix: **cochecito** 'a little car' (**coche** 'car'), **mujercita** 'little woman' (**mujer** 'woman')

-dor forms agent nouns from verbs: **hablador** 'talker' (**hablar** 'to talk'), **regulador** 'regulator' (**regular** 'to regulate'), which are sometimes used as adjectives: **hablador** 'talkative', **regulador** 'regulating'

-ejo is a pejorative suffix: **librejo** 'worthless book' (**libro** 'book'), **lugarejo** 'Podunk' (**lugar** 'place')

-ería attaches to noun stems to denote
- *a.* a place where something is made or sold: **zapatería** 'shoestore' (**zapato** 'shoe'), **pastelería** 'pastry shop' (**pastel** 'pastry')
- *b.* a profession, business, or occupation: **carpintería** 'carpentry' (**carpintero** 'carpenter'), **ingeniería** 'engineering' (**ingeniero** 'engineer')
- *c.* a group: **chiquillería** 'bunch of children' (**chiquillo** 'little kid')

-ero
- *a.* attaches to nouns to indicate a person who makes, sells, or is in charge of something: **librero** 'bookseller' (**libro** 'book'), **zapatero** 'shoemaker' (**zapato** 'shoe'), **carcelero** 'jailer' (**cárcel** 'jail')
- *b.* attaches to nominal stems to form adjectives: **guerrero** 'warlike' (**guerra** 'war'), **conejero** 'for hunting rabbits' (**conejo** 'rabbit')

-ez, -eza are used to make abstract nouns from adjectival bases: **vejez** 'old age' (**viejo** 'old'), **niñez** 'childhood' (**niño** 'child'), **grandeza** 'greatness' (**grande** 'large, great'), **rareza** 'rarity' (**raro** 'rare')

-ía forms abstract nouns from adjectival bases: **valentía** 'courage' (**valiente** 'brave'), **cobardía** 'cowardice' (**cobarde** 'coward')

-ico is a diminutive suffix: **ratico** 'little while' (**rato** 'while'), **momentico** 'brief moment' (**momento** 'moment')

-(i)ento attaches to adjectives to indicate attenuation, as in **amarillento** 'yellowish' (**amarillo** 'yellow'), or an undesirable quality, as in **hambriento** 'hungry' (**hambre** 'hunger')

-illo is sometimes a diminutive suffix: **politiquillo** 'insignificant politician' (**político** 'politician'), **chiquillo** 'little kid' (**chico** 'child')

-ísimo attaches to adjectives to indicate an extreme degree of a quality: **hermosísimo** 'very beautiful' (**hermoso** 'beautiful')

-ito	is a diminutive suffix: **librito** 'small book' (**libro** 'book'), **casita** 'little house' (**casa** 'house')
-izo	forms adjectives from nominal stems, indicating a tendency or attenuation: **rojizo** 'reddish' (**rojo** 'red'), **olvidadizo** 'forgetful' (**olvidar** 'to forget')
-mente	is the adverbial ending attached to the feminine form of the adjective: **generosamente** 'generously' (**generoso** 'generous'), **claramente** 'clearly' (**claro** 'clear')

-ón *a.* is an augmentative adjectival suffix: **barrigón** 'potbellied' (**barriga** 'belly'), **cabezón** 'large-headed' (**cabeza** 'head')

        b. attaches to verb stems to denote sudden actions: **tirón** 'pull, jerk' (**tirar** 'to pull'), **apretón** 'push' (**apretar** 'to push')

-oso	forms adjectives from nouns, indicating abundance or character: **rocoso** 'rocky' (**roca** 'rock'), **tormentoso** 'stormy' (**tormenta** 'storm')
-ote, -ota	is an augmentative and pejorative suffix attached to nouns: **discursote** 'long, boring speech' (**discurso** 'speech'), **narizota** 'big ugly nose' (**nariz** 'nose')
-udo	forms adjectives from nouns, indicating an excess: **peludo** 'hairy' (**pelo** 'hair'), **panzudo** 'big-bellied' (**panza** 'belly')
-ura	forms abstract nouns from adjectives: **negrura** 'blackness' (**negro** 'black'), **altura** 'height' (**alto** 'high')
-uzco	forms adjectives from other adjectives, indicating attenuation: **blancuzco** 'whitish' (**blanco** 'white'), **negruzco** 'blackish' (**negro** 'black')

Spanish Regular Verbs

First Conjugation

infinitive	**hablar**
pres. indic.	hablo, hablas, habla, hablamos, habláis, hablan
pres. subj.	hable, hables, hable, hablemos, habléis, hablen
pret. indic.	hablé, hablaste, habló, hablamos, hablasteis, hablaron
imp. indic.	hablaba, hablabas, hablaba, hablábamos, hablabais, hablaban

imp. subj.	hablara, hablaras, hablara, habláramos, hablarais, hablaran, *or*
	hablase, hablases, hablase, hablásemos, hablaseis, hablasen
fut. indic.	hablaré, hablarás, hablará, hablaremos, hablaréis, hablarán
cond.	hablaría, hablarías, hablaría, hablaríamos, hablaríais, hablarían
imper.	habla (tú), hable (usted), hablemos (nosotros), hablad (vosotros), hablen (ustedes)
pres. part.	hablando
past part.	hablado

Second Conjugation

infinitive	**comer**
pres. indic.	como, comes, come, comemos, coméis, comen
pres. subj.	coma, comas, coma, comamos, comáis, coman
pret. indic.	comí, comiste, comió, comimos, comisteis, comieron
imp. indic.	comía, comías, comía, comíamos, comíais, comían
imp. subj.	comiera, comieras, comiera, comiéramos, comierais, comieran, *or*
	comiese, comieses, comiese, comiésemos, comieseis, comiesen
fut. indic.	comeré, comerás, comerá, comeremos, comeréis, comerán
cond.	comería, comerías, comería, comeríamos, comeríais, comerían
imper.	come (tú), coma (usted), comamos (nosotros), comed (vosotros), coman (ustedes)
pres. part.	comiendo
past part.	comido

Third Conjugation

infinitive	**vivir**
pres. indic.	vivo, vives, vive, vivimos, vivís, viven
pres. subj.	viva, vivas, viva, vivamos, viváis, vivan
pret. indic.	viví, viviste, vivió, vivimos, vivisteis, vivieron
imp. indic.	vivía, vivías, vivía, vivíamos, vivíais, vivían
imp. subj.	viviera, vivieras, viviera, viviéramos, vivierais, vivieran, *or*
	viviese, vivieses, viviese, viviésemos, vivieseis, viviesen
fut. indic.	viviré, vivirás, vivirá, viviremos, viviréis, vivirán
cond.	viviría, vivirías, viviría, viviríamos, viviríais, vivirían
imper.	vive (tú), viva (usted), vivamos (nosotros), vivid (vosotros), vivan (ustedes)
pres. part.	viviendo
past part.	vivido

Spanish Irregular and Orthographic Changing Verbs

The superscript number or numbers listed as part of a verb entry indicate that the verb is to be conjugated like the model verb in this section that has the corresponding number. Only the tenses that have irregular forms or spelling changes are given, and these irregular forms and spelling changes are shown in boldface type.

1. **pensar**
   pres. indic. **pienso, piensas, piensa,** pensamos, pensáis, **piensan**
   pres. subj.   **piense, pienses, piense,** pensemos, penséis, **piensen**
   imper.   **piensa** (tú), **piense** (usted), pensemos (nosotros), pensad (vosotros), **piensen** (ustedes)

2. **perder**
   pres. indic. **pierdo, pierdes, pierde,** perdemos, perdéis, **pierden**
   pres. subj.   **pierda, pierdas, pierda,** perdamos, perdáis, **pierdan**
   imper.   **pierde** (tú), **pierda** (usted), perdamos (nosotros), perded (vosotros), **pierdan** (ustedes)

3. **discernir**
   pres. indic. **discierno, disciernes, discierne,** discernimos, discernís, **disciernen**
   pres. subj.   **discierna, disciernas, discierna,** discernamos, discernáis, **disciernan**
   imper.   **discierne** (tú), **discierna** (usted), discernamos (nosotros), discernid (vosotros), **disciernan** (ustedes)

4. **adquirir**
   pres. indic. **adquiero, adquieres, adquiere,** adquirimos, adquirís, **adquieren**
   pres. subj.   **adquiera, adquieras, adquiera,** adquiramos, adquiráis, **adquieran**
   imper.   **adquiere** (tú), **adquiera** (usted), adquiramos (nosotros), adquirid (vosotros), **adquieran** (ustedes)

5. **contar**
   pres. indic. **cuento, cuentas, cuenta,** contamos, contáis, **cuentan**
   pres. subj.   **cuente, cuentes, cuente,** contemos, contéis, **cuenten**
   imper.   **cuenta** (tú), **cuente** (usted), contemos (nosotros), contad (vosotros), **cuenten** (ustedes)

6. **volver**
   pres. indic. **vuelvo, vuelves, vuelve,** volvemos, volvéis, **vuelven**
   pres. subj.   **vuelva, vuelvas, vuelva,** volvamos, volváis, **vuelvan**

imper.	**vuelve** (tú), **vuelva** (usted), volvamos (nosotros) volved (vosotros), **vuelvan** (ustedes)
past part.	**vuelto**

7. dormir

pres. indic.	**duermo, duermes, duerme,** dormimos, dormís, **duermen**
pres. subj.	**duerma, duermas, duerma, durmamos, durmáis, duerman**
pret. indic.	dormí, dormiste, **durmió,** dormimos, dormisteis, **durmieron**
imp. subj.	**durmiera, durmieras, durmiera, durmiéramos, durmierais, durmieran,** or **durmiese, durmieses, durmiese, durmiésemos, durmieseis, durmiesen**
imper.	**duerme** (tú), **duerma** (usted), **durmamos** (nosotros), dormid (vosotros), **duerman** (ustedes)
pres. part.	**durmiendo**

8. sentir

pres. indic.	**siento, sientes, siente,** sentimos, sentís, **sienten**
pres. subj.	**sienta, sientas, sienta, sintamos, sintáis, sientan**
pret. indic.	sentí, sentiste, **sintió,** sentimos, sentisteis, **sintieron**
imp. subj.	**sintiera, sintieras, sintiera, sintiéramos, sintierais, sintieran,** or **sintiese, sintieses, sintiese, sintiésemos, sintieseis, sintiesen**
imper.	**siente** (tú), **sienta** (usted), **sintamos** (nosotros), sentid (vosotros), **sientan** (ustedes)
pres. part.	**sintiendo**

9. pedir

pres. indic.	**pido, pides, pide,** pedimos, pedís, **piden**
pres. subj.	**pida, pidas, pida, pidamos, pidáis, pidan**
pret. indic.	pedí, pediste, **pidió,** pedimos, pedisteis, **pidieron**
imp. subj.	**pidiera, pidieras, pidiera, pidiéramos, pidierais, pidieran,** or **pidiese, pidieses, pidiese, pidiésemos, pidieseis, pidiesen**
imper.	**pide** (tú), **pida** (usted), **pidamos** (nosotros), pedid (vosotros), **pidan** (ustedes)
pres. part.	**pidiendo**

10. reír

pres. indic.	**río, ríes, ríe,** reímos, reís, **ríen**
pres. subj.	**ría, rías, ría, riamos, riáis, rían**
pret. indic.	reí, reíste, **rió,** reímos, reísteis, **rieron**

imp. subj.	**riera, rieras, riera, riéramos, rierais, rieran,** or **riese, rieses, riese, riésemos, rieseis, riesen**
imper.	**ríe** (tú), **ría** (usted), **riamos** (nosotros), reíd (vosotros), **rían** (ustedes)
pres. part.	**riendo**
past part.	**reído**

11. **reñir**

pres. indic.	**riño, riñes, riñe,** reñimos, reñís, **riñen**
pres. subj.	**riña, riñas, riña, riñamos, riñáis, riñan**
pret. indic.	reñí, reñiste, **riñó,** reñimos, reñisteis, **riñeron**
imp. subj.	**riñera, riñeras, riñera, riñéramos, riñerais, riñeran,** or **riñese, riñeses, riñese, riñésemos, riñeseis, riñesen**
imper.	**riñe** (tú), **riña** (usted), **riñamos** (nosotros), reñid (vosotros), **riñan** (ustedes)
pres. part.	**riñendo**

12. **seguir**

pres. indic.	**sigo, sigues, sigue,** seguimos, seguís, **siguen**
pres. subj.	**siga, sigas, siga, sigamos, sigáis, sigan**
pret. indic.	seguí, seguiste, **siguió,** seguimos, seguisteis, **siguieron**
imp. subj.	**siguiera, siguieras, siguiera, siguiéramos, siguierais, siguieran,** or **siguiese, siguieses, siguiese, siguiésemos, siguieses, siguiesen**
imper.	**sigue** (tú), **siga** (usted), **sigamos** (nosotros), seguid (vosotros), **sigan** (ustedes)
pres. part.	**siguiendo**

13. **erguir**

pres. indic.	**yergo, yergues, yergue,** erguimos, erguís, **yerguen** or **irgo, irgues, irgue,** erguimos, erguís, **irguen**
pres. subj.	**yerga, yergas, yerga, irgamos, irgáis, yergan** or **irga, irgas, irga, irgamos, irgáis, irgan**
pret. indic.	erguí, erguiste, **irguió,** erguimos, erguisteis, **irguieron**
imp. subj.	**irguiera, irguieras, irguiera, irguiéramos, irguierais, irguieran,** or **irguiese, irguieses, irguiese, irguiésemos, irguieseis, irguiesen**
imper.	**yergue** or **irgue** (tú), **yerga** or **irga** (usted), **irgamos** (nosotros), erguid (vosotros), **yergan** or **irgan** (ustedes)
pres. part.	**irguiendo**

14. **elegir**

pres. indic.	**elijo, eliges, elige,** elegimos, elegís, **eligen**
pres. subj.	**elija, elijas, elija, elijamos, elijáis, elijan**

pret. indic.	elegí, elegiste, **eligió,** elegimos, elegisteis, **eligieron**
imp. subj.	**eligiera, eligieras, eligiera, eligiéramos, eligierais, eligieran,** or **eligiese, eligieses, eligiese, eligiésemos, eligieseis, eligiesen**
imper.	**elige** (tú), **elija** (usted), **elijamos** (nosotros), elegid (vosotros), **elijan** (ustedes)
pres. part.	**eligiendo**

15. **tañer**

pret. indic.	tañí, tañiste, **tañó,** tañimos, tañisteis, **tañeron**
imp. subj.	**tañera, tañeras, tañera, tañéramos, tañerais, tañeran,** or **tañese, tañeses, tañese, tañésemos, tañeseis, tañesen**
pres. part.	**tañendo**

16. **bullir**

pret. indic.	bullí, bulliste, **bulló,** bullimos, bullisteis, **bulleron**
imp. subj.	**bullera, bulleras, bullera, bulléramos, bullerais, bulleran,** or **bullese, bulleses, bullese, bullésemos, bulleseis, bullesen**
pres. part.	**bullendo**

17. **gruñir**

pret. indic.	gruñí, gruñiste, **gruñó,** gruñisteis, **gruñeron**
imp. subj.	**gruñera, gruñeras, gruñera, gruñéramos, gruñerais, gruñeran,** or **gruñese, gruñeses, gruñese, gruñésemos, gruñeseis, gruñesen**
pres. part.	**gruñendo**

18. **creer**

pret. indic.	creí, creíste, **creyó,** creímos, creísteis, **creyeron**
imp. subj.	**creyera, creyeras, creyera, creyéramos, creyerais, creyeran,** or **creyese, creyeses, creyese, creyésemos, creyeseis, creyesen**
pres. part.	**creyendo**
past part.	**creído**

19. **huir**

pres. indic.	**huyo, huyes, huye,** huimos, huís, **huyen**
pres. subj.	**huya, huyas, huya, huyamos, huyáis, huyan**
pret. indic.	hui, huiste, **huyó,** huimos, huisteis, **huyeron**
imp. subj.	**huyera, huyeras, huyera, huyéramos, huyerais, huyeran,** or **huyese, huyeses, huyese, huyésemos, huyeseis, huyesen**

imper.	**huye** (tú), **huya** (usted), **huyamos** (nosotros), huid (vosotros), **huyan** (ustedes)
pres. part.	**huyendo**

20. **argüir**

pres. indic.	**arguyo, arguyes, arguye,** argüimos, argüís, **arguyen**
pres. subj.	**arguya, arguyas, arguya, arguyamos, arguyáis, arguyan**
pret. indic.	argüí, argüiste, **arguyó,** argüimos, argüisteis, **arguyeron**
imp. subj.	**arguyera, arguyeras, arguyera, arguyéramos, arguyerais, arguyeran,** or **arguyese, arguyeses, arguyese, arguyésemos, arguyeseis, arguyesen**
imper.	**arguye** (tú), **arguya** (usted), **arguyamos** (nosotros), argüid (vosotros), **arguyan** (ustedes)
pres. part.	**arguyendo**

21. **errar**

pres. indic.	**yerro, yerras, yerra,** erramos, erráis, **yerran**
pres. subj.	**yerre, yerres, yerre,** erremos, erréis, **yerren**
imper.	**yerra** (tú), **yerre** (usted), erremos (nosotros), errad (vosotros), **yerren** (ustedes)

22. **oler**

pres. indic.	**huelo, hueles, huele,** olemos, oléis, **huelen**
pres. subj.	**huela, huelas, huela,** olamos, oláis, **huelan**
imper.	**huele** (tú), **huela** (usted), oled (vosotros), **huelan** (ustedes)

23. **avergonzar**

pres. indic.	**avergüenzo, avergüenzas, avergüenza,** avergonzamos, avergonzáis, **avergüenzan**
pres. subj.	**avergüence, avergüences, avergüence, avergoncemos, avergoncéis, avergüencen**
pret. indic.	**avergoncé,** avergonzaste, avergonzó, avergonzamos, avergonzasteis, avergonzaron
imper.	**avergüenza** (tú), **avergüence** (usted), **avergoncemos** (nosotros), avergonzad (vosotros), **avergüencen** (ustedes)

24. **degollar**

pres. indic.	**degüello, degüellas, degüella,** degollamos, degolláis, **degüellan**
pres. subj.	**degüelle, degüelles, degüelle,** degollemos, degolléis, **degüellen**
imper.	**degüella** (tú), **degüelle** (usted), degollemos (nosotros), degollad (vosotros), **degüellen** (ustedes)

25. **averiguar**

pres. subj.   **averigüe, averigües, averigüe, averigüemos, averigüéis, averigüen**

pres. indic. **averigüé,** averiguaste, averiguó, averiguamos, averiguasteis, averiguaron

imper.   averigua (tú), **averigüe** (usted), **averigüemos** (nosotros), averiguad (vosotros), **averigüen** (ustedes)

26. **continuar**

pres. indic. **continúo, continúas, continúa,** continuamos, continuáis, **continúan**

pres. subj.   **continúe, continúes, continúe,** continuemos, continuéis, **continúen**

imper.   **continúa** (tú), **continúe** (usted), continuemos (nosotros), continuad (vosotros), **continúen** (ustedes)

27. **reunir**

pres. indic. **reúno, reúnes, reúne,** reunimos, reunís, **reúnen**

pres. subj.   **reúna, reúnas, reúna,** reunamos, reunáis, **reúnan**

imper.   **reúne** (tú), **reúna** (usted), reunamos (nosotros), reunid (vosotros), **reúnan** (ustedes)

28. **enviar**

pres. indic. **envío, envías, envía,** enviamos, enviáis, **envían**

pres. subj.   **envíe, envíes, envíe,** enviemos, enviéis, **envíen**

imper.   **envía** (tú), **envíe** (usted), enviemos (nosotros), enviad (vosotros), **envíen** (ustedes)

29. **prohibir**

pres. indic. **prohíbo, prohíbes, prohíbe,** prohibimos, prohibís, **prohíben**

pres. subj.   **prohíba, prohíbas, prohíba,** prohibamos, prohibáis, **prohíban**

imper.   **prohíbe** (tú), **prohíba** (usted), prohibamos (nosotros), prohibid (vosotros), **prohíban** (ustedes)

30. **buscar**

pres. subj.   **busque, busques, busque, busquemos, busquéis, busquen**

pret. indic. **busqué,** buscaste, buscó, buscamos, buscasteis, buscaron

imper.   busca (tú), **busque** (usted), **busquemos** (nosotros), buscad (vosotros), **busquen** (ustedes)

31. **trocar**

pres. indic.	**trueco, truecas, trueca,** trocamos, trocáis, **truecan**
pres. subj.	**trueque, trueques, trueque, troquemos, troquéis, truequen**
pret. indic.	**troqué,** trocaste, trocó, trocamos, trocasteis, trocaron
imper.	**trueca** (tú), **trueque** (usted), **troquemos** (nosotros), trocad (vosotros), **truequen** (ustedes)

32. **convencer**

pres. indic.	**convenzo,** convences, convence, convencemos, convencéis, convencen
pres. subj.	**convenza, convenzas, convenza, convenzamos, convenzáis, convenzan**
imper.	convence (tú), **convenza** (usted), **convenzamos** (nosotros), convenced (vosotros), **convenzan** (ustedes)

33. **esparcir**

pres. indic.	**esparzo,** esparces, esparce, esparcimos, esparcís, esparcen
pres. subj.	**esparza, esparzas, esparza, esparzamos, esparzáis, esparzan**
imper.	esparce (tú), **esparza** (usted), **esparzamos** (nosotros), esparcid (vosotros), **esparzan** (ustedes)

34. **cocer**

pres. indic.	**cuezo, cueces, cuece,** cocemos, cocéis, **cuecen**
pres. subj.	**cueza, cuezas, cueza, cozamos, cozáis, cuezan**
imper.	**cuece** (tú), **cueza** (usted), **cozamos** (nosotros), coced (vosotros), **cuezan** (ustedes)

35. **conocer**

pres. indic.	**conozco,** conoces, conoce, conocemos, conocéis, conocen
pres. subj.	**conozca, conozcas, conozca, conozcamos, conozcáis, conozcan**
imper.	conoce (tú), **conozca** (usted), **conozcamos** (nosotros), conoced (vosotros), **conozcan** (ustedes)

36. **placer**

pres. indic.	**plazco,** places, place, placemos, placéis, placen
pres. subj.	**plazca, plazcas, plazca, plazcamos, plazcáis, plazcan**
imper.	place (tú), **plazca** (usted), **plazcamos** (nosotros), placed (vosotros), **plazcan** (ustedes)

37. yacer
pres. indic.   **yazco** or **yazgo** or **yago,** yaces, yace, yacemos, yacéis, yacen
pres. subj.   **yazca, yazcas, yazca, yazcamos, yazcáis, yazcan,** or **yazga, yazgas, yazga, yazgamos, yazgáis, yazgan** or **yaga, yagas, yaga, yagamos, yagáis, yagan**
imper.   yace or **yaz** (tú), **yazca** or **yazga** or **yaga** (usted), **yazcamos** or **yazgamos** or **yagamos** (nosotros), yaced (vosotros), **yazcan** or **yazgan** or **yagan** (ustedes)

38. conducir
pres. indic.   **conduzco,** conduces, conduce, conducimos, conducís, conducen
pres. subj.   **conduzca, conduzcas, conduzca, conduzcamos, conduzcáis, conduzcan**
pret. indic.   **conduje, condujiste, condujo, condujimos, condujisteis, condujeron**
imp. subj.   **condujera, condujeras, condujera, condujéramos, condujerais, condujeran,** or **condujese, condujeses, condujese, condujésemos, condujeseis, condujesen**
imper.   conduce (tú), **conduzca** (usted), **conduzcamos** (nosotros), conducid (vosotros), **conduzcan** (ustedes)

39. lucir
pres. indic.   **luzco,** luces, luce, lucimos, lucís, lucen
pres. subj.   **luzca, luzcas, luzca, luzcamos, luzcáis, luzcan**
imper.   luce (tú), **luzca** (usted), **luzcamos** (nosotros), lucid (vosotros), **luzcan** (ustedes)

40. llegar
pres. subj.   **llegue, llegues, llegue, lleguemos, lleguéis, lleguen**
pret. indic.   **llegué,** llegaste, llegó, llegamos, llegasteis, llegaron
imper.   llega (tú), **llegue** (usted), **lleguemos** (nosotros), llegad (vosotros), **lleguen** (ustedes)

41. negar
pres. indic.   **niego, niegas, niega,** negamos, negáis, **niegan**
pres. subj.   **niegue, niegues, niegue, neguemos, neguéis, nieguen**
pret. indic.   **negué,** negaste, negó, negamos, negasteis, negaron
imper.   **niega** (tú), **niegue** (usted), **neguemos** (nosotros), negad (vosotros), **nieguen** (ustedes)

42.   **colgar**
   pres. indic.   **cuelgo, cuelgas, cuelga,** colgamos, colgáis, **cuelgan**
   pres. subj.   **cuelgue, cuelgues, cuelgue, colguemos, colguéis, cuelguen**
   pret. indic.   **colgué,** colgaste, colgó, colgamos, colgasteis, colgaron
   imper.   **cuelga** (tú), **cuelgue** (usted), **colguemos** (nosotros), colgad (vosotros), **cuelguen** (ustedes)

43.   **jugar**
   pres. indic.   **juego, juegas, juega,** jugamos, jugáis, **juegan**
   pres. subj.   **juegue, juegues, juegue, juguemos, juguéis, jueguen**
   pret. indic.   **jugué,** jugaste, jugó, jugamos, jugasteis, jugaron
   imper.   **juega** (tú), **juegue** (usted), **juguemos** (nosotros), jugad (vosotros), **jueguen** (ustedes)

44.   **distinguir**
   pres. indic.   **distingo,** distingues, distingue, distinguimos, distinguís, distinguen
   pres. subj.   **distinga, distingas, distinga, distingamos, distingáis, distingan**
   imper.   distingue (tú), **distinga** (usted), **distingamos** (nosotros), distinguid (vosotros), **distingan** (ustedes)

45.   **coger**
   pres. indic.   **cojo,** coges, coge, cogemos, cogéis, cogen
   pres. subj.   **coja, cojas, coja, cojamos, cojáis, cojan**
   imper.   coge (tú), **coja** (usted), **cojamos** (nosotros), coged (vosotros), **cojan** (ustedes)

46.   **dirigir**
   pres. indic.   **dirijo,** diriges, dirige, dirigimos, dirigís, dirigen
   pres. subj.   **dirija, dirijas, dirija, dirijamos, dirijáis, dirijan**
   imper.   dirige (tú), **dirija** (usted), **dirijamos** (nosotros), dirigid (vosotros), **dirijan** (ustedes)

47.   **abrazar**
   pres. subj.   **abrace, abraces, abrace, abracemos, abracéis, abracen**
   pret. indic.   **abracé,** abrazaste, abrazó, abrazamos, abrazasteis, abrazaron
   imper.   abraza (tú), **abrace** (usted), **abracemos** (nosotros), abrazad (vosotros), **abracen** (ustedes)

48. **empezar**

pres. indic.	**empiezo, empiezas, empieza,** empezamos, empezáis, **empiezan**
pres. subj.	**empiece, empieces, empiece, empecemos, empecéis, empiecen**
pret. indic.	**empecé,** empezaste, empezó, empezamos, empezasteis, empezaron
imper.	**empieza** (tú), **empiece** (usted), **empecemos** (nosotros), empezad (vosotros), **empiecen** (ustedes)

49. **forzar**

pres. indic.	**fuerzo, fuerzas, fuerza,** forzamos, forzáis, **fuerzan**
pres. subj.	**fuerce, fuerces, fuerce, forcemos, forcéis, fuercen**
pret. indic.	**forcé,** forzaste, forzó, forzamos, forzasteis, forzaron
imper.	**fuerza** (tú), **fuerce** (usted), **forcemos** (nosotros), forzad (vosotros), **fuercen** (ustedes)

50. **asir**

pres. indic.	**asgo,** ases, ase, asimos, asís, asen
pres. subj.	**asga, asgas, asga, asgamos, asgáis, asgan**
imper.	ase (tú), **asga** (usted), **asgamos** (nosotros), asid (vosotros), **asgan** (ustedes)

51. **bendecir**

pres. indic.	**bendigo, bendices, bendice,** bendecimos, bendecís, **bendicen**
pres. subj.	**bendiga, bendigas, bendiga, bendigamos, bendigáis, bendigan**
pret. indic..	**bendije, bendijiste, bendijo, bendijimos, bendijisteis, bendijeron**
imp. subj.	**bendijera, bendijeras, bendijera, bendijéramos, bendijerais, bendijeran** or **bendijese, bendijeses, bendijese, bendijésemos, bendijeseis, bendijesen**
fut. indic.	bendeciré, bendecirás, bendecirá, bendeciremos, bendeciréis, bendecirán
cond.	bendeciría, bendecirías, bendeciría, bendeciríamos, bendeciríais, bendecirían
imper.	**bendice** (tú), **bendiga** (usted), **bendigamos** (nosotros), bendecid (vosotros), **bendigan** (ustedes)
pres. part.	**bendiciendo**
past part.	bendecido

52. **caer**

pres. indic.	**caigo,** caes, cae, caemos, caéis, caen
pres. subj.	**caiga, caigas, caiga, caigamos, caigáis, caigan**

pret. indic.	caí, caíste, **cayó,** caímos, caísteis, **cayeron**
imp. subj.	**cayera, cayeras, cayera, cayéramos, cayerais, cayeran,** or **cayese, cayeses, cayese, cayésemos, cayeseis, cayesen**
imper.	cae (tú), **caiga** (usted), **caigamos** (nosotros), caed (vosotros), **caigan** (ustedes)
pres. part.	**cayendo**
past part.	**caído**

53. decir[1]

pres. indic.	**digo, dices, dice,** decimos, decís, **dicen**
pres. subj.	**diga, digas, diga, digamos, digáis, digan**
pret. indic.	**dije, dijiste, dijo, dijimos, dijisteis, dijeron**
imp. subj.	**dijera, dijeras, dijera, dijéramos, dijerais, dijeran,** or **dijese, dijeses, dijese, dijésemos, dijeseis, dijesen**
fut. indic.	**diré, dirás, dirá, diremos, diréis, dirán**
cond.	**diría, dirías, diría, diríamos, diríais, dirían**
imper.	**di** (tú), **diga** (usted), **digamos** (nosotros), decid (vosotros), **digan** (ustedes)
pres. part.	**diciendo**
past part.	**dicho**

54. hacer

pres. indic.	**hago,** haces, hace, hacemos, hacéis, hacen
pres. subj.	**haga, hagas, haga, hagamos, hagáis, hagan**
pret. indic.	**hice, hiciste, hizo, hicimos, hicisteis, hicieron**
imp. subj.	**hiciera, hicieras, hiciera, hiciéramos, hicierais, hicieran,** or **hiciese, hicieses, hiciese, hiciésemos, hicieseis, hiciesen**
fut. indic.	**haré, harás, hará, haremos, haréis, harán**
cond.	**haría, harías, haría, haríamos, haríais, harían**
imper.	**haz** (tú), **haga** (usted), **hagamos** (nosotros), haced (vosotros), **hagan** (ustedes)
past part.	**hecho**

55. oír

pres. indic.	**oigo, oyes, oye,** oímos, oís, **oyen**
pres. subj.	**oiga, oigas, oiga, oigamos, oigáis, oigan**
pret. indic.	oí, oíste, **oyó,** oímos, oísteis, **oyeron**

---

1. The compound verbs of *decir* have the same irregularities with the exception of the following: The future and conditional forms of the compound verbs *contradecir, desdecir,* and *predecir* are used interchangeably in both their irregular and regular forms (see 51 **bendecir**). However, their past participles are always irregular (see 74 **Irregular Past Participles**).

imp. subj.	**oyera, oyeras, oyera, oyéramos, oyerais, oyeran,** or **oyese, oyeses, oyese, oyésemos, oyeseis, oyesen**
imper.	**oye** (tú), **oiga** (usted), **oigamos** (nosotros), oíd (vosotros), **oigan** (ustedes)
pres. part.	**oyendo**
past part.	**oído**

56. poner

pres. indic.	**pongo,** pones, pone, ponemos, ponéis, ponen
pres. subj.	**ponga, pongas, ponga, pongamos, pongáis, pongan**
pret. indic.	**puse, pusiste, puso, pusimos, pusisteis, pusieron**
imp. subj.	**pusiera, pusieras, pusiera, pusiéramos, pusierais, pusieran,** or **pusiese, pusieses, pusiese, pusiésemos, pusieseis, pusiesen**
fut. indic.	**pondré, pondrás, pondrá, pondremos, pondréis, pondrán**
cond.	**pondría, pondrías, pondría, pondríamos, pondríais, pondrían**
imper.	**pon** (tú), **ponga** (usted), **pongamos** (nosotros), poned (vosotros), **pongan** (ustedes)
past part.	**puesto**

57. salir

pres. indic.	**salgo,** sales, sale, salimos, salís, salen
pres. subj	**salga, salgas, salga, salgamos, salgáis, salgan**
fut. indic.	**saldré, saldrás, saldrá, saldremos, saldréis, saldrán**
cond.	**saldría, saldrías, saldría, saldríamos, saldríais, saldrían**
imper.	**sal** (tú),[2] **salga** (usted), **salgamos** (nosotros), salid (vosotros), **salgan** (ustedes)

58. tener

pres. indic.	**tengo, tienes, tiene,** tenemos, tenéis, **tienen**
pres. subj.	**tenga, tengas, tenga, tengamos, tengáis, tengan**
pret. indic.	**tuve, tuviste, tuvo, tuvimos, tuvisteis, tuvieron**
imp. subj.	**tuviera, tuvieras, tuviera, tuviéramos, tuvierais, tuvieran,** or **tuviese, tuvieses, tuviese, tuviésemos, tuvieseis, tuviesen**
fut. indic.	**tendré, tendrás, tendrá, tendremos, tendréis, tendrán**

2. The compound *sobresalir* is regular in the familiar imperative: *sobresale.*

cond.	**tendría, tendrías, tendría, tendríamos, tendríais, tendrían**
imper.	**ten** (tú), **tenga** (usted), **tengamos** (nosotros), tened (vosotros), **tengan** (ustedes)

59. **traer**

pres. indic.	**traigo,** traes, trae, traemos, traéis, traen
pres. subj.	**traiga, traigas, traiga, traigamos, traigáis, traigan**
pret. indic.	**traje, trajiste, trajo, trajimos, trajisteis, trajeron**
imp. subj.	**trajera, trajeras, trajera, trajéramos, trajerais, trajeran,** or **trajese, trajeses, trajese, trajésemos, trajeseis, trajesen**
imper.	trae (tú), **traiga** (usted), **traigamos** (nosotros), traed (vosotros), **traigan** (ustedes)
pres. part.	**trayendo**
past part.	**traído**

60. **valer**

pres. indic.	**valgo,** vales, vale, valemos, valéis, valen
pres. subj.	**valga, valgas, valga, valgamos, valgáis, valgan**
fut. indic.	**valdré, valdrás, valdrá, valdremos, valdréis, valdrán**
cond.	**valdría, valdrías, valdría, valdríamos, valdríais, valdrían**
imper.	**val** or vale (tú), **valga** (usted), **valgamos** (nosotros), valed (vosotros), **valgan** (ustedes)

61. **venir**

pres. indic.	**vengo, vienes, viene,** venimos, venís, **vienen**
pres. subj.	**venga, vengas, venga, vengamos, vengáis, vengan**
pret. indic.	**vine, viniste, vino, vinimos, vinisteis, vinieron**
imp. subj.	**viniera, vinieras, viniera, viniéramos, vinierais, vinieran,** or **viniese, vinieses, viniese, viniésemos, vinieseis, viniesen**
fut. indic.	**vendré, vendrás, vendrá, vendremos, vendréis, vendrán**
cond.	**vendría, vendrías, vendría, vendríamos, vendríais, vendrían**
imper.	**ven** (tú), **venga** (usted), **vengamos** (nosotros), venid (vosotros), **vengan** (ustedes)
pres. part.	**viniendo**

62. **dar**

pres. indic.	**doy,** das, da, damos, dais, dan

pres. subj.	**dé,** des, **dé,** demos, deis, den
pret. indic.	**di, diste, dio, dimos, disteis, dieron**
imp. subj.	**diera, dieras, diera, diéramos, dierais, dieran,** or **diese, dieses, diese, diésemos, dieseis, diesen**
imper.	da (tú), **dé** (usted), demos (nosotros), dad (vosotros), den (ustedes)

63. estar

pres. indic.	**estoy, estás, está,** estamos, estáis, **están**
pres. subj.	**esté, estés, esté,** estemos, estéis, **estén**
pret. indic.	**estuve, estuviste, estuvo, estuvimos, estuvisteis, estuvieron**
imp. subj.	**estuviera, estuvieras, estuviera, estuviéramos, estuvierais, estuvieran,** or **estuviese, estuvieses, estuviese, estuviésemos, estuvieseis, estuviesen**
imper.	**está** (tú), **esté** (usted), estemos (nosotros), estad (vosotros), **estén** (ustedes)

64. ir

pres. indic.	**voy, vas, va, vamos, vais, van**
pres. subj.	**vaya, vayas, vaya, vayamos, vayáis, vayan**
imp. indic.	**iba, ibas, iba, íbamos, ibais, iban**
pret. indic.	**fui, fuiste, fue, fuimos, fuisteis, fueron**
imp. subj.	**fuera, fueras, fuera, fuéramos, fuerais, fueran,** or **fuese, fueses, fuese, fuésemos, fueseis, fuesen**
imper.	**ve** (tú), **vaya** (usted), **vayamos** (nosotros), id (vosotros), **vayan** (ustedes)
pres. part.	**yendo**

65. ser

pres. indic.	**soy, eres, es, somos, sois, son**
pres. subj.	**sea, seas, sea, seamos, seáis, sean**
imp. indic.	**era, eras, era, éramos, erais, eran**
pret. indic.	**fui, fuiste, fue, fuimos, fuisteis, fueron**
imp. subj.	**fuera, fueras, fuera, fuéramos, fuerais, fueran,** or **fuese, fueses, fuese, fuésemos, fueseis, fuesen**
imper.	**sé** (tú), **sea** (usted), **seamos** (nosotros), sed (vosotros), **sean** (ustedes)

66. andar

pret. indic.	**anduve, anduviste, anduvo, anduvimos, anduvisteis, anduvieron**

imp. subj.   **anduviera, anduvieras, anduviera,**
anduviéramos, anduvierais, anduvieran, or
anduviese, anduvieses, anduviese,
anduviésemos, anduvieseis, anduviesen

67. **caber**

pres. indic.   **quepo,** cabes, cabe, cabemos, cabéis, caben

pres. subj.   **quepa, quepas, quepa, quepamos, quepáis,**
quepan

pret. indic.   **cupe, cupiste, cupo, cupimos, cupisteis, cupieron**

imp. subj.   **cupiera, cupieras, cupiera, cupiéramos,**
cupierais, cupieran, or **cupiese, cupieses, cupiese,**
cupiésemos, cupieseis, cupiesen

fut. indic.   **cabré, cabrás, cabrá, cabremos, cabréis, cabrán**

cond.   **cabría, cabrías, cabría, cabríamos, cabríais,**
cabrían

imper.   cabe (tú), **quepa** (usted), **quepamos** (nosotros), cabed
(vosotros), **quepan** (ustedes)

68. **haber**

pres. indic.   **he, has, ha, hemos,** habéis, **han**

pres. subj.   **haya, hayas, haya, hayamos, hayáis, hayan**

pret. indic.   **hube, hubiste, hubo, hubimos, hubisteis,**
hubieron

imp. subj.   **hubiera, hubieras, hubiera, hubiéramos,**
hubierais, hubieran, or **hubiese, hubieses,**
hubiese, hubiésemos, hubieseis, hubiesen

fut. indic.   **habré, habrás, habrá, habremos, habréis, habrán**

cond.   **habría, habrías, habría, habríamos, habríais,**
habrían

69. **poder**

pres. indic.   **puedo, puedes, puede,** podemos, podéis, **pueden**

pres. subj.   **pueda, puedas, pueda,** podamos, podáis, **puedan**

pret. indic.   **pude, pudiste, pudo, pudimos, pudisteis,**
pudieron

imp. subj.   **pudiera, pudieras, pudiera, pudiéramos,**
pudierais, pudieran, or **pudiese, pudieses,**
pudiese, pudiésemos, pudieseis, pudiesen

fut. indic.   **podré, podrás, podrá, podremos, podréis, podrán**

cond.   **podría, podrías, podría, podríamos, podríais,**
podrían

pres. part.   **pudiendo**

70. **querer**

pres. indic.	**quiero, quieres, quiere,** queremos, queréis, **quieren**
pres. subj.	**quiera, quieras, quiera,** queramos, queráis, **quieran**
pret. indic.	**quise, quisiste, quiso, quisimos, quisisteis, quisieron**
imp. subj.	**quisiera, quisieras, quisiera, quisiéramos, quisierais, quisieran,** or **quisiese, quisieses, quisiese, quisiémos, quisieseis, quisiesen**
fut. indic.	**querré, querrás, querrá, querremos, querréis, querrán**
cond.	**querría, querrías, querría, querríamos, querríais, querrían**
imper.	**quiere** (tú), **quiera** (usted), queramos (nosotros), quered (vosotros), **quieran** (ustedes)

71. **saber**

pres. indic.	**sé,** sabes, sabe, sabemos, sabéis, saben
pres. subj.	**sepa, sepas, sepa, sepamos, sepáis, sepan**
pret. indic.	**supe, supiste, supo, supimos, supisteis, supieron**
imp. subj.	**supiera, supieras, supiera, supiéramos, supierais, supieran,** or **supiese, supieses, supiese, supiésemos, supieseis, supiesen**
fut. indic.	**sabré, sabrás, sabrá, sabremos, sabréis, sabrán**
cond.	**sabría, sabrías, sabría, sabríamos, sabríais, sabrían**
imper.	sabe (tú), **sepa** (usted), **sepamos** (nosotros), sabed (vosotros), **sepan** (ustedes)

72. **ver**[3]

pres. indic.	**veo,** ves, ve, vemos, veis, ven
pres. subj.	**vea, veas, vea, veamos, veáis, vean**
pret. indic.	**vi, viste, vio, vimos, visteis, vieron**
imp. indic.	**veía, veías, veía, veíamos, veíais, veían**
imp. subj.	**viera, vieras, viera, viéramos, vierais, vieran** or **viese, vieses, viese, viésemos, vieseis, viesen**
imper.	ve (tú), **vea** (usted), **veamos** (nosotros), ved (vosotros), **vean** (ustedes)
past part.	**visto**

---

3. The verb *prever* differs orthographically in the second- and third-person forms of the present indicative (*prevés, prevéis, prevé, prevén*), the first- and third-person singular forms of the preterit indicative (*preví, previó*), and the familiar imperative form (*prevé*).

73. Defective Verbs

The following verbs are used only in the forms that have an **i** in the ending: **abolir, agredir, aterirse, empedernirse, transgredir.**

The verb **atañer** is used only in the third person, most frequently in the present indicative: atañe, atañen.

The verb **concernir** is used only in the third person of the following tenses:

pres. indic.	**concierne, conciernen**
pres. subj.	**concierna, conciernan**
imp. indic.	concernía, concernían
imp. subj.	concerniera *or* concerniese, concernieran *or* concerniesen
fut. indic	concernirá, concernirán
cond.	concerniría, concernirían

The verb **roer** (also **corroer**) has three forms in the first person of the present indicative: **roo, royo, roigo,** all of which are infrequently used. In the present subjunctive the preferable form is **roa, roas, roa,** etc., although the forms **roya** and **roiga** are found.

The verb **soler** is used most frequently in the present and imperfect indicative. It is less frequently used in the present subjunctive.

pres. indic.	**suelo, sueles, suele,** solemos, soléis, **suelen**
pres. subj.	**suela, suelas, suela,** solamos, soláis, **suelan**
imp. indic.	solía, solías, solía, solíamos, solíais, solían

74. Additional Irregular Past Participles
absolver—**absuelto**
abrir—**abierto**
anteponer—**antepuesto**
circunscribir—**circunscrito**
componer—**compuesto**
contradecir—**contradicho**
cubrir—**cubierto**
decir—**dicho**
deponer—**depuesto**
descomponer—**descompuesto**
describir—**descrito**
descubrir—**descubierto**
desdecir—**desdicho**
desenvolver—**desenvuelto**
deshacer—**deshecho**
devolver—**devuelto**
disolver—**disuelto**

disponer—**dispuesto**
encubrir—**encubierto**
entreabrir—**entreabierto**
entrever—**entrevisto**
envolver—**envuelto**
escribir—**escrito**
exponer—**expuesto**
freír—**frito** (often regular, **freído**)
hacer—**hecho**
imponer—**impuesto**
imprimir—**impreso** (often regular, **imprimido**)
indisponer—**indispuesto**
inscribir—**inscrito**
interponer—**interpuesto**
morir—**muerto**
oponer—**opuesto**
poner—**puesto**
posponer—**pospuesto**
predecir—**predicho**
predisponer—**predispuesto**
prescribir—**prescrito**
presuponer—**presupuesto**
prever—**previsto**
proponer—**propuesto**
proscribir—**proscrito**
proveer—**provisto** (often regular, **proveído**)
pudrir—**podrido**
reabrir—**reabierto**
recubrir—**recubierto**
reescribir—**reescrito**
rehacer—**rehecho**
reponer—**repuesto**
resolver—**resuelto**
revolver—**revuelto**
romper—**roto**
satisfacer—**satisfecho**
sobreponer—**sobrepuesto**
suscribir—**suscrito**
superponer—**superpuesto**
suponer—**supuesto**
transcribir—**transcrito**
trasponer—**traspuesto**
ver—**visto**
volver—**vuelto**
yuxtaponer—**yuxtapuesto**

Aa

a PREP **voy — Londres** I'm going to London; **te lo doy — ti** I'm giving it to you; **se sentó — la sombra** she sat down in the shade; **tumbarse —l sol** to lie down in the sun; **una soga —l cuello** a rope around his neck; **lo miraba — la luz de una vela** she looked at him by the light of a candle; **— dos pesetas cada uno** at two pesetas each; **— las tres y media** at three-thirty; **sentarse — la mesa** to sit down at the table; **prestar dinero —l 15%** to lend money at 15%; **en grupos de — cinco** in groups of five; **cocina — gas** gas cooker; **fotos — todo color** full-color photos; **nadie le gana — testaruda** no one touches her for stubbornness; **terminaron — puñetazos** they ended up fighting; **¡— jugar!** let's play! **¿— qué vienen?** what are they coming for? **veo — mi mamá** I see my mother

AA [Alcohólicos Anónimos] F AA

abacá M manila

abad -esa M abbot; F abbess

abadejo M cod

abadía F abbey

abajo ADV (dirección) down; (posición relativa) below; **mirar para —** to look down; **el piso de —** the apartment below; **véase —** see below; **— de** under, underneath; **Stefan está — del coche** Stefan is under/ underneath the car; **¡— el rey!** down with the king! **— firmante** undersigned; **echar —** to knock down; **río —** downstream; **venirse —** to go to ruin

abalanzarse[47] VI **— sobre** to lunge at, to swoop down upon

abanderado -da MF standard-bearer

abandonado ADJ abandoned; **es una persona muy abandonada** she's very unkempt

abandonar VT (a una persona, a una familia) to leave, to desert; (el hogar, un partido) to abandon; (una competencia, el poder) to give up; (una competencia, a un enamorado, el hábito de fumar) to quit; (en los naipes) to fold; (un curso) to drop out of

abandono M (descuido) neglect; (acción de abandonar, condición de abandonado) abandonment; **— de funciones** dereliction of duties

abanicar[30] VT (contra el calor) to fan; (en béisbol) to swing and miss

abanico M (accesorio) fan; (rango) array; (en béisbol) swing and a miss; **abrirse en —** to fan out

abaratar VT (bajar el precio) to lower the price of; (desprestigiar) to cheapen

abarcar[30] VT (categorías) to embrace, to encompass; (tiempo) to span

abarrotería F Méx grocery store

abarrotero -ra MF Méx grocer

abarrotes M PL Méx groceries; **tienda de —** Méx grocery store

abastecedor -ora MF supplier

abastecer[35] VT (un ejército, una ciudad) to supply; (una tienda) to stock

abastecimiento M supply

abasto M supply; **mercado de —s** farmers' market; **yo sola no doy —** I can't cope alone

abatido ADJ dejected, despondent, downcast

abatimiento M dejection, despondency

abatir VT (bajar) to lower; (derribar) to knock down; (desanimar) to depress; (matar a tiros) to shoot; **—se** to swoop down

abdicar[30] VI/VT to abdicate

abdomen M abdomen

abdominal ADJ abdominal; M sit-up

abecedario M alphabet

abedul M birch

abeja F bee; **— asesina** killer bee

abejón M bumblebee

abejorro M bumblebee

aberración F aberration

abertura F (acción) opening; (cualidad) openness

abeto M fir

abierto ADJ (no cerrado, no determinado, destapado) open; (franco) frank; **— de par en par** wide open

abierto ver abrir

abigarrado ADJ motley

abigeato M cattle rustling

abismal ADJ abysmal

abismo M abyss, chasm; **— generacional** generation gap

ablandar VT to soften

abnegación F self-denial

abobado ADJ silly

abocar[30] VI to turn onto; **—se a** to devote oneself to

abochornar VT (avergonzar) to embarrass; **—se** to become embarrassed

abocinar VT to flare

abofetear VT to slap

abogacía F legal profession; **estudiar —** to study law

abogado -da MF lawyer, attorney; **— tributarista** tax attorney, tax lawyer

abogar[40] VI **— por** to advocate, to plead for

abolengo M ancestry

abolición F abolition

abolir[73] VT to abolish

abollado ADJ dented

abolladura F dent

abollar VT to dent; —**se** to become dented
abolsarse VI to sag
abombar VT to make bulge
abominable ADJ abominable, loathsome
abominación F abomination
abominar VI to detest
abonado -da MF subscriber
abonar VT (suscribir) to subscribe; (pagar) to make a payment; (poner fertilizante) to fertilize; —**se** to subscribe; — **a una cuenta** credit an account
abono M (a una revista) subscription; (para una temporada deportiva) season ticket; (de autobús) pass; (para la tierra) fertilizer; (de dinero) payment
abordar VT (un avión, un buque) to board; (un problema) to tackle, to approach; (a una persona) to accost
aborigen ADJ aboriginal; MF native inhabitant; — **australiano** Australian aborigine
aborrascarse[30] VI to become stormy
aborrecer[35] VT to abhor, to loathe
aborrecible ADJ hateful, abhorrent
aborrecimiento M abhorrence
abortador -ora MF abortionist
abortar VI (naturalmente) to miscarry, to have a miscarriage; VI/VT (intencionadamente) to abort
abortero -ra MF abortionist
aborto M (espontáneo) miscarriage; (provocado) abortion; — **espontáneo** spontaneous abortion
abotargarse[40] VI to bloat
abotonar VT to button; —**se** to button up
abovedar VT (una iglesia) to vault, to cover with a vault; (una calle) to arch, to cover as a vault
abozalar VT to muzzle
abracadabra M abracadabra
abrasador ADJ burning
abrasar VT to burn; —**se** to be consumed
abrasión F abrasion; — **cutánea** dermabrasion
abrasivo ADJ abrasive
abrazadera F clamp
abrazar[47] VT (rodear con los brazos) to hug, to embrace; (rodear una cosa sujetando) to clasp; (una opinión) to espouse
abrazo M hug, embrace
abrevadero M trough
abrevar VT (dar de beber) to water; (beber) to drink
abreviación F abbreviation
abreviar VT to abbreviate, to abridge
abreviatura F abbreviation
abridor M opener
abrigado ADJ (ropa) warm; (lugar) sheltered
abrigar[40] VT (refugiados) to shelter; (emociones) to harbor; —**se** to bundle up
abrigo M (refugio) shelter; (prenda de vestir) coat, wrap; — **impositivo** tax shelter

abril M April
abrillantar VT to make shiny
abrir[74] VI/VT (una puerta) to open; VT (un candado) to unlock; (un grifo) to turn on; — **el apetito** to whet one's appetite; — **la sesión** call a meeting to order; — **paso** to make way; M SG **abrebotellas** bottle opener; M SG **abrelatas** can opener; VI (el cielo) to clear up; —**se** to open up; —**se paso** to press through; **en un — y cerrar de ojos** in the twinkle of an eye
abrochar VT to fasten; —**se** to buckle [up]
abrogación F repeal
abrogar[40] VT to repeal
abrojo M bur, sticker
abrumador ADJ overwhelming, overpowering
abrumar VT to overwhelm, to weigh down; —**se** to become foggy
abrupto ADJ abrupt
absceso M abscess
absolución F acquittal
absolutamente ADV, INTERJ absolutely
absoluto ADJ absolute; **en —** absolutely not
absolver[6,74] VT to absolve, to acquit
absorbente ADJ absorbent
absorber VT to absorb
absorción F absorption
absorto ADJ absorbed, engrossed
abstemio -mia ADJ abstemious; MF teetotaler
abstención F abstention
abstenerse[58] VI to abstain; — **de** to abstain from, to refrain from, to forego
abstinencia F abstinence
abstracción F abstraction
abstracto ADJ abstract
abstraer[59] VT to abstract
abstraído ADJ lost in thought
absurdo ADJ absurd, preposterous; M absurdity
abuchear VI/VT to boo, to jeer
abucheo M boo, jeer
abuelo -la M grandfather; F grandmother; —**s** grandparents
abulia F apathy
abultado ADJ bulgy
abultar VI to bulge
abundancia F abundance, plenty
abundante ADJ abundant, plentiful
abundar VI to abound; — **en** to abound in
aburrido ADJ (sin entretenimiento) bored; (pesado) boring, tiresome
aburrimiento M boredom
aburrir VT to bore; —**se** to become bored
abusar VT — **de** to abuse; (sexualmente) to molest
abuso M abuse; — **conyugal** spousal abuse; — **de confianza** breach of trust; — **de drogas** drug abuse; — **de sustancias** substance abuse
abyecto ADJ abject

acá ADV (en este lugar) here; (hacia este lugar) over here, *lit* hither; — **y allá** here and there
acabado ADJ finished; M finish
acabar VT to finish; VI to end; (llegar al orgasmo) *vulg* to come; — **de comer** to have just eaten; — **por** to end up by; — **con** (la corrupción) to put an end to; (las cucarachas) to get rid of; **él y yo hemos acabado** he and I are through; **se acabaron los dulces** the candy is all gone; **se nos acabaron las ideas** we ran out of ideas; **y se acabó** and that's that
academia F (corporación, escuela militar) academy; (centro privado de enseñanza) private school
académico ADJ academic
acallar VT to silence, to quiet
acalorado ADJ heated
acaloramiento M **sufrió un** — he got too hot
acalorarse VI/VT (sofocarse) to overheat; (emocionarse) to get excited
acampada F camping trip
acampante MF camper
acampar VT to camp
acanalar VT to groove
acantilado ADJ sheer, steep; M bluff, cliff
acantonarse VT to be quartered
acaparar VT (productos) to hoard; (atención) to capture; (monopolizar) *fam* to hog; — **el mercado** to corner the market
acaramelar VT to candy
acariciar VT to caress; — **una esperanza** to harbor a hope
ácaro M mite
acarrear VT (transportar) to transport; (transportar en carro) to cart; (ocasionar) to bring about
acarreo M transport
acaso ADV perhaps; **por si** — just in case
acatamiento M compliance
acatar VT to abide by, to comply with
acatarrar VI to chill; —**se** to catch cold
acaudalado ADJ wealthy
acceder VI — **a** (un pedido) to accede to; VI (una invitación) to accept
accesibilidad F accessibility
accesible ADJ accessible, convenient
acceso M (entrada) access; (de ira) fit; — **a internet** Internet access; — **denegado** access denied; — **remoto** remote access, remote login; **de** — **prohibido** off limits
accesorio ADJ & M accessory
accidentado -da ADJ (viaje) eventful; (terreno) uneven; MF accident victim
accidental ADJ accidental
accidentarse VI to have an accident
accidente M (suceso imprevisto) accident; (del terreno) feature; (automovilístico) wreck; — **de tránsito** traffic accident; **por** — by accident

acción F (acto) action; (valor de bolsa) share of stock; — **de gracias** thanksgiving; **buenas acciones** good deeds; **acciones preferenciales** preferred stock; **acciones ordinarias** common stock
accionable ADJ actionable
accionar VT to operate
accionista MF shareholder, stockholder
acebo M holly
acechar VT (emboscar) to lie in ambush; (amenazar) to stalk
acecho M **rondar en** — to prowl; **estar al** — to lie in wait
aceitar VT to oil
aceite M oil; — **de linaza** linseed oil; — **de oliva** olive oil; — **de ricino** castor oil; — **vegetal** vegetable oil
aceitera F (recipiente) oilcan; (fábrica) oil factory
aceitoso ADJ oily
aceituna F olive
aceleración F acceleration
acelerador M accelerator
acelerar VT to accelerate, to speed up; VI to accelerate, to step on the gas; — **en vacío** to rev, to race; —**se** *Am* to get nervous
acémila F pack animal
acento M (pronunciación, signo) accent; (intensidad mayor, de voz) stress
acentuar[26] VT (aumentar) to accentuate; (poner tilde) to accent; (reforzar la voz) to stress; —**se** to accentuate
acepción F gloss, meaning
aceptable ADJ acceptable
aceptación F acceptance
aceptar VT to accept; — **entrega** to take delivery
acequia F irrigation ditch
acera F sidewalk
acerado ADJ made of steel
acerar VT to steel
acerca PREP — **de** about, concerning
acercamiento M approach
acercar[30] VT to bring near; **os acerco a la estación** I'll give you a ride to the station; —**se** to come near, to approach
acería F steel mill
acero M steel; — **inoxidable** stainless steel
acérrimo ADJ bitter
acertado ADJ right
acertar[1] VT to hit; VI to be right; — **con** to hit upon; — **a pasar** to happen to go by; **no** — to miss the mark
acertijo M riddle, conundrum
acervo M heritage
acetaminofén M acetaminophen
acetona F acetone
achacar[30] VI to blame
achacoso ADJ infirm, ailing

achaparrado ADJ (planta) stunted; (persona) squat

achaque M affliction, ailment; —**s** aches and pains

achicado ADJ weak-kneed

achicar[30] VT (de tamaño) to make small; (un vestido) to take in; (agua) to bail; —**se** (acobardarse) to feel intimidated; (empequeñecerse) to get smaller

achicoria F chicory

aciago ADJ unlucky

acicalado ADJ clean-cut

acicalarse VI to dress up

acicate M incentive

acidez F (de una solución) acidity; (del vinagre) sourness; — **de estómago** heartburn

ácido M acid; —**s grasos** fatty acids; ADJ (propio del ácido) acidic; (fruta) sour, tart

acierto M (contestación) right answer; (elección) felicitous choice

aclamación F acclamation, acclaim; **por** — by acclamation

aclamar VT to acclaim, to hail

aclaración F clarification

aclarar VT (con explicaciones) to clarify; (con agua) to rinse; (la voz) to clear; VI to dawn; **aclaró después de la tormenta** it cleared up after the storm; —**se** to lighten

aclimatar VT to acclimate

acné M acne

acobardar VT to intimidate

acogedor ADJ (persona) hospitable; (cuarto) cozy

acoger[45] VT (una sugerencia) to receive; (a un refugiado) to shelter; —**se** to take refuge; —**se a la ley** to have recourse to the law

acogida F reception

acogimiento M reception

acolchar VT to pad

acollarar VT to collar

acometer VT (atacar) to attack; (emprender) to undertake

acometida F attack

acomodado ADJ well-off

acomodador -ora MF usher

acomodar VT (arreglar) to arrange; (ajustar) to adjust; (adaptar) to adapt; —**se** (ponerse cómodo) to make oneself comfortable; (adaptarse) to adapt oneself

acomodo M position; **no tengo** — I can't find a comfortable position

acompañamiento M (acción, música) accompaniment; (grupo de personas que acompaña) retinue; (comida) side dish; (tenis) follow-through

acompañante ADJ accompanying; MF (compañero) companion; (en música) accompanist

acompañar VI/VT to accompany (también en música); (escoltar) to escort; (en una carta) to enclose; —**se de** to be accompanied by; **esperemos que el tiempo acompañe** let's hope the weather cooperates; **te acompaño en el sentimiento** my thoughts are with you

acompasado ADJ (rítmico) rhythmical; (mesurado) measured

acomplejado ADJ self-conscious

acondicionar VT to prepare

acongojado ADJ grief-stricken

acongojar VT to distress; —**se** to become distressed

aconsejable ADJ advisable

aconsejar VT to advise, to counsel

acontecer[35] VI to take place

acontecimiento M event; **todo un** — quite a happening; **a esta altura de los** —**s** at this point in the proceedings

acopiar VT to stockpile

acopio M (acción de guardar) storing; (cosas guardadas) stockpile

acoplamiento M coupling; — **universal de cardán** universal joint

acoplar VT to couple; —**se** (piezas complementarias, partes) to couple, to join; (altavoces) to have feedback

acople M coupling, connection

acorazado ADJ armored; M battleship, warship

acorazar[47] VT to armor

acordado VI agreed-upon

acordar[5] VT to agree; VI — **en** to arrange to; —**se [de]** to remember

acorde M chord; ADJ in agreement; **en** — **con** in agreement with

acordeón M accordion

acordonar VT (un zapato) to lace; (un lugar) to rope off, to seal off; (una moneda) to mill

acorralar VT (meter en un corral) to corral; (arrinconar) to corner

acortamiento M shortening

acortar VT to shorten

acosar VT (perseguir) to harry; (atacar) to beset; (atormentar) to badger; (importunar sexualmente) to harass

acoso M (de presa) hunting down, pursuit; (de una persona) harassment, hounding

acostar[5] VT to put to bed; —**se** to go to bed; —**se con** to sleep with

acostumbrado ADJ (normal) accustomed; (habitual) customary; **estar** — **a** to be used / accustomed to

acostumbrar VT to accustom; (soler) to be accustomed to; —**se [a]** to get accustomed [to]; **acostumbraban ir al teatro** they used to go to the theater

acotación F (anotación) marginal note; (en una obra de teatro) stage directions

acotar VT (un terreno) to mark off; (un texto) to

make marginal notes on
acre ADJ acrid, pungent, sharp; M acre
acrecentamiento M growth, increase
acrecentar[1] VT to grow; — **se** to grow
acreditar VT (una cuenta) to credit; (a un
profesional) to accredit; — **a una cuenta** to
credit an account; **a quien pueda — ser el
dueño de** to whoever can prove to be the
owner of
acreedor -ora ADJ deserving; **saldo** — positive
balance; MF creditor
acribillar VI (a balazos) to riddle [with]; (a
pedradas) to pelt
acrílico ADJ & M acrylic
acritud F acrimony
acrobacia F (arte) acrobatics; (pirueta) stunt
acróbata MF acrobat
acrobático ADJ acrobatic
acrofobia F acrophobia
acrónimo M acronym
acta F (de nacimiento) certificate; (de una
reunión) minutes; (de un congreso)
proceedings
actitud F attitude, mind-set
activar VT to activate
actividad F activity
activismo M activism
activista MF activist
activo ADJ active; **en** — working; M assets; —
líquido liquid assets; — **convertible**
convertible assets
acto M (solemne, sexual, dramático) act; (acción)
action; — **seguido** immediately after; —
fallido Freudian slip; **en el** — on the spot;
hacer — de presencia to show up
actor M actor, performer; — **de carácter**
character actor
actriz F actor, actress, performer
actuación F (acción) acting; (rendimiento,
desempeño) performance
actual ADJ current, present
actualidad F present time; —**es** latest news; **de**
— up-to-date
actualización F (de información) update; (de
ordenador) upgrade
actualizado ADJ (al día) up-to-date; (al minuto)
up-to-the-minute
actualizar[47] VT to update; (programa de
ordenador) to upgrade; (pantalla de
ordenador) to refresh
actualmente ADV presently, currently
actuar[26] VI (comportarse) to act; (dar una
representación) to perform
actuario -ria MF (judicial) clerk; (de seguros)
actuary
acuarela F watercolor
acuario M aquarium
acuartelar VT to quarter
acuático ADJ aquatic

acuchillar VT (penetrar) to stab; (cortar) to slash
acuclillado ADJ squatting
acuclillarse VI to squat
acudir VI (ir) to go; (asistir) to attend; — **a** to
turn to; — **al llamado** to respond to the call;
— **al socorro de** to go to the rescue of; — **en
masa** to flock
acueducto M aqueduct
acuerda, acuerde ver acordar
acuerdo M agreement; — **comercial** trade
agreement; — **contractual** contractual
agreement; — **global** package deal
agreement; **estar de** — to be in agreement;
ponerse de — to come to an agreement; **de**
— **con** in accordance with
acumulación F (de dinero) accumulation; (de
tensión) buildup
acumulador M storage battery
acumular VT (desperdicios) to accumulate;
(fortuna) to amass; (deudas) to accumulate, to
run up; —**se** to collect; **rabia acumulada**
pent-up rage
acumulativo ADJ cumulative
acuñación F coinage, minting
acuñar VT (monedas, una expresión) to coin;
(meter cuñas) to wedge
acuoso ADJ watery
acupuntor -ora MF acupuncturist
acupuntura F acupuncture
acurrucarse[30] VI to nestle, to huddle
acusación F accusation, charge
acusado -da MF accused; (en un juicio)
defendant
acusador -ora MF accuser
acusar VT (culpabilizar) to accuse; (detectar) to
detect; (revelar) to betray; (entre niños) to
tattle, to tell; — **el golpe** to feel the blow; —
recibo to acknowledge receipt
acuse M acknowledgment
acusetas MF SG tattletale
acusica MF tattletale
acústica F acoustics
acústico ADJ acoustic
adagio M adage
adaptabilidad F resilience, adaptability
adaptación F adaptation
adaptador M adapter
adaptar VT to adapt
adecuado ADJ appropriate
adecuar VT to adapt; —**se a** to be suitable for
adefesio M sight, hideous thing
adelantado ADJ (economía, alumno) advanced;
(reloj) fast; (tren) ahead of time, ahead of
schedule; **por** — in advance
adelantamiento M (de una fecha) bringing
forward; (de un coche) overtaking
adelantar VT (una fecha, dinero) to advance; (la
mano) to move forward; (un coche) to pass;
(una noticia) to have a scoop; VI (un reloj) to

gain; — **en** to make progress in; —**se** (sacar ventaja) to get ahead; (actuar antes) to go first; (innovar) to be ahead; (hablar antes de tiempo) to get ahead of oneself

adelante ADV forward; — **con los faroles** let's get started; — **de mí** in front of me; **de aquí en** — from now on; **hacia** — forward; **ir** — to go ahead; **más** — later; **sacar** — to make prosper; **seguir** — to go on; INTERJ go for it!

adelanto M (de la ciencia) advance, breakthrough; (de un coche) passing; (pago) advance; **el** — **de los relojes** setting the clocks forward

adelfa F oleander

adelgazar[47] VI to lose weight; VT to lose; (hacer perder peso) to make one lose weight; (hacer menos espeso) to thin; (hacer parecer delgado) to make one look thinner; — **cinco kilos** to lose five kilos; —**se** to get thinner

ademán M gesture; **hacer un** — **a alguien** to motion to someone

además ADV moreover, besides, in addition; — **de deberme dinero** besides / in addition to owing me money

adentrarse VI — **en** (un asunto) to go deeply into; (un lugar) to go deep into, to penetrate into; (una edad) to enter

adentro ADV inside; **ir para/hacia** — to go inside; **hablar para sus** —**s** to talk to oneself; **con lo de** — **para afuera** inside out

aderezar[47] VT (embellecer) to adorn; (condimentar) to season, to garnish

aderezo M (adorno) adornment; (de un alimento) seasoning; (de una ensalada) dressing

adeudar VT (deber) to owe; — **una cuenta** to debit an account

adeudo M (endeudamiento) indebtedness; (a una cuenta) debit

adherencia F adhesion

adherir[8] VI to adhere; —**se a** (una cosa) to stick to; (una huelga) to join; (una idea) to subscribe to

adhesión F (a una cosa) adhesion; (a una doctrina) adherence

adhesivo ADJ adhesive; M (pegamento) cement, adhesive; (calcomanía) sticker

adicción F addiction

adición F addition

adicional ADJ additional

adictivo ADJ addictive, habit-forming

adicto -ta ADJ addicted; MF addict; — **al trabajo** workaholic

adiestramiento M training

adiestrar VT to train

adinerado ADJ wealthy, well-to-do, moneyed

adiós INTERJ good-bye; **hacer** — **con la mano** to wave good-bye

adiposo ADJ fatty

aditivo M additive

adivinanza F riddle

adivinar VT to guess

adivino -na MF fortune-teller

adjetivo ADJ & M adjective

adjudicación F award

adjudicar[30] VT to award; —**se** to be awarded

adjuntar VT (incluir en una carta) to enclose; (añadir) to add, to attach, to append

adjunto ADJ (unido) attached; (incluido) enclosed; (asistente) adjunct; ADV herewith; M attachment

adminículo M gadget

administración F administration, management; — **pública** civil service; — **intermedia** middle management

administrador -ora MF administrator, manager; — **de cuentas** account manager; — **de un sitio web** webmaster

administrar VT (un medicamento) to administer; (una empresa) to administer, to manage; (justicia) to dispense; —**se** to budget

administrativo ADJ administrative

admirable ADJ admirable

admiración F admiration

admirador -ora MF admirer; (de una estrella de cine) fan

admirar VT to admire; —**se** to be amazed; —**se de** to wonder at

admisible ADJ admissible, allowable

admisión F (aceptación) admission; (reconocimiento) acknowledgment

admitir VT (dejar entrar, reconocer) to admit; (aceptar) to accept; (permitir) to allow

ADN [ácido desoxirribonucleico] M DNA

adobar VT (aderezar carne) to season; (curtir una piel) to tan; (encurtir) to pickle

adobe M adobe

adobo M sauce for seasoning

adoctrinar VT to indoctrinate

adolecer[35] VI — **de** to suffer from

adolescencia F adolescence

adolescente ADJ adolescent; MF adolescent, teenager

adonde ADV REL **esa es la casa** — **vamos** that's the house [that] we're going to, that's the house where we're going

adónde ADV INTERR & PRON where

adopción F adoption

adoptar VT to adopt

adoptivo ADJ adoptive

adoquín M cobblestone

adorable ADJ adorable

adoración F (a una persona) adoration; (a un dios) worship

adorador -ora MF worshiper

adorar VT (a una persona) to adore; (a un dios) to worship

adormecer[35] VT (dar sueño) to make drowsy;

(entumecer) to numb; **—se** (de sueño) to become drowsy; (de frío) to go numb

adormilado ADJ sleepy

adornar VT to adorn, to embellish

adorno M adornment, ornament, decoration

adquirir[4] VT (un bien) to acquire; (una característica) to take on

adquisición F (compra) acquisition; (nuevo miembro) addition; (compra de una compañía) takeover

adquisitivo ADJ purchasing

adrede ADV on purpose

adrenalina F adrenaline

aduana F (control) customs; (edificio) customshouse

aduanero -ra ADJ customs; **control —** customs control; MF customs officer

aducir[38] VT to adduce

adueñarse VI to take possession

adulación F flattery

adulador -ora ADJ flattering; MF flatterer

adular VI/VT to flatter

adulón -ona ADJ flattering; MF *fam* brown-noser

adulterar VT to adulterate

adulterio M adultery

adúltero -ra MF adulterer

adulto -ta ADJ & MF adult

adusto ADJ stern

advenedizo ADJ upstart

advenimiento M advent

adverbio M adverb

adversario -ria MF adversary, opponent

adversidad F adversity

adverso ADJ adverse

advertencia F (aviso) notice; (amonestación) warning, admonition

advertir[8] VT (avisar) to warn; (notar) to notice; (notificar) to advise, to tip off

Adviento M Advent

advierta, advierte *ver* advertir

adyacente ADJ adjacent

aéreo ADJ aerial; **correo —** airmail

aeróbico ADJ aerobic

aeróbic M aerobics

aerobio ADJ aerobic

aerodeslizador M hovercraft

aerodinámica F aerodynamics

aerodinámico ADJ aerodynamic, streamlined

aeródromo M airport

aeroespacial ADJ aerospace

aerolínea F airline

aeronáutica F aeronautics

aeronave F aircraft

aeropuerto M airport

aerosol M (suspensión) aerosol; (aparato) spray can

aerotransportado ADJ airborne

aerotransportar VT to airlift

afabilidad F affability, friendliness

afable ADJ affable, friendly

afamado ADJ famed

afán M eagerness

afanar VT *fam* to swipe; VI **—se** to work hard

afanoso ADJ hardworking

afasia F aphasia

afear VT to make ugly; **—se** to become ugly

afección F condition

afectación F affectation

afectado ADJ (dañado, lastimado) affected, stricken; (artificial) affected, unnatural

afectar VT to affect

afecto M affection, fondness; **— a** fond of

afectuoso ADJ affectionate, loving

afeitado -da ADJ clean-shaven; M shave

afeitadora F shaver

afeitar VT to shave

afelpado ADJ & M plush

afeminado ADJ effeminate, sissy

aferrado ADJ stubborn, obstinate

aferrar VT (agarrar) to grasp; (atar) to grapple; **—se** to cling

affaire M affair

Afganistán M Afghanistan

afgano -na ADJ & MF Afghan, Afghani

afianzado ADJ (garantizado) bonded; (apuntalado, amarrado) secured, firmed up

afianzar[47] VT (una pared) to secure; (un préstamo) to secure, to guarantee; (una amistad) to build up

afiche M poster

afición F (inclinación) inclination; (afecto) fondness; (hinchada) fans

aficionado -da ADJ **— a** fond of; MF (no profesional) amateur; (hincha) fan

aficionarse VI **— a** to become fond of

afilado ADJ sharp; M sharpening

afilador -ora MF grinder, sharpener

afilar VT to sharpen, to grind

afiliación F affiliation; **sin — política** nonpartisan

afiliarse VI **— con** to affiliate oneself with

afín ADJ kindred, related

afinación F tune-up

afinado ADJ in tune

afinador -ora MF tuner

afinar VT (una destreza) to perfect; (un plan) to fine-tune; (un piano) to tune; **—se** to become thinner

afinidad F (afecto) affinity; (parentesco) kinship

afirmación F (aseveración) assertion; (aseveración positiva) affirmation

afirmar VT (decir) to assert, to declare; (aseverar) to affirm; (sujetar) to secure; **—se** to steady oneself

afirmativa F affirmative answer

afirmativo ADJ affirmative

aflicción F affliction, woe

afligir[46] VT (dar dolor) to afflict; (entristecer) to distress

aflojar VT (una soga) to slacken, to loosen; (la vigilancia) to relax; — **el dinero** to hand over the money; VI to ease up, to slack off; —**se** to work loose, to loosen up

afluencia F influx

afluente M tributary

afluir[19] VI (río) to flow [into]; (turistas) to flock

afortunadamente ADV fortunately, luckily

afortunado ADJ fortunate, lucky

afrecho M bran

afrenta F affront

afrentar VT to offend

África F Africa

africano -na ADJ & MF African

afroamericano -na ADJ & MF African American

afrodisíaco M aphrodisiac

afrontar VT to face

afuera ADV (de un edificio) outdoors; (de un recipiente) outside; F PL **las** —**s** outskirts

agachar VT to lower; —**se** to crouch, to stoop

agalla F (de pez) gill; (de roble) gallnut; **tener** —**s** to have guts/spunk

agarrado ADJ tight-fisted

agarrar VT (sujetar) to seize, to grasp, to grab; (capturar) to catch; (adherirse) to grip; — **por sorpresa** to catch by surprise; —**le la onda a algo** to get the swing of something; —**se una neumonía** to catch a case of pneumonia; —**se** to hold on; —**se de** to latch onto; **agarré por la calle ocho** I took Eighth Street; **agarró y se fue** he up and went

agarre M (también golf) grip

agarrón M grab

agarrotarse VI (el cuerpo) to stiffen up; (un motor) to seize [up]

agasajar VT to entertain

agasajo M (acogida) welcome; (regalo) gift

agazaparse VI to crouch

agencia F agency, bureau; — **de empleo** employment agency; — **de publicidad** advertising agency; — **de viajes** travel agency; — **gubernamental** government agency

agenciar VT to wrangle

agenda F (cuaderno) daily planner; (orden del día) agenda

agente MF (representante) agent; (espía) operative; — **de policía** police officer; — **de compras** purchasing agent

ágil ADJ agile, nimble

agilidad F agility

agilizar VT to expedite

agitación F (acción de agitar, nerviosismo) agitation; (protesta) turmoil, unrest

agitado ADJ (estado) agitated; (vida) eventful, hectic; (mar) choppy; (sueño) uneasy

agitador -ora M (aparato) agitator; MF (rebelde) agitator, troublemaker

agitar VT (sacudir) to agitate, to shake up; (incitar a la protesta) to agitate; —**se** (ponerse nervioso) to get worked up; (moverse) to thrash around

aglomeración F crowd

aglomerado M particle board

aglomerarse VI to crowd together

agnóstico -ca ADJ & MF agnostic

agobiado ADJ (por los enemigos) embattled; (por el trabajo) overwhelmed

agobiante ADJ overwhelming

agobiar VT (con una carga excesiva) to weigh down; (con trabajo) to overwhelm; (con impuestos) to burden

agolparse VI to crowd together

agonía F throes of death; **ser un** —**s** to be a whiner

agonizante ADJ dying

agonizar[47] VI to be in the throes of death

agorafobia F agoraphobia

agorero -ra ADJ ominous; MF soothsayer

agosto M August; **hacer su** — to make hay while the sun shines

agotado ADJ (persona) worn-out, tired out; (libro) out-of-print; (mercancía) out-of-stock

agotador ADJ exhausting

agotamiento M (de una persona) exhaustion; (de un recurso) depletion

agotar VT (recurso) to exhaust, to use up, to deplete; (energía) to sap; (a una persona) to wear down; —**se** (acabarse) to be all gone; (venderse) to sell out; (secarse) to dry up; (libro) to go out of print

agraciado ADJ attractive

agraciar VT to grace

agradable ADJ (persona) agreeable, pleasant, congenial; (situación) pleasant, enjoyable

agradar VT to please

agradecer[35] VT (dar gracias) to thank; (sentir gratitud) to be grateful for; **se agradece** thank you

agradecido ADJ thankful, grateful

agradecimiento M thankfulness, appreciation; (en un libro) acknowledgment

agradezca, agradezco ver agradecer

agrado M pleasure; **de su** — to his liking

agrandamiento M enlargement

agrandar VT to enlarge

agrario ADJ agrarian

agravar VT to aggravate, to make worse; —**se** to get worse

agraviar VT to outrage

agravio M outrage

agredir[73] VT to assault

agregado -da MF (funcionario de embajada) attaché; (profesor) adjunct; M (mezcla) aggregate

agregar[40] VT to add
agresión F (violencia) aggression; (ataque) assault; — **con lesiones** assault and battery
agresividad F (actitud) aggressiveness; (propensión violenta) aggression
agresivo ADJ aggressive
agresor -ora MF aggressor, assailant
agreste ADJ (recio) rough; (silvestre) wild
agriar[28] VT to make sour; —**se** to go sour
agrícola ADJ agricultural
agricultor -ora MF agriculturist, farmer
agricultura F agriculture, farming
agridulce ADJ (sabor) sweet-and-sour; (memoria) bittersweet
agrietarse VI (cristales) to crack; (los labios) to chap
agrimensor -ora MF surveyor
agrimensura F surveying
agrio ADJ sour
agrisarse VI to gray
agropecuario ADJ agricultural
agrumarse VI to lump
agrupación F group
agrupamiento M grouping
agrupar VT (objetos, personas) to group; (documentos digitales) to queue
agua F water; — **con gas** sparkling water; — **corriente** running water; — **de colonia** cologne; — **de grifo** tap water; — **de manantial** spring water; — **dulce** fresh water; —**marina** aquamarine; — **mineral** mineral water; — **oxigenada** hydrogen peroxide; — **potable** drinking water; — **salada** salt water; —**s abajo** downstream; —**s arriba** upstream; —**s negras** sewer water; **hacer** — *fam* to take a leak; **se me hace** — **la boca** my mouth is watering
aguacate M avocado
aguacero M shower, cloudburst, downpour
aguada F watering hole
aguadero M watering hole
aguado ADJ (fruta) watery; (vino, sopa) watered-down
aguantar VT (miserias) to endure; (a una persona molesta) to bear, to stand; (un peso) to bear; (la respiración) to hold; VI (mantenerse) to stand; (durar) to last; (esperar) to wait; (no pudrirse) to keep; **aguántate** grin and bear it
aguante M (para el trabajo) endurance, stamina; (para el vino) tolerance
aguar[25] VT (añadir agua, despojar de fuerza) to water down; (estropear) to spoil; — **una fiesta** to ruin a party; —**se** to become diluted; MF SG **aguafiestas** killjoy, wet blanket
aguardar VI to wait; VT to wait for, to await
aguardentoso ADJ hoarse
aguardiente M brandy

aguarrás M turpentine
agudeza F (visual) sharpness, keenness; (del ingenio) quickness; (para los negocios) acumen; (dicho agudo) witticism
agudo ADJ (dolor, enfermedad, ángulo) acute; (vista, mente) sharp, keen; (mentón) pointed; (voz) high-pitched; (chiste) witty
agüero M portent, omen; **de mal** — portentous
aguijada F goad
aguijar VT to goad
aguijón M (de planta) spur; (de insecto) sting, stinger
aguijonear VT (a un buey) to goad, to prod; (insecto) to sting
águila F eagle; **es un** — he is sharp
aguilucho M eaglet
aguinaldo M Christmas bonus
aguja F (de coser, tejer, tocadiscos, pino, velocímetro) needle; (de reloj) hand; (riel móvil) railroad switch; (chapitel) steeple, spire; — **de croché** crochet hook; — **de punto** knitting needle; — **de zurcir** darning needle; — **hipodérmica** hypodermic needle; **como una** — **en un pajar** like a needle in a haystack
agujerear VT to pierce
agujero M (orificio) hole; (vacío legal) loophole; (déficit) shortfall; — **negro** black hole; **tapar** —**s** (reparar orificios) to plug holes; (pagar deudas) to pay debts
aguzar[47] VT to sharpen; — **el oído** to prick up one's ears
ahechaduras F PL chaff
ahí ADV there; **por** — over there, thereabouts; **de** — hence; — **te quiero ver** I want to see you in that situation
ahijado -da M godson; F goddaughter
ahínco M **trabajar con** — to work hard
ahogamiento M drowning
ahogar[40] VT (asfixiar en agua) to drown; (inundar con combustible) to flood; (asfixiar por falta de aire) to smother; (reprimir) to stifle; (asfixiar por presión al cuello) to throttle, to strangle, to choke; — **las penas bebiendo** to drown one's sorrows in drink; —**se** (en agua) to drown; (por falta de aire) to asphyxiate
ahogo M (por calor, falta de aire) suffocation; (por un esfuerzo) breathlessness; **vivir sin** —**s** to live a comfortable life
ahondar VT (hoyo) to deepen; (asunto) to dig deeper into; —**se** to become deeper
ahora ADV now; — **bien** now then; — **mismo** right now; — **sí** now we're cooking; **por** — for the present, for now; **hasta** — to date, up to now, so far
ahorcar[30] VT to hang; *fam* to string up
ahorita ADV (ahora mismo) right now; (dentro de poco) in a second

ahorrar VT (dinero) to save; (molestias) to spare
ahorrativo ADJ frugal, thrifty
ahorro M thriftiness; —**s** savings; —**s de toda la vida** life savings
ahuecar[30] VT to hollow out; — **la voz** to speak in a hollow voice
ahumado ADJ smoked; M smoking
ahumar VT to smoke
ahuyentar VT to drive away, to scare away; —**se** to get scared
airado ADJ irate
airarse VI to get angry
airbag M airbag
aire M air; (melodía) tune; (manera de ser) manner; — **acondicionado** air conditioning; — **libre** outdoors; **al** — **libre** outdoors; **andar con el culo al** — to walk around buck naked; **cambiar de** —**s** to change surroundings; **darse** —**s** to posture; **en el** — up in the air; **estar en el** — to be on the air; **tener** — **de** to look like; **tomar** — to breathe in, to get some air
airear VT to air out
airoso ADJ graceful; **salir** — to come out smelling like a rose
aislacionismo M isolationism
aislado ADJ (persona) isolated; (lugar) secluded
aislador M insulator; ADJ insulating
aislamiento M (acción de aislarse) isolation; (cosa que aísla) insulation; (soledad) seclusion
aislante M insulator
aislar[28] VT (separar) to isolate; (envolver) to insulate; (rechazar socialmente) to ostracize
ajar VT (una planta) to wither; (las manos) to make rough; (la piel) to age
ajedrez M chess
ajeno ADJ (de otro) belonging to someone else; (extraño) alien; — **a un peligro** oblivious to a danger; — **a mi voluntad** beyond my control; — **a mi experiencia** foreign to my experience
ajetrearse VI to bustle about
ajetreo M bustle, hustle and bustle
ají M chile
ajo M garlic
ajonjolí M sesame
ajuar M (de novia) trousseau; (mobiliario) furnishings
ajustado ADJ tight, snug; — **a la ley** in accordance with the law
ajustar VT (una prenda) to adjust; (un contrato) to tweak; (una tuerca) to tighten; — **cuentas** to settle accounts; VI to fit tight; —**se a derecho** to be in accordance with the law
ajuste M (de horarios, planes) adjustment; (del cinturón) tightening; (de una máquina) fine-tuning; (de cuentas) settlement; (de una prenda) alteration; **hacer** —**s** to tinker with
ala F (de ave) wing; (de sombrero) brim; (en

fútbol) winger; **cortarle las** —**s a alguien** to clip someone's wings
alabanza F praise
alabar VT to praise
alabeo M warp
alacena F pantry
alacrán M scorpion
alamar M (adorno) frog; (presilla) clasp
alambique M still
alambrada F wire fence
alambrado M (barrera) wire fence; (acción de alambrar) wiring
alambrar VT to wire
alambre M wire; — **de púas** barbed wire
alameda F poplar grove
álamo M poplar tree
alancear VT to wound with a lance, to spear
alano M mastiff
alarde M show; **hacer** — **de** to boast of, to show off
alardear VI — **de** to boast about
alargar[40] VT (hacer más largo) to lengthen; (un brazo, un guiso) to stretch [out]; — **la vista** to peer into the distance; —**se** to go on [longer than expected]
alargue M (fútbol) extra time
alarido M scream, howl
alarma F alarm; — **antirrobo** burglar alarm; — **contra incendios** fire alarm
alarmante ADJ alarming
alarmar VT to alarm
alba F dawn
albacea MF executor
albanés -esa ADJ & MF Albanian
Albania F Albania
albañal M sewer
albañil M mason, bricklayer
albañilería F masonry
albaricoque M apricot
albatros M albatross
alberca F (depósito) reservoir; (piscina) *Méx* swimming pool
albergar[40] VT (refugiar) to shelter; (hospedar) to lodge; (ser sede de) to house; (guardar rencor, un secreto) to harbor; —**se** (protegerse) to take shelter; (alojarse) to lodge
albergue M lodging; **dar** — (a un refugiado) to give refuge; (a un criminal) to harbor
albinismo M albinism
albino -na MF albino
albóndiga F meatball
albor M dawn
alborada F dawn
albornoz M bathrobe
alborotador -ora ADJ rowdy; MF troublemaker
alborotar VT (el pelo) to muss; (la casa) to mess up; (una turba) to rouse; (a los niños) to excite; —**se** to get excited
alboroto M hubbub, fuss

alborozado ADJ joyful
alborozar⁴⁷ VT to gladden; —**se** to rejoice
alborozo M joy
albricias F PL & INTERJ congratulations
álbum M album
alcachofa F artichoke
alcahuete -ta MF (soplón) tattletale; (mediador, encubridor) procurer
alcaide M warden
alcalde -esa MF mayor
alcaldía F (edificio) city hall; (oficio) mayoralty
álcali M alkali
alcalino ADJ alkaline
alcance M (de una persona) reach; (de los deseos) attainment; (de un misil) range; (de una ley) scope; **de corto[s] —[s]** of meager intellect; **al —** at hand, within reach; **a su —** within his reach; **al — del oído** within hearing; **dar — a** to catch up with; **de gran —** far-reaching; **de largo —** long-range
alcancía F piggybank
alcanfor M camphor
alcantarilla F (para agua sucia) sewer; (para lluvias) gully, gutter
alcantarillado M sewage system
alcanzar⁴⁷ VT (llegar, cumplir) to reach; (igualar) to catch up with; (pasar, poner en la mano) to pass; (herir a balazos) to get; **no alcanzo a verlo** I can't quite see it; **no me alcanza el dinero** I don't have enough money; **alcancé a conocer a mi abuela** I was born soon enough to meet my grandmother
alcaparra F caper
alcaucil M artichoke
alcázar M fortress
alce M (europeo, asiático) elk; (norteamericano) moose
alcoba F bedroom
alcohol M alcohol; **— etílico** ethyl alcohol; **— para fricciones** rubbing alcohol
alcohólico -ca ADJ & MF alcoholic
alcoholismo M alcoholism
alcornoque M (árbol) cork tree; (persona) blockhead
alcuza F oilcan
aldaba F (para llamar) knocker; (para cerrar) bolt
aldabón M large knocker
aldea F village, hamlet
aldeano -na MF villager; ADJ **joven aldeana** village girl
aleación F alloy
alear VT (metales) to alloy; VI (aves) to flap wings
aleatorio ADJ random
aleatorizar VT to randomize
aleccionar VT to teach a lesson
aledaños M PL vicinity
alegar⁴⁰ VT (aducir) to adduce; (pretender) to

claim
alegato M (a favor de) plea; (en contra de) allegation
alegoría F allegory
alegrar VT (a una persona) to gladden; (una fiesta) to brighten up; —**se** to be glad; (por efecto del alcohol) to get tipsy
alegre ADJ (contento) joyful, cheerful, lighthearted; (ebrio) tipsy, lit
alegría F joy, merriment, cheer
alejamiento M (distanciamiento) withdrawal; (separacion de un cargo) dismissal
alejar VT (distanciar) to move away; (ahuyentar) to scare off; —**se** (físicamente) to move away; (emocionalmente) to withdraw
alelar VT to stupefy
alemán -ana ADJ & MF German; M (lengua) German
Alemania F Germany
alentador ADJ encouraging
alentar¹ VT (animar) to encourage, to cheer up; VI to breathe
alergeno/alérgeno M allergen
alergia F allergy
alérgico ADJ allergic
alergólogo -ga MF allergist
alero -ra MF (baloncesto) forward; M eaves
alerón M (de avión) aileron, flap; (de coche) spoiler
alerta ADJ & F alert
alertar VT to alert
aleta F (de pez) fin; (de ballena) fluke; (de buceador, delfín) flipper
aletargado ADJ sluggish, lethargic
aletargarse⁴⁰ VI to fall into lethargy, to become lethargic
aletazo M flap of a wing
aletear VI to flap, to flutter
aleteo M flapping, flutter
alevín M small fry
alevosía F treachery
alevoso ADJ treacherous
alfabetismo M literacy; **— digital** computer literacy
alfabetización F literacy; **— digital** computer literacy
alfabetizar⁴⁷ VI (enseñar) to teach to read and write; VT (ordenar) alphabetize
alfabeto M alphabet
alfalfa F alfalfa
alfanumérico ADJ alphanumeric
alfarería F pottery
alfarero -ra MF potter
alféizar M windowsill
alfeñique M (golosina) sugar paste; (persona) weakling
alférez MF second lieutenant; **— de fragata** ensign
alfil M bishop

alfiler M pin; — **de corbata** tie tack; **no cabe un** — it's totally full
alfiletero M pincushion
alfombra F (de pared a pared) carpet; (suelta) rug
alfombrar VT to carpet
alfombrilla F (en el suelo) mat; (para ordenador) mouse pad
alforja F saddlebag
alga F seaweed; —**s** algae
algarabía F uproar
algarrobo M locust tree
algazara F merriment
álgebra F algebra
algo PRON something; — **es** — something is better than nothing; **por** — **será** there must be reason; ADV somewhat, slightly
algodón M cotton; — **de azúcar** cotton candy; **se crió entre algodones** he had a protected childhood
algoritmo M algorithm
alguacil M (de policía) sheriff, marshal; (en un tribunal) bailiff
alguien PRON INDEF somebody, someone; **vino** — **a hablarte** someone came to talk to you; (en preguntas) anybody, anyone; **¿— lo vio?** did anyone see him?
alguno ADJ some; —**s** some, a few; **sin ruido** — without a sound; **en alguna parte** somewhere; **de alguna manera** somehow; **en algún momento** sometime; **¿lo has visto alguna vez?** have you ever seen him? **¿hay alguna forma de hacer esto?** is there any way to do this? PRON someone, something
alhaja F jewel (también persona); —**s** jewelry
alhajero M jewelry box
alharaca F fuss
alhelí M wallflower
aliado-da ADJ allied; MF ally
alianza F (con aliados, socios) alliance
aliar[28] VT to ally
alias M alias, assumed name; (uso policial) a k a
alicaído ADJ crestfallen
alicates M PL pliers
aliciente M inducement
aliento M (aire respirado) breath; (ánimo) encouragement; **cobrar** — to catch one's breath; **contener el** — to hold one's breath; **sin** — out of breath, breathless
aligerar VT to lighten; — **el paso** to quicken one's pace
alijo M cache, stash
alimentación F (comida) nourishment, food; (acción de dar de comer) feeding; — **intravenosa** intravenous feeding
alimentador M feeder; — **de hojas** paper feeder; — **de impresora** printer feeder
alimentar VT (a una persona) to feed, to nourish; (un fuego) to stoke
alimentario ADJ alimentary; **canal** — alimentary canal
alimenticio ADJ (nutritivo) nutritious, nourishing; (relativo a los alimentos) alimentary; **industria alimenticia** food industry; **pensión alimenticia** alimony
alimento M food, nourishment
alineación F (deportes) lineup; (coche) alignment; — **a la derecha** right justification; — **a la izquierda** left justification
alinear VT (objetos) to line up; (a un deportista) to put in the lineup; —**se con** to align oneself with
aliño M condiment, seasoning
alisar VT (tela) to smooth; (pelo) to straighten
alistamiento M enlistment
alistar VT to enlist
aliviar VT (aligerar) to lighten; (mitigar) to alleviate, to relieve; (tranquilizar) to relieve; —**se** (mejorarse) to get better; (hacer sus necesidades) to relieve oneself
alivio M relief (también golf); — **de la deuda** debt relief
aljaba F quiver
aljibe M cistern
allá ADV there, over there; **más** — farther, beyond; **el más** — the hereafter; — **tú** that's your problem
allanamiento M raid; — **de morada** forcible entry
allanar VT (la tierra) to level, to smooth; (una dificultad) to iron out; (una casa) to raid; — **el camino** to smooth the way
allegado-da ADJ close to; MF relative
allegar[40] VT to gather; —**se** to arrive
allí ADV (espacial) there; (temporal) then; **por** — through there
alma F soul; **con toda el** — from the bottom of one's heart; **hasta el** — to the bone; **ni un** — not a soul; **no me cabía el** — **en el cuerpo** I was overjoyed; **se me fue el** — **al piso** my heart sank
almacén M (depósito) warehouse, storehouse, depot; (negocio) department store; **grandes almacenes** department store
almacenaje M storage
almacenamiento M storage; — **de datos** data storage; — **masivo** mass storage, bulk storage
almacenar VT to store, to stock up on; — **como** to save as
almacenista MF wholesaler
almáciga F nursery
almádena F sledgehammer
almanaque M (anuario) almanac; (calendario) calendar
almeja F clam

almendra F almond
almendro M almond tree
almiar M haystack
almíbar M syrup
almidón M starch
almidonado ADJ (persona) stiff; (camisa) starched
almidonar VT to starch
almirante M admiral
almohada F pillow; **consultarlo con la** — to sleep on it
almohadilla F (para sellos) cushion; (en las patas de los perros) pad; — **eléctrica** heating pad
almohadón M cushion
almohaza F currycomb
almohazar[47] VT to groom
almorranas F PL piles, hemorrhoids
almorzar[49] VT to lunch, to eat lunch
almuerzo M lunch
alocado ADJ wild
áloe M aloe vera
alojamiento M (residencia) lodging, accommodations; (militar) quarters; — **web** web hosting
alojar VT (a un invitado) to lodge, to accommodate; (a unos huérfanos) to house; (a las tropas) to quarter; —**se** (una bala) to lodge; (una persona) to board, to room
alondra F lark
alpaca F alpaca
alpinismo M mountain climbing
alpinista MF mountain climber, mountaineer
alpino ADJ alpine
alpiste M birdseed
alquería F farmhouse
alquilar VT to rent; **se alquila** for rent
alquiler M (pago mensual) rent; (acción de alquilar) renting; **coche de** — rental car; **dar en** — to hire out
alquitrán M tar
alquitranar VT to tar
alrededor ADV around; — **de la casa** around the house; M —**es** (de un área) surroundings; (de una ciudad) outskirts
alta F discharge; **dar de** — to discharge
altamente ADV highly
altanería F haughtiness
altanero ADJ haughty
altar M altar
alteración F alteration; **alteraciones al orden público** public disturbances
alterar VT to alter; — **el ánimo** to upset; —**se** to get upset
altercado M altercation
altercar[30] VT — **con** to quarrel with
alternador M alternator
alternancia F alternation
alternar VT to alternate; — **con** to rub elbows

with
alternativa F alternative
alternativo ADJ (cambiante) alternating; (optativo) alternative
alterno ADJ alternate; **alterna y continua** AC/DC
alteza F highness
altibajos M PL ups and downs
altillo M attic
altímetro M altimeter
altiplano M high plateau
altisonante ADJ high-sounding
altitud F altitude
altivez F haughtiness
altivo ADJ haughty
alto ADJ (que está arriba) high; (que tiene altura vertical) tall; **altas finanzas** high finance; — **contraste** high contrast; **de alta calidad** high-quality; **de alta fidelidad** high-fidelity; **de** — **nivel** high-level; **de alta potencia** high-powered; **de** — **riesgo** high-risk; **de alta velocidad** high-speed; **en voz alta** aloud; **en** — **grado** to a great extent; **en alta mar** on the high seas; M **altavoz** loudspeaker; M **altoparlante** loudspeaker; M (altura) height; (piso) upper story; — **el fuego** cease-fire; ADV loud; **hablar** — to talk loud; **cotizarse** — to be set high; INTERJ halt!
altruismo M altruism
altura F (de persona, edificio, ola, epidemia) height; (de avión) altitude; (sobre el nivel del mar, lugar alto) elevation; **a estas** —**s** at this stage; **a la** — **de la calle ocho** at Eighth Street; **a la** — **de las circunstancias** equal to the circumstances
alubia F bean
alucinación F hallucination
alucinar VT (causar alucinaciones) to hallucinate; (fascinar) to fascinate; (deslumbrar) to bowl over; VI (sufrir alucinaciones) to hallucinate
alucinógeno M hallucinogen
alud M avalanche
aludir VI — **a** to allude to, to refer to
alumbrado M lighting; — **público** street lighting; ADJ lit
alumbramiento M childbirth
alumbrar VT encender, to light up; (dar a luz) to give birth to
aluminio M aluminum
alumnado M student body
alumno -na MF (de enseñanza primaria) pupil; (de enseñanza secundaria) student
alusión F allusion
aluvión M (de preguntas, pedidos) barrage; (de personas) flood
alza F appreciation; — **de precios** boost in prices

alzado ADJ elevated; MF insurgent
alzamiento M (acción de alzar) raising; (insurrección) uprising
alzaprima F crowbar
alzar[47] VT (la mano, la voz, una casa) to raise; (a un niño) to lift up; **— la vista** to look up; **—se** to rise up in rebellion; **—se con** to make off with
amabilidad F kindness; **¿tendría la — de . . . ?** would you mind . . . ?
amable ADJ kind, nice
amado -da MF beloved
amaestrador -ora MF trainer
amaestramiento M training
amaestrar VT to train
amagar[40] VI/VT threaten; **amagó que iba a llover** it looked like it was going to rain; **amagó con golpearla** he made as if he was going to hit her
amago M **hacer —** to make as if
amague M (baloncesto) fake, juke
amalgamar VT to amalgamate
amamantar VT to nurse, to breast-feed
amanecer[35] VI to dawn; **— enfermo** to wake up ill; **amanecí en Londres** I woke up in London; M dawn, sunrise, daybreak
amanerado ADJ effete
amansar VT to tame
amante MF lover; **— de** fond of
amañar VT (una elección) to rig; (un documento) to tamper with
amapola F poppy
amar VT to love
amargar[40] VT to embitter
amargo ADJ bitter
amargor M bitterness
amargura F bitterness
amarillear VI/VT to yellow, to turn yellow
amarillento ADJ yellowish
amarillo -lla ADJ yellow; MF (esquirol) scab
amarra F cable, rope; **—s** moorings; **soltar —s** to cast off
amarrar VT (un barco) to moor; (una cosa) to secure, to tie down
amartillar VT (pegar con martillo) to hammer; (un arma) to cock
amasar VT (masa) to knead; (una fortuna) to amass
amateur ADJ INV & MF amateur
amatista F amethyst
Amazonas M Amazon River
Amazonia M Amazon Forest
ambages M PL **hablar sin —** to not mince words, to speak plainly
ámbar M amber
ambición F ambition
ambicionar VT to have the ambition to
ambicioso ADJ (emprendedor) ambitious; (codicioso) overambitious

ambidiestro ADJ ambidextrous
ambiental ADJ (limpieza) environmental; (temperatura) ambient
ambiente ADJ ambient; M (condiciones biológicas) environment; (atmósfera) atmosphere, ambience, ambiance; (sector social) milieu
ambigüedad F ambiguity
ambiguo ADJ ambiguous
ámbito M (ambiente) scene; (alcance) scope; (esfera) sphere
ambivalente ADJ ambivalent
ambos ADJ & PRON both
ambulancia F ambulance
ambulante ADJ itinerant
ambulatorio ADJ ambulatory
ameba F amoeba
amedrentar VT to scare
amén INTERJ amen; **decir —** to approve without discussion; **— de** besides
amenaza F threat, menace
amenazador ADJ threatening
amenazante ADJ threatening
amenazar[47] VT to threaten; **— con** to threaten to
amenidad F (cualidad de ameno) pleasantness
amenizar[47] VI to make entertaining
ameno ADJ enjoyable, entertaining
América F America
americano -na ADJ & MF American; F sport coat
ametrallador -ora MF gunner; F machine gun
ametrallar VT to strafe, to machine-gun
amianto M asbestos
amigable ADJ friendly
amígdala F (faríngea) tonsil; (cerebral) amygdala
amigdalitis F tonsillitis
amigo -ga ADJ friendly; **— de** fond of; **— de lo ajeno** thieving; MF friend
amiguismo M cronyism
aminoácido M amino acid
aminorar VT to lessen
amistad F (relación) friendship; (amigo) friend; **trabar —** to strike up a friendship
amistoso ADJ friendly, amicable
amnesia F amnesia
amniocentesis F amniocentesis
amnistía F amnesty
amo -ma M (de esclavo, sirviente) master; (de animal) owner; F (de esclavo, de sirviente) mistress; (de animal) owner; **ama de leche** wet nurse; **ama de llaves** housekeeper; **ama de casa** homemaker
amodorrado ADJ drowsy
amodorrar VI to make drowsy; **—se** to become drowsy
amolar[5] VT to annoy
amoldar VT to mold
amonestación F admonition, warning

amonestar VT to admonish, to warn
amoníaco M ammonia
amontonamiento M pile
amontonar VT to pile up
amor M love; — **propio** self-esteem; **de mil**
—**es** gladly; **hacerle el** — **a** to make love to;
por el — **de Dios** for God's sake; **por** — **al**
arte unremunerated
amoral ADJ amoral
amoratado ADJ (de golpes) black-and-blue; (de
frío, por falta de oxígeno) blue
amordazar[47] VT (a una persona) to gag; (a un
perro, a los críticos) to muzzle
amorfo ADJ amorphous
amorío M love affair
amoroso ADJ loving, amorous
amortajar VT to shroud
amortiguador M shock absorber
amortiguar[25] VT (un sonido) to muffle, to
absorb; (un golpe) to cushion, to absorb; (un
dolor) to deaden, to dull
amortización F (desvalorización periódica)
depreciation; (recuperación de una inversión)
recovery; (reembolso gradual) amortization,
paying off
amortizar[47] VT (recuperar a plazos) to amortize;
(depreciar) to depreciate
amoscarse[30] VI to get peeved
amostazarse[47] VI to get peeved
amotinarse VI (en un barco) to mutiny; (en una
cárcel) to riot
amparar VT (proteger) to protect; (refugiar) to
shelter; —**se** to protect oneself
amparo M (protección) protection; (refugio)
shelter; **al** — **de** under the protection of
amperio M ampere
ampicilina F ampicillin
ampliación F (de una foto) enlargement; (de
una casa) extension
ampliar[28] VT (una foto) to enlarge; (una calle) to
extend; (una explicación) to expand; (un
volumen) to amplify; — **una imagen** to
zoom in
amplificador M amplifier
amplificar[30] VT (un sonido) to amplify; (una
imagen) to magnify
amplio ADJ (información, tiempo) ample; (piso)
spacious, roomy; (región, resonancia,
sonrisa) broad; (vestido) full; **de amplias
miras** open-minded
amplitud F (de comprensión) breadth; (de onda)
amplitude
ampolla F (de la epidermis) blister; (vasija) vial
ampollar VT to blister
ampuloso ADJ bombastic
amputar VT to amputate
amueblar VT to furnish
amuleto M amulet, charm
anacronismo M anachronism

ánade M duck
anadear VI to waddle
anadeo M waddle
anaerobio ADJ anaerobic
anal ADJ anal
anales M PL annals
analfabetismo M illiteracy
analfabeto -ta ADJ & MF illiterate
analgésico ADJ & M analgesic
análisis M analysis; — **costo-beneficio**
cost-benefit analysis; — **de mercado** market
analysis; — **de orina** urinalysis
analista MF analyst
anotación F (béisbol) run; (básquetbol) point;
(fútbol americano) touchdown; (glosa) note
analítico ADJ analytical, analytic
analizador M parser
analizar[47] VT (datos) to analyze; (secuencia) to
parse
analogía F analogy
analógico ADJ (relativo a la analogía) analogical;
(no digital) analog
análogo ADJ analogous
ananá[s] M SG pineapple
anaquel M shelf
anaranjado ADJ & M (color) orange
anarquía F anarchy
anarquista MF anarchist
anatema M anathema
anatomía F anatomy
anatómico ADJ anatomical
anca F haunch, rump
ancho ADJ wide, broad; **a sus anchas** at his
ease; **me viene** — it's too wide for me; M
width, breadth; **a lo** — widthwise; **tiene un
metro de** — it's one meter wide
anchoa F anchovy
anchura F width, breadth
ancianidad F old age
anciano -na ADJ elderly, aged; MF old person
ancla F anchor
anclar VI/VT to anchor
andada F **volver a las** —**s** to backslide
andador -ora MF walker
Andalucía F Andalusia
andaluz -za ADJ & MF Andalusian; M (dialecto)
Andalusian
andamiaje M (para construcción) scaffolding;
(fundamento) framework
andamio M scaffold
andanada F broadside; **una** — **de insultos** a
barrage of insults
andante ADJ walking
andanzas F PL adventures
andar[66] VI to walk; (coche, motor, reloj) to run;
(el tiempo) to pass; (un aparato) to work; —
con cuidado to be careful; — **en coche** to
travel by car, to ride in a car; — **mal** to be in
bad shape, to be a mess; — **mal del corazón**

to have heart trouble; **—se por las ramas / con vueltas** to beat around the bush; **no —se con rodeos** to make no bones about it; **en eso ando** that's what I'm up to; **¡andando!** move on! **¿dónde anda a estas horas?** where is he at this hour? **¡ándale!** *Méx* (apresúrate) come on! (de acuerdo) OK; M gait

andariego ADJ fond of walking

andas F **llevar en —** RP to carry on one's shoulders

andén M (de tren) platform; (para peatones) sidewalk

Andes M PL Andes

andino ADJ Andean

Andorra F Andorra

andorrano -na ADJ & MF Andorran

andrajo M rag, tatter

andrajoso ADJ ragged, tattered

andrógino ADJ androgynous

anduve, anduviera, anduviese *ver* andar

anécdota F anecdote

anegar[40] VT to flood

anejo ADJ attached; M accompanying volume

anemia F anemia; **— falciforme** sickle cell anemia; **— por deficiencia de hierro** iron deficiency anemia

anémico ADJ anemic

anestesia F (acción de anestesiar) anesthesia; (sustancia) anesthetic

anestesiar VT to anesthetize

anestésico ADJ & M anesthetic

anestesiología F anesthesiology

anestesiólogo -ga MF anesthesiologist

anestesista MF anesthesiologist

aneurisma M aneurysm

anexar VT (un territorio) to annex; (con una carta) to enclose

anexión F annexation

anexo ADJ attached; M (de un edificio) annex, extension; (a una ley) rider

anfeta F *fam* speed

anfetamina F amphetamine

anfibio ADJ & M amphibian

anfiteatro M amphitheater

anfitrión -ona M host (también informático); F hostess

ángel M angel; **— de la guarda** guardian angel

angelical ADJ angelic

angélico ADJ angelic

angina F **—s** tonsillitis; **— del pecho** angina pectoris; **— laríngea** laryngeal angina

angiocardiografía F angiocardiography

angiograma M angiogram

angioplastia F angioplasty

anglosajón -ona ADJ & MF Anglo-Saxon

Angola F Angola

angolano -na, angoleño -ña, angolés -esa ADJ & MF Angolan

angostar VT to narrow, to contract

angosto ADJ narrow

angostura F (cualidad de angosto) narrowness; (desfiladero) narrows

anguila F eel; **— eléctrica** electric eel

angular ADJ angular

ángulo M (figura geométrica, enfoque) angle; (rincón, esquina) corner; **— muerto** blind spot; **— recto** right angle

anguloso ADJ angular

angustia F (desasosiego) anguish, anxiety, distress; (congoja) heartache; (desazón existencial) angst

angustiado ADJ (desasosegado) anguished, anxious; (acongojado) distraught

angustiante ADJ nerve-wracking

angustiar VT to distress; **—se** to feel distressed

angustioso ADJ distressing

anhelante ADJ longing

anhelar VT to long for, to yearn for

anhelo M longing, yearning

anidar VI to nest

anillas F PL gymnastics rings

anillo M ring; **— de boda** wedding ring; **me queda como — al dedo** it fits me like a glove

ánima F soul of the departed

animación F (viveza) animation, liveliness; (en películas) animation

animado ADJ (vivo) animate; (bullicioso) lively

animador -ora MF (de un espectáculo) host; (de un equipo) cheerleader

animal ADJ & M animal

animar VT (dar vida) to animate, to enliven; (incitar) to encourage, to urge on; (dar aliento) to cheer up; **—se** (alegrarse) to cheer up; (atreverse) to gather courage

ánimo M (espíritu) spirit; (aliento) encouragement; (humor) mood; (intención) intention; **no estoy de — para eso** I'm not in the mood for that; INTERJ hang in there!

animosidad F animosity

animoso ADJ spirited

aniñado ADJ childlike

aniquilar VT to annihilate, to wipe out

anís M anise

aniversario M anniversary

ano M anus

anoche ADV last night

anochecer[35] VI to get dark; **anochecimos en París** night found us in Paris; M nightfall, dusk

anomalía F anomaly

anómalo ADJ anomalous

anonadado ADJ dumbfounded

anonadar VT (aniquilar) to annihilate; (vencer) overwhelm; (desconcertar) to dumbfound; **—se** to become dumbfounded

anónimo ADJ anonymous, nameless; M

anonymous letter
anorak M anorak
anorexia F anorexia
anoréxico ADJ anorexic
anormal ADJ abnormal; MF freak
anotación F (nota) annotation, notation; (en fútbol) goal
anotar VT (apuntar) to note; (marcar un tanto) to score; —**se** to sign up
anquilosarse VT (las articulaciones) to become stiff; (una institución) to become stagnant
ansia F (deseo) eagerness; (congoja) anguish
ansiar[28] VT to covet
ansiedad F anxiety
ansioso ADJ (ávido) anxious, eager; (inquieto) fretful
antagonismo M antagonism
antagonista MF antagonist
antagonizar[47] VT to antagonize
antaño ADV in the old days
antártico ADJ antarctic
Antártida F Antarctica
ante PREP before; — **este problema** in the face of this problem; — **todo** above all; M suede
anteanoche ADV night before last
anteayer ADV day before yesterday
antebrazo M forearm
antecedente ADJ & M antecedent; —**s** (profesionales) background; (criminales) record; —**s delictivos** criminal record
antecesor -ora MF (antepasado) ancestor; (predecesor) predecessor
antedatar VT to backdate
antedicho ADJ aforesaid
antelación LOC ADV **con** — beforehand
antemano LOC ADV **de** — beforehand
antena F (de radio) antenna, aerial; (de insecto) antenna, feeler
anteojera F blinder
anteojos M PL glasses, spectacles; — **de sol** sunglasses; — **bifocales** bifocals
antepasado -da MF ancestor, forebear
antepecho M sill
anteponer[56, 74] VT (poner delante, poner antes) to place before; (dar preferencia) to give priority to
anterior ADJ (en el tiempo) previous; (en el espacio) anterior, front; — **a** prior to
anterioridad F **con** — before
anteriormente ADV (antes) previously, formerly; (en la parte delantera) in front
antes ADV (previamente) before, formerly; (más temprano) sooner; **llegó** — he arrived sooner; — **de** before; — **la muerte** I'd rather die; — **bien** rather; — **de impuestos** pretax; — **del cierre** before closing; **lo** — **posible** ASAP, as soon as possible
antesala F (habitación) anteroom; (preludio) prelude; (béisbol) third base

antesalista MF third baseman
antiaborto ADJ INV antiabortion, right-to-life
antiácido ADJ & M antacid
antiaéreo ADJ antiaircraft
antialérgico ADJ antiallergic
antibacteriano ADJ antibacterial
antibalas ADJ INV bulletproof
antibalístico ADJ (misil) antiballistic; (chaqueta) bulletproof
antibiótico ADJ & M antibiotic; — **de amplio espectro** broad-spectrum antibiotic
antibloqueo ADJ INV antilock
anticipación LOC ADV **con** — in advance
anticipado LOC ADV **por** — in advance
anticipar VT (una fecha) to move up; (dinero) to advance; (el porvenir) to anticipate; —**se a los acontecimientos** to jump the gun
anticipo M advance, deposit
anticoagulante M anticoagulant
anticoncepción F contraception
anticonceptivo ADJ & M contraceptive
anticongelante M antifreeze
anticonvulsivo M anticonvulsant
anticuado ADJ antiquated, out-of-date
anticuerpo M antibody
antideportivo ADJ unsportsmanlike
antidepresivo ADJ & M antidepressant
antidiarreico M antidiarrheal
antidiurético M antidiuretic
antídoto M antidote
antieconómico ADJ wasteful
antiespasmódico M antispasmodic
antiestético ADJ unsightly
antígeno M antigen
antigualla F old piece of junk
antiguano -na ADJ & MF Antiguan
Antigua y Barbuda F Antigua and Barbuda
antigüedad F (cualidad de antiguo) antiquity; (objeto) antique; (tiempo en un cargo) seniority
antiguo ADJ (era, historia) ancient; (ropa) old; (mueble) antique; **a la antigua** in the old style; **la antigua capital** the former capital; **más** — with more seniority
antihigiénico ADJ unsanitary
antihistamínico M antihistamine
antiinflamatorio ADJ & M anti-inflammatory
Antillas F PL West Indies
antílope M antelope
antimonio M antimony
antimonopolio ADJ INV antitrust
antioxidante ADJ & M antioxidant
antiparras F PL goggles
antipatía F antipathy
antipático ADJ unfriendly, unkind
antipoliomielítico ADJ antipolio
antipsicótico M antipsychotic
antirreflejante ADJ anti-glare
antisemitismo M anti-Semitism

antiséptico ADJ & M antiseptic
antisocial ADJ antisocial
antítesis F antithesis
antitoxina F antitoxin
antitranspirante M antiperspirant
antitrust ADJ INV antitrust
antiviral M antiviral
antojadizo ADJ whimsical
antojarse VI **se le antojó comer salchicha** he took a notion to eat sausage; **esa tarea se me antoja difícil** that task seems hard to me
antojo M (deseo) whim, craving; (mancha de nacimiento) birthmark
antología F anthology, reader
antónimo M antonym
antorcha F torch
antracita F anthracite
ántrax M anthrax
antro M (bar) dive, joint; **— de perdición** den of iniquity
antropología F anthropology
antropólogo -ga MF anthropologist
anual ADJ annual, yearly
anualidad F annuity; **— variable** variable annuity
anuario ADJ annual; M yearbook
anudar VT to knot; **se le anudó la garganta** he got all choked up
anulación F (de un contrato) cancellation; (de un matrimonio) annulment
anular VT (un matrimonio) to annul; (un contrato, un evento) to cancel; (una sentencia) to overrule, to overturn; (un talón) to void; (un comando de computadora) to undo; **— una selección previa** to deselect; M ring finger
anunciador -ora MF announcer
anunciante MF advertiser
anunciar VT (información) to announce; (un producto) to advertise
anuncio M (de información) announcement; (de un producto) advertisement; **— clasificado** classified advertisement, want ad; **— publicitario** advertisement, ad; **poner un — to place an ad**
anzuelo M fishhook; **morder/picar el — to** take the bait
añadidura F addition; **por — in addition**
añadir VT to add
añejo ADJ aged, vintage
añicos M **hacerse — to break into a thousand pieces**
añil M indigo, bluing
año M year; (de la escuela) grade; (de vino) vintage; **— bisiesto** leap year; **— luz** light-year; **de cuarenta —s** aged forty; **del — hasta la fecha** year-to-date; **el — en curso** the current year; **el — pasado** last year; **en los —s veinte** in the 1920s; **entrado en —s** getting on in years; **¿cuántos —s tienes?** how old are you?
añojo -ja MF yearling
añoranza F longing; (del hogar) homesickness
añorar VT to long for, to be homesick for
añoso ADJ old
añublo M blight
aorta F aorta
apabullar VT (impresionar) to bowl over; (derrotar) to crush
apacentar[1] VI to graze, to pasture
apacible ADJ good-natured, laid-back
apaciguar[25] VT (pacificar) to pacify; (aplacar) to mollify, to appease; **—se** to calm down
apadrinar VT to sponsor; (en un bautismo) to act as godfather to; (en una boda) to act as best man for; (en un duelo) to second
apagado ADJ (no llamativo) flat; (no intenso) dull
apagar[40] VT (un fuego) to put out, to extinguish; (una luz) to turn off, to turn out; (motor) to turn off, to kill; (una computadora) to power down; (una vida) to kill, to snuff out; (la sed) to quench; **—se** (luz) to go out; (un color) to fade; (una voz) to trail off; (un volcán) to become extinct
apagón M blackout, outage
apalabrarse VI **— con** to make a verbal agreement with
apalancamiento M leverage
apalear VT to thrash
aparador M sideboard, buffet, cupboard
aparato M (de gimnasia artística) apparatus; (para ejercicio) machine; (de cocina) appliance; (de teléfono) telephone; (máquina, dirigencia política) machine; (boato) pomp; **— circulatorio** circulatory system; **— de televisión** television set; **— ortodóntico** braces; **— ortopédico** leg brace
aparatoso ADJ pompous
aparcamiento M (lugar para aparcar) parking lot; (acción de aparcar) parking
aparcar[30] VI/VT to park; MF SG **aparcacoches** valet
aparcero -ra MF sharecropper
aparear VT (animales) to mate; (calcetines) to match, to pair; **—se** (animales) to mate; (en un baile) to pair off
aparecer[35] VI (ponerse a la vista, publicarse) to appear; (hacer acto de presencia) to show up; **se me apareció un ángel** an angel appeared to me
aparejar VT (un cuarto, un ejército) to prepare; (problemas) to entail; (una embarcación) to rig
aparejo M (de caballo) harness; (de buque) rigging; (para pescar) tackle; **—s** equipment
aparentar VT to feign; VI to show off; **aparenta**

la edad que tiene she looks her age
aparente ADJ apparent
aparezca, aparezco ver aparecer
aparición F (fantasma) apparition; (acción de aparecer) appearance
apariencia F (aspecto) appearance; (fingimiento) pretense, semblance; **las —s engañan** appearances are deceiving; **guardar las —s** to keep up appearances
apartado M section; — **postal** post office box; ADJ (recóndito) secluded; (distante) distant; **muy —** far apart
apartamento M apartment
apartamiento M separation
apartar VT (separar) sort out; **aparta las monedas de veinticinco centavos** set aside the quarters; (mover) to move away; **apartó la silla de la pared** he moved the chair away from the wall; (empujar) to push away/aside; **lo apartó de un empujón** she pushed him away; (aislar) to take aside; **lo aparté para hablarle** I took him aside to talk to him; (retirar) to take off; **apartó la cacerola del fuego** she took the pan off the fire; (alejar del cargo) to remove from office; **apartaron al ministro de su cargo** they removed the minister from his post; **apartó la vista** he looked away; VI **—se** to stray; **se apartaron del buen camino** they strayed from the straight and narrow; **los resultados se apartan de lo esperado** the results depart/deviate from the norm; **se apartó para que no lo atropellara el coche** he got out of the way so the car wouldn't hit him
aparte ADJ separate; ADV **bromas —** kidding aside; **dejar —** to exclude; **punto y —** new paragraph; M aside; PREP **— de** (además de) besides; (salvo) except for
apasionado ADJ (amor, hombre) passionate; (defensa, comentario) impassioned
apasionante ADJ exciting
apasionar VT **eso me apasiona** I love that; **—se por** to be passionate about
apatía F apathy
apático ADJ apathetic
apear VT to get down; **—se** to dismount
apechugar[40] VI **— con** to put up with
apedrear VT to stone
apegado ADJ attached
apegarse[40] VI to become attached
apego M attachment
apelación F appeal
apelar VI/VT to appeal
apellidarse VI to have the surname of
apellido M surname, last name
apelotonarse VI (una almohada) to ball up; (gente) to bunch together
apenado ADJ (dolorido) grieved; (avergonzado) embarrassed
apenar VT to grieve, to pain; **—se** to be grieved
apenas ADV hardly, scarcely, barely; **— llegó, se desmayó** no sooner had he arrived than he fainted; **— comienza la reunión** the meeting is just starting
apéndice M (órgano, parte de un libro) appendix; (añadido) appendage
apendicectomía F appendectomy
apendicitis F appendicitis
apercibir VT to warn; **—se de** to notice
aperitivo M appetizer
apero M farm implement
apertura F (transparencia) openness; (oportunidad) opening; **a la —** at the opening
apesadumbrado ADJ doleful
apestar VT (hacer heder) to stink up; (causar la peste) to plague; VI to stink, to reek
apestoso ADJ (hediondo) smelly; (apestado) pestilent
apetecer[35] VI **no me apetece ir contigo** I don't feel like going with you
apetecible ADJ appetizing
apetito M appetite
apetitoso ADJ appetizing
apiadarse VI **— de** to pity, to take pity on
ápice M apex; (de la lengua) tip; **no apartarse ni un —** not to diverge a jot
apio M celery
apisonadora F steamroller
apisonar VT to pack down
aplacamiento M appeasement
aplacar[30] VT (a una persona) to appease, to mollify; (miedo) to allay; (sed, pasión) to quench; **—se** to relent
aplanadora F steamroller
aplanamiento M flattening, leveling
aplanar VT (un terreno) to level, to flatten; (con una aplanadora) to roll
aplastado ADJ flattened
aplastamiento M crushing
aplastante ADJ (derrota) crushing; (victoria) sweeping
aplastar VT (achatar) to squash, to crush; (derrotar) to plaster, to stomp; (una revolución) to squelch, to smash, to crush; **—se** to crumple
aplaudir VI/VT to applaud
aplauso[s] M SG/PL applause
aplazamiento M postponement, deferral; (de un proceso legal) continuance
aplazar[47] VT to postpone, to put off
aplicable ADJ applicable
aplicación F (acción de aplicarse) application; (de un castigo) administration; (de computadora) application, app; **— de fondo** background application
aplicado ADJ (conocimiento, ciencia) applied; (trabajador) industrious

aplicador M applicator
aplicar[30] VT to apply; —**se** to work hard, to apply oneself
aplomado ADJ (equilibrado) poised; (vertical) plumb
aplomar VT to plumb
aplomo M poise
apnea M apnea; — **obstructiva del sueño** sleep apnea
apocado ADJ timid
apocalipsis MF (desastre) apocalypse; (Biblia) Revelation
apocamiento M timidity
apocarse[30] VI to become intimidated
apodar VT to nickname
apoderado -da MF proxy, agent
apoderarse VI — **de** to take possession of, to seize
apodo M nickname
apogeo M apogee; **en su** — (una fiesta) in full swing; (un estilo) in its heyday, at its peak
apolillado ADJ (comido por las polillas) moth-eaten; (anticuado) antiquated
apología F apology
apoplejía F apoplexy
aporrear VT to club, to cudgel
aportación F contribution
aportar VT (evidencia) to provide; (dinero) to contribute
aporte M contribution
aposento M chamber
apostador -ora MF bettor
apostar[5] VI/VT (a los caballos) to bet, to wager; (a un centinela) to station, to post; — **por** (caballo) to bet on; (cambio) to commit to
apóstol M apostle
apóstrofe MF apostrophe, invocation
apóstrofo M (ortografía) apostrophe
apostura F bearing
apoyar VT (sostener) to rest; (respaldar) to support, to back; (votar por) to second; (respaldar un argumento) to buttress; —**se en** (recostarse contra) to lean on, to prop against; (basarse en) to be based on; M SG **apoyabrazos** armrest
apoyo M support
apreciable ADJ (digno de aprecio) esteemed; (perceptible) noticeable; (registrable) appreciable
apreciablemente ADV significantly
apreciación F appreciation
apreciado ADJ (amigo) dear; (tesoro) valued, prized
apreciar VT (valorar) to appreciate; (percibir) to notice; (registrar) to measure; (considerar) to take into consideration; (sentir afecto) to cherish; —**se** (un fenómeno) to be noticeable; (moneda) to appreciate
aprecio M appreciation

aprehender VT (a un delincuente) to apprehend; (contrabando) to seize; (una idea) to grasp
aprehensión F (arresto) apprehension; (incautación) seizure
apremiante ADJ pressing
apremiar VT to pressure
apremio M pressure
aprender VI/VT to learn; — **de memoria** to memorize, to learn by heart
aprendiz -za MF (de un oficio) apprentice, trainee; (de una lengua, canto) learner
aprendizaje M (de un oficio) apprenticeship; (acto de aprender) learning
aprensión F apprehension, misgivings
aprensivo ADJ apprehensive
apresar VT (aprisionar) to imprison; (incautar) to seize
aprestar VT to prepare; —**se a** to get ready to
apresurado ADJ hasty, hurried
apresurar VT to hurry, to hasten
apretado ADJ (zapato) tight; (beso) hard; (racimo) compact; (síntesis) succinct; (jornada) busy; (situación) difficult, dangerous
apretar[1] VT (un botón) to press; (un gatillo) to squeeze; (un tornillo) to tighten; (los dientes, puños) to clench; (a un bebé) to clasp; **me apretó para que le diera dinero** he pressured me to give him money; **ese profesor nos aprieta mucho** that teacher demands a lot of us; VI (zapatos) to be tight, to pinch; (sol) to be intense; (esforzarse) to try hard, to bear down; —**se** to crowd together
apretón M squeeze; — **de manos** handshake
aprieta, apriete ver apretar
aprieto M jam, fix, predicament; **en —s** in need, hard-pressed, in dire straits; **estar en un —** to be in a tight spot, to be in trouble, to be in a pickle; **poner en —s** to embarrass
aprisa ADV quickly
aprisco M (para el ganado) fold
aprisionar VT to trap
aprobación F (aceptación) approval; (adopción, promulgación) passage, adoption; (calificación) passing grade; — **de crédito** credit approval
aprobar[5] VT (una medida, una opinión) to approve of; (una ley) to pass, to approve; (un examen) to pass; (un crédito) to sign off on; VI to pass
aprontar VT to ready
apropiación F appropriation; — **indebida** embezzlement
apropiadamente ADV properly, appropriately
apropiado ADJ appropriate, suitable
apropiarse VT — **de** to appropriate
aprovechable ADJ usable
aprovechado ADJ opportunistic

aprovechamiento M use

aprovechar VT (una ocasión) to take advantage of; (el espacio) to utilize; (la enseñanza) to profit from; VI to be useful; **—se de** to take advantage of; INTERJ **¡que aproveche!** enjoy your meal!

aproximación F (acercamiento) approach; (estimado) rough estimate

aproximado ADJ approximate

aproximar VT to bring near; **—se** to approach; **— a** to approximate

aprueba, apruebe ver aprobar

aptitud F aptitude; **—es musicales** musical aptitude

apto ADJ apt, suitable; **— para menores** for general audiences

apuesta F bet, wager

apuesto ADJ good-looking

apuntalar VT to prop up, to shore up

apuntar VT (señalar) to point out; (dirigir sobre un blanco) to aim; (matricular) to enroll; (escribir) to write down, to note; (ayudar a un actor) to prompt; (marcar puntos) to score; VI (una flecha) to point; (canas) to sprout; **— a un blanco** to aim at a target; **me apunto para ir con vosotros** I'm game to go with you

apunte M notation; **—s** notes; **tomar —s** to take notes; **llevar el — a alguien** to pay attention to someone

apuñalar VT to stab

apurado ADJ (situación) difficult; (persona) in dire straits; (apresurado) in a hurry

apurar VT (consumir) to drink up; (apremiar) to put under pressure; **—se** Am to hurry

apuro M predicament, fix; (prisa) hurry; **estar en —s** to be in distress

aquejado ADJ stricken

aquejar VT to afflict, to trouble

aquel ADJ that; **aquella chica se llama María** that girl is named María; **aquellas ciudades son antiguas** those cities are old; PRON that one; **— es el mayor** that one is the oldest; **aquellos son mis hijos** those are my children; **de mis dos hijos, Juan y Pedro, este es gordo y — es flaco** of my two sons, Juan and Pedro, the latter is fat and the former is thin; **en/por — entonces** back then

aquí ADV here; **está por —** it is around here; **ven por —** come this way; **hasta —** this far; **de — a cuatro horas** four hours from now; **de — en adelante** from now on; **de — para allá** to and fro, back and forth; **— y ahora** here and now

aquietar VT to quiet; **—se** (los nervios) to calm down; (una tormenta) to subside

ara LOC ADV **en —s de** for the sake of

árabe MF (persona) Arab; M (caballo) Arabian;

(lengua) Arabic; ADJ (caballo) Arabian; (costumbre, arte) Arab

Arabia Saudí, Arabia Saudita F Saudi Arabia

arácnido M arachnid

arado M plow

Aragón M Aragon

aragonés -esa ADJ Aragonese; MF (persona) Aragonese; M (dialecto) Aragonese

arancel M (impuesto) tariff; (lista de honorarios) list of fees

arancelario ADJ **acuerdo —** tariff agreement

arándano M blueberry; **— rojo** cranberry

arandela F washer

araña F (arácnido) spider; (candelabro) chandelier

arañar VT (rayar) to scratch; (herir con garras) to claw, to scratch; (raspar) to scrape, to score

arañazo M scratch

arañero M warbler

arar VI/VT to plow, to till

arbitraje M arbitration

arbitrar VT (un desacuerdo) to arbitrate; (un partido) to referee, to officiate; (un partido de béisbol) to umpire

arbitrariedad F (acción) arbitrary action; (cualidad) arbitrariness

arbitrario ADJ arbitrary

arbitrio M (libre albedrío) free will; (capricho) whim; (decisión) discretion; (deseos) wishes

árbitro -tra MF (del buen gusto) arbiter; (de conflictos) arbitrator; (de encuentros deportivos) referee

árbol M tree; (mástil) mast; **— de Navidad** Christmas tree; **— de levas** camshaft; **— genealógico** family tree

arbolado ADJ woody, wooded

arboleda F grove, clump

arbóreo ADJ arboreal

arbusto M shrub, bush

arca F ark; **— de Noé** Noah's ark; **las —s municipales** municipal coffers

arcada F arcade, archway; **tener/dar —s** to gag

arcaico ADJ archaic

arcaísmo M archaism

arcano ADJ arcane

arce M maple [tree]

arcén M shoulder of a road

archienemigo -ga MF archenemy

archipiélago M archipelago

archisabido ADJ very well-known

archivado ADJ on file

archivador M filing cabinet

archivar VT (guardar en un archivo) to file; (arrumbar) to shelve

archivo M (repositorio de documentos) archive; (fichero de ordenador) file; (acción de archivar) filing; **— comprimido** compressed file; **— cookie** cookie; **— corrupto** corrupted file; **— de datos** data

file; — **de lectura/escritura** read/write file
arcilla F clay
arco M (geométrico, eléctrico) arc; (estructura arquitectónica) arch; (arma, varilla de violín) bow; — **iris** rainbow
arder VT to burn; **la cosa está que arde** things are really getting hot; **el trigo se ardió** the wheat spoiled
ardid M scheme, artifice
ardiente ADJ (deseo) ardent; (calor, fuego, deseo) burning
ardilla F squirrel; — **de tierra** gopher; — **listada** chipmunk
ardite M **no valer un** — not to be worth a penny
ardor M (de pasión) ardor; (de fuego) heat; (por ácido) burning; — **de estómago** heartburn
arduo ADJ arduous, grueling
área F area; — **de penales** (fútbol) penalty area, box
arena F (tierra) sand; (plaza) arena; — **movediza** quicksand
arenero M sandbox
arenga F harangue
arengar[40] VT to harangue
arenisca F sandstone
arenisco ADJ sandy
arenoso ADJ sandy
arenque M herring
arete M earring
argamasa F mortar
Argelia F Algeria
argelino -na ADJ & MF Algerian
Argentina F Argentina
argentino -na ADJ Argentine, Argentinian; (como la plata) silvery; MF Argentine, Argentinian
argolla F iron ring
argón M argon
argot M slang
argucias F PL trickery
argüir[20] VT to argue
argumentar VT to argue
argumento M (razonamiento) argument; (conjunto de sucesos) plot
aridez F dryness
árido ADJ (seco) arid, dry, barren; (aburrido) dry; —**s** dry goods
ariete M (militar) battering ram; (fútbol) center forward
arisco ADJ surly
arista F (borde) edge; (de trigo) beard; **limar** —**s** to overcome difficulties
aristocracia F aristocracy
aristócrata MF aristocrat
aristocrático ADJ aristocratic
aritmética F arithmetic
aritmético ADJ arithmetical
arma F (instrumento bélico) arm, weapon; (división del ejército) branch; — **blanca** sharp weapon; — **de fuego** firearm; **a las** —**s** to arms; **de** —**s tomar** resolute; **tomar las** —**s** to take up arms
armada F armada, fleet
armado ADJ armed; **a mano armada** at gunpoint; M assembly, putting together
armador -ora MF (naviero) shipowner; (en fútbol) playmaker; (en vóleibol) setter
armadura F (cobertura de hierro) armor; (de un edificio) framework; (de gafas) frame; (de música) key signature
armamento M armament
armar VT (proveer de armas) to arm; (abastecer una embarcación) to equip; (reforzar) to reinforce; (ensamblar) to assemble, to put together; (levantar una tienda de campaña) to pitch; — **jaleo** to whoop it up; — **relajo** to make a mess; —**se de** to arm oneself with; — **una pendencia** to pick a fight, to start a quarrel
armario M (de ropa) wardrobe, closet; (de cocina) cabinet, armoire
armatoste M unwieldy object
armazón MF framework, skeleton
Armenia F Armenia
armenio -nia ADJ & MF Armenian
armería F (depósito) armory; (tienda) gun shop
armiño M ermine
armisticio M armistice
armonía F harmony
armónico ADJ & M harmonic
armonioso ADJ harmonious
armonizar[47] VI/VT to harmonize, to blend
ARN [ácido ribonucleico] M RNA
arnés M harness
aro M (de rueda) rim; (de baloncesto) hoop; **no tocó ni** — it was an airball
aroma M (olor agradable) aroma; (del vino) bouquet
aromático ADJ aromatic
arpa F harp
arpía F shrew
arpillera F burlap
arpón M harpoon
arponear VT to harpoon
arqueado ADJ arched
arquear VT to arch
arqueología F archaeology
arqueológico ADJ archaeological
arquero -ra MF (tirador de flechas) archer; (guardametas) goalkeeper
arquetipo M archetype
arquitecto -ta MF architect
arquitectónico ADJ architectural
arquitectura F architecture
arrabal M outlying slum
arraigar[40] VT to take root
arrancar[30] VT (una planta) to uproot; (el pelo) to

tear out; (un diente) to pull; (un vicio) to eradicate; (una flor) to pick; (una confesión) to extract; **— de** to wrest from; VI/VT (un vehículo) to start; **arrancó para el valle** he took off for the valley; **arrancó a sudar** he began to sweat; **sus problemas arrancan de su niñez** his problems are rooted in his childhood; **—se los cabellos** to tear one's hair [out]

arranque M (proceso de arrancar) starting; (dispositivo para arrancar) starter; (decisión, empuje) gumption; **— de ira** fit of rage

arrasar VT (destruir) to level, to raze; (derrotar) to crush; **— con** to obliterate; VI to win

arrastrado ADJ wretched

arrastrar VT (mover por el suelo) to drag; (llevarse consigo) to sweep away; (atraer) to draw; (soportar) to bear; (pronunciar lentamente) to draw out; **— los pies** (moverse con dificultades) to shuffle; (ser renuente) to stall; VI (cortinas) to hang down to the floor; **—se** (una serpiente) to slither; (una lagartija, un insecto) to crawl; (una persona) to grovel; **— y soltar** to drag and drop, to drag and release; M SG **arrastrapiés** shuffle

array M array

arrayán M myrtle

arrear VT to drive, to herd

arrebatar VT (quitar) to snatch away, to wrest away; (quemar) to burn on the outside; **—se** to have a fit

arrebatiña F mad scramble

arrebato M fit, outburst

arreciar VI to increase in intensity

arrecife M reef

arreglar VT (poner en orden, concertar, adaptar música) to arrange; (ordenar) to tidy up; (reparar) to fix, to repair; (resolver) to settle; **— cuentas** to settle accounts; **ya te arreglo** I'll fix you; **—se** (embellecerse) to fix oneself up; (llevarse bien con) to get along with; (entablar relaciones amorosas) to start dating; (reconciliarse) to make up; (conformarse) to make do; (despejarse) to clear up; **arreglárselas** to cope, to manage

arreglo M arrangement; **con — a** in accordance with; **no tiene —** it can't be helped; **llegar a un —** to settle; **—s** alterations

arrellanarse VI to lounge, to loll

arremangado ADJ turned up, rolled up

arremangar[40] VT to roll up; **—se** to roll up one's sleeves, to knuckle down

arremeter VI to attack; **— contra** to lunge at

arremetida F thrust, lunge

arremolinarse VT (viento) to whirl around; (agua) to eddy

arrendajo M bluejay

arrendamiento M rental

arrendar VI/VT to rent, to lease; **se arrienda** for lease

arrendatario -ria MF tenant

arreo M adornment; **—s** tack, harness

arrepentido ADJ repentant, rueful

arrepentimiento M (contrición) repentance; (disgusto) regret

arrepentirse[8] VI (de los pecados) to repent; (de los errores) to regret

arrestar VT to arrest

arresto M arrest

arriar[28] VT (la bandera) to lower; (un cabo) to slacken

arriate M flower bed

arriba ADV above; **¡—!** get up! **¡— las manos!** stick 'em up! **¡— Juan!** long live Juan! **de — abajo** from top to bottom; **lleno hasta —** full to the brim; **te vas para —** you are doing well; **viven —** they live upstairs

arribar VI LIT to arrive; (buque) to put into port

arribista MF social climber

arribo M LIT arrival

arriendo M leasing, rental

arriero -ra MF animal driver

arriesgado ADJ (peligroso) risky; (valiente) daring

arriesgar[40] VT to risk; **—se** to take a chance

arrimar VT (acercar) to bring near; (golpear) to strike; **—se a** (apoyarse) to lean on; (acercarse) to get near

arrinconar VT (acorralar) to corner; (poner en un rincón) to put in a corner; (abandonar) to abandon

arritmia F arrhythmia

arrobamiento M rapture

arrobarse VI to be enraptured

arrodillarse VI to kneel

arrogancia F arrogance

arrogante ADJ arrogant

arrogarse[40] VT to claim

arrojadizo ADJ for throwing

arrojar VT (lanzar) to throw, to hurl; (expulsar) to throw out; (botar) to throw away; (vomitar) to throw up, to vomit; (proyectar una luz) to shed, to throw; **— un saldo de** to show a balance of; **—se** to hurl oneself

arrojo M boldness, daring

arrollador ADJ overwhelming

arrollar VT (enrollar) to roll up; (arrastrar) to run over; (derrotar) to defeat

arropar VT (con ropa) to wrap up; (en la cama) to tuck in; **—se** to pull up the covers

arroyo M stream, creek

arroz M rice; **— integral** brown rice

arrozal M rice field

arruga F wrinkle

arrugar[40] VT to wrinkle; **— el ceño** to knit one's brow; **—se** (pasar a tener arrugas) to get wrinkles; (asustarse) to be afraid

arruinar VT (estropear) to ruin; (destruir) to destroy, to ravage; (aguar) to spoil; (dejar en la quiebra) to bankrupt, to ruin; —**se** to go to ruin

arrullar VI (una paloma) to coo; VT (a un enamorado) to whisper sweet nothings to; (a un niño) to rock to sleep, to lull to sleep

arrullo M (de la tórtola) cooing; (del agua) babbling

arrumbar VT (arrinconar) to put aside; (marginalizar) to marginalize

arsenal M (depósito) arsenal; (astillero) navy yard

arsénico M arsenic

arte M SG art; F PL arts; M (destreza) skill, ability; (actividad manual) craft; **bellas —s** fine arts; **el — por el —** art for art's sake; **malas —s** wiles; **no tener ni — ni parte en algo** to have nothing to do with something; **por — de** by means of; **por — de magia** by magic

artefacto M (aparato) contrivance, device; (bomba) bomb

arteria F artery

arterial ADJ arterial

arteriosclerosis F arteriosclerosis

artero ADJ artful, wily

artesanía F (trabajo, obra) craft; (habilidad) craftsmanship

artesano -na MF artisan; M craftsman; F craftswoman

ártico ADJ arctic

articulación F (acción de articular) articulation; (juntura) joint

articular VT (pronunciar) to articulate, to enunciate; (unir) to join

artículo M (de revista) article; (de diccionario) article, entry; — **de fondo** editorial; — **definido** definite article; **hacer el —** to give a sales pitch

artífice MF (autor) architect; M (artesano) craftsman; F craftswoman

artificial ADJ artificial

artificio M artifice

artificioso ADJ affected, contrived

artillería F artillery

artillero -ra MF (militar) gunner; (en fútbol) striker

artimaña F trick, wile

artista MF (plástica) artist; (drama, música) performer

artístico ADJ artistic

artritis F arthritis

artroscopia F arthroscopy

artroscópico ADJ arthroscopic

artrosis F degenerative joint disease

Aruba F Aruba

arveja F pea

arzobispo M archbishop

arzón M saddletree

as M ace (también atleta)

asa F handle

asado ADJ roasted; M (carne asada) roast; (carne asada al aire libre) barbecue; (acción de asar) roasting

asador -ora M spit; MF barbecue cook

asalariado -da MF wage earner

asaltante MF mugger

asaltar VT (a una persona) to assault, to assail; (un banco) to hold up; (con preguntas) to assail; —**le a uno una idea** to be struck by an idea

asalto M (ataque) assault; (de un banco) holdup, stickup; **tomar por —** to storm

asamblea F assembly, gathering

asar VT to roast; — **a la parrilla** to grill; — **con adobo** to barbecue

asbesto M asbestos

ascendencia F ancestry

ascendente ADJ (que incrementa) ascending, rising; (que sube) upward

ascender² VT (a un empleado) to promote; (una montaña) to climb; VI to ascend; — **a** to amount to

ascendiente MF ancestor

ascenso M (acción de ascender) ascent; (en el trabajo) promotion

ascensor M elevator

asceta MF ascetic

ascético ADJ ascetic

ascienda, asciende *ver* ascender

asco M disgust, revulsion; **hacer —s a** to reject; **me da —** it makes me sick, it disgusts me; **ese hombre está hecho un —** that man is a mess; **su acné me da —** his acne is a turnoff

ascórbico ADJ ascorbic; **ácido —** ascorbic acid

ascua F ember; **estar en —s** to be on pins and needles; **tener a alguien en —s** to string someone along

aseado ADJ well-groomed

asear VT to clean up

asediar VT to besiege

asedio M siege

asegurable ADJ insurable

asegurador -ora MF underwriter

asegurar VT (una victoria) to assure; (una frontera, una cerradura) to secure; (con un contrato de seguros) to insure; —**se [de]** to make sure [of]; **te lo aseguro** I assure you

asemejarse VI — **a** to resemble

asentaderas F PL buttocks

asentamiento M (de una comunidad) settlement; (de un edificio) settling

asentar VT (datos) to enter; (una población) to establish; —**se** (posarse) to settle; (madurar) to settle down

asentimiento M assent, acquiescence

asentir⁸ VI to assent, to acquiesce; — **con la cabeza** to nod

aseo M (acción de asearse) cleaning; (cualidad de aseado) cleanliness; (cuarto de baño) bathroom; (servicio) toilet, restroom
aséptico ADJ aseptic
asequible ADJ (disponible) available; (barato, económico) affordable
aserción F assertion
aserradero M sawmill, lumber mill
aserrado ADJ serrated; M sawing
aserrar[1] VT to saw
aserrín M sawdust
aserto M assertion
asesinar VT to murder; (a una figura pública) to assassinate
asesinato M murder, killing; (de una figura pública) assassination
asesino-na ADJ murderous; MF killer, murderer; (de una figura pública) assassin; — **en serie** serial killer
asesor-ora MF consultant, advisor/adviser
asesoramiento M (profesional, legal) consulting, advising; (académico) counseling; — **de crédito** credit counseling
asesorar VT to advise
asesor-ora MF aide
asestar VT — **un golpe** to inflict/deal a blow
aseveración F assertion
aseverar VT to assert
asexual ADJ asexual
asfalto M asphalt
asfixia F suffocation, asphyxiation, asphyxia
asfixiar VT to suffocate, to smother
así ADV so, thus, like this; — — so-so; — **como** in the same way that; — **de grande** that big; — **que** so that; ¿— **que no vienes?** so you're not coming?
Asia F Asia
asiático-ca ADJ & MF Asian
asidero M hold; **eso no tiene — en la realidad** that has no basis in reality
asiduo ADJ (lector) assiduous; (cliente) steady
asiento M (lugar donde sentarse, parte de una silla, válvula) seat; (de nóminas) entry, record; **tomar —** to take a seat
asignación F (acción de asignar) assignment; (acción de dar fondos) appropriation; (lo asignado) allotment; (pago) allowance
asignar VT (una tarea) to assign; (fondos) to allot, to allocate, to earmark
asignatura F subject
asilado-da MF inmate; — **político-ca** political refugee
asilar VT (a un político) to give asylum to; (un animal) to shelter
asilo M (para los perseguidos) asylum; (para huérfanos, ancianos) home
asimétrico ADJ asymmetric, asymmetrical
asimilar VT (vitaminas, un grupo étnico) to assimilate; (información) to absorb

asimismo ADV likewise
asintomático ADJ asymptomatic
asir[50] VT to grasp, to grip; —**se a** to hold onto
asistencia F (presencia, personas presentes) attendance; (ayuda) assistance, aid; (servicio de averías) roadside assistance; (deporte) assist; — **médica** health care; — **social** (ayuda) welfare; (profesión) social work
asistente-ta ADJ assistant; MF assistant, helper; — **social** social worker
asistir VT — **a** (estar presente) to attend; (ayudar) to help, to assist
asma F asthma
asmático ADJ asthmatic
asno M ass, donkey
asociación F association; — **de propietarios** homeowners' association
asociado-da MF associate
asociar VT to associate; —**se** to join; —**se con** to fall in with
asolamiento M desolation
asolar VT to desolate, to devastate
asomar VI to show; VT to poke out, to stick out; —**se a** to look out
asombrar VT to astonish, to amaze, to astound; —**se** to be astonished
asombro M astonishment, amazement
asombroso ADJ astonishing, amazing
asomo LOC ADV **ni por —** by no means
asonancia F assonance
aspa F (de hélice) blade; (de ventilador) vane
aspartamo M aspartame
aspecto M (faceta) aspect, feature; (apariencia) looks
aspereza F roughness, harshness; **con —** sharply; **limar —s** to smooth over disagreements
áspero ADJ (terreno, mano) rough; (lucha) bitter; (tiempo, voz) harsh
aspiración F (ambición) aspiration, ambition; (respiración) breathing in; (succión) suction
aspiradora F vacuum cleaner
aspirante MF applicant, candidate
aspirar VT (inhalar) to breathe in, to inhale; (a un empleo) to apply for; — **a** to aspire to
aspirina F aspirin
asqueado ADJ disgusted
asquear VT to disgust
asquerosidad F nastiness; **¡estás hecho una —!** you're gross!
asqueroso ADJ nasty, disgusting, gross
asta F (de toro) horn; (de ciervo) antler; (de bandera) flagpole; (de lanza) shaft; **a media —** at half mast
asterisco M asterisk, star
asteroide M asteroid
astigmatismo M astigmatism
astilla F (de madera) chip, splinter; (de vidrio) sliver; —**s** kindling

astillar VT to chip, to splinter
astillero M shipyard
astringente ADJ & M astringent
astro M (del cielo) celestial body; (de cine) movie star
astrofísica F astrophysics
astrología F astrology
astronauta MF astronaut
astronáutica F astronautics
astronomía F astronomy
astronómico ADJ (relativo a las estrellas) astronomical; (muy elevado) astronomic, astronomical
astrónomo -ma MF astronomer
astucia F (listeza) cunning, guile; (treta) trick
asturiano -na ADJ & MF Asturian; (dialecto) Asturian
Asturias F SG Asturias
astuto ADJ shrewd, wily, cunning
asueto M (día libre) day off; (licencia) time off
asumir VT (una responsabilidad) to assume, to shoulder; (una mala noticia) to accept; — **un cargo** to take office
asunción F assumption; — **presidencial** presidential inauguration
asunto M (cuestión) matter; (tema de una obra) theme
asustadizo ADJ easily frightened, jumpy
asustado ADJ frightened, scared
asustar VT to frighten, to scare; —**se** to become frightened
atacante ADJ attacking; MF assailant
atacar[30] VT to attack, to assault; —**se de risa** to have a laughing fit
atado M bundle
atadura F **sin** —**s** with no strings attached
atajador M tackle
atajar VT (interrumpir) to cut off; VI (cortar camino) to take a shortcut
atajo M shortcut
atalaya F watchtower
atañer[15, 73] VI to concern, to pertain to
ataque M (de violencia, asma) attack; (de rabia, de tos) fit; (de epilepsia) seizure; (en fútbol americano) offensive series; — **cardíaco** heart attack; — **de nervios** nervous breakdown; — **relámpago** blitz
atar VT (sujetar) to tie, to bind; — **cabos** to put two and two together; —**se los zapatos** to tie one's shoes
atardecer[35] VI to get dark; M late afternoon, dusk, evening; **al** — at dusk
atareado ADJ busy
atarearse VI to busy oneself
atascadero M (lodazal) quagmire; (de tránsito) bottleneck
atascado ADJ stuck
atascar[30] VT (un tubo) to stop up; (una máquina) to jam; (el tráfico) to obstruct; —**se** (un

vehículo) to get stuck; (una máquina) to get jammed
ataúd M coffin, casket
ataviar[28] VT to attire, to array; —**se** to dress up
atavío M attire, garb
ateísmo M atheism
atemorizar[47] VT to frighten
atención F attention; (médica) care; (acto de cortesía) courtesy; — **al cliente** customer care; — **médica a largo plazo** long-term care; — **prenatal** prenatal care; — **primaria** primary care; **a la** — **de** to the attention of; **llamar la** — (hacer notar) to call attention; (ser llamativo) to attract attention; (interesar) to interest; INTERJ watch out!
atender[2] VT (a un enfermo) to take care of, to look after; (una súplica) to heed; (a un cliente) to serve; (el trabajo) to attend to, to take care of; VI to pay attention to
atenerse[58] VI — **a los hechos** to bear the facts in mind, to limit oneself to the facts; — **a la ley** to abide by the law
atentado M (asesinato) assassination; (ataque fracasado) assassination attempt; (con bomba) bombing; **un** — **contra** an affront to
atentamente ADV (con atención) attentively; (despedida en cartas) yours truly / yours sincerely
atentar[1] VI — **contra la vida de alguien** to make an attempt on someone's life
atento ADJ (que presta atención) attentive; (amable) thoughtful
atenuar[26] VT (la violencia) to attenuate; (una luz) to dim; —**se** to abate
ateo -a MF atheist
aterciopelado ADJ velvety
aterido ADJ stiff with cold
aterirse[73] VI to become stiff with cold
aterrador ADJ terrifying
aterrar VT to terrify
aterrizaje M landing; — **forzoso** crash landing
aterrizar[47] VI/VT to land
aterrorizar[47] VT (intimidar) to terrorize; (dar miedo) to terrify
atesorar VT (memorias) to treasure; (dinero) to hoard
atestado ADJ crowded, crammed
atestar VT (certificar) to attest to; (llenar) to jam, to pack
atestiguar[25] VT to bear witness, to testify
atiborrar VT to stuff; —**se** to stuff one's face
atienda, atiende ver atender
atiesar VT to stiffen
atildado ADJ spruced up
atinar VT (acertar) to hit the mark; (adivinar) to guess right; **no** — **a decir palabra** not to manage to get a word out
atípico ADJ atypical

atisbar VT (mirar con disimulo) to peek at, to peep at; (vislumbrar) to catch a glimpse of; VI to peek

atisbo M glimpse, hint

atizar[47] VT (fuego) to poke, to stoke; (pasiones) to stir up, to stoke

atlántico ADJ Atlantic; M **Océano Atlántico** Atlantic Ocean

atlas M atlas

atleta MF athlete

atlético ADJ athletic

atletismo M track and field

atmósfera F atmosphere

atmosférico ADJ atmospheric

atolladero M quagmire

atolondrado ADJ scatterbrained; (muchacha) ditsy

atómico ADJ atomic

atomizador M atomizer

atomizar[47] VT to atomize

átomo M atom

atónito ADJ dumbfounded

atontado ADJ stupefied

atontar VT to stupefy

atorar VT to jam; —**se** to choke

atormentar VT to torment; —**se por** to agonize over

atornillar VT to bolt

atracadero M dock

atracar[30] VT (amarrar) to dock; (robar) to hold up, to mug; —**se** to gorge oneself

atracción F attraction

atraco M holdup, stickup

atracón M **darse un** — to gorge

atractivo ADJ attractive, fetching; M (capacidad de atraer) attractiveness, appeal; (cosa que atrae) attraction; — **sexual** sex appeal

atraer[59] VT to attract

atragantarse VI to choke

atraiga, atraigo, atrajo, atrajera, atrajese ver atraer

atrancar[30] VT to bolt, to bar

atrapada F catch

atrapar VT (en una trampa) to trap, to ensnare, to catch; (una pelota, el interés) to catch

atrás ADV — **de la casa** behind the house; **cuatro años** — four years back; **hacia** — backward; **para** — back/backwards; **quedarse** — to fall behind

atrasado ADJ (de tiempo) late; (en el pago) in arrears, behind; (país) backward; (un libro de biblioteca) overdue; **tengo sueño** — I'm behind in my sleep; **el reloj anda** — the clock is slow; **feliz cumpleaños** — belated happy birthday

atrasar VT (un plazo) to delay; (un objeto) to push back; (un reloj) to turn back; VI (un reloj) to run slow; —**se** to fall behind, to lag

atraso M (condición de atrasado) backwardness;

(pago) back payment; (de trabajo) backlog; **con dos meses de** — two months in arrears

atravesar[1] VT (cruzar) to cross; (estar tendido) to span; (penetrar) to impale, to run through; — **un momento difícil** to go through a difficult moment; **se me atravesó un caballo** a horse crossed in front of me; —**se en la cama** to lie crossways in bed

atraviesa, atraviese ver atravesar

atrayendo ver atraer

atreverse VI to dare, to go for it; ¡**atrévete!** go for it!

atrevido ADJ (audaz) bold, daring; (insolente) insolent

atrevimiento M (cualidad de atrevido) boldness, daring, audacity; (acción atrevida) daring act

atribución F attribution; **atribuciones** powers

atribuir[19] VT (imputar) to attribute, to ascribe; (conferir) to confer; VI —**se** to claim

atribular VT to distress; —**se** to be distressed

atributo M attribute

atribuya, atribuye, atribuyendo, atribuyera, atribuyese ver atribuir

atril M stand

atrincherar VT to entrench

atrio M atrium

atrocidad F atrocity

atrofia F atrophy

atrofiar VT to atrophy, to stunt

atronador ADJ thunderous, deafening

atronar[5] VI to make a racket

atropellar VT (a un peatón) to run over, to run down; (los derechos de alguien) to trample upon

atropello M (arrollamiento) running over; (ultraje) outrage; (abuso) trampling

atroz ADJ (modales, crimen) atrocious; (dolor) excruciating; (ofensa) grievous

atuendo M getup

atún M tuna

aturdido ADJ bewildered; **estar** — to be in a daze

aturdimiento M bewilderment

aturdir VT to bewilder, to daze

atusar VT to smooth, to fix

audacia F audacity, boldness

audaz ADJ audacious, bold

audible ADJ audible

audición F audition; — **radial** radio program

audiencia F (tribunal) court; (público) audience; (en un pleito, proceso legal) hearing

audífono M (para sordos) earphone; (para música) headphone

audio M audio; —**libro** audio book

audiología F audiology

audiovisual ADJ audiovisual; M audiovisual presentation

auditar VI/VT to audit

auditivo ADJ auditory
auditor -ora MF auditor
auditoría F (revisión) audit; (trabajo de auditor) auditing
auditorio M (público) audience; (local) auditorium
auge M (del mercado) boom; (de una moda) heyday; (de una carrera) peak
augurar VT to foretell; **no — nada bueno** not to bode well
aula F (de clase) classroom; (de conferencia) lecture hall
aullar VI to howl
aullido M howl
aumentar VT to augment, to increase; **— los salarios** to raise pay; VI (precios) to rise, to escalate; (población) to grow; (violencia) to escalate
aumento M increase; (de expectativas) buildup; (de población) growth; (de precios) rise, upturn; (de peso) gain; **— por mérito** merit raise; **— salarial / de sueldo** pay raise
aun ADV even; **— así** even so; **— cuando** even though/if
aún ADV still
aunque CONJ though, although
aura F aura
áureo ADJ golden
aureola F halo
auricular M (de teléfono) receiver; **—es** headphones, earphones
aurora F dawn, aurora; **— boreal** aurora borealis, northern lights
auscultar VT to listen to with a stethoscope
ausencia F absence
ausentarse VT to absent oneself
ausente ADJ absent, missing
ausentismo M absenteeism
auspicios M PL auspices
austeridad F austerity
austero ADJ austere, stern
Australia F Australia
australiano -na ADJ & MF Australian
Austria F Austria
austríaco -ca ADJ & MF Austrian
autenticar[30] VT to authenticate
autenticidad F authenticity
auténtico ADJ authentic
autismo M autism
autista ADJ autistic
auto M (coche) auto; (orden judicial) writ; **— de choques** bumper car
autoadhesivo M decal; (para el parachoques) bumper sticker
autoayuda F self-help
autobiografía F autobiography
autobomba M RP fire engine
autobús M bus
autocine M drive-in movie theater

autocompasión F self-pity
autocontrol M self-control
autócrata MF autocrat
autóctono ADJ indigenous
autodestructivo ADJ self-destructive
autodeterminación F self-determination
autodisciplina F self-discipline
autoedición F desktop publishing
autoescuela F driving school
autoestima F self-esteem
autogobierno M self-government
autogol M own goal
autógrafo M autograph
autoimagen F self-image
automático ADJ automatic
automatización F automation
automatizar[47] VT (mecanizar) to automate; (hacer automáticamente) to do automatically
automóvil M automobile
automovilista MF motorist
automovilístico ADJ automotive
autonomía F autonomy; (de un vehículo) range
autonómico ADJ autonomic
autónomo ADJ (independiente) autonomous, independent; (que trabaja por su cuenta) self-employed; (que se presenta solo) stand-alone
autopista F freeway, turnpike; **— de la información** information superhighway
autopropulsado ADJ self-propelled
autopsia F autopsy
autor -ora MF author
autoridad F authority
autoritario ADJ (tiránico) authoritarian; (respetado) authoritative
autorización F authorization
autorizar[47] VT (permitir) to authorize; (dar propiedad intelectual) to license
autosatisfacción F self-satisfaction
autoservicio M (sistema de venta) self-service; (tienda) convenience store
autosuficiencia F self-reliance
autosuficiente ADJ (independiente) self-sufficient; (presumido) smug
autovía F freeway
auxiliar VT to help; ADJ auxiliary; MF assistant; **— de vuelo** flight attendant
auxilio M help
avalancha F avalanche
avalar VT to guarantee, to cosign
avaluar[26] VT to appraise
avalúo M appraisal
avance M (acción de avanzar, adelanto) advance, headway; (sinopsis de película) trailer
avanzada F scouting party
avanzado ADJ advanced
avanzar[47] VI (ir hacia adelante) to advance; (progresar) to make headway; **a medida que avanzaba la mañana** as the morning

progressed; VT (un vehículo) to move forward; (una grabación) to fast-forward

avaricia F avarice

avariento ADJ avaricious, miserly

avaro ADJ miserly, avaricious

avasallar VT to subjugate

avatar M (vicisitud) vicissitude; (encarnación de un dios, personaje digital) avatar

ave F bird; — **de corral** poultry; — **de rapiña** bird of prey; — **canora** songbird; — **zancuda** wading bird

avecindarse VI to take up residence

avellana F hazelnut

avellano M hazel

avena F oats

avenencia F agreement

avenida F avenue

avenir[61] VI to reconcile; —**se a** to come around to; —**se bien** to get along

aventadora F fan, blower

aventajar VT (ser mejor) to be superior to; (sobrepasar) to get ahead of

aventón M **dar un** — *Méx* to give a lift

aventura F (suceso) adventure; (relación amorosa) fling, affair

aventurado ADJ (arriesgado) risky; (atrevido) daring

aventurar VT (arriesgar) to risk; (sugerir) to venture; —**se a** to dare to

aventurero -ra ADJ adventurous; MF adventurer

avergonzado ADJ (tímido) abashed; (arrepentido) ashamed, embarrassed

avergonzar[23] VT to shame, to embarrass; —**se** to be ashamed/embarrassed

avería F (de frutas) damage, bruise; (de coche) breakdown, mechanical trouble

averiado ADJ (un coche) broken-down; (un televisor) on the blink; (un ascensor) out of service; (fruta) bruised, damaged

averiarse[28] VI (fruta) to become damaged; (un coche) to break down

averiguar[25] VT to find out, to ascertain

aversión F aversion, dislike

avestruz MF ostrich

avezado ADJ seasoned

aviación F aviation

aviador -ora MF aviator

aviar[28] VT to fix

avidez F eagerness

ávido ADJ eager, avid

avinagrado ADJ sour

avinagrar VT to sour; —**se** to become sour

avío M tidying up; —**s de pescar** fishing tackle

avión M (máquina) airplane; (ave) martin; — **comercial** airliner; — **a reacción** jet airplane; — **caza** fighter airplane

avisar VT (notificar) to advise; (alertar) to alert

aviso M notice; — **publicitario** advertisement;

estar sobre — to be forewarned; **poner sobre** — to forewarn; **sin previo** — without warning

avispa F wasp

avispado ADJ (despierto) lively; (inteligente) smart

avisparse VI to wise up

avispero M wasp's nest; **alborotar el** — to stir up a wasp's nest

avispón M hornet

avistar VT to catch sight of

avivar VT (una llama) to fan; (una fiesta) to enliven; (un fuego, un debate) to fuel

avizorar VT to spy on

axila F underarm

ay INTERJ (de dolor) ouch; (de decepción) oh, no; (de sorpresa desagradable) oh; ¡— **de mí!** poor me; ¡**ay, no!** oh, no!

ayer ADV yesterday

ayuda F (asistencia) help; (después de una catástrofe) relief; — **en línea** online help

ayudante -ta MF assistant, helper, aide; — **de médico** physician's assistant

ayudantía F assistantship

ayudar VT to help, to aid

ayunar VI to fast

ayunas F PL **en** — (antes de comer) without having eaten; (despistado) clueless; **estoy en** — I am fasting

ayuno M fast, fasting

ayuntamiento M (gobierno) municipal government; (edificio) city hall

azabache M jet; ADJ jet-black, raven

azada F hoe

azadón M hoe

azafato -ta MF (en aviones) flight attendant; (en ferias) host

azafrán M saffron

azahar M orange blossom

azar M chance; **al** — by chance, at random

azaroso ADJ (arriesgado) risky; (aleatorio) random

azerbaiyano -na, azerbaijano -na ADJ & MF Azerbaijani, Azerbaijanian

Azerbaiyán F Azerbaijan

azogar[40] VT to silver

azogue M (sustancia) quicksilver, mercury; (niño inquieto) restless child; **tener** — **en el cuerpo** to be restless

azorar VT (alarmar) to alarm; (avergonzar) to embarrass

azotaina F flogging

azotar VT (con azote) to whip, to lash, to flog; VI/VT (el viento) to whip, to buffet; (el sol) to beat down; (la lluvia) to sting

azote M (instrumento) whip; (golpe) lash; (aflicción) scourge; (golpe de viento) buffet

azotea F flat roof

azteca ADJ, MF Aztec

azúcar MF sugar; — **moreno** -**na** brown sugar
azucarar VT to sugar
azucarera F (fábrica) sugar mill; *Am* (recipiente) sugar bowl
azucarero M sugar bowl
azucena F white lily
azufre M sulfur, sulphur
azul ADJ blue; — **acero** steel blue; — **celeste** sky blue; — **claro** light blue; — **marino** navy blue
azulado ADJ bluish
azular VT to color blue
azulear VI (tener color azul) to be blue; (ponerse azul) to become blue; VT (dar color azul) to color blue
azulejar VT to tile
azulejo M tile
azuzar[47] VT (a un perro) to sic; (a una persona) to egg on

Bb

baba F drivel, drool, slobber; (de un caracol, de agua estancada) slime; **se le cae la — por el coche nuevo** he's drooling over the new car
babear VI to drivel, to drool
babero M bib
babor M portside
babosa F slug
babosear VI/VT to slobber [on]
baboso ADJ (caracol) slimy; (persona que babea) driveling; (persona tonta) idiotic; (adulador) fawning
babuino M baboon
baca F luggage rack
bacalao M cod
bache M (pozo) pothole; (momento) bad time; (de aire) air pocket
bacheado ADJ bumpy
bachiller -**ra** M (graduado) high school graduate; (alumno) high school student
bachillerato M baccalaureate
bacilo M bacillus
backgammon M backgammon
bacteria F bacteria
bacteriano ADJ bacterial
bacteriología F bacteriology
badajo M bell clapper
badana F sheepskin
bagaje M baggage
bagatela F trifle
bagazo M pulp
Bahamas F PL Bahamas
bahameño -**ña** ADJ & MF Bahamian

bahía F (geography) bay; (computer) slot
Bahrein M Bahrain
bahreiní ADJ & MF Bahraini
bailador -**ora** MF folk dancer; ADJ dancing
bailar VI/VT to dance; **me bailan los pantalones** my pants are falling off; **me tocó — con la más fea** I was left holding the bag; **que me quiten lo bailado** I enjoyed it anyway
bailarín -**ina** MF dancer
baile M (actividad) dance; (fiesta) dance, ball; — **aeróbico** aerobic dance; — **de máscaras** masked ball; — **folklórico** folk dance; — **zapateado** clog dance
bailongo M hop
bailotear VI to dance around
baivel M bevel
baja F (de temperatura, presión) drop; (de precios) decline; (de guerra) casualty; (del ejército) discharge, dismissal; (del trabajo) leave; **dar de** — to discharge; **darse de** — to call in sick
bajada F (acción de bajar, pendiente) descent; (de un caballo) dismount; — **contra-reloj** downhill ski race
bajar VI (descender) to go down; (correr) to run down; (de un árbol) to climb down; (de un caballo) to get down; (de un ómnibus) to step off, to get off; (en calidad) to worsen; (la marea) to ebb; (una creciente) to subside; VT (las escaleras) to go down; (un avión de un tiro) to shoot down; (comida con agua) to wash down; (la cabeza) to lower; (un cargamento) to let down; (el volumen) to turn down; (focos) to dim; (la voz) to lower, to soften; (los precios) to cut; — **de categoría** to demote; — **el cursor** to scroll down; — **en picado** to dive; —**se los pantalones** to pull down one's pants
bajeza F (cualidad) baseness; (acción) vile act
bajío M shoal
bajista ADJ (bolsa) bearish; MF (músico) bassist
bajo ADJ (nubes, estante, precio, voz grave) low; (persona) short; (voz débil) soft; (río) lower; (vista, persianas) lowered; (acto) base; **baja espalda** small of the back; **de baja calidad** low-end; **de baja ley** base; **de — precio** low-cost; **de — presupuesto** low-budget; **de —s ingresos** low-income; PREP under; — **contrato** under contract; — **control** under control, in hand; — **cuerda** under-the-table; — **fianza** on bail; — **fuego** under fire; — **sospecha** under a cloud; — **tierra** underground; **poner — llave** to lock up; **por lo — under** one's breath; M (en un coro, contrabajo) bass; (de pantalón) cuff; **hacer los —s** to cuff; ADV low
bala F (de pistola) bullet; (atletismo) shot; (de cañón) ball

balada F ballad
baladí ADJ trivial
balance M (cálculo) balance; (documento) balance sheet; (número de víctimas) toll; (movimiento) sway; **hacer un —** to take stock
balancear VT to swing; VI to sway; **—se** to sway
balanceo M (de un cuerpo) swinging, swing; (de un barco) rolling, roll
balancín M seesaw
balanza F scale; **— comercial** balance of trade; **— de pagos** balance of payments
balar VI to bleat
balasto M ballast
balazo M (disparo) shot; (herida) bullet wound
balbucear VI (un adulto) to stammer; (un bebé) to babble
balbuceo M (tartamudeo) stammer; stammering; (de bebé) babble, babbling
balcón M balcony
balde M pail, bucket; **de —** gratis; **en —** in vain
baldear VT to flush
baldío ADJ (terreno) fallow; (acción) useless
baldosa F (en una casa) floor tile; (en una calle) flagstone
balido M bleat, bleating
balística F ballistics
balístico ADJ ballistic
ballena F (animal) whale; (para corsé) whalebone
ballenato M whale calf
ballet M ballet
balneario M (de veraneo) seaside resort; (con aguas medicinales) spa
balón M ball; **baloncesto** basketball; **balonmano** handball; **— de angioplastia** angioplasty balloon; **se le fue el —** (fútbol americano) he fumbled; (fútbol) he lost the ball; M **balonvolea** volleyball
balsa F (embarcación) raft, balsa; (lago) pond
bálsamo M balsam, balm
baluarte M bulwark, stronghold
bambolear VT to sway, to swing; **—se** to sway, to swing
bamboleo M swinging, swaying
bambú M bamboo
banal ADJ banal; **una respuesta —** a pat answer
banana F banana
banano M (tree) banana tree; (fruit) banana
banca F (industria) banking; (en el juego) bank; **— electrónica** e-banking; **— en línea** online banking; **— por internet** Internet banking
bancario-ria ADJ bank, banking; MF banker
bancarrota F bankruptcy
banco M (establecimiento) bank; (asiento) bench; (de peces) school; (de arena) shoal, spit; (de suplentes) bench; **— de datos** data

bank; **— de niebla** fog bank; **Banco Mundial** World Bank
banda F (de músicos) band; (cinta ancha, también de computadora) band; (cinta de vestido) sash; (de delincuentes) gang, band, ring; (dibujo) stripe; (de neumático) tread; (lindero) side, edge, border; (de un barco) side; (en deporte) sideline; **— ancha** broadband; **— de frecuencia** frequency band; **— horaria** time slot; **— magnética** magnetic strip; **— sonora** soundtrack
bandada F (de aves) flock, flight; (de peces) school
bandeja F tray; **me lo sirvieron en — [de plata]** they served it to me on a silver platter
bandera F flag; **jurar la —** to pledge allegiance to the flag
banderín M pennant
banderola F pennant
bandido-da MF (delincuente) bandit, outlaw; (niño terrible) rascal
bando M (decreto) edict; (partido) camp
bandolero-ra MF bandit
Bangladesh M Bangladesh
bangladeshí, bangladesí ADJ & MF Bangladeshi
banjo M banjo
banquero-ra MF banker
banqueta F (taburete) stool; (acera) *Méx* sidewalk
banquete M banquet
banquetearse VI to feast
banquillo M bench (también en fútbol)
bañar VT (a un bebé) to bathe; (una torta) to ice, to frost; **—se** (en una bañera) to take a bath; (en el mar) to swim
bañera F bathtub
bañista MF bather
baño M (acción) bath; (cuarto) bathroom, lavatory; (de torta) icing, frosting; **darse un —** (bañarse) to take a bath; (nadar) to take a swim; **— de asiento** sitz bath; **— de esponja** sponge bath; **— [de] María** double boiler; **— de remolino** whirlpool bath; **— de sangre** bloodbath
bar M bar
barahúnda F ruckus, racket
baraja F pack/deck of cards
barajada F shuffle
barajar VI/VT (naipes) to shuffle; (alternativas) to weigh
baranda F railing, guard rail
barandal M banister
barandilla F rail, railing
barata F *Méx* sale
baratear VT to sell cheap
baratija F trinket, knickknack
barato ADJ cheap
baratura F cheapness

barba F beard; **—s** whiskers; **hacer algo en las —s de alguien** to do something right under someone's nose
barbacoa F barbecue
barbadense ADJ & MF Barbadian
barbado ADJ bearded
Barbados M Barbados
barbaridad F atrocity; **una — de** a lot of; **¡qué —!** what nonsense!
barbarie F savagery
bárbaro -ra ADJ (salvaje) barbarous, barbaric; (estupendo) cool, super; MF barbarian
barbecho M fallow land
barbería F barbershop
barbero -ra MF barber
barbilla F chin
barbitúrico M barbiturate
barbudo ADJ bearded
barca F rowboat
barcaza F barge
barco M boat; **— petrolero** oil tanker
bardo M bard
bario M barium
barítono ADJ & M baritone
barlovento M windward
barniz M (para madera) varnish; (para cerámica) glaze; (de cultura) veneer
barnizar[47] VT (madera) to varnish; (cerámica) to glaze
barómetro M barometer
barón M baron
barquero -era M boatman; F boatwoman
barquillo M rolled wafer
barquinazo M **dar —s** to lurch
barra F (de hierro, arena, chocolate, en un bar) bar; (en gimnasia) crossbar; (signo ortográfico) slash; **— de estado** status bar; **— de herramientas** toolbar; **— de jabón** bar of soap; **— de menú** menu bar; **— de tareas** task bar; **— espaciadora** space bar; **— invertida** backslash
barrabasada F mischief
barraca F (de feria) stall, stand; (casucha) hovel; (depósito) shed
barracuda F barracuda
barranca M ravine
barranco M gully, ravine
barrena F (de un taladro) bit; (de un avión) tailspin; **entrar en —** to go into a tailspin
barrenar VT to drill
barredora F sweeper
barrendero -ra MF street sweeper
barrer VI/VT (pasar escoba) to sweep; (derrotar) to defeat decisively; M SG **barreminas** minesweeper
barrera F (protección) barrier; (valla) barrier, bar; **— arancelaria** tariff barrier; **— comercial** trade barrier; **— de coral** barrier reef; **— del sonido** sound barrier

barrica F vat
barricada F barricade
barrida F sweep
barrido M (acción de barrer) sweeping; (movimiento) sweep
barriga F (abdomen) belly; (panza) paunch; **rascarse la —** to do nothing
barrigón ADJ potbellied
barril M barrel, keg, drum
barrio M neighborhood, quarter; **— residencial** residential neighborhood; **—s bajos** slums
barritar VI to trumpet
barro M (lodo) mud; (arcilla) clay; (acné) pimple; **de —** earthen
barroco ADJ & M baroque
barroso ADJ muddy
barrote M bar
barruntar VT to suspect
barrunto M suspicion
bártulos M PL stuff
barullo M hubbub
basal ADJ basal
basalto M basalt
basar VT to base; **—se en** (depender de) to rely on; (fundamentar en) to be based on
basca F nausea
báscula F scale
base F (apoyo, área militar, en química, en béisbol) base; (punto de partida) basis; (de maquillaje) foundation; (de una campaña) plank; MF (baloncesto) point guard; **—s de concurso** contest rules; **— de datos** database; **— de lanzamiento** launching pad; **con — en** on the basis of; **en — a** on the basis of; **las —s** (de un partido) base, grass roots; (de un sindicato) rank and file; **salario — base** salary; **tener una — sólida** to be on a strong footing; **—s llenas** (béisbol) bases loaded; **— por bolas [intencional]** [intentional] base on balls
basic M (lenguaje de programación) BASIC
básico ADJ (fundamental) basic; (sin lujos) no-frills, bare-bones
básquet M basketball
básquetbol M basketball
bastante ADJ & PRON enough, sufficient; **tiene bastante dinero como para ser feliz** she has enough money to be happy; ADV (suficientemente) enough; **me lo has dicho bastante** you've told me that enough times; (mucho) quite a lot; **la herida me duele bastante** my injury is hurting a lot; (algo) quite, pretty; **la película estuvo bastante bien** the movie was quite good
bastar VI to be enough, to suffice; **¡basta!** enough!
bastardilla F italics
bastardo -da ADJ & MF *ofensivo* bastard

bastedad F coarseness
bastidor M (de teatro) wing; (para bordado) frame; (de coche) chassis; (de ventana) sash; **entre —es** (en teatro) offstage; (en privado) behind the scenes
bastimentos M PL provisions
basto ADJ coarse, crude; M suit in the Spanish deck of cards
bastón M cane, walking stick; **— de esquí** ski pole
basura F rubbish, garbage, trash
basural M *Am* dump
basurero -ra MF (persona) garbage collector; M (lugar) dump
bata F (para llevar en casa) robe, housecoat; (de laboratorio) lab coat; (de pacientes) hospital gown; **— de baño** bathrobe
batahola F racket, din
batalla F battle; (de un carro) wheelbase; **— naval** sea battle; **ropa de —** everyday clothing; **trabar —** to engage in battle
batallar VI to battle
batallón M battalion
batata F sweet potato
bate M baseball bat; **al —** at bat
batea F tray
bateador -ora MF batter; **— ambidiestro -ra** switch hitter; **— designado -da** designated hitter; **— emergente** pinch hitter
batear VT to bat, to hit; **— un jonrón** to hit a homerun; **— un sencillo** to hit a single
batería F (de coche, artillería, béisbol) battery; (de cocina) pots and pans; (musical) drums; **— de iones de litio** lithium-ion battery
baterista MF drummer
batiburrillo M hodgepodge
batido M shake, milk shake
batidor M whisk, beater
batidora F mixer
batintín M gong
batir VT (una alfombra) to beat; (un terreno) to comb; (mantequilla) to cream, to churn; (un récord) to break; (huevos) to beat; (crema) to whip; (alas) to flap, to beat; **— palmas** to clap, to applaud; **—se en duelo** to duel; **—se en retirada** to retreat
batuta F baton; **llevar la —** to call the shots
baudio M baud
baúl M trunk
bautismo M baptism, christening; **— de fuego** baptism of fire
bautizar[47] VT to baptize, to christen
bautizo M christening, baptism
baya F berry
bayeta F cleaning cloth
bayo ADJ bay
bayoneta F bayonet
baza F card trick; **meter — en una conversación** to participate in a

conversation
bazar M bazaar
bazo M spleen
bazofia F slop
bazuca F bazooka
beagle M beagle
beato ADJ (bendito) blessed; (piadoso) beatified; (santurrón) overly pious
bebé M baby, infant
bebedero M (en un corral) drinking trough; (en el campo) watering hole; (para personas) water fountain
bebedor -ora MF drinker
beber VI/VT to drink
bebercio M *fam* booze
bebida F drink, beverage
beca F scholarship, fellowship
becario -ria MF scholar, fellow
becerro M (animal) calf; (piel) calfskin
becuadro M natural sign
befa F jeer
befar VT to jeer at
beicon M *Esp* bacon
beige ADJ & M beige
béisbol M baseball
beisbolista M baseball player
beldad F beauty
belga ADJ & MF Belgian
Bélgica F Belgium
Belice M Belize
beliceño -ña ADJ & MF Belizean
bélico ADJ warlike
belicoso ADJ (guerrero) bellicose; (peleador) feisty
beligerante ADJ & MF belligerent
bellaco M rascal, scoundrel
bellaquería F mischief
belleza F beauty
bello ADJ beautiful
bellota F acorn
bemol M (música) flat; **tener —es** to be tricky
bencina F benzine
bendecir[51] VT to bless
bendición F (parte de la misa) benediction; (acción de bendecir) blessing; (beneficio) boon, blessing
bendito ADJ (agua) holy; (alma) blessed; **— sea** may he be blessed; **dormir como un —** to sleep like a log; **es un —** he is a saint
benefactor -ora MF benefactor, patron
beneficencia F charity; **— pública** welfare
beneficiar VT to benefit; **—se de** to benefit from
beneficiario -ria MF (de una herencia, perdón, acto de bondad) beneficiary; (de un cheque) payee
beneficio M benefit (también espectáculo); **—s adicionales** perks; **—s por fallecimiento** death benefits

beneficioso ADJ beneficial
benéfico ADJ beneficent
benemérito ADJ worthy of esteem
benevolencia F benevolence
benévolo ADJ benevolent
bengala F flare
bengalés -esa ADJ & MF Bangladeshi
benigno ADJ benign
Benín M Benin
beninés -esa ADJ & MF Beninese
benjamín -ina MF youngest child
beodo ADJ drunk
berbiquí M carpenter's brace
berenjena F eggplant
bermejo ADJ reddish
bermellón M vermilion
berrear VI (animal) to bellow, to bawl; (bebé) to squall
berrido M (de animal) bellowing, bawling; (de bebé) squall, squalling
berrinche M tantrum
berro M watercress
berza F cabbage
besar VT to kiss
beso M kiss
bestia F beast
bestial ADJ bestial
best-seller M best seller
besuquear VT to kiss repeatedly; **—se** to make out
betabel M *Méx* beet
betabloqueador M beta blocker
betabloqueante M beta blocker
betún M shoe polish
Biblia F Bible
bíblico ADJ biblical
bibliografía F bibliography
biblioteca F (edificio) library; (anaquel) bookcase
bibliotecario -ria MF librarian
bicarbonato M bicarbonate; **— de sosa/soda** bicarbonate of soda
bíceps M SG bicep[s]
bicho M (insecto) bug (también en informática); (animal) *fam* critter; **— raro** odd bird; **mal —** creep; **¿qué — te ha picado?** what's gotten into you? **—s** vermin
bici F bike
bicicleta F bicycle; **— de montaña** mountain bike; **— estática** stationary bike
bicúspide ADJ bicuspid
biela F connecting rod
Bielorrusia F Belarus
bien ADV well; **—aventurado** blessed; **— arreglado** well-groomed; **— conocido** well-known; **— hecho** well-made, well-done; **— poco** very little; **agarrarse —** to hold on tight; **ahora —** now then; **apretar —** to press hard; **está —** she is fine;

más — rather; **me doy — cuenta** I'm perfectly aware; **pues —** now; **qué —** how wonderful; **si —** although; **ya está —** that's enough; M good; **—es** property, assets; **—es consumibles** consumable goods; **—es inmuebles** real estate; **—es muebles** personal property; **—es raíces** real estate; **—estar** well-being, welfare; **—hechor** benefactor; **persona de —** a good person; INTERJ OK!
bienio M biennium
bienvenida F welcome
bienvenido ADJ welcome
bifurcación F (en un camino) fork, forking; (en un programa de computadora) branch
bifurcarse[30] VI to fork, to branch off
bigamia F bigamy
bigote M (de hombre) mustache; (de animal) whisker
bikini M bikini
bilateral ADJ bilateral
bilingüe ADJ & MF bilingual
bilingüismo M bilingualism
bilis F bile
billar M (juego) billiards, pool; (mesa) pool table
billete M (de viaje, para espectáculos) ticket; (de banco) bill, banknote; (financiero) note; **— de ida solo** one-way ticket; **— de ida y vuelta** return ticket
billetera F billfold
billón M trillion
bimestral ADJ bimonthly
bimestre M two-month period
binario ADJ binary
bingo M bingo
binomial ADJ binomial
binomio M binomial
biodegradable ADJ biodegradable
biofeedback M biofeedback
biografía F biography
bioingeniería F bioengineering
biología F biology
biológico ADJ biological
biólogo -ga MF biologist
biombo M folding screen
biopsia F biopsy
bioquímica F biochemistry
biorritmo M biorhythm
biotecnología F biotechnology
bipartidista ADJ bipartisan
bipolar ADJ bipolar
birlar VT *fam* to pinch, to swipe
Birmania F Burma
birmano -na ADJ & MF Burmese, from Myanmar
birrete M mortarboard
bis M encore
bisabuelo -la M great-grandfather; F great-grandmother

bisagra F hinge
bisecar[30] VT to bisect
biselado ADJ beveled
biselar VT to bevel
bisemanal ADV biweekly
bisexual ADJ bisexual, *fam* switch-hitter
bisiesto ADJ **año** — leap year
bisnieto -ta M great-grandson; F
    great-granddaughter
bisonte M bison, buffalo
bistec M beefsteak
bisturí M scalpel
bisutería F costume jewelry
bit M bit
bizarría F gallantry
bizarro ADJ gallant
bizco ADJ cross-eyed
bizcocho M (pastel) sponge cake; (pastelillo)
    pastry
bizcochuelo M sponge cake
bizquear VI to be cross-eyed
black-jack M blackjack
blanca ADJ half note
blanco ADJ (color) white; (tez) fair; M (color)
    white (también clara de huevos, ojos); (de
    tiro) target; (de una burla) butt; — **fácil**
    sitting duck; **dar en el** — to hit the target; **en**
    — (hoja de papel, mente) blank; (sin dormir)
    sleepless; **en** — **y negro** in black and white
blancura F whiteness; (de tez) fairness
blancuzco ADJ whitish
blandir VT to brandish, to wield
blando ADJ (sin dureza, sin rigor) soft;
    (sensiblero) mushy
blandura F softness
blanqueador ADJ whitening; M bleach,
    whitener
blanquear VT (una pared) to whitewash;
    (dinero) to launder; (verduras) to blanch;
    —**se** to whiten
blanquecino ADJ whitish
blanqueo M whitening
blasfemar VI to blaspheme
blasfemia F blasphemy
blasón M coat of arms
blasonar VI to boast
blazer M blazer
blindado ADJ armored
blindaje M armor
blindar VT to armor
bloc M writing tablet, pad of paper
blog M blog
bloguear VI to blog
bloguero -ra MF blogger
bloque M block (también de motor, político);
    (edificio) building; **en** — together
bloquear VT (carretera, asalto, pase, virus
    digital) to block; (puerto) to blockade;
    (cuentas bancarias) to freeze; —**se** to choke

bloqueo M (deporte) block; (computadoras)
    block, blocking; (militar) blockade
blues M PL blues
bluff M bluff
blusa F blouse, top
boa F boa constrictor
boato M pomp
bobada F (tontería) foolish act; (fruslería) trifle
bobalicón -ona ADJ goofy; MF nincompoop
bobear VI to fool around, to monkey around
bobería F (cualidad) foolishness; (dicho) foolish
    remark; (hecho) foolish act
bobina F (de hilo) bobbin; (de alambre, de
    coche) coil; (de película) reel
bobinar VT to reel
bobo -ba ADJ (tonto) dumb, dimwitted, silly;
    (estupefacto) flabbergasted; MF dimwit,
    booby, fool
boca F mouth (también de río); (de un arma de
    fuego) muzzle; (del estómago) pit; (de una
    cueva) opening; —**calle** intersection; — **a** —
    mouth-to-mouth; — **abajo** face down; —
    arriba face up; **a** — **de jarro** at close range;
    callarse la — to shut up
bocadillo M snack; *Esp* sandwich
bocado M (de comida) bite, morsel, mouthful;
    (de una brida) bit
bocanada F (de líquido) mouthful; (de humo)
    puff; (de aire) sniff
bocazas MF SG loudmouth
boceto M sketch
bochorno M (calor) oppressive heat;
    (vergüenza) embarrassment
bochornoso ADJ (caluroso) sultry, oppressive,
    muggy; (vergonzoso) embarrassing
bocina F (de coche) horn; (megáfono)
    megaphone
bocinazo M honk, toot
bocio M goiter
boda F wedding; —**s de oro** golden anniversary;
    —**s de plata** silver anniversary
bodega F (despensa subterránea) cellar; (para
    vinos) wine cellar; (vinería) winery; (espacio
    en un barco, avión) hold; (tienda de
    comestibles) *Carib, Am Central* grocery store
bodeguero -ra MF (viñatero) wine producer;
    (almacenero) *Carib, Am Central* grocer
bofe M [de animal] lung; **echar los** —**s** to tire
    oneself out
bofetada F slap
boga LOC ADV **en** — in vogue, fashion
bogar[40] VI/VT to row
bogey M bogey
bohemio -mia ADJ & MF (nacionalidad)
    Bohemian; (estilo) bohemian
boicot M boycott
boicotear VT to boycott
boicoteo M boycott
boina F beret

bol M bowl

bola F (golf, tenis, béisbol) ball; (canica) marble; (de helado) dip; (de algodón) wad; (jugada de béisbol) ball; — **blanca** cue ball; **en —s** in the buff; **no dar pie con** — to be lost; **no dar ni** — not to pay attention; — **de nudillos** knuckleball; **darle una base por —s** to walk someone; **sacar una base por —s** to walk; — **de break** break point; — **de partido** match-ball; — **de ruptura** break point

bolera F bowling alley

boleta F (de lotería) ticket; (de votación) *Méx* ballot

boletín M bulletin

boleto M ticket; — **de ida solo** one-way ticket; — **de ida y vuelta** return ticket

boliche M (juego) bowling; (bolera) bowling alley

bolígrafo M ballpoint pen; — **computadora portátil** pen computer; — **ordenador portátil** pen computer

bolita F pellet

Bolivia F Bolivia

boliviano -na ADJ & MF Bolivian

bollo M bun, roll

bolo M bowling pin; **jugar a los —s** to bowl

bolsa F (saco) bag; (cartera) purse; (órgano) sac; (marsupio) pouch; — **de valores** stock market; — **de aire** airbag; — **de estudio** scholarship; — **de miseria** pocket of poverty; **hace —s** it pooches out

bolsillo M pocket; **de** — pocket-sized

bolsista MF stockbroker

bolso M (grande) bag; (pequeño) purse

bomba F (para agua, gasolina) pump; (artefacto explosivo) bomb; (noticia, mujer) *fam* bombshell; — **atómica** atomic bomb; — **de hidrógeno** hydrogen bomb; — **de neutrones** neutron bomb; — **de tiempo** time bomb; — **fétida** stink bomb; — **incendiaria** incendiary bomb; — **inteligente** smart bomb; **lo pasamos** — we had a blast

bombacha F *RP* panties, underpants

bombardear VT to bombard

bombardeo M bombardment, bombing

bombardero -ra MF (tripulante) bombardier; M (avión) bomber

bombear VT to pump

bombero -ra MF firefighter

bombilla F lightbulb

bombo M (en música) bass drum; (en béisbol) fly ball; **dar** — to extol; **con —s y platillos** with great fanfare

bombón M (chocolate) bonbon; (mujer atractiva) *fam* dish

bombonería F candy store

bonachón ADJ (amable) good-natured;

(inocente) naive

bonaerense ADJ from the city of Buenos Aires; MF person from Buenos Aires

bonanza F (buen tiempo) fair weather; (prosperidad) prosperity

bondad F goodness, kindness; —**es** virtues; **tenga la** — **de** would you please

bondadoso ADJ kind, kindly

boniato M sweet potato

bonito ADJ pretty; M tuna

bono M (título de deuda) bond; (vale) voucher

boñiga F dung

boqueada F gasp

boquear VI to gasp

boquete M opening

boquiabierto ADJ (de boca abierta) openmouthed; (asombrado) astonished

boquilla F (para cigarros) cigarette holder; (para trompeta) mouthpiece; **defender de** — to pay lip service to

bórax M borax

borbollar VI to bubble

borbollón M (burbujeo) bubbling; (alboroto) commotion; **a borbollones** bubbling over

borbotar VI to bubble, to gurgle

borboteo M bubbling, gurgling

bordado M embroidery, needlework

bordar VI/VT to embroider

borde M (de una superficie) edge, border; (de un vaso) rim, brim; (de un desastre) brink; (de una calle) *Méx* curb

bordear VT (rodear) to skirt, to go along the edge of; (adornar) to trim

bordillo M curb

bordo LOC ADV **a** — on board

bordó, bordeaux ADJ INV & M maroon

borla F (de birrete) tassel; (de algodón) powder puff

boro M boron

borra F dregs

borrachera F (estado) drunkenness; (juerga) drunken spree

borrachín -ina M drunkard

borracho -cha ADJ drunk, wasted; **no lo hago ni** — I would never do such a thing; MF drunkard, wino

borrado M erasure

borrador M (bosquejo) rough draft; (goma) eraser

borrar VT (texto escrito) to erase; (texto digital) to cut, to erase; —**se de un club** to withdraw from a club

borrasca F squall

borrego M lamb

borrico M (asno) donkey; (persona) *pey* ass

borrón M blot, blotch, smudge; **hacer** — **y cuenta nueva** to start over at square one

borronear VT to smudge

borroso ADJ (imagen) blurry, blurred;

(memoria) fuzzy
boscaje M thicket
Bosnia-Herzegovina F Bosnia and Herzegovina
bosnio-nia ADJ & MF Bosnian
bosque M forest, woods
bosquecillo M grove
bosquejar VT to sketch, to outline
bosquejo M sketch, outline
bosta F dung
bostezar[47] VI to yawn
bostezo M yawn
bota F (calzado) boot; (para vino) leather wine bag
botadura F launch
botánica F botany
botánico ADJ botanical
botar VT (una pelota) to bounce; (un buque) to launch; (basura) to throw out
botarate M fool
bote M (jarro) can; (embarcación) boat; (rebote) bounce; — **de basura** garbage can; — **de remos** rowboat; — **de salvamento** lifeboat; **de — en / a —** filled to overflowing; (tenis) — **pronto** half volley
botella F bottle
botero-ra M boatman; F boatwoman
botija F earthen jug
botijo M earthen jar
botín M (de guerra) booty, plunder; (de ladrón) loot, haul
botiquín M (en el baño) medicine cabinet; (de primeros auxilios) first-aid kit
botón M (de aparato, de camisa) button; (remache) stud; (de planta) bud; **botones** bellboy, page; — **de inicio** start button
bótox M botox
Botsuana F Botswana
botsuano-na MF Botswanan
botulismo M botulism
bouquet M bouquet
boutique F boutique
bóveda F (techo) arched roof, vault; — **celeste** the vault of heaven
bowling M bowling
box M (para coches de carrera) pit
boxeador-ora MF boxer, prizefighter
boxear VI/VT to box
boxeo M boxing
bóxer M boxer
boya F (en el mar) buoy; (corcho) float
boyante ADJ buoyant
boyar VI to buoy
bozal M muzzle
bozo M fuzz on the lip
bracear VI to move one's arms
bracero-ra MF migrant worker
bragas F PL underpants, panties
bragueta F fly

brainstorming M brainstorming
bramar VI (ciervo, cochino) to bellow; (león, viento) to roar
bramido M (de ciervo, cochino) bellow; (de león, viento) roar
brandy M brandy
brasa F ember
brasero M brazier
Brasil M Brazil
brasileño-ña ADJ & MF Brazilian
brasilero-ra ADJ & MF Brazilian
bravata F act of bravado
bravío ADJ wild
bravo ADJ (animal, río) wild; (terreno) rugged; (persona) brave; (barrio) tough; INTERJ bravo!
bravucón-ona ADJ bullying; MF bully
bravuconería F bullying
bravura F (de bestia) fierceness; (de persona) courage
braza F fathom
brazada F (cantidad) armful; (en natación) stroke
brazalete M bracelet
brazo M arm (también de silla); (de cornamenta) branch; (de balanza) beam; — **de mar** sound; — **derecho** right-hand man; —**s** day laborers; **con los —s abiertos** with open arms; **con los —s cruzados** with crossed arms; **ir del —** to go arm in arm; **luchar a — partido** to fight to the end
brea F pitch, tar
brecha F (en un muro) breach, gap; (entre generaciones) gap
brécol M broccoli
bregar[40] VI to struggle, to toil
breña F scrub
breve ADJ (cuento) brief, short; (bikini) scanty; **en —** shortly
brevedad F brevity, shortness; **a la —** as soon as possible
bribón-ona ADJ roguish; MF rascal, rogue, scoundrel
brida F bridle
brigada F brigade
brillante ADJ brilliant, bright; M diamond, gem
brillantez F brilliance
brillantina F glitter
brillar VI (oro) to shine; (ojos) to sparkle, to twinkle; (nieve) to glisten; — **por su ausencia** to be conspicuous by its absence
brillo M (de metal, piedras preciosas) shine, luster, sparkle; (de los ojos) twinkle; (de nieve) glistening; (del pelo, plumas) sheen; (de diamantes) sparkle; (de una pantalla) brightness; **dar —** to give luster; **sacar —** to polish
brilloso ADJ shiny
brincar[30] VI to hop, to skip
brinco M hop, skip

brindar VI (beber) to toast; (proporcionar) to provide; — **por alguien** to toast someone; —**se a hacer algo** to volunteer to do something
brindis M toast
brío M spirit
brioso ADJ spirited
brisa F breeze
británico ADJ British
brizna F blade of grass
broca F drill bit
brocado M brocade
brocal M (borde) rim; (boca de pozo) curb
brocha F paintbrush; **de — gorda** coarse
broche M (alhaja) brooch; (sujetador) clasp, clip; (para el pelo) barrette; — **de oro** grand finale
brocheta F skewer
brócoli, bróculi M broccoli
broma F (chiste) joke; (réplica) jest, wisecrack; — **pesada** practical joke; —**s aparte** kidding aside; **en** — in jest; **gastar una** — to play a joke; **ni en** — no way; **no estoy para** —**s** I'm not in the mood for kidding
bromear VI to joke, to kid
bromista MF wag, joker
bromo M bromine
bromuro M bromide
bronca F row; **armar una** — to cause a disturbance, to raise a rumpus; **echarle la** — **a alguien** to bawl someone out; **tener** — to be angry
bronce M bronze
bronceado ADJ (cubierto de bronce) bronzed; (tostado) tanned; (de color bronce) bronze; M suntan
broncear VT (un objeto) to bronze; —**se** to get a tan
bronco ADJ (voz) gruff; (terreno) rough; (caballo) wild
bronquial ADJ bronchial
bronquio M bronchial tube
bronquitis F bronchitis
brotar VI (planta) to sprout; (enfermedad eruptiva) to break out; (agua) to gush, to flow, to issue
brote M (de una enfermedad) outbreak; (retoño) sprout, spear
broza F brushwood
bruces LOC ADV **de** — face down
brujería F witchcraft, devilry
brujo-ja M wizard, sorcerer; F witch
brújula F compass
bruma F mist
brumoso ADJ misty
brunch M brunch
bruneano-na ADJ & MF Bruneian
Brunéi M Brunei
bruñir[17] VT to burnish
bruscamente ADV (girar, responder) sharply;

(hablar) brusquely
brusco ADJ (descortés) brusque, curt; (repentino) sudden
brusquedad F (descortesía) brusqueness; (lo repentino) suddenness
brutal ADJ brutal
brutalidad F brutality
bruto -ta ADJ (ignorante) ignorant; (maleducado, burdo) uncouth; (violento) brutish; (sin descuentos) gross; **a lo** — roughly; **en** — in the rough; **recaudar en** — to gross; MF (ignorante) blockhead; (persona violenta) brute; (mal educado) lout, brute
bucal ADJ oral
bucear VI (sumergirse) to scuba dive; (indagar) to explore
buceo M scuba diving
buche M (en las aves) crop; (bocado) mouthful
bucle M (de pelo) curl, ringlet; (en informática) loop
budín M pudding
budismo M Buddhism
budista ADJ, MF Buddhist
bueno ADJ good; **buena fe** good faith; **a la buena de Dios** haphazardly; **de buenas a primeras** out of the blue; **estar** — to be sexy; **hace buen tiempo** it is fine weather; **lo** — the good thing; **por las buenas o por las malas** by hook or by crook; **ser** — **con los números** to be good at figures; INTERJ OK! —**s días** good day/morning; **buenas noches** good night/evening; **buenas tardes** good afternoon
buey M ox, steer
búfalo M buffalo, bison
bufanda F scarf, muffler
bufar VI to snort; **está que bufa** he is incensed
bufete M (despacho) lawyer's office; (negocio) practice
buffet M buffet
bufido M snort
bufón -ona MF buffoon, jester
bufonear VI to clown
buhardilla F (desván) attic, garret
búho M owl
buhonero -ra MF peddler
buitre M vulture, buzzard
buje M bushing
bujía F spark plug
bulbo M bulb
bulldog M bulldog
bulevar M boulevard
Bulgaria F Bulgaria
búlgaro -ra ADJ & MF Bulgarian
bulimia F bulimia
bulla F uproar, fuss, bustle
bulldozer M bulldozer
bullicio M uproar, racket, bustle
bullicioso ADJ boisterous, rowdy

bullir[16] VI (hervir) to boil; (hacer burbujas) to bubble; (ajetrearse) to bustle; (moverse) to stir
bullón M puff
bullpen M bullpen
bulto M (paquete) bundle; (tumor) lump, growth; (silueta) shape; (saliente) bulge; **a —** approximately; **escurrir el —** to slack off
bungaló M bungalow
bungee M bungee jumping
búnker M bunker
buñuelo M fritter
buque M ship; **— de carga** freighter
burbuja F bubble
burdel M brothel, *fam* whorehouse
burdo ADJ coarse
burgués ADJ bourgeois
burguesía F bourgeoisie, middle class
burla F ridicule, mockery; **hacer — a alguien** to mock someone
burlar VT to mock; **—se de** to scoff at, to make fun of
burlesco ADJ burlesque
burlón ADJ mocking
burocracia F bureaucracy
burócrata MF bureaucrat
burrez F stupidity
burro M (animal) donkey, ass; (persona) dunce; ADJ dense
bursátil ADJ **mercado —** stock market
bursitis F bursitis
burundés -esa ADJ & MF Burundian
Burundi M Burundi
bus M bus; **— en serie** serial bus
busca LOC ADV **en — de** in search of
buscar[30] VT (objetos perdidos) to seek, to look for, to search for; (datos, palabras) to look up; (provocar) to provoke; (la verdad) to seek after; (minerales) to prospect for; (talento) to scout for; **—se problemas** to invite trouble; **— y reemplazar** to search and replace; **tú te lo buscaste** you asked for it; **ir a —** to fetch; M SG **buscapersonas** beeper, pager
búsqueda F search; **— del tesoro** treasure hunt; **— hacia atrás** backward search; **— por palabra clave** keyword search
busto M bust
butaca F (en la casa) armchair; (en el teatro) seat
Bután M Bhutan
butanés -esa ADJ & MF Bhutanese
butano M butane
buzo M diver
buzón M mailbox; **— de sugerencias** suggestion box
bypass M bypass operation, coronary bypass
byte M byte

Cc

cabal ADJ (completo) complete; (exacto) exact; (honrado) upright; **estar uno en sus —es** to be in one's right mind
cabalgar[40] VI to ride horseback
caballa F mackerel
caballada F herd of horses
caballejo M nag
caballeresco ADJ chivalrous
caballería F (tropas) cavalry; (equino) equine; (condición de caballero) knighthood
caballeriza F stable
caballerizo M groom
caballero M (señor) gentleman; (hidalgo) knight; **— andante** knight errant; ADJ gentlemanly
caballerosidad F chivalry
caballeroso ADJ chivalrous, gentlemanly
caballete M (soporte de madera) sawhorse; (de la nariz) bridge; (de pintor) easel; (de tejado) ridge
caballo M (animal) horse; (en ajedrez) knight; (heroína) *fam* smack; **a —** on horseback; **— de carreras** racehorse; **— de batalla** hobbyhorse; **— de fuerza** horsepower; **— de Troya** Trojan horse
cabaña F (casucha) hovel; (casa de campo) cabin, cottage; (conjunto de ganado) livestock
cabaret M cabaret
cabecear VI (mover la cabeza) to nod; (dormirse) to nod off; (un barco) to bob, to pitch; VT (balón) to head
cabeceo M (de la cabeza) nodding; (de un barco) pitching
cabecera F (de cama) headboard; (de mesa) head
cabecilla MF ringleader
cabellera F head of hair
cabello M hair; **traido por los —s** far-fetched
caber[67] VI to fit; **no cabe duda** there is no doubt; **no cabe nadie más** there is no room for anybody else; **no — uno en sí** to be puffed up with pride; **no cabe en lo posible** it is absolutely impossible; **¿en qué cabeza cabe?** who would believe that?
cabestrillo M sling
cabestro M halter
cabeza F head; **— de chorlito** scatterbrain, airhead; **— de playa** beachhead; **— de puente** bridgehead; **— de turco** scapegoat, fall guy; **— de serie** seed; **— rapada** skinhead; **a la —** at the forefront; **caerse de —** to fall head first; **echarse de —** to plunge headlong; **ir a la —** to lead the way; **por —** each; **romperse la —** to rack one's brains; **la**

fama se le fue a la — fame went to his head; **sentar** — to settle down; **tiene la** — **cuadrada** she's a square

cabezada F nod; **dar —s** to nod off

cabezal M magnetic head

cabezazo M (golpe) head butt; (jugada de fútbol) header

cabezón ADJ (de cabeza grande) big-headed; (testarudo) pig-headed; (con mucho alcohol) strong

cabezudo ADJ (de cabeza grande) big-headed; (testarudo) pig-headed

cabida F capacity; **dar** — to include; **tener** — **en** to fit in

cabina F (de pasajeros) cabin; (de piloto) cockpit; (de camión) cab; (de teléfono, control) booth

cabizbajo ADJ crestfallen, downcast

cable M cable; — **coaxial** coaxial cable; **—s del ordenador / de la computadora** media

cableado M wiring

cablevisión F cable television

cabo M (parte extrema) end; (hilo) thread; (cuerda) rope; (saliente de la costa) cape; MF (rango militar) corporal; — **suelto** loose end; **al** — **de** at the end of; **atar —s** to put two and two together; **de** — **a rabo** from beginning to end; **llevar a** — to carry out

cabotaje M coastal trade

Cabo Verde M Cape Verde

caboverdiano -na ADJ & MF Cape Verdean

cabra F goat; — **montés** mountain goat; **[loco] como una** — completely crazy

cabrá, cabría ver caber

cabrearse VI to get mad

cabrestante M winch

cabrillas F PL whitecaps

cabrio M rafter

cabrío ADJ **macho** — he-goat

cabriola F caper

cabriolar VI to cavort

cabritilla F kid [leather]

cabrito M kid [goat]

cabrón -ona M (macho de cabra) he-goat; (cornudo) cuckold; (hijo de puta) *ofensivo* bastard; F (hija de puta) *ofensivo* bitch; MF (cobarde) wimp

caca F poop; **hacer** — to poop

cacahuate M *Méx* peanut

cacahuete M *Esp* peanut

cacao M cocoa

cacarear VI to cackle, to squawk

cacareo M cackling, squawking

cacatúa F cockatoo

cacería F hunt; — **de brujas** witch hunt

cacerola F saucepan

cacha F (de navaja) handle; (nalga) thigh, butt; **hasta la** — completely

cachalote M sperm whale

cacharro M (vasija) earthen pot; (coche viejo) clunker, jalopy

cachaza F slowness

cachazudo ADJ slow

caché M (en informática) cache; (distinción) cachet; — **de memoria** memory cache

cachear VT to body-search, to frisk

cachet M artist's fee

cachetada F slap

cachete M cheek

cachiporra F blackjack

cachivaches M PL stuff, odds and ends

cacho M hunk

cachondo ADJ *fam* horny

cachorro M (de oso, lobo, tigre, león) cub; (de perro) puppy

cacique -ca M (de indios) chief, chieftain; MF (caudillo) political boss

cacofonía F cacophony

cacto/cactus M cactus

cada ADJ each; — **uno** each one; — **vez más** more and more; — **vez menos gente** fewer and fewer people; — **vez menos harina** less and less flour; — **vez peor** worse and worse; **doscientas pesetas** — **una** two hundred pesetas each/apiece

cadalso M gallows

cadáver M (para enterrar) corpse; (para disecar) cadaver

cadavérico ADJ ghastly

caddie, caddy MF caddie

cadena F (serie de piezas) chain; (de televisión) network; (cordillera) mountain range; — **alimenticia** food chain; — **de montaje** assembly line; — **perpetua** life sentence; **—s** shackles; **tirar la** — to flush

cadencia F cadence

cadera F hip

cadete M cadet

cadmio M cadmium

caducar[30] VI to lapse, to expire

caducidad F expiration

caduco ADJ (deciduo) deciduous; (decrépito) decrepit

caer[52] VI to fall; (desplomarse) to fall down; (colgar) to hang; (ir a parar) to end up; **al** — **la noche** at nightfall; — **en desgracia** to fall into disfavor, to fall out of favor; — **en desuso** to fall into disuse; — **en cama** to fall ill; — **en cuenta** to catch on; — **en ruina** to fall into disrepair; **—le bien/mal a uno** (una persona) to make a good/bad impression; (una comida) to agree with; **—le en suerte a uno** to fall to one's lot; — **tan bajo** to fall so low; **caiga quien caiga** let fall who may; **dejar** — to drop; **está al** — he's about to show up; **—se** (persona) to fall down; (computadora, ordenador) to crash; **se cayó el sistema** the system crashed; **—se de culo** to fall on one's bottom

café M (bebida) coffee; (color) brown; (establecimiento) coffee shop, café
cafeína F caffeine
cafetal M coffee plantation
cafetera F coffeepot
cafetería F snack bar, cafeteria, diner
cafetero -ra MF coffee dealer; ADJ **industria cafetera** coffee industry
cafeto M coffee bush
cagada F (acción de cagar) *vulg* dump; (desacierto) *vulg* screw-up; **este libro es una —** *fam* this book sucks
cagalera F *vulg* the trots, the shits
cagar[40] VI/VT *vulg* to shit, to take a crap; **—la** *vulg* to screw up, to fuck up; **me cago en diez / la mar** *fam* I'll be damned; **me cago en tu madre** *ofensivo* fuck you! **me cagué la chaqueta** *vulg* I fucked up my jacket; **—se de miedo** *vulg* to shit a brick, to be scared shitless
caída F (acción de caer) fall, tumble, spill; (de presión arterial) drop; (de un ordenador) crash; (de una cortina) hang; (de precios) drop; **— libre** free fall; **— del sol** sunset; **— en picado** nosedive; **—s del sistema** system crashes
caído ADJ (orejas) floppy; (arco del pie) fallen; **los —s** the fallen
caiga, caigo *ver* caer
caimán M alligator
caja F box; **— boba** *fam* boob tube; **— chica** petty cash; **— de ahorros** savings bank; **— de bateo** batter's box; **— de cambios** transmission; **— de escalera** stairwell; **— de fusibles** fuse box; **— de herramientas** toolkit; **— de jubilaciones** pension fund; **— de música** music box; **— de seguridad** safe deposit box; **— de reloj** watchcase; **— fuerte** safe; **— negra** flight recorder; **— registradora** (aparato) cash register, till; (mostrador) checkout counter; **— tonta** idiot box; **— torácica** rib cage; **entrar en —** (comenzar) to get going; (establecerse) to settle down
cajero -ra MF cashier; (en un banco) teller; **— automático** ATM
cajetilla F pack [of cigarettes]
cajilla F pack [of cigarettes]
cajón M (para transportes) crate; (parte de un mueble) drawer; **eso es de —** that's a foregone conclusion
cajuela F *Méx* car trunk
cal F lime; **cerrar a — y canto** to close hermetically
calabacín M zucchini
calabaza F (grande y redonda) pumpkin; (pequeña y/o alargada) squash; (vaciada) gourd; **dar —s** to turn down
calabozo M dungeon

calado M draft
calamar M squid
calambre M cramp
calamidad F calamity
calamina F calamine
calandria F lark
calar VT (agujerear) to perforate; (empapar) to soak, to drench; **— a alguien** to see through someone; **— hondo** to resonate; **—se** to get drenched
calavera F skull; M libertine
calcar[30] VT (sobre papel) to trace; (imitar) to copy
calcetería F hosiery
calcetín M sock
calcinar VT to bake
calcio M calcium
calco M (acción de calcar) tracing; **es el — de su padre** he's the spitting image of his father
calcomanía F decal
calculador ADJ calculating
calculadora F calculator
calcular VT (computar) to calculate, to figure; (sopesar) to weigh; (prever) to reckon
cálculo M (cómputo) calculation; (aritmética) arithmetic; (integral, diferencial) calculus; **— biliar** gallstone; **— renal** kidney stone
caldear VT to warm up; **— los ánimos** to get everyone upset
caldera F (en una máquina de vapor) boiler; (recipiente con asas) kettle; (de calefacción) furnace
calderón M hold
caldo M broth, stock; **— de cultivo** culture medium
calefacción F heat, heating; **— central** central heating
calendario M calendar
caléndula F marigold
calentador M heater; **— de agua** water heater
calentamiento M warming; (en deportes) warm-up; **— global** global warming
calentar[1] VI/VT (poner caliente) to warm, to heat; **—se** (ponerse caliente, prepararse para un partido) to warm up, to heat up; (excitarse sexualmente) *fam* to get horny
calentura F (fiebre) fever; (excitación sexual) *fam* horniness
calesa F buggy
caletre M **no tener —** to have no brains
calibrador M caliper
calibrar VT to gauge, to calibrate
calibre M (de pistola, tubo) caliber; (de alambre) gauge; (calibrador) caliper
calicó M calico
calidad F quality; **baja —** low quality; **de —** of good quality; **de — inferior** substandard; **estoy aquí en — de representante** I'm here in my capacity as representative

cálido ADJ warm
caliente ADJ (agradable) warm; (excesivo) hot; (excitado sexualmente) *fam* horny
calificación F (nota) grade, mark; (acción de asignar notas) grading; (comparación) rating; — **crediticia** credit rating; **le dieron la** — **de genio** they called him a genius
calificar[30] VT (juzgar la calidad) to rate, to adjudge; (asignar nota) to grade; —**se como** to be characterized as
calificativo ADJ qualifying; M label
caligrafía F (letra) penmanship; (arte) calligraphy
calina F haze
callado ADJ silent, quiet; **estarse** — to keep quiet
callar VT (no manifestar, no dejar decir) to quiet; VI (no hablar) to remain silent; (dejar de hablar) to go quiet; —**se la boca** to shut up, to pipe down
calle F (de ciudad) street; (golf) fairway; — **abajo** down the street; — **arriba** up the street; — **de sentido único** one-way street; **hacer la** — *fam* to cruise for johns, to turn tricks; **no pisar la** — to stay home
calleja F narrow street
callejear VI to walk the streets
callejero ADJ **perro** — stray dog; **caos** — chaos in the streets
callejón M alley; — **sin salida** blind alley, dead end
callo M callus, corn
calloso ADJ callous
calma F calm; — **chicha** absolute calm; **mantener la** — (no enojarse) to keep one's temper; (no ponerse nervioso) to stay calm; **tomar las cosas con** — to take things easy
calmante ADJ & M sedative
calmar VT (nervios) to calm; (dolor) to sooth; (miedo) to allay, to quell; (sed) to quench; —**se** (una persona) to calm down; (una tormenta, la ira) to subside, to abate
calmo ADJ calm
calmoso ADJ easygoing
calor M (temperatura alta) heat; (temperatura templada) warmth; (actitud acogedora) warmth; **hace** — **hoy** it's hot today; **los** —**es** hot flashes; **tengo** — I'm hot
caloría F calorie
calumnia F calumny, slander
calumniar VT to slander, to malign
calumnioso ADJ slanderous
caluroso ADJ (día) hot; (recepción) warm
calva F bald spot
calvario M **mi vida es un** — *fam* my life is hell
calvicie F baldness
calvo ADJ bald, baldheaded; **ni tanto ni tan** — *fam* it ain't necessarily so; **quedarse** — to go bald

calza F long sock
calzada F pavement
calzado M footwear
calzador M shoehorn
calzar[47] VT (poner zapatos) to shoe; (hacer zapatos para) to make shoes for; — **a la familia** to buy shoes for the family; **calzo 42** I take size 10; —**se** to put on shoes
calzones M PL (de mujer) panties; (de hombre) shorts
calzonazos M SG henpecked man
calzoncillos M PL underpants, briefs; — **largos** long johns
cama F bed; — **de agua** waterbed; — **doble** double bed; — **elástica** trampoline; — **individual** twin bed; **guardar** — to be confined to bed; **meterse en la** — **con** to sleep with
camada F litter
camafeo M cameo
camaleón M chameleon
cámara F (espacio) chamber; (de neumático) inner tube; (fotográfica) camera; — **de comercio** chamber of commerce; — **de diputados** lower house; — **de gas** gas chamber; — **digital** digital camera; — **de oxígeno** oxygen tent; — **frigorífica** cold-storage locker; — **legislativa** legislature; — **hiperbárica** hyperbaric chamber; **en** — **lenta** in slow motion; MF (persona que maneja una cámara) camera operator
camarada MF comrade
camarero -ra M (restaurante) waiter, server; (coche cama) steward; F (restaurante) waitress, server; (coche cama) stewardess; (hotel) maid; MF (béisbol) second baseman
camarilla F clique
camarógrafo -fa M cameraman; F camerawoman
camarón M shrimp
camarote M cabin, stateroom
cambalache M (intercambio) fraudulent swap; (tienda) secondhand store
cambalachear VI/VT to swap fraudulently
cambiante ADJ (que cambia) changing; (propenso a cambiar) changeable; (temperamento) volatile
cambiar VI/VT to change; VT (una cosa por otra) to exchange, to swap, to trade; — **de marcha** to shift gears; — **de opinión/parecer** to change one's mind; — **de sitio** to move places
cambiario ADJ **sistema** — foreign exchange system
cambio M (acción de cambiar) change; (marcha) gear; (cotización) exchange rate; (de ferrocarril) railway switch; (béisbol) changeup; — **de velocidad** (en béisbol)

change-up; — **de lado** (tenis) changeover; — **de divisas** foreign exchange; — **para peor** a turn for the worse; — **y fuera** over and out; **a — [de]** in return [for]; **en —** on the other hand

cambista MF money changer

Camboya F Cambodia

camboyano -na ADJ & MF Cambodian

camellear VT to push [drugs]

camello -lla MF (animal) camel; (vendedor de droga) pusher

camerino M dressing room

Camerún M Cameroon

camerunés -esa ADJ & MF Cameroonian

camilla F stretcher, litter

camillero -ra MF hospital orderly

caminante MF walker, wayfarer

caminar VI/VT to walk; (baloncesto) to travel

caminata F long walk; (por un lugar agreste) hike

camino M (carretera) road; (itinerario, dirección a seguir) way; — **de** on the way to; — **de mesa** table runner; — **de rosas** bed of roses; **abrirse —** to make way; **a medio —** halfway; **en — [a]** on the way [to]; **llevar por mal —** to lead astray; **mostrar el —** to lead the way; **ponerse en —** to set out; **señalar el —** to show the way

camión M (de cargas) truck; (para transporte de personas) *Méx* bus; — **de la basura** garbage truck; — **de mudanzas** moving van; — **de remolque** tow truck, wrecker; — **de reparto** delivery truck, — **volteador** dump truck

camionero -ra MF truck driver; *Méx* bus driver

camioneta F (furgoneta) van, minivan; (camioncito) pickup truck; (coche sin maletero) station wagon

camisa F shirt; — **de fuerza** straitjacket; **meterse en — de once varas** to get into a jam

camiseta F (exterior) T-shirt; (interior) undershirt

camisón M nightgown

camorrista MF hell-raiser; ADJ rowdy

campamento M (de refugiados, exploradores) camp; (recreativo) campground

campana F bell; **tocar una —** to ring a bell

campanario M belfry, bell tower

campanilla F (campana pequeña) small bell; (flor) bluebell; (órgano en la boca) uvula

campanilleo M ringing

campánula F bellflower

campaña F campaign; — **publicitaria** advertising campaign; **hacer —** to campaign; **el ejército estaba de —** the army was on the front

campechano ADJ straightforward

campeón -ona MF champion

campeonato M championship; — **Mundial de Fútbol** Soccer World Cup

campero ADJ **hombre —** a man from the country

campesino -na MF peasant; ADJ **casa campesina** peasant house

campestre ADJ rural

camping M (lugar) campground; (actividad) camping

campiña F open country

campista MF camper

campo M (fuera de la ciudad) country, countryside; (para cultivos, deportes, ámbito del saber) field; (grupo en un conflicto) camp; — **abierto** range; MF —**corto** (béisbol) shortstop; — **de acción** field of action; — **de batalla** battlefield; — **de concentración** concentration camp; — **de golf** golf course; — **de juego** athletic field; — **de tiro** shooting range; — **libre** free rein; — **magnético** magnetic field; — **minado** minefield; — **petrolífero** oil field; — **visual** visual field; **a — traviesa** cross-country; —**santo** churchyard

campus M campus

camuflaje M camouflage

camuflar VT to camouflage

can M dog

cana F white hair; **echar una — al aire** to go out for a good time

Canadá M Canada

canadiense ADJ & MF Canadian

canal M (cauce artificial de agua) canal; (estrecho marítimo, banda de frecuencia) channel; (emisora) station; — **de parto** birth canal; — **radicular** root canal

canalé M ribbed fabric

canalizar[47] VT to channel

canalla MF *ofensivo* scum, lowlife

canalón M spout

canana F cartridge belt

canapé M (mueble) divan; (aperitivo) canape, starter

canario -ria M canary; ADJ of/from the Canary Islands; MF Canary Islander

canasta F basket (también en baloncesto)

canasto M hamper

cancelación F cancellation

cancelar VT (contrato, sello) to cancel; (deuda) to pay off; (evento) to call off

cáncer M cancer; — **de mama** breast cancer; — **de colon** colorectal cancer

cancerígeno ADJ carcinogen

canceroso -sa MF cancer patient; ADJ cancerous

cancha F (de baloncesto, tenis) court; (de fútbol) field; **¡abran —!** gangway! **falta —** there's no room

canciller MF (de Alemania, de universidades) chancellor; (de EEUU) secretary of state

canción F song; — **de cuna** lullaby
candado M padlock
candela F (vela) candle; (fuego) fire
candelabro M candelabrum
candelero M candlestick; **en el** — in the limelight
candente ADJ red-hot
candidato -ta MF candidate
candidatura F (hecho de ser candidato) candidacy; (conjunto de candidatos) ticket
candidez F innocence
cándido ADJ naive
candil M oil lamp
candilejas F PL footlights
candor M innocence
canela F (especia) cinnamon; (árbol) cinnamon tree
canesú M yoke of a shirt
cangrejo M crab
canguro M kangaroo; MF *Esp* baby-sitter
caníbal ADJ & MF cannibal
canica F toy marble
caniche M poodle; — **enano** toy poodle
canilla F (espinilla) shin; (pantorrilla) calf; (grifo) faucet
canino ADJ canine; **tener un hambre canina** to be ravenous; M canine [tooth]
canje M exchange
canjear VT (prisioneros, libros) to exchange; (un cupón) to redeem
cano ADJ gray-haired
canoa F canoe
canon M (regla, modelo) canon; (canción) round
canónigo M canon
canoso ADJ gray-haired
cansado ADJ (fatigado) tired, weary; (fatigoso) wearing, tiring
cansancio M weariness
cansar VT (fatigar) to tire, to tire out; (aburrir) to bore; —**se** to get tired
cantante MF singer
cantar VI/VT (hacer música) to sing; VT (anunciar) to call out; (revelar secretos) to squeal; — **a tono** to sing on key; —**le a alguien las cuarenta** to give someone a piece of one's mind; — **victoria** to declare victory; **en menos que canta un gallo** before you can say Jack Robinson; M epic poem; **eso es otro** — that's another story
cántaro M pitcher; **llover a** —**s** to rain cats and dogs
cantera F quarry
cantero M *RP* flower bed
cántico M chant
cantidad F quantity, amount; (de dinero) amount, sum; — **a pagar** amount payable; — **debida** amount due; — **pagada** amount paid; — **de gente** a lot of people
cantimplora F canteen, water bottle

cantina F (lugar donde comer) mess hall, mess, canteen; (bar) tavern
cantinela F chant
cantinero -ra MF bartender
canto M (cosa cantada) song; (piedra) pebble; — **de cisne** swan song; — **llano** chant; — **rodado** rounded pebble; **de** — on edge
cantor -ora MF singer
canturrear VI to hum
canturreo M hum, humming
caña F (planta gramínea) reed; (de azúcar) cane; (cerveza) *Esp* beer; (vaso) *Esp* beer glass; — **de pescar** fishing pole; **dale** — floor it
cañada F (barranco) ravine; (arroyo) brook
cáñamo M hemp
cañaveral M reed patch
cañería F (en la calle) piping; (en la casa) plumbing
caño M (tubo) pipe; (grifo) spout; (de arma) barrel; **de doble** — double-barreled
cañón M (arma) cannon; (pieza hueca) barrel; (cañada profunda) canyon; (de pluma, bolígrafo) shaft
cañonero M gunboat
caoba F mahogany
caos M chaos
caótico ADJ chaotic
capa F (prenda) cape, cloak; (de pintura, animal) coat; (de tierra) layer; (de hielo) sheet; — **de ozono** ozone layer; — **freática** water table; **de** — **y espada** cloak and dagger
capacidad F capacity; —**es** aptitude, ability, capability; — **de almacenamiento de disco** disk capacity
capacitación F training; — **para empleados** in-service training
capacitar VT (entrenar) to train; (habilitar) to qualify
capar VT to castrate
caparazón M shell
capataz -za MF boss, overseer
capaz ADJ (habilidoso) capable, able; (apto) apt; (espacioso) spacious, roomy; (competente) competent
capear VT to ride out, to weather
capellán M chaplain
caperuza F pointed hood
capilar ADJ & M capillary
capilla F chapel; **estar en** — (castigado) to be in the doghouse; (en ascuas) to be on pins and needles
capital M (dinero) capital; (de préstamo) principal; — **de riesgo** venture capital; — **inicial** start-up funds; **el gran** — big business; F capital [city]; ADJ main
capitalino ADJ **atmósfera capitalina** capital city atmosphere
capitalismo M capitalism
capitalista MF capitalist; ADJ capitalistic

capitalización F capitalization
capitalizar[47] VT (aportar capital) to capitalize; (aprovechar) to capitalize on
capitán -ana MF captain
capitanear VT to captain
capitel M capital
capitolio M capitol
capitulación F (militar) capitulation, surrender; **capitulaciones matrimoniales** prenuptial agreement
capitular VI to capitulate
capítulo M chapter
capó M hood [of a car]
capo M mafia boss
capota F top [of a car]
capote M cloak; (de coche) *Méx* hood; **decir para su —** to say under one's breath
capricho M caprice, whim, notion
caprichoso ADJ (impredecible) capricious; (impulsivo) whimsical, fanciful; (malcriado) willful
cápsula F capsule
captación F (de agua) collection; (de clientes) attraction; (de inversiones, fondos) raising
captar VT (un concepto) to grasp; (atención, interés) to capture; (una emisión) to receive; (una indirecta) to get; **— la onda** to get the drift
captor -ora MF captor
captura F (acción de capturar) capture; (pesca capturada) catch; (fútbol americano) sack; **— de video/vídeo** video capture
capturar VT to capture; (pescado) to catch
capucha F (de cabeza) hood, cowl; (de lapicero) cap
capuchina F nasturtium
capuchino M cappuccino
capullo M (de insecto) cocoon; (de flor) bud; (tonto) *vulg* dickhead
caqui M khaki
cara F (rostro) face; (de cubo) surface; (de papel, moneda) side; (morro) nerve; **— a —** face to face; **— o cruz** heads or tails; **dar la —** to face up to things; **de — al sur** facing south; **decir en la —** to tell to one's face; **de dos —s** two-sided; **la otra — de la moneda** the other side of the coin; **poner buena —** to put on a good face; **se le ve en la —** it's written all over his face; **tener — [dura]** to have a lot of nerve; **un ojo de la —** an arm and a leg; **volverle la — a** to snub
carabinero -ra MF (oficial de aduana) border patrol officer; (agente de policía) police officer; M (crustáceo) red prawn
caracol M (molusco) snail; (concha) snail shell; INTERJ **¡—es!** *fam* darn!
carácter M (temperamento, signo) character; (rasgo) characteristic; (índole) kind
característica F characteristic, feature; (en informática) feature
característico ADJ characteristic
caracterización F (descripción) characterization, description; (retrato) portrayal
caracterizar[47] VT to characterize
carajo INTERJ *vulg* shit! **irse al —** *vulg* to go to hell; **no sabe un —** *vulg* he doesn't know shit; **¿qué — quieres?** *vulg* what the fuck do you want? **un artista del —** *vulg* a shitty artist; M *Esp vulg* dick
caramba INTERJ *fam* darn! good grief! heck!
carámbano M icicle
carambola F carom; **por —** indirectly
caramelo M (azúcar fundido) caramel; (dulce pequeño) bonbon
caramillo M reed pipe
carátula F (máscara) mask; (portada) title page
caravana F (en el desierto, convoy) caravan; (remolque) trailer
caray INTERJ *fam* shoot! darn!
carbohidrato M carbohydrate
carbón M (sustancia) coal; (pedazo) piece of coal; **— de leña** charcoal
carboncillo M charcoal drawing
carbonera F coal bin
carbono M carbon
carburador M carburetor
carburante M fuel
carca ADJ old-fashioned; MF *fam* fossil, old fogey
carcaj M quiver
carcajada F burst of laughter, guffaw
carcamal M *fam* fossil, old fogey
cárcel F jail, prison
carcelero -ra MF jailer
carcinógeno M carcinogen
carcinoma M carcinoma; **— de célula basal** basal cell carcinoma
carcomido ADJ worm-eaten
carda F card, comb
cardán M universal joint
cardar VT (lana) to card, to comb; (pelo) to rat, to tease
cardenal M (pájaro, prelado) cardinal; (moretón) bruise
cardíaco -ca ADJ cardiac; MF heart patient
cardinal ADJ cardinal
cardioangiograma M cardioangiogram
cardiograma M cardiogram
cardiología F cardiology
cardiólogo -ga MF cardiologist
cardiopulmonar ADJ cardiopulmonary
cardiovascular ADJ cardiovascular
cardo M thistle
cardumen M school of fish
carear VT to bring face to face; **—se** to meet face to face
carecer[35] VI **— de** to lack
carencia F (falta) lack; (deficiencia alimenticia)

deficiency
carenciado ADJ disadvantaged
carente ADJ lacking; — **de** lacking in
carero ADJ expensive
carestía F (escasez) scarcity; (costo alto) high cost
careta F mask
carezca, carezco *ver* carecer
carga F (cosa cargada) load, freight; (de la prueba, impuesto) burden; (hipoteca) lien; (de encendedor) refill; (de explosivo, electricidad) charge; (de programas) upload; — **de municiones** round of ammunition; — **útil** payload; **volver a la** — to insist
cargado ADJ (bebida) stiff; (pausa) pregnant; (cartucho) live; — **de deudas** deep in debt; — **de espaldas** stooping
cargador M (de batería) charger; (de arma de fuego) clip, magazine
cargamento M cargo, load, shipment
cargar[40] VT (cargamentos, dados, arma, programa de ordenador) to load; (batería, a una cuenta, en baloncesto) to charge; (de obligaciones) to burden with; (a un niño) to carry; (a un estudiante) *Esp* to flunk; (molestar) to bother; — **a alguien de responsabilidades** to saddle someone with responsibilities; — **al hombro** to shoulder; — **de combustible** to fuel; — **un programa** to upload; VI to charge; — **con la culpa** to be saddled with blame; — **sobre** to charge, to attack
cargo M (función en una empresa) position; (en una factura, a una cuenta) charge; (acusación) count, charge; — **de conciencia** guilt feelings; —**s atrasados** back charges; — **de tramitación** handling charges; **a mi** — under my charge; **hacerse** — **de** (responsabilizarse de) to take charge of; (ser consciente de) to understand; **investir de un** — to induct into office; **los niños están a** — **de la maestra** the children are under the care of the teacher; **la maestra está a[l]** — **de los niños** the teacher is in charge of the children
cargoso ADJ fussy
carguero ADJ freight-carrying
cariado ADJ decayed
caribeño ADJ Caribbean
caricatura F (dibujo) caricature; (con texto) cartoon
caricaturista MF cartoonist
caricaturizar[47] VT to caricature
caricia F caress
caridad F charity
caries F INV cavity, tooth decay
carillón M chimes
cariño M (amor) affection, fondness; (apodo) honey; **darle** —**s a alguien** to send love to

someone; **ella y el perro se hacen** —**s** she and the dog nuzzle each other; **hacer algo con** — to do something with great care; **tenerle** — **a alguien** to be fond of someone
cariñoso ADJ affectionate, loving
carisma M charisma
caritativo ADJ charitable
cariz M complexion; **no me gusta el** — **que está tomando la situación** I don't like the look of this
carmesí ADJ INV & M crimson
carmín M (carmesí) crimson; (lápiz de labios) lipstick
carnal ADJ carnal
carnaval M carnival
carne F (para comer) meat; (de animal vivo, de persona, de tomate) flesh; — **de cañón** cannon fodder; — **de cerdo** pork; — **de cordero** mutton; — **de gallina** (comida) chicken; (reacción de la piel) goose bumps; — **de res** beef; — **de venado** venison; — **y hueso** flesh and blood; **como** — **y uña** *fam* thick as thieves; **en** — **viva** raw; **metido en** —**s** overweight
carnear VT to butcher
carnero M ram
carnet/carné M — **de conducir** driver's license; — **de identidad** ID
carnicería F (tienda) butcher's shop; (matanza) carnage, bloodbath
carnicero -ra MF butcher; ADJ (carnívoro) carnivorous; (cruel) cruel
carnívoro ADJ carnivorous
carnoso ADJ fleshy
caro ADJ expensive, high-priced, *fam* pricey; ADV at a high price
carona F saddle pad
carótida F carotid artery
carozo M *RP* pit, stone
carpa F (pez) carp; (tienda) tent
carpeta F (para documentos, también de ordenador) folder; (cartera) portfolio
carpintería F (oficio) carpentry; (taller) carpenter's shop
carpintero -ra MF carpenter
carraspear VI to clear one's throat
carraspera F scratchy throat
carrera F (conjunto de estudios) major; (trayectoria profesional) career; (competición) race; (en las medias) run; (recorrido corto) run, dash; (en fútbol americano, béisbol) run; (de pistón) stroke; — **a pie** footrace; — **de caballos** horse race; — **de relevos** relay race; **a la** — running; **hacer** — to succeed in a profession; **tomar** — to get a running start; — **impulsada** (en béisbol) run batted in; — **limpia** (en béisbol) earned run; — **sucia** (en béisbol) unearned run

carreta F wagon
carrete M (de película) reel; (de hilo) bobbin; (de alambre) spool
carretera F highway; — **de circunvalación** bypass; — **de peaje** toll road
carretero ADJ **sistema** — highway system
carretilla F (de una rueda) wheelbarrow; (de más de una rueda) dolly; **de** — by memory
carretón M large wagon
carril M (de ferrocarril) rail; (de calle) lane
carrillo M cheek, jowl; **a dos/cuatro —s** voraciously
carrillón M chimes
carrizo M reed
carro M (automóvil) car; (vehículo de dos ruedas, de golf) cart; (de máquina de escribir) roll; — **alegórico** parade float; — **blindado** armored car; — **de guerra** chariot; **poner el** — **delante de los bueyes** to put the cart before the horse; **subirse al** — to get on the bandwagon
carrocería F auto body
carroña F carrion
carroza F (de caballos) coach; (de desfile) parade float; (fúnebre) hearse
carruaje M carriage, coach
carta F (misiva) letter; (naipe) card; (de restaurante) menu; (constitución) charter; (mapa) chart; — **blanca** freehand; — **con anexos** cover letter; — **de agradecimiento** thank-you letter; — **de remisión** cover letter; — **de renuncia** resignation letter; **a la** — à la carte; **echarle las —s a alguien** to do a card-reading for someone; **tomar —s en la situación** to take charge of a situation
cartearse VI to correspond
cartel M poster, placard; **en** — showing; — **de la droga** drug cartel
cartelera F (de periódico) entertainment section; (publicitaria) billboard; (tablón para anuncios) bulletin board
cárter M oil pan
cartera F (para dinero) wallet, billfold; (para papeles) briefcase; (escolar) satchel; (bolsa) handbag; (de valores) portfolio
carterista MF pickpocket
cartero -ra MF letter carrier; M mailman, postman
cartílago M cartilage
cartilla F (para aprender a leer) reader; (de información) booklet; — **de racionamiento** ration book; — **de examen de vista** eye chart
cartografiar[28] VT to chart
cartón M cardboard, pasteboard; — **de cigarrillos** carton of cigarettes
cartuchera F cartridge belt
cartucho M (de pistola) cartridge, shell; (de

monedas) roll; (de dinamita) stick; — **de fogueo** blank cartridge; — **de tinta / tóner** toner cartridge; **quemar el último** — to exhaust one's resources
cartulina F thin cardboard
casa F (edificio) house; (hogar) home; (negocio) business firm; — **de ancianos** old folks' home; — **de citas** cheap motel for rendezvous; — **de empeños** pawnshop; — **de la moneda** mint; — **de muñecas** dollhouse; — **de pompas fúnebres** funeral home; — **de putas** *vulg* whorehouse; — **de reposo** rest home; — **de rehabilitación** halfway house; — **de subastas** auction house; — **embrujada** haunted house; — **rodante** house trailer; — **solariega** manor house; **de** — **en** — from house to house; **en** — at home; **entró como Perico por su** — he made himself right at home; **estás en tu** — make yourself at home; **ir a** — to go home; **la** — **paga** on the house; **poner una** — to set up a household; **quedarse en** — to stay home; **tirar la** — **por la ventana** to live it up
casaca F riding jacket
casadero ADJ marriageable
casado ADJ married
casamentero -ra MF matchmaker
casamiento M wedding, marriage ceremony
casar VT to marry off; —**se** to get married, to wed; —**se con** to get married to; **no —se con nadie** to remain independent
cascabel M (campanita) jingle bell; (de víbora) rattle; **ser un** — to be lively; **ponerle el** — **al gato** to stick one's neck out
cascada F cascade, waterfall
cascajo M old wreck
cascar[30] VT (quebrar) to crack; (dar bofetadas) to slap around; —**se** to crack open; M SG
cascanueces nutcracker; MF SG
cascarrabias crab, grouch; ADJ INV grouchy
cáscara F (de huevo, fruto seco) shell; (de granos, arvejas) husk; (de fruto seco) hull; (de fruta) rind; (de naranja, manzana) peel
casco M (de ciclista, militar) helmet; (de obrero) hard hat; (de barco) hull; (de naranja) shell; (uña del pie de caballería) hoof; — **urbano** built-up area
cascote M rubble
caserío M (aldea) hamlet; (casa) *Esp* farmhouse
casero -ra ADJ (doméstico) domestic; (hecho en casa) homemade; MF (cuidador) caretaker; M (propietario) landlord; F landlady
caseta F (en un mercado) booth, stall; (de guardia) guardhouse; (de perro) doghouse
casete MF cassette
casi ADV almost, nearly; — **diez mil** almost/ nearly ten thousand; — **lo hago** I almost did it; — **siempre** almost always; — **nadie**

hardly anyone; — **nunca** hardly ever
casilla F (en el tablero de ajedrez) square; (en una tabla) box; (en un casillero) pigeonhole, cubbyhole; — **de perro** doghouse; **sacarle a alguien de sus —s** to drive someone up the wall
casino M (club) men's club; (lugar de apuestas) casino
caso M case; — **de fuerza mayor** act of God; — **perdido** (persona incapacitada) basket case; (persona incorregible) lost cause; **en — de** in the event of; **en — de que** in case that; **el — es que** the deal is that; **en todo** — in any case, at any rate; **en último** — as a last resort; **eso no viene al** — that is beside the point; **hacer — [de]** to pay attention [to]; **hacer — omiso de** to disregard; **no hay** — there's no point; **pongamos por** — let's suppose that; **venir al** — to come to the point
caspa F dandruff
casquillo M (de bala) case; (de lámpara) socket
cassette MF cassette
casta F caste
castaña F chestnut; — **de cajú** cashew
castañetear VI to chatter; — **con los dedos** to snap one's fingers
castañeteo M (de dientes) chattering; (de dedos) snapping
castaño M (árbol) chestnut tree; (color, madera) chestnut; ADJ chestnut-colored, brown
castañuela F castanet
castellano ADJ & MF Castilian; M (lengua) Castilian
castidad F chastity
castigar[40] VT to chastise, to punish
castigo M chastisement, punishment; ¡**qué** —! what a nuisance!
Castilla F Castile
castillo M castle; — **de arena** sandcastle; **—s en el aire** *fam* pie in the sky
casting M casting
castizo ADJ traditional
casto ADJ chaste
castor M beaver
castrar VT (a un hombre, animal) to castrate; (a una mascota) to neuter, to fix; (a mascotas hembras) to spay
casual ADJ chance, accidental
casualidad F chance, coincidence; **da la** — **que** it so happens that; **oír por** — to overhear; **por** — by chance
casucha F shack
cata F — **de vinos** wine-tasting
catalán -ana ADJ (del catalán) Catalan; (de Cataluña) Catalonian; MF Catalan; M (lengua) Catalan
catalejo M spyglass
catalizador M catalyst
catalogar[40] VT to catalog/catalogue

catálogo M catalog, catalogue
Cataluña F Catalonia
catar VT to taste
catarata F (cascada) cataract, waterfall; (de los ojos) cataract
catarí ADJ & MF Qatari
catarro M cold
catástrofe F catastrophe
catatonia F catatonia
catecismo M catechism
cátedra F (puesto de profesor) chair, professorship; (enseñanza) teaching; (división académica) department; **sentar** — to hold forth, to pontificate
catedral F cathedral
catedrático -ca MF [full] professor
categoría F category; **de** — important; **de** — **mundial** world-class; **de poca** — third-rate
caterpillar M caterpillar
catéter M catheter
cateterización F catheterization
cateterizar VT to catheterize
cátodo M cathode
catolicismo M Catholicism
católico -ca ADJ Catholic; MF Catholic
catorce NUM fourteen
catre M cot
cátsup M catsup, ketchup
cauce M channel; — **de río** riverbed
cauchero -ra MF rubber gatherer; ADJ **industria cauchera** rubber industry
caucho M rubber; — **sintético** synthetic rubber
caución F security payment
caudal M (de bienes) wealth; (de agua) volume of water
caudaloso ADJ mighty
caudillo M leader
causa F (motivo) cause; (proceso) case; — **noble** worthy cause; — **perdida** lost cause; **a** — **de** on account of, because of; **con conocimiento de** — wittingly; **hacer** — **común** to work together
causante ADJ causing; MF instigator
causar VT to cause; — **problemas** to make trouble
cáustico ADJ caustic
cautela F caution
cautelar ADJ preventive
cauteloso ADJ cautious, wary
cauterizar[47] VT to cauterize
cautivar VT (capturar) to capture; (atraer) to captivate
cautiverio M captivity
cautivo -va MF captive
cauto ADJ cautious, wary
cava F (acción de cavar) digging; (sótano) cellar; (vino) cava
cavar VT to dig
caverna F cavern, cave

cavidad F cavity
cavilar VI to muse
cayado M shepherd's crook, staff
cayendo, cayera, cayese, cayeron ver caer
cayo M key
caza F (acción de cazar) hunt, hunting; (conjunto de animales) wild game; — **mayor** big game; — **menor** small game; **andar a la — de** to hunt for; **dar — a** to hunt down; M (avión) fighter
cazador -ora ADJ hunting; MF hunter; F Windbreaker™
cazar⁴⁷ VI/VT (buscar presas) to hunt; (matar presas) to shoot, to bag; (atrapar presas) to trap; MF SG **cazatalentos** talent scout, headhunter; M **cazatorpedero** destroyer, torpedo boat
cazo M (cacerola) pan; (cucharón) ladle, dipper
cazoleta F pipe bowl
cazuela F (recipiente) casserole; (cazo) pan
CD M CD; — **ROM** CD-ROM
cebada F barley
cebador M pump primer
cebar VT (un animal) to fatten; (bombas) to prime; (anzuelos) to bait; —**se** to vent one's anger
cebo M (para peces) bait, lure; (para animales) feed
cebolla F onion
cebollar M onion patch
cebollino M scallion
cebra F (animal) zebra; (paso) crosswalk
cecear VI to lisp
ceceo M lisp
cecina F jerky
cedazo M sieve
ceder VT (propiedad) to cede, to assign; (un sitio) to yield, to give up; VI (el frío) to diminish; (la resistencia) to give way
cedro M cedar
cédula F document; — **de identidad** identification card
céfiro M zephyr
cegar⁴¹ VT to blind
ceguera F blindness; — **cromática** color blindness
ceja F (sobre el ojo) eyebrow; (en una encuadernación) tab; **quemarse las —s** to cram for an exam; **cejijunto** with thick eyebrows
cejar VI to back down
celada F ambush
celador -ora MF (en una escuela) school monitor; (en un barrio) security officer
celar VT to guard
celda F cell
celebración F (fiesta) celebration; (acto solemne) performance
celebrar VT (una fiesta) to celebrate; (una

reunión) to hold; (un rito) to perform
célebre ADJ famous, noted
celebridad F celebrity
celeste ADJ (relativo al firmamento) celestial; (del color del cielo) azure, light blue
celestial ADJ celestial, heavenly
célibe ADJ celibate; MF unmarried person
cellisca F sleet; **caer** — to sleet
celo M (diligencia) zeal; (excitación sexual) heat; **estar en** — to be in heat; —**s** jealousy; **tener** —**s** to be jealous
celofán M cellophane
celosía F window lattice
celoso ADJ (que tiene celos) jealous; (diligente) zealous
célula F cell; — **adiposa** fat cell; — **estaminal embrional** stem cell
celular ADJ cellular; M mobile phone
celulitis F cellulite
celuloide M celluloid
celulosa F cellulose
cementar VT to cement
cementerio M cemetery, graveyard
cemento M cement; — **armado** reinforced concrete
cena F supper, dinner
cenagal M quagmire, swamp
cenagoso ADJ marshy, swampy
cenar VI to eat supper, to eat dinner; **vamos a — pescado** we're having fish for dinner
cencerro M cowbell
cenicero M ashtray
ceniciento ADJ ashen
cenit M zenith
cenizas F PL ashes, cinders
censar VI/VT to take a census [of]
censo M census
censor -ora MF censor; — **de cuentas** auditor
censura F (reprobación) censure; (control) censorship
censurador ADJ censuring
censurar VT (criticar) to censure; (examinar) to censor
centavo M cent
centella F sparkle; **pasar como una** — to go by in a flash
centelleante ADJ sparkling
centellear VI to sparkle, to scintillate
centelleo M sparkle
centenar M group of a hundred; —**es** hundreds
centenario M centennial; ADJ centenarian
centeno M rye
centésimo ADJ & M hundredth
centígrado ADJ centigrade
centímetro M centimeter
céntimo M cent
centinela MF sentry, sentinel
centrado ADJ (un tablón) true; (un cuadro) centered; (una persona) focused; M truing

central ADJ central; F plant; **— de teléfonos** telephone exchange; **— eléctrica** power plant; **— lechera** milk processing plant; **— nuclear** nuclear power plant

centralita F switchboard

centralizar[47] VT to centralize; **—se** to become centralized

centrar VT to center; **—se** to focus, to be focused

céntrico ADJ central

centrífugo ADJ centrifugal

centrípeto ADJ centripetal

centro M center (también de baloncesto); (de ciudad) downtown; **— comercial** shopping center; **— de gravedad** center of gravity; **— de mesa** centerpiece; MF **—campista** (fútbol) midfield player

Centroamérica F Central America

centroamericano -na M Central American

ceñido ADJ tight

ceñir[11] VT (rodear) to gird; (abrazar) to encircle; **— la corona** to be crowned; VI (estar apretado) to be tight; **—se a** (limitarse) to limit oneself to; (arrimarse) to get close to

ceño M **fruncir el —** to frown, to scowl

cepa F (de árbol) stump; (de viña) stock; (de bacteria) strain; **de pura —** of good stock

cepillar VT (dientes, pelo) to brush; (madera) to plane, to shave

cepillo M (para pelo, dientes) brush; (para madera) carpenter's plane; **— de dientes** toothbrush

cepo M (para cazar) trap; (para inmovilizar coches) boot

cera F wax; **— de oídos** earwax; **— para muebles** polish

cerámica F (arte) ceramics; (conjunto de artículos) pottery, earthenware

cerámico ADJ ceramic

cerbatana F blowpipe

cerca ADV near, nearby, close; **— de** near, close to; **de —** close up; F fence

cercado M (terreno cercado) enclosure; (cerca) fence

cercanía F proximity, nearness, closeness

cercano ADJ (lugar) near, nearby; (pariente) close; **— Oriente** Near East

cercar[30] VT (rodear con una cerca) to fence, to enclose; (sitiar) to besiege

cercenar VT (cortar) to chop off; (reducir) to curtail, to encroach upon

cerciorarse VI **— [de]** to make sure [of]

cerco M (sitio) siege; (cerca) fence

cerdo -da M (animal, persona sucia) hog, pig; (carne) pork; F (puerca) sow; (de cepillo) bristle

cerdoso ADJ bristly

cereal M cereal; **—es** breakfast cereal; **cultivo — cereal** crop

cerebral ADJ cerebral

cerebro M (órgano, genio) brain; (organizador de un plan) mastermind; **lavarle el — a** to brainwash

ceremonia F ceremony

ceremonial ADJ & M ceremonial

ceremonioso ADJ ceremonious

cereza F cherry

cerezo M cherry tree

cerilla F match

cerner[2] VT to sift; **—se** (un ave) to hover; (un desastre) to loom

cernícalo M kestrel

cero M (cifra) zero; (en deportes) nothing, goose egg, zip; (en tenis) love; **— absoluto** absolute zero; **partir de —** to start from scratch; **ser un — a la izquierda** to be a nobody

cerrado ADJ (no abierto) closed; (tonto) dense; (poco comunicativo) reserved; (intransigente) closed-minded; (anguloso) sharp; M enclosure

cerrador -ora MF closer

cerradura F lock; **— de combinación** combination lock

cerrajería F locksmith's shop

cerrajero -ra MF locksmith

cerrar[1] VT (la puerta, un cajón) to close, to shut; (un trato) to close, to clinch; (un terreno) to enclose; (el gas, un grifo) to turn off; (una fábrica) to shut down, to close; **— filas** to close ranks; **— el paso** to block passage; VI to close; **—se** (una flor, una tienda) to close; (un plazo) to end; **—se el cielo** to become overcast

cerrazón F (de la mente) closed-mindedness; (del cielo) stormy skies

cerro M hill

cerrojo M bolt

certamen M contest; **— de belleza** beauty contest

certero ADJ sure

certeza F certainty

certidumbre F certainty

certificación F certification

certificado ADJ certified; M certificate; **— de nacimiento** birth certificate

certificar[30] VT (la autenticidad) to certify; (una carta) to register

cervatillo M fawn

cervecera F brewery

cervecería F bar

cerveza F beer; **— de barril** draft beer

cervical ADJ cervical

cérvix M cervix

cerviz F cervix

cesar VI to cease; **— de trabajar** to stop working; **— en un cargo** to resign from a position; **— a** to dismiss

cesárea F cesarean [section]

cese M cessation; — **el fuego** ceasefire; — **de actividades** shutdown
cesión F (de propiedad) assignment; (de derechos) waiver
césped M (ante una casa) lawn; (hierba, también para tenis) grass
cesta F basket
cestería F basketry
cesto M (cesta) basket; (para ropa) hamper
cetrino ADJ olive-colored
chabacano ADJ (modales) crude; (gustos) tacky; M *Méx* apricot
chacal M jackal
chacha F servant girl
cháchara F small talk
chacota F joke; **tomarse algo a la** — to take lightly
chacra F (establecimiento agrícola) small farm; (terreno) small plot
Chad M Chad
chadiano -na ADJ & MF Chadian
chal M shawl, wrap
chala F *Am* husk; **quitar la** — to husk
chalán M horse trader
chalé M cottage
chaleco M waistcoat, vest; — **antibalas** bulletproof vest; — **de fuerza** straitjacket; — **salvavidas** life jacket
chalupa F small canoe; *Méx* tortilla with sauce
chamaco -ca M *Méx* boy; F *Méx* girl
chamarra F sheepskin jacket
chambergo M wide-brimmed hat
chambón ADJ clumsy
champán/champaña M champagne
champiñón M mushroom
champú M shampoo
chamuscadura F scorch
chamuscar[30] VT to scorch, to singe; — **se** to get scorched, to get singed
chamusquina F scorching, singeing
chance MF chance
chancearse VI — **de** to make fun of
chancho M hog
chanchullo M *fam* monkey business
chancleta F thong, flipflop; **tirar la** — to kick up one's heels
chanclo M galosh, overshoe; — **s** rubbers
chándal M sweatsuit
chantaje M blackmail
chantajear VT to blackmail
chanza F jest
chao INTERJ bye-bye
chapa F (de metal) sheet metal; (de policía) badge; (de botella) bottle top; (de prostituta) trick; (de madera) veneer; — **en la puerta** shingle on the door; **hacer** — **s** to turn tricks; **hacerle** — **y pintura a un coche** to fix the bodywork and paint of a car
chapado ADJ — **a la antigua** old-fashioned

chapalear VI to splash
chapar VT to plate
chaparral M dry rangeland, chaparral
chaparro M scrub oak; ADJ *Méx* short
chaparrón M cloudburst
chaperón -ona MF chaperon[e]; **ir de** — to chaperon[e]
chapitel M spire, steeple
chapotear VI to splash
chapoteo M splash, splashing
chapucear VT to botch, to bungle
chapucería F (trabajo, obra) botched job; (cualidad) sloppiness
chapucero ADJ shoddy, slipshod
chapurrear VT to speak a language poorly
chapuz M dive
chapuza F botched job
chapuzar[47] VI to dive
chaqueta F jacket; — **de sport** sport jacket
charada F charades
charca F pond
charco M puddle, pool; **cruzar el** — to cross the ocean
charcutería F (tienda) delicatessen; (industria) sausage-making
charla F chat, talk
charlar VI to chat, to gab
charlatán -ana ADJ talkative; MF (parlanchín) chatterbox, windbag; (curandero) charlatan, quack
charlotear VI to chatter, to jabber
charloteo M chatter, jabber
charol M (barniz) varnish; (cuero barnizado) patent leather
charolar VT to varnish
charqui M beef jerky
charro ADJ flashy, tawdry
chárter M charter flight
chascar VT (los nudillos, un hueso) to crack; (los labios) to smack; (la lengua) to click
chascarrillo M funny anecdote
chasco M (broma) prank, practical joke; (decepción) dud; **llevarse un** — to be disappointed
chasis M frame, chassis
chasquear VT (decepcionar) to disappoint; (una cerradura, la lengua) to click; (un látigo) to crack; (los labios) to smack; (los dedos) to snap; — **se** to be disappointed
chasquido M (de látigo, madera, articulaciones) crack; (de labios) smack; (de la lengua, una cerradura) click; (de los dedos) snap
chata F bedpan
chatarra F scrap iron
chatarrería F junkyard
chatear VI to chat
chato ADJ (nariz) snub-nosed; (zapatos, pecho) flat; — **como una tabla** as flat as a pancake
chaucha F green bean

chaval -la M *Esp* boy; F *Esp* girl
chaveta F cotter pin; **perder la** — *fam* to go
  bonkers
che INTERJ *RP* say! hey!
checo -ca ADJ & MF Czech
chef MF chef
cheque M check; — **de viajero** traveler's check;
  — **de caja** bank check; — **sin fondos** bad
  check, worthless check
chequear VT to check
checar VT to check
chequera F checkbook
chic ADJ INV & M chic
chicha F (bebida alcohólica) *Am* corn liquor;
  (carne) *Esp fam* meat; **de** — **y nabo** two-bit;
  ni — **ni limonada** neither fish nor fowl
chicharra F (insecto) cicada; (timbre) buzzer
chiche M *Am vulg* tit, boob
chichi M *Am vulg* tit, boob; *Esp vulg* beaver, cunt
chichón M bump, lump, knot
chicle M chewing gum; — **de globo** bubblegum
chico -ca ADJ small, little; M boy; F girl; **mis** —**s**
  my kids
chicote M *Am* whip
chicotear VT *Am* to whip
chicoteo M *Am* whipping
chiflado ADJ *fam* nuts, cuckoo, loony; MF
  (persona loca) *fam* basket case, loon
chifladura F craziness
chiflar VI (silbar) to whistle; VT (volver loco) to
  drive crazy; —**se** to go crazy
chiflido M whistle
chifón M chiffon
chile M chile
Chile M Chile
chileno -na ADJ & MF Chilean
chillar VI (persona) to shriek; (puerta, ratón) to
  squeak; (cerdo) to squeal
chillido M (de persona) shriek; (de puerta,
  ratón) squeak; (de cerdo) squeal
chillón ADJ (sonido) shrill; (color) loud, gaudy,
  flashy
chimenea F (salida de humo) chimney; (hogar)
  fireplace; (de volcán, baño, mina) vent; (de
  fábrica) smokestack
chimpancé M chimpanzee
china F (porcelana) china; (piedra) pebble
China F China
chinche F (insecto) bedbug; (chincheta)
  thumbtack; MF (persona molesta) pain
chinchilla F chinchilla
chinchorro M rowboat
chingar[40] VT (fastidiar) *vulg* to screw with;
  (estropear) *vulg* to screw up; VI/VT *Méx vulg* to
  fuck
chino -na ADJ Chinese; M (lengua) Chinese; MF
  Chinese; **vi a un chino** I saw a Chinese
  person; **los chinos no están de acuerdo**
  the Chinese don't agree; **eso es** — that's

  Greek to me
chip M (de ordenador, en golf) chip; (de papa/
  patata) potato chip; — **de silicio** silicon chip
Chipre M Cyprus
chipriota ADJ & MF Cypriot[e]
chiquilín -ina M little boy; F little girl
chiquito ADJ tiny, wee
chiripa F stroke of good luck; **por/de** — by a
  fluke
chirivía F parsnip
chirona F jail
chirriante ADJ squeaky
chirriar[28] VI (puerta, freno) to squeak; (ave,
  freno) to screech
chirrido M (de puerta, freno) squeak; (de ave,
  freno) screech
chisgarabís M pipsqueak
chisguete M squirt
chisme M (rumor) gossip, piece of gossip;
  (objeto) *fam* gizmo, thingamajig
chismear VI to gossip
chismoso -sa ADJ gossipy; MF gossip
chispa F (partícula incandescente) spark;
  (ingenio) wit; **echar** —**s** to be furious; **pasar**
  echando —**s** to whiz by
chispeante ADJ (que echa chispas) sparkling;
  (ingenioso) witty
chispear VI (echar chispas) to spark; (lloviznar)
  to sprinkle
chisporrotear VI (fuego) to sputter; (cigarrillo)
  to fizzle; (carne) to sizzle
chisporroteo M (de fuego) sputter; (de carne)
  sizzle
chiste M (verbal) joke; (visual) cartoon;
  (ocurrencia) wisecrack; — **verde** dirty joke;
  no le veo el — I don't see the humor in it
chistera F top hat
chistoso ADJ funny, amusing, humorous
chivar VI/VT to snitch [on], to rat [on]
chivatar VI/VT to squeal [on], to snitch [on]
chivato -ta MF (delator) informer, snitch, stool
  pigeon; (chivito) kid
chivo M kid; — **expiatorio** scapegoat; **estar**
  como un — to be crazy as a loon
chocante ADJ shocking, jarring
chocar[30] VI (golpearse) to bump, to collide;
  (antagonizar) to clash; VT (sorprender) to
  shock; (destrozar) to wreck; — **los cinco** to
  shake hands
chocarrería F coarseness
chochear VI to be in one's dotage
chochera F senility, dotage
chochez F senility, dotage
chocho ADJ senile; **estar** — to be in one's
  dotage; **estar** — **con** to dote on; M *vulg* cunt
choclo M ear of corn
chocolate M (planta, dulce) chocolate; (bebida)
  cocoa, drinking chocolate; (hachís) *Esp* pot
chocolatera F chocolate pot

chocolatina F chocolate bar
chófer, chofer MF chauffeur, driver
cholo -la MF (mestizo) person of mixed race; (indio) Europeanized Indian
chopo M poplar
choque M (de objetos móviles) collision, bump, crash; (eléctrico, emocional, cultural) shock; — **insulínico** insulin shock
chorizo M sausage
chorlito M plover
chorrear VI/VT (poco) to drip; (mucho) to gush
chorro M spurt, jet; **a —s** in buckets
chotearse VI — **de** to make fun of
choteo M mocking
chovinismo M chauvinism
choza F hut, shack, hovel
chubasco M squall, shower
chuchería F trinket, knickknack
chueco ADJ *Am* crooked
chuleta F (papel para copiar) cheat sheet; (golf) divot; — **de cerdo** pork chop; — **de ternera** veal cutlet
chulo -la M (proxeneta) pimp; (dandi) dandy, dude; (bravucón) tough guy; MF working-class resident of Madrid; ADJ (fanfarrón) boastful; (bonito) cute
chupada F (de cigarro) puff; (de bebida) sip
chupar VI/VT (succionar) to suck; (fumar) to puff [on]; VT (absorber) to absorb; (vivir a costa de) to sponge off; **chupársela** *vulg* to suck off; **chúpate esa** put that in your pipe and smoke it; M SG **chupasangre** leech
chupete M pacifier
chupetín M *RP* lollipop, sucker
churrasco M *Am* barbecued steak
churro M fritter
chusma F rabble, riffraff
chut M hard shot
chutar VI (drogas) to shoot up; VT (un balón) to shoot; *Esp* — **la bola** to kick the ball hard
chute M narcotic fix
chuzo M watchman's pike
CIA F CIA
cianotipo M blueprint
cianuro M cyanide
cibercafé M cybercafe
ciberespacio M cyberspace
cibernética F cybernetics
ciberpunk MF cyberpunk
cicatero ADJ stingy
cicatriz F scar
cicatrizar VI (formar cicatriz) to form a scar; (curarse) to heal up
cíclico ADJ cyclical
ciclista MF bicycle rider, cyclist, biker
ciclo M cycle; —**motor** moped; — **vital** life cycle; — **de auditoría** audit cycle; — **de facturación** billing cycle; — **presupuestario** budget cycle

ciclón M cyclone
ciclotrón M cyclotron
cicuta F hemlock
ciego ADJ (no vidente) blind; (por borrachera) plastered; (por drogas) high; **quedarse** — to go blind; **a ciegas** blindly
cielo M (firmamento) sky; (paraíso) heaven; **a —abierto** under the open sky; **minería a —abierto** open pit mining; — **raso** ceiling; **¡—s!** good heavens! **estar en el séptimo —** to be in seventh heaven; **me cayó del —** it's a godsend; **poner el grito en el —** *fam* to hit the ceiling
ciempiés M centipede
cien, ciento NUM hundred; **por ciento** percent
ciénaga F swamp, mire, marsh
ciencia F (campo de investigación) science; (conocimiento) knowledge; (arte) art; — **ficción** science fiction; —**s políticas** political science; **a — cierta** with certainty; **las —s ocultas** the occult; **no tiene —** there's nothing to it
cieno M mud, mire
científico -ca ADJ scientific; MF scientist
cierra, cierre *ver* cerrar
cierre M (traba) clasp, fastener; (cremallera) zipper; (acción de cerrar) closing, closure; — **patronal** lockout; **al —** (noticias) at press time; (acciones) at the close
ciertamente ADV certainly
cierto ADJ certain; (verdadero) true; (seguro) sure; **en — sentido** in a sense; **hasta — punto** to a certain extent; **por —** by the way; INTERJ you're right!
ciervo -va M (animal) deer; (macho) stag; — **volante** stag beetle; F (hembra) doe, hind
cierzo M north wind
cifra F (numeral) digit; (número) figure; (clave) cipher, key; — **aproximada** ballpark estimate; **poner en —** to encode
cifrado M encryption; — **de datos** data encryption
cifrar VT to write in code, to encrypt; — **las esperanzas en** to place one's hopes on; **el monto se cifra en veinte millones de pesos** the figure amounts to twenty million pesos
cigarra F cicada
cigarrera F cigar case, cigarette case
cigarrillo M cigarette
cigarro M (cigarrillo) cigarette; (puro) cigar
cigoto M zygote
cigüeña F stork
cigüeñal M crankshaft
cilíndrico ADJ cylindrical
cilindro M cylinder
cima F summit
cimarrón -ona ADJ wild; MF runaway slave
címbalo M cymbal

cimbel M decoy
cimbrar VT to sway, to vibrate
cimentar VT (una casa) to lay the foundation of; (una victoria) to secure
cimiento M foundation
cinc M zinc
cincel M chisel
cincelar VT to chisel
cincha F cinch, girth
cinchar VT to cinch, to girth
cinco NUM five
cincuenta NUM fifty
cine M cinema, movies
cineasta MF filmmaker
cinematografía F cinematography, movie-making
cinematografiar[28] VI/VT to film
cinematográfico ADJ cinematographic; **industria cinematográfica** motion-picture industry
cinestesia F kinesthesia
cingalés -esa ADJ & MF Sri Lankan
cínico -ca ADJ cynical; MF cynic
cinismo M cynicism
cinta F (de adorno) ribbon; (adhesiva) tape; (cinematográfica) film; — **aislante** electrical tape; — **de vídeo** videotape; — **magnetofónica** recording tape; — **métrica** tape measure; — **rodante** treadmill; — **transportadora** conveyor belt
cinto M belt
cintura F (de persona) waist; (de cosa) middle
cinturón M belt; — **de seguridad** safety belt
ciprés M cypress
circo M circus
circonio M zirconium
circuitería F circuitry
circuito M circuit; — **cerrado** closed circuit; — **impreso** circuit board; — **integrado** integrated circuit
circulación F (de sangre, de bienes) circulation; (de vehículos) traffic; **poner en** — to circulate
circular VI to circulate; **hay que** — **por la derecha** you have to drive on the right; F circular letter
circulatorio ADJ circulatory; **problemas —s** cardiovascular problems; **atasco** — traffic jam
círculo M circle; — **vicioso** vicious circle
circuncidar VT to circumcise
circundante ADJ surrounding
circundar VT to surround
circunferencia F circumference
circunlocución F circumlocution
circunscribir[74] VT to circumscribe
circunspecto ADJ circumspect
circunstancia F circumstance
circunstancial ADJ circumstantial

cirio M candle
cirro M cirrus
cirrosis F cirrhosis
ciruela F plum; — **pasa** prune
ciruelo M plum tree
cirugía F surgery; — **de corazón abierto** open-heart surgery; — **plástica/estética** plastic surgery, cosmetic surgery
cirujano -na MF surgeon
cisne M swan
cisterna F cistern
cita F (romántica) date; (con el médico) appointment; (textual) quotation, quote; — **a ciegas** blind date; **darse** — to meet
citación F citation, summons
citar VT (a un testigo) to summon; (a un autor) to cite, to quote; —**se con** (el médico) to make an appointment with; (un amigo) to make a date with
citología F (ciencia) cell biology, cytology; (toma de células vaginales) pap smear
cítrico ADJ citric; M citrus
ciudad F city
ciudadanía F citizenship
ciudadano -na MF citizen
Ciudad del Vaticano F Vatican City
ciudadela F citadel
cívico ADJ civic
civil ADJ (no criminal, no religioso) civil; (no militar) civilian
civilidad F civility
civilización F civilization
civilizador ADJ civilizing
civilizar[47] VT to civilize; —**se** to become civilized
cizalla F metal shears
cizaña F **sembrar** — to sow discord
clamar VT/VI to demand; — **por** to clamor for
clamor M clamor, outcry
clamorear VI/VT to shout
clamoreo M shouting
clamoroso ADJ clamorous
clan M clan
clandestino ADJ clandestine
claqué M tap dance
clara F egg white; — **de huevo** egg white
claraboya F skylight
clarear VI (aclararse) to become clear; (amanecer) to grow light; (desenturbiarse) to thin; VT to illuminate; —**se** to grow light
claridad F (de ideas) clarity; (de la luz) brightness, lightness
clarificar[30] VT to clarify, to clear
clarín M bugle
clarinete M clarinet
clarividente MF & ADJ clairvoyant
claro ADJ clear; (franco) straightforward; (iluminado) light, bright; **azul** — light blue; **a las claras** clearly; ADV clearly; INTERJ of

course! M (espacio) gap; (en un bosque) clearing; — **de luna** moonlight

clase F (tipo) kind, sort; (grupo social, sesión docente, alumnado) class; (aula) classroom; — **alta** upper class; — **media** middle class; — **obrera** working class; — **turista** economy class; **dar** — to teach a class; **toda** — **de** all sorts of

clasicismo M classicism

clásico ADJ (destacado, consabido) classic; (de un período histórico) classical; M classic

clasificación F (taxonómica) classification; (deportiva) qualification; — **descendiente** descending sort

clasificado M want ad

clasificar[30] VT (ordenar) to classify; (en deportes) to qualify; —**se para** to qualify for; —**se segundo** to come in second

claustro M cloister; — **de profesores** university faculty

claustrofobia F claustrophobia

claustrofóbico ADJ claustrophobic

cláusula F clause

clausura F closing

clausurar VT (una sesión) to bring to a close, to conclude; (una tienda) to close [down]

clavadista MF diver

clavado ADV exactly; M (de clavos) nailing; (en una piscina) dive; **tirarse un** — to dive

clavar VT (perforar con un clavo) to nail, to drive a nail into; (pinchar) to stick, to poke; —**le la mirada / los ojos a alguien** to stare at someone; — **los frenos** to stomp on the brakes; **me clavaron** I got a raw deal

clave F (sistema de signos) code; (tabla de correspondencias) key; (signo musical) clef; (clavicémbalo) harpsichord; (de mapa) legend; — **de fa** bass clef; — **de seguridad** password; — **de sol** treble clef; ADJ key

clavel M carnation

clavetear VT to put pegs on

clavicémbalo M harpsichord

clavícula F collarbone, clavicle

clavija F (de guitarra) peg; (de enchufe) pin

clavo M (pieza de metal) nail; (capullo) clove; (de zapato) spike; **dar en el** — to hit the nail on the head

claxon M car horn

clearing M clearing

clemencia F clemency, mercy

clemente ADJ forgiving, merciful

cleptomanía F kleptomania

cleptómano -na MF kleptomaniac

clerecía F (funciones) ministry; (clérigos) clergy

clerical ADJ clerical

clérigo M clergyman, minister

clero M clergy

clic M click; **hacer** — to click; **hacer doble** — to double-click

cliché M (placa fotográfica) photographic plate; (expresión muy usada) cliché

cliente MF, **clienta** F (de un profesional) client; (de un negocio) customer; (de un restaurante) patron; (de un hotel) guest

clientela F clientele, customer base

clientelismo M patronage

clima M climate

climático ADJ climatic; **cambio** — climate change

climatización F air conditioning

clímax M climax

clinch M clinch

clínica F clinic

clínico ADJ clinical

clip M paper clip

clítoris M clitoris

cloaca F sewer

clon M clone

clonación F cloning

clonaje M cloning

clonar VT to clone

cloquear VI to cluck

cloqueo M cluck, clucking

clorhidrato M hydrochloride; — **de Ritalina** Ritalin hydrochloride

cloro M chlorine

clorofila F chlorophyll

cloroformo M chloroform

cloruro M chloride

club M club (también palo de golf); — **nocturno** nightclub

coacción F compulsion, coercion; **bajo** — under duress

coagulación F (de sangre) clotting; (por productos químicos) coagulation

coagulante M coagulant

coagular VI (con productos químicos) to coagulate; (sangre) to clot

coágulo M clot

coalición F coalition

coartada F alibi

coartar VT (una libertad) to restrict; (a una persona) to inhibit; (la creatividad) to strangle

cobalto M cobalt

cobarde ADJ cowardly; MF coward

cobardía F cowardice

cobertizo M shed

cobertor M cover

cobertura F (de nieve, aérea) cover; (de seguros, noticias, televisión) coverage; — **extendida** extended coverage

cobija F (cubierta) cover; (manta) blanket

cobijar VT to shelter; —**se** to seek shelter

cobra F cobra

cobrador -ora MF (persona) collector; M (perro) retriever

cobranza F collection

cobrar VT (impuestos) to collect; (una factura) to

charge; (un cheque) to cash; (el sueldo) to earn; (víctimas) to claim; — **al entregar** to collect on delivery; — **ánimo** to take heart; — **caro** to charge a lot; — **de más** to overcharge; — **de menos** to undercharge; — **valor** to gain importance; **a** — receivable; **vas a** — you're in for it

cobre M (elemento) copper; (utensilios) copper utensils

cobrizo ADJ copper-colored

cobro M collection, charge; — **excesivo** overcharge

coca F (planta, hoja) coca; (cocaína) *fam* coke

cocaína F cocaine

cóccix M coccyx

cocear VI/VT to kick

cocer[34] VI/VT (huevos) to boil; (verduras) to cook; (cerámica) to fire; — **al vapor** to steam; **a medio** — half-cooked; **romper a** — to break into a boil; **¿qué se cuece aquí?** what's up?

coche M (automóvil, vagón) car; (autobús) coach; (vehículo tirado por caballerías) carriage; — **bomba** car bomb; — **cama** sleeper; —**-comedor** dining car; — **de bebé** stroller, baby carriage; — **de bomberos** fire engine; — **de choque** bumper car; — **de golf** golf cart; — **de línea** city bus; — **deportivo** sports car; — **fúnebre** hearse; **ir en** — to go by car, to drive; **pasear en** — to go on a drive

cochera F carport

cochinada F (asquerosidad) filthy action; (maldad) dirty trick

cochinilla F woodlouse

cochino -na ADJ filthy; MF pig

cocido M stew

cociente M quotient; — **intelectual** IQ

cocina F (habitación) kitchen; (electrodoméstico) range, stove; (arte) cuisine, cookery

cocinar VI/VT to cook; (tramar) to cook up

cocinero -ra MF cook

cócker MF cocker spaniel

coco M (fruto) coconut; (cabeza) *fam* dome; (fantasma) bogeyman; **comerse el** — to get all worked up

cocodrilo M crocodile

cóctel M (bebida) cocktail, mixed drink; (fiesta) cocktail party

codazo M jab with the elbow; **dar —s** to elbow

codear VI/VT to elbow, to jab; —**se** to nudge one another; —**se con** to rub elbows with

codeína F codeine

codicia F (avaricia) greed; (deseo sexual) lust

codiciar VT (una cosa) to covet; (a una persona) to lust after

codicioso ADJ covetous, greedy

codificación F coding, encoding

codificar[30] VT (mensaje) to codify, to encrypt; (programa de computadora) to code

código M code; — **abierto** open code; — **de acceso** access code; — **de barras** bar code; — **de país** country code; — **fuente** source code; — **genético** genetic code; — **impositivo** tax code; — **postal** zip code

codo M elbow; — **a** — side by side; — **de tenista** tennis elbow; **empinar el** — to drink too much; **hablar por los —s** to talk one's head off; **hasta los —s** up to one's elbows

codorniz F quail

coeficiente M coefficient; — **de inteligencia** intelligence quotient

coerción F coercion

coetáneo ADJ contemporary

coexistencia F coexistence; — **pacífica** peaceful coexistence

cofre M coffer

coger[45] VT (a un criminal, una pelota) to catch; (con las manos) to grasp; (flores) to gather; to pick; (a un empleado) to hire; (una emisora) to receive; (cosas del suelo) to pick up; (espacio) to take up; (un pez) to land, to catch; (un camino, tren, curso) to take; (poseer sexualmente) *Am vulg* to screw, to fuck; — **por/de sorpresa** to catch by surprise; — **el sueño** to fall asleep; — **hacia el castillo** to turn toward the castle; —**le miedo a algo** to become scared of something; —**le el tranquillo a algo** to get into the swing of things; —**se un resfriado** to come down with a cold; **coge y le dice** he up and says

cognado ADJ & M cognate

cognitivo ADJ cognitive

cogollo M heart

cogote M neck

cohabitar VI (amigos) to live [with]; (una pareja) to cohabitate

cohecho M bribe

coheredero -ra MF joint heir

coherencia F (consecuencia) consistency; (lógica) coherence

coherente ADJ (consecuente) consistent; (lógico) coherent; (con significado) meaningful; **lo que dices no es** — you're not making any sense

cohesión F cohesion

cohesivo ADJ coherent

cohete M rocket

cohetería F rocketry

cohibición F inhibition

cohibido ADJ inhibited, self-conscious

cohibir VT to inhibit

coincidencia F coincidence

coincidir VI to coincide

coito M coitus

cojear VI to limp; **saber de qué pie cojea alguien** to know someone's weaknesses

cojera F limp
cojín M cushion
cojinete M bushing; — **de bolas** ball bearing
cojo ADJ lame, crippled
cojones M PL (testículos) *vulg* balls, nuts; (valor) guts, grit; **estoy hasta los** — I've had it; **¿qué** — **quieres?** *vulg* what the hell do you want? **tener** — to be brave; **tu doctorado me lo paso por los** — *vulg* I don't give a shit about your doctorate
cojonudo ADJ (estupendo) cool; (valeroso) gutsy
cok M coke
col F cabbage; —**es de Bruselas** Brussels sprouts
cola F (de perro, ave, avión) tail; (de vestido) train; (hilera de gente) line; (secuencia de datos o programas) queue; (pegamento) glue; — **de caballo** ponytail; **hacer** — to stand in line; **no pegar ni con** — not to go together; **traer** — to have consequences
colaboración F collaboration
colaborador -ora MF (con el gobierno) collaborator; (de periódico) contributor
colaborar VI to collaborate; (con un periódico) to contribute
colación F **sacar a** — to bring up
colacionar VT to collate
colador M (para té) strainer; (para verduras) colander
colágeno M collagen
colapso M (de puente, edificio) collapse; (de nervios) breakdown; (de mercado) crash
colar[5] VT (té) to strain; (metal líquido) to pour; VI to go through, to slip through; **esa excusa no va a** — that excuse won't wash; —**se en una fiesta** to crash a party
colateral ADJ collateral
colcha F bedspread
colchón M (para dormir) mattress; (para emergencias) cushion
colchoneta F mat
colear VI (un perro) to wag the tail; (un tema) to be pending; (un auto) to fishtail
colección F collection
coleccionar VT to collect
coleccionista MF collector
colecta F charity collection
colectividad F collective, community
colectivo M (grupo) collective; (autobús) *Am* bus
colector M (de aguas negras) sewer; (eléctrico) collector; (de coche) manifold
colega MF colleague
colegio M (escuela privada) private school; (escuela primaria) elementary school; (centro de educación secundaria) high school; (asociación profesional) association, college
colegir[14] VI to gather
cólera F rage, wrath; **montar en** — to fly into a rage; M cholera

colérico ADJ irritable, choleric
colesterol M cholesterol
coleta F pigtail
coletilla F tag
coleto M **decir para su** — to say to oneself
colgadero M hanger; ADJ hanging
colgado ADJ high and dry
colgadura F drapery; —**s** hangings
colgante ADJ hanging; M pendant
colgar[42] VT (suspender, ahorcar) to hang; (un teléfono, un abrigo) to hang up; VI (un espejo) to hang; (un andrajo) to dangle; (un asunto) to be pending; **esa falda te cuelga por atrás** that dress hangs down in the back; —**se [un ordenador]** to crash; —**se de** to get hooked on; —**se del teléfono** to tarry on the phone
colibrí M hummingbird
cólico M colic
coliflor F cauliflower
colilla F cigarette butt
colina F hill, knoll
colindante ADJ neighboring
colindar VI — **con** to border [on], to adjoin
colirio M eyedrops
coliseo M coliseum
colisión F collision
collage M collage
collar M (de perlas) necklace; (de perro) collar; — **antipulgas** flea collar
collera F horse collar
collie M collie
colmar VT (un vaso) to fill; (una demanda) to satisfy; — **de alabanzas** to lavish praise upon
colmena F beehive
colmillo M (de persona) eyetooth, cuspid; (de elefante) tusk; (de víbora) fang
colmo M — **de la locura** height of folly; **¡eso es el** —! that takes the cake; **para** — to top it all
colocación F (ubicación) placement; (puesto) position
colocar[30] VT (poner, encontrar lugar para) to place; (casar) to marry off; (invertir) to invest; —**se** (drogarse) to get stoned; (encontrar empleo) to get a job; (ubicarse) to place oneself
coloide M colloid
Colombia F Colombia
colombiano -na ADJ & MF Colombian
colon M colon
colón M (moneda) colon
colonia F (territorio, grupo de insectos) colony; (comunidad de inmigrantes) community, settlement; (vivienda) development; (perfume) cologne
colonial ADJ colonial
colonización F colonization
colonizador -ora MF colonist

colonizar[47] VT to colonize, to settle

colono -na MF (habitante de una colonia) colonist, settler; (arrendatario) tenant farmer

colonoscopia F colonoscopy

coloquial ADJ colloquial

coloquio M colloquium

color M (tono) color; (pintura) paint; (maquillaje) rouge; (de naipes) flush; **—es primarios** primary colors; **a todo —** full color; **persona de —** person of color

coloración F coloring

colorado ADJ & M red; **ponerse —** to blush

colorante ADJ & M coloring

coloreado ADJ colored; M coloring

colorear VT to color

colorete M rouge

colorido M (de un caballo) coloring; (de un comentario, paisaje) color; ADJ colorful

colosal ADJ (grande) colossal; (estupendo) wonderful

colostomía F colostomy

columbrar VT to glimpse

columna F column; **— de dirección** steering column; **— vertebral** spinal column, backbone

columnista MF columnist

columpiar VI/VT to swing

columpio M swing

colza F (planta) rape; (aceite) rapeseed oil

coma F (signo) comma; M (falta de conciencia) coma

comadre F (mujer chismosa) gossip; (partera) midwife; (parienta) godmother of one's child

comadreja F weasel

comadrona F (mujer chismosa) gossip; (partera) midwife

comandancia F command

comandante MF (rango militar) major; (militar que ejerce el mando) commander; **— en jefe** commander in chief

comandar VT to command; **— un avión** to pilot an airplane

comando M (grupo militar) commando; (orden dada al ordenador) command

comarca F district

comatoso ADJ comatose

comba F (de una pared) bulge; (de madera) warp; **saltar a la —** to jump rope

combar VI (una pared) to sag; (madera) to warp; (trayectoria de pelota) to curve

combate M combat, fight; **fuera de —** out of combat / the competition

combatiente MF combatant

combatir VI/VT to combat

combativo ADJ combative

combinación F (mezcla) combination; (billete) transfer ticket

combinar VT to combine; **—se para hacer algo** to agree to do something; **esos colores no combinan** those colors don't match

combo M combo

combustible ADJ combustible; M fuel

combustión F combustion

comedero M trough

comedia F (obra teatral) comedy; (farsa) farce; **— de situación** situation comedy, sitcom; **hacer la — de** to play the part of

comediante MF comedian

comedido ADJ moderate; *Am* obliging

comedirse[9] VI to show restraint; **— a hacer algo** *RP* to volunteer to do something

comedor M (habitación) dining room; (de empresa) cafeteria

comensal MF [fellow] diner

comentador -ora MF commentator

comentar VI/VT to comment [on], to remark [on]

comentario M (análisis) commentary; (observación) comment, remark

comentarista MF commentator

comenzar[48] VI/VT to begin, to start; **— a comer** to begin to eat; **— preguntando** to begin by asking

comer VI/VT to eat; (al mediodía) to have lunch; (en ajedrez) to take; (en el juego de damas) to jump; **dar de —** to feed; **sin —lo ni beberlo** through no fault of one's own; **—se** (corroer) to eat away; (terminar la comida) to eat up; **—se las eses** to drop one's esses; **—se las palabras** to eat one's words; **—se un semáforo en rojo** to run a red light

comercial ADJ & M commercial

comercialización F marketing, merchandising

comercializar[47] VT (volver comercial) to commercialize; (vender) to market, to merchandise

comerciante MF merchant, trader, dealer

comerciar VI to trade

comercio M commerce, trade; **— electrónico** e-business; **— exterior** foreign trade; **— minorista** retail trade; **— mayorista** wholesaler

comestible ADJ edible; M PL groceries

cometa M (cuerpo celeste) comet; F (juguete) kite

cometer VT to commit

cometido M purpose, objective

comezón F itch, itching; **tener —** to itch

cómic M comic book

comicios M PL polls

cómico -ca ADJ comic, comical; MF comedian

comida F (ocasión) meal; (alimento) food; (al mediodía) lunch; **— basura** junk food; **— macrobiótica** health food; **— rápida** fast food

comience, comienza *ver* comenzar

comienzo M beginning; **a —s de** toward the beginning of; **al —** at first, initially; **desde un/el —** from the start

comilla F quotation mark; **entre —s** in quotes

comilón -ona MF big eater; F binge

comino M cumin; **me importa un —** *fam* I don't give a hoot; **no vale un —** *fam* it's not worth a hoot

comisaría F **— de policía** police station, precinct

comisario -ria MF (comisionado) commissioner; (jefe de policía) police chief

comisión F (acción de cometer, porcentaje ganado) commission; (comité) committee

comisionar VT to commission

comistrajo M bad food

comisura F **— de los labios** corner of the mouth

comité M committee

comitiva F retinue

como ADV (del mismo modo que) as, like; **ella pinta — yo** she paints like I do; (aproximadamente) about; **pesa — diez kilos** it weighs about ten kilos; CONJ (puesto que) since; **— no tenemos dinero** since we have no money; **— no me pagues** if you don't pay me; **era — que muy viejo** he was, like, real old; **— que te voy a permitir** as if I would let you; **— quieras** as you please; **— si** as if; **¡— si me lo fuera a creer!** a likely story!

cómo ADV INTERR & PRON (de qué manera) how; (¿perdón?) excuse me? what? **¡— brillan las estrellas!** how the stars are shining! **¡— no!** of course! **¿a — me lo vende?** what does that cost?

cómoda F chest of drawers, dresser, bureau

comodidad F (cualidad) comfort; (cosa cómoda) convenience; **—es** amenities

comodín M joker, wild card

cómodo ADJ (mueble) comfortable; (horario) convenient; (persona) lazy

Comoras F PL Comoros

compactar VT to compact

compacto ADJ compact

compadecer[35] VT to pity; **—se de** to take pity on

compadre M (amigo) pal, crony; (pariente) godfather of one's child

compañero -ra MF (camarada) companion; (de un zapato) mate; **— de clase** classmate; **— de cuarto** roommate; **— de equipo** teammate

compañía F company; **— de importación y exportación** import-export company; **— fantasma** bogus company; **— recién establecida** start-up; **en — de** in the company of

comparable ADJ comparable

comparación F comparison

comparar VI/VT to compare; **—se con** to compare [oneself] with

comparativo ADJ comparative

comparecencia F appearance

comparecer[35] VI to appear

compartimiento M compartment

compartir VT (bienes) to share; (tiempo) to divide

compás M (instrumento de geometría) compass; (ritmo) beat; (espacio entre barras) measure, bar; (división de música) time signature; **marcar el —** to beat time

compasión F compassion

compasivo ADJ compassionate, sympathetic

compatibilidad F compatibility

compatible ADJ compatible

compatriota MF compatriot

compeler VT to compel

compendiar VT to summarize

compendio M digest, condensation

compenetración F bonding

compensación F compensation

compensar VT (un daño) to compensate; (un gasto) to offset; **compensa su falta de inteligencia con mucha disciplina** he makes up for his lack of intelligence with a lot of discipline; **te voy a — por esto** I'll make it up to you

competencia F (pugna, competición, competidores) competition; (cualidad de competente) competence

competente ADJ competent

competición F athletic competition, meet

competidor -ora ADJ competing; MF (comercial) competitor; (deportivo) athlete, participant

competir[9] VI to compete, to vie

competitividad F competitiveness

competitivo ADJ competitive

compilador M compiler

compilar VT to compile

compinche M chum, crony

compita, compite, compitiendo, compitiera, compitiese *ver* competir

complacencia F satisfaction

complacer[36] VT to please, to gratify; **—se [en]** to take pleasure [in]

complaciente ADJ (que complace) obliging; (que consiente) indulgent

complejidad F complexity

complejo ADJ complex; M complex; **— de inferioridad** inferiority complex

complementar VT to complement, to supplement

complementario ADJ complementary

complemento M complement; **— alimenticio** dietary supplement; **— directo** direct object; **— indirecto** indirect object; **—s** fringe benefits

completar VT (terminar) to complete; (en fútbol americano) to complete [passes]; **—se** to be completed

completo ADJ (terminado) complete; (lleno) full; **hoy tenemos el —** today we have a full house; **por —** completely

complexión F build

complicación F complication

complicado ADJ complicated

complicar[30] VT to complicate; **—le a alguien la vida** to give someone trouble

cómplice MF accomplice

complicidad F complicity

complot M plot

compondrá, compondría ver componer

componenda F (arreglo provisional) quick fix; (arreglo ilegal) shady deal

componente ADJ & M component

componer[56, 74] VT (un grupo) to compose, to make up; (imprenta) to set; (un coche descompuesto) to fix; (música) to compose; **—se de** to be composed of; **componérselas** to deal with one's problems alone

componga, compongo ver componer

comportamiento M conduct, behavior

comportarse VI/VT to conduct oneself, to behave

composición F composition

compositor -ora MF composer

compostura F (arreglo) repair; (dignidad) composure

compra F purchase; **— apalancada** LBO; **ir de —s** to go shopping; **— hostil** hostile takeover

comprador -ora MF (comercial) buyer, purchaser; (en una tienda) shopper

comprar VT to buy, to purchase; **compró su silencio** he gave her hush money

comprender VT (entender) to understand, to comprehend; (abarcar) to cover, to include

comprensible ADJ comprehensible, understandable

comprensión F (intelectual) understanding, comprehension; (emocional) sympathy, understanding

comprensivo ADJ understanding

compresa F compress

compresión F compression; **— de archivos** file compression

comprimido ADJ compressed; M tablet

comprimir VT to compress

comprobación F verification, check

comprobante M proof; **— de compra** proof of purchase

comprobar[5] VT (verificar) to verify, to check; (probar) to prove; (darse cuenta) to realize

comprometer VT (obligar) to commit; (poner en peligro) to jeopardize, to compromise; **—se** (prometer) to promise; (tomar partido) to commit oneself; (para casarse) to get engaged

comprometido ADJ (obligado) obligated; (arriesgado) risky; (implicado) compromised;

(con planes de casarse) engaged; (entregado, dedicado) committed, engaged

compromiso M (ideología, obligación, promesa) commitment; (acuerdo) agreement; (cita) appointment, engagement; (de matrimonio) engagement; (solución negociada) compromise; **no me pongas en —** don't compromise me; **sin — de compra** without obligation to buy

comprueba, compruebe ver comprobar

compuerta F sluice gate, floodgate

compuesto ADJ (ojos, tiempo, interés) compound; **estar — de** to be composed of; M compound

compuesto ver componer

compulsión F compulsion

compulsivo ADJ compulsive

compungirse[46] VI to feel sorry

computación F computing

computadora F computer; **— personal** personal computer; **— de escritorio** desktop computer; **— de mano** palmtop, handheld computer; **— digital** digital computer; **— portátil** laptop computer; **— torre** tower model

computar VT to compute

computarizar[47] VT to computerize

cómputo M computation

comulgar[40] VI (recibir el sacramento) to take Communion; (estar de acuerdo) to agree

común ADJ common; **en —** in common; **por lo —** generally; **el — de las gentes** the majority of the people

comuna F commune

comunicable ADJ communicable

comunicación F (interacción) communication; (ponencia) presentation; **se nos cortó la —** we got disconnected

comunicado M communiqué, report

comunicar[30] VI/VT to communicate; **—se con** (entenderse) to communicate with; (ponerse en contacto con) to reach; (desembocar en) to open into

comunicativo ADJ communicative

comunidad F community; **— internauta** Internet community; **— virtual** virtual community

comunión F communion

comunismo M communism

comunista ADJ & MF communist

comunitario ADJ (en común) communal; **espíritu —** community spirit; **presupuesto —** European Union budget

con PREP with; **— lo que come, tendría que estar obesa** given what she eats, she should be obese; **— mucho** by far; **— que le digas alcanza** just telling him is enough; **— tal [de] que** provided that; **— todo** all things considered

conato M attempt
concavidad F hollow
cóncavo ADJ concave
concebible ADJ conceivable
concebir[9] VT (engendrar) to conceive; (entender) to conceive of
conceder VT (dar) to grant; (admitir) to concede, to allow
concejal MF councilor
concejo M council
concentración F (densidad, atencíon, cantidad) concentration; (manifestación) rally, demonstration
concentrar VT to concentrate; —**se** (prestar atención) to concentrate, to focus; (manifestar) to rally
concepción F conception
concepto M (idea) concept; (artificio) conceit
conceptual ADJ conceptual
concernir[73] VT to concern
concertación F agreement
concertar[1] VT (arreglar) to arrange; (concretar) to finalize; (planear) to concert; —**se** to agree
concesión F (admisión) concession; (otorgamiento) grant; (permiso comercial) franchise
concesionario M dealership
concha F (de molusco) shell; (genitales femeninos) Am vulg pussy
conchabarse VI to conspire
conciba, concibe, concibiendo, concibiera, concibiese ver concebir
conciencia F (moral) conscience; (mental) consciousness, awareness; **tomar** — **de** to come to grips with; — **de marca** brand awareness
concienzudo ADJ conscientious, thorough
concierto M (música) concert; (armonía) harmony; (acuerdo) agreement
conciliación F conciliation
conciliar VT (personas) to conciliate; (ideas) to reconcile; — **el sueño** to fall sleep
concilio M council
concisión F conciseness
conciso ADJ concise, brief
conciudadano -na MF fellow citizen
concluir[19] VI/VT to conclude
conclusión F conclusion
concluya, concluye, concluyendo, concluyera, concluyese ver concluir
concluyente ADJ conclusive
concomitante ADJ attendant
concordancia F agreement
concordar[5] VI to agree
concordia F concord
concretamente ADV specifically; **tiene un perro,** — **un chihuahua** he has a dog, a chihuahua, to be precise
concretar VT (cerrar) to finalize; (especificar) to be specific about; (realizar) to realize; —**se a** to focus on
concreto ADJ concrete; **en** — specifically; M Am concrete
concubina F concubine
concurrencia F (reunión) gathering; (asistencia) attendance
concurrido ADJ well-attended
concurrir VI (confluir) to come together; (asistir) to attend
concursante MF contestant
concurso M (para un premio) contest; (en una licitación) call for bids; (para un puesto de trabajo) competitive examination; — **de belleza** beauty pageant
concusión F graft
concusionario -ria MF grafter
condado M county
conde M count
condecoración F decoration
condecorar VT to decorate
condena F (castigo) sentence; (crítica) condemnation; **¡qué** —**!** what a pain!
condenación F condemnation
condenado ADJ (perdido) damned; (sentenciado) sentenced; **está** — **a muerte** he's on death row
condenar VT (criticar) to condemn; (sentenciar) to sentence; **eso le condenó al fracaso** that doomed him to failure; —**se** to go to hell
condensación F condensation
condensar VI to condense
condesa F countess
condescendencia F (tolerancia) acquiescence; (superioridad) condescension
condescender[2] VI (acomodarse) to acquiesce; (dignarse) to condescend
condición F condition; — **social** social station; **a** — **de que** on the condition that; **condiciones** (físicas) condition; (de un contrato) terms, provisos
condicional ADJ & M conditional
condicionamiento M conditioning
condicionar VT to condition
condimentar VT to season
condimento M condiment, seasoning
condiscípulo -la MF classmate
condolencias F PL condolences; **dar las** — **to** offer one's condolences
condolerse[6] VI to offer one's condolences
condominio M condominium
condón M condom, rubber
cóndor M condor
conducción F (de electricidad) conduction; (de un difunto o prisionero) transport
conducente ADJ conducive
conducir[38] VT (a un grupo) to lead; (una orquesta, electricidad) to conduct; (un coche) to drive, to steer; —**se** to behave

conducta F (moral) conduct, behavior; (biológica) behavior; — **de alto riesgo** high-risk behavior

conducto M (de agua) conduit; (anatómico) duct; — **de aire** airway; **por** — **de** through

conductor-ora ADJ (de electricidad) conductive; M (de electricidad) conductor; MF (de coches) driver; (en baloncesto) point guard

conductual ADJ behavioral

conduje, condujera, condujese ver conducir

conectar VI/VT to connect

conectividad F connectivity

conector M connector; — **en serie** serial connector

conejillo M — **de Indias** guinea pig

conejo M rabbit; (genitales femeninos) Esp vulg pussy

conexión F connection

confabulación F collusion

confección F (fabricación de ropa) dressmaking, tailoring; (calidad) workmanship; **de** — ready-made

confeccionar VT (productos) to manufacture; (ropa) to tailor, to sew

confederación F confederation

confederado-da ADJ & MF confederate

confederar VI to form a confederacy

conferencia F (discurso) lecture; (reunión) conference; — **de prensa** press conference; **dar una** — to give a lecture

conferenciante MF lecturer, speaker

conferenciar VI to confer

conferencista MF lecturer, speaker

conferir[8] VT to confer, to bestow; (un título) to confer

confesar[1] VI/VT to confess

confesión F confession

confesionario M confessional

confesor-ora MF confessor

confiabilidad F reliability

confiable ADJ reliable

confiado ADJ (seguro de sí) confident; (crédulo) trusting

confianza F confidence, trust; **en** — in confidence; **tener** — to be confident; **tener** — **en** to have confidence in; **tomar** —**s** to be overly familiar with

confianzudo ADJ overfamiliar

confiar[28] VT (un secreto) to confide; (un valor, bien) to entrust; — **en** to rely on; **confío que Dios me proteja** I trust that God will protect me

confidencia F confidence

confidencial ADJ confidential; **altamente** — top-secret

confidente MF (amigo) confidant; M (mueble) love seat

confiesa, confiese ver confesar

configuración F configuration

configurar VT to configure (también computadoras); —**se** to take shape

confinamiento M confinement

confinar VT to confine

confines M PL bounds, confines

confirmación F confirmation

confirmar VT to confirm

confiscación F (de una propiedad) confiscation, seizure; (de un monto) forfeiture

confiscar[30] VT to confiscate

confitar VT to candy

confite M candy

confitería F confectionery

confitura F confection

conflictivo ADJ (persona, tema) contentious; (región) volatile

conflicto M conflict

confluencia F (de calles) junction; (de ríos) confluence

conformación F creation, establishment

conformar VT to adapt; —**se** to go along; —**se con** to settle for

conforme ADJ in agreement, content; — **a** in accordance with; CONJ — **amanece** as dawn breaks

conformidad F conformity, agreement; **estar de/en** — **con** to be in accordance with

conformismo M conformity

confort M comfort

confortable ADJ comfortable

confortar VT to comfort

confraternidad F fraternity, fellowship

confraternizar[47] VI to fraternize

confrontación F confrontation

confrontar VT (a un enemigo) to confront; (dos listas) to compare

confundido ADJ confused, mixed-up

confundir VT to confuse, to perplex, to baffle; —**se** (personas) to become confused; (cosas) to mingle

confusión F (mental) confusion; (de cosas) clutter, disarray

confuso ADJ (que no comprende, desordenado) confused; (difícil de comprender) confusing

congelación F freezing; — **salarial** pay freeze

congelado ADJ frozen

congelador M freezer

congelar VT to freeze

congeniar VI — **con** to get along with

congénito ADJ congenital

congestión F congestion

conglomeración F conglomeration

conglomerado M conglomeration

Congo M Congo

congoja F anguish, grief

congoleño-ña ADJ & MF Congolese

congregación F (feligreses) congregation; (orden) order

congregar⁴⁰ VI to congregate
congresista MF (legislador) member of Congress; (asistente a un congreso) conference attendee, conventioneer
congreso M (cuerpo legislativo, edificio) congress; (reunión periódica) conference, convention
congresual ADJ congressional
congruencia F congruence
conífera F conifer
conjetura F conjecture, surmise
conjeturar VT to conjecture, to surmise
conjugación F conjugation
conjugar⁴⁰ VT to conjugate
conjunción F conjunction
conjuntamente ADV jointly
conjuntivitis F conjunctivitis, pinkeye
conjunto M (grupo de cosas) set; (totalidad) total, aggregate; (de ropa) outfit; — **musical** ensemble; **en** — as a whole, all told; ADJ joint
conjuración F conspiracy
conjurado-da MF conspirator
conjurar VT (conspirar) to conspire, to plot; (evitar, cancelar) to ward off
conjuro M incantation, spell
conllevar VT to entail, to involve
conmemoración F commemoration
conmemorar VT to commemorate
conmemorativo ADJ commemorative, memorial
conmigo PRON with me
conmiseración F commiseration
conmoción F commotion; — **cerebral** brain concussion, cerebral concussion
conmovedor ADJ moving, touching
conmover⁶ VT to move, to touch
conmovido ADJ moved, touched
conmutador M switch
conmutar VT to commute
connatural ADJ inborn
connotación F connotation
cono M cone
conocedor-ora ADJ who know[s], aware; **muy** — **de la situación** well aware of the situation; MF connoisseur, expert
conocer³⁵ VT to know (también en sentido carnal); (reconocer) to recognize; (tratar por primera vez) to meet; — **el paño** to know the ropes; **se conoce que** it is clear that
conocido-da ADJ well-known; MF acquaintance
conocimiento M knowledge, acquaintance; — **de embarque** bill of lading; **perder el** — to lose consciousness; **poner en** — to inform; —**s** knowledge
conozca, conozco ver conocer
conque CONJ so
conquista F conquest
conquistador-ora MF conqueror; ADJ conquering

conquistar VT (un terreno) to conquer; (el amor de alguien) to win
consabido ADJ habitual
consagración F consecration
consagrar VT (declarar consagrado) to consecrate; (dedicar) to devote
consciente ADJ conscious; — **del problema** aware of the problem
conscribir VT to draft
consecución F attainment, achievement
consecuencia F (hecho que resulta de otro) consequence; (cualidad de consecuente) consistency; **a** — **de** as a result of
consecuente ADJ (que se sigue de) consequent, logical; (fiel en sus actos) consistent
consecutivo ADJ consecutive
conseguible ADJ obtainable
conseguir¹² VT (un derecho) to attain, to get; (un objetivo) to achieve; (un puesto de trabajo) to land, to get; — **hacer algo** to manage to do something
consejero-ra MF (asesor) adviser; (miembro del consejo) board member; **consejero-ra delegado-da** Esp CEO
consejo M (opinión) counsel, advice; (comité) council; — **de guerra** court-martial
consenso M consensus
consentimiento M consent, acquiescence
consentir⁸ VT (permitir) to consent to, to acquiesce to; (mimar) to pamper, to indulge; — **en** to permit
conserje MF (limpiador) janitor; (portero) superintendent; (recepcionista) hotel clerk
conserva F canned food; **en** — canned
conservación F conservation, preservation
conservador-ora MF (en política) conservative; (de museo) curator; ADJ (de tradiciones) conservative; (de alimentos) preservative
conservadurismo M conservatism
conservante M preservative
conservar VT (guardar) to keep; (mantener) to retain; (preservar) to preserve; (ahorrar) to conserve
conservatorio M conservatory
considerable ADJ considerable
considerablemente ADV significantly
consideración F consideration; **de** — considerable; **tomar/tener en** — to take into consideration
considerado ADJ considerate, thoughtful
considerar VT to consider
consiga ver conseguir
consigna F (eslogan) motto, watchword; (orden) order
consignación F consignment; **a/en** — on consignment
consignar VT to consign
consignatario-ria MF consignee

consigo PRON with oneself/himself/herself/ themselves

consigo, consiguiendo, consiguiera, consiguiese *ver* conseguir

consiguiente ADJ consequent; **por —** consequently

consistencia F consistency

consistente ADJ (firme) consistent; **— de** consisting of

consistir VI **— en** to consist of

consocio -cia MF fellow member

consola F console; **— de juegos** game console

consolación F consolation

consolar[5] VT to console

consolidación F consolidation

consolidar VT to consolidate

consonante ADJ & F consonant

consorcio M consortium

consorte MF consort

conspicuo ADJ conspicuous

conspiración F conspiracy, plot

conspirador -ora MF conspirator, plotter

conspirar VI to conspire, to plot

constancia F (en el amor) constancy; (en el esfuerzo) perseverance; (en el trabajo) steadiness; (prueba) documentary proof

constante ADJ & F constant; **—s vitales** vital signs

constar VI to be stated; **aquí consta que me debes cien dólares** here it states that you owe me a hundred dollars; **— de** to consist of, to be composed of; **hacer —** to mention; **me consta que** I am aware that; **que conste** let it be known

constatar VT to verify

constelación F constellation

consternación F consternation, dismay

consternar VT to dismay

constipación F constipation

constipado ADJ *Esp* (resfriado) suffering from a cold; *Am* (seco de vientre) constipated; M *Esp* head cold

constitución F constitution

constitucional ADJ constitutional

constituir[19] VT to constitute

constitutivo ADJ (constituyente) constituent; (inherente) inherent; **— de un delito** which constitutes a crime

constituya, constituye *ver* constituir

constituyente ADJ constituent

constreñimiento M constraint

constreñir[11] VT (limitar) to constrain; (apretar) to constrict, to constrain

constricción F constriction

construcción F (actividad de construir, cosa construida) construction, building; (gramatical) construction

constructivo ADJ constructive

constructor -ora MF builder; F construction

company

construir[19] VI/VT to construct, to build

construye, construyendo, construyera, construyese *ver* construir

consuelo M consolation, comfort, solace

consuetudinario ADJ (acción) habitual; (derecho) common

cónsul MF consul

consulado M consulate

consulta F (acción de consultar) consultation; (pregunta) question; (consultorio) doctor's office

consultar VT to consult; **—lo con la almohada** to sleep on it

consultivo ADJ consultative

consultor ADJ consulting

consultoría F consulting firm

consultorio M doctor's office

consumado ADJ consummate, accomplished

consumar VT to consummate

consumidor -ora MF consumer; ADJ consuming

consumir VT to consume; **—se** (agua) to boil off; (neumático) to wear out; **—se de** to be consumed by

consumismo M consumerism

consumo M consumption

consunción F consumption

contabilidad F accounting, bookkeeping

contable MF accountant, bookkeeper

contactar VI/VT to contact; **—[se] con** to get in contact/touch with

contacto M contact; **— visual** eye contact; **en — con** in touch with

contado M **al —** in cash; ADJ **—s** few

contador -ora ADJ counting; M (de dinero) counter; (de electricidad) meter; **— Geiger** Geiger counter; MF accountant; **— público -ca** CPA

contaduría F accountant's office

contagiar VT to infect

contagio M (de enfermedad) contagion; (de ordenador) infection

contagioso ADJ contagious, catching, infectious

contaminación F (del agua, de la comida) contamination; (del medio ambiente) pollution; **— sonora** noise pollution

contaminante M contaminate

contaminar VT (agua, alimentos, cultura) to contaminate; (el medio ambiente) to pollute; **—se** (agua) to become contaminated; (medio ambiente) to become polluted

contar[5] VI/VT (medir una cantidad) to count; (decir historias) to tell; **el hotel cuenta con una piscina** the hotel has a swimming pool; **cuento con mi hermano** I count on my brother; **esto no cuenta** this doesn't count; **¿me lo vas a contar a mí?** you can say that again; **tienes que — el tiempo** you have to watch the time; M SG **cuentakilómetros** (marcador de kilómetros) odometer; (velocímetro) speedometer

contemplación F contemplation

contemplar VT (mirar, tener en cuenta) to contemplate; (consentir) to spoil; VI to contemplate

contemporáneo ADJ contemporary

contención F containment

contender[2] VI to contend

contendrá, contendría ver contener

contenedor M container

contenedorizar VT containerize

contener[58] VT (un líquido) to contain; (risa, lágrimas) to hold back; (entusiasmo) to restrain; (el aliento) to hold

contenga, contengo ver contener

contenido ADJ restrained; M content[s]

contentar VT to satisfy; —**se** to be satisfied

contento ADJ (conforme) content, contented; (feliz) happy; M contentment

conteo M count

contera F (de paraguas) tip; (de bolígrafo) cap

contestación F answer, reply

contestador M answering machine

contestar VT to answer; VI to talk back, to mouth off

contexto M context

contextura F (de un objeto) makeup; (de persona) build

contienda F (guerra) conflict; (encuentro deportivo) competition

contiene, contienes ver contener

contigo PRON with you

contiguo ADJ contiguous; **estar — a** to adjoin

continental ADJ continental

continente M (masa geográfica) continent; (opuesto a isla) mainland; ADJ continent

contingencia F contingency

contingente ADJ & M contingent

continuación F (de una acción) continuation; (de una película) sequel; (tenis) follow-through; **a —** after that; **a — hubo una guerra** there ensued a war

continuado ADJ continuing

continuar[26] VI/VT to continue

continuidad F continuity

continuo ADJ (ininterrumpido) continuous; (repetido) continual

contonearse VI (mujer) to swing one's hips; (hombre) to swagger

contoneo M (de mujer) swinging of the hips; (de hombre) swagger

contorno M (forma) outline, contour; (tamaño de árbol, persona) girth

contorsión F contortion

contra PREP against; M **los pro y los —** the pros and cons; **en —** against; F drawback; **llevarle la — a alguien** to contradict someone

contraatacar[30] VI/VT to counterattack

contraataque M (militar) counterattack; (en baloncesto) fast break

contrabajo M double bass; MF double bass player

contrabandear VI/VT to smuggle

contrabandista MF smuggler

contrabando M (actividad) smuggling; (mercancías) contraband; **hacer —** to smuggle

contracción F contraction

contrachapado M plywood

contractual ADJ contractual

contracultura F counterculture

contradecir[53, 74] VT to contradict

contradicción F contradiction

contradictorio ADJ contradictory

contraejemplo M counterexample

contraer[59] VT (enfermedad) to contract; (derechos) to limit; (deudas) to incur; — **matrimonio** to get married

contraespionaje M counterespionage

contrafuerte M (de muro) buttress; (de zapato) counter

contrahecho ADJ deformed

contralor M (control) comptroller, controller; (auditor) auditor

contralto M (voz) alto; MF (persona) alto

contramandar VT to countermand

contramedida F countermeasure

contraoferta F counteroffer

contraorden F countermand

contrapartida F compensation

contrapelo LOC ADV **a —** against the grain

contrapesar VT to counterbalance

contrapeso M counterbalance

contraproducente ADJ counterproductive

contrariar[28] VT to annoy; —**se** to get annoyed

contrariedad F (fastidio) annoyance; (dificultad) snag

contrario ADJ (opuesto) opposite; (discrepante) conflicting; **al —** on the contrary; **de lo —** otherwise; **llevar la contraria** to be contrary; **por el —** on the contrary; **soy — al doblaje de películas** I'm against the dubbing of films; **todo lo —** just the opposite

contrarrestar VT to counteract

contrarrevolución F counterrevolution

contraseña F password, watchword

contrastar VI/VT to contrast

contraste M contrast

contrata F contract

contratación F hiring; **— externa** outsourcing

contratar VT (a un empleado) to hire; (un servicio) to contract for; —**se** to be hired; **— y despedir** hire and fire

contratiempo M mishap

contratista MF contractor, builder

contrato M contract; **— de alquiler** rental

agreement; **por —** by contract
contravenir[61] VT to contravene
contraventana F shutter
contribución F (regalo, participación) contribution; (impuesto) tax; **— alternativa mínima** alternative minimum tax
contribuir[19] VT to contribute
contribuya, contribuye, contribuyendo, contribuyera, contribuyese *ver* contribuir
contribuyente MF taxpayer
contrincante MF opponent
contrito ADJ contrite
control M (dominio, dirección) control; (contralor médico) checkup; (vigilancia) check; (puesto) checkpoint; **— de calidad** quality control; **— de daños** damage control; **— de la natalidad** birth control; **— fronterizo** border control; **— paternal** parental control; **— remoto** remote control; **bajo —** under control
controlador -ora MF comptroller; M driver; **— de impresora** printer driver
controlar VT (restringir) to control; (vigilar) to check on
controversia F controversy
controvertido ADJ controversial
contumacia F obstinacy
contumaz ADJ stubborn
contundente ADJ (argumento) forceful; (objeto) blunt; (prueba) convincing; (victoria) resounding
contusión F bruise, contusion
contuve, contuviera, contuviese *ver* contener
convalecencia F convalescence
convalecer[35] VI to convalesce
convaleciente MF convalescent
convección F convection
convencer[32] VT (por lógica) to convince; (por insistencia) to persuade
convencimiento M (creencia) conviction; (acción) convincing
convención F convention
convencional ADJ conventional
convendrá, convendría, convenga, convengo *ver* convenir
convenido ADJ agreed-upon
conveniencia F (algo cómodo) convenience; (algo aconsejable) desirability; **a su —** at your convenience
conveniente ADJ (cómodo) convenient; (aconsejable) advisable
convenio M agreement; **— colectivo** collective bargaining; **— comercial** business agreement
convenir[61] VI (ser apropiado) to be suitable; (llegar a un acuerdo) to agree
convento M convent

convergencia F convergence
converger[45] VI to converge
conversación F conversation; **trabar — con** to engage in a conversation with
conversar VI to converse
conversión F conversion; **— de dos puntos** two-point conversion
converso -sa MF convert
convertible ADJ convertible
convertidor M converter
convertir[8] VT to convert; **—se en** to become
convexo ADJ convex
convicción F conviction
convicto -ta ADJ convicted; MF convict
convidar VT to invite; *Am* to offer
convierta, convierte *ver* convertir
convincente ADJ convincing, compelling
convine, conviniendo, conviniera, conviniese *ver* convenir
convirtiendo, convirtiera, convirtiese *ver* convertir
convite M (invitación) invitation; (banquete) banquet
convivencia F (coexistencia) coexistence; (cohabitación) cohabitation, living together
convivir VI (coexistir) to coexist; (cohabitar) to cohabitate, to live together
convocación F convocation
convocar[30] VT to convoke, to call together; (una reunión, un concurso) to convene
convocatoria F (anuncio) announcement; (llamamiento) call
convoy M convoy
convoyar VT to convoy
convulsión F convulsion
conyugal ADJ conjugal, marital
cónyuge MF spouse
coñac M cognac, brandy
coñazo M (molestia) *vulg* pain in the butt
coño M *vulg* pussy, cunt; **en el quinto —** in the boondocks; INTERJ *fam* damn!
cooperación F cooperation
cooperar VI to cooperate
cooperativa F cooperative, co-op
cooperativista MF member of a cooperative
cooperativo ADJ cooperative
coordenada F coordinate
coordinación F coordination
coordinado ADJ coordinate
coordinador -ora MF coordinator; ADJ coordinating
coordinar VT to coordinate
copa F (vaso) goblet, wineglass; (de árbol) top; (de sombrero) crown; (palo de la baraja) card in the suit of *copas*; (trofeo, parte de un sujetador) cup; **ir de —s** to go for a drink; **— del Mundo** World Cup
copago M copayment
copete M (de pelo) tuft; (de plumas) crest; **estar**

hasta el — to be fed up
copia F (réplica) copy; (de foto) print; — **de respaldo** backup copy; — **de respaldo automático** automatic backup copy; — **de seguridad** backup copy; — **en papel** hard copy; — **impresa** hard copy
copiadora F copy machine
copiar VT (reproducir) to copy; (en un examen) to cheat
copión-ona MF copycat
copioso ADJ copious, plentiful
copla F (canción) popular song; (estrofa) stanza
copo M (de nieve) snowflake; (de lana, algodón) wad; —**s de maíz** cornflakes
copropietario-ria MF joint owner
coprotagonista MF costar
cópula F (acto sexual) coupling, mating; (verbo) copula
copulación F copulation
copular VI to copulate
copyright M copyright
coque M coke
coqueta F (mujer) coquette; (mueble) dressing table
coquetear VI to flirt, to dally
coquetería F flirtation
coqueto ADJ flirtatious
coraje M (valentía) courage; (enojo) anger
coral M (marino) coral; (musical) chorale
coralino ADJ coral
coraza F armor
corazón M (órgano) heart; (de manzana) core; (vocativo) honey; **con el — en la boca** (cansado) really tired; (nervioso) on edge; **de buen —** kindhearted; **de todo —** wholeheartedly; **romperle el — a alguien** to break someone's heart
corazonada F hunch
corbata F necktie, tie, cravat
corcel M charger, steed
corchea F eighth note; — **con puntillo** dotted eighth note
corchete M (en costura) hook and eye; (paréntesis recto) square bracket; (llave) brace
corcho M (para botella) cork; (para pescar) float
corcova F hump, hunchback
corcovear VI to buck
cordaje M strings
cordel M string
cordero M (animal) lamb; (piel, cuero) lambskin
cordial ADJ cordial
cordillera F mountain range
cordobés-esa ADJ from Cordoba; MF person from Cordoba
cordón M (cinta) cord; (al borde de la calle) *Am* curb; — **de apertura** ripcord; — **de zapatos** shoelace, shoestring; — **policial** police cordon; — **umbilical** umbilical cord
cordoncillo M ridge, rib

cordura F sanity
Corea F Korea; — **del Norte** North Korea; — **del Sur** South Korea
coreano-na ADJ & MF Korean
corear VI/VT to chant
coreografía F choreography
cornada F goring
cornear VT to gore
corneja F crow
córner M corner kick
corneta F cornet; MF bugler
cornisa F cornice, ledge
corno M horn; — **francés** French horn
cornudo ADJ horned; M cuckold
coro M (cantantes) choir, chorus; (música) chorus; (parte de la iglesia) loft; **cantar a —** to sing in unison
corolario M corollary
corona F crown
coronación F coronation
coronar VT to crown
coronario ADJ coronary
coronel M colonel
coronilla F crown of the head; **estar hasta la — ** to be fed up
corpiño M (almilla) bodice; (sujetador) *Am* bra
corporación F guild
corporal ADJ corporal, bodily
corporativo ADJ corporate
corpulento ADJ stout, corpulent
corpus M corpus
corpúsculo M corpuscle
corral M (de granja) barnyard, farmyard; (para ganado) corral, pen
correa F (de cuero) leather strap; (de ventilador) belt; (de perro) leash
corrección F (acción de corregir) correction; (cualidad de correcto) correctness
correctamente ADV correctly, properly
correcto ADJ (apropiado) correct, proper; (acertado) right
corrector-ora MF editor; — **de pruebas** proofreader
corredizo ADJ sliding
corredor-ora ADJ running; MF (persona que corre, también en deportes) runner; (deportista automovilístico, ciclista) racer; (intermediario) broker, agent; M (pasillo) hallway, corridor
correduría F brokerage
corregir[14] VT (errores) to correct; (exámenes) to grade; —**se** (en lo moral) to mend one's ways; (en los errores) to correct oneself
correlación F correlation
correlacionar VT to correlate
correlato M correlate
correo M mail; (edificio) post office; — **aéreo** air mail; — **certificado** certified mail; — **de voz** voice mail; — **electrónico** e-mail; —

electrónico basura junk e-mail, spam;
echar al — to mail
correoso ADJ tough
correr VI (persona, agua, calle) to run; (coche) to
go fast; (una puerta) to slide; (dinero, tiempo)
to pass; **— con los gastos** to take on the
costs; VT (una cortina) to draw; (una carrera,
un riesgo) to run; **—se** (moverse) to scoot
over; (desteñir) to run, to bleed; (manchar) to
smear; (tener orgasmo) *Esp fam* to come
correría F foray
correspondencia F correspondence
corresponder VI (ser adecuado, estar en
consonancia) to correspond; (pertenecer) to
belong; VT (amor, favores) to reciprocate; **a
mí me corresponde llamarla** it's up to me
to call her, it behooves me to call her
correspondiente ADJ corresponding; MF
correspondent
corresponsal MF correspondent
corretaje M broker's/agent's commission
corretear VI to run around
corrida F (acción de correr) running;
(competición) race; (orgasmo) *Esp* orgasm;
(de banco) run; **— de toros** bullfight; **de —**
without stopping
corrido ADJ (experimentado) worldly;
(continuo) uninterrupted; **de —** without
stopping; M ballad
corriente ADJ (que corre) running; (común)
usual; (franco) frank; **el — mes** the current
month; **estar al —** to be up to date; F (de
agua, electricidad) current; (de dinero) flow;
(de pesimismo) wave; (de aire) draft; (de
computadora) streaming; **— alterna**
alternating current; **— continua** direct
current; **— del Golfo** Gulf Stream; **al —** in
the loop; **dejarse llevar por la —** to
conform; **llevarle la — a alguien** to humor
someone
**corrija, corrijo, corrigiendo, corrigiera,
corrigiese, corrigió** *ver* corregir
corrillo M group of gossips
corro M circle of people
corroborar VT to corroborate
corroer[73] VT to corrode
corromper VT (a una persona) to corrupt; (un
alimento) to rot; **—se** (una persona) to
become corrupt; (un alimento) to rot
corrompido ADJ corrupt
corrosión F corrosion
corrupción F corruption
corrupto ADJ corrupt
corsé M corset
cortada F shortcut
cortado ADJ (abreviado, sucinto) clipped;
(tímido) shy; M (café) coffee with some milk;
(desnivel) slope; (tenis) backspin, slice
cortador -ora MF (persona) cutter; F (aparato)

cutter; **cortadora de césped** lawn mower
cortadura M cut
cortante ADJ (comentario, instrumento)
cutting; (frío, viento) biting; (tono,
instrumento) sharp
cortar VT to cut (también un texto digital); (un
vestido, el uso de algo) to cut out; (a un
locutor, una rama, el gas) to cut off; (un árbol)
to cut down; (las uñas) to clip; (el césped) to
mow; **— el paso** to block; **— por lo sano** to
take drastic action; M SG **cortacésped** lawn
mower; M SG **cortacircuitos** circuit
breaker; M SG **cortafuego** fire line; M SG
cortafuegos firewall; M SG **cortapapeles**
paper cutter; M SG **cortaplumas** penknife;
M SG **cortauñas** nail clipper; VI (el frío) to
bite; (la piel) to crack; **—se** (lastimarse) to cut
oneself; (intimidarse) to be intimidated;
(cuajarse) to curdle, to sour; **—se el pelo** to
get a haircut; **— y pegar** cut and paste
corte M (de un traje, herida) cut; (acción de
cortar) cutting; (de televisión) commercial
break; (estilo) style; **— de pelo** haircut; **—
transversal** cross section; **— y confección**
dressmaking; **eso me da —** that embarrasses
me; F (real, judicial) court; (séquito) retinue;
las —s Spanish parliament; **hacer la —** to
court
cortedad F shortness
cortejar VT to court, to woo
cortejo M (séquito) entourage; (acción de
cortejar) courtship
cortés ADJ courteous, polite
cortesano -na MF courtier
cortesía F courtesy, politeness
córtex M cortex
corteza F (de árbol) bark; (de pan, de la Tierra)
crust; (de queso, fruta) rind; **— cerebral**
cerebral cortex
corticoesteroide M corticosteriod
cortijo M country house
cortina F (de ventana) curtain; (de lluvia) sheet;
— de humo smoke screen
cortisona F cortisone
corto ADJ (breve) short; (tonto) short on brains;
(encogido) bashful; **— de vista**
short-sighted; **a — plazo** in the short run, in
the short term; **quedarse —** to come up
short; **vestirse de —** to wear a short dress; M
short [film]; M **—circuito** short circuit
cosa F thing; **como quien no quiere la —**
without realizing it; **como si tal —** as cool as
a cucumber; **¡cómo son las —s!** what a
surprise; **decir una — por otra** to tell a lie;
esperamos — de cinco minutos we
waited about five minutes; **las —s como son**
let's be honest; **las —s de la vida** that's life;
no es gran — it's no big deal; **otra —**
something else

cosecha F crop, harvest; **de su** — of his invention; **vino** — **1975** wine of 1975 vintage
cosechadora F combine
cosechar VT (cultivos) to harvest; (resultados) to reap
coser VI/VT to sew
cosignatario -**ria** MF cosigner
cosmético ADJ & M cosmetic
cósmico ADJ cosmic
cosmología F cosmology
cosmonauta MF cosmonaut
cosmopolita ADJ cosmopolitan
cosmos M cosmos
cosmovisión F worldview
coso M doodad
cosquillas F **hacer** — to tickle; **tener** — to be ticklish
cosquillear VT to tickle
cosquilleo M tickle
cosquilloso ADJ ticklish
costa F (del mar) coast, shore; **a toda** — at all costs; —**s** costs
Costa de Marfil F Ivory Coast
costado M side; **al** — alongside; **de** — edgewise; **por los cuatro** —**s** from all sides
costal M sack
costanero ADJ coastal
costar[5] VI/VT to cost; — **trabajo** to be difficult; — **un dineral** to cost a fortune; — **un ojo de la cara** to cost an arm and a leg
Costa Rica F Costa Rica
costarricense, costarriqueño -**ña** ADJ & MF Costa Rican
coste M cost; — **de [la] vida** cost of living; **al** — at cost
costear VT to defray costs; VI to sail along the coast
costero ADJ coastal
costilla F rib; **lo hizo a** —**s de su padre** he did it at his father's expense
costo M cost; — **adicional** added cost, extra cost; — **de [la] vida** cost of living; **al** — at cost; — **de mantenimiento** maintenance cost; — **de operación** operating cost
costoso ADJ costly
costra F (de pan) crust; (de herida) scab
costroso ADJ (pan) crusty; (heridas) scabby
costumbre F (hábito) habit; (tradición) custom; **de** — habitual; **tener la** — **de** to have the habit of; **está más cansado que de** — he's especially tired today
costura F (acción de coser) sewing; (línea de puntadas) stitching; (unión de dos piezas) seam; **alta** — high fashion, haute couture
costurero -**ra** M (caja) sewing box; (sastre) tailor; F seamstress
costurón M (puntada) large stitch; (cicatriz) large scar
cota F (nivel del agua) height above sea level; (estándar) benchmark
cotejar VT to check against
cotejo M comparison
cotidiano ADJ everyday
cotización F price quote, price quotation
cotizar[47] VT to quote
coto M — **de caza** game preserve; **poner** — **a** to put an end to
cotorra F (loro) parrot; (persona) chatterbox
cotorrear VI to chatter
covacha F small cave
coyote M coyote
coyuntura F (articulación) joint; (situación) juncture; **aprovechar la** — to take advantage of the situation
coz F kick; **dar coces** to kick
crack M (cocaína) crack; (deportista) ace
cráneo M cranium, skull
craso ADJ crass
cráter M crater
crayola® F crayon
creación F creation
creacionismo M creationism
creador -**ora** MF creator; ADJ creative
crear VI/VT to create
creatividad F creativity
creativo ADJ creative
crecer[35] VI (un niño) to grow; (masa, río) to rise; (madera, mar) to swell; (la luna) to wax
crecida F rise of a river
crecido ADJ (adulto) grown; (grande) large; (demasiado alto) overgrown
creciente ADJ (que crece) growing; (luna) crescent; M (luna) crescent; (marea) high tide; (de un río) flood
crecimiento M growth
credencial F credential
credibilidad F credibility
crédito M (solvencia, unidad de estudios) credit; (hecho de creer) credence; (fama) reputation; (préstamo) loan; — **al consumidor** consumer credit; — **rotativo** revolving credit; **dar** — **a** to believe; —**s** film credits; **vender a** — to sell on credit
credo M creed
crédulo ADJ credulous, gullible
creencia F belief
creer[18] VI/VT (tomar como cierto) to believe; (opinar) to think, to feel; —**se** to fall for; **¿quién se cree que es?** who does he think he is? **se cree artista** he fancies himself an artist; **¡ya lo creo!** I should say so!
creíble ADJ credible, believable
crema F cream (también cosmético); — **de espárragos** cream of asparagus; — **para [los] labios** lip balm, Chapstick®
cremallera F (de coche) rack; (de prenda) zipper; — **y piñón** rack and pinion
cremar VT to cremate

cremoso ADJ creamy
creosota F creosote
crepitación F crackle
crepitar VI to crackle
crepúsculo M twilight
crespo ADJ wiry, kinky
crespón M crepe
cresta F (de ola, montaña) crest; (de ave) tuft; (de gallo) comb
creyendo, creyera, creyese, creyó ver creer
creyente MF believer; ADJ believing
crezca, crezco ver crecer
cría F (acción de criar) breeding; (camada) litter; (animal joven) young
criada ver criado
criadero M — **de peces** hatchery; — **de pollos** chicken farm
criado -da MF servant; F maid
criador -ora MF breeder
crianza F (de animales) breeding; (de hijos) upbringing; (modales) manners
criar²⁸ VT (animales) to breed; (hijos) to bring up, to rear, to raise; **estar criando malvas** fam to be pushing up daisies; —**se** to grow up
criatura F (ser extraño) creature; (bebé) baby
criba F sieve
cribar VT to sift
crimen M (delito grave) serious crime, felony; (asesinato) murder; — **de guerra** war crime
criminal ADJ & MF criminal
criminalidad F serious crime
crin F mane
criogénico ADJ cryogenic
criollo ADJ (nacido en América) born in Spanish America; (tradicionalmente americano) traditionally Spanish American; M (lengua) creole
críquet M cricket
crisálida F chrysalis
crisantemo M chrysanthemum
crisis F crisis; — **de la edad madura** midlife crisis
crisma F crown of the head
crisol M crucible, melting pot
crisparse VI (un músculo) to contract; (los puños) to clench; (los nervios) to be on edge
cristal M (mineral, vidrio fino) crystal; (vidrio de ventana) Esp glass, pane; (lente) lens; — **labrado** cut glass
cristalería F (objetos) glassware; (establecimiento) glassware store; (fábrica) glassworks
cristalino ADJ (de cristal) crystalline; (transparente) crystal-clear; M lens of the eye
cristalizar⁴⁷ VI/VT to crystallize
cristiandad F Christendom
cristianismo M Christianity
cristiano -na ADJ & MF Christian; **hablar en —** (claramente) to speak clearly; (español) to

speak Spanish
criterio M criterion
crítica F criticism; (de un libro) review
criticar³⁰ VT to criticize
crítico -ca ADJ critical; MF critic; (de un libro) reviewer
criticón -ona ADJ critical; MF faultfinder
Croacia F Croatia
croar VI to croak
croata ADJ & MF Croatian
crocante ADJ crisp, crunchy
croché, crochet M crochet; **hacer —** to crochet
croissant M croissant
crol M (estilo de natación) crawl, freestyle
cromado ADJ chroming
cromo M chromium, chrome
cromosoma M chromosome
crónica F (narración de eventos) chronicle; (reportaje) feature; — **policial** police report
crónico ADJ chronic
cronista MF (deportivo) reporter; (histórico) chronicler
cronología F chronology
cronológico ADJ chronological
cronometrador -ora MF timer, timekeeper
cronometraje M timing
cronometrar VT to time
cronómetro M chronometer, stopwatch
croquet M croquet
croquis M rough sketch
cross M cross-country race
cruasán M croissant
cruce M (acción, lugar) crossing; (de dos calles) crossroads, intersection; (de razas) crossbreeding; (de palabras) blend; (animal híbrido) cross; — **peatonal** crosswalk
crucero M (buque de guerra) cruiser; (viaje de placer) cruise
cruceta F crosspiece
crucial ADJ crucial
crucificar³⁰ VT to crucify
crucifijo M crucifix
crucigrama M crossword puzzle
crudo ADJ (comida, seda) raw; (tiempo, invierno, imágenes) harsh; (petróleo, lenguaje) crude; **agua cruda** hard water; **color —** yellowish white
cruel ADJ cruel, mean
crueldad F cruelty, meanness
cruento ADJ grisly, gruesome
crujido M (de puerta, piso) creak; (de un tallo al quebrarse) crack; (de hojas) rustle; (de un fuego) crackle
crujiente ADJ (manzana, tocino) crisp, crispy; (nueces) crunchy
crujir VI (puerta, piso) to creak; (dientes) to grate; (hojas) to rustle; (nueces) to crunch; (fuego) to crackle
cruz F (cristiana) cross; (de moneda) tails;

hacerse cruces to dread
cruzada F crusade
cruzado M (soldado) crusader; ADJ (tenis) crosscourt; (boxeo) cross; (traje) double-breasted
cruzamiento M (de piernas, razas) crossing; (de calles) crossroads; (de razas) cross
cruzar[47] VT (la calle) to cross; (un cheque) to write across; —**le la cara a alguien** to backhand someone's face; **cruzo los dedos** I'll keep my fingers crossed; —**se con alguien** to bump into someone; —**se de brazos** to fold one's arms; **se me cruzó un ciervo** a deer crossed in front of me
cuaderno M notebook; — **de bitácora** logbook; — **de espiral** spiral notebook
cuadra F (establo) stable; (distancia) *Am* block
cuadrado ADJ square; **estar** — to be fat; M square; **es [un]** — he's a square; **dos al** — two squared; **elevar al** — to square
cuadrangular ADJ (geometría) quadrangular; M (béisbol) home run
cuadrar VT (estar en ángulo recto) to square; VI (corresponder) to fit; (ser conveniente) to be convenient; (ser iguales) to balance, to add up; — **con** to be in agreement with
cuadricular VT to divide into squares
cuadrilátero ADJ quadrilateral; M (en boxeo) ring; (polígono) quadrilateral
cuadrilla F (de ladrones) gang; (de obreros) crew; (baile) square dance
cuadro M (cuadrado) square; (pintura) picture; (de bicicleta) frame; (de jardín) bed; (en tela) checker; (de fútbol) team; — **clínico** symptoms; — **interior** (béisbol) infield; — **sinóptico** summary table; **a/de** —**s** checked
cuadrúpedo ADJ & M quadruped
cuajada F curd
cuajar VI (leche) to curdle; (queso, cemento) to set; (gelatina) to jell; (un grupo, una organización) to come about; —**se** to curdle; **la cosa no cuajó** that didn't pan out
cuajarón M clot
cual PRON REL which; **el/la** — (cosa) which; (persona) who; **lo** — which; **sea** — **sea** whichever it may be; ADV like; — **hoja al viento** like a leaf in the wind
cuál PRON INTERR which; **¿cuáles son los tuyos?** which ones are yours?
cualidad F quality, trait
cualitativo ADJ qualitative
cualquiera ADJ INDEF any; **de cualquier manera/forma** anyhow; **en cualquier lado** anywhere; PRON INDEF (cosa) any; (persona) anyone; — **que sea su nacionalidad** whatever his nationality may be; — **que elijas** whichever one you choose; — **podría hacer eso** anyone could do that
cuando ADV REL when; — **menos** at least; —

mucho at most; **se rompió** — **lo usaba** it broke while she was using it; PREP — **la guerra** during the war
cuándo ADV INTERR & PRON when
cuantía F (cantidad) quantity; (importancia) importance
cuántico ADJ quantum
cuantificar[30] VT to quantify
cuantioso ADJ considerable
cuantitativo ADJ quantitative
cuanto ADJ REL any; **lee** — **libro ve** she reads any book she sees; PRON REL **unos** —**s** a few; CONJ **hice** — **pude** I did as much as I could; ADV — **antes** as soon as possible; — **más trabajo, menos consigo** the more I work, the less I accomplish; **en** — as soon as possible; **en** — **a** regarding; **en** — **que** as
cuánto ADJ, ADV & PRON INTERR (dinero, agua) how much; (personas, libros) how many; **¿cada** —**?** how often? **¿** — **piensas quedarte?** how long do you plan to stay?
cuarenta NUM forty; **cantarle las** — **a alguien** to bawl someone out; — **iguales** (tenis) deuce
cuarentena F quarantine; **una** — **de libros** forty-odd books
cuarentón -ona MF person in his or her forties
cuaresma F Lent
cuarta F (marcha) fourth gear; (palmo) span of a hand
cuartear VT (una res) to quarter; (los labios) to chap; —**se** to chap
cuartel M barracks; — **general** headquarters; **no dar** — to give no quarter
cuartelada F military coup
cuartelazo M military coup
cuarteto M quartet
cuartilla F sheet of paper
cuarto ADJ one-fourth, quarter; M (habitación) room; (cantidad) quarter, one-fourth; — **de baño** bathroom; — **de estar** living room; — **de final** quarter finals; — **oscuro** darkroom; **¡ni que ocho** —**s!** no way! **tres** —**s** three-fourths
cuarzo M quartz
cuásar M quasar
cuate M *Méx* pal, buddy
cuatrero -ra MF cattle rustler
cuatrillizo -za MF quadruplet
cuatro NUM four; — **ojos** four-eyes; **más de** — a good number
cuba F (barril) cask, barrel; (tina) tub, vat
Cuba F Cuba
cubano -na ADJ & MF Cuban
cubeta F (recipiente rectangular) tray; (balde) pail; — **de hielo** ice tray
cúbico ADJ cubic
cubículo M cubicle
cubierta F (de libro) cover; (cosa para cubrir)

covering; (neumático) tire; (de buque) deck
cubierto M place setting; — **de plata**
silverware; **a** — sheltered
cubierto *ver* cubrir
cubismo M cubism
cúbito M ulna
cubo M (cuerpo geométrico, tercera potencia)
cube; (balde) bucket; (de rueda) hub; (juguete)
building block; — **de basura** trash can
cubrir[74] VT (con una manta) to cover; (con
carteles) to plaster; (una vacante) to fill; (con
pintura) to coat; (con crema batida) to
smother; (de niebla) to shroud; —**se**
(nublarse) to fog up; (ponerse el sombrero) to
put on one's hat
cucaracha F cockroach
cuchara F (cubierto) spoon; (de excavadora)
bucket; (para helado) scoop; — **sopera** soup
spoon; **meter la** — to butt in
cucharada F (lo que cabe en una cuchara)
spoonful; (medida) tablespoonful; (de helado)
dip
cucharadita F teaspoonful
cucharear VT to spoon
cucharita F teaspoon
cucharón M (para helado) scoop, dipper; (para
sopa) ladle
cuchichear VI/VT to whisper
cuchicheo M whisper
cuchilla F (cuchillo grande) large knife, cleaver;
(de afeitar, de licuadora) blade; (de patín)
runner
cuchillada F (golpe) stab, slash; (herida) stab
wound, gash
cuchillería F (conjunto de cuchillos) cutlery;
(tienda) cutlery store
cuchillo M knife; **pasar a** — to kill with a knife
cuclillas LOC ADV **en** — squatting; **sentarse en**
— to squat
cuclillo M cuckoo
cuco ADJ cute
cucú INTERJ cuckoo
cucurucho M (de papel) paper cone; (para
helado) ice-cream cone; (capirote) hood
cuelga, cuelgue *ver* colgar
cuello M (del cuerpo) neck; (de una prenda)
collar; — **de botella** bottleneck; — **uterino**
cervix; — **vuelto** turtleneck; **estoy hasta el**
— **en deudas** I'm up to my neck in debts
cuenca F (de un río) basin; (del ojo) eye socket
cuenco M earthen bowl
cuenta F (cálculo) count, calculation; (factura)
bill, check; (relación de ingresos y gastos)
account; (bolita) bead; (depósito bancario)
bank account; — **conjunta** joint account; —
corriente checking account; — **de ahorros**
savings account; — **de contrapartida**
contra account; — **de crédito** charge
account; — **de depósito en garantía**

charge account; — **de gastos** expense
account; — **de mercado monetario** escrow
account; — **en un paraíso fiscal** offshore
account; —**s por/a cobrar** accounts
receivable; —**s por/a pagar** accounts
payable; — **regresiva/atrás** countdown;
abrir/cerrar una — to open/close an
account; **a fin de** —**s** when all is said and
done; **ajustar** —**s** to settle old scores; **caí en**
[la] — **de que** it just dawned on me that; **dar**
— **de** to finish off; **dar** —**s** to give an
accounting; **darse** — to realize; **en** — **de**
margen on margin; **en resumidas** —**s** in
short; **eso corre por mí** — that is my
responsibility; **habida** — **de** bearing in
mind; **más de la** — more than necessary;
pasar la — to call in a favor; **tomar/tener**
en — to take into account; **trabajar por** —
propia to freelance; M SG **cuentagotas**
eyedropper
cuenta, cuente *ver* contar
cuento M story, tale; — **chino** tall tale; — **de**
hadas fairy tale; — **de nunca acabar**
never-ending story; **déjese de** —**s** come to
the point; **traer a** — to bring up; **venir a** —
to be to the point
cuerda F (soga) cord, rope; (de arco) bowstring;
(de guitarra) string; (de reloj) spring; — **floja**
tightrope; —**s vocales** vocal cords; **bajo** —
under the table; **contra las** —**s** on the ropes;
dar — **a** to wind; **no le des** — don't get him
started
cuerdo ADJ sane
cuerno M horn (también instrumento de
viento); (de caracol) feeler; (de ciervo) antler;
— **de la abundancia** horn of plenty; **coger**
el toro por los —**s** to take the bull by the
horns; **irse al** — *vulg* to go to hell; **poner** —**s**
a to be unfaithful to
cuero M (piel de animal) hide; (piel curtida)
leather; — **cabelludo** scalp; **en** —**s** naked
cuerpo M body; (torso) torso; **¡**— **a tierra!** hit
the deck! — **de bomberos** fire department;
— **de policía** police force; — **de prensa**
press corps; — **docente** teaching staff; **a** —
de rey in great luxury; — **extraño** foreign
body; **dar** — **a** to flesh out; **de** — **entero**
through and through; **ganó por tres** —**s de**
ventaja he won by three lengths; **ir de** — to
have a bowel movement
cuervo M crow, raven
cuesta F slope; — **abajo** downhill; — **arriba**
uphill; **a** —**s** piggyback
cuesta, cueste *ver* costar
cuestión F question; **en** — **de segundos** in a
matter of seconds; **poner en** — to question;
ser — **de** to be a matter of
cuestionable ADJ questionable
cuestionador ADJ questioning

cuestionar VT to question
cuestionario M questionnaire
cueva F cave
cuidado M (atención) care; (preocupación)
worry; — **con el perro** beware of the dog; —
de la casa housekeeping; — **dental** dental
care; — **posparto** postnatal care; —
prenatal prenatal care; — **terminal**
end-of-life care; **al** — **de** under the care of;
con — carefully; **eso me trae sin** — I don't
care about that; **tener** — to be careful; **un**
enfermo de — a severely ill patient; INTERJ
look out!
cuidador -ora MF caregiver, caretaker
cuidadoso ADJ careful
cuidar VT to take care of, to look after; — **de** to
take care of; — **la casa** to keep house; —
niños to babysit; —**se de** to beware of
culata F (anca) haunch; (de rifle) butt; (de motor)
cylinder head
culatazo M (golpe) blow with the butt of a rifle;
(rebote al disparar) recoil
culear VI/VT *Am vulg* to fuck, to screw
culebra F snake
culebrear VI to slither
culebrilla F shingles
culinario ADJ culinary
culminación F (de carrera, ceremonia)
culmination, high point; (de un sueño)
fulfillment
culminante ADJ climactic
culminar VI to culminate
culo M (trasero) *vulg* ass, butt; (ano) anus; — **de**
botella bottle bottom; — **del mundo**
boondocks; — **veo,** — **quiero** I want
everything I see; **caerse de** — (desplomarse)
to fall on one's butt; (sorprenderse) to be
astounded; **dar por el** — (fastidiar) to
bother; (sodomizar) to sodomize; **nacer de**
— to be lucky; **lamer** —**s** *fam* to suck up to
someone, *vulg* to brown-nose; **rascarse el** —
vulg to fart around; **romperse el** — *vulg* to
bust one's ass
culpa F (responsabilidad) fault, blame;
(sentimiento) guilt; **echar la** — **a** to blame;
por — **de** because of; **tener la** — to be to
blame
culpabilidad F guilt
culpable ADJ guilty; MF culprit
culpar VT to blame
cultivable ADJ (planta) cultivable; (tierra) arable
cultivado ADJ (tierra) cultivated; (perlas,
persona) cultured
cultivador -ora MF (persona) cultivator; F
(aparato) cultivator
cultivar VT (cosecha) to grow, to raise; (la tierra)
to farm; (relaciones, inteligencia) to cultivate;
(microbios) to culture
cultivo M (de plantas) growing; (de la tierra)

farming; (de microbios) culture; (de
relaciones) cultivation; **de** — cultured
culto ADJ educated, cultured; M worship;
libertad de — freedom of religion
cultura F culture; — **general** general
knowledge
cultural ADJ cultural
culturismo M body-building
cumbre F summit
cumpleaños M SG birthday
cumplido ADJ (cortés) polite; (perfecto) perfect;
M compliment; **hacer algo de** — to do
something out of duty; **hacer un** — to pay a
compliment
cumplimiento M (de un contrato)
performance; (de una promesa, obligación)
fulfillment; (de un plazo) expiration
cumplir VT (una obligación) to fulfill, to
discharge; (una promesa) to keep, to honor;
(una condena) to complete, to serve; — **diez**
años to turn ten; **hacer** — to enforce; VI
(vencer) to expire; — **con** to meet [a goal];
me cumple informarle que it is my duty
to inform you that
cúmulo M (grupo) host; (tipo de nube) cumulus
cuna F (que se mece) cradle; (con barandas) crib
cundir VI (extenderse) to spread; (rendir) to go a
long way
cuneta F roadside ditch; **en la** — out to pasture
cunilinguo M cunnilingus
cuña F (pieza para hender) wedge; (bacinilla)
bedpan
cuñado -da M brother-in-law; F sister-in-law
cuño M die-stamp; **de** — **hispano** with a
Hispanic stamp
cuota F (cantidad que le corresponde a uno)
quota, allotment; (cantidad que hay que
pagar) dues; (mensualidad) installment; —**s**
del coche car payments; —**s sindicales**
union dues
cupé M coupé
cupe, cupiera, cupiese *ver* caber
cupo M (cantidad) quota; (capacidad) *Am* room
cupón M coupon
cúpula F dome
cura F cure, remedy; M priest
curable ADJ curable
curación F cure
curanderismo M faith healing
curandero -ra MF healer
curar VT (una enfermedad, carne) to cure; (una
herida) to heal; —**se** to heal; —**se en salud**
to take precautionary measures
curiosear VI to look around; (en asuntos ajenos)
to pry
curiosidad F curiosity
curioso ADJ curious
Curita® F *Am* adhesive bandage, Band-aid®
currículo/currículum M résumé; — **vitae** CV

curro M *Esp* job
curruca F warbler
curry M curry
cursar VT (estudios) to take; (mensaje, invitación) to send
cursi ADJ (afectado) affected; (de mal gusto) tacky
cursillo M (individual) tutorial; (corto) short course
cursivo ADJ cursive; **escribir en cursiva** to write in cursive
curso M (de río, enfermedad, acontecimientos, moneda) course; (período docente) academic year; (grupo de estudiantes) class; (libro) textbook; — **legal** legal currency; **el mes en** — the current month
cursor M cursor
curtiduría F tannery
curtiembre F tannery
curtir VT (cuero) to tan; (cutis) to weather; (el carácter) to harden; —**se** (envejecerse) to get weathered; (acostumbrarse) to become accustomed to hardships
curva F curve (también béisbol); — **de campana** bell curve
curvatura F curvature
curvo ADJ curved
cúspide F summit
custodia F custody, keeping; **en** — (un monto de dinero) in escrow; (un prisionero) in custody
custodiar VT to guard
custodio -dia MF guardian
cutáneo ADJ cutaneous
cutícula F cuticle
cutis M facial skin
cuyo ADJ REL whose
cyborg M cyborg

Dd

dádiva F gift
dadivoso ADJ generous
dado ADJ given; M die; **jugar a los** —**s** to throw dice
dador -ora MF giver; — **de sangre** blood donor
daga F dagger
dalia F dahlia
daltónico ADJ color-blind
dama F lady; (en el juego de mesa) king; **jugar a las** —**s** to play checkers; — **de honor** bridesmaid
damajuana F demijohn
damasco M (fruta) apricot; (árbol) apricot tree
damisela F damsel
dandi M dandy

danés -esa ADJ Danish; MF Dane; M (lengua) Danish
danza F dance; — **del vientre** belly dance; **en** — in action
danzante MF dancer
danzar[47] VI/VT to dance
dañar VT to harm, to damage; —**se** to suffer harm
dañino ADJ harmful
daño M damage, harm; — **colateral** collateral damage; — **emergente** actual damage; — **físico** bodily harm; —**s materiales** property damage; —**s y perjuicios** damages; **hacer** — to harm
dañoso ADJ harmful
dar[62] VT (un regalo) to give; (un golpe, naipes) to deal; (sal) to add; (una fiesta) to throw; (la hora) to strike; (un olor) to give off; (la alarma) to raise; (un paseo) to take; — **a** (un edificio) to face; (una calle) to lead to; — **a conocer** to announce; — **a entender** to intimate; — **con** to hit upon, to find; — **de alta** to discharge, to release from the hospital; — **de baja** to discharge; — **de comer** to feed; — **de sí** to perform at capacity; **esta tela da de sí** this fabric gives; — **en la pared** to hit the wall; —**le con** to scrub with; **lo misma da** it makes no difference; **¿qué más da?** what difference does it make? **dale que dale** on and on; **hoy no doy una** today I can't get anything right; **le doy cincuenta años** he must be about fifty; **me da rabia/miedo** that makes me angry/afraid; **no me da el tiempo para ir al cine** I don't have time to go to the movies; **que no le dé el sol** don't let the sun shine on it; **y dale** enough already; —**se a la bebida** to indulge in drinking; —**se por conforme** to be satisfied; —**se prisa** to hurry; **dárselas de** to boast of being; **en este lugar se dan las flores silvestres** in this location wildflowers are found
dardo M dart
dársena F dock
datar VT to date; — **de** to date from
dátil M date
dato M piece of information; —**s** data
d.C. ADV AD
de PREP — **la familia** of the family; — **Madrid** from Madrid; **habló** — **la guerra** he talked about the war; **el hombre** — **gafas** the man with glasses; **el mejor estudiante** — **la clase** the best student in the class; **fácil** — **hacer** easy to do; **más** — **tres** more than three; **llevar** — **la mano** to lead by the hand; — **regreso a España** upon returning to Spain; — **venta en farmacias** on sale in pharmacies; **ancianos** — **respeto** older people to be respected; — **lo más lindo**

really pretty; **tonto — mí** silly me

dé *ver* **dar**

deambular VI to amble, to saunter; — **por** (el bosque) to wander about; (el internet) to surf

deán M dean

debacle M debacle

debajo ADV under, underneath; PREP — **de** under, below; **por — de** under

debate M debate

debatir VT to debate; —**se** to struggle

debe M debit

deber VT **deben apoyarme** they should support me; **debe de ser** it must be; **deberías sentarte** you should sit down; VT to owe; **me debes una** you owe me one; **me debo a mis alumnos** I'm devoted to my students; M duty; —**es** homework

debidamente ADV duly

debido ADJ due; — **a** due to, owing to; **a su — tiempo** in due time

débil ADJ (sin fuerza) weak; (endeble) frail, feeble; (sonido) faint

debilidad F (falta de fuerza) weakness; (cualidad de endeble) frailty; (de un sonido) faintness

debilitamiento M weakening

debilitante ADJ debilitating

debilitar VT to weaken, to debilitate

débito M debit

debutar VI to make a debut

década F decade

decadencia F (moral) decadence, decay; (cultural, económica) decline

decadente ADJ decadent

decaer[52] VI (fuerza) to weaken; (energía) to ebb; (salud) to fail; (ánimo) to flag

decaimiento M (decadencia) decline; (debilidad) weakness

decano -na ADJ senior; MF dean

decapitar VT to behead, to decapitate

decatlón M decathlon

decena F —**s de candidatos** tens of candidates

decencia F decency

decenio M decade

decente ADJ decent; **muy —** rather good

decepción F disappointment

decepcionante ADJ disappointing

decepcionar VT to disappoint

decibelio M decibel

decidido ADJ resolute, determined; **una decidida preferencia** a decided preference

decidir VI/VT to decide; —**se** to make up one's mind; —**se a** to resolve to

deciduo ADJ deciduous

décima F tenth

decimal ADJ decimal

décimo ADJ & M tenth

decir[53, 74] VT (palabras, oraciones) to say; (una mentira, un chiste, la verdad) to tell; — **tonterías** to talk nonsense; **con —te que**

suffice it to say that; **este tipo no me dice nada** this guy leaves me cold; **¡que me lo digan a mí!** you're telling me that? VI to say; **diga** hello (al contestar el teléfono); **es —** that is to say; **he dicho** I have spoken; **no es prometedor que digamos** it's hardly promising; **no me digas** you don't say; **querer —** to mean; M saying

decisión F decision; **tomar una —** to make a decision

decisivo ADJ decisive

declaración F (de amor, independencia, guerra) declaration; (de un hecho) statement; (de un testigo) deposition; — **de derechos** bill of rights; — **de impuestos / de la renta** tax return; — **de impuestos sobre la renta** income tax return; — **jurada** affidavit; — **de la misión** mission statement; — **errónea/ falsa** misstatement; — **sobre la privacidad** privacy statement

declarar VT (amor, independencia, ingresos) to declare; (un hecho) to state; — **culpable** to find guilty; **os declaro marido y mujer** I pronounce you man and wife; VI (como testigo) to testify; —**se** (un amante) to declare one's love; —**se culpable** to plead guilty; —**se en huelga** to go on strike; —**se en quiebra** to declare bankruptcy

declinar VI/VT to decline

declive M (pendiente) slope, drop; (decadencia) decline

decoración F decoration; — **de interiores** interior decorating

decorado M (de casa) decoration; (de escenario) scenery

decorar VT to decorate

decorativo ADJ decorative

decoro M decorum, propriety

decorosamente ADV decorously, properly

decoroso ADJ decorous, proper

decrépito ADJ decrepit

decrepitud F decrepitude

decretar VT to decree

decreto M (disposición ejecutiva) decree; (ley) act

dedal M thimble

dedicación F dedication

dedicar[30] VT (la vida) to dedicate, to devote; (un libro) to dedicate; —**se** to dedicate oneself; (a los estudios) to apply oneself

dedicatoria F dedication

dedo M (de la mano) finger; (del pie) toe; — **anular** ring finger; — **índice** index finger; — **mayor / del corazón** middle finger; — **meñique** little finger; — **pulgar** thumb; **chuparse el —** to be a fool; **chuparse los —s** to lick one's fingers; **cruzar los —s** to keep one's fingers crossed; **elegir a —** to appoint directly; **hacer —** to hitch a ride; **no**

mover un — not to lift a finger

deducción F deduction; — **impositiva** tax deduction

deducible ADJ deductible

deducir[38] VT (concluir) to deduce, to conclude; (descontar) to deduct

defecación F bowel movement

defecar[30] VI/VT to defecate

defección F defection

defecto M defect, flaw; **por** — by default

defectuoso ADJ defective, faulty

defender[2] VT (un fuerte) to defend; (una causa) to champion; (los derechos) to stand up for, to stick up for; **se defiende en francés** he can hold his own in French

defendible ADJ defensible

defensa F defense (también deportes); MF (fútbol) defender; — **individual** man-to-man defense; — **en zonas** zone defense; **aprende** — **personal** he's learning self-defense; **lo dijo en** — **propia** he said it in self-defense

defensivo ADJ defensive; **a la defensiva** on the defensive

defensor-ora MF (en la guerra) defender; (de una causa) champion

deferencia F deference

deficiencia F deficiency

deficiente ADJ deficient

déficit M deficit, shortfall; — **presupuestario** budget deficit

defienda, defiende ver defender

definición F definition; — **por penales** penalty shoot-out

definido ADJ definite

definir VT to define

definitivamente ADV definitely; once and for all; — **voy a comprar una impresora** I am definitely going to buy a printer; **lo arreglaremos todo** — we will take care of everything once and for all

definitivo ADJ (superior) definitive; (final) final; **en definitiva** all things considered

deflación F deflation

deflector M baffle

deforestación F deforestation

deformación F deformation

deformar VT to deform; —**se** to become deformed

deforme ADJ deformed, misshapen

deformidad F deformity

defraudar VT (cometer fraude) to defraud; (decepcionar) to disappoint

defunción F death

degenerado-da ADJ & MF degenerate

degenerar VI to degenerate

degenerativo ADJ degenerative

deglución F swallowing

degollar[24] VT to slash someone's throat

degradación F degradation

degradar VT (envilecer) to degrade, to debase; (rebajar el rango) to demote; —**se** to degrade

degüello M throat-slashing; **lucha a** — fight to the death

dehesa F pasture

deidad F deity

dejada F — **de volea** drop shot, stop-volley

dejadez F slovenliness

dejado ADJ slovenly

dejar VT (abandonar, no comer, legar) to leave; (a un enamorado) to leave, to dump; (permitir) to let; (soltar) to let go; — **de** to stop; — **caer** to drop; — **pasar** to pass up; **déjame en paz** leave me alone; **me dejó atónito** it left/rendered me speechless; **no dejes de venir** don't fail to come; **te lo dejo en mil dólares** I'll sell it to you for one thousand dollars; —**se** to let oneself go; —**se crecer la barba** to grow a beard; **déjate de joder** give me a break

deje M slight accent

dejo M (sabor) aftertaste; (acento) slight accent; (toque) hint; **tener un** — **de** to smack of

delantal M apron

delante ADV in front; — **de** in front of, ahead of

delantera F (de carrera) lead; (de vestido) front; **llevar la** — to be in the lead; **tomar la** — to take the lead

delantero-ra ADJ (pata) front; MF (línea, deportista) forward; M front

delatar VT to inform against, to squeal on; — **la edad** to betray one's age

delator-ora MF accuser, informer

delegación F delegation

delegado-da MF delegate

delegar[40] VT to delegate

deleitar VT to delight; —**se en algo** to revel in something; —**se la vista con** to feast one's eyes on

deleite M delight

deletrear VT to spell; — **mal** to misspell

deleznable ADJ despicable

delfín M dolphin

delgadez F thinness

delgado ADJ thin, slender, slim

deliberación F deliberation

deliberadamente ADV deliberately

deliberado ADJ deliberate

deliberar VI/VT to deliberate

delicadeza F (tacto) gentleness; (fineza) delicacy; **con** — gently; **tuvo la** — **de llamar** he was kind enough to call

delicado ADJ (suave, frágil, controvertido) delicate; (enfermizo) frail; (exquisito) dainty; (quisquilloso) squeamish

delicatessen F PL delicacies

delicia F delight

delicioso ADJ delicious, delectable

delimitar VT to delimit
delincuencia F crime
delincuente ADJ & MF delinquent, criminal; —
   juvenil juvenile delinquent
delineador M eyeliner
delinear VT to delineate, to outline
delirante ADJ delirious, raving
delirar VI to be delirious, to rave
delirio M delirium; — **paranoico** paranoid
   delusion; —**s de grandeza** delusions of
   grandeur
delito M crime, offense
deltoides M SG deltoids
demacrado ADJ drawn, gaunt, haggard
demagogo -ga MF demagogue
demanda F (de mercancías) demand; (de
   seguros) insurance claim; (pleito) lawsuit;
   por — on demand; **entablar una** — to file a
   lawsuit
demandado -da MF (en un pleito) defendant;
   (en un arbitraje) respondent
demandante MF plaintiff
demandar VT (pedir) to ask for; (poner pleito) to
   sue, to file a suit against
demarcar[30] VT to demarcate
demás ADJ (restante) remaining; PRON the
   others, the rest; **lo** — the rest; **y** — and
   whatnot; ADV **por lo** — moreover; **por** —
   useless
demasía LOC ADV **en** — excessively
demasiado ADV too; too much; **eso es** — **para**
   mí that's too much for me; **él es** — **alto** he's
   too tall; ADJ too much; too many; — **dinero**
   too much money; **demasiadas cosas** too
   many things
demencia F (locura) insanity; (senilidad)
   senility; (enfermedad mental) dementia
demente ADJ demented, insane, deranged
democracia F democracy
demócrata MF democrat; **Partido** —
   Democratic Party
democrático ADJ democratic; (del Partido —)
   Democrat, Democratic
democratización F democratization
demografía F demographics
demográfico ADJ demographic
demoler[6] VT to demolish, to tear down
demonio M demon; **al** — **con los libros** vulg to
   hell with books; **mandar al** — vulg to tell
   someone to go to hell; **¿qué** —**s haces?** what
   the heck are you doing? **un frío del** — bitter
   cold
demora F delay
demorar VT to delay; —**se** to linger
demostración F (prueba) demonstration; (de
   un programa digital) demo; — **de fuerza**
   show of force
demostrar[5] VT (mostrar) to demonstrate, to
   show; (comprobar) to prove, to demonstrate

demostrativo ADJ demonstrative
demudar VT to change, to alter
demuestra, demuestre ver demostrar
denegación F (de una petición) denial
dengue M dengue fever
denigrar VT to denigrate, to disparage
denodado ADJ untiring
denominación F (valor) denomination;
   (nombre) designation
denominador M denominator; — **común**
   common denominator
denominar VT to designate, to term
denostar[5] VT to revile
denotación F denotation
denotar VT to denote
densidad F density; **alta** — high density
denso ADJ (sólido) dense; (líquido) heavy
dentado ADJ (rueda) toothed; (montaña) ragged
dentadura F set of teeth; — **postiza** false teeth
dental ADJ dental
dentellada F (mordedura) bite; (señal de diente)
   tooth mark; **a** —**s** biting
dentífrico M toothpaste, dentifrice
dentista MF dentist
dentro ADV inside; (tenis) in; PREP — **de la casa**
   inside the house; — **de la ley** within the law;
   — **de quince días** (en el plazo de) within two
   weeks; (al cabo de) in two weeks; **por** —
   within
denuncia F (acusación) denunciation; (de mina,
   de seguro) claim
denunciar VT (un hecho negativo) to denounce;
   (una mina) to claim; (un delito) to report
deparar VT (tener preparado) to have in store;
   (proporcionar) to afford; **el destino me**
   deparaba una sorpresa fate had a surprise
   in store for me
departamento M (división) department; (piso)
   small apartment; (provincia) province
departir VI lit to commune
dependencia F (hecho de depender)
   dependence; (habituación) dependency;
   (filial) branch office
depender VI to depend; — **de** to depend on
dependiente -ta ADJ dependent; MF sales clerk,
   salesperson
depilación F hair removal
depilar VT to remove hair; (con cera) to wax
depilatorio ADJ & M depilatory
deplorable ADJ deplorable
deplorar VT to deplore
deponer[56, 74] VT (las armas) to lay down; (a un
   ministro) to depose, to remove; VI to defecate
deportar VT to deport
deporte M sport; **me gusta el** — I like sports/
   athletics
deportista ADJ athletic; MF athlete
deportivo ADJ athletic; **revista deportiva**
   sports magazine

deposición F (de un testigo) deposition; (de un ministro) removal; (movimiento de vientre) bowel movement

depositante MF depositor

depositar VT to deposit; —**se** to settle

depositario -ria MF repository

depósito M (en el banco) deposit; (de gasolina) tank; (de agua) reservoir; (de armas) depot, dump; (de mercancías) stock room, storehouse; — **de cadáveres** morgue; — **de garantía** security deposit; **hacer un** — to make a deposit; **en** — on consignment

depravado ADJ depraved

depreciar VI to depreciate

depredador -ora MF predator

depresión F depression

depresor M depressor; — **de lengua** tongue depressor

deprimente ADJ depressing

deprimido ADJ depressed

deprimir VT to depress

deprisa ADV quickly

depuración F (de agua) purification; (de un programa) debugging

depurador M debugger

depurar VT to purify; (un programa) to debug

derby M derby

derecha F (política) right wing; (tenis) forehand; **a la** — to the right; **de** —**s** right-wing

derechista ADJ right-wing; MF rightist

derecho ADJ (no izquierdo) right; (recto) straight; **ponerse** — to hold oneself erect, to stand up straight; ADV straight; **volver** — **a casa** to go straight home; **todo** — straight ahead; M (preceptos, disciplina) law; (prerrogativa) right; — **al trabajo** right to work; — **consuetudinario** common law; — **de admisión** fee; —**s del cliente** customer rights; — **internacional** international law; —**s** fees; —**s aduaneros** tax on imports; —**s civiles** civil rights; —**s de autor** royalties; —**s de la mujer** women's rights; —**s de los animales** animal rights; —**s mineros** mineral rights; **estar en su** — to be entitled; **poner al** — to put on right side out; **registrar los** —**s** to copyright

derechura F straightness

deriva F drift; **ir a la** — to be adrift

derivación F derivation

derivado M (subproducto) by-product; (palabra) derivative

derivar VT to derive

dermabrasión F dermabrasion

dermatología F dermatology

dermatólogo -ga MF dermatologist

derogación F repeal

derogar[40] VT to repeal

derramamiento M spill, spilling; — **de sangre** bloodshed

derramar VT (un líquido) to spill; (sangre, lágrimas) to shed; —**se** to spill over, to run over

derrame M spill; — **cerebral** stroke, cerebral hemorrhage

derredor LOC ADV **en** — all around

derrengar[40] VT (dañar la espalda) to sprain one's back; (cansar) to exhaust

derretir[9] VT to melt; —**se por alguien** to be crazy about someone

derribar VT (un edificio) to demolish, to tear down; (a una persona) to knock down; (un gobierno) to topple, to overthrow; (un avión) to shoot down, to down

derrocamiento M overthrow

derrocar[30] VT (un gobierno) to overthrow, to topple; (a un dictador) to depose

derrochador -ora ADJ extravagant; MF (de dinero) spendthrift; (de recursos) squanderer

derrochar VT (dinero) to squander; (salud) to radiate

derroche M (de recursos) waste, extravagance; (de color) profusion

derrota F defeat

derrotar VT to defeat

derrotero M course

derrubio M washout

derruido ADJ dilapidated

derrumbadero M precipice

derrumbamiento M collapse

derrumbar VT to demolish; —**se** (edificio) to collapse; (túnel, caverna) to cave in

derrumbe M (de tierra) landslide; (de un edificio) collapse

desabotonar VT to unbutton, to undo

desabrido ADJ (comida) tasteless; (persona) *Am* dull; *Esp* surly

desabrigado ADJ exposed; **no salgas tan** — put on some warm clothes before you go out

desabrochado ADJ undone, unfastened

desabrochar VT (botones) to undo; (ganchos) to unhook; (hebillas, cinturones) to unbuckle; (botones) to unbutton; —**se** to come undone

desacato M disrespect; — **al tribunal** contempt of court

desacelerar VI to decelerate

desacierto M mistake

desaconsejable ADJ inadvisable

desaconsejar VT to caution against

desacoplar VT to uncouple, to disconnect

desacostumbrado ADJ unusual

desacostumbrar VT to break of a habit; —**se** to lose a habit

desacreditar VT to discredit

desactivación F deactivation

desactivar VT (explosivo, situación) to defuse; (mecanismo) to disable; (virus) to deactivate

desacuerdo M disagreement; **estar en** — to be at odds

desafiante ADJ defiant
desafiar[28] VT (retar) to challenge, to dare; (enfrentar) to defy
desafilado ADJ dull
desafilar VT to dull; —**se** to become dull
desafinado ADJ out of tune, off-key
desafinar VT to be out of tune
desafío M (reto) challenge; (desobediencia) defiance
desafortunadamente ADV unfortunately
desafortunado ADJ unfortunate, unlucky
desafuero M (de un diputado) withdrawal of immunity; (atropello) outrage
desagradable ADJ disagreeable, unpleasant
desagradar VT to displease
desagradecido ADJ ungrateful
desagrado M displeasure
desagraviar VI to make amends, to redress
desagravio M redress
desaguadero M drainpipe
desaguar[25] VI to drain
desagüe M (acción de desaguar) drainage; (de lavabo) drain, drainpipe; (en la azotea) gutter
desaguisado M mess
desahogado ADJ (cómodo) comfortable; (espacioso) spacious
desahogar[40] VT (aliviar) to relieve; —**se** to pour out one's feelings
desahogo M relief; **vivir con** — to live an easy life
desairar VT to slight, to snub, to rebuff
desaire M slight, snub, rebuff
desajustar VT to loosen; —**se** to come loose
desalentado ADJ despondent
desalentador ADJ disheartening
desalentar[1] VT to discourage, to dishearten; —**se** to get discouraged
desaliento M discouragement, dismay
desaliñado ADJ disheveled, slovenly, unkempt
desaliño M slovenliness
desalmado ADJ heartless
desalojar VT (una piedra) to dislodge; (un tribunal) to clear; (un edificio) to evacuate; (a un inquilino) to evict; (una vivienda) to vacate
desamparado ADJ helpless, forlorn
desamparar VT to forsake
desamparo M abandonment, helplessness
desamueblado ADJ unfurnished
desangrar VT to bleed; —**se** to bleed to death
desanimado ADJ (persona) discouraged; (jornada) dull
desanimar VT to discourage
desánimo M discouragement
desaparecer[35] VI (perderse) to disappear, to vanish; (morir) to pass away
desaparezca, desaparezco ver desaparecer
desaparición F disappearance; (muerte) demise
desapasionado ADJ dispassionate
desapego M detachment

desapercibido ADJ unnoticed
desaprobación F disapproval
desaprobar[5] VT to disapprove of
desarmado ADJ unarmed
desarmar VT (quitar las armas) to disarm; (desmontar) to take apart
desarme M disarmament
desarraigar[40] VT to uproot
desarreglar VT to disturb, to mess up
desarreglo M (trastorno, enfermedad) disorder; (desorden) mess
desarrollador-ora MF developer
desarrollar VT (aumentar) to develop; (extender algo enrollado) to unroll; (llevar a cabo) to carry out; (aclarar) to elaborate, to flesh out; —**se** to unfold
desarrollo M development; (de una ecuación) expansion; **en** — developing
desarticulado ADJ disjointed
desaseado ADJ slovenly
desaseo M slovenliness
desasir[50] VT to let go of
desasosiego M uneasiness
desastrado ADJ (desaseado) untidy; (funesto) ill-fated
desastre M disaster
desastroso ADJ disastrous
desatado ADJ (ambición) unfettered; (zapatos) untied
desatar VT (un nudo) to untie, to loosen; (una ola de violencia) to unleash; —**se** to come untied; —**se en insultos** to let out a string of insults
desatascador M plunger
desatascar[30] VT (un inodoro) to unclog; (un objeto atrapado) to dislodge
desatención F lack of attention
desatender[2] VT (no ocuparse de algo) to neglect; (ignorar) to ignore
desatendido ADJ (descuidado) neglected; (ignorado) ignored
desatento ADJ inattentive
desatinado ADJ imprudent
desatornillar VT to unscrew
desatracar[30] VI/VT to cast off, to shove off
desavenencia F discord
desayunar VT **desayuné huevos** I had eggs for breakfast; —**se** to have breakfast; —**se [con que]** to find out [that]
desayuno M breakfast
desazón F uneasiness
desbandarse VI to disband
desbaratar VT (un plan) to disrupt; (un hechizo) to break; —**se** to break down
desbocado ADJ (caballo) runaway; (collar) loose
desbordamiento M overflow
desbordante ADJ overflowing
desbordar VI (derramar) to overflow; VT (abrumar) to overwhelm; —**se** to overflow, to

spill over
desbravar VT to break
descabalgar[40] VI to dismount
descabellado ADJ harebrained
descabezar[47] VT to behead; — **un sueño** to take a nap
descafeinado ADJ decaffeinated
descalabrar VT (la cabeza) to split someone's head open; (a una persona) to hurt
descalabro M disaster
descalcificación F decalcification
descalificar VT to disqualify
descalzar[47] VT to take off someone's shoes; —**se** to take off one's shoes
descalzo ADJ barefoot
descaminado ADJ **andar/ir**— to be on the wrong track
descamisado ADJ (sin camisa) shirtless; (pobre) poor
descansar VI/VT to rest; — **en paz** to rest in peace; —**se en** to rely on
descanso M (acción de descansar) rest; (de escalera) landing; (intermisión, receso) break; (en fútbol) halftime; **en** — at ease
descapotable ADJ & M convertible
descarado ADJ shameless, impudent, brazen; **a la descarada** shamelessly
descarga F (de batería, agua, armas) discharge; (de buques) unloading; (emocional) outpouring; (de electricidad) shock; (de internet) download
descargar[40] VT (una batería, agua) to discharge; (un buque, un arma de fuego) to unload; (bomba) to drop; (un programa de computadora) to download; —**se** (una batería) to drain; (ira) to vent
descargo M **en su** — in his defense
descarnado ADJ (realidad) stark; (cara) emaciated
descaro M effrontery, impudence, nerve
descarriar[28] VT to lead astray; —**se** to go astray
descarrilarse VI to derail, to jump the track
descartar VT (un naipe) to discard; (una posibilidad) to dismiss, to discard
descarte M discard; **por** — by elimination
descascararse VI (en jirones) to peel; (en fragmentos) to chip, to flake
descendencia F (linaje) descent; (descendientes) descendants
descendente ADJ descending, downward
descender[2] VI to descend; — **de** to descend from
descendiente MF descendant
descenso M descent
descentralización F decentralization
descienda, desciende *ver* descender
descifrado M deciphering
descifrar VT to decipher
descodificación F decoding, decryption

descodificar[30] VT to decode, to decrypt
descolgar[42] VT (una cortina) to take down; (un teléfono) to pick up; —**se con** to come up with; —**se de** to come down from
descollar[5] VI to excel
descolorido ADJ (persona) pale; (cosa) colorless
descomponer[56, 74] VT (disgustar) to upset; (dar diarrea) to give diarrhea; (dar náuseas) to make nauseous; (separar) to break down; (cadáveres) to decompose; (un reloj) to break; — **en factores** to factor; —**se** (productos químicos) to break down; (cadáveres) to decompose; (un reloj) to break; (sentir náuseas) to be nauseous; (tener diarrea) to have diarrhea; (disgustarse) to go to pieces
descomposición F (de cadáveres) decomposition; (de productos químicos) breaking down; (diarrea) diarrhea
descomprimir VT to decompress
descompuesto ADJ (roto) broken; (caótico) chaotic; (con diarrea) having diarrhea
descomunal ADJ enormous
desconcertado ADJ disconcerted
desconcertante ADJ disconcerting
desconcertar[1] VT to disconcert, to puzzle, to baffle; —**se** to become disconcerted
desconchar VT to chip
desconcierto M confusion
desconectado ADJ disconnected
desconectar VT to disconnect
desconexión F (acción de desconectar) disconnecting; (incomunicación) disconnect
desconfiado ADJ mistrustful, suspicious
desconfianza F mistrust
desconfiar[28] VT to distrust, to mistrust, to be wary of
descongelación F thawing
descongestionante M decongestant
descongestionar VT to decongest
desconocer[35] VT (no reconocer) to fail to recognize; (no saber) not to know; **te desconozco** you are not acting like yourself today
desconocido-da ADJ unknown; MF stranger
desconocimiento M ignorance
desconsideración F thoughtlessness
desconsiderado ADJ thoughtless, inconsiderate
desconsolado ADJ disconsolate, dejected
desconsolador ADJ disheartening
desconsolar[5] VT to dishearten; —**se** to become disheartened
desconsuelo M dejection
descontaminación F decontamination
descontaminar VT to decontaminate
descontar[5] VT (bajar el precio) to discount; (excluir) to exclude; (quitar) to dock
descontentadizo ADJ hard to please
descontentar VT to displease

descontento ADJ & M discontent
descorazonado ADJ disheartened
descortés ADJ discourteous, impolite
descortesía F discourtesy, impoliteness
descortezar[47] VT to strip the bark from
descoser VT to rip; —**se** to come unsewn
descosido ADJ unsewn; M unsewn place;
hablar como un — to talk one's head off
descostrar VT to remove the crust from
descoyuntado ADJ dislocated, out of joint
descoyuntar VT to dislocate; —**se** to become
dislocated
descrédito M discredit
descreído -da ADJ unbelieving; MF unbeliever
descreimiento M unbelief
describir[74] VT to describe
descripción F description
descriptivo ADJ descriptive
descrito ver describir
descuartizar[47] VT to quarter
descubierto ADJ (destapado) uncovered; (sin
sombrero) hatless; **al** — in the open; **estar al**
— to be exposed; **poner al** — to expose, to
lay bare; **en** — overdrawn; M overdraft
descubierto ver descubrir
descubridor -ora MF discoverer
descubrimiento M discovery
descubrir[74] VT (hallar) to discover; (destapar) to
uncover; —**se** to take off one's hat; — **el**
pastel to spill the beans
descuento M discount; — **por grupo** group
discount; **con** — at a discount; **los** —**s** extra
time, injury time
descuidado ADJ (en una tarea) careless,
negligent; (en el aspecto personal) slovenly
descuidar VT to neglect; **descuida, yo me**
ocupo de eso don't worry, I'll take care of
that; —**se** to be negligent
descuido M (falta de cuidado) neglect; (acción
descuidada) oversight; **al** — offhand; **por** —
by chance
desde PREP (origen) from; (tiempo) since; —
Madrid from Madrid; — **el martes** since
Tuesday; — **luego** of course; — **el principio**
from the start; — **el vamos** from the get-go;
— **entonces** ever since
desdecirse[53, 74] VI (contradecirse) to contradict
oneself; (retractarse) to retract
desdén M disdain, scorn
desdentado ADJ toothless
desdeñar VT to disdain, to scorn
desdeñoso ADJ disdainful, scornful
desdicha F misfortune; **por** — unfortunately
desdichado ADJ wretched
desdoblamiento M division
desdoblar VT (desplegar) to unfold; (dividir) to
divide
deseabilidad F desirability
deseable ADJ desirable

desear VT to desire
desecación F drying
desecar[30] VT to dry, to desiccate; —**se** to dry up,
to desiccate
desechable VT disposable, throwaway
desechar VT (ropa vieja) to discard; (una oferta)
to refuse; (una posibilidad) to dismiss
desecho M waste material; —**s** refuse, waste
desembalar VT to unpack
desembarazar[47] VT to rid of; —**se** to get rid of
desembarcadero M dock
desembarcar[30] VI (de un buque) to disembark,
to go ashore; (de un avión) to deplane
desembarco M landing
desembarque M landing
desembocadura F mouth
desembocar[30] VI to flow; — **en** to flow into; **la**
calle Ocho desemboca en la avenida A
Eighth Street feeds into Avenue A
desembolsar VT to disburse, to pay out
desembolso M disbursement, outlay
desembragar[40] VI/VT to disengage [the clutch]
desempacar[30] VT to unpack
desempañar VT to wipe clean
desempate M (tenis) tie-break; **[partido de]**
desempate playoff [game]
desempeñar VT to redeem; — **un cargo** to
perform the duties of a position; — **un papel**
to play a part; —**se** to get out of debt
desempeño M (de un cargo o papel)
performance; (de una cosa en prenda)
redemption
desempleado ADJ unemployed
desempleo M unemployment
desempolvar VT to dust off
desencadenar VT (quitar las cadenas) to
unchain; (provocar, causar) to trigger, to
spark
desencajado ADJ (mandíbula) dislocated;
(mirada) wild; **estaba** — **en el funeral** he
was deeply disturbed at the funeral
desencajar VT (un cajón) to unstick; (la
mandíbula) to dislocate
desencantar VT (desilusionar) to disillusion;
(quitar un hechizo) to remove a spell from
desencanto M disillusion
desenchufar VI/VT to unplug
desenfadado ADJ uninhibited
desenfado M lack of inhibition
desenfrenadamente ADV with wild abandon
desenfrenado ADJ (sin moderación) unbridled,
wanton, rampant; (muy rápido) reckless
desenganchar VT to unhook
desengañar VT to disabuse; —**se** (de un error)
to become disabused; (de una ilusión) to
become disillusioned
desengaño M disillusion
desengranar VT to take out of gear
desenlace M (de un libro) ending; (de un suceso)

outcome

desenmarañar VT to disentangle

desenmascarar VT to unmask, to expose

desenredar VT (el cabello) to disentangle; (una historia) to disentangle

desenrollar VT to unroll

desenroscar VT to untwist

desentenderse[2] VI to pay no attention

desentendido ADJ **hacerse el —** to pretend not to notice/know

desenterrar[1] VT (un tesoro) to unearth, to dig up; (un cadáver) to disinter

desentonado ADJ out of tune

desentonar VI (cantar mal) to sing off key; (estar fuera de lugar) to be out of place

desentrañar VT to unravel

desenvoltura F self-assurance

desenvolver[6, 74] VT (desenrollar) to unroll; (quitar la envoltura) to unwrap; **—se** to behave

desenvuelto ADJ self-assured

deseo M desire, wish; (sexual) desire; **pedir un — ** to make a wish

deseoso ADJ desirous

desequilibrado -da ADJ unbalanced; MF unbalanced person

desequilibrar VT to unbalance

desequilibrio M imbalance

deserción F desertion; **— escolar** school dropout rate

desertar VI/VT to desert; **— de** to defect from

desértico ADJ desert

desertor -ora MF (militar) deserter; (escolar) drop-out

desesperación F desperation

desesperadamente ADV desperately

desesperado ADJ desperate

desesperanza F despair, hopelessness

desesperanzado ADJ hopeless

desesperanzar[47] VT to discourage, to deprive of hope; **—se** to despair

desesperar VI to despair; VT to drive crazy

desestabilizar[47] VT to destabilize

desestimación F rejection

desestimar VT to reject

desfachatez F audacity

desfalcar[30] VT to embezzle

desfalco M embezzlement

desfallecer[35] VI (debilitarse) to grow weak; (desmayarse) to faint

desfallecimiento M (debilidad) weakness; (desmayo) faint

desfavorable ADJ unfavorable

desfibrilación F defibrillation

desfibrilador M defibrillator

desfibrilar VT to defibrillate

desfigurar VT (el rostro) to disfigure; (una estatua) to deface

desfiladero M narrow passage

desfilar VI (coches) to file by; (soldados, modelos) to parade

desfile M parade

desgana F (falta de apetito) lack of appetite; (falta de entusiasmo) lack of enthusiasm

desganado ADJ apathetic, without enthusiasm

desgarbado ADJ ungainly, gawky

desgarrado ADJ (prenda, músculo) torn; (grito) heartrending

desgarradura F tear

desgarrar VT (rasgar) to tear; (un escándalo) to dredge up; **—le el corazón a alguien** to break someone's heart; **—se** to tear, to pull

desgarro M muscle pull

desgarrón M tear

desgastar VT to wear away; **—se** to get worn away

desgaste M wear and tear

desglosar VT (una suma) to itemize; (un tema) to break down

desglose M (de una suma) itemization; (de un tema) breakdown

desgracia F (infortunio) misfortune; (infelicidad) unhappiness; **—s personales** casualties; **caer en —** to fall into disgrace/ disfavor

desgraciadamente ADV unfortunately

desgraciado -da ADJ (desafortunado) unfortunate; (infeliz) unhappy; MF (persona desafortunada) unfortunate person; (hombre despreciable) *vulg* bastard; F (mujer desgraciada) *vulg* bitch

desgranar VT (granos) to thrash, to thresh; (guisantes) to shell

desgravable ADJ tax-deductible

desgreñado ADJ disheveled, unkempt

desgreñar VT to dishevel; **—se** to muss up one's hair

desguazar[47] VT to scrap

deshabitado ADJ (territorio) uninhabited; (casa) vacant

deshacer[54, 74] VT (una acción, comando a la computadora) to undo; (una cama) to strip; (un plato, un jarrón) to destroy; (un sólido en un líquido) to dissolve; (un nudo) to untie; **— la maleta** to unpack the suitcase; **—se de** to get rid of; **—se en elogios** to rave about

deshaga, deshago, deshará, desharía *ver* deshacer

desharrapado ADJ ragged

deshecho *ver* deshacer

deshelar[1] VT to thaw

desheredar VT to disinherit

deshice, deshiciera, deshiciese *ver* deshacer

deshielo M thaw

deshierbar VT to weed

deshilachar VT to unravel, to fray

deshojado ADJ leafless

deshojar VT to strip of leaves; **—se** (un árbol) to

shed leaves; (un libro) to lose pages
deshonestidad F (falta de honradez)
dishonesty; (falta de recato) immodesty
deshonesto ADJ (no honrado) dishonest; (no
modesto) immodest
deshonra F dishonor, disgrace
deshonrar VT to dishonor, to disgrace
deshonroso ADJ dishonorable
deshora LOC ADV **a** — at an inopportune time;
comer a — to eat between meals
deshuesar VT (un fruto) to stone; (un animal) to
bone
deshumanizar[47] VT to dehumanize
deshumidificador M dehumidifier
desidia F indolence
desierto ADJ (lugar) deserted; (premio)
unawarded; M (región árida) desert; (región
poco fértil y no habitada) wilderness
designación F (acción de designar, nombre)
designation; (nombramiento) appointment
designar VT to designate; (a un funcionario) to
appoint
designio M design
desigual ADJ (pelea) one-sided; (actuación)
uneven; (números) not equal; (rango)
unequal; (terreno) uneven
desigualdad F inequality; (del terreno)
roughness
desilusión F disillusion, disappointment
desilusionar VT to disillusion, to disappoint;
—**se** to become disillusioned/disappointed
desinencia F ending
desinfección F disinfection
desinfectante ADJ & M disinfectant
desinfectar VT to disinfect
desinfestación F disinfestation
desinflado ADJ (globo, persona) deflated;
(neumático) flat; M flat tire
desinflar VT to deflate
desinformación F (falta de información)
disinformation; (mala información)
misinformation
desinformar VT to misinform
desinhibido ADJ uninhibited
desinstalar VT to uninstall
desintegración F disintegration; — **atómica**
atomic decay
desintegrarse VI to disintegrate; (material
radiactivo) to decay
desinterés M (falta de interés) lack of interest;
(generosidad) unselfishness
desinteresado ADJ (apático) disinterested;
(generoso) unselfish, selfless
desistir VI to desist
deslavado ADJ faded
deslavar VT (quitar color) to fade; (lavar
ligeramente) to wash superficially
desleal ADJ (persona) disloyal, faithless;
(competencia) unfair

desleír[10] VT to mix with a liquid
deslindar VT to mark off
desliz M slipup
deslizamiento M slide, glide
deslizar[47] VT (un patín) to slip, to slide, to glide;
(una tarjeta) to swipe; —**se** (un patín) to slide,
to glide; (un error) to slip by
deslucido ADJ (actuación) dull; (color) dingy
deslucir[39] VT (un espectáculo) to tarnish; (color)
to make dingy
deslumbramiento M dazzle
deslumbrante ADJ dazzling
deslumbrar VT to dazzle; —**se** to be dazzled
deslustrar VT to tarnish
deslustre M tarnish
desmadejado ADJ (fatigado) exhausted;
(desgarbado) ungainly
desmadejar VT to exhaust
desmán M abuse
desmantelar VT to dismantle
desmañado ADJ awkward, clumsy
desmayar VI to lose courage; —**se** to faint, to
pass out
desmayo M faint, swoon; **peleó sin** — he
fought unflaggingly
desmedido ADJ excessive
desmejorar VI (empeorar el aspecto) to look
worse; (debilitarse) to get worse
desmembrar VT to dismember
desmentido M denial
desmentir[8] VT to deny
desmenuzar[47] VT (pan) to crumble;
(zanahorias) to mince
desmerecer[35] VI — **en valor** to not do justice;
no — **de** to compare favorably with
desmesurado ADJ (esfuerzo) inordinate;
(orejas) too large
desmigajar VT to crumb, to crumble
desmitificar[30] VT to debunk
desmochar VT to top, to cut the top off of
desmontar VT (limpiar un monte) to clear;
(desarmar) to dismantle, to take apart;
(derribar de una caballería) to throw; —**se** to
dismount
desmoralizar[47] VT to demoralize; —**se** to
become demoralized
desmoronar VT to crumble
desmovilizar[47] VT to demobilize
desnatar VT to skim
desnaturalizado ADJ (madre) unnatural;
(aceite) denatured
desnudar VT to undress; —**se** to get undressed
desnudez F nakedness
desnudo ADJ nude, naked
desnutrición F malnutrition
desnutrido ADJ underfed, undernourished
desobedecer[35] VT to disobey
desobediencia F disobedience; — **civil** civil
disobedience

desobediente ADJ disobedient

desocupación F (paro) unemployment; (abandono de vivienda) vacating

desocupado ADJ (asiento, casa) unoccupied, empty; (tiempo) idle; (que no trabaja) unemployed

desocupar VT to vacate; —**se** to become free

desodorante M deodorant

desodorizar VT to deodorize

desoír⁵⁵ VT to turn a deaf ear to

desolación F desolation

desolado ADJ desolate, bleak

desolar VT to lay waste to, to desolate; —**se** to be desolated

desollar⁵ VT to skin; — **vivo** to skin alive

desorbitado ADJ (precio, reacción) out of proportion; (ojos) bulging

desorden M disorder, disarray; — **público** public disturbance; **en** — in disarray

desordenado ADJ (persona, situación) messy; (persona, estilo de vida) wild; (cuarto) untidy, disorderly; (archivo) disorganized

desordenar VT to mess up

desorganización F disorganization

desorganizado ADJ disorganized

desorientar VT (marear, hacer perder) to disorient; (confundir) to confuse; —**se** to lose one's bearings, to become disoriented

desovar VT to spawn

desoxidar VT to deoxidize

despabilado ADJ (despierto) wide-awake; (listo) on the ball

despabilar VT (cortar el pabilo) to trim the wick of; (despertar) to awaken; —**se** to wake up

despachar VT (problemas) to dispatch; (una carta) to mail; (a un cliente) to take care of; (mercancías) to ship; (a una víctima) to bump off; (un pedido) to fill; — **al público** to sell to the public; —**se a su gusto** to speak one's mind

despacho M (oficina) office; (comunicación) dispatch; (envío de cartas) mailing; (envío de mercancías) shipping

despachurrar VT to squash

despacio ADV slow, slowly

desparasitar VT to worm

desparejo ADJ uneven

desparpajo M (desenvoltura) ease; (descaro) impudence

desparramar VT to scatter; —**se** to be scattered

desparramo M (lío) commotion; (de libros) clutter

despatarrarse VT (caerse) to sprawl; (abrirse de piernas) to spread one's legs

despecho M spite; **por** — out of spite

despectivo ADJ derogatory, pejorative

despedazar⁴⁷ VT to tear to pieces

despedida F farewell; — **de soltero** bachelor party

despedir⁹ VT (decir adiós) to see off; (echar de un empleo) to fire, to dismiss; (emitir un dolor) to emit, to give off; **despídeme de tus padres** say good-bye to your parents for me; —**se [de]** to take leave [of], to say good-bye [to]

despegar⁴⁰ VT (dos cosas pegadas) to detach; VI (un avión) to take off; (un cohete) to blast off; —**se** to become detached

despegue M (de avión) takeoff; (de cohete) blastoff, liftoff

despeinado ADJ unkempt

despejado ADJ (el cielo) clear, cloudless; (un camino) clear; (la frente) with one's hair pulled back; (una persona) bright

despejador M (fútbol americano) punter

despejar VT (el campo, una pelota) to clear; (en fútbol americano) to punt; VI (una duda, el cielo) to clear up; —**se** to sober up

despellejar VT to skin

despensa F pantry

despeñadero M cliff

despeñar VT to push off a precipice; —**se** to fall down a precipice

despepitar VT (una granada) to seed; (una manzana) to core; —**se por una cosa** to be crazy about something

desperdiciar VT to waste; —**se** to go to waste

desperdicio M waste; —**s** scraps

desperdigar⁴⁰ VT to scatter; —**se** to be scattered

desperezarse⁴⁷ VI to stretch

desperezo M stretch

desperfecto M damage; — **mecánico** mechanical breakdown

despertador M alarm clock

despertar¹ VT (a una persona) to awaken, to wake up; (sospecha) to arouse; (interés, deseo) to kindle; —**se** to wake up

despiadado ADJ merciless, heartless, ruthless

despida, despide, despidiendo, despidiera, despidiese *ver* despedir

despido M dismissal, termination; — **temporal de un empleado** layoff

despierta, despierte *ver* despertar

despierto ADJ (no dormido) awake; (vivaracho) alert

despilfarrador ADJ wasteful

despilfarrar VT to squander

despilfarro M waste

despistado ADJ absent-minded, out of it

despistar VT (confundir) to throw off the track; (deshacerse de) to lose; —**se** to get confused

desplantador M trowel

desplante M rude remark

desplazado -da MF displaced person

desplazamiento M (de tropas) movement; (de refugiados) displacement

desplazar⁴⁷ VT to displace; —**se** to move

desplegar[41] VT (papel plegado) to unfold; (una bandera) to unfurl; (tropas) to deploy; (interés) to display

despliegue M display

desplomarse VI (edificio, precios) to collapse; (una persona) to slump; (esperanzas) to be dashed

desplome M collapse

desplumar VT (un ave) to pluck; (a un incauto) to fleece

despoblado ADJ uninhabited; — **de árboles** treeless; M open country

despojar VT to despoil; —**se** to shed leaves

despojos M PL (de batalla) spoils; (mortales) remains

desportilladura F chip

desportillar VT to chip

desposeer VT to dispossess

déspota MF despot

despótico ADJ despotic

despotismo M despotism

despotricar[30] VI to rant

despreciable ADJ (vil) contemptible, despicable, worthless; (insignificante) negligible

despreciar VT (menospreciar) to despise, to look down on; (rechazar) to snub

desprecio M (menosprecio) contempt, disdain; (rechazo) snub

desprender VT (un cierre) to unfasten; (algo prendido) to detach; (gases) to give off; —**se de algo** to part with something; —**se la ropa** to undo one's clothes; **de lo dicho se desprende que** from what has been said it follows that

desprendimiento M (de retina) detachment; (de energía) release; (de tierra) landslide; (generosidad) generosity

despreocupado ADJ carefree

desprestigiar VT to discredit; —**se** to lose one's prestige

desprestigio M loss of prestige

desprevenido ADJ unprepared; **tomar** — to take by surprise

desproporcionado ADJ disproportionate, out of proportion

despropósito M nonsense

desprovisto ADJ — **de** lacking in

después ADV after, afterward; — **de** after; — **de todo** after all; — **de horas hábiles** after hours

despuntar VI/VT to blunt; —**se** to become blunt

desquiciar VT to unhinge; —**se** to come unhinged

desquitarse VI to get even

desquite M getting even, revenge

desregular VT to deregulate

destacable ADJ notable, noteworthy

destacado ADJ outstanding

destacamento M military detachment, military detail

destacar[30] VT (tropas) to detach; (una cualidad) to highlight, to accentuate; VI to stand out; —**se** to stand out

destajo LOC ADV **a** — by the job

destapar VT (una cacerola) to take the top off; (un plan, a un niño en cama) to uncover; —**se** (en la cama) to uncover; (desnudarse) to bare all

destartalado ADJ dilapidated

destellar VI to flash

destello M flash

destemplado ADJ (persona) feverish; (sonido) out of tune

desteñido ADJ washed-out

desteñir[11] VI/VT to fade; VI to run; —**se** to fade

desternillarse VI — **de risa** to die laughing

desterrado -da ADJ exiled, banished; MF (persona) exile

desterrar[1] VT to exile, to banish

destetar VT to wean

destierro M exile, banishment

destilación F distillation

destilar VT to distill

destilería F distillery

destinar VT (determinar el destino) to destine; (dirigir) to address; (asignar) to commit

destinatario -ria MF addressee, recipient

destino M (hado) destiny, fate, lot; (uso) use; (final de viaje) destination

destitución F dismissal

destituir[19] VT to dismiss

destornillador M screwdriver

destoxificación F detoxification

destrabar VT to untie

destreza F dexterity, skill

destripar VT to gut

destronar VT to dethrone

destrozar[47] VT (estropear) to ruin; (causar grandes daños) to destroy; (derrotar) to rout

destrozo M damage

destrucción F destruction

destructible ADJ destructible

destructivo ADJ destructive

destructor -ra ADJ destructive; M (buque) destroyer; MF (persona) destroyer

destruir[19] VT (destrozar) to destroy, to obliterate; (estropear) to ruin

destruya, destruya, destruyendo, destruyera, destruyese ver destruir

desunir VT to divide; —**se** to come apart

desusado ADJ (no frecuente) unusual; (no usado) obsolete

desuso M disuse, obsolescence; **caer en** — to fall into disuse

desvaído ADJ faded

desvainar VT to hull, to husk

desvalido ADJ helpless

desvalijar VT (un cuarto) to ransack; (a una persona) to clean out

desvalimiento M helplessness

desván M attic

desvanecer[35] VT (un color) to fade; (un contorno) to blur; —**se** (una persona) to faint; (un color, arrugas) to fade; (un sonido) to trail off

desvanecido ADJ (una persona) fainted; (un color) faded; (un contorno) blurred

desvanecimiento M (de una persona) fainting; (de colores) fading; (de un contorno) blurring

desvariar[28] VI to rave

desvarío M raving

desvelado ADJ sleepless

desvelar VT to keep awake; —**se** to be sleepless

desvelo M (falta de sueño) sleeplessness; —**s** (esfuerzos) efforts

desvencijado ADJ dilapidated, rickety; **estoy** — I'm all beat up

desventaja F disadvantage; **estar en** — to be at a disadvantage

desventura F misfortune

desventurado ADJ unfortunate

desvergonzado ADJ shameless

desvergüenza F shamelessness

desvestir[9] VT to undress; —**se** to get undressed, to undress

desviación F (de una norma) deviation, divergence; (en ruta) detour; (de fondos) diversion; (de la columna vertebral) curvature; — **estándar** standard deviation

desviar[28] VT (la vista) to avert; (fondos, tráfico) to divert; (un golpe) to ward off; (una conversación) to steer; (un tren) to sidetrack; —**se de** (un camino) to stray from; (una norma) to deviate from

desvío M (camino secundario) side road; (desviación) detour

desvirtuar[26] VT to distort; —**se** to become distorted

desvivirse VI — **por hacer algo** to bend over backward to do something; — **por alguien** to go out of one's way for someone

detallado ADJ detailed

detallar VT to detail, to go into detail about

detalle M (pormenor) detail; (venta al por menor) retail; (lista) list; **¡qué —!** how thoughtful! **con/al/en** — in detail

detallista ADJ (cuidadoso) meticulous; (considerado) thoughtful; M (comercio) retail; MF retailer

detección F detection

detectar VT to detect

detective M detective; — **privado** private eye

detector M detector; — **de incendios** smoke detector; — **de mentiras** lie detector; — **de metales** metal detector

detención F (arresto) detention, arrest; (de un

vehículo) stop; — **domiciliaria** house arrest; — **ilegal** false arrest

detendrá, detendría ver detener

detener[58] VT (arrestar) to detain, to arrest; (parar) to stop; —**se** to stop; —**se en** to linger on; —**se a pensar** to stop to think

detenga, detengo ver detener

detenidamente ADV closely

detenido ADJ thorough

detenimiento LOC ADV **con** — with care

detergente ADJ & M detergent

deteriorado ADJ in disrepair

deteriorar VT to deteriorate

deterioro M deterioration, disrepair

determinación F determination; — **del grupo sanguíneo** blood typing

determinado ADJ (cierto) certain; **es lo que suponen determinadas personas** that is what certain people suppose; (específico) definite, specific; **pidió una cantidad determinada** he asked for a specific amount

determinante ADJ determining; M determiner

determinar VT to determine

detestable ADJ detestable

detestar VT to detest

detiene, detienes ver detener

detonación F detonation; **hacer detonaciones** to backfire

detonar VI/VT to detonate

detrás ADV behind; — **de** (en el espacio) behind; (en el tiempo) after; **por** — behind

detritus M INV debris

detuve, detuviera, detuviese ver detener

deuce M deuce

deuda F debt; — **incobrable** bad debt

deudor -ora ADJ & MF debtor; — **hipotecario** mortgagor

devaluación F devaluation

devanar VT to spool; —**se los sesos** to rack one's brain

devaneo M (pasatiempo) idle pursuit; (amorío) fling

devastador ADJ devastating

devastar VT to devastate

devengar[40] VT to earn

devoción F devotion

devolución F (de un producto) return; (de poder político) devolution

devolver[6, 74] VT (dar al dueño) to return; (enviar por correo) to send back; — **al remitente** to return to sender; — **la llamada** to call back; VI (vomitar) to throw up

devorar VT to devour

devoto ADJ (pío) devout; (que muestra devoción) devoted

devuelto, devuelva, devuelve ver devolver

dextrosa F dextrose

di ver dar, decir

día M day; — **a** — day-to-day; — **tras** — day after

day; **al** — up-to-date; **al otro** — on the next
day; **de** — by day; **de todos los** —**s**
everyday; **el** — **de mañana** in the future;
hoy — nowadays; **no veo el** — I can't wait;
ponerse al — to catch up; **por** — by the day;
todo el — all day; **todos los** —**s** every day;
un — **sí y otro no** every other day; **vivir al**
— to live from hand to mouth
diabetes F SG diabetes
diablo M devil; **irse al** — *vulg* to go to hell;
pobre — poor devil; **¿por qué** —**s dices**
eso? *fam* why the heck are you saying that?
diablura F devilry, mischief
diabólico ADJ (ritual) diabolic, devilish;
(perverso) diabolical
diácono M deacon
diacrítico ADJ & M diacritic
diafragma M diaphragm
diagnosis F diagnosis
diagnosticar[30] VT to diagnose
diagnóstico ADJ diagnostic; M diagnosis
diagonal ADJ & F diagonal
diagrama M diagram; — **de flujo** flow chart; —
de pastel pie chart
dial M dial
dialéctica F dialectic
dialéctico ADJ dialectic
dialecto M dialect
dialectología F dialectology
diálisis F dialysis
dialogar[40] VI to dialogue, to hold talks
diálogo M dialogue, conversation; **fue un** — **de**
sordos they talked past each other
diamante M diamond; — **en bruto** diamond in
the rough
diámetro M diameter
diana F bull's-eye
diapasón M tuning fork
diapositiva F slide
diario ADJ daily; M (periódico) newspaper; (de
sucesos personales) journal, diary; (de
navegación) log; **a** — every day; **de** —
everyday; **llevar un** — to keep a diary
diarrea F diarrhea
diastólico ADJ diastolic
diatriba F diatribe
dibujante MF illustrator
dibujar VT to draw; —**se** to appear, to loom
dibujo M (arte de dibujar, cosa dibujada)
drawing; (diseño) design; — **al carbón**
charcoal drawing; —**s animados** animated
cartoon
dicción F diction
diccionario M dictionary
dice, dicen *ver* decir
dicha F happiness
dicharachero ADJ witty
dicho ADJ aforementioned; M saying
dicho *ver* decir

dichoso ADJ happy; **todo el** — **día** the whole
blessed day
diciembre M December
diciendo *ver* decir
dicotomía F dichotomy
dictado M (ejercicio) dictation; (orden) dictate;
escribir al — to take dictation
dictador -ora MF dictator
dictadura F dictatorship
dictamen M (opinión) report; (judicial) ruling
dictaminar VI (dar una opinión) to report;
(fallar) to rule
dictar VT to dictate; — **clase** to teach class; —
sentencia to rule
diecinueve NUM nineteen
dieciocho NUM eighteen
dieciséis NUM sixteen
diecisiete NUM seventeen
diente M (de persona, sierra) tooth; (de víbora)
fang; (de rueda dentada) cog; (de tenedor)
prong; — **de león** dandelion; — **de leche**
baby tooth; —**s postizos** false teeth; **entre**
—**s** under one's breath; **tener buen** — to
have a good appetite
diera, diese *ver* dar
diesel M diesel
diestra F right hand
diestro -tra ADJ (habilidoso) skillful, deft; (no
zurdo) right-handed; MF right-handed
person; **a diestra y siniestra** on all sides
dieta F (ingesta) diet; (dinero para gastos) per
diem; **estar a** — to be on a diet
dietético ADJ dietary
dietista MF dietitian
diez NUM ten
diezmar VT to decimate
diezmo M tithe; **pagar el** — to tithe
difamación F (oral) slander; (escrita) libel
difamar VT to defame, to malign; (oralmente) to
slander; (por escrito) to libel
difamatorio ADJ slanderous
diferencia F difference; **a** — **de** unlike; **hacer**
—**s entre** to treat differently; **partir la** — to
split the difference
diferenciación F differentiation, distinction
diferencial ADJ & M (distancia, pieza de coche)
differential; F (matemática) differential
diferenciar VT to differentiate; —**se de** to differ
from
diferente ADJ different
diferir[8] VT (aplazar) to defer; VI (ser diferente) to
differ
difícil ADJ difficult, hard
difícilmente ADV (apenas) hardly; (con
dificultad) with difficulty
dificultad F difficulty
dificultar VT to make difficult
dificultoso ADJ difficult
difteria F diphtheria

difundir VT (luz) to diffuse; (noticias) to broadcast
difunto -ta ADJ & MF deceased
difusión F (de luz) diffusion; (de noticias) broadcasting
difuso ADJ diffuse
diga *ver* decir
digerible ADJ digestible
digerir[8] VT to digest
digestible ADJ digestible
digestión F digestion
digestivo ADJ digestive
digesto M digest
digital ADJ digital
digitalizar[47] VT to digitalize, to digitize
digitar VI/VT to type
dígito M digit
dignarse VI to deign
dignatario -ria MF dignitary
dignidad F dignity
digno ADJ (respetable) worthy; (orgulloso) dignified; — **de confianza** trustworthy; — **de elogio** praiseworthy
digo *ver* decir
digresión F digression
dije M charm
dije, dijera, dijese *ver* decir
dilación F delay; **sin** — without delay
dilatación F (de un metal, parte dilatada) expansion; (del ojo) dilation
dilatar VT (pupilas, capilares) to dilate; (metal, músculo) to expand; (tiempo, plazo) to defer; (prolongar) to prolong; —**se en un asunto** to dwell on a subject
dilema M dilemma
diletante MF dilettante
diligencia F (laboriosidad) diligence, industry; (vehículo) stagecoach; (tarea) errand; — **debida** due diligence
diligente ADJ diligent, industrious
dilucidar VT to elucidate
diluido ADJ dilute
diluir[19] VT (una solución) to dilute; (pintura, sopa) to thin
diluvio M deluge
dimensión F dimension
dimes M PL — **y diretes** gossip; **andar en** — **y diretes** to quibble
diminutivo ADJ & M diminutive
diminuto ADJ (tamaño) diminutive; (cantidad) minute
dimisión F resignation
dimitir VI to resign
Dinamarca F Denmark
dinámica F dynamics
dinámico ADJ dynamic
dinamismo M vigor
dinamita F dynamite
dinamitar VT to dynamite

dínamo M dynamo
dinastía F dynasty
dineral M fortune
dinero M money; — **contante y sonante** ready cash, hard cash; — **de plástico** plastic, credit card; — **sucio** dirty money
dinosaurio M dinosaur
diodo M diode; — **electroluminiscente** light-emitting diode
Dios M God; **dios** god; — **dirá** we'll see; — **los cría y ellos se juntan** birds of a feather flock together; — **mediante** God willing; ¡— **mío!** my God! — **te lo pague** may God reward you; — **y su madre** everybody and their dog; **a la buena de** — any old way; **como** — **manda** as it should be; ¡**por** —! oh, my! **que** — **te oiga** I hope you're right
diosa F goddess
diploma M diploma
diplomacia F diplomacy
diplomático -ca ADJ diplomatic; MF diplomat
diptongo M diphthong
diputación F council
diputado -da MF representative
dique M (presa) dike; (al lado de un río) levee; — **seco** dry dock
dirá *ver* decir
dirección F (sentido, rumbo) direction; (domicilio) address; (administración) management; (administración de una escuela) principal's office; (mecanismo, acción de conducir) steering; — **asistida** power steering; — **de correo electrónico** e-mail address
directiva F (orden) directive; (norma) guidelines; (junta de directores) board of directors
directrices F PL guidelines
directivo -va ADJ leadership; MF officer
directo ADJ (sin desviaciones, intermediarios) direct; (derecho) straight; **en** — live
director -ora MF (de una empresa) director, manager; (de una escuela) principal; (de orquesta) conductor; — **de correos** postmaster; — **general** CEO; — **técnico** coach
directorio M (índice) directory; (junta directiva) board of directors; — **[de] raíz** root directory; — **padre** parent directory
diría *ver* decir
dirigente MF leader; — **sindical** union leader
dirigible M dirigible
dirigir[46] VT (una obra teatral) to direct; (una empresa) to manage; (una orquesta) to conduct; (a un turista) to guide; (un saludo, una carta, una pregunta, una crítica) to address; —**se a** (hablar con) to address; (ir a) to go to; (tratar de) to be aimed at
discapacidad F disability

discapacitado ADJ disabled
discar[30] VI/VT *Am* to dial
discernimiento M discernment, insight
discernir[3] VT to discern
disciplina F discipline
disciplinar VT to discipline
discípulo -la MF disciple
disco M (cartílago, objeto plano y circular) disk; (fonográfico) record; — **compacto** compact disc; — **comprimido** compressed disk; — **de iniciación** boot disk; — **duro** hard disk; — **duro interno** internal hard disk; — **volador** Frisbee®; **es un — rayado** he's a broken record
díscolo ADJ unruly
disconforme ADJ dissatisfied
discontinuo ADJ discontinuous
discordancia F discord
discordia F discord
discoteca F (lugar donde bailar) discotheque; (colección de discos) record collection
discreción F discretion; **a —** at one's own discretion
discrepancia F discrepancy
discrepar VI to disagree; — **de** to take issue with
discreto ADJ (prudente) discreet; (separado) discrete; **un partido —** a sorry game
discriminación F discrimination; — **por edad** age discrimination; — **positiva** affirmative action; — **sexual** sexual discrimination
discriminar VI to discriminate; — **a** to discriminate against
disculpa F (excusa) excuse; (perdón) apology
disculpable ADJ excusable
disculpar VT (excusar) to excuse; (perdonar) to forgive, to pardon; —**se** to apologize
discurrir VI (transcurrir) to pass; (exponer) to discourse
discursear VI to make speeches
discurso M (enunciado) discourse; (disertacíon pública) speech, address; — **de apertura** keynote address
discusión F (charla) discussion; (riña) argument
discutible ADJ debatable, questionable
discutir VT (hablar sobre) to discuss; (oponerse a) to dispute; VI (reñir) to argue
disecar[30] VT (cortar) to dissect; (preparar para conservar) to stuff
diseminación F dissemination
diseminar VT to disseminate
disensión F dissension, dissent
disenso M dissent
disentería F dysentery
disentir[8] VI to dissent, to disagree
diseñador -ora MF designer
diseñar VT to design
diseño M design; — **de interiores** interior design; — **de página** page layout; — **gráfico** graphic design

disertación F lecture
disertar VI to lecture
disfraz M (para ocultarse) disguise; (de carnaval) costume
disfrazar[47] VT to disguise
disfrutar VI/VT to enjoy; — **de** to enjoy
disfrute M enjoyment
disfunción F dysfunction
disgustado ADJ (molesto) upset; (enojado) angry
disgustar VT to upset; —**se** (molestarse) to get upset; (enfadarse) to get angry
disgusto M (desagrado) unpleasantness; (discusión) quarrel; **a —** (con desgana) against one's will; (con incomodidad) uncomfortably; (en disconformidad) in conflict; **esa niña no da más que —s** that girl keeps us upset all the time
disidente ADJ & MF dissident
disimulado ADJ **hacerse el —** to pretend not to notice
disimular VI (fingir) to dissemble; (ocultar) to conceal
disimulo M (fingimiento) dissimulation; (ocultamiento) concealment
disipación F dissipation
disipar VT (niebla, calor) to dissipate; (dudas) to dispel; (miedo) to allay; (dinero) to squander; —**se** to dissipate; (miedo, dudas) to allay, to lift
dislexia F dyslexia
dislocación F dislocation
dislocar[30] VT to dislocate; —**se** to get dislocated
disminución F (acción de disminuir) decrease, lessening; (desprecio) belittling; (de ventas) dip, decrease
disminuir[19] VT (menguar) to diminish, to decrease, to lessen; (despreciar) to belittle
disminuya, disminuye, disminuyendo, disminuyera, disminuyese *ver* disminuir
disolución F dissolution
disoluto ADJ dissolute, loose
disolvente M solvent; — **de pintura** paint thinner
disolver[6, 74] VT (sal) to dissolve; (reunión) to break up
disonancia F discord
dispar ADJ disparate
disparar VT (un arma de fuego) to shoot, to fire; (una cámara) to click; (la inflación) to trigger; VI (en fútbol) to shoot; —**le a alguien** to shoot at someone; —**se** (aumentar) to take off; (salir) to shoot out
disparatado ADJ absurd
disparatar VI to talk nonsense
disparate M absurdity, nonsense; **decir —s** to talk nonsense; **un — de plata** a ton of money; **puros —s** *vulg* pure bullshit
disparo M (acción de disparar) shooting; (tiro,

herida) shot, gunshot; (tiro de fútbol) shot at goal
dispensa F dispensation
dispensación F dispensation
dispensar VT to dispense; — **de** to exempt from
dispensario M dispensary
dispersar VT to disperse
dispersión F dispersal
disperso ADJ (diseminado) dispersed, scattered; (distraído) absent-minded, distracted; (no concentrado) disperse
display M display
displicencia F flippancy
displicente ADJ (comportamiento) flippant; (actitud) cavalier
dispon, dispondrá, dispondría ver disponer
disponer[56, 74] VT (colocar) to arrange; (preparar) to prepare, to dispose; (mandar) to order; — **de** to have; —**se** to set about; —**se para** to get ready for
disponga, dispongo ver disponer
disponibilidad F availability
disponible ADJ (asiento, taxi) available; (dinero) on hand; (inventario) in stock
disposición F (voluntad) disposition; (colocación) arrangement; (de ánimo) mood; **a — de** at the disposal of
dispositivo M device; — **analógico** analog device; — **de almacenamiento** storage device; — **de salida** output device; — **intrauterino** intrauterine device
dispuesto ADJ ready; **bien —** willing; **no estar — a** to be unwilling to
dispuesto, dispuse, dispusiera, dispusiese ver disponer
disputa F (controversia) dispute; (riña) argument
disputar VI/VT to dispute; —**se el poder** to vie/ challenge/contend for power; —**se la posición** to jockey for position
disquete M floppy disk; — **de iniciación** bootable diskette
disquetera F disk drive
distancia F distance; **a —** at arm's length; **guardar —s** to keep at a distance; **¿a qué — está?** how far away is it?
distanciarse VT to distance oneself
distante ADJ distant
distar VI **dista mucho de** it's a far cry from; **dista diez kilómetros de** it's ten kilometers from
distender[2] VT (aflojar) to relax; (dilatar) to expand
distensión F distension; — **muscular** muscle strain
distinción F distinction
distinguido ADJ distinguished
distinguir[44] VT to distinguish
distintivo ADJ distinctive, distinguishing; M

distinguishing characteristic
distinto ADJ (diferente) different; (claro) distinct
distorsión F distortion
distorsionar VT to distort
distracción F distraction
distraer[59] VT (la atención) to distract; (fondos, mano de obra) to divert; —**se** (divertirse) to entertain oneself; (dispersarse) to become distracted, *fam* to space out
distraído ADJ distracted, absent-minded; **hacerse el —** to play dumb
distribución F distribution
distribuidor -ora MF (persona) distributor; M (pieza de un motor) distributor
distribuir[19] VT to distribute
distrito M district
Distrito de Columbia M District of Columbia
distrofia F dystrophy; — **muscular** muscular dystrophy
disturbio M disturbance, trouble
disuadir VT (mediante palabras) to dissuade; (mediante acciones) to deter
DIU [dispositivo intrauterino] M IUD
diurético ADJ & M diuretic
diurno ADJ (actividad) daytime; (animal) diurnal
divagación F rambling
divagar[40] VI to ramble on, to digress
diván M divan; (de psiquiatra) couch
divergencia F divergence
divergir[46] VI to diverge
diversidad F diversity
diversión F (pasatiempo) amusement, entertainment, fun; (hecho de distraer la atención) diversion
diverso ADJ diverse; —**s** various
diverticulitis F diverticulitis
divertido ADJ amusing, entertaining
divertir[8] VT to amuse, to entertain; —**se** to have a good time, to have fun
dividendo M dividend
dividir VT to divide; (un territorio) to partition
divierta, divierte ver divertir
divieso M boil
divinidad F divinity
divino ADJ divine; **estuvo —** it was heavenly; **lo pasé —** I had a wonderful time
divirtiendo, divirtiera, divirtiese, divirtió ver divertir
divisa F (señal) emblem; (moneda) currency; (moneda extranjera) foreign currency
divisar VT to make out, to catch sight of
división F division; (de un territorio) partition
divisorio ADJ dividing
divorciar VT to divorce; —**se** to get divorced
divorcio M divorce
divulgación F dissemination; — **financiera** financial disclosure
divulgar[40] VT (un secreto) to divulge;

(información) to disseminate
dobladillo M hem; **hacer —s** to hem
doblado ADJ (hipócrita) hypocritical; M (de tela, papel) folding; (de tubos) bending
doblaje M dubbing
doblar VT (una sábana) to fold; (el capital) to double; (una esquina) to turn; (la voz de un actor) to dub; VI (un coche) to turn; (una campana) to knell; **—se** to bend over
doble ADJ double (también en tenis); **— agente** double agent; **— falta** double fault; **— indemnización** double indemnity; **— matanza** double play; **— pulsación** double click; **— personalidad** split personality; **— visión** double vision; **de — caño** double-barreled; **de — filo** double-edged; **de — sentido** two-way; MF (persona muy parecida, actor sustituto) double; M (repique) knell; **—s** doubles; **—s mixtos** mixed doubles; **el —** double
doblegar[40] VT to break
doblete M double
doblez M fold; F deceitfulness
doce NUM twelve
docena F dozen; **— del fraile** baker's dozen
docente ADJ teaching
dócil ADJ (persona, animal) docile, pliant; (pelo) manageable
docto ADJ learned
doctor -ora MF doctor; **— en medicina** MD
doctorado M doctorate
doctrina F doctrine
documentación F documentation (también para computadoras)
documental ADJ & M documentary
documentar VT to document
documento M document; **— de instrucciones previas** living will; **— de voluntad anticipada** living will
dogma M dogma
dogmático ADJ dogmatic
dogo M pug
dólar M dollar
dolencia F ailment
doler[6] VI to ache, to hurt; **me duele el brazo** my arm aches, my arm is sore; **—se de** (compadecerse) to feel sorry for; (arrepentirse) to regret
doliente ADJ aching; MF mourner
dolor M (físico) pain, ache; (espiritual) sorrow, pain; **— de barriga** bellyache; **— de cabeza** headache; **— de espalda** backache; **— de muela** toothache; **— de oídos** earache; **— de garganta** sore throat; **—es del crecimiento** growing pains; **— de garganta** sore throat; **—es de parto** labor pains
dolorido ADJ aching, sore
doloroso ADJ painful

doma F (de caballos) breaking; (de leones) taming
domado ADJ (caballo) broken; (león) tamed
domador -ora MF (de perros) trainer; (de leones) lion tamer
domar VT (caballos, personas) to break; (leones) to tame
domesticar[30] VT to domesticate, to tame
doméstico -ca ADJ domestic; MF servant
domiciliarse VI to take up residence; **¿dónde se domicilia usted?** where do you reside?
domicilio M (casa) dwelling; (dirección) address
dominación F domination
dominador ADJ (predominante) dominant; (tiránico) domineering, overbearing
dominante ADJ (predominante) dominant; (tiránico) domineering, overbearing
dominar VT (tener bajo su autoridad, ser más alto) to dominate; (reprimir) to control, to rein in; (tener sometido a su voluntad) to domineer
domingo M Sunday; **— de Ramos** Palm Sunday; **— de Pascua** Easter Sunday
Dominica F Dominica
dominicano -na ADJ & MF Dominican [de la República Dominicana]
dominio M (sobre una tierra, derecho de usar una cosa) dominion; (de sí mismo) control; (de una lengua) mastery, command; (hecho de dominar) domination; (ámbito, campo) domain; **— público** public domain
dominiqués -esa ADJ & MF Dominican [de Domínica]
dominó M (pieza) domino; (juego) dominoes
domo M dome
don M (gracia) gift; (título, jefe mafioso) don; **un — nadie** a nobody
dona F *Méx* doughnut, donut
donación F donation
donador -ora MF donor
donaire M grace
donante MF donor; **— universal** universal donor
donar MF to donate
doncella F *lit* maiden
donde ADV REL where; **de —** whence, from which; **ir — el herrero** to go to the blacksmith's shop; **— no** otherwise; **—quiera** wherever; **donde no comas, no te dejo salir a jugar** if you don't eat, I won't let you go out to play
dónde ADV INTERR where
donoso ADJ graceful
donut M *Esp* doughnut, donut
doña F doña
dopamina F dopamine
dopar VT to dope
dorado ADJ (cubierto de oro) gilt; (de color oro) golden; M dolphin fish

dorar VT to gild; — **la píldora** to sweeten the pill
dormido ADJ asleep
dormir[7] VI/VT to sleep; — **a** to put to bed; — **a un paciente** to anesthetize a patient; — **la mona** to sleep it off; — **la siesta** to take a nap; **se me ha dormido el brazo** my arm has fallen asleep; —**se** to fall asleep
dormitar VI to doze, to snooze
dormitorio M bedroom
dorso M back, reverse
dos NUM two; — **puntos** colon; — **veces** twice; **cada** — **por tres** constantly; **en un** — **por tres** in a jiffy; **los** — both of them
DOS M DOS
doscientos NUM two hundred
dosel M canopy
dosificar[30] VT to dose
dosis F (de medicamento) dose; (de droga) hit
dotación F (de fondos) endowment; (de personal) complement
dotar VT to endow
dote F dowry; —**s** talents
doy ver dar
draga F dredge
dragado M dredging
dragar[40] VT (para limpiar) to dredge; (para buscar objetos) to drag; M SG **dragaminas** minesweeper
dragón M (animal fantástico) dragon; (planta) snapdragon
drama M drama
dramático ADJ dramatic
dramatizar[47] VT to dramatize
dramaturgo -ga MF playwright, dramatist
drapear VI to drape
drástico ADJ drastic
drenaje M drainage
drenar VI/VT to drain
dribbling M dribble, dribbling
driblar VI/VT to dribble
drible M dribble
dril M drill
drive M drive
drive-in M drive-in
driver M driver
droga F drug; — **anticancerosa** anticancer drug; — **de recreo** recreational drug; —**s de diseño** designer drugs; **tomar** —**s** to do drugs; MF **drogadicto -ta** drug addict
drogar[40] VT to drug
drogata MF junkie
drogota MF junkie
droguería F (tienda) drugstore; (industria) drug industry
droguero -ra MF druggist
dropar VI to drop
ducado M dukedom
ducha F shower; — **vaginal** vaginal douche

ducharse VI to shower
ducho ADJ skillful
dúctil ADJ (metal) ductile; (persona) flexible, supple
duda F doubt; **en** — in doubt; **fuera de** — beyond doubt; **no cabe** — there's no doubt; **poner en** — to cast doubt on; **sin** — without a doubt, undoubtedly; **sin lugar a** —**s** without doubt; **tengo una** — I have a question
dudar VT (no creer) to doubt; (vacilar) to hesitate; — **de** to have doubts about
dudoso ADJ doubtful; **de dudosa honestidad** of dubious honesty
duela F stave
duela, duele ver doler
duelo M (combate) duel; (luto) mourning; (pena) grief; (dolientes) mourners; **estar de** — to be in mourning
duende M (gnomo) goblin, gremlin; (gracia) charm
dueño -ña MF owner; **me sentí** — **de la situación** I felt like I was in control of the situation; M landlord; F landlady
duerma, duerme ver dormir
dueto M duet
dulce ADJ (sabor, personalidad) sweet; (clima) pleasant; (agua) fresh; —**amargo** bittersweet; M (cosa dulce) sweet; (mermelada) preserves, conserve
dulcería F confectionery
dulcificar[30] VT to sweeten
dulzón ADJ unpleasantly sweet
dulzor M sweetness
dulzura F sweetness
duna F dune
dúo M duet; **decir a** — to say in unison
duodeno M duodenum
dúplex M duplex
duplicado ADJ & M duplicate; **por** — in duplicate
duplicar[30] VT to duplicate
duplicidad F duplicity
duque M duke
duquesa F duchess
durabilidad F durability
duración F duration; (de una película, vocal) length; — **de la vida** lifespan
duradero ADJ (ropa) durable, serviceable; (pilas) long-lasting
durante PREP during; — **el mandato de los Demócratas** under the Democrats; — **muchos años** for/over many years
durar VI/VT to last
duraznero M peach tree
durazno M (fruto) peach; (árbol) peach tree
dureza F (de metal) hardness; (del clima, de la expresión, de una tempestad) severity; (del invierno) harshness; (de un boxeador)

toughness; (del cuero) stiffness
durmamos, durmiendo *ver* dormir
durmiente ADJ sleeping; M railroad tie, sleeper
durmiera, durmiese *ver* dormir
duro ADJ (metal, golpe, droga, agua) hard;
(clima, tormenta) severe; (invierno,
expresión, sonido) harsh; (soldado) tough;
(grifo) stuck; (viento) strong; (autoridad)
inflexible; (pan) stale; (cuero) stiff; — **de
corazón** hard-hearted; — **de
entendederas** slow on the uptake; **a duras
penas** barely; M five-peseta coin; **no tengo
un** — I'm flat broke
DVD M DVD

Ee

e CONJ and
ebanista MF cabinetmaker
ébano M ebony
ebrio ADJ drunk, inebriated
ebullición F boiling
eccema M eczema
echar VT (una pelota, redes) to throw, to cast;
(yemas, hojas) to sprout; (a un empleado) to
fire; (humo, olor) to give off; (un líquido) to
pour; (a un borracho) to throw out; — **abajo**
to knock down; — **a la basura** to throw
away; — **al mar** to put to sea; — **al correo** to
mail; — **anclas** to drop anchor; — **a pique**
to sink; — **carnes** to get fat; — **de menos** to
miss; — **de ver** to notice; — **mano de** to
seize upon; — **la culpa** to blame; — **por la
borda** to jettison; — **raíces** to take root; —
sangre to bleed; — **suertes** to draw lots; —
una carta to mail a letter; — **una siesta** to
take a nap; — **un vistazo a** to glance at, to
take a look at; **te echo una carrera** I'll race
you; — **le el muerto a alguien** to pass the
buck to someone; — **se** to lie down; —**se a** to
start to; —**se a correr** to bolt; —**se a perder**
to spoil; —**se a reír** to burst out laughing;
—**se a un lado** to dodge; —**se atrás** to back
down/off; —**se para atrás** to lean back
ecléctico ADJ eclectic
eclesiástico ADJ & M ecclesiastic
eclipsar VT (ocultar) to eclipse; (superar) to
eclipse, to outshine, to overshadow; —**se** to
fade
eclipse M eclipse; — **de sol** solar eclipse; — **de
luna** lunar eclipse
eco M echo; **hacer** — to echo; **hacerse** — **de** to
repeat
ecocardiograma M echocardiogram
ecología F (medio ambiente) environment;

(ciencia) ecology
ecológico ADJ (ambiental) environmental,
ecological; (bueno para la naturaleza)
eco-friendly
ecologista ADJ environmental; MF
environmentalist
economato M commissary
economía F (actividades de producción)
economy; (ciencia) economics; (familiar)
finances; — **doméstica** home economics;
—**s** savings; **hacer** —**s** to be thrifty
económico ADJ (relativo a la economía)
economic; (frugal) frugal, thrifty; (barato)
economical
economista MF economist
economizar[47] VT to economize, to save
ecosistema M ecosystem
ecuación F equation
ecuador M equator
Ecuador M Ecuador
ecualizar[47] VT to equalize
ecuatoriano -na ADJ & MF Ecuadorian
ecuménico ADJ ecumenical
edad F age; — **avanzada** ripe old age; — **de
merecer** marriageable age; — **de Piedra**
Stone Age; — **del consentimiento sexual**
age of consent; — **Media** Middle Ages; —
mental mental age
edición F (ejemplar) edition; (acción de editar)
publication; — **de sobremesa** desktop
publishing
edicto M edict
edificación F building
edificar[30] VT (construir) to build; (infundir
sentimientos morales) to edify, to uplift
edificio M building
editar VT to edit, to publish
editor -ora ADJ publishing; MF editor
editorial ADJ publishing; F publishing house; M
editorial
editorializar[47] VI to editorialize
edredón M comforter
educación F (escolar) education; (social)
breeding; — **a distancia** distance learning;
— **cívica** civics; — **especial** special
education; — **en línea** e-learning; — **física**
physical education; — **para adultos**
continuing education; — **superior** higher
education
educado ADJ (cortés) well-bred; (instruido)
educated
educador -ora MF educator
educar[30] VT (desarrollar conocimientos) to
educate; (entrenar) to train
educativo ADJ educational
edulcorante M sweetener
EEUU [Estados Unidos] M SG/PL USA
efectivamente ADV actually; **más de los que**
— **encuentran** more than they actually find;

INTERJ exactly
efectividad F effectiveness; **tener** — to be valid, to become valid
efectivo ADJ (eficaz) effective; (real) actual; **hacer** — (un cheque) to cash; (una deuda) to pay off; (una amenaza) to make good on; M cash; **en** — in cash; **—s** troops
efecto M (resultado) effect, result; (letra comercial) bill of exchange; (rotación) English, spin; **en** — in fact; **llevar a** — to carry out; **surtir** — to work; — **invernadero** greenhouse effect; **—s especiales** special effects; **—s personales** personal effects; **perder** — to wear off; **rebotar con** — to glance off; **a estos** **—s** to this effect; **para los** **—s** to all intents and purposes; **por** — **de** as a consequence of
efectuar[26] VT to effect; **—se** to be carried out
eficacia F efficacy, effectiveness; — **de una ley** force of law
eficaz ADJ effective
eficiencia F efficiency
eficiente ADJ efficient
efigie F effigy; **quemar en** — to burn in effigy
efímero ADJ ephemeral, fleeting
efusivo ADJ effusive
egipcio -cia ADJ & MF Egyptian
Egipto M Egypt
égloga F pastoral
ego M ego
egocéntrico ADJ egocentric, self-centered
egoísmo M selfishness
egoísta ADJ selfish; MF selfish person
egotismo M egotism
egresado -da MF graduate
eje M (de la Tierra) axis; (de un vehículo) axle; — **del pistón** piston rod; **eso me parte por el** — that messes up my plans
ejecución F (de un condenado) execution; (de un plan, una orden) carrying out, execution; (de una tarea) performance; (de una propiedad) foreclosure
ejecutable ADJ executable
ejecutar VT (a un condenado) to execute; (un plan, una orden) to carry out; (una tarea, música) to perform; (una propiedad) to foreclose on
ejecutivo -va ADJ & MF executive; — **de empresa** corporate officer
ejemplar ADJ exemplary, model; M (libro) copy; (individuo) specimen
ejemplario M handout
ejemplificar[30] VT to exemplify
ejemplo M (cosa típica) example; (modelo) model; **a** — **de** on the example of; **dar** — to set an example; **por** — for example
ejercer[32] VT (una profesión) to practice; (influencia, fuerza) to exert; (poder) to wield
ejercicio M exercise; (de una profesión) practice;

hacer — to exercise; — **contable** accounting period; — **físico** physical exercise; **—s de Kegel** Kegel exercises; **en** — active
ejercitar VT (la vista, los músculos) to exercise; (a soldados) to drill; (a alumnos) to train; **—se** to train
ejército M army; **el** — the military
ejido M common
ejote M *Méx* green bean
el ART DEF M the; — **de la derecha** the one on the right; — **que** the one that; — **que sepa** whoever knows
él PRON PERS M SG (como sujeto) he; — **dijo** he said; (como objeto) him; **para** — for him; **le di el libro a** — I gave the book to him; **estamos hablando de** — we're talking about him; **el libro de** — his book
elaboración F (de miel, comida) making; (de un método) development; (de un informe) drafting
elaborado ADJ elaborate
elaborar VT (un método) to elaborate, to develop; (comida) to make; (un informe) to draft
elasticidad F elasticity
elástico ADJ (sustancia) elastic; (cuerpo) supple; (horario) flexible; M elastic
elección F (votación) election; (selección) choice, selection; **no tuve** — I had no choice
electo ADJ elect
elector -ora ADJ electoral; MF elector
electoral ADJ electoral
electricidad F electricity; — **estática** static electricity
electricista MF electrician
eléctrico ADJ (aparato) electric; (instalación, corriente) electrical
electrificar[30] VT to electrify
electrizado ADJ electrified
electrizante ADJ electrifying
electrizar[47] VT (suministrar electricidad) to electrify; (emocionar) to galvanize, to electrify
electrocardiograma M electrocardiogram
electrocutar VT to electrocute
electrodo M electrode
electrodoméstico M electrical appliance
electroencefalograma M electroencephalogram
electroimán M electromagnet
electrólisis F electrolysis
electromagnético ADJ electromagnetic
electrón M electron
electrónica F electronics
electrónico ADJ electronic
elefante M elephant
elegancia F elegance
elegante ADJ (armonioso) elegant; (bien

vestido) stylish, classy
elegibilidad F eligibility
elegible ADJ eligible
elegir[14] VT (seleccionar) to choose, to select;
(votar) to elect
elemental ADJ (sencillo) elementary; (básico)
elemental
elemento M element
elenco M cast
elevación F elevation; **tirar por** — to throw
high in the air
elevado ADJ (pensamiento, estilo) elevated;
(fiebre, montaña) high; (precios) high; M
(béisbol) fly ball
elevador M elevator
elevar VT (en una jerarquía) to elevate; (precios,
voz, objeto) to raise; (el espíritu) to uplift; —
la vista to look up; — **al cuadrado** to
square; — **al cubo** to cube; —**se a** to go up to,
to rise to; **el rascacielos se eleva sobre la
ciudad** the skyscraper towers over the city
elfo M elf
eliminación F elimination
eliminar VT to eliminate
eliminatoria F (atletismo, natación) heat; —**s**
(fútbol) playoffs
elíptico ADJ elliptical
elite/élite F elite
elitista ADJ & MF elitist
ella PRON PERS F SG (como sujeto) she; — **dijo**
she said; (como objeto) her; **para** — for her;
le di el libro a — I gave the book to her; **el
libro de** — her book
ellas PRON PERS F PL (como sujeto) they; —
dijeron they said; (como objeto) them; **para**
— for them; **les di el libro a** — I gave them
the book; **el libro de** — their book
ello PRON NEUTRO it; — **es que** the fact is that
ellos PRON M PL (como sujeto) they; — **dijeron**
they said; (como objeto) them; **para** — for
them; **les di el libro a** — I gave them the
book; **el libro de** — their book
elocuencia F eloquence
elocuente ADJ eloquent; **las estadísticas son**
—**s** the statistics speak for themselves
elogiar VT to praise
elogio M praise
elote M *Méx* corn on the cob
elucidación F elucidation
elucidar VT to elucidate
eludir VT to elude, to avoid, to dodge
emanación F emanation, flow
emanar VI/VT to emanate
emancipación F emancipation
emancipar VT to emancipate; —**se** to become
free
emascular VT to emasculate
embadurnar VT to daub
embajada F embassy

embajador-ora MF ambassador
embalador-ora MF packer
embalaje M packing, packaging
embalar VT to pack; VI to accelerate
embaldosar VT to tile
embalsamar VT (a un muerto) to embalm; (un
animal) to stuff
embalse M reservoir
embanderar VT to adorn with flags
embarazada ADJ pregnant
embarazar[47] VT (impedir) to hamper;
(fecundar) to make pregnant; —**se** to get
pregnant
embarazo M (obstáculo) impediment; (estado
de embarazada) pregnancy
embarazoso ADJ embarrassing, awkward
embarcación F boat, embarkation, craft
embarcadero M wharf, pier
embarcar[30] VT (pasajeros) to embark;
(mercancías) to load; —**se** to embark, to go
aboard; —**se en** to embark upon
embargar[40] VT to seize; **estar embargado de
emoción** to be overcome with emotion
embargo M embargo; — **judicial** seizure;
imponer un — to embargo; **sin** —
nevertheless, however
embarque M (de mercancías) loading; (de
pasajeros) embarkation
embarrado ADJ smeared with mud
embarrar VT to smear with mud, to muddy
embate M lashing
embaucador M confidence man
embaucar[30] VT to dupe
embeber VT to soak up; —**se** to be absorbed
embelesar VT to enrapture
embeleso M rapture
embellecer[35] VI/VT to beautify
embestida F charge
embestir[9] VI/VT to charge
embetunar VT to polish
emblanquecer[35] VI/VT to whiten
emblema M emblem
embobar VT to amaze; —**se** to be amazed
embolia F embolism; — **cerebral** cerebral
embolism
émbolo M piston, plunger
embolsar VT (dinero) to pocket; (una compra) to
bag
emborrachar VT (a una persona) to intoxicate;
(el carburador) to flood; —**se** to get drunk
emborronar VT (manchar) to blot; (hacer
impreciso) to blur
emboscada F ambush; **tender una** — to lie in
ambush
emboscar[30] VT to ambush; —**se** to lie in ambush
embotamiento M (efecto de embotar) dullness,
bluntness; (acción de embotar) dulling
embotar VT to dull
embotelladora F bottling plant

embotellamiento M (de cerveza) bottling; (de tráfico) traffic jam, bottleneck

embotellar VT (cerveza) to bottle; (tráfico) to bottle up

embozar⁴⁷ VT to conceal

embragar⁴⁰ VI to engage the clutch

embrague M clutch

embriagado ADJ drunken

embriagar⁴⁰ VT to intoxicate; —se to become intoxicated

embriaguez F intoxication, drunkenness

embridar VT to bridle

embrión M embryo

embrionario ADJ embryonic

embriónico ADJ embryonic

embrollar VT (involucrar) to embroil; (confundir) to muddle

embrollo M muddle

embromar VT to kid

embrujar VT to bewitch

embrujo M spell

embrutecer³⁵ VT to stupefy

embudo M funnel

embuste M lie

embustero -ra MF liar, trickster

embutido M sausage

embutir VT to cram, to jam

emergencia F emergency

emergente ADJ emergent, emerging

emerger⁴⁵ VI (surgir) to emerge; (salir del agua) to surface

emigración F (de personas) emigration; (de animales) migration

emigrante ADJ & MF emigrant

emigrar VI (personas) to emigrate; (animales) to migrate

eminencia F eminence; — gris gray eminence

eminente ADJ eminent

emisario -ria MF emissary; M outlet

emisión F (de acciones, billetes) issue; (de un olor) discharge; (de programas) broadcast; (de gas) emission

emisor ADJ emitting; M transmitter

emisora F radio/television station

emitir VT (un olor, vapor) to emit; (juicios) to pronounce; (dinero, acciones) to issue; VI/VT (programas) to broadcast; —se to be on the air; el programa se emite en horas de la mañana the program airs in the morning

emoción F emotion; ¡qué —! what a thrill!

emocional ADJ emotional

emocionante ADJ (conmovedor) touching; (apasionante) exciting

emocionar VT (apasionar) to excite; (conmover) to move, to touch; —se (estar ilusionado) to be excited; (estar conmovido) to be touched

emoticón M emoticon

emoticono M emoticon

emotivo ADJ emotional

empacador -ora MF packer

empacar³⁰ VT (regalos, mercancías) to pack; (algodón) to bale

empachar VI to cause indigestion; —se to suffer indigestion; —se de to get sick on, to stuff oneself with

empacho M (indigestión) indigestion; (cohibición) inhibition; no tener — en to have no qualms about

empalagar⁴⁰ VI/VT to cloy

empalagoso ADJ cloying, saccharine

empalar VT to impale

empalizada F stockade, palisade

empalmar VT to splice; — con to join

empalme M (de caminos) junction; (de cuerdas) splice; — genético gene splicing

empanada F turnover, pie

empanar VT to bread

empañado ADJ (vidrio) misty, foggy; (metal, reputación) tarnished

empañar VT (vidrio) to fog up; (metal, reputación) to tarnish

empapado ADJ soggy, sopping wet

empapamiento M soaking

empapar VT (mojar) to soak, to drench; (recoger con algo) to soak up; —se (mojarse) to get soaked; (enterarse) to find out all about

empapelado M wallpapering

empapelar VT to paper, to wallpaper; — las calles to plaster the streets

empaque M (acción de empacar) packing; (envoltorio) packaging

empaquetadura F gasket

empaquetar VT to pack, to package; —se to get dolled up

emparedado M sandwich

emparejar VT (una carga, un partido) to even up; VI/VT (los enamorados) to pair up; (calcetines, zapatos) to match up

emparentado ADJ akin, related

emparentar VT to relate by marriage; —se to become related by marriage

empastar VT to fill

empaste M filling

empatar VI to tie; — una marca to tie a record

empate M tie, draw

empatía F empathy

empecinado ADJ stubborn

empedernido ADJ (criminal) hardened; (mujeriego) incorrigible; (solterón) confirmed

empedernirse⁷³ VI to become hardened

empedrado M (acción) paving with stones; (cosa) cobblestone pavement; ADJ paved with stones

empedrar¹ VT to pave with stones

empeine M (del pie) instep; (del vientre) groin

empellón M shove; a empellones with shoves, shoving

empeñar VT to pawn; — **la palabra** to pledge; —**se** (endeudarse) to go into debt; (obstinarse) to insist; (esforzarse) to apply oneself; —**se en** to engage in

empeño M (prenda) pawn; (insistencia) insistence; (deseo) desire; (esfuerzo) exertion; **poner** — **en** to strive for

empeorar VT to make worse, to aggravate; VI to worsen; —**se** to get worse

empequeñecer[35] VT to make smaller; VI to get smaller

emperador -triz M emperor; F empress

emperifollarse VI to deck oneself out, to doll oneself up

empezar[48] VI/VT to begin, to start; — **a** to start to; — **de cero** to start from scratch; **para** — for starters; **no tengo ni para** — **con él** I can't touch him; — **por** to begin with; **empezamos mal** we got off to a bad start; **un paquete sin** — an unopened box; **por algo se empieza** you have to start somewhere

empinado ADJ steep

empinar VT to raise; — **el codo** to drink; —**se** (una persona) to stand on tiptoes; (un caballo) to rear; (una torre) to tower

empírico ADJ empirical

empizarrar VT to cover with slate

emplastar VT to plaster

emplasto M plaster

emplazamiento M (colocación) placement; (lugar) location

empleado -da MF employee; — **temporal** temp

emplear VT (usar) to employ, to use; (dar trabajo) to employ; —**se en** to be employed in

empleo M (ocupación) employment, work; (puesto de trabajo) job; (utilización) use

emplumado ADJ feathery

emplumar VT (adornar) to adorn with feathers; (pegar plumas en el cuerpo) to tar and feather; VI (echar plumas) to grow feathers

empobrecer[35] VI/VT to impoverish

empollar VT (huevos) to hatch, to brood; VI/VT (para un examen) to cram

empollón -ona MF *fam* egghead, overachiever

empolvar VT to cover with dust; —**se** (con cosméticos) to powder oneself; (con polvo) to get dirty

emponzoñar VT to poison

empotrado ADJ built-in

emprendedor ADJ enterprising

emprender VT (una tarea) to undertake; (un viaje) to embark on; —**la con alguien** to attack someone

empresa F (cosa que se emprende) undertaking; (compañía) company, enterprise; **libre** — free enterprise; — **privada** private

enterprise; — **pública** public company; — **tiburón** raider

empresarial ADJ —**es** business administration studies; **grupo** — business group

empresario -ria MF entrepreneur

empréstito M loan

empujar VT (mover) to push; (mover con violencia) to shove; (apresurar) to hurry

empuje M (ánimo) drive; (fuerza de propulsión) thrust; (fuerza hacia arriba) lift

empujón M shove, push; **dar empujones** to jostle

empuñadura F (espada) hilt; (cuchillo) handle; (palo de golf, raqueta) grip

empuñar VT to grasp

emular VT to emulate

en PREP in; — **Asturias** in Asturias; (sobre una superficie) on, upon; — **la mesa** on the table; **sentarse** — **el suelo** to sit down on the floor; **me lo vendió** — **mil pesetas** she sold it to me for a thousand pesetas; — **la parada del autobús** at the bus stop; — **la noche** at night; **ir** — **tren** to go by train

enaguas F PL petticoat

enajenación M (locura) insanity; (transferencia) transfer

enajenar VT (trasladar) to transfer; (alienar) to alienate; —**se** to become alienated

enaltecer[35] VT to extol

enamorado -da ADJ in love; MF lover

enamoramiento M crush

enamorar VT to make fall in love; —**se [de]** to fall in love [with]

enanismo M dwarfism

enano -na MF (personaje imaginario, persona deforme) dwarf; (persona pequeña bien proporcionada) midget

enarbolar VT (una bandera) to raise on high; (un garrote) to brandish

enardecer[35] VT to inflame; —**se** to become inflamed

enardecimiento M inflaming

encabezado M header

encabezamiento M heading

encabezar[47] VT (una carta, una obra, un gobierno) to head; (un desfile) to lead

encabritarse VI (un caballo) to rear [up]; (una persona) to get furious

encadenar VT (poner en cadenas) to chain; (unir) to link

encajar VI/VT (colocar) to fit; VI (un gol) to allow; **el policía me encajó una multa** the policeman stuck me with a fine; **tu historia no encaja** your story doesn't hold water

encaje M (tejido) lace; (reserva bancaria) reserve; (acción de encajar) fitting together

encajonar VT (meter en una caja) to box; (apretar) to squeeze in

encallar VI to run aground, to strand; (una

ballena) to beach; VT to ground
encamarse VI — **con** to go to bed with, to sleep with
encaminar VT to direct; —**se hacia** to head for
encanecer[35] VI to go gray; VT to cause to go gray
encanijado ADJ sickly
encanijarse VI to become sickly
encantado ADJ (contento) delighted; (hechizado) enchanted; — **de conocerla** pleased to meet you
encantador -ora ADJ charming, delightful; MF charmer
encantamiento M enchantment
encantar VT to enchant; **eso me encanta** I love that
encanto M (encantamiento) enchantment; (atractivo) charm; **un** — **de persona** a delightful person; **como por** — as if by magic
encapotado ADJ overcast
encapotarse VI to become overcast
encapricharse VI — **con/de/por** to become infatuated with
encapuchar VT (a una persona) to hood; (un bolígrafo) to put the top on
encaramar VT to raise; —**se** to climb up on; —**se al primer puesto** to rise to first place
encarar VT to face; **me encaró el fusil** he pointed the rifle at me; —**se con** to face
encarcelamiento M imprisonment
encarcelar VT to imprison, to jail, to incarcerate
encarecer[35] VI (subir de precio) to increase in price; VT (rogar) to beg
encarecidamente ADV earnestly
encargado -da ADJ on order; MF person in charge; — **de curso** lecturer
encargar[40] VT (responsabilizar) to put in charge; (pedir) to order; (mandar) to commission, to order; — **a alguien una tarea** to charge someone with a task; —**se de** to take care of
encargo M (pedido) order; (tarea) assignment, charge, errand; **construido por/de** — custom-built; **hecho por** — made to order
encariñarse VI — **de** to become fond of
encarnación F incarnation
encarnado ADJ (color) red; (uña) ingrown
encarnar VT (un ideal) to embody; (a un personaje) to play; **se me encarnó una uña** one of my nails got ingrown
encarnizado ADJ fierce
encarnizarse[47] VI — **con alguien** to attack someone viciously
encarte M insert
encasillar VT to pigeonhole
encauzamiento M channeling
encauzar[47] VT to channel
encefalitis F encephalitis; — **espongiforme bovina** mad cow disease
encendedor M cigarette lighter
encender[2] VT (un cigarro, fuego) to light; (un

fósforo) to strike; (una luz, radio) to switch on, to turn on; (una computadora) to power on, to power up; (pasión) to arouse; VI —**se** (una persona, sexualmente) to become aroused; (una lámpara) to turn on
encendido ADJ (rojo) bright; (excitado) aroused; M ignition
encerado M (pizarrón) blackboard; (acción de encerar) waxing; (capa de cera) wax coating; ADJ waxed
encerar VT to wax, to polish
encerrar[1] VT (palabras entre paréntesis) to enclose; (una oveja) to pen; (a una persona) to lock up; (un contenido) to contain; (un peligro) to involve; —**se** (aislarse) to isolate oneself; (obstinarse) to become fixated
encestar VI to make a basket
enchapar VT (metal) to plate; (madera) to veneer
enchilada F enchilada
enchufar VT (un aparato eléctrico) to plug in; (a un protegido) to fix up; — **un tubo con otro** to fit one pipe into another
enchufe M (entrada eléctrica) socket, plug-in, electrical outlet; (situación ventajosa) connection
encías F PL gums
enciclopedia F encyclopedia
encienda, enciende *ver* encender
encierra, encierre *ver* encerrar
encierro M (confinamiento) confinement; (lugar) enclosure
encima ADV (arriba) on top; (además) in addition; — **de** on top of, atop; **por** — **de** above; **sacarse de** — to get rid of; **orinarse** — to urinate on oneself; **ya tenía el coche** — the car was already on top of me; **no lleves tanto dinero** — don't carry so much money on you; **se nos vienen** — **los exámenes** the exams are upon us; **mi madre siempre me está** — my mother is always on me; **lo leí por** — I scanned it
encimera F counter
encina F oak
encinta ADJ pregnant
enclaustrar VT to cloister
enclavarse VI to be located
enclave M enclave
enclenque ADJ (endeble) sickly; (desvencijado) rickety
encoger[45] VI/VT to shrink; —**se** (una prenda) to shrink; (una persona) to be intimidated; —**se de hombros** to shrug one's shoulders
encogido ADJ (tímido) shy; M (encogimiento) shrinkage, shrinking
encogimiento M (acción de encoger) shrinkage, shrinking; — **de hombros** shrug
encolar VT to glue
encolerizar[47] VT to incense; —**se** to become

incensed, to lose one's temper

encomendar[1] VT to entrust; —**se** to commend oneself

encomienda F (encargo) assignment, task; (colonial) encomienda [colonial land grant]

enconar VT to inflame; VI —**se** (discusión) to become inflamed; (herida) to fester

encono M animosity

encontrado ADJ contrary, opposing

encontrar[5] VT (hallar) to find; (verse con) to meet; — **a** to run into; —**se** (estar ubicado) to be located; (hallarse) to feel; —**se con** (verse por acuerdo) to meet with; (verse, por coincidencia) to run into; (enterarse) to find out; **vas a encontrarte la casa en obras** you'll find the house under construction

encontronazo M collision

encordado M strings

encordar[5] VT to string

encorvado ADJ stoop-shouldered

encorvamiento M slouch, stoop

encorvar VT to stoop; —**se** to bend over

encostrarse VI to scab

encrespar VT (el pelo) to curl; (el mar) to make choppy; —**se** (el pelo) to get curly; (el mar) to get choppy

encrucijada F crossroads

encuadernación F (oficio) bookbinding; (producto) binding

encuadernar VT to bind

encuadrar VT to frame; **la poesía de esta época se encuadra en tres tendencias** the poetry of this period can be classified into three tendencies

encubierto ADJ covert

encubrimiento ADJ (de un delincuente) concealment; (de un escándalo) cover-up

encubrir[74] VT (un secreto) to conceal; (un escándalo) to cover up, to hush up

encuentra, encuentre ver encontrar

encuentro M (casual) encounter; (planeado) meeting; (partido) game; (de atletismo) meet; **salir al — de** (ir a encontrar) to go out to meet; (contradecir) to counter

encuerar VT to strip

encuesta F survey, poll

encuestado -da MF respondent

encuestar VI/VT to survey, to poll

encumbrado ADJ elevated, lofty

encumbramiento M elevation

encumbrar VT to elevate

encurtido M pickle

encurtir VT to pickle

ende LOC ADV **por** — hence

endeble ADJ (persona) feeble; (material, argumento) flimsy; (mesa) rickety

endémico ADJ endemic

endemoniado ADJ (poseído por el diablo) possessed by the devil; (niño) devilish;

(pregunta) tough

enderezar[47] VT to straighten; **enderézate** stand up straight; **la niña se enderezó con los años** the girl straightened out after a few years

endeudamiento M indebtedness

endeudarse VI to get into debt

endiablado ADJ devilish

endocrino ADJ endocrine

endocrinología F endocrinology

endodermo M endoderm

endomingado ADJ dressed in one's Sunday best

endorfina F endorphin

endosante MF endorser

endosar VT to endorse

endoso M endorsement

endrogar VT to drug

endulzante M sweetener

endulzar[47] VT to sweeten; **se endulzó el tiempo** the weather became milder

endurecer[35] VT to harden, to stiffen; VI —**se** (músculos) to get hard; (pegamento) to set

endurecimiento M hardening

enebro M juniper

eneldo M dill

enema MF enema

enemigo -ga ADJ & MF enemy; **buques** —**s** enemy ships; **ser — de algo** to dislike something

enemistad F enmity

enemistar VT to cause enmity between; —**se con** to become an enemy of

energético ADJ **política energética** energy policy

energía F energy; — **eólica** wind power; — **hidráulica** water power; — **nuclear** nuclear energy; — **solar** solar energy; — **térmica** thermal energy

enérgicamente ADV strongly

enérgico ADJ (persona) energetic; (protesta, medida, tono) forceful

enero M January

enervar VT (debilitar) to enervate; (irritar) to irritate

enfadado ADJ angry

enfadar VT to anger; *fam* to piss off; VI —**se** to get angry

enfado M anger

enfadoso ADJ annoying

enfardar VT to bale

énfasis M emphasis

enfático ADJ emphatic

enfatizar[47] VT to emphasize

enfermar VT to sicken; VI to become sick; —**se** to become ill

enfermedad F (malestar) sickness, illness; (cardiovascular, de Parkinson) disease; (social) ill; — **contagiosa** contagious disease; — **coronaria** heart disease; — **de**

altura altitude sickness; — **de Alzheimer** Alzheimer's disease; — **de las vacas locas** mad cow disease; — **del legionario** legionnaire's disease; — **de Lou Gehrig** Lou Gehrig's disease; — **de Lyme** Lyme disease; — **de Parkinson** Parkinson's disease; — **degenerativa articular** degenerative joint disease; — **mental** mental illness; — **parasitaria** parasitic disease; — **por radiación** radiation sickness; — **venérea** venereal disease

enfermería F infirmary

enfermero -ra M male nurse; F nurse

enfermizo ADJ (persona) sickly, infirm; (obsesión, aspecto) unhealthy; (imaginación) sick

enfermo -ma ADJ sick, ill; **me tiene — que vengan tarde** I'm sick of them coming late; MF patient; — **del corazón** heart patient

enfisema M emphysema

enflaquecer[35] VI to get thin

enfocar[30] VT (los ojos) to focus; (un faro) to point; (una cámara) to train; (un tema) to approach

enfoque M (método) approach; (acción de enfocar) focusing

enfrentamiento M clash, confrontation

enfrentar VT (enemigos) to confront; (una dificultad) to face, to tackle; — **a dos personas** to pit two people against each other; **—se con** to clash with

enfrente ADV opposite; — **de** in front of, opposite

enfriamiento M (del aire) cooling; (de una persona) chill; (de la economía, las relaciones) cooling off

enfriar[28] VT to cool, to chill; VI **—se** to cool off

enfundar VT to sheathe

enfurecer[35] VT to infuriate, to enrage; VI **—se** to become enraged, to rage

enfurruñado ADJ sulky

enfurruñarse VI to sulk

engalanar VT (una mesa) to decorate; (a una muchacha) to dress up; **—se** to dress up

enganchar VT (bueyes) to hitch; (una red) to snag; (un teléfono) to hook up; (a los televidentes, a un adicto) to hook; VI **—se** to get hooked

enganche M (del gas, teléfono) connection, hookup; (de drogas) addictiveness; (de vagones) coupling; (de caballos) team; (primer pago) *Méx* down payment

enganchón M snag

engañador ADJ deceitful

engañar VT (mentir) to deceive; (ser infiel) to cheat on; — **el hambre** to ward off hunger; **—se** to deceive oneself

engaño M deceit, deception

engañoso ADJ (una persona) deceitful; (un

hecho) misleading

engastar VT to set

engaste M setting

engatusar VT to coax, to cajole

engendrar VT (emociones) to engender; (hijos) to father

englobar VT to encompass

engomar VT to glue

engordar VI to get fat, to put on weight; VT to make fat, to fatten; **esta semana he engordado dos kilos** I gained two kilos this week

engorroso ADJ irksome

engoznar VT to hinge

engranado ADJ meshed, interlocking; **estar —** to be in gear

engranaje M gears, gearing; **el — del partido** the party apparatus

engranar VT (meter una marcha) to put in gear, to throw into gear; (encajar) to mesh; — **la marcha atrás** to put [the car] in reverse

engrandecer[35] VT (a una persona) to aggrandize; (un palacio) to make more grandiose

engrapar VT to staple, to cramp

engrasar VT (untar) to grease; (manchar) to make greasy; (sobornar) to grease someone's palm; **—se** to get greasy

engrase M grease job

engreído ADJ conceited

engreírse[10] VI to become conceited

engrillar VT to shackle

engrosar VT (una manifestación) to swell; (un volumen) to grow; (una persona) to get fat

engrudo M paste

engullir[16] VT to gobble

enhebrar VT (un hilo) to thread; (cuentas) to string; — **idioteces** to string together a bunch of idiocies

enhorabuena F congratulation; INTERJ congratulations

enigma M (misterio) enigma, conundrum; (adivinanza) riddle; (problema) puzzle

enjabonar VT (poner jabón) to soap, to lather; (adular) to flatter

enjaezar[47] VT to harness

enjalbegar[40] VT to whitewash

enjambre M swarm

enjaular VT (un animal) to cage; (a una persona) to jail

enjuagar[40] VT to rinse; (ropa) to rinse out; (platos) to rinse off

enjuague M (limpieza) rinse, rinsing; (trama) scheme; — **bucal** mouthwash

enjugar[40] VT (la frente) to wipe; (lágrimas) to wipe away

enjuiciar VT to prosecute, to try

enjuto ADJ dry; (delgado) thin

enlace M (de trenes, web) link; (químico) bond;

(boda) marriage; (persona) liaison; —
  muerto dead link
enladrillado M brick pavement
enladrillar VT to brick, to pave with bricks
enlatar VT to can
enlazar[47] VT (unir) to link (también en la web);
  (sujetar con lazo) to rope, to lasso; VI to
  connect; **—se** to connect
enlodar VT to muddy; **—se** to get muddy
enloquecedor ADJ maddening
enloquecer[35] VT to drive crazy; VI to go crazy;
  —se to go crazy
enlosado M flagstone pavement
enlosar VT to pave with flagstones
enmantecar[30] VT to butter
enmarañar VT (pelo) to entangle; (problema) to
  complicate
enmarcar[30] VT (un cuadro) to frame; **se
  enmarca dentro de** it takes place in the
  context of
enmascarar VT to mask
enmendar[1] VT (una ley) to amend; (un texto) to
  revise; **— la situación** to mend matters; **no
  me enmiendes la plana** don't correct me;
  VI **—se** to mend one's ways
enmienda F (de una ley) amendment; (de un
  texto) revision
enmohecer[35] VT to mold; **—se** to get moldy, to
  mold
enmudecer[35] VT to silence; VI to go silent
ennegrecer[35] VI/VT to blacken
ennoblecer[35] VT to ennoble
enojadizo ADJ hotheaded
enojado ADJ angry, mad
enojar VT to anger; **—se** to get angry
enojo M anger
enojoso ADJ bothersome
enorgullecer[35] VT to fill with pride; **—se de** to
  take pride in
enorme ADJ enormous
enormemente ADV vastly
enramada F bower
enrarecido ADJ thin, rare
enrarecimiento M rarity, thinness
enredadera F creeper
enredar VT (enmarañar) to entangle;
  (complicar) to complicate; (involucrar) to mix
  up; VI to cause trouble; **—se** to get tangled
  up; **—se con** to become involved with
enredijo M tangle, snarl
enredo M (enredijo) snarl; (lío) mess;
  (amancebamiento) affair
enredoso ADJ complicated
enrejado M (de metal) grating, grate; (de
  varillas) lattice
enrejar VT to install a grate on
enrevesado ADJ involved
enriquecer[35] VT to enrich; **—se** to become rich
enriquecimiento M enrichment

enrojecer[35] VI/VT to redden
enrollar VT (manga, alfombra) to roll up; (hilo,
  cuerda, cinta) to wind up; **—se con** to
  become involved with
enronquecer[35] VT to make hoarse; VI to become
  hoarse
enroscar[30] VT (soga) to coil, to roll up; (tuerca)
  to screw in; (tapa) to screw on; **—se** (vid) to
  twine; (serpiente) to coil up
ensacar[30] VT to sack
ensalada F salad
ensalzar[47] VT to extol
ensanchar VT to widen; **—se** (una calle) to
  widen; (una falda) to flare
ensanche M (de una calle) widening; (de una
  ciudad) expansion
ensangrentado ADJ gory, bloody
ensangrentar VT to smear blood on; **—se** to get
  covered with blood
ensartar VT (cuentas) to string; (aguja) to
  thread; (con un pincho) to pierce; (historias)
  to rattle off
ensayar VT (probar) to try out; (intentar) to try;
  (analizar un metal) to assay; (practicar una
  obra teatral) to rehearse
ensayo M (intento) trial, attempt; (de teatro)
  rehearsal; (obra literaria) essay; (nuclear)
  testing; (de un metal) assay; **— clínico**
  clinical trial; **— general** dress rehearsal; **por
  — y error** by trial and error
enseguida ADV at once, immediately
ensenada F cove
enseña F ensign, flag
enseñanza F teaching, education; **—s** teachings
enseñar VT (mostrar) to show; (instruir) to
  teach; **— a** to teach how to
enseres M PL household utensils
ensillar VT to saddle, to saddle up
ensimismarse VI to lose oneself in thought
ensoberbecer[35] VT to make haughty; **—se** to
  become haughty
ensombrecer[35] VT (oscurecer) to make
  shadowy; (entristecer) to sadden
ensoñación F dream
ensordecedor ADJ deafening
ensordecer[35] VT to deafen
ensortijar VT to curl
ensuciar VT to dirty, to sully; **—se** (mancharse)
  to get dirty; (defecar) to soil oneself
ensueño M reverie, dream
entablar VT (relaciones) to establish; (un
  conflicto) to start; (una conversación) to
  strike up; (una demanda) to file; (una pelea)
  to pick
entablillar VT to splint
entallar VT to take in
entarimar VT to floor with planks
ente M (ser) entity; (excéntrico) weirdo;
  (agencia) agency

enteco ADJ sickly
entender² VT (comprender) to understand; (oír) to hear; (ser homosexual) *Esp* to be homosexual; **— de** to know about; **—se con** (comunicar) to communicate with; (llevarse bien) to get along with; **dar a —** to intimate; **yo me entiendo** I know what I'm doing; **se entiende** of course
entendido -da ADJ (comprendido) understood; (experto) expert; **tengo — que** I understand that; **caridad mal entendida** misguided charity; MF expert
entendimiento M understanding
enterado ADJ informed; **darse por —** to acknowledge; **estar — de** to be privy to
enterar VT to inform; **—se [de]** to find out [about]; **recién me entero** I just found out; **para que te enteres** just so you know
entereza F fortitude
enternecedor ADJ touching
enternecer³⁵ VT to touch; **—se** to be touched
entero ADJ (completo) entire, whole; (número) whole; **se mantuvo — durante el funeral** he held himself together during the funeral; M integer, whole number
enterramiento M (de un cable) burying; (de un difunto) burial
enterrar¹ VT (cable, muerto) to bury; (balón) to dunk
entibiar VT to make lukewarm; **—se** to become lukewarm
entidad F entity; **de —** significant; **— bancaria** banking institution
entienda, entiende *ver* entender
entierro M burial, funeral
entintar VT to stain with ink
entoldar VT to cover with an awning
entomología F entomology
entonación F intonation
entonar VT to sing; VI to sing in tune; **— con** to go well with; **—se** to get tipsy
entonces ADV then; **desde —** ever since; **hasta — until** then; **el — presidente** the then president; CONJ (así que) so
entornado ADJ half-open
entornar VT (una puerta) to leave ajar; (los ojos) to close partially
entorno M (lo que rodea) surroundings; (medio ambiente, informático) environment; **— de trabajo** work environment
entorpecer³⁵ VT (los sentidos) to dull; (el paso) to hinder; **—se** to become sluggish
entorpecimiento M (de los sentidos) dullness; (del paso) hindrance
entrada F (sitio por donde se entra, de un actor) entrance; (acción de entrar, artículo de diccionario) entry; (asistentes a un espectáculo) gate; (oportunidad para actuar) opening; (billete, derecho, precio de entrar)

admission; (llegada) arrival; (primer plato) appetizer; (pago inicial) down payment; (tiempo en béisbol) inning; **—s** cash receipts; **— de coches** driveway; **— de datos** data input; **— por partida doble** double entry; **de —** from the start
entramado M lattice
entrante ADJ (alcalde) incoming; (año) next; M recess
entrañable ADJ (amistad) close; (persona) endearing
entrañas F PL (intestinos) entrails, *fam* guts; (sentimientos) heart, core; **— de la tierra** bowels of the earth; **de mis —** of my own flesh and blood
entrar VI (ir hacia adentro) to go in; (comenzar el día de trabajo) to come in; (caber) to fit; **dejar —** to let in; **hacer — en razón** to bring to reason; **— a medicina** to go into medicine; **— en calor** to warm up; **— en coma** to go into a coma; **— en/a un cuarto** to enter a room; **— en materia** to get to the meat of a matter; **— en vigencia/vigor** to go into effect; **me entró miedo** I became afraid; **me entró sueño** I got sleepy; **no sé cómo —le a esa chica** I don't know how to approach that girl; **la física no me entra** I can't learn physics; **no entra entre mis favoritos** it is not included among my favorites; **la semana que entra** next week; **este vestido no me entra** this dress doesn't fit me; **seis entra dos veces en doce** six goes into twelve two times; **hazle —** show him in; VT (datos) to enter, to input
entre PREP (dos) between; (muchos) among; **— vaso y vaso** between glasses; **— dientes** under one's breath
entreabierto ADJ ajar, half-open
entreabrir⁷⁴ VT (puerta) to crack open; (los ojos) to half-open
entreacto M intermission
entrecano ADJ graying
entrecejo M space between the eyebrows
entrecortado ADJ (voz) faltering; (respiración) irregular
entrecortarse VI to falter
entrecruzar⁴⁷ VT to interlace; **—se** to cross
entredicho LOC ADV **en —** in doubt
entrega F (de un paquete) delivery; (de un manuscrito) submission; (al vicio) surrender; (de una novela) installment; (de revista) issue; **a la —** on delivery; **por —s** serial; **— a domicilio** home delivery; **— de premios** presentation of awards; **— el mismo día** same-day delivery; **— gratuita** free delivery; **— inicial** down payment
entregar⁴⁰ VT (un paquete) to deliver; (a un rehén, prisionero) to hand over; (a un delincuente) to turn in; (a una hija en

matrimonio) to give; (premios) to hand out,
to present; (tarea escolar) to hand in; (el
coche) to trade in; —**se** [a] (la policía) to
surrender [to]; (a una misión) to dedicate
oneself to
entrelazar[47] VT to intertwine
entremés M (obra de teatro) interlude; (comida)
hors d'oeuvre
entremeter VT to insert; —**se en** (meterse) to
get mixed up in; (inmiscuirse) to meddle in
entremetido-da ADJ meddlesome, nosy; MF
meddler, busybody
entremezclar VT to intermingle
entrenador-ora MF trainer, coach; — **en jefe**
head coach
entrenamiento M training
entrenar VI/VT to train
entrepierna F (del cuerpo) crotch; (de
pantalón) inseam
entrepiso M mezzanine
entresacar[30] VT (seleccionar) to cull;
(adelgazar) to thin
entresuelo M (de hotel) mezzanine; (de cine)
balcony
entretanto ADV meanwhile
entretejer VT (el pelo, una tela) to weave; (una
historia) to weave together
entretener[58] VT (hacer atrasar) to delay;
(distraer) to distract; (divertir) to entertain;
—**se** (divertirse) to amuse oneself;
(detenerse) to delay
entretenido ADJ entertaining
entretenimiento M entertainment,
amusement
entrever[72, 74] VT (apenas) to catch a glimpse of;
(a lo lejos) to make out
entreverar VT to mix, to intersperse; —**se** to
meddle
entrevía F gauge
entrevista F interview; — **de salida** exit
interview
entrevistar VT to interview; —**se con** to have
an interview with
entristecer[35] VT to sadden; —**se** to become sad
entrometerse VI to meddle, to interfere
entrometido-da ADJ meddlesome, nosy; MF
meddler, busybody
entronque M (ferroviario) junction;
(parentesco) relationship
entropía F entropy
entumecido ADJ (dedo, diente) numb;
(músculo) stiff
entumecimiento M (de los dedos, dientes)
numbness; (de los músculos) stiffness
enturbiar VT (el agua) to muddy; (una decisión)
to muddle; (el juicio, la alegría) to cloud; —**se**
(agua) to get muddy; (alegría) to be marred
entusiasmado ADJ enthusiastic, excited
entusiasmar VT to excite; —**se** to be excited

entusiasmo M enthusiasm, excitement
entusiasta MF enthusiast; ADJ enthusiastic
enumerar VT to enumerate
enunciado M utterance
enunciar VT (palabras) to enunciate; (una
teoría) to articulate, to enunciate
envainar VT to sheathe
envalentonar VT to embolden, to make bold;
—**se** to become bold
envanecer[35] VT to make vain; —**se** to become
vain
envarado ADJ stiff, staid
envaramiento M stiffness
envasar VT to package; — **al vacío** to
vacuum-pack
envase M packaging
envejecer[35] VT to make old; **ese maquillaje te
envejece** that makeup makes you look older;
VI to grow old, to age
envejecimiento M aging
envenenamiento M poisoning
envenenar VT to poison
envergadura F (de un avión) wingspan; (de un
ave) wingspread; (de un evento, proyecto)
importance
envés M SG back
enviado-da MF (político) envoy; (periodístico)
correspondent
enviar[28] VT to send; — **por fax** to fax
enviciar VT to corrupt; —**se con** to get hooked
on
envidia F envy
envidiable ADJ enviable
envidiar VT to envy
envidioso ADJ envious, jealous
envilecer[35] VT to debase
envío M (acción) shipping; (mercancía)
shipment; (manuscrito) submission; — **de
anotación** touchdown pass; — **rápido**
express delivery
envite M bet
envoltorio M (cosa envuelta) bundle;
(envoltura) wrapper
envoltura F wrapping, wrapper; — **de plástico
transparente** shrinkwrap
envolver[6, 74] VT (involucrar) to involve; (cubrir)
to wrap; (atrapar) to entangle; (rodear) to
surround; —**se** to become involved
envuelto, envuelva, envuelve ver envolver
enyesar VT (enlucir con yeso) to plaster;
(escayolar) to put in a cast
enzima F enzyme
épica F epic
epicentro M epicenter
épico ADJ epic
epidemia F epidemic
epidémico ADJ epidemic
epidermis F epidermis
epifanía F epiphany

epiglotis F epiglottis
epilepsia F epilepsy
epiléptico ADJ epileptic
epílogo M epilogue
episódico ADJ episodic
episodio M episode
epitafio M epitaph
epítome M epitome
época F (momento) time, period; (período histórico) age; (temporada) season; (período geológico) epoch
epopeya F epic poem
equidad F equity
equidistante ADJ equidistant
equilibrado ADJ balanced; M balancing
equilibrar VT to balance; — **un presupuesto** to balance a budget
equilibrio M equilibrium, balance; **perder el** — to lose one's balance; **hacer —s** to do a balancing act
equino ADJ & M equine
equinoccio M equinox
equipaje M baggage, luggage
equipamiento M equipment
equipar VT to equip, to outfit
equiparar VT to equate
equipo M (materiales) equipment; (grupo) team; — **de vida** life-support system; — **deportivo** sweatsuit; — **de esquí** ski gear
equitación F (arte) horsemanship; (actividad) riding
equitativo ADJ equitable
equivalente ADJ equivalent
equivaler[60] VI to be equivalent; **lo que equivale a decir** which amounts to saying
equivocación F mistake
equivocado ADJ mistaken, wrong; **estar —** to be wrong/mistaken
equivocar[30] VT to mistake; **—se** to be mistaken, to make a mistake, to miscalculate; **—se de sala** to choose the wrong room; **si no me equivoco** unless I'm mistaken; **me equivoqué de baño** I went into the wrong bathroom
equívoco ADJ (ambiguo) equivocal; (moralmente dudoso) questionable; M misunderstanding
era F (período) era, age; (lugar donde se trilla) threshing floor; (parcela) plot
era, eras ver ser
erario M treasury
erección F erection
eréctil ADJ erectile
erecto ADJ (cabeza) erect; (postura) upright
eres ver ser
ergonomía F ergonomics
ergonómico ADJ ergonomic
erguido ADJ erect, upright
erguir[13] VT to lift, to raise; **—se** to rise

erial M uncultivated land
erigir[46] VT (construir) to erect; (fundar) to found; **—se en** to set oneself up as
Eritrea F Eritrea
eritreo -a ADJ & MF Eritrean
erizado ADJ bristly; — **de** bristling with
erizar[47] VT to set on end; **—se** to bristle
erizo M hedgehog; — **de mar** sea urchin; **ser un —** to be a grouch
ermitaño -ña MF (persona) hermit; M (cangrejo) hermit crab
erógeno ADJ erogenous
erosión F erosion
erótico ADJ erotic
erotismo M eroticism
erradicación F eradication
erradicar[30] VT to eradicate, to root out
errado ADJ erroneous, in error
errante ADJ wandering
errar[21] VT to miss; — **el cálculo** to miscalculate; VI (estar equivocado) to be mistaken; (vagar) to roam, to rove, to wander
errata F misprint, typographical error
errático ADJ erratic
erróneo ADJ erroneous
error M error, mistake; — **de hecho** factual error; — **de imprenta** misprint; — **no forzado** unforced error; — **tipográfico** typo
eructar VI to belch, to burp
eructo M belch, burp
erudición F erudition, learning, scholarship
erudito -ta ADJ (persona) erudite; (obra) scholarly, learned; MF scholar
erupción F eruption; **hacer —** to erupt
es ver ser
esbelto ADJ slender
esbozar[47] VT to outline; — **una sonrisa** to give a hint of a smile
esbozo M sketch, outline; — **de una sonrisa** hint of a smile
escabechar VT to pickle
escabroso ADJ (agreste) rugged; (espinoso) thorny; (sórdido) lurid, sordid
escabullirse[16] VI (ladrones) to slip away, to steal away; (lagartijas) to scurry away/off; — **de** to wriggle out of
escafandra F (para el agua) scuba gear; (para el espacio) spacesuit
escala F (escalera, escalafón) ladder; (serie de grados, notas, serie ascendente) scale; (parada) stopover; — **de sueldos** salary range, wage scale; **hacer — en** to stop over at; — **salarial** wage scale, pay scale; **a — nacional** nationwide; **a/de gran —** large-scale; **sin —s** nonstop
escalada F (de una montaña) climb; (de violencia) escalation
escalador -ora MF climber

escalar VT (subir) to scale, to climb; (cambiar de tamaño) scale

escaldadura F scald

escaldar VT (la piel) to scald; (las verduras) to blanch; —**se** to get scalded

escalera F (en un edificio) stairs, staircase; (portátil) ladder; (de naipes) straight; — **mecánica** escalator; — **de caracol** spiral/ winding staircase; — **de color** straight flush; — **de incendios** fire escape; — **real** royal flush

escalfar VT to poach

escalinata F grand staircase

escalofriante ADJ chilling, hair-raising

escalofrío M chill; —**s** the shivers

escalón M (peldaño) step, stair; (de escalera de mano, de escalafón) rung; (terraza) rung; (formación militar) echelon

escalonar VT (distribuir) to stagger; (aterrazar) to terrace

escalope M scallop

escama F (de animal) scale; (de piel, corteza) flake

escamar VT to scale

escamoso ADJ (animal) scaly; (piel) flaky

escamotear VT (esconder) to palm; (robar) to snatch; (eludir) to shirk

escampar VI to clear up

escandalizar[47] VT (chocar) to scandalize; (causar escándalo) to cause a scandal; —**se** to be shocked

escándalo M (suceso vergonzoso) scandal; (riña) uproar

escandaloso ADJ (chocante) scandalous, shocking; (ruidoso) raucous

escandir VT *lit* to scan

escaneado M scanning

escanear VT to scan

escáner M scanner; — **color** color scanner

escaño M seat in parliament

escapada F (escape) escape

escapar VI (de un lugar, una situación) to escape; (de alguien, de una responsabilidad) to run away; —**se** (persona) to escape; (gas) to leak; **se me escapó una sonrisa** I inadvertently smiled; **Matilde se me está escapando de las manos** Matilde is getting out of hand

escaparate M shop window

escapatoria F (de un lugar) escape, way out; (legal) loophole

escape M (fantasía, escapatoria) escape; (de coche) exhaust; (de gas, agua) leak

escápula F scapula

escarabajo M beetle

escaramuza F skirmish

escaramuzar[47] VI to skirmish

escarbar VI/VT to dig, to scratch; — **en los archivos** to dig around in the files; —**se los dientes** to pick one's teeth

escarcha F frost

escarchar VI to frost

escardar VT to weed

escarlata ADJ INV & M (color) scarlet; F (enfermedad) scarlet fever

escarlatina F scarlet fever

escarmentar[1] VI to learn one's lesson; VT to teach a lesson

escarmiento M lesson; **que te sirva de** — let that be a lesson to you

escarnecer[35] VT to deride

escarnio M derision

escarpa F steep slope

escarpado ADJ steep, precipitous; M steep slope

escasear VI to be scarce

escasez F (falta) shortage; (carestía) scarcity, want

escaso ADJ sparse, scarce; **una docena escasa** a scant dozen; — **de** short on; — **de personal** short-handed

escatimar VT to skimp on; **no** — **gastos** to spare no expense

escena F (fragmento de una obra de teatro, episodio) scene; (escenario) stage; **montar una** — to make a scene; **en** — on stage; **poner en** — to stage; **entrar en** — to go on stage

escenario M stage

escénico ADJ **pánico** — stage fright

escenificación F staging

escepticismo M skepticism

escéptico -ca ADJ skeptical; MF skeptic

escisión F split

esclarecer[35] VT to elucidate

esclavitud F slavery

esclavizar[47] VT to enslave

esclavo -va MF slave

esclerosis F sclerosis; — **múltiple** multiple sclerosis

esclusa F (de un canal) lock; (de una presa) floodgate, sluice gate

escoba F broom

escobilla F whisk broom

escocer[34] VI to sting

escocés -esa ADJ Scottish; **[cuadros]** escoceses plaid; MF Scot; M (whisky) Scotch; (lengua) Scots

Escocia F Scotland

escoger[45] VT to choose

escolar MF pupil; ADJ **año** — school year

escoliosis F scoliosis

escollo M (arrecife) reef; (obstáculo) obstacle

escolta F (policial) escort; MF (persona) escort; (baloncesto) shooting guard

escoltar VT to escort

escombros M PL rubble, debris

esconder VT to hide; VI —**se** to hide

escondidas LOC ADV **a** — on the sly; **entrar a** — to sneak in; **meter algo a** — to sneak something in; **jugar a las** — to play hide and seek

escondite M (en un juego) hiding place; (de ladrón) hideout; (de cazador) blind; **jugar al** — to play hide and seek

escondrijo M hiding place

escopeta F shotgun

escoplo M chisel

escora F listing

escorar VI to list

escorbuto M scurvy

escoria F (de metales) slag; (de la sociedad) scum, dregs

escorpión M scorpion

escotado ADJ low-cut

escote M (parte del vestido) neckline; (parte del cuerpo) cleavage; **pagar a** — to go Dutch

escotilla F hatch

escozor M smarting sensation; — **vaginal** vaginal itching

escribiente MF clerk

escribir[74] VI/VT to write; **¿cómo se escribe?** how do you spell it? — **a máquina** to type

escrito ADJ written; — **a máquina** typewritten; **no** — unwritten; **por** — in writing; M document

escrito *ver* escribir

escritor -ora MF writer, author

escritorio M (mueble) desk; (oficina) office

escritura F (acción de escribir) writing; (certificado de propiedad) deed; — **de traspaso** conveyance; — **de venta** bill of sale

escroto M scrotum

escrúpulo M scruple, qualm; **sin** —**s** unscrupulous

escrupuloso ADJ scrupulous

escrutar VT (a una persona) to scrutinize; (el horizonte) to scan; (votos) to count

escrutinio M (examen) scrutiny; (recuento) vote count

escuadra F (de buques, soldados) squadron; (instrumento) square

escuadrilla F (de aviones) flight of aircraft; (de buques) squadron

escuadrón M squadron; — **de la muerte** death squad

escualidez F (delgadez) skinniness; (suciedad) squalor

escuálido ADJ (sucio) squalid; (delgado) thin

escuchar VT to listen to; (oír) to hear; VI to listen; — **a hurtadillas** to eavesdrop

escudar VT to shield

escudo M (arma defensiva) shield; (moneda de Portugal) escudo; — **de armas** coat of arms

escudriñar VT (a una persona) to scrutinize, to peer at; (el horizonte) to scan

escuela F school; — **industrial** trade school; — **normal** school of education; — **pública**

public school; — **primaria** elementary school; — **secundaria** secondary school; **tener** — to have good technique

escueto ADJ (explicación) succinct; (verdad) simple

esculpir VI/VT to sculpture, to sculpt

escultor -ora MF sculptor

escultura F sculpture

escupir VI/VT to spit

escupitajo M spit

escurridizo ADJ (acera) slippery; (ladrón) elusive, slippery

escurrir VI/VT (platos, verduras) to drain; (ropa) to wring out; —**se** to slink away

ese ADJ DEM that, those; **esa chica se llama Matilde** that girl is called Matilde; **esas ciudades son antiguas** those cities are old; PRON that one, those; **ese es el mayor** that one is the oldest; **esos son mis hijos** those are my children

esencia F essence

esencial ADJ essential; **lo** — the gist, the bottom line, the name of the game

esfera F (cuerpo sólido) sphere; (espacio, ámbito) realm, sphere; (de reloj) face, dial; — **de influencia** sphere of influence

esférico ADJ spherical; M soccer ball

esfínter M sphincter

esforzado ADJ valiant

esforzarse[49] VI to try hard, to exert oneself; — **por** to strive to, to make an effort to

esfuerzo M effort

esfumar VT to tone down; —**se** to vanish, to fizzle out

esgrima F fencing; **practicar** — to fence

esgrimir VT (armas) to brandish, to wield; (argumentos) to employ

eslabón M chain link; — **perdido** missing link

eslabonar VT to link

eslavo -va ADJ Slavic; MF Slav

eslogan M slogan

eslovaco ADJ & MF Slovakian; M (lengua) Slovakian

Eslovaquia F Slovakia

Eslovenia F Slovenia

esloveno -na ADJ & MF Slovene; M (lengua) Slovene

esmaltar VT to enamel

esmalte M enamel; — **de uñas** nail polish

esmeradamente ADV carefully

esmerado ADJ careful, painstaking

esmeralda F emerald

esmerarse VI to take pains

esmerilado ADJ frosted; M frosting

esmerilar VT to frost

esmero M care

esmirriado ADJ scrawny

esmoquin M tuxedo

esnifar VT to snort

esnob M snob
esnórquel M snorkel
eso PRON DEM that; — **es verdad** that's true; — **sí** granted; **a** — **de las tres** at about three o'clock; **de —, nada** no way! yeah, right! **en** — **llega y me dice** at that moment he arrives and says to me; **y** — **que le dije que viniese temprano** even when I told him to come early
esófago M esophagus
esotérico ADJ esoteric
espaciado M pitch, spacing; — **de palabras** word spacing
espacial ADJ spatial; **nave** — spaceship
espaciar VT to space; —**se** to space out
espacio M (capacidad) space, room; (superficie) expanse; (separación entre líneas) space, spacing; (en un formulario) blank space; (porción de tiempo) span; — **aéreo** aerospace; — **entre caracteres** letterspacing; — **exterior** outer space; — **noticioso** newscast; **a doble** — double-spaced; **a un** — single-spaced; **por** — **de una semana** for a week
espacioso ADJ spacious, roomy
espada F sword; —**s** (palo de naipes) swords; — **de doble filo** double-edged sword; **estar entre la** — **y la pared** to be between a rock and a hard place
espalda F back; — **mojada** *pey* wetback; **a** —**s de alguien** behind someone's back; **caerse de** —**s** to fall on one's back; **nadar [de]** — to do the backstroke; **tener las** —**s anchas** to take a lot of abuse; **volver las** —**s** to turn one's back
espaldar M chair back
espantadizo ADJ easily scared
espantado ADJ frightened
espantajo M scarecrow
espantar VT to frighten, to scare; (ahuyentar) to frighten away, to scare away; —**se** to get scared; M SG **espantapájaros** scarecrow
espanto M fright, dread; **estás hecho un** — you look a sight; **estoy curado de** — nothing surprises me anymore
espantoso ADJ frightful, dreadful
España F Spain
español -ola ADJ Spanish; MF Spaniard; M (lengua) Spanish
esparadrapo M surgical tape
esparcimiento M (recreo) relaxation; (reparto) spreading
esparcir[33] VT to scatter, to spread; —**se** to amuse oneself
espárrago M asparagus
espasmo M spasm, jerk
espasmódico ADJ spasmodic, jerky
espástico ADJ spastic
espátula F spatula

especia F spice
especial ADJ & M special; **en** — in particular, especially
especialidad F specialty, specialization
especialista MF specialist
especialización F specialization
especializar[47] VT to specialize; —**se en** to specialize in, to major in
especialmente ADV (de forma particular) specially; **esto lo hice** — **para ti** I made this specially for you; (en especial) especially; **este tipo es** — **bueno** this kind is especially good
especie F (clase) kind; (categoría biológica) species; —**s en peligro de extinción** endangered species; **pagar en** — to pay in kind; **una** — **de** a kind of
especiero M spice rack
especificar[30] VT to specify
específico ADJ & M specific
espécimen M specimen
espectacular ADJ spectacular
espectáculo M (escándalo) spectacle; (actuación pública) show; (vista) sight; **dar el** — to make a spectacle of oneself
espectador -ora MF (de un espectáculo) spectator; (de un suceso) onlooker
espectro M (fantasma) specter; (de la luz, de un antibiótico) spectrum
especulación F speculation
especulador -ora MF speculator
especular VT to speculate; ADJ mirror; **imagen** — mirror image
especulativo ADJ speculative
espejismo M (en el desierto) mirage; (ilusión) illusion
espejo M mirror; — **de cuerpo entero** full-length mirror; — **retrovisor** rearview mirror
espeluznante ADJ hair-raising
espeluznar VT to terrify; —**se** to be terrified
espera F (acción de esperar) wait; (aplazamiento) extension; **estar en** — **de** to be waiting for
esperanza F hope; — **de vida** life expectancy; **con una** — **de voto del 12,5%** expected to get 12.5% of the vote
esperanzado ADJ hopeful
esperanzador ADJ hopeful
esperanzar[47] VT to give hope to
esperar VT (tener esperanza) to hope; (estar embarazada, anticipar) to expect; (aguardar) to wait for; VI to wait; **como era de** — not surprisingly; **era de** — it was to be expected; **espera sentado** don't hold your breath; **estoy esperando un milagro** I'm hoping for a miracle; **todavía espera confirmación** it still awaits confirmation
esperma MF sperm
espermicida M spermicide

esperpento M fright, grotesque person or thing
espesar VT to thicken
espeso ADJ (pelo, sopa, niebla) thick; (cejas) bushy
espesor M thickness
espesura F (espesor) thickness; (lugar poblado de matorrales) thicket
espetar VT (decir bruscamente) to blurt out; (pinchar) to skewer
espeto, espetón M spit
espía MF spy
espiar[28] VI to spy; VT to spy on
espichar VI *fam* to croak, to bite the dust
espiga F spike
espigar[40] VT to glean; VI to grow spikes; —**se** to grow tall
espina F (de planta) thorn; (de pez) fish bone; — **dorsal** spinal column; **me quedé con la** — I was left wondering
espinaca F spinach
espinal ADJ spinal
espinazo M spine, backbone
espinilla F (en la pierna) shin; (de animal) shank; (acné, comedón) blackhead
espino M thorny shrub
espinoso ADJ thorny
espionaje M espionage
espiración F expiration
espiral ADJ & F spiral
espirar VI/VT to exhale, to breathe out, to expire
espíritu M (ánima, fantasma, intención de una ley) spirit; (alma) soul; — **fuerte** free spirit; — **deportivo** sportsmanship; — **emprendedor** can-do attitude, entrepreneurship; — **Santo** Holy Spirit
espiritual ADJ & M spiritual
espiritualidad F spirituality
espita F spigot
espléndido ADJ (estupendo) splendid; (dispendioso) lavish
esplendor M splendor
esplendoroso ADJ magnificent
espliego M lavender
espolear VT to spur
espoleta F bomb fuse
espolón M (de gallo, planta, estímulo) spur; (de buque) ram
espolvorear VT to dust, to sprinkle
esponja F (animal, utensilio) sponge; (borracho) souse
esponjado ADJ spongy
esponjar VT to make spongy; —**se** to become spongy
esponjoso ADJ spongy
esponsales M PL betrothal
espontaneidad F spontaneity
espontáneo ADJ spontaneous
espora F spore
esposar VT to handcuff

esposo-sa M husband; F wife; **esposas** handcuffs
espuela F spur
espulgar[40] VT to delouse
espuma F (de cerveza) froth; (de jabón) suds, lather; (de la boca) foam; (de colchón) foam rubber; (de mar) foam, spray; **echar** — **por la boca** to foam at the mouth; **hacer** — to make suds
espumar VT (quitar la espuma) to skim; (formar espuma) to foam
espumarajo M foam; **echar** —**s por la boca** to foam at the mouth
espumillón M tinsel
espumoso ADJ foamy
esputo M sputum
esquela F note; — **mortuoria** death notice
esquelético ADJ skeletal
esqueleto M (huesos) skeleton; (armazón) framework; **mover el** — (bailar) to dance; (moverse) to move
esquema M outline; **romperle los** —**s a alguien** (planes) to ruin one's plans; (conceptos) to shatter one's preconceptions
esquí M (tabla) ski; (deporte) skiing; — **acuático** (tabla) water ski; (deporte) waterskiing; **hacer** — **acuático** to water-ski
esquiar[28] VI to ski
esquila F (cencerro) cowbell; (acción de esquilar) shearing
esquilador-ora MF sheep shearer
esquilar VT to shear, to clip
esquileo M shearing
esquimal ADJ & MF Eskimo; M (lengua) Eskimo
esquina F corner; **en cada** — everywhere
esquinero ADJ **mesa esquinera** corner table; M cornerback
esquirol M strikebreaker; *pey* scab
esquivar VT (a una persona) to avoid; (un golpe) to dodge
esquivo ADV (tímido) shy, coy; (huraño) aloof; (reservado) elusive; (indirecto) evasive
esquizofrenia F schizophrenia
estabilidad F stability
estabilización F stabilization
estabilizar[47] VT to stabilize
estable ADJ (mesa) stable; (precio) firm; (huésped) long-term
establecer[35] VT to establish; (averiguar) to ascertain; — **una cita** to set up an appointment; —**se** to settle
establecimiento M establishment
establezca, establezco *ver* establecer
establishment M establishment
establo M stable
estaca F (con punta) stake; (gruesa) club
estacada F stockade; **dejar en la** — to leave in the lurch
estacar[30] VT (atar) to stake; (delimitar) to

stake off

estación F (de tren, autobús, radio) station; (del año) season; — **bípeda** bipedal stance; — **de bomberos** fire station; — **de esquí** ski resort; — **de servicio** gas/filling station; — **de trabajo** workstation; — **espacial** space station

estacional ADJ seasonal

estacionamiento M (acción) parking; (lugar) parking lot

estacionar VT (tropas) to station; (un vehículo) to park; —**se** (un coche) to park; (precios) to level off

estacionario ADJ stationary

estadía F stay

estadio M (recinto deportivo) stadium; (fase) stage

estadista M statesman; F stateswoman

estadística F (ciencia) statistics; —**s** (datos numéricos) statistics

estado M (situación, unidad política) state; — **civil** marital status; — **de cuenta** bank statement; — **de alarma** state of emergency; — **de ánimo** state of mind; — **de excepción** martial law; — **de guerra** state of war; — **de sitio** state of siege; — **mayor** chiefs of staff; — **policíaco** police state; **de** — **sólido** solid state; **en** — **interesante** expecting; **en** — **vegetativo** in a vegetative state, brain-dead

Estados Unidos M PL/SG United States

estadounidense ADJ & MF American

estafa F swindle, scam, racket

estafador -ora MF swindler, racketeer

estafar VT to swindle

estalactita F stalactite

estalagmita F stalagmite

estallar VI (una bomba) to explode; (un globo) to burst; (una guerra) to break out; (una persona) to snap; — **de risa** to burst out laughing; — **en una carcajada** to burst out laughing; **hacer** — to set off

estallido M (explosión) explosion; (ruido) bang, report

estampa F (de revista) illustration; (imagen) image; (apariencia) appearance; **de buena** — good-looking; **la viva** — **de la madre** the spitting image of her mother; **la viva** — **de la desolación** the very picture of desolation

estampado ADJ printed; M (tela) print; (acción) printing

estampar VT (en tela, papel) to print; (con un molde, en metal) to stamp; —**le un beso a alguien** to plant a kiss on someone

estampida F stampede

estampido M bang

estampilla F stamp

estampillar VT to stamp

estancado ADJ stagnant

estancamiento M stagnation (también

económico)

estancar[30] VT to stem; to dam; to block; —**se** to stagnate

estancia F (estadía) stay; (habitación) hall; (hacienda) RP cattle ranch

estanco ADJ waterproof; M government store

estándar ADJ & M standard

estandarización F standardization

estandarizar[47] VT to standardize

estandarte M standard, banner

estanque M pond

estante M (tabla) shelf; (mueble) bookcase

estantería F (mueble) bookcase; (de biblioteca) stack

estañar VT to tin-plate

estaño M tin

estar[63] VI to be; — **a tres kilómetros de aquí** to be three kilometers from here; — **bien** to be all right; — **mal/enfermo del corazón** to have heart trouble; — **de más** to be unnecessary; — **para** to be about to; — **por** (a favor de) to be in favor of; (a punto de) to be about to; — **trabajando duro** to be working hard; **¿a cuántos estamos?** what day of the month is it? **ahí está** that's it; **¿está Alice?** is Alice there? **están muy buenos tus zapatos nuevos** your new shoes are nice; **estate tranquilo** don't worry; **no** — to be out; **cuarto de** — living room

estatal ADJ **compañía** — state-run company

estático ADJ static

estatua F statue

estatura F (importancia) stature; (altura física) height

estatutario ADJ statutory

estatuto M (ley) statute; (de una sociedad) bylaw; — **de quiebras** bankruptcy law

este ADJ DEM this, these; **esta chica se llama Hilary** this girl is called Hilary; **estas ciudades son antiguas** these cities are old; PRON DEM this one, these; — **es el mayor** this one is the oldest; **estos son mis hijos** these are my children; M & ADJ east; **hacia el** — eastward

estela F (de una embarcación) wake; (de humo, polvo) trail; **dejar una** — to leave a trail

estelar ADJ stellar

estenotipista MF court reporter

estentóreo ADJ booming

estepa F steppe

estera F mat

estercolar VT to fertilize with manure

estercolero M dunghill

estéreo ADJ & M stereo; **en** — in stereo

estereotipo M stereotype

estéril ADJ (gasa, esfuerzo) sterile; (mujer) barren

esterilidad F sterility

esterilizar[47] VT to sterilize

esternón M sternum, breastbone
esteroide M steroid; — **anabólico** anabolic steroid
estertor M death rattle
estética F aesthetics
estético ADJ aesthetic
estetoscopio M stethoscope
estibador M stevedore, longshoreman
estibar VT to stow
estiércol M manure
estigma M stigma
estigmatizar[47] VT to stigmatize
estilarse VI to be in style; **eso no se estila aquí** that's not done here
estilística F stylistics
estilístico ADJ stylistic
estilo M (literario, estético, caligráfico) style; (de natación) stroke; — **de vida** lifestyle; — **espalda** backstroke; — **indirecto** reported speech; — **libre** freestyle; — **mariposa** butterfly stroke; — **pecho** breaststroke; — **perrito** dog paddle; **cosas por el** — things like that
estima F esteem, regard
estimación F (cálculo) estimate; (estima) estimation
estimado ADJ esteemed; — **Sr.** Dear Sir
estimar VT (apreciar) to esteem; (determinar el valor) to estimate; (opinar) to think
estimulación F stimulation
estimulante ADJ stimulating; M stimulant
estimular VT (despertar, excitar) to stimulate; (alentar) to encourage
estímulo M stimulus
estío M *lit* summer
estipendio M stipend
estipulación F stipulation
estipular VT to stipulate
estirado ADJ stuck-up
estirar VT (alargar) to stretch; — **el cuello** to crane one's neck; — **la pata** *fam* to kick the bucket; (crecer) to grow; —**se** to stretch
estirón M growth spurt; **pegar un** — to have a growth spurt
estirpe F lineage
estival ADJ **vacaciones** —**es** summer vacation
esto PRON DEM this; — **es** that is to say; **a todo** — meanwhile; **en** — at this point
estocada F thrust; **lanzar una** — to thrust
estofa F type; **de baja** — low-class
estofado M stew
estofar VT to stew
estoico -ca ADJ & MF stoic
estolón M runner
estómago M stomach
Estonia F Estonia
estonio -nia ADJ & MF Estonian; M (lengua) Estonian
estopa F tow

estorbar VT (obstaculizar) to hinder, to impede; (molestar) to be a nuisance
estorbo M (obstáculo) hindrance, impediment; (molestia) nuisance
estornino M starling
estornudar VI to sneeze
estornudo M sneeze
estoy *ver* estar
estrado M bench
estrafalario ADJ bizarre, outlandish
estragar[40] VT (físicamente) to devastate; (moralmente) to corrupt
estrago M havoc; **hacer** —**s** to wreak havoc
estrangular VT to strangle
estratagema F stratagem
estrategia F strategy; (de negocios, deportes) game plan; — **de salida** exit strategy
estratégico ADJ strategic
estrato M stratum, layer; — **social** social class
estratosfera F stratosphere
estrechamente ADV closely
estrechamiento M constriction
estrechar VT (angostar) to narrow; (abrazar) to embrace; **la estrechó en sus brazos** he held her in his arms; —**se** to get narrower; —**se la mano** to shake hands
estrechez F (cualidad de estrecho) narrowness; (acción de estrechar) narrowing; (aprietos) dire straits
estrecho ADJ narrow; **la falda le quedaba estrecha** the skirt was too tight for her; M strait
estrella F star; — **binaria** binary star; — **de cine** movie star; — **de mar** starfish; — **fugaz** shooting star, falling star; **ver las** —**s** to see stars
estrellado ADJ (como una estrella) starlike; (cubierto de estrellas) starry
estrellar VT (aplastar) to smash; (romper) to crack; —**se** (avión) to crash; (intento) to fail; —**se contra** to smash into
estremecer[35] VT to make shudder; **el terremoto estremeció París** the earthquake rocked Paris; —**se** to shudder
estremecimiento M shudder
estrenar VT (un vestido) to wear for the first time; (una película, obra de teatro) to debut; (una bicicleta) to try out for the first time; (un título) to use for the first time; —**se** to debut
estreno M (de una película) premiere; (de un objeto) first use; (de una actividad) debut
estreñido ADJ (constipado) constipated; (antipático) uptight
estreñimiento M constipation
estreñir[11] VT to constipate; —**se** to become constipated
estrépito M racket, clatter; **causar** — to clatter
estrepitoso ADJ noisy
estrés M stress

estresante ADJ stressful, high-pressure
estresar VT to stress [out]
estría F (en la piel) stretch mark; (en una columna) flute; (en mármol) striation
estriado ADJ (piel) covered with stretch marks; (columna) fluted; (piedra) streaked
estriar[28] VT to flute; —**se** to get stretch marks
estribación F spur
estribar VI — **en** (apoyarse en) to lean on; (radicar en) to lie in
estribillo M refrain
estribo M (de silla, oído) stirrup; (de coche) running board; **perder los** —**s** to fly off the handle
estribor M starboard
estricnina F strychnine
estricto ADJ strict
estridente ADJ strident
estrofa F verse, stanza
estrógeno M estrogen
estropajo M scrubber; **tengo la boca que es un** — my mouth is as dry as a bone
estropajoso ADJ sinewy
estropear VT to ruin
estructura F structure
estructuración F structuring
estructural ADJ structural
estructurar VT to structure
estruendo M din, racket
estruendoso ADJ thunderous
estrujamiento M (para romper) crushing; (para sacar jugo) squeezing
estrujar VT (aplastar) to crush; (apretar) to squeeze
estrujón M squeeze
estuario M estuary
estucar[30] VT to stucco
estuche M (para joyas) jewelry box; (para pastillas) pill box; (para lentes) glasses case
estuco M stucco
estudiantado M student body
estudiante MF student
estudiantil ADJ **vida** — student life
estudiar VI/VT to study
estudio M (acción de estudiar, investigación, habitación) study; (taller de artista) studio; (apartamento pequeño) studio apartment; **en** — under study; — **del impacto ambiental** environmental impact study
estudioso -sa ADJ studious; MF scholar
estufa F (para calentar) heater, stove; (para cocinar) stove
estupefaciente ADJ & M narcotic
estupefacto ADJ stunned, speechless
estupendo ADJ stupendous, terrific; **me la pasé** — **en la casa de Hilary** I had a great time at Hilary's house
estupidez F stupidity; **estupideces** nonsense
estúpido ADJ stupid

estupor M stupor
estupro M statutory rape
estuve, estuviera, estuviese ver estar
etanol M ethanol
etapa F stage; **por** —**s** by stages
etcétera CONJ et cetera, and so forth
éter M ether
eternidad F eternity
eternizarse[47] VI to drag on
eterno ADJ eternal, everlasting
ética F ethics
ético ADJ ethical
etimología F etymology
etíope ADJ & MF Ethiopian
Etiopia F Ethiopía
etiqueta F (de comportamiento) etiquette; (en una lata, botella) label; (en una prenda) tag; — **adhesiva** sticker; — **de identificación** name tag; — **de precio** price tag; **nos trataron con** — they treated us very formally; **vestirse de** — to dress formally
etiquetar VT (latas, botellas, personas) to label; (prendas) to tag
etnicidad F ethnicity
étnico ADJ ethnic
etnografía F ethnography
etnología F ethnology
ETS [enfermedad de transmisión sexual] F STD
eucalipto M eucalyptus
eufemismo M euphemism
euforia F euphoria
eunuco M eunuch
euro M euro
Europa F Europe
europeo -a ADJ & MF European
euskera M Basque [language]
eutanasia F euthanasia
evacuación F (de un lugar) evacuation; (del vientre) bowel movement; (de agua) drainage
evacuar VT (un lugar, a una persona) to evacuate; (el vientre) to void; (agua) to drain; VI to defecate
evadir VT to evade; —**se** to escape
evaluación F evaluation; — **del rendimiento** performance review
evaluar[26] VT (analizar) to evaluate, to assess; (tasar) to estimate; (calificar) to test
evangélico ADJ evangelical
evangelio M gospel
evaporación F evaporation
evaporar VT to evaporate; —**se** to vanish
evasión F (fiscal) evasion; (de prisioneros, de la realidad) escape; — **de capitales** capital flight; — **de impuestos** tax evasion
evasiva F **salirse con** —**s** to beat around the bush
evasivo ADJ evasive
evasor -ora MF evader

evento M event
eventual ADJ (posible) possible; (temporal) temporary
evidencia F evidence; **dejar/poner en — a alguien** to show someone up; **quedar/ponerse en —** to become apparent
evidenciar VT to make evident; **—se** to become evident
evidente ADJ evident, obvious
evidentemente ADV & INTERJ obviously
evitar VT (eludir) to avoid; (ahorrar) to spare
evocación F evocation
evocar[30] VT (una memoria) to evoke; (a los espíritus) to conjure up
evolución F evolution
evolucionar VI to evolve
evolutivo ADJ evolutionary
ex MF *fam* ex
exacerbar VT (intensificar) to exacerbate; (irritar) to aggravate
exactamente ADV & INTERJ exactly, precisely; **llegaron — a las tres** they arrived exactly at three
exactitud F accuracy, precision
exacto ADJ exact, precise, accurate; INTERJ exactly
exageración F exaggeration
exagerado ADJ exaggerated; **Jorge es un —** Jorge always exaggerates
exagerar VI/VT to exaggerate
exaltación F (elogio) praise; (excitación) excitement
exaltar VT to exalt; **—se** to get excited
examen M (inspección) examination; (prueba) examination, test, exam; **— de ingreso** entrance examination; **— dérmico de alergias** scratch test; **— final** final examination; **— físico** physical examination; **— médico** medical exam, checkup; **dar un —** to take a test; **poner un —** to give a test
examinar VT (inspeccionar) to examine; (someter a un examen) to test
exasperar VT to exasperate, to aggravate
excavación F (geológica) excavation; (arqueológica) dig
excavador -ora MF (persona) excavator; F (aparato) excavator, earthmover
excavar VT to excavate, to dig
excedente ADJ & M surplus
exceder VT (sobrepasar) to exceed; (superar) to surpass; **— de** to go beyond
excelencia F excellence; **por —** par excellence
excelente ADJ excellent, great
excentricidad F eccentricity
excéntrico ADJ eccentric
excepción F exception; **a — de** with the exception of
excepcional ADJ exceptional
excepto ADV & PREP except

exceptuar[26] VT to except
excesivo ADJ excessive
exceso M excess; **— de costos** overrun; **— de equipaje** excess baggage; **beber en —** to drink to excess; **comer en —** to overeat
excitación F (de músculos) excitement; (sexual) arousal
excitante ADJ stimulating
excitar VT (un nervio) to excite; (impulso sexual) to arouse; **—se** (sexualmente) to get aroused; (átomos) to be excited
exclamación F exclamation
exclamar VT to exclaim
excluir[19] VT to exclude
exclusión F exclusion
exclusivo ADJ exclusive
excomulgar[40] VT to excommunicate
excrecencia F excrescence
excreción F excretion
excremento M excrement
excretar VT to excrete
excursión F excursion, outing
excusa F excuse
excusable ADJ excusable
excusado M *Méx* toilet
excusar VT to excuse
exención F exemption
exento ADJ exempt; **— de impuestos** tax-exempt
exequias F PL funeral rites
exfoliación F exfoliation
exhalar VI/VT (aire) to exhale, to breathe out; (un olor) to give off; **— un suspiro** to sigh
exhaustivo ADJ exhaustive, thorough
exhausto ADJ exhausted
exhibición F (manifestación) exhibition; (despliegue) display
exhibicionismo M exhibitionism
exhibir VT (fotos) to exhibit; (mercancías) to display; (el carnet de identidad) to show; **—se** to show off; **le gusta exhibirse en traje de baño** she likes to show off in her bathing suit; **esa película ya no se exhibe** that movie is not showing anymore
exhortar VT to exhort, to urge
exhumación F exhumation
exigencia F demand
exigente ADJ demanding, exacting
exigir[46] VT to demand; **exigen a alguien que sepa inglés** they require someone who knows English
exiguo ADJ meager; **exigua mayoría** scant majority
exiliado -da MF exile
exiliar VT to exile
exilio M exile
eximido ADJ exempt; **— por la cláusula del abuelo** grandfathered
eximio ADJ illustrious

eximir VT (de impuestos) to exempt; (de sospecha) to clear; (de una responsabilidad) to excuse

existencia F existence; **complicarle la — a alguien** to cause someone trouble; **la lucha por la —** the fight for survival; **—s** stock on hand; **en —** in stock, on hand

existencial ADJ existential

existente ADJ extant, existing

existir VI to exist

éxito M success; (musical) hit; **— de taquilla** blockbuster; **tener —** to be successful; **tiene — con las mujeres** he's popular with women

exitoso ADJ successful

éxodo M exodus

exonerar VT to exonerate

exorbitante ADJ exorbitant

exorcisar VT to exorcise

exorcismo M exorcism

exótico ADJ exotic

expandir VT (dilatar) to expand, to spread; (propagar) to disseminate; **—se** to expand, to spread

expansión F (crecimiento) expansion; (diversión) relaxation

expansivo ADJ (que crece) expansive; (efusivo) effusive

expatriado-da MF expatriate

expatriar VT to expatriate, to exile

expectación F anticipation

expectativa F (esperanza) expectation; (posibilidad) prospect; **estar a la — de algo** to be on pins and needles; **— de vida** life expectancy

expectorante M expectorant

expectorar VI/VT to expectorate, to cough up

expedición F (viaje) expedition; (de documentos) issuing; (de mercancías) delivery

expedicionario-ria ADJ expeditionary; MF member of an expedition

expedidor-ora ADJ shipping; MF shipper

expediente M (administrativo) file, dossier; (policial, académico, médico) record

expedir[9] VT (enviar) to dispatch; (emitir) to issue

expeler VT to expel

expendedor-ora MF vendor; **— automático** vending machine

experiencia F experience

experimentación F experimentation

experimentado ADJ experienced

experimental ADJ experimental

experimentar VI (hacer experimentos) to experiment; VT (sufrir, tener experiencia) to experience

experimento M experiment

experto-ta ADJ & MF expert; **— en**

computación wizard, *fam* techie

expiación F atonement

expiar[28] VT to atone for

expirar VI to expire

explanada F (terreno junto al mar) esplanade; (terreno nivelado) leveled area

explayarse VI to become extended; **— sobre** to enlarge upon

explicable ADJ explainable, explicable

explicación F explanation

explicar[30] VT to explain; **—se** to make oneself clear; **no me explico por qué** I can't figure out why

explicativo ADJ explanatory

explícito ADJ explicit

exploración F exploration

explorador-ora ADJ exploring; MF (expedicionario) explorer; (militar) scout

explorar VI/VT to explore; (con fines diagnósticos) to scan; (con fines militares) to scout

exploratorio ADJ exploratory

explosión F explosion; **hacer —** to explode

explosivo ADJ & M explosive

explotación F exploitation

explotar VT (sacar provecho) to exploit; (hacer explosión) to explode

expondrá, expondría *ver* exponer

exponente M exponent

exponer[56, 74] VT (al sol, al peligro) to expose; (al público) to exhibit, to display; (explicar) to state, to set forth; **—se al peligro** to expose oneself to danger

exponga, expongo *ver* exponer

exportación F (acción) exportation, export; (cosa) export

exportador-ora ADJ exporting; MF exporter

exportar VI/VT to export

exposición F (feria) exposition; (de arte) exhibition; (explicación) explanation; (al sol, a una influencia, al peligro) exposure

expresar VT to express

expresión F expression; **valga la —** so to speak

expresividad F expressiveness

expresivo ADJ expressive

expreso ADJ (explícito) express; (rápido) fast; M express train; **café —** espresso

exprimidor M juicer

exprimir VT (naranjas) to squeeze; (zumo) to squeeze out

expropiar VT to expropriate

expuesto ADJ exposed; **lo —** what has been said

expuesto *ver* exponer

expulsar VT to expel; (de un bar) to throw out; (de un partido) to eject

expulsión F expulsion

expuse, expusiera, expusiese *ver* exponer

exquisito-ta ADJ (arte) exquisite; (comida) delicious

extasiado ADJ rapt
extasiarse[28] VI to be enraptured
éxtasis M ecstasy (también droga)
extender[2] VT (el brazo, radio de acción, gratitud) to extend; (un tapete, una masa, un idioma) to spread; (un cheque) to draw up; **—se** to extend; **la fiesta se extendió hasta las 3** the party lasted until 3 o'clock
extendido ADJ (brazos) outstretched; (costumbre) widespread
extensión F (del antebrazo, de significado, telefónica) extension; (de terreno) expanse; (de un texto) length; (eléctrica) extension cord; **por —** by extension; **tener mucha —** to be widespread
extensivo ADJ extensive; **hacer —** to extend
extenso ADJ (calendario, plan, grupo) extensive; (narración, programa de radio) extended
extenuado ADJ exhausted
exterior ADJ (de fuera) exterior, outer; (mundo) outside; (política) foreign; M (parte de afuera) exterior, outside; (aspecto) outward appearance; (fútbol americano) end; **en —es** on location
exteriorizar[47] VT to externalize
exterminación F extermination
exterminar VT to exterminate
exterminio M extermination
externo ADJ external
extienda, extiende ver extender
extinción F extinction
extinguidor M fire extinguisher
extinguir[44] VT (un fuego) to extinguish, to put out; (una especie) to make extinct, to wipe out; **—se** (animal, volcán) to go extinct
extinto ADJ extinct
extintor M fire extinguisher
extirpación F removal
extirpar VT to remove
extorsión F extortion
extorsionar VT to extort money from
extorsionista MF racketeer
extra ADJ extra; **horas —s** overtime; MF (actor) extra; M (cosa accesoria) extra; F (pago extraordinario) bonus
extrabursátil ADJ over-the-counter
extracción F extraction
extracto M (resumen) abstract; (de café) extract
extradición F extradition
extraditar VT to extradite
extraer[59] VT (esencia) to extract; (minerales) to mine; (un diente) to pull
extraiga, extraigo, extraje, extrajera, extrajese ver extraer
extrajudicial ADJ out-of-court
extramarital ADJ extramarital
extranjero -ra ADJ foreign; MF foreigner; **en el — abroad**
extrañar VT (sorprender) to surprise; (echar de

menos) to miss; **no es de — que** it's no wonder that; **no me extraña** it doesn't surprise me; **—se** to be surprised
extrañeza F surprise
extraño -ña ADJ (persona, costumbre) strange; (partícula) foreign; MF stranger
extraoficial ADJ unofficial
extraordinario ADJ extraordinary
extrapolar VI/VT to extrapolate
extrasensorial ADJ extrasensory
extraterrestre ADJ & M alien, extraterrestrial
extravagancia F (cualidad de extravagante) extravagance; (comportamiento extravagante) outrageous behavior
extravagante ADJ flamboyant, outrageous
extraviar[28] VT (perder) to misplace; (confundir) to lead astray; **—se** to lose one's way, to get lost
extravío M loss
extrayendo ver extraer
extremadamente ADV extremely
extremado ADJ extreme
extremar VT to maximize
extremidad F extremity
extremo ADJ (máximo, mínimo, extraordinario) extreme; (más lejano) farthest; **con — cuidado** with utmost care; M (punto más alejado) extreme; (de una región) end; **llegar al — de** to go so far as to; **— Oriente** Far East; **extrema izquierda** far left; F **extrema unción** last rites
extrovertido -da ADJ extroverted; MF extrovert
exuberante ADJ (vegetación, jóvenes) exuberant; (mujer) voluptuous
exudar VI/VT to exude
exultante ADJ exhilarated, exultant
exultar VI to exult
eyacular VI/VT to ejaculate
eyectar VT to eject

Ff

fábrica F factory, plant; (de acero, textiles) mill
fabricación F manufacture, manufacturing
fabricante MF manufacturer; (de coches) maker
fabricar[30] VT (producir) to manufacture, to make; (construir) to build; (inventar) to concoct, to fabricate
fabril ADJ manufacturing
fábula F (relato) fable; (mentira) falsehood
fabuloso ADJ (imaginario) imaginary; (magnífico) awesome, fabulous
facción F faction; **facciones** facial features
faceta F facet
facha F **estaba hecho una —** he was a sight

fachada F facade
facial ADJ facial
fácil ADJ (sencillo) easy; (promiscuo) easy, loose; — **de entender** self-explanatory; — **de usar** user-friendly
facilidad F ease; (habilidad) facility, knack
facilitar VT (hacer más fácil) to facilitate; (proporcionar) to furnish
facsímil M fax
factible ADJ feasible
fáctico ADJ factual
factor M factor; —**es de riesgo** risk factors
factoría F trading post
factura F bill, invoice; — **detallada** itemized invoice
facturable ADJ billable
facturación F billing
facturar VT (importe) to invoice; (equipaje) to check
facultad F (habilidad) faculty; (autoridad) authority; (división de una universidad) college; — **de odontología** dental school
facundia F gift of gab
faena F (trabajo corporal) chore; (labor) task; (molestia) nuisance
fagot M bassoon
fairway M fairway
faisán M pheasant
faja F (cinta) sash; (prenda interior) girdle; (de tierra) ribbon, strip
fajar VT (ceñir) to gird; (envolver) to wrap up; (golpear) to thrash
fajo M (de dinero) wad; (de papel, paja) sheaf
falacia F fallacy
falaz ADJ fallacious
falda F (prenda de vestir) skirt (también mujeres); (de una montaña) slope
faldón M (de una camisa) tail, shirttail; (de un saco) coattail
falible ADJ fallible
falla F (en un argumento) flaw; (en un motor) miss; (de una máquina) failure; (geológica) fault; **las Fallas** Valencian holiday
fallar VI (no funcionar) to fail; (un motor) to miss; VI/VT (un juez) to find, to rule
fallecer[35] VI to pass away, to decease
fallecimiento M passing, decease
fallo M (de un programa) bug, glitch; (de la memoria) lapse; (de un juez) ruling, finding
falo M phallus
falsear VT to falsify
falsedad F (dicho falso) falsehood; (condición de falso) falseness
falsificación F (de dinero) counterfeit; (de un documento) forgery
falsificar[30] VT (documento) to falsify, to fake; (dinero) to counterfeit; (una firma) to forge; (libros de contabilidad) to cook
falso ADJ (dato) false, untrue; (sentimientos)

fake, phony; (dinero) counterfeit; (promesa) hollow; (amigo) faithless, two-faced; (excusa) made-up; **falsa alarma** false alarm; **jurar en** — to perjure oneself; **paso en** — a false step; **salida en** — false start
falta F (defecto) fault; (carencia) lack, want; (ausencia) absence, miss; (jugada ilícita) foul; (de ortografía) mistake; — **de aire** shortness of breath, breathlessness; — **de pago** default; — **de respeto** disrespect; — **personal** (baloncesto) personal foul; — **de pie** foot fault; **a** — **de** for want of, in the absence of; **cometer** — to commit a foul; **hacer** — to be necessary; **me haces** — I miss you; **sin** — without fail
faltar VI (ausentarse) to be absent; (no haber) to be lacking; — **a la palabra** to break a promise; — **a la verdad** to misstate oneself; —**le el respeto a** to disrespect; — **poco para las cinco** to be almost five o'clock; **me falta tiempo** I don't have enough time; **¡no faltaba más!** (con indignación) that's the last straw! (no hay de qué) don't mention it! (no te molestes) I wouldn't hear of it
falto ADJ lacking; — **de esperanza** devoid of hope
fama F (condición de conocido) fame; (reputación) reputation; **de** — **mundial** world-famous
famélico ADJ ravenous
familia F family; — **nuclear** nuclear family; **en** — in the family; **jefe de** — head of household; **la señora de Juan tuvo** — John's wife had a baby
familiar ADJ (muy conocido) familiar; (de familia) familial; **tamaño** — family-size; **coche** — family car; **vida** — family life; MF relative; —**es** next of kin
familiaridad F familiarity
familiarizar[47] VT to familiarize, to acquaint; —**se** to acquaint oneself, to become familiar with
famoso ADJ famous
fanático -ca ADJ fanatic; MF fanatic, zealot; (de deportes) freak
fanatismo M fanaticism
fanega F bushel
fanfarria F fanfare
fanfarrón -ona MF braggart, show-off; ADJ blustering
fanfarronear VI to bluster
fanfarronería F bluster, swagger
fango M mire
fangoso ADJ miry
fantasear VI to fantasize
fantasía F (imaginación) imagination; (imagen) fantasy; **de** — fake, artificial
fantasioso ADJ (niño) imaginative; (idea) fanciful

fantasma M ghost, phantom
fantasmagórico ADJ ghostly
fantástico ADJ fantastic
farándula F show business
fardo M (paquete) bundle; (de heno, algodón) bale
farfolla F husk
farfulla F jabber
farfullar VI to jabber
faringe F pharynx
faríngeo ADJ pharyngeal
farmacéutico -ca ADJ pharmaceutical; MF pharmacist, druggist
farmacia F pharmacy, drugstore
fármaco M medicine, pharmaceutical
farmacología F pharmacology
faro M (torre) lighthouse; (luz de alerta) beacon; (luz del coche) light; — **delantero** headlight
farol M (portátil) lantern; (del alumbrado público) street lamp, streetlight; (con pie de hierro) lamppost; (jactancia, envite) bluff; **darse** — to show off, to put on airs
farra F spree; **ir de** — to go on a spree
farsa F (engaño) sham, hoax; (obra teatral, imitación ridícula) farce, mockery
farsante MF fraud, fake
fascículo M installment
fascinación F fascination
fascinante ADJ fascinating, riveting
fascinar VI/VT to fascinate
fascismo M fascism
fascista ADJ & MF fascist
fase F phase
fastidiado ADJ irked
fastidiar VT to irk
fastidio M annoyance
fastidioso ADJ annoying, wearisome
fatal ADJ (mortal) fatal; (terrible) terrible; **mujer** — femme fatale; ADV very badly; **me fue** — **en el examen** I did very poorly on the exam
fatalidad F (desgracia) misfortune; (destino) destiny
fatídico ADJ ill-fated
fatiga F fatigue, exhaustion; — **ocular** eye strain; —**s** hardships
fatigado ADJ tired, weary
fatigar[40] VT to tire out
fatigoso ADJ (cansado) tiring; (aburrido) tiresome
fauces F PL jaws
faul M foul
fauna F fauna
favor M favor; **a** — **de** in favor of; **por** — please
favorable ADJ favorable
favorecer[35] VT to favor
favorezca, favorezco ver favorecer
favoritismo M favoritism
favorito -ta ADJ favorite; MF favorite; (en una

elección) front-runner; (de la maestra) pet
fax M fax
faxear VT to fax
faz F face
FBI M FBI
fe F faith; — **de bautismo** baptismal certificate; — **de erratas** list of errors; — **de nacimiento** birth certificate; **buena** — good faith; **de buena** — in good faith; **dar** — **de** to vouch for
fealdad F ugliness
febrero M February
febril ADJ (con fiebre) feverish; (actividad) feverish, hectic
fecal ADJ fecal
fecha F date; — **de vencimiento** date due, due date
fechado ADJ dated
fechar VT to date
fechoría F misdeed
fecundación F fertilization
fecundar VT (un huevo) to fertilize; (una hembra) to impregnate
fecundo ADJ fertile
federación F federation
federal ADJ federal
felación F fellatio
felicidad F happiness; ¡—**es!** congratulations
felicitación F congratulation; ¡**felicitaciones!** congratulations!
felicitar VT to congratulate
feligrés -esa MF parishioner; **feligreses** congregation
felino ADJ feline; M cat
feliz ADJ happy
felizmente ADV happily
felpa F plush
felpudo M doormat
femenino ADJ (como una mujer, relativo al género gramatical) feminine; (de la mujer) female
feminidad F femininity
feminismo F feminism
feminista MF feminist
fémur M femur
fenómeno M phenomenon
feo ADJ (cara) ugly, homely; (dentadura) bad; (accidente) nasty
féretro M coffin
feria F (mercado) market; (exposición) fair; (espectáculo) carnival; (celebración) holiday
feriante MF trader at fairs, stallholder
fermentación F fermentation
fermentar VT (leche) to ferment; (cerveza) to brew
fermento M ferment
ferocidad F ferocity
feroz ADJ ferocious, fierce
férreo ADJ (puente) iron; (disciplina) harsh

ferretería F (tienda) hardware store; (artículos) hardware
ferrocarril M railroad, railway
ferroviario -ria ADJ railroad; MF railroad employee
ferry M ferryboat
fértil ADJ fertile
fertilidad F fertility
fertilización F fertilization
fertilizante M fertilizer
fertilizar[47] VT to fertilize
ferviente ADJ fervent
fervor M fervor, zeal
fervoroso ADJ zealous
festejar VT to celebrate
festejo M celebration
festín M feast; **darse un** — to treat oneself
festival M festival
festividad F festivity
festivo ADJ festive, celebratory; **día** — holiday
festón M scallop
festonear VT to scallop
fetal ADJ fetal
fetiche M fetish
fétido ADJ foul-smelling
feto M fetus
feudal ADJ feudal
feudo M manor
fiabilidad F reliability
fiable ADJ reliable
fiador -ora MF guarantor, voucher; (prestamista) backer; (de un preso) bondsman
fiambre M (carne) cold cut; (cadáver) *fam* stiff
fianza F (de un préstamo) security, guaranty; (de un preso) bail
fiar[28] VT (garantizar) to vouch for; **—se de** to trust
fiasco M fiasco
fibra F fiber; **— de vidrio** fiberglass; **— óptica** optical fiber
fibrosis F fibrosis; **— cística** cystic fibrosis
fibroso ADJ fibrous
ficción F fiction
ficha F (de teléfono) token; (de dominó) domino; (de damas) checker; (en poker, ruleta) chip; (tarjeta) index card; MF (delincuente) delinquent, criminal
fichar VT to open a file on; VI to punch in
fichero M (de computadora) file; (archivador) filing cabinet; **— de datos** data file
ficticio ADJ (no real) fictitious; (novelesco) fictional
fidedigno ADJ trustworthy
fideicomisario -ria MF trustee
fideicomiso M trusteeship
fidelidad F (de un amante) fidelity, faithfulness; (de una traducción) closeness; (a la bandera) allegiance
fideo M noodle

fiduciario -ria ADJ & MF fiduciary
fiebre F fever; **— aftosa** foot-and-mouth disease; **— amarilla** yellow fever; **— de candilejas** stage fright; **— del oro** gold rush; **— reumática** rheumatic fever; **— tifoidea** typhoid fever; **tener —** to run a fever
fiel ADJ (leal) faithful; (exacto) true, accurate; M pointer on a scale; **los —es** the congregation
fieltro M (tela) felt; (sombrero) felt hat
fiera F beast; **ponerse hecho una —** to go berserk
fiereza F ferocity
fiero ADJ (salvaje) fierce; (muy grande) huge
fiesta F (festejo) party; (día feriado) holiday; **aguar una —** to ruin a party
fiestero -ra ADJ fond of parties; MF merrymaker, party animal
figura F figure
figurado ADJ figurative
figurar VI (aparecer) to appear, to figure; (lucirse) to show off; **—se** to imagine; **¡figúrate!** imagine!
figurativo ADJ figurative
figurín M fashion plate
figurón M dummy
fijación F fixing; **— de precios** pricing
fijador M hairspray
fijar VT (un cartel) to fix, to fasten; (una fecha) to set; (precios) to peg; **—se en** (notar) to notice; (prestar atención) to pay attention to, to focus on
fijo ADJ (sujeto, incambiado) fixed; (inmóvil) fixed, stationary; (firme) firm; (definitivo) definite; (permanente) permanent
fila F (uno detrás del otro) row, file; (hombro a hombro) rank; (de espera) line; (de documentos) queue; **— india** single file; **cerrar —s** to close ranks; **romper —s** to break ranks
filamento M filament
filantropía F philanthropy
filarmónica F philharmonic
filarmónico ADJ philharmonic
fildear VT to field
fildeo M fielding
filete M (de carne) fillet; (de un plato) rim
filetear VT to fillet
filiación F (membresía) affiliation; (datos personales) personal information; (lazo de parentesco) filiation; **— política** political affiliation
filial ADJ filial; F affiliate, subsidiary
filibusterismo M filibustering
filigrana F filigree
Filipinas F Philippines
filipino -na ADJ & MF Filipino, Filipina
filme M film, movie
filmación F filming, shooting

filmar VT to film, to shoot
filo M (de una navaja) cutting edge; (biológico) phylum; **de doble —** two-edged; **al — de las dos** at around two o'clock
filón M seam, vein, pocket
filoso ADJ sharp
filosofía F philosophy
filosófico ADJ philosophical
filósofo -fa MF philosopher
filtración F (purificación) filtration; (pérdida) leak; (percolación) seepage
filtrar VT (purificar) to filter; (perder) to leak; (clasificar) to screen; **—se** (gotear) to leak through; (percolarse) to seep
filtro M filter; **— de aire** air filter; **— de amor** love potion
fin M (conclusión, objetivo) end; **— de año** New Year's Eve; **el — del mundo** (lugar apartado) boondocks; **— de semana** weekend; **— de siglo** turn of the century; **al —** at last; **al — y al cabo** at any rate; **a — de que** so that; **a — de mes** toward the end of the month; **de — de año** year-end; **en —** in conclusion; **poner — a** to put an end to; **por —** at last, finally; **sin —** (ilimitado) myriad; (continuo) endless
finado ADJ late
final ADJ final, last; F (deportiva) final; M (de una historia) ending; (de un terreno) end; (de una carrera) finish; (de una filmación) wrap
finalidad F objective, purpose
finalista MF finalist
finalización F completion
finalizar[47] VT to finish; **— una sesión** lo log off/out
finalmente ADV at last, finally
financiación F (para una compra) financing; (para un proyecto) funding
financiamiento M (para una compra) financing; (para un proyecto científico) funding; **— por el propietario** owner financing
financiar VT (una compra) to finance; (un proyecto) to underwrite, *fam* to bankroll
financiero -ra ADJ financial; MF financier
finanza F finance; **—s** finances
finca F (inmueble) property; (granja) farm, country estate
finés -esa MF Finn; M (lengua) Finnish; ADJ Finnish
fineza F (atención) courtesy; (suavidad) smoothness
fingir[46] VI/VT (sorpresa) to feign; (un ataque al corazón) to fake; **fingió que la quería** he pretended to love her
finiquito M settlement
finito ADJ finite
finlandés -esa MF Finn; M (lengua) Finnish; ADJ Finnish
Finlandia F Finland

fino ADJ (vino, arena, pelo, metal) fine; (sentidos) keen, sharp; (medias) sheer; (hielo, alambre, voz) thin; (modales) smooth, refined
finta F fake, juke
firma F (compañía) firm; (rúbrica) signature; **— consultora** consulting firm
firmamento M sky
firmante MF signer
firmar VI/VT (documento, carta) to sign; (contrato) to enter
firme ADJ (estructura) firm; (control) tight; (colores) fast; (amarras) secure; (mano) steady, sure; (resistencia) stiff; (apoyo, resistencia) strong, staunch, steadfast; **mantenerse —** to stand one's ground; **¡—s!** attention!
firmemente ADV firmly
firmeza F (de una estructura) firmness; (de la mano) steadiness; (de la resistencia) stiffness; (del apoyo) strength; **con —** firmly
fiscal ADJ fiscal; MF public prosecutor, district attorney
fiscalía F prosecution
fiscalización F (de comportamiento) supervision; (de gastos) oversight
fiscalizar[47] VT (comportamiento) to supervise; (gastos) to oversee
fisgar[40] VI to snoop
fisgón -ona ADJ snooping; MF snoop
fisgonear VI to snoop
físico -ca ADJ physical; MF (persona) physicist; M (cuerpo) physique; F physics
fisiología F physiology
fisiológico ADJ physiological
fisioterapia F physical therapy
fisonomía F features
fístula F fistula
fisura F fissure
fiyano ADJ Fijian
Fiyi M Fiji
flácido, fláccido ADJ (sin firmeza) limp, flaccid; (gordo) flabby
flaco ADJ thin, skinny; **su lado —** his weakness
flacura F thinness
flagrante ADJ gross; **en — delito** in the act
flamante ADJ brand-new
flamear VI (llamear) to flame; (ondear) to flap
flamenco -ca ADJ Flemish; MF Flemish person; M (lengua) Flemish; (ave) flamingo; (baile) flamenco
flamígero ADJ flaming
flan M caramel custard
flanco M (de un animal, ejército) flank; (de un neumático) sidewall
flanquear VT to flank
flaquear VI (intención) to waver; (salud) to wane
flaqueza F weakness
flash M (noticias, visión, memoria digital) flash;

(lámpara) flashbulb, flash
flashback M flashback
flatulencia F flatulence
flauta F flute; — **dulce** recorder
flautín M piccolo
flecha F arrow
flechar VT to wound with an arrow
flechazo M (herida) wound from an arrow; (enamoramiento) love at first sight
fleco M (de una alfombra) fringe; (de pelo) bangs
flema F phlegm
flequillo M bangs
fletamento M charter
fletar VT to charter
flete M (contratación) charter; (envío) transport; (precio de transporte) freight; (encuentro sexual) *Esp* one-night stand
flexibilidad F (ductilidad) flexibility; (libertad) latitude
flexible ADJ (material) flexible; (cuerpo humano) limber, supple; (opinión) pliant, pliable
flojear VT to slacken
flojedad F laxity, looseness; (debilidad) weakness
flojera F (debilidad) weakness; (pereza) laziness
flojo ADJ (suelto) loose, slack; (holgazán) lazy; (inferior) crummy; (débil) weak; (sin fundamento) flimsy
floppy M floppy disk
flor F flower, blossom, bloom; (cumplido) compliment; — **de la edad** prime of life; — **de Pascua** poinsettia; — **y nata** the cream of the crop; **a** — **de** flush with; **en** — in bloom
flora F flora (también bacteriana); — **intestinal** intestinal flora
floración F blooming, blossoming
floral ADJ flowery
floreado ADJ flowery
florear VT (adornar con flores) to decorate with flowers; (adornar) to adorn
florecer[35] VI (echar flores) to flower, to bloom; (prosperar) to flourish, to thrive
floreciente ADJ (próspero) flourishing, prosperous; (florecido) blooming
florecimiento M flourishing
floreo M flourish
florería F florist's shop
florero M flower vase
florete M fencing foil
florido ADJ flowery
florista MF florist
floritura F flourish
flota F fleet
flotador M (para nadar) float; (de un avión) pontoon; ADJ floating
flotante ADJ floating, buoyant
flotar VI (estar suspendido, variar en valor) to float; (moverse en la superficie) to drift; (ir

por el aire) to waft
flote M flotation; **a** — afloat; **poner a** — to set afloat
fluctuación F fluctuation; (amplitud de variación) range
fluctuar[26] VI to fluctuate
fluidez F (cualidad de fluido) fluency; (cualidad de diluido) thinness
fluido ADJ (que fluye) fluid, flowing; (no vacilante) fluent; M fluid
fluir[19] VI to flow
flujo M (de agua) flow; (vaginal) discharge; (de datos) streaming; — **continuo de datos de audio** audio streaming; — **continuo de datos de vídeo** video streaming; — **de caja** cash flow; — **de trabajo** work flow
flúor M (elemento gaseoso) fluorine; (sal) fluoride
fluorescente ADJ fluorescent
fluoruro M fluoride
fluvial ADJ **transporte** — river transportation
fluyente ADJ flowing
FMI [Fondo Monetario Internacional] M IMF
fobia F phobia
foca F seal
foco M (punto central) focus; (bombilla) bulb; (lámpara potente) spotlight
fofo ADJ mushy
fogata F (fuego abierto) bonfire; (en un campamento) campfire
fogonazo M flash
fogoso ADJ fiery, spirited
folclor, folclore M folklore
folclórico/folklórico ADJ folkloric; **cuento** — folktale
foliculitis F folliculitis
folículo M follicle
folio M folio
folíolo M leaflet
follaje M foliage
follar VT *vulg* to fuck, to screw
folleto M pamphlet, brochure
follón M (confusión) mess; (alboroto) ruckus
fomentar VT (estudio) to promote; (amistad) to foster; (discordia) to foment; (apoyo) to drum up
fomento M encouragement
fonda F inn
fondear VI to anchor
fondillos M PL seat of pants
fondista MF (posadero) innkeeper; (corredor) long-distance runner
fondo M (parte más profunda) bottom; (parte posterior) rear; (del mar) bed; (de un cuadro, foto) background; (de dinero) fund; (de una biblioteca) holdings; (de un jardín) backyard; — **común** pool; — **de contingencia** contingency fund; — **especulativo** hedge

fund; — **físico** endurance; — **musical** background music; — **mutuo** mutual fund; —**s** funds; —**s administrados** managed funds; — **sin comisión de entrada** no-load fund; **a** — in depth; **carrera de** — long-distance race; **de cuatro en** — four abreast; **de** — (exhaustivo) in depth; (subyacente) underlying; **sin** — bottomless; **tocar** — to hit rock bottom
fonética F phonetics
fonético ADJ phonetic
fonógrafo M phonograph
fonología F phonology
fontanería F plumbing
fontanero -ra MF plumber
footing M jogging
forajido -da MF outlaw
foráneo ADJ foreign; **influencia foránea** outside influence
forastero -ra MF stranger, outsider
forcejear VI to struggle
forcejeo M struggle
fórceps M PL forceps
forense ADJ forensic; MF forensic scientist
forestal ADJ forest; **división** — forestry division
forja F (fogón) forge; (acción de forjar) forging; (taller) blacksmith's shop
forjado ADJ wrought
forjar VT (metales, un acuerdo) to forge; (un acuerdo) to hammer out; (un documento) to frame
forma F (figura) form, shape; (manera) manner; — **de pago** mode of payment; — **de pensar** mind-set; **ponerse en** — to get in shape; **no hay** — no way; **dar** — **a** to shape
formación F formation
formal ADJ (que atañe a la forma) formal, serious; (fiable) reliable
formaldehído M formaldehyde
formalidad F (convencionalidad) formality; (fiabilidad) reliability
formalismo M formality
formalizar[47] VT to make official; —**se** to settle down
formar VT (crear) to form; (reunir tropas) to muster; (entrenar) to train; —**se** (montañas) to form; (estudiantes) to be educated
formatear VT to format
formateo M formatting
formativo ADJ formative
formato M format; — **de archivo/fichero** file format; — **de texto enriquecido** rich text format
formidable ADJ formidable
formón M wood chisel
fórmula F formula
formulación F (acción de formular) formulation; (fórmula) formula; (redacción) wording
formular VT to formulate; (un plan, una pregunta) to frame; (un documento) to word
formulario M form
fornicar[30] VI to fornicate
fornido ADJ stout, sturdy
foro M forum; (de un escenario) back
forrado ADJ (con un forro) lined; (bien provisto) flush
forraje M forage, fodder
forrajear VI to forage
forrar VT (un saco) to line; —**se** to line one's pockets
forro M lining; (de un libro) jacket
fortalecer[35] VT to fortify, to strengthen
fortalecimiento M strengthening
fortaleza F (construcción) fortress, fort; (fuerza) fortitude
fortificación F fortification
fortificar[30] VT to fortify
fortuito ADJ fortuitous, accidental
fortuna F fortune; **por** — fortunately; **probar** — to try one's luck; **hacer** — to become rich
forúnculo M boil
forzar[49] VT to force, to coerce; — **la entrada** to break into
forzoso ADJ (por la fuerza) forcible; (inevitable) necessary; (aterrizaje) forced
fosa F (sepultura) grave; (de la nariz) cavity; (en el fondo del mar) trench
fosfato M phosphate
fósforo M (sustancia) phosphorus; (cerilla) match
fósil ADJ & M fossil
foso M (de un castillo) moat; (de un taller, teatro) pit
foto F snapshot, photo
fotocopia F photocopy
fotocopiadora F photocopier
fotocopiar VI/VT to photocopy
fotoeléctrico ADJ photoelectric
fotogénico ADJ photogenic
fotografía F (foto) photograph; (arte) photography; — **digital** digital photography
fotografiar[28] VT to photograph
fotógrafo -fa MF photographer
fotón M photon
fotosíntesis F photosynthesis
foul M foul
frac M tails
fracasar VI (un proyecto) to fail; (de una película) to bomb; (una embarcación) to break up
fracaso M (de un proyecto) failure; (de una película) flop, bomb
fracción F fraction
fractura F fracture, break; — **fina** hairline fracture
fracturar VT to fracture, to break; **se fracturó**

la cadera she broke her hip
fragancia F fragrance
fragante ADJ fragrant; **en —** in the act
fragata F frigate
frágil ADJ (delicado) delicate; (quebradizo) fragile, brittle; (una paz) tenuous
fragilidad F (condición de quebradizo) brittleness, delicacy; (debilidad) frailty
fragmentación F fragmentation
fragmento M fragment; (de metal, piedra) scrap; (de una conversación) snatch; (de un texto) extract, excerpt
fragoso ADJ rugged
fragua F (fogón) forge; (taller) blacksmith's shop
fraguar[25] VT to forge; (una trama) to hatch; VI (cemento, yeso) to set
fraile M friar
frambuesa F raspberry
frambueso M raspberry bush
francamente ADV **—, me horroriza** frankly / to be honest, it horrifies me; **lo pasaban — bien** they were doing pretty well; **—, es ridículo** it is simply ridiculous
francés -esa ADJ French; M (lengua) French; (hombre) Frenchman; F (mujer) Frenchwoman
franchute -uta MF *pey* frog
Francia F France
franco ADJ (sincero) frank, candid; (exento) free; **una franca mayoría** a clear majority; **un tratado — -americano** a Franco-American treaty
francotirador -ora MF sniper
franela F flannel
franja F ribbon
franquear VT (una frontera) to cross; (una carta) to frank; **—se** to be frank
franqueo M postage
franqueza F (personal) frankness; (institucional) openness
franquicia F (concesión) franchise; (exención) exemption
frasco M (recipiente de vidrio) flask; (de medicina, perfume) bottle; (de mermelada) jar
frase F phrase
frasear VI/VT to phrase
fraternal ADJ fraternal, brotherly
fraternidad F fraternity
fraternizar[47] VI fraternize
fraterno ADJ fraternal
fraude M fraud
fraudulento ADJ fraudulent
frazada F blanket
frecuencia F frequency; **con —** frequently
frecuentar VT to frequent; (una tienda) to patronize
frecuente ADJ frequent
fregadero M sink

fregado M scrubbing
fregar[41] VT to scour, to scrub
fregona F (persona) scrubwoman, drudge; (utensilio) mop
freír[10, 74] VI/VT to fry
frenar VT (un coche) to brake; (la inmigración) to restrain; (los impulsos) to bridle; VI to brake, to apply the brakes
frenesí M frenzy; (de actividad) flurry
frenético ADJ frantic
freno M (de coche) brake; (de caballo) bit; (contra el contrabando) curb
frente F forehead; **el sudor de la —** the sweat of one's brow; M (parte delantera, zona de combate, zona meteorológica) front; (de un edificio) face; **— a** (ante) in the face of; (al otro lado) facing; **— a —** face to face; **de —** head-on; **en — de** in front of; **hacer —** to face; **pasar al —** to come to the fore
fresa F (fruta) strawberry; (herramienta) mill
fresadora F milling machine
fresar VT to mill
frescachona F buxom woman
fresco ADJ (reciente, descansado, insolente) fresh; (frío) cool, brisk; (poco abrigado) light; (no cocinado) raw; (pintura) wet; M (frío) coolness; (pintura) fresco
frescor M (de verduras) freshness; (del aire) coolness
frescura F (de verduras, de carácter) freshness; (del tiempo) coolness; (comentario) impudent remark
fresno M ash tree
friabilidad F looseness
frialdad F coldness, coolness
fricción F friction, rubbing
friccionar VT to rub
friega F rubbing, massage
frigidez F frigidity
frigorífico M (electrodoméstico) refrigerator; (cámara) refrigeration chamber
frijol M bean
frío ADJ (de temperatura, de temperamento) cold; (helado) frigid; M cold; **tener —** to be cold
friolento ADJ sensitive to cold
friolera F **la — de $50,000** a trifling $50,000
fritada F dish of fried food
frito ADJ fried; M dish of fried food
fritura F (acción de freír) frying; (comida frita) dish of fried food
frivolidad F frivolity
frívolo ADJ frivolous
fronda F foliage
frondoso ADJ leafy
frontal ADJ (ataque) frontal; (colisión) head-on
frontera F frontier, border
fronterizo ADJ frontier
frontón M (juego) jai alai; (pista) jai alai court

frotación F rubbing
frotar VI/VT to rub
frote M rub
frotis M smear
fructífero ADJ fruitful
fructificar[30] VI to bear fruit
fructosa F fructose
frugal ADJ frugal
frunce M (volante) ruffle; (defecto) pucker
fruncir[33] VT to gather; — **el ceño** to frown, to knit one's brow; — **los labios** to purse one's lips
fruslería F trifle
frustración F frustration
frustrar VT (los planes) to frustrate, to thwart, to foil; (las esperanzas) to shatter, to dash; —**se** to fail, to miscarry
fruta F fruit
frutero -era MF fruit vendor; M fruit dish
fruto M fruit; —**s del mar** seafood
fue ver ser, ir
fuego M fire; (para un cigarro) light; — **antiaéreo** antiartillery fire; —**s artificiales** fireworks; **abrir el** — to begin to fire; **alto el** — cease-fire; **bajo** — under fire; **arma de** — firearm; **entre dos** —**s** between a rock and a hard place; **hacer** — to fire; **prender/poner/pegar** — **a** to set fire to
fuelle M bellows
fuel-oil M fuel oil
fuente F (surtidor) fountain; (manantial, referencia) spring; (caracteres de imprenta) font; **de buena** — from the horse's mouth
fuera ADV (en el exterior) outside; (tenis) out; — **de** outside of; — **de borda** outboard; — **de combate** out of commission; — **de juego** (fútbol) offside; — **de límites** (golf) out of bounds; — **de línea** offline; — **de serie** one of a kind; — **de servicio** out of service; INTERJ out!
fuera, fuéramos ver ser, ir
fuero M (jurisdicción) jurisdiction; (privilegio) privilege, charter
fuerte ADJ (hombre, bebida) strong; (ruido) loud; (cuero) tough; (personalidad) forceful; (estantería) sturdy; (plato) hearty; M (castillo) fort; (talento especial) strong point; ADV (tirar) strongly; (respirar) heavily; (gritar) loud; **soplar** — to bluster; **pisar** — to stomp; **atar** — to tie tight
fuerza F (de una máquina) force; (de una persona, animal) strength; — **aérea** air force; — **bruta** brute force; — **de la naturaleza** force of nature; — **de tarea** task force; — **de voluntad** willpower; —**s armadas** armed forces; **a** — **de** by dint of; **con** — strongly; **hacer** — to press on; **por la** — by force; **sacar** — **de flaqueza** to pull oneself

together
fuerza, fuerce ver forzar
fuese, fuésemos ver ser, ir
fuga F (escape) escape, flight; (de la cárcel) jailbreak; (de gas) leak; (de capitales) drain, flight
fugarse[40] VI to flee, to escape; — **con el dinero** to abscond with the money
fugaz ADJ fleeting
fugitivo -va ADJ fugitive; MF fugitive
fui, fuimos ver ser, ir
fulano -na MF so-and-so; —, **zutano y mengano** Tom, Dick, and Harry; F tart, tramp
fulgor M radiance
fulgurar VI to flash
full M full house
fullero -ra MF (tramposo) cheat; (en naipes) card sharp
fulminante M cap; ADJ devastating
fulminar VT to strike with lightning; to thunder; **lo fulminó con la mirada** she gave him a withering look
fumadero M crackhouse
fumador -ora MF smoker
fumar VI/VT to smoke; —**se mucho dinero** to blow a lot of money
fumigar[40] VT to fumigate, to fog
función F (uso) function; (representación) performance; (cargo) office; — **de búsqueda** search function
funcional ADJ functional; **una casa** — a practical/livable house
funcionamiento M operation, working
funcionar VI to function, to work; (motor) to run
funcionario -ria MF government employee, official; — **de préstamos** loan officer
funda F (de un mueble) cover; (de una almohada) pillowcase, slip; (de navaja) sheath
fundación F foundation
fundador -ora MF founder
fundamental ADJ (básico) fundamental; (importante) crucial
fundamentalmente ADV fundamentally, mainly
fundamentar VT to base, to support; —**se en/ sobre** to be based on, to be supported by
fundamento M foundation, basis; —**s** fundamentals
fundar VT (un instituto) to found, to establish; (un argumento) to base
fundición F (fábrica) foundry; (acción de fundirse) fusing
fundido ADJ molten; M (en cinematografía) fade-in/fade-out
fundidor -ora MF foundry worker
fundir VT (combinar) to fuse; (derretir) to melt; (moldear) to mold; —**se** (combinarse) to fuse;

(romperse una bombilla) to burn out
fúnebre ADJ (relativo a funerales) funeral;
(lúgubre) funereal
funeral ADJ & M funeral
funerario -ria ADJ funeral; F funeral parlor; MF
funeral director
funesto ADJ ill-fated, unlucky
fungible ADJ fungible
fungicida M fungicide
funicular M cable car
funky ADJ funky
furgón M (vagón) boxcar; (camioneta de policía)
police van; — **blindado** armored vehicle; —
de cola caboose
furia F fury
furibundo ADJ furious, livid
furioso ADJ (persona) furious; (tempestad) fierce
furor M fury; **hacer** — to be all the rage
furtivo ADJ furtive, stealthy
fuselaje M fuselage
fusible M electric fuse
fusil M rifle
fusilamiento M execution by firing squad
fusilar VT to execute with firearms
fusión F (de hielo) melting; (nuclear) fusion;
(empresarial) merger; (de documentos
digitales) merge; **fusiones y
adquisiciones** mergers and acquisitions
fusionar VT (metales) to fuse; (compañías,
documentos digitales) to merge
fusta F crop
fustigar[40] VT (golpear) to lash, to whip;
(criticar) to lash out at
fútbol M soccer; — **americano** football
futbolista MF soccer player
fútil ADJ futile, trivial
futilidad F triviality
futuro ADJ future; M future; —**s** futures

Gg

gabacho -cha ADJ & MF (francés) *pey* frog;
(americano) *pey* American
gabán M overcoat
gabardina F trench coat
gabinete M (ministerial) cabinet;
(administrativo) office
Gabón M Gabon/Gabun
gabonés -esa ADJ & MF Gabonese
gacela F gazelle
gaceta F gazette
gacetilla F short news item
gachas F PL — **de avena** oatmeal
gachí F bimbo

gacho ADJ (orejas) drooping; (cabeza) bowed;
(ojos) lowered
gachupín -ina MF *Méx pey* Spaniard
gafar VT to jinx
gafas F PL glasses
gafe M jinx
gaffe M gaffe, faux pas
gag M gag
gaita F bagpipe
gaje M —**s del oficio** occupational hazards
gajo M (de planta) branch; (de naranja) section
gala F (cena) banquet; —**s** finery; **hacer** — **de** to
boast of, to flaunt; **vestirse de** — to dress up
galán M (pretendiente) gallant, suitor; (en cine)
leading man
galante ADJ gallant
galantear VT to court
galanteo M courting
galantería F (caballerosidad) gallantry;
(cumplido) compliment
galardón M award
galaxia F galaxy
galera F galley (también prueba de imprenta);
RP top hat
galerada F galley proof
galería F (salón) gallery; (pasillo) corridor;
(tiendas) mall, gallery; (de coro) loft;
(subterráneo) tunnel; —**s** *Esp* department
store
Gales M Wales
galés -esa ADJ & MF Welsh
galgo M greyhound
Galicia F Galicia
gallardete M pennant
gallardía F (elegancia) elegance; (valentía)
bravery
gallardo ADJ (elegante) elegant; (valiente) brave
gallego -ga ADJ Galician; M (lengua) Galician;
MF Galician
gallera F cockpit
galleta F (salada) cracker; (dulce) cookie
gallina F (pollo) chicken; (hembra adulta) hen;
MF coward; — **ciega** blind man's bluff; **la** —
de los huevos de oro the goose that laid the
golden egg
gallinero M (de gallinas) chicken coop; (de
teatro) gallery; **alborotar el** — to raise a
ruckus
gallito ADJ cocksure, cocky; M braggart
gallo M cock, rooster; (de la voz) break; **tener**
—**s en la garganta** to have a frog in one's
throat; **en menos que canta un** — before
you can say Jack Robinson
galón M (de líquido) gallon; (de tela) stripe
galopar VI/VT to gallop
galope M gallop; **al** — at a gallop
galvanizar[47] VT to galvanize
gama F gamut, range
gamba F large shrimp

gamberro -rra MF (rebelde, pandillero) punk, hoodlum; *Esp* (en fútbol) hooligan

Gambia F Gambia

gambiano -na ADJ & MF Gambian

gamo M buck

gamuza F (animal) chamois (también piel); (piel de venado) buckskin, deerskin; (piel de vaca) suede

gana F urge; **con —s** with a vengeance; **de buena —** willingly; **tener —s de** to feel like; **tengo —s [de ir al baño]** I have to go [to the bathroom]; **no me da la —** I just don't feel like it

ganadería F (cría) cattle breeding; (ganado) livestock

ganadero -ra M cattleman; F cattlewoman; ADJ **industria ganadera** cattle industry

ganado M livestock; **— ovino** sheep; **— porcino** swine; **— vacuno** cattle

ganador -ora MF winner; ADJ winning

ganancia F profit, gain, return; **—s** (recaudación de un evento) proceeds; (de un juego) winnings; (de un negocio) earnings; **—s pre-impositivas** before-tax earnings

ganapán M (obrero) menial worker; (trabajo) bread and butter

ganar VI/VT (una guerra, la lotería) to win; (kilos, eficacia) to gain; VT (un sueldo) to earn; (tiempo, espacio) to save; (tierra) to reclaim; **dejarse — por algo** to give in to something; **nos ganaron el partido** they beat us; **—se la vida** to make a living

ganchillo M crochet

gancho M hook (también en boxeo, baloncesto); (rama) snag; (para sujetar) clip; (atractivo) lure; **echar a uno el —** to hook someone; **tener —** to be attractive

gandul -la MF loafer

ganga F bargain, steal

gangoso ADJ twangy

gangrena F gangrene

gangrenarse VI to gangrene

gángster M gangster

ganguear VI to twang

ganso M (animal) goose; (macho) gander; (tonto) *fam* ding-a-ling

ganzúa F picklock

gañido M yelp

gañir[17] VI to yelp

garabatear VI/VT to scribble

garabato M scribble; **hacer —s** to scribble

garaje M garage

garante MF voucher

garantía F (de producto) guarantee, warranty; (de promesa) security, guaranty; (de un derecho) guarantee; (comercial) backing; **— de devolución de dinero** money-back guarantee; **— de préstamo** loan guarantee

garantizar[47] VT (producto) to guarantee, to

warranty; (promesa) to warrant

garañón M stud, horse

garbanzo M chickpea

garbo M grace

garboso ADJ graceful

garfio M hook

garganta F (faringe) throat; (cuello) neck; (valle estrecho) gorge

gárgara F gargle; **hacer —s** to gargle

gargarismo M gargle

garita F sentry box

garito M gambling house

garra F (de ave) claw; (de león) paw with claws; **caer en las —s de alguien** to fall into someone's clutches

garrafa F decanter

garrapata F tick

garrapatear VI/VT to scribble

garrapiñar VT to candy

garrocha F pole

garrote M club

garrucha F pulley

gárrulo ADJ garrulous

garza F heron

gas M gas; **—es** (de motor) fumes; (de intestino) gas; **— ionizado** plasma; **— lacrimógeno** tear gas; **— mostaza** mustard gas; **— natural** natural gas; **— nervioso** nerve gas; **a todo —** at full speed

gasa F (tela) gauze; (para heridas) dressing

gaseosa F soda, soft drink

gaseoso ADJ gaseous

gasoducto M pipeline

gasolina F gasoline, gas

gasolinera F gas station

gastado ADJ (neumático) smooth; (ropa) worn-out, shabby

gastador -ora ADJ extravagant, wasteful; MF spendthrift

gastar VT (dinero, tiempo) to spend; (energía) to expend; (neumáticos, ropa) to wear out, to use up; **— una broma** to play a trick; **—se** to wear out

gasto M (desembolso) expense, expenditure; (desgaste) wear; **—s de desplazamiento** travel costs; **—s del hogar** household expenses; **—s de subsistencia** living expenses; **—s de viaje** travel expenses; **—s menores** incidentals

gástrico ADJ gastric

gastritis F gastritis

gastroenteritis F gastroenteritis

gastrointestinal ADJ gastrointestinal

gastronomía F gastronomy

gatas LOC ADV **a —** on all fours

gatear VI to creep, to crawl

gatillo M (de arma de fuego) trigger; (de dentista) forceps

gatito M kitten

gato M (felino) cat; (aparato para levantar) jack; — **montés** wildcat, mountain lion; **aquí hay** — **encerrado** I smell a rat; **a gatas** on all fours; **dar** — **por liebre** to sell someone a pig in a poke

gaucho M gaucho

gaveta F small drawer

gavilán M hawk

gavilla F (de maíz) sheaf; (de maleantes) gang

gaviota F seagull

gayola F *fam* big house

gazmoñería F prudery

gazmoño -ña MF prude; ADJ prudish

gaznate M gullet

gazpacho M *Esp* gazpacho

geco M gecko

géiser M geyser

gel M gel

gelatina F gelatin

gélido ADJ frigid

gema F gem, jewel

gemelo -la ADJ & MF identical twin; **—s** (mellizos) identical twins; (binoculares) binoculars, opera glasses; (botón) studs

gemido M (de dolor) moan, groan; (de queja) whine

gemir[9] VI (gruñir) to moan, to groan; (lloriquear) to whine

gen, gene M gene; — **recesivo** recessive gene

genealogía F genealogy

generación F generation

generador M generator

general ADJ & MF general; **por lo** — generally

generalidad F generality

generalización F (de un concepto) generalization; (de una moda) spreading

generalizar[47] VI/VT to generalize; **—se** to become widespread

generalmente ADV generally, usually

generar VT generate

genérico ADJ generic

género M (clase) kind; (gramatical) gender; (tela) material; (literario) genre; (biológico) genus; — **humano** human race; **—s** dry goods

generosidad F generosity

generoso ADJ generous

genética F genetics

genético ADJ genetic

genial ADJ brilliant

genio MF (persona inteligente) genius; M (inteligencia) genius, brilliance; (temperamento) temperament, nature; (mal humor) temper; **de mal** — mean; **de buen** — good-natured

genital ADJ genital; M PL **—es** genitals

geniudo ADJ quick-tempered

genocidio M genocide

genoma M genome

gente F people; — **de campo** country folk; — **de color** persons of color; — **en obra** men at work; — **joven** young people; — **menuda** small fry; **buena** — good person

gentil ADJ (cortés) gracious; (no judío) gentile; MF gentile

gentileza F graciousness

gentío M crowd

gentuza F rabble, riffraff

genuino ADJ genuine

geocéntrico ADJ geocentric

geoestacionario ADJ geostationary

geofísica F geophysics

geografía F geography

geográfico ADJ geographical

geología F geology

geológico ADJ geological

geometría F geometry

geométrico ADJ geometric

geopolítico ADJ geopolitical

Georgia F Georgia

georgiano -na ADJ & MF Georgian

geotérmico ADJ geothermal

geranio M geranium

gerencia F management

gerente MF manager

geriatría F geriatrics

geriátrico ADJ geriatric

germánico ADJ Germanic

germen M germ

germinar VI to germinate, to sprout

gerundio M gerund, present participle

gestación F gestation

gesticular VI (con ademanes) to gesture; (con movimientos exagerados) to gesticulate

gestión F (acción) step, measure; (dirección empresarial, digital) management; (administración política) administration; **—es** negotiations; — **de datos** data management; **hacer gestiones para** to take steps to

gestionar VT (negociar) to negotiate; (administrar) to administer, to manage

gesto M (con la cara) face; (con las manos) gesture; **hacerle —s a alguien** to make faces at someone

gestor -ora MF agent

Ghana F Ghana

ghanés -esa ADJ & MF Ghanaian

giba F hump, hunch

gibón M gibbon

Gibraltar M Gibraltar

gibraltareño -ña ADJ & MF Gibraltarian

giga F jig

gigabyte M gigabyte

gigahercio M gigahertz

gigante ADJ giant, gigantic; MF giant

gigantesco ADJ gigantic

gilipollas MF INV *ofensivo* idiot, schmuck

gimnasia F gymnastics
gimnasio M gymnasium, gym
gimotear VI to whimper
gimoteo M whimper
ginebra F gin
ginecología F gynecology
ginecólogo -ga MF gynecologist
gingivitis F gingivitis
gira F tour
girar VI/VT (una llave, un volante, un coche, a la derecha) to turn; VI (un trompo, un disco) to revolve, to spin, to whirl; VT (dinero) to wire
girasol M sunflower
giratorio ADJ rotary, revolving
giro M (movimiento circular) rotation, spin; (cambio de dirección) turn; (expresión) turn of phrase; (monetario) draft, remittance; — **de cheques sin fondos** check kiting; — **postal** money order
giroscopio M gyroscope
gitano -na ADJ & MF gypsy
glacial ADJ glacial, bitter
glaciar M glacier
gladiador M gladiator
glamoroso ADJ glamorous
glamour M glamour
glándula F gland; —**s sudoríparas** sweat glands
glandular ADJ glandular
glaseado M (de torta) glaze; ADJ (papel) glossy
glasear VT to glaze
glaucoma M glaucoma
glicerina F glycerin
global ADJ (mundial) global; (de conjunto) blanket, overall
globalización F globalization
globo M (esfera) globe; (de árbol de Navidad) ball; (lleno de gas) balloon; (en tenis) lob; — **ocular** eyeball; — **terráqueo** globe
globulina F globulin
glóbulo M globule; — **rojo** red cell; — **blanco** white cell
gloria F glory
glorieta F (pérgola) arbor; (rotonda) traffic circle
glorificar[30] VT to glorify
glorioso M glorious
glosa F gloss
glosar VT to gloss
glosario M glossary
glotal ADJ glottal
glótico ADJ glottal
glotis F glottis
glotón -ona ADJ gluttonous; MF glutton
glotonería F gluttony
glucosa F glucose
gluglutear VI to gobble
gluten M gluten
gobernabilidad F governability

gobernación F (acción de gobernar) governing; (entidad gubernamental) government
gobernador -ora ADJ governing; MF governor
gobernante ADJ governing; MF ruler
gobernar[1] VI/VT to govern, to rule; (un buque) to steer
gobierno M government
goce M enjoyment
gofre M waffle
gol M goal; — **de campo** (fútbol americano) field goal; — **del empate** (fútbol) equalizer; — **en contra** (fútbol) own goal
goleador -ora MF (artillero) shooter; (máximo anotador) top scorer
goleta F schooner
golf M golf
golfo -fa M (mar) gulf; (sinvergüenza) rascal; F pey tramp
gollería F delicacy
golondrina F swallow
golosina F sweet, goody, tidbit
goloso ADJ sweet-toothed
golpazo M bang, whack
golpe M (físico) blow, knock, whack; (emocional) blow; (estafa) sting; (robo) holdup; (golf) stroke; (de viento) buffet; (con el codo) jab; (con los nudillos) rap; — **bajo** low blow; — **cortado** (tenis) backspin, slice; — **cruzado** (tenis) crosscourt shot; — **de aproximación** (golf) approach shot; — **de calor** heat stroke; — **de derecha** (tenis) forehand; — **de estado** coup; — **de gracia** coup de grâce; — **de penalidad** (golf) penalty stroke; — **de sol** sunstroke; **de** — suddenly; **de un** — all at once
golpear VI/VT (pegar) to strike, to hit; (llamar) to knock, to rap; (dar una paliza) to beat, to batter; (patear) to kick; (codear) to jab
golpecito M tap
golpetear VI (dedos) to tap; (lluvia) to patter; (motor) to knock; (algo suelto) to rattle
golpeteo M (con los dedos) tap; (de lluvia) patter; (de un motor) knock; (de algo suelto) rattle
goma F (chicle) gum; (caucho) rubber; (neumático) tire; (en béisbol) home; — **de borrar** eraser; — **de mascar** chewing gum; — **elástica** rubber band; —**espuma** foam
gomero M rubber tree
gomoso ADJ slimy
gónada F gonad
góndola F gondola
gong M gong
gonorrea F gonorrhea, fam the clap
gordinflón ADJ pey fatso
gordito ADJ chubby
gordo ADJ fat; **se armó la gorda** all hell broke loose; **hacer la vista gorda** to turn a blind eye

gordura F (cualidad) fatness; (sebo) fat
gorgojo M weevil
gorila M (primate) gorilla; (portero) bouncer; (guardaespaldas) bodyguard
gorjear VI (ave) to warble, to chirp, to twitter; (niño) to gurgle
gorjeo M (de ave) warble, twitter, chirp; (de niño) gurgle
gorra F cap; **de** — at someone else's expense; **vivir de** — to sponge
gorrino M piglet
gorrión M sparrow
gorro M cap
gorrón M sponge, sponger
gorronear VI/VT to mooch, to freeload
gospel M gospel
gota F (de líquido) drop; (de sudor) bead; (enfermedad) gout; — **a** — drop by drop; —**s oftálmicas** eyedrops; **ser dos** —**s de agua** to be like two peas in a pod; **sudar la** — **gorda** (transpirar) to sweat profusely; (trabajar) to work hard
gotear VI (caer gota a gota) to drip; (rápidamente) to dribble, to trickle; (salirse) to leak; (llover) to sprinkle
goteo M drip (también intravenoso); (rápido) dribble, trickle
gotera F leak
gotero M dropper
gótico ADJ Gothic; M (lengua) Gothic
gourmet ADJ & MF gourmet
gozar⁴⁷ VT to enjoy; — **de** to enjoy
gozne M hinge
gozo M pleasure, enjoyment
gozoso ADJ enjoyable
grabación F recording
grabado M (en piedra) engraving; (con ácido) etching
grabador-ora MF (persona) engraver; F (aparato) tape recorder; (empresa) recording company
grabar VI/VT (en piedra) to engrave; (con ácido) to etch; (en cinta magnetográfica) to record, to tape; (en computadora) to write; — **en la memoria** to etch/imprint on one's memory
gracejo M wit
gracia F (garbo, desenvoltura) grace, gracefulness; (humor) humor; (monería) antic; (favor) favor; (indulto) pardon; ¡—**s**! thanks! thank you! —**s a Dios** thank God; **caer en** — to please; **dar** —**s** to say the blessing; **dar las** —**s** to thank; **hacer** — to amuse; **tener** — to be funny
grácil ADJ supple, graceful
gracioso ADJ (chistoso) amusing, funny; (gentil) gracious
grada F step, bleachers
gradación F gradation
graderías F PL bleachers

grado M (de temperatura, de parentesco, de un ángulo, de universidad) degree; (militar) rank; (de alcohol) proof; **de buen** — willingly; **en alto** — to a great extent; **en mayor o menor** — to some extent; **quemadura de primer** — first-degree burn
graduación F (de una escuela) graduation, commencement; (militar) military rank; (de alcohol) proof; (de un lente óptico) correction
graduado-da MF graduate
gradual ADJ gradual
graduar²⁶ VT (ajustar) to adjust; (regular) to calibrate; —**se** to graduate, to get a degree
graffiti M graffiti
grafiar²⁸ VT to graph
gráfica F (arte) graphics; (representación) graph, chart; — **de pastel** pie graph
graficar³⁰ VT to chart
gráfico-ca ADJ graphic; **acento** — written accent; M (representación) graph, chart; MF (empleado) printer
grafito M graphite
grama F lawn
gramática F grammar
gramatical ADJ grammatical
gramo M gram
grana ADJ & F scarlet
granada F (fruta) pomegranate; (proyectil) grenade; — **de mano** hand grenade
Granada F Grenada
granadino-na ADJ & MF Grenadian
granado M pomegranate tree; ADJ notable
granate M garnet
Gran Bretaña F Great Britain
grande ADJ (de tamaño) large, big; (de importancia) great; **un gran poeta** a great poet; **divertirse en** — to have a whale of a time; **a** —**s alturas** at high altitudes; **de gran alcance** far-reaching; **de/a gran escala** large-scale; **en gran parte** in large measure, largely; **gran almacén** department store
grandeza F greatness; **delirios de** — delusions of grandeur
grandiosidad F grandeur
grandioso ADJ grandiose, grand
granero M (edificio) granary, grain barn; (recipiente) bin, crib; **el** — **de América** the breadbasket of America
granito M granite
granizada F hailstorm
granizar⁴⁷ VI to hail
granizo M hail
granja F farm
granjearse VI to win for oneself
granjero-ra MF farmer
grano M (de una foto, arena, semilla) grain; (cereal) cereal, grain; (barrito) pimple; — **de**

café coffee bean; **ir al** — to come to the point
granuja MF ragamuffin
granular VT to granulate; —**se** to become granulated
granuloso ADJ granular
grapa F (para sujetar madera) clamp; (para sujetar papel) staple
grapadora F stapler
grasa F (aceite) grease; (animal) fat
grasiento ADJ greasy
graso ADJ (cutis) oily; (leche) fatty; (pelo) greasy
grasoso ADJ greasy
gratificación F bonus
gratificar[30] VT to gratify
gratis ADJ INV & ADV free
gratitud F gratitude, thankfulness
grato ADJ pleasant
gratuito ADJ (gratis) free; (arbitrario) wanton, gratuitous
grava F gravel
gravamen M (impuesto) tax, assessment; (carga sobre una propiedad) lien, encumbrance
gravar VT (con un impuesto) to tax, to assess; (con una carga) to encumber
grave ADJ (enfermedad, decisión) grave, serious; (sonido) low, deep; (injuria) grievous; (personalidad) earnest
gravedad F (fuerza de atracción) gravity; (de una situación) seriousness; (de una tormenta) severity; (de la voz) depth; (de una personalidad) earnestness
gravemente ADV (herido) seriously; (enfermo) seriously, gravely
gravitación F gravitation
gravitatorio ADJ gravitational
gravoso ADJ burdensome
graznar VI (cuervo) to caw, to croak; (pato) to quack; (ganso) to honk
graznido M (de cuervo) caw, croak; (de pato) quack; (de ganso) honk
Grecia F Greece
greda F clay
green M green
gregario ADJ gregarious
gremial ADJ **acuerdo** — union agreement
gremio M (conjunto de personas) trade; (asociación histórica) guild; (sindicato) trade union
greña F mop of hair
grey F flock, fold
griego -ga ADJ & MF Greek
grieta F crevice, crack
grifo M faucet, spigot, tap
grillete M fetter, shackle
grillo M (insecto) cricket; —**s** (grilletes) shackles
grima F uneasiness; **dar** — (disgustar) to be upsetting; (asquear) to be disgusting
gringo -ga ADJ & MF *pey* American
gripe, gripa F flu, influenza; — **asiática**

Asiatic flu
gris ADJ & M gray
grisáceo ADJ grayish
gritar VI/VT (vociferar) to shout, to yell; (chillar) to scream
gritería F shouting
grito M (voz alta) shout, cry; (chillido) scream; **el último** — the last word; **estar en un** — to be in agony; **pedir a** —**s** to clamor for; **poner el** — **en el cielo** to hit the ceiling
grosella F currant
grosellero M currant
grosería F (cualidad) rudeness; (hecho, dicho) profanity, something rude
grosero ADJ (descortés) rude, ill-mannered, boorish; (vulgar) vulgar, profane; (sin arte) coarse, unrefined
grosor M thickness
grotesco ADJ grotesque
grúa F (máquina) crane; (guinche, remolcadora) wrecker, tow truck
grueso -sa ADJ (persona) thick-set, heavy; (tabla) thick; (palabra, arena) coarse; M (grosor) thickness; (mayoría) majority; F gross
grulla F crane
grumo M lump
grumoso ADJ lumpy
gruñido M (de perro) growl, snarl; (de cerdo) grunt; (humano) grumble
gruñir[17] VI (el cerdo) to grunt; (el perro) to growl, to snarl; (el ser humano) to grumble
gruñón -ona ADJ grumpy; MF grumpy person
grupa F rump; **volver** —**s** to turn around
grupo M group; — **de apoyo** support group; — **de presión** lobby; — **étnico** ethnicity; — **paritario** peer group; — **sanguíneo** blood type; — **de usuarios** user group
gruta F grotto, cavern
guacal M crate
guacamole M *Méx* guacamole
guacho M (cría de ave) chick; *Am* (animal huérfano) orphan
guadaña F scythe
guagua F (fruslería) trifle; *Carib* bus; *Chile* baby; LOC ADV **de** — for nothing, free
guaje -ja MF urchin
guano M guano, bird dung
guantada F slap
guante M glove (también en deporte); **arrojar el** — to challenge; **echarle el** — **a alguien** to capture someone; **te queda como un** — it fits you like a glove
guantelete M gauntlet
guantera F glove compartment
guapetón -ona MF *fam* fox
guapo ADJ (hombre) good-looking, handsome; (mujer) good-looking, pretty; (valiente) brave; ¡**hola**—! hey, good-looking!

guarapo M cane syrup
guarda MF (guardián) guard; F (almacenamiento) storage
guardameta MF (fútbol) goalkeeper
guardar VT (almacenar) to keep, to store; (observar) to observe; (datos) to save; (proteger) to guard; — **como** to save as; — **rencor** to hold a grudge; — **un secreto** to keep a secret; —**se de** to guard against; M SG **guardabarros** fender; M SG **guardacostas** Coast Guard cutter; MF SG **guardaespaldas** bodyguard; M SG **guardafangos** fender; M SG **guardapelo** locket; M SG **guardarropa** (armario, ropa) wardrobe; (en un local) cloakroom; MF SG **guardabosque[s]** forest ranger, forester; MF SG **guardafrenos** brake operator; MF SG **guardagujas** switch operator; MF SG **guardameta** goalie
guardería F nursery, day-care center
guardia MF (vigilante) guard; (en baloncesto) point guard; — **civil** civil guard; F (vigilancia) guard; **bajar la** — to let down one's guard; **de** — (militar) on duty, on watch; (médico) on call; **en** — en garde; **hacer/montar** — to stand guard
guardián -ana MF guardian, keeper
guarecerse[35] VT to take shelter
guarida F den, lair
guarismo M cipher
guarnecer[35] VT (un plato) to garnish; (un vestido) to trim; (una fortaleza) to man, to garrison
guarnición F (de tropas) garrison; (de comida) trimmings; **guarniciones** harness
guarro ADJ filthy; M pig
guasa LOC ADV **de/a** — in jest, as a joke
guasón -ona MF joker
guata F padding
Guatemala F Guatemala
guatemalteco -ca ADJ & MF Guatemalan
guau INTERJ woof
guay ADJ *Esp* cool, great
guayaba F guava
guayabera F tropical pleated shirt
gubernamental ADJ governmental
gubernativo ADJ governmental
gubia F gouge
guedeja F shock of hair
guepardo M cheetah
guerra F war, warfare; **dar** — to aggravate; **en pie de** — at war; — **fría** cold war
guerrear VI to war
guerrero -ra MF warrior; **operación guerrera** war operation; **espíritu** — warrior spirit
guerrilla F guerrilla army
guerrillero -ra MF guerrilla
gueto M ghetto
guía MF (persona) guide, leader; F (cosa o

animal) guide; — **para padres** parenting guide; — **telefónica** telephone directory
guiar[28] VT to guide, to lead; —**se por** to follow
guijarro M pebble
guinche M *Am* (grúa) winch; (remolque) tow truck
guinda F cherry
guindilla F *Esp* small hot pepper
Guinea F Guinea
guineano -na ADJ & MF Guinean
guingán M gingham
guiñada F wink
guiñapo M rag
guiñar VI/VT to wink
guiño M wink
guión M (ortografía) hyphen; (libreto) script, screenplay
guionista MF screenwriter
guirnalda F garland; (de Navidad) tinsel
guisa F a — **de** by way of
guisado M stew, hash
guisante M pea
guisar VI/VT (cocer) to cook; (en olla) to stew
guiso M stew, casserole
guitarra F guitar
gula F gluttony
gusano M worm; — **de seda** silkworm
gustar VT (agradar) to be pleasing to; **ella me gusta** I like her; **le gustan los perros** he likes dogs; **no me gustan las fiestas** I dislike parties; **te guste o no te guste** whether you like it or not; **cuando gustes** whenever you want; — **de** (preferir) to be fond of; (saborear) to taste
gusto M (sentido, sabor, sentido estético) taste; (agrado) pleasure; (preferencia personal) like; **a** — at ease; **a mi** — to my liking; **dar** — to be a pleasure; **darle el** — **a alguien** to humor someone; **darse el** — to indulge oneself; **de mal** — in bad taste; **el** — **es mío** the pleasure is mine; **estar a** — to be comfortable; **mucho** — nice to meet you; **por** — for fun; **tener el** — **de** to have the pleasure of; **tomarle el** — **a una cosa** to become fond of something
gustoso ADJ (que gusta de) fond of; (agradable) pleasant; ADV willingly
Guyana F Guyana
guyanés -esa ADJ & MF Guyanese

Hh

ha, has *ver* haber
haba F (frijol) bean; (frijol verde) lima bean
habano M cigar

haber[68] v AUX to have; — **comido cuatro veces en un día** to have eaten four times in a day; **habérselas con** (un problema) to grapple with; (una persona) to have it out with; **ha de llegar mañana** he is to arrive tomorrow; **hay** there is, there are; **hay viento** it is windy; **hubo un problema** there was a problem; **había gente** there were people; **hay que** it is necessary to; **no hay de qué** don't mention it; **no hay forma** no way; **no hay problema** no problem; **¿qué hay?** what's up? **todo lo habido y por haber** everything possible; M (hacienda) assets; (columna en una cuenta) credit; **—es** earnings

habichuela F bean; — **verde** string bean

hábil ADJ adept, able; **día —** workday

habilidad F ability, skill

habilidoso ADJ deft, skillful

habilitar VT (equipar) to outfit; (autorizar) to authorize

habitación F (vivienda) dwelling; (cuarto) room

habitante MF (de un país, región) inhabitant; (de un barrio) resident

habitar VT to inhabit

hábitat M habitat

hábito M habit (también vestimenta religiosa); **—s de compra** buying habits

habitual ADJ habitual, usual

habituar[26] VT to accustom; **—se** to get used to

habla F (lenguaje) speech; (variedad local) dialect; — **infantil** baby talk; **al —** in communication with; **quedarse sin —** to be left speechless

hablador ADJ talkative

habladurías F idle talk, gossip

hablante ADJ speaking; **castellano—** Castilian-speaking; MF speaker; **castellano—** Castilian speaker

hablar VI/VT to talk; — **de política** to talk about politics; — **hasta por los codos** to talk one's head off; — **no cuesta nada** talk is cheap; — **por teléfono** to talk on the phone; — **solo / para sí** to talk to oneself; to speak; — **francés** to speak French; — **sin rodeos** to speak one's mind; — **por señas** to use sign language; **hablando mal y pronto** pardon my French; **no —se** not to be on speaking terms; **no me hagas —** don't get me started on it; **hablando en serio, ¿qué es lo que quieres?** seriously, what do you want?

hablilla F malicious tale

habrá, habría ver haber

hacedor -ora MF maker

hacendado -da MF landowner

hacendoso ADJ industrious, diligent

hacer[54, 74] VT (crear) to do, to make; (causar) to make; (resolver) to do; (decir) to go; **la vaca hace 'mu'** the cow goes moo; — **clic** to click; — **economías** to scrimp; — **frío/calor/ viento** to be cold/hot/windy; — **una oferta** make an offer; — **un pastel** to make a cake; — **un crucigrama** to do a crossword puzzle; — **un gol** to score a goal; **me hizo llorar** he made me cry; **hace mucho tiempo** a long time ago; **hace poco** a short while ago; **hizo como si estuvieras presente** he acted as if you were here; **a lo hecho, pecho** you've got to face the music; **la hiciste buena** you've really screwed up; **¿qué le vamos a hacer?** that's life; **¿qué se hizo de Juan?** whatever became of Juan? **haz el trabajo** do the work; **hecho a pedido** built to order; **—se rico** to become rich; **—se el tonto** to play the fool; **—se el listo** to pull a stunt; **—se pasar por el jefe** to pose as the boss; **—se a un lado** to step aside; **—se amigo de** to befriend; **—se a la oscuridad** to get used to the dark; **—se cargo** to take over; **—se [del] rogar** to play hard to get

hacha F (grande) ax[e]; (pequeña) hatchet

hachís M hashish

hacia PREP (en dirección a) toward; (aproximadamente) about; — **abajo** downward; — **adelante** forward; — **adentro** inward; — **afuera** outward; — **arriba** upward; — **atrás** backward; — **el este** eastward; — **la izquierda** to the left; **dar —** to face

hacienda F (bienes) estate; (establecimiento agropecuario) ranch; (impositiva) Internal Revenue Service

hacina F shock

hacinar VT (liar) to shock; (atestar) to crowd in

hada F fairy

hado M fate

haga, hago ver hacer

Haití M Haiti

haitiano -na ADJ & MF Haitian

halagar[40] VT to flatter, to compliment

halago M flattery, compliment

halagüeño ADJ (palabras) flattering; (perspectiva) promising

halcón M falcon

hálito M breath

halitosis F halitosis

hallar VT to find; **—se** to be; **—se en un aprieto** to be in a pickle; **—se mal de salud** to be in a bad way

hallazgo M finding; **ese documento fue un — sensacional** that document was a real find

halo M halo

halógeno ADJ & M halogen

halterofilia F weight training, weightlifting

hamaca F hammock

hambre F (deseo de comer) hunger; (hambruna) famine; **tener —** to be hungry; **pasar —** to go hungry; **morirse de —** to starve

hambrear VI/VT to starve
hambriento ADJ (con hambre) hungry; (famélico) famished, starving
hambruna F famine
hamburguesa F hamburger
hampa F underworld
hámster M hamster
hándicap M handicap
handicapar VT to handicap
hangar M hangar
hará, haría ver hacer
haragán -ana ADJ indolent; MF loafer
haraganear VI to loaf
haraganería F laziness
harapiento ADJ ragged, tattered
harapo M rag, tatter
hardware M hardware
harén M harem
harina F (fina) flour; (gruesa) meal; — **de avena** oat flour; — **de maíz** cornmeal; **es** — **de otro costal** that's another kettle of fish
hartar VT to satiate; —**se** (de comida) to have one's fill; (de aburrimiento) to get fed up
hartazgo M surfeit, excess
harto ADJ (satisfecho) full; **estar** — to be fed up; **ese asunto me tiene** — I'm sick and tired of the whole business
hasta PREP (temporal) till, until; (espacial) [up] to; — **ahora** to date / so far; — **cierto punto** to a certain extent; — **luego** good-bye, see you later; — **pronto** see you later; **caminó** — **la esquina** he walked to the corner; **lo llenó** — **el borde** he filled it up to brim; **estar** — **la coronilla** to be fed up; ADV even; — **mi madre lo notó** even my mother noticed it; — **que** until
hastiado ADJ jaded
hastial M gable
hastiar[28] VT to cloy, to tire; —**se** to grow weary of
hastío M tedium
hato M (envoltorio) bundle; (rebaño) herd
hay ver haber
haya F beech
haya, hayamos ver haber
hayuco M beechnut
haz[1] M (de leña) bundle; (de luz) beam; (de flechas) sheaf
haz[2] ver hacer
hazaña F deed, exploit, feat
hazmerreír M laughingstock
he VT IMPERSONAL **he aquí la lista** here's the list
he, hemos ver haber
hebilla F buckle
hebra F (de hilo) thread; (vegetal) fiber
hebreo -a ADJ & MF Hebrew
heces F PL (de vino, café) dregs; (excremento) feces

hechicería F enchantment
hechicero -ra ADJ bewitching; M sorcerer; F sorceress
hechizar[47] VT (embrujar) to bewitch, to enchant; (fascinar) to enthrall
hechizo M charm, spell
hecho M fact; **los** —**s de la noche del 17** the events of the night of the 17th; **de** — in fact
hecho ver hacer
hechura F cut
hectárea F hectare
heder[2] VI to stink, to reek
hediondez F stench
hediondo ADJ stinking, smelly
hedonismo M hedonism
hedor M stink, stench
hegemonía F hegemony
helada F (frente frío) freeze; (escarcha) frost
heladera F refrigerator
heladería F ice-cream parlor
helado ADJ (muy frío) frozen, freezing; (con hielo) icy; M ice cream
helar[1] VI/VT to freeze
helecho M fern
hélice F (espiral) helix; (de avión) propeller; (de barco) screw, propeller
helicóptero M helicopter
helio M helium
hematoma M hematoma
hembra F (de animal) female; (de venado) doe; (de ballena, foca) cow; (de ave) hen
hemisferio M hemisphere (también cerebral)
hemofilia F hemophilia
hemoglobina F hemoglobin
hemorragia F hemorrhage; — **cerebral** cerebral hemorrhage; — **vaginal** vaginal bleeding
hemorroide F hemorrhoid
henchir[9] VT to swell
hender[2] VI/VT to cleave, to split
hendido ADJ cleft, split
hendidura F (quebradura) crack; (geológica) fissure
henil M hayloft
heno M hay; **fiebre de** — hay fever
hepatitis F hepatitis
heraldo M herald
herbicida M weedkiller, herbicide
herbívoro ADJ herbivorous; M herbivore
herboso ADJ grassy
heredad F homestead
heredar VI/VT (recibir) to inherit; (dar) to bequeath
heredero -ra M heir; F heiress; —**s y cesionarios** heirs and assigns
hereditario ADJ hereditary
hereje MF heretic
herejía F heresy
herencia F (económica) inheritance; (cultural)

heritage; (genética) heredity
herida F (lastimadura) injury; (abierta) wound; — **de bala** gunshot wound; — **perforada** puncture wound; **respirar por la** — to reopen an old wound
herido ADJ (lastimado) injured; (con herida abierta) wounded
herir[8] VI/VT (lastimar) to injure; (con herida abierta) to wound; (sentimientos) to hurt
hermafrodita MF hermaphrodite
hermanastro -tra M stepbrother; F stepsister
hermandad F (de hombres) brotherhood; (de mujeres) sisterhood
hermanito -ta M little brother; F little sister
hermano -na MF sibling; M brother (también religioso); — **mayor** older brother; — **menor** younger brother; F sister (también religiosa); — **mayor** older sister; — **menor** younger sister
herméticamente ADV tight, tightly
hermético ADJ hermetic, airtight; (a prueba de agua) watertight; (que no revela secretos) secretive
hermosear VT to beautify
hermoso ADJ beautiful, lovely
hermosura F beauty
hernia F hernia
héroe M hero
heroico ADJ heroic
heroína F (droga) heroin; (personaje) heroine
heroísmo M heroism
herpes M (erupción) herpes; (en la boca) cold sore; — **febril** fever blister
herradura F horseshoe
herraje M ironwork
herramienta F tool
herrar[1] VT (un caballo) to shoe; (una vaca) to brand
herrería F blacksmith's shop
herrero -ra MF blacksmith
herrumbre F rust
hervidero M swarm
hervidor M kettle
hervir[8] VI/VT to boil; — **a fuego lento** to simmer; — **de** to be swarming with; **me hervía la sangre** I was seething
hervor M boiling; **levantar el** — to come to a boil
heterodoxo ADJ unorthodox
heterogéneo ADJ heterogeneous
heterosexual ADJ heterosexual; *fam* straight
hexágono M hexagon
hiato M hiatus
hibernar VI to hibernate
hibridación F hybridization
híbrido ADJ & M hybrid
hice, hiciera *ver* hacer
hidalgo M nobleman
hidalguía F (nobleza) nobility; (generosidad)

generosity
hidrato M hydrate
hidráulico ADJ hydraulic
hidroavión M hydroplane, seaplane
hidrocarburo M hydrocarbon
hidroeléctrico ADJ hydroelectric
hidrofobia F hydrophobia
hidrógeno M hydrogen
hiedra F ivy
hiel F gall
hielo M ice; — **seco** dry ice; **romper el** — to break the ice
hiena F hyena
hierba F (pasto) grass; (especia) herb; (marihuana) *fam* weed; —**buena** mint; **mala** — weed; **y otras** —**s** and so on
hierro M iron (también de golf); — **corrugado** corrugated iron; — **forjado** wrought iron; — **fundido** cast iron; —**s** handcuffs
hígado M liver; **malos** —**s** ill will
higiene F hygiene
higiénico ADJ hygienic
higienista MF hygienist
higo M fig; **me importa un** — I couldn't care less
higuera F fig tree
hijastro -tra M stepson; F stepdaughter
hijo -ja M son; — **de perra** *ofensivo* son of a bitch; — **de puta** *ofensivo* son of a bitch; — **de su madre** *fam* son of a gun; **John Smith** — John Smith Jr.; **sin** —**s** childless; F daughter; **hija de puta** *ofensivo* bitch
hilachas F loose threads
hilado M spinning
hilandería F (fábrica) spinning mill; (técnica) spinning
hilandero -ra MF spinner
hilar VI/VT to spin; — **fino** to split hairs
hilaridad F mirth
hilera F row, line
hilo M (para coser) thread; (para tejer, hilar) yarn; (alambre) filament; — **de agua** trickle; — **de pensamiento** train of thought; — **de perlas** string of pearls; — **de voz** thin voice; — **dental** floss; **al** — in a row; **mover** —**s** to pull strings; **seguir el** — **de** to keep track of; **pender de un** — to be hanging by a thread; **perder el** — to lose track
hilván M basting
hilvanar VT to baste, to tack
himen M hymen
himno M (religioso) hymn; (patriótico) anthem
hincapié M emphasis; **hacer** — to emphasize
hincar[30] VT — **los dientes en** to sink one's teeth into; —**se** to kneel
hincha MF (aficionado) supporter; F (antipatía) *Esp* grudge
hinchado ADJ (inflamado) swollen, bloated; (exagerado) inflated

hinchar VT (un río) to swell; (un globo) to blow up; — **por el equipo de Uruguay** to pull for the Uruguayan team; —**se** (cuerpo) to swell; (pulmones) to inflate; (mejillas) to bulge; (de orgullo) to puff up; (el pan) to rise

hinchazón F swelling

hindi M Hindi

hindú ADJ & MF Hindu

hinojos LOC ADV **de** — on one's knees

hipar VI hiccup

hiperactivo ADJ hyperactive, overactive

hiperdocumento M hyperdocument

hiperenlace M hyperlink

hipermedia M hypermedia

hipermercado M superstore

hipermétrope ADJ farsighted

hipersensible ADJ (a la luz) hypersensitive; (a la crítica) touchy

hipertensión F hypertension, high blood pressure

hiperventilar VI to hyperventilate

hipervínculo M hyperlink

hipnosis F hypnosis

hipnoterapia F hypnotherapy

hipnotizar VI/VT to hypnotize, to mesmerize

hipo M (espasmo) hiccup; (sollozo) sob; **tengo** — I have the hiccups

hipoalérgico ADJ hypoallergenic

hipocondríaco -ca, hipocondriaco -ca ADJ & MF hypochondriac

hipocresía F hypocrisy

hipócrita ADJ hypocritical, two-faced; MF hypocrite

hipódromo M racetrack

hipogloso M halibut

hipoglucemia F hypoglycemia

hipopótamo M hippopotamus

hipoteca F mortgage; — **con tasa de interés ajustable** adjustable-rate mortgage; — **de tasa fija** fixed-rate mortgage

hipotecar[30] VT to mortgage

hipotecario ADJ **banco** — mortgage bank

hipótesis F hypothesis

hipotiroidismo M hypothyroidism

hiriente ADJ (comentario) catty, hurtful

hirviente ADJ boiling

hisopo M swab

hispánico -ca ADJ Hispanic

hispano -na ADJ Hispanic, Spanish-speaking; MF (por su lengua) Spanish-speaking person; (por su etnia) Hispanic

Hispanoamérica F Spanish America

hispanoamericano ADJ Spanish-American

histamina F histamine

histerectomía F hysterectomy

histérico ADJ hysterical

historia F (el pasado, estudio del pasado) history; (relato) story; — **clínica** case history, medical history; **dejarse de** —**s** to stop fooling around; **esa es otra** — that's another story; **la** — **se repite** history repeats itself; **pasar a la** — to be a thing of the past

historiador -ora MF historian

historial M record; — **de crédito** credit history

histórico ADJ (de importancia histórica) historic; (pertinente a la historia) historical

historietas F PL funnies

histrionismo M histrionics

hito M landmark, milestone; **de** — **en** — fixedly; **marcar un** — to be a milestone

hobby M hobby

hocicar[30] VI/VT (un cerdo) to root; (un caballo) to nose

hocico M snout, muzzle

hockey M hockey

hogaño ADV *lit* nowadays

hogar M (lumbre) hearth, fireplace; (casa, asilo) home

hogareño ADJ domestic; **persona hogareña** homebody

hoguera F bonfire, campfire

hoja F (de planta) leaf; (de mesa plegable) flap; (de papel) sheet; (de libro) page; (de navaja) blade; — **clínica** medical chart; — **de afeitar** razor blade; — **de depósito** deposit slip; — **de ejercicios** worksheet; — **de metal** foil; **echar** —**s** to leaf; — **de servicio** record; F —**lata** tin plate

hojaldre M puff pastry

hojarasca F fallen leaves

hojear VT to page through, to flip through, to browse

hojuela F flake; —**s de maíz** cornflakes

hola INTERJ hello, hi

Holanda F Holland

holandés -esa ADJ Dutch; M (hombre) Dutchman; (lengua) Dutch; F Dutchwoman

holding M holding company

holgado ADJ (vida) comfortable; (pantalón) loose-fitting, baggy; (cuarto) roomy

holganza F (haraganería) idleness; (diversión) leisure

holgar[42] VI to loaf; **huelga decir** it is needless to say

holgazán -ana ADJ lazy, idle; MF idler, loafer, slouch

holgazanear VI to idle, to loaf

holgazanería F laziness

holgura F (de movimiento) ease; (financiera) comfort; (de la ropa) looseness

holístico ADJ holistic

hollejo M skin

hollín M soot, smut

holocausto M holocaust

hombre M man; — **anuncio** sandwich man; — **de bien** man of good will; — **de familia** family man; — **de las cavernas** caveman; — **de la calle** man on the street; — **de**

negocios businessman; **— del saco** bogeyman; **— de paja** straw man; **— lobo** werewolf; **— orquesta** one-man band; **— rana** frogman; **es bien —** he's a real he-man; INTERJ come on!

hombrera F shoulder pad

hombro M shoulder; **encogerse de —s** to shrug; **cargar al —** to shoulder; **en/a —s** piggyback; **poner el —** to lend a hand

hombruno ADJ mannish

home M home

homenaje M homage, tribute

homeopatía F homeopathy

homeopático ADJ homeopathic

homicida MF murderer

homicidio M homicide, murder; **— culposo/ involuntario** manslaughter; **— sin premeditación** manslaughter

homofobia F homophobia

homofóbico ADJ homophobic

homogeneizar[47] VT to homogenize

homogéneo ADJ homogeneous

homólogo -ga MF counterpart

homóplato M shoulder blade

homosexual ADJ homosexual; *fam* gay

honda F sling, slingshot

hondo ADJ deep; M hollow

hondonada F hollow, dell

hondura F depth; **meterse en —s** to get in over one's head

Honduras F Honduras

hondureño -ña ADJ & MF Honduran

honestidad F (castidad) chastity, modesty; (honradez) honesty

honesto ADJ (casto) chaste, modest; (honrado) honest, straightforward

hongo M (seta) mushroom; (moho) fungus; **aburrirse como un —** to be bored stiff

honor M honor; **con —es** with honors; **tener el — de** to have the honor of; **hacerle los —es a** to be appreciative of

honorable ADJ honorable

honorario ADJ honorary; M PL fee

honra F honor

honradez F honesty

honrado ADJ honest

honrar VT (respetar) to honor; (dignificar) to do credit to

honroso ADJ honorable

hora F hour; **— de dormir** bedtime; **— oficial** standard time; **— punta** rush hour; **—s extra[s]** overtime; **a esta —** at this time; **¿a qué —?** at what time? **a todas —s** at all hours; **a última —** at the last minute; **decir la —** to tell time; **en —** on time; **es — de** it is time to; **es — de que me vaya** it's time for me to go; **kilómetros por —** kilometers per hour; **no ver la — de** to be dying to; **por —** by the hour; **¿qué — es?** what time is it? **ya**

era — it was about time

horadar VT to bore

horario M (agenda) schedule, timetable; (manecilla del reloj) hour hand; **— de trabajo** work schedule

horca F (cadalso) gallows; (tridente) pitchfork; **— de ajos** string of garlic

horcajadas LOC ADV **a —** astraddle, astride

horda F horde

horizontal ADJ horizontal

horizonte M (del cielo) horizon; (de una ciudad) skyline

horma F (de zapato) shoe last; (de queso) wheel

hormiga F ant; **— blanca** termite

hormigón M concrete

hormigonera F cement mixer

hormiguear VI (moverse en grandes cantidades) to swarm; (dar sensación de hormigueo) to tingle

hormigueo M tingle

hormiguero M anthill

hormona F hormone; **— del crecimiento** growth hormone

hornada F batch

horneado M baking

hornear VI/VT to bake

hornilla F burner

horno M (industrial) furnace; (doméstico) oven; (para cerámica) kiln; **— de microondas** microwave oven; **alto —** blast furnace; **el — no está para bollos** it's not a good time; **recién salido del —** brand-new

horóscopo M horoscope

horquilla F (para el pelo) hairpin; (horca) pitchfork

horrendo ADJ (asesinato) horrific, ghastly; (vestido) hideous, ghastly

horrible ADJ horrible

horripilante ADJ gruesome, hair-raising

horror M (miedo, repulsión) horror; (monstruosidad) abomination; (espectáculo) sight; **tenerle — a** to be scared of

horrorizar[47] VT to horrify, to shock, to appall

horroroso ADJ appalling, awful

hortaliza F vegetable; **—s** produce

hortera ADJ tacky, uncool, cheesy

horticultura F horticulture

hosco ADJ sullen, surly

hospedaje M lodging

hospedar VT to lodge, to accommodate; **—se** to lodge, to room

hospicio M (para peregrinos) hospice; (para huérfanos) orphanage

hospital M hospital

hospitalario ADJ hospitable

hospitalidad F hospitality

hostal M hostel

hostería F inn, hostelry

hostia F (oblea) host, wafer; (golpe) whack; **¡—s!**

vulg shit! **me cago en la —** *vulg* goddammit!
hostigamiento M harassment
hostigar[40] VT to harass, to harry
hostil ADJ hostile
hostilidad F hostility
hotel M hotel
hotelero -ra MF hotel keeper
hoy ADV today; **— [en] día** nowadays; **de — en adelante** from now on; **— por —** at present
hoya F river basin
hoyo M hole (también de golf); (muy profundo) pit; **— en uno** (golf) hole in one
hoyuelo M dimple
hoz F sickle
hozar[47] VI to root
HTML M HTML
hube, hubiera, hubo *ver* haber
hucha F piggy bank
hueco ADJ (vacío) hollow; (vanidoso) vain, affected; **palabras huecas** empty words; M (entre los dientes) gap; (cavidad) hollow; (de ascensor) shaft
huelga F strike, work stoppage; **— de hambre** hunger strike; **declararse en —** to strike; **en — on** strike
huelguista MF striker
huella F (rastro) trace, trail; (de pie) footprint, track; (de rueda) track; **— dactilar/digital** fingerprint; **seguir las —s de alguien** to follow in someone's footsteps
huérfano -na ADJ & MF orphan
huerta F (de verduras) large vegetable garden; (de árboles frutales) large orchard; **la — valenciana** the farming region of Valencia
huerto M (de verduras) vegetable garden; (de árboles frutales) orchard
hueso M (de animal) bone; (de fruta) stone, pit; **calado hasta los —s** soaked to the bone; **la sin —** the tongue; **no dejarle un — sano a alguien** to break someone's bones; **un — duro de roer** a hard pill to swallow
huésped MF (invitado) guest; (anfitrión) host (también de parásitos)
hueste F host
huesudo ADJ bony
hueva F spawn
huevo M egg; **— de Pascua** Easter egg; **— duro** hard-boiled egg; **— estrellado/frito** fried egg; **— pasado por agua** soft-boiled egg; **—s** (testículos, valentía) *vulg* balls; **—s revueltos** scrambled eggs; **ir pisando —s** to walk on eggshells; **me importa un —** *vulg* I don't give a shit; **¡y un —!** *vulg* my ass!
huida F flight
huir[19] VI to flee, to fly
hule M oilcloth
hulla F soft coal; **— blanca** hydroelectric power
humanidad F (cualidad y condición) humanity; (conjunto de los seres humanos) humankind;

—es humanities
humanismo M humanism
humanitario ADJ (organización, ayuda) humanitarian; (generoso) humane
humano ADJ (del hombre) human; (generoso) humane; M human
humareda F cloud of smoke
humeante ADJ (hoguera) smoking; (sopa) steaming
humear VI (echar humo) to give off smoke; (echar vapor) to give off steam
humedad F (del aire) humidity; (de un paño) dampness; (en la tierra) moisture; (en una pared) moisture stain
humedal M wetland
humedecer[35] VT (sello, ojo) to moisten; (paño) to dampen; **se le humedecieron los ojos** his eyes grew teary
húmedo ADJ (trapo) damp; (aire) humid; (tierra) moist; (tiempo) wet, soggy
humero M flue, funnel
humidificar[30] VT to humidify
humildad F (actitud) humility; (condición) lowliness
humilde ADJ (actitud) humble; (condición) low, lowly, mean
humillación F humiliation
humillar VT (insultar) to humiliate; (disminuir) to humble; **—se** to grovel
humo M (de combustión) smoke; (de gases tóxicos) fume; (de agua) vapor, steam; **—s** conceitedness; **bajarle los —s a alguien** to cut someone down to size; **echar —** to put out smoke, **estar que echa** to be fuming; **hacerse —** to vanish into thin air
humor M (actitud risueña) humor; (estado de ánimo) mood
humorada F witty remark
humorismo M (humor) humor; (profesión) comedy
humorista MF comedian
humorístico ADJ humorous
humoso ADJ smoky
hundimiento M (acción de hundirse) sinking; (hoyo) sinkhole
hundir VT (hacer naufragar) to sink, to scuttle; (arruinar) to destroy; (enterrar) to bury; **—se** (barco) to sink; (empresa, edificio, precios) to collapse; (tierra) to subside; (sol) to go down
húngaro -ra MF Hungarian
Hungría F Hungary
huracán M hurricane
huraño ADJ sullen, unsociable
hurgar[40] VI (en una bolsa) to rummage; (en la basura) to scavenge; **—se las narices** to pick one's nose
hurón M ferret
huronear VI to ferret out
hurra INTERJ hurrah

hurtadillas LOC ADV **a** — stealthily
hurtar VT to steal, to swipe; — **el cuerpo** to dodge; —**se** to hide
hurto M (robo) theft, larceny; (robo en tiendas) shoplifting; — **con escalo** break-in
husky M (perro) husky
husmear VT (un pedazo de carne) to sniff at; (a un delincuente) to smell out; (peligro) to smell; (en los asuntos ajenos) to nose around, to poke around
husmeo M sniff
huso M spindle; — **horario** time zone
huy INTERJ (de sorpresa) wow; (de pena) oh
huya, huye, huyendo, huyera, huyese ver huir

Ii

iba, ibas ver ir
ibérico ADJ Iberian
iberoamericano -na ADJ Ibero-American
ibuprofeno M ibuprofen
iceberg M iceberg
ictericia F jaundice
ictérico ADJ jaundiced
ID [investigación y desarrollo] F R&D
ida F outward journey; —**s y venidas** comings and goings
idea F (reflexión) idea, thought; (intuición) inkling
ideal ADJ & M ideal
idealismo M idealism
idealista ADJ idealistic; MF idealist
idear VT (un método) to devise, to think out, to plan; (un plan) to conceive; (una solución) to engineer; (un complot) to hatch
ídem PRON & ADV ditto
idéntico ADJ identical
identidad F identity
identificación F identification
identificar[30] VT to identify
ideología F ideology
ideológico ADJ ideological
idilio M idyll
idioma M language
idiosincrasia F idiosyncrasy
idiota ADJ idiotic, lamebrained; MF fam idiot, dork, twerp
idiotez F idiocy
ido[1] ADJ out of it
ido[2] ver ir
idolatrar VT to idolize
idolatría F idolatry
ídolo M idol
idóneo ADJ (calificado) expert; (ideal) ideal
iglesia F church

iglú M igloo
ignición F ignition
ignifugar[40] VT to fireproof
ignorancia F ignorance
ignorante ADJ ignorant, uneducated; MF ignoramus
ignorar VT (no saber) to be unaware of; (hacer caso omiso de) to ignore, to disregard; (despreciar) to shrug off, to discount
igual ADJ (idéntico) equal; (semejante) same, alike; (derecho) even; **me da** — it's all the same to me; **al** — **que** just like; M equal sign
igualar VT (alisar) to level; (ser igual a) to equal; (hacer iguales) to equalize; (compararse con) to match
igualdad F equality
igualmente ADV (de manera igual) equally; **quedaron** — **sorprendidos** they were similarly surprised; **¡que te vaya bien!** — I hope things go well for you! likewise
ijada F loin
ijar M loin
ilegal ADJ illegal, unlawful, lawless
ilegítimo ADJ illegitimate
ileso ADJ unharmed, unhurt
ilícito ADJ illicit
ilimitado ADJ (crédito) unlimited; (energía) boundless; (horizonte) limitless
iluminación F (luz) illumination, lighting; (moral, académica) enlightenment
iluminado ADJ lit
iluminar VT (con luz) to illuminate, to brighten; (con conocimiento) to enlighten; —**se** to light up
ilusión F (idea o imagen falsa) illusion; (deseo) dream, fond hope; (entusiasmo) thrill; — **óptica** optical illusion; **me da** — I'm looking forward to
ilusionado ADJ excited
iluso ADJ naive
ilusorio ADJ illusory
ilustración F illustration; **la** — the Enlightenment
ilustrador -ora MF illustrator
ilustrar VT (dibujar) illustrate; (educar) to enlighten
ilustre ADJ illustrious
imagen F (representación, reputación) image; (foto, televisión) picture; (unidad de película fotográfica) frame; — **especular** mirror image; **la** — **del tacto** the soul of tact; — **por resonancia magnética** magnetic resonance imaging; **imágenes por ultrasonido** ultrasound imaging
imaginable ADJ conceivable
imaginación F imagination
imaginar VT (crear una imagen mental) to imagine, to picture; (idear) to dream up
imaginario ADJ imaginary

imaginativo ADJ imaginative
imán M magnet
imantar VT to magnetize
imbatible ADJ unbeatable
imbécil ADJ idiotic; MF *ofensivo* imbecile, moron
imbuir[19] VT to imbue
imitación F imitation
imitador -ora MF (copión) imitator; (mímico) mimic; **un — de Elvis** an Elvis impersonator
imitar VT (copiar) to imitate; (hacer mímica) to mimic; (representar a un personaje) to impersonate
impaciencia F impatience
impaciente ADJ impatient; *fam* antsy
impactar VI/VT to impact
impacto M impact
impagado ADJ unpaid
impala M impala
impar ADJ odd, uneven
imparcial ADJ (sin prejuicios) impartial, unbiased, neutral; (justo) evenhanded; (apartidario) nonpartisan
imparcialidad F impartiality
impartir VT to impart
impasible ADJ impassive
impasse M impasse
impávido ADJ undaunted
impeachment M impeachment
impecable ADJ (perfecto) flawless; (limpio) spick and span
impedimento M (obstáculo) impediment, hindrance; (incapacidad) handicap
impedir[9] VT to impede, to prevent, to hinder; (acceso) to bar
impeler VT (empujar) to impel; (inducir) to drive
impenetrable ADJ impenetrable
impensable ADJ unthinkable
imperante ADJ prevailing
imperar VI to prevail
imperativo ADJ & M imperative
imperceptible ADJ imperceptible
imperdible ADJ that shouldn't be missed; **una película —** a must-see movie; M safety pin
imperecedero ADJ undying
imperfecto ADJ & M imperfect
imperial ADJ imperial
imperialismo M imperialism
impericia F lack of skill
imperio M (organización política) empire; (gobierno) rule; **— industrial** manufacturing empire
imperioso ADJ (mandón) imperious; (necesario) imperative
impermeabilizar[47] VT to waterproof
impermeable ADJ (al agua) waterproof; (a la crítica) impervious; M raincoat, slicker
impersonal ADJ impersonal
impertinencia F (actitud) impertinence, impudence; (réplica) backtalk
impertinente ADJ impertinent, impudent
impétigo M impetigo
ímpetu M impetus
impetuoso ADJ impetuous, brash
impida, impide, impidiendo, impidiera, impidiese *ver* impedir
impío ADJ godless
implacable ADJ implacable, relentless
implantación F (de un diente) implantation; (de una costumbre, sistema) establishment, introduction
implantar VT to implant
implante M implant; **— dental** dental implant
implementación F implementation
implementar VT to implement
implemento M implement
implicación F (lógica) implication; (en un delito) involvement
implicar[30] VT (involucrar) to implicate, to involve; (conllevar) to entail
implícitamente ADV implicitly, by implication
implícito ADJ implicit
implorar VI/VT to implore
impondrá, impondría *ver* imponer
imponente ADJ (impresionante) imposing; (espantoso) forbidding
imponer[56, 74] VT to impose, to force upon; (gravar) to assess; **—se** to get one's way
imponible ADJ taxable
impopular ADJ unpopular
importación F import
importancia F importance
importante ADJ (persona) important, (cantidad) substantial; (tema, asunto) weighty; (suceso, ocasión) momentous
importar VI (ser importante) to matter; **me importa un comino** I don't give a hoot; **no importa** it makes no difference; VT (introducir productos) to import
importe M amount
importunar VT to besiege
importuno ADJ inopportune
imposibilidad F impossibility
imposibilitar VT to make impossible
imposible ADJ impossible
imposición F (de ideas) imposition; (de impuestos) assessment
impositivo ADJ **sistema —** tax system
impostor -ora MF impostor, fraud
impotencia F impotence
impotente ADJ (sin poder) powerless; (sin libido) impotent
impreciso ADJ inaccurate
impredecible ADJ unpredictable
impregnar VT to impregnate
impremeditado ADJ unpremeditated
imprenta F (arte, oficio) printing; (máquina) press, printing press

imprescindible ADJ indispensable
impresión F (efecto en el ánimo) impression; (acción de imprimir) printing; (huella) imprint
impresionante ADJ (logro) impressive, imposing; (edificio) grand, imposing; (panorama) breathtaking
impresionar VT to impress; —**se** to be overwhelmed; **para**— for show
impreso M printed matter
impresor -ora MF (persona) printer; F (aparato) printer; **impresora de burbuja** bubble-jet printer; **impresora de inyección de tinta** ink-jet printer; **impresora en serie** serial printer; **impresora gráfica** plotter; **impresora láser** laser printer; **impresora local** local printer
imprevisible ADJ unpredictable
imprevisto ADJ unforeseen; M unforeseen event
imprimir[74] VI/VT (producir un impreso) to print; (marcar con presión) to imprint
improbable ADJ improbable, unlikely
improductivo ADJ unproductive
impromptu M impromptu
impropio ADJ (inadecuado) unbecoming; (atípico) atypical
improvisación F improvisation, role-playing
improvisado ADJ impromptu
improvisando ADV ad lib
improvisar VI/VT to improvise
improviso LOC ADV **de**— all of a sudden
imprudencia F (actitud) recklessness; (acción) reckless act
imprudente ADJ unwise, ill-advised
impublicable ADJ unprintable
impúdico ADJ immodest
impuesto M tax, duty; —**a la herencia** inheritance tax; —**s atrasados** back taxes; — **de tasa única** flat tax; — **de sucesión** inheritance tax; —**s** taxation; — **sobre ingresos** income tax; — **sobre las donaciones** gift tax; — **sobre las ventas** sales tax; — **sobre rentas** income tax
impuesto *ver* imponer
impugnar VT to contest, to dispute
impulsar VT (empujar) to propel, to drive; (estimular) to boost
impulsivo ADJ impulsive
impulso M (estímulo) boost; (deseo espontáneo) impulse, urge
impune ADJ unpunished
impunidad F impunity
impureza F impurity
impuro ADJ (sustancia) impure; (pensamiento) impure, unclean
impuse, impusiera, impusiese *ver* imponer
inacabado ADJ unfinished
inaccesible ADJ inaccessible

inaceptable ADJ (inadmisible) unacceptable; (insuficiente) inadequate
inacostumbrado ADJ unwonted
inactividad F inactivity
inactivo ADJ inactive
inadaptado -da ADJ maladjusted; MF misfit
inadecuado ADJ unsuitable
inadmisible ADJ (comportamiento) unacceptable; (pruebas) inadmissible
inadvertido ADJ unnoticed, unobserved
inagotable ADJ (recursos) inexhaustible; (optimismo) unfailing
inaguantable ADJ unbearable
inalámbrico ADJ cordless, wireless
inalterable ADJ unalterable, unchangeable
inalterado ADJ unchanged
inamovible ADJ immovable
inanición F starvation
inanimado ADJ inanimate
inapetencia F lack of appetite
inapreciable ADJ (invalorable) invaluable; (muy pequeño) too small to be seen
inapropiado ADJ unsuitable
inasequible ADJ inaccessible
inaudible ADJ inaudible
inaudito ADJ (historia, situación) unheard-of, unprecedented; (sufrimiento) untold
inauguración F (de un gobierno) inauguration; (de un monumento) dedication
inaugurar VT (un gobierno) to inaugurate; (un monumento) to dedicate
inca ADJ & MF Inca
incalculable ADJ untold
incandescencia F glow
incandescente ADJ incandescent, glowing
incansable ADJ untiring, tireless
incapacidad F inability
incapacitar VT to disable, to incapacitate
incapaz ADJ incapable
incautación F seizure
incauto ADJ unwary
incendiar VT to set fire to; VI/VT to burn; —**se** to catch fire, to burn down
incendiario -ria ADJ incendiary; MF arsonist
incendio M fire, blaze, conflagration; — **doloso** arson; — **forestal** forest fire
incentivo M incentive, inducement
incertidumbre F uncertainty, suspense
incesante ADJ incessant, ceaseless
incesto M incest
incestuoso ADJ incestuous
incidencia F incidence
incidental ADJ incidental
incidente M incident
incidir VI — **en un asunto** to affect/influence a situation
incienso M incense
incierto ADJ uncertain
incinerar VT to incinerate

incipiente ADJ incipient
incisión F incision
incisivo ADJ incisive; M incisor
incitar VT to incite, to whip up
incivilizado ADJ uncivilized
inclemencia F **las —s del tiempo** foul weather
inclemente ADJ inclement, foul
inclinación F (tendencia) inclination, bent, disposition; (acción de inclinar) tilting; (posición inclinada) tilt; (de un techo) slant; (del terreno) slope; (de opinión) bias
inclinar VT (ladear) to tilt; (bajar) to hang; **— la cabeza** to hang one's head; **—se** (doblarse en la cintura) to bend over; (tener tendencia a) to tend; (hacer una reverencia) to bow
incluido ADJ included; **con todo —** all-inclusive
incluir[19] VT (incorporar) to include; (abarcar) to include, to comprise; **incluyéndote a ti, somos cuatro** including you, there are four of us
inclusión F inclusion; **con — de** including
inclusive ADV even
inclusivo ADJ inclusive
incluso ADV even
incluya, incluye, incluyendo, incluyera, incluyese ver incluir
incobrable ADJ noncollectible, uncollectable
incógnita F unknown [quantity]
incógnito LOC ADV **de —** incognito
incoherente ADJ incoherent
incoloro ADJ colorless
incomestible ADJ inedible
incomformista ADJ & MF nonconformist
incomible ADJ inedible
incomodar VT to inconvenience
incomodidad F uneasiness
incómodo ADJ (silla) uncomfortable; (situación) awkward, inconvenient; (baúl) cumbersome; (silencio) uneasy; (que siente molestia) ill at ease
incomparable ADJ incomparable, peerless
incompatible ADJ incompatible
incompetente ADJ incompetent
incompleto ADJ incomplete
incomprensible ADJ incomprehensible
incomunicación F disconnect, miscommunication
inconcebible ADJ inconceivable
inconcluso ADJ unfinished
incondicional ADJ unconditional, unqualified
inconexo ADJ disconnected
inconformista MF nonconformist
inconfundible ADJ unmistakable
inconsciente ADJ (sin sentido) unconscious, senseless; (ignorante) unaware, oblivious
inconsecuencia F inconsistency
inconsecuente ADJ inconsistent
inconsolable ADJ heartbroken

inconstancia F inconstancy
inconstante ADJ inconstant, changeable
inconstitucional ADJ unconstitutional
incontable ADJ countless
incontenible ADJ uncontrollable
incontinente ADJ incontinent
incontrolable ADJ uncontrollable
incontrovertible ADJ incontrovertible
inconveniencia F inconvenience
inconveniente ADJ improper; M inconvenience, downside
incorporación F (inclusión) inclusion; (asimilación) incorporation
incorporado ADJ built-in
incorporar VT (incluir) to include; (asimilar) to incorporate; (agregar) to build into; **—se** (erguirse) to sit up
incorrectamente ADV incorrectly, wrongly
incorrecto ADJ incorrect, wrong
incorregible ADJ incorrigible
incredulidad F disbelief
incrédulo ADJ incredulous
increíble ADJ (inverosímil) incredible, unbelievable; (extraordinario) amazing
incrementar VT to augment
incremento M increment, increase
incriminar VT to incriminate
incrustación F inlay
incrustado ADJ (en piedra) embedded; (joyas) inlaid
incrustar VT (piedra) to embed; (oro) to inlay; **—se en** to become embedded in
incubadora F incubator
incuestionable ADJ unquestionable
inculcar[30] VT to inculcate, to instill
inculto ADJ (sin modales) uncultured, unrefined; (sin instrucción) uneducated
incumbencia F **no es de tu —** it's none of your business
incumplimiento M (de contrato) breach; (de deberes) nonperformance; (de deudas) default; (de metas) failure to accomplish; (de promesas) failure to keep
incumplir VT (contratos) to breach; (deberes) to fail to perform; (deudas) to default on; (metas) to fail to accomplish; (promesas) to renegue on, to fail to keep
incurable ADJ incurable
incurrir VI **— en** (una deuda, un gasto) to incur; (un error) to fall into
incursión F raid, foray
incursionar VI to foray
indagación F investigation, probe
indagar[40] VI/VT to investigate, to inquire into
indebido ADJ improper
indecencia F indecency
indecente ADJ indecent
indecible ADJ unspeakable
indecisión F indecision

indeciso ADJ (que no ha decidido) undecided; (que suele vacilar) wishy-washy

indecoroso ADJ improper

indefendible ADJ indefensible

indefenso ADJ defenseless

indefinible ADJ indefinable

indefinido ADJ (plazo) indefinite; (silueta) undefined

indeleble ADJ indelible

indelicado ADJ indelicate

indemnización F (resarcimiento) indemnity; (de guerra) reparation; (de un pleito) recovery; — **por despido** severance pay

indemnizar[47] VT to indemnify

independencia F independence; (de un individuo) self-reliance

independiente ADJ independent

indescriptible ADJ indescribable

indeseable ADJ undesirable, unwelcome

indestructible ADJ indestructible

indeterminado ADJ indeterminate, undetermined

indexación F indexing

indexar VT to index

India F India

indicación F (señal) indication; (instrucción) instruction; **indicaciones** directions

indicador M pointer, indicator; — **clave** key indicator; —**es anticipados** leading indicators

indicar[30] VT (señalar) to indicate, to point out; (registrar) to read, to register; (mostrar) to show

indicativo ADJ & M indicative

índice M (lista alfabética) index; (tabla de materias) table of contents; (dedo) index finger; — **de confianza del consumidor** consumer confidence index; — **de mortalidad** mortality rate; — **de precios al consumidor** consumer price index

indicio M clue, sign

Indico M **Océano** — Indian Ocean

indiferencia F indifference; (frialdad) coolness

indiferente ADJ (apático) indifferent, unconcerned; (frío) cool; (sin entusiasmo) lukewarm; (no conmovido) unmoved; **esa chica me es** — I don't care about that girl

indígena ADJ indigenous; MF native

indigente ADJ destitute, indigent

indigestión F indigestion

indignación F indignation

indignado ADJ indignant

indignar VT to make indignant; —**se** to become indignant

indigno ADJ unworthy

índigo M indigo

indio -dia ADJ & MF Indian

indirecta F hint

indirecto ADJ (estilo, consecuencia) indirect; (ruta) roundabout

indisciplinado ADJ unruly

indiscreción F indiscretion

indiscreto ADJ indiscreet

indiscutible ADJ unquestionable

indispensable ADJ indispensable

indisponer[56, 74] VT to indispose; —**se** to become indisposed

indispuesto ADJ (disgustado) upset; (enfermo) indisposed

indistinto ADJ indistinct, vague

individual ADJ (derechos) individual; (habitación) single; —**es** singles

individualidad F individuality

individualismo M individualism

individualista ADJ & MF individualist

individuo ADJ & M individual

indivisible ADJ indivisible

indiviso ADJ undivided

indocumentado -da ADJ (carta) undocumented; (persona) without identity papers; MF illegal immigrant

índole F type

indolencia F indolence

indolente ADJ indolent

indoloro ADJ painless

indomable ADJ indomitable

indomado ADJ unbroken

Indonesia F Indonesia

indonesio -sia ADJ & MF Indonesian

inducción F induction

inducir[38] VT to induce, to prompt

indudable ADJ undeniable; unquestionable

indudablemente ADV undoubtedly

indulgencia F indulgence

indulgente ADJ indulgent, lenient

indultar VT to pardon

indulto M pardon

indumentaria F apparel

industria F industry, trade; — **petrolera** oil industry

industrial ADJ industrial; MF industrialist

industrialización F industrialization

industrioso ADJ industrious

inédito ADJ unpublished

inefable ADJ ineffable

ineficaz ADJ ineffective, ineffectual

ineficiente ADJ inefficient

inelegible ADJ ineligible

ineludible ADJ inescapable, unavoidable

inempleable ADJ unemployable

inepto ADJ inept

inequívoco ADJ unequivocal

inercia F inertia

inerte ADJ inert

inescrutable ADJ inscrutable

inesperado ADJ unexpected

inestabilidad F instability

inestable ADJ (personalidad, estructura)

unstable; (andar) unsteady
inestimable ADJ inestimable, invaluable
inevitable ADJ (conclusión) inevitable; (accidente) unavoidable
inexacto ADJ inaccurate
inexcusable ADJ inexcusable
inexistente ADJ nonexistent
inexorable ADJ inexorable
inexperto ADJ (trabajador) inexperienced, unskilled; (ojo) untrained
inexplicable ADJ inexplicable
inexpresivo ADJ inexpressive, wooden
infalible ADJ (a toda prueba) infallible, foolproof; (confiable) unfailing
infame ADJ infamous
infamia F infamy
infancia F childhood
infante -ta MF (hijo -ja del rey) infante -ta; M (soldado) infantryman
infantería F infantry; — **de marina** marine corps
infantil ADJ (como niño) childlike; (aniñado) childish, infantile
infarto M infarction, heart attack; — **cardíaco** heart attack; — **cerebral** stroke, cerebral infarction; — **del miocardio** myocardial infarction
infección F infection; — **del tracto urinario** urinary tract infection; — **respiratoria alta** upper respiratory infection
infeccioso ADJ infectious
infectar VT to infect; —**se** to become infected
infecto ADJ foul, repugnant
infelicidad F misery
infeliz ADJ unhappy, wretched, miserable; MF poor wretch
inferencia F inference
inferior ADJ (en calidad) inferior, subpar; (en posición) lower
inferioridad F inferiority
inferir[8] VT to infer
infernal ADJ (calor) infernal; (ruido) unholy
infertilidad F infertility
infestación F infestation
infestar VT to infest
infiel ADJ unfaithful, faithless, untrue
infierno M (bíblico) hell; (lugar caliente) inferno; **en el quinto** — in the middle of nowhere
infinidad F infinity; **una** — **de** a large number of
infinitivo ADJ & M infinitive
infinito ADJ infinite; M infinity
inflación F inflation; — **básica** core inflation
inflado ADJ bloated; M pumping up
inflamable ADJ flammable
inflamación F inflammation
inflamar VT to inflame; —**se** to become inflamed

inflar VT (neumáticos) to inflate, to pump up; (globos) to blow up; (precios) to balloon
inflexible ADJ (rígido) inflexible; (testarudo) unbending, adamant
infligir[46] VT to inflict
influencia F influence, pull, clout; (sobre las masas) sway
influir[19] VI — **en/sobre** to influence; (las masas) to sway
influjo M influence
influya, influye, influyendo, influyera, influyese ver influir
influyente ADJ influential
infomercial M infomercial
información F information; (periodística) story
informal ADJ (no formal) informal, casual; (poco fiable) unreliable
informante MF (para un estudio) informant; (de la policía) informer
informar VT (enterar) to inform, to appraise; (un militar) to debrief; (un periodista) to report; (un abogado) to advise; —**se** to become informed
informática F computer science, information technology
informático -ca ADJ computing; MF computer specialist
informativo ADJ informative; M (televisión, radio) news program
informatizar[47] VT to computerize
informe M (de noticias) report; (militar) debriefing; — **de crédito** credit report; —**s de guía** information; ADJ shapeless
infortunio M misfortune
infracción F (de reglamentos) infraction, infringement; (de contrato) breach; (de tránsito) violation; (en deportes) penalty
infractor -ora MF lawbreaker
infraestructura F infrastructure
infrarrojo ADJ & M infrared
infrascrito -ta MF undersigned
infravalorado ADJ underrated, undervalued
infringir[46] VT to infringe, to breach, to violate
infructuoso ADJ fruitless, unsuccessful
ínfulas F PL airs; **darse** — to put on airs
infundado ADJ groundless, unfounded
infundir VT to infuse, to imbue
infusionar VT to steep
ingeniar VT to contrive; **ingeniárselas para** to contrive to
ingeniería F engineering; — **genética** genetic engineering; — **química** chemical engineering
ingeniero -ra MF engineer; — **civil** civil engineer; — **electricista** electrical engineer; — **en computación** computer engineer; — **informático** computer engineer
ingenio M (mental) ingenuity, cleverness; (verbal) wit; (artefacto) artifact; — **de azúcar**

(refinería) sugar refinery, sugar mill; (plantación) sugar plantation

ingeniosidad F ingenuity

ingenioso ADJ ingenious, resourceful

ingenuidad F ingenuousness, naiveté

ingenuo -nua ADJ (inocente) naive, ingenuous; (crédulo) gullible; MF dupe

ingerir VI/VT to ingest

ingestión F ingestion

ingle F groin

inglés -esa ADJ English; M Englishman; (lengua) English; F Englishwoman

ingobernable ADJ unruly

ingratitud F ingratitude

ingrato -ta ADJ thankless, ungrateful; MF ingrate

ingrávido ADJ weightless

ingrediente M ingredient; **ese libro tiene todos los —s de un éxito** that book has all the makings of a best seller

ingresar VT (datos) to input; (dinero en una cuenta) to deposit; VI (a un hospital) to be admitted; (a un sistema) to log in

ingreso M (permiso para entrar) entrance, entry; (depósito bancario) deposit; (renta) income; **—s** (de una firma) earnings; (del estado) revenue; **— bruto** gross income; **— neto ajustado** adjusted net income; **—s discrecionales** discretionary income; **—s disponibles** disposable income

inhábil ADJ unskilled

inhabilidad F inability

inhabilitar VT to disqualify

inhalación F inhalation; **— de humo** smoke inhalation

inhalar VI/VT to breathe in, to inhale

inherente ADJ inherent

inhibición F inhibition

inhibidor ADJ inhibiting; M inhibitor

inhibir VT to inhibit

inhospitalario ADJ inhospitable

inhóspito ADJ inhospitable

inhumano ADJ inhuman

iniciación M initiation, induction

inicial ADJ initial; (pago) up-front; F (letra) initial; (béisbol) first base

inicialista MF first baseman

inicializar[47] VT to initialize

inicialmente ADV initially

iniciar VT (conversaciones) to initiate; (en un grupo) to induct; (software) to launch; (computadora) to boot up; (negociaciones) to enter

iniciativa F initiative

inicio M beginning, start

inimitable ADJ inimitable

ininflamable ADJ fireproof

ininteligible ADJ unintelligible

ininterrumpido ADJ unbroken, uninterrupted

injerencia F interference

injertar VT to graft

injerto M graft; **— óseo** bone graft

injugable ADJ unplayable

injuria F (insulto) insult, verbal abuse; (daño) damage

injuriar VT to insult, to abuse verbally

injurioso ADJ insulting, injurious, verbally abusive

injustamente ADV unjustly, unfairly, wrongly

injusticia F (desigualdad) injustice; (acto injusto) wrong; (error judicial) miscarriage of justice

injustificable ADJ unjustifiable

injustificado ADJ uncalled-for, unwarranted

injusto ADJ unjust, unfair

inmaculado ADJ immaculate, spotless

inmaduro ADJ immature

inmanejable ADJ unmanageable

inmaterial ADJ immaterial

inmediaciones F PL vicinity

inmediato ADJ immediate, instant; **de —** at once

inmensidad F immensity, vastness

inmenso ADJ immense, vast

inmerso ADJ (en agua) submerged; (en el trabajo) absorbed; (en un tema, una situación) immersed

inmerecido ADJ unearned

inmigración F immigration

inmigrante ADJ & MF immigrant

inmigrar VI to immigrate

inminente ADJ imminent, impending

inmiscuir[19] VI to mix; **—se** to meddle

inmodestia F immodesty

inmodesto ADJ immodest

inmoral ADJ immoral

inmoralidad F immorality

inmortal ADJ & MF immortal

inmortalidad F immortality

inmóvil ADJ motionless, immobile

inmovilizar[47] VT (impedir los movimientos) to immobilize; (contra el suelo) to pin

inmueble M building

inmune ADJ immune

inmunidad F immunity

inmunodeficiencia F immunodeficiency

inmutable ADJ unchangeable, immutable

innato ADJ innate, inborn

innecesario ADJ unnecessary, needless

innegable ADJ undeniable

innoble ADJ ignoble

innocuo ADJ innocuous, harmless

innovación F innovation

innovador -ora ADJ innovating, innovative; MF innovator

innovar VI to innovate; VT to modernize

innumerable ADJ innumerable, countless

inocencia F innocence

inocente ADJ innocent, guiltless; MF dupe
inocuo ADJ innocuous, harmless
inodoro ADJ odorless; M toilet, commode
inofensivo ADJ inoffensive, harmless
inolvidable ADJ unforgettable
inoperable ADJ inoperable
inoportuno ADJ inopportune, untimely
inorgánico ADJ inorganic
inoxidable ADJ rustproof
inquietante ADJ distressing, worrisome
inquietar VT to worry
inquieto ADJ (movedizo) restless; (preocupado) uneasy
inquietud F (intranquilidad) restlessness; (preocupación) alarm, concern
inquilino -na MF (de un apartamento) tenant, renter; (de una pensión) lodger
inquina F spite
inquirir[4] VI/VT to inquire
inquisición F inquisition
inquisitivo ADJ inquisitive
insaciable ADJ insatiable
insalubre ADJ unhealthy, unsanitary
insatisfactorio ADJ unsatisfactory
insatisfecho ADJ dissatisfied, unhappy
inscribir[74] VT (grabar) to inscribe; (matricular) to register, to enroll; —**se** to register, to enroll
inscripción F (grabado) inscription; (matriculación) registration, enrollment
insecticida M insecticide
insectívoro ADJ insectivorous
insecto M insect
inseguridad F insecurity; **la — urbana** the lack of safety in cities / the city
inseguro ADJ (personalidad) insecure; (vehículo) unsafe; (andar) unsteady; (computadora) vulnerable to hacking
inseminación F insemination
insensato -ta ADJ foolish; MF fool
insensibilizar[47] VT to desensitize
insensible ADJ (cruel) insensitive, callous; (imperturbable) unfeeling, thick-skinned; (entumecido) numb
inseparable ADJ inseparable
inserción F insertion
insertar VT to insert
inservible ADJ useless
insidioso ADJ insidious
insigne ADJ famous
insignia F insignia, badge
insignificante ADJ insignificant, unimportant
insincero ADJ insincere
insinuación F (sugerencia) insinuation; (comentario sexual) innuendo
insinuante ADJ suggestive
insinuar[26] VT to insinuate, to suggest; —**se** to insinuate oneself
insípido ADJ insipid, flavorless

insistencia F (machaconería, testarudez) insistence; (perseverancia) persistence
insistente ADJ (testarudo, repetitivo) insistent; (perseverante) persistent
insistir VI/VT (repetir) to insist; (perseverar) to persist; — **en** to insist on; — **sobre** to harp on
insolación F (por sol) sunstroke; (por calor) heatstroke
insolencia F (falta de respeto) insolence; (comentario) smart remark
insolente ADJ insolent, sassy
insólito ADJ (situación) unusual; (accidente) freak, freakish
insoluble ADJ insoluble
insolvente ADJ insolvent
insomne ADJ wakeful, unable to sleep
insomnio M insomnia
insoportable ADJ (persona, conducta) unbearable, impossible; (dolor) excruciating, unbearable
insospechado ADJ unsuspected
insostenible ADJ untenable
inspección F (revisación) inspection; (encuesta) canvass
inspeccionar VT to inspect, to survey
inspector -ora MF inspector
inspiración F (idea) inspiration; (inhalación) inhalation
inspirar VI/VT to inspire; VI to inhale, to breathe in
instalación F (de programas, fontanería) installation; (de aparatos electrónicos) setup; **instalaciones** fixtures
instalar VT (programas, fontanería) to install; (aparatos electrónicos) to set up; —**se** to take up residence
instancia LOC ADV **a —s de** at the request of
instantánea F snapshot
instantáneo ADJ instantaneous
instante M instant; **al —** right away
instar VT to enjoin
instauración F establishment
instigador -ra MF instigator
instigar[40] VT to instigate, to abet
instintivo ADJ instinctive
instinto M instinct; — **suicida** death wish
institución F institution; — **benéfica** charity
institucional ADJ institutional
instituir[19] VT to institute
instituto M (institución, agencia) institute; (escuela secundaria) high school
institutriz F governess
instrucción F instruction, schooling
instructivo ADJ instructive
instructor -ora MF instructor
instruir[19] VT to instruct, to school
instrumental ADJ instrumental
instrumentar VT (un plan) to implement; (música) to do the instrumentation for

instrumento M instrument; — **de cuerda**
string instrument; — **de metal** brass
instrument; — **de percusión** percussion
instrument; — **de viento** wind instrument;
—**s quirúrgicos** surgical instruments
insubordinado ADJ insubordinate
insuficiencia F (incapacidad) insufficiency;
(falla de los órganos) failure; — **cardíaca
congestiva** congestive heart failure; —
coronaria coronary failure; — **renal** kidney
failure, renal failure; — **respiratoria**
respiratory failure
insuficiente ADJ insufficient, inadequate
insufrible ADJ insufferable
insulina F insulin
insulso ADJ bland
insultar VT to insult
insulto M insult, put-down
insuperable ADJ (resultado) insuperable;
(obstáculo) insurmountable
insurgente ADJ & MF insurgent
insurrección F insurrection
insurrecto -ta ADJ rebellious; MF rebel
intachable ADJ blameless
intacto ADJ intact, unbroken
intangible ADJ intangible
integración F (de razas) integration; (de
elementos) incorporation
integral ADJ (parte) integral; ADJ (harina)
whole-grain
integrante ADJ integral
integrar VT (crear) to form; (ser miembro de) to
be a member of
integridad F integrity
íntegro ADJ (objeto) whole; (texto) unabridged;
(comportamiento) upright
intelecto M intellect
intelectual ADJ & MF intellectual
inteligencia F intelligence (también militar);
(persona) mind; — **artificial** artificial
intelligence
inteligente ADJ intelligent, bright, smart
inteligible ADJ intelligible
intemperie LOC ADV **a la** — exposed to the
weather
intención F intention, intent
intencional ADJ intentional
intendente MF (civil) administrator; (militar)
quartermaster general
intensidad F intensity
intensificar[30] VT to intensify; —**se** (frío) to
intensify; (violencia) to escalate
intensivo ADJ intensive
intenso ADJ (actividad) intense; (debate) fierce;
(calor) severe
intentar VI/VT to try; VT to attempt
intento M (tentativa) try, attempt; (propósito)
intention
interacción F interaction

interactivo ADJ interactive
interactuar[26] VI to interact
intercalación F insertion
intercalar VT to insert
intercambiador M interchange
intercambiar VI/VT to exchange
intercambio M exchange
interceder VI to intercede
interceptación F interception (también en
fútbol americano)
interceptar VT intercept (también en fútbol
americano)
intercesión F intercession
intercesor -ora MF advocate
interés M (intelectual, financiero) interest;
(preocupación) concern; (participación
comercial) stake; — **compuesto** compound
interest; — **mutuo** mutual interest;
intereses ocultos hidden agenda
interesado ADJ (atento) interested;
(preocupado) concerned; (egoísta)
self-serving
interesante ADJ interesting
interesar VT to interest; —**se por** to become
interested in
interestatal ADJ interstate
interestelar ADJ interstellar
interface MF interface
interfaz MF interface; — **digital de
instrumentos musicales** musical
instrument digital interface
interferencia F (en los negocios ajenos)
interference; (en una transmisión)
interference, static; — **externa** outside
interference
interferir[8] VT to jam; VI to interfere
interferón M interferon
ínterin M interim; **en el** — meanwhile
interino ADJ acting, interim
interior ADJ (habitación) inside; (mundo, vida)
inner; (zona geográfica) inland; (mercado,
comercio) domestic; M (parte) inside part,
interior; **el** — **de la caja** the inside of the
box; (de un país) the country, the provinces;
una ciudad del — a provincial town
interiorizar[47] VT to internalize
interjección F interjection
interlineal ADJ interlinear
interlock M interlock
interlocutor -ora MF interlocutor
interludio M interlude
intermediario -ria M middleman; MF
(mensajero) go-between; ADJ intermediary
intermediarista MF second baseman
intermedio -a ADJ intermediate; M
intermission; **por** — **de** through; F (béisbol)
second base
interminable ADJ interminable, unending,
endless

intermitente ADJ intermittent; M turn signal

internación F inpatient care

internacional ADJ international

internado -da M (escuela) boarding school; (práctica) internship; MF (alumno) boarding student; (en un hospital) patient

internalizar[47] VT to internalize

internar VT (en una cárcel) to intern; (en un hospital) to admit, to hospitalize; (en un hospital psiquiátrico) to commit

internauta MF Internet user

internet M Internet, web; — **inalámbrico** wireless Internet; — **móvil** mobile Internet

internista MF internist

interno -na ADJ (correo) internal; (mercado) domestic; MF (persona que vive internada) inmate; (residente médico) intern

interpersonal ADJ interpersonal

interponer[56, 74] VT to interpose; —**se** to intervene

interpretación F (de un texto) interpretation; (artística) performance, rendition

interpretar VT (ideas) to interpret; (música) to perform; (intenciones) to construe

intérprete MF (traductor, explicador) interpreter; (músico) artist, performer

interracial ADJ interracial

interrelacionado ADJ interrelated

interrogación F interrogation

interrogador -ora MF questioner; ADJ questioning

interrogar[40] VI/VT (la policía) to interrogate; (con intensidad) to grill; (a un testigo) to question, to cross-examine

interrogativo ADJ interrogative

interrogatorio M interrogation, questioning

interrumpir VI/VT (cortar) to interrupt; VT (servicios) to disrupt, to cut off; (producción de un modelo) to discontinue; (en una conversación) to intrude, to cut in; (software) to abort

interrupción F interruption; (en una conversación) intrusion; (de producción) stoppage; (software) abort

interruptor M switch

intersección F intersection

intersticio M interstice

intervalo M (período) interval; (en el teatro) intermission, interlude

intervención F intervention; — **de teléfono** wiretap

intervendrá, intervendría, intervenga, intervengo ver intervenir

intervenir[61] VI to intervene; — **un teléfono** to wiretap

interventor -ora ADJ controlling, intervening; MF (en las elecciones) observer; (en lo fiscal) auditor

intervine, interviniendo, interviniera,

interviniese ver intervenir

interviú F interview

intestino ADJ & M intestine; — **delgado** small intestine; — **grueso** large intestine; —**s** bowels

intimar VI to become friendly

intimidad F intimacy

intimidar VT (una persona) to intimidate; (una tarea) to daunt

íntimo ADJ intimate, close

intitular VT to entitle; —**se** to be entitled

intolerable ADJ intolerable

intolerancia F intolerance, bigotry; — **a la lactosa** lactose intolerance

intolerante ADJ intolerant, narrow-minded

intoxicación F intoxication, poisoning; — **con plomo** lead poisoning; — **por alimentos** food poisoning

intoxicar[30] VT to poison, to intoxicate

intransigente ADJ intransigent, uncompromising

intransitivo ADJ intransitive

intravenoso ADJ IV [intravenous]

intrepidez F fearlessness

intrépido ADJ (sin miedo) intrepid, fearless; (aventurero) adventurous

intriga F intrigue

intrigante MF schemer; ADJ scheming

intrigar[40] VI/VT to intrigue, to scheme

intrincado ADJ intricate

intrínseco ADJ intrinsic

introducción F introduction

introducir[38] VT (incorporar) to introduce; (colocar) to put in, to insert

introduzca, introduzco ver introducir

introspección F introspection

introvertido -da ADJ introverted; MF introvert

intrusión F intrusion

intrusivo ADJ intrusive

intruso -sa ADJ intruding; MF intruder

intubación F intubation

intuición F intuition

intuir[19] VT to sense

intuitivo ADJ intuitive

inundación F flood

inundar VI/VT (de agua, de pedidos) to inundate, to flood; (de regalos) to shower

inusitado ADJ unusual

inútil ADJ (medida) useless, pointless; (esfuerzo) futile; (persona) worthless, good-for-nothing

inutilidad F uselessness; (de un esfuerzo) futility

inutilizar[47] VT to render useless, to put out of commission

invadir VI/VT to invade

invalidar VT to render invalid

inválido -da ADJ (discapacitado) invalid; (nulo) void; MF invalid

invalorable ADJ priceless, invaluable

invariable ADJ invariable
invasión F invasion
invasivo ADJ invasive
invasor -ora MF invader; ADJ invading
invencible ADJ invincible
invención F invention (también mentira); (mental) construct
inventar VT (un dispositivo) to invent; (una historia) to fabricate, to make up
inventariar[28] VT to inventory
inventario M inventory
inventiva F ingenuity
inventivo ADJ inventive
invento M invention
inventor -ora MF inventor
invernadero M greenhouse, hothouse; **efecto** — greenhouse effect
invernal ADJ wintry
invernar[1] VI to winter
inverosímil ADJ unlikely, farfetched
inversión F (trasposición) inversion; (financiera) investment
inversionista MF investor
inverso ADJ inverse, reverse; **a la inversa** the other way around
inversor -ora[8] MF investor
invertir[8] VT (dar vuelta) to invert, to reverse; VI/VT (dinero) to invest
investidura F inauguration, investment
investigación F (policial) investigation, inquiry; (científica) research
investigador -ora MF investigator; (científico) researcher
investigar[40] VI/VT (policía) to investigate, to look into; (científico) to research
investir[9] VI/VT to invest; — **de un cargo** to induct into office
invicto ADJ unbeaten
invierno M winter
invierta, invierte, invirtiendo, invirtiera, invirtiese, invirtió ver invertir
invisible ADJ (no visible) invisible; (oculto) unseen
invitación F invitation
invitado -da MF guest
invitar VI/VT to invite
invocación F invocation
invocar[30] VT (razones, argumentos) to invoke; (espíritus) to conjure
involucrar VT (implicar) to implicate; (consistir de) to involve
involuntario ADJ (automático) involuntary; (accidental) inadvertent
inyección F (en medicina) injection, shot; (en coches) fuel injection
inyectado ADJ — **de sangre** bloodshot
inyectar VT to inject
ion, ión M ion
ionizar[47] VT to ionize

ir[64] VI to go; — **a caballo** to ride horseback; — **a pie** to walk; — **[a] por** to fetch; — **aprendiendo** to learn gradually; — **corriendo** to run; — **de mal en peor** to go from bad to worse; — **en coche** to drive/ride in a car; — **tirando** to scrape along; **no me va ni me viene** it's all the same to me; **¿cómo te va?** how are you? **los platos no van aquí** the plates don't belong here; **¡vaya!** well now! **¡vaya a saber uno!** go figure! **¡vamos!** let's go! come on! **¡vaya hombre!** what a man! **¡ve a freír espárragos!** take a hike! **va por dos años que me casé** it's going on two years since I got married; **voy a comer** I'm going to eat; **va y se come un hongo venenoso** she goes and eats a poisonous mushroom; **en lo que va del año** since the beginning of the year; **ya van siete veces que me lo dice** that makes seven times that she's told me; **voy a ir de rojo** I'm going dressed in red; **para que no vayas a creer** lest you should think; **no vayas a caerte** don't fall; **¡qué va!** no way! —**se** to go away, to leave; —**se a la quiebra** to go broke; —**se a las manos** to come to blows; —**se a pique** to founder; —**se de vacaciones** to take a vacation
ira F ire, wrath
Irak M Iraq
Irán M Iran
iraní ADJ & MF Iranian
iraquí ADJ & MF Iraqi
irascible ADJ irascible, quick-tempered
iridiscente ADJ iridescent
iris M iris
Irlanda F Ireland
irlandés -esa MF Irish; ADJ Irish
IRM [imagen por resonancia magnética] F MRI
ironía F irony
irónico ADJ ironic, wry
irracional ADJ irrational, unreasonable
irradiar VT to radiate, to irradiate
irreal ADJ unreal
irreconocible ADJ unrecognizable
irrecuperable ADJ irretrievable
irreflexivo ADJ thoughtless
irrefutable ADJ irrefutable
irregular ADJ (situación) irregular; (borde, filo) ragged; (pulso) unsteady; (superficie) rough, uneven; (comportamiento) erratic, haphazard
irregularidad F irregularity
irremediable ADJ hopeless
irremplazable ADJ irreplaceable
irreparable ADJ irreparable
irreprochable ADJ irreproachable, flawless
irresistible ADJ irresistible
irrespetuoso ADJ disrespectful

irresponsabilidad F irresponsibility
irresponsable ADJ irresponsible
irreverente ADJ irreverent
irreversible ADJ irreversible
irrevocable ADJ irrevocable
irrigación F irrigation
irrigar⁴⁰ VI/VT to irrigate
irritable ADJ irritable
irritación F irritation
irritante ADJ (molesto) irritating, grating; (agresivo) abrasive
irritar VI/VT to irritate, to aggravate
irrumpir VI to burst into
isla F island, isle; —**s Fiyi** Fiji Islands; —**s Malvinas** Falkland Islands; —**s Marshall** Marshall Islands; —**s Salomón** Solomon Islands; —**s Vírgenes** Virgin Islands
islam, Islam M Islam
islámico ADJ Islamic
islamismo M Islam
islandés -esa MF Icelander; ADJ Icelandic
Islandia F Iceland
isleño -ña MF islander
isobara F isobar
isométrico ADJ isometric
isótopo M isotope
Israel M Israel
israelí ADJ & MF Israeli
istmo M isthmus
Italia F Italy
italiano -na ADJ & MF Italian
itálico ADJ italic; F **itálica** italics
ítem M item
itinerante ADJ itinerant
itinerario M itinerary
IVA [impuesto al valor añadido/agregado] M sales tax, VAT
izar⁴⁷ VT to hoist, to raise
izquierda F left (también política); (mano) left hand; **a la** — to the left
izquierdista ADJ & MF leftist
izquierdo ADJ left

Jj

jab M jab
jabalí M [wild] boar
jabalina F javelin
jabón M soap
jabonera F soap dish
jabonoso ADJ soapy
jaca F nag
jacinto M hyacinth
jactancia F boastfulness
jactancioso ADJ boastful, blustering

jactarse VI to boast, to brag
jacuzzi M Jacuzzi™, hot tub
jade M jade
jadear VI to pant, to gasp
jadeo M panting, gasping
jaez M harness
jaguar M jaguar
jalar VI/VT to pull, to tug
jalea F jelly
jaleo M (lío) mess; (barahúnda) ruckus
jam M jam session
Jamaica F Jamaica
jamaicano -na ADJ & MF Jamaican
jamaiquino -na ADJ & MF Jamaican
jamás ADV never
jamelgo M hack
jamón M ham
jamona F buxom woman
Japón M Japan
japonés -esa ADJ & MF Japanese
jaque M check; — **mate** checkmate; **tener a uno en** — *fam* to have someone by the short hairs
jaqueca F migraine
jarabe M syrup; — **de ipecacuana** ipecac syrup
jarana F revelry; **ir de** — to paint the town red
jarcia F rigging
jardín M (de flores) garden; (de césped) yard; (béisbol) outfield; — **de niños** kindergarten; — **infantil** nursery
jardinero -ra MF (de oficio) gardener; (en béisbol) outfielder
jarra F (cántaro) jug, pitcher; (taza) mug; **en** —**s** akimbo
jarro M pitcher, jug
jarrón M vase
jaspe M (piedra silícea) jasper; (mármol) veined marble
jaula F cage, coop
jauría F pack
jazmín M jasmine
jazz M jazz
jeans M PL jeans
jefatura F headquarters
jefe MF, **jefa** F (laboral) boss; (militar) commander; (departamental) chair, head; (policial) chief; — **del estado mayor** chief of staff; — **de departamento** department head
jején M gnat
jengibre M ginger
jerarquía F hierarchy
jerez M sherry
jerga F jargon, slang
jerigonza F (sinsentido) gibberish, gobbledygook; (juego lingüístico) pig Latin
jeringa F syringe
jeringar⁴⁰ VT to annoy
jeroglífico ADJ & M hieroglyphic

jersey M sweater
jesuita ADJ & M Jesuit
Jesús INTERJ God bless you! gesundheit!
jeta F (hocico) snout; (cara) mug
jet-set M jet set
jilguero M goldfinch
jinete M rider
jinetear VI to ride horseback
jingle M jingle
jirafa F giraffe
jobar INTERJ holy cow! holy Moses! holy mackerel!
jóckey M jockey
jocoso ADJ jocular
joder VI/VT (tener relaciones sexuales) *vulg* to fuck; VT (dañar) *vulg* to fuck up; (fastidiar) *vulg* to jerk around; INTERJ *vulg* fuck! shit! ¡no jodas! (vete) buzz off! (¿en serio?) are you for real? no kidding! (no molestes) stop bothering me!
jodido ADJ (maldito) *vulg* fucking; (estropeado) *vulg* fucked up
jofaina F basin
jogging M jogging
jolgorio M rumpus
jonrón M home run
Jordania F Jordan
jordano -na ADJ & MF Jordanian
jornada F (día laboral) workday; (coloquio) colloquium
jornal M daily wage
jornalero -ra MF day laborer
joroba F hump
jorobado -da ADJ & MF hunchback
jorobar VT (molestar) to hassle; (estropear) to gum up
jota F jay; **no saber ni —** to know zilch
joven ADJ young; MF young person
jovial ADJ jolly
joya F jewel; (persona apreciada) gem; **—s** jewelry
joyería F jewelry store, jeweler's
joyero -ra MF jeweler
joystick M joystick
juanete M bunion
jubilación F (retiro) retirement; (pagos) pension; **— anticipada** early retirement
jubilado ADJ retired; MF retiree
jubilar VT to pension, to retire; **—se** to retire
jubileo M jubilee
júbilo M glee
jubiloso ADJ jubilant, joyous
judaísmo M Judaism
judicial ADJ judicial
judío -ía ADJ Jewish; MF Jew; F bean; **judía blanca** navy bean; **judía pinta** pinto bean; **judía verde** green bean
juego M (actividad recreativa) play; (deporte) game; (conjunto de piezas) set; (muebles) suite; **— de apuestas** gambling; **— de damas** checkers; **ofimático** office suite; **— de palabras** pun, play on words; **—s Olímpicos** Olympic Games; **estar en —** to be at stake; **hacer —** to match
juerga F binge; **irse de —** to go on a binge, to party
juerguista MF merrymaker
jueves M Thursday
juez MF, **jueza** F (en un tribunal) judge; (en deportes) referee; **— de paz** justice of the peace; **— de línea** linesman; **— de silla** judge, umpire
jugada F play, move; **— de tres puntos** three-point play
jugador -ora MF (deportista) player; (apostador) gambler
jugar⁴³ VI to play; (apostar) to gamble; **— a la baraja / a los naipes** to play cards; **— con fuego** to play with fire; **— en casa** to play a home game; **— limpio** to play fair; **—se** to risk
jugarreta F bad turn
jugo M juice
jugoso ADJ juicy
juguete M plaything, toy
juguetear VI to toy with, to fiddle with
juguetón -ona ADJ playful
juicio M (criterio) judgment; (proceso) trial; **— por quiebra** bankruptcy proceedings; **perder el —** to lose one's mind; **a mi —** in my estimation
juicioso ADJ sensible, judicious
juke-box M jukebox
julio M July
jumbo ADJ jumbo; M jumbo jet
jumper M jumper
junco M (planta) rush, reed; (barco chino) junk
jungla F jungle
junio M June
junta F (reunión) meeting; (concejo) council; (juntura) joint; (pieza de motor) gasket; **— directiva** board of directors
juntar VT (tubos) to attach; (flores) to gather, to pick; (ganado) to round up, to wrangle; **— polvo** to gather dust; **— valor** to muster courage; **—se** (acumularse) to gather; (asociarse) to band together; (reunirse) to come together
junto ADJ together; LOC ADV **— a** next to; **— con** together with
juntura F (lugar) juncture; (articulación) joint
jurado -da MF (individuo) juror; M (grupo) jury
juramentar VI/VT to swear in; **—se** to be sworn in
juramento M oath; **— hipocrático** Hippocratic oath
jurar VI/VT to swear, to vow; **— en falso** to perjure oneself; **— la bandera** to pledge

allegiance to the flag
jurídico ADJ legal
jurisdicción F jurisdiction
jurisprudencia F (doctrina) jurisprudence; (derecho) law
justa F joust, tilt
justamente ADV (exactamente) precisely; (con justicia) fairly
justicia F justice
justificación F justification
justificar[30] VT to justify
justo ADJ (ecuánime) just; (equitativo) equitable; (pío) righteous, upright; ADV exactly, right; — **después de** right after; — **en ese momento** exactly at that moment
juvenil ADJ (inmaduro) juvenile; (de apariencia joven) youthful
juventud F youth
juzgado M court
juzgar[40] VI/VT to judge, to pass judgment [on]; — **mal** to misjudge

Kk

kaki M khaki
kart M go-cart
kayak M kayak
Kazajstán M Kazakhstan
kazako -ka ADJ & MF Kazak[h]
Kenia F Kenya
keniata ADJ & MF Kenyan
kermés F bazaar
keroseno M kerosene
ketchup M catsup, ketchup
kg *ver* kilogramo
kilo M kilo
kilobyte M kilobyte
kilogramo M kilogram
kilometraje M mileage
kilómetro M kilometer
kilovatio M kilowatt; F —**-hora** kilowatt-hour
Kirguistán M Kyrgyzstan
Kiribati M Kiribati
kosher ADJ kosher
Kuwait M Kuwait
kuwaití ADJ & MF Kuwaiti

Ll

la ART DEF F the; — **del sombrero verde** the one with the green hat, that one with the

green hat; PRON PERS it, her; PRON REL — **que** she who, the one that
laberinto M labyrinth, maze
labia F gift of gab
labial ADJ labial
labihendido N harelipped
labio M (de la boca) lip; (de los genitales) labium; —**s agrietados** chapped lips; — **leporino** cleft lip, harelip; **con** — **leporino** harelipped
labor F (trabajo) labor; (tarea) task; (manualidad) handiwork
laboral ADJ work-related; **legislación** — labor legislation
laboratorio M laboratory
laborioso ADJ (trabajoso) laborious; (trabajador) hardworking
laborterapia F occupational therapy
labrado ADJ carved
labrador -ora MF (persona) farmhand; M (perro) labrador
labranza F plowing
labrar VT to till; —**se una carrera** to carve out a career
laca F lacquer
lacar[30] VT to lacquer
lacayo M lackey, flunky
laciar VT RP to straighten
lacio ADJ straight
lacónico ADJ (persona) laconic; (comentario) terse
lacra F (física) scar; (moral) blight
lacre M sealing wax
lacrimógeno ADJ tear-producing
lactancia F lactation; — **materna** breast-feeding
lactar VT to nurse
lácteo ADJ (como la leche) milky; (hecho de leche) dairy
lactosa F lactose
LAD [lipoproteína de alta densidad] F HDL
ladeado ADJ (torcido) awry, askew; (asimétrico) lopsided
ladear VT (una superficie) to tilt; (la cabeza) to cock; (un avión) to bank; (ignorar) to snub, to ignore; —**se** to tilt, to lean
ladeo M tilt
ladera F hillside
ladilla F crab louse
ladillo M sidebar
ladino ADJ artful
lado M side; — **a** — side by side; **al** — nearby; ¡a un —! gangway! **de** — sideways; **hacerse a un** — to move over
ladrar VI (perro) to bark; VI/VT (persona) to snap [at]
ladrido M bark, barking
ladrillo M brick
ladrón -ona MF (de casas) burglar; (con violencia) robber; (con astucia) thief; (de

tiendas) shoplifter
lagartija F (animal) lizard; (ejercicio) push-up
lagarto M alligator; — **varano** monitor lizard
lago M lake
lágrima F tear, teardrop
lagrimear VI to weep
laguna F (de agua) lagoon; (de la memoria, conocimiento) gap; (legal) loophole
laico -ca MF layperson; ADJ lay
laja F slab
lamentable ADJ (desafortunado) lamentable, regrettable; (ruinoso) woeful
lamentablemente ADV unfortunately
lamentación F lamentation
lamentar VT (una acción) to lament, to regret; (una muerte) to grieve; —**se** to lament, to wail
lamento M lament, lamentation
lamer VT (pasar la lengua) to lick; (rozar) to lap; — **culos** *fam* to brownnose; MF SG **lameculos** brownnoser
lamida F lick
lámina F (de vidrio, metal) sheet; (de metal) plate; (grabado) print
laminar VT to laminate
lámpara F lamp
lamparilla F night-light
lampiño ADJ (sin pelo) hairless; (sin barba) beardless
lana F wool; — **de acero** steel wool
lanar ADJ wool-bearing
lance M incident
lancear VT to lance, to spear
lanceta F lancet, lance
lancha F launch, boat; — **a motor** motorboat
langosta F (crustáceo) lobster; (insecto) locust
langostino M prawn
languidecer[35] VI to languish, to wilt
languidez F languor
lánguido ADJ languid, listless
lanilla F flannel
lanolina F lanolin
lanudo ADJ wooly, shaggy
lanza F lance, spear; **romper una — por alguien** to stick one's neck out for someone
lanzadera F shuttle
lanzador -ora MF (beisbol) pitcher
lanzamiento M (de un cohete, producto) launch; (de suministros) drop; (de una roca grande) heave; (de una pelota, en béisbol) pitch; (en tenis) toss
lanzar[47] VT (un cohete) to launch; (un producto) to launch, to roll out; (una pelota) to throw; (una bala) to fire; (algo pesado) to heave; (lodo) to sling; VI/VT (vomitar) to puke; —**se** to launch forth/out; — **un tiro libre** to shoot a free throw; M SG —**llamas** flamethrower
lanzazo M thrust with a lance
Laos M Laos

laosiano -na ADJ & MF Laotian
lápida F (piedra) stone tablet; (de sepultura) gravestone, tombstone
lapidar VT to stone
lapidario ADJ & M lapidary
lápiz M pencil; — **de color** crayon; — **de labios** lipstick
lapso M lapse, span
lapsus M lapse, slip of the tongue
laptop M laptop
laquear VT to lacquer
largar[40] VT (soltar) to cough up; —**se** *fam* to scram, to buzz off, to shove off
largo ADJ (camino, cuento) long; (discurso) lengthy; **de — alcance** long-range; **¡— de aquí!** scram! M —**metraje** feature film; **a la larga** in the long run; **a lo —** lengthwise; M length
larguero M crossbar
largueza F generosity
larguirucho ADJ lanky
largura F length
laringe F larynx
laringitis F laryngitis
larva F larva
lascivia F (deseo) lust; (perversión) lewdness
lascivo ADJ (pervertido) lascivious, lewd; (cachondo) *fam* horny
láser M laser
lástima F pity; **¡qué —!** what a shame!
lastimadura F hurt
lastimar VT (herir) to hurt; (insultar) to hurt one's feelings; —**se** to get hurt
lastimoso ADJ pitiful
lastrar VT to ballast
lastre M ballast
lata F (envase) tin can, can; (con tapa) canister; (pesadez) bore; **dar la —** to be a nuisance
latente ADJ latent, dormant
lateral ADJ lateral, side
látex M latex
latido M (individual) beat, throb; (colectivo) beating; (del corazón) heartbeat
latifundio M large estate
latigazo M (golpe) lash; (chasquido) crack of a whip
látigo M whip
latín M Latin
latino -na ADJ (relativo a los hispanos) Latino; (relativo a la lengua latina) Latin; M Latino; F Latina
Latinoamérica F Latin America
latinoamericano ADJ Latin American
latir VI to beat, to throb
latitud F latitude (también flexibilidad)
latón M brass
latrocinio M larceny
laudable ADJ laudable
laurel M laurel; **dormirse sobre los —es** to

rest on one's laurels
lava F lava
lavable ADJ washable
lavabo M (retrete) lavatory, toilet; (recipiente) sink
lavadero M laundry; — **automático** Laundromat™
lavado M wash, washing; — **de cerebro** brainwashing; — **de dinero** money laundering; — **en seco** dry cleaning
lavadora F washing machine
lavanda F lavender
lavandera F washerwoman
lavandería F laundry
lavar VI/VT to wash; (ropa) to launder; —**se** to wash up; —**se las manos** to wash one's hands; M SG **lavaplatos/lavavajillas** dishwasher
lavativa F enema
lavatorio M washroom
laxante M laxative
laxitud F laxity
laxo ADJ lax
lazada F bowknot
lazar⁴⁷ VT to lasso
lazarillo M (persona) guide for the blind; (perro) guide dog
lazo M (soga) lasso, rope; (vuelta) loop; (nudo corredizo) noose; (relación) tie, bond
LBD [lipoproteína de baja densidad] F LDL
le PRON PERS — **dije** I told you/him/her; — **vi** *Esp* I saw him/you; **se** — **murió el perro** hls/her dog died on him/her
leal ADJ loyal, trusty
lealtad F loyalty, allegiance; — **de marca** brand loyalty
lección F lesson, assignment; **darle una** — **a alguien** to teach someone a lesson
lechada F whitewash
leche F (de vaca) milk; (semen) *vulg* come; — **desnatada** skim milk; — **en polvo** powdered milk; — **entera** whole milk; — **homogeneizada** homogenized milk; — **malteada** malted milk; **¿qué —s quieres?** *Esp fam* what the hell do you want? **mala** — nasty disposition; **ir a toda** — to barrel along; **ese tío es la** — that guy's a case; **es un mala** — *fam* he's a nasty creep
lechería F dairy
lechero -ra ADJ dairy; M milkman; F milkmaid
lecho M bed (también de río)
lechón M suckling pig
lechoso ADJ milky
lechuga F lettuce
lechuza F screech owl, barn owl
lector -ora MF reader; — **de código de barras** bar code reader; M — **de tarjetas** card reader
lectura F (acción) reading; (material) reading matter

leer¹⁸ VI/VT to read
legación F legation
legado M legacy, bequest
legajo M file
legal ADJ legal, lawful
legalidad F (conjunto de normas) law; (cualidad de legal) legality
legalización F (de un documento) authentication; (de una actividad) legalization; — **de una validación testamentaria** probate
legalizar⁴⁷ VT to legalize
legar⁴⁰ VT to will, to bequeath
legendario ADJ legendary
leggings M PL leggings
legible ADJ (descifrable) legible; (fácil de leer) readable
legión F legion
legionario M legionnaire
legionelosis F legionnaire's disease
legislación F legislation
legislador -ora MF legislator, lawmaker
legislar VI/VT to legislate
legislativo ADJ legislative
legislatura F legislature
legitimidad F legitimacy
legítimo ADJ legitimate, lawful, rightful
lego -ga MF layperson; ADJ lay
legua F league
leguleyo -ya MF *pey* shyster
legumbre F legume
leído ADJ well-read
lejanía F distance
lejano ADJ (distancia) distant, faraway; (parentesco) remote
lejía F (producto de limpieza) bleach; (de sosa) lye
lejos ADV far away, far; **a lo** — in the distance; — **de** far from; **desde** — from afar
lelo ADJ silly
lema M (frase típica) motto; (propaganda política) slogan
lencería F lingerie
lengua F (órgano) tongue; (idioma) language; — **materna** mother tongue
lenguado M sole
lenguaje M language (también en informática); — **compilador** compiler language; — **corporal** body language; — **[de] máquina** machine language; — **de programación** programming language; — **de signos** sign language; — **ensamblador** assembly language
lenguaraz ADJ gossipy
lengüeta F (de un instrumento de viento) reed; (de un zapato) tongue
lengüetazo M lick
lentamente ADV slowly
lente MF lens; — **filtrador** filter lens; —**s**

eyeglasses; **—s de contacto** contact lenses;
—s negros/oscuros sunglasses, shades
lenteja F lentil
lentitud F slowness
lento ADJ (despacioso) slow; (tonto) dull;
(letárgico) sluggish; ADV slowly
leña F firewood
leñador -ora MF woodcutter, lumberjack
leñera F woodshed
leño M log
leñoso ADJ woody
león M lion; **— marino** sea lion
León M Leon
leona F lioness
leonés ADJ Leonese
leopardo M leopard
lepra F leprosy
lerdo ADJ slow
lesbiano -na ADJ lesbian; F lesbian
lesión F injury, lesion; **— ocular** eye injury
lesionar VT to injure; **—se** to get injured
Lesotho M Lesotho
letal ADJ lethal
letárgico ADJ lethargic
letargo M lethargy
letón -ona ADJ & MF Latvian
Letonia F Latvia
letra F (del alfabeto) letter; (caligrafía)
handwriting; (de una canción) lyrics, words;
— bastardilla/cursiva italics; **— chica**
fine print; **— de cambio** bill of exchange; **—
de imprenta** block letter; **— manuscrita**
longhand; **sin —s** uneducated
letrado ADJ learned, literate
letrero M sign
letrina F latrine
leucemia F leukemia
leudar VI to rise; VT to leaven
leva F (de tropas) levy; (de motor) cam
levadura F leaven, yeast
levantamiento M (revuelta) uprising;
(suspensión) suspension; **— de pesas**
weight-lifting
levantar VT (la mano) to raise; (una caja) to lift;
(un interruptor) to switch; (del piso) to pick
up; (perdices) to flush; (a un dormido) to
wake up, to rouse; (un edificio) to put up; **—
el campamento** to break camp; **— falso
testimonio** to bear false witness; **— la
mesa** to clear the table; **— la sesión** to
adjourn the meeting; **— vuelo** to take flight;
—se (de la cama) to get up, to rise, to arise;
(de una silla) to stand up, to get up; (un
edificio) to go up
levar VT **— anclas** to weigh anchor
leve ADJ (brisa) light; (resfrío) mild; (problema)
slight
levedad F (de una brisa) lightness; (de un resfrío)
mildness

levemente ADV lightly
léxico M lexicon, dictionary; ADJ lexical
lexicografía F lexicography
ley F law, statute; **— de prescripción** statute of
limitations; **— de [los] rendimientos
decrecientes** law of diminishing returns; **—
marcial** martial law; **de buena —** of good
quality
leyenda F (mitología) legend; (texto que
acompaña una figura) caption
leyendo, leyera, leyese, leyeron ver leer
liar[28] VT (paquetes) to bundle; (cigarros) to roll;
—se to get involved
libanés -esa ADJ & MF Lebanese
Líbano M Lebanon
libelo M libel
libélula F dragonfly
liberación F (de un país ocupado) liberation; (de
pecados) deliverance; (de presos) release
liberal ADJ & MF liberal
liberalidad F liberality
liberalismo M liberalism
liberalización F liberalization
liberar VT (de un deber) to relieve; (a un pueblo)
to liberate; (del sufrimiento) to deliver; (a un
preso) to free, to release
Liberia F Liberia
liberiano -na ADJ & MF Liberian
líbero M sweeper
libertad F liberty, freedom; **— condicional**
parole; **— de expresión** free speech; **poner
en —** to set free; **poner en — bajo fianza** to
let out on bail; **poner en — condicional** to
parole
libertador -ora MF liberator
libertar VT to liberate
libertinaje M licentiousness
libertino -na MF libertine
Libia F Libya
libidinoso ADJ libidinous
libido F libido
libio -bia ADJ & MF Libyan
libra F pound (también moneda)
librar VT (a un preso) to free, to set free; (de una
obligación) to release; (un cheque) to write;
(una letra de cambio) to draft; (una guerra) to
wage; **—se de** to get rid of
libre ADJ (persona) free; (asiento) vacant;
(camino) clear; (traducción) loose; (de una
obligación) exempt; **— albedrío** free will; **—
cambio/comercio** free trade; **— de cargos**
toll-free; **— de gravámenes** free and clear;
— de intereses interest-free; **— de
impuestos** duty-free, tax-free; **— de virus**
virus-free; **— pensador** freethinker
librería F bookstore
librero -ra MF bookseller
libresco ADJ bookish
libreta F small notebook; **— de direcciones**

address book
libreto M libretto
libro M book; — **de bolsa** pocket book; — **de
cocina** cookbook; — **de texto** textbook; —
electrónico e-book; — **en rústica**
paperback; — **mayor** ledger
licencia F (carnet de conducir, libertad poética)
license; (permiso) leave; (permiso para
ausentarse) leave of absence; — **de sitio** site
license; — **por maternidad** maternity leave
licenciado -da MF college graduate
licenciar VT to discharge; —**se** to graduate from
college
licenciatura F bachelor's degree
licencioso ADJ licentious
liceo M high school
licitación F bid
lícito ADJ lawful, permissible
licor M liqueur, cordial
licuadora F blender
líder MF leader
liderar VT to head up
liderar VT to lead
liderazgo M (de una organización, condición de
líder) leadership; (en una competencia) lead
lidiar VI/VT to contend, to grapple
liebre F hare; **levantar la** — to let the cat out of
the bag
Liechtenstein M Liechtenstein
liechtensteiniano -na MF Liechtensteiner
lienzo M canvas
liftado M top spin
lifting M face-lift
liga F (alianza, grupo deportivo) league; (cinta
elástica) garter; — **mayor** major league
ligado M slur
ligadura F ligature
ligamento M ligament
ligar[40] VT (atar) to bind; (conectar notas) to slur;
VI (conquistar sexualmente) to score; —**se** to
bind; —**se las trompas** to have one's tubes
tied
ligeramente ADV lightly
ligereza F (de peso) lightness; (de
temperamento) levity
ligero ADJ (poco pesado) light; (rápido) swift;
(pequeño) slight; **a la ligera** lightly
ligue M (amistad casual) pickup; (conquista
sexual) score
liguero M garter belt
lija F sandpaper
lijar VI/VT to sandpaper, to sand
lila ADJ & MF lilac
lima F (fruta) lime; (árbol) lime tree; — **de uñas**
nail file
limar VI/VT to file
limero M lime tree
limitación F (restricción) limitation; (defecto)
shortcoming

limitar VT (restringir) to limit; (gastos) to curb;
—**se a** to limit oneself to
límite M (restricción) limit; (de una región)
boundary; (de la paciencia) bounds; — **de
edad** age limit; — **de tiempo** time limit; —
de velocidad speed limit
limítrofe ADJ bordering
limo M slime
limón M lemon
limonada F lemonade
limonero M lemon tree
limosna F alms, handout
limpiador M cleanser
limpiar VI/VT to clean; VT (una superficie) to
wipe; (la piel) to cleanse; (un camino, una
pantalla de computadora, la reputación) to
clear; (animales) to dress; (zapatos) to shine;
(un derrame) to mop up, to wipe up; (dejar sin
dinero) to clean out; M SG
limpiaparabrisas windshield wiper; M SG
limpiavidrios squeegee
límpido ADJ limpid
limpieza F (pulcritud) cleanliness, neatness;
(operación militar) mop-up; — **étnica** ethnic
cleansing
limpio ADJ (casa) clean, neat; (piel, conciencia)
clear; (juego) fair; (sin dinero) broke; **pasar
en** — to make a clean copy
limusina F limousine
linaje M lineage, ancestry
linaza F linseed
lince M (animal) lynx; (persona astuta) sly fox;
con ojos de — sharp-eyed
linchar VT to lynch
lindante ADJ neighboring
lindar VI to border, to adjoin
linde MF boundary
lindero ADJ adjoining; M boundary
lindo ADJ pretty; **un día** — a nice day; **de lo** — a
lot
línea F (raya, cola) line; (en béisbol) line drive; —
aérea airline; — **de banda** (fútbol) sideline;
— **de conducta** course of action; — **de
crédito** credit line; — **de fondo** baseline; —
de golpeo line of scrimmage; — **de meta**
goal line; — **de montaje** assembly line; —
ofensiva offensive line; **batear una** — to
line out; **en** — online
lineal ADJ linear
linfa F lymph
linfocito M lymphocyte
linfoma M lymphoma
lingüista MF linguist
lingüística F linguistics
lingüístico ADJ linguistic
linimento M liniment
lino M (tela) linen; (fibra) flax
linóleo M linoleum
linterna F (a pilas, de bolsillo) flashlight; (de un

faro) lantern

lío M (bulto) bundle; (enredo, molestia) mess, hassle; (amorío) affair, fling; **armar un —** to raise a ruckus; **meterse en un —** to get oneself into a mess

liofilizar VI/VT to freeze-dry

liposucción F liposuction

liquidación F (ajuste de cuentas, de bienes) settlement, liquidation; (rebaja) sale, clearance sale; (pago completo) payment in full

liquidar VT (bienes, mercancías) to liquidate, to sell off; (una cuenta, herencia) to settle; (a una persona) *fam* to waste, to off, to whack

liquidez F liquidity

líquido ADJ & M liquid; **— amniótico** amniotic fluid

lira F (moneda) lira

lírica F lyric poetry

lírico ADJ lyric, lyrical

lirio M iris, lily; **— de los valles** lily of the valley

lirismo M lyricism

lisiado ADJ (descapacitado) handicapped; (lesionado) injured

lisiar VT to handicap

liso ADJ (neumático) bald; (camino) even, smooth; (terreno) flat; (pelo) straight; **azul — solid blue**

lisonja F flattery

lisonjear VI/VT to flatter

lisonjero -ra MF flatterer; ADJ flattering

lista F (de palabras) list; (de miembros) roster; (de alumnos) roll; (banda) stripe; (de precios) schedule, list; **— de control** checklist; **— de correo** mailing list; **— de espera** waiting list; **— negra** blacklist; **pasar —** to call the roll

listado ADJ striped; M listing, printout

listo ADJ (preparado) ready, set; (inteligente) clever, smart; **hacerse el —** to pull a stunt

listón M (tabla) board; (en salto de altura) crossbar

lisura F smoothness

litera F (cama en el tren, barco) berth; (cama superpuesta) bunk bed

literal ADJ literal

literario ADJ literary

literato -ta MF writer

literatura F literature

litigante MF litigant

litigio M (pleito) lawsuit; (acción de litigar) litigation

litio M lithium

litoral ADJ seaside; M seaboard, seacoast

litro M liter

Lituania F Lithuania

lituano -na ADJ & MF Lithuanian

liviano ADJ (leve) light; (promiscuo)

promiscuous

lívido ADJ livid

living M living room

llaga F sore

llama F (fuego) flame; (animal) llama

llamada F (de teléfono, a la acción) call; (grito) hail; (nota al pie) footnote; **— de cobro revertido / por cobrar** collect call

llamado M (acción de convocar) call; (petición) appeal

llamador M knocker

llamamiento M (conversación) call; (exhortación) appeal; **hacer un —** to appeal

llamar VT (un nombre, una huelga, por teléfono) to call; (a la puerta) to knock; (gritar) to hail; **— la atención** to call attention; **me llamo Juan** my name is Juan

llamarada F blaze, flare

llamativo ADJ (impactante) striking, bold; (chabacano) gaudy, flashy

llameante ADJ flaming

llamear VI to flare, to flame

llana F trowel

llano ADJ (sencillo) plain; (liso) flat, smooth, level; (de poca profundidad) shallow; M plain

llanta F (reborde metálico) rim; (neumático) tire

llanto M crying, weeping

llanura F plain, prairie

llave F (para puertas) key; (de armas de fuego) lock; (en lucha libre) lock, hold; (grifo) faucet, tap; (interruptor) light switch; (de gas) cock; **— de tuercas** wrench; **— inglesa** pipe wrench; **— maestra** master key

llavero M key ring

llegada F arrival

llegar[40] VI (arribar) to arrive, to get there/here; (alcanzar) to reach; **— a las manos** to come to blows; **— a ser** to become; **— a un acuerdo** to strike a deal; **— a un arreglo** to cut a deal; **— tarde** to be late

llenar VT (un recipiente) to fill; (un formulario) to fill out; **— el tanque** to tank up, to gas up; **—se** to fill up; **—se de** to get filled with; **—se de oro** to make a killing

lleno ADJ full; **— de** full of; **de —** totally; M **un — completo** a full house

llevadero ADJ bearable

llevar VT (transportar) to carry, to take; (transportar en coche) to drive; (tener puesto) to wear; (contener) to hold; (inducir) to lead, to drive; **— a cabo** to carry out; **— la cuenta** to keep score; **— la ventaja** to have an advantage; **— los libros** to keep the books; **— un mes aquí** to have been here one month; **le llevo dos años a mi hermano** I'm two years older than my brother; **llevo las de perder** the odds are against me; **—se** to carry away, to take away; **—se bien con** to get along with

llorar VI (con ruido) to cry, to bawl; (con lágrimas) to weep; VT (una pérdida) to lament; (una muerte) to mourn

lloriquear VI to whimper

lloriqueo M whimper

llorón-ona ADJ weeping; MF crybaby, whiner

lloroso ADJ tearful, weeping

llovedizo ADJ **agua llovediza** rainwater

llover[6] VI/VT to rain; — **a cántaros** to rain cats and dogs; **llueva o truene** rain or shine

llovizna F drizzle

lloviznar VI to drizzle, to mist

lluvia F (precipitación) rain; (de preguntas, críticas) barrage; (de protestas, flechas, piedras) volley; (de golpes, chispas) shower; — **ácida** acid rain; — **de ideas** brainstorming; — **torrencial** driving rain

lluvioso ADJ rainy

lo PRON PERS — **bueno** the good thing; — **de la protesta** the matter of the protest; — **que quiero** what I want; **sé** — **bueno que eres** I know how good you are; **yo** — **vi** I saw it/him/you

loable ADJ laudable, praiseworthy

loar VT to laud

lobato M wolf cub

lobbista, lobista MF lobbyist

lobby M lobby

lobezno M wolf cub

lobo M wolf

lobotomía F lobotomy

lóbrego ADJ gloomy

lóbulo M lobe

local ADJ local; M premises

localidad F (pueblo) town, locality; (en un teatro) seat

localización F location

localizar[47] VT (encontrar) to locate; (limitar) to localize

loción F lotion

loco-ca ADJ insane, mad, crazy; — **de remate** stark raving mad; MF lunatic, insane person; M madman

locomotora F locomotive, train engine

locuaz ADJ garrulous, loquacious

locura F madness, insanity

locutor-ora MF radio announcer

lodazal M quagmire

lodo M mud

lodoso ADJ muddy

logaritmo M logarithm

logia F lodge

lógica F logic

lógicamente ADV logically

lógico ADJ (razonado) logical; (bien fundado) sound

logística F logistics

lograr VT to achieve, to accomplish; **logré convencerle** I managed to / succeeded in convincing him

logro M (lo conseguido) accomplishment, achievement; (hazaña) feat

lola F *fam* boob

loma F knoll

lombriz F (de tierra) earthworm; (de estómago) tapeworm

lomo M (de animal) back ridge; (corte de carne) loin

lona F canvas

longaniza F cured sausage

longevidad F longevity

longevo ADJ long-lived

longitud F (distancia angular) longitude; (largo) length; — **de onda** wavelength

lonja F (mercado) commodity exchange; (tajada) slice of meat

loquería F *fam* booby hatch, funny farm

loquero-ra MF (psiquiatra) *fam* shrink; M (manicomio) *fam* funny farm

lord M lord

loro M parrot

losa F (lápida) slab; (baldosa) flagstone

lote M lot

lotería F lottery

loza F (basta) crockery; (fina) china

lozanía F freshness, bloom

lozano ADJ fresh, blooming

LSD MF LSD

lubina F bass

lubricante ADJ & M lubricant

lubricar[30] VI/VT to lubricate

lucero M morning star; — **del alba** morning star

lucha F (pugna, contienda) struggle; (pelea) fight; — **libre** wrestling

luchador-ora MF fighter; (en lucha libre) wrestler

luchar VI/VT (contra un enemigo) to fight; (con un problema) to struggle; (en lucha libre) to wrestle; — **por** to strive for

lucidez F lucidity

lúcido ADJ lucid, clear-headed

luciérnaga F firefly, glowworm

lucio M pike

lucir[39] VI (mostrarse) to look; (favorecer, sentar bien) to look good on, to suit; VT (llevar) to model, to sport; (alardear de) to flaunt; —**se** (sobresalir) to excel; (ostentar) to show off

lucrativo ADJ lucrative, profitable

lucro M **sin fines de** — not for profit

luctuoso ADJ sad, mournful, dismal

luego ADV afterward, then, next; — **de** after; **desde** — of course; **hasta** — so long

lugar M place; — **común** platitude; — **de nacimiento** birthplace, place of birth; — **de trabajo** workplace; **dar** — **a** to give rise to; **no hay** — there's no room; **en** — **de** instead of

lúgubre ADJ mournful, gloomy
lujo M luxury; **darse un —** to indulge oneself; **con — de detalles** in great detail
lujoso ADJ (ropa) luxurious; (hotel) plush
lujuria F lust
lujurioso ADJ lustful
lumbago M lumbago
lumbar ADJ lumbar
lumbre F (fuego) fire; (luz) light
luminosidad F brilliance, luminosity
luminoso ADJ luminous
luna F (satélite) moon; (espejo) large mirror; — **de miel** honeymoon; **estar en la —** to be distracted; — **llena** full moon
lunar ADJ lunar; M (en la piel) mole; (en una tela) polka dot
lunático -ca ADJ & MF lunatic
lunes M Monday
lupa F magnifying glass
lúpulo M hops
lupus M lupus
lustrar VT to shine, to polish
lustre M luster, shine
lustroso ADJ (revista) glossy; (pelo) shiny, sleek
luto M mourning
luxación F dislocation
Luxemburgo M Luxembourg
luxemburgués -esa MF Luxembourger; ADJ Luxembourgian
luz F light (también aparato); (del sol) sunshine; (abertura) aperture; — **trasera** taillight; — **verde** green light; **dar a —** to give birth; **sacar a —** to disclose

Mm

macabro ADJ grim
macanudo ADJ cool
Macao M Macao
macarrones M PL macaroni
Macedonia F Macedonia
macedonio -nia ADJ & MF Macedonian
maceta F flower pot
machacar[30] VT (aplastar) to pound, to crush; (insistir) to harp on; (en baloncesto) to dunk
machacón ADJ persistent
machetazo M hack with a machete
machete M machete
machismo M [male] chauvinism
macho M (animal masculino) male; (mulo) he-mule; (varón) man; (hombre muy varonil) he-man; — **cabrío** he-goat; — **y hembra** hook and eye; ADJ (masculino) male; (fuerte) strong; INTERJ man!
machote ADJ butch

machucar[30] VT to bruise
macilento ADJ pale
macizo ADJ massive; M plateau
Madagascar M Madagascar
madama F madam
madeja F skein
madera F wood (también en golf); (árboles maderables) timber; (para construcción) lumber; — **contrachapada** plywood; — **flotante** driftwood; — **noble** hardwood; —**s** woodwinds; **tocar —** to knock on wood
maderaje M woodwork
madero M trunk
madrastra F stepmother
madre F mother; — **de alquiler** surrogate mother; — **patria** mother country; —**perla** mother-of-pearl; — **política** mother-in-law; —**selva** honeysuckle; **ciento y la —** everybody and their dog
madriguera F burrow, hole
madrileño -ña ADJ & MF [person] from Madrid
madrina F godmother
madrugada F early morning hours; **a las dos de la —** at two in the morning
madrugador -ra ADJ & MF early bird
madrugar VI to get up early; — **con gripe** to wake up with a cold
maduración F (animales, personas) maturation, maturing; (frutos) ripening; (vino) aging
madurar VI to mature, to grow up
madurez F (de persona) maturity; (de fruta) ripeness
maduro ADJ (persona) mature; (fruta) ripe
maestría F master's degree; — **en administración de empresas** master of business administration
maestro -tra MF (docente) [school]teacher; (artesano) master; (director) maestro
mafia F mafia
mafioso -sa MF mafioso
magia F magic
mágico ADJ magic, magical
magisterio M (actividad) teaching; (conjunto de los maestros) teachers; (profesión) teaching profession
magistrado -da MF magistrate
magistral ADJ masterful, masterly
magma M magma
magnánimo ADJ magnanimous
magnate MF magnate, tycoon
magnesia F magnesia
magnesio M magnesium
magnético ADJ magnetic
magnetismo M magnetism
magnetizar[47] VT to magnetize
magnificar[30] VT to magnify
magnificencia F magnificence
magnífico ADJ (palacio) magnificent; (día)

glorious
magnitud F magnitude
magno ADJ great
magnolia F magnolia
magnolio M magnolia tree
mago M magician, wizard
magro ADJ lean
magulladura F bruise, contusion
magullar VI/VT (machucar) to bruise; (mutilar) to mangle
mahonesa F mayonnaise
maicena® F cornstarch
maíz M corn, maize
maizal M cornfield
majadería F stupidity
majadero ADJ stupid
majar VT to pound
majestad F majesty
majestuoso ADJ majestic, stately
majo ADJ (atractivo) good-looking; (agradable) charming
mal M (maldad) evil; (enfermedad) malady, affliction; (daño) harm; — **de altura** altitude sickness; — **de ojo** evil eye; ADV wrong, badly; — **aconsejado** misguided; — **adquirido** ill-gotten; — **hablado** foulmouthed; **hablar** — **de alguien** to speak ill of someone; **hacer** — to do wrong; **lo hice mal** I did it badly
malabarista MF juggler
malandanza F misfortune
malaria F malaria
Malasia F Malaysia
malasio -sia ADJ & MF Malaysian
Malawi M Malawi
malawiano -na ADJ & MF Malawian
malbaratar VT to undersell
malcontento ADJ discontented
malcriado ADJ spoiled
malcriar VT to spoil
maldad F evil, wickedness
maldecir[51] VI/VT to curse
maldición F curse
maldito ADJ accursed; ¡— **sea!** *fam* damn it!
Maldivas F PL Maldives
maldivo -va ADJ & MF Maldivian
maleable ADJ malleable
maleante MF gangster, hoodlum
malear VT to corrupt
maleducado ADJ ill-mannered, ill-bred
maleficio M evil spell
maléfico ADJ evil
malentendido M misunderstanding
malestar M (de estómago) upset; (físico) discomfort; (espiritual) malaise; (social) unrest
maleta F suitcase, bag; **hacer la** — to pack one's suitcase
maletero M car trunk

maletín M briefcase
malévolo ADJ (persona) malevolent; (comentario) snide
maleza F (en el monte) underbrush, scrub; (en un jardín) weeds
malformación F malformation
malgache ADJ & MF Madagascan
malgastar VI/VT to waste, to throw away
malgasto M waste
malhechor -ora MF evildoer, criminal
malhumorado ADJ grumpy, ill-humored
Mali, Malí M Mali
malí ADJ & MF Malian
malicia F malice
malicioso ADJ malicious, spiteful
malignidad F malignancy
maligno ADJ (persona) vicious, evil; (tumor) malignant
malinterpretar VI/VT to misunderstand
malla F (de armadura) mail; (de metal) mesh
malo ADJ bad; (calidad, letra) poor; (enfermo) ill; **mal estado** disrepair; **mal humor** bad mood; **mala fama** ill repute; **mala fe** bad faith; **mala hierba** weed; **mala pasada** bad turn; **mala racha** slump; **mala suerte** bad luck
malograr VT to spoil, to ruin; —**se** to fail, to miscarry
malpagar[40] VI/VT to underpay
malparto M miscarriage
malsano ADJ unhealthy, unwholesome
malta F malt
Malta F Malta
maltés -esa ADJ & MF Maltese
maltratar VT to mistreat, to abuse
maltrato M mistreatment, abuse
maltrecho ADJ battered
malvado ADJ wicked, evil
malvavisco M marshmallow
malversación F misuse, misappropriation
malversar VT to misuse, to embezzle
mamá F mama, mamma, mom
mamada F suck; (felación) *vulg* blow job
mamado ADJ drunk
mamar VI (un bebé) to suckle, to nurse; VI/VT to suck; —**la** *vulg* to blow
mamario ADJ mammary
mamarracho M sight
mami F mommy
mamífero ADJ mammalian, mammal; M mammal
mamografía F mammography
mampara F partition
mamut M mammoth
manada F (de ballenas) pod; (de vacas) herd; (de lobos) pack
manantial M (naciente) spring; (fuente inagotable) wellspring
manar VI to stream out

mancha F (marca) stain, spot; (de tinta) blot; (cosa borrosa) blur; (aceitosa) smear, smudge; (menoscabo) tinge; (en la piel) blemish

manchado ADJ spotted

manchar VI/VT (ensuciar) to spot; (menoscabar) to stain, to blemish

manchón M large spot

mancilla F blemish

mancillar VT to defile, to sully

manco ADJ one-armed

mancuerna F dumbbell

mandado M errand

mandamás M *fam* big enchilada, big kahuna

mandamiento M commandment

mandante MF principal

mandar VI/VT (dar órdenes) to command, to order; (enviar) to send; — **buscar a** to send for; — **decir** to send word; **¿quién manda?** who's in charge? —**se hacer un traje** to have a suit made; **¿mande?** (hola) hello; (perdón) excuse me? what?

mandarina F tangerine

mandatario -ria MF (mediante contrato) agent; (abogado) attorney; (de estado) head of state

mandato M (orden) command, order; (cargo político) term, mandate

mandíbula F (quijada) jaw; (hueso) jawbone

mandil M apron

mandioca F manioc

mando M (de un estado) rule; (de un aparato) control; — **a distancia** remote control

mandolina F mandolin

mandón -ona ADJ bossy, domineering; MF bossy person, control freak

mandonear VI/VT to domineer, to boss around

manea F hobble

manear VT to hobble

manecilla F clock hand

manejable ADJ manageable

manejar VT (un vehículo) to drive, to steer; (un negocio) to run, to manage; (una máquina) to operate

manejo M (de un negocio) running, management; (de asuntos) handling; (de una máquina) operation

manera F manner, way; **a — de** like; **de alguna — somehow**; **de cualquier —** anyway; **de ninguna —** on no account; **de — que** so that

manga F (de una camisa) sleeve; (de una nave) beam; (de agua) hose; (tenis) set; — **de viento** windsock; **en —s de camisa** in shirtsleeves; **ser de — ancha** to be broad-minded; **sacar algo de la —** to pull something out of a hat

manganeso M manganese

mangle M mangrove

mango M (agarradera) handle, grip; (fruta, árbol) mango

mangosta F mongoose

manguera F hose

manguito M muff

maní M peanut

manía F (moda, estado patológico) mania; (hábito) bad habit; (tic) tic

maníaco -ca ADJ maniacal; MF maniac

maníaco-depresivo ADJ manic-depressive

maniatar VT to tie the hands; (manear) to hobble

maniático ADJ (que tiene manías) crotchety; (melindroso) fastidious

manicomio M *pey* insane asylum

manicura F manicure

manicurar VT to manicure

manido ADJ hackneyed

manifestación F (muestra) manifestation; (protesta) demonstration

manifestante MF demonstrator

manifestar[1] VI/VT to manifest, to show; (expresar) to air; (protestar en público) to demonstrate; (declarar) to state

manifiesta, manifieste *ver* manifestar

manifiesto ADJ & M manifest; **poner de —** to underscore; M (dogma) manifesto; — **de vuelo** manifest

manija F handle

maniobra F (militar) maneuver; (para llamar la atención) stunt; — **de Heimlich** Heimlich maneuver

maniobrar VI/VT to maneuver

manipulación F (de la opinión pública) manipulation; (de alimentos) handling

manipular VT (influir) to manipulate; (tocar con las manos) to handle

maniquí M (muñeco) mannequin; MF (modelo) model

manivela F crank

manjar M delicacy

mano F hand (también de naipes); (de pintura) coat; (fútbol) handball; — **a —** one on one; — **de obra** workforce; —**s a la obra** let's get to work; —**s de mantequilla** butterfingers; **a — (presente)** at hand; (con la mano) by hand; **a — armada** at gunpoint; **dar una —** to lend a hand; **dar una — de pintura** to put on a coat of paint; **darle una — a alguien** to lend someone a hand; **darse la — (saludo)** to shake hands; (señal de afecto) to hold hands; **de primera —** firsthand; **de segunda —** secondhand; **estar a — con alguien** to be even with someone; **hecho a —** handmade; **poner las —s en el fuego por alguien** to go out on a limb for someone; **quedar a —** to break even; **se le fue la —** he got carried away; **ser —** to lead [in a card game]; **tener buena — con/para algo** to have a knack for something; **tomarse de la —** to hold hands

manojo M (de monedas) handful; (de llaves) bunch

manómetro M pressure gauge
manopla F (guante) mitten; (en béisbol) glove
manosear VT (a una persona) to fondle, to grope; (tocar una cosa) to feel, to finger
manoseo M feel, grope
manotazo M swat; **tirarle un — a alguien** to take a swipe at someone
manotear VI to swat at
mansalva LOC ADV **a —** at will
mansedumbre F gentleness, meekness
mansión F mansion
manso ADJ (humilde) meek; (domesticado) tame; (apacible) gentle
manta F (gruesa) blanket, cover; (liviana) throw
manteca F lard, shortening; *RP* butter; **— de cacao** cocoa butter
mantecoso ADJ rich, buttery
mantel M tablecloth
mantendrá, mantendría *ver* mantener
mantener[58] VT (conservar, sostener) to maintain; (dejar prolongadamente) to keep; (alimentar, costear a alguien) to provide for; (apoyar a lo largo del tiempo) to sustain; **— a flote** to buoy up; **— el orden público** to keep the peace; **— en secreto** to keep under wraps; **— en suspenso** to keep in suspense; **— la calma** to remain calm; **—se** (quedarse) to remain; (ganarse la vida) to support oneself; **—se al corriente** to keep abreast; **—se al tanto** to stay informed; **—se en contacto** to keep in touch; **—se firme** to stand pat, to stick to one's guns
mantenga, mantengo *ver* mantener
mantenimiento M maintenance, upkeep
mantequera F (platillo) butter dish; (aparato para hacer mantequilla) churn
mantequilla F butter; **— de maní** peanut butter
mantiene, mantienes *ver* mantener
mantilla F mantilla
manto M mantle (también geológico); (de juez) robe
mantón M shawl
mantra M mantra
mantuve, mantuviera, mantuviese *ver* mantener
manual ADJ & M manual
manubrio M handlebar
manufactura F manufacture
manufacturar VT to manufacture
manufacturero -ra ADJ manufacturing; MF manufacturer
manuscrito ADJ written by hand; M manuscript
manutención F maintenance
manzana F (fruta) apple; (de ciudad) block; **— de la discordia** bone of contention
manzanar M apple orchard
manzano M apple tree
maña F (destreza) skill, knack; (artimaña) cunning
mañana F (división del día) morning; (futuro) tomorrow; ADV tomorrow; **— por la —** tomorrow morning
mañanero -ra MF early bird
mañoso ADJ tricky
mapa M map; **— de memoria** memory map; **— en relieve** relief map
mapache M raccoon
maple M maple
maqueta F mock-up
maquillaje M makeup
maquillar[se] VI/VT to put on makeup
máquina F (aparato) machine; (motor) engine; **— de búsqueda** search engine; **— de coser** sewing machine; **— de escribir** typewriter; **— de lavar** washing machine; **— de vapor** steam engine; **— expendedora** vending machine; **— fotográfica** camera
maquinación F scheming, plotting
maquinador -ora MF schemer
maquinal ADJ automatic
maquinar VI/VT to plot, to scheme
maquinaria F (aparato) machinery, apparatus; (del gobierno) machine
maquinilla F clipper; **— de afeitar** razor
maquinista M (de locomotora) locomotive engineer; (obrero) machinist
mar MF sea; **— de fondo** undercurrent; **llover a mares** to rain cats and dogs; **en alta —** on the high seas; **un — de cosas** a lot of things; **hacerse a la —** to put to sea
maraca F maraca
maraña F (de hilos) tangle, snarl; (de pelo) mat
marañón M cashew
maratón M marathon
maravilla F (portento) wonder, marvel; (flor) marigold; **a las mil —s** wonderfully
maravillar VT to amaze; **—se** to be amazed, to marvel
maravilloso ADJ marvelous, wonderful
marca F (récord) record; (de ganado) brand; (de producto) brand, brand name, label; (de coche) make; **— comercial** name brand; **— de nacimento** birthmark; **— de fábrica** trademark; **— genérica** generic brand; **— registrada** registered trademark; **de —** name-brand
marcadamente ADV sharply
marcado ADJ (acento) thick; (contraste) sharp, stark; (descenso) steep; (parecido) strong
marcador M (lapicero) marker; (en deporte) scoreboard; **— de libros** bookmark; **— genético** genetic marker; **¿cómo va el —?** what's the score?
marcar[30] VT (una respuesta) to mark; (ganado) to brand; (el ritmo) to beat; (la hora) to say; (un tanto) to score; (medida) to read, to show; (un número telefónico) to dial; **— para**

seleccionar to highlight; — **un gol** to score a goal

marcha F (caminata, pieza musical) march; (partida) leaving; (progreso) course; (modo de andar) gait; (cambio en un coche) gear; (animación) nightlife; — **atrás** reverse; **ponerse en** — to get going; **puesta en** — beginning; **sobre la** — as you go

marchante MF (vendedor) art dealer; (cliente) customer

marchar VI (soldado) to march; (máquina, vehículo) to run; —**se** to go away

marchista MF walker

marchitar VT to wither; —**se** to wither, to shrivel up

marchito ADJ withered, shriveled up

marcial ADJ martial

marco M (de un cuadro, de una puerta, de referencia) frame; (moneda) mark

marea F tide; — **baja** low tide; — **alta** high tide

mareado ADJ (en un barco) seasick; (en un coche) carsick; (de alegría) giddy; (con vértigo) dizzy, lightheaded

marear VT (dar vértigo) to make dizzy; (en un barco) to make seasick; —**se** (tener vértigo) to get dizzy; (en un barco) to get seasick

marejada F tidal wave

maremoto M tidal wave

mareo M (en un barco) seasickness; (en un vehículo) motion sickness; (vértigo) dizziness

marfil M ivory

marfileño -ña ADJ & MF Ivorian

margarina F margarine

margarita F daisy; **echar —s a los cerdos** to cast pearls before swine

margen M (de un papel) margin; (de la sociedad) fringe; MF (de un río) bank; — **de error** margin of error; — **de ganancia** profit margin, markup; — **de seguridad** margin of safety; **al** — on the outside

marginación F (de un grupo) marginalization; (de un individuo) isolation; **hay cierta** — **entre entre los colegas** there is a certain distance among the colleagues; **la** — **de ciertos grupos minoritarios** the marginalization of certain minorities

marginado -da ADJ & MF outcast

marginal ADJ marginal

marginar VT to marginalize

mariachi M mariachi

marica ADJ (homosexual) *ofensivo* queer; (cobarde) sissy; M (homosexual) *ofensivo* queer, fruit; (cobarde) sissy, pansy

maricón ADJ (homosexual) *ofensivo* queer; (cobarde) sissy; M (homosexual) *ofensivo* queer, fruit; (cobarde) sissy

marido M husband

mariguana, marihuana F marijuana; *fam* grass, pot

marimacho ADJ (niña) tomboyish; (mujer) butch; MF (niña) tomboy; (mujer) butch

marimba F marimba

marina F navy; — **mercante** merchant marine

marinar VT to marinate

marinero -ra ADJ (buque) seaworthy; (nación) seafaring; MF sailor

marino -na ADJ marine; MF sailor; (oficial) naval officer

marioneta F marionette

mariposa F (insecto) butterfly (también en natación); (tuerca) wing nut; — **nocturna** moth

mariquita F ladybug

mariscal M marshal; — **de campo** (militar) field marshal; (fútbol americano) quarterback

mariscos M PL shellfish

marítimo ADJ maritime

marketing M marketing

marmita F pot

mármol M marble

marmóreo ADJ marble

marmota F groundhog

maroma F rope

marqués M marquis

marquesa F marquise

marrano M hog

marrón ADJ brown

marroquí ADJ & MF Moroccan

Marruecos M Morocco

marshalés -esa ADJ & MF Marshallese

marsopa F porpoise

martes M Tuesday

martillar VI/VT to hammer

martillo M hammer (también hueso del oído, pieza de revólver); (de juez) gavel; — **neumático** jackhammer

martinete M (martillo grande) pile driver; (pieza de piano) piano hammer

martini M martini

mártir MF martyr

martirio M martyrdom

martirizar[47] VT to martyr, to torment

marxismo M Marxism

marzo M March

mas CONJ but

más ADJ more; PREP plus; ADV more; (más tiempo) longer; — **allá de** beyond; — **bien** rather; — **de tres** more than three; — **o menos** more or less; — **que nada** primarily; — **que nunca** more than ever; — **que tú** more than you; **a lo** — at best; **a** — **tardar** at the latest; **de** — extra; **el** — **allá** the hereafter; **es de lo** — **simpático** he's really nice; **es** — furthermore; **está de** — it is superfluous; **otro** — yet another; **por** — **que** no matter how much; **y** — **todavía** and then some

masa F mass; (de agua) body; (de harina) batter;

(para amasar) dough; **en —** en masse, in large numbers; **las —s** the masses; **— de hojaldre** puff pastry
masacrar VT to massacre, to slaughter
masacre M massacre
masaje M massage
masajear VT to massage
masajista M masseur; F masseuse
mascar[30] VI/VT (chicle) to chew; (con ruido) to crunch
máscara F mask; **— de gas** gas mask
mascarada F masquerade
mascota F (animal doméstico) pet; (emblema de un equipo) mascot
masculino ADJ (como un hombre, género gramatical) masculine; (del hombre) male
mascullar VI/VT to mumble
masilla F putty
masivo ADJ massive
masón M mason
masonería F masonry
masoquismo M masochism
mastectomía F mastectomy
máster M master; **— en administración de empresas** master of business administration
masticar[30] VT to chew
mástil M (en un barco) mast; (para una bandera) flagpole, flagstaff
mastín M mastiff
masturbarse VI to masturbate
mata F bush; **— de pelo** head of hair
matadero M slaughterhouse
matador ADJ horrendous; M bullfighter
matanza F slaughter, killing
matar VT to kill; (animales) to butcher, to slaughter; **— a tiros** to gun down; **— de hambre** to starve; VT **matasellar** to cancel a stamp; M SG **matamoscas** flyswatter; M SG **matasellos** postmark; M SG **matasanos** quack [doctor]
mate M (en ajedrez) checkmate; (planta, bebida) mate; ADJ (pintura) flat; **hacer un —** (baloncesto) to dunk the ball
matemática, matemáticas F mathematics
matemático -ca ADJ mathematical; (exacto) precise; MF mathematician
materia F (sustancia) matter; (tema de estudio) school subject; (tema) topic; **— extraña** extraneous matter; **— fecal** fecal matter; **— gris** gray matter; **— prima** raw material
material ADJ (necesidades) material; (autor) real; M material
materialismo M materialism
maternal ADJ (instinto) maternal; (amor) motherly
maternidad F (relacionado con el nacimiento) maternity; (estado de ser madre) motherhood
materno ADJ maternal
matiné M matinee

matiz M (de un color) tint, shade, hue; (de ironía) tinge; (de sentido) nuance
matizar[47] VT (mezclar colores) to blend, to tinge; (moderar) to qualify
matón -ona MF (persona que intimida a los pequeños) bully; (pandillero, peleador) thug
matorral M (mata) thicket; (región) bush
matraz M flask
matriarca F matriarch
matrícula F (alumnado) enrollment, matriculation; (de un coche) registration; (placa) license plate; (costo de la universidad) tuition fees
matriculación F matriculation
matricular VT to matriculate, to enroll
matrilineal ADJ matrilineal
matrimonial ADJ marital
matrimonio M (estado civil) matrimony, marriage; (pareja) married couple
matriz F (en matemáticas) matrix; (bidimensional) array; (útero) womb; (plantilla) stencil; **casa —** main office
matrona ADJ frumpy, matronly; F matron
matutino ADJ of the morning
maullar VI to mew
maullido M mew
mauriciano -na ADJ & MF Mauritian
Mauricio M Mauritius
Mauritania F Mauritania
mauritano -na MF Mauritanian
maxilar M jawbone
máxima F maxim
maximizar VT to maximize
máximo ADJ & M maximum; (autoridad) ultimate; (cuidado) utmost; **— histórico** all-time high
maya ADJ & MF Maya, Mayan
mayo M (mes) May; (palo) maypole
mayonesa F mayonnaise
mayor ADJ (de tamaño) greater, larger; (de edad) older, elder; (rango, clave) major; **al por —** wholesale; **dedo —** middle finger; **el — número de votos** the most votes; M (adulto) adult
mayoral M boss
mayordomo M butler
mayoreo M wholesale
mayoría F majority; **— de edad** legal age, majority; **en su —** largely
mayorista MF wholesale dealer
mayoritario ADJ majority
mayúsculo -la ADJ (letra) capital; (problema) major; F capital letter
mazmorra F dungeon
mazo M mallet
mazorca F (con maíz) ear of corn; (sin maíz) corncob
me PRON PERS **él — vio** he saw me; **él — habló** he talked to me; **se — murió el perro** my

dog died on me
meadero M *fam* john
mear VI/VT *fam* to pee, to piss
mecánico -ca ADJ mechanical; MF mechanic; F mechanics
mecanismo M mechanism; **— de seguridad** safety device
mecanografía F typewriting
mecanografiar²⁸ VI/VT to type
mecanógrafo -fa MF typist
mecedora F rocking chair, rocker
mecenas MF SG/PL patron, sponsor
mecenazgo M patronage
mecer³² VI/VT (cuna) to rock; (columpio) to swing
mecha F (de una vela) wick; (de explosivos) fuse; (de pelo) lock; **—s** (en el pelo) highlights
mechar VT (rellenar con tocino) to lard; (robar) to shoplift
mechero -ra MF shoplifter; M burner; **— Bunsen** Bunsen burner
mechón M lock, strand
medalla F medal
médano M dune
media F (hasta el muslo) stocking; (hasta la cintura) pantyhose; (calcetín) sock; (promedio) mean; M PL (medios de comunicación) media
mediación F mediation
mediador -ora MF mediator
mediados LOC ADV **a — de mayo** in mid-May
mediana F median
mediano ADJ (intermedio en tamaño) medium; (intermedio en calidad) average; **de tamaño** **— middle-sized; de mediana edad** middle-aged
medianoche F midnight
mediante PREP by means of
mediar VI (en un asunto) to mediate, to intervene; (tiempo) to intervene; **mediaba febrero** it was mid-February
medible ADJ measurable
medicación F medication
medicamento M medicine, drug
medicar VT to medicate; **—se** to self-medicate
medicina F medicine; **— defensiva** defensive medicine; **— familiar** family practice
medición F (de una cantidad) measurement; (de un terreno) survey
médico -ca MF doctor, physician; **— forense** coroner, medical examiner; **— general** general practitioner; **— tratante** attending physician; ADJ medical
medida F (dimensión) measure; (acto de medir) measurement; **— cautelar** restraining order; **— para áridos** dry measure; **a — que** as; **en la — en que** to the extent that; **hacer a la —** to make to measure; **hecho a la —** made-to-measure; **tomar —s** to take

measures; **tomarle las —s a alguien** to measure someone
medidor M gauge, meter
medieval ADJ medieval
medio ADJ (la mitad) half; **— pastel** half a cake; (promedio) average; **el ciudadano —** the average man; **—día** (hora) noon, midday; (hora de comer) lunch hour, noon hour; (punto cardinal) south; (territorio) the south; **— hermano** half-brother; **a media asta** at half-mast; **a — camino** halfway; **clase media** middle class; **el americano —** the average American; **media hora** half an hour; **mi media naranja** my better half; **temperatura media** mean temperature; **— tiempo** (fútbol) halftime; **de — tiempo** part-time; **media volea** (tenis) half-volley; **hacer una cosa a medias** to do something halfway; **ir a medias** to go halves; M (centro) middle; (ambiente) medium; **—s** means, resources; **— ambiente** environment; **—s de comunicación** media; **— de transporte** means of transport; **en [el] — de** in the middle of; **en — de la calle** in the middle of the street; **meterse de por —** to intervene; **por — de** by means of; **por todos los —s** by all possible means; ADV half; **a — derretir** half-melted
medioambiental ADJ environmental
mediocre ADJ mediocre; (actuación) lackluster
mediocridad F mediocrity
medir⁹ VI/VT to measure; VT (consecuencias) to gauge; (terreno) to survey; **— a pasos** to step off; **—se** to be moderate
meditación F meditation
meditar VI to meditate, to ponder
mediterráneo ADJ Mediterranean
médium MF medium, psychic
medroso ADJ fearful
médula F marrow, pith; **— espinal** spinal cord; **— ósea** bone marrow
medusa F jellyfish, man-of-war
megabyte M megabyte
megáfono M megaphone
megahercio, megahertz M megahertz
megalomanía F megalomania
mejilla F cheek
mejor ADJ better; **el —** the best; **en el — de los casos** at best; **te deseo lo —** I wish you the best; ADV better; **a lo —** maybe; **tanto —** so much the better
mejora F improvement
mejoramiento M improvement
mejorar VT to improve, to improve upon; (software, aparato) to upgrade; (las posibilidades de uno) to better; VI (ventas) to pick up; **—se** to get better/well
mejoría F improvement
melancolía F melancholy, gloom

melancólico ADJ melancholy, gloomy

melanoma M melanoma

melaza F molasses

melena F mane

melindre M affectation

melindroso ADJ affected, finicky

mella F notch; **hacer** — to make a dent

mellar VT to notch

mellizo -za ADJ & MF twin

melocotón M peach

melocotonero M peach tree

melodía F melody

melódico ADJ (agradable al oído) melodious; (relativo a la melodía) melodic

melodioso ADJ melodious

melodrama M melodrama

melómano -na ADJ music-loving; MF music lover

melón M melon, cantaloupe

membrana F (en un órgano) membrane; (en las patas de los patos) web

membrete M letterhead

membrillo M (fruta) quince; (árbol) quince tree

membrudo ADJ stout

memorable ADJ memorable

memorándum M memorandum

memoria F (facultad de recordar, recuerdo) memory; (obra autobiográfica) memoir; (actas) proceedings; — **de acceso directo** random access memory [RAM]; — **de caché** cache memory; — **de ROM** read-only memory; — **de sólo lectura** read-only memory [ROM]; — **expandida** expanded memory; **intermedia** buffer; — **residente** internal memory; **de** — by heart; **hacer** — to try to remember/recollect

memorial M memorial

memorizar[47] VI/VT to memorize

mención F mention

mencionar VT to mention

mendigar[40] VI to beg

mendigo -ga MF beggar

mendrugo M large crumb

menear VT (las caderas) to wiggle, to wriggle, to shake; (la cola) to wag

meneo M (de las caderas) wiggle; (de la cola) wag

menesteroso ADJ needy, destitute

mengua F diminution, waning

menguante ADJ waning

menguar[25] VI (luna) to wane; (energía) to flag; (provisiones) to dwindle

meningitis F meningitis

menjurje M concoction

menopausia F menopause

menor ADJ (de tamaño) smaller; (de cantidad) lesser, smaller; (de edad) younger; (de importancia, en música) minor; **el** — (de tamaño) the smallest; (de cantidad) the least, the smallest; (de edad) the youngest; MF — **de**

edad minor; **al por** — retail

menos ADV (no contables) less; (contables) fewer; — **de** less than, fewer than; — **de lo que se esperaba** less than expected, fewer than expected; — **mal** just as well; **a** — **que** unless; **al** — at least; **dar de** — to shortchange; **echar de** — to miss; **lo** — the least; **no es para** — there is good reason; **por lo** — at least; **signo de** — minus sign; **venir a** — to decline; **el que trabaja** — the one who works the least; **no puede** — **que hacerlo** he cannot help doing it; **tienes** — **que yo** you have less than I; **trabaja** — **que yo** she works less than I; PREP (salvo) except, but; **las cinco** — **cuarto** quarter to five; ADJ & PRON less, least; — **agua** less water; — **problemas** fewer problems; M minus

menoscabar VT to impair, to undermine

menoscabo M impairment

menospreciar VI/VT (despreciar) to despise; VT (burlarse de) to belittle, to demean

menosprecio M contempt

mensaje M message; — **de error** error message; — **de texto** text message

mensajería F carrier; — **instantánea** instant messaging

mensajero -ra MF messenger, courier

menstruación F menstruation

menstruar VI to menstruate

mensual ADJ monthly

mensualidad F (recibida) monthly allowance; (pagada) monthly installment

mensuario ADJ monthly

mensurable ADJ measurable

menta F mint, peppermint; — **verde** spearmint

mental ADJ mental

mentalidad F mentality

mente F mind

mentecato -ta ADJ foolish, simple; MF simpleton

mentir[8] VI to lie

mentira F lie, falsehood

mentirilla F fib, white lie

mentiroso -sa ADJ lying; MF liar

mentón M chin

mentor -ora MF mentor

menú M menu (también de computadoras); — **abatible** pull-down menu; — **del día** daily special; — **de inicio** start menu; — **emergente** pop-up menu

menudeo LOC ADV **al** — retail

menudo ADJ (pequeño) small; (insignificante) insignificant; **a** — often, frequently; **dinero** — small change; — **perro** that's some dog; M (entrañas) entrails

meñique ADJ & M little finger, *fam* pinkie; **dedo** — little finger

meollo M (médula) marrow; (parte sustancial de un asunto) marrow, pith, core; (seso) brain

mequetrefe M runt, pipsqueak
mercachifle M peddler, huckster
mercadear VT to market
mercadeo M merchandising; — **de nicho** niche marketing
mercader M merchant
mercadería F merchandise
mercado M market, marketplace; — **alcista** bull market; — **bajista** bear market; — **de divisas** currency exchange; — **de prueba** test market; — **de pulgas** flea market; — **de valores** stock market; — **extrabursátil** aftermarket; — **libre** free market; — **negro** black market; — **secundario** aftermarket
mercadotecnia F marketing
mercancía F merchandise, goods
mercante ADJ merchant
mercantil ADJ mercantile
merced LOC ADV — a thanks to; **a [la]** — **de** at the mercy of
mercenario -ria ADJ & MF mercenary
mercería F notions store
mercurio M mercury, quicksilver
merecedor ADJ deserving
merecer³⁵ VT to deserve, to merit
merecido M deserved punishment, due
merendar¹ VI to have a snack
merendero M picnic area
merezca, merezco ver merecer
meridiano ADJ & M meridian
meridional ADJ southern; MF southerner
merienda F afternoon snack
mérito M merit
meritorio ADJ meritorious, worthy
merluza F hake
merma F decrease
mermar VI/VT to decrease, to dwindle
mermelada F (de fresa, pera) jam; (de cítricos) marmalade
mero ADJ mere; **la mera idea** the very idea; M grouper
merodear VI to loiter
mes M month
mesa F (mueble) table; (consejo) board; (formación geológica) mesa; — **de noche** nightstand; **levantar la** — to clear the table; **poner la** — to set the table
mesada F monthly allowance
mesero -ra M waiter; F waitress
meseta F plateau
mesón M inn, lodge
mesonero -ra MF innkeeper
mestizo -za ADJ (persona de raza mezclada) *pey* half-breed; (perros) mongrel; MF (de raza mezclada) *pey* half-breed; (mezcla de europeo e india) mestizo; (perro de raza mezclada) mongrel
mesura F moderation
mesurado ADJ (persona, opinión) moderate; (respuesta) measured

meta F (objetivo) goal; (en una carrera) finish line
metabólico ADJ metabolic
metabolismo M metabolism
metafísica F metaphysics
metafísico ADJ metaphysical
metáfora F metaphor
metafórico ADJ metaphorical
metal M metal; — **precioso** precious metal
metálico ADJ metallic; M cash
metalurgia F metallurgy
metamorfosis F metamorphosis
metano M methane
metástasis F metastasis
metastatizar VI to metastasize
meteorito M meteorite
meteoro M meteor
meteorología F meteorology
meteorológico ADJ meteorological; **parte** — weather report
meteorólogo -ga M weatherman; F weatherwoman
meter VT (en una bolsa) to put [into], to stick [into]; (un lío) to force [into]; (invertir) to invest; — **el estómago** to suck in one's stomach; — **la pata** to make a mistake; — **miedo** to scare; — **ruido** to make noise; — **un gol** to score a goal; —**se** to meddle; —**se a bailar** to begin to dance; —**se con** to mess with; —**se en camisa de once varas** to get oneself into a fix
metódico ADJ methodical
método M method
metodología F methodology
metralleta F portable machine gun
métrico ADJ metric
metro M (medida, ritmo poético) meter; (cinta de medir) measuring tape; (tren subterráneo) subway, metro
metrónomo M metronome
metrópoli F metropolis
metropolitano ADJ metropolitan; M subway
mexicano -na ADJ & MF Mexican
México M Mexico
mezcla F (de ingredientes) mixture, mix; (en albañilería) mortar; (de café, especias) blend
mezclador -ora MF (persona) mixer; F (aparato) mixer
mezclar VT (ingredientes) to mix, to blend; (naipes) to shuffle; (números) to scramble; —**se** (combinarse) to mix; (tener trato con) to mingle; (entrometerse) to meddle
mezcolanza F hodgepodge
mezquindad F (crueldad) meanness; (tacañería) stinginess
mezquino ADJ (cruel) mean, mean-spirited, petty; (insignificante) small, petty; (tacaño) tight, stingy

mezquita F mosque
mi ADJ POS my
mí PRON PERS me; **es para —** it's for me; **me vio a —** he saw me; **me la dio a —** he gave it to me
miau M meow
mico M long-tailed monkey
micra F micron
micro M (autobús) bus; (micrófono) microphone
microbio M microbe, germ
microbiología F microbiology
microcirujía F microsurgery
microcomputadora F microcomputer
microeconomía F microeconomics
microficha F microfiche
microfilm M microfilm
micrófono M microphone
Micronesia F Micronesia
micronesio -sia ADJ & MF Micronesian
microonda F microwave; M SG **—s** microwave oven
microordenador M microcomputer
microorganismo M microorganism
microprocesador M microprocessor
microscópico ADJ microscopic
microscopio M microscope; **— electrónico** electron microscope
mida, mide, midiendo, midiera, midiese ver medir
miedo M fear; **— al escenario** stage fright; **tener —** to be afraid
miedoso ADJ fearful
miel F honey
miembro M (integrante) member, (extremidad) limb; **— viril** penis
mienta, miente ver mentir
mientras CONJ (durante) while, as; (siempre y cuando) as long as; **— que** while; **— tanto** meanwhile; ADV in the meantime
miércoles M Wednesday
mierda F (excremento) vulg shit, crap; (droga) vulg shit; (persona o cosa despreciable) vulg piece of shit, piece of crap; **una — de coche** vulg a crappy/shitty car; **mandar a alguien a la —** vulg to tell somebody to go to hell; **¡—!** vulg shit! **¡vete a la —!** vulg go fuck yourself!
mies F grain; **—es** fields of grain
miga F crumb; **hacer buenas —s** to get along well
migaja F crumb
migración F migration
migrante ADJ migrant
migraña F migraine
migrar VI to migrate
migratorio ADJ migratory
mil NUM thousand; **— millones** billion; **llegamos a las — y quinientas** we got there very late
milagro M miracle, wonder

milagroso ADJ miraculous
milano M kite
milenio M millennium
milicia F militia
miligramo M milligram
mililitro M milliliter
milímetro M millimeter
militancia F (actitud) militance; (actitud) militancy
militante ADJ & MF militant
militar ADJ military; MF soldier; VI to militate
milla F mile
millaje M mileage
millar M thousand
millón M million
millonario -ria MF millionaire
millonésimo ADJ & M millionth
mimar VT to pamper, to spoil, to coddle
mimbre M wicker
mímico ADJ mimic; F mimicry
mimo M (trato cariñoso) caressing, cuddling; MF (actor) mime
mimoso ADJ cuddly
mina F (yacimiento) mine; (explosivo) [land] mine; (de un lápiz) lead; (fuente) storehouse
minado M mining
minar VT (sembrar minas) to mine; (socavar) to undermine; VI (cavar) to burrow
mineral M mineral; (de oro) ore; ADJ mineral
minería F mining
minero -ra MF miner; ADJ mining
mingitorio M urinal
miniatura F miniature
mini-break M (tenis) mini-break
minicomputadora F minicomputer
minifalda F miniskirt
minifundio M subsistence farm
minimizar[47] VT (gastos) to minimize; (a una persona) to belittle; VI (un incidente) to play down
mínimo ADJ (cantidad) least; (tamaño) smallest; M minimum; **como —** at least; **en lo más —** at all
minino M kitty
miniordenador M minicomputer
ministerial ADJ cabinet, ministerial
ministerio M (religioso) ministry; (gubernamental) ministry, department
ministro -tra MF minister, secretary; **— de justicia** attorney general
minoría F minority
minoridad F minority
minorista MF retailer
minoritario ADJ minority
mintiendo, mintiera, mintiese, mintió ver mentir
minucioso ADJ (detalle) minute; (trabajo) thorough; (persona) fastidious
minúsculo ADJ (tamaño) small, minuscule;

(cantidad) negligible; **letra minúscula** lowercase letter

minusvalía F disability

minusválido -da ADJ disabled; MF disabled person

minutas F (honorarios) lawyers' fees; (actas) minutes

minutero M minute hand

minuto M minute

mío ADJ & PRON mine; **este libro es —** this book is mine; **un amigo —** a friend of mine

miope ADJ shortsighted, nearsighted

miopía F nearsightedness, myopia

mira F (dispositivo de arma) gun sight; (intención) intention; **con —s a** with a view to

mirada F gaze, look; **— asesina** dirty look; **— de soslayo** side glance; **— fija** stare

mirador M vantage point, overlook

miramiento M consideration

mirar VI/VT to look [at]; (un partido, televisión) to watch; **— de soslayo** to look askance [at]; **— fijamente** to stare [at]; **¡mira [tú]!** you don't say!

miríada F myriad

mirilla F peephole

mirlo M blackbird

mirón M (curioso) onlooker; (erótico) voyeur

mirto M myrtle

misa F mass

misantropía F misanthropy

misántropo -pa MF misanthrope

misceláneo ADJ miscellaneous

miserable ADJ (vil, pobre) wretched, unhappy; (insignificante) paltry; (tacaño) miserly

miseria F (desgracia) misery; (pobreza) poverty, squalor; (cantidad despreciable) trifle

misericordia F mercy

misericordioso ADJ merciful, gracious

mísero ADJ miserable

misil M missile; **— balístico** ballistic missile; **— crucero** cruise missile

misión F mission (también religiosa)

misionero -ra MF missionary

mismo ADJ same; **ese — día** that very day; **se nombró a sí —** he named himself; **lo —** the same thing; **me da lo —** it's all the same to me; **yo —** I myself

misoginia F misogyny

misterio M mystery

misterioso ADJ mysterious

místico -ca ADJ mystical; MF mystic

mitad F half; **por la —** in half; **en la — de** in the middle of; **a — de[l] camino** midway

mítico ADJ mythic, mythical

mitigar[40] VT to mitigate

mitin M political meeting

mito M myth

mitocondria F mitochondria

mitología F mythology

mitológico ADJ mythological

mixto ADJ mixed; **escuela mixta** coed school

mobiliario M furniture

mocasín M (zapatilla, culebra) moccasin; (zapato sin cordones) loafer

mochar VT to chop off

mochila F backpack, knapsack

moción F motion

moco M (interno) mucus; (líquido) *fam* snot; (sólido) *fam* booger

mocoso -sa ADJ snotty; MF *fam* brat, punk

moda F fashion; **de —** fashionable, in style; **ponerse de —** to catch on

modales M PL manners

modalidad F form, variant; **ganó oro en la — de espalda** she won gold in the backstroke; **la — italiana es más conocida** the Italian form is better known

Moldavia F Moldova

modelar VI/VT to model

modelo ADJ & MF model

módem M modem

moderación F moderation, restraint

moderado -da ADJ (posición política) moderate; (invierno) mild; (precio) reasonable; (respuesta) measured; (clima) temperate; MF moderate

moderar VT (restringir) to moderate, to restrain; (presidir) to moderate

modernidad F (actualidad) modern age; (actualidad) modern world

modernismo M (cualidad de moderno) modernity, modernness; (tendencia artística) modernism

modernización F modernization

moderno ADJ modern

modestia F modesty

modesto ADJ modest

módico ADJ moderate, reasonable

modificación F modification

modificar[30] VT to modify

modismo M idiom

modista MF dressmaker

modo M (manera) mode, manner, way; (categoría gramatical) mood; (de computadora/ordenador) mode; **— a prueba de fallos/errores** safe mode; **— de ahorro** power-save mode; **— de dormir** sleep mode; **— de entrega** mode of delivery; **— de reescritura** overwrite mode; **a — de** by way of; **del mismo —** in like manner, similarly; **de ningún —** by no means; **de — que** so that; **de otro —** otherwise; **de ningún —** not at all; **de todos —s** anyway; **en cierto —** in a way; **ni —** no dice; **no hay —** no way

modorra F drowsiness

modulación F modulation

modular VT to modulate

módulo M (componente) module; (unidad) unit
mofa F jeer, ridicule
mofarse VI — **de** to make fun of, to scoff at
mofeta F skunk
moflete M fat cheek, jowl
mohair M mohair
mohín M grimace
moho M mold, mildew
mohoso ADJ moldy
mojado -da ADJ wet; MF (inmigrante ilegal) *pey* wetback
mojadura F wetting
mojar VT (humedecer) to wet; (sumergir) to dip; —**se** to get wet; *vulg* to get laid
mojigatería F prudery
mojigato -ta ADJ prudish; MF prude
mojo M dip
mojón M (hito) landmark; (zurullo) turd
molar ADJ molar
moldavo -va ADJ & MF Moldovan
molde M (norma) mold, cast; (tortera) cake pan; (patrón) pattern; (de imprenta) die; **letras de** — block letters
moldeado M molding
moldear VT to mold, to cast
moldura F molding
mole F mass
molécula F molecule
molecular ADJ molecular
moler[6] VI/VT to mill, to grind; — **a palos** to beat thoroughly
molestar VT to bother, to pester; **no te molestes** don't bother
molestia F bother, nuisance; **no te tomes la** — don't go to the trouble
molesto ADJ (que molesta) bothersome, irksome; (que está molesto) uneasy, uncomfortable
molibdeno M molybdenum
molienda F grinding
molinero -ra MF miller
molinete M (puerta) turnstile; (juguete) pinwheel
molinillo M mill, grinder
molino M mill; — **de viento** windmill
mollete M muffin
molusco M mollusk
momentáneo ADJ momentary
momento M (tiempo) moment; (impulso) momentum; **al** — immediately; **a cada** — continually; **en todo** — all the time; **no veo el** — I can't wait
momia F mummy
Mónaco M Monaco
monada F (acción graciosa) antic; (persona atractiva) *fam* peach
monarca MF monarch
monarquía F monarchy
monárquico -ca MF monarchist; ADJ

monarchical
monasterio M monastery
mondar VT to pare; —**se los dientes** to pick one's teeth; M SG **mondadientes** toothpick
moneda F (dinero metálico) coin; (divisa) currency; — **corriente** common currency; — **de curso legal** legal tender; — **falsa** counterfeit money
monegasco -ca ADJ & MF Monegasque
monería F antic
monetario ADJ monetary
mongol -la ADJ & MF Mongolian
Mongolia F Mongolia
mongoloide ADJ mongoloid
monigote M puppet
monitor -ora M (aparato) monitor; — **[a] color** color monitor; MF (persona) monitor
monitorear VT to monitor
monitoreo M monitoring
monitorización F monitoring; — **fetal** fetal monitoring
monja F nun
monje M monk
mono -na MF (simio) monkey; — **araña** spider monkey; M (mimo) mimic; (prenda de trabajo) overalls, coverall; (síndrome de abstinencia) withdrawal symptoms; **dormir la mona** to sleep it off; ADJ cute
monogamia F monogamy
monokini M topless swimsuit
monólogo M monologue, monolog
mononucleosis F mononucleosis
monopatín M (tabla) skateboard; (con manillar) scooter; (de nieve) snowboard
monopolio M monopoly
monopolizar[47] VT (un producto) to monopolize; (un mercado) to corner
monotonía F monotony
monótono ADJ monotonous
monseñor M monsignor
monserga F nonsense
monstruo M (ser imaginario, persona perversa) monster; (persona grotesca) freak; ADJ INV monstrous
monstruosidad F monstrosity
monstruoso ADJ monstrous
monta F mount; **de poca** — of little value
montaje M (de un aparato) assembly, set up; (de una película) editing
montante M (total) total; (ventana de puerta) transom; (columna) upright
montaña F mountain; — **rusa** roller coaster
montañés -esa ADJ mountain; MF mountain dweller
montañismo M mountaineering
montañoso ADJ mountainous
montar VT (ir a caballo, en bicicleta) to ride; (un aparato) to assemble; (una película) to edit; (subirse al caballo) to mount, to get on; — **en**

cólera to fly into a rage; **— una escena** to make a scene; **—se a caballo** to mount a horse

montaraz ADJ coarse

monte M (montaña) mount; (zona agreste) wilderness; **— de piedad** pawnshop

montés ADJ (salvaje) wild; (de la montaña) of the mountains

montículo M mound; (béisbol) pitcher's mound

monto M amount; **— debido** amount due; **— pagado** amount paid

montón M (pila) pile, heap; (de papel) stack; (de nieve) drift; (de flores) basketful; (de gente) bunch; **a montones** in abundance; **del —** run-of-the-mill

montura F (animal) mount; (silla) saddle; (armazón de gafas) frame, rim

monumental ADJ monumental

monumento M monument

moño M (de pelo) bun; (adorno) bow

mopa F mop

moquearse VI to become snotty

moquillo M distemper

MOR [movimentos oculares rápidos] M PL REM

mora F (fruta) blackberry, mulberry; (tardanza) delay, delinquency; **en —** in default, past due

morada F dwelling, abode

morado ADJ purple; **ojo —** black eye

morador-ora MF dweller

moral ADJ moral; F (principios éticos) morals; (estado de ánimo) morale; M mulberry tree

moraleja F moral

moralidad F morality

moralista MF moralist

moralizar[47] VI/VT to moralize

morar VI to dwell, to abide

mórbido ADJ morbid

morbilidad F (predisposición a la enfermadad) morbidity

morbosidad F (que produce enfermedad) morbidity

morboso ADJ (mórbido) morbid; (atractivo) sexy

morcilla F blood sausage

mordacidad F sharpness

mordaz ADJ (comentario) cutting, sharp; (persona) sharp-tongued

mordaza F (de la boca) gag; (de un torno) vise jaw

mordedor ADJ biting, snappy

mordedura F bite

morder[6] VI/VT to bite; **—se la lengua** to bite one's tongue

mordida F (mordisco) bite; (soborno) bribe, kickback

mordiscar[30] VI/VT to nibble; to nip

mordisco M nibble, nip

mordisquear VI/VT to nip; to nibble

mordisqueo M nibble

moreno ADJ (piel) dark, dark-skinned, swarthy; (pelo) dark, brunette

moretón M bruise

morfina F morphine

morgue F morgue

moribundo ADJ dying, moribund

morir[7, 74] VI (persona, animal) to die; (calle) to end; **—se de envidia** to eat one's heart out; **—se de hambre** to starve; **—se de miedo** to die of fear; **—se de risa** to die laughing; **—se por algo** to crave something; **—se por alguien** to be crazy about someone

morisco ADJ Moorish

moro-ra ADJ Moorish; MF Moor; **—s y cristianos** (personas) Moors and Christians; (plato) beans and rice; **no hay —s en la costa** the coast is clear

morocho ADJ dark-haired, brunet, brunette

moroso ADJ delinquent, deadbeat

morrear VI to make out

morriña F homesickness

morro M (monte) knoll; (caradura) gall, nerve; (de un avión) nose; (de animal) snout

morrón M bell pepper

morsa F walrus

mortaja F shroud

mortal ADJ mortal, deadly; MF mortal

mortalidad F mortality

mortandad F death toll

mortecino ADJ fading

mortero M mortar

mortífero ADJ deadly

mortificación F mortification, chagrin

mortificar[30] VT to mortify, to chagrin

mortuorio ADJ mortuary; **casa mortuaria** funeral home

mosaico M mosaic

mosca F (insecto) fly; (dinero) dough; **— muerta** hypocrite; **no se oía volar una —** you could have heard a pin drop

mosquear VT (crear desconfianza) to cause distrust; (hacer enfadar) to enrage; **—se** (desconfiar) to distrust; (enfadarse) to become enraged

mosquitero M (pantalla de ventana) window screen; (red) mosquito net

mosquito M mosquito

mostacho M mustache, moustache

mostaza F mustard

mostrador M counter

mostrar[5] VT to show; **—se reticente** to appear reticent

mostrenco ADJ stray

mota F speck, speckle

mote M nickname

moteado ADJ speckled, spotted

motear VT to speck, to speckle

motejar VI **— de** to brand as

motel M motel

motín M (en un barco) mutiny; (de prisioneros) riot

motivación F motivation

motivar VT (impulsar) to motivate; (causar) to cause

motivo M (causa) motive, reason; (figura repetida) motif, theme; **con — de** on the occasion of

moto F bike, motorcycle

motocicleta F motorcycle

motociclista MF biker, motorcyclist

motor ADJ of motion; M motor, engine; **— de reacción** jet engine; **— de búsqueda** search engine; **— de combustión interna** internal combustion engine; **— fuera de borda** outboard engine

motriz ADJ **fuerza —** motive power

movedizo ADJ restless

mover[6] VT to move; **— palancas** to pull strings; **—se** to move, to budge

movible ADJ movable

movido ADJ (vida, fiesta) eventful; (foto) blurred; **— por gas** powered by gas

móvil M (motivo) motive; (teléfono) mobile telephone; (adorno, juguete) mobile; ADJ (que se mueve) mobile; (que puede ser movido) movable; **un blanco —** a moving target

movilidad F mobility

movilización F mobilization

movilizar[47] VI/VT to mobilize

movimiento M (cambio de posición) movement, motion, (organización, pieza de reloj) movement; (comercial) traffic; **—s oculares rápidos** REM [rapid eye movements]; **los rojos tienen poco —** the red ones don't sell well; **un cuerpo en —** a moving body

Mozambique M Mozambique

mozambiqueño -ña ADJ & MF Mozambican

mozárabe ADJ Mozarabic

mozo -za ADJ young; **en mis años —s** in my youth; M (joven) young man; (sirviente) servant; F (joven) young woman; (sirvienta) servant; **— de cordel** porter; **buen —** handsome man

mucama F chambermaid

muchacho -cha M boy, youngster; F (chica) girl; (de servicio) maid

muchedumbre F crowd, throng

mucho ADJ a lot of; (cosas contables) many; (cosas incontables, en oraciones interrogativas y/o negativas) much; **¿tienes — tiempo?** do you have much time? **no tenemos — tiempo** we don't have much time; **tenemos —s problemas** we have many problems; ADV much; (demasiado) too much; **hace — que no lo veo** I haven't seen

him for a long time; **ni con —** not by a long shot; **ni — menos** not by any means; **por — que** no matter how much; PRON a lot, many; (en preguntas y oraciones negativas) much; **¿había —s?** were there many?

mucoso ADJ mucous

muda F (de ropa, voz) change; (de plumas, piel de serpiente) molt

mudable ADJ fickle

mudanza F move

mudar VT (condiciones, clima) to change; (el pelo) to shed; (la piel, plumas) to molt; **—se [de casa]** to move [house]; **—se de ropa** to change clothes

mudez F dumbness, muteness

mudo -da ADJ (incapaz de hablar) mute, dumb; (por emoción) speechless; (película) silent; MF mute

mueble M piece of furniture; **—s** furniture

mueblería F (tienda) furniture store; (fábrica) furniture factory

mueca F grimace; **hacer —s** to grimace

muela F (diente) molar tooth; (piedra) grindstone; **— del juicio** wisdom tooth; **— impactada** impacted molar

muelle M (para embarcaciones) wharf, pier; (resorte) spring; **— en espiral** coil; **— real** mainspring

muera, muere ver morir

muérdago M mistletoe

muerte F death; **— cerebral** brain death; **— súbita** (fútbol) sudden death; (tenis) tie-break; **dar —** to kill; **sus clases son la —** his classes are unbearable; **de mala —** disreputable

muerto ADJ dead, lifeless; **— de cansancio** dead tired; **— de hambre** famished; **estoy — de sed** I'm parched; **echarle el — a uno** to pass the buck; **ni —** not in a million years

muerto ver morir

muesca F notch, indentation

muestra F (ejemplo) sample (también en computadoras); (señal) sign, token; **— de orina** urine specimen; **dar —s de impaciencia** to show impatience

muestra, muestre ver mostrar

muestrear VT to sample (también para computadoras)

muestreo M sampling

mueva, mueve ver mover

mugido M moo, lowing

mugir[46] VI to moo, to low

mugre F dirt, grime, crud

mugriento ADJ grimy, dirty

mujer F (género) woman; (esposa) wife; **— de negocios** businesswoman; **— de la vida** prostitute

mujeriego ADJ womanizing; M womanizer, *fam* player

mujerzuela F *pey* slut
mula *ver* mulo
mulato -ta ADJ & MF mulatto
muleta F crutch
muletilla F cliché
mullido ADJ fluffy
mullir[16] VT to fluff
mulo -la MF mule (también en el tráfico de drogas)
multa F fine, penalty; (de tránsito) ticket
multar VT to fine; (en tránsito) to ticket
multianual ADJ multiyear
multicultural ADJ multicultural
multilateral ADJ multilateral
multimedia M & ADJ INV multimedia
multipantalla ADJ multiscreen
múltiple ADJ multiple
multiplicación F multiplication
multiplicar[30] VI/VT to multiply; —**se** to breed
multiplicidad F multiplicity
múltiplo M multiple
multitarea F multitasking
multitud F multitude, throng
mundano ADJ mundane, worldly
mundial ADJ global, worldwide; **la guerra** — the world war
mundo M world; **todo el** — everybody; **tener** — to be worldly; **el tercer** — the third world; **el** — **al revés** the world upside-down
munición F ammunition, munition
municipal ADJ municipal; **servicios** —**es** city services
municipalidad F municipality
municipio M municipality; (ayuntamiento) city hall
muñeca F (juguete) doll; (articulación del brazo) wrist; — **de trapo** ragdoll
muñeco M (juguete) boy doll; (de ventrílocuo) dummy; — **de nieve** snowman
muñón M stump
mural ADJ & M mural
muralla F wall
murciélago M bat
muriendo, muriera, muriese *ver* morir
murmullo M (voz baja) murmur; (ruido de agua) babble
murmuración F gossip
murmurar VI/VT (voz) to murmur; VI (agua) to babble
muro M wall; — **de contención** retaining wall
murria F the blues; **tener** — to have the blues
musa F muse
musaraña F shrew
muscular ADJ muscular
músculo M muscle
musculoso ADJ muscular
muselina F muslin
museo M museum
musgo M moss

musgoso ADJ mossy
música F music; — **de cámara** chamber music; — **folclórica** folk music; — **incidental** incidental music
musical ADJ & M musical
músico -ca ADJ musical; MF musician
musitar VI to mutter
muslo M thigh
mustio ADJ (triste) sad, humble; (marchito) limp; (deslucido) faded
musulmán -ana ADJ & MF Muslim, Moslem
mutación F mutation
mutante ADJ & MF mutant
mutilar VT to mutilate, to mangle; (a un ser vivo) to maim, to mutilate; (una estatua) to deface
mutuo ADJ mutual
muy ADV very; **estás** — **grande para eso** you're too big for that
Myanmar M Myanmar

Nn

nabo M turnip
nácar M mother-of-pearl
nacarado ADJ pearly
nacer[35] VI (un bebé) to be born; (una calle) to begin; — **de** (río) to spring from; — **de nuevo** to have a new lease on life
naciente ADJ (tendencia) incipient; (sol) rising; M (de río) origin
nacimiento M (alumbramiento) birth; (pesebre) nativity scene; (naciente) origin [of a river]; — **del pelo** hairline
nación F nation
nacional ADJ & MF national
nacionalidad F nationality
nacionalismo M nationalism
nacionalista ADJ & MF nationalist
nacionalizar[47] VT to nationalize
nada PRON nothing; *fam* squat, zilch; — **del otro mundo** nothing special; — **en absoluto** nothing at all; **como si** — as if nothing had happened; **de** — you are welcome, don't mention it; **no es por** —, **pero** I hope you don't mind my saying this, but; **no sirve para** — it's useless; **no tener** — **que ver con** to have nothing to do with; **no tengo** — **de dinero** I don't have any money; **para** — in the least; **quedar en la** — to fall through; **salir de la** — to come out of nowhere; ADV not at all; **no me gusta [para]** — I don't like it at all; (tenis) **quince a** — forty love; F (existencial) nothingness
nadador -ora MF swimmer

nadar VI/VT to swim; — **en la abundancia** to be in the lap of luxury

nadería F trifle, nothing

nadie PRON nobody; — **más** no one else; **no vi a** — **en el parque** I didn't see anyone in the park; **un don** — a nobody

nafta F gasoline

nailon M nylon

naipe M playing card

nalgada F smack on the bottom

nalgas F PL buttocks

Namibia F Namibia

namibio -bia ADJ & MF Namibian

nana F (canción de cuna) lullaby; (lastimadura) boo-boo; (niñera) babysitter

nanosegundo M nanosecond

nanotecnología F nanotechnology

napalm M napalm

napias F PL *fam* snout

naranja F (fruta) orange; ADJ INV & M (color) orange; — **de ombligo** navel orange; **mi media** — my better half

naranjal M orange grove

naranjo M orange tree

narcisismo M narcissism

narciso M narcissus, daffodil

narcolepsia F narcolepsy

narcótico ADJ & M narcotic

narcotizar[47] VT to drug

narcotraficante MF drug trafficker

narcotráfico M drug trafficking

nariz F nose; — **chata** pug nose; **sonarse la** — to blow one's nose; F PL **narices** nostrils; **se dio de narices contra la ventana** he bumped his nose on the window; **estoy hasta las narices** I've had it up to here

narración F narration

narrador -ora MF narrator

narrar VT to narrate, to recount

narrativa F narrative

narrativo ADJ narrative

NASA F NASA

nasal ADJ nasal

nata F skin of boiled milk; *Esp* cream

natación F swimming

natal ADJ (relativo al nacimiento) natal; (suelo) native; **mi ciudad** — my hometown

natalidad F birth rate

natilla[s] F SG/PL custard

nativo -va ADJ & MF native

nato ADJ **es un músico** — he's a born musician

natural ADJ (no artificial) natural; (nacido en un lugar) native; (nacido fuera del matrimonio) illegitimate; (sin afectación) unaffected; M nature; **al** — unprocessed

naturaleza F nature; — **muerta** still life

naturalidad F naturalness

naturalista MF naturalist

naturalización F naturalization

naturalizar[47] VT to naturalize; —**se** to become naturalized

naturalmente ADV (de forma natural) naturally; (desde luego) of course

naufragar[40] VI (un barco) to shipwreck; (una empresa) to fail

naufragio M shipwreck

náufrago -ga MF shipwrecked person

Nauru M Nauru

nauruano -na ADJ & MF Nauruan

náusea F nausea; —**s** morning sickness; **dar** —**s** to nauseate; **hasta la** — ad nauseam; **tener** —**s** to be nauseated, to be sick to one's stomach

nauseabundo ADJ nauseating

nauseoso ADJ (que siente náuseas) nauseous, queasy; (que provoca náuseas) nauseating

náutica F navigation

náutico ADJ nautical

navaja F (de explorador) jackknife, pocketknife; (de barbero) razor

navajazo M (golpe) stab with a jackknife; (herida) stab wound

naval ADJ naval

navarro ADJ & MF Navarrese

nave F (embarcación) vessel; (parte de una catedral) nave; — **espacial** spaceship

navegable ADJ navigable

navegación F (de mar, río) navigation; (deportiva) boating; (en internet) surfing, browsing

navegador M browser; — **web** web browser

navegante MF navigator; ADJ navigating

navegar[40] VI/VT (buque) to navigate; (barco a vela) to sail; (en internet) to browse, to surf

Navidad F Christmas

navideño ADJ **fiesta navideña** Christmas party

navío M ship

nazi MF Nazi

neblina F mist

neblinoso ADJ misty

nebulosidad F cloudiness

nebuloso ADJ (poco claro) nebulous; (que tiene niebla) foggy

necesario ADJ necessary

neceser M toiletry bag

necesidad F (urgencia, sensación de falta) need; (cosa necesaria) necessity; **hacer sus** —**es** to relieve oneself; **de primera** — indispensable; **por** — out of necessity

necesitado ADJ needy

necesitar VT to need

necio -cia ADJ asinine, foolish; MF *pey* clod

necrología F necrology

necrosis F necrosis

néctar M nectar

nectarina F nectarine

nefasto ADJ unholy

nefritis F nephritis
negación F (partícula gramatical) negation; (rechazo) denial
negar[41] VT (decir que no es verdad) to deny; (no consentir) to refuse; (no reconocer) to disavow; **—se [a]** to refuse [to]
negativa F (rechazo verbal) denial; (falta de cooperación) refusal
negativo ADJ negative; **signo —** minus sign; M [photographic] negative
negligencia F (falta de atención) negligence, neglect; (médica) malpractice
negligente ADJ negligent, neglectful
negociación F negotiation; **— laboral** collective bargaining
negociador -ora MF negotiator; ADJ negotiating
negociante MF businessperson
negociar VI/VT (acordar) to negotiate; (comerciar) to trade
negocio M (tienda, actividad comercial) business; (transacción) business deal, business transaction; **— de ventas por correo** mail-order business; **— principal** core business; **hombre de —s** businessman; **mujer de —s** businesswoman; **hacer —** to make a profit
negrear VI to appear black; VT to blacken
negrilla F boldface
negritas F PL boldface type
negro -ra ADJ black (también café sin leche); (futuro) bleak; **pasarlas negras** to undergo hardships; F (nota) quarter-note; MF (persona) person of color, black person
negrura F blackness
negruzco ADJ blackish
némesis F nemesis
nene -na M baby boy; F baby girl
nenúfar M water lily
neologismo M neologism
neón M neon
neonatal ADJ neonatal
neozelandés -esa MF New Zealander
Nepal M Nepal
nepalés -esa ADJ & MF Nepali
nepalí ADJ & MF Nepalese
nepotismo M nepotism
nervado ADJ veined
nervio M nerve; **— pellizcado** pinched nerve; **— pinzado** pinched nerve; **perder los —s** to lose one's cool; **tener los —s de punta** to be on edge
nerviosismo M nervousness
nervioso ADJ (relativo a los nervios) nervous; (inquieto) nervous, jumpy
nervudo ADJ sinewy, wiry
neto ADJ (mejoría) distinct; (ganancia) net
neumático M tire; ADJ pneumatic
neural ADJ neural

neuralgia F neuralgia
neurastenia F neurasthenia
neurocirugía F neurosurgery
neurocirujano -na MF neurosurgeon
neurólogo -ga MF neurologist
neurona F neuron, nerve cell
neurosis F neurosis
neurótico -ca ADJ & MF neurotic
neurotransmisor M neurotransmitter
neutral ADJ neutral
neutralidad F neutrality
neutralizar[47] VT to neutralize
neutro ADJ neutral; (género) neuter
neutrón M neutron
nevada F snowfall
nevado ADJ snowy
nevar[1] VI to snow
nevera F icebox, refrigerator
nevisca F snow flurry
ni CONJ & ADV **— con mucho** not by a long shot; **— hablar** forget it; **— habló conmigo** he didn't even talk to me; **— idea** [it] beats me; **— modo** no way; **— que esto fuera un hotel** it's not like this is a hotel; **— siquiera** not even; **— soñar** fat chance; **— trabaja — estudia** he neither works nor studies; **— una palabra** not a word; **no tiene amigos — enemigos** he has no friends nor enemies; **no es rico — mucho menos** he's not even close to being rich
Nicaragua F Nicaragua
nicaragüense ADJ & MF Nicaraguan
nicho M niche, recess
nicotina F nicotine
nidada F (huevos) nest of eggs; (crías) hatch, brood
nido M nest
niebla F fog
niega, niegue ver negar
nieto -ta M grandson; F granddaughter; **—s** grandchildren
nieve F snow (también droga en polvo)
Níger M Niger
Nigeria F Nigeria
nigeriano -na ADJ & MF Nigerian
nigerino -na ADJ & MF Nigerien
nigua F chigger
nihilismo M nihilism
nilón M nylon
nimio ADJ insignificant
ninguno ADJ & PRON **no tengo —** I have none / I don't have any; **ningún amigo mío** no friend of mine; **no tengo ningún libro** I don't have any books; **— de los dos** neither one; **de ningún modo** in no way
niñera F (ocasional) babysitter; (permanente) nanny
niñería F childish act
niñez F (infancia) childhood; (de niño) boyhood;

(de niña) girlhood
niño -ña M child, kid, boy; F child, kid, girl; **niña del ojo** pupil [of the eye]; ADJ childish
níquel M nickel
niquelado ADJ nickel-plated
níspero M loquat
nitidez F sharpness
nítido ADJ sharp
nitrato M nitrate
nitrógeno M nitrogen
nitroglicerina F nitroglycerine
nivel M level (también herramienta); (grado jerárquico) echelon; — **de cobertura** coverage level; — **de mar** sea level; — **de vida** standard of living; **a** — straight; **a** — **de** level with
nivelar VT (emparejar) to level; (aplanar) to grade
níveo ADJ snowy
no ADV no; — **quiero** I don't want to; — **acreditado** unlicensed; — **afiliado** unaffiliated; — **ajustado** unadjusted; — **autorizado** unauthorized; — **comercial** noncommercial; — **confirmado** unconfirmed; — **conforme** nonconforming; — **declarado** undeclared; — **disponible** unavailable; — **divulgado** undisclosed; — **esencial** nonessential; — **especificado** unspecified; — **ético** unethical; — **gubernamental** nongovernmental; — **negociable** nonnegotiable; — **reembolsable** nonrefundable; — **relacionado** unrelated; — **residente** nonresident; — **restringido** unrestricted; — **solicitado** unsolicited; — **tributable** nontaxable; — **bien llegaron** no sooner had they arrived; — **sólo** not only; — **sea que** lest; **a** — **ser que** unless
noble ADJ noble; M nobleman; F noblewoman
nobleza F nobility
nocaut M knockout
noche F (período sin luz) night; (horas de la noche) nighttime; —**buena** Christmas Eve; —**vieja** New Year's Eve; — **y día** day and night; **de** — at night; **de la** — **a la mañana** overnight; **esta** — tonight; **por la** — at night
noción F notion; **no tener ni** — to have no clue
nocivo ADJ harmful, noxious
nocturno ADJ (que actúa de noche) nocturnal; (que sucede todas las noches) nightly
nodo M node
nodriza F wet nurse
nódulo M node
nogal M walnut tree
nómada MF nomad
ningunear VT to dismiss
nomás ADV Am aquí — close by; **así** — just like that; **entre** — come right in
nombramiento M (civil) appointment;

(militar) commission
nombrar VT (a un funcionario) to name, to appoint; (a un oficial militar) to commission
nombre M name; — **completo** full name; — **de acceso** login name; — **de pila** first name; — **de soltera** maiden name; — **del usuario** username; **en** — **de** on behalf of; **eso no tiene** — that's unheard of; **hacerse un** — to make a name for oneself
nomenclatura F nomenclature
nomeolvides M SG forget-me-not
nómina F payroll
nominación F nomination
nominal ADJ nominal
nominar VT to nominate
non ADJ odd; M odd number
nopal M prickly pear
noquear VT to knock out
norcoreano -na ADJ & MF North Korean
nordeste ADJ & M northeast
nórdico ADJ Nordic
noreste ADJ & M northeast
norma F norm, standard; —**s industriales** industry standards
normal ADJ (estándar, común) normal, standard; F (escuela) teacher's college; (línea) perpendicular line
normalidad F normalcy, normality; **con toda** — normally; **todo volvió a la** — everything returned to normal
normalizar[47] VT to normalize
normalmente ADV normally, usually
normativa F norm
noroeste ADJ & M northwest
norte ADJ & M north
norteamericano -na ADJ & MF (de América del Norte) North American; (de EEUU) American
norteño -ña ADJ northern; MF northerner
Noruega F Norway
noruego -ga ADJ & MF Norwegian; M (lengua) Norwegian
nos PRON us; **él** — **vio** he saw us; — **dio el libro** he gave us the book, he gave the book to us
nosotros -as PRON we; **para** — for us
nostalgia F nostalgia
nostálgico ADJ nostalgic
nota F (musical) note; (anotación) annotation; (calificación) grade, mark; — **al pie de página** footnote; **de** — of note; **exagerar la** — to overdo something
notable ADJ notable, noteworthy, remarkable
notablemente ADV (destacadamente) notably; (visiblemente) noticeably
notación F notation
notar VT (percibir) to note, to notice; (señalar) to note
notariar VT to notarize
notario -ria MF notary
noticia F piece of news; —**s** news; **tener** —**s de**

alguien to hear from someone
noticiario M newscast, news bulletin
noticiero M newscast
notificación F (informe) notification; (policial) summons; — **de despido** pink slip
notificar[30] VT to notify
notorio ADJ (conocido públicamente) well-known; (evidente) obvious
novato -ta MF (profesional) novice; (policía, atleta) rookie
novecientos NUM nine hundred
novedad F novelty; —**es** news; **sin** — all's well
novedoso ADJ novel
novela F novel; — **policial** detective novel
novelesco ADJ fictional
novelista MF novelist
noveno ADJ ninth
noventa NUM ninety
noviazgo M engagement
novicio -cia MF novice
noviembre M November
novillo -lla M steer; **hacer** —**s** to play hooky; F heifer
novio -via M (comprometido) fiancé; (no formal) boyfriend; (de boda) bridegroom; F (comprometida) fiancée; (no formal) girlfriend; (de boda) bride
novocaína F novocaine
nubarrón M thunderhead
nube F (atmosférica) cloud; (de humo) billow; **poner por las** —**s** to praise to the skies; **está en las** —**s** his head is in the clouds; **los precios están por las** —**s** prices have gone through the roof
nublado ADJ (cielo) cloudy, overcast; (los ojos, de emoción) misty; (los ojos, por falta de sueño) bleary
nublar VT to blur; —**se** (el cielo) to become overcast; (los ojos) to cloud over
nubosidad F (de un concepto) nebulousness; (del cielo) cloudiness
nuboso ADJ cloudy
nuca F nape
nuclear ADJ nuclear
núcleo M (de célula, átomo) nucleus; (de reactor) core; (de sistema operativo) kernel
nudillo M knuckle
nudismo M nudism
nudista ADJ & MF nudist
nudo M knot (también en la madera, medida de velocidad); (de una obra teatral) turning point; (en el pelo) tangle; (en plantas) node; (en la garganta) lump; — **corredizo** slipknot; — **de rizo** square knot
nudoso ADJ knotty, gnarled
nuera F daughter-in-law
nuestro ADJ POS our; — **hijo** our son; PRON ours; **esto es** — this is ours
nuevamente ADV again

nueve NUM nine
nuevo ADJ new; **de** — again; **¿qué hay de** — ? what's new?
nuez F walnut; — **de Adán** Adam's apple; — **moscada** nutmeg
nulidad F (legal) nullity; (persona) nonentity
nulo ADJ null and void, invalid
numeral ADJ & M numeral
numerar VT to number
numérico ADJ numerical
número M (dígito) number; (en un espectáculo) act; (de una revista) issue; (cifra) figure; — **de serie** serial number
numeroso ADJ numerous
nunca ADV never, not ever; **no viene** — he never comes, he doesn't ever come; **más que** — more than ever; **casi** — hardly ever; **peor que** — worse than ever
nupcial ADJ nuptial, bridal
nupcias F PL nuptials
nutria F otter
nutrición F nutrition
nutrido ADJ **el congreso tuvo una nutrida concurrencia** the conference was well attended
nutriente M nutrient
nutrir VT to nourish
nutritivo ADJ nutritious, nourishing

Ññ

ñandú M rhea
ñato ADJ *Am* pug-nosed
ñoño ADJ bland
ñu M gnu

Oo

o CONJ or; — **se casa** — **lo mato** either he gets married or I'll kill him; — **sea** that is
oasis M oasis
obedecer[35] VI/VT to obey; **esto obedece a que** this is due to the fact that
obedezca, obedezco *ver* obedecer
obediencia F obedience
obediente ADJ obedient
obertura F musical overture
obesidad F obesity
obeso ADJ obese
obispo M bishop
obituario M obituary

objeción F objection
objetable ADJ objectionable
objetar VI/VT to object, to take exception [to]
objetividad F objectivity
objetivo ADJ objective; M (lente) objective; (meta) aim, objective
objeto M object
oblea F wafer
oblicuo ADJ (inclinado) oblique; (sesgado) biased
obligación F (deber) obligation, duty; (deuda) obligation; (título financiero) bond
obligado ADJ (forzado) forced; (obligatorio) compulsory, obligatory; **me vi — a comprar otro coche** I was forced / had to buy another car
obligar[40] VT to force, to compel, to oblige; **—se [a]** to obligate oneself [to]
obligatorio ADJ obligatory, compulsory
oboe M oboe
obra F (artística, literaria, de construcción) work; (lugar de construcción) construction site; **— maestra** masterpiece; **en —s** under construction
obrar VI to act; **obra en nuestro poder** we acknowledge receipt of
obrero -ra MF worker; ADJ working
obscenidad F obscenity; **—es** filth
obsceno ADJ obscene
obscuridad ver oscuridad
obsequiar VT to present, to give; **me obsequió perfume** he gave me perfume
obsequio M gift
obsequioso ADJ obsequious
observación F (mirada) observation; (comentario) remark
observador -ora MF observer; ADJ observant
observancia F observance
observar VI/VT (mirar) to observe; (hacer un comentario) to remark, to observe
observatorio M observatory
obsesión F obsession
obsesionado ADJ obsessed
obsesionar VT to obsess; **—se con** to obsess over, to be obsessed with
obsesivo-compulsivo ADJ obsessive-compulsive
obstaculizar VT to impede
obstáculo M (impedimento) obstacle, hindrance, impediment; (en carreras) hurdle
obstante LOC PREP **no — tu oposición** notwithstanding your opposition; LOC ADV **no —, voy a ir** nevertheless, I am going to go
obstar VT to preclude
obstetra MF obstetrician
obstetricia F obstetrics
obstinación F obstinacy
obstinado ADJ obstinate, bullheaded
obstinarse VI to be obstinate
obstrucción F (de justicia, de un caño) obstruction, blockage; (del intestino) obstruction, occlusion; **— intestinal** intestinal obstruction
obstruir[19] VT (un movimiento, procedimiento) to obstruct, to block; (un aparato) to jam; VI **—se** to get jammed
obtención F acquisition
obtendrá, obtendría ver obtener
obtener[58] VT (bienes) to obtain, to get; (permiso) to secure; (con dificultad) to procure
obtenga, obtengo, obtiene, obtienes ver obtener
obturador M (de una cámara fotográfica) shutter; (de un coche) choke
obtuve, obtuviera, obtuviese ver obtener
obviamente ADV obviously
obviar VT to obviate, to circumvent
obvio ADJ obvious
ocasión F (vez, instancia) occasion; (oportunidad) opportunity; (ganga) bargain; **de —** reduced
ocasional ADJ occasional
ocasionar VT to occasion, to cause
ocaso M sunset, twilight
occidental ADJ occidental, western; MF westerner
occidente M west
oceánico ADJ oceanic
océano M ocean
oceanografía F oceanography
ocelote M ocelot
ochenta NUM eighty
ocho NUM eight
ochocientos NUM eight hundred
ocio M (diversión) leisure; (inacción) idleness
ociosidad F idleness
ocioso ADJ (inactivo) idle; (no usado) unused
oclusión F occlusion
octágono M octagon
octano M octane
octava F octave
octavilla F tract
octavo ADJ & M eighth
octeto M byte
octógono M octagon
octubre M October
ocular M eyepiece; ADJ **infección —** eye infection
oculista MF oculist, eye doctor
ocultar VT to conceal; (información) to withhold
ocultismo M the occult
oculto ADJ (invisible) unseen; (sobrenatural) occult; (escondido) hidden, under wraps
ocupación F (trabajo) occupation; (capacidad) occupancy
ocupado ADJ (persona, teléfono) busy; (asiento, aseo) occupied
ocupante MF occupant

ocupar VT (usar) to occupy; (contratar) to employ; **—se de** to take care of, to address

ocurrencia F witticism, quip

ocurrente ADJ witty

ocurrir VI to occur

oda F ode

odiar VI/VT to hate

odio M hatred, hate

odioso ADJ (tarea) odious; (persona) hateful, obnoxious

odontología F dentistry

odre M wineskin

OEA [Organización de Estados Americanos] F OAS

oeste ADJ & M west

ofender VI/VT to offend; **—se** to get offended, to take offense

ofensa F offense

ofensiva F (militar) offensive; (deportiva) offense; (fútbol americano) offensive series

ofensivo ADJ offensive, obnoxious

oferta F (oportunidad) offer; (rebaja) special offer; **— de apertura** opening bid; **en —** on sale; **— de prueba** trial offer; **— pública inicial** initial public offering

offset M offset

oficial -la ADJ official; MF (militar) officer; (obrero calificado) skilled worker; **— general** high-ranking officer

oficialismo M party in power

oficialista ADJ in power

oficiar VI to officiate; **— de** to serve as

oficina F (despacho) office; (dependencia gubernamental) bureau; **— central** home office, headquarters; **— en el hogar** home office

oficinista MF office worker

oficio M (actividad laboral) trade, craft; (comunicación oficial) official communication; **tiene mucho —** he knows his stuff; **buenos —s** good offices

oficioso ADJ (entrometido) officious; (no oficial) unofficial, off-the-record

ofrecer[35] VT (un regalo) to offer; (en una subasta) to bid; (una cena) to give; **— resistencia** to put up resistance; **¿qué se le ofrece a usted?** how can I help you?

ofrecimiento M (acción de ofrecer) offering; (oferta) offer

ofrenda F offering

oftalmólogo -ga MF ophthalmologist

ofuscar[30] VT to bewilder

ogro M ogre

ohmio M ohm

oído M (facultad) hearing; (órgano) inner ear; (musical) ear; **— medio** middle ear; **al —** confidentially; **de —** by ear

oiga, oigo ver oír

oír[55] VI/VT (percibir) to hear; (atender) to listen; **— decir que** to hear that; **— hablar de** to hear about; **— misa** to attend mass; **¡oye!** listen! hey!

ojal M buttonhole

ojalá INTERJ **— estuviera aquí** I wish he were here; **— que venga** I hope that he comes

ojeada F glimpse

ojear VT to glimpse

ojera F dark circle under the eye

ojeriza F animosity

ojeroso ADJ with dark circles under the eyes

ojiva F (arco) pointed arch; (explosivo) warhead

ojo M (órgano, centro de huracán, instinto, yema de patata) eye; **¡—!** careful! look out! **a — de buen cubero** as a rule of thumb; **a —s vistas** clearly; **me costó un — de la cara** it cost me an arm and a leg; **¿no tienes —s en la cara?** are you blind? **dichosos los —s que te ven** you're a sight for sore eyes; **— de buey** porthole; **— de la cerradura** keyhole; **— de lince** eagle-eye; **— morado** black eye; **— por —** an eye for an eye

ola F wave; (de un olor) waft; (de protesta) storm

oleada F wave, surge

oleaje M swell, surge

óleo M oil painting

oleoducto M oil pipeline

oleoso ADJ oily

oler[22] VI/VT to smell (también sospechar); **— a** to smell of

olfatear VI/VT to scent, to sniff

olfateo M sniff, sniffing

olfato M (facultad) sense of smell; (instinto) nose

olfatorio ADJ olfactory

olimpíada F Olympiad; **—s** Olympic Games

olímpico ADJ Olympian

oliva F olive

olivar M olive grove

olivo M olive tree

olla F pot; **— de grillos** snake pit; **— podrida** stew of mixed vegetables and meat

olmo M elm

olor M smell, odor

oloroso ADJ odorous

olvidadizo ADJ forgetful

olvidar VI/VT to forget; **—se [de]** to forget; **se me olvidó algo** I forgot something

olvido M oblivion; **caer en el —** to be forgotten; **echar al —** to cast into oblivion; **tus —s** your forgetfulness

Omán M Oman

omaní ADJ & MF Omani

ombligo M navel

OMC [Organización Mundial del Comercio] F WTO

omisión F omission; **por —** by default

omiso ADJ **hacer caso — [de]** to ignore

omitir VT (eliminar) to omit, to leave out; (no notar) to overlook

ómnibus M bus
omnipotente ADJ omnipotent
omnisciencia F omniscience
omnisciente ADJ omniscient
omnívoro ADJ omnivorous
omóplato M scapula
OMS [Organización Mundial de la Salud] F
WHO
once NUM eleven
oncología F oncology
onda F wave; — **corta** shortwave; — **expansiva**
shock wave; — **sonora** sound wave;
agarrarle la — a algo to get in the swing of
things; **captar la** — to get the drift
ondeado ADJ wavy
ondeante ADJ flying
ondear VI to wave
ondulación F ripple, ruffle, roll
ondulado ADJ (pelo) wavy; (paisaje) rolling
ondulante ADJ undulating
ondular VI to undulate; VI/VT to wave
ónix M onyx
omnipotencia F omnipotence
onomatopeya F onomatopoeia
ONU [Organización de las Naciones Unidas]
F UN
onza F ounce
opacar[30] VT (oscurecer) to dull; (eclipsar) to
overshadow
opaco ADJ (no transparente) opaque; (no
brillante) dull
ópalo M opal
opción F option; **opciones** stock options; — **de**
venta put option
opcional ADJ optional
OPEP [Organización de Países
Exportadores de Petróleo] F OPEC
ópera F (composición) opera; (teatro) opera
house
operable ADJ operable
operación F operation
operador -ora M (en matemáticas) operator; MF
(de teléfono) operator
operar VI/VT (usar maquinaria) to operate; VT
(intervenir quirúrgicamente) to operate on;
(llevar a cabo) to carry out; VI (hacer cuentas)
to do mathematical operations
operario -ria MF operator, operative
operativo ADJ (que funciona) operative;
(vigente) in effect; M *Am* — **policial** police
operation
opiáceo M opiate
opinar VI/VT to hold an opinion, to think
opinión F opinion, view, feeling; **cambiar de**
— to change one's mind
opio M opium
oponente MF (en un debate) opponent; (en una
película) costar
oponer[56, 74] VT to oppose; —**se** to conflict; —**se**

a to oppose, to be against
oponga, opongo *ver* oponer
oporto M port wine
oportunidad F (chance) opportunity, chance;
(pretexto) opening; (fútbol americano) down
oportunista ADJ & MF opportunistic
oportuno ADJ (conveniente) opportune, timely;
(adecuado) appropriate
oposición F opposition; **oposiciones**
competitive examinations
opositor -ora MF opponent
opresión F oppression
opresivo ADJ oppressive
opresor -ora MF oppressor
oprimir VT (al pueblo) to oppress; (un botón) to
press; (un enlace digital) to click
optar VI to choose; — **por** to choose
optativo ADJ optional
óptico -ca ADJ optical; MF optician; F optics
optimismo M optimism
optimista ADJ optimistic; MF optimist
optimizar VT to optimize
óptimo ADJ optimal
optometría F optometry
optometrista MF optometrist
opuesto ADJ opposite, contrary; **se mostró** —
al casamiento he was against the marriage;
dos fuerzas opuestas two opposing forces;
lo — the opposite; **dirección opuesta** the
opposite/reverse direction
opulencia F opulence
opulento ADJ (decoración) opulent; (sociedad)
affluent
opuse, opusiera, opusiese *ver* oponer
oración F (frase) sentence; (plegaria) prayer
oráculo M oracle
orador -ora MF orator, speaker
oral ADJ oral
orangután M orangutan
orar VI/VT to pray
oratoria F oratory
oratorio M oratory
órbita F (de los cuerpos celestes) orbit; (de los
ojos) eye socket
orbitador M orbiter
orbital ADJ orbital
orbitar VI/VT to orbit
orca F killer whale
orden M (limpieza, secuencia) order; —
ascendente ascending order; — **de**
clasificación sort order; — **del día** order of
the day; **perturbar el** — **público** to disturb
the peace; **sin** — **ni concierto** haphazard; F
(mando) command, order; (grupo religioso)
order; — **de cateo** warrant; — **de compra**
purchase order; — **judicial** court order; **a**
sus órdenes at your service
ordenación F (arreglo) ordering, organization;
(de un cura) ordination; (informatización)

computerization
ordenado ADJ orderly, neat
ordenador M *Esp* computer; — **de mano** palmtop; — **de sobremesa** desktop computer; — **digital** digital computer; — **portátil** laptop computer; — **torre** tower computer
ordenamiento M (arreglo) ordering, putting in order; (conjunto de leyes) legal code; — **territorial** land use
ordenanza F ordinance; MF orderly
ordenar VT (arreglar) to sort, to put in order; (mandar) to order, to command; (conferir órdenes religiosos) to ordain; —**se** to become ordained
ordeñar VT to milk
ordeño M milking
ordinal ADJ ordinal
ordinariez F vulgarity
ordinario ADJ (corriente) ordinary; (vulgar) vulgar
orear VT to air out
orégano M oregano
oreja F [outer] ear; (de un martillo) claw; (en un utensilio) flap; **aguzar la —** to prick up one's ears; **sonreír de — a —** to smile from ear to ear; **estar hasta las —s en algo** to be up to one's neck in something
orejera F earmuff
orfanato M orphanage
orfebre MF (con oro) goldsmith; (con plata) silversmith
orgánico ADJ organic
organigrama M organizational chart, flow chart
organismo M organism
organista MF organist
organización F organization
organizado ADJ organized
organizador -ora MF organizer
organizar[47] VT (una reunión, evento) to organize; (un ataque) to stage; (una fiesta) to give, to throw
organizativo ADJ organizational, organizing
órgano M organ
orgía F orgy
orgullo M pride; **es mi —** she's my pride and joy
orgulloso ADJ proud
orientación F (vocacional, psicológica) orientation, guidance; (de velas) trim; (de estudios) track; (de un objeto) lie; (del terreno) lay; — **horizontal** landscape; — **vertical** portrait
orientado ADJ oriented; — **al cliente** customer-oriented
oriental ADJ oriental, eastern; MF oriental
orientar VT to orient; —**se** to get one's bearings
oriente M Orient, east
orificio M orifice

origen M origin; (de un problema, conflicto) source; (antecedentes familiares) birth
original ADJ original; M (de una pintura) original; (de una cinta magnética) master
originalidad F originality
originar VT to originate, to give rise to; —**se** to originate, to arise
originario ADJ (original) original; — **de** (de cierto origen) coming from, native of
orilla F (de un lago, mar) shore, bank; (de una cama) edge; (de una prenda) hem
orillar VT (una calle) to border; (una prenda) to hem
orín M rust; M PL **orines** urine
orina F urine
orinal M chamber pot
orinar VI/VT to urinate
oriundo ADJ **ser — de** (persona) to hail from; (cosa) to originate in
orla F (de un uniforme) trimming; (de una alfombra) fringe
orlar VT to fringe
orlón™ M Orlon™
ornamentación F ornamentation
ornamental ADJ ornamental
ornamentar VT to ornament, to embellish
ornamento M ornament
ornar VT to adorn
ornitología F ornithology
oro M gold; — **blanco** white gold; — **en lingotes** gold bullion; — **negro** black gold; — **puro** solid gold; **prometer el — y el moro** to promise the moon
orondo ADJ self-satisfied
oropel M tinsel
oropéndola F oriole
orquesta F orchestra
orquestar VT to orchestrate
orquídea F orchid
ortiga F nettle
ortodoncia F orthodontics
ortodoxo ADJ orthodox
ortografía F orthography, spelling
oruga F caterpillar
orujo M rape
orzuelo M sty
osadía F boldness, daring
osado ADJ bold, daring
osamenta F skeleton
osar VI/VT to dare
oscilación F oscillation
oscilar VI to oscillate, to seesaw; — **entre** to range between
oscurecer VI (ponerse oscuro) to get dark; VT (poner oscuro) to darken; (volver poco inteligible, ocultar) to obscure; —**se** to get darker
oscuridad F (lugar sin luz) dark, darkness; (condición de oscuro) darkness; (falta de

claridad conceptual, anonimato) obscurity
oscuro ADJ (sin luz) dark; (turbio) murky; (poco claro, poco conocido) obscure; **lentes —s** dark glasses; **gris —** dark gray; **a oscuras** in the dark
óseo ADJ bony
osezno M bear cub
osificarse VI to ossify
ósmosis F osmosis
oso -sa M bear; F she-bear; **— blanco/polar** polar bear; **— hormiguero** anteater
ostentación F ostentation, show, display; **hacer — de** to flaunt
ostentar VI/VT to display, to show off, to flaunt
ostentoso ADJ ostentatious, showy
osteoartritis F osteoarthritis
osteoporosis F osteoporosis
ostión M large oyster
ostra F oyster
OTAN [Organización del Tratado del Atlántico Norte] F NATO
otero M hillock
otitis F otitis; **— externa** swimmer's ear
otoñal ADJ autumnal
otoño M autumn, fall
otorgamiento M grant
otorgar⁴⁰ VT (permiso) to grant, to concede; (premio) to award
otro ADJ (uno adicional) another; (uno diferente) other; **otra vez** again; **otra cosa** something else; **— más** another one; **al — día** the next day; **de — modo** otherwise; **en otra parte** somewhere else; **la otra cara de la moneda** the flip side; **por otra parte** on the other hand; PRON (uno más) another one; (una persona diferente) someone else; (una cosa diferente) something else
out ADV & M out; **— forzado** force out
ovación F ovation, acclaim
oval ADJ oval
ovalado ADJ oval
óvalo M oval
ovárico ADJ ovarian
ovario M ovary
oveja F (ovino) sheep; (hembra) ewe
ovejero M sheepdog
overoles M PL overalls
ovillar VT to ball; **—se** to curl up into a ball
ovillo M ball of yarn; **hacerse un —** to curl up
OVNI [objeto volador no identificado] M UFO
ovoide N egg-shaped
ovulación F ovulation
ovular VI to ovulate
óvulo M egg
oxidación F oxidation, rusting
oxidado ADJ oxidized, rusty
oxidar VI/VT to oxidize, to rust
óxido M (compuesto químico) oxide;

(herrumbre) rust
oxígeno M oxygen
oye, oyendo, oyera, oyese ver oír
oyente MF (que oye) listener, hearer; (alumno no oficial) auditor
ozono M ozone

Pp

pabellón M (puesto de feria) pavilion; (parte de un edificio) wing; (bandera) flag; (sección de hospital) ward; **— de la oreja** outer ear
pabilo M wick
paca F bale
pacana F (fruto) pecan; (árbol) pecan tree
pacer³⁵ VI to pasture, to graze; VT to crop, to graze
paciencia F patience; **con —** patiently; **tener —** to be patient
paciente ADJ & MF patient; **— ambulatorio -ria** outpatient; **— externo -na** outpatient; **— de alto riesgo** high-risk patient
pacificación F pacification
pacificar³⁰ VT to pacify
pacífico ADJ peaceful; M **Océano Pacífico** Pacific Ocean
pacifismo M pacifism
pactar VT (hacer un pacto) to make a pact / an agreement; (decidir de común acuerdo) to agree; VI **— con el diablo** to sell one's soul to the devil
pacto M pact, covenant
paddock M (de caballos) paddock; (de coches) pit
padecer³⁵ VI/VT to suffer; **— de cáncer** to suffer from cancer
padecimiento M suffering
padezca, padezco ver padecer
padrastro M (marido de la madre) stepfather; (uñero) hangnail
padre M father; **—s** parents, folks; **— de familia** male head of the household; **—nuestro** the Lord's Prayer; **John Smith, —** John Smith Sr.; **ser —** to become a father; ADJ **un lío —** a real mess
padrino M (de bautizo) godfather; (de boda) best man; (en un duelo) second
paella F paella
paga F (salario) pay; (para un niño) allowance; **— de tiempo y medio** time-and-a-half pay; **— por mérito** merit pay
pagadero ADJ payable, due
pagado ADJ paid; **— de sí mismo** self-satisfied
pagador -ora MF payer
paganismo M paganism
pagano -na ADJ & MF pagan

pagar⁴⁰ VT (cuentas, deudas) to pay; (préstamo) to pay off; (mercancías) to pay for; —**se de** to be proud of; — **el pato** to be left holding the bag; **pagan justos por pecadores** the just pay for the sins of others; — **a plazos** to pay in installments; — **al contado** to pay cash; — **con la misma moneda** to pay in kind; — **en especie** to pay in kind

pagaré M promissory note

página F page; — **de estilo** stylesheet; — **web** web page

paginar VT to paginate

pago M payment; — **en efectivo** cash payment; ADJ paid

paila F large pan

país M country; — **de origen** country of origin; — **en desarrollo** developing country; — **exportador de petróleo** oil-exporting country

paisaje M landscape, scenery

paisajismo M landscape architecture

paisano -na M countryman; F countrywoman

paja F straw (también para beber de un vaso); **a humo de —s** thoughtlessly; **hacerse una** — *vulg* to jack off; **no caberle a alguien una** — **por el culo** to be self-satisfied; **por un quítame allá esas —s** for a trifle

pajar M hayloft

pájaro M bird; — **carpintero** woodpecker; — **pinto** cautious person; **un** — **francés** a French guy

paje M page

pajizo ADJ straw-colored

pajonal M *Am* grassland

pala F (para cavar) shovel; (para recoger basura) dustpan; (de hélice, remo) blade; (de zapato) upper; (para remar, de ping-pong) paddle; — **mecánica** power shovel; **lo tuvimos que recoger con —** he was exhausted

palabra F (unidad léxica) word; (facultad) speech; — **clave** key word; —**s mayores** a big deal; **cuatro —s** a few words; **cumplir con la —** to keep one's word; **dejar con la — en la boca** to cut someone off in midsentence; **en pocas —s** in a nutshell; **faltar a la —** to break a promise; **la última —** the final say; **ni una —** not a word; **no dijo —** he didn't breathe a word; **un hombre de —** a man of his word; **tener la —** to have the floor; **tomar la —** to take the floor; **traducción — por —** word-for-word translation; **tragarse/comerse las propias —s** to eat one's words

palabrerío M verbiage

palabrero ADJ long-winded

palabrota F curse word, four-letter word; —**s** profanity

palacio M palace

paladar M palate; — **hendido** cleft palate; —

óseo hard palate

paladear VT to relish

paladín M champion, crusader

palanca F (para levantar algo) lever; (para abrir algo) crowbar; (fuerza) leverage; — **de cambios** gearshift lever; — **de juegos** joystick; — **del regulador** throttle lever; **hacer —** to use leverage

palangana F basin

Paláu M Palau

palco M box

palenque M fence

paleontología F paleontology

Palestina F Palestine

palestino -na MF Palestinian; ADJ Palestinian

paleta F (de pintor) palette; (de albañil) trowel; (de ping-pong, para mezclar, batir) paddle; (hélice) blade; (de caramelo) lollipop, sucker; (de helado) Popsicle™

paletilla F shoulder

paleto -ta MF hayseed, hick

paliar VT to alleviate

paliativo M palliative

palidecer³⁵ VI to turn pale

palidez F pallor, paleness

pálido ADJ pallid, pale

palillo M (de dientes) toothpick; (de tambor) drumstick; (para comida china) chopstick; **tocar todos los —s** to try everything

palique M chitchat

paliza F beating, whipping; **dar una —** to beat, to whip

palma F (árbol) palm [tree]; (hoja) palm leaf; (de la mano) palm [of the hand]; **batir —s** to clap; **llevarse la —** to take the prize; **conocer como la — de la mano** to know like the back of one's hand

palmada F (en la espalda) slap; (aplauso) clap; (en el trasero) spank; **dar una —** (en la espalda) to slap; (en el trasero) to spank

palmear VT to slap on the back

palmera F palm tree

palmípedo M web-footed bird

palmo M span; — **a —** inch by inch

palmotear VT to slap on the back

palo M (de madera) stick; (de barco) mast; (de naipes) suit; (fútbol) goalpost; —**s** (fútbol americano) goalposts; — **de golf** golf club; — **de escoba** broomstick; **dar —s** to hit with a stick; **de tal — tal astilla** a chip off the old block

paloma F dove, pigeon

palomar M pigeon loft

palomilla F wing nut

palomita F (béisbol) fly ball; —**s** popcorn; **hacer —** to pop corn

palote M rolling pin

palpable ADJ palpable

palpar VT to feel

palpitación F palpitation
palpitante ADJ palpitating; **una cuestión** — a burning question
palpitar VI to palpitate
palta F *Am* avocado
paludismo M malaria
pampa F *Am* prairie
pamplinas F PL baloney, hogwash
pan M bread; (pieza) loaf of bread; — **comido** piece of cake, cinch; — **de cada día** everyday occurrence; — **rallado/molido** bread crumbs; **al** —, — **y al vino, vino** to call a spade a spade; **contigo,** — **y cebolla** love is all we need; **ganarse el** — to make a living
pana F corduroy
panacea F panacea, magic bullet
panadería F bakery
panadero -ra MF baker
panal M honeycomb
Panamá M Panama
panameño -ña ADJ & MF Panamanian
panamericano ADJ Pan-American
panceta F *RP* bacon
páncreas M SG pancreas
panda M panda bear
pandearse VT to buckle, to sag
pandemia F pandemic
pandémico M pandemic
pandeo M sag
pandereta F tambourine
pandilla F gang, band
panecillo M roll
panegírico M eulogy
panel M panel; — **de control** control panel
panera F breadbasket
panfleto M pamphlet
pánico ADJ & M panic
panoja F ear of corn
panorama M (paisaje) panorama; (horizonte) outlook
panorámico ADJ panoramic
panqueque M pancake
pantaletas F PL panties
pantalla F (de lámpara) lampshade; (para películas) screen; (de monitor) screen, display; (para actividades ilícitas) cover, front; **la** — **grande** the silver screen; — **dividida** split screen; — **táctil** touchscreen, touch-sensitive display
pantalón M pants, trousers; — **corto** shorts; **pantalones** pants, trousers; **llevar bien puestos los pantalones** to be master in one's own home
pantano M swamp, marsh
pantanoso ADJ swampy, marshy
panteón M vault
pantera F panther
pantomima F mime, pantomime
pantorrilla F calf

pantufla F slipper
panty M pantyhose
panza F paunch, belly
panzudo ADJ potbellied
pañal M diaper; **estar en** —**es** to be in its infancy
paño M (de tela) cloth; (de lana) woolen cloth; (para limpiar) rag; — **higiénico** sanitary napkin; — **mortuorio** pall; — **de manos** towel; — **de cocina** dishcloth; — **de mesa** tablecloth; **ella es mi** — **de lágrimas** I always cry on her shoulder; —**s menores** underwear
pañuelo M (de nariz) handkerchief; (de cuello) scarf
papa M pope; F *Am* potato; **no saber ni** — not to know a thing; —**s fritas** French fries
papá M papa, dad
papacito M (padre) daddy; (hombre apuesto) hunk
papada F double chin
papado M papacy
papagayo M parrot
papaíto M daddy
papal ADJ papal
papar VT to eat; MF SG **papamoscas** (pájaro) flycatcher; (tonto) half-wit; MF SG **papanatas** twerp
paparruchas F PL baloney, bull
papaya F papaya
papel M (para escribir) paper; (dramático) role, part; — **aluminio** aluminum foil; — **carbón** carbon paper; — **cuadriculado** graph paper; — **de cartas** stationery; — **de estaño** tinfoil; — **de estraza** brown paper; — **de lija** sandpaper; — **de seda** tissue paper; — **encerado** wax paper; — **higiénico** toilet paper; — **moneda** paper money; — **tisú** tissue paper; **desempeñar un** — to play a role; **en el** — on paper; **hacer buen** — to cut a good figure
papeleo M paperwork
papelera F (fábrica) paper factory; (cubo) wastepaper basket
papelería F stationery store
papeleta F (para escribir) slip of paper; (para votar) ballot
paperas F PL mumps
papito M daddy
páprika F paprika
papú ADJ & MF Papua New Guinean
paquete M (envuelto) package; (atado) bundle; (programas de ordenador) package; — **de programas de productividad** office suite; — **turístico** package tour
Paquistán M Pakistan
paquistano -na ADJ & MF Pakistani
par ADJ even; M (de cosas idénticas) pair; (de cosas diferentes) couple; (título nobiliario)

peer; (en golf) par; **a la** — at par; **sin** — peerless; **de** — **en** — wide-open
para PREP in order to, for; **lo hice** — **ganar dinero** I did it in order to earn money; **demasiado** — **mí** too much for me; **trabajo** — **mi padre** I work for my father; — **ser perro es inteligente** for a dog he's smart; — **mi sorpresa** to my surprise; **voy** — **Madrid** I'm going to Madrid; — **las dos** by two o'clock; — **atrás** backwards; — **empezar** for starters; — **llevar** to go; ¿— **qué?** what for? — **que** so that, so as to; — **siempre** forever; — **su información** FYI [for your information]; **habla** — **sí** he talks to himself; — **mis adentros** to myself; — **morirse de risa** hilarious; **no es** — **tanto** it's no big deal; **sin qué ni** — **qué** without rhyme or reason
parabién M congratulations; **dar el** — to congratulate
parada F (acción de parar) stop; (de perro de caza) point; (de taxis) stand; (militar) parade; (relevo de guardia) changing of the guard; (de balón) parry; (en fútbol americano) tackle
paradero M whereabouts
paradigma M paradigm
parado ADJ (inmóvil) stationary; (sin trabajo) unemployed, idle; **salir bien** — to come out on top
paradoja F paradox
paradójico ADJ paradoxical
parafernalia F paraphernalia
parafina F paraffin
parafrasear VI/VT to paraphrase
paráfrasis F paraphrase
paraguas M SG umbrella
Paraguay M Paraguay
paraguayo -**ya** ADJ & MF Paraguayan
paraíso M paradise
paraje M spot
paralelo -**la** ADJ & M parallel; F parallel line; **hacer** —**s** to draw parallels; **barras paralelas** parallel bars
parálisis F (inmovilidad física, espiritual) paralysis; (condición médica) paralysis, palsy; — **cerebral** cerebral palsy
paralítico -**ca** ADJ & MF paralytic
paralización F (de tránsito) gridlock; (del cuerpo) paralysis
paralizar[47] VT (movimiento) to paralyze; (negociaciones) to stall; —**se** to gridlock
paramédico -**ca** ADJ & MF paramedic
parámetro M parameter
paramilitar ADJ & MF paramilitary
páramo M cold highland, moor
parangón M comparison; **sin** — incomparable
parangonar VT to compare
paraninfo M auditorium
paranoia F paranoia

paranoico -**ca** ADJ & MF paranoid
paranormal ADJ paranormal
parapléjico -**ca** MF paraplegic
parapsicología F parapsychology
parar VI/VT (detener) to stop; (motor) to stall; VT (un pase de pelota) to block; (un golpe) to parry; — **de hacer algo** to stop doing something; **y para de contar** and that's it; — **en seco** to stop short; **ir a** — to end up; **habló sin** — he talked nonstop; —**se** (detenerse) to stop; (erguirse) Am to stand up; —**se a pensar** to stop to think; M SG
parabrisas windshield; M SG **paracaídas** parachute; M SG **paracaídas dorado** golden parachute; M **paracaidismo** parachuting; M SG **parachoques** bumper; M SG
pararrayos lightning rod; M **parasol** parasol; MF **paracaidista** parachutist
parasítico ADJ parasitic
parásito M parasite
parcela F parcel, plot
parcelación F subdivision
parcelar VT to parcel [out]
parche M (para remendar, informático) patch; (de tambor) drumhead; (médico) Band-aid®; — **de ojo** eye patch
parcial ADJ partial
pardillo M linnet
pardo ADJ (color) gray-brown; (mulato) mulatto
pareado M couplet
parear VT to match
parecer[35] VI to seem; — **que** to seem like, to look like; **¿qué te parece?** what do you think? —**se a** to resemble, to look like; M (opinión) opinion; (aspecto) appearance; **al** — apparently; **a mi** — to my mind / way of thinking; **del mismo** — like-minded
parecido ADJ alike, similar; **bien** — good-looking; M similarity, resemblance
pared F wall; **poner a alguien contra la** — to corner; **subirse por las** —**es** to be furious; **de** — **a** — wall-to-wall; **reloj de** — wall clock
paredón M execution wall
pareja F (de personas) couple; (de cosas) [matching] pair; (compañero) partner
parejo ADJ (hermanos) alike; (carrera) even; (dientes) straight; **correr [al]** — to go hand in hand
parental ADJ parental
parentela F kin
parentesco M kinship, relation
paréntesis M parenthesis
parezca, parezco ver parecer
pargo M red snapper
paria MF pariah, outcast
paridad F parity
pariente MF, **parienta** F relative, relation; — **consanguíneo** blood relative
parir VI/VT to give birth [to]

parlamentar VI to parley
parlamentario -ria ADJ parliamentary; MF member of parliament
parlamento M (en una obra de teatro) speech; (negociación) parley; (cuerpo legislativo) parliament
parlanchín ADJ talkative; MF chatterbox
parlotear VI to chatter, to rattle on
parloteo M chatter
paro M (huelga breve) stoppage; (falta de trabajo) unemployment; (ave) tit; — **cardiaco** cardiac arrest; — **laboral** work stoppage
parodia F parody
parodiar VT to parody
parpadear VI (un ojo, pantalla) to blink; (una vela) to flicker; (una estrella) to twinkle
parpadeo M (del ojo) blink; (de una vela) flicker; (de una estrella) twinkle; (de una pantalla) blinking
párpado M eyelid
parque M park; — **automotor** fleet of cars; — **de atracciones** amusement park; — **zoológico** zoo
parra F grapevine
párrafo M paragraph; **echar un — con** to have a chat with
parral M grape arbor
parranda F binge, spree; **andar de —** to go out partying
parrandear VI to revel
parrandero -ra MF party animal
parrilla F (sobre el fuego) grill; (en el horno) broiler; (de calles) grid; (de coche) grille
parrillada F barbecue dish
párroco M parish priest
parroquia F (distrito) parish; (iglesia) parish church
parroquial ADJ parochial
parroquiano -na MF (de iglesia) parishioner; (de tienda) regular
parte F (sección) part; (lugar) place; (papel en una obra teatral) lines; (persona legal) party; — **integrante** built-in part; — **interesada** interested party; —**s pudendas** private parts, *fam* privates; **a otra —** somewhere else; **a —s iguales** fifty-fifty; **de un tiempo a esta —** for some time; **de — de** on behalf of; **de — a —** completely; **echar a mala —** to take amiss; **en —** partly; **en gran —** in large measure; **en otra —** elsewhere; **en/por todas —s** everywhere; **formar — de** to be part of; **ir por —s** to proceed by steps; **la mayor — de** most of; **la — del león** the lion's share; **no está en ninguna —** it's nowhere to be found; **no va a ninguna —** it's going nowhere; **por otra —** on the other hand; **tomar — en** to take part in; M report; **dar —** to report; **dar — de enfermo** to call

in sick; **dar — de un crimen** to report a crime
partera F midwife
partición F (of a country) partition; (of a cell) division
participación F (en un proyecto) participation, involvement; (en un negocio) interest; — **de nacimiento** birth announcement
participante MF (en un grupo) participant; (en una carrera) entrant; (en un concurso) contestant
participar VI to participate; VT to announce; — **de/en** to participate in, to share in
partícipe MF participant
participio M participle
partícula F particle
particular ADJ (específico) particular; (poco usual) peculiar; (privado) private; **en —** in particular; **clases —es** private lessons; M (detalle) particular; (asunto) matter; MF private citizen
partida F (fondos) appropriation; (grupo de personas) party; (cantidad de mercancía) parcel, lot; (de ajedrez) game; (acción de partir) departure; — **de nacimiento** birth record; **jugar una mala —** to play a mean trick; **por — doble** double-entry
partidario -ria MF (de una medida) supporter, advocate; (de un partido político) partisan
partidista ADJ & MF partisan
partido M (grupo político) party; (de golf) round; (de tenis, fútbol) game, match; **es un buen —** he's a good match; **sacar — de** to take advantage of; **tomar —** to take sides; **¿cómo va el —?** what's the score? ADJ split, cleft
partir VT (dividir) to divide; (repartir) to share; (quebrar) to break; **eso me parte por el eje** that screws me up; **que te parta un rayo** go jump in the lake; VI (salir) to depart, to leave; **a — de entonces** since then; **a — del lunes** starting Monday; —**se de risa** to die of laughter
partisano -na MF partisan
partitura F musical score
parto M childbirth, delivery; — **prematuro** premature birth; **estar en trabajo de —** to be in labor
parvulario M kindergarten, nursery
párvulo -la MF nursery school child
pasa F raisin
pasable ADJ passable
pasada F (acción de pasar) passing; (con una máquina) pass; **una mala —** a mean trick; **de — by the way
pasadizo M secret passage
pasado M past; ADJ (anterior) past; (demasiado maduro) overripe; — **mañana** day after tomorrow; **el año —** last year; **el — mes de**

septiembre last September
pasador M (de un cierre) pin; (de la puerta) latch
pasaje M (sitio por donde se pasa, fragmento de texto) passage; (billete) ticket; (precio de un viaje) fare; (conjunto de los pasajeros) passengers
pasajero -ra ADJ fleeting, transitory; MF (en un coche, tren) passenger; (en un taxi) fare
pasante M (tenis) passing shot; MF (compañía) intern
pasaporte M passport
pasar VI (no querer jugar, ir de un lado a otro, seguir su proceso, transcurrir) to pass; (ocurrir) to happen; — **a ser** to become; — **de moda** to go out of style; — **hambre** to go hungry; — **por** to pass by; — **por alto** to pass over; — **una tarjeta por un lector** to swipe a card; —**le por la cabeza a alguien** to occur to someone; **pasan de los 80 años** they're over 80 years old; **te pasaste de la casa** you missed the house; —**se** to spoil; —**se de la raya** to cross the line; —**se de sol** to get too much sun; —**se de listo** to outsmart oneself; **se me pasó ir a buscarte** I totally forgot to pick you up; **me la paso bien** I have a good time; VT (la sal, una prueba, la plancha, una pelota) to pass; (un sofocón) to endure; (una tarde) to spend; — **las de Caín** to go through hell; — **en limpio** to make a new copy; — **por alto** to overlook; — **los 50 kmh** to exceed 50 kmh; — **revista** to pass in review; **nos pasó un Volvo** a Volvo passed us; **no lo paso** I can't stand him; M **tienen un buen** — they have a comfortable life; M **pasamano** (de barco) guard rail, gangway; (de escalera) banister, railing; M **pasatiempo** pastime
pasarela F (en un barco) gangplank; (en un desfile de modas) runway
Pascua F (fiesta cristiana) Easter; (fiesta judía) Passover; — **Florida / de Resurrección** Easter Sunday; — **de Navidad** Christmas
pase M (deporte) pass; — **cruzado** cross; — **de anotación** touchdown pass; — **de cabeza** header; — **pantalla** screen pass
pasear VI (a pie) to take a walk; (en bici, a caballo) to go on a ride; (en coche) to go for a drive, to go on a ride; —**se** to parade, to take a walk; —**se a caballo** to go horseback riding; VT (un perro) to walk a dog
paseo M (a pie) walk, stroll; (a caballo, en bicicleta) ride; (en coche) drive, ride; (calle donde se pasea) mall; (recreativo) outing; **irse a** — to go jump in a lake; **dar un** — (a pie) to take a walk; (a caballo, en bicicleta) to go on a ride; (en coche) to go on a drive
pasillo M (de un teatro) aisle; (de un edificio) hallway, corridor; (para vuelo aéreo) corridor; — **de dobles** alley

pasión F passion
pasivo ADJ passive; **voz pasiva** passive voice; M (en un negocio) liabilities; (de una cuenta) debit side
pasmado ADJ astounded
pasmar VT to astound, to stun; —**se** to be astounded, to be stunned
pasmo M astonishment
pasmoso ADJ astonishing, stunning
paso M (acción de pasar, lugar donde pasar) pass; (de pie, de danza, distancia, de un proceso) step; (velocidad) pace; (de caballerías) walk; (de tornillo) pitch; (de coche) wheelbase; — **elevado** overpass; — **a nivel** grade crossing; — **de tortuga** snail's pace; — **a** — step by step; **dar** — (dejar pasar) to let pass; (dejar actuar) to make possible; **dar** —**s** to take steps; **hacer** —**s** to travel; **de** — by the way, in passing; **estar de** — to be passing through; **marcar el** — to set the pace; **al** — **que** while; **salir del** — to get out of a difficulty; **dicho sea de** — incidentally; **a cada** — at every turn; — **del tiempo** passage of time; **abrir** — **para** to make way for; **abrirse** — to plow through, to press through; ADJ dried
pasta F (de almidón) paste; (de harina) dough; (de fideos) pasta; (de libro) hard cover, binding; (dinero) *fam* dough; **de buena** — of good disposition; — **dentífrica/dental** toothpaste
pastar VI/VT to pasture, to graze
pastel M (torta) cake; (tarta) pie; (pintura, cuadro) pastel; — **de cumpleaños** birthday cake; — **de limón** lemon pie; — **de carne** meat pie; **descubrir el** — to spill the beans; ADJ pastel
pastelería F (establecimiento) pastry shop; (conjunto de pasteles) pastry
pastelero -ra M pastry cook
pasterizar, pasteurizar[9] VT to pasteurize
pastilla F (de medicina) tablet, pill; (para la tos) drop; (de jabón) bar
pastizal M grassland
pasto M (terreno) pasture, grassland; (hierba) grass; **ser** — **de** to be a victim of
pastor -ora MF (de ovejas) shepherd; (sacerdote protestante) pastor, minister; M — **alemán** German shepherd
pastoral ADJ pastoral; F pastoral letter
pastoril ADJ pastoral
pastoso ADJ pasty
pastura F feed
pat M putt
pata F (de animal, mueble) foot, leg; (de pollo) drumstick; (de un enchufe) pin; — **palmada** webfoot; — **de gallo** crow's feet; **en cuatro** —**s** on all fours; **a [la]** — **coja** skipping on one leg; **estirar la** — *fam* to kick the bucket; **mala** — bad luck; **metedura de** — faux pas;

meter la — to slip up; **—s arriba** upside down; ADJ **patihendido** cloven-hoofed; **patitieso** dumbfounded; **patizambo** (hacia adentro) knock-kneed; (hacia afuera) bow-legged

patada F kick (también en deportes); **libros a —s** tons of books; **en dos —s** in a jiffy; **dar —s** to kick; **echar a —s** to kick out; — **lateral** (fútbol americano) onside kick

patalear VI (en el aire) to kick; (en el suelo) to stamp

pataleo M (en el aire) kick; (en el suelo) stamp

pataleta F fit; **tener una** — to throw a fit

patán M boor

patata F *Esp* potato; **—s fritas** French fries; — **caliente** hot potato

pateador M kicker

patear VT (algo, a alguien) to kick; (el suelo) to stamp; VI to tramp around; VI/VT (en golf) to putt; VI to kick; — **al arco** to shoot at goal

patentar VT to patent

patente ADJ & F patent; **se hizo** — **su ignorancia** he betrayed his ignorance; — **en trámite** patent pending

paternal ADJ (del padre) paternal; (como un padre) fatherly

paternidad F paternity, fatherhood; **prueba de** — paternity test

paterno ADJ paternal

patético ADJ moving

patetismo M pathos

patíbulo M gallows scaffold, gallows

patilla F (de gafas) arm; **—s** (de pelo) sideburns

patín M (tabla) skate; (de trineo) runner; — **de ruedas** roller skate; — **de cuchilla / de hielo** ice skate

patinaje M skating

patinar VI (una persona) to skate; (un coche sobre hielo) to skid; (un embrague) to slip; (en un examen) to blank out

patinazo M (de embrague) slip; (de coche) skid

patio M (de casa) patio, courtyard; (de escuela) playground

pato M (ave) duck; (macho) drake; **pagar el** — to take the rap

patochada F blunder

patógeno M pathogen

patología F pathology

patológico ADJ pathological

patoso ADJ clumsy

patotero-ra MF *Am* hooligan

patraña F tall tale

patria F fatherland, homeland

patriarca M patriarch

patriarcal ADJ patriarchal

patrimonial ADJ inherited, patrimonial

patrimonio M patrimony; — **cultural** cultural heritage; — **neto** net worth; — **personal** personal assets

patriota MF patriot

patriótico ADJ patriotic

patriotismo M patriotism

patrocinador-ora MF sponsor

patrocinar VT to sponsor

patrocinio M sponsorship; — **empresarial** corporate backing

patrón-ona MF (protector) patron; (jefe) employer; (de navío) skipper; M (dueño de pensión) landlord; (de costura) pattern; (punto de referencia) yardstick, standard; (de planta) stock; (de un parásito) host; — **de oro** gold standard; F (dueña de pensión) landlady

patronal ADJ management; **asociación** — employers' association; F management

patronato M board of trustees

patrono-na MF patron

patrulla F (grupo de policías o soldados) patrol, squad; (coche) squad car

patrullar VI/VT to patrol

patrullero-ra M patrol car, squad car; MF patrol officer

pausa F (musical) pause, rest; **trabajar con** — to work slowly; **hacer** — to pause

pauta F guideline

pavimentar VT to pave

pavimento M pavement

pavo M turkey; — **real** peacock; ADJ silly

pavón M peacock

pavonearse VI to strut, to swagger

pavoneo M strut, swagger

pavor M dread

pavoroso ADJ frightful

payasada F clownish act or remark; **—s** antics, horseplay

payasear VI to clown around, to horse around

payaso M (de circo) clown; (persona poco seria) buffoon; **hacer el** — to clown around

paz F peace; **estamos en** — we are even; **[que] en** — **descanse** may she rest in peace; **hacer las paces** to make up; **dejar en** — to leave alone

PC M PC

peaje M (tasa) toll; (cabina donde se paga) tollbooth

peatón-ona MF pedestrian

peca F freckle

pecado M sin; — **mortal** mortal sin

pecador-ora MF sinner; ADJ sinful

pecaminoso ADJ sinful

pecar[30] VI to sin; — **contra** to transgress against; — **de bueno** to be too good; — **de generoso** to be generous to a fault; — **de oscuro** to be exceedingly unclear

pecera F (pequeña) fish tank, fishbowl; (grande) aquarium

pechera F (de camisa) front; (de delantal) bib

pecho M (parte del cuerpo) chest; (mama) breast; **dar el** — to nurse; **nadar** — to do the

breaststroke; **tomar a —[s]** to take to heart; **sacar —** to puff out one's chest
pechuga F breast
pechugona ADJ buxom
pecio M flotsam and jetsam
pecoso ADJ freckled
pectoral ADJ & M pectoral
peculado M embezzlement
peculiar ADJ peculiar
peculiaridad F peculiarity
pedagogía F pedagogy, education
pedagógico ADJ pedagogical, teaching
pedagogo -ga MF pedagogue
pedal M pedal
pedalear VI/VT to pedal
pedante ADJ pedantic; MF pedant
pedazo M piece; **— de idiota** absolute idiot; **él es un — de pan** he's a saint; **hacer —s** to tear to pieces; **caerse a —s** to fall to pieces; **— por —** piece by piece
pederasta M pederast, pedophile
pedófilo -la MF pedophile
pederastia F pederasty
pedernal M flint
pedestal M pedestal
pedestre ADJ pedestrian
pediatra MF pediatrician
pediatría F pediatrics
pedido M (comercial) order; (petición) request; **hacer un —** to place an order; **— fijo** standing order; **— pendiente** back order; **— urgente** rush order
pedigrí M pedigree
pedigüeño -ña MF mooch, moocher; ADJ **no seas —** stop mooching
pedir[9] VT (requerir) to ask for, to request; (exigir) to demand; (encargar) to order, to requisition; **— limosna** to beg; **— prestado** to borrow; **— socorro** to cry for help; **— un deseo** to make a wish; **— que** to ask/pray that; **— la mano de una mujer** to ask a woman's hand in marriage; **— por alguien** to ask to speak to someone
pedo M fart; **tener/cogerse un —** to be drunk; **tirarse —s** to fart
pedofilia F pedophilia
pedrada F **dar una —** to hit with a stone; **matar a —s** to stone to death
pedregal M rocky ground
pedregoso ADJ stony
pedrería F precious stones
pedrusco M boulder
pedúnculo M stem
pega F snag
pegadizo ADJ catchy
pegado ADJ (adherido) stuck; (contiguo) adjoining, contiguous; **quedarse —** to get an electric shock; **— al televisor** glued to the television

pegajoso ADJ sticky, tacky
pegamento M glue
pegar[40] VT (con el puño) to hit, to strike; (algo con pegamento) to stick, to glue; (botones) to sew on; **— con** to match; **— contra** to touch; **— un cuadrangular** to hit a homerun; **— un grito** to yell; **— un sencillo** to hit a single; **— un susto** to give a scare; **— un salto** to jump; **—le a la bola** to hit the ball; **—le un tiro a alguien** to shoot someone; **—se** (adherir) to stick together, to cling; (contagiarse) to be contagious; **—se a** to latch onto; **no — un ojo** not to sleep a wink
pegote M glob
pegotear VT to gum up
peinado M (estilo) coiffure, hairdo; (acción) combing
peinador -ora MF hairdresser
peinar VT to comb (también registrar); (en una peluquería) to style; **— a contrapelo** to rub the wrong way
peine M comb
pelada F bald spot
pelado ADJ (sin pelo) hairless; (pobre) poor; (sin cáscara) peeled; (sin árboles) treeless; (sin plumas) plucked; (sin dinero) broke
pelador M peeler
pelaje M coat, fur
pelar VT (el pelo) to cut the hair of; (las plumas) to pluck the feathers from; (frutas, verduras, huevo) to peel; (a un jugador) to fleece; **duro de —** hard to deal with; **el agua está que pela** the water is really hot; **—se** to peel; M SG **pelagatos** nobody
peldaño M step, stair
pelea F (de palabra) fight, quarrel; (de obra) fight, scrape; (de boxeo) fight; **— a puñetazos** fistfight; **— de perros** dogfight
pelear VI (con palabras) to fight, to quarrel; (con obras) to fight, to scuffle; **—se con alguien** to have a fight with someone
pelechar VI (perder la piel) to shed; (mejorar) to get better
pelele M (persona sin carácter) wimp; (muñeca) straw doll
peletería F (tienda) fur store; (comercio) fur trade
pelícano M pelican
película F film (también membrana); (obra cinematográfica) motion picture, film, movie; **de —** extraordinary; **dar una —** to show a film; **— muda** silent film
peligrar VI to be in danger
peligro M danger, peril; **ese muchacho es un —** that boy is dangerous; **en —** in danger; **poner en —** to imperil/endanger/jeopardize
peligroso ADJ dangerous, perilous
pellejo M (piel de animal) hide, pelt; (odre) wineskin; **salvar el —** to save one's skin; **ser**

todo — to be skin and bones; **jugarse el** — to risk one's life

pellizcar[30] VT to pinch

pellizco M pinching

pelma MF jerk

pelo M (de persona) hair; (de animal) fur; (de alfombra) pile; **con —s y señales** with every possible detail; **de medio** — low-class; **eso me viene al** — that suits me perfectly; **montar en** — to ride bareback; **ni un** — not at all; **no tener —s en la lengua** not to mince words; **se le ponen los —s de punta** his hair stands on end; **se salvó por un** — he was saved by the skin of his teeth; **tomarle el** — **a alguien** to tease someone, to pull someone's leg; **traído de los —s** far-fetched; ADJ **pelirrojo** redheaded

pelón ADJ bald

pelota F (objeto) ball (también testículo); (juego) ballgame; — **vasca** jai-alai; **en —s** naked; **pasar la** — (dar el balón) to pass the ball; (dar la responsabilidad) to pass the buck

pelotear VI to rally

peloteo M rally

pelotera F brawl

pelotero -ra MF (jugador de béisbol) baseball player; (juego para niños) ball pit

pelotón M (pelota grande) large ball; (de tierra seca) clod; (de ciclistas) pack; (de soldados) platoon; (de fusilamiento) firing squad

peltre M pewter

peluca F wig

peludo ADJ (persona) hairy; (animal) furry; (perro) shaggy

peluquería F (para hombres) barbershop; (para mujeres) salon

peluquero -ra MF (de hombres) barber; (de mujeres) hairdresser

peluquín M toupee

pelusa F (de tela, ropa) lint, fluff; (de melocotón, de la piel) fuzz; (de plantas) hair; (de polvo) dust bunny

pelvis F pelvis

pena F (castigo) penalty; (tristeza) sorrow; (vergüenza) embarrassment; — **de muerte** death penalty, capital punishment; **—s** hardships; **a duras —s** with great difficulty; **me da** — it grieves me; **hecho una** — looking like a mess; **¡qué —!** what a shame! **sería una** — **perder** it would be a shame to lose; **so** — **de** on pain of; **valer la** — to be worthwhile

penacho M (de plumas) tuft, crest; (de humo) plume

penal ADJ penal; M penitentiary

penalidad F (penuria) hardship; (castigo) penalty

penalizar[47] VT to penalize

penalti, penalty M penalty kick

penar VI to suffer; VT to punish

penco M plug, nag

pendejo -ja M (pelo púbico) pubic hair; MF (persona licenciosa) *pey* swine; (persona tonta) *fam* dummy; M (hombre despreciable) *pey* schmuck

pendencia F wrangle, fight

pendenciero ADJ quarrelsome

pender VI to hang, to dangle

pendiente F slope, incline; M *Esp* earring; ADJ (aretes) dangling; (negocio) pending, unfinished; (pago) outstanding; **quedo** — **de tu llamada** I look forward to your call

pendón M banner

péndulo M pendulum

pene M penis

penetración F penetration

penetrante ADJ (mirada, sonido) penetrating, piercing; (frío) biting; (comentario) cutting; (inteligencia) keen

penetrar VT (pasar al interior) to penetrate, to pierce; (comprender) to comprehend

penicilina F penicillin

península F peninsula

peninsular ADJ peninsular

penitencia F (religiosa) penance; (castigo) detention; **¡estás en —!** you're grounded!

penitenciaría F penitentiary

penitente ADJ & MF penitent

penoso ADJ (triste) painful, grievous; (difícil) trying; (que da vergüenza) embarrassing

pensador -ora MF thinker; ADJ reflective

pensamiento M (facultad, acción, efecto) thought; (flor) pansy

pensante ADJ thinking

pensar[1] VI/VT to think; — **en** to think about/ over; — **hacer algo** to intend to do something; **eso da que** — that seems questionable; **no lo pienses dos veces** don't think twice

pensativo ADJ pensive, thoughtful

pensión F (asignación periódica) pension, allowance; (comidas) board; (hostal) boardinghouse; — **completa** room and board; **tener en** — to have as a boarder

pensionado M boarding school

pensionar VT to pension

pensionista MF (que vive en una pensión) boarder; (que cobra una pensión) pensioner

pentágono M pentagon

pentagrama M musical staff

penthouse M penthouse

penúltimo ADJ next to the last, penultimate

penumbra F semi-darkness, dimness

penuria F (escasez) shortage; (pobreza) poverty

peña F boulder; — **folclórica** folklore club

peñasco M crag

peñascoso ADJ craggy

peñón M crag

peón -ona MF (obrero) unskilled laborer, farmhand; — **caminero** road worker; M (en ajedrez) pawn; (en damas) piece
peonada F gang of laborers
peonaje M gang of laborers
peonza F toy top
peor ADJ worse, worst; **este libro es** — this book is worse; **el** — **libro** the worst book; ADV worse; **trabaja** — he works worse; — **que** worse than; — **que nunca** worse than ever; **en el** — **de los casos** if worst comes to worst; **lo** — the worst [thing]; **tanto** — so much the worse
pepa F **es un viva la** — it's bedlam
pepino M cucumber
pepita F (simiente) seed; (tumor de gallina) pip; (masa de oro) nugget
pequeñez F (cualidad de pequeño) smallness; (cosa insignificante) trifle
pequeño -ña ADJ (de poco tamaño) small, little; (de corta edad) young; (de poca importancia) trivial
pera F pear; **pedirle** —**s al olmo** to ask the impossible
peral M pear tree
perca F perch; — **americana** black bass
percal M percale
percance M accident, mishap
percatarse VI (darse cuenta) to realize; (notar) to notice
percebe M barnacle
percepción F perception
perceptible ADJ perceptible, noticeable
perceptivo ADJ perceptive
percha F (para el armario) clothes hanger; (palo para colgar cosas) peg; (palo para aves) perch; (perchero) coat rack
perchero M coat rack
percibir VT (experimentar) to perceive, to sense; (recibir) to collect
percudir VT to make grimy; —**se** to get grimy
percusión F percussion
percutor M firing pin
perdedor -ora MF loser
perder[2] VT (dejar de tener algo, extraviar) to lose, to mislay, to misplace; (echar a perder) to spoil, to ruin; (ser derrotado) to lose; (no aprovechar) to waste; (no llegar a tiempo, no disfrutar) to miss; — **el conocimiento** to lose consciousness; — **el tiempo** to waste time; — **los estribos** to fly off the handle; — **hojas** to shed leaves; — **pie** to lose one's footing; — **terreno** to lose ground; **echarse a** — to spoil; **el vaso pierde agua** the glass leaks water; **llevo las de** — the odds are against me; —**se** (extraviarse) to lose one's way, to get lost; (apartarse del buen camino) to go astray, to stray; **se han perdido las llaves** the keys have gotten lost; —**se de**

vista to disappear; —**[se] una oportunidad** to pass up / miss an opportunity; — **el balón** (fútbol americano) to fumble; (fútbol) to lose the ball
perdición F perdition, damnation
pérdida F (acción de perder, cosa perdida) loss; (de dinero dado en prenda) forfeiture; **entrar en** — to nosedive; — **de tiempo** waste of time; — **de balón** (fútbol americano) fumble, turnover; (fútbol) loss of ball possession; —**s cubiertas** covered losses; —**s totales** total loss
perdido -da ADJ (extraviado) lost, missing; (aislado) isolated; (promiscuo) promiscuous; **un borracho** — an utter drunkard; **estar** — **por alguien** to be crazy about someone; M degenerate; F **pey** slut
perdigón M (pollo de perdiz) young partridge; (bolita de plomo) birdshot, buckshot
perdiz F partridge
perdón M (privado) forgiveness; (oficial) pardon; **con** — **de los presentes** present company excepted; **no tener** — to be unforgivable; INTERJ excuse me
perdonar VT (en privado) to forgive; (oficialmente) to pardon
perdurable ADJ lasting
perdurar VI to last
perecedero ADJ perishable
perecer[35] VI to perish
peregrinación F pilgrimage
peregrinar VI to go on a pilgrimage
peregrino -na MF pilgrim; ADJ far-fetched
perejil M parsley
perenne ADJ perennial
pereza F laziness, idleness, sloth
perezoso ADJ lazy, idle; M (animal) sloth
perfección F perfection; **a la** — to perfection, perfectly
perfeccionamiento M perfecting
perfeccionar VT to perfect
perfeccionista MF perfectionist
perfectamente ADV perfectly; **tú hablas español** — you speak Spanish quite well
perfecto ADJ perfect, flawless; **es un** — **tarado** he's an utter idiot; **es un** — **desconocido** he's a complete stranger
perfil M profile; **de** — from the side
perfilar VT to outline; —**se** (marcarse) to be outlined; (definirse) to become clear
perforación F (de una superficie) perforation; (de un pozo) drilling; (de la piel) piercing
perforar VT (agujerear) to perforate; (buscar petróleo) to drill
perfumar VT to perfume, to scent
perfume M perfume, scent
perfumería F perfumery
pergamino M parchment
pérgola F arbor

pericia F expertness, know-how
perico M (loro) parakeet; (cocaína) *fam* snow
periferia F periphery, fringe
periférico ADJ & M peripheral
perilla F (adorno, remate) knob; (pelo de barbilla) goatee; **me viene de —s** it's exactly what I need
perímetro M perimeter
periódico M newspaper; — **mensual** monthly periodical; ADJ periodic
periodismo M journalism
periodista MF journalist
periodístico ADJ journalistic
período M period (también menstruación); (de materia radiactiva) half-life; — **de prueba** (para un trabajo) probationary period; (para una mercancía) trial period; — **glaciar** ice age
peripecia F vicissitude
peripuesto ADJ dressed up, dolled up, decked out
periquito M parakeet
periscopio M periscope
perista MF fence
perito -ta ADJ expert, practiced; MF technician
peritonitis F peritonitis
perjudicar[30] VT to harm
perjudicial ADJ harmful, detrimental
perjuicio M harm
perjurar VT to swear; VI to commit perjury; **—se** to commit perjury
perjurio M perjury
perla F (de nácar) pearl; (persona) gem; (de sudor) head; (de sabiduría) nugget; (frase inoportuna) blooper; **me viene de —s** it suits me perfectly
perlado ADJ pearly
permanecer[35] VI to remain, to stay
permanencia F (carácter de permanente) permanence; (acción de permanecer) stay
permanente ADJ permanent
permanezca, permanezco *ver* permanecer
permeable ADJ permeable
permear VT to permeate
permisible ADJ permissible
permisivo ADJ permissive
permiso M (para ir al baño) permission; (para faltar al servicio militar) furlough; (para faltar al trabajo) leave; (para casarse, conducir) license, permit; — **de trabajo** work permit; **con** — excuse me
permitir VT (dar permiso) to permit, to allow; (posibilitar) to enable; **—se** (una libertad) to take the liberty of; (un lujo) to allow oneself; **¿me permite?** may I?
permuta F exchange
permutación F permutation
permutar VT to exchange
pernetas LOC ADV **en** — barelegged

pernicioso ADJ pernicious
pernicorto ADJ short-legged
perno M bolt, pin
pero CONJ but; ADV **muy** — **muy lindo** very, very pretty; M objection; **no hay** — **que valga** there are no buts about it
perogrullada F platitude
perorar VI to hold forth
perorata F lecture
peróxido M peroxide
perpendicular ADJ perpendicular
perpetrar VT to perpetrate
perpetuar[26] VT to perpetuate
perpetuo ADJ perpetual
perplejidad F perplexity, bewilderment
perplejo ADJ perplexed, bewildered; VT **dejar** — to perplex
perrera F (lugar donde guardar perros) pound; (rabieta) tantrum
perrero -ra MF dogcatcher; ADJ dog-loving
perro M dog; — **caliente** hot dog; — **callejero** stray dog; — **cobrador** retriever; — **de caza** hunting dog; — **de lanas** poodle; — **esquimal** husky; — **faldero** lapdog; — **guía** guide dog; — **guardián** watchdog, guard dog; — **pastor** sheepdog; — **policía** police dog; **hijo de perra** *vulg* son of a bitch; ADJ miserable; **en la perra vida** never
perruno ADJ canine
persa ADJ & MF Persian; M (lengua) Persian
persecución F (religiosa) persecution; (policial) pursuit, chase
perseguidor -ora MF (que sigue) pursuer; (que acosa) persecutor
perseguir[12] VT (seguir para alcanzar) to pursue, to chase; (seguir para encontrar) to track down; (acosar) to hound; (tratar de destruir) to persecute
perseverancia F perseverance
perseverar VI to persevere
Persia F Persia
persiana F blind, shade
persiga, persigo, persigue, persiguiendo, persiguiera, persiguiese *ver* perseguir
persistencia F persistence
persistente ADJ persistent
persistir VI to persist
persona F person; — **influyente** player; — **legal** legal entity; **en** — in person; — **mayor** adult
personaje M (persona importante) personage; (de obra literaria) character; **es todo un** — he's quite a character
personal ADJ personal; M personnel, staff
personalidad F personality
personalmente ADV personally
personificar[30] VT to personify, to embody
perspectiva F (punto de vista, distancia, técnica de dibujo) perspective; (panorama) view,

vista; (posibilidad) prospect; **tener en —** to have planned
perspicacia F insight, sharpness
perspicaz ADJ perspicacious, perceptive
persuadir VT to persuade
persuasión F persuasion
persuasivo ADJ persuasive
pertenecer[35] VI to belong
perteneciente ADJ belonging
pertenencias F PL belongings
pertenezca, pertenezco *ver* pertenecer
pértiga F pole
pertinente ADJ pertinent, relevant
pertrechos M PL military supplies
perturbación F disturbance
perturbar VT to perturb, to disturb
Perú M Peru
peruano -na ADJ & MF Peruvian
perversidad F (distorsión) perversity; (maldad) wickedness
perversión F perversion
perverso ADJ (distorsionante) perverse; (malvado) wicked
pervertido -da MF pervert
pervertir[8] VT (enviciar) to pervert; (distorsionar) to distort; **—se** to become perverted
pesa F (para pesar) weight; (para hacer ejercicio) dumbbell; **—s y medidas** weights and measures
pesadez F (cualidad de pesado) heaviness; (tedio) tiresomeness; (persona pesada) tiresome person
pesadilla F nightmare
pesado -da ADJ (que pesa mucho, difícil de digerir) heavy; (aburrido) tiresome; (robusto) heavy-set; (tardo) slow; MF bore, pest
pesadumbre F grief, sorrow
pésame M condolence, expression of sympathy
pesar VT (apenar) to sadden; (medir el peso de) to weigh; (recaer sobre) to weight down; VI (tener peso, importancia) to weigh; M grief, sorrow; LOC ADV **a — de** in spite of
pesaroso ADJ (triste) sad; (arrepentido) repentant
pesca F (acción de pescar) fishing; (lo pescado) catch; **ir de —** to go fishing
pescadería F fish market
pescado M fish
pescador -ora MF fisherman
pescar[30] VI/VT (capturar peces) to fish; (sacar del agua, coger, comprender, sorprender, pillar) to catch; (obtener) to land, to nail
pescozón M blow to the back of the head
pescuezo M neck
pesebre M (para pienso) manger, crib; (belén) nativity scene
peseta F peseta
pesimismo M pessimism

pesimista MF pessimist
pésimo ADJ dismal, wretched
peso M (fuerza, importancia) weight; (cosa opresiva) burden; (cosa pesada) load; **vender al —** to sell by weight; **levantar en —** to lift off the ground
pesquería F fishery
pesquero ADJ fishing; M fishing boat
pesquisa F inquiry
pestaña F (del ojo) eyelash; (en costura) fringe; (de papel, texto) tab; **quemarse las —s** to burn the midnight oil
pestañear VI to blink; **sin —** unflinchingly
pestañeo M blink
peste F (enfermedad) plague; (persona molesta) pest; (hedor) stench; **— bubónica** bubonic plague; **— negra** black death; **hablar —s de alguien** to speak badly of someone
pestilencia F pestilence
pestillo M deadbolt, latch
petaca F (para tabaco) tobacco pouch; (para whisky) flask
pétalo M petal
petardear VI to backfire
petardeo M backfire
petate M bundle; **liar el —** to pack up and go
petición F petition, request
peticionar VT to petition
petirrojo M robin
pétreo ADJ stony
petróleo M petroleum, oil; **— crudo** crude oil
petrolero -ra ADJ oil, petroleum; **plataforma —** oil rig; M oil tanker; F oil company
petrolífero ADJ (que contiene petróleo) oil-bearing; (que produce petróleo) oil-producing; (relativo al petróleo) oil
petulancia F smugness
petulante ADJ smug
petunia F petunia
peyorativo ADJ pejorative
peyote M peyote
pez M fish; **— dorado** goldfish; **— espada** swordfish; **— gordo** *fam* fat cat, big shot; **— vela** sailfish; **— volador** flying fish; **como — en el agua** perfectly at ease; F pitch
pezón M nipple
pezuña F hoof
phishing M phishing
piadoso ADJ pious, saintly
piafar VI to stamp
pianista MF pianist, piano player
piano M piano; **— de cola** grand piano; **— vertical** upright piano
pianola F player piano
piar[28] VI to peep, to chirp
pica F (lanza) pike; (palo de baraja) spade
picada F (de insecto) bite; (de avión) nosedive; **caer en —** to dive
picadillo M meat [and vegetable] hash

picado ADJ (mar) rough, choppy; (carne) chopped; (de viruela) poked; M (de avión) nosedive; **caer en** — to dive

picador M picador; ADJ stinging

picadora F grinder; **— de carne** meat grinder

picadura F (de serpiente) bite; (de insecto) sting, bite

picante ADJ (especia) spicy, hot; (queso) sharp; (obsceno) risqué; M (especia fuerte) strong seasoning; (cualidad) spiciness

picar³⁰ VI/VT (un pez) to bite; (un ave) to peck; (comer en pequeñas cantidades) to nibble; VT (tomates) to chop up; (carne) to mince; (una vaca) to goad, to poke; (la curiosidad) to pique; (con espuelas) to spur; VI (una comida picante) to sting; (el sol) to burn; (la piel) to itch, to smart; (un avión) to dive; **— alto** to aim high; **—se** to spoil; **—se heroína** to shoot up heroin; **se pica el mar** the sea is getting rough; **se me picó un diente** I got a cavity; M SG **picapleitos** *pey* shyster; M **picaporte** latch

picardía F mischief

picaresco ADJ picaresque

pícaro -ra MF rogue, rascal; ADJ roguish, mischievous

picazón F (en la piel) itch; (en la garganta) tickle; **provoca** — it causes itching

picea F spruce

pichi M jumper

pichón M (paloma) pigeon; (cría de ave) chick

picnic M picnic

pico M (de ave) beak, bill; (de montaña) peak; (herramienta) pick; (de tetera) spout; **cuarenta y** — forty-odd; **cerrar el** — to shut one's mouth; **tener el** — **de oro** to be very eloquent

pícolo M piccolo

picotazo M peck

picotear VI/VT (aves) to peck; (personas) to nibble

pictórico ADJ pictorial

pida, pide, pidiendo, pidiera, pidiese *ver* pedir

pídola F leapfrog

pie M (del cuerpo, de calcetín, de cama, medida) foot; (de foto) caption; (de copa) stem; (de lámpara) stand; (de página) bottom; (para un actor) cue; (de árbol) trunk; (de mueble) leg; **— de atleta** athlete's foot; **— de autor** byline; **— de imprenta** printer's mark; **— zambo** clubfoot; **a** — on foot; **un soldado de a** — a footsoldier; **— de banco** silly remark; **a** — **juntillas** firmly; **al** — **de la letra** to the letter; **caer de** — to have good luck; **con un** — **en el estribo** with one foot out of the door; **dar** — (a una crítica) to give rise to; (a un actor) to cue; **de/en** — standing; **en** — **de guerra** (enojado) on the warpath;

(belicoso) on a war footing; **estar de** — to be standing; **estar en** — **de igualdad con** to be on a par with; **esto no tiene ni** —**s ni cabeza** I can't make heads or tails of this; **ir a** — to walk; **perder** — to lose one's footing; **ponerse de** — to stand up

piedad F (cualidad de pío) piety; (misericordia) mercy; **tener** — to show mercy

piedra F stone; **— angular** cornerstone, keystone; **— caliza** limestone; **— de afilar** whetstone; **— de toque** touchstone; **— pómez** pumice; **— preciosa** gemstone; **ser — de escándalo** to be an object of scandal

piel F (humana) skin; (animal) hide, pelt; (para confección) fur; **— de gallina** goosebumps; **— de naranja** cellulite

piensa, piense *ver* pensar

pienso M feed; **ni por** — no way

pierda, pierde *ver* perder

pierna F leg; **— de ternera** leg of lamb; **dormir a** — **suelta** to sleep like a log

pieza F (de artillería, de tela, de música, de teatro) piece; (habitación) room; **— de repuesto** replacement part; **de una** — astonished; **menuda** — a piece of work

pífano M fife

pifia F goof, miscue

pifiar VT to goof up, to miscue

pigmento M pigment

pigmeo -a MF pygmy

pija F *Mex vulg* cock, dick

pijama M pajamas

pila F (recipiente) basin; (bautismal) baptismal font; (cúmulo) pile, heap, stack; (generador) battery; **— atómica** atomic reactor

pilar M pillar

píldora F pill; **—s para dormir** sleeping pills

pillaje M pillage, plunder

pillar VT (saquear) to pillage, to plunder; (atrapar, coger) to catch; (en un juego infantil) to tag

pillo -lla ADJ (travieso) naughty; (taimado) sly; MF (adulto) scoundrel; (niño) scamp

pilluelo -la MF urchin

pilón M (fuente) large basin; (soporte) pylon

pilotar, pilotear VT to pilot, to fly

pilote M pile, stilt

piloto MF (conductor) pilot; (llama pequeña de gas) pilot light; **— automático** autopilot; **— de pruebas** test pilot

pimentar VT to pepper

pimentero M pepper shaker

pimentón M paprika

pimienta F pepper; **— blanca** white pepper; **— de cayena** red pepper; **— negra** black pepper

pimiento M pepper, bell pepper; **— verde** green pepper

pimpollo M (de rosa) rosebud; (de vid) shoot

PIN M PIN
pináculo M pinnacle
pinar M pine grove
pincel M artist's brush
pincelada F stroke; **dar las últimas —s** to put on the final touches
pinchadura F flat tire
pinchar VT (perforar) to prick, to puncture; (apuñalar) to poke; (inyectar) to inject; (intervenir un teléfono) to wiretap; (provocar) to needle; VI to have a flat; **ni corta ni pincha** he doesn't count; M SG **pinchadiscos** disk jockey, DJ
pinchazo M (acción de pinchar) puncture, prick; (neumático) flat tire; (puñalada) stab; (de teléfono) wiretap
pinche ADJ *Méx vulg* fucking
pincho M (palo afilado) spike; (de rotisería) spit
pingajo M (harapo) tatter; (harapiento) person dressed in rags
ping-pong M ping-pong
pingüe ADJ abundant
pingüino M penguin
pino M (árbol) pine; (ejercicio) handstand; **en el quinto —** in the boondocks
pinta F (mancha) dot; (aspecto) looks; (medida de líquidos) pint
pintada F grafitti
pintado ADJ (animales, plantas) colorful; **ese traje te queda —** you look great in that suit
pintar VT (colorear) to paint; (describir) to depict; **este marcador no pinta** this marker won't write; **no — nada** to count for nothing; **las cosas no pintaban bien** things did not look well; **—se** to put on makeup
pintarrajear VT to daub, to smear with paint; **—se** to put on too much makeup
pinto ADJ paint, dapple[d]
pintor -ora MF painter; **— de brocha gorda** house painter
pintoresco ADJ picturesque, colorful
pintorrear VT to smear with paint
pintura F (acción de pintar, obra) painting; (sustancia) paint; **— al óleo** oil painting; **— en aerosol** spray paint; **— fresca** wet paint
pinza F (de cangrejo) claw; (de médico) clamp; (de vestido) dart; (instrumento) clothespin; **—s** tweezers
piña F (fruto del pino) pinecone; (ananás) pineapple; (bomba) hand grenade
piñata F piñata
piñón M (semilla del pino) pine nut; (rueda del engranaje) pinion; (de bicicleta) sprocket
pío ADJ pious; INTERJ peep; **ni —** not a word
piojo M louse; **como —s en costura** like sardines
piojoso ADJ lousy
pionero -ra MF pioneer

pipa F (para fumar) pipe; (semilla) sunflower seed; **pasarlo —** to have a great time
pipí M pee; **hacer —** *fam* to pee
pipiolo -la MF novice
pique M (rivalidad) rivalry; (desavenencia) falling-out; **echar a —** to sink; **irse a —** to capsize
piquete M picket (también de huelga)
piquetear M to picket
piragua F dugout canoe
pirámide F pyramid
pirata MF pirate; **— informático -ca** hacker
piratear VT to pirate
piratería F piracy
piromanía F pyromania
pirómano -na MF pyromaniac
piropo M compliment
pirotecnia F pyrotechnics
pirulí M sucker, lollipop
pisada F (paso) footstep; (huella) footprint; **seguir las —s de** to follow in the footsteps of
pisar VT (oprimir con el pie) to step on, to tread on; (apisonar) to mash; **jamás pisó una plaza de toros** he never set foot in a bullring; **ir pisando huevos** to walk on eggshells; VI to step on; **— fuerte** to throw one's weight around; M SG **pisapapeles** paperweight
piscifactoría F fishery, fish farm
piscina F swimming pool
piso M (suelo) floor; (planta) story; (vivienda) apartment; **de — a techo** from the ground up
pisotear VT to tramp on, to trample, to stomp on
pisotón M stamp; **dar un —** to stamp, to step on
pista F (rastro) track, scent; (noticia) clue; (de aterrizaje) runway; (de circo) arena, ring; (de patinaje) skating ring; (de tenis) court; (de baile) floor; (de carreras) track, racetrack; **seguir la —** to track; **— para bicicletas** bike lane
pistola F (revólver) pistol; (para pintura) gun
pistolera F holster
pistolero MF gunner; M gunman; F gun woman
pistón M (válvula) piston; (explosivo) cap
pitada F drag, puff
pitar VI to toot, to whistle; VI/VT (rechiflar) to boo
pitazo M honk
pitido M (silbido) whistle, toot; (en deportes) whistle
pitillo M cigarette
pito M (silbato) whistle; (pene) *fam* dick; **no vale un —** *fam* it is not worth a damn; **entre —s y flautas** when all is said and done; **¿qué —s toca?** what's his role here?
pitón M (serpiente) python; (punta de cuerno)

tip of a bull's horn

pituitario ADJ pituitary

pivot MF *Am* (baloncesto) center

pivotar VI to pivot

pivote M pivot; — **central** kingpin

píxel M pixel

pizarra F (roca) slate; (pizarrón) blackboard, chalkboard

pizarrón M blackboard, chalkboard

pizca F (de sal) pinch, dash; (de evidencia) shred; (de verdad) grain; (de suciedad) speck; **no entiendo ni —** I don't understand a bit/jot

pizza F pizza

placa F (fotográfica) plate; (de policía) badge; (condecoración, sarro) plaque; (de coche) license plate; (de computadora/ordenador) board, card; — **lógica** logic board; — **madre** motherboard

placaje M tackle

placar³⁰ VI/VT to tackle

placebo M placebo

placenta F placenta, afterbirth

placentero ADJ pleasant

placer³⁶ M pleasure, enjoyment; VT *lit* to please

plácido ADJ placid

plaf INTERJ plop

plaga F (enfermedad) plague; (persona, insecto) pest

plagar⁴⁰ VT to infest; **—se de** to become infested with

plagio M plagiarism

plan M (proyecto) plan; (ligue) pickup; — **de estudios** curriculum; — **de juego** game plan; — **de salud administrado** managed care; **se vistió en — de vampiresa** she was dressed to kill

plana F newspaper page; — **mayor** top brass; **enmendar la — a uno** to correct a person's mistakes

plancha F (electrodoméstico) iron; (lámina) metal plate; (parrilla) griddle; **hacer la —** to float; **tirarse una —** to fall flat on one's face

planchado M ironing

planchar VT to iron, to press; **me dejó planchado** it left me speechless

plancton M plankton

planeador M glider

planeamiento M planning

planear VI/VT to plan; VI (volar) to glide, to plane; VT (madera) to plane

planeo M gliding

planeta M planet

planetario M planetarium

planificación F organization, planning; — **familiar** family planning; — **para contingencias** contingency planning

planificador M planner, scheduler; — **de rutas** trip planner

planificar³⁰ VI/VT to plan

planilla F (de sueldos) payroll; (digital) worksheet; *Am* — **de cálculo** spreadsheet

plano ADJ flat, even; M (superficie) plane; (de un edificio) plan; (de calles) map; — **inclinado** inclined plane; **caer de —** to fall flat; **de —** flatly; **primer —** foreground

planta F (vegetal) plant; (del pie) sole; — **baja** ground floor

plantación F plantation

plantar VT (una planta, cruz) to plant; (a un novio) to dump; (a un colega) to make wait; **—se** to stand firm, to refuse to move; — **una bofetada a alguien** to give someone a slap; **dejar plantado** to stand up

planteamiento M (enfoque) approach; (exposición) presentation; **es un — poco provechoso** it is not a very beneficial approach

plantear VT (presentar) to present; **me planteó sus planes** she explained her plans to me; (provocar) to give rise to; **eso plantea un problema** that gives rise to a problem; **—se** to occur to; **¿te has planteado lo que pasa si te quedas sin trabajo?** have you thought about what will happen if you become unemployed?

plantel M (personal) staff; (almáciga) nursery

plantilla F (pieza suelta) insole; (patrón para calcar) pattern, stencil; (digital) template

plantío M grove

plasma M plasma (también de pantalla)

plasmar VT (captar) to capture; (dar forma plástica o sensible) to mold, to shape; **—se** to materialize

plasta ADJ tiresome; F (cosa informe) lump; (persona) bore

plástico ADJ & M plastic

plata F (metal, color, objeto de plata) silver; *Am* (dinero) money; **hablar en —** to speak in plain language

plataforma F platform (también política y digital); — **de lanzamiento** launching pad; — **petrolífera** oil rig; — **continental** continental shelf

platanar M banana grove

plátano M (fruta) banana; (para cocinar) plantain; (bananero) banana tree; (árbol ornamental) plane tree

platea F main floor of a theater

plateado ADJ & M (color) silver; M (acción de platear) silver-plating

platear VT to silver-plate

platero -ra MF silversmith

plática F chat

platicar³⁰ VI to chat

platija F flounder

platillo M (plato pequeño) saucer; (instrumento musical) cymbal; — **volador** flying saucer

platino M platinum

plato M (recipiente) plate; (comida) dish; (béisbol) home plate; — **fuerte** main dish/course; — **hondo** bowl; — **sopero** soup dish

plausible ADJ plausible

playa F beach

playboy M playboy

plaza F (espacio amplio) plaza, public square; (puesto de trabajo) job; **de cuatro —s** four-seater; — **de toros** bullring; — **mayor** main square

plazo M term; **a corto —** short-term; **a largo —** long-term, long-range; **a — fijo** fixed-term; **a —s** on credit; **cumplir un —** to meet a deadline

plazoleta F court

plazuela F court

pleamar M high tide

plebe F rabble

plebeyo -ya ADJ & MF plebeian

plegable ADJ folding

plegadera F paper folder

plegadizo ADJ folding

plegar⁴¹ VT to fold; —**se [a]** (ceder) to yield [to]; (unirse) to join

pleitesía F compliance

pleito M (pelea) dispute; (demanda judicial) litigation, lawsuit; **poner —** to sue

plenamente ADV fully

plenario ADJ & M plenary

plenitud F — **de la vida** prime of life

pleno ADJ complete; **en — día** in broad daylight; **en — invierno** in the dead of winter; **en — rostro** right on the face; **en — verano** in midsummer; **en plena vista** in plain sight; M full session

pliego M leaflet

pliegue M (en papel) fold; (en tela) pleat

plomada F plumb

plomería F plumbing

plomero -ra MF plumber

plomizo ADJ leaden

plomo M (metal, color) lead; (pesa) lead weight; (perdigón) shot; **a —** plumb; **caer a —** to fall vertically; **sin —** unleaded; ADJ INV tiresome

pluma F (de ave) feather, quill; (para escribir) pen; — **fuente** fountain pen

plumaje M plumage

plumero M dust mop, duster

plumífero ADJ feathery

plumón M down

plural ADJ & M plural

pluralidad F plurality

pluriempleo M moonlighting

pluscuamperfecto ADJ & N pluperfect

plutonio M plutonium

pluvial ADJ **aguas —es** rainwater

pluviómetro M rain gauge

PNB [producto nacional bruto] M GNP

población F (conjunto de personas) population; (acción de poblar) settlement; (pueblo) town

poblado M hamlet

poblador -ora MF settler

poblar⁵ VT (habitar) to populate; (colonizar) to settle; —**se de** to become covered with

pobre ADJ poor; MF **los —s** the poor

pobrecito -ta MF poor thing

pobreza F (miseria) poverty; (escasez) scarcity

pocilga F pigsty, pigpen

pocillo M cup

poción F potion

poco ADJ (no mucho) little; **poca paciencia** little patience; **al — rato** after a little while; (no muchos) few; —**s pasajeros** few passengers; **al — tiempo** shortly; **a los —s meses** after a few months; **de pocas luces** stupid; **en pocas palabras** in a nutshell; ADV little; **trabaja —** he works little; — **caritativo** not very charitable; — **conocido** little known; — **a** — little by little; — **más o menos** about; **hace —** a short while ago; **por — me caigo** I almost fell; **tener en —** to hold in low esteem; PRON a little, a bit; **un —** a little bit, a little while; **como —** at least; **unos —s** a few

poda F trim

podadera F pruning hook

podar VT to prune, to trim

poder⁶⁹ VI to be able to; **no puedo llegar antes de las cinco** I can't get there before five; **¿puedo sentarme?** may I be seated? **puede que venga** she may come; **a más no —** to the utmost; **no puedo más** I can't go on; **nadie puede con ella** nobody can deal with her; **no puede menos que venir** he can't help but come; **no puede menos que hacerlo** he cannot help doing it; M (fuerza) power; (escrito que da autoridad) proxy, power of attorney; — **ejecutivo** executive branch; — **judicial** judiciary branch; — **legislativo** legislative branch; **por —** by proxy

poderío M power, might

poderoso ADJ powerful, mighty

podiatra MF podiatrist

podiatría F podiatry

podio M podium

podólogo -ga MF podiatrist

podrá, podría ver poder

podredumbre F rot

podrido ADJ rotten

podrir ver pudrir

poema M poem

poesía F (género lírico) poetry; (poema) poem

poeta MF, **poetisa** F poet

poética F poetics

poético ADJ poetic

polaco -ca ADJ Polish; M (lengua) Polish; MF Pole

polaina F legging
polar ADJ polar
polaridad F polarity
polarización F polarization
polca F polka
polea F pulley
polémica F polemic, controversy
polémico ADJ polemic
polen M pollen
poli MF cop; F *fam* cops
policía F (en conjunto) police; (mujer) policewoman; M policeman; MF police officer
policíaco ADJ police
policial ADJ police; **parte —** police report
poliéster M polyester
poliestireno M Styrofoam™
poligamia F polygamy
políglota ADJ & MF polyglot
polígrafo M polygraph
poliinsaturado ADJ polyunsaturated
polilla F moth
polímero M polymer
polinizar[47] VT to pollinate
polio F polio
pólipo M polyp
política F (actividad relativa al gobierno) politics; (conjunto de orientaciones) policy; **— exterior** foreign policy
político -ca ADJ (relativo a la política) political; (diplomático) politic; MF politician
poliuretano M polyurethane
póliza F policy; **— de seguros** insurance policy
polizón -ona MF stowaway
polizonte M *pey* cop
polla F (cría de ave) pullet; (pene) *vulg* cock, dick; **¡y una —!** *vulg* bullshit!
pollada F brood
pollera F (mujer) woman who raises and sells chickens; (falda) *Am* skirt
pollo M (cría de ave) young chicken; (carne) chicken
polo M (punto geográfico) pole; (juego) polo; **— acuático** water polo; **— de atención** focus of attention; **— Norte** North Pole
Polonia F Poland
poltrona F easy chair
polvareda F cloud of dust; **levantar una —** (causar escándalo) to raise a ruckus; (causar una nube de polvo) to kick up the dust
polvera F compact
polvo M (suciedad) dust; (partículas) powder; **— de hornear** baking powder; **echarse un —** *fam* to get laid; **juntar —** to gather dust; **limpio de — y paja** net
pólvora F gunpowder
polvoriento ADJ dusty
polvorín M (almacén de pólvora) magazine; (situación explosiva) powder keg
pomada F salve

pomelo M grapefruit
pómez F pumice
pomo M doorknob
pompa F (boato) pomp; (burbuja) soap bubble; **—s fúnebres** funeral ceremony
pomposo ADJ pompous
pómulo M cheekbone
pon *ver* poner
ponchado M (béisbol) strikeout
ponchar VT (un neumático) to puncture; **— a alguien** (en béisbol) to strike someone out; **—se** (un neumático) to become punctured; (en béisbol) to strike out
ponche M (bebida) punch; (en béisbol) strikeout
ponchera F punch bowl
poncho M poncho
ponderación F (acción de ponderar) pondering; (valor relativo) weighting
ponderar VT (considerar) to ponder, to consider; (exagerar) to exaggerate; (ajustar valores) to weight
pondrá, pondría *ver* poner
ponencia F presentation
poner[56, 74] VT to put, to place; (la mesa, un reloj) to set; (huevos) to lay; (azúcar) to add; (un examen) to give; (el televisor) to turn on; (un pleito) to file; **— a alguien a hacer algo** to assign someone to do something; **— en claro** to clarify; **— en limpio** to recopy, to make a clean copy; **— nombre a un niño** to name a child; **— sangre** to give a transfusion; **cada uno pone mil pesetas** each person contributes a thousand pesetas; **pongamos que** let us suppose that; **¿qué pone ahí?** what does it say there? **—se** (volverse) to become; (el sol) to set; (ropa) to put on; (sexualmente) to get turned on; **—se a** to begin to; **—se al corriente** to become informed; **—se de acuerdo** to come to an agreement; **—se de pie** to stand up; **—se por delante en el marcador** (deporte) to take the lead
póney M pony
ponga, pongo *ver* poner
poniente M (oeste) west; (viento del oeste) west wind
pontón M pontoon
ponzoña F poison
ponzoñoso ADJ poisonous
pool M pool
popa F poop, stern
populacho M mob
popular ADJ (conocido y citado) popular; (del pueblo) folk
popularidad F popularity
populoso ADJ populous
popurrí M (de perfume) potpourri; (musical) medley
poquito *ver* poco

por PREP — **barco** by boat; — **casualidad** by chance; — **Dios** by God; — **etapas** by stages; — **las buenas** o — **las malas** by hook or by crook; — **litro** by the liter; ¿— **qué?** why? for what reason? **multiplicar** — to multiply by; **lo agarró** — **la garganta** he grabbed him by the throat; **mi amor** — **ella** my love for her; — **poco tiempo** for a short time; — **primera vez** for the first time; — **vía de argumento** for the sake of argument; — **ejemplo** for instance; — **el momento** for the time being; **hazlo** — **mí** do it for my sake; **trabaja** — **mí** work on my behalf; **no me gustan** — **su olor** I don't like them because of their smell; **lo supe** — **él** I found out through him; **pasé** — **Londres** I passed through London; **un viaje** — **la costa** a trip along the coast; — **lo que cuentas** from what you're telling me; — **adelantado** in advance; — **escrito** in writing; — **la mañana** in the morning; — **lo general** in general; — **rachas** in spurts; **está** — **Badajoz** it's near Badajoz; — **fin** at last; — **el mes de marzo** around the month of March; — **ciento** percent; — **consiguiente** consequently; — **escrito** in writing; — **poco se muere** he almost died; **está** — **hacer** it is yet to be done; **él está** — **hacerlo** (a favor de) he is in favor of doing it; (a punto de) he is about to do it; **recibir** — **esposa** to take as a wife; **tener** — to consider, to think of as

porcelana F porcelain, china
porcentaje M percentage; — **de bateo** (béisbol) batting average
porche M porch, stoop
porcino ADJ **ganado** — swine; M pig
porción F (parte) portion, share; (de alimento) helping
pordiosear VT to panhandle
pordiosero -ra MF panhandler
porfía F obstinacy
porfiado ADJ willful
porfiar[28] VT to insist
pormenor M detail
pormenorizar[47] VT to detail, to go into detail about
porno M porn
pornografía F pornography
pornográfico ADJ pornographic
poro M pore
poroso ADJ porous
poroto M *Am* bean
porque CONJ because
porqué M reason; **el** — **de su tristeza** the reason for his sadness
porquería F (suciedad) filth; (acción despreciable) dirty trick; (cosa de mala calidad) crud; (comida de mala calidad) junk food; (persona despreciable) *pey* douchebag,

dirtbag
porra F club, cudgel
porrista MF cheerleader
porro M joint
portada F (de un libro) title page; (de una revista) front cover
portador -ora MF (de enfermedad) carrier; (de cheque) bearer; — **del féretro** pallbearer
portal M portal, doorway; — **de videos/vídeos** video portal
portar VT to carry; —**se** to behave; —**se mal** to misbehave; M SG **portaaviones** aircraft carrier; M SG **portaequipajes** luggage bin; M **portaestandarte** standard-bearer; M **portafolio** briefcase; M SG **portalámparas** socket; M SG **portaligas** garter belt; M SG **portamonedas** coin purse; M **portaobjeto** slide; M SG **portapapeles** clipboard; MF **portavoz** spokesperson
portátil ADJ portable
portazo M slam; **dar un** — to slam the door
porte M (envío) freight; (por correo) postage; (aspecto) bearing, carriage; (capacidad de carga) capacity; (tamaño) size; — **de armas** the carrying of arms; **enviar** — **pagado** to send prepaid
portear VT to carry
portentoso ADJ portentous
porteño -ña MF (de Buenos Aires) person from Buenos Aires; (de un puerto) person from a port city; ADJ (de Buenos Aires) from Buenos Aires; (de un puerto) from a port city
portería F (de un edificio) entrance area; (en fútbol) goal
portero -ra MF (de un edificio) doorkeeper, superintendent; (en fútbol) goalkeeper; M — **automático** intercom
portón M gate
portuario ADJ harbor, port; **trabajador** — dockworker
Portugal M Portugal
portugués -esa ADJ & MF Portuguese; M (lengua) Portuguese
porvenir M future
pos LOC PREP **en** — **de** after
posada F inn, lodge
posaderas F PL *fam* rear end
posadero -ra MF innkeeper
posar VT (la mano, los ojos) to rest; VI (en el suelo) to sit down; (como modelo) to pose; —**se** (partículas) to settle; (mariposa) to alight; (pájaro) to perch
posdata F postscript
pose F pose
poseedor -ora MF possessor
poseer[18] VT to possess
poseído ADJ possessed
posesión F possession
posesivo ADJ & M possessive

poseyendo, poseyera, poseyese, poseyó *ver* poseer

posfechar VT to postdate

posguerra F postwar period

posibilidad F possibility

posibilitar VT (hacer posible) to make possible; (permitir) to allow, to permit

posible ADJ possible; **hacer lo** — to do one's best; **es** — it's possible

posición F (ubicación) position; (opinión) stance; (rango) standing; — **de negociación** bargaining position; — **del misionero** missionary position; — **fetal** fetal position

posicionamiento M (acción de posicionar, también de productos) placement, positioning; (actitud política) position, stance

posicionarse VI to position oneself

positivo ADJ & M positive

poso M (de vino) dregs; (de café) grounds

posparto M postpartum

posponer^{56, 74} VT (aplazar) to postpone, to defer, to put off; (relegar) to put after

posta F (relevo) relay; (perdigón) buckshot

postal ADJ postal; F postcard

poste M (palo) post; (en fútbol) upright, goalpost

póster M poster

postergar^{40} VT (para un ascenso) to pass over; (posponer) to postpone

posteridad F posterity; **eso quedará para la** — that will remain for all eternity

posterior ADJ (espacial) back, rear; (anatómico) posterior; (temporal) later; **nuestro divorcio fue** — **a la compra del negocio** our divorce came after we purchased the business

posterioridad LOC ADV **con** — later, subsequently

posteriormente ADV (atrás) in the back; (después) afterward[s]; **vocal pronunciada** — vowel pronounced in the back [of the mouth]

postigo M shutter

postizo ADJ false; **familia postiza** adoptive family; M hairpiece

postnasal ADJ postnasal

postrado ADJ prostrate, prone

postrar VT to prostrate

postre M dessert; **a la** — at last

postulado M postulate

postulante MF candidate

postular VT to postulate

póstumo ADJ posthumous

postura F posture (también opinión)

potable ADJ drinkable, potable

potasio M potassium

pote M (cilíndrico) jar; (panzudo) jug

potear VI/VT to putt

potencia F (sexual) potency; (de una fuerza, nación) power; **es un asesino en** — he's a

potential murderer; — **naval** sea power; **de alta** — high-powered; **segunda** — the second power

potencial ADJ & M potential

potenciar VT (a una persona) to empower; (proyectos, relaciones) to promote, to support

potentado -da MF potentate

potente ADJ potent, powerful

potranco -ca M colt; F filly

potrero M pasture; *Am* cattle ranch, stock farm

potro M (caballo) colt; (en gimnasia) vaulting horse; — **de tormento** rack

pozo M (de agua, petróleo) well; (hoyo profundo) pit; (minero) mine shaft; **sacar del** — to rescue; — **negro** sink; — **sin fondo** bottomless pit; — **séptico** septic tank

práctica F (repetición, costumbre) practice; (destreza) skill; **en la** — in practice; **poner en** — to put into practice; — **comercial desleal** deceptive practice

prácticamente ADV (casi) practically, virtually; (de forma práctica) practically; (en la práctica) in practice

practicante ADJ practicing; MF (que practica) practitioner; (asistente de médico) physician's assistant

practicar^{30} VI/VT (una habilidad) to practice; (un agujero) to make

práctico ADJ (sencillo) practical; (adiestrado) skillful; M — **de puerto** harbor pilot

pradera F prairie, grassland

prado M meadow, pasture

pragmático ADJ pragmatic

preadolescente ADJ & MF preteen, preadolescent

preámbulo M preamble

preaprobado ADJ preapproved

precalentamiento M warmup

precanceroso ADJ precancerous

precario ADJ precarious, *fam* touch-and-go

precaución F precaution

precaverse VT to take precautions

precavido ADJ cautious

precedencia F precedence

precedente ADJ preceding; M precedent; **sin** — unprecedented; **sentar** — to set a precedent

preceder VI/VT to precede

precepto M precept

preciado ADJ (estimado) prized; (valioso) valuable

preciarse VI — **de** to be proud of

precintar VT to seal

precinto M seal

precio M price; **poner** — **a** to put a price on; **no tener** — to be priceless; — **de compra** purchase price; — **de lista** list price; — **de mercado** market price; — **de referencia** bench price; — **justo en el mercado** fair

market price; — **sugerido** suggested retail price; — **sugerido por el fabricante** manufacturer's suggested retail price; — **vigente** going price
preciosista ADJ precious
precioso ADJ (metal, piedra, objeto de gran valor) precious; (muy bonito) beautiful, adorable
precipicio M precipice, cliff
precipitación F precipitation (también atolondramiento)
precipitado ADJ precipitate, hasty, rash; M precipitate
precipitar VI to precipitate; VT to hurl; —**se** (apresurarse) to be hasty; (arrojarse) to plunge, to plummet; (depositarse) to precipitate; (adelantarse) to come to a head
precisamente ADV precisely, exactly, just; — **de eso te quería hablar** that is just what I wanted to talk to you about; (de hecho) as a matter of fact; —, **se alojó en este hotel** as a matter of fact he stayed in this hotel
precisar VT (determinar) to determine precisely; (necesitar) to need
precisión F precision, accuracy; **precisiones** clarifications
preciso ADJ precise, accurate; **es — que vengas** you must come; **en este — instante** at this very moment
precoz ADJ (niño) precocious; (diagnóstico) early
precursor-ora MF precursor, forerunner
predecesor-ora MF predecessor
predecir[53, 74] VT to predict, to foretell
predestinar VT to predestine
predeterminado ADJ predetermined
predicación F preaching
predicado ADJ & M predicate
predicador-ora MF preacher
predicar[30] VI/VT to preach
predicción F prediction
predilección F predilection
predilecto ADJ favorite, pet
predio M piece of land
predisponer[56, 74] VT to predispose
predisposición F predisposition
predominante ADJ predominant, prevailing
predominar VI to predominate
predominio M predominance
preeclampsia F preeclampsia
preeminente ADJ foremost
preempacado ADJ prepacked
preescolar ADJ nursery; MF nursery school child
preestablecido ADJ preset
preestreno M preview
preexistente ADJ preexisting
prefacio M preface
preferencia F preference; (en el tráfico) right of way; **de** — predominantly

preferente ADJ (tratamiento) preferential; (acciones) preferred
preferible ADJ preferable
preferido ADJ preferred, favorite
preferir[8] VT to prefer
prefiera, prefiere ver preferir
prefijar VT to prefix
prefijo M prefix
prefiriendo, prefiriera, prefiriese ver preferir
pregonar VT (noticias) to make public; (mercancías) to hawk
pregrabado ADJ prerecorded
pregunta F question; **hacer una** — to ask a question; —**s frecuentes** frequently asked questions
preguntar VI/VT to ask, to inquire; — **por** (pedir información) to inquire about; (pedir para hablar) to ask for; —**se** to wonder
preguntón ADJ inquisitive
prehistórico ADJ prehistoric
prejuicio M prejudice, bias
prejuzgar[40] VT to prejudge
preliminar ADJ & M preliminary
preludiar VT to prelude
preludio M prelude
prematrimonial ADJ premarital
prematuro ADJ (bebé) premature; (muerte) untimely
premeditado ADJ premeditated
premenstrual ADJ premenstrual
premiar VT to reward; **las obras premiadas** the award-winning works
première M premiere
premio M (galardón) prize, award; (de la moneda) appreciation; **Juan Pérez,** — **nacional de poesía** Juan Pérez, winner of the national poetry award; — **gordo** jackpot
premisa F premise
premonición F premonition
prenatal ADJ prenatal
prenda F (fianza) pawn, pledge; (de vestir) article of clothing, garment; **dejar en** — to pawn; **en** — **de** as a token of
prendar VT to charm; —**se de** to fall in love with
prendedor M brooch, pin
prender VT (agarrar) to grab; (sujetar) to clasp; (enganchar) to fasten; (detener) to arrest; (arraigar) to take root; (encender) to turn on, to switch on; — **fuego** to set on fire; **la vacuna no prendió** the vaccination didn't take
prensa F press; **tener mala** — to have bad press
prensar VT to press
prensil ADJ prehensile
prenupcial ADJ prenuptial
preñada ADJ pregnant
preñar VT (a una hembra animal) to impregnate;

(a una mujer) *vulg* to knock up
preñez F pregnancy
preocupación F worry, concern
preocupado ADJ worried, concerned, anxious
preocupante ADJ worrisome
preocupar VT to worry, to concern; **—se de** to worry about; **—se por** to be concerned about
preocupón -ona MF worrywart
preparación F preparation
preparado ADJ ready; M preparation
preparar VT to prepare; **—se** to get ready, to brace oneself; **— el cuerpo de un difunto** to embalm a body
preparativo ADJ preparatory; M preparation
preparatorio ADJ preparatory; **escuela preparatoria** preparatory school
preponderancia F preponderance
preponderante ADJ preponderant
preponderar VI to predominate
preposición F preposition
prepucio M foreskin
prerrequisito M prerequisite
prerrogativa F prerogative
presa F (animal de caza) prey, quarry; (dique) dam
presagiar VT to forebode
presagio M omen, sign
présbita, présbite ADV & MF farsighted
prescindible ADJ dispensable
prescindir VI **— de** to dispense with, to do without
prescribir[74] VT to prescribe
prescripción F prescription
presencia F presence; **— de ánimo** presence of mind
presenciar VT to witness
presentable ADJ presentable
presentación F (de un tema) presentation; (de una persona) introduction
presentador -ora MF (de programa de televisión) host; (de noticiero) anchor
presentar VT (una idea) to present; (a una persona) to introduce; (la declaración de impuestos, una demanda) to file; (un informe) to submit; (documentos) to produce; (una queja) to lodge; (una renuncia) to tender; **—se** (aparecer) to appear; (hacerse conocer) to introduce oneself
presente ADJ present; M (tiempo) present; (regalo) present, gift; **al —** at the present time; **tener —** to bear in mind; **en el — [contrato]** herein; **por la — [carta]** hereby
presentimiento M presentiment, foreboding, hunch
presentir[8] VT to have a presentiment of
preservación F (protección) preservation; (ahorro) conservation
preservar VT (proteger) to preserve; (ahorrar) to conserve

preservativo M condom
presidencia F presidency
presidencial ADJ presidential
presidente MF, **presidenta** F (de un país) president; (de una reunión, junta) chair
presidiario -ria MF prisoner
presidio M prison
presidir VI to preside; VT to preside over
presilla F loop
presión F pressure; **— atmosférica** atmospheric pressure; **— arterial** blood pressure; **— arterial alta** high blood pressure, hypertension; **— de aire** air pressure
presionar VT (un botón) to press; (al gobierno) to lobby
preso -sa MF prisoner, inmate
prestación F provision; **prestaciones** benefits
prestador -ora MF lender
prestamista MF (de dinero) lender; (en un montepío) pawnbroker
préstamo M loan; **— convencional** conventional loan; **— garantizado** guaranteed loan
prestar VT to loan, to lend; **— ayuda** to give help; **— atención** to pay attention; **— juramento** to take an oath; **— servicio** to render service
prestatario -ria MF borrower
prestidigitación F sleight of hand
prestigio M prestige
prestigioso ADJ prestigious
presumido ADJ conceited, presumptuous
presumir VT (suponer) to presume; VI (ostentar) to show off; **— de valiente** to boast of one's valor
presunción F presumption
presuntamente ADV allegedly
presunto ADJ (dueño, autor de una obra) presumed; (autor de un crimen) alleged; **— heredero** heir apparent
presuntuoso ADJ presumptuous
presuponer[56, 74] VT to presuppose
presupuestación F budgeting
presupuestario ADJ budget, budgetary
presupuesto M (de gastos e ingresos) budget; (de costos) estimate; **— equilibrado** balanced budget
presuroso ADJ hasty
pretencioso ADJ pretentious
pretender VI (sostener) to claim, to purport; **— ser** to claim to be; **— al trono** to pretend to the throne; VT (intentar) to attempt
pretendiente MF, **pretendienta** F (al trono) pretender; (a un puesto) aspirant; M (de una mujer) suitor, admirer
pretensión F pretension
pretérito ADJ past; M past tense; **— perfecto** present perfect

pretexto M pretext, pretense; **so — de** under pretense of
pretil M railing
pretina F waistband
prevalecer[35] VI to prevail
prevaleciente ADJ prevalent
prevé, prevea, preveía *ver* prever
prevención F (protección) prevention; (recelo) caution
prevenido ADJ forewarned
prevenir[61] VT (precaver) to prevent; (prever) to foresee; (advertir) to warn; **— contra** to protect oneself against
preventivo ADJ preventive, precautionary
prever[72, 74] VT to foresee, to anticipate
previamente ADV previously
previo ADJ previous, prior; **— examen de salud** after undergoing a health examination
previsible ADJ foreseeable
previsión F foresight, anticipation
previsto *ver* prever
previsualización F previewing
prieto ADJ swarthy
prima F (cuota de seguro) premium; (recargo) surcharge; (pago extraordinario) bonus
primario ADJ primary
primate M primate
primavera F spring
primaveral ADJ springlike
primero ADJ & ADV first; **primer ministro** prime minister; **primer piso** second floor; **primer plano** foreground; **primera base** (posición) first base; (jugador) first baseman; **primera enseñanza** primary education; **primera persona** first person; **primer tiempo** first half; **—s auxilios** first aid; **a primera vista** at first sight; **de primer grado** first degree; **de primera** top-notch; **de primera mano** firsthand; **por primera vez** for the first time; **— del mes** first of the month; **Juan llegó —** Juan arrived first; F (marcha) first gear; (clase en un avión) first class
primicia F (fruto primero) first fruit; (noticia) scoop
primitivo ADJ primitive
primo -ma MF (hijo de tío) cousin; (persona incauta) sucker, dupe; **— hermano** first cousin; **— segundo** second cousin; ADJ prime
primogénito -ta ADJ & MF firstborn
primogenitura F birthright
primor M (esmero) care; (cosa fina) lovely thing
primordial ADJ primordial
primoroso ADJ exquisite
princesa F princess
principal ADJ principal, main; **la causa — de muerte** the leading cause of death; **el dormitorio —** the master bedroom

principalmente ADV mainly, principally
príncipe M prince
principesco ADJ princely
principiante MF beginner; ADJ beginning
principiar VT to commence
principio M (fundamento, regla de conducta) principle, tenet; (hecho de empezar, tiempo, lugar) beginning, start; **a —s de** toward the beginning of; **— activo** active ingredient; **al —** at the beginning, at first; **de — a fin** from beginning to end; **desde el —** from the beginning; **en —** in principle
pringar[40] VT (ensuciar) to get greasy; (mojar) to dip
pringoso ADJ greasy
pringue MF grease
prioridad F (autoridad, preferencia) priority, precedence; (en el tráfico) right of way
prioritario ADJ having priority, most important
prisa F haste, hurry; **a toda —** at full speed; **correr —** to be urgent; **darse —** to hurry; **las —s comienzan a la una** the rush starts at one; **tener —** to be in a hurry; **sin —** leisurely
prisión F prison; **— perpetua** life in prison
prisionero -ra MF prisoner; **— de guerra** prisoner of war
prisma M prism
prismáticos M PL binoculars
privacidad F privacy
privación F privation; **pasar privaciones** to suffer want
privado ADJ private; **en —** in private
privar VT to deprive; **—se de** to deprive oneself of
privativo ADJ exclusive
privatización F privatization
privatizar[47] VT to privatize
privilegiado ADJ privileged
privilegiar VT to favor, to give a privilege to
privilegio M privilege
pro M advantage; **en — de** in favor of; **en — y en contra** for and against
proa F prow, bow
proaborto ADJ INV pro-choice
probabilidad F (chance) likelihood; (en estadística) probability; **tienes pocas —es de ganar** you have little chance of winning; **¿qué —es tiene?** what are her odds?
probable ADJ probable, likely; **lo más — es que haya venido** in all likelihood he came
probador M dressing room
probar[5] VT (alimento, bebida) to taste, to try, to sample; (una hipótesis) to prove; (una guitarra) to try out; (un coche) to test-drive; **—se un vestido** to try on a dress; **— fortuna** to try one's luck; **prueba a venir más temprano** try to come earlier; **no — bocado** not to eat a bite

probatorio ADJ probationary
probeta F test tube
problema M problem; **él sólo da —s** he's nothing but trouble
problemático -ca ADJ problematic; F problems
procedencia F origin
procedente ADJ **— de** from
proceder VI to proceed; **— de** to come from; **— a** to proceed to; **— contra** to take action against
procedimiento M procedure; **—s** proceedings
procesable ADJ actionable
procesado -da MF accused; M processing
procesador ADJ processing; M processor; **— de textos** word processor
procesamiento M prosecution; **— de datos** data processing; **— de textos** word processing
procesar VT to prosecute, to try
procesión F procession; **la — va por dentro** he doesn't let it show
proceso M (etapas) process; (juicio) trial, legal proceedings
proclama F proclamation
proclamación F proclamation
proclamar VT to proclaim; **—se campeón** to be proclaimed winner
proclive ADJ prone
procrear VI/VT to procreate
proctología F proctology
procurador -ora MF attorney
procurar VT (intentar) to endeavor; (obtener) to procure, to obtain
prodigar⁴⁰ VT to lavish; **—se** to be lavish
prodigio M prodigy
prodigioso ADJ prodigious
pródigo -ga ADJ (derrochador) prodigal; (muy generoso) lavish; MF spendthrift
producción F (acción de producir) production; (cantidad producida) production, yield; **— masiva** mass production
producir³⁸ VT (efectos, mercancías, películas) to produce; (fruta, resultados) to yield, to bear; **—se** to happen
productividad F productivity
productivo ADJ (rendidor) productive; (exitoso) successful
producto M product; **— interno bruto** gross national product
productor -ora MF producer; ADJ **un país — de petróleo** an oil-producing country
produje, produjera, produjese ver producir
pro-elección ADJ INV pro-choice
proeza F exploit
profanación F desecration
profanar VT to profane, to desecrate
profano ADJ profane
profecía F prophecy
proferir⁸ VT to utter

profesar VT to profess
profesión F profession
profesional ADJ & MF professional; **— de la salud** health care provider
profesionista MF *Méx* professional
profesor -ora MF (universitario) professor; (de enseñanza secundaria) teacher; (de tenis) instructor
profesorado M faculty
profeta MF prophet
profético ADJ prophetic
profetizar⁴⁷ VI/VT to prophesy
profilaxis F prevention
prófugo -ga ADJ & MF fugitive
profundidad F (del mar, de comprensión, de un armario) depth; (sabiduría) profundity
profundizar⁴⁷ VT to deepen; VI to go into deeply
profundo ADJ (idea, comentario, razonamiento) profound; (mar, pozo, armario, voz) deep
profuso ADJ profuse
progesterona F progesterone
programa M (de boxeo) card; (de televisión) show, program; (de un curso) syllabus; (de un congreso) program; **— antivirus** antivirus program, antivirus software; **— de protección contra virus** virus protection software; **— de instalación** setup program, install program; **— instalador** setup program, install program; **— para recuperar datos borrados** undelete utility; **—s almacenados en circuitos integrados** firmware
programable ADJ programmable
programación F programming
programador -ora MF programmer
programar VT (una computadora) to program; (un evento) to schedule
progresar VT to progress, to advance
progresión F progression
progresista ADJ & MF progressive
progresivo -va ADJ & MF progressive
progreso M progress
prohibición F prohibition, ban
prohibido ADJ forbidden; **prohibida la entrada** no admittance; **— el paso** no trespassing
prohibir²⁹ VT to prohibit, to ban; **se prohíbe fumar** no smoking
prohijar VT to adopt
prójimo -ma MF fellow human
prole F offspring
proletariado M proletariat
proletario -ria ADJ & MF proletarian
proliferación F proliferation, spread
prolífico ADJ prolific
prolijo ADJ (verboso) wordy; (esmerado) overly careful
prologar⁴⁰ VT to preface

prólogo M prologue, foreword, preface
prolongación F prolongation
prolongado ADJ extended
prolongar[40] VT to prolong; —**se** to wear on
promediar VT to average
promedio M average, mean; **de/en**— on average; — **de carreras limpias permitidas** earned run average
promesa F promise; **romper una**— to break a promise; **una joven**— a promising young player
prometedor ADJ promising
prometer VT to promise; VI to show promise
prometido-da ADJ engaged; M fiancé; F fiancée
prominente ADJ prominent
promiscuo ADJ promiscuous
promisorio ADJ promissory; **un futuro**— a promising future
promoción F (oferta comercial) promotion; (conjunto de personas) class
promocional ADJ promotional
promocionar VT to promote, to publicize
promontorio M promontory
promotor-ora MF (de un producto) promoter; (de bienes inmuebles) developer
promover[6] VT (ideas, producto, a un alumno) to promote; (la paz, una causa) to foster, to further
promulgación F enactment
promulgar[40] VT to promulgate, to enact
pronombre M pronoun
pronominal ADJ pronominal
pronosticar[30] VT to forecast
pronóstico M (del tiempo, de la economía) forecast; (de una enfermedad) prognosis
prontitud F promptness, dispatch
pronto ADJ (rápido) quick; (listo) ready; ADV soon, promptly; **de**— suddenly; ¡**hasta**—! see you soon! **tan**— **como** as soon as
pronunciación F pronunciation
pronunciado ADJ pronounced
pronunciamiento M declaration, pronouncement
pronunciar VT (un sonido, una sentencia) to pronounce; (un discurso) to make, to deliver; —**se** (acusarse) to be pronounced; (expresarse) to declare one's opinion
propagación F propagation, spread
propaganda F (de ideas) propaganda; (de mercancías) advertising, publicity; **hacer**— to advertise
propagar[40] VT to propagate
propalar VT to spread
propano M propane
propasarse VI to go too far
propensión F propensity
propenso ADJ prone
propiciar VT to favor
propicio ADJ propitious, auspicious

propiedad F (cualidad, pertenencia, finca) property; (derecho de dueño) ownership; (corrección) precision; — **mayoritaria** majority ownership; — **privada** private property; —**es** estate; —**es colindantes** adjoining properties
propietario-ria M (de una tienda) proprietor, owner; (de un apartamento) landlord; F (de una tienda) owner; (de un apartamento) landlady; — **ausente** absentee landlord
propina F tip, gratuity; **dar [una]**— to tip
propinar VT — **una paliza** to give a beating
propio ADJ (correcto) proper; **el significado**— the proper meaning; (típico) like; **no es**— **él quejarse así** it's not like him to complain like that; (conveniente) appropriate; **una expresión propia** an appropriate expression; (que le pertenece) own; **su**— **hijo** his own son; **un hijo**— a son of his own; **por tu**— **bien** for your own good; (mismo) same; **al**— **tiempo** at the same time
propondrá, propondría ver proponer
proponente MF proponent
proponer[56, 74] VT to propose; —**se** to set out to
proponga, propongo ver proponer
proporción F proportion, ratio; **proporciones** dimensions
proporcional ADJ proportional, proportionate
proporcionar VT (ajustar a proporción) to proportion; (brindar) to furnish, to provide
proposición F (lógica) proposition; (de matrimonio) proposal; **proposiciones deshonestas** indecent proposals
propósito M purpose, intent; **a**— (adecuado) apropos; (voluntariamente) on purpose, intentionally, deliberately; (además) by the way, incidentally; **a**— **de** apropos of
propuesta F proposal
propuesto ver proponer
propugnar VT to urge
propulsar VT to propel
propulsión F propulsion; — **a chorro** jet propulsion
propulsor-ora ADJ propelling; MF promoter
propuse, propusiera, propusiese ver proponer
prorratear VT to prorate
prórroga F (plazo) extension of time; (de un préstamo) renewal; (fútbol americano) overtime; (fútbol) extra time
prorrogar[40] VT (un pago) to put off, to defer; (un plazo) to extend; (un préstamo) to renew
prorrumpir VI to burst; — **en llanto** to burst into tears; — **en carcajadas** to burst out laughing
prosa F prose
prosaico ADJ prosaic
proscribir[74] VT to banish, to disenfranchise
proscripción F banishment

proseguir[12] VI to proceed
prosódico ADJ prosodic
prospectar VT to prospect
prospector-ora MF prospector
prosperar VI to prosper, to flourish, to thrive
prosperidad F prosperity
próspero ADJ prosperous
próstata F prostate [gland]
prostitución F prostitution
prostituir[19] VT to prostitute
prostituto-ta MF prostitute
protagonista MF protagonist
protagonizar[47] VT to star in
protección F protection; — **al consumidor** consumer protection; — **contra copias** copy protection; — **contra grabación** write protection; — **contra lectura** read protect; — **por contraseña** password protection
proteccionista ADJ & MF protectionist
protector-ora ADJ protective; MF protector; — **de pantalla** screen saver; — **de tensión** surge protector; — **sobrecargas de voltaje** surge protector; — **solar** sunblock
protectorado M protectorate
proteger[45] VT (a alguien vulnerable) to protect; (a un artista) to sponsor; — **contra grabación** to write-protect
protegido-da MF protégé[e]; — **por contraseña** password protected
proteína F protein
prótesis F prosthesis; — **de cadera** hip prosthesis
protesta F protest
protestante MF Protestant
protestar VI/VT to protest
protocolo M protocol
protón M proton
protoplasma M protoplasm
prototipo M prototype
protozoario M protozoan
protuberancia F protuberance, bulge, bump
protuberante ADJ bulging
provecho M (beneficio) benefit; (eructo) burp; **¡buen** —**!** bon appétit! **sacar** — [**de**] to benefit [from], to profit [from]
provechoso ADJ beneficial, advantageous
proveedor-ora MF (de un servicio) provider; (de un producto) supplier, vendor; — **de acceso** access provider; — **de acceso a internet** Internet access provider
proveer[18, 74] VT to provide; — **de** to provide with; —**se de** to provide oneself with
provenga, provengo ver provenir
proveniente ADJ — **de** coming from
provenir[61] VI to arise; — **de** to stem from
proverbio M proverb
providencia F providence
providencial ADJ providential
provincia F province

provincial ADJ provincial
provinciano-na ADJ & MF provincial
provine, proviniendo, proviniera, proviniese, provino ver provenir
provisión F provision, supply, store
provisional ADJ temporary, provisional
provisorio ADJ temporary
provocación F provocation
provocar[30] VT (ira) to provoke; (sexualmente) to excite; (un incendio) to start; (una respuesta) to elicit
provocativo ADJ provocative
proxeneta MF procurer, pimp, panderer
proximidad F proximity, nearness; **en las** —**es** in the vicinity
próximo ADJ (posterior) next; (cercano) near, nearby; **el lunes** — **pasado** last Monday; **de próxima aparición** forthcoming
proyección F projection
proyectar VT (un plan) to project; (una película) to screen; (una sombra) to cast; —**se** to overhang, to jut
proyectil M projectile
proyecto M (idea) project; (arquitectónico) plan; — **de ley** bill
proyector M (para películas) projector; (en el teatro) spotlight
prudencia F prudence
prudente ADJ prudent
prueba F (de imprenta, argumento irrefutable) proof; (argumento parcial) evidence; (intento, dificultad) trial, test; (examen) test, examination; (de ropa) fitting; — **beta** beta test; — **de detección** screening test; — **de doble incógnita** double-blind test; — **de embarazo** pregnancy test; — **de esfuerzo** stress test; — **de esfuerzo máximo** exercise electrocardiogram; — **de fuego** trial by fire; — **de ingresos** means test; — **de paternidad** paternity test; — **de Rorschach** Rorschach test; **a** — on approval; **a** — **de fallos** foolproof; **a** — **de incendio** fireproof; **poner a** — to put to the test
prueba, pruebe ver probar
psicoanálisis M psychoanalysis
psicodélico ADJ & M psychedelic
psicología F psychology
psicológico ADJ psychological
psicólogo-ga MF psychologist
psicópata MF psychopath
psicosis F psychosis
psicosomático ADJ psychosomatic
psicoterapia F psychotherapy
psicótico ADJ psychotic
psiquiatra MF psychiatrist
psiquiatría F psychiatry
psíquico ADJ psychic
psoriasis F psoriasis
púa F (con punta aguda) spike; (de alambre)

barb; (de guitarra) pick; (de erizo) quill; (de tridente) prong

puaf, puaj INTERJ yuck, ugh

pubertad F puberty

publicación F publication

publicar[30] VT to publish; (revelar) to divulge

publicidad F publicity, advertising; — **de cebo y anzuelo** bait-and-switch advertising; — **engañosa** false advertising; — **exterior** outdoor advertising; **hacer** — to advertise

publicitario -ria MF advertising agent; ADJ publicity

público ADJ public; M (testigo) public; (en un espectáculo) audience; **en** — in public

publirreportaje M infomercial

puchero M (vasija) pot; (guiso) stew; (gesto) pout; **hacer** —**s** to pout

puck M puck

pude, pudiendo, pudiera, pudiese ver poder

pudiente ADJ wealthy

pudín M pudding

pudor M (sexual) modesty; (emocional) reserve

pudrir[74] VI to rot

pueblerino ADJ provincial

pueblo M (población) town; (nación) people, folk

pueda, puede ver poder

puente M bridge (también dental, de gafas, de nariz); (fin de semana) long weekend; — **aéreo** (regular) shuttle; (de emergencia) airlift; — **cardiopulmonar** cardiopulmonary bypass, coronary bypass; — **colgante** suspension bridge; — **levadizo** drawbridge

puénting M bungee jumping

pueril ADJ childish

puerta F (de casa) door; (de aeropuerto, de ciudad) gate; (entrada) entrance; — **de acceso** gateway; **vender de** — **en** — to sell door to door; **dar a alguien con la** — **en las narices** to slam the door in someone's face; **llamar a la** — to knock on the door; — **trasera** back door; **a** — **cerrada** behind closed doors

puerto M port (también en informática); — **de acceso** gateway; — **de entrada** port of entry; — **de ratón** mouse port; — **paralelo** parallel port; — **serie/serial** serial port; — **USB** USB port; **llegar a buen** — to bring to a satisfactory conclusion

puertorriqueño -ña ADJ & MF Puerto Rican

pues CONJ (puesto que) since, for; ADV (entonces) then; — **bien** well then, now

puesta F — **al día** update; — **del sol** sunset, setting of the sun; — **en marcha** (de un proyecto) setting in motion; (de un coche) starting; — **en libertad** freeing

puestero -ra MF vendor, seller

puesto ADJ **bien** — (casa) well-appointed; (persona) well made-up; **llevar** — to have on; M (posición) place; (de venta) booth, stand; (de trabajo) post, position; — **de socorros** first-aid station; **quedarse con lo** — to be left with only the clothes on one's back; CONJ — **que** since

puesto ver poner

pugilato M boxing

pugilista MF boxer, prizefighter

pugna F struggle; **estar en** — **con** to be in conflict with

pugnaz ADJ feisty

puja F (del viento) push; (en una subasta) bid

pujanza F vigor

pujar VI (para dar a luz) to push; (en una subasta) to bid; — **por** to strive to

pujo M contraction

pulcritud F neatness

pulcro ADJ neat

pulga F flea; **tener malas** —**s** to be ill-tempered

pulgada F inch

pulgar M thumb

pulido ADJ polished; M polishing

pulimento M (de modales) refinement; (de metales) buffing; (polvo para pulir) scouring powder

pulir VT (metal, un discurso) to polish; (madera) to sand

pulla F taunt, dig

pulmón M lung; — **de acero** iron lung

pulmonar ADJ pulmonary; **capacidad** — lung capacity

pulmonía F pneumonia

pulpa F pulp

púlpito M pulpit

pulpo M octopus

pulque M *Méx* pulque

pulquería F *Méx* pulque bar

pulsación F (de corazón) pulse; (de ratón de computadora) click; (de tecla) keystroke

pulsar VT (una tecla) to press; (cuerdas de guitarra) to pluck; (la opinión pública) to gauge; — **y arrastrar** to click and drag

púlsar M pulsar

pulsera F (alhaja) bracelet; (de reloj) watchband; **reloj de** — wristwatch

pulso M (pulsación) pulse; (firmeza de mano) steadiness; **echar un** — to arm-wrestle; **tomar el** — to take the pulse; **a** — with great effort

pulular VI to swarm, to teem with

pulverizar[47] VT to pulverize

puma F mountain lion, cougar, puma

puna F cold, arid tableland of the Andes

punitivo ADJ punitive

punk ADJ & M punk

punkero -ra MF punk

punta F (de cuchillo) point; (de la lengua, de un

lápiz) tip; (de calcetín) toe; — **de lanza** spearhead; **una — de** a bunch of; **a — de cuchillo** at knifepoint; — **de flecha** arrowhead; **de —** on end; **iba caminando de —s** he was tiptoeing; **sacar — a un lápiz** to sharpen a pencil; **en la — de la lengua** on the tip of the tongue; **me pone los nervios de —** it makes me nervous; M **—pié** kick; ADJ **puntiagudo** sharp, pointed

puntada F stitch, prick

puntal M (de un edificio) prop; (de la economía) mainstay

puntear VT (una guitarra) to pluck; (un mapa) to make dots on; (una lista) to check off

puntería F aim; **tener buena —** to be a good shot

puntero M pointer

puntilla F point lace; **de —s** on tiptoe

punto M (puntuación) period; (de cinturón) notch; (marca, signo) point, dot; (anotación, tema, lugar) point; (puntada) stitch; — **álgido** fever pitch; — **culminante** (de una carrera) peak; (de una historia) climax; (de negociaciones) critical stage; — **de apoyo** foothold; — **de condensación** dewpoint; — **de congelación** freezing point; — **de ebullición** boiling point; — **de juego** game point; — **de manga** set point; — **de origen** point of origin; — **de partida** point of departure; — **de partido** match-point; — **de referencia** point of reference, benchmark; — **de vista** viewpoint, point of view; — **extra** (fútbol americano) point after touchdown; — **muerto** (en un negocio) stalemate, deadlock; (en un coche) neutral; — **y coma** semicolon; **al —** at once; **a — ready; a — de** on the point/verge of; **cogerle el —** to figure out; **dos —s** colon; **el — medio** the halfway mark; **en —** on the dot; **hacer —** to knit; **hasta cierto —** to a certain extent; **poner los —s sobre las íes** to dot one's i's and cross one's t's

puntuación F punctuation

puntual ADJ (en hora) punctual, prompt; (específico) specific

puntualidad F punctuality

puntualizar⁴⁷ VT to point out

puntuar²⁶ VT to punctuate

punzada F (de dolor) stab; (de remordimiento, hambre) pang, twinge

punzante ADJ sharp, piercing

punzar⁴⁷ VT to prick

punzón M (en papel) hole punch; (en cuero) awl

puñado M handful; **a —s** by the handful

puñal M dagger

puñalada F stab; **coser a —s** to stab to death

puñetazo M punch, slug; **dar un —** to punch; **dar un — en la mesa** to bang on the table

puño M (mano cerrada) fist; (en una manga) cuff; (de espada) handle; **arreglarlo con los —s** to duke it out; **de mi — y letra** by my own hand

pupa F *Esp* boo-boo

pupila F pupil

pupilo -la MF ward

pupitre M school desk

puré M purée; — **de patatas/papas** mashed potatoes; **hacer —** to smash

pureza F purity

purga F (política) purge; (medicinal) purgative

purgación F atonement

purgante ADJ & M purgative, laxative

purgar⁴⁰ VT (el vientre, a un rival) to purge; (frenos) to bleed; (pecados) to atone for

purgatorio M purgatory

purificar³⁰ VT to purify

purista ADJ & MF purist

puritano ADJ puritanical

puro ADJ pure; **lo hizo de — bueno** he did it out of sheer kindness; **a pura fuerza** by sheer force; **la pura verdad** the plain truth; **son puras mentiras** that's a lot of bull; **de purasangre** thoroughbred; M cigar

púrpura ADJ & M purple

pus M pus

puse, pusiera, pusiese *ver* poner

puta F (prostituta) *ofensivo* whore, hooker; (mujer fácil) *ofensivo* slut; **de — madre** *vulg* very good; **de la gran —** *vulg* huge; **¡— madre!** *vulg* fuck! shit!

putañero M john

putón M *ofensivo* slut

putrefacto ADJ putrid, decayed

putter M putter

Qq

Qatar M Qatar

quásar M quasar

que PRON REL that; (con antecedente no humano) which; (con antecedente humano) who, whom; **el/la —** the one that; **lo — tú dices** what you say; **vino la suegra, lo — complicó la visita** the mother-in-law came, which complicated the visit; CONJ that; **no creo — haya tiempo** I don't think [that] there's time; **estoy — me muero** I feel like I'm about to die; **Carlos es más alto — Luis** Carlos is taller than Luis; **más/menos —** more/less than; **déjalo aquí — lo voy a necesitar después** leave it here because I will need it later; **por mucho —** no matter how much; **a — gana** I bet he'll win; **— yo sepa** as far as I know

qué ADJ INTERR & PRON what, which; **¿— libro**

vas a usar? what/which book are you going to use? **¿— dices?** what are you saying? **no sé — dijo** I don't know what he said; **¡— bonito!** how beautiful! **¡— de gente!** what a lot of people! **¿y eso —?** so what! **no hay de —** don't mention it; **¿— sé yo?** what do I know? **¿— tal?** how are you? **¡— más da!** what's the difference! **¡— va!** *fam* oh yeah? yeah right! **¡a mí —!** so what!

quebrada F (valle) ravine; (arroyo) creek
quebradizo ADJ breakable, brittle
quebrado ADJ (roto) broken; (rajado) cracked; (sin dinero) broke; M fraction
quebrantar VT (una casa, la salud) to weaken; (la ley) to violate
quebranto M weakening
quebrar[1] VT (romper) to break; (rajar) to crack; VI (irse a la bancarrota) to go bankrupt, to go under, to fail; **—se** to break [up]; **se quebró la muñeca** he broke his wrist; **—se uno la cabeza** to rack one's brain
queda F **toque de —** curfew
quedar VI (permanecer) to remain; (no haberse terminado) to be left; **queda leche en el vaso** there's milk in the glass; (estar ubicado) to be located; **la iglesia queda en la esquina** the church is located on the corner; (sentar bien la ropa) to suit; **— bien** to come out well; **— en** to agree to; **—se** to remain, to stay; **—se con una cosa** (comprar) to take/buy something; (llevarse) to take something
quehacer M chore, errand
queja F (protesta) complaint; (oficial) grievance
quejarse VI (protestar) to complain; (protestar ruidosamente) to gripe, to squawk; (protestar incesantemente) to whine
quejica ADJ whiny; MF nag, whiner
quejido M (de tono grave) moan, groan; (de tono agudo) squawk
quejoso ADJ whiny
quema F burning
quemado -da MF burn victim
quemador M burner
quemadura F (lugar quemado) burn; (sensación) burning; (enfermedad de plantas) blight
quemar VT to burn (también cedés); **—se** (un edificio) to burn up/down; (al sol) to sunburn
quemazón F burning sensation
quepa, quepamos *ver* caber
querella F lawsuit
querellante MF plaintiff
querellarse VI to file suit
querer[70] VI/VT (desear) to want; (amar) to love; **como quieras** as you please; **cuando quieras** whenever you want; **no quiso hacerlo** he refused to do it; **quiere llover** it is about to rain; **sin —** unwillingly; **— decir** to mean; **lo quiero mucho** I want it badly

querido -da ADJ beloved, dear; MF (enamorado) sweetheart; (como tratamiento) dear, darling
queroseno M kerosene
querrá, querría *ver* querer
quesería F dairy, cheese factory
queso M cheese; **— crema / de untar** cream cheese; **— suizo** swiss cheese
quiche M quiche
quicio M hinge; **sacar a uno de —** to drive someone up the wall
quiebra F bankruptcy (también moral); (de un mercado) crash; (de un comercio) failure; **— bancaria** bank failure
quiebra, quiebre *ver* quebrar
quiebre M break
quien PRON REL who, whom; **Juan, — recién cumplió cuarenta años** Juan, who just turned forty; **— hizo eso** whoever did that; **a — corresponda** to whom it may concern; **—quiera** whoever; **de —** whose; **con —** with whom
quién PRON INTERR & PRON who; **¿— es?** who is it? **no sé — entró** I don't know who came in; **¿a — se lo diste?** who did you give it to? to whom did you give it?
quiera, quiere *ver* querer
quieto ADJ still
quietud F stillness
quijada F jaw
quilate M carat
quilla F keel
química F chemistry
químico -ca ADJ chemical; MF chemist
quimioterapia F chemotherapy
quince NUM fifteen (también en tenis)
quincena F (de cosas) group of fifteen; (de días) two-week period
quincenal ADV biweekly
quincha F thatch
quinchar VT to thatch
quinesiología F kinesiology
quingombó M okra
quinientos NUM five hundred
quinina F quinine
quinqué M oil lamp
quinta F (casa) villa; (reclutamiento) draft
quinto ADJ, ADV, & M fifth
quiosco M kiosk, newsstand
quiquiriquí INTERJ cock-a-doodle-doo
quirófano M surgery, operating room
quiropráctico -ca ADJ chiropractic; MF chiropractor; F chiropractic
quirúrgico ADJ surgical
quise, quisiera, quisiese *ver* querer
quisquilloso ADJ particular, fussy
quiste M cyst
quitar VT (una mancha) to remove; (una prenda de vestir) to take off; (despojar de) to take away; M SG **quitaesmalte** nail polish

remover; M SG **quitanieves** snowplow; M SG **quitamanchas** spot remover; VI **—se** to take off; **—se a alguien de encima** to get rid of someone; **quítate de ahí** move over

quite M **salir al — de** to go to the rescue of

quizá, quizás ADV perhaps, maybe

Rr

rabadilla F (coxis) tailbone; (de un ave) rump

rábano M radish; **me importa un —** I couldn't care less

rabia F (enfermedad) rabies; (enojo) rage; **me tiene —** he hates me; **dar —** to anger

rabiar VI to rage, to fume; **guapa a —** drop-dead beautiful

rabieta F tantrum

rabino -na MF rabbi

rabioso ADJ (hidrofóbico, apasionado) rabid, mad; (enojado) mad, furious

rabo M (cola) tail; (pene) *fam* dick; (cabo) stem; **mirar con el — del ojo** to look out of the corner of one's eye; **con el — entre las piernas** with his tail between his legs

rabón ADJ bobtail

racha F (de suerte) streak; (de viento) gust

racial ADJ racial

racimo M (de plátanos, personas) bunch; (de uvas) cluster

raciocinio M reasoning

ración F (de guerra) ration, allowance; (de comida) portion

racional ADJ rational (también número)

racionalizado ADJ (justificado) rationalized; (reestructurado) streamlined

racionalizar[47] VT (una acción) to rationalize; (un negocio) to streamline

racionamiento M rationing

racionar VT to ration

racismo M racism

racista ADJ & MF racist

radar M radar

radiación F radiation

radiactivo ADJ radioactive

radiador M radiator

radial ADJ radial

radiante ADJ radiant

radiar VT (calor) to radiate; (por radio) to broadcast

radical ADJ (extremo) radical; (células) root; M (en química) radical; (en gramática) root

radicalismo M radicalism

radicar[30] VI to be located; **— en** to lie in; **—se** to take up residence

radio M (hueso, segmento de un círculo) radius; (elemento radiactivo) radium; F (aparato, difusión) radio; (emisora) radio station; **— de acción** sphere of influence

radiodifusión F broadcasting

radiodifusora F radio station

radioescucha MF radio listener

radiofónico ADJ radio

radiografía F x-ray

radiografiar[28] VT (hacer rayos x) to x-ray; (examinar con cuidado) to examine carefully

radiología F radiology

radiólogo -ga MF radiologist

radiotelescopio M radio telescope

radioterapia F radiation therapy

radiotransmisor M radio transmitter

radón M radon

raer[52] VI/VT to scrape [off]; (un artículo de ropa) to wear out

ráfaga F (de viento) gust, blast; (de luz) flash; (de ametralladora) burst

raído ADJ threadbare

raigón M stump

raíz F root; **— cuadrada** square root; **a — de** due to; **arrancar de —** to uproot; **cortar de —** to nip in the bud; **echar raíces** to take root

raja F (de melón) slice; (de falda) slit; (del trasero) *vulg* crack; (de leña) stick

rajadura F (en piedra, metal) crack; (en tela) rent, rip

rajar VT (una piedra) to crack; (un tronco) to split; **—se** (partir) to split open; (acobardarse) to chicken out, to blink; ADV **a rajatabla** strictly

ralea F ilk

ralear VI to thin out

ralentización F (de la economía) slump; (de un motor) idle

rallador M grater

rallar VT to grate, to shred

ralo ADJ sparse, thin

RAM M RAM

rama F branch, limb; (delgada) twig; **andarse por las —s** to beat around the bush; **algodón en —** raw cotton

ramaje M foliage

ramal M (de soga) strand; (de vía férrea) branch, spur

ramera F *pey* whore

ramificarse[30] VI to divide into branches, to branch off

ramillete M bouquet, bunch, spray

ramo M (de flores) bouquet; (de una ciencia) branch; (de una actividad) line; **— de olivo** olive branch

rampa F ramp

ramplón ADJ vulgar

rana F frog

ranchero -ra MF rancher; **música ranchera**

Mexican country music

rancho M (comida para soldados) mess; (comida mala) swill; (finca) ranch; (choza) hut; **hacer — aparte** to keep to oneself

rancio ADJ rancid; **de — abolengo** of ancient lineage

rango M (militar) rank; (categoría) standing

ranilla F frog [of a hoof]

ránking M (tenis) ranking

ranura F (corte) groove; (para insertar monedas, cartas) slot; **— para accesorios** accessory slot, expansion slot

rapar VT (pelo) to shave off; (cabeza) to shave

rapaz ADJ (animal) predatory; (destructivo) rapacious

rape M **cortar al —** to crop

rapé M snuff

rapear VI to rap

rápidamente ADV (con mucha velocidad) fast; (en poco tiempo) quickly

rapidez F (de un coche) speed; (de un movimiento) rapidity, quickness

rápido ADJ (con mucha velocidad) fast; (en poco tiempo) quick; M **—s** rapids; ADV (con mucha velocidad) fast; (en poco tiempo) quickly

rapiña F pillage

raptar VT to kidnap, to abduct

rapto M (secuestro) abduction, kidnapping; (arrebato) fit

raqueta F racket (también de tenis)

raquítico ADJ feeble, sickly

raramente ADV seldom, rarely

rareza F (escasez) rarity; (cosa rara) oddity; (cualidad de extraño) strangeness

raro ADJ (infrecuente) rare; (extraño) strange, funny; **rara vez** seldom, rarely; **sentirse —** to feel funny; **gas —** rare gas; **tierra rara** rare earth

ras LOC ADV **a — de la tierra** low to the ground

rascar[30] VT to scratch; **—se el culo** *vulg* to fart around; M SG **rascacielos** skyscraper

rasgado ADJ **ojos —s** slit eyes

rasgadura F tear, rip

rasgar[40] VT to tear, to rip

rasgo M (propiedad) trait, feature; **a grandes —s** in broad strokes

rasgón M tear

rasguñar VT to scratch

rasguño M scratch

raso ADJ (superficie) smooth; (cucharada) level; **al —** in the open air; M satin

raspado M scrape

raspador M scraper

raspadura F scrape

raspar VT to scrape

raspón M scrape

rastra F harrow; **a —s** dragging, pulling

rastrear VT (a un animal) to trail, to track, to trace; (un terreno) to search

rastreo M sweep, search

rastrero ADJ (planta) creeping; (persona) contemptible

rastrillar VT to rake

rastrillo M rake

rastro M (huella) track, trail; (olor) scent; (mercado) flea market; **ni —s** no trace

rastrojo M stubble

rasurado M shave

rasurador -ora MF razor

rasurar VT to shave

rata F rat

ratear VT to pilfer

ratería F petty larceny, pilferage

ratero -ra MF pickpocket

ratificación F ratification

ratificar[30] VT to ratify

rato M while; **—s perdidos** leisure hours; **a cada —** frequently; **a —s** from time to time; **pasar el —** to kill time; **pasar un buen —** (divertirse) to have a pleasant time; (permanecer) to spend a long time; **un largo —** a great while

ratón M mouse (también de computadora); **— almizclero** muskrat; **— en serie** serial mouse

ratonera F mousetrap

raudal LOC ADV **a —es** in great quantities

raudo ADJ swift

raya F (línea) line; (linde) boundary; (lista) stripe; (en el pelo) part; (en un pantalón) crease; (de ortografía) dash; (en un zapato) scuff; (pez marino) stingray; **tener a —** to hold in check; **pasarse de la —** to be out of line, to cross the line

rayado ADJ (papel) lined; (vestido) striped; **hablaba como disco —** he talked like a broken record

rayar VT (papel) to rule, to make lines on; (disco, espejo) to scratch; (zapatos) to scuff; **— el alba** to dawn; **— en** to border on

rayo M (de luz) ray, beam, streak; (de relámpago) flash of lightning; (de rueda) spoke; (de esperanza) ray, flicker; **— láser** laser beam; **—s infrarrojos** infrared rays; **—s X** x-rays

rayón M rayon

raza F (de personas) race; (de animal) breed

razón F (facultad) reason; (proporción) ratio; **— social** company name; **a — de** at the rate of; **¡con —!** no wonder! **entrar en —** to listen to reason; **te doy la —** I admit you're right; **perder la —** to lose one's mind; **tener —** to be right

razonable ADJ reasonable

razonamiento M reasoning

razonar VI (pensar) to reason; (argüir) to argue

reabastecer[35] VT to replenish

reabrir[74] VT to reopen

reacción F reaction; **— en cadena** chain

reaction; — **nuclear** nuclear reaction
reaccionar VI to react
reaccionario ADJ & MF reactionary
reacio ADJ averse, reluctant
reacondicionar VT to rebuild
reactivo M reagent
reactor M reactor; — **nuclear** nuclear reactor
readaptación F readjustment
readaptar VT to readjust
reafirmar VT to reaffirm; —**se** to reassert
reagrupar VT to regroup
reajustar VT to readjust
reajuste M readjustment
real ADJ (verdadero) real, actual; (del rey) royal; M fairground
realce M **dar** — to enhance
realeza F royalty
realidad F reality, actuality; **en** — really, actually; **en** — **no es abogado** he's not really a lawyer; — **virtual** virtual reality
realismo M realism
realista ADJ (auténtico) realistic; (partidario del rey) royalist; MF (no idealista) realist; (partidario del rey) royalist
realización F (de un sueño) realization, fulfillment; (de una tarea) completion; (de una película) production
realizador -ora MF (director) director; (productor) producer
realizar[47] VT (un sueño) to realize, to fulfill; (película) to produce
realmente ADV really
realzar[47] VT (mejorar) to enhance; (destacar) to accentuate; (intensificar) to heighten
reanimación F resuscitation; — **cardiopulmonar** cardiopulmonary resuscitation
reanimar VT (devolver fuerzas) to revive; (dar ánimos) to rally
reanudación F renewal; — **del juego** (fútbol) restart of play
reanudar VT (una amistad) to renew; (una reunión) to resume; (un partido del fútbol) to restart
reaparecer[35] VI to reappear
reasumir VT to resume
reata F lariat, lasso
reavivar VT to revive
rebaja F markdown, price cut; **con** — at a discount, on sale; **de** —**s** cut-rate
rebajado N on sale, reduced
rebajar VT (precios) to cut, to lower, to slash; (una bebida) to water down; (una crítica) to tone down; VI/VT (los cambios) to downshift; —**se** to lower oneself; —**se a** to stoop to
rebanada F slice
rebanar VT to slice
rebaño M flock, fold
rebasar VT (un coche) to overtake; (un límite) to

exceed
rebatir VT to refute
rebato M alarm
rebelarse VI to rebel, to revolt
rebelde ADJ (niño) rebellious; (pelo) unruly; MF rebel
rebeldía F rebelliousness, defiance; (no comparecencia) default
rebelión F rebellion
rebenque M whip
rebobinar VT to rewind
reborde M edge
rebosante ADJ (de líquido) brimming, overflowing; (de salud) flush, glowing; — **de alegría** overjoyed
rebosar VI (líquido) to overflow, to brim over; (de alegría) to bubble over; (de salud) to glow
rebotar VI/VT (en baloncesto) to rebound, to bounce; (chocar) to bounce; (cambiar de dirección una bala) to ricochet; (cambiar de dirección una pelota) to carom
rebote M (en baloncesto) rebound, bounce; (de bala) ricochet
rebotear VI (en baloncesto) to rebound
rebozar[47] VT to cover with batter; —**se** to muffle up
rebozo M shawl; **sin** — frankly
rebullir[16] VI to stir
rebuscado ADJ (estilo) overly elaborate; (persona) affected
rebuscar[30] VT (espigar) to glean; VI — **en** (la memoria) to search through; (un cajón) to rummage in
rebuznar VI to bray
rebuzno M bray, braying
recabar VT to raise
recado M (mensaje) message; (quehacer) errand; — **de escribir** writing materials
recaer[52] VI to relapse; — **sobre** to fall to
recaída F relapse
recalar VI to make a stop at
recalcar[30] VT to accentuate
recalcitrante ADJ obstinate
recalentar[1] VT (volver a calentar) to warm over; (calentar en exceso) to overheat
recamar VT to embroider
recámara F (de un arma de fuego) chamber; *Méx* (dormitorio) bedroom
recapitular VI/VT to recapitulate, to sum up
recargado ADJ busy
recargar[40] VT to overload, to burden
recargo M (emocional) burden; (de precio) surcharge, premium; — **por mora** late fee
recatado ADJ (cauteloso) cautious; (modesto) modest
recato M (cautela) caution; (modestia) modesty
recaudación F collection, levy; — **de fondos** fundraising
recaudador -ora MF tax collector

recaudar VT (impuestos) to collect, to levy; (fondos) to raise; — **en bruto** to gross; — **fondos** to raise funds; **lo recaudado** proceeds

recaudo M **estar a buen** — to be in a safe place

rección F government

recelar VT to suspect; — **de** to be suspicious of

recelo M misgivings

receloso ADJ mistrustful

recepción F reception

receptáculo M receptacle, holder

receptor M receiver (también en fútbol americano); (en béisbol) catcher; — **abierto** wide receiver; — **cerrado** tight end

recesión F recession

receta F (de cocina) recipe; (de médico) prescription

recetar VT to prescribe

rechazar[47] VT (una propuesta, un plan) to reject; (un ataque) to repel, to repulse; (una invitación) to decline, to turn down, to refuse; (una acusación) to deny; (a un amante) to spurn, to reject

rechazo M (de un amante) rejection; (de un ataque) repulse; (de una oferta) refusal; (de una acusación) denial

rechifla F whistling, booing

rechiflar VT to whistle, to boo

rechinamiento M (de una puerta) creaking, squeaking; (de los dientes) grinding

rechinante ADJ squeaky

rechinar VI (una puerta) to squeak, to creak; VI/VT (los dientes) to grind; **eso me rechina** that grates on my nerves

rechoncho ADJ plump, chubby, roly-poly

recibidor-ora MF receiver; M reception room

recibimiento M reception

recibir VT (premio) to receive, to get; (visitas) to receive, to welcome; (una noticia trágica) to take; — **noticias de** to hear from; —**se** to graduate; —**se de médico** to graduate from medical school

recibo M receipt; **de** — acceptable; **al** — **de** upon receipt of; **acusar** — to acknowledge receipt; **acuse de** — acknowledgment of receipt

reciclaje M recycling

reciclar VI/VT to recycle

recidiva F relapse

recién ADV recently; — **casado** newlywed; — **comprado** brand-new; — **llegado** newly arrived; — **nacido** newborn; — **me entero** it's news to me

reciente ADJ recent

recinto M enclosure

recio ADJ strong, rugged

recipiente M container

recíproco ADJ reciprocal

recitación F recitation

recital M recital

recitar VT to recite, to speak

reclamación F (protesta) protest; (demanda) claim

reclamante MF claimant

reclamar VT (protestar) to protest; (demandar) to claim; VI (aves) to call

reclamo M (reclamación) claim; (queja) complaint; (voz de animal) call, cry; (dispositivo) bird call; (señuelo) decoy

reclinar VT to lean; —**se** to recline

recluir[19] VT to confine; —**se** to be a recluse

recluso-sa MF (preso) inmate; (ermitaño) recluse

recluta F recruitment; MF (voluntario) recruit; (forzoso) conscript

reclutamiento M (voluntario) recruitment; (forzoso) conscription

reclutar VT (voluntariamente) to recruit; (por la fuerza) to draft, to conscript

recobrar VI to recover, to recuperate; VT to recover, to regain

recodo M bend, turn

recoger[45] VT (el cabello) to gather; (un cuarto) to tidy up; (citas en un texto) to collect; (la mesa) to clear; (polvo) to sweep up; (a un desamparado) to shelter; (los frutos del campo) to glean; —**se** (retirarse) to retire, to withdraw; (acumularse) to gather

recogida F (del cabello) gathering; (de un cuarto) tidying up; (de la mesa) clearing; (de un desamparado) sheltering

recogido ADJ (apartado) secluded; (tranquilo) peaceful, quiet

recogimiento M (aislamiento) seclusion; (meditación) meditation

recolección F (de frutos, datos) collecting, gathering; (de carga) pickup; (cosecha) harvest

recolectar VT to gather, to forage

recomendable ADJ advisable

recomendación F recommendation

recomendar[1] VT to recommend

recomienda, recomiende ver recomendar

recompensa F recompense, reward

recompensar VT to recompense, to reward

reconcentrar VI to concentrate intensely; —**se** to concentrate, to become absorbed in thought

reconciliación F reconciliation

reconciliar VT to reconcile

recóndito ADJ remote

reconfortante ADJ heartwarming, comforting

reconfortar VT to comfort

reconocer[35] VT (identificar) to recognize; (admitir) to admit, to acknowledge; (explorar) to reconnoiter

reconocible ADJ recognizable

reconocimiento M (identificación) recognition; (admisión, agradecimiento)

acknowledgment; (exploración) scouting; —
de habla speech recognition; — **de voz**
voice recognition; — **visual** visual
recognition; **hacer un** — to reconnoiter
reconozca, reconozco *ver* reconocer
reconsiderar VT to reconsider
reconstrucción F reconstruction
reconstruir[19] VT to reconstruct, to rebuild
**reconstruya, reconstruye,
reconstruyendo, reconstruyera,
reconstruyese** *ver* reconstruir
recopilación F collection, compilation
recopilar VT to compile
récord M record
recordar[5] VT (acordarse) to remember, to
recollect, to recall; (hacer acordar) to remind
recordatorio M reminder
recorrer VT (andar una distancia) to cover;
(examinar) to go over, to look over
recorrido M (ruta) run, route; (distancia)
distance
recortado ADJ jagged
recortar VT (pelo, hilos, presupuesto) to trim;
(uñas, periódicos) to clip; (una película) to
shorten; —**se** to be outlined
recorte M (de pelos, hilos) trimming; (de uñas,
periódicos) clipping; (de sueldo, de gastos)
cut; (de recursos) cutback; (sobrante)
trimming; — **salarial** pay cut
recostar[5] VT (sobre) to lay; (contra) to lean; —**se**
to recline
recoveco M (en un camino) turn; (rincón)
cranny
recreación F recreation
recrear VT to entertain; —**se** to amuse oneself
recreativo ADJ recreational; **actividades
recreativas** leisure activities; **sala
recreativa** game room
recreo M (recreación) recreation, relaxation;
(tiempo de descanso) recess; (lugar de juego)
playground
recriminar VT to recriminate
recrudecer[35] VI to flare up
recrudecimiento M flareup
recta F (de una pista) straight; (en béisbol)
fastball; — **final** final stretch
rectangular ADJ rectangular
rectángulo M rectangle
rectificar[30] VT to rectify
rectitud F uprightness, righteousness
recto ADJ (no curvo) straight; (honrado) upright,
righteous; (estricto) strict; **todo** — straight
ahead; M rectum
rector -ora MF university president, chancellor
recua F herd
recubrir[74] VT to cover; — **con pintura** to coat
with paint
recuento M account; — **sanguíneo** blood
count

recuerda, recuerde *ver* recordar
recuerdo M (acción de recordar, cosa recordada)
memory, recollection; (objeto que hace
recordar) souvenir, token; —**s** regards; **dale
—s a tu hermana** say hi to your sister
recular VI (retroceder) to move backward;
(retroceder en un coche) to back up;
(retroceder ante un desafío) to back down
recuperación F (salarial, de salud) recovery; (de
datos, documentos guardados) retrieval; (de
objetos, datos, documentos perdidos)
recovery
recuperar VT (una cosa perdida) to recover;
(datos, documentos guardados) to retrieve;
(tiempo perdido) to make up for; (dinero
perdido) to recoup; —**se** to recuperate
recurrente ADJ MF (que reclama) complainant;
ADJ (repetitivo) recurring, recurrent
recurrir VT to appeal; — **a** to resort to, to have
recourse to
recurso M (acción de recurrir) recourse;
(reclamación) appeal; —**s** resources; —**s
humanos** HR [human resources]; —**s
naturales** natural resources
recusar VT (a una persona) to reject; (a un juez)
to challenge
red F (para pescar, de tenis) net; (malla tejida)
mesh; (de conexiones, para computadora)
network; (para engañar) snare; (internet)
World Wide Web, Internet; — **[de área]
local** local area network
redacción F (ensayo) composition; (acción de
redactar) drafting; (en un periódico) editorial
department
redactar VT (un ensayo) to draft; (trabajo
escolar) to compose
redactor -ora MF editor
redada F (de peces) catch, haul; (policial) raid
redar VT to throw a net
redecilla F hairnet
redención F redemption
redil M sheepfold, sheep pen; **volver al** — to
come back into the fold
redimir VT (a un pecador) to redeem; (a un
esclavo) to set free
rédito M (de ahorros) interest; (de acciones)
yield
redituar[26] VT to yield
redoblar VT (esfuerzos) to double; VI/VT (un
tambor) to roll
redoble M drumroll
redoma F flask
redonda F whole note; **a la** — all around
redondear VT (una figura) to make round; (una
cifra) to round up
redondel M ring
redondez F roundness
redondo ADJ round; **en** — all around; **caer** — to
collapse; **salir** — to turn out perfect

reducción F reduction, cutback; — **de sueldo** cut in salary; **hacer — de personal** to cut back on personnel

reducidor-ora MF *Am* fence

reducir[38] VT (una cantidad) to reduce; (un hueso) to set; (actividades) to curtail, to cut down on; (costos) to cut; (personal) to downsize, to cut back on; —**se a** to boil down to

reduje, redujera, redujese *ver* reducir

redundante ADJ redundant

reduzca, reduzco *ver* reducir

reedificar[30] VT to rebuild

reelección F reelection

reelegir[14] VT reelect

reembolsar VT to reimburse, to refund

reembolso M reimbursement, refund

reemplazable ADJ replaceable

reemplazar[47] VT to replace

reemplazo M replacement, substitute

reencarnación F reincarnation

reescribir[74] VT to rewrite

reestructuración F restructuring

reexpedir[9] VT to forward

referencia F reference

referéndum M referendum

referente LOC ADV — **a** relative to

referir[8] VT (narrar) to narrate; —**se a** to refer to

refiera, refiere *ver* referir

refinación F refinement

refinado ADJ refined, genteel

refinamiento M refinement

refinanciar VI/VT to refinance

refinar VT to refine

refinería F refinery

refiriendo, refiriera, refiriese *ver* referir

reflector M (en una bicicleta) reflector; (en deportes) floodlight; (militar, policial) searchlight

reflejar VT (luz) to reflect; (imagen) to mirror; —**se** to be reflected

reflejo M (luz) reflection; (movimiento) reflex; —**s** frosting; ADJ reflex

reflexión F reflection

reflexionar VI to reflect; — **sobre** to think over

reflexivo ADJ (gramatical) reflexive; (pensativo) thoughtful

reflujo M (de agua) ebb; (gástrico) reflux

reforma F (política) reform; (religiosa) reformation

reformador-ora MF reformer

reformar VT (un gobierno, a un delincuente) to reform; (ropa) to make alterations in; —**se** to mend one's ways

reformatorio M reformatory

reformista MF reformer

reforzado ADJ reinforced; M reinforcement

reforzar[49] VT (una construcción) to reinforce; (las defensas) to beef up; (un argumento) to bolster, to buttress

refracción F refraction

refractario ADJ refractory

refrán M proverb, saying

refrenar VT (un caballo) to rein in; (emociones) to restrain, to check

refrendar VT (una sentencia) to uphold; (un documento) to countersign, to endorse

refrendario-ria MF endorser

refrendo M endorsement

refrescante ADJ refreshing

refrescar[30] VT to refresh (también pantalla de computadora); (el tiempo) to get cool; —**se** to cool off

refresco M (bebida) soft drink; (comida ligera) refreshment

refriega F fray, scuffle

refrigeración F refrigeration

refrigerador ADJ refrigerating; M refrigerator

refrigerante ADJ cooling; M coolant

refrigerar VT to cool, to refrigerate

refrigerio M refreshment

refrito ADJ (comida) refried; M (obra) rerun

refuerzo M (acción de reforzar) reinforcement; (de tela) backing; (de una vacuna) booster

refugiado-da MF refugee

refugiar VT to shelter; —**se** to take shelter

refugio M refuge, shelter; — **antiaéreo** bomb shelter; — **fiscal** tax shelter

refulgente ADJ resplendent

refundir VT to recast

refunfuñar VI to grumble, to mutter

refunfuño M grumbling, muttering

refunfuñón-ona ADJ grouchy, grumpy; MF grouch

refutar VT to refute

regadera F watering can

regadío M (tierra irrigada) irrigated land; (riego) irrigation

regalar VT (dar como presente) to give as a gift; (vender barato, donar) to give away; (agasajar) to regale

regaliz M licorice

regalo M (presente) present, gift; (para los sentidos) treat, delight

regañar VI (un perro) to snarl; VT (a un niño) to scold, to go off on; (constantemente) to nag; LOC ADV **a regañadientes** reluctantly

regaño M scolding, reprimand

regañón-ona ADJ nagging, scolding; MF scold

regar[41] VT (campos) to irrigate; (flores) to water

regate M dribble

regatear VI (precios) to haggle, to bargain; (fútbol) to dribble

regateo M bargaining

regazo M lap

regeneración F regeneration; — **audible** audible feedback

regente MF, **regenta** F regent; F regent's wife; ADJ ruling

reggae M reggae
régimen M (gobierno) regime; (dieta) diet; — **de vida** lifestyle
regimiento M regiment
regio ADJ (propio del rey) regal; (excelente) swell
región F region
regional ADJ regional
regir[14] VT to govern (también en sintaxis); VI to be in force; —**se por** to be guided by
registrador -ora MF (empleado) recorder, registrar; M — **de vuelo** flight recorder
registrar VT (examinar) to search; (dejar constancia) to record, to register; (inscribir) to log; — **al desnudo** to strip-search
registro M (de la voz, lingüístico) register; (de nacimientos) record, register; (del equipaje) search; (de un órgano) stop; (en la computadora) log; — **al desnudo** strip search
regla F (norma) rule; (utensilio para medir) ruler; (menstruación) period; **en** — in order; **por** — **general** as a general rule
reglamentación F (acción de reglamentar) regulation; (conjunto de reglas) regulations
reglamento M regulations; —**s y disposiciones administrativas** rules and regulations
regocijar VT to gladden; —**se** to rejoice
regocijo M joy, rejoicing
regodearse VI (en la desgracia propia) to wallow; (en la desgracia ajena) to gloat
regodeo M (en la desgracia propia) wallowing; (en la desgracia ajena) gloating
regordete ADJ plump
regresar VI to return
regreso M return; **estar de** — to be back
reguero M trail; **correr como un** — **de pólvora** to spread like wildfire
regulación F (acción de regular) regulation; (de una máquina) adjustment
regulador M regulator, governor, throttle; — **de voltaje** dimmer
regular VT (reglamentar) to regulate; (ajustar una máquina) to adjust; ADJ regular; **una paliza** — quite a beating; ADV so-so
regularidad F regularity
regularizar[47] VT (reglamentar) to regulate; (formalizar) to formalize; —**se** to become regular
regurgitar VI/VT to regurgitate
rehabilitación F rehabilitation
rehabilitador ADJ remedial
rehabilitar VT to rehabilitate
rehacer[54, 74] VT to remake; —**se** to recover
rehén MF hostage
rehuir[19] VT (a una persona) to shun; (responsabilidades) to shirk
rehusar[26] VT to refuse; —**se a** to refuse to
reimpresión F reprint

reina F queen
reinado M reign
reinante ADJ (política, opinión) prevailing; (monarca) ruling
reinar VI to reign
reincidencia F (episodio) relapse; (cualidad) recidivism
reincidir VI to relapse
reiniciar VT to reboot, to reset
reino M (territorio de un rey) kingdom, realm; (período de reinado) reign; (división biológica) kingdom; (ámbito) realm
reinserción F reinsertion; — **laboral** reemployment
reinstaurar VT to reinstate
reintegrar VT to rebate; —**se a** to return to
reintegro M rebate
reinvertir VI/VT to reinvest, to roll over
reír[10] VI to laugh; —**se de** to laugh at
reiterar VT to reiterate
reivindicación F (demanda) demand; (rehabilitación) vindication; (responsabilidad) responsibility; **la** — **del atentado** the responsibility for the act
reivindicar[30] VT (vengar) to vindicate; (responsabilizarse) to take responsibility, to claim
reja F (enrejado) grate, grating; (pieza de arado) plowshare; **entre** —**s** behind bars
rejilla F (para equipaje) luggage rack; (de coche) grille
rejuvenecer[35] VT to rejuvenate; VI to become rejuvenated
relación F (conocido) relation, connection; (trato) relationship, involvement; (relato) account, report; (lista) list; **relaciones** (conocidos) connections; (trato) dealings; **relaciones públicas** public relations; **con** — **a** in relation to
relacionado ADJ related, germane
relacionar VT to relate, to connect; —**se con** to relate to
relajación F relaxation
relajamiento M relaxation
relajante ADJ (actividad) relaxing; (droga) sedative; M — **muscular** muscle relaxant
relajar VT to relax; —**se** (abandonarse moralmente) to become lax; (tranquilizarse) to chill [out], to relax
relajo M (aflojamiento) relaxation; (desorden) mess
relamerse VI to lick one's lips
relámpago M lightning
relampaguear VI (el cielo) to lightning; (los ojos, cosa reluciente) to flash
relampagueo M flash of lightning
relatar VT to relate, to recount
relatividad F relativity
relativo ADJ relative; — **a** relative to

relato M (informe) account; (cuento) story, tale
relé M relay
relegar[40] VT to relegate
relevancia F importance
relevante ADJ important
relevar VT (a un trabajador, guardia) to relieve
relevista MF (atletismo) relay runner; (béisbol) reliever; **— de cierre** (béisbol) closer
relevo M (soldado) relief; **carrera de —s** relay race
relicario M reliquary, locket
relieve M relief; **de —** (mapa) relief; (persona) prominent; **poner de —** to emphasize; **letras en —** raised letters
religión F religion
religioso-sa ADJ religious; M monk; F nun
relinchar VI to neigh
relincho M neigh
reliquia F relic
rellenado M filling
rellenar VT (un vaso) to refill, to replenish; (un tanque de gasolina) to fill, to fill up; (un formulario) to fill out; (un hueco) to fill in; (una almohada) to stuff
relleno ADJ (un pimiento) stuffed; (la cara) full, round; (la figura, el cuerpo) plump; M (de comida) stuffing, dressing; (de un colchón) padding
reloj M (de pared) clock; (de muñeca, bolsillo) watch; (de horno) timer; **— de pulsera** wristwatch; **— de sol** sundial; **— despertador** alarm clock; **contra —** against the clock; **como un —** regularly, like clockwork
relojería F (tienda) watch shop; (actividad) clock-making
relojero-ra MF watchmaker
reluciente ADJ shining
relucir[39] VI to shine; **sacar a —** to bring up
relumbrar VI to glare
relumbre M glare
REM M REM
remachar VT (una victoria, un clavo) to clinch; (un remache) to rivet
remache M (acción de remachar) riveting; (clavo) clinching; (tachuela, clavija) rivet
remanente M remainder
remar VI/VT to row, to paddle
remarcado VT mark-up
rematador-ora MF auctioneer
rematar VT (acabar) to finish; (matar) to finish off; (perfeccionar) to give the finishing touches to; (subastar) to auction; VI (patear un balón) to take a shot
remate M (de una obra) finishing touch; (tiro) shot; (subasta) auction; (tenis) smash; **— de un chiste** punch line; **loco de —** stark raving mad
remedador-ora MF mimic

remedar VT to mimic, to ape, to mock
remediar VT to remedy
remedio M remedy, cure; **sin —** unavoidable; **no tiene —** it can't be helped; **no tengo más —** I can't help it; **el — es peor que la enfermedad** the remedy is worse than the disease
remedo M mockery
remendar[1] VT (ropa) to mend, to patch; (calcetines) to darn; (zapatos) to repair
remendón-ona MF cobbler
remero-ra MF rower
remesa F (de mercancías) shipment; (de dinero) remittance
remiendo M (de ropa) patch; (de zapatos) repair
remilgado ADJ fussy, prim
remilgo M fussiness, primness
reminiscencia F reminiscence
remisión F remission
remitente MF sender
remitir VT (enviar) to remit; (dirigir a otra parte de un texto) to refer; **—se** (ceder) to yield; **a las pruebas me remito** the evidence speaks for itself
remo M (pala) oar, paddle; (deporte) rowing
remodelación F (de una casa) remodeling; (de una ciudad) redevelopment, renewal; (de una organización) reorganization
remodelar VI/VT to remodel
remojar VT to soak
remojo M soaking; **poner en —** to soak
remojón M soaking
remolacha F beet
remolcador M tugboat
remolcar[30] VT to tow
remolino M (de viento) whirlwind; (de agua) whirlpool, eddy; (de pelo) cowlick; (juguete) pinwheel; **— de gente** throng, crowd
remolón-ona ADJ dallying; MF dallier
remolonear VI to dally
remolque M (acción de remolcar) tow; (vehículo remolcado) towed vehicle; (vehículo que remolca) tow truck; (caravana de camión) trailer; **llevar a —** to tow
remontada F (deporte) comeback
remontar VT (una cometa) to fly; (una pendiente, un río) to go up; **—se** to rise; **el globo se remonta** the balloon goes up; **el coche se remonta a los años 20** the car dates from the '20s; **para comprenderlo, debemos remontarnos a su juventud** in order to understand him, we must go back to his youth
remorder[6] VT to gnaw at
remordimiento M remorse
remoto ADJ remote, distant; **no tiene la más remota idea** he doesn't have the slightest idea
remover[6] VT (un cargo, un obstáculo) to

remove; (un asunto problemático) to stir up
remuneración F remuneration, compensation
remunerar VT remunerate, compensate
remunerado ADJ gainful
renacentista ADJ Renaissance
renacer[35] VI to be reborn
renacimiento M (resurgimiento) revival; (período histórico) Renaissance
renacuajo M (cría de rana) tadpole; (hombre esmirriado) shrimp
renal ADJ renal
rencilla F quarrel
rencor M rancor; **guardar —** to bear a grudge
rencoroso ADJ resentful
rendición F surrender
rendido ADJ exhausted
rendija F crack
rendimiento M (lo rendido) yield, output; (productividad) performance; **— previo** past performance
rendir[9] VT (someter) to subdue; (producir) to yield; (fatigar) to fatigue; **— homenaje** to pay homage; **— cuentas a** to answer to; VI (obtener buenos resultados) to perform well; **—se** (darse por vencido) to surrender, to give in; (fatigarse) to become fatigued
renegado -da MF renegade
renegar[41] VT (negar) to deny insistently; (repudiar) to renounce; **— de** to gripe about
renegociar VI/VT to renegotiate
renglón M line; **a — seguido** immediately following
rengo ADJ lame
renguear VI to limp
renguera F limp
reno M reindeer
renombrado ADJ renowned
renombre M renown; **de —** of note
renovable ADJ renewable
renovación F renewal; **— urbana** urban renewal
renovador -ora ADJ (artista) innovating; (baño) refreshing; MF innovator
renovar[5] VT (un edificio) to renovate; (ataques, temores) to renew
renquear VT to limp
renta F (de una persona) income; (de un gobierno) revenue; (alquiler) rent; **— anual** annuity; **—s internas** internal revenue; **vivir de la —** to live on the interest
rentabilidad F profitability; **cuentas y depósitos de alta —** high-return accounts and deposits
rentable ADJ (negocio, inversión) profitable; (idea) viable
renuencia F reluctance
renuente ADJ reluctant, loath; **ser — a** to be loath to
renueva, renueve ver renovar

renuevo M sprout
renuncia F (dimisión) resignation; (a un derecho) waiver; (a una herencia) renunciation
renunciar VI **— a** (un cargo) to resign; (la ciudadanía) to renounce; (un derecho) to relinquish, to waive
reñido ADJ contested
reñir[11] VI (discutir) to quarrel, to bicker, to argue; (pelear) to fight, to scuffle; (rezongar) to scold
reo -a MF defendant, accused
reojo M **mirar de —** to look out of the corner of one's eye
reorganización F reorganization
reorganizar[47] VT to reorganize, to regroup
repaginar VT to repaginate
repantigarse[40] VI to lounge
reparación F (compensación) reparation, redress; (arreglo) repair
reparador -ra ADJ refreshing; M serviceman; F service woman
reparar VT (arreglar) to repair; (compensar) to redress; **— en** to notice
reparo M **no tener —s en** to have no qualms about; **sin —s** freely; **hacer —s** to object
repartición F distribution
repartir VT (tierras, un botín) to distribute; (volantes) to hand out; (periódicos) to deliver; (naipes) to deal; (días libres) to space out
reparto M (de tierras) distribution; (de periódicos) delivery; (de naipes) dealing; (ruta de entrega) route; (lista de actores) cast; **— proporcional** apportionment
repasar VI (una lección) to review, to go over again; (en la memoria) to retrace; (leer por encima) to skim
repaso M review
repelente ADJ repellent
repeler VT to repel, to repulse
repente M **de —** suddenly
repentinamente ADV suddenly
repentino ADJ sudden
repercusión F repercussion
repercutir VI to have repercussions
repertorio M repertoire
repetición F (reiteración) repetition; (en tenis) let
repetido ADJ repeated; **repetidas veces** repeatedly
repetir[9] VI/VT (reiterar) to repeat; VI (eructar) to belch; (tomar una segunda ración) to have seconds; **— como loro** to parrot; **—se** to recur
repicar[30] VI/VT to ring
repique M ringing, ring
repiquetear VI/VT to ring
repiqueteo M ringing
repisa F shelf

repita, repitiendo, repitiera, repitiese, repito ver repetir
replegar[41] VT to fold; **—se** to retreat
repleto ADJ replete
réplica F (contestación) reply, comeback; (copia) replica; (temblor secundario) aftershock
replicación F replication
replicar[30] VI/VT (responder) to reply, to rejoin; (reproducirse) to replicate
repliegue M (pliegue marcado) crease; (retirada) retreat
repollo M cabbage
reponer[56, 74] VT (reemplazar) to replace; (restituir) to restore; (replicar) to reply; (una obra de teatro) to revive; (una película) to show again; **—se** to recover one's health
reportaje M feature story
reportar VT (beneficios) to yield; VI (en una organización) to answer to; **—se enfermo** to call in sick
reportero-ra MF reporter
reposado ADJ quiet, calm
reposar VI to repose, to rest; **dejar—** to let steep; M SG **reposacabezas** headrest; M SG **reposapiés** footrest
reposición F (reemplazo) replacement; (de una obra de teatro) revival
reposo M (descanso) repose, rest; (sosiego) calm
repostería F (establecimiento) pastry shop; (actividad) baking
repostero-ra MF pastry cook
reprender VT to reprimand, to scold, to rebuke
reprensión F rebuke
represa F (dique) dam; (reservorio de agua) reservoir
represalia F reprisal
represar VT to dam
representación F (interpretación) representation; (delegación) delegation; (de un papel) portrayal; (de una obra de teatro) performance
representante MF (legislativo) representative; (comercial) agent
representar VT (una imagen) to represent, to depict; (una obra de teatro) to perform; (un personaje) to portray; **tiene treinta años, pero no los representa** he's thirty years old, but he doesn't look it; **tu presencia representa mucho para mí** your presence means a lot to me
representativo ADJ representative
represión F (psicológica) repression; (política) repression, suppression, crackdown
represivo ADJ repressive
reprimenda F reprimand, rebuke
reprimido ADJ repressed, pent-up
reprimir VT (impulsos) to repress; (una tendencia) to check; (enemigos políticos) to suppress, to crack down on; (una rebelión) to quell

reprobación F reproof
reprobar[5] VT to reprove; VI/VT (no aprobar un examen) to flunk, to fail
reprochar VT to reproach, to rebuke
reproche M reproach, rebuke
reproducción F reproduction
reproducir[38] VI/VT to reproduce; **—se** to reproduce, to breed
reproductor-ora ADJ breeding; **aparato—** VCR; MF breeding animal
reproduje, reprodujera, reprodujese, reproduzca, reproduzco ver reproducir
reptar VI to crawl
reptil M reptile
república F republic
republicano-na ADJ & MF republican; (del Partido Republicano) Republican
repudiar VT (a la sociedad) to repudiate; (a un hijo) to disown; (una herencia) to renounce
repuesto M spare part; **de—** spare
repugnancia F repugnance, disgust, revulsion
repugnante ADJ repugnant, disgusting, loathsome
repugnar VI to be repugnant; VT to disgust, to cloy
repulir VT to polish up
repulsa F rebuff, repulse
repulsar VT to repulse
repulsivo ADJ repulsive, creepy
repuntar VI to rally
reputación F reputation
reputado ADJ reputable
requemar VT to burn
requerimiento M request
requerir[8] VT to require
requesón M cottage cheese
requiebros M PL advances
requisa F requisition
requisar VT (interceptar, incautar) to commandeer, to requisition; (registrar) to search
requisito M requirement, requisite
res F animal; **— lanar** sheep; **— vacuna** cow
resabio M (dejillo) aftertaste; (vicio) bad habit
resaca F (de mar) undertow; (malestar físico) hangover
resaltar VI (sobresalir) to stand out; (poner de relieve) to highlight
resarcir[33] VT to compensate for
resbaladizo ADJ slippery, slick
resbalar VI (deslizar) to slip; (ser/estar resbaladizo) to be slippery; **—se** to slip
resbalón M slip; **darse un—** to slip
resbaloso ADJ (que resbala) slippery; Méx fam (inmoral) sleazy
rescatar VT (a un secuestrado) to ransom; (a una persona en peligro) to rescue
rescate M (para un secuestrado) ransom; (de una

persona en peligro) rescue
rescindir VT to rescind
rescoldo M embers
resecar[30] VT to dry; **—se** to dry out
reseco ADJ dried-up, parched
resentido ADJ resentful
resentimiento M resentment, grudge; **guardar —** to hold a grudge, to have hard feelings
resentirse[8] VI to hurt, to suffer; **— de** to resent
reseña F book review
reseñar VT to review
reserva F (de provisiones, de oro, de jugadores, del ejército) reserve; (de localidades, de hotel, de indios) reservation; (de animales) preserve; **sin —s** without reservations; **tener —s** to have reservations
reservación F Am reservation
reservado ADJ (distante) aloof; (discreto) reserved
reservar VT to reserve; **me reservo mi opinión** I'll spare you my opinion
resfriado M common cold; **estoy —** I've got a cold
resfriarse VI to catch cold
resfrío M cold, head cold
resguardar VT to shelter; **—se de** to seek shelter from
resguardo M (abrigo) shelter; (comprobante) deposit slip
residencia F residence
residencial ADJ (para vivir) residential; (en las afueras) suburban
residente ADJ & MF resident
residir VI to reside
residuo M residue
resignación F resignation
resignarse VI to resign oneself
resina F resin
resistencia F (fuerza opuesta) resistance; (de la calefacción) element; (aguante) endurance, stamina
resistente ADJ resistant, tough
resistir VT (una tentación) to resist; (un ataque) to withstand; **—se a un arresto** to resist arrest; VI to resist, to hold [up]
resollar[5] VI (por enfermedad) to wheeze; (después de un esfuerzo) to pant; (por alivio) to sigh
resolución F (acción de resolver) resolution; (ánimo) determination, resolve; **— óptica** optical resolution
resolver[6, 74] VT (decidir) to decide; (solucionar) to solve; **—se a** to resolve to
resonancia F resonance
resonar[5] VI (sonidos) to resound, to boom; (una polémica) to resonate
resoplar VI (con enfado) to huff and puff; (un caballo) to snort

resoplido M (con enojo) puff; (de caballo) snort
resorte M spring
respaldar VT to back, to stand behind
respaldo M (parte de una silla) back; (apoyo) support, backing; **— automático** automatic backup; **— de archivos** backup; **— global** global backup
respectivo ADJ respective
respecto LOC ADV **— a/de** with respect to, concerning; **a ese —** on that score; **con — a** with regard to, regarding, vis-à-vis
respetable ADJ respectable
respetar VT to respect
respeto M respect, regard; **con todo —** with all due respect; **faltar el/al —** to slight, to disregard
respetuoso ADJ respectful
respingado M upturned
respingar[40] VI (dar respingos) to buck; (asustarse) to shy away
respingo M (salto) buck; (susto) start
respiración F respiration, breathing; **— boca a boca** mouth-to-mouth resuscitation
respirar VI/VT (inhalar y exhalar) to breathe; (sentir alivio) to breathe easy; **dejar —** to give a breather
respiratorio ADJ respiratory
respiro M (acto de respirar) breathing; (descanso) respite; **dame un —** I need a break
resplandecer[35] VI (brillar) to glare; (de felicidad) to glow
resplandeciente ADJ resplendent, radiant
resplandor M brilliance, radiance
responder VI (reaccionar) to respond; VT (contestar) to answer; (corresponder) to correspond
respondón ADJ saucy
responsabilidad F (obligación de aceptar consecuencias) responsibility; (obligación de informar) accountability
responsabilizar VT to hold liable, to hold responsible
responsable ADJ (que debe aceptar las consecuencias) responsible; (obligado legalmente) liable; (que tiene que informar) accountable
respuesta F response, answer
resquebrajadura F crack
resquebrajar VI to crack
resquicio M (rendija) crack; (laguna legal) loophole
resta F subtraction
restablecer[35] VT (un servicio) to reestablish; (una costumbre) to revive; **—se** to recover
restador -ora MF receiver
restante ADJ remaining
restañar VT to stanch/staunch
restar VT (sustraer) to subtract; (quitar) to take

away from; (quedar) to remain; — **importancia a** to make light of
restauración F restoration
restaurante M restaurant
restaurar VT (el gobierno) to restore; (muebles) to refurbish
restitución F restitution
restituir[19] VT to pay back, to give back
resto M (lo demás) rest; (sobrante) remainder; (tenis) return of service; **—s** (de un edificio) remains; (de una comida) leftovers; **echar el —** to go all out
restorán M restaurant
restregar[41] VT to scrub, to scour
restricción F restriction
restringir[46] VT to restrict, to constrain
resucitación F resuscitation, revival
resucitar VT to resuscitate, to revive
resuello M (por enfermedad) wheeze; (por fatiga) panting
resuelto ADJ (de carácter decidido) resolute, strong-willed; (de actitud decidida) resolved
resuelto, resuelva, resuelve *ver* resolver
resulta LOC ADV **de —s** as a result
resultado M (de una operación matemática) result; (de un suceso) outcome; (de un partido) score; **— final** (fútbol) final score; **—s científicos** findings; **—s electorales** returns; **como —** as a result; **dar buen —** to pan out; **dar por —** to result in
resultante ADJ resulting, consequent
resultar VI to result; **— de** to result from; **resulta que** it turns out that; **resultó ser un idiota** he turned out to be an idiot, he proved to be an idiot
resumen M summary, abstract; **en —** in sum, in brief
resumir VT to summarize, to sum up; **—se a** to be condensed to, to boil down to
resurgimiento M revival
resurgir[46] VI to arise again
resurrección F resurrection
retablo M altarpiece
retaguardia F rear guard
retal M remnant
retama F broom
retar VT to challenge
retardar VI/VT to retard
retardo M lag
retazo M remnant
retén M (aparato) retainer; (de vigilancia) checkpoint
retención F retention; **— de líquido** fluid retention; **— impositiva** tax withholding
retendrá, retendría *ver* retener
retener[58] VT (una pelota, la atención) to hold; (salarios, fondos) to garnish, to withhold
retenga, retengo *ver* retener
retina F retina

retintín M (en los oídos) ringing; (de cascabeles) jingle
retirada F (de tropas) retreat, withdrawal; (de un diplomático, producto) recall
retirar VT (apartar) to move away; (dinero) to withdraw; (algo dicho) to take back, withdraw; (un producto) to recall; **—se** (para dormir, de un empleo, de la carrera militar) to retire; (un ejército) to retreat, to pull back
retiro M (refugio) retreat; (jubilación) retirement; (de fondos) withdrawal; **— de deuda** debt retirement
reto M challenge
retocar[30] VT to retouch, to touch up
retomar VT to take up again
retoñar VI to sprout
retoño M sprout, shoot, bud
retoque M retouching
retorcer[34] VT (una toalla mojada) to wring out; (la muñeca) to wrench, to twist; **—se** (de dolor) to writhe; (de inquietud) to squirm
retorcido ADJ (persona) devious; (rama) gnarled
retorcimiento M (de dolor) writhing; (de inquietud) squirming
retórica F rhetoric
retornar VT to return
retorno M (de un viajero) return (también en un teclado); (de una costumbre, moda) revival; **— de línea automático** word wrap
retozar[47] VI (en juegos infantiles) to frolic, to romp; (en juegos eróticos) to cavort
retozo M frolic, romp
retractarse VI to take back one's words
retraer[59] VT (las garras) to retract; **—se** to withdraw
retraído ADJ shy
retraimiento M shyness
retrasado ADJ (falto de desarrollo) backward; (deficiente mental) retarded
retrasar VT (atrasar) to delay; (un reloj) to set back; **—se** to fall behind
retraso M delay, lag
retratar VT (describir) to portray; (pintar un retrato) to paint a portrait
retrato M (pintura) portrait; (descripción) portrayal
retreta F retreat
retrete M lavatory
retribución F (acción de retribuir) remuneration; (pago) salary
retro ADJ retro
retroactivo ADJ retroactive
retroalimentación F feedback
retroceder VI (recular) to step back; (por miedo) to recoil, to shrink back; (en un coche) to back up; (al mecanografiar) to backspace; (dar marcha atrás) to backtrack; (tropas) to retreat, to fall back; (una inundación) to recede
retroceso M (pérdida) step back; (de un arma de

fuego) recoil; (económico) recession; (en un teclado) backspace

retrogradismo M backwardness

retrógrado ADJ backward

retroiluminación F backlighting

retroiluminado ADJ backlit

retroproyector M overhead projector

retrovirus M retrovirus

retrucar[30] VT to counter

retruécano M play on words

retumbar VI to rumble, to roll

retumbo M rumble

retuve, retuviera, retuviese ver retener

reubicar[30] VT to relocate

reuma M rheumatism

reumatismo M rheumatism

reumatoide ADJ rheumatoid

reunificación F reunification

reunión F (de negocios) meeting; (informal) get-together; (de ex-alumnos) reunion

reunir[27] VT (juntar) to gather; (convocar) to reunite, to bring together; (coleccionar) to collect; (juntar coraje) to muster; (juntar dinero) to raise; **—se** (formal) to meet; (informal) to get together; (un gentío) to gather

revancha F (venganza) revenge; (en deportes) return game

revelación F revelation

revelado M film development

revelador ADJ revealing

revelar VT (un secreto) to reveal; (película) to develop; (un escándalo) to expose; (información) to disclose; **—se** to show oneself

revendedor -ora MF (de mercadería) middleman; (de entradas) scalper

revender VT (vender de nuevo) to resell; (entradas) to scalp

reventar[1] VI/VT (estallar) to burst, to bust; (morir) to die; (fastidiar) to annoy

reventón M (acción de reventar) bursting; (de un neumático) blowout

reverberar VI to reverberate

reverdecer[35] VI (ponerse verde de nuevo) to become green again; (renovarse) to gain new strength

reverencia F (adoración) reverence; (gesto) bow

reverenciar VT to revere

reverendo -da ADJ & MF reverend

reverente ADJ reverent

reverso M reverse

revertir[8] VI to revert; **— en beneficio de** to be of benefit to

revés M (lado opuesto) reverse; (en tenis) backhand; (contratiempo) setback, downturn; **al —** (con lo de adelante hacia atrás) backwards; (con lo de arriba hacia abajo) upside down; (con lo de adentro hacia

afuera) inside out; **dar vuelta al —** to turn inside out

revestimiento M overlay; (de piso) flooring; (de pared exterior) siding; (de pared interior) paneling

revestir[9] VT (un camino) to surface; (una pared) to cover; (conllevar) to be marked by

revisar VT (examinar) to review, to go over; (un coche) to service

revisión F (de un libro) review; (de una película vieja) revival; (médica, mecánica) checkup

revisor -ora MF (en un tren, autobús) conductor; (de un texto) proofreader

revista F (inspección) inspection; (de tropas) muster; (publicación) magazine, journal, periodical; (espectáculo) revival; **— de historietas** comic book; **— electrónica** e-zine; **pasar —** to pass in review

revistar VT to inspect

revitalizar VT to revitalize

revivir VI/VT to revive

revocación F (de un derecho, de un fallo) revocation; (de una ley) repeal

revocar[30] VT (un fallo) to reverse; (una ley) to repeal; (una pared) to plaster

revolcar[31] VT (derribar) to knock over; **—se** (cerdos) to wallow; (niños) to roll around

revolear VT to roll

revolotear VI to flutter, to flit

revoltijo M (de cosas) jumble; (de pelo) muss

revoltoso -sa ADJ unruly, disorderly; MF troublemaker

revolución F (cambio radical) revolution; (giro) revolution, turn; **revoluciones por minuto** revolutions per minute

revolucionario -ria ADJ revolutionary, earthshaking; MF revolutionary

revolver[6, 74] VT (remover) to stir up; (registrar) to rummage in; (desordenar) to mess up; (huevos) to scramble; (ensalada) to toss; **eso me revuelve el estómago** that makes my stomach turn; **—se en la cama** to toss and turn in bed

revólver M revolver, pistol

revuelo M stir, commotion

revuelta F revolt

revuelto ADJ (el mar) rough; (el ánimo) restless; (el pelo) disheveled; **huevos —s** scrambled eggs

rey M king; **los —es Magos** the Wise Men

reyerta F melee, squabble

rezagarse[40] VI to straggle behind, to lag behind

rezar[47] VI/VT (a Dios) to pray; (un letrero) to say

rezo M prayer

rezongar[40] VI/VT (murmurar) to grumble; (quejarse) to gripe

rezongón -ona ADJ grumpy; MF grouch

rezumar VT to ooze

ría, ríe ver reír

riachuelo M brook
riada F flash flood
ribazo M steep bank
ribera F shore, bank; (de río) riverbank
ribereño ADJ on the bank
ribete M (de uniforme) trimming; (de alfombra) binding; (de ropa) piping; (de mosaico) border; **tener —s de** to have hints of
ribetear VT (un uniforme) to trim; (una alfombra) to bind; (un diseño) to border
ricacho ADJ very rich
rico ADJ (persona) rich, wealthy, affluent; (suelo) rich; (adorno) exquisite; (manjar) delicious; (niño) cute
ridiculizar[47] VT to ridicule, to deride
ridículo ADJ (sin sentido) ridiculous; (absurdo, risible) ludicrous; **hacer el —** to act the fool; **poner en —** to ridicule; **ponerse en —** to make a spectacle of oneself
riego M irrigation
riel M rail
rienda F rein; **dar — suelta** to give a free hand
riendo, riera, rieron, riese ver reír
riesgo M risk; **— ocupacional** occupational hazard/risk; **en —** at risk; **correr un —** to run a risk
rifa F raffle
rifar VT to raffle
rifirrafe M free-for-all
rifle M rifle
rigidez F rigidity
rígido ADJ rigid
rigor M (exactitud) rigor; (dureza) harshness; **en — in** reality; **de —** indispensable
riguroso ADJ (estricto) rigorous; (duro) harsh
rima F rhyme
rimar VI/VT to rhyme
rimbombante ADJ grandiose
rímel M mascara
rin M rim
rincón M (ángulo) corner; (lugar retirado) nook, alcove
rinconera F (estantería) corner cupboard; (mesa) corner table
rinda, rinde, rindiendo, rindiera, rindiese ver rendir
ring M boxing ring
ringlera F row
rinoceronte M rhinoceros
rinoplastia F rhinoplasty, *fam* nose job
rinovirus M rhinovirus
riña F (discusión) quarrel; (pelea) scrap, fight, spat
riñón M (órgano) kidney; (región lumbar) lower back
río M river; **— abajo** downstream
rió ver reír
ripio M rubble
riqueza F wealth; **—s** riches

risa F (carcajada) laugh; (acción, sonido de reír) laughter; **reventar/desternillarse de —** to burst with laughter; **morirse de —** to die laughing; **¡qué —!** what a joke!
risco M crag, bluff
risible ADJ laughable
risita F (burlona) snicker; (ahogada) chuckle
risotada F guffaw, gale of laughter
ristra F string
risueño ADJ (sonriente) smiling; (alegre) cheerful
rítmico ADJ rhythmical
ritmo M rhythm; **— cardíaco** heart rate; **— de vida** pace of life
rito M rite
ritual ADJ & M ritual
rival ADJ & MF rival
rivalidad F rivalry; **— entre hemanos** sibling rivalry
rivalizar[47] VI to rival; **— con** to compete with
rizado ADJ curly; M curling
rizar[47] VT (pelo) to curl, to crimp; (agua) to ripple
rizo M (en el pelo) curl, ringlet; (en el agua) ripple, ruffle; (pirueta de avión) loop
robar VT (a una persona) to rob; (un objeto, dinero) to steal; **—se una base** to steal a base
roble M oak tree
robledal M oak grove
robo M (violento) robbery; (furtivo) theft; **— a mano armada** armed robbery, holdup; **— con allanamiento** burglary; **— de base** base steal; **— de identidad** identity theft
robot M robot
robótica F robotics
robusto ADJ (fuerte) robust; (grueso) stout, stocky; (sólido) sturdy
roca F rock
roce M (de una bala) graze; (de dos superficies) rub, rubbing; (con la ley, la policía) brush
rociada F (acción de rociar) sprinkling, spraying; (de insultos) volley
rociar[28] VI/VT (con agua) to spray, to sprinkle; (con jugo, aliño) to baste
rocín M nag
rocío M (del alba) dew; (en aerosol) spray, mist
rock M rock
rocoso ADJ rocky
rodada F (superficial) track; (profunda) rut
rodadura F rolling
rodaja F flat round slice
rodaje M (de un coche) running; (de una película) shoot
rodante ADJ rolling
rodar[5] VI (girar) to roll; (caer) to tumble down; (vagar) to roam; (filmar) to shoot
rodear VT (cercar) to surround; (cubrir) to wrap around; (evitar) to go around
rodeo M (desvío) detour; (modo de expresarse)

circumlocution; (espectáculo) rodeo
rodilla F knee; **de —s** on one's knees; **hincarse de —s** to kneel down
rodillo M (para pintar) roller; (para cocinar) rolling pin; (para caminos) road roller
rododendro M rhododendron
roedor M rodent
roer[73] VI/VT to gnaw
rogar[42] VT to pray, to beg, to beseech; **hacerse [del]** — to play hard to get; **se ruega no molestar** please do not disturb
rojez F redness
rojizo ADJ reddish
rojo ADJ & M red; **al — vivo** red-hot
rol M role
roletazo M ground ball; **lo sacaron con un —** he grounded out
rollizo ADJ plump; M log
rollo M (de papel, de película, de grasa) roll; (de árbol) log; (de cuerda) reel; (de tela) bolt; (discurso aburrido) long story; (mentira) lie; (lío) mess, hassle; (relación amorosa) affair; (manuscrito) scroll; (de alambre) coil; **dar el — to** hassle
ROM M ROM
romance ADJ Romance; M (lengua románica) Romance language; (español) Spanish language; (relación amorosa) romance; (composición métrica) ballad; **en buen —** in plain language
románico ADJ (arte) Romanesque; (lengua) Romance
romano -na ADJ & MF Roman
romanticismo M (corriente literaria) romanticism; (sentimentalismo) romance
romántico -ca ADJ & MF romantic
rombo M diamond
romería F pilgrimage
romero ra MF (persona) pilgrim; M rosemary
romo ADJ (sin punta) blunt; (sin filo) dull
romper[74] VI/VT (un jarrón) to break; VT (relaciones) to sever; **— a** to start to; **— con** to break up with; **— el alba** to dawn; **— filas** to break ranks; **— un contrato** to break a contract; **rompió las aguas / la fuente** her water broke; **de rompe y rasga** coarse; M SG **rompecabezas** jigsaw puzzle; M SG **rompehuelgas** strikebreaker; M SG **rompeolas** breakwater
rompible ADJ breakable
rompientes M PL surf
rompimiento M (con el pasado) break; (de una promesa) breach
rompope M *Méx* eggnog
ron M rum
roncar[30] VI to snore
roncha F (de sarampión) spot; (de mosquito) bite
ronco ADJ hoarse, raspy
ronda F (de policía) patrol, beat; (de niños)

circle; (de bebidas, de negociaciones, de golf) round
rondar VT (patrullar) to patrol; (acercarse) to hang around; (cantar serenatas) to serenade; **rondaba los cuarenta** she was around forty years old
ronquera F hoarseness
ronquido M snore
ronronear VI to purr
ronroneo M purr
ronzal M halter
roña F (enfermedad de plantas) scab; (sarna) mange; MF (tacaño) skinflint
roñoso ADJ (planta) scabby; (animal) mangy; (persona) stingy
ropa F clothing, clothes; **— blanca** linens; **— vieja** stew made from leftover meat
ropaje M apparel
ropería F checkroom
ropero M (armario) wardrobe; (cuarto) closet
roque M castle
rorro M baby
rosa F (flor) rose; (marca) blemish; **— de los vientos** mariner's compass; ADJ INV (rosado) rose-colored, pink; (homosexual) *fam* gay
rosado ADJ (saludable) rosy; (de color de rosa) rose-colored, pink; M rosé wine
rosal M rosebush
rosario M rosary
rosbif M roast beef
rosca F (de tornillo) screw; (pan) ring-shaped roll; **pasarse de —** to go off the deep end
roséola F roseola
rostro M (cara) face; (morro) nerve
rotación F rotation
rotar VI/VT to rotate
rotativo ADJ (movimiento) rotary; (cultivos) rotating; M newspaper
rotatorio ADJ rotary
roto ADJ (averiado) broken; (cansado) exhausted; (ropa, voz) ragged
roto *ver* romper
rotor M rotor
rótula F kneecap
rotular VT to label
rótulo M (título) title; (etiqueta) label
rotundo ADJ resounding; **una negativa rotunda** a categorical denial
rotura F (de un aparato) break; (de un órgano, tubo) rupture; **— de servicio** (tenis) service break
roturar VT to plow
round M (en boxeo) round
rozadura F chafing
rozamiento M friction
rozar[47] VT (herir levemente) to graze; (arañar) to scrape; (irritar) to rub, to chafe; (limpiar un terreno) to clear; **—se con alguien** to have dealings with someone; **rozaba en los**

cuarenta she was almost forty years old
Ruanda F Rwanda
ruandés -esa ADJ & MF Rwandan
rubéola/rubeola F rubella
rubí M (piedra preciosa) ruby; (en un reloj) jewel
rubicundo ADJ (permanente) ruddy; (temporal) flush
rubio -a ADJ & MF blond
rubor M (de la piel) blush, flush; (de las mejillas) bloom, glow
ruborizarse[47] VI to blush
rúbrica F (trazo) flourish; (título) title
rucio ADJ gray
rudeza F rudeness, coarseness
rudo ADJ rude, coarse; — **golpe** hard blow
rueca F spinning wheel
rueda F (de coche) wheel; (de personas) circle; (rodaja) slice; — **de prensa** news conference; **ir sobre —s** to be smooth sailing
ruedo M (de un circo) ring; (de vestido) hem
ruego M (plegaria) prayer; (petición) plea, entreaty
rufián M (matón) ruffian; (proxeneta) pimp
rugby M rugby
rugido M roar
rugir[46] VI (animal) to roar; (estómago) to growl
rugoso ADJ rough
ruibarbo M rhubarb
ruido M noise; — **de fondo** background noise; **mucho — y pocas nueces** much ado about nothing
ruidoso ADJ noisy, loud
ruin ADJ (persona, cosa) vile; (animal) puny
ruina F (destrucción) destruction; (edificio derruido, estado de pobreza) ruin; (persona) wreck; (perjuicio) downfall; **en —s** in ruins
ruindad F (actitud) vileness; (acto) vile act
ruinoso ADJ ruinous
ruiseñor M nightingale
rulero M RP roller, curler
ruleta F roulette
rulo M roller, curler
Rumania F Romania, Rumania
rumano -na ADJ & MF Romanian, Rumanian
rumba F rumba
rumbear VI (dirigirse a) to head in a certain direction; (bailar) to dance the rumba
rumbo M course, route; — **a** toward
rumiar VI (meditar, comer el rumen) to ruminate; (reflexionar) to ruminate, to mull over, to brood over
rumor M rumor
runrún M (rumor) rumor; (sonido sordo) humming
ruptura F (de relaciones) break; (de órganos internos) rupture
rural ADJ rural
Rusia F Russia
ruso -sa ADJ & MF (persona) Russian; M (lengua) Russian
rústico ADJ (rural) rustic, rural; (tosco) coarse; **en rústica** paperback
ruta F (itinerario) route; (carretera) highway; (en informática) path
rutina F routine

Ss

sábado M Saturday
sábalo M shad
sábana F bed sheet
sabana F savannah
sabañón M chilblain
saber[71] VI/VT to know; (tener sabor) to taste; — **nadar** to know how to swim; **supo la verdad** he found out the truth; **las vacaciones me han sabido a poco** my vacation was too short; — **a ciencia cierta** to know for sure; — **de biología** to know all about biology; **a** — namely; **hacer** — to let know; **para que sepas** for your information; **sabérselas todas** to know the ropes; **vaya a** — who knows? **no sabe un comino** he doesn't know squat; — **a** to taste like; **sabe bien** it tastes good; M knowledge, learning; **a mi leal** — **y entender** as far as I know; M SG **sabelotodo** know-it-all
sabiduría F wisdom
sabiendas LOC ADV **a** — knowingly
sabiondo -da ADJ & MF wise guy; know-it-all
sabio -bia ADJ wise, sage; MF (estudioso) scholar; (sabedor) sage, wise person
sable M saber
sabor M taste, flavor
saborear VT to savor, to relish
sabotaje M sabotage
sabotear VT to sabotage
sabrá, sabría ver saber
sabroso ADJ (comida) savory, tasty; (cuento) juicy
sabueso M (perro) bloodhound; (detective) sleuth
sacador -ora MF (en deportes) server
sacar[30] VT (cosas de la maleta, a pasear) to take out; (manchas, dinero del banco) to get out; (los zapatos) to take off; (malas notas, carnet de conducir) to get; (una copia) to make; (una foto) to take; (una conclusión) to draw; (la lengua, la cabeza por la ventana) to stick out; (una pelota de tenis) to serve; (una asignatura escolar) Esp to pass; — **ampollas** to blister; — **brillo** to polish up; — **provecho [de]** to benefit [from]; — **a bailar** to ask to dance; — **a colación** to broach; — **a luz** to divulge; —

de un apuro to bail out; **me saca de quicio** he gets my goat, he gets on my nerves; **— el cuerpo** to dodge; **— el mejor partido de** to make the best of; **—le el jugo a algo** to make the most of; **— en limpio** to deduce; **—se el sombrero** *Am* to take off one's hat; **¡sáquese de allí!** *Am* get out of there! **— punta** to sharpen; **— a alguien** (béisbol) to get someone out; M SG **sacabocados** punch; M SG **sacacorchos** corkscrew; M SG **sacamuelas** quack dentist; M SG **sacapuntas** pencil sharpener

sacarina F saccharine

sacarosa F sucrose

sacerdocio M priesthood

sacerdote M priest

saciar VT to satiate; **—se** to be satiated

saco M (bolsa) sack; (chaqueta) blazer, sport coat; (aparato de boxeo) punching bag; (parte de órgano interno) sac; **— de dormir** sleeping bag; **— de noche** overnight bag; **echar en — roto** to waste one's effort

sacramento M sacrament

sacrificar[30] VT (en un rito religioso) to sacrifice; (una mascota) to put to sleep

sacrificio M sacrifice (también en béisbol)

sacrilegio M sacrilege

sacrílego ADJ sacrilegious

sacristán M sexton

sacro M sacrum

sacudida F (sacudón) shake, jolt; (de terremoto) tremor; (de la cabeza) toss; (eléctrica) shock

sacudir VT (sarandear) to shake; (las alfombras) to beat; (el polvo) to dust; **ir sacudiéndose** to rattle along, to jolt along; **—se de alguien** to get rid of someone

sádico ADJ sadistic

sadismo M sadism

sadomasoquismo M sadomasochism

saeta F arrow

safari M safari

sagaz ADJ shrewd, astute

sagrado ADJ sacred, holy; **Sagradas Escrituras** Holy Scripture

sahumar VT to perfume with incense

sahumerio M burning of incense

sainete M one-act farce; **esa familia es un —** that family is a complete mess

sal F (mineral) salt; (gracia) wit; **— de Epsom** Epsom salt; **— gorda** cooking salt; **— yodada** iodized salt; **— de mesa** table salt; **dar —** to spice up; **— y pimienta** (condimentos) salt and pepper; (gracia) life, spark

sal *ver* salir

sala F (de estar) parlor, living room; (grande) hall, large room; **— de justicia** courtroom; **— de clase** classroom; **— de chat** chat room; **— de cuidados intensivos** intensive

care unit; **— de espera** waiting room; **— de directorio** boardroom; **— de lectura** reading room; **— de operaciones** operating room; **— de recuperación** recovery room

salado ADJ (con sal) salty, savory; (gracioso) witty; *Am* (caro) expensive; M (acción) salting

salamandra F salamander

salar VT to salt; **—se** to become salty

salarial ADJ salary, wage

salario M pay, wages; **— base** base pay; **— bruto** gross pay; **— de subsistencia** living wage; **— mínimo** minimum wage

salchicha F sausage

saldar VT to settle

saldo M (resultado final) balance; (venta especial) sale; **—s** (restos) remnants; **— pendiente** balance due

saldrá, saldría *ver* salir

salegar[40] VT to give salt to; M salt lick

salero M (dispensador) salt cellar, salt shaker; (gracia) charm

saleroso ADJ charming

salga, salgo *ver* salir

salida F (partida) departure; (puerta) exit, way out; (comienzo de una carrera) start; (militar) sally; (eléctrica, de computadora) output; (de una crisis) way out; **este artículo tiene mucha —** this article sells well; **dar la —** to start a race; **— del sol** sunrise; **— de emergencia** emergency exit; **— en falso** false start

saliente ADJ (roca) salient, projecting; (gobierno) outgoing; M salient, projection, overhang

salina F salt mine

salino ADJ saline

salir[57] VI (del interior al exterior, para divertirse) to go out; (de un país) to depart, to leave; (del trabajo) to quit; (de un programa de computadora) to exit, to quit; (manchas de tinta) to come out; (un anillo del dedo) to come off; (el sol) to rise; (una publicación) to appear; (flores) to sprout; **— a bolsa** to go public; **— del armario** *Esp* to come out; **— del clóset** *Am* to come out; **trabajando no se puede — de pobre** you can't work your way out of poverty; **salió a su madre** she takes after her mother; **— a la luz** to surface; **— adelante** to overcome difficulties; **— bien** to turn out well; **— con** to date; **— ganando** to come out ahead; **— mal** to go wrong; **¿a cuánto sale?** how much is it? **no me sale ser amable con él** I can't bring myself to be nice to him; **—se** (gotear) to leak; (rebosar) to overflow; (proyectarse) to stick out

salitre F saltpeter

saliva F saliva

salmón M salmon

salmonela F salmonella
salmuera F brine
salobre ADJ salty
salomonense ADJ & MF Solomon Islander
salón M (de estar) living room, parlor; (de conferencias) hall; — **de belleza** beauty salon; — **de clase** classroom; — **de exposición y ventas** showroom; — **de exhibición** exhibition hall; — **de té** tearoom
salpicadero M dashboard
salpicadura F spatter, splash, splatter
salpicar[30] VI/VT (humedecer) to sprinkle, to spatter, to splash; (adornar) to punctuate; (dispersar) to intersperse
salpicón M meat salad
salpimentar[1] VT to salt and pepper
salsa F (blanca) sauce; (picante) salsa; **en su** — in her element; — **tártara** tartar sauce; — **de soya** soy sauce; — **de tomate** ketchup
saltar VI/VT (brincar) to jump, to leap; (una cerca) to jump over, to vault; (un renglón) to skip; (una ley) to ignore; VI (los fusibles) to trip; — **a la vista** to be obvious; — **sobre** to pounce on; **se le saltaron los ojos** his eyes bugged out; **se le saltó un botón** one of his buttons popped off; **se me saltaban las lágrimas** it brought tears to my eyes; M SG **saltamontes** grasshopper
salteador -ora MF bandit
saltear VT to stir-fry
salto M jump, leap; — **alto** high jump; — **con esquí** ski jump; — **con pértiga** pole vault; — **de agua** waterfall; — **de cama** dressing gown; — **de línea** return; — **de línea forzado** hard return; — **de línea suave** soft return; — **de longitud** broad jump; — **de página** page break; — **de página forzado** forced page break, hard page break; — **de página suave/automático** soft page break; — **del ángel** swan dive; — **mortal** somersault; — **triple** triple jump; **a — de mata** from hand to mouth; **dar un** — (saltar) to jump; (el corazón) to skip a beat
saltón ADJ (que salta) jumping; (que resalta) bulging; M grasshopper
salubridad F sanitation
salud F health; — **mental** mental health; — **pública** public health; **curarse en** — to take precautions; INTERJ cheers!
saludable ADJ healthy, healthful
saludar VT (decir hola) to greet; (dar la bienvenida) to salute, to hail; (en el ejército) to salute; (hacer un gesto amistoso con la mano) to wave
saludo M (hola) greeting, salutation; (gesto) wave; (militar) salute; **retirar el — a alguien** to stop speaking to someone; **—s** best wishes, regards

salva F salvo
salvación F salvation
salvado M (harina) bran; (béisbol) save
salvador -ora MF savior; ADJ saving
salvadoreño -ña ADJ & MF Salvador[i]an
salvaguarda F safeguard
salvaguardar VT to safeguard
salvajada F (acción) savage act; (comentario) savage remark
salvaje ADJ (feroz) savage; (no domesticado) wild; MF savage
salvajismo M savagery
salvamento M (de gente) rescue; (de bienes, propiedades) salvage; (béisbol) save
salvar VT (la vida, el alma) to save; (de un peligro) to rescue; (propiedad) to salvage; (un obstáculo) to clear; (un camino difícil) to negotiate; — **el pellejo** to save one's skin; **el puente salva el río** the bridge spans the river; —**se** to pull through; —**se por poco** to have a narrow escape; **sálvese quien pueda** every man for himself; M SG **salvapantallas** screen saver; M SG **salvavidas** (aparato) life preserver, life jacket; MF (persona) lifeguard
salvia F sage
salvo ADJ safe; **a** — safe; M —**conducto** safe-conduct; PREP save, except; — **en caso de desastre** barring a disaster
Samoa F Samoa
samoano -na ADJ & MF Samoan
sanar VI/VT to heal; M **sanalotodo** cure-all
sanatorio M (para convalecientes) sanatorium; (para enfermos) hospital
sanción F sanction
sancionar VT to sanction
sandalia F sandal
sandez F (acción) stupidity, foolishness; (dicho) foolish remark
sandía F watermelon
saneamiento M sanitation
sanear VT to drain
sangrar VI/VT to bleed; VT (un árbol) to tap; (un párrafo) to indent
sangre F blood; — **fría** coolness under pressure; **a — fría** in cold blood; **hacerse mala** — to get upset; **eso lo llevo en la** — that's in my blood; **de — caliente** warm-blooded; — **azul** blue blood; **sudar** — to sweat bullets; **de pura** — thoroughbred; **chupar la — a alguien** to be a parasite on someone
sangría F (bebida) wine punch; (acción de sangrar) bleeding; (espacio tipográfico) indentation; (pérdida) drain
sangriento ADJ (manchado de sangre, que provoca pérdida de sangre) bloody; (sanguinario) bloodthirsty
sanguijuela F leech
sanguinario ADJ bloody, vicious
sanguíneo ADJ blood; **grupo** — blood group

sanidad F public health
sanitario -ria ADJ sanitary; M —**s** bathroom fittings; MF public health worker
sanmarinense ADJ & MF San Marinese
sanmarinés -esa ADJ & MF San Marinese
sano ADJ (persona) healthy; (juicio) sound; (dieta) healthful; (vaso) unbroken; — **y salvo** safe and sound; **en su** — **juicio** of sound mind
sánscrito M Sanskrit
sanseacabó INTERJ **te quedas y** — you're staying and that's that
santalucense ADJ & MF St. Lucian
santiamén LOC ADV **en un** — in a jiffy, lickety-split
santidad F sanctity, holiness
santificar[30] VT to sanctify
santiguarse[25] VI to cross oneself
santo -ta ADJ saintly, holy; **esperar todo el** — **día** to wait the whole blessed day; MF saint; **día del** — saint's day; **quedarse para vestir** —**s** to be a spinster; **¿a** — **de qué?** for what reason? **¡por todos los** —**s!** my goodness!
santotomense ADJ & MF São Tomean
santuario M sanctuary
santurrón -ona ADJ & MF goody-goody
saña F fury
sañudo ADJ furious
sapo M toad (también hombre feo); **echar** —**s y culebras** to swear, to curse; **sentirse como un** — **de otro pozo** to feel like a fish out of water
saque M (tenis) service, serve; — **de inicio** (fútbol) kickoff; — **de banda** throw-in; — **de esquina** corner kick; — **de meta** goal kick; — **de puerta** goal kick; — **inicial** kick-off; — **ganador** ace; — **y volea** (tenis) serve and volley
saquear VT to sack, to plunder, to pillage
saqueo M sacking, plundering, pillaging
sarampión M measles; — **alemán** rubella
sarape M *Méx* serape
sarcasmo M sarcasm
sarcástico ADJ sarcastic
sarcófago M sarcophagus
sarcoma M sarcoma
sardina F sardine
sardo -da ADJ & MF Sardinian
sardónico ADJ sardonic
sargento -ta MF sergeant; F battle-ax[e]
sarmentoso ADJ gnarled
sarmiento M vine
sarna F mange
sarnoso ADJ mangy
sarpullido M rash
sarro M tartar, plaque
sarta F string; **una** — **de mentiras** a pack of lies; **una** — **de idiotas** a bunch of idiots

sartén F frying pan, skillet
sastre -tra MF tailor
sastrería F tailor shop
satánico ADJ satanic
satélite M satellite; — **artificial** man-made satellite
satén M satin
sátira F satire
satírico ADJ satirical
satirizar[47] VT to satirize
satisfacción F satisfaction
satisfacer[54, 74] VT (un deseo) to satisfy; (una deuda) to pay; —**se** to be satisfied
satisfactorio ADJ (aceptable) satisfactory; (exitoso) successful
satisfaga, satisfago, satisfará, satisfaría *ver* satisfacer
satisfecho ADJ contented, satisfied
satisfecho, satisfice, satisficiera, satisficiese *ver* satisfacer
saturar VT (una solución) to saturate; (un mercado) to glut; (líneas de teléfono) to overload
sauce M willow; — **llorón** weeping willow
saudí, saudita ADJ & MF Saudi Arabian
savia F sap
saxofón M saxophone
sazón F season; **a la** — at that time; **en** — ripe
sazonar VT (condimentar) to season, to flavor; (madurar) to ripen
scooter M scooter
scout MF scout
se PRON PERS — **coronó a sí mismo** he crowned himself; — **lavó la cara** he washed his face; **besaron** they kissed each other; — **habla español** Spanish is spoken; — **lo puede combatir** it can be fought
sé *ver* saber
sea, seas *ver* ser
sebo M tallow, fat
seborrea F seborrhea
secador M hair dryer
secadora F clothes dryer
secante ADJ drying
secar[30] VT (la ropa) to dry; (las manos) to dry off; —**se** (planta) to dry up; (río) to run dry; (madera) to season
sección F (militar) platoon; (de un almacén) department; (un texto) section
seccionar VT to section
seco ADJ (ropa) dry; (río) dried-up; (planta) withered; (respuesta) curt, brief; **en** — on dry land; **parar en** — to stop short; **quedar** — to fall dead; **estar** — to be broke; **lavar en** — to dry-clean; **a secas** plain
secreción F secretion
secretar VT to secrete
secretaría F secretariat
secretariado M (profesión) secretarial

profession; (secretaría) secretariat; (conjunto de secretarias) secretarial pool

secretario-ria MF secretary; — **general** secretary general

secretear VI to whisper

secreto ADJ (oculto) secret; (policía) undercover; M (cosa oculta) secret; (condición de oculto) secrecy; — **a voces** open secret; **en** — in secret; — **bancario** account holder confidentiality

secta F sect

sector M sector

sectorial ADJ sectorial

secuaz M henchman

secuela F consequence; —**s** aftermath

secuencia F (de acontecimientos) sequence; (de datos) string

secuenciar VT to sequence

secuestrador-ora MF kidnapper

secuestrar VT (a una persona) to kidnap, to abduct; (una propiedad) to seize; (un avión) to hijack

secuestro M (de una persona) kidnapping; (de propiedad) seizure; (de un avión) hijacking

secular ADJ secular

secundar VT (apoyar) to second; (imitar) to imitate; (seguir) to follow suit

secundaria F secondary school

secundario ADJ secondary

sed F thirst; **tener** — to be thirsty

seda F silk; **como una** — (suave) soft as silk; (afable) sweet-tempered

sedación F sedation

sedán M sedan

sedante ADJ & M sedative

sedar VT to sedate

sedativo ADJ & M sedative

sede F (gubernamental) seat; (religiosa) see; — **central** headquarters

sedentario ADJ sedentary

sedería F (conjunto de artículos de seda) silk goods; (tienda de sedas) silk shop

sedero-ra MF (que vende) silk dealer; (que fabrica) silk weaver; ADJ **industria sedera** silk industry

sedición F sedition

sediento ADJ thirsty; **estar** — **de** to thirst for

sedimento M sediment

sedoso ADJ silken, silky

seducción F seduction

seducir[38] VT (corromper) to seduce; (atraer) to entice; (persuadir con argucias) to lure

seductivo ADJ alluring

seductor-ora ADJ alluring; M seducer; F seductress

sefardí ADJ Sephardic; MF Sephardi; M (variedad del español) Sephardi

sefardita ADJ & MF Sephardi

segador-ora MF (persona) mower, reaper; F (máquina) mower, reaper

segar[41] VT (hierba) to mow; (mies) to reap

seglar ADJ secular; M layman; F laywoman

segmento M segment

segregar[40] VT (separar) to segregate; (producir secreciones) to secrete

seguido ADJ in a row; **dos horas seguidas** two hours in a row; ADV straight through; **trabajaron** — they worked continuously

seguidor-ora MF follower

seguimiento M (persecución) pursuit; (atención continuada) follow-up

seguir[12] VT (camino, instrucciones) to follow; (estudios) to pursue; (progreso de un avión) to track; **sigue trabajando** he keeps on working, he continues to work; **sigue allí** he is still there; **de lo anterior se sigue que** from the preceding it follows that; — **los pasos de** to follow in the footsteps of; —**le la corriente a alguien** to play along with someone; — **el tren** to keep up; — **el hilo de** to keep track of; — **la pista de** to trail

según PREP according to; — **se mire** depending on how you see it; — **pasa el tiempo** as time goes by; — **tus instrucciones** per your instructions; CONJ as; — **se informa** reportedly; **lo haré** — **me digas** I will do it as you tell me to

segundero M second hand

segundo-da ADJ & ADV second; MF second in command; — **tiempo** (fútbol) second half; — **servicio** (tenis) second serve; **segunda base** (posición en béisbol) second base; M (jugador) second baseman; **segunda hipoteca** second mortgage; **segunda intención** ulterior motive; **de segunda mano** secondhand, preowned; **de segunda** second-rate

segundón-ona MF (hijo) second-born child; (persona mediocre) also-ran

seguramente ADV certainly, surely; **lenta pero** — slowly but surely

seguridad F (contra el delito) security; (contra accidentes) safety; — **en sí mismo** self-confidence; — **social** social security

seguro ADJ (a prueba de delincuentes) secure; (que no ofrece o siente duda) sure, certain; (libre de peligro) safe; (firme) stable; **es** — **que** it is certain that; **su** — **servidor** yours truly; — **de sí mismo** self-assured; M (contrato contra riesgos) insurance; (dispositivo) safety device, restraint; — **contra accidentes** accident insurance; — **contra daños a terceros** liability insurance; — **contra incendios** fire insurance; — **contra inundaciones** flood insurance; — **contra todo riesgo** comprehensive insurance; — **de discapacidad** disability insurance; — **de**

vida life insurance; — **de vida a término** term life insurance; — **de vida permanente** whole life insurance; — **médico** health insurance; **en** — in safety; **sobre** — without risk

seis NUM six

selección F selection, choice; — **de texto** highlighting; — **natural** natural selection; — **nacional** national team

seleccionado M — **nacional** national team

seleccionar VT to select, to choose

selectivo ADJ selective

selecto ADJ select, choice

sellar VT (poner sello) to stamp; (precintar) to seal

sello M (de correo) stamp; (de documento oficial) seal; (instrumento) seal, stamp; (de discos) label; — **de goma** rubber stamp; — **fiscal** revenue stamp

selva F (templada o fría) forest; (tropical) jungle; — **virgen** virgin forest

semáforo M traffic light

semana F week; **entre** — during the week

semanal ADJ weekly

semanario M weekly publication

semántica F semantics

semblante M countenance

semblanza F biographical sketch

sembrado M sown ground

sembradora F planting machine

sembrar¹ VT (plantar) to sow, to plant; (esparcir) to scatter; (minas) to lay; (pánico, alegría) to spread

semejante ADJ similar, like; — **afirmación** such a statement; **un tipo** — such a guy; M fellow human being

semejanza F resemblance, similarity; **a** — **de** in the manner of

semejar VT to resemble

semen M semen, sperm

semental ADJ stud; M stud, stallion

semestral ADJ biannual

semestre M semester

semianual ADJ biannual

semicírculo M semicircle

semiconductor M semiconductor

semifinal ADJ & F semifinal

semilla F seed

semillero M seedbed; — **de vicios** hotbed of vice

seminario M (religioso) seminary; (universitario) seminar

semítico ADJ Semitic

senado M senate

senador-ora MF senator

sencillez F simplicity; **con** — simply

sencillo ADJ (no complicado, humilde) simple; (fácil) easy, simple; (sin adornos) plain; (no afectado) straightforward; M (béisbol) single

senda F (construida) path, pathway; (natural) track, trail

sendero M (construido) path, pathway; (natural) track, trail

sendos ADJ **tenían** — **sombreros** each one had a hat

Senegal M Senegal

senegalés -esa ADJ & MF Senegalese

senil ADJ senile

senilidad F senility

seno M (pecho) breast; (hueco) sinus; (útero) womb; (en matemática) sine; — **de la familia** bosom of the family

sensación F (física) sensation; (mental) feeling, impression; **tengo la** — **de que** I have the feeling that; **fue la** — **de la fiesta** she was the life of the party

sensacional ADJ sensational

sensatez F common sense

sensato ADJ sensible, level-headed

sensibilidad F (modo de pensar) sensibility; (percepción) sensitiveness

sensibilizar⁴⁷ VT to sensitize

sensible ADJ (que siente) sensitive; (notable) perceptible; **tengo el brazo muy** — **por el accidente** my arm is very tender because of the accident; **Juana es muy** — **en estas ocasiones** Juana is very emotional on these occasions

sensiblería F sentimentality

sensiblero ADJ sentimental, mushy

sensitivo ADJ sensitive

sensor M sensor

sensorial ADJ sensory

sensual ADJ (carnal) sensual; (de los sentidos) sensuous

sensualidad F sensuality

sentada F (acto de sentarse) sitting; (protesta) sit-in; **de una** — at one sitting

sentado ADJ **dar por** — to take for granted

sentar¹ VT to seat; — **bien** to agree with; **me sentó muy mal lo que dijo** what he said did not sit well with me; **este peinado te sienta** this hairdo becomes you; **no te sienta ese traje** that suit does not fit you; — **precedente** to set a precedent; —**se** to sit down

sentencia F (dicho) maxim; (fallo) ruling; (condena) sentence; (indemnización) award

sentenciar VT (condenar) to sentence; (fallar) to rule

sentido ADJ heartfelt; M (facultad) sense; (significado) meaning; (dirección) way; — **común** common sense; — **de la vista** sense of sight; — **del gusto** sense of taste; — **del humor** sense of humor; — **del oído** sense of hearing; — **del olfato** sense of smell; — **del tacto** sense of touch; **aguzar el** — to prick up one's ears; **de un solo** — one-way; **de dos**

—s two-way; **dejar sin —** to render unconscious; **en cierto —** in a sense; **perder el —** to faint; **quedar —** to have one's feelings hurt; **sin —** meaningless; **tener —** to make sense

sentimental ADJ sentimental

sentimentalismo M sentimentality

sentimiento M feeling, sentiment

sentir[8] VT (percibir) to feel; (oír) to hear; (lamentar) to regret; **—se** to feel; **—se capaz de** to feel up to; **—se de los pies** to have pains in the feet

seña F (gesto) sign; (rasgo) trait; (marca) mark; **—s** name and address; **por más —s** as an additional proof; **—s de vida** life signs; **hablar por —s** to use sign language; **hacer —s** to signal

señal F (de tráfico, de violencia, de vida, de la cruz) sign; (de violencia) mark; (de radio) signal; (pago anticipado) deposit; **en — de** in token of

señalar VT (marcar, señalar) to mark; (mostrar, mencionar) to point out; (fijar) to fix; **—se** to distinguish oneself

señor M (título) Mr.; (forma de tratamiento) sir; (dueño) *lit* master, lord; **el Señor** the Lord; **un gran —** a great man

señora F (dama) lady; (forma de tratamiento) madam, ma'am; (título) Mrs., Ms.; (esposa) wife

señorear VI to dominate

señoría F lordship; **su —** Your Honor

señorial ADJ lordly

señorío M (dominio) dominion; (dignidad) lordship

señorita F miss; **toda una —** quite a young lady

señorito M (joven) master; (dandi) dandy

señuelo M decoy, lure

sepa, sepamos *ver* saber

separación F separation

separado ADJ (apartado) separate; (estado civil) separated; **por —** separately

separar VT (apartar) to separate; (clasificar) to sort out; (despedir de un cargo) to remove; **—se** to separate, to part company

separata F offprint, reprint

septentrional ADJ northern

septicemia F blood poisoning

septiembre, setiembre M September

séptimo ADJ & M seventh

sepulcro M tomb

sepultar VT to bury, to inter

sepultura F (acción) burial; (lugar) grave, tomb; **dar —** to bury

sepulturero -ra MF gravedigger

sequedad F dryness

sequía F drought

séquito M retinue, entourage

ser[65] VI to be; **— de Valencia** to be from

Valencia; **— de madera** to be made of wood; **a no — que** unless; **así es** that's right; **érase una vez** once upon a time; **es decir** that is to say; **es de esperar** it is to be expected; **es más** what's more; **la boda es hoy** the wedding takes place today; **son las nueve** it is nine o'clock; **somos cuatro** there are four of us; V AUX to be; **fue elegido presidente** he was elected president; M (entidad viviente) being; (esencia) essence; (existencia) existence; **un — humano** a human being

serbio -bia ADJ Serbian; MF (persona) Serb, Serbian; M (lengua) Serbian

serenar VI to quiet; **—se** (el alma) to become serene, to calm down; (el tiempo) to clear up

serenata F serenade; **dar —** to serenade

serenidad F serenity, peace of mind

sereno ADJ (mar, alma) serene; (cielo) clear; **al —** in the night air; M night watchman

serie F series; **— de instrucciones** (en un programa de computadora) macro; **en — ** serial; **— ofensiva** offensive series

seriedad F seriousness, earnestness

serio ADJ (problema) serious; (persona) earnest, serious; **en —** seriously

sermón M (prédica) sermon; (reprimenda) lecture

sermonear VI/VT (predicar) to preach; (reprender) to lecture

serpentear VI to wind, to meander

serpiente F snake

serrado ADJ serrated

serranía F mountainous region

serrano -na M mountain man; F mountain woman; ADJ **zona serrana** mountain region

serrín M sawdust

serrucho M handsaw

servicial ADJ helpful

servicio M (también en tenis) service; (sirvientes) servants; (para un comensal) place setting; (aseo) restroom, facilities; **— a la habitación** room service; **— de ayuda al usuario** helpdesk; **— de contestador** answering service; **— de entrega** delivery service; **— directo** ace; **— militar** military service; **a su —** at your service; **de — pesado** heavy-duty; **estar en —** to be in commission; **poner en —** to commission, to put into service

servidor -ora MF (persona) servant; **un —** yours truly; **su seguro —** yours truly; M (ordenador) server; **— remoto** remote server

servidumbre F servitude

servil ADJ (personalidad) servile; (trabajo) menial

servilleta F napkin

servir[9] VI to serve; **— de** to serve as; **— para** to be used for; **para —le** at your service; **no — para nada** to be of no use; **¿en qué le**

puedo —? how can I help you? **—se de** to make use of; **sírvase usted hacerlo** please do it

sésamo M sesame; **¡ábrete —!** open sesame!

sesenta NUM sixty

sesgado ADJ biased

sesgar[40] VT (una tela) to cut on the bias; (una opinión) to slant; (las estadísticas) to skew

sesgo M (en la tela) bias; (de los ojos, de orientación) slant; **al —** obliquely

sesión F (reunión, período) session; (de fotografía) sitting; (de una película) showing; **— de ejercicio** workout

seso M brain; **de poco —** foolish; **devanarse los —s** to rack one's brain

sestear VI to take a nap

sesudo ADJ (persona) brainy; (explicación) intelligent; (testarudo) *Méx* stubborn

set M set

seta F mushroom

setenta NUM seventy

seto M hedge

sétter M setter

seudónimo M pseudonym, pen name

severidad F severity, harshness

severo ADJ severe, stern, harsh

sevillano -na ADJ & MF Sevillian; F PL Sevillian dances

sexar VT to sex

sexismo M sexism

sexista MF sexist

sexo M (género, acto) sex; (órganos) genitals; **el bello —** the fair sex; **— seguro** safe sex

sexto ADV, ADJ & M sixth

sexual ADJ sexual

sexualidad F sexuality

sexy ADJ sexy

Seychelles F PL Seychelles

SFA [Sistema de frenos antibloqueo] M ABS

shock M shock

short, shorts M shorts

si CONJ if; **yo voy — tú vas** I'm going if you're going; **no sé — viene o no** I don't know whether she's coming or not; **¡— ya te lo dije!** but I already told you! **— bien** although; **por — acaso** just in case; **— Dios quiere** God willing; **— no me equivoco** unless I'm mistaken

sí ADV yes; *fam* yeah; **¿—?** really? **— que fui** I did go; **creo que —** I think so; M consent; **me dio el —** she said yes; PRON himself, herself, itself, oneself, themselves; **de por —** in itself; **estar sobre —** to be on the alert; **volver en —** to come to; **pagado de —** self-satisfied; **estar fuera de —** to be beside oneself; **hablar para —** to talk to oneself; **dio todo de —** she gave her all; **cada cual para —** every man for himself

sicario M hitman

sicomoro M sycamore

SIDA [síndrome de inmunodeficiencia adquirida] M AIDS

siderurgia F steel industry

sidra F cider

siega F (de la hierba) mowing; (de las mieses) reaping

siembra F (acción de sembrar) sowing; (época) sowing time

siempre ADV always; **— nos has apoyado** you've always been very supportive of us; **desde —** since forever; **para/por —** forever; **por — jamás** forevermore; **— que** (en cualquier momento) whenever; (con tal que) provided that; **— y cuando** provided that; **como —** as usual; **hoy no eres el mismo de —** you're not yourself today

sien F temple

sienta, siente *ver* sentar, sentir

sierpe F *lit* serpent

sierra F (herramienta) saw; (cordillera) small mountain range; **— de cadena** chainsaw

siesta F siesta, afternoon nap; **dormir la —** to take an afternoon nap

siete NUM seven

sífilis F syphilis

sifón M (para líquidos) siphon; (tubo) trap

siga, sigamos *ver* seguir

sigilo M stealth

sigla F acronym

siglo M century

signatario -ria MF signer

significación F (sentido) meaning; (importancia) significance

significado M meaning, sense

significar[30] VT to mean, to signify

significativo ADJ significant, meaningful

signo M sign; **— de admiración** exclamation point; **— de igual** equal sign; **— de interrogación** question mark; **— de más** plus sign; **— de menos** minus sign; **— de multiplicación** multiplication sign; **—s vitales** vital signs

sigo, siguiendo *ver* seguir

siguiente ADJ following; **al día —** the next day

siguiera, siguiese *ver* seguir

sílaba F syllable

silbar VI (soplar aire) to whistle; (rechiflar) to hiss

silbato M whistle (también en fútbol)

silbido M whistle

silenciador M (de arma) silencer; (de coche) muffler

silenciar VT to silence

silencio M silence, quiet; **guardar —** to keep quiet

silenciosamente ADV quietly

silencioso ADJ silent, quiet

silicio M silicon

silla F chair; (de montar) saddle; — **de ruedas** wheelchair; — **eléctrica** electric chair; — **plegadiza** folding chair
sillín M saddle, seat
sillón M (mueble) armchair
silo M silo
silogismo M syllogism
silueta F silhouette
siluro M catfish
silvestre ADJ wild
silvicultura F forestry
sima F chasm
simbiosis F symbiosis
simbólico ADJ symbolic
simbolismo M symbolism
simbolizar[47] VT to symbolize
símbolo M symbol; — **de status** status symbol; — **sexual** sex symbol
simetría F symmetry
simétrico ADJ symmetrical
simiente F seed
símil M simile
similar ADJ similar
similitud F resemblance, similarity
simio M ape
simpatía F friendliness; **no le tengo mucha —** I don't like him much
simpático ADJ (amistoso) nice, friendly, congenial; (sistema nervioso) sympathetic
simpatizante ADJ supporting, sympathizing; MF supporter, sympathizer
simpatizar[47] VI (con alguien) to like; (con una idea) to be sympathetic toward
simple ADJ (no complicado) simple; (mero) mere; (tonto) simpleminded
simplemente ADV simply, merely
simpleza F (sencillez) simplicity; (estupidez) stupidity
simplicidad F simplicity
simplificar[30] VT to simplify
simplista ADJ (intepretación) simplistic; (explicación) glib, simplistic
simplón -ona ADJ simpleminded; MF simpleton
simposio M symposium
simulación F simulation
simulacro M — **de batalla** mock battle; — **de incendio** fire drill
simulador -ora MF simulator; M — **de vuelo** flight simulator
simular VT to simulate, to feign
simultanear VI perform simultaneously
simultáneo ADJ simultaneous
sin PREP without; — **aliento** out of breath; — **amueblar** unfurnished; — **azúcar** sugar-free; — **comentarios** no comment; — **compromiso** without obligation; — **condiciones** unconditionally, with no strings attached; — **culpa** no-fault; — **declarar** unreported; — **derecho** nonvoting; — **duda** without doubt, undoubtedly; — **embargo** nevertheless; — **escrúpulos** unscrupulous; — **excepciones** across the board; — **falta** without fail; — **garantía** unsecured; — **intereses** interest-free; — **lujos** no-frills; — **marcar** unmarked; — **peligro** safely; — **percances** safely; — **problemas** trouble-free; — **receta** over-the-counter; — **restricciones** open-ended; — **riesgo** risk-free; — **seguro médico** uninsured; — **sentido** meaningless
sinagoga F synagogue
sincerarse VI to clear the air, to come clean
sinceridad F sincerity
sincero ADJ (personalidad) sincere; (opinión) candid; (agradecimiento) heartfelt, wholehearted
sincrónico ADJ (proceso) synchronous; (enfoque lingüístico) synchronic
sincronización F timing
sincronizar[47] VT to synchronize
sindical ADJ (relativo al síndico) trustee; (relativo al sindicato) union; **dirigente —** union leader
sindicar[30] VT to unionize, to syndicate
sindicato M (de trabajadores) syndicate, trade union, labor union; (de bancos) syndicate
síndico -ca MF receiver, trustee
síndrome M syndrome; — **de abstinencia** withdrawal symptoms; — **de choque tóxico** toxic shock syndrome; — **de Down** Down's syndrome; — **de muerte infantil súbita** crib death, sudden infant death syndrome
sinergia F synergy
sinfín M **un — de cosas** a lot of things
sinfonía F symphony
Singapur M Singapore
singapurense ADJ & MF Singaporean
singular ADJ (número) singular; (excepcional) unique
siniestro ADJ sinister; M disaster
sinnúmero M myriad
sino CONJ but; **no vino — que llamó** she didn't come but instead called; **no tengo dos — tres** I have not two but three; **no es — madera** it's only wood
sinónimo ADJ synonymous; M synonym
sinopsis F synopsis
sinrazón F injustice
sinsabor M trouble
sinsonte M mockingbird
sintamos ver sentir
sintaxis F syntax
síntesis F synthesis; — **de habla** speech synthesis; — **de habla** voice synthesis
sintético ADJ (producto) synthetic; (fibras) man-made
sintetizador M synthesizer
sintetizar[47] VT to synthesize

sintiendo, sintiera, sintiese *ver* sentir
síntoma M symptom
sintonía F tuning; **en** — on the same wavelength
sintonizador M tuner
sintonizar[47] VT (una emisora) to tune in; (un sintonizador) to fine-tune; **los dos sintonizan bien** the two are on the same wavelength
sinuoso ADJ (camino) sinuous, winding; (comportamiento) devious
sinusitis F sinusitis
sinvergüenza MF creep
siquiera ADV at least; **dame** — **unos días** give me a few days at least; **ni** — not even
sirena F (ninfa, bocina) siren; (mitad mujer, mitad pez) mermaid
Siria F Syria
sirio -ria ADJ & MF Syrian
sirve, sirviendo, sirviera, sirviese *ver* servir
sirviente MF, **sirvienta** F servant
sisar VT to pilfer, to swipe
sisear VI to hiss
siseo M hiss, hissing
sísmico ADJ seismic
sistema M system; — **binario** binary system; — **de asistencia de salud** health care system; — **de cifrado** encryption system; — **de reconocimiento óptico de caracteres** optical character recognition; — **experto** expert system; — **inmune** immune system; — **mundial de posicionamiento** global positioning system; — **nervioso central** central nervous system; — **operativo** operating system; — **solar** solar system
sistemático ADJ systematic
sistematizar[47] VI/VT to systematize
sistémico ADJ systemic
sistólico ADJ systolic
sitial M — **de honor** seat of honor
sitiar VT to besiege
sitio M (espacio vacío) room; (ubicación) place, site; (asedio) siege; **no hay** — there's no room; **esto no está en su** — this is out of place; — **web** website; **poner** — **a** to lay siege to; **poner a alguien en su** — to put someone in his place
sito ADJ situated
situación F (circunstancia) situation; (legal, financiera, social) status
situado ADJ situated; **estar** — to be located
situar[26] VT to locate, to place; —**se** to be located
sketch M sketch, skit
slalom M slalom
smog M smog
smoking M dinner jacket
so PREP — **pena de** under penalty of; — **pretexto de** under the pretext of; INTERJ whoa; ADV — **tonto** you stupid idiot!

sobaco M armpit
sobar VT (la masa) to knead; (a una persona) to fondle; (un traje) to wear out
soberanía F sovereignty
soberano -na ADJ & MF sovereign
soberbia F pride, haughtiness
soberbio ADJ (orgulloso) proud, haughty; (magnífico) magnificent
sobornar VT to bribe
soborno M (acción) bribery; (mordida) bribe, *fam* payola
sobra F surplus; —**s** leftovers, leavings; **de** — **sabes** you know full well; **está de** — it is superfluous; **las piezas de** — spare parts
sobrado ADJ more than enough
sobrante ADJ leftover, remaining; surplus
sobrar VI (dinero, libros) to be left over, to remain; (personas) to be in the way
sobre PREP (encima de) above, over; (en contacto con) on, upon; (acerca de) about; **un préstamo** — **su coche** a loan on his car; — **todo** above all, especially; — **las 9:30** at about 9:30; — **marchar** — **Madrid** to march toward Madrid; M (para cartas) envelope; (de sopa) packet; — **manila** manila envelope; **irse al** — to hit the sack
sobreactuar[26] VI to ham it up
sobrealimentador M supercharger
sobrecalificado ADJ overqualified
sobrecarga F overload; — **de voltaje** power surge; — **sensorial** sensory overload
sobrecargar[40] VT to overload
sobrecogedor ADJ awesome
sobrecoger[45] VI/VT to awe; —**se** to be in awe; —**se de pánico** to be panic-stricken
sobrecogimiento M awe
sobrecompensar VI to overcompensate
sobrecorrección F overcorrection
sobredosis F overdose
sobreendeudado N debt-ridden
sobreentenderse[2] VI to be understood
sobreentendido ADJ understood; M assumption
sobreestimar VT to overestimate
sobreexcitado ADJ overexcited, wired
sobreexcitar VT to overexcite
sobreextendido ADJ overextended
sobregirar VT to overdraw
sobregiro M overdraft
sobrehumano ADJ superhuman
sobrellevar VT to bear, to endure
sobremanera ADV beyond measure
sobremesa F after-dinner conversation
sobrenadar VI to float
sobrenatural ADJ supernatural
sobrenombre M nickname
sobrepasar VT to exceed
sobrepeso M overweight
sobreponer[56, 74] VT to superimpose; VI — **a**

(valer más que) to outweigh; (recuperarse) to get over

sobreproteger[45] VT to overprotect, to smother

sobrepujar VT to surpass

sobresaliente ADJ outstanding; MF understudy

sobresalir[57] VI (ser notable) to stand out; (estar en un plano más saliente) to project, to jut out; (ser excelente) to excel

sobresaltar VT to startle, frighten; —**se** to be startled, to start

sobresalto M start, scare

sobrestante M foreman

sobresueldo M extra pay

sobretasa F surtax

sobretodo M overcoat

sobrevenir[61] VI to happen unexpectedly

sobrevivencia F survival

sobreviviente MF survivor; ADJ surviving

sobrevivir VI/VT to survive

sobriedad F sobriety

sobrino -na M nephew; F niece; — **nieto** great-nephew; **sobrina nieta** great-niece

sobrio ADJ sober

socarrar VT to singe

socarrón ADJ sarcastic

socarronería F sarcasm

socavar VT (excavar por debajo) to dig under; (debilitar) to undermine, to undercut

socavón M sinkhole; shaft, tunnel

sociable ADJ sociable, gregarious

social ADJ social

socialismo M socialism

socialista ADJ & MF socialist

socializar[47] VT to socialize

sociedad F (grupo humano) society; (firma) company, partnership; — **anónima** corporation; — **de consumo** consumer society; **alta** — high society

socio -cia MF (de una firma) partner; (de un club) member; — **minoritario** minority partner; — **principal** senior partner; — **comercial** trading partner

socioeconómico ADJ socioeconomic

sociología F sociology

sociópata MF sociopath

socorrer VT to help

socorro INTERJ & M help; **acudir al** — **de** to go to the rescue of; **pedir** — to cry out for help

soda F soda

sodio M sodium

sodomía F sodomy

soez ADJ vulgar

sofá M sofa, couch; —-**cama** sleeper, sofa bed

sofisma M fallacy

sofisticado ADJ sophisticated

sofocante ADJ suffocating, oppressive

sofocar[30] VI/VT (ahogar) to suffocate; (una rebelión) to quash, to quell, to suppress; (un incendio) to put out

sofoco M suffocation

softball M softball

software M software; — **de fuente abierta** open source software

soga F rope; **estar con la** — **al cuello** to have a rope around one's neck

sois *ver* ser

soja F (planta) soy; (semilla) soybean

sojuzgar[40] VT to subjugate, to subdue

sol M sun; **de** — **a** — from sunrise to sunset; **hace** — it is sunny; **tomar el** — to sunbathe; **ella es un** — she's a gem; **arrimarse al** — **que más calienta** to know which side one's bread is buttered on

solamente ADV only, solely

solana F sunny place

solapa F lapel

solapado ADJ underhanded

solar M (terreno) lot; (casa ancestral) manor; ADJ solar

solaz M *lit* recreation

soldado -da MF soldier; — **raso** private; — **de línea** regular soldier

soldador M soldering iron

soldadura F (acción de adherir con estaño) soldering; (resultado) solder; (acción de adherir sin estaño) welding; (resultado) weld; — **autógena** arc welding

soldar[5] VI/VT (con estaño) to solder; (sin estaño) to weld; —**se** to mend

soleado ADJ sunny

solear VT to put in the sun; —**se** to sun oneself

soledad F solitude, loneliness

solemne ADJ solemn; — **disparate** downright foolishness

solemnidad F solemnity

solenoide M solenoid

soler[6, 73] VI **suelo levantarme a las siete** I usually get up at seven; **solía acostarme tarde** I used to go to bed late; **no suele importarle** he usually doesn't mind

solferino ADJ reddish-purple

solicitante MF applicant

solicitar VT (permiso) to request; (un puesto, una beca) to apply for

solícito ADJ solicitous

solicitud F (para beca, puesto) application; (de información, permiso) request; — **de préstamo** loan application; **a** — **de** at the request of

solidaridad F solidarity

solidario ADJ supportive, sympathetic

solidez F solidity

solidificar[30] VT to solidify

sólido ADJ (materia) solid; (mueble) sturdy; (argumento) strong; M solid

solista MF soloist

solitario -ria ADJ solitary; MF (persona) recluse; M (juego de cartas, brillante) solitaire; F

tapeworm
sollozar[47] VI to sob
sollozo M sob
solo ADJ (desamparado) lonely, lonesome; (no acompañado) alone; **tengo un — coche** I have only one car; **a solas** alone; **habla solo** he talks to himself; **ni una sola palabra** not a single word; ADV just, only; **— quiero saber** I just/only want to know; M solo
solomillo M sirloin
solsticio M solstice
soltar[5] VT (a un prisionero) to let go, to release; (el vientre) to loosen; (una carcajada) to let out; (bombas) to drop; (un disparate) to say; **— amarras** to cast off; **— el hervor** to come to a boil; **— tacos** to swear; **—se** to loosen up; **—se el pelo** to kick up one's heels
soltero -ra ADJ single, unmarried; M bachelor; F unmarried woman
solterón -ona M old bachelor; F *pey* spinster
soltura F ease; **hablar con —** to speak fluently
soluble ADJ soluble
solución F solution; **— salina** saline solution
solucionar VT to solve
solventar VT to settle
solvente ADJ & M solvent
somalí ADJ & MF Somalian
Somalia F Somalia
sombra F (de una figura) shadow; (protección del sol) shade; (para ojos) eye shadow; **hacer — to** overshadow; **dar — to** shade; **no fiarse ni de su propia — to** be scared of one's own shadow; **a la — in** the shade; **sin — de duda** without a shadow of a doubt
sombreado ADJ (protegido del sol) shady; (oscuro) shadowy
sombrear VT to shade
sombrerería F millinery
sombrerero -ra MF milliner
sombrero M hat; **— de copa** top hat; **— hongo** derby
sombrilla F parasol
sombrío ADJ (oscuro) dark; (triste) somber, gloomy
somero ADJ (agua) shallow; (discusión) superficial
someter VT (proponer algo) to submit; (poner bajo dominio) to subject; **—se a** to undergo
sometimiento M (propuesta) submission; (dominio) subjection
somnífero M sleeping pill
somnolencia F drowsiness, sleepiness
somnoliento ADJ drowsy
somos *ver* ser
son M sound; LOC ADV **al — de** to the sound of; **venimos en — de paz** we come in peace
son *ver* ser
sonaja F rattle
sonajero M rattle

sonámbulo -la MF sleepwalker
sonar[5] VI (hacer un sonido) to sound; (mencionarse) to be mentioned; (ser familiar) to sound familiar; **— a** to sound like; VT (bocina) to sound; (tambor) to beat; (campana, timbre) to ring; **—se la nariz / los mocos** to blow one's nose; **suena que** it is rumored that; M sonar
sonda F (de médico) catheter; (cohete) probe; **— de alimentación** feeding tube; **tirar una — to** sound
sondear VT (medir la oportunidad) to sound, to fathom; (investigar la opinión) to sound out
sondeo M survey
soneto M sonnet
sonido M sound
sonoridad F (de la voz) sonority; (de un instrumento) tone; (de un sonido lingüístico) voicing
sonoro ADJ sonorous
sonreír[10] VI to smile
sonriente ADJ smiling
sonrisa F smile
sonrojarse VI to blush
sonrojo M blush, flush
sonrosado ADJ rosy
sonsacar[30] VT to extract
soñador -ora MF dreamer
soñar[5] VI/VT to dream; **— con** to dream of; **— despierto** to daydream; **— que** to dream that; **ni — fam** fat chance
soñoliento ADJ sleepy
sopa F (líquido) soup; (pan mojado) sop; **estar hecho una — to** be sopping wet; **— crema** cream soup
sopapo M smack
sopera F soup tureen
sopesar VT to weigh
sopetón LOC ADV **de — all** of a sudden
soplador -ora MF blower
soplar VI/VT (el viento) to blow; (la sopa) to blow on; (en un examen) to whisper the answers
soplete M blowtorch
soplo M breath, puff; **en un — in** a jiffy; **— cardíaco** heart murmur
soplón -ona MF informer, snitch, stool pigeon
sopor M lethargy
soportar VT (un peso) to support, to bear; (una molestia, a una persona) to stand, to bear; (un programa de computadora) to support
soporte M (de un peso, de un programa) support; (de una bicicleta) kickstand; **— técnico** technical support
soprano M (voz) soprano; F (cantante) soprano
sorber VI/VT to sip; **—se los mocos** to sniffle
sorbete M sherbet
sorbo M sip; **de un — in** one gulp
sordera F deafness
sórdido ADJ sordid, tawdry, sleazy

sordina F mute
sordo -da ADJ (persona) deaf; (dolor) dull;
(sonido) dull, muffled; **hacer oídos —s** to
turn a deaf ear; MF deaf person; **hacerse el**
— to pretend not to hear
sordomudo -da ADJ deaf and dumb; MF
deaf-mute
sorna F irony
sorprendente ADJ surprising, startling
sorprendentemente ADV surprisingly
sorprender VT to surprise; **—se** to be surprised
sorpresa F surprise; **— de cumpleaños** party
favor; **para mi —** to my surprise; **pillar por**
— to catch by surprise
sortear VT (elegir al azar) to draw lots, to raffle;
(esquivar) to dodge
sorteo M drawing, raffle
sortija F (anillo) ring; (de pelo) ringlet
sortilegio M spell, charm
SOS M SOS
sosa F soda
sosegado ADJ composed, sedate
sosegar[41] VT to calm, to quiet; **—se** to quiet
down, to compose oneself
sosiego M quiet, calm
soslayo LOC ADV **de —** oblique, slanting; **mirar**
de — to look out of the corner of one's eye
soso ADJ (comida) tasteless, insipid; (persona)
dull
sospecha F suspicion
sospechar VT to suspect
sospechoso -sa ADJ suspicious; MF suspect
sostén M (apoyo, sustento) support, prop;
(persona que sostiene) supporter, provider;
(prenda) brassiere; **— de la familia**
breadwinner
sostendrá, sostendría ver sostener
sostener[58] VT (una nota musical) to hold, to
sustain; (una familia) to support; (un peso) to
support, to hold; (una opinión) to claim, to
uphold
sostenga, sostengo ver sostener
sostenible ADJ sustainable
sostenido ADJ sustained; M sharp
sostiene, sostienes, sostuve, sostuviera,
sostuviese ver sostener
sota F jack, knave
sótano M cellar, basement
soto M thicket
soy ver ser
soya F (semilla) soybean; (planta) soy
squash M squash
Sr. M Mr.
Sra. F (casada) Mrs.; (sin indicación de estado
civil) Ms.
S.R.C. [se ruega contestar] LOC RSVP
status M status
stop M stop sign
strip-tease M striptease

striptisero -ra MF stripper
su ADJ POS (de él) his; (de ella) her; (de usted,
ustedes) your; (de ellos, ellas) their
suave ADJ (pelo, piel) soft; (tiempo, droga) mild;
(brisa, persona, animal) gentle; (coñac)
smooth; **hablan —** they speak gently
suavemente ADV lightly, gently
suavidad F (de pelo, piel) softness; (de coñac)
smoothness; (de tiempo, droga) mildness; (de
brisa, persona, animal) gentleness
suavizante M fabric softener
suavizar[47] VT to soften
suazi ADJ & MF Swazi
Suazilandia F Swaziland
subalterno -na ADJ & MF subordinate
subarrendar VI/VT to sublet
subasta F auction
subastador -ora MF auctioneer
subastar VT to sell at auction, to auction
subcomité M subcommittee
subconsciente ADJ subconscious
subcontratar VT to subcontract, to contract
out, to farm out
subdesarrollado ADJ underdeveloped
súbdito -ta MF subject
subdividir VT subdivide
subdivisión F subdivision
subempleado ADJ underemployed
subestimar VT to underestimate
subgerente MF assistant manager
subida F (de precios, de río) rise; (de montaña)
climb; (de drogas) high; (cuesta) slope; **—s y**
bajadas ups and downs
subido ADJ (color) bright; **— de tono** risqué
subíndice M subscript
subir VI (los precios) to rise, to go up; (la marea)
to surge; (a un tren) to board; (a un autobús,
coche) to get into; VT (algo del sótano) to
bring up; (una montaña) to climb; (precios) to
raise; **— a la red** to upload; **—se** to ride up;
el vino se me sube a la cabeza wine goes
to my head; M **subibaja** seesaw
súbitamente ADV suddenly
súbito ADJ sudden
subjetividad F subjectivity
subjetivo ADJ subjective
subjuntivo ADJ & M subjunctive
sublevación F revolt
sublevar VT (instigar) to incite to rebellion;
(indignar) to infuriate; **—se** to revolt
sublime ADJ sublime
submarino ADJ underwater; M submarine
suboficial M noncommissioned officer
subordinado -da ADJ & MF subordinate
subordinar VT to subordinate
subproducto M by-product
subproletariado M underclass
subrayado ADJ underlined; M underscore,
underlining

subrayar VT (con una línea) to underline, to underscore; (enfatizar) to emphasize, to underscore
subrepticio ADJ surreptitious
subrutina F subroutine
subsanar VT (una deficiencia) to remedy; (un error) to correct
subsecretario -ia MF undersecretary; — **de justicia** solicitor general
subsidiar VT to subsidize
subsidiario ADJ subsidiary
subsidio M subsidy
subsiguiente ADJ subsequent
subsistencia F survival
subsistir VI to subsist, to survive
subteniente MF second lieutenant
subterfugio M subterfuge
subterráneo ADJ subterranean, underground; M subway
subtítulo M (de un capítulo, película) subtitle; (pie de foto) caption
subtotal M subtotal
suburbano -na ADJ of shantytowns; MF shantytown resident
suburbio M shantytown
subvaluar[26] VT to underestimate
subvención F subsidy
subvencionar VT to subsidize
subversivo ADJ subversive
subyacente ADJ underlying
subyacer[37] VI to underlie
subyugar[40] VT (dominar) to subjugate; (hechizar) to charm
succión F suction
sucedáneo -a ADJ & MF substitute
suceder VI to happen, to occur; — **al trono** to succeed to the throne; VT to succeed
sucesión F (herencia, secuencia) succession; (heredero) descendant
sucesivo ADJ successive; **en lo** — in the future
suceso M (evento) event, occurrence; (incidente) incident
sucesor -ora MF successor
suciedad F (porquería) dirt, filth; (cualidad de sucio) filthiness
sucinto ADJ concise
sucio ADJ (baño, ropa) dirty, filthy; (trabajo, chiste) dirty; (conciencia) guilty; **blanco** — off-white; **este traje es** — this suit gets dirty easily
sucumbir VI to succumb
sucursal F branch, subsidiary
sudadera F sweatshirt
sudado ADJ sweaty
Sudáfrica F South Africa
sudafricano -na ADJ & MF South African
Sudamérica F South America
sudamericano -na ADJ & MF South American
Sudán M Sudan

sudanés -esa ADJ & MF Sudanese
sudar VT to sweat; — **la gota gorda** to sweat blood
sudeste ADJ southeast, southeastern; M southeast
sudoeste ADJ southwest, southwestern; M southwest
sudor M sweat
sudoración F sweating
sudoroso ADJ sweaty
Suecia F Sweden
sueco -ca ADJ Swedish; M (lengua) Swedish; MF Swede; **hacerse el** — to pretend not to understand
suegro -a M father-in-law; F mother-in-law
suela F (de zapato) sole; (pez) flounder
suela, suele ver soler
sueldo M salary
suelo M (tierra) soil, ground; (piso) floor; **arrastrar por el** — to drag; **por los** —**s** at rock-bottom
suelta, suelte ver soltar
suelto ADJ (no atado) loose, unattached; (flojo) loose; (libre) free; M loose change
suena, suene ver sonar
sueña, sueñe ver soñar
sueño M (acto de dormir) sleep; (acto de soñar) dream; (ganas de dormir) sleepiness; **en** —**s** dreaming; **conciliar el** — to get to sleep; **tener** — to be sleepy; **ni en** —**[s]** never; **perder el** — to lose sleep; — **húmedo** wet dream; — **profundo** sound sleep; **estar en el séptimo** — to be deeply asleep
suero M serum; — **de leche** buttermilk; — **fisiológico** saline solution
suerte F (destino) fate; (fortuna) luck; (clase) kind; **de** — in luck; **dejar a su** — to leave to his own devices; **echar** —**s** to cast lots; **mala** — (desgracia) bad luck; (lo siento) too bad; **tener** — to be lucky; **tentar a la** — to court danger; **tocarle algo en** — **a alguien** to be one's lot
suertudo -da ADJ lucky; MF lucky devil
suéter M sweater
suficiencia F adequacy; **¡tiene una** —! she's so arrogant!
suficiente ADJ (adecuado) sufficient, adequate; (arrogante) smug; M (calificación mínima) lowest passing grade; PRON enough; **ser** — to be enough; **tiempo más que** — ample time
sufijo M suffix
sufragar[40] VT to defray; — **los gastos** to meet the expenses
sufragio M suffrage
sufrido ADJ (madre) long-suffering; (tela) durable
sufrimiento M suffering
sufrir VI/VT (pasar apremios) to suffer; VT (soportar) to stand; (una lesión) to sustain;

(un cambio) to undergo; (una pena) to grieve; — **de** to suffer from; — **de los pies** to have foot pains
sugerencia F suggestion
sugerir[8] VT to suggest
sugestión F suggestion
sugiere, sugirió, sugiriendo, sugiriera, sugiriese *ver* sugerir
suicida MF suicide [victim]
suicidarse VI to commit suicide
suicidio M suicide
suite F suite
Suiza F Switzerland
suizo -za ADJ & MF Swiss; M sweet roll
sujeción LOC ADV **con** — **a** subject to
sujetar VT (fijar) to attach; (unir) to hold; (someter) to subdue, to hold down; —**se** to hold on; M SG **sujetalibros** bookend; M SG **sujetapapeles** paper clip
sujeto ADJ held by; — **a** subject to; M (de oración, de experimento) subject; (individuo) individual
sulfato M sulfate
sulfurarse VI to hit the roof
sulfúrico ADJ sulfuric
sulfuro M sulfide
suma F (resultado aritmético) sum; (operación aritmética) addition; (cantidad) amount, sum; **en** — in sum
sumadora F adding machine
sumamente ADV extremely
sumar VT to add, to add up; —**se a** to join
sumario M brief; ADJ summary
sumergible ADJ waterproof
sumergir[46] VT to submerge, to dip; —**se** to dive; —**se en** to immerse oneself in
sumidero M (socavón) sinkhole; (desagüe) drain
suministrar VT to furnish, to supply with
suministro M provision, supply; — **de energía** power supply; —**s** supplies, provisions
sumir VT to immerse
sumisión F submission
sumiso ADJ submissive
súmmum M ultimate, acme; **el** — **de la moda** the cat's meow
sumo ADJ utmost, paramount; **a lo** — at the most
suntuoso ADJ sumptuous, luxurious
supe, supiera, supiese *ver* saber
súper ADJ & ADV super; F (gasolina) high-octane gasoline; M (supermercado) supermarket
superabundancia F overabundance, glut
superación F (de expectativas) surpassing; (de límites) exceeding; (de un récord) breaking; (de una dificultad) overcoming
superar VT (las expectativas) to surpass; (un límite) to exceed; (una dificultad) to overcome, to surmount; (una prueba) to pass;

(a un rival) to outdo; —**se** to improve oneself
superávit M surplus
supercomputadora F supercomputer
superdirecta F overdrive
superdotado ADJ gifted
superego M superego
superestrella F superstar
superficial ADJ (conocimiento, herida, persona) superficial; (persona) shallow
superficialidad F shallowness
superficie F (parte exterior) surface; (de una figura geométrica) area
superfluo ADJ superfluous
superíndice M superscript
superintendente MF superintendent
superior ADJ (mejor) superior; (más alto) higher; (más grande, intenso) greater; MF superior
superioridad F superiority
superlativo ADJ & M superlative
supermercado M supermarket
superordenador M supercomputer
superponer[56, 74] VT to superimpose
superpotencia F superpower
superproducción F overproduction
supersónico ADJ supersonic
superstición F superstition
supersticioso ADJ superstitious
supervisar VT to supervise
supervisión F supervision
supervisor -ora MF supervisor
supervivencia F survival; **la** — **del más apto** the survival of the fittest
superviviente ADJ surviving; MF survivor
superyó M superego
supino ADJ supine
suplantar VT to supplant
suplementar VT to supplement
suplementario ADJ supplemental
suplemento M supplement
suplente ADJ & MF substitute
súplica F entreaty, plea
suplicar[30] VT to plead, to beseech
suplicio M ordeal
suplir VT (sustituir) to substitute for; (compensar) to make up for
supondrá, supondría *ver* suponer
suponer[56, 74] VT (dar por sentado) to suppose, to presume, to surmise; (implicar) to involve; **es de** — **que ya esté preparado** presumably he's already prepared
suponga, supongo *ver* suponer
suposición F supposition, surmise
supositorio M suppository
supremacía F supremacy
supremo ADJ supreme
supresión F (de una idea) suppression; (de una palabra) deletion
suprimir VT (una idea) to suppress; (la

esclavitud) to abolish; (una palabra) to delete
supuestamente ADV supposedly, allegedly
supuesto ADJ (hipotético) supposed; (alegado) alleged, ostensible; **dar por** — to assume; **por** — of course; M supposition, assumption
supuesto *ver* suponer
supuración F discharge
supurante ADJ festering, running
supurar VI to fester, to discharge
supuse, supusiera, supusiese *ver* suponer
sur ADJ & M south; **hacia el** — southward; **rumbo al** — southward
surcar[30] VT to plow
surco M (en la tierra) furrow; (en un camino) rut; (en un disco) groove; (en el rostro) wrinkle
surcoreano -na ADJ & MF South Korean
sureño -ña ADJ southern; MF southerner
sureste ADJ southeast, southeastern; M southeast
surfear VI/VT to surf (también en el internet)
surfing M surfing; **hacer** — to surf
surgimiento M rise
surgir[46] VI (situación) to arise; (manantial) to rise; (problema) to emerge, to crop up
Surinam M Surinam, Suriname
surinamés -esa ADJ & MF Surinamer
surmenage M burnout
suroeste ADJ southwest, southwestern; M southwest
surrealismo M surrealism
surrealista ADJ surreal, surrealistic; MF surrealist
surtido M stock, assortment; ADJ assorted
surtidor M (bomba) pump; (chorro, pieza de carburador) jet
surtir VT to provide; — **efecto** to produce the desired effect; — **un pedido** to fill an order
susceptible ADJ susceptible
suscitar VT to stir up
suscribir[74] VT (una opinión) to subscribe to, to endorse; (un seguro) to underwrite; —**se a** to subscribe to
suscripción F subscription
suscriptor -ora MF (de un revista) subscriber; (en el mercado de acciones) underwriter
susodicho ADJ above-mentioned
suspender VT (colgar) to suspend, to hang; (interrumpir) to suspend, to stop; (cancelar) to cancel; (castigar) to suspend; VI/VT (no aprobar) to fail, to flunk
suspense M suspense
suspensión F suspension
suspenso ADJ hanging; **quedarse** — to freeze; M (en un examen) failure; (en una película) suspense; **en** — in suspense
suspensorio M jock [strap]
suspicaz ADJ suspicious
suspirar VT to sigh; — **por** to yearn for
suspiro M sigh

sustancia F substance; — **peligrosa** hazardous substance
sustancial ADJ substantial
sustancioso ADJ substantial
sustantivo M noun; ADJ substantive
sustentable ADJ sustainable
sustentar VT to sustain
sustento M (alimento) sustenance; (apoyo) support; **ganarse el** — to earn a living
sustitución F substitution; — **protésica de la cadera** hip replacement
sustituible ADJ replaceable
sustituir[19] VI/VT to substitute for, to replace; **Juan sustituyó a María** John substituted for Mary; **sustituí la leche por agua** I replaced the milk with water
sustituto -ta MF substitute
sustituya, sustituye, sustituyendo, sustituyera, sustituyese *ver* sustituir
susto M scare, fright
sustracción F subtraction
sustraer[59] VT to take away; —**se a** to avoid
susurrar VI/VT (una persona, el viento) to whisper; (agua) to murmur, to ripple; (hojas) to rustle
susurro M (de una persona, del viento) whisper; (del agua) murmur; (de las hojas) rustle
sutil ADJ subtle
sutileza F (delicadeza) subtlety; (fineza excesiva) nicety, quibble
sutilizar[47] VT to quibble over
sutura F suture
suyo ADJ & PRON POS (de él) his; (de ella) her; (de usted, de ustedes) your; (de ellos, de ellas) their; PRON (de él) his; (de ella) hers; (de usted, de ustedes) yours; (de ellos, de ellas) theirs; **salirse con la suya** to get one's own way; **hacer de las suyas** to be up to one's tricks; **los** —**s** his/her/your/their family
swing M swing

Tt

tabaco M tobacco
tábano M horsefly
tabaquismo M smoking
taberna F tavern, saloon
tabernero -ra MF bartender
tabicar[30] VT to partition
tabique M partition
tabla F (madera) board, plank; (teatro) stage; (pliegue) pleat; (gráfica) table, chart; — **de surf** surfboard; — **de planchar** ironing board; —**s** (escenario) stage; —**s de la ley** the tables of the law; —**s de multiplicar**

multiplication tables; — **periódica** periodic table; — **de contenidos** table of contents; — **de cortar** cutting board; **hacer —s** to tie
tablado M stage
tablero M (para juegos de mesa) board; (de instrumentos) panel, instrument panel; (de coche) dashboard; (pizarra) blackboard; (para noticias) bulletin board; — **de mando** control panel
tableta F (de aspirina) tablet; (de chocolate) bar
tablilla F (de arcilla) tablet; (de cama) slat; (para fracturas) splint
tabloide M tabloid
tablón M plank
tabú M taboo
tabulador M tab
tabular VT (en una tabla, planilla) to tabulate, to chart; (en la computadora) to tab
taburete M stool, footstool
TAC [tomografía axial computarizada] F CAT scan
tacañería F stinginess, tightness
tacaño -ña ADJ stingy, miserly; MF miser, penny-pincher
tacha F (mancha visible) blemish; (al honor) blot
tachado M strikethrough
tachar VT (borrar) to cross out, to delete; (acusar) to accuse of
tachón M crossing out
tachonar VT to stud
tachuela F tack, thumbtack
tácito ADJ tacit
taciturno ADJ taciturn
taco M (de artillería) wad; (palo de billar) billiard cue; (comida ligera) snack; (palabrota) swear word; (comida) *Méx* taco; **—s** (en el zapato) cleats; **soltar —s** *Esp* to swear
tacómetro M tachometer
tacón M heel
taconear VI to click one's heels
taconeo M clicking
táctica F tactic
táctil ADJ tactile
tacto M (acción de tocar) touch; (sentido) sense of touch; (diplomacia) tact; **con mucho —** gently
TAE [tasa anual equivalente] F APR
tahúr -ura MF gambler
tailandés -esa ADJ & MF Thai, Thailander
Tailandia F Thailand
taimado ADJ sly, devious
Taiwán M Taiwan
taiwanés -esa ADJ & MF Taiwanese
tajada F (de pan, jamón) slice; (de carne) slab; **sacar —** to take one's cut
tajante ADJ (inequívoco) unequivocal; (cortante) sharp
tajar VT to slice
tajear VI/VT to slash

tajo M (corte) slash, hack; (cañón) gorge; (separación) gap
tal ADJ such; — **cual** just so; — **vez** perhaps; **un — García** a certain García; **a — grado** to such an extent; **de — palo — astilla** a chip off the old block; **en — caso** in such a case; CONJ — **como** like, just as; **con — [de] que** provided that; ADV **¿qué —?** how is it going? PRON **y —** and so on; **como si —** as if nothing had happened
taladrar VT to bore, to drill
taladro M drill
talante M temperament
talar VT (un árbol) to chop down; (un bosque) to lumber
talco M talcum
talento M talent
talentoso ADJ talented, gifted
talismán M charm
talla F (altura) height; (moral, intelectual) stature; (de ropa) size; (de madera) carving
tallado M carving
tallar VT (piedra) to carve; (madera) to whittle, to carve; (naipes) to deal
tallarín M noodle
talle M (cintura) waist, waistline; **tiene buen —** she has a good figure; **corto de —** short-waisted
taller M (para trabajo manual, enseñanza artística, congresos) workshop; (de artista plástico) studio; (de mecánico) garage, shop
tallo M stalk, stem
talón M (de pie, calcetín) heel; (de cheque) stub; — **de Aquiles** Achilles' heel; **girar sobre los talones** to turn on one's heels; **pisarle los talones a alguien** to be hot on someone's heels
talonario M checkbook
talonear VI to walk briskly
tamal M tamale
tamaño M size; **de — mediano** medium-sized; **de — natural** life-sized; ADJ such a big, so big a; **tamaña injusticia** such a big injustice
tambalearse VI (un borracho) to stagger; (un boxeador) to reel; (un viejo) to dodder; (un objeto) to wobble
tambaleo M stagger
también ADV also, too, as well; **este — me gusta** I like this one too, I like this one as well, I also like this one
tambor M (instrumento musical, pieza de máquina) drum; (músico) drummer; (cilindro) cylinder; **a — batiente** with fanfare
tamborilear VI to drum, to tap
tamborilero -ra MF drummer
tamiz M sieve
tamizar[47] VT to sift
tampoco CONJ either; **no lo hizo —** he did not

do it either; **ni yo** — me either/neither
tampón M tampon
tan ADV **es** — **rica** she is so rich; — **alto como**
Juan as tall as Juan; — **pronto como** as soon
as; **es** — **idiota** he's such an idiot; **vecinos** —
simpáticos such nice neighbors
tanda F (de personas) group; (de galletas) batch;
(de ejercicios) set
tándem M tandem
tanga F thong
tangente ADJ & F tangent; **salirse por la** —
(irse de tema) to go off on a tangent; (evadir)
to beat around the bush
tangerina F tangerine
tangible ADJ tangible
tango M tango
tanque M tank
tantán M African drum
tantear VT (calcular) to estimate roughly;
(averiguar) to sound out, to feel out;
(apuntar) to score; (palpar) to grope
tanteo M (cálculo) estimate; (número de tantos)
score; **al** — approximately
tanto ADJ, PRON, & ADV **lloró** — **que se le**
enrojecieron los ojos he cried so much his
eyes got red; **yo tengo** — **como tú** I have as
much as you do; **me quiere** — he loves me
so; **no te quiero** — I don't love you that
much; **a cada** —**s pasos** every so many
steps; **cuarenta y** —**s** forty-odd; **a** — **el kilo**
at so much per kilo; **el** — **por ciento** at such
and such a percentage; **estar al** — to be in the
know; **no es para** — it's not such a big deal;
— **da** it's all the same; — **como** as much as; —
en la ciudad como en el campo both in
the city and in the country; **entre/mientras**
— meanwhile; **mantenerse al** — to stay
informed; **otros** —**s** just so many more; **por**
lo — therefore; **a las tantas** until late at
night; M (en los deportes) point
Tanzania F Tanzania
tanzano -**na** ADJ & MF Tanzanian
tañer[15] VT *lit* (una guitarra) to play; VI (una
campana) to ring, to toll
tañido M (de guitarra) twang; (de campanas) toll
tapa F (de botella) cap; (de libro) cover; (de
coche) hood; (de olla, bote) lid, top; *Esp*
(comida) bar snack
tapadera F (de recipiente) lid; (de un fraude)
cover
tapado ADJ stuffy
tapar VT (una olla) to cover; (una salida) to
block; (un caño) to plug up, to stop up;
(encubrir) to cover up for; M SG **tapacubos**
hubcap; M SG **tapajuntas** flashing; M SG
taparrabos loincloth
tapete M runner
tapia F garden wall
tapiar VT to board up

tapicería F (para paredes) tapestry; (para
muebles) upholstery; (tienda de textiles de
decoración) tapestry shop; (arte) tapestry
making; (tienda de textiles para muebles)
upholstery shop
tapioca F tapioca
tapir M tapir
tapiz M (para pared) tapestry, wall hanging;
(para muebles) upholstery
tapizar[47] VT to upholster
tapón M (de botella) stopper; (de lavabo) plug;
(de corcho) cork; (en baloncesto) block; — **de**
oído earplug; **tapones** (en el zapato de
fútbol) cleats
taponar VT (baloncesto) to block
taponazo M pop of a cork
taquigrafía F shorthand
taquígrafo -**fa** MF stenographer
taquilla F ticket office, box office
tarambana MF dork, knucklehead
tarántula F tarantula
tararear VI/VT to hum
tarareo M hum, humming
tarascada F (mordedura) snap, bite; (réplica)
rude answer
tardanza F lateness
tardar VI to take time; ¿**cuánto tarda el**
trámite de divorcio? how long does it take
to get divorced? —**se** to take a long time; **tu**
padre se tarda your father is taking a long
time; **a más** — at the latest
tarde F (después del almuerzo) afternoon; (hacia
el anochecer) evening; **buenas** —**s** good
afternoon; ADV late; **ya es** — it is late; — **o**
temprano sooner o later; **más** — later on;
llegar — to be late
tardío ADJ late
tardo ADJ *lit* slow
tarea F (trabajo) task, chore; (escolar) homework
tarifa F (impuesto) tariff; (lista de precios) list of
prices; (de transporte) fare; (precio
estipulado) rate
tarima F platform
tarjeta F card (también dispositivo de
computadora); — **amarilla** yellow card; —
bancaria bank card; — **comercial** business
card; — **de circuito integrado** smart card;
— **de sonido** sound card; — **gráfica**
graphics card; — **inteligente** smart card; —
postal postcard; — **de cobro automático /**
— **de débito** debit card; — **de crédito** credit
card; — **de Navidad** Christmas card; — **roja**
red card; **marcar** — to punch in
tarro M jar
tarta F tart, pie
tartajear VI to stutter
tartamudear VI to stutter, to stammer
tartamudeo M stammer, stutter
tartamudez F stuttering

tartamudo -da MF stutterer, stammerer; ADJ
stuttering, stammering
tártaro M tartar
tartera F round baking pan
tarugo M (trozo de madera) piece of wood;
(tonto) blockhead
tasa F (índice) rate; (impuesto) tax; — **de**
desempleo unemployment rate; — **de**
interés interest rate; — **de mortalidad**
death rate; — **de natalidad** birth rate; — **de**
ocupación occupancy rate; — **de paro**
unemployment rate; — **prima** prime rate
tasación F valuation, appraisal
tasajo M jerky
tasar VT to appraise, to assess
tatarabuelo -la M great-great-grandfather; F
great-great-grandmother
tataranieto -ta M great-great-grandson; F
great-great-granddaughter
tatuaje M tattoo
tatuar²⁶ VT to tattoo
tauromaquia F bullfighting
taxi M taxi, taxicab
taxidermia F taxidermy
taxista MF taxi driver, cab driver
taxonomía F taxonomy
Tayikistán M Tajikistan
tayiko -ka ADJ & MF Tajik
taza F (de té, café) cup; (del inodoro) bowl
tazón M (para beber) mug; (para comer) bowl
té M (bebida) tea; (fiesta) tea party
te PRON PERS you; **yo** — **amo** I love you; — **digo**
mañana I'll tell you tomorrow; **no** — **mires**
en el espejo don't look at yourself in the
mirror
teatral ADJ theatrical
teatro M theater; — **de títeres** puppet show; **no**
hagas — don't make such a production
techado M (techo) roof; (acción de techar)
roofing
techar VT to roof
techo M (exterior) roof; (interior) ceiling; — **de**
cristal glass ceiling
techumbre F roof
tecla F key; — **de alt** alt key; — **de alternativa**
gráfica alt gr key; — **de borrado** delete key;
— **de cambio** shift key; — **de comando**
command key; — **de control** control key; —
de escape escape key; — **de fin** end key; —
de función function key; — **de**
mayúsculas shift key; — **de ordenación**
sort key; — **de reinicio** reset key; — **de**
retorno return key; — **de retroceso**
backspace key, return key; — **de tabulación**
tab key; — **fin** end key; **dar uno en la** — to
hit the nail on the head
teclado M keyboard; — **numérico** keypad
teclear VT (pulsar las teclas) to key in, to type;
(hacer ruido) to click

tecleo M keying in, clicking
técnica F (método) technique; (tecnología)
technology
técnico -ca ADJ technical; MF (en mecánica)
technician; (de fútbol) coach
tecnología F technology; — **de punta**
cutting-edge technology
tecnológico ADJ technological
tectónica F tectonics
tedio M boredom
tedioso ADJ tedious
tee M tee
teja F (de cerámica) tile; (de madera u otros
materiales) shingle
tejado M roof
tejar M tile factory; VT to cover with tiles
tejedor -ora MF weaver
tejer VI/VT (cesta, tela) to weave; (suéter) to knit;
M **tejemaneje** (fraude) hanky-panky;
(actividad) goings-on
tejido M (tela) textile, fabric; (de células) tissue;
(acción de hilar) weaving; (acción y efecto de
tejer) knitting
tejo M disk
tejón M badger
tela F (paño) cloth, fabric; (lienzo para pintar)
canvas; (de araña) web; (dinero) money; —
adhesiva adhesive tape; — **de cebolla**
onion skin; **en** — hardbound; **poner en** —
de juicio to call into question
telar M loom
telaraña F cobweb, spider's web
tele F TV
telebobo -ba MF couch potato
telecomunicación F telecommunication
teleconferencia F teleconference
teledifusión F telecast
teledirección F remote guidance
teleférico M cable car
telefonazo M buzz, ring
telefonear VI/VT to telephone, to phone
telefónico ADJ **llamada telefónica** telephone
call
telefonista MF telephone operator
teléfono M (aparato) telephone, phone;
(número) telephone number
telegrafiar²⁸ VI/VT to telegraph, to wire
telegráfico ADJ telegraphic
telégrafo M telegraph
telegrama M telegram
telemarketing M telemarketing
telemercadeo M telemarketing
telémetro M range finder
telenovela F soap opera
teleobjetivo M zoom lens
telepatía F telepathy
telescopio M telescope
telespectador -ora MF viewer
telesquí M ski lift

teletipo M Teletype™
teletrabajo M telecommuting
televidente MF television viewer
televisar VT to televise
televisión F television; — **de alta definición** high-definition television
televisivo ADJ (apto para la televisión) televisable; (relativo a la televisión) television
televisor M television set; — **a/en color** color television
telón M theater curtain; — **de acero** iron curtain
tema M (de una obra literaria, musical) theme; (de conversación) topic, subject; (de un CD) song, track
temario M agenda
temático ADJ thematic
temblar¹ VI (la mano, la tierra) to tremble; (la voz) to shake, to quaver; (de frío) to shiver; (de miedo) to shudder; (la luz) to flicker
temblequear VI to dodder
temblón ADJ trembling
temblor M (acción de temblar) trembling; (de tierra) tremor; (de una llama) flicker; (de la voz) quaver; (de frío) shiver; (de miedo) shudder; — **de tierra** earthquake
tembloroso ADJ (mano) shaky; (llama) flickering; (voz) quavering; (de miedo) shuddering; (de frío) shivering
temer VI/VT to fear, to be afraid [of]; — **por** to fear for; **mucho me temo que** I fear that
temerario ADJ rash, reckless
temeridad F temerity, recklessness
temeroso ADJ fearful
temible ADJ dreadful, dread
temor M fear
témpano M (bloque de hielo) block of ice; (persona fría) cold fish
temperamento M temperament, disposition
temperancia F temperance
temperatura F temperature
tempestad F tempest, storm; **una — en un vaso de agua** a tempest in a teapot
tempestuoso ADJ tempestuous, stormy
templado ADJ (clima) moderate, temperate; (ánimo) serene; (actitud) moderate
templanza F temperance
templar VT (moderar, dar fuerza) to temper; (calentar) to warm up; (una guitarra) to tune
temple M (dureza) temper; (coraje) mettle; **de mal** — in a bad mood
templo M temple
temporada F season (también de fútbol); — **baja** off-season; — **de caza** hunting season
temporal ADJ (relativo al tiempo) temporal; (secular) worldly; (no permanente) temporary; M storm; **capear el** — to weather the storm
tempranero -ra ADJ early rising; MF early riser

temprano ADJ & ADV early
tenacidad F tenacity
tenaz ADJ tenacious
tenazas F PL (de cangrejo) pincers; (de mecánico) pliers; (de dentista) forceps; (para hielo) tongs
tendedero M clothesline
tendencia F tendency; (orientación) orientation; (de la moda) trend; **de** — **mayoritaria** mainstream; — **a la baja** downturn; — **al alza** upturn, upward trend
tender² VT (un mantel) to spread out; (la ropa) to hang out; (la mano) to extend; (un cable) to lay; (una trampa) to set; VI — **a** to tend to; —**se** to stretch out
tendero -ra MF (de una tienda) storekeeper; (de una tienda de comestibles) grocer
tendido M (de cables) laying; (de ropa mojada) hanging out; (conjunto de cables) cables
tendinitis F tendonitis
tendón M tendon, sinew; — **de Aquiles** Achilles' tendon
tendrá, tendría ver tener
tenebroso ADJ (oscuro) dark; (sombrío) gloomy
tenedor -ora M table fork; MF holder, payee; — **de libros** bookkeeper
teneduría F — **de libros** bookkeeping
tener⁵⁸ VT to have; **tiene el pelo castaño** she has brown hair, her hair is brown; — **en cuenta** to bear in mind; — **en mucho** to esteem highly; — **por** to consider; — **que** to have to; — **ganas** to feel like; **tengo escrita la carta** I have the letter written; — **éxito** to be successful; — **miedo** to be afraid; — **sueño** to be sleepy; — **frío** to be cold; — **hambre** to be hungry; **tiene cinco años** she is five years old; —**se** to stand straight; **no** — **más remedio** to have no other choice; — **que ver con** to have to do with
tenería F tannery
tenga, tengo ver tener
tenia F tapeworm
teniente MF lieutenant
tenis M (juego) tennis; M PL (zapatos) sneakers, tennis shoes
tenista MF tennis player
tenor M (voz, estilo) tenor; (tono) tone, tenor; ADJ **saxofón** — tenor saxophone
tensión F tension
tenso ADJ (nervioso) tense; (extendido) taut
tentación F temptation
tentáculo M tentacle
tentador ADJ tempting
tentar¹ VT to tempt; — **a la suerte** to court danger; — **por todos los medios** to try everything
tentativa F attempt, try
tentativo ADJ tentative
tentempié M snack

tenue ADJ (tela) delicate; (luz) tenuous, dim, faint; (sonido) feeble
tenuidad F faintness, softness
teñir[11] VT (de color) to dye; (de emoción) to tinge
teología F theology
teológico ADJ theological
teólogo -ga MF theologian
teoría F theory; **en —** in theory
teórico ADJ theoretical
tepe M sod
tequila M tequila
terabyte M terabyte
terapeuta MF therapist
terapéutico ADJ therapeutic
terapia F (médica) therapy; (psicológica, marital) counseling; **— de electroshock** shock therapy; **— electroconvulsiva** shock therapy; **— hormonal** hormone therapy; **— ocupacional** occupational therapy
tercero ADJ third; **tercera base** third base; **tercera persona** third person; **tercera edad** old age; **tercer mundo** third world; M (en un contrato) third party; (en béisbol) third baseman
terciar VI/VT to arbitrate
tercio M third
terciopelo M velvet
terco ADJ obstinate, stubborn
tergiversación F distortion, misrepresentation
tergiversar VT (palabras) to distort; (datos) to skew
termal ADJ thermal
térmico ADJ heat, thermal
terminación F (de un proyecto) termination, completion; (de una palabra, cuento) ending; (de un piso) finish
terminal ADJ terminal; MF (de aeropuerto, de omnibus) terminal; M (de computadora, eléctrica) terminal
terminante ADJ (negativa) flat; (prohibición) absolute
terminar VI/VT (completar) to finish, to conclude; VI (tener como final) to end; **— por** to end up; **no termino de entender** I still can't understand; **terminó con las ratas** he got rid of the rats; **sin —** unfinished
término M (final) end; (período de tiempo) period; (límite) boundary; (palabra) term; **— medio** medium; **a —** (trabajo) with a deadline; (embarazo) full-term; **en primer —** first of all; **en —s generales** in general terms; **en último —** as a last resort; **estar en buenos —s** to be on good terms; **por — medio** on average; **poner —** to end
terminología F terminology
termita F termite
termo M thermos
termodinámico ADJ thermodynamic
termómetro M thermometer

termonuclear ADJ thermonuclear
termostato M thermostat
ternero -ra MF (animal) calf; F (carne) veal
terneza F tenderness
terno M three-piece suit
ternura F tenderness
terquedad F obstinacy, stubbornness
terraplén M embankment
terrateniente MF landholder
terraza F (terreno) terrace; (de casa) veranda; (delante de un bar) deck; (azotea) flat roof
terremoto M earthquake
terrenal ADJ earthly
terreno M (campo) piece of land, tract of land; (lote) lot; (formación geológica) terrain; (campo científico) field; **— de juego parejo** level playing field; **ganarle — a alguien** to gain on someone; **perder —** to lose ground; **tantear el —** to put out feelers; **todo —** with four-wheel drive
terrestre ADJ terrestrial, earthly
terrible ADJ terrible, awful
terrier M terrier
territorio M territory
terrón M (de tierra) clod; (de azúcar) lump
terror M terror, dread
terrorismo M terrorism
terrorista ADJ & MF terrorist
terso ADJ (liso) smooth; (pulido) polished
tersura F smoothness
tertulia F social gathering
tesis F thesis; **— doctoral** dissertation
tesón M determination
tesonero ADJ determined
tesorería F treasury
tesorero -ra MF treasurer
tesoro M (riqueza) treasure; (tesorería) treasury
test M test
testaferro M straw man
testamentaria F (gestiones) execution; (bienes) estate
testamento M testament, will
testarudez F stubbornness
testarudo ADJ stubborn, headstrong
testículo M testicle
testificar[30] VI to testify
testigo MF witness; **— de cargo** witness for the prosecution; **— ocular** eyewitness; M proof
testimoniar VI to give testimony
testimonio M testimony, proof, evidence; **levantar falso —** to bear false witness; **en — de su amor** as a testament to his love
testosterona F testosterone
teta F (de animal) teat; (de mujer) *vulg* tit, jug
tétanos M SG tetanus, lockjaw
tetera F teapot, teakettle
tetilla F nipple
tetina F nipple
tetraciclina F tetracycline

tetrapléjico -ca ADJ & MF quadriplegic
tétrico ADJ gloomy
teutónico ADJ Teutonic
textear VT to text
textil ADJ & M textile
texto M (algo escrito) text; (libro escolar) textbook; — **listo para cámara** camera-ready copy
textual ADJ verbatim
textura F texture
tez F complexion
ti PRON PERS you; **para** — for you; **te lo doy a** — I give it to you
tía F (pariente) aunt; (prostituta) *pey* hooker; *fam* (mujer) woman, chick; — **abuela** great-aunt
tibieza F (poco fervor, afecto) lukewarmness; (calor) warmth
tibio ADJ (ni caliente ni frío) tepid, lukewarm; (templado) warm
tiburón M shark
tic M twitch, tic
tictac M **hacer** — to tick
tiempo M (cronológico) time; (climático) weather; (gramatical) tense; (de un partido de cuatro tiempos) quarter; (de un partido de dos tiempos) half; — **compartido** timeshare; — **completo** full-time; — **de descuento** extra time; — **extra** overtime; — **libre** leisure hours, free time; — **parcial** part-time; — **pretérito** past tense; — **real** real time; — **suplementario** (fútbol americano) overtime; (fútbol) extra time; — **y medio** time and a half; **a** — on time; **al mismo** — at the same time; **antes de** — ahead of time; **a su** — in due course; **a un** — at the same time; **con** — in advance; **de medio** — half-time; **en aquel** — back then; **en mis** —**s** in my day; **hace buen** — the weather is nice; **hace mucho** — a long time ago; **mal** — rough weather; **motor de dos** —**s** two-stroke motor; **perder el** — to goof off, to waste time; **tener** — **de sobra** to have time to spare; **todo el** — all the time; **tomar el** — to clock
tienda F (de venta) store; (de campaña) tent; — **minorista** retail store; — **virtual** online store
tienda, tiende *ver* tender
tiene, tienes *ver* tener
tientas LOC ADV **a** — blindly; **andar a** — to feel one's way
tiento M care; **coger el** — to get the hang of something
tierno ADJ (fácil de cortar) tender; (joven) young; (cariñoso) affectionate
tierra F (planeta) earth; (superficie) land; (país) country; (suelo) soil; — **adentro** inland; —**s altas** highlands; —**s bajas** lowlands; — **batida** clay; — **de cultivo** farmland; — **de**

nadie no-man's-land; — **firme** mainland; —**s raras** rare earths; **bajo** — underground; **caer a** — to fall to the ground; **dar en** — **con alguien** to overthrow someone; **echar por** — to knock down; **por** — overland
tieso ADJ (articulación) stiff; (persona) erect; **quedarse** — *fam* to kick the bucket
tiesto M flowerpot
tiesura F stiffness
tifoideo -a ADJ & F typhoid
tifón M typhoon
tifus M (causado por salmonella) typhoid fever; (causado por rickettsia) typhus
tigre M tiger
tijera[s] F SG/PL (instrumento para cortar) scissors; (patada de fútbol) scissor kick
tijereta F scissor kick
tijeretada F snip
tijeretazo M snip
tijeretear VT to snip
tildar VT to brand
tilde F (en la ñ) tilde; (en las vocales) accent [mark]
tilín M *fam* ding-a-ling
timador M confidence man
timbrar VT to stamp
timbrazo M ring
timbre M (aparato) buzzer, doorbell; (cualidad de la voz) timbre; (sello) stamp; (impuesto) stamp tax; (insignia heráldica) crest
timidez F timidity, shyness
tímido ADJ timid, shy, bashful
timo M confidence game, scam; — **en pirámide** Ponzi scheme
timón M helm, rudder
timonear VT to steer
timonel M pilot
timorato ADJ timorous, faint-hearted
tímpano M eardrum
tina F (bañera) tub; (de tintorero) vat
tinaja F large earthen jar
tinglado M (armazón) shed; (plataforma) platform
tinieblas F PL darkness; **en** — in the dark
tinitus M tinnitus
tino M (buen juicio) good judgment; (puntería) marksmanship
tinta F ink; **medias** —**s** wishy-washiness
tinte M (sustancia) dye, stain; (matiz) tint
tintero M inkwell; **eso se me quedó en el** — I never got to that
tintín M clink
tintinear VI to tinkle, to clink
tintineo M tinkle, tinkling
tinto ADJ red
tintorería F dry cleaner
tintorero -ra MF dry cleaner
tintura F (en medicina) tincture; (tinte) dye, tint
tiñoso ADJ scabby

tío -a M (hermano de la madre o el padre) uncle;
— **abuelo** great-uncle; (tipo) guy; F
(hermana de la madre o el padre) aunt; (tipa)
woman, gal; (prostituta) *pey* whore
tíovivo M merry-go-round
tipear, tipiar VI/VT to type
típico ADJ typical
tiple M treble
tipo -pa M (especie, imprenta) type; (tío) *fam*
guy, dude; *Am* rate of interest; — **de cambio**
rate of exchange; — **de interés** interest rate;
— **de letra** typeface, font; — **de letra por
omisión** base font; **un buen** — (hombre
guapo) a good-looking fellow; (buena
persona) a regular guy; **tiene buen** — he's
good looking; F (tía) *pey* woman, broad
tipografía F printing
tipología F typology
tira F (de papel, tocino, tela) strip; (de cuero,
zapato) strap; — **cómica** comic strip
tirada F (de una pelota) throw; (de una
publicación) issue, print run; (distancia)
stretch; **de una** — all at once
tirador -ora MF (persona que dispara) shooter;
M (tirachinas) slingshot; (pomo de la puerta)
knob
tiranía F tyranny
tiránico ADJ tyrannical
tirano -na ADJ tyrannical; MF tyrant
tirante ADJ (cable) taut; (relaciones) strained; M
(de caballería) trace; (de vestido) strap;
(apoyo) brace, strut; — **s** suspenders
tirantez F tension, strain
tirar VT (pelota) to throw, to toss, to pitch;
(derechos, dinero) to throw away; (una bala)
to shoot; (una moneda) to flip, to toss; (dados)
to cast; (una cuerda) to pull, to tug; VI/VT (en
baloncesto) to shoot; VI — **a puerta** to shoot
at goal; —**se** (echarse) to lie down; (en fútbol)
to fake a foul; — **al suelo** to throw down; — **a**
to tend toward; — **abajo** to knock over; — **de**
to tug at; — **la cadena** to flush; — **la casa
por la ventana** to live it up; — **la
chancleta** to kick up one's heels; —**se
pedos** to fart; —**se solo** to go it alone;
tirárselas de to pretend to be; **no me tira
la política** I'm not attracted to politics; **el
coche tira a un lado** the car pulls to one
side; **ir tirando** to get along; **trabajar con
él es un constante tira y afloja** working
with him is a roller-coaster; M **tirabuzón**
(sacacorchos) corkscrew; (espiral) coil; M SG
tirachinas slingshot
tiritar VI (de frío) to shiver; (de miedo) to
shudder
tiro M (lanzamiento) throw; (disparo) shot;
(deporte) shooting; (de cocaína) hit; (de
dados) roll; (de caballos) team; (de chimenea)
draft; (fútbol) shot; — **al arco** archery; — **al**

blanco target practice; — **de esquina**
corner kick; — **de penalidad** penalty kick;
— **en suspensión** jump shot; — **libre**
(baloncesto) free throw; (fútbol) free kick;
errar el — to miss the mark; **matar a** —**s** to
gun down; **ni a** —**s** absolutely not; **pegarle
un** — **a alguien** to shoot someone; **me
salió el** — **por la culata** the plan backfired
on me
tiroides ADJ & M thyroid
tirón M (tironeo) jerk, tug, pull; (atracción
fuerte, lesión de un músculo) pull; **de un** —
all at once; **un** — **de orejas** a slap on the
wrist
tironear VI/VT to jerk, to tug at
tirotear VI to shoot; —**se** to exchange shots
tiroteo M (tiros) shooting, gunfire; (entre
bandos) shootout
tirria F dislike; **tenerle** — **a una persona** to
have a strong dislike for someone
tisana F herbal tea
tísico ADJ consumptive
tisis F consumption
titánico ADJ titanic
titanio M titanium
títere M (marioneta) puppet; (persona) puppet,
dupe; —**s** puppet show; **no dejar** — **con
cabeza** to leave no one standing
titilación F flicker
titilar VI to flicker, to twinkle
titileo M twinkle
titubear VI (vacilar) to hesitate, to waver;
(oscilar) to totter, to dodder
titubeo M hesitation
titular VT to entitle; —**se** to graduate; ADJ
permanent; M (de periódico) headline; MF (de
cargo) incumbent
titularidad F tenure
título M (de una obra, persona, liga) title;
(derecho) claim, legal right; (universitario)
degree, diploma; — **de propiedad** title
deed; —**s de crédito** credits; **a** — **de** by way
of
tiza F chalk
tiznado ADJ sooty
tiznar VT to smear with soot
tizne M soot
tizón M (leña) burning log; (parásito) smut
TNT M TNT
toalla F towel; **tirar la** — to throw in the towel
toallero M towel rack
tobillo M ankle
tobogán M slide
tocado M headdress; ADJ touched
tocador M (mueble) dressing table, vanity table;
(habitación) *lit* boudoir
tocante a PREP concerning
tocar[30] VT (con los dedos) to touch; (un
instrumento musical) to play; (una campana)

to ring; (un timbre) to buzz; (a la puerta) to knock; (la bocina) to honk, to blast; (una alarma) to sound; (mencionar) to touch upon; — **en** to stop over in; —**le a uno** to be one's turn; — **fondo** to hit bottom; — **la pelota** (béisbol) bunt; M SG **tocadiscos** record player

tocayo -ya MF namesake

tocino M bacon

tocón M stump

todavía ADV still, as yet, yet; — **está aquí** she's still here; ¿— **no has comido?** have you not eaten yet? — **no ha llegado** she still has not arrived, as yet she has not arrived; **me dio** — **más** she gave me even more

todo ADJ all; (cada uno) every, each; — **hombre** every man; —**s los días** every day; **a** — **correr** at top speed; **a toda costa** at all costs; **a toda marcha** in high gear; **a toda vela** under full sail; **a toda velocidad** at full speed; **a** — **volumen** at full blast; **de** — **corazón** wholeheartedly; **de** —**s modos** still, anyway, all the same; **del** — entirely; **en** — **caso** in any case, at any rate, in any event; **es** — **un personaje** he's quite a character; **por** — **lados** everywhere; — **el día** all day; — **el tiempo** all the time; — **el mundo** everyone; **todas las noches** nightly; **toda la noche** all through the night; **toda clase de** all sorts of; **en/por todas partes** everywhere, far and wide; **con toda el alma** from the bottom of one's heart; **con toda sinceridad** in all earnestness; PRON **de una vez por todas** once and for all; **se vale** anything goes; —**s** everybody; —**s juntos** all together; ADV — **derecho** straight ahead; — **lo contrario** quite the opposite; — **recto** straight ahead; — **sucio** all dirty; — **o nada** all or nothing; **ante** — first of all; **así y** — in spite of that; **con** — in spite of that; **del** — completely; **sobre** — especially; M whole; —**poderoso** almighty; **el** — **es más que la suma de las partes** the whole is more than the sum of its parts

toga F (de catedrático) gown; (de juez) robe

Togo M Togo

togolés -esa ADJ & MF Togolese

toldería F Indian village

toldo M awning, canopy

tolerancia F tolerance

tolerante ADJ tolerant, broad-minded

tolerar VT to tolerate; **no lo puedo** — I can't stand it

tolete M oarlock

toma F (de una ciudad) taking; (cinematográfica) take; (de juramento) administration; (de teléfono) jack; — **de agua** faucet; — **de corriente** electric outlet; — **de poder** takeover; — **y daca** give-and-take

tomar VT (una pastilla) to take; (un juramento) to administer; (un vestido) to take in; (a un empleado) to hire; (una bebida) to drink; — **a pecho** to take to heart; — **asiento** to take a seat; — **desprevenido** to take by surprise; — **el sol** to sunbathe; —**lo a mal** to take the wrong way; — **el pelo a** to make fun of, to kid, to pull someone's leg; — **medidas** to take action; — **posesión** to take possession; — **una decisión** to make a decision; —**le las medidas a alguien** to measure someone for clothes; —**se de la mano** to hold hands; —**se la molestia** to bother to

tomate M tomato

tomillo M thyme

tomo M volume

tomografía F scan; — **axial computarizada** CAT scan; — **cerebral** brain scan

ton LOC ADV **sin** — **ni son** for no reason

tonada F tune

tonel M (barril) barrel; (persona) pey fatso

tonelada F ton

tóner M toner

Tonga F Tonga

tongano -na ADJ & MF Tongan

tongo M setup

tonicidad F tone; — **muscular** muscle tone

tónico -ca ADJ & M tonic; F (tono) tone; (agua) tonic [water]

tono M (al hablar) tone; (musical) pitch; (intervalo musical) step; — **de ocupado** busy signal; — **menor** minor key; — **muscular** muscle tone; **a** — on key; **bajar el** — to lower the volume; **darse** — to put on airs; **de buen** — in good taste; **fuera de** — out of place; **subido de** — risqué

tontear VI to fool around

tontería F (cualidad de tonto) stupidity; (hecho o dicho tonto) foolishness, nonsense

tonto -ta ADJ (ingenuo) foolish; (de poca inteligencia) stupid, dumb; **a tontas y a locas** haphazardly; MF (persona ingenua) fool; (persona de poca inteligencia) fam dummy, blockhead, dimwit; — **de capirote** dunce; **hacer[se] el** — to play the fool

topacio M topaz

topar VT to butt; —**se con** to bump into

tope M (de precios) ceiling, cap; (de tren) bumper; (de puerta) doorstop; **a** — a lot; **hasta el** — to the maximum; **estar hasta el** — to be completely full

topetazo M butt

tópico M (lugar común) cliché; (tema) topic; ADJ topical

topless ADJ topless

topo M mole (también espía)

toque M (con la mano) touch; (de campana) ringing; (de tambor) beat; (de trompeta) blare; (de pintura) dab; — **de queda** curfew;

— **de pelota** (béisbol) bunt; **dar los últimos —s** to put the finishing touches; **dar —s** to dab; **un— femenino** a woman's touch
toquetear VI/VT (mercancías) to finger; (por placer sexual) *vulg* to grope, to feel up/off
toqueteo M feel
tórax M thorax
torbellino M whirlwind
torcedura F twist, sprain, strain
torcer³⁴ VT (el cuello) to twist; (una articulación) to sprain, to strain; (tergiversar) to distort; **—le el pescuezo a alguien** to wring someone's neck; VI (un río) to bend
torcido ADJ crooked, bent
tordo M thrush
torear VT (lidiar) to fight a bull; (provocar) to provoke
torero -ra MF bullfighter
tormenta F storm; **— de arena** sandstorm; **— eléctrica** electrical storm
tormento M torment
tormentoso ADJ stormy
tornadizo ADJ changeable
tornado M tornado, twister
tornar VI (regresar) to return; VT (cambiar) to turn; **— a hacer algo** to do something again
tornasolado ADJ iridescent
tornear VT to turn on a lathe
torneo M tournament
tornillo M screw; **— de banco** vise; **faltarle a uno un—** to have a screw loose
torniquete M (eje giratorio) turnstile; (contra hemorragia) tourniquet
torno M (para levantar cosas pesadas) hoist, winch; (para cerámica) lathe, pottery wheel; **en — [a]** around
toro M bull; **coger/agarrar el — por los cuernos** to take the bull by the horns
toronja F grapefruit
torpe ADJ (poco habilidoso) clumsy, awkward; (lento) slow, sluggish
torpedear VT to torpedo
torpedero -ra MF (en béisbol) shortstop; M (barco) torpedo boat; (avión) torpedo plane
torpedo M torpedo
torpeza F (falta de habilidad) clumsiness; (lentitud) slowness, sluggishness
torpor M torpor
torrar VT to roast
torre F (de castillo) tower; (de buque de guerra) turret; (en ajedrez) castle; **— de control** control tower; **— de marfil** ivory tower; **— de perforación** oil derrick; **— de vigilancia** watchtower
torrencial ADJ torrential
torrente M torrent; **— de lágrimas** flood of tears; **— sanguíneo** bloodstream
torreón M large tower

torreta F turret
tórrido ADJ torrid
torsión F torsion
torso M torso
torta F (postre) cake; (bofetada) slap
tortícolis F kink
tortilla F (de huevo) omelet; (de harina) *Méx* tortilla; **se dio vuelta la—** the tables have turned
tortillera F *ofensivo* dyke
tórtola F turtledove
tortuga F tortoise, turtle; **— marina** sea turtle; **a paso de—** at a snail's pace
tortuoso ADJ (camino) tortuous; (carácter) devious
tortura F torture
torturante ADJ torturous
torturar VT to torture
torvo ADJ fierce
tos F cough; **— ferina** whooping cough
tosco ADJ coarse, crude
toser VI to cough
tosquedad F coarseness, crudeness
tostada F toast
tostado ADJ (pan) toasted; (café) roasted; M (acción de tostar pan) toasting; (color, bronceado) tan; (acción de tostar café) roasting
tostador -ora MF toaster
tostar⁵ VT (pan) to toast; (piel) to tan; (café) to roast
total ADJ & M total; **en—** all together; **—, a mí no me importa** anyway, I don't care
totalidad F **la— del dinero** all the money; **en su—** as a whole
totalitario ADJ totalitarian
totalmente ADV totally, perfectly
tour M tour
tóxico ADJ toxic
toxina F toxin
traba F (estorbo) hindrance; (de caballo) hobble
trabajador -ora ADJ (esforzado) hardworking; (proletario) working; MF worker
trabajar VI/VT to work; **— un taxi** to drive a taxi; VI (una tienda) to be open; **— duro** to work hard; **— horas extras** to work overtime
trabajo M (actividad) work; (acción de trabajar) working; (empleo) job; (informe académico) paper; **— manual** manual labor; **da mucho—** it's a lot of work; **sin—** unemployed
trabajoso ADJ laborious
trabar VT (una puerta) to jam; (un caballo) to hobble; (a un boxeador) to clinch; (una salsa) to thicken; (negociaciones) to impede; **— amistad con alguien** to strike up a friendship with someone; **— batalla** to join battle; **— conversación** to strike up a conversation; M SG **trabalenguas** tongue

twister
tracción F traction
tractocamión M tractor-trailer
tractor M tractor
tradición F tradition
tradicional ADJ traditional
traducción F translation
traducir[38] VI/VT to translate
traductor-ora MF translator
traduje, tradujera, tradujese, traduzca, traduzco ver traducir
traer[59] VT (venir con) to bring; (llevar puesto) to have on; (contener) to feature; **— a colación** to bring up; **— a mal a alguien** to mistreat someone; **este niño se las trae** this child is something else; **¿qué te traes entre manos?** what are you up to? **—se secretos** to have secrets
tráfago M bustle
traficante MF dealer
traficar[30] VI to traffic, to trade
tráfico M traffic
tragar[40] VI/VT (ingerir) to swallow; (comer) *fam* to stuff one's face; (consumir gasolina) to guzzle; (aguantar) to stand; (hacer desaparecer) to engulf; **—se algo** to swallow [accidentally]; **no me lo trago** I don't buy that; M **tragaluz** skylight; M/F SG
tragamonedas/tragaperras slot machine
tragedia F tragedy
trágico ADJ tragic
trago M (lo tragado) swallow; (bebida alcohólica) shot, slug; **a —s** (beber) in sips; (poco a poco) little by little; **echar/tomar un —** to take a drink; **pasar un mal —** to suffer a difficulty
traición F (política) treason; (personal) betrayal; (acto desleal) treachery; **a —** by treachery
traicionar VT to double-cross
traicionero ADJ treacherous
traidor-ora ADJ treacherous; MF (político) traitor; (personal) betrayer
traiga, traigo ver traer
trailer M trailer
traílla F leash
traje M (conjunto) suit; (de fiesta) gown; **— de baño** swimsuit
traje, trajera, trajese ver traer
trajeado ADJ **bien —** well-dressed
trajín M hustle and bustle
trajinar VI to rush around
trama F (argumento) plot; (intriga) scheme; (conjunto de hilos) woof
tramador-ora MF plotter
tramar VT (con hilos) to weave; (intrigar) to plot, to scheme
tramitación F processing
tramitar VT to take steps to obtain
trámite M procedure, paperwork
tramo M (de carretera) stretch; (de puente) span;

(de hielo) patch; (de escalera) flight
tramoyista MF stagehand
trampa F (de caza) trap, snare; (engaño) trick; **— de arena** (golf) sand trap; **hacer —** to cheat, to trick; **tender una —** to set a trap
trampear VI to cheat
trampilla F trapdoor
trampolín M (de piscina) springboard; (de circo) trampoline
tramposo-sa ADJ deceitful; MF cheat
tranca F crossbar
trance M (momento difícil) pass, difficult moment; (estado mental) trance; **el último —** the last moment of life; **a todo —** at any cost
tranco M stride; **a —s** hurriedly; **en dos —s** in a jiffy
tranquera F wooden fence
tranquilidad F tranquillity, calm, quiet
tranquilizante M tranquilizer
tranquilizar[47] VT to quiet, to calm down; **—se** to calm down, to wind down
tranquilo ADJ (silencioso) quiet, peaceful; (apacible) calm, cool; (despreocupado) calm, at ease; (no excitable) sedate, laid-back; (sin olas) smooth, tranquil
transacción F transaction; **— comercial** business transaction; **transacciones** trading; **transacciones a precio de mercado** arm's-length transactions
transar VI to compromise
transatlántico ADJ transatlantic; M transatlantic liner
transbordar VI to transfer
transbordo M transfer
transcribir[74] VT to transcribe
transcripción F transcript
transcultural ADJ cross-cultural
transcurrir VI to elapse
transcurso M passing, passage; **en el — de un año** in the course of a year
transeúnte MF passerby, transient
transexual ADJ & MF transsexual
transferencia F transfer; **— electrónica** wire transfer
transferible ADJ transferable
transferir[8] VT to transfer (también en computadora)
transformación F transformation
transformador M transformer
transformar VT to transform
transfusión F transfusion; **dar una — de sangre** to give a transfusion
transgénico ADV genetically modified
transgredir[73] VT to transgress
transgresión F transgression
transgresor-ora MF lawbreaker
transición F transition
transigir[46] VI to compromise

transistor M transistor
transitable ADJ passable
transitar VI/VT to travel
transitivo ADJ transitive
tránsito M (acción de viajar) transit, passage; (tráfico) traffic; **de/en** — in transit
transitorio ADJ transitory
transmisible ADJ communicable
transmisión F transmission; — **automática** automatic transmission; — **por la web** webcast
transmisor M transmitter; ADJ transmitting
transmitir VI/VT (enviar) to transmit; (una enfermedad) to communicate; (por radio o televisión) to broadcast; — **por la web** to webcast
transnacional ADJ transnational
transparencia F (visual) transparency; (institucional) openness
transparente ADJ transparent
transpiración F perspiration, sweating
transpirar VI/VT to transpire, to perspire
transportación F transportation, transport
transportar VT (mercancías, gente) to transport; (mercancías) to ship, to haul
transporte M (acción) transport, transportation; (vehículo de transporte) transport [vessel]; — **de locura** fit of madness; — **público** mass transit
transportista MF teamster, trucker
transversal ADJ transverse; F transversal
transverso ADJ transverse
tranvía M (transporte urbano) streetcar, trolley; (tren de cercanías) local train
trapacería F racket
trapacero -ra MF racketeer
trapeador M mop
trapear VI/VT Am to mop
trapecio M trapeze
trapezoide ADJ & M trapezoid
trapiche M sugar mill
trapisonda F trick
trapo M rag; —**s** fam duds; **a todo** — at full speed; **tratar a alguien como un** — to treat someone like dirt; —**s sucios** dirty laundry
tráquea F trachea, windpipe
traqueotomía F tracheotomy
traquetear VI (hacer sonido) to rattle, to clatter; (llevar a todos lados) to drag from place to place
traqueteo M rattle, clatter
tras PREP (temporal) after; (espacial) after, behind, in back of; **correr** — to run after; **día** — **día** day after day; **una vez** — **otra** time after time
trascendencia F (concepto filosófico) transcendence; (importancia) importance
trascendental ADJ (que sobrepasa la realidad) transcendental; (importante) important

trascendente ADJ (que sobrepasa la realidad) transcendental; (importante) important
trascender VT (sobrepasar) to transcend; VI (surgir) to emerge; (extender) to extend
trasegar[41] VT (vino) to pour from one container to another; (objetos) to move around; (papeles) to shuffle
trasero ADJ (punto, asiento) rear, back; (pata) hind; M (de persona) fam rear, rear end, bottom
traslación F transfer
trasladar VT (a un empleado) to transfer; (una reunión) to postpone; —**se** to travel
traslado M transfer
traslapo M overlap
trasnochar VI to stay up late
traspapelar VT to mislay, to misplace; —**se** to become mislaid
traspasar VT (pasar por) to transfix; (ir más allá de) to go beyond; (pasar un límite) to transgress, to cross over; (una propiedad) to transfer
traspaso M transfer
traspié M stumble, slip; **dar un** — to stumble
trasplantar VT to transplant
trasplante M transplant
trasponer[56, 74] VT to transpose
trasquilar VT (una oveja) to shear; (a una persona) to fleece
trastabillar VI to stumble
trastazo M bump
traste M (de guitarra) fret, stop; (trasero) buttocks; **dar al** — **con** to destroy; **irse al** — to go down the drain
trasto M piece of junk; —**s** stuff
trastocar[30] VT to disrupt
trastornar VT (alterar psíquicamente) to disturb; (alterar el funcionamiento) to disrupt; —**se** to go crazy
trastorno M (molestia) trouble; (patología) disorder; — **bipolar** bipolar disorder; — **de Asperger** Asperger's syndrome; — **de déficit de atención** attention deficit disorder; — **de la alimentación** eating disorder; — **de la personalidad** personality disorder; — **de personalidad múltiple** multiple personality disorder; — **del sueño** sleep disorder
trasudar VI/VT to perspire
trata F trade; — **de blancas** white slave trade
tratable ADJ (curable) treatable; (amistoso) approachable
tratado M (acuerdo) treaty; (libro) treatise
tratamiento M (acción de tratar) treatment; (fórmula de cortesía) form of address; — **de canal** root canal; — **de convalecencia** aftercare; — **de residuos** waste treatment; — **de textos** Esp word processing; — **postoperatorio** aftercare

tratante MF dealer, trader
tratar VT (una enfermedad, a un paciente, un asunto) to treat; VI (intentar) to try; — **como** to treat like; — **con** to have dealings with; — **de** to try to, to attempt; — **sobre** to be about; **lo trató de imbécil** she called him an idiot; —**le a uno de** to address someone as; — **en** to deal in; —**se con** to have to do with; —**se de** to be a question of, to be about
trato M (acuerdo) treatment; (acción de tratar) dealings; (convenio) deal; (comercio) trade; (modales) manners; ¡— **hecho!** it's a deal! **tener buen** — to have good manners; **cerrar un** — to strike a bargain
trauma M trauma
traumático ADJ traumatic
traumatismo M trauma
través LOC ADV **a/al** — **de** through, across; **a** — **de las declaraciones** throughout the declarations; **de** — across; **mirar de** — to look askance [at]
travesaño M crossbar (también en fútbol)
travesía F crossing, sea voyage, passage
travestí, travesti MF cross-dresser, transvestite
travestido -da MF transvestite
travesura F mischief, prank; —**s** naughtiness; **hacer** —**s** to play pranks
traviesa F railway tie
travieso ADJ mischievous, naughty
trayecto M course, route
trayectoria F (de proyectil) trajectory, path; (profesional) career, track record
trayendo ver traer
traza F (huella) trace; (aspecto) appearance; **tiene** —**s de no acabar nunca** it looks as if it will never end
trazado M (de ciudad) layout; (de edificio) blueprint; (de un plan) outline
trazador M — **gráfico** plotter
trazar⁴⁷ VT (un dibujo) to trace, to sketch; (un plan) to outline; (un edificio) to blueprint; — **el curso** to plot a course
trazo M stroke
trébol M clover
trece NUM thirteen
trecho M stretch; **a** —**s** at intervals; **de** — **en** — at intervals
tregua F (de guerra) truce; (descanso) lull, respite
treinta NUM thirty (también en tenis)
treintañero -ra MF thirtysomething
tremendo ADJ (extraordinario) tremendous; (terrible) terrible
trementina F turpentine
tremolar VI (bandera) to flutter; (voz) to trill
trémolo M quaver
trémulo ADJ tremulous, trembling
tren M train; — **de aterrizaje** landing gear; —

de carga / de mercancías freight train; — **de cercanías** local train; — **de vida** lifestyle; — **expreso** express train; **a todo** — at top speed; **perder el** — to miss the boat; **seguir el** — to keep up
trenza F braid
trenzar⁴⁷ VT to braid
trepador -ora ADJ (planta) climbing; (ciclista) climber; MF social climber; F climbing plant
trepar VI to climb
trepidar VI to tremble
tres NUM three
trescientos NUM three hundred
treta F trick, wile
triaje M triage
triangular ADJ triangular
triángulo M triangle; — **recto** right triangle
tribu F tribe
tribulación F tribulation
tribuna F (de orador) rostrum; (para el público) grandstand
tribunal M (sala del juez) court, courtroom; (cuerpo de jueces) panel of judges
tributable ADJ taxable
tributar VT to pay tribute with; VI to pay taxes
tributario ADJ & M tributary
tributo M (pago obligatorio) tribute; (impuesto) tax
triceps M triceps
triciclo M tricycle
tridimensional ADJ three-dimensional
trifulca F fight
trigo M wheat
trigueño ADJ (tez) swarthy; (pelo) dark-blond
trillado ADJ trite
trilladora F threshing machine
trillar VT to thresh
trillizo -za ADJ & MF triplet
trilogía F trilogy
trimestral ADJ quarterly
trimestre M quarter
trinar VI to trill; **está que trina** she is furious
trinchante M carving knife
trinchar VT to carve
trinche M pitchfork
trinchera F (fosa) trench; (gabardina) trench coat
trinchero M carving table
trineo M sleigh, sled
trinitense ADJ & MF Trinidadian
trino M trill
trinquete M ratchet
trío M trio
tripas F PL guts; **hacer de** — **corazón** to pluck up one's courage
triple ADJ triple; M (también en béisbol) triple; (baloncesto) three-point basket
triplicar³⁰ VT to triple, to treble
trípode M tripod

triptongo M triphthong
tripulación F crew
tripulante MF crew member
tripular VT to man
triquiñuela F caper
triquitraque M firecracker
triscar[30] VI to frisk
triste ADJ sad, sorrowful
tristeza F sadness, sorrow
tristón ADJ glum
tritón M newt
trituradora F (para desechos) garbage disposal unit; (para papel) paper shredder
triturar VI/VT (documentos) to shred; (granos) to grind
triunfador -ora MF winner; ADJ triumphant
triunfal ADJ triumphal
triunfante ADJ triumphant
triunfar VT to triumph
triunfo M triumph
trivial ADJ trivial, commonplace, trite
trizas F PL hacer — to tear into shreds
trocar[31] VT (transformar) to change into; (cambiar una cosa por otra) to exchange
trocear VT to divide into pieces
trocha F trail
trofeo M trophy
troje M granary
trola F whopper
trole M trolley
trolebús M trolley bus
tromba F waterspout; **salir en** — to storm out
trombón M trombone
trombosis F thrombosis; — **coronaria** coronary thrombosis
trompa F (de elefante) trunk; (instrumento musical) horn; — **de Eustaquio** eustachian tube; — **de Falopio** fallopian tube
trompada F blow with the fist
trompeta F trumpet
trompetazo M trumpet blast
trompetear VI to trumpet
trompo M spinning top
tronada F thunderstorm
tronar[5] VI to thunder
tronchar VT to chop off
tronco M (de árbol) trunk, log; (del cuerpo) trunk, torso; — **del encéfalo** brain stem; **dormir como un** — to sleep like a log
tronera F (de buque) gun port; (de mesa de billar) pocket
trono M throne (también wáter)
tropa F (en el ejército) troop; (oficiales) rank and file; —**s de asalto** storm troops; —**s de choque** shock troops
tropel LOC ADV **en** — in droves
tropezar[48] VI to stumble, to trip; —**[se] con alguien** to run into someone; — **con algo** to come across something

tropezón M stumble, trip; **salir a tropezones** to stumble out; **darse un** — to stumble
tropical ADJ tropical
trópico M tropic
tropiezo M stumble
troquel M die
trotar VI to trot, to jog
trote M trot; **al** — at a trot; **no estoy para estos** —**s** I'm too old for this
troza F log
trozar[47] VT to cut up
trozo M (de roca, madera, torta) piece; (de un texto) section; (de carbón) lump; (de carne) slab
trucha F trout
truco M clever trick
truculento ADJ gruesome
trueno M thunder
trueque M (intercambio) exchange; (transacción sin dinero) bartering
truhán -ana MF scoundrel
truja F cigarette
trust M trust
tu ADJ POS your
tú PRON PERS you
tuba F tuba
tuberculosis F tuberculosis
tubería F (tubo) pipe; (conjunto de tubos) piping
tubo M (cilindro hueco) tube; (de agua, órgano) pipe; (digestivo) tract; — **de ensayo** test tube; — **de escape** tailpipe; — **digestivo** gastrointestinal tract
tubular ADJ tubular
tuerca F nut
tuerto ADJ one-eyed
tuétano M marrow; **hasta los** —**s** through and through
tufillo M whiff
tufo M (humo) fumes; (hedor) stench
tugurio M hovel; —**s** slums
tulipán M tulip
tullido -da ADJ crippled; MF *pey* cripple
tullir VT to cripple; —**se** to become crippled
tumba F (panteón) tomb; (sepultura) grave; **soy una** — my lips are sealed
tumbar VT to knock down, to flatten; —**se** to lie down, to stretch out
tumbo M tumble, somersault; **dar** —**s** (persona) to stagger; (coche) to bump along
tumor M tumor; — **cerebral** brain tumor; — **maligno** malignancy
tumorectomía F lumpectomy
tumulto M (alboroto) tumult, uproar; (muchedumbre) mob
tumultuoso ADJ tumultuous
tuna F (fruta) prickly pear; *Esp* (grupo de cantantes) minstrel group
tunante -ta MF scamp
tunda F thrashing

túnel M tunnel
tunesino -na ADJ & MF Tunisian
Túnez M Tunisia
tungsteno M tungsten
túnica F tunic; — **de laboratorio** lab gown
tupido ADJ dense, compact
tupir VT (hacer tupido) to compact; (cubrir) to cover; —**se** to stuff oneself
turba F (muchedumbre) mob; (carbón fósil) peat
turbación F confusion
turbamulta F throng
turbante M turban
turbar VT to disturb; —**se** to become disturbed
turbina F turbine
turbio ADJ (pasado, secreto) dark; (agua, materia) murky
turbocompresor M turbocharger
turborreactor M turbojet
turbulencia F turbulence
turbulento ADJ turbulent
turco -ca ADJ Turkish; MF Turk; M (lengua) Turkish
turcomano -na ADJ & MF Turkmen
turismo M (actividad) tourism; (conjunto de turistas) tourists; **hacer** — to go sightseeing
turista MF tourist
turístico ADJ (relativo al turismo) tourist; **atracción turística** tourist attraction; **clase turística** coach class
Turkmenistán M Turkmenistan
turnarse VI to take turns
turno M (vuelta) turn; (de trabajo) shift; (en béisbol) at bat
turquesa F turquoise
Turquía F Turkey
turrón M nougat
tutear VT to address as "tú"
tutela F guardianship
tutelar VT to have charge of
tutor -ora MF (de un menor) guardian; M (de planta) prop
tutorial M tutorial
Tuvalu M Tuvalu
tuvaluano -na ADJ & MF Tuvaluan
tuve, tuviera, tuviese *ver* tener
tuyo ADJ & PRON POS your, yours; **el amigo** — your friend; **esto es** — this is yours
tweed M tweed

Uu

u CONJ or
ubicación F location
ubicar[30] VT (situar) to locate; (identificar) to place; —**se** to be located

ubicuo ADJ ubiquitous
ubre F udder
UCP [unidad central de proceso] F CPU
Ucrania F Ukraine
ucraniano -na ADJ & MF Ukrainian
UE [Unión Europea] F EU
ufanarse VI to glory [in], to be proud [of]
ufano ADJ proud
Uganda F Uganda
ugandés -esa ADJ & MF Ugandan
ujier M bailiff
úlcera F (lesión superficial) sore; (en el estómago) ulcer; (en la boca) canker, canker sore
ulcerar VI to ulcerate
ulceroso ADJ ulcerous
ulterior ADJ ulterior
últimamente ADV of late
ultimar VT to finalize
ultimátum M ultimatum
último ADJ (palabra, capítulo) last, final; (destino) ultimate; (más reciente) latest; **estar en las últimas** to be on one's last legs; **la última palabra** the last word; **en los** —**s tiempos** lately; **en última instancia** ultimately; **a última hora** at the last moment; **por** — finally
ultrajante ADJ outrageous
ultrajar VT to outrage
ultraje M outrage, indignity
ultraligero M ultralight
ultramar LOC ADV **de** — overseas
ultramoderno ADJ ultramodern
ultrasonido M ultrasound
ultratumba LOC ADV **de** — from beyond the grave
ultravioleta ADJ & M ultraviolet
ulular VI (viento) to howl; (búho) to hoot
ululato M (viento) howling; (búho) hooting
umbral M threshold, doorstep; — **de rentabilidad** breakeven point
umbrío ADJ shady
un, uno, una ART INDEF a, an; **un hombre** a man; **un actor** an actor; **una mujer** a woman; **una manzana** an apple; NUM one; **de a** — one at a time; **es la una** it is one o'clock; PRON one; **uno por uno** one by one; —**s** some; **unos cuantos** some; **uno tiene que cuidarse** you've got to take care of yourself; **yo tengo uno** I have one; **uno tras otro** one after the other; **uno más** (tenis) let; **uno al lado del otro** side by side; **los unos a los otros / el uno al otro** one another / each other
unánime ADJ unanimous
unanimidad F unanimity
uncir[33] VT (a un buey) to yoke; (a un carro) to hitch
ungüento M ointment, salve

único ADJ (solo) only; **una única vez** a single time; (extraordinario) unique; **eres — you're one of a kind**
unidad F (indivisibilidad) unity; (ejemplar) unit; (fracción militar) unit, outfit; (de computadora) drive; — **central de proceso/procesamiento** central processing unit; — **de cuidado coronario** coronary care unit; — **de cuidados intensivos** intensive care unit; — **de disco duro** hard disk drive; — **de disquete** diskette drive; — **monetaria** currency unit
unido ADJ united; **una familia unida** a close-knit family
unificar[30] VT to unify
uniformar VT (estandarizar) to standardize; (dar uniformes) to furnish with uniforms
uniforme ADJ & M uniform
uniformidad F uniformity
unilateral ADJ unilateral
unión F (acción de unir, cosas unidas) union; (lugar en que se unen dos cosas) junction; (indivisibilidad) unity
unir VT (una nación) to unite; (dos construcciones) to join; (cinta magnética, genes) to splice; (caños) to couple; VI/VT (con lazos) to bind
unisex ADJ INV unisex
unísono ADJ unison; **al — in unison**
unitario ADJ (partidario de la unidad) unitarian; (que tiene unidad) unitary
universal ADJ universal
universidad F (de enseñanza e investigación) university; (de enseñanza) college
universitario -ria ADJ university; (relativo a los deportes) collegiate; MF college student
universo M universe
untar VT (la piel con crema) to oil; (el pan con mantequilla) to spread on; (la cara con pintura) to smear; —**le la mano a alguien** to grease someone's palm
untuoso ADJ (graso) oily; (zalamero) slick, unctuous
uña F (de dedo) fingernail; (de gato) claw; — **encarnada** hangnail; **como — y carne** thick as thieves; **con —s y dientes** tooth and nail
uñero M hangnail
uranio M uranium
urbanidad F refinement, polish
urbanismo M (modo de vida) urbanism; (planificación) city planning
urbanización F development
urbanizar[47] VT to build up
urbano ADJ (relativo a la ciudad) urban; (refinado) suave; **autobús — city bus**
urbe F metropolis
urdimbre F warp
urdir VT (una tela) to weave; (una historia) to

concoct; (un plan) to devise, to work out
uretra F urethra
urgencia F (prisa) urgency; (crisis médica) emergency; **con — urgently; —s emergency room**
urgente ADJ urgent, pressing
urgir[46] VT to urge; VI to be urgent
úrico ADJ uric
urinario ADJ urinary; M urinal
URL M URL
urna F (para cenizas) urn; (electoral) ballot box; **acudir a las —s** to go to the polls
urólogo -ga MF urologist
urraca F (ave) magpie; (persona acaparadora) packrat
urticaria F hives
Uruguay M Uruguay
uruguayo -ya ADJ & MF Uruguayan
usado ADJ (utilizado) used; (desgastado) worn
usar VT (emplear) to use; (ponerse) to wear; —**se** to be in use; **sin — unused**
USB M USB
uso M (empleo) use; (costumbre) usage, custom; **al — de la época** according to the custom of the time
usted PRON PERS you; —**es** you, you all, y'all
usual ADJ usual
usuario -ria MF (de un servicio) user; (en una biblioteca) borrower
usufructo M enjoyment
usufructuar[26] VT to enjoy the use of
usura F usury
usurero -ra MF usurer, loan shark
usurpar VT to encroach upon, to usurp
utensilio M utensil
uterino ADJ uterine
útero M uterus, womb
útil ADJ useful, helpful; M PL —**es** utensils
utilidad F usefulness, utility
utilitario ADJ utilitarian
utilización F use, utilization
utilizar[47] VT (emplear) to utilize; (explotar) to use
utopía F utopia
uva F grape
úvula F uvula
uvular ADJ uvular
Uzbekistán M Uzbekistan
uzbeko -ka ADJ & MF Uzbek

Vv

va, vamos ver ir
vaca F cow; — **marina** sea cow
vacación F vacation; **de vacaciones** on

vacation
vacante ADJ vacant; F vacancy, opening
vaciar[28] VT (una botella) to empty; (una naranja) to hollow out; (una estatua) to cast; (una computadora) to dump
vacilación F hesitation
vacilante ADJ (dudoso) vacillating, hesitating; (tembloroso) shaky
vacilar VI to vacillate, to hesitate, to waver; — [**con**] *fam* to make fun [of]
vacío ADJ (envase) empty; (casa) vacant; (comentarios) idle; (expresión) blank; M (condición) emptiness; (lugar) void; (espacio sin aire) vacuum; **envasado al —** vacuum-packed; **hacer el —** to give the cold shoulder
vacuna F (inoculación) vaccine; (enfermedad) cowpox
vacunación F vaccination
vacunar VI/VT to vaccinate
vacuno ADJ bovine
vadear VT to ford
vado M ford, crossing
vagabundear VI to wander idly
vagabundo-da ADJ vagabond, vagrant; MF (pordiosero) tramp, bum; (trabajador errante) drifter, transient; (en la playa) beachcomber
vagancia F vagrancy
vagar[40] VI to wander, to roam
vagina F vagina
vaginal ADJ vaginal
vaginitis F vaginitis
vago-ga ADJ (idea) vague; (silueta) shadowy; (impresión) faint, vague; (persona) lazy; MF vagrant, tramp
vagón M railway car; — **restaurante** dining car
vaguedad F faintness
vahído M dizzy spell
vaho M steam
vaina F (de una espada) sheath; (de legumbres) pod, shell; (molestia) nuisance; (cosa mal recordada) thing
vainilla F vanilla
vaivén M swaying, swinging; **vaivenes** ups and downs
vajilla F tableware, dishes; — **de barro** earthenware; — **de porcelana** chinaware
vale M voucher; INTERJ oh well, OK
valedero ADJ valid
valenciano-na ADJ & MF Valencian
valentía F courage, valor, bravery
valentón-ona ADJ cocky; MF cocky person
valer[60] VT (tener un determinado valor) to be worth; VI (ser válido) to be valid; (estar permitido) to be allowed; (ser de utilidad) to be useful; — **la pena** to be worthwhile; — **más que** to outweigh; —**se de** to avail oneself of; —**se por sí mismo** to be

self-sufficient; **¿cuánto vale?** how much is it? **hacer — los derechos** to assert one's rights; **hacerse —** to stand up for oneself; **le valió una paliza** that earned him a beating; **más vale solo que mal acompañado** better alone than in poor company; **no hay pero que valga** no buts about it; **más vale tarde que nunca** better late than never; **no vale ni un comino** it's not worth a hoot; **no vale** that's not fair; **¡vale!** OK! **¡válgame Dios!** gracious! **todo vale** anything goes
valeroso ADJ valorous, brave
valga, valgo *ver* valer
valía F worth
validez F validity
válido ADJ (entrada, cupón) valid; (cheque) good; (argumento) solid
valiente ADJ valiant, brave, courageous
valija F (para viajes) valise, suitcase; (para el correo) pouch
valioso ADJ valuable
valla F (en un jardín) fence; (en carreras) hurdle
vallar VT to fence
valle M valley, vale
valor M (precio) value, worth; (valentía) valor, mettle; — **contable** book value; —**es** securities; —**es en cartera** holdings; — **nominal** face value, par value; —**es respaldados por hipoteca** mortgage-backed securities; **armarse de —** to muster up one's courage
valoración F valuation
valorar VT (apreciar) to value; (determinar el valor) to appraise; (aumentar el valor) to make more valuable
valorizar[47] VT to make more valuable; —**se** to become more valuable
vals M waltz
valsar VI to waltz
valuación F valuation, appraisal
valuar[26] VT to appraise
valva F valve
válvula F valve; — **reguladora de aceleración** throttle
vampiresa F vamp
vampiro M vampire
vanagloria F boastfulness
vanagloriarse VI to boast
vanaglorioso ADJ boastful
vándalo-la MF vandal
vanguardia F vanguard; **a la —** at the forefront
vanidad F vanity, conceit
vanidoso ADJ vain
vano ADJ vain; **en —** in vain
Vanuatu M Vanuatu
vanuatuense ADJ & MF Vanuatuan
vapor M (de agua) vapor, steam; (buque) steamship; —**es** fumes; **cocer al —** to steam; **echar —** to give off steam

vapulear VT to thrash
vapuleo M thrashing
vaquería F cowshed
vaqueriza F cowshed
vaquero -ra M cowboy; **—s** blue jeans; F cowgirl; ADJ **botas vaqueras** cowboy boots
vaqueta F cowhide
vaquilla F heifer
vara F (rama) stick; (palo) rod
varadero M dry dock
varar VT to beach, to strand; VI to run aground
varear VT to whip with a stick
variable ADJ variable, changeable; F variable
variación F variation
variado ADJ varied
variante F variant
variar[28] VI/VT to vary
varicela F chicken pox
várices, varices F PL varicose veins
varicoso ADJ varicose
variedad F variety, assortment
varilla F (palo delgado) small rod; (para azotar) switch; (de paraguas) rib
vario ADJ varied; **—s** various, several
variopinto ADJ variegated
varita F wand
varón M male [person]
varonil ADJ (masculino) manly; (hombruno) mannish
vasco -ca ADJ & MF Basque; M (lengua) Basque
vascuence ADJ Basque; M (lengua) Basque
vascular ADJ vascular
vasectomía F vasectomy
vaselina F Vaseline™
vasija F vessel
vaso M (de vidrio) glass; (de papel, plástico) cup; (corto y grueso) tumbler; (sanguíneo) vessel; **— de precipitado** beaker
vástago M (de planta) shoot, sprout; (de persona) offspring; (de motor) rod
vasto ADJ vast
vataje M wattage
vaticinar VT to foretell
vaticinio M prediction
vatio M watt
vaya, vayamos, ve ver ir
vea, veamos ver ver
vecindad F (cercanía) vicinity; (barrio) neighborhood
vecindario M neighborhood
vecino -na MF (cercano, contiguo) neighbor; (residente de una zona) resident; ADJ neighboring
vector M vector
vedar VT to prohibit
vega F fertile plain
vegan ADJ & MF vegan
vegetación F vegetation
vegetal ADJ vegetable; M vegetable, plant

vegetar VI to vegetate
vegetariano -na ADJ & MF vegetarian
vehemencia F vehemence
vehemente ADJ vehement
vehículo M vehicle
veía, veíamos ver ver
veinte NUM twenty
veintena F (aproximadamente) group of [about] twenty; (exactamente) score
veinticinco NUM twenty-five
veintiuno NUM twenty-one; M (juego de naipes) blackjack
vejancón -ona M codger; F old woman
vejar VT to humiliate
vejestorio -ria M codger; F old woman
vejete M codger
vejez F old age
vejiga F (órgano) bladder; (ampolla) blister
vela F (período de vigilancia) vigil, watch; (de cera) candle; (de un navío) sail; **a toda —** under full sail; **en —** without sleep; **hacerse a la —** to set sail
velada F (noche) evening; (fiesta) evening party
velador M nightstand
velar VI (no dormir) to keep vigil, to stay awake; (cubrir con velo) to veil; (exponer a la luz una película fotográfica) to expose; **— por** to look after
velatorio M wake
veleidoso ADJ fickle
velero M sailboat; ADJ swift-sailing
veleta F weathervane; MF fickle person
vello M (del cuerpo) body hair; (de frutas) fuzz
vellón M fleece
velloso ADJ fuzzy
velludo ADJ hairy
velo M veil; **— del paladar** soft palate
velocidad F velocity, speed; **— de transferencia** transfer rate; **a toda —** at full speed
velocímetro M speedometer
velorio M wake
veloz ADJ swift, fast
ven ver venir
vena F (vaso sanguíneo, veta) vein; (estado de ánimo) mood; (de locura) streak; **estar en —** to be in the mood, to be inspired
venado M (animal) deer; (macho) stag; (carne) venison
vencedor -ora ADJ winning; MF winner, victor
vencer[32] VT (a un enemigo) to conquer, to vanquish; (a un equipo) to defeat, to beat; (obstáculos) to overcome; (en valor, inteligencia) to surpass; VI **—se** (un plazo) to expire; (un colchón) to cave in
vencido ADJ (derrotado) defeated; (a pagar) due, overdue, past due; **darse por —** to give up, to surrender
vencimiento M (de una deuda) maturity; (de un

contrato) expiration
venda F (para una herida) bandage; (sobre los ojos) blindfold
vendaje M bandage; — **quirúrgico** surgical dressing
vendar VT (una herida) to bandage; (los ojos) to blindfold
vendaval M gale
vendedor -ora MF vendor, seller, salesperson; — **mayorista** wholesaler
vender VI/VT (comercializar) to sell; (traicionar) to betray; —**se a** to go over to; **se vende** for sale
vendetta F vendetta
vendible ADJ marketable
vendimia F vintage
vendrá, vendría ver venir
veneciana F venetian blind
veneno M (sustancia dañina) poison; (ponzoña de víbora) venom
venenoso ADJ (planta) poisonous; (víbora) venomous
venerable ADJ venerable
veneración F veneration, reverence
venerar VT (a una persona) to venerate, to revere; (a Dios) to worship
venéreo ADJ venereal
venezolano -na ADJ & MF Venezuelan
Venezuela F Venezuela
venga, vengamos ver venir
vengador -ora ADJ avenging; MF avenger
venganza F vengeance, revenge, payback
vengar[40] VT to avenge; —**se de** to retaliate for, to avenge, to take revenge
vengativo ADJ vindictive, vengeful
venida F coming
venidero ADJ forthcoming
venir[61] VI to come; — **a colación** to come up [in conversation]; — **al caso / a cuento** to be relevant; — **bien** to be convenient; —**le a uno bien** to be suitable to someone; —**se** *fam* to come [sexually]; —**se abajo** to collapse; **¿a qué viene eso?** what is the point of that? **el año que viene** next year; **lo mejor está por** — the best is yet to come; **no me vengas con excusas** no excuses; **venga lo que venga** come what may
venta F sale; — **al por mayor** wholesale; — **al por menor** retail; — **de liquidación** fire sale; **en** — for sale; **poner a la** — to put up for sale
ventaja F (también en tenis) advantage; (en una carrera) head start; — **al resto** ad out; — **al saque** ad in; — **al servicio** ad in
ventajoso ADJ advantageous
ventana F window (también digital); **tirar por la** — to throw out the window
ventanal M large window
ventanilla F [de coche, avión] window; (de la

nariz) nostril
ventarrón M gale, high wind
ventear VI to sniff the wind
ventilación F (aireado) ventilation; (hueco para el aire) vent
ventilado ADJ airy
ventilador M (abertura) ventilator; (aparato) electrical fan
ventilar VT to ventilate, to air out; (una cuestión) to air
ventisca F blizzard
ventisquero M (lugar ventoso) place prone to blizzards; (lugar nevado) snowfield
ventolera F gust of wind; **darle a uno la** — **de** to take a notion to
ventosear VI to break wind
ventoso ADJ windy, breezy
ventrículo M ventricle
venturoso ADJ fortunate; **futuro** — bright future
veo ver ver
ver[72, 74] VI/VT (un paisaje) to see; (televisión, espectáculos) to watch; (un programa de computadora) to view; **a** — let's see; **eso aún está por** —**se** that is still to be seen; **no lo puedo** — I can't stand him; **no veo la hora de terminar** I'm dying / I can't wait to finish; **no tener nada que** — **con** not to have anything to do with; **te veo preocupado** you look worried; **a mi modo de** — in my opinion; —**se obligado a** to be obliged to; **vérselas con algo** to confront something; **vérselas negras** to have a hard time
vera LOC ADV **a la** — beside
veracidad F truthfulness
veranear VI to spend the summer
veraneo M summer vacation
veraniego ADJ summer
verano M summer
veras LOC ADV **de** — really; **¿de** —? oh really? oh yeah?
veraz ADJ truthful
verbal ADJ verbal
verbena F carnival
verbo M verb
verborrágico ADJ long-winded
verboso ADJ verbose, wordy
verdad F truth; **¿—?** really? — **a medias** half-truth; **de** — indeed; **una pistola de** — a real pistol; **faltar a la** — to fib
verdaderamente ADV really, truly
verdadero ADJ true, real
verde ADJ green (también inmaduro, sin experiencia, ecologista); (chiste) off-color; — **oliva** olive-green; **ponerse** — to stuff oneself; M green; **poner** — **a alguien** to run someone down
verdear VI/VT to turn green

verdín M scum
verdor M greenness
verdoso ADJ greenish
verdugo M executioner, hangman
verdugón M welt
verdulero -ra MF vegetable vendor
verdura F (hortaliza) vegetable; (verdor) *lit* verdure; **—s** produce
vereda F (en el campo) path; (para peatones) *Am* sidewalk; **entrar en —** to toe the line
veredicto M verdict
verga F (percha para vela) yard; (pene) *vulg* dick
vergonzoso ADJ (que da vergüenza) shameful, disgraceful; (que siente vergüenza) sheepish, bashful
vergüenza F (humillación) shame; (incomodidad) embarrassment; (escándalo) disgrace; **tener —** to be ashamed; **tener — ajena** to cringe; **es una —** it's a shame; **me dan — mis dientes** I'm embarrassed about my teeth; **me da — decírtelo** I'm embarrassed to tell you
vericueto M twists and turns
verídico ADJ truthful, true
verificación F verification, cross-check
verificar[30] VT to verify, to check; **—se** to take place
verja F grate
vermú M vermouth
vernáculo ADJ & M vernacular
verruga F wart; **— genital** genital wart
versado ADJ versed
versalillas F PL small caps
versalitas F PL small caps
versar VI **— sobre** to deal [with], to treat
versátil ADJ versatile
versículo M Bible verse
versión F (de un texto) version; (traducción) translation; (de una canción) rendition; **— beta** beta version; **— impresa** printout; **— original** original [of a film]
verso M line [of poetry]; **— libre** free verse; **— suelto/blanco** blank verse
versus PREP versus
vértebra F vertebra
vertebrado ADJ & M vertebrate
vertebral ADJ spinal
vertedero M dump, landfill
verter[2] VT (echar líquido) to pour; (vaciar) to pour out; (derramar) to spill; **— en** to empty into; **—se** to spill
vertical ADJ (en ángulo recto) vertical; (erguido) upright; (empinado) sheer
vertido M (acción) dumping; (lo vertido) waste; **— de petróleo** oil spill
vertiente F (pendiente) slope; (cuenca) watershed; ADJ flowing
vertiginoso ADJ dizzy, giddy
vértigo M (falta de equilibrio) vertigo; (frenesí) hectic pace
vertigoso ADJ dizzy, giddy
vesícula F gall bladder
vestíbulo M (de un edificio) vestibule, lobby; (de una casa) hallway
vestido M dress; **— de noche** evening gown; **— de novia** bridal dress
vestidura F attire
vestigio M vestige, trace, remnant
vestimenta F attire, dress; (estrafalaria) getup
vestir[9] VT to dress, to clothe; **—se** to get dressed; **—se de gala** to dress up
vestuario M (ropa) wardrobe; (en el teatro) costumes; (lugar para vestirse) changing room
veta F (de minerales) vein, seam; (de madera) grain; (de humor) strain
vetar VT to veto
veteado ADJ veined
veterano -na ADJ & MF veteran
veterinario -ria MF veterinarian; ADJ veterinary; F veterinary medicine
veto M veto
vetusto ADJ ancient
vez F time; **a la —** at the same time; **a su —** in turn; **a veces** sometimes; **cada — más** more and more; **cada — que** whenever; **de — en cuando** from time to time; **de una —** (por entero) all at once; (por fin) one and for all; **de una — por todas** once and for all; **en — de** instead of, in lieu of; **por primera —** for the first time; **otra —** again; **una — [que]** once; **una — tras otra** over and over; **una y otra —** over and over again; **raras veces** seldom; **hacer las veces de** to take the place of
vía F (camino) road; (de ferrocarril) track; (medio de acceso) avenue; **— de transmisión local** local bus; **— Láctea** Milky Way; **— navegable** waterway; **— respiratoria** airway; **—s urinarias** urinary tract; **por — de** by means of; **en —s de** in the process of; PREP via
viabilidad F viability
viable ADJ viable
viaducto M tunnel
viajante MF traveler; **— de comercio**; M traveling salesman; F saleswoman
viajar VI (por tierra, aire) to travel, to journey; (por mar) to voyage; (con drogas) to trip
viaje M (por tierra, aire) trip, journey; (por mar) voyage; (en coche, caballo) ride; (por efecto de las drogas) trip; **— de ida y vuelta** round trip; **buen —** have a nice trip; **de — out of town**
viajero -ra MF traveler
viandante MF passerby
viático M (de viaje) per diem; (religioso) last rites
víbora F viper; **— de cascabel** rattlesnake

vibración F (de una cuerda) vibration; (de la lengua) trill
vibrador M vibrator
vibrante ADJ vibrating
vibrar VI/VT to vibrate
vicegobernador -ora MF lieutenant governor
vicepresidente MF, **vicepresidenta** F vice president
vicerrector -ora MF provost
viceversa ADV vice versa
viciado ADJ (aire) stale; (costumbre) stuffy; (corrupto) foul
viciar VT (estropear) to foul; (corromper) to corrupt
vicio M (mala costumbre) vice, bad habit; **de —** unjustifiably; **quitarse el — de** to wean oneself of
vicioso ADJ (persona) dissolute; (gasto) unjustifiable; (gramática) faulty
vicisitud F vicissitude
víctima F (de un crimen) victim; (en un accidente) casualty, victim
victimizar[47] VT to victimize
victoria F victory
victorioso ADJ victorious
vid F vine, grapevine
vida F life; **— media** half-life; **— mía** sweetheart; **— nocturna** nightlife; **— sentimental** love life; **así es la —** that's life; **de toda la —** lifelong; **de — o muerte** life-and-death; **en la — voy a hacer eso** I would never do that; **esto es —** this is the life; **ganarse la —** to earn a living; **mujer de mala —** fam hooker; **sin —** lifeless
vidente MF seer; ADJ seeing
vídeo, video M (aparato) VCR; (técnica) video; (cinta) videocassette
videocámara F camcorder
videocasete F videocassette
videoclip M videoclip
videoconferencia F videoconference
videoconsola F video console
videojuego M video game
vidriado M glaze; ADJ glazed
vidriar VT to glaze
vidriera F show window
vidriero -ra MF glazier, glassmaker
vidrio M (sustancia) glass; (en una ventana) pane; **pagar los —s rotos** to be left holding the bag
vidrioso ADJ glassy
vieira F scallop
viejo -ja ADJ old; (chiste) stale; M (anciano) old man; (padre) father; **— amigo** longtime friend; **— verde** dirty old man; **los —s** the old folks; F (anciana) old woman; (madre) mother
viento M wind; **hace —** it is windy; **a los cuatro —s** in all directions

vientre M (abdomen) abdomen; (barriga) belly; (útero) womb
viernes M Friday
Vietnam M Vietnam
vietnamita ADJ & MF INV Vietnamese
viga F (de madera) beam, rafter; (de metal) girder
vigencia F **entrar en —** to go into effect; **estar en —** to be in force
vigente ADJ effective, in force
vigésimo NUM twentieth
vigía F lookout, reef; MF lookout
vigilancia F (cuidado) vigilance; (en una tienda) surveillance
vigilante ADJ vigilant; M watchman; F watchwoman
vigilar VI/VT to keep watch [over]; VT to keep an eye on; (policía) to stake out
vigilia F vigil, watch
vigor M vigor; **en —** in force; **entrar en —** to become effective
vigorizar[47] VT to invigorate
vigoroso ADJ vigorous
VIH [virus de inmunodeficiencia humana] M HIV
vil ADJ vile, base, low
vileza F villainy, baseness
vilipendiar VT to revile
villa F (aldea) village; (casa) country house
villancico M Christmas carol
villanía F villainy
villano -na ADJ villainous; MF villain
vilo LOC ADV **en —** (en el aire) suspended; (en ascuas) in suspense
vinagre M vinegar
vinculación F connection
vincular VT to link (también para páginas web); **—se** to link up
vínculo M link, tie; (en la web) link
vindicar[30] VT to vindicate
vine, viniendo, viniera, viniese ver venir
vinilo M vinyl
vino M wine; **— blanco** white wine; **— espumoso** sparkling wine; **— rosado** rosé wine; **— tinto** red wine
viña F vineyard
viñatero -ra MF winegrower
viñedo M vineyard
viola F viola
violación F (de la ley) violation, infringement; (sexual) rape
violado ADJ & M violet
violar VT (una ley) to violate, to break; (una mujer) to rape, to ravish; (una promesa) to breach; (una cerradura) to pick; (derechos) to infringe upon; (mandamientos) to trespass against
violencia F violence; **— doméstica** domestic violence

violentar VT (a una persona) to manhandle; (una casa) to break into; —**se** to get mortified

violento ADJ (deporte, tratamiento) violent, rough; (marido) abusive; (entrada) forcible; (ataque) vicious

violeta ADJ & M violet

violín M (para música clásica) violin; (para música folclórica) fiddle

violinista MF violinist

violonchelo M cello

VIP M VIP

virada F veer

viraje M swerve

viral ADJ viral

virar VI/VT (vehículo) to swerve, to veer; VI (barco) to tack

virgen ADJ & MF virgin; ADJ (cassette) blank; (selva) undisturbed

virginal ADJ virginal

viril ADJ virile, manly

virilidad F virility, manliness

virología F virology

virreinato M viceroyalty

virrey M viceroy

virtual ADJ virtual

virtud F (moral) virtue; (práctica) asset

virtuosismo M virtuosity

virtuoso-sa ADJ (moral) virtuous; ADJ & MF (artístico) virtuoso

viruela F smallpox

virulento ADJ virulent

virus M virus (también de computadoras); — **de inmunodeficiencia humana** human immunodeficiency virus

viruta F wood shaving

visa F visa

visado M visa

visar VT to endorse

visceral ADJ visceral

viscoso ADJ viscous

visera F visor

visibilidad F visibility

visible ADJ visible

visigodo-da ADJ Visigothic; MF Visigoth

visillo M window shade

visión F (capacidad de ver, lo visto) vision; (persona fea) sight; — **en túnel** tunnel vision

visionario-ria ADJ & MF visionary

visita F (acción de visitar) visit; (persona) visitor, caller; (a un edificio) tour; (en una página web) hit; — **de médico** house call

visitación F visitation

visitador-ora MF visitor, caller; (inspector) inspector; (vendedor de medicamentos) pharmaceutical sales representative

visitante MF caller, visitor; ADJ visiting (también en fútbol)

visitar VT (a un amigo, país) to visit; (a un paciente) to make a house call

vislumbrar VT to make out

viso M slip

visón M mink

víspera LOC ADV **en —s de** on the eve of

vista F (panorama) view, vista; (visión) eyesight; **a la** — in sight; — **cansada** eye strain; **a primera** — at first sight; **a simple** — with the naked eye; **bajar la** — to lower one's eyes; **conocer de** — to know by sight; **con —s a** with a view to; **en** — **de** considering; **hacer la** — **gorda** to look the other way; **¡hasta la** —! good-bye; **perder de** — to lose sight of; **tener a la** — to have before one's eyes; **tener** — **a** to look out on

vistazo M glance, glimpse, look; **dar/echar un** — **a** to glance over

visto ADJ **bien** — well thought of; **mal** — looked down upon; — **que** whereas; M — **bueno** approval; **dar el** —**bueno** to approve

visto *ver* ver

vistoso ADJ showy

visual ADJ visual

visualizador M display

visualizar[47] VT (en la imaginación) to visualize; (en pantalla) to display

vital ADJ vital; **fuerzas** —**es** life force

vitalicio ADJ life, for life; M lifetime pension

vitalidad F vitality

vitamina F vitamin

viticultor-ora MF winegrower

vítor M cheer

vitorear VI/VT to cheer

vitral M stained-glass window

vitrina F (ventana) shop window; (armario) showcase

vituperación F vituperation

vituperar VT to revile

vituperio M vituperation

viudo-da M widower; F widow; **viuda negra** black widow spider

vivacidad F vivacity

vivaracho ADJ vivacious

vivaz ADJ vivacious, lively

víveres M PL provisions

vivero M nursery

viveza F (vivacidad) liveliness; (inteligencia) cleverness

vívido ADJ vivid

vivienda F (casa) dwelling; (alojamiento) housing; — **unifamiliar** single-family home

viviente ADJ living

vivir VI/VT to live; **vive una vida normal** he leads a normal life; **vivieron felices y comieron perdices** they lived happily ever after; **¡viva!** hurrah! **¡viva el rey!** long live the king!

vivisección F vivisection

vivo ADJ (viviente) alive, living; (ágil) lively;

(vistoso, intenso) vivid; (listo) clever; **en —** before a live audience; **en — y en directo** live; **de viva voz** by word of mouth
vocablo M word
vocabulario M vocabulary
vocación F (profesional) vocation, calling; (religioso) call
vocal ADJ (de la voz) vocal; (no consonántico) vowel; F vowel; MF member
vocálico ADJ vocalic
vocear VI/VT (gritar) to cry out; (anunciar) to page
vocerío M clamor
vocero -ra MF spokesperson
vociferante ADJ vociferous
vociferar VI to clamor
vodevil M vaudeville
vodka M vodka
volado ADJ (drogado) high; (escrito arriba) superscript
volador ADJ flying
volante ADJ flying; M (en un vestido) ruffle, frill; (en un coche) steering wheel; (en un motor) flywheel; (folleto) leaflet, handbill
volar[5] VI/VT to fly; **— por su cuenta** to fly solo; **ir volando** to hurry; VT (un puente) to blow up; VI (hojas) to blow; **—se** (hacer explosión) to blow up; (enojarse) to lose one's temper; (irse volando) to fly away; (drogarse) *fam* to get stoned
volátil ADJ volatile
volcada F **hacer una —** (baloncesto) to dunk the ball
volcán M volcano
volcánico ADJ volcanic
volcar[31] VT (voltear) to tip over, to knock over; (derramar) to spill; (vaciar) to empty; VI to roll over; **—se** (un coche) to tip over, to overturn; (en baloncesto) to dunk
volea F (en vóleibol) volley; (en béisbol) fly ball; (en tenis) volley
volear VI/VT to volley
voleibol, vóleibol M volleyball
volición F volition
volqueta F *Am* dump truck
volquete M dump truck
voltaje M voltage
voltear VT (una lámpara) to knock over, to turn over; (la cara) to turn away
voltereta F somersault, tumble; **dar una —** to somersault; **dar —s** to tumble
voltio M volt
voluble ADJ (malhumorado) moody; (mercado de valores) volatile
volumen M volume
voluminoso ADJ voluminous, bulky
voluntad F will; **a —** at will; **buena —** good will, willingness; **mala —** ill will; **por su propia —** of his own volition

voluntario -ria ADJ voluntary; MF volunteer
voluntarioso ADJ (bien dispuesto) willing; (testarudo) willful
voluptuoso ADJ voluptuous
voluta F scroll; **—s de humo** spirals of smoke
volver[6, 74] VI (regresar al punto de partida) to return, to come back; (ir de nuevo) to return, to go back, to go again; **— a comer** to eat again; **— del revés** to turn inside out; **— en sí** to regain consciousness; **—se** (regresar) to go back; (ponerse) to become; **—se contra** to turn against; **—se atrás** to turn back; **—se hacia** to go toward; **—se loco** to go crazy; VT (la cara) to turn away; (la página) to turn; **— las espaldas** to turn one's back
vomitar VI/VT to vomit, to throw up
vómito M vomit
voraz ADJ voracious, ravenous
vórtice M vortex
vos PRON *fam RP, Am Central* you
vosotros -as PRON PERS *Esp* you, you guys; (sur de EEUU) you all, y'all
votación F voting
votante MF voter
votar VI (emitir el voto) to vote; VT (elegir) to vote for; (aprobar) to vote into law; **— a/por** to vote for; **— a favor** to vote in favor; **— en contra** to vote against; **— es un deber importante** voting is an important duty
voto M (opinión) vote; (promesa) vow; **— de confianza** vote of confidence
voy *ver* ir
voz F (sonido, aptitud, voto) voice; (en un diccionario) headword; **a — en cuello** at the top of one's lungs, **alzar la —** to raise one's voice; **correr la —** to be rumored; **en — alta** aloud; **en — baja** quietly, softly; **a voces** shouting; **dar voces** to shout
vozarrón M loud voice
vudú M voodoo
vuela, vuele *ver* volar
vuelco M **dar un —** to overturn, to turn over; **todo daría un —** everything would change radically; **me dio un — el corazón** my heart skipped a beat
vuelo M (en avión) flight; (de una falda) flare; **al —** on the fly; **de alto —** prestigious; **levantar/alzar el —** to fly away
vuelta F (movimiento circular) turn; (regreso, devolución) return; (carrera ciclista) tour; (en una pista) lap; (curva) twist; (de un collar) loop; (en deportes) round; (dinero) change; **— de tuerca** unforeseen event; **a la — de la esquina** around the corner; **a — de correo** by return mail; **dar —** to turn upside down; **dar — al revés** to turn inside out; **dar — a una página / una llave** to turn a page / a key; **dar —s** to spin; **dar —s en la cama** to toss and turn; **dar — a algo** to turn

something upside down; **dar la** — to turn around; **dar una** — to take a walk, to take a spin; **darse** — to roll over; **estar de** — (de regreso) to be back; (desencantado) to be jaded; **me da —s la cabeza** my head is spinning; **no tiene — de hoja** there are no two ways about it

vuelto M *Am* change

vuelto, vuelva, vuelve *ver* volver

vuestro ADJ POS *Esp* — **hermano** your brother; **un amigo** — a friend of yours; PRON **el** — yours

vulgar ADJ (común) ordinary; (tosco) vulgar

vulgaridad F vulgarity

vulgo M common people

vulnerable ADJ vulnerable

vulva F vulva

Ww

wafle M waffle

waflera F waffle iron

wáter M toilet

web F web, Internet, World Wide Web

whisky M whisk[e]y; — **escocés** scotch

wifi [fidelidad inalámbrica] F Wi-Fi™

windsurf M windsurfing

wok M wok

Xx

xenofobia F xenophobia

xilofón, xilófono M xylophone

Yy

y CONJ and

ya ADV (desde antes) already; (ahora) now; (pronto) soon; **¡—!** enough! — **era hora** it was about time; **¡— lo creo!** I should say so! — **no** no longer; — **que** since; — **sea que** whether; — **te arreglo** I'll fix you; — **verás** mark my words; — **voy** I am coming

yacer[37] VI to lie

yacimiento M (de minerales) deposit; (de petróleo) field

yanqui ADJ & MF *pey* American

yapa F freebie

yarda F yard (también en fútbol americano)

yate M yacht

yegua F mare

yelmo M helmet

yema F (de huevo) egg yolk; (de una planta) bud, shoot; — **de huevo** egg yolk; — **del dedo** fingertip

Yemen M Yemen

yemení ADJ & MF Yemeni

yen M yen

yendo *ver* ir

yerba *ver* hierba

yermo ADJ (estéril) barren; (desolado) bleak, stark

yerno M son-in-law

yesca F tinder

yeso M (mineral) gypsum; (en construcción, medicina) plaster [of Paris]; (escayola) cast

Yibuti M Djibouti

yibutiano -na ADJ & MF Djiboutian

yo PRON PERS I; M (ego) ego

yodo M iodine

yoduro M iodide

yoga M yoga

yogur M yogurt

yo-yo M yo-yo

yuan M yuan

yuca F (ornamental) yucca; (comestible) manioc

yudo M judo

yugo M yoke

Yugoslavia F Yugoslavia

yugoslavo -va ADJ & MF Yugoslavian

yugular ADJ & F jugular

yunque M anvil

yunta F yoke

yuppie MF yuppie

yuxtaponer[56, 74] VT juxtapose

Zz

zacate M grass (también en tenis)

zafar VT to release; **—se** (soltarse) to slip off; (no cumplir) to cop out; **—se de un aprieto** to squirm out of a difficulty

zafio ADJ boorish

zafiro M sapphire

zafra F [sugar] harvest

zaga LOC ADV **a la** — behind; F **ir a la** — to be behind; **quedar a la** — to fall behind

zaguán M vestibule, hall

zaino ADJ chestnut-colored

zalamería F (tacto) smoothness; (lisonja) flattery

zalamero -ra MF flatterer; ADJ (empalagoso)

smooth, unctuous; (lisonjero) flattering
Zambia F Zambia
zambiano -na ADJ & MF Zambian
zambo ADJ knock-kneed
zambullida F dive, plunge
zambullir[16] VT to plunge, to dip; —**se** to dive, to plunge
zanahoria F carrot
zanca F leg of a wading bird
zancada F stride; **dar** —**s** to stride
zancadilla F intentional tripping; **hacer una** — to trip
zanco M stilt
zancudo ADJ long-legged, lanky; M *Am* mosquito
zángano M drone (también holgazán)
zangolotear VI/VT to jiggle
zangoloteo M jiggle
zanja F ditch, trench
zanjar VT to settle
zapapico M pickax[e]
zapata F brake shoe
zapatear VI to tap the feet in dancing
zapateo M tapping with the feet in dance
zapatería F shoe store
zapatero -ra MF (fabricante) shoemaker; (vendedor) shoe dealer; (remendón) cobbler
zapatilla F (pantufla) slipper; (de vestir) pump; —**s** sneakers
zapato M shoe; —**s con tacos** (fútbol americano) cleats; —**s con tapones** (fútbol) cleats; —**s del mismo par** matching shoes
zar M czar
zarandear VT to jiggle; —**se** to flop around
zarandeo M jiggle
zarcillo M (arete) earring; (de planta) tendril
zarigüeya F opossum
zarpa F claw
zarpar VI to sail, to set sail
zarpazo M blow with a claw; **dar** —**s** to claw
zarza F bramble, briar
zarzamora F blackberry
zepelín M blimp, zeppelin
zigoto M zygote
zigzag M zigzag
zigzaguear VI to zigzag, to weave one's way
Zimbabue M Zimbabwe
zimbabuo -bua ADJ & MF Zimbabwean
zirconio M zirconium
zócalo M baseboard; *Méx* main square
zodíaco M zodiac
zombi M zombie
zona F (área) zone; (culebrilla) shingles; — **de anotación/ensayo** (fútbol americano) end zone; — **de calentamiento** (béisbol) bullpen; — **de strike** (béisbol) strike zone; — **gris** gray area; — **tampón** buffer zone
zonificación F zoning
zonzo ADJ silly, foolish

zoo M zoo
zoología F zoology
zoológico ADJ zoological; M zoo
zoom M (de cámara fotográfica) zoom lens; (de computadora) zoom
zopenco -ca MF dolt, numbskull
zorrillo M skunk
zorro -a MF (animal) fox; F (hembra) vixen; (prostituta) *pey* prostitute; ADJ (astuto) foxy, cunning; (promiscuo) loose
zorzal M thrush
zozobra F anxiety, worry
zozobrar VI to founder
zueco M clog
zumbar VI (hacer sonidos los insectos) to buzz, to drone, to hum; (hacer ruido las máquinas) to whir, to whiz; (tintinear los oídos) to ring; (dar golpe) to sock
zumbido M (sonido de insectos) buzz, drone, hum; (sonido de máquina) whir, whiz; (sonido en los oídos) ring
zumo M fruit juice
zurcido M (remiendo) darn; (acción de remendar) darning
zurcir[33] VT to darn
zurdo -da ADJ left-handed, southpaw; MF *fam* southpaw
zuro M corncob
zurra F whipping
zurrar VT to whip, to thrash
zurullo M turd
zutano -na M so-and-so, what's-his-name; F so-and-so, what's-her-name

Inglés–Español · English–Spanish

Lista de abreviaturas / List of Abbreviations

adj	adjetivo	adjective
adv	adverbio, adverbial	adverb, adverbial
Am	América	America
art	artículo	article
Carib	Caribe	Caribbean
conj	conjunción	conjunction
def	definido	definite
dem	demostrativo	demonstrative
f	femenino	feminine
fam	familiar	familiar
indef	indefinido	indefinite
interj	interjección	interjection
interr	interrogativo	interrogative
inv	invariable	invariable
lit	literario	literary
loc	locución	locution
m	masculino	masculine
Mex	México	Mexico
n	sustantivo	noun
num	numeral	numeral
pej, pey	peyorativo	pejorative
pl	plural	plural
poss	posesivo	possessive
prep	preposición, preposicional	preposition, prepositional
pron	pronombre	pronoun
rel	relativo	relative
RP	Río de la Plata	River Plate
sg	singular	singular
Sp	España, español	Spain, Spanish
v aux	verbo auxiliar	auxiliary verb
vi	verbo intransitivo	intransitive verb
vt	verbo transitivo	transitive verb
vulg	vulgar	vulgar

Pronunciación inglesa

I. VOCALES

Símbolo fonético	Ortografía inglesa	Explicación
[i]	see, pea	como la *i* en hilo
[ɪ]	bit	el sonido más aproximado es la *i* en *virtud*, pero la [ɪ] inglesa es más abierta, tirando a *e*
[e]	late, they	equivale aproximadamente a *ei*
[ɛ]	set	semejante a la *e* de *perro*, pero más abierta
[ɝ]	work, bird	como la *u* de *cud* (ver abajo) pero articulada simultáneamente con una *r*
[æ]	sat	sonido intermedio entre *e* y *a*
[ɑ]	hot	como la vocal de *pan*
[ɔ]	saw, laud	sonido intermedio entre *a* y *o*
[o]	low, mode	equivale aproximadamente a *ou*
[ʊ]	book, pull	como la *u* de *turrón*, pero más abierta
[u]	June, moon	como la *u* de *uno*
[ʌ]	cud	una *e* muy relajada
[ə]	adept	una *e* muy relajada y átona
[ɚ]	teacher	una *e* átona relajada articulada simultáneamente con una *r*

II. DIPTONGOS

Símbolo fonético	Ortografía inglesa	Explicación
[aɪ]	pie, aisle	como *ai* en *aire*
[aʊ]	now, foul	como *au* en *causa*
[ɔɪ]	boy	como *oy* en *hoy*
[ju]	use	como *iu* en *ciudad*

III. CONSONANTES

Símbolo fonético	Ortografía inglesa	Explicación
[b]	bat	semejante a la *b* española
[d]	day	semejante a la *d* española, pero articulada en los alvéolos y con más tensión
[f]	fun, photo	como la *f* española

[g]	go	como la g de *goma*, pero con más tensión
[h]	hat	muy suave como la j de los dialectos caribeños del español
[j]	year	como la i del diptongo de *hielo*
[k]	cat, kill	como la c de *carro*, pero seguida de aspiración en posición inicial de sílaba (sobre todo tónica)
[l]	let	como la l de *lado*
[ɫ]	ball	como la l final catalana
[m]	much	como la m española
[n]	no	como la n española
[p]	pea	como la p española, pero seguida de aspiración en posición inicial de sílaba (sobre todo tónica)
[r]	red	no tiene equivalente en español; se pronuncia con la punta de la lengua enrollada hacia arriba, sin tocar el paladar
[s]	sea	como la s hispanoamericana (no la castellana)
[t]	tea	como la t española pero articulada en los alvéolos y seguida de aspiración en posición inicial de sílaba (sobre todo tónica)
[v]	very	se articula con los dientes incisivos superiores colocados en el labio inferior
[w]	weed	equivale a la u del diptongo de *fui*
[z]	zero, rose	como la s de *mismo* cuando se sonoriza, pero aun más sonora
[ɒ]	latter, ladder	como la r de *para*
[θ]	thin	como la z del español castellano en *zagal*
[ð]	this	como la d de *cada*
[ʃ]	sheet, machine, notation	una s muy palatal como en francés *chapeau* o italiano *lasciare*
[ʒ]	measure, beige	como la ll argentina en *valle*, cuando es sonora
[tʃ]	church	como la ch de *charla*
[ʤ]	judge	como la y de *inyectar*
[ṇ]	eaten, button	representa la n silábica, articulada sin la vocal anterior
[ŋ]	ring	como la n española en *mango* y *banco*
[ḷ]	rental	representa la l silábica, articulada como la l final catalana
[hw]	where	combinación de los sonidos [h] y [w] arriba descritos

Notas sobre gramática inglesa

El sustantivo

Género. En la gramática inglesa el género solo desempeña un papel importante en el sistema pronominal, p. ej. **he runs** 'él corre', **she runs** 'ella corre', **I see him** 'lo veo', **I see her** 'la veo'. En los sustantivos que designan a personas, se emplean varios métodos para distinguir entre los sexos, v. gr. el agregado de un sufijo, como en **actor** 'actor', **actress** 'actriz', el agregado de una palabra, como en **baby boy** 'niño', **baby girl** 'niña', **she-bear** 'osa', **male nurse** 'enfermero', o el uso de palabras completamente distintas, como en **uncle** 'tío', **aunt** 'tía'.

Número. Generalmente se forma el plural añadiendo **-s** al singular: **paper, papers** 'papel, papeles', **book, books** 'libro, libros', **chief, chiefs** 'jefe, jefes'.

Los sustantivos que terminan en **-ss, -x, -sh, -z** y **-o** añaden **-es** para formar el plural: **kiss, kisses** 'beso, besos', **box, boxes** 'caja, cajas', **dish, dishes** 'plato, platos', **buzz, buzzes** 'zumbido, zumbidos', **hero, heroes** 'héroe, héroes' (excepción: **piano, pianos**). Esto vale también para **-ch** cuando se pronuncia [č], como en **arch, arches** 'arco, arcos', pero no cuando se pronuncia [k], como en **monarch, monarchs** 'monarca, monarcas'.

Los sustantivos que terminan en **-fe,** y ciertos sustantivos que terminan en **-f,** cambian estas letras en **v** y añaden **-es** en el plural: **leaf, leaves** 'hoja, hojas', **life, lives** 'vida, vidas', **wife, wives** 'esposa, esposas', **knife, knives** 'cuchillo, cuchillos' (pero **reef, reefs** 'arrecife, arrecifes').

Para formar el plural de los sustantivos terminados en **-y** precedida de consonante se cambia la **-y** en **-ies: fly, flies** 'mosca, moscas', **family, families** 'familia, familias'. En cambio, los sustantivos terminados en **-y** precedida de vocal forman el plural añadiendo **-s** al singular: **day, days** 'día, días'.

Ciertos sustantivos forman el plural de una manera irregular: **man, men** 'hombre, hombres', **woman, women** 'mujer, mujeres', **mouse, mice** 'ratón, ratones', **louse, lice** 'piojo, piojos', **goose, geese** 'ganso, gansos', **tooth, teeth** 'diente, dientes', **foot, feet** 'pie, pies', **ox, oxen** 'buey, bueyes'.

Ciertos sustantivos que terminan en **-is** forman el plural cambiando la **i** de la terminación en **e: axis, axes** 'eje, ejes', **crisis, crises** 'crisis' (sg., pl.).

El adjetivo

El adjetivo inglés es invariable en cuanto a género y número. Normalmente se coloca delante del sustantivo: **an interesting woman** 'una mujer interesante', **a large man** 'un hombre grande', **beautiful birds** 'aves hermosas'.

Los comparativos y superlativos. Aunque no hay una regla general, por lo común los adjetivos monosílabos, los adjetivos acentuados en la última sílaba y algunos bisílabos comunes forman el comparativo de aumento y el superlativo añadiendo **-er** y **-est** (como **tall**). Los demás adjetivos van precedidos de **more** (para el comparativo) y **most** (para el superlativo) (como **careful**). Nótese que (1) si la palabra termina en **-e** muda, se añaden **-r** y **-st** en vez de **-er** y **-est** (ver **wise**), (2) los adjetivos terminados en **-y** cambian esta letra en **i** (ver **happy**), (3) los adjetivos terminados en consonante (menos **r**) precedida de vocal doblan la consonante (ver **fat**):

Positivo	Comparativo	Superlativo
tall alto	**taller** más alto	**the tallest** el más alto
careful cuidadoso	**more careful** más cuidadoso	**the most careful** el más cuidadoso
wise sabio	**wiser** más sabio	**the wisest** el más sabio
happy feliz	**happier** más feliz	**the happiest** el más feliz
fat gordo	**fatter** más gordo	**the fattest** el más gordo

Los adjetivos siguientes forman el comparativo y el superlativo de una manera irregular:

good	**better**	**best**
bad, ill	**worse**	**worst**
much	**more**	**most**

El adverbio

Muchos adverbios se forman añadiendo **-ly** al adjetivo: **courteous** 'cortés', **courteously** 'cortésmente', **bold** 'atrevido', **boldly** 'atrevidamente'. Existen las irregularidades ortográficas siguientes en la formación de los adverbios que terminan en **-ly**: (1) los adjetivos terminados en **-ble** cambian la **-e** en **-y**: **possible, possibly**, (2) los terminados en **-ic** añaden **-ally**: **poetic, poetically**, (3) los terminados en **-ll** añaden solo **-y**: **full, fully**, (4) los terminados en **-ue** pierden la **-e** final: **true, truly**, (5) los terminados en **-y** cambian la **-y** en **i**: **happy, happily**.

La mayor parte de los adverbios forman el comparativo y el superlativo con los adverbios **more** 'más' y **most** 'el/la más'. Asimismo los adverbios monosílabos añaden **-er** y **-est**:

Positivo	Comparativo	Superlativo
boldly	**more boldly**	**most boldly**
generously	**more generously**	**most generously**
soon	**sooner**	**soonest**
early	**earlier**	**earliest**
late	**later**	**latest**
fast	**faster**	**fastest**

Los adverbios siguientes forman el comparativo y el superlativo de una manera irregular:

well	better	best
badly	worse	worst
little	less	least
far	farther, further	farthest, furthest

Sufijos comunes del inglés

-dom   a partir de bases nominales, forma sustantivos con los sentidos de dominio, jurisdicción, estado, condición: **kingdom** 'reino' (**king** 'rey'), **martyrdom** 'martirio' (**martyr** 'mártir'), **freedom** 'libertad' (**free** 'libre')

-ee   a partir de verbos, forma sustantivos indicando a la persona que recibe una acción: **addressee** 'destinatario' (**to address** 'dirigir'), **employee** 'empleado' (**to employ** 'emplear').

-eer   a partir de bases diversas, forma sustantivos que denotan oficio u ocupación: **auctioneer** 'subastador' (**to auction** 'subastar'), **puppeteer** 'titiritero' (**puppet** 'títere')

-en   *a.*   forma adjetivos que denotan la sustancia de que está hecha una cosa: **golden** 'dorado' (**gold** 'oro'), **wooden** 'de madera' (**wood** 'madera')
    b.   forma verbos a partir de adjetivos: **to whiten** 'blanquear' (**white** 'blanco'), **to darken** 'oscurecer' (**dark** 'oscuro')

-er   *a.*   forma sustantivos a partir de verbos para indicar agente: **player** 'jugador' (**to play** 'jugar'), **speaker** 'hablante' (**to speak** 'hablar'), **baker** 'panadero' (**to bake** 'hornear')
    b.   forma sustantivos a partir de sustantivos para denominar al residente de un lugar: **New Yorker** 'neoyorquino' (**New York** 'Nueva York'), **islander** 'isleño' (**island** 'isla')

-ess   se usa para formar el género femenino de ciertos sustantivos: **princess** 'princesa' (**prince** 'príncipe'), **countess** 'condesa' (**count** 'conde')

-fold   indica el número de veces que se repite algo: **twofold** 'dos veces' (**two** 'dos'), **hundredfold** 'cien veces' (**hundred** 'cien')

-ful   *a.*   forma adjetivos a partir de sustantivos para indicar la presencia de una cualidad: **hopeful** 'esperanzado' (**hope** 'esperanza'), **careful** 'cuidadoso' (**care** 'cuidado'), **willful** 'voluntarioso' (**will** 'voluntad')
    b.   forma adjetivos a partir de verbos para indicar tendencia: **forgetful** 'olvidadizo' (**to forget** 'olvidar')

    c. forma sustantivos a partir de sustantivos indicando la capacidad: **handful** 'puñado' (**hand** 'mano'), **spoonful** 'cucharada' (**spoon** 'cuchara')

-hood   forma abstractos a partir de sustantivos concretos: **motherhood** 'maternidad' (**mother** 'madre'), **childhood** 'niñez' (**child** 'niño'), **likelihood** 'probabilidad' (**likely** 'probable')

-ing   *a.* forma adjetivos a partir de verbos: **running water** 'agua corriente' (**to run** 'correr'), **drinking water** 'agua potable' (**to drink** 'beber'), **waiting room** 'sala de espera' (**to wait** 'esperar'), **washing machine** 'máquina lavadora' (**to wash** 'lavar')

    b. se usa para formar sustantivos que expresan la acción de un verbo: **understanding** 'entendimiento' (**to understand** 'entender'), **supplying** 'abastecimiento' (**to supply** 'abastecer')

    c. se usa para formar sustantivos que denominan una cosa que desempeña una acción: **clothing** 'ropa' (**to clothe** 'vestir'), **covering** 'cobertura' (**to cover** 'cubrir')

-ish   forma adjetivos a partir de sustantivos indicando semejanza o atenuación: **boyish** 'como un niño' (**boy** 'niño'), **womanish** 'como mujer, mujeril' (**woman** 'mujer'), **whitish** 'blancuzco' (**white** 'blanco')

-less   se agrega a sustantivos para indicar falta de algo: **childless** 'sin hijos' (**child** 'hijo'), **penniless** 'sin dinero' (**penny** 'centavo'), **endless** 'interminable, sin fin' (**end** 'fin')

-like   se añade a sustantivos para indicar semejanza: **lifelike** 'que parece vivo' (**life** 'vida'), **childlike** 'infantil' (**child** 'niño'), **tigerlike** 'como un tigre' (**tiger** 'tigre')

-ly   *a.* se añade a adjetivos para formar adverbios: **slowly** 'lentamente' (**slow** 'lento'), **happily** 'felizmente' (**feliz** 'happy')

    b. deriva adjetivos a partir de sustantivos indicando una cualidad: **motherly** 'maternal' (**mother** 'madre'), **gentlemanly** 'caballeroso' (**gentleman** 'caballero'), **friendly** 'amistoso' (**friend** 'amigo')

    c. deriva adjetivos o adverbios de tiempo a partir de sustantivos: **daily** 'diario', 'diariamente' (**day** 'día'), **weekly** 'semanal', 'semanalmente' (**week** 'semana')

-ness   forma nombres de cualidades a partir de adjetivos: **goodness** 'bondad' (**good** 'bueno'), **darkness** 'oscuridad' (**dark** 'oscuro'), **foolishness** 'tontería' (**fool** 'tonto')

-ship	se emplea para derivar sustantivos a partir de sustantivos y verbos para denotar
a.	cualidades abstractas: **friendship** 'amistad' (**friend** 'amigo')
b.	arte o destreza: **horsemanship** 'equitación' (**horseman** 'jinete')
c.	dignidad, oficio, cargo o título: **professorship** 'cátedra' (**professor** 'catedrático'), **lordship** 'señoría' (**lord** 'señor')
d.	la duración de una acción: **courtship** 'cortejo' (**to court** 'cortejar')

-some   se añade a verbos para formar adjetivos que expresan tendencia excesiva: **tiresome** 'aburrido' (**to tire** 'aburrir'), **quarrelsome** 'pendenciero' (**to quarrel** 'discutir')

-th   es el sufijo que forma números ordinales a partir de los cardinales: **fifth** 'quinto' (**five** 'cinco'), **tenth** 'décimo' (**ten** 'diez')

-ward   se añade a sustantivos y adverbios para indicar movimiento hacia un lugar: **homeward** 'hacia casa' (**home** 'casa'), **downward** 'hacia abajo' (**down** 'abajo')

-wise,   se añaden a sustantivos para indicar dirección o posición: **edgewise** 'de
-ways   lado' (**edge** 'borde'), **lengthwise** 'a lo largo' (**length** 'largo'), **sideways** 'de lado' (**side** 'lado')

-y *a.*	es un sufijo diminutivo: **doggy** 'perrito' (**dog** 'perro'), **Johnny** 'Juanito' (**John** 'Juan')
b.	se añade a sustantivos para formar adjetivos que indican abundancia: **rocky** 'rocoso' (**rock** 'roca'), **rainy** 'lluvioso' (**rain** 'lluvia'), **hairy** 'peludo' (**hair** 'pelo'), **angry** 'enojado' (**anger** 'enojo')
c.	se añade a sustantivos para formar adjetivos que expresan semejanza: **rosy** 'rosado' (**rose** 'rosa')

Verbos irregulares de la lengua inglesa

Se denominan verbos irregulares los que no forman el pretérito o el participio pasivo con la adición de **-d** o **-ed** al presente. Obsérvese que en ciertos verbos (aquí señalados con asterisco) coexiste la forma regular al lado de la irregular. Las formas poco usadas aparecen entre paréntesis.

Presente	*Pretérito*	*Participio pasivo*
*abide	(abode)	abided
am, is, are	was, were	been
arise	arose	arisen
*awake	awoke	awoken

Presente	Pretérito	Participio pasivo
bear	bore	borne
beat	beat	beaten
become	became	become
befall	befell	befallen
beget	begat	begotten
begin	began	begun
behold	beheld	beheld
bend	bent	bent
*beseech	(besought)	(besought)
beset	beset	beset
bet	bet	bet
bid 'ofrecer'	bid	bid
bid 'mandar'	bade	bidden
bind	bound	bound
bite	bit	bitten, bit
bleed	bled	bled
blow	blew	blown
break	broke	broken
breed	bred	bred
bring	brought	brought
build	built	built
*burn	burnt	burnt
burst	burst	burst
buy	bought	bought
cast	cast	cast
catch	caught	caught
choose	chose	chosen
cling	clung	clung
*clothe	(clad)	(clad)
come	came	come
cost	cost	cost
creep	crept	crept
cut	cut	cut
deal	dealt	dealt
dig	dug	dug
*dive	dove	dived
do	did	done
draw	drew	drawn
*dream	dreamt	dreamt
drink	drank	drunk
drive	drove	driven
*dwell	dwelt	dwelt
eat	ate	eaten
fall	fell	fallen

Verbos irregulares

Presente	Pretérito	Participio pasivo
feed	fed	fed
feel	felt	felt
fight	fought	fought
find	found	found
*fit	fit	fit
flee	fled	fled
fling	flung	flung
fly	flew	flown
forbear	(forbore)	(forborne)
forbid	forbade	forbidden
foresee	foresaw	foreseen
foretell	foretold	foretold
forget	forgot	forgotten
forgive	forgave	forgiven
forsake	forsook	forsaken
freeze	froze	frozen
get	got	got, gotten
give	gave	given
go	went	gone
grind	ground	ground
grow	grew	grown
hang[1]	hung	hung
have, has	had	had
hear	heard	heard
*hew	hewed	hewn
hide	hid	hidden, hid
hit	hit	hit
hold	held	held
hurt	hurt	hurt
keep	kept	kept
*kneel	knelt	knelt
*knit	knit	knit
know	knew	known
lay	laid	laid
lead	led	led
*lean	(leant)	(leant)
*leap	leapt	leapt
*learn	(learnt)	(learnt)
leave	left	left
lend	lent	lent
let	let	let

1. Es regular cuando significa 'ahorcar'.

Presente	Pretérito	Participio pasivo
lie[2]	lay	lain
*light	lit	lit
lose	lost	lost
make	made	made
mean	meant	meant
meet	met	met
mistake	mistook	mistaken
*mow	mowed	mown
pay	paid	paid
*plead	pled	pled
put	put	put
quit	quit	quit
read [rid]	read [rɛd]	read [rɛd]
rend	rent	rent
*rid	rid	rid
ride	rode	ridden
ring	rang	rung
rise	rose	risen
run	ran	run
*saw	sawed	sawn
say	said	said
see	saw	seen
seek	sought	sought
sell	sold	sold
send	sent	sent
set	set	set
*sew	sewed	sewn
shake	shook	shaken
*shave	shaved	shaven
*shear	sheared	shorn
shed	shed	shed
shine[3]	shone	shone
shoe	shod	shod
shoot	shot	shot
*show	showed	shown
shrink	shrank (shrunk)	shrunk (shrunken)
shut	shut	shut
sing	sang	sung
sink	sank	sunk
sit	sat	sat
slay	slew	slain

2. Es regular cuando significa 'mentir'.
3. Suele ser regular cuando es transitivo, en el sentido 'pulir, dar brillo'.

Verbos irregulares

Presente	Pretérito	Participio pasivo
sleep	slept	slept
slide	slid	slid
sling	slung	slung
slink	slunk	slunk
slit	slit	slit
*smell	(smelt)	(smelt)
smite	smote	smitten
*sow	sowed	sown
speak	spoke	spoken
*speed	sped	sped
*spell	(spelt)	(spelt)
spend	spent	spent
*spill	(spilt)	(spilt)
spin	spun	spun
spit	spat, spit	spat, spit
split	split	split
*spoil	(spoilt)	(spoilt)
spread	spread	spread
spring	sprang, sprung	sprung
stand	stood	stood
*stave	(stove)	(stove)
steal	stole	stolen
stick	stuck	stuck
sting	stung	stung
stink	stank	stunk
*strew	strewed	strewn
stride	strode	stridden
strike	struck	struck, stricken
string	strung	strung
*strive	strove	striven
swear	swore	sworn
*sweat	sweat	sweat
sweep	swept	swept
*swell	swelled	swollen
swim	swam	swum
swing	swung	swung
take	took	taken
teach	taught	taught
tear	tore	torn
tell	told	told
think	thought	thought
throw	threw	thrown
thrust	thrust	thrust
tread	trod	trodden

Presente	Pretérito	Participio pasivo
understand	understood	understood
undertake	undertook	undertaken
undo	undid	undone
uphold	upheld	upheld
upset	upset	upset
*wake	woke	woken
wear	wore	worn
weave	wove	woven
*wed	wed	wed
weep	wept	wept
*wet	wet	wet
win	won	won
wind	wound	wound
withdraw	withdrew	withdrawn
withhold	withheld	withheld
withstand	withstood	withstood
wring	wrung	wrung
write	wrote	written

Aa

a [ə, e] INDEF ART un *m*, una *f*; **what — fool!** ¡qué tonto! **such — fool** tan tonto; **I'm — teacher / Catholic** soy maestro / católico
AA [Alcoholics Anonymous] [éé] N AA *f*
aback [əbǽk] ADV **to be taken —** estar desconcertado
abandon [əbǽndən] VT abandonar; N **with wild —** desenfrenadamente
abandonment [əbǽndənmənt] N abandono *m*, desamparo *m*
abashed [əbǽʃt] ADJ humillado, avergonzado
abate [əbét] VI/VT (trend, payments) disminuir, mitigar[se]; (storm) calmarse, atenuarse
abbey [ǽbi] N abadía *f*
abbot [ǽbət] N abad *m*
abbreviate [əbríviet] VT abreviar
abbreviation [əbriviéʃən] N (act of abbreviating) abreviación *f*; (short form) abreviatura *f*
abdicate [ǽbdɪket] VI/VT abdicar
abdomen [ǽbdəmən] N abdomen *m*, vientre *m*
abdominal [æbdámənl] ADJ abdominal; **— distension** distensión abdominal *f*
abduct [æbdʌ́kt] VT secuestrar, raptar
abduction [æbdʌ́kʃən] N secuestro *m*, rapto *m*
aberration [æbəréʃən] N anomalía *f*, aberración *f*
abet [əbét] VT instigar
abeyance [əbéəns] ADV LOC **in —** pendiente, en suspenso
abhor [əbhɔ́r] VT aborrecer
abhorrence [əbhɔ́rəns] N aborrecimiento *m*
abhorrent [əbhɔ́rənt] ADJ aborrecible
abide [əbáɪd] VT (tolerate) soportar; VI (dwell) morar, permanecer; **to — by** acatar, atenerse a
ability [əbílɪDi] N (skill) habilidad *f*; (aptitude) capacidad *f*
abject [ǽbdʒékt] ADJ abyecto; **in — poverty** en extrema miseria
ablaze [əbléz] ADV en llamas
able [ébəl] ADJ hábil, capaz; **—-bodied** de cuerpo sano; **to be — to** (be capable of) poder; (have an acquired skill) saber
abnegate [ǽbnɪget] VT renunciar
abnormal [æbnɔ́rməl] ADJ anormal
aboard [əbɔ́rd] ADV a bordo; **all —!** (train) ¡viajeros al tren! (ship) ¡pasajeros a bordo! **to go —** embarcarse, abordar
abode [əbód] N morada *f*
abode [əbód] *see* abide
abolish [əbálɪʃ] VT abolir, suprimir
abolition [æbəlíʃən] N abolición *f*
abominable [əbámənəbəl] ADJ abominable

abomination [əbamənéʃən] N (action, thing) abominación *f*; (condition, vice) horror *m*
aboriginal [æbərídʒənəl] ADJ aborigen
aborigine [æbərídʒəni] N aborigen *mf*; **Australian —** aborigen australiano -na *mf*
abort [əbɔ́rt] VT (fetus) abortar; VI/VT (mission) suspender; (software) interrumpir; N (software) interrupción *f*
abortion [əbɔ́rʃən] N aborto *m*
abortionist [əbɔ́rʃənɪst] N abortador -ora *mf*, abortero -ra *mf*
abortive [əbɔ́rDɪv] ADJ frustrado
abound [əbáʊnd] VI abundar; **to — with** abundar en
about [əbáʊt] PREP (concerning) acerca de, tocante a; (near, surrounding) alrededor de, por; **to be — one's business** atender a su negocio; ADV más o menos, alrededor de; **at — ten o'clock** a eso de las diez, sobre las diez; **to be — to do something** estar por / para hacer algo, estar a punto de hacer algo; **I'm all — transparency** insisto en la transparencia
above [əbʌ́v] PREP **you could see the towers — the buildings** se veían las torres sobre los edificios; **everyone — five years of age** todos los de más de cinco años; **he's — me in the company** es mi superior en la compañía; **to be — suspicion** estar libre de toda sospecha; **I thought you were — such things** no pensaba que te rebajarías a eso; ADV **the apartment —** el apartamento de arriba; **books of fifty pages and —** libros de cincuenta páginas y más; **the remark quoted —** la observación anteriormente citada; **— all** sobre todo; **—-mentioned** susodicho, ya mencionado
abrasion [əbréʒən] N abrasión *f*
abrasive [əbrésɪv] ADJ (material) abrasivo; (person, tone) irritante
abreast [əbrést] ADV al lado; **to keep —** mantenerse al corriente; **four —** de cuatro en fondo
abridge [əbrídʒ] VT abreviar
abroad [əbrɔ́d] ADV en el extranjero; **to go —** ir al extranjero
abrupt [əbrʌ́pt] ADJ abrupto
ABS [antilock braking system] [ébíés] N SFA *m*
abscess [ǽbsɛs] N absceso *m*
abscond [æbskánd] VI fugarse
absence [ǽbsəns] N (nonpresence) ausencia *f*; (lack) falta *f*; **in the — of** a falta de
absent [ǽbsənt] ADJ ausente; **—-minded** distraído, despistado; **to be — from school** faltar a la escuela
absentee [æbsəntí] N ausente *mf*; **— landlord** propietario -ria ausente *mf*
absenteeism [æbsəntíɪzəm] N ausentismo *m*
absolute [ǽbsəlút] ADJ (ruler, certainty)

absoluto; (prohibition) terminante
absolutely [æbsəlútli] ADV absolutamente; —
not en absoluto; INTERJ —! ¡sí, señor! ¡claro!
absolve [æbzálv] VT absolver
absorb [əbzɔ́rb] VT (liquid) absorber; (shock)
amortiguar; (people, information) asimilar;
he is —ed in his work está absorto en su
trabajo
absorption [əbzɔ́rpʃən] N absorción f
abstain [æbstén] VI abstenerse; — **from**
abstenerse de
abstention [æbsténʃən] N abstención f
abstinence [æbstənəns] N abstinencia f
abstract [æbstrækt] ADJ abstracto; N (summary)
resumen m, extracto m; **in the** — en
abstracto
abstraction [æbstrǽkʃən] N abstracción f
absurd [əbsɤ́d] ADJ absurdo, disparatado
absurdity [əbsɤ́DIDi] N (quality) absurdo m;
(action) disparate m
abundance [əbándəns] N abundancia f
abundant [əbándənt] ADJ abundante
abuse[1] [əbjús] N (of privileges) abuso m; (of
authority) abuso m, desmán m; (physical)
maltrato m; (verbal) injuria f
abuse[2] [əbjúz] VT (privileges) abusar de;
(physically) maltratar; (verbally) injuriar
abusive [əbjúsiv] ADJ (physically) violento;
(verbally) injurioso
abysmal [əbízməɫ] ADJ abismal; — **results**
resultados desastrosos m pl
abyss [əbís] N abismo m
A/C [air conditioning] [ésí] N aire
acondicionado m
academic [ækədémɪk] ADJ (university)
académico; (school) escolar; N profesor -ora
universitario -ria mf
academy [əkǽɒəmi] N academia f
accede [æksíd] VI acceder; **to** — **to** acceder a
accelerate [ækséləret] VI/VT acelerar
acceleration [æksɛləréʃən] N aceleración f
accelerator [æksélərɒɚ] N acelerador m
accent[1] [æksɛnt] N (pronunciation) acento m;
(written) tilde f, acento escrito/ortográfico m
accent[2] [æksént] VT (syllable) acentuar
accentuate [ækséntʃuet] VT (differences, facts,
syllables) acentuar, recalcar; (beauty) realzar
accept [æksépt] VT aceptar
acceptable [ækséptəbəɫ] ADJ aceptable
acceptance [ækséptəns] N (action) aceptación f;
(approval) aprobación f
access [æksɛs] N acceso m; — **code** código de
acceso m; — **provider** proveedor -ora de
acceso mf; — **denied** acceso denegado m; VT
acceder a
accessibility [æksɛsəbíliDi] N accesibilidad f
accessible [æksésəbəɫ] ADJ accesible
accessory [æksésəri] ADJ accesorio; N (to
clothes, to gadgets) accesorio m; (to a crime)

cómplice mf; — **slot** ranura para accesorios f
accident [æksɪDənt] N accidente m; (mishap)
percance m; — **insurance** seguro contra
accidentes m; **by** — por casualidad
accidental [æksɪdéntɫ] ADJ (injury) accidental;
(discovery, meeting) casual, fortuito
acclaim [əklém] VT aclamar; N aclamación f,
ovación f
acclamation [ækləméʃən] N aclamación f
acclimate [ækləmet] VI/VT (to physical
conditions) aclimatar[se]; (to an ambience)
acostumbrar[se]
accolade [ækəled] N elogio m
accommodate [əkámədet] VT (adjust) tener en
cuenta; (lodge) hospedar, alojar; (contain)
tener capacidad para; VI **to** — **oneself**
adaptarse
accommodation [əkamədéʃən] N (adjustment)
acomodación f, adaptación f; —**s** (lodging)
alojamiento m; (facilities) comodidades f pl
accompaniment [əkámpənimənt] N
acompañamiento m
accompanist [əkámpənɪst] N acompañante mf
accompany [əkámpəni] VI/VT acompañar
accomplice [əkámplɪs] N cómplice mf
accomplish [əkámplɪʃ] VT (objective) lograr;
(mission) completar
accomplished [əkámplɪʃt] ADJ (actor, athlete)
consumado; (musician) talentoso
accomplishment [əkámplɪʃmənt] N
(achievement) logro m; (skill) habilidad f;
(completion) realización f
accord [əkɔ́rd] N acuerdo m, convenio m; **of
one's own** — voluntariamente; VT otorgar,
conceder
accordance [əkɔ́rdn̩s] ADV LOC **in** — **with** de
acuerdo con, de conformidad con
according to [əkɔ́rDɪŋ] ADV LOC según
accordingly [əkɔ́rDɪŋli] ADV (therefore) por
consiguiente; (correspondingly) como
corresponde
accordion [əkɔ́rDiən] N acordeón m
accost [əkɔ́st] VT abordar
account [əkáunt] N (bill) cuenta f; (story) relato
m, relación f; — **manager** administrador
-ora de cuentas mf; —**s payable** cuentas por/
a pagar f pl; —**s receivable** cuentas por/a
cobrar f pl; **to open [close] an** — abrir
[cerrar] una cuenta; **on** — **of** a causa de,
debido a; **on my** — por mí; **on one's own** —
por cuenta propia; **on no** — de ninguna
manera; **of no** — de ningún valor; **to take
into** — tener en cuenta; VI **to** — **for** dar
cuenta de; **how do you** — **for that?** ¿cómo
se explica eso?
accountability [əkauntəbíliDi] N
responsabilidad f
accountable [əkáuntəbəɫ] ADJ responsable
accountant [əkáuntn̩t] N Am contador -ra mf; Sp

contable *mf*
accounting [əkáʊntɪŋ] N contabilidad *f*; — **firm** empresa de contadores públicos *f*; — **period** ejercicio contable *m*
accredit [əkrέdɪt] VT acreditar
acculturate [əkʌ́ltʃəret] VI/VT aculturar[se]
accumulate [əkjúmjəlet] VI/VT acumular[se]
accumulation [əkjumjəléʃən] N acumulación *f*
accuracy [ǽkjəəsi] N (of measure, instrument) precisión *f*, exactitud *f*; (of a translation) fidelidad *f*
accurate [ǽkjəɪt] ADJ (measure, instrument) preciso, exacto; (translation) fiel
accursed [əkə́sɪd] ADJ maldito
accusation [ækjuzéʃən] N acusación *f*
accuse [əkjúz] VT acusar
accused [əkjúzd] ADJ acusado; N acusado -da *mf*, reo -a *mf*, procesado -da *mf*
accuser [əkjúzə] N acusador -ra *mf*
accustom [əkʌ́stəm] VT acostumbrar, habituar; **to — oneself** acostumbrarse, habituarse; **to be —ed to** tener la costumbre de, estar acostumbrado a
AC/DC [alternating current / direct current] [ésidísi] ADJ (electricity) alterna y continua; (sexuality) bisexual
ace [es] N (cards, athlete, aviator) as *m*; (tennis) saque ganador *m*, servicio directo *m*; VT (a test) sacarse la máxima nota en
acetaminophen [əsɛDəmínəfən] N acetaminofén *m*
acetone [ǽsəton] N acetona *f*
ache [ek] N dolor *m*; —**s and pains** achaques *m pl*; VT doler; **my stomach —s** me duele el estómago
achieve [ətʃív] VT (a goal) conseguir, lograr; (a level) alcanzar
achievement [ətʃívmənt] N (attainment) consecución *f*; (success) logro *m*, realización *f*
Achilles tendon [əkɪliz téndən] N tendón de Aquiles *m*
aching [ékɪŋ] ADJ doliente, dolorido
achy [éki] ADJ dolorido
acid [ǽsɪd] ADJ ácido; N ácido *m*; (hallucinogen) LSD *m*; — **rain** lluvia ácida *f*; — **test** prueba de fuego *f*
acidic [əsíDɪk] ADJ ácido
acidity [əsíDɪDi] N acidez *f*
acknowledge [æknálɪʤ] VT (merits) reconocer; (faults) admitir, reconocer; (help) agradecer; **to — receipt** acusar recibo
acknowledgment [æknálɪʤmənt] N (of merits) reconocimiento *m*; (of merits, faults) reconocimiento *m*, admisión *f*; (gratefulness) agradecimiento *m*; — **of receipt** acuse de recibo *m*
acme [ǽkmi] N súmmum *m*
acne [ǽkni] N acné *m*
acorn [ékɔrn] N bellota *f*

acoustics [əkústɪks] N acústica *f*
acquaint [əkwént] VT informar, familiarizar; **to — oneself with** informarse de, familiarizarse con; **to be —ed with** (a person, city, country) conocer; (a piece of news) estar enterado de
acquaintance [əkwéntn̥s] N (with facts) conocimiento *m*; (a person) conocido -a *mf*
acquiesce [ækwiés] VT asentir, condescender; (unwillingly) consentir
acquiescence [ækwiésəns] N asentimiento *m*, consentimiento *m*, condescendencia *f*
acquire [əkwáɪr] VT (knowledge, skill, purchase) adquirir; (fortune, information) obtener; (disease) contraer
acquisition [ækwəzíʃən] N (knowledge, skill, purchase) adquisición *f*; (fortune, information) obtención *f*
acquisitive [əkwízɪDɪv] ADJ codicioso
acquit [əkwít] VT absolver
acquittal [əkwíDl̥] N absolución *f*
acre [ékə] N acre [0.405 hectares] *m*
acrid [ǽkrɪd] ADJ acre
acrimony [ǽkrəmoni] N acritud *f*
acrobat [ǽkrəbæt] N acróbata *mf*
acrobatic [ækrəbǽDɪk] ADJ acrobático; N —**s** acrobacia *f*
acronym [ǽkrənɪm] N acrónimo *m*, sigla *f*
acrophobia [ækrəfóbiə] N acrofobia *f*
across [əkrɔ́s] PREP **to lay one stick — the other** poner dos palos cruzados; **there's a bridge — that river** hay un puente sobre ese río; **he came — his old love letters** encontró sus viejas cartas de amor; **the library is — the street** la biblioteca está al otro lado de la calle; — **the board** de manera uniforme, sin excepciones; ADV **cut the boards —** corta los tablones a lo ancho; **five hundred miles —** de quinientas millas de ancho; **the meaning doesn't come —** el significado no se entiende
acrylic [əkrílɪk] ADJ & N acrílico *m*
act [ækt] N (deed, part of play) acto *m*; (part of show) número *m*; (law) ley *f*, decreto *m*; — **of God** caso de fuerza mayor *m*; VI (behave) actuar, comportarse; (take measures) obrar; (play a part, chemical process) actuar; (represent) representar; (function) funcionar; **to — up** (child) portarse mal; (car) funcionar mal; **to — out** (event) representar; (feelings) exteriorizar
acting [ǽktɪŋ] N actuación *f*; (in a drama) representación *f*; ADJ (interim) interino; (substitute) suplente
action [ǽkʃən] N (practical measure, plot of a play) acción *f*; (deed) acto *m*; (functioning) funcionamiento *m*; **to take —** tomar medidas
actionable [ǽkʃənəbl̥] ADJ accionable, procesable

activate [ǽktɪvet] VT activar
active [ǽktɪv] ADJ activo
activism [ǽktɪvɪzəm] N activismo *m*
activist [ǽktɪvɪst] N activista *mf*
activity [æktívɪDi] N actividad *f*
actor [ǽktɚ] N actor *m*
actress [ǽktrɪs] N actriz *f*
actual [ǽktʃuəł] ADJ verdadero, real
actually [ǽktʃuəli] ADV en realidad,
efectivamente
actuary [ǽktʃuɛri] N actuario -ria *mf*
acuity [əkjúɪDi] N agudeza *f*
acumen [ǽkjəmən] N perspicacia *f*, agudeza *f*
acupuncture [ǽkjupʌŋktʃɚ] N acupuntura *f*
acupuncturist [ǽkjupʌ́ŋktʃɚɪst] N acupuntor
-ora *mf*
acute [əkjút] ADJ (pain, illness) agudo;
(observation) perspicaz, penetrante
AD [édí] ADV d.C.
ad [æd] N anuncio publicitario *m*; — **in** (tennis)
ventaja al saque *f*, ventaja al servicio *f*; — **out**
(tennis) ventaja al resto *f*; — **lib** ADJ
improvisado; ADV improvisando; **to — lib** VI
improvisar
adamant [ǽDəmənt] ADJ inflexible, firme
Adam's apple [ǽDəmz æpəł] N nuez de Adán *f*
adapt [ədǽpt] VT adaptar; VI **to — to** adaptar[se]
a, acomodar[se] a
adaptation [æDæptéʃən] N adaptación *f*
adapter [ədǽptɚ] N adaptador *m*
add [æd] VT añadir, agregar; (find sum) sumar;
—**ed cost** costo adicional *m*; **to — to**
aumentar; **to — up** (find sum) sumar; (make
sense) cuadrar; N —**-on** accesorio *m*
addict [ǽDɪkt] N adicto -ta *mf*
addicted [ədíktɪd] ADJ adicto
addiction [ədíkʃən] N adicción *f*
addition [ədíʃən] N (of numbers) suma *f*; (to a
collection, staff) adición *f*, adquisición *f*; (to a
building) anexo *m*; **in — [to]** además [de]
additional [ədíʃənəł] ADJ adicional
additive [ǽDɪtɪv] N aditivo *m*
address¹ [ədrés] N (street) dirección *f*, domicilio
m; (speech) discurso *m*; — **book** libreta de
direcciones *f*; **form of** — tratamiento *m*
address² [ədrés] VT (write the address) dirigir;
(speak to) dirigirse a; (deal with) ocuparse de
addressee [ædrɛsí] N destinatario -ria *mf*
adduce [ədús] VT aducir
adept [ədépt] ADJ hábil
adequacy [ǽDɪkwəsi] N suficiencia *f*
adequate [ǽDɪkwɪt] ADJ (sufficient) suficiente;
(acceptable) aceptable
adhere [ædhír] VI adherirse; **to — to** adherirse a
adherence [ædhírəns] N adhesión *f*
adhesion [ædhíʒən] N (thing or tissue that
adheres) adherencia *f*; (act of sticking
together) adhesión *f*
adhesive [ædhísɪv] ADJ adhesivo; — **tape** cinta

adhesiva *f*
adjacent [ədʒésənt] ADJ adyacente
adjective [ǽdʒɪktɪv] ADJ & N adjetivo *m*
adjoin [ədʒɔ́ɪn] VT lindar con, colindar con;
—**ing** colindante; VI estar contiguo a
adjourn [ədʒɚ́n] VT **to — the meeting** levantar
la sesión; **meeting —ed** se levanta la sesión
adjournment [ədʒɚ́nmənt] N levantamiento de
la sesión *m*
adjudge [ədʒʌ́dʒ] VT (declare) declarar; (deem)
calificar
adjudicate [ədʒúDɪket] VI arbitrar; VT declarar
adjunct [ǽdʒʌŋkt] ADJ adjunto; N agregado -da
mf
adjust [ədʒʌ́st] VT (fix) ajustar, graduar; (adapt a
machine) regular; —**ed net income** ingreso
neto ajustado *m*; VI ajustarse, adaptarse
adjustable [ədʒʌ́stəbəł] ADJ ajustable; —**-rate
mortgage** hipoteca con tasa de interés
ajustable *f*
adjustment [ədʒʌ́stmənt] N ajuste *m*; (to a
machine) regulación *f*
administer [ædmínɪstɚ] VT (a business)
administrar, gestionar; (a punishment)
aplicar; (an oath) tomar[le]
administration [ædmɪnɪstréʃən] N
administración *f*; (period in power) gestión *f*;
(of punishment) aplicación *f*; (of an oath)
toma *f*
administrative [ædmínɪstreDɪv] ADJ
administrativo
administrator [ædmínɪstreDɚ] N
administrador -ra *mf*; (civil) intendente *mf*
admirable [ǽdmɚəbəł] ADJ admirable
admiral [ǽdmɚəł] N almirante *m*
admiration [ædmɚéʃən] N admiración *f*
admire [ædmáɪr] VT admirar
admirer [ædmáɪrɚ] N admirador -ora *mf*;
(suitor) pretendiente *mf*
admissible [ædmísəbəł] ADJ admisible
admission [ædmíʃən] N (acceptance) admisión
f; (access, ticket price) entrada *f*; (confession)
confesión *f*
admit [ædmít] VT (allow entry) admitir; (to a
hospital) internar; (acknowledge) reconocer,
admitir
admittance [ædmítn̩s] N entrada *f*; **no** —
prohibida la entrada
admonish [ædmánɪʃ] VT amonestar
admonition [ædməníʃən] N (warning)
advertencia *f*; (reproof) amonestación *f*
adobe [ədóbi] N (mud) adobe *m*; (house) casa de
adobe *f*
adolescence [ædlɛ́səns] N adolescencia *f*
adolescent [ædlɛ́sənt] ADJ & N adolescente *mf*
adopt [ədápt] VT (child, custom) adoptar;
(suggestion) aprobar
adoption [ədápʃən] N (of a child, custom)
adopción *f*; (of a suggestion) aprobación *f*

adoptive [ədáptɪv] ADJ adoptivo
adorable [ədɔ́rəbəł] ADJ adorable, precioso
adoration [æpərésən] N adoración f
adore [ədɔ́r] VT adorar; **I — playing tennis** me encanta jugar al tenis
adorn [ədɔ́rn] VT adornar, ornar
adornment [ədɔ́rnmənt] N adorno m
adrenal [ədrínl] ADJ suprarrenal
adrenaline [ədrénəlɪn] N adrenalina f
adrift [ədríft] ADJ & ADV a la deriva
adult [ədʌ́łt] ADJ & N adulto -ta mf
adulterate [ədʌ́łtəret] VT adulterar
adulterer [ədʌ́łtərə] N adúltero -ra mf
adultery [ədʌ́łtəri] N adulterio m
advance [ædvǽns] VI (move forward) avanzar; (make progress) avanzar, progresar; (bring forward) adelantar; VT (promote) promover; (propose) proponer; (pay beforehand) adelantar, anticipar; N (movement) avance m; (progress) adelanto m; (loan) adelanto m, anticipo m; **—s** (sexual) requiebros m pl; **in —** por adelantado, con anticipación
advanced [ædvǽnst] ADJ (idea, stage) avanzado; (country) adelantado
advancement [ædvǽnsmənt] N (movement) avance m; (rank) ascenso m; (knowledge) progreso m
advantage [ædvǽntɪdʒ] N ventaja f (also tennis); **it would be to your —** te convendría; **to take — of** aprovecharse de
advantageous [ædvæntédʒəs] ADJ ventajoso, provechoso
advent [ædvɛnt] N advenimiento m
adventure [ædvéntʃə] N aventura f
adventurer [ædvéntʃərə] N aventurero -ra mf
adventuresome [ædvéntʃəsəm] ADJ atrevido, osado
adventurous [ædvéntʃəəs] ADJ (seeking adventure) aventurero, intrépido; (daring) atrevido, audaz
adverb [ædvɜb] N adverbio m
adversary [ædvəseri] N adversario -ria mf
adverse [ædvɜ́s] ADJ adverso
adversity [ædvɜ́sɪDi] N adversidad f
advertise [ædvətaɪz] VT anunciar, hacer publicidad/propaganda para; VI hacer propaganda/publicidad; **to — for a cook** poner un anuncio buscando cocinero
advertisement [ædvətáɪzmənt] N anuncio publicitario m, aviso m
advertiser [ædvətaɪzə] N anunciante mf
advertising [ædvətaɪzɪŋ] N publicidad f; **— agency** agencia de publicidad f; **— campaign** campaña publicitaria f; **— agent** agente publicitario -ria mf
advice [ædváɪs] N consejo m; (expert) asesoramiento m
advisable [ædváɪzəbəł] ADJ aconsejable, recomendable

advise [ædváɪz] VI/VT (counsel) aconsejar, advertir; VT (inform) avisar, informar; (expertly) asesorar
adviser, advisor [ædváɪzə] N consejero -ra mf, asesor -ora mf
advocacy [ædvəkəsi] N defensa f
advocate[1] [ædvəkɪt] N (promoter) partidario -ria mf; (defender) defensor -ora mf, intercesor -ora mf; (lawyer) abogado -da mf
advocate[2] [ædvəket] VT abogar por, defender
aerial [ériəł] ADJ aéreo; N antena f
aerobic [ɛróbɪk] ADJ (exercise) aeróbico; (air-breathing) aerobio; N **—s** aeróbic m
aerodynamic [ɛrodaɪnǽmɪk] ADJ aerodinámico; N **—s** aerodinámica f
aeronautics [ɛrənɔ́Dɪks] N aeronáutica f
aerosol [érəsɑł] N aerosol m
aerospace [érospes] N espacio aéreo m; ADJ aeroespacial
aesthetic [ɛsθɛ́Dɪk] ADJ estético; N **—s** estética f
affable [ǽfəbəł] ADJ afable
affair [əfɛ́r] N (social) acontecimiento social m; (business) asunto m, negocio m; (love) aventura amorosa f, affaire m
affect [əfɛ́kt] VT (have effect on) afectar; (move) conmover; (feign) fingir
affectation [æfɛktéʃən] N afectación f, melindre m
affected [əfɛ́ktɪd] ADJ (moved) afectado, conmovido; (feigned) fingido, artificioso, melindroso
affection [əfɛ́kʃən] N afecto m, cariño m
affectionate [əfɛ́kʃənɪt] ADJ afectuoso, cariñoso
affidavit [æfɪdévɪt] N declaración jurada f
affiliate[1] [əfíliet] VT afiliar; VI afiliarse, asociarse
affiliate[2] [əfíliɪt] N filial f
affiliation [əfɪliéʃən] N (relation) afiliación f; (membership) filiación f; **political —** filiación política f
affinity [əfínɪDi] N afinidad f
affirm [əfɜ́m] VT afirmar
affirmation [æfəméʃən] N afirmación f
affirmative [əfɜ́məDɪv] ADJ afirmativo; **— action** discriminación positiva f; N **reply in the —** dar una respuesta afirmativa
affix[1] [əfíks] VT fijar; **to — one's signature** poner su firma, firmar
affix[2] [ǽfɪks] N afijo m
afflict [əflíkt] VT aquejar; **to be —ed with** padecer de, sufrir de
affliction [əflíkʃən] N (misery) aflicción f; (ailment) achaque m, mal m
affluent [ǽfluənt] ADJ (society) opulento; (person) rico
afford [əfɔ́rd] VT **I cannot — a car** no me alcanza el dinero para un coche; **he cannot — to waste time** no puede darse el lujo de perder tiempo; **I cannot — the risk** no me puedo permitir ese riesgo; **we will — you**

every opportunity se te darán todas las oportunidades
affordable [əfɔ́rDəbəl] ADJ asequible
affront [əfrʌ́nt] N afrenta *f*
Afghan, Afghani [ǽfgæn/æfgǽni] ADJ & N afgano -na *mf*
Afghanistan [æfgǽnɪstæn] N Afganistán *m*
afire [əfáɪr] ADJ & ADV en llamas
afloat [əflót] ADJ & ADV flotando, a flote
afraid [əfréd] ADJ asustado; **to be — [of]** temer, tener miedo [a]
afresh [əfréʃ] ADV de nuevo, desde el principio
Africa [ǽfrɪkə] N África *f*
African [ǽfrɪkən] ADJ & N africano -na *mf*
African American [ǽfrɪkənəmérɪkən] ADJ & N afroamericano -na *mf*
after [ǽftɚ] PREP (temporal) después de, tras; (spatial) detrás de; **— all** después de todo; ADV después; CONJ después [de] que
afterbirth [ǽftɚbɚθ] N placenta *f*
aftercare [ǽftɚkɛr] N (post-illness) tratamiento de convalecencia *m*; (postoperative) tratamiento post-operatorio *m*
after-hours [ǽftɚ áurz] ADV después de horas hábiles
afterlife [ǽftɚlaɪf] N el más allá *m*
aftermarket [ǽftɚmɑrkɪt] ADJ de mercado secundario; N (for merchandise) mercado secundario *m*; (for stocks) mercado extrabursátil *m*
aftermath [ǽftɚmæθ] N secuelas *f pl*
afternoon [ǽftɚnún] N tarde *f*; INTERJ **good —!** ¡buenas tardes!
aftershave [ǽftɚʃev] N loción para después del afeitado *f*
aftershock [ǽftɚʃak] N réplica *f*
aftertaste [ǽftɚtest] N (in the mouth) dejo *m*; (bad memory) resabio *m*
aftertax profit [ǽftɚtækspráfɪt] N ganancia neta *f*
afterthought [ǽftɚθɔt] N **it was just an —** se nos ocurrió después
afterward, afterwards [ǽftɚwɚd[z]] ADV después, posteriormente
again [əgén] ADV otra vez, de nuevo; **— and —** repetidas veces; **to fall —** volver a caerse
against [əgénst] PREP contra; **— the grain** a contrapelo; **— all odds** a pesar de todo
age [edʒ] N (of a person) edad *f*; (era) era *f*, época *f*; **— of consent** edad de consentimiento sexual *f*; **— discrimination** discriminación por edad *f*; **— limit** límite de edad *m*; **old —** vejez *f*; **of —** mayor de edad; **to come of —** llegar a la mayoría de edad; **under —** menor de edad; VI/VT envejecer
aged[1] [edʒd] ADJ (wine) añejo; **— forty** de cuarenta años
aged[2] [édʒɪd] ADJ anciano
ageless [édʒlɪs] ADJ (everlasting) eterno; (not

showing age) siempre joven; (classic) clásico
agency [édʒənsi] N agencia *f*; **through the — of** por mediación de
agenda [ədʒéndə] N orden del día *m*, agenda *f*
agent [édʒənt] N agente *mf*; (commercial) representante *mf*, gestor -ora *mf*; (legal) apoderado -da *mf*
aggrandize [əgrǽndaɪz] VT engrandecer
aggravate [ǽgrəvet] VT (worsen) exacerbar, agravar; (annoy) irritar, exasperar, exacerbar
aggregate [ǽgrɪgɪt] N conjunto *m*; (rock) agregado *m*; ADJ total, global
aggression [əgréʃən] N (attack) agresión *f*; (propensity to violence) agresividad *f*
aggressive [əgrésɪv] ADJ (violent) agresivo; (dynamic) emprendedor
aggressiveness [əgrésɪvnɪs] N agresividad *f*
aggressor [əgrésɚ] N agresor -ra *mf*
aghast [əgǽst] ADJ horrorizado
agile [ǽdʒəl] ADJ ágil
agility [ədʒílɪDi] N agilidad *f*
aging [édʒɪŋ] N (of a person) envejecimiento *m*; (of wine) maduración *f*
agitate [ǽdʒɪtet] VT (shake) agitar; (perturb) turbar; (campaign) alborotar
agitation [ædʒɪtéʃən] N agitación *f*
agitator [ǽdʒɪteDɚ] N agitador -ra *mf*
agnostic [ægnástɪk] ADJ & N agnóstico -ca *mf*
ago [əgó] ADV **many years —** hace muchos años; **long —** hace mucho tiempo
agog [əgág] ADJ planchado, boquiabierto
agonize [ǽgənaɪz] VI sufrir angustiosamente; **to — over** atormentarse por
agony [ǽgəni] N (pain) dolor *m*, tormento *m*; (anguish) angustia *f*
agoraphobia [ægɚəfóbiə] N agorafobia *f*
agrarian [əgrériən] ADJ agrario
agree [əgrí] VI (be in agreement) estar de acuerdo; (in grammar, mathematics) concordar; (color, food) sentarle bien; **to — upon** acordar, convenir, pactar; **they —d to meet the next day** quedaron en reunirse al día siguiente, acordaron reunirse al día siguiente; **the two sides —d to a truce** los dos bandos pactaron una tregua
agreeable [əgríəbəl] ADJ (nice) agradable; (willing) conforme
agreement [əgrímənt] N (concord, document) acuerdo *m*, concertación *f*, convenio *m*; (grammatical) concordancia *f*; **to be in —** estar de acuerdo; **to come to an —** ponerse de acuerdo, pactar
agricultural [ægrɪkʌ́ltʃəɚl] ADJ (related to crops) agrícola; (related to crops and cattle) agropecuario
agriculture [ǽgrɪkʌltʃɚ] N agricultura *f*
aground [əgráund] ADV **to run —** encallar, varar
ahead [əhéd] ADV delante; **— of time**

adelantado, con antelación; **to go** — ir
adelante, adelantarse; **to get** — prosperar;
our team is — nuestro equipo va primero;
the years — los años venideros
aid [ed] N (help) asistencia f; (assistant) ayudante
mf; VT ayudar; **to** — **and abet** instigar
aide [ed] N (high-ranking) asesor -ora mf;
(low-ranking) ayudante mf
**AIDS [acquired immune deficiency
syndrome]** [edz] N SIDA m
ail [eł] VI/VT **what** —**s you?** ¿qué tienes? ¿qué te
aflige? **he's** —**ing** está enfermo
aileron [élərɑn] N alerón m
ailing [élɪŋ] ADJ (person) achacoso, enfermizo;
(economy) debilitado
ailment [éłmənt] N achaque m, dolencia f
aim [em] N (with a weapon) puntería f;
(objective) objetivo m; VT (a weapon) apuntar;
(a question, blow) dirigir; **to** — **to please**
tratar de agradar
aimless [émlɪs] ADJ (purposeless) sin propósito;
(directionless) sin rumbo
air [ɛr] N aire m; —**bag** airbag m, bolsa de aire f;
—**brake** freno neumático m; **to** —
condition poner aire condicionado; —
conditioner acondicionador de aire m; —
conditioning aire acondicionado m,
climatización f; —**craft** aeronave f; —**craft
carrier** portaaviones m sg; —**field**
aeródromo m; — **force** fuerza aérea f;
—**head** cabeza de chorlito mf; —**lift** puente
aéreo m; —**line** línea aérea f, areolínea f; —
mail correo aéreo m; —**plane** avión m; —
piracy piratería aérea f; —**port** aeropuerto
m; — **power** fuerza aérea f; — **pressure**
presión de aire f; — **raid** ataque aéreo m; —
rifle escopeta de aire comprimido f; —**ship**
dirigible m; — **strike** bombardeo aéreo m;
—**strip** pista de aterrizaje f; —**-to-** —
aire-aire; — **traffic control** control del
tráfico aéreo m; —**way** conducto de aire m,
vía respiratoria f; **up in the** — en el aire,
incierto; **in the open** — al aire libre; **to be
on the** — estar en el aire, emitirse; **to put on
—s** presumir, darse ínfulas; **to vanish into
thin** — evaporarse; VT (an opinion)
manifestar; **to** —**lift** aerotransportar; **to** —
out orear, ventilar; ADJ aéreo; —**borne**
(troops) aerotransportado; (particles)
transportado por el aire; — **conditioned** con
aire acondicionado, climatizado; —**tight**
hermético
aisle [aɪł] N pasillo m; (of a church) nave lateral f
ajar [ədʒár] ADJ entornado, entreabierto
aka [ékéé] ADV (also called) también conocido
como; (in police usage) alias
akin [əkín] ADJ (related) emparentado; (similar)
semejante
à la mode [ɑlɑmód] ADV con helado

alarm [əlárm] N (warning) alarma f; (worry)
inquietud f; — **clock** despertador m; **to
sound an** — tocar a rebato; VT (worry)
alarmar; (frighten) asustar
alarming [əlármɪŋ] ADJ alarmante
Albania [ælbéniə] N Albania f
Albanian [ælbéniən] ADJ & N albanés -esa mf
albatross [ǽłbətrɑs] N albatros m
albinism [ǽłbɪnɪzəm] N albinismo m
albino [ælbáɪno] N albino -na mf
album [ǽłbəm] N álbum m
alcohol [ǽłkəhɔł] N alcohol m
alcoholic [ælkəhɔ́lɪk] ADJ & N alcohólico -ca mf
alcoholism [ǽłkəhɔlɪzəm] N alcoholismo m
alcove [ǽłkov] N rincón m
ale [eł] N cerveza inglesa f
alert [əlɝ́t] ADJ (vigilant) alerta; (awake)
despierto; **to be** — (on guard) estar alerta;
(lively) ser despierto; N alerta f; VT alertar,
avisar
alfalfa [ælfǽłfə] N alfalfa f
algae [ǽłdʒi] N algas f pl
algebra [ǽłdʒəbrə] N álgebra f
Algeria [ældʒíriə] N Argelia f
Algerian [ældʒíriən] ADJ & N argelino -na mf
algorithm [ǽłgərɪðəm] N algoritmo m
alias [éliəs] N alias m sg
alibi [ǽləbaɪ] N coartada f
alien [élіən] N (visitor from space) extraterrestre
mf; (foreigner) extranjero -ra mf; ADJ ajeno
alienate [éliənet] VT (people) alienar, alejar;
(property) enajenar
alight [əláɪt] VI (rider) apearse; (bird, insect)
posarse
align [əláɪn] VI/VT alinear[se]
alignment [əláɪnmənt] N alineación f
alike [əláɪk] ADJ parecido, igual; **to be** —
parecerse, ser iguales; ADV del mismo modo
alimentary [ælіméntəri] ADJ alimenticio; —
canal canal alimentario m
alimony [ǽləmoni] N pensión alimenticia f
alive [əláɪv] ADJ (living) vivo; — **with** lleno de;
the symphony came — **under his
direction** la sinfonía cobró vida bajo su
dirección
alkali [ǽłkəlaɪ] N álcali m
alkaline [ǽłkəlɪn] ADJ alcalino
all [ɔ̀ł] ADJ todo; — **the time** todo el tiempo; N
todo m; **to give one's** — dar todo de sí; PRON
todo; **is that** —? ¿eso es todo? — **or nothing**
todo o nada; ADV completamente, todo; — **at
once** (uninterrupted) de una vez; (sudden) de
repente; —**-inclusive** con todo incluido; —-
time high máximo histórico m; — **told** en
conjunto; **he's** — **dirty** está todo sucio; **it is**
— **over** se acabó; **not at** — de ninguna
manera; **nothing at** — nada en absoluto;
once [and] for — de una vez por todas;
she's — **right** está bien; INTERJ — **right**

bueno

allay [əlé] VT (fear, doubt) calmar, disipar; (anger) aplacar

allegation [æligéʃən] N acusación *f*

allege [əléʤ] VT (state) afirmar; (claim) alegar

alleged [əléʤd] ADJ (event) supuesto; (perpetrator) presunto

allegedly [əléʤɪdli] ADV supuestamente, presuntamente

allegiance [əlíʤəns] N lealtad *f*, fidelidad *f*; **to pledge — to the flag** jurar la bandera

allegory [æligɔri] N alegoría *f*

allergen [ǽlə·ʤɪn] N alergeno/alérgeno *m*

allergic [əlɔ́·ʤɪk] ADJ alérgico

allergist [ǽlə·ʤɪst] N alergólogo -ga *mf*

allergy [ǽlə·ʤi] N alergia *f*

alleviate [əlíviet] VT (suffering) aliviar; (hunger) paliar

alley [ǽli] N callejón *m*; (tennis) pasillo de dobles *m*; **right up her —** ideal para ella

alliance [əláiəns] N alianza *f*

allied [əláid, ǽlaid] ADJ aliado

alligator [ǽligɛɾə·] N caimán *m*; Am lagarto *m*

alliterate [əlíɾəret] VI hacer aliteración

allocate [ǽləket] VT asignar

allot [əlát] VT asignar

allotment [əlátmənt] N asignación *f*, cuota *f*

allow [əláʊ] VI/VT (permit) permitir; (make possible) posibilitar; (admit) admitir; **to — for** tener en cuenta

allowable [əláʊəbəɫ] ADJ admisible, permisible

allowance [əláʊəns] N (regular payment) asignación *f*, pensión *f*; (monthly payment) mensualidad *f*; (for a child) paga *f*, mesada *f*; (payment for a particular purpose) pago *m*; (food) ración *f*; **to make — for** tener en cuenta

alloy[1] [ǽlɔi] N aleación *f*

alloy[2] [əlɔ́i] VT alear

allude [əlúd] VI aludir; **to — to** aludir a

allure [əlúr] VI/VT seducir, atraer; N atractivo *m*

alluring [əlúrɪŋ] ADJ seductivo, atractivo

allusion [əlúʒən] N alusión *f*

ally[1] [ǽlai] N aliado -da *mf*

ally[2] [əlái] VT **to — oneself with** aliarse con

almanac [ɔ́ɫmənæk] N almanaque *m*

almighty [ɔlmáiDi] ADJ todopoderoso

almond [ɔ́mənd] N almendra *f*; **— tree** almendro *m*

almost [ɔ́ɫmost] ADV casi; **I — fell down** por poco me caigo

alms [ɔmz] N limosna *f*

aloe vera [ǽlovírə] N áloe *m*

alone [əlón] ADJ solo; **— among his contemporaries** único entre sus contemporáneos; ADV solo, solamente; **she — knew that** solo ella sabía eso; **all — a solas**; **to leave — no** tocar, dejar en paz

along [əlɔ́ŋ] PREP **he was walking — the**

street andaba por la calle; **all — the coast** a lo largo de toda la costa; **— with** junto con; **all —** desde el principio; **to carry — with oneself** llevar consigo; **to go — with** acceder a, conformarse con; **to get — with** llevarse bien con

alongside [əlɔ́ŋsáid] PREP al lado de; **— the boat** al lado del bote; ADV al lado, al costado; **the dog ran —** el perro corría al costado

aloof [əlúf] ADJ reservado, esquivo; ADV apartado

aloud [əláʊd] ADV en voz alta

alphabet [ǽɫfəbɛt] N alfabeto *m*, abecedario *m*

alphanumeric [ǽɫfənumérɪk] ADJ alfanumérico

alpine [ǽɫpain] ADJ alpino

already [ɔlrédi] ADV ya

also [ɔ́ɫso] ADV también, además; **—-ran** (horse, candidate) caballo/candidato vencido *m*

alt [ǽlt] *see* alternate[1]

altar [ɔ́ɫtə·] N altar *m*; **—piece** retablo *m*

alter [ɔ́ɫtə·] VI/VT (change) alterar; (neuter) capar, castrar

alteration [ɔ̀ɫtəréʃən] N (change) alteración *f*, cambio *m*; **—s** arreglos *m pl*, reformas *f pl*

altercation [ɔ̀ɫtə·kéʃən] N altercado *m*

alternate[1] [ɔ́ɫtə·nɪt] ADJ alternativo, alterno; **— route** ruta alternativa *f*; **— spelling** ortografía alterna *f*; **he visits us on — Mondays** nos visita un lunes sí y otro no; **alt key** tecla de alt *f*; **alt gr key** tecla de alternativa gráfica *f*; N suplente *mf*

alternate[2] [ɔ́ɫtə·net] VI/VT alternar

alternation [ɔ̀ɫtə·néʃən] N alternancia *f*

alternative [ɔ̀ɫtɔ́·nəDiv] ADJ alternativo; **— minimum tax** contribución alternativa mínima *f*; N alternativa *f*

alternator [ɔ́ɫtə·neDə·] N alternador *m*

although [ɔlðó] CONJ aunque, si bien

altimeter [æltímiDə·] N altímetro *m*

altitude [ǽɫtitud] N altura *f*, altitud *f*; **— sickness** mal de altura *m*

alto [ǽɫto] N contralto *mf*; ADJ alto

altogether [ɔ̀ɫtəgéðə·] ADV (completely) completamente; (all included) en total

altruism [ǽɫtruizəm] N altruismo *m*

aluminum [əlúmənəm] N aluminio *m*; **— foil** papel de aluminio *m*

always [ɔ́ɫwez] ADV siempre

Alzheimer's disease [ɔ́ɫtshaimə·z dɪziz] N enfermedad de Alzheimer *f*

a.m. [éém] ADV de la mañana

am [æm] *see* be

amalgamate [əmǽɫgəmet] VI/VT (metals) amalgamar[se]; (companies) fusionar[se]

amass [əmǽs] VT acumular, amasar

amateur [ǽmətʃə·] ADJ amateur; N amateur *mf*; aficionado -da *mf*

amaze [əméz] VT maravillar, asombrar

amazement [əmézmənt] N asombro *m*

amazing [əmézɪŋ] ADJ asombroso, increíble
Amazon [ǽməzɑn] N (region) Amazonia f; (river) Amazonas m sg
ambassador [æmbǽsəDɚ] N embajador -ora mf
amber [ǽmbɚ] N ámbar m; ADJ (quality) ambarino; (material) de ámbar; (color) [de] color ámbar
ambidextrous [æmbɪdékstrəs] ADJ ambidiestro
ambience, ambiance [ǽmbiəns] N ambiente m
ambient [ǽmbiənt] ADJ ambiental; — **temperature** temperatura ambiente f
ambiguity [æmbɪgjúɪDi] N ambigüedad f
ambiguous [æmbígjuəs] ADJ ambiguo
ambition [æmbíʃən] N ambición f, aspiración f
ambitious [æmbíʃəs] ADJ ambicioso
ambivalent [æmbívələnt] ADJ ambivalente
amble [ǽmbəl] VI deambular
ambulance [ǽmbjələns] N ambulancia f
ambulatory [ǽmbjələtɔri] ADJ ambulatorio
ambush [ǽmbuʃ] N emboscada f, celada f; **to lie in** — tender una emboscada; VT emboscar
ameliorate [əmíliəret] VI/VT mejorar
amen [ámén] INTERJ amén
amenable [əménəbəl] ADJ bien dispuesto
amend [əménd] VT enmendar; **to make** —**s [for]** compensar [por]
amendment [əméndmənt] N enmienda f
amenities [əménɪDiz] N PL comodidades f pl
America [əmɛ́rɪkə] N América f
American [əmɛ́rɪkən] ADJ & N (continental) americano -na mf; (USA) americano -na mf, norteamericano -na mf, estadounidense mf
amethyst [ǽməθɪst] N amatista f
amiable [émiəbəl] ADJ amable
amicable [ǽmɪkəbəl] ADJ amistoso, amigable
amid [əmíd] PREP en medio de, entre
amino acid [əmínoǽsɪd] N aminoácido m
amiss [əmís] ADV **something is** — algo anda mal
ammonia [əmónjə] N amoníaco m
ammunition [æmjəníʃən] N munición f
amnesia [æmníʒə] N amnesia f
amnesty [ǽmnɪsti] N amnistía f
amniocentesis [æmniosɪntísɪs] N amniocentesis f
amniotic [æmniáDɪk] ADJ amniótico; — **fluid** líquido amniótico m
amoeba [əmíbə] N ameba f
among [əmʌ́ŋ] PREP entre
amoral [emɔ́rəl] ADJ amoral
amorous [ǽmərəs] ADJ (sexually aroused) excitado; (in love) enamorado
amorphous [əmɔ́rfəs] ADJ amorfo
amortization [æmɚDɪzéʃən] N amortización f
amortize [ǽmɚtaɪz] VT amortizar
amount [əmáunt] N (of a substance) cantidad f; (of money) suma f, importe m; — **due** cantidad debida f, monto debido m; — **paid** cantidad pagada f, monto pagado m; —

payable cantidad a pagar f; VI (add up to) ascender [a]; **that** —**s to stealing** eso equivale a robar
ampere [ǽmpír] N amperio m
amphetamine [æmfɛ́Dəmin] N anfetamina f
amphibian [æmfíbiən] N anfibio m
amphibious [æmfíbiəs] ADJ anfibio
amphitheater [ǽmfəθiəDɚ] N anfiteatro m
ampicillin [æmpɪsílɪn] N ampicilina f
ample [ǽmpəl] ADJ (in quantity) suficiente; (in size) amplio
amplifier [ǽmpləfaɪɚ] N amplificador m
amplify [ǽmpləfaɪ] VT (an explanation) ampliar; (a sound) amplificar
amplitude [ǽmplɪtud] N amplitud f
amputate [ǽmpjətet] VT amputar
amuck, amok [əmʌ́k] ADV **to run** — (kill people) perpetrar un ataque homicida; (go crazy) volverse loco
amulet [ǽmjəlɪt] N amuleto m
amuse [əmjúz] VT (make laugh) divertir; (help pass time) entretener; **to** — **oneself** divertirse, entretenerse
amusement [əmjúzmənt] N diversión f, entretenimiento m
amusing [əmjúzɪŋ] ADJ (entertaining) divertido; (funny) gracioso, chistoso
amygdala [əmígdələ] N amígdala f
an [ən, æn] INDEF ART un m, una f
anabolic [ænəbálɪk] ADJ anabólico; — **steroid** esteroide anabólico m
anachronism [ənǽkrənɪzəm] N anacronismo m
anaerobic [ænəróbɪk] ADJ anaerobio
anal [énl] ADJ anal; (neurotic) rígido, neurótico
analgesic [ænlʤízɪk] N & ADJ analgésico m
analogical [ænəláʤɪkəl] ADJ analógico
analogous [ənǽləgəs] ADJ análogo
analogue, analog [ǽnəlɔg] ADJ analógico; — **device** dispositivo analógico m
analogy [ənǽləʤi] N analogía f
analysis [ənǽlɪsɪs] N análisis m
analyst [ǽnəlɪst] N analista mf
analytic, analytical [ænəlíDɪk[əl]] ADJ (approach) analítico; (person) analítico, analista
analyze [ǽnəlaɪz] VT analizar
anarchist [ǽnɚkɪst] N anarquista mf
anarchy [ǽnɚki] N anarquía f
anathema [ənǽθəmə] N anatema m
anatomical [ænətámɪkəl] ADJ anatómico
anatomy [ənǽDəmi] N anatomía f
ancestor [ǽnsɛstɚ] N antepasado -da mf, ascendiente mf
ancestral [ænséstrəl] ADJ ancestral, de los antepasados; — **home** casa solariega f
ancestry [ǽnsɛstri] N linaje m, ascendencia f, abolengo m
anchor [ǽŋkɚ] N ancla f; —**man** presentador m; —**woman** presentadora f; **to drop** — anclar,

echar anclas; vt (a boat) anclar; (an argument) basar; vi echar anclas, fondear

anchovy [æntʃovi] N anchoa f

ancient [énʃənt] ADJ antiguo; *pej* vetusto

and [ænd] CONJ y; (before i, hi) e; — **so forth** etcétera, y así sucesivamente

Andalusia [ændəlúʒə] N Andalucía f

Andalusian [ændəlúʒən] ADJ & N andaluz -za *mf*

Andes [ændiz] N Andes *m pl*

Andorra [ændɔ́rə] N Andorra f

Andorran [ændɔ́rən] ADJ & N andorrano -na *mf*

androgynous [ændrádʒənəs] ADJ andrógino

anecdote [ǽnɪkdot] N anécdota f

anemia [əními ə] N anemia f

anemic [ənímɪk] ADJ anémico

anesthesia [ænɪsθíʒə] N anestesia f

anesthesiologist [ænəsθiziáləʤɪst] N anestesiólogo -ga *mf*, anestesista *mf*

anesthesiology [ænɪsθiziáləʤi] N anestesiología f

anesthetic [ænɪsθéDɪk] ADJ anestésico; N (substance) anestesia f

anesthetize [ənésθətaɪz] vt anestesiar

aneurysm [ǽnjərɪzəm] N aneurisma *m*

anew [ənú] ADV de nuevo, otra vez

angel [énʤəɬ] N ángel *m*

angelic [ænʤélɪk] ADJ angélico, angelical

anger [ǽŋgɚ] N enojo *m*, enfado *m*; vt enojar, enfadar

angina pectoris [ænʤáɪnəpéktɚɪs] N angina de pecho f

angiocardiography [ænʤiokɑrDiágrəfi] N angiocardiografía f

angiogram [ǽnʤiogræm] N angiograma *m*

angioplasty [ǽnʤiəplæsti] N angioplastia f; — **balloon** balón de angioplastia *m*

angle [ǽŋgəɬ] N (geometrical) ángulo *m*; (point of view) punto de vista *m*, perspectiva f; vi pescar

Anglo-Saxon [ǽŋglosǽksən] ADJ & N anglosajón -ona *mf*

Angola [æŋgólə] N Angola f

Angolan [æŋgólən] ADJ & N angolano -na *mf*, angoleño -ña *mf*

angry [ǽŋgri] ADJ enojado, enfadado

angst [áŋkst] N angustia f

anguish [ǽŋgwɪʃ] N angustia f, ansia f, congoja f

angular [ǽŋgjələ] ADJ angular; (face) anguloso

animal [ǽnəməɬ] ADJ & N animal *m*; — **rights** derechos de los animales *m pl*

animate[1] [ǽnəmɪt] ADJ animado

animate[2] [ǽnəmet] vt (enliven) animar; (encourage) alentar; —**d cartoon** dibujo animado *m*

animation [ænəméʃən] N animación f

animosity [ænəmúsiDi] N animosidad f, ojeriza f, encono *m*

anise [ǽnɪs] N anís *m*

ankle [ǽŋkəɬ] N tobillo *m*

annals [ǽnɬz] N anales *m pl*

annex[1] [ǽnɛks] N anexo *m*

annex[2] [ənéks] vt anexar

annexation [ænɛkséʃən] N anexión f

annihilate [ənáɪəlet] vt aniquilar

anniversary [ænəvɚ́səri] N aniversario *m*

annotate [ǽnətet] vt anotar

annotation [ænətéʃən] N (action, result) anotación f; (result) nota f

announce [ənáuns] vt (make known) anunciar, dar a conocer; (declare) anunciar

announcement [ənáunsmənt] N (of an engagement, birth, candidacy) anuncio *m*; (of a conference or competition) convocatoria f

announcer [ənáunsɚ] N anunciador -ra *mf*; (on radio) locutor -ora *mf*

annoy [ənɔ́i] vi/vt fastidiar, contrariar

annoyance [ənɔ́iəns] N fastidio *m*, contrariedad f

annual [ǽnjuəɬ] ADJ anual; N (book) anuario *m*; (plant) planta anual f

annuity [ənjúiDi] N anualidad f, renta anual f

annul [ənʌ́ɬ] vt anular

annulment [ənʌ́ɬmənt] N anulación f

anomalous [ənámələs] ADJ anómalo

anomaly [ənáməli] N anomalía f

anonymous [ənánəməs] ADJ anónimo

anorak [ǽnəræk] N anorak *m*

anorexia [ænəréksiə] N anorexia f

anorexic [ænəréksɪk] ADJ anoréxico

another [ənʌ́ðɚ] ADJ otro; — **day** otro día; PRON otro; **I want** — quiero otro; **one** — el uno al otro, los unos a los otros

answer [ǽnsɚ] N (to a question) respuesta f, contestación f; (to a problem) solución f; vi contestar, responder; **to** — **for** ser responsable de/por; vt contestar

answering [ǽnsɚɪŋ] ADJ — **machine** contestador automático *m*; — **service** servicio telefónico contratado *m*, servicio de contestador *m*

ant [ænt] N hormiga f; —**eater** oso hormiguero *m*; —**hill** hormiguero *m*

antacid [æntǽsɪd] N & ADJ antiácido *m*

antagonism [æntǽgənɪzəm] N antagonismo *m*

antagonist [æntǽgənɪst] N antagonista *mf*

antagonize [æntǽgənaɪz] vt antagonizar

antarctic [æntárktɪk] ADJ antártico

Antarctica [æntárktɪkə] N Antártida f

antecedent [æntəsídn̩t] ADJ & N antecedente *m*

antelope [ǽntəlop] N antílope *m*

antenna [ænténə] N antena f

anterior [æntíriɚ] ADJ anterior

anthem [ǽnθəm] N himno *m*

anthology [ænθáləʤi] N antología f

anthracite [ǽnθrəsaɪt] N antracita f

anthrax [ǽnθræks] N ántrax *m*

anthropologist [ænθrəpáləʤɪst] N antropólogo -ga *mf*

anthropology [ænθrəpáIədʒi] N antropología f
anthropomorphize [ænθrəpəmɔ́rfaIz] VI/VT antropomorfizar
antiabortion [æntiəbɔ́rʃən] ADJ antiaborto inv
antiaircraft [æntiérkræft] ADJ antiaéreo
antiallergic [æntiəlɜ́-dʒIk] ADJ antialérgico
antibacterial [æntibæktíriəł] ADJ antibacteriano
antiballistic [æntibəlístIk] ADJ antibalístico
antibiotic [æntIbaIáDIk] N & ADJ antibiótico m
antibody [æntIbaDi] N anticuerpo m
anticancer [æntikænsə-] ADJ anticanceroso f
anticipate [æntísəpet] VI/VT (foresee) prever; (jump the gun) anticiparse [a]
anticipation [æntIsəpéʃən] N previsión f; **with great** — con gran expectación
anticlimactic [æntikləmǽktIk] ADJ decepcionante
anticoagulant [æntikoǽgjələnt] ADJ & N anticoagulante m
anticonvulsant [æntikənvʌ́łsənt] ADJ & N anticonvulsivo m
antics [æntIks] N payasadas f pl, monerías f pl, monadas f pl
antidepressant [æntidIprésənt] ADJ & N antidepresivo m
antidiarrheal [æntidaIəríəł] ADJ & N antidiarreico m
antidiuretic [æntidaIəréDIk] ADJ & N antidiurético m
antidote [æntIdot] N antídoto m
antifreeze [æntIfriz] N anticongelante m
antigen [æntIdʒən] N antígeno m
anti-glare [æntiglér] ADJ antirreflejante
Antigua and Barbuda [æntígæændbɑrbúDə] N Antigua y Barbuda f
Antiguan [æntígən] ADJ & N antiguano -ana mf
antihistamine [æntihístəmin] N & ADJ antihistamínico m
anti-inflammatory [æntiInflǽmətɔri] ADJ & N antiinflamatorio m
antilock [æntilɑk] ADJ antibloqueo; — **brakes** frenos antibloqueo mpl
antimony [æntəmoni] N antimonio m
antioxidant [æntiáksIDənt] N antioxidante m
antipathy [æntípəθi] N antipatía f
antiperspirant [æntipɜ́-spə-ənt] N antitranspirante m
antipsychotic [æntisaIkáDIk] ADJ & N antipsicótico m
antiquated [æntIkweDId] ADJ (custom) anticuado; (word) desusado
antique [æntík] ADJ antiguo; N antigüedad f
antiquity [æntíkwIDi] N antigüedad f
anti-Semitism [æntisémItIzəm] N antisemitismo m
antiseptic [æntIséptIk] ADJ & N antiséptico m
antisocial [æntisóʃeł] ADJ antisocial
antispasmodic [æntispæzmáDIk] ADJ & N

antiespasmódico m
antithesis [æntíθəsIs] N antítesis f
antitoxin [æntitáksIn] N antitoxina f
antitrust [æntitrʌ́st] ADJ antimonopolio, antitrust
antiviral [æntiváIrəł] ADJ & N antiviral m
antivirus [æntivaIrəs] ADJ antivirus
antler [æntlə-] N asta f, cuerno m
antonym [æntənIm] N antónimo m
antsy [æntsi] ADJ (impatient) impaciente; (anxious) ansioso
anus [énəs] N ano m
anvil [ænvəł] N yunque m
anxiety [æŋzáIIDi] N ansiedad f, angustia f
anxious [æŋkʃəs] ADJ (worried) ansioso, preocupado; (desirous) ansioso, deseoso
any [éni] ADJ & PRON cualquier[a], cualesquier[a], alguno; — **woman** cualquier mujer, una mujer cualquiera; — **houses** unas casas cualesquiera; lit cualesquiera casas; **in** — **case** en todo caso; **do you have** — **money?** ¿tienes dinero? **I don't have** — no tengo; **do you like** — **of these?** ¿te gusta alguno de estos?
anybody [énibaDi] PRON alguien, cualquiera; — **could do that** cualquiera podría hacer eso; **is** — **here?** ¿hay alguien aquí? **he does not know** — no conoce a nadie
anyhow [énihaU] ADV de todos modos, en todo caso
anymore [énimɔ́r] ADV **he doesn't work** — ya no trabaja, no trabaja más
anyone [éniwʌn] PRON alguien, cualquiera; — **could do that** cualquiera podría hacer eso; **is** — **here?** ¿hay alguien aquí? **he does not know** — no conoce a nadie
anyplace [éniples] ADV en cualquier parte/lugar; **you can buy it** — se puede comprar en cualquier lugar; **he's not going** — no va a ninguna parte
anything [éniθIŋ] PRON cualquier cosa, algo; — **is fine** cualquier cosa me viene bien; — **you wish** todo lo que quieras; **do you have** — **for a cough?** ¿tienes algo para la tos? **I don't know** — no sé nada
anytime [énitaIm] ADV en cualquier momento
anyway [éniwe] ADV de todos modos, de cualquier manera, en todo caso
anywhere [énihwer] ADV en cualquier parte / lugar; **you can buy it** — se puede comprar en cualquier lugar; **he's not going** — no va a ninguna parte
aorta [eɔ́rDə] N aorta f
apart [əpárt] ADV **they are three miles** — están a tres millas de distancia; **they kept him** — **from the group** lo apartaron del grupo; **each factor viewed** — cada factor visto por separado; **to take** — desarmar, desmontar; **to tear** — despedazar, hacer

pedazos; **to tell** — distinguir
apartment [əpártmənt] N apartamento *m*; *Sp*
  piso *m*
apathetic [æpəθέDɪk] ADJ apático
apathy [æpəθi] N apatía *f*, abulia *f*
ape [ep] N simio *m*; VT remedar
aperture [æpə·tʃə·] N abertura *f*; (of a pipe) luz *f*
apex [épɛks] N (of tongue) ápice *m*; (of a
  mountain) cumbre *f*
aphasia [əféʒə] N afasia *f*
aphrodisiac [æfrədíziæk] N afrodisíaco *m*
apiece [əpís] ADV cada uno
apnea [æpniə] N apnea *f*
apocalypse [əpákəlɪps] N apocalipsis *mf*
apogee [æpədʒi] N apogeo *m*
apologetic [əpɑlədʒέDɪk] ADJ lleno de disculpas
apologize [əpɑ́lədʒaɪz] VI disculparse
apology [əpɑ́lədʒi] N (expression of regret)
  disculpa[s] *f* [*pl*]; (justification) apología *f*
apoplexy [æpəpleksi] N apoplejía *f*
apostle [əpásəł] N apóstol *m*
apostrophe [əpástrəfi] N (punctuation)
  apóstrofo *m*; (invocation) apóstrofe *m*
app [æp] N (computer software) aplicación *f*
appall [əpáł] VT horrorizar
appalling [əpálɪŋ] ADJ horroroso
apparatus [æpərǽDəs] N (single) aparato *m*;
  (group) maquinaria *f*
apparel [əpǽrəł] N indumentaria *f*, ropa *f*; (fine)
  ropaje *m*
apparent [əpǽrənt] ADJ (visible) visible; (clear)
  obvio, evidente; (seeming) aparente
apparition [æpəríʃən] N aparición *f*, fantasma *m*
appeal [əpíł] N (legal) apelación *f*, recurso *m*;
  (request) llamamiento *m*, llamado *m*;
  (attraction) atractivo *m*; VT apelar, recurrir
  [contra]; VI **to — to** atraer
appear [əpír] VI (show up) aparecer[se]; (seem)
  parecer, aparentar; (be published) salir;
  (come before a judge) comparecer
appearance [əpírəns] N (looks) apariencia *f*,
  traza *f*, estampa *f*; (act of appearing) aparición
  f; (coming before a judge) comparecencia *f*
appease [əpíz] VT aplacar, apaciguar
appeasement [əpízmənt] N aplacamiento *m*,
  apaciguamiento *m*
appellate [əpélɪt] N — **court** tribunal de
  apelaciones *m*
append [əpénd] VT adjuntar
appendage [əpéndɪdʒ] N apéndice *m*
appendectomy [æpɪndéktəmi] N
  apendicectomía *f*
appendicitis [əpɛndəsáɪdɪs] N apendicitis *f*
appendix [əpéndɪks] N apéndice *m*
appetite [æpɪtaɪt] N apetito *m*
appetizer [æpɪtaɪzə·] N aperitivo *m*
appetizing [æpɪtaɪzɪŋ] ADJ apetecible, apetitoso
applaud [əplɔ́d] VI/VT aplaudir
applause [əplɔ́z] N aplauso[s] *m* [*pl*]

apple [æpəł] N manzana *f*; — **grove** manzanar
  m; — **of my eye** niña de mis ojos *f*; —**sauce**
  compota de manzana *f*; — **tree** manzano *m*;
  Adam's — nuez de Adán *f*
appliance [əplárəns] N aparato *m*; (electric)
  aparato electrodoméstico *m*,
  electrodoméstico *m*
applicable [æplɪkəbəł] ADJ aplicable
applicant [æplɪkənt] N aspirante *mf*, solicitante
  mf
application [æplɪkéʃən] N (act of applying,
  computer software) aplicación *f*; (form)
  solicitud *f*, formulario *f*
applicator [æplɪkeDə·] N aplicador *m*
apply [əplái] VT aplicar; **to — for** solicitar, pedir;
  are you —ing for the scholarship? ¿te
  presentas para la beca? ¿estás solicitando la
  beca? **to — oneself** aplicarse, dedicarse
appoint [əpɔ́ɪnt] VT (designate) nombrar,
  designar; (furnish) amueblar, equipar; **a well**
  —ed house una casa bien amueblada
appointee [əpɔɪntí] N persona nombrada *f*
appointment [əpɔ́ɪntmənt] N (designation)
  nombramiento *m*, designación *f*;
  (engagement) cita *f*; **doctor's** — cita/hora
  con el médico *f*; —**s** mobiliario *m sg*,
  accesorios *m pl*
apportion [əpɔ́rʃən] VT repartir
  proporcionalmente
apportionment [əpɔ́rʃənmənt] N reparto
  proporcional *m*
appraisal [əprézəł] N (of a property) tasación *f*,
  valuación *f*; (of a situation) evaluación *f*
appraise [əpréz] VT (a property) avaluar,
  valorar, tasar; (a situation) evaluar
appreciable [əpríʃəbəł] ADJ apreciable
appreciate [əpríʃiet] VT (value) apreciar,
  estimar; (recognize) darse cuenta, percibir;
  (thank) agradecer; **to — in value** apreciarse
appreciation [əpriʃiéʃən] N (esteem) aprecio *m*;
  (thanks) agradecimiento *m*; (monetary value)
  apreciación *f*, alza *f*
apprehend [æprɪhénd] VT (arrest) aprehender;
  (understand) comprender
apprehension [æprɪhénʃən] N (arrest)
  aprehensión *f*; (worry) aprensión *f*
apprehensive [æprɪhénsɪv] ADJ aprensivo
apprentice [əpréntɪs] N aprendiz -iza *mf*; VT
  poner de aprendiz
apprenticeship [əpréntɪsʃɪp] N aprendizaje *m*
apprise [əpráɪz] VT informar
approach [əprótʃ] N (act of approaching)
  aproximación *f*; (method) enfoque *m*,
  acercamiento *m*; (means of access) acceso *m*,
  entrada *f*; — **shot** golpe de aproximación *m*;
  VI (go nearer) acercar, aproximarse; (in
  golf) aprochar; VT (a problem) abordar,
  enfocar; **to — someone about a problem**
  plantearle a alguien un problema

approachable [əprótʃəbəł] ADJ tratable
approbation [æprəbéʃən] N aprobación *f*
appropriate[1] [əprópriit] ADJ apropiado, adecuado
appropriate[2] [əprópriet] VT apropiarse; (funds) asignar
appropriation [əpropriéʃən] N (act of seizing) apropiación *f*; (assignment of funds) asignación *f*; (assigned funds) partida *f*
approval [əprúvəł] N aprobación *f*; **on** — a prueba
approve [əprúv] VI/VT aprobar
approximate[1] [əpráksəmɪt] ADJ aproximado
approximate[2] [əpráksəmet] VT aproximarse a
approximately [əpráksəmɪtli] ADV aproximadamente
APR [annual percentage rate] [épíár] N TAE *f*
apricot [æprɪkɑt] N albaricoque *m*; *Am* damasco *m*; *Mex* chabacano *m*
April [éprəł] N abril *m*
apron [éprən] N (for a cook) delantal *m*; (for a workman) mandil *m*
apropos [æprəpó] ADV a propósito; ADJ oportuno, pertinente; — **of** a propósito de
apt [æpt] ADJ (prone, able) capaz; (suited) pertinente; **is he** — **to be at home?** ¿estará en casa?
aptitude [æptɪtud] N aptitud *f*, capacidad *f*
aquamarine [ɑkwəmərín] N aguamarina *f*
aquarium [əkwériəm] N (tank) acuario *m*, pecera *f*; (building) acuario *m*
aquatic [əkwɑ́ɾɪk] ADJ acuático
aqueduct [ǽkwɪdʌkt] N acueducto *m*
Arab [ǽrəb] ADJ & N árabe *mf*
Arabic [ǽrəbɪk] ADJ árabe, arábigo; N (language) árabe *m*
arable [ǽrəbəł] ADJ cultivable
Aragonese [ærəgəníz] ADJ & N aragonés -esa *mf*
arbiter [árbɪɾɚ] N árbitro -ra *mf*
arbitrariness [árbɪtrɛrɪnɪs] N arbitrariedad *f*
arbitrary [árbɪtrɛri] ADJ arbitrario; — **action** arbitrariedad *f*
arbitrate [árbɪtret] VI/VT (mediate) arbitrar [en], terciar [en]; (submit to mediation) someter al arbitraje
arbitration [ɑrbɪtréʃən] N arbitraje *m*
arbitrator [árbɪtreɾɚ] N árbitro -tra *mf*
arbor [árbɚ] N pérgola *f*, glorieta *f*
arboreal [ɑrbóriəł] ADJ arbóreo
arc [ɑrk] N arco *m*
arcade [ɑrkéd] N (series of arcs) arcada *f*; (shops) galería *f*; (video game center) sala de juegos electrónicos *f*
arcane [ɑrkén] ADJ arcano
arch [ɑrtʃ] N arco *m*; (curved roof) bóveda *f*; —**way** arcada *f*; VI/VT arquear[se]
archaeological [ɑrkiəládʒɪkəł] ADJ arqueológico
archaeology, archeology [ɑrkiáləʤi] N

arqueología *f*
archaic [ɑrkéɪk] ADJ arcaico
archaism [árkeɪzəm] N arcaísmo *m*
archbishop [ɑrtʃbíʃəp] N arzobispo *m*
archenemy [ártʃénəmi] N archienemigo -ga *mf*
archer [ártʃɚ] N arquero -ra *mf*
archery [ártʃəri] N tiro al arco *m*
archetype [árkɪtaɪp] N arquetipo *m*
archipelago [ɑrkəpéləgo] N archipiélago *m*
architect [árkɪtɛkt] N arquitecto -ta *mf*; (creator) artífice *mf*
architectural [ɑrkɪtéktʃɚəł] ADJ arquitectónico
architecture [árkɪtɛktʃɚ] N arquitectura *f*
archive [árkaɪv] N archivo *m*
arctic [árktɪk] ADJ ártico
ardent [árdn̩t] ADJ ardiente
ardor [árdɚ] N ardor *m*, fervor *m*
arduous [árdʒuəs] ADJ arduo
are [ɑr] *see* be
area [ériə] N (space) área *f*; (region) zona *f*; (of a geometric figure) superficie *f*, área *f*
arena [ərínə] N (for sports) estadio *m*; (in a circus) pista *f*
Argentina [ɑrdʒəntínə] N Argentina *f*
Argentinian [ɑrdʒəntíniən] ADJ & N argentino -na *mf*
argon [árgɑn] N argón *m*
argue [árgju] VT (reason) argüir, argumentar; VI (bicker) discutir, reñir
argument [árgjəmənt] N (reason) argumento *m*; (altercation) disputa *f*, discusión *f*
arid [ǽrɪd] ADJ árido
arise [əráɪz] VI (get up) levantarse; (appear) surgir; (result) provenir, resultar
arisen [ərízən] *see* arise
aristocracy [ærɪstɑ́krəsi] N aristocracia *f*
aristocrat [ərístəkræt] N aristócrata *mf*
aristocratic [ərɪstəkrǽdɪk] ADJ aristocrático
arithmetic[1] [əríθmətɪk] N aritmética *f*
arithmetic[2] [ærɪθmɛ́dɪk] ADJ aritmético
ark [ɑrk] N arca *f*; **Noah's** — arca de Noé *f*
arm [ɑrm] N brazo *m*; —**chair** sillón *m*, butaca *f*; —**pit** sobaco *m*, axila *f*; —**rest** (in a car) apoyabrazos *m sg*; (on a sofa) brazo *m*; — **in** — del brazo; **at** —**'s length** a distancia; —**'s-length transactions** transacciones a precio de mercado *f pl*; **with open** —**s** con los brazos abiertos; —**s** armas *f pl*; VT armar; —**ed forces** fuerzas armadas *f pl*; —**ed robbery** robo a mano armada *m*
armada [ɑrmáɖə] N armada *f*, flota *f*
armament [árməmənt] N armamento *m*
Armenia [ɑrmíniə] N Armenia *f*
Armenian [ɑrmíniən] ADJ & N armenio -nia *mf*
armful [ármfuł] N brazada *f*
armistice [ármɪstɪs] N armisticio *m*
armoire [ɑrmwár] N armario *m*
armor [ármɚ] N (of a knight) armadura *f*; (on a vehicle) blindaje *m*; (on insects) coraza *f*; VT (a

car) blindar; (a tank) acorazar
armored [ármə-d] ADJ (van) blindado; (tank) acorazado
armory [árməri] N armería f
army [ármi] N ejército m; (multitude) muchedumbre f
aroma [ərómə] N aroma m
aromatic [ærəmǽDIk] ADJ aromático
arose [əróz] see arise
around [əráUnd] ADV **there were books all** — había libros por todos lados; **there is a supermarket** — **here** hay un supermercado por aquí; **it was the only farm for miles** — era la única granja en millas a la redonda; **the tree is forty centimeters** — el árbol tiene cuarenta centímetros de circunferencia; **I'll show you** — te enseño el lugar; **the wheels turned** — las ruedas giraban; **turn** — date la vuelta; **she finally came** — al final la convencimos; **he hasn't been** — no ha estado por aquí; — **five o'clock** a eso de las cinco; PREP **a ribbon** — **her wrist** una cinta alrededor de su muñeca; **tie a string** — **your finger** átate un hilo al dedo; **stay** — **the house** quédate cerca de la casa; **we drove** — **the block** dimos vuelta a la manzana; **he wandered** — **the park** deambuló por el parque; **the church** — **the corner** la iglesia a la vuelta de la esquina; **a town with mountains** — **it** un pueblo rodeado de montañas; **motion** — **its axis** movimiento en torno a su eje; — **-the-clock** veinticuatro horas al día; **we walked** — **town** dimos una vuelta por el pueblo
arouse [əráUz] VI despertar; VT (suspicion) despertar; (sexual response) excitar
arraign [ərén] VT hacer comparecer ante un juez
arrange [əréndʒ] VT arreglar
arrangement [əréndʒmənt] N (array) arreglo m; (placement) disposición f; (agreement) acuerdo m; **to make** — **s [for]** hacer arreglos [para]
array [əré] N (arrangement) abanico m, selección f; (placement of troops) orden m, formación f; (attire) gala f; (in software) vector m; VT (troops) formar; (attire) ataviar
arrears [ərírz] ADV LOC **in** — atrasado; N atrasos m pl
arrest [ərést] N arresto m, detención f; VI/VT arrestar, detener
arrhythmia [əríðmiə] N arritmia f
arrival [əráɪvəł] N llegada f; lit arribo m; **the new** — **s** los recién llegados
arrive [əráɪv] VI llegar; lit arribar
arrogance [ǽrəgəns] N arrogancia f
arrogant [ǽrəgənt] ADJ arrogante
arrow [ǽro] N flecha f; lit saeta f; — **head** punta de flecha f

arsenal [ársənl] N arsenal m
arsenic [ársənɪk] N arsénico m
arson [ársən] N incendio doloso m
art [art] N arte m [sg] f [pl]; (works) obras f pl; (skill) destreza f; **fine** — **s** bellas artes f pl; **master of** — **s** maestría en humanidades f; — **deco** art déco m
arterial [artíriəł] ADJ arterial
arteriosclerosis [artiriosklərósɪs] N arteriosclerosis f
artery [árDəri] N arteria f
artful [ártfəł] ADJ (aesthetic) artístico; (deceitful) artero, astuto
arthritis [arθráɪDɪs] N artritis f
arthroscopic [arθrəskápɪk] ADJ artroscópico
arthroscopy [árθrəskapi] N artroscopia f
artichoke [árDɪtʃok] N alcachofa f
article [árDɪkəł] N artículo m; — **of clothing** prenda de vestir f
articulate[1] [artíkjəlɪt] ADJ (clear) claro; (eloquent) elocuente; **he's very** — se expresa muy bien
articulate[2] [artíkjəlet] VI/VT (pronounce, join) articular; (express) enunciar
articulation [artɪkjəléʃən] N articulación f
artifact [árDəfækt] N artefacto m, ingenio m
artifice [árDəfɪs] N artificio m
artificial [arDəfíʃəł] ADJ artificial; (affected) afectado; — **insemination** inseminación artificial f; — **intelligence** inteligencia artificial f
artillery [artíłəri] N artillería f
artisan [árDɪzən] N artesano -na mf, artífice mf
artist [árDɪst] N (painter, sculptor) artista mf; (performer) intérprete mf
artistic [artístɪk] ADJ artístico
Aruba [ərúbə] N Aruba f
as [æz] CONJ — **for me** en lo que a mí respecta; — **if** como si; — **is** en la condición en que está; — **it were** por decirlo así; — **of** a partir de; — **per** según; — **the illness worsened** a medida que empeoraba la enfermedad; — **yet** hasta ahora, todavía; **the same** — lo mismo que; **it broke** — **I was using it** se rompió cuando lo usaba; **we talked** — **he knitted** — we talked tejía mientras conversábamos; **he played** — **never before** jugó como nunca; PREP — **a child, I always felt loved** de niño, siempre me sentí querido; — **a teacher, I must be tough** como maestro, tengo que ser estricto; ADV tan, tanto; — **large** — tan grande como; — **long** — **you wish** todo el tiempo que quieras; — **much** — tanto como; — **well** también; **it's not** — **important** no es tan importante
ASAP [as soon as possible] [ésæp] ADV lo antes posible
asbestos [æzbéstəs] N asbesto m, amianto m
ascend [əsénd] VI ascender; — **ing order** orden

ascendente *m*
ascent [əsént] N ascenso *m*
ascertain [æsɚtén] VT averiguar, establecer
ascetic [əsɛ́DIk] ADJ ascético; N asceta *mf*
ascorbic [əskɔ́rbɪk] ADJ ascórbico
ascribe [əskráɪb] VT atribuir, imputar
aseptic [əsɛ́ptɪk] ADJ aséptico
asexual [esékʃuəɫ] ADJ asexual
ash [æʃ] N (residue, remains) ceniza *f*; (species of tree) fresno *m*; —**tray** cenicero *m*; — **Wednesday** miércoles de ceniza *m*
ashamed [əʃémd] ADJ avergonzado; **to be** — tener vergüenza, avergonzarse
ashen [ǽʃən] ADJ ceniciento
ashore [əʃɔ́r] ADV (movement) a tierra; (location) en tierra; **to go** — desembarcar
Asia [éʒə] N Asia *f*
Asian [éʒən] ADJ & N asiático -ca *mf*
Asiatic [eʒiǽDIk] ADJ — **flu** gripe asiática *f*
aside [əsáɪd] ADV **all kidding** — bromas aparte; **his father took him** — su padre lo llamó aparte; **he threw his coat** — tiró su saco a un lado; PREP — **from** aparte de, además de; N (theater) aparte *m*
asinine [ǽsənaɪn] ADJ necio
ask [æsk] VT (inquire) preguntar; (request) pedir; **to** — **a question** hacer una pregunta; **to** — **about** preguntar por; **to** — **for** pedir; **to** — **for someone** pedir para hablar con alguien; **to** — **a woman's hand in marriage** pedir la mano de una mujer; **what's your** —**ing price?** ¿cuánto pides? **you** —**ed for it** te lo has buscado
askance [əskǽns] ADV **to look** — (obliquely) mirar de soslayo/través/reojo; (suspiciously) mirar con recelo
askew [əskjú] ADJ ladeado, torcido
asleep [əslíp] ADJ dormido; **to fall** — dormirse; **my arm is** — se me ha dormido/entumecido el brazo
asparagus [əspǽrəgəs] N espárrago *m*
aspartame [ǽspɚtem] N aspartamo *m*
aspect [ǽspɛkt] N aspecto *m*
aspen [ǽspɪn] N álamo temblón *m*
Asperger's disorder [ǽspɚgɚzdɪsɔ́rDɚ] N trastorno de Asperger *m*
asphalt [ǽsfɑɫt] N asfalto *m*
asphyxia [æsfíksiə] N asfixia *f*
aspiration [æspəréʃən] N aspiración *f*
aspire [əspáɪr] VI aspirar
aspirin [ǽsprɪn] N aspirina *f*
ass [æs] N (animal) asno *m*, burro *m*, borrico *m*; (fool) *fam, pej* borrico -ca *mf*, idiota *mf*; (body part) *vulg* culo *m*; —**hole** *vulg* hijo de puta *m*; **to bust one's** — *vulg* romperse el culo
assail [əséɫ] VT (physically) asaltar, atacar; (verbally) atacar
assailant [əsélənt] N atacante *mf*, agresor -ora *mf*

assassin [əsǽsɪn] N asesino -na *mf*
assassinate [əsǽsənet] VT asesinar
assassination [əsæsənéʃən] N asesinato *m*
assault [əsɑ́ɫt] N asalto *m*, agresión *f*; — **rifle** rifle de asalto *m*; — **and battery** agresión con lesiones *f*; VT asaltar, agredir; (sexually) violar
assay[1] [æsé] VT (situation) examinar, analizar; (metal) ensayar
assay[2] [ǽse] N ensayo *m*
assemble [əsɛ́mbəɫ] VI/VT (call together) reunir[se], congregar[se]; VT (put together) armar, montar
assembly [əsɛ́mbli] N (meeting) asamblea *f*, reunión *f*; (putting together) montaje *m*, armado *m*; — **language** lenguaje ensamblador *m*; — **line** cadena de producción *f*, línea de montaje *f*
assent [əsɛ́nt] N asentimiento *m*; VI asentir
assert [əsɚ́t] VT (declare) aseverar, afirmar; **to** — **one's rights** hacer valer los derechos de uno; **to** — **oneself** obrar con firmeza
assertion [əsɚ́ʃən] N (declaration) aseveración *f*, afirmación *f*, aserto *m*; **an** — **of ownership** una afirmación de los derechos de propiedad
assess [əsɛ́s] VT (evaluate for tax purposes) tasar; (impose tax) gravar, imponer; (measure performance) evaluar
assessment [əsɛ́smənt] N (estimate) avalúo *m*, tasación *f*; (tax) imposición *f*, gravamen *m*; (testing) evaluación *f*
asset [ǽsɛt] N (useful thing) ventaja *f*; (useful quality) virtud *f*; —**s** activo *m*, bienes *m pl*; (on balance sheet) haber *m*, activo *m*; **personal** —**s** bienes muebles *m pl*; **real** —**s** bienes inmuebles *m pl*
assiduous [əsídʒuəs] ADJ (constant) asiduo; (industrious) diligente
assign [əsáɪn] VT (allot) asignar; (appoint, designate) designar; (transfer property) ceder
assignment [əsáɪnmənt] N (act of assigning) asignación *f*; (task) encargo *m*, encomienda *f*; (mission) misión *f*; (transfer of property) cesión [de bienes] *f*; (homework) tarea *f*; (lesson) lección *f*
assimilate [əsíməlet] VI/VT asimilar[se]
assist [əsíst] VI/VT ayudar, asistir; N (in sports) asistencia *f*
assistance [əsístəns] N ayuda *f*, asistencia *f*
assistant [əsístənt] N ayudante *mf*, asistente -ta *mf*; ADJ auxiliar; — **manager** subgerente *mf*
assistantship [əsístəntʃɪp] N ayudantía *f*
associate[1] [əsóʃiɪt] ADJ asociado; N (acquaintance) compañero -ra *mf*; (co-worker) colega *mf*; (employee) empleado -da *mf*
associate[2] [əsóʃiet] VI/VT asociar[se]; **to be** —**d with** asociarse con
association [əsosiéʃən] N asociación *f*

assonance [ǽsənəns] N asonancia *f*
assorted [əsɔ́rDɪd] ADJ variado, surtido
assortment [əsɔ́rtmənt] N (act of assorting) clasificación *f*; (selection of wares) surtido *m*; (selection of tools, etc.) colección *f*
assume [əsúm] VT (responsibility, role) asumir; (right) arrogarse; (suppose) dar por sentado, suponer; **—d name** alias *m*
assumption [əsʌ́mpʃən] N (premise) suposición *f*, supuesto *m*; (unstated belief) sobreentendido *m*; (seizure) toma *f*; (acceptance of duties) asunción *f*
assurance [əʃúrəns] N (promise) promesa *f*, palabra *f*; (reassurance) palabras de apoyo *f pl*; (certainty) certeza *f*; (confidence) confianza *f*
assure [əʃúr] VT (give confidence) asegurar; (encourage) infundir confianza
assuredly [əʃúrɪdli] ADV seguramente, sin duda
asterisk [ǽstərɪsk] N asterisco *m*
asteroid [ǽstərɔɪd] N asteroide *m*
asthma [ǽzmə] N asma *m*
asthmatic [æzmǽDɪk] ADJ asmático
astigmatism [əstígmətɪzəm] N astigmatismo *m*
astonish [əstánɪʃ] VT asombrar, pasmar
astonishing [əstánɪʃɪŋ] ADJ asombroso, pasmoso
astonishment [əstánɪʃmənt] M asombro *m*, pasmo *m*
astound [əstáʊnd] VT pasmar, asombrar
astraddle [əstrǽdl̩] ADV a horcajadas
astray [əstré] ADV **to go —** perderse, extraviarse; **to lead —** (seduce) llevar por mal camino, seducir; (perplex) confundir
astride [əstráɪd] ADV a horcajadas
astringent [əstríndʒənt] ADJ & N astringente *m*
astrology [əstrálədʒi] N astrología *f*
astronaut [ǽstrənɔt] M astronauta *mf*
astronautics [æstrənɔ́Dɪks] N astronáutica *f*
astronomer [əstránəmɚ] N astrónomo -ma *mf*
astronomic [æstrənámɪk] ADJ astronómico
astronomical [æstrənámɪkəl̩] ADJ astronómico
astronomy [əstránəmi] N astronomía *f*
astrophysics [æstrofízɪks] N astrofísica *f*
Asturian [æstúriən] ADJ & N asturiano -na *mf*
Asturias [æstúriəs] N Asturias *f sg*
astute [əstút] ADJ astuto, sagaz
asylum [əsáɪləm] N asilo *m*
asymmetric, asymmetrical [esɪmétrɪk[əl]] ADJ; asimétrico
asymptomatic [esɪmptəmǽDɪk] ADJ asintomático
at [æt] PREP **— the end of the story** al final de la historia; **— five o'clock** a las cinco; **— high altitude** a grandes alturas; **— last** por fin, al fin; **— once** enseguida; **— the table** a/ en la mesa; **— five dollars a kilo** a cinco dólares el kilo; **— Easter** en Pascua; **— home** en casa; **— war** en guerra; **wait — the door** espera en la puerta; **he is — peace with**

himself está en paz consigo mismo; **the children are — play** los niños están jugando; **look — that** mira eso; **amazed —** pasmado por; **he laughed — me** se rió de mí
ate [et] *see* eat
atheism [éθiɪzəm] N ateísmo *m*
atheist [éθiɪst] N ateo -a *mf*
athlete [ǽθlit] N deportista *mf*; (track and field) atleta *mf*; **—'s foot** pie de atleta *m*
athletic [æθléDɪk] ADJ deportivo; (concerning track and field; well-built) atlético
athletics [æθléDɪks] N deporte *m*; (track and field) atletismo *m*
Atlantic [ætlǽntɪk] ADJ atlántico; **— Ocean** Océano Atlántico *m*
atlas [ǽtləs] N atlas *m*
ATM [automatic teller machine] [étiém] N cajero automático *m*
atmosphere [ǽtməsfɪr] N (air) atmósfera *f*; (mood) ambiente *m*
atmospheric [ætməsfírɪk] ADJ atmosférico
atom [ǽDəm] N átomo *m*; **— bomb** bomba atómica *f*
atomic [ətámɪk] ADJ atómico; **— age** era atómica *f*; **— energy** energía atómica *f*; **— number** número atómico *m*; **— weight** peso atómico *m*
atomize [ǽDəmaɪz] VT atomizar
atomizer [ǽDəmaɪzɚ] N atomizador *m*
atone [ətón] VI **to — for** expiar, purgar
atonement [ətónmənt] N expiación *f*, purgación *f*
atop [ətáp] PREP encima de
atrium [étriəm] N (of office building, hotel) vestíbulo *m*, patio central *m*; (of church) atrio *m*
atrocious [ətróʃəs] ADJ atroz
atrocity [ətrásɪDi] N atrocidad *f*, barbaridad *f*
atrophy [ǽtrəfi] N atrofia *f*; VI/VT atrofiar[se]
attach [ətǽtʃ] VI/VT (pipe, cable) unir[se], juntar; (paper) sujetar; (wages) retener; (significance) atribuir; (an electronic file) adjuntar; **to be —ed to someone** estar apegado a alguien
attaché [ætæʃé] N agregado -da *mf*
attachment [ətǽtʃmənt] N (act of attaching) unión *f*; (pipe, cable) conexión *f*; (of wages) retención *f*; (significance) atribución *f*; (to an e-mail) adjunto *m*; (affection) apego *m*, cariño *m*; (accessory) accesorio *m*
attack [ətǽk] N ataque *m*, acometida *f*; VI/VT atacar, acometer
attain [ətén] VT (rank) alcanzar; (ambition) lograr *m*, realizar *f*; VI (age) llegar a
attainment [əténmənt] N (rank) alcance *m*; (ambition) logro *m*, realización *f*
attempt [ətémpt] N tentativa *f*, intento *m*; (murder) atentado *m*; VT tratar [de], intentar
attend [əténd] VT (meeting) asistir a, acudir a; VI **to — to** (a sick person) atender, cuidar; (a

speaker) prestar atención; —**ing physician**
médico -ca tratante *mf*
attendance [əténdəns] N asistencia *f*
attendant [əténdənt] N (at a gas station)
encargado -da *mf*; (servant) sirviente -ta *mf*;
ADJ concomitante
attention [əténʃən] N atención *f*; (courtesy)
atenciones *f pl*; — **deficit disorder**
trastorno de déficit de atención *m*; **to pay** —
prestar atención; **to pay** — **to** atender a; **to
call** — llamar la atención; INTERJ —! ¡firmes!
attentive [əténtɪv] ADJ (focused) atento;
(courteous) cortés
attenuate [əténjuet] VT atenuar
attest [ətést] VT (bear witness to) atestiguar;
(manifest) demostrar; VI certificar, dar fe,
atestar
attic [ǽdɪk] N desván *m*, altillo *m*
attire [ətáɪr] N atavío *m*, vestidura *f*; VT ataviar
attitude [ǽdɪtud] N (mental) actitud *f*; (physical)
postura *f*; (insolence) insolencia *f*, descaro *m*
attorney [ətɚ́ni] N abogado -da *mf*, mandatario
-ria *mf*; — **General** Ministro -tra de Justicia
mf
attract [ətrǽkt] VT atraer; **to** — **attention**
llamar la atención
attraction [ətrǽkʃən] N (act, power) atracción
f; (charm) atractivo *m*; (of customers)
captación *f*
attractive [ətrǽktɪv] ADJ atractivo; (beautiful)
atractivo, agraciado
attractiveness [ətrǽktɪvnɪs] N atractivo *m*
attribute[1] [ǽtrəbjut] N atributo *m*
attribute[2] [ətríbjut] VT atribuir
attribution [ætrəbjúʃən] N atribución *f*
attrition [ətríʃən] N (wearing out) desgaste *m*;
(casualties) bajas *f pl*; **war of** — guerra de
agotamiento *f*
atypical [etípɪkəɫ] ADJ atípico
auburn [ɔ́bɚn] N & ADJ castaño rojizo *m*
auction [ɔ́kʃən] N subasta *f*, remate *m*; — **house**
casa de subastas *f*; VI/VT subastar, rematar
auctioneer [ɔkʃənír] N subastador -ra *mf*,
rematador -ra *mf*
audacious [ɔdéʃəs] ADJ audaz, atrevido
audacity [ɔdǽsɪdi] N audacia *f*, desfachatez *f*,
atrevimiento *m*
audible [ɔ́dəbəɫ] ADJ audible; — **feedback**
regeneración audible *f*
audience [ɔ́diəns] N público *m*, auditorio *m*; (TV,
radio) audiencia *f*
audio [ɔ́dio] ADJ de audio; — **book** audiolibro *m*;
— **frequency** audiofrecuencia *f*; —**visual**
audiovisual; —**visuals** audiovisuales *m pl*; N
audio *m*
audiology [ɔdiálədʒi] N audiología *f*
audit [ɔ́dɪt] VI/VT (class) asistir de oyente;
(accounts) auditar; N auditoría *f*; — **cycle**
ciclo de auditoría *m*

auditing [ɔ́dɪtɪŋ] N auditoría *f*
audition [ɔdíʃən] N audición *f*; VI dar una
audición [para]
auditor [ɔ́dɪdɚ] N (of accounts) auditor -ora *mf*,
contralor -ora *mf*; (of a class) oyente *mf*
auditorium [ɔdɪtɔ́riəm] N auditorio *m*,
paraninfo *m*
auditory [ɔ́dɪtɔri] ADJ auditivo
augment [ɔgmént] VT incrementar, aumentar
August [ɔ́gəst] N agosto *m*
aunt [ænt] N tía *f*
aura [ɔ́rə] N aura *f*
aurora [ərɔ́rə] N aurora *f*; — **borealis** aurora
boreal *f*
auspices [ɔ́spɪsɪz] N auspicios *m pl*
auspicious [ɔspíʃəs] ADJ propicio
austere [ɔstír] ADJ austero
austerity [ɔstérɪdi] N austeridad *f*
Australia [ɔstréljə] N Australia *f*
Australian [ɔstréljən] ADJ & N australiano -na
mf
Austria [ɔ́striə] N Austria *f*
Austrian [ɔ́striən] ADJ & N austríaco -ca *mf*
authentic [ɔθéntɪk] ADJ auténtico
authenticate [ɔθéntɪket] VT autenticar
authentication [ɔθentɪkéʃən] N legalización *f*
authenticity [ɔθentísɪdi] N autenticidad *f*
author [ɔ́θɚ] N (professional) escritor -ra *mf*;
(creator) autor -ora *mf*
authoritarian [əθɔrɪtérian] ADJ autoritario
authoritative [əθɔ́rɪtedɪv] ADJ (official)
autorizado; (dictatorial) autoritario
authority [əθɔ́rɪdi] N autoridad *f*; (permission)
autorización *f*; **to have on good** — saber de
buena fuente; **it's not within your** — no
está dentro de tus facultades
authorization [ɔθɚɪzéʃən] N autorización *f*
authorize [ɔ́θəraɪz] VT autorizar, habilitar
autism [ɔ́tɪzəm] N autismo *m*
autistic [ɔtístɪk] ADJ autista
auto [ɔ́do] *see* automobile, automatic
autobiography [ɔdobaɪágrəfi] N autobiografía *f*
autocrat [ɔ́dəkræt] N autócrata *mf*
autograph [ɔ́dəgræf] N autógrafo *m*
autoimmune [ɔdoɪmjún] ADJ autoinmune
automated [ɔ́dəmedɪd] ADJ automatizado
automatic [ɔdəmǽdɪk] ADJ automático;
(response) maquinal; — **backup** (copy) copia
de respaldo automático *f*; (process) respaldo
automático *m*; — **pilot** piloto automático *m*;
— **transmission** transmisión automática *f*
automation [ɔdəméʃən] N automatización *f*
automobile [ɔ́dəməbiɫ] N automóvil *m*
automotive [ɔdəmódɪv] ADJ (sport)
automovilístico; (industry) automotor,
automotriz
autonomic [ɔdənámɪk] ADJ autonómico
autonomous [ɔtánəməs] ADJ autónomo
autonomy [ɔtánəmi] N autonomía *f*

autopilot [ɔ́DopaIlət] N piloto automático *m*
autopsy [ɔ́tapsi] N autopsia *f*
autumn [ɔ́Dəm] N otoño *m*
autumnal [ɔtʌ́mnəł] ADJ otoñal
auxiliary [ɔgzíləri] ADJ & N auxiliar *mf*
avail [əvéł] VI/VT servir; **to — oneself of** aprovecharse de; N utilidad *f*; **of no —** de ninguna utilidad; **to no —** en vano
availability [əveləbílIDi] N (of a person, taxicab, funds) disponibilidad *f*; (of merchandise) existencias *f pl*
available [əvéləbəł] ADJ disponible, asequible
avalanche [ǽvəlæntʃ] N avalancha *f*, alud *m*
avarice [ǽvərIs] N avaricia *f*
avaricious [ævəríʃəs] ADJ avaro, avariento
avatar [ǽvətɑr] N avatar *m*
avenge [əvéndʒ] VT vengar
avenger [əvéndʒɚ] N vengador -ra *mf*
avenue [ǽvənu] N avenida *f*; (means of access) vía *f*
aver [əvɚ́] VT afirmar
average [ǽvrIdʒ] N promedio *m*; **on —** de promedio; ADJ medio, mediano; **just —** (person) del montón; (thing) nada del otro mundo; VT promediar; **he —s 20 miles an hour** hace un promedio de 20 millas por hora
averse [əvɚ́s] ADJ reacio; **he's not — to a glass of wine** no se opone a una copa de vino
aversion [əvɚ́ʒən] N aversión *f*
avert [əvɚ́t] VT (eyes) desviar, apartar; (danger) evitar
aviation [eviéʃən] N aviación *f*
aviator [évieDɚ] N aviador -ra *mf*
avid [ǽvId] ADJ ávido
avocado [ævəkáDo] N aguacate *m*; *Am* palta *f*
avocation [ævəkéʃən] N pasatiempo *m*
avoid [əvɔ́Id] VI/VT (stay away from) evitar; (dodge) esquivar
avow [əváU] VT confesar
avowal [əváUəł] N confesión *f*
avuncular [əvʌ́ŋkjələ] ADJ propio de un tío; **— attitude** actitud paternal y amistosa
await [əwét] VT aguardar
awake [əwék] ADJ despierto; VI/VT despertar[se]
awaken [əwékən] VI/VT despertar[se]
award [əwɔ́rd] N premio *m*, galardón *m*; (judicial) adjudicación *f*; VT otorgar, adjudicar
aware [əwér] ADJ consciente, enterado; **I'm — of that** eso me consta
awareness [əwérnIs] N conciencia *f*
away [əwé] ADV **far —** lejos; **— from his family** lejos de su familia; **she looked —** apartó la vista; **she's —** no está; **he's been painting — all day** se ha pasado todo el día pintando; **right —** ahora mismo, ahorita; **ten miles —** a diez millas de distancia; **to give —** regalar; **to go —** irse; **to take —** quitar; **to blow —** (destroy) [hacer] volar;

(astonish) dejar atónito
awe [ɔ] N sobrecogimiento *m*; **to be in —** sobrecogerse; VT sobrecoger
awesome [ɔ́səm] ADJ (awe-inspiring) sobrecogedor; (impressive) fabuloso
awestruck [ɔ́strʌk] ADJ pasmado
awful [ɔ́fəł] ADJ terrible, horroroso; ADV espantoso
awhile [əhwáIł] ADV un rato
awkward [ɔ́kwɚd] ADJ (clumsy) torpe, desmañado; (embarrassing) embarazoso; (unwieldy) incómodo
awl [ɔ́ł] N punzón *m*
awning [ɔ́nIŋ] N toldo *m*
awoke [əwók] *see* wake
awoken [əwókn̩] *see* wake
awry [ərái] ADJ (clothes) mal puesto; (hat) ladeado; **my plans went —** mis planes fracasaron rotundamente
ax, axe [æks] N hacha *f*; VT eliminar
axis [ǽksIs] N eje *m*
axle [ǽksəł] N eje *m*
Azerbaijan [æzɚbaIdʒán] N Azerbaiyán *m*
Azerbaijani, Azerbaijanian [æzɚbaIdʒáni[ən]] ADJ & N azerbaijano -na *mf*, azerbaiyano -na *mf*
Aztec [ǽztɛk] ADJ & N azteca *mf*
azure [ǽʒɚ] ADJ [azul] celeste; N azul celeste *m*

Bb

babble [bǽbəł] N (baby talk) balbuceo *m*; (chatter) parloteo *m*; (murmur) murmullo *m*; VI (to talk like a baby) balbucear; (to chatter) parlotear; (to murmur) murmurar
baboon [bæbún] N babuino *m*
baby [bébi] N bebé *mf*; **who's the — in your family?** ¿quién es el menor/benjamín en tu familia? **— blue** celeste *m*; **— boomer** persona nacida entre 1946 y 1965 *f*; **— carriage** cochecito de bebé *m*; **— food** comida para bebés *f*; **— girl** nena *f*; **— sister** hermanita *f*; **— sitter** niñera *f*; **— talk** habla infantil *f*; **— tooth** diente de leche *m*; **to —sit** cuidar niños; **she had a —** dio a luz; VT mimar
baccalaureate [bækəlɔ́riət] N bachillerato *m*
bachelor [bǽtʃələ] N soltero *m*; **—'s degree** licenciatura *f*; **— of Arts** (degree) licenciatura en filosofía y letras *f*; (person) licenciado -da en filosofía y letras *mf*
bacillus [bəsíləs] N bacilo *m*
back [bæk] N (human body part) espalda *f*; (animal body part) lomo *m*; (opposite side) dorso *m*; (of chair) respaldo *m*, espaldar *m*;

—**ache** dolor de espalda *m*; —**bone** columna vertebral *f*, espinazo *m*; —**pack** mochila *f*; **behind one's** — a espaldas de uno; **he has no** —**bone** no tiene carácter; **in** — **of** detrás de, tras; **in the** — **of the house** atrás de la casa; **to fall on one's** — caer de espaldas; **to turn one's** — volver las espaldas; ADJ — **charges** cargos atrasados *m pl*; — **door** puerta trasera *f*; — **issues** números atrasados *m pl*; — **order** pedido pendiente *m*; — **taxes** impuestos atrasados *m pl*; **on the** — **burner** en suspenso; —-**and-forth movement** movimiento de vaivén *m*; VT respaldar, apoyar; VI dar marcha atrás; **to** — **down** echarse [para] atrás, recular; **to** — **up** (in a car) dar marcha atrás; (a file) hacer una copia de seguridad de; ADV (look) atrás / para atrás; (fall) de espaldas; **to** — **off** echarse atrás; — **and forth** de aquí para allá; **he ran** — **to the house** volvió corriendo a la casa; **he's** — **from work** está de vuelta del trabajo

backbite [bǽkbaɪt] VI/VT difamar

back date [bǽk det] VT antedatar

backer [bǽkɚ] N (financial) fiador -ra *mf*; (political) partidario -ria *mf*

backfire [bǽkfaɪr] VI (automobile) petardear, hacer detonaciones; (plan) ser contraproducente; N petardeo *m*

backgammon [bǽkgæmən] N backgammon *m*

background [bǽkgraʊnd] N (of a picture) fondo *m*; (experience) antecedentes *m pl*; (software) — **application** aplicación de fondo *f*; — **noise** ruido de fondo *m*; **I have a** — **in computers** tengo conocimientos de informática; **I know what goes on in the** — sé lo que pasa entre bastidores; **a humble** — orígenes humildes *m pl*

backhand [bǽkhænd] N revés *m*

backing [bǽkɪŋ] N (support) respaldo *m*, apoyo *m*; (guarantee) garantía *f*; (fabric) refuerzo *m*

backlash [bǽklæʃ] N reacción violenta *f*

backlighting [bǽklaɪDɪŋ] N retroiluminación *f*

backlit [bǽklɪt] ADJ retroiluminado

backlog [bǽklɑg] N atraso *m*

backpack [bǽklɑg] N mochila *f*; VI viajar con mochila

backseat [bǽksít] N asiento trasero *m*

backslash [bǽkslæʃ] N barra invertida *f*

backslide [bǽkslaɪd] VI volver a las andadas, reincidir

backspace [bǽkspes] N (action) retroceso *m*; (key) tecla de retroceso *f*; VI apretar la tecla de retroceso

backspin [bǽkspɪn] N efecto *m*, cortado *m*

backstage [bækstédʒ] ADV entre bastidores

backtrack [bǽktræk] VI retroceder, dar marcha atrás

backup [bǽkʌp] N (support) respaldo *m*; (copy) copia de seguridad *f*

backward [bǽkwɚd] ADV hacia atrás, para atrás; — **search** búsqueda hacia atrás *f*; **to go** — recular; ADJ (underdeveloped) atrasado; (reactionary) retrógrado

backwardness [bǽkwɚdnɪs] N (underdevelopment) atraso *m*; (conservatism) retrogradismo *m*; (timidity) timidez *f*

backyard [bǽkjárd] N patio trasero *m*

bacon [békən] N tocino *m*, *Sp* beicon *m*

bacteria [bæktíriə] N bacteria[s] *f* [*pl*]

bacterial [bæktíriəł] ADJ bacteriano

bacteriology [bæktiriáləʤi] N bacteriología *f*

bad [bæd] ADJ malo; (man) perverso; (teeth) feo; (drug) dañoso; (flood) grave; (fruit) podrido; (very good) *vulg* de puta madre; — **blood** enemistad *f*; — **check** cheque sin fondos *m*; — **debt** deuda incobrable *f*; — **faith** mala fe *f*; **to go from** — **to worse** ir de mal en peor; **he has a** — **heart** está enfermo del corazón; **to look** — tener mal aspecto; *fam* quedar mal; ADV mal; **not** — no está nada mal; **too** — ¡qué pena! VT **to** —**mouth** difamar [a]

bade [bed] *see* bid

badge [bæʤ] N insignia *f*, chapa *f*

badger [bǽʤɚ] N tejón *m*; VT acosar

badly [bǽdli] ADV (do) mal; (want) mucho; (hurt) gravemente

baffle [bǽfəł] VT (confuse) confundir; (frustrate) desconcertar; N deflector *m*

bag [bæg] N bolsa *f*, bolso *m*; (suitcase) maleta *f*; (under eyes) ojera *f*; — **lady** vagabunda *f*; —**pipe** gaita *f*; VT (groceries) empacar, embolsar; (prey) cazar

baggage [bǽgɪʤ] N (suitcases) equipaje *m*; (impediments) bagaje *m*; — **car** vagón de equipajes *m*; — **check** contraseña de equipajes *f*; — **claim** recogida de equipaje *f*; — **tag** etiqueta *f*; — **inspection** revisión de equipaje *f*

baggy [bǽgi] ADJ flojo, holgado

Bahamas [bəháməz] N Bahamas *f pl*

Bahamian [bəhémiən] ADJ & N bahameño -ña *mf*

Bahrain [bɑrén] N Bahréin *m*

Bahraini [bɑréni] ADJ & N bahreiní *mf*

bail [beł] N fianza *f*; —**out** rescate financiero *m*; **to let out on** — poner en libertad bajo fianza; VT pagar la fianza; **to** — **someone out** pagarle la fianza a alguien; **to** — **someone out of a predicament** sacar a alguien de un apuro; **to** — **out water** achicar, vaciar; VI **to** — **out** (of a plane) tirarse con paracaídas de un avión; (of a situation) abandonar

bailiff [bélɪf] N ujier *mf*

bait [bet] N cebo *m*; VT (prepare hook) cebar; (attract customers) seducir; (harass) acosar; — **and switch advertising** publicidad de cebo y anzuelo *f*

bake [bek] VI/VT (in an oven) hornear; (in the sun) calcinar, abrasar; **I'm baking in this heat** me estoy asando, me muero de calor

baker [békə-] N panadero -ra *mf*; **—'s dozen** la docena del fraile *f*

bakery [békəri] N panadería *f*

baking [békɪŋ] N (act of baking) horneado *m*; (activity) repostería *f*; **— powder** polvo de hornear *m*; **— soda** bicarbonato de sodio *m*

balance [bǽləns] N (instrument) balanza *f*; (equilibrium) equilibrio *m*; (debit, credit) saldo *m*, balance *m*; **— due** saldo pendiente *m*; **— sheet** balance *m*; **— of payments** balanza de pagos *f*; **— of trade** balanza comercial *f*; **to lose one's —** perder el equilibrio; VT equilibrar, hacer equilibrio con; **to — the risks with the benefits** sopesar los riesgos y los beneficios; VI (accounts) cuadrar; **—ed budget** presupuesto equilibrado *m*; **to — a budget** equilibrar un presupuesto

balanced [bǽlənst] ADJ equilibrado

balancing [bǽlənsɪŋ] N equilibrado *m*

balcony [bǽłkəni] N balcón *m*; (in a theater) palco *m*, entresuelo *m*

bald [bɔłd] ADJ (person) calvo, pelón; (mountain) pelón; (tire) liso; **— eagle** águila americana de cabeza blanca *f*; **—headed** calvo; **— spot** calva *f*; **he went —** se quedó calvo

baldness [bɔ́łdnɪs] N calvicie *f*

bale [beł] N paca *f*, fardo *m*; VT empacar, enfardar

balk [bɔk] VI oponerse, rehusarse a

ball [bɔł] N (tennis, baseball, golf) pelota *f*, bola *f*; (baseball, opposite of strike) bola *f*; (basketball, football, soccer) balón *m*; (billiards) bola *f*; (of string, thread) ovillo *m*; (cannon) bala [de cañón] *f*; (dance) baile *m*; **— and chain** grillete *m*; **— bearing** cojinete de bolas *m*; **— game** juego de pelota *m*; (baseball) partido de béisbol *m*; **—park estimate** cifra aproximada *f*; **—s** (testicles) *vulg* pelotas *f pl*, *vulg* huevos *m pl*; *Sp vulg* cojones *m pl*; VT (string) ovillar; (have sex with) *Sp vulg* follar; *Am vulg* coger, culear

ballad [bǽləd] N balada *f*; (historical) romance *m*

ballast [bǽləst] N lastre *m*; (railroad) balasto *m*; VT lastrar

ballerina [bælərínə] N bailarina de ballet *f*

ballet [bælé] N ballet *m*

ballistic [bəlístɪk] ADJ balístico; **— missile** misil balístico *m*; N **—s** balística *f*

balloon [bəlún] N globo *m*; **— mortgage** hipoteca con pago final mayor *f*; VI (travel in a balloon) pasear en globo; VI/VT (grow) inflar[se]

ballot [bǽlət] N (system of voting) votación *f*; (paper) papeleta *f*; *Mex* boleta *f*; **— box** urna *f*

balm [bam] N bálsamo *m*

balmy [bámi] ADJ templado

baloney [bəlóni] N pamplinas *f pl*, paparruchas *f pl*

balsa [bɔ́łsə] N (wood) madera balsa *f*; (raft) balsa *f*

balsam [bɔ́łsəm] N (resin) bálsamo *m*; (tree) especie de abeto *m*

bamboo [bæmbú] N bambú *m*

ban [bæn] N prohibición *f*; (church) excomunión *f*; VT prohibir

banal [bénl] ADJ banal

banana [bənǽnə] N plátano *m*, banana *f*; **— grove** platanar *m*; **— split** banana split *m*; **— tree** plátano *m*, banano *m*

band [bænd] N (group) banda *f*, pandilla *f*; (group of musicians) banda *f*, conjunto *m*; (cloth) banda *f*; (ribbon) cinta *f*; (leather) tira *f*; **to join the —wagon** subirse al carro/tren; **—width** amplitud de banda *f*; VI/VT **to — together** unirse, juntarse

bandage [bǽndɪdʒ] N venda *f*, vendaje *m*; VT vendar

Band-aid® [bǽnded] N Curita® *f*, parche *m*

bandit [bǽndɪt] N bandido -da *mf*, bandolero -ra *mf*, salteador -ora *mf*

bang [bæŋ] N (blow) golpe *m*, golpazo *m*; (sound) estampido *m*, estallido *m*; **—s** fleco *m*, flequillo *m*; **I get a — out of seeing my grandkids** me emociona ver a mis nietos; VI/VT (hit) golpear; (make noise) hacer estrépito; (screw) *Sp vulg* follar; *Am vulg* coger, culear

Bangladesh [bæŋglədéʃ] N Bangladesh *m*

Bangladeshi [bæŋglədéʃi] ADJ & N bangladeshí *mf*, bangladesí *mf*, bengalés -esa

banish [bǽnɪʃ] VT desterrar

banishment [bǽnɪʃmənt] N destierro *m*, proscripción *f*

banister [bǽnɪstə-] N barandal *m*, pasamano[s] *m*, balaustrada *f*

banjo [bǽndʒo] N banjo *m*

bank [bæŋk] N (financial institution) banco *m*; (in gambling) banca *f*; (of a body of water) orilla *f*, ribera *f*, margen *m*; (slope) escarpa *f*; **— card** tarjeta bancaria *f*; **— account** cuenta bancaria *f*; **— check** cheque de caja *m*; **— failure** quiebra bancaria *f*; **—note** billete *m*; **— statement** estado de cuenta *m*; **— vault** cámara *f*; ADJ bancario, de banco; VT (money) depositar en un banco; VI (snow, sand) amontonar; (airplane) ladear; **to — on** contar con; **to —roll** financiar

banker [bǽŋkə-] N (bank owner) banquero -ra *mf*; (bank employee) bancario -ria *mf*

banking [bǽŋkɪŋ] N (activity) actividad bancaria *f*; (industry) banca *f*; ADJ bancario, de banco

bankrupt [bǽŋkrʌpt] ADJ en bancarrota, en quiebra; VT arruinar, quebrar

bankruptcy [bǽŋkrʌptsi] N bancarrota *f*, quiebra *f*; **— law** estatuto de quiebras *m*; —

proceedings juicio por quiebra *m*; **to go into** — declararse en quiebra
banner [bǽnə-] N estandarte *m*, pendón *m*; ADJ sobresaliente
banquet [bǽŋkwɪt] N banquete *m*, gala *f*
baptism [bǽptɪzəm] N (sacrament) bautismo *m*; (action) bautizo *m*
baptize [bǽptaɪz] VT bautizar
bar [bɑr] N (of iron, sand, soap, of a tavern) barra *f*; (of chocolate) barra *f*, tableta *f*; (vertical rod) barrote *m*; (obstacle) barrera *f*, obstáculo *m*; (in music) compás *m*; (saloon) bar *m*; —**bell** barra para pesas *f*; —**code** código de barras *m*; —**code reader** lector de código de barras *m*; — **graph** gráfica de barras *f*; —**keeper/tender** tabernero -ra *mf*, cantinero -ra *mf*; —**room** bar *m*; —**room brawl** pelea de borrachos *f*; **behind** —**s** tras las rejas; **to be admitted to the** — recibirse de abogado; VT (door, exit) atrancar; (access) impedir; (from membership) excluir; — **none** sin excepción; —**ring a disaster** salvo en caso de desastre
barb [bɑrb] N púa *f*; —**ed wire** alambre de púas *m*; *Sp* alambre de espino *m*
Barbadian [bɑrbéɪdiən] ADJ & N barbadense *mf*
Barbados [bɑrbéɪdos] N Barbados *m*
barbarian [bɑrbériən] ADJ & N bárbaro -ra *mf*
barbaric [bɑrbǽrɪk] ADJ bárbaro
barbarous [bɑ́rbə-əs] ADJ bárbaro
barbecue [bɑ́rbɪkju] N (meat dish) barbacoa *f*, asado *m*, parrillada *f*; — **sauce** adobo de barbacoa *m*; VI/VT asar con adobo
barber [bɑ́rbə-] N peluquero *m*, barbero *m*; —**shop** peluquería *f*, barbería *f*
barbiturate [bɑrbítʃə-ɪt] N barbitúrico *m*
bard [bɑrd] N bardo *m*
bare [bɛr] ADJ (legs, walls) desnudo; (pantry) vacío; —**back** a pelo; —-**bones** básico; —**faced** descarado; —**foot** descalzo; **the** — **necessities** lo imprescindible; —**headed** con la cabeza descubierta; —**legged** con las piernas desnudas; — **majority** escasa mayoría *f*; **to lay** — poner al descubierto; **with his** — **hands** con las propias manos
barely [bérli] ADV apenas
bargain [bɑ́rgɪn] N (agreement) trato *m*; (inexpensive purchase) ganga *f*, ocasión *f*; — **basement** sección de ofertas *f*; **into the** — por añadidura; **to strike a** — cerrar un trato; VI (haggle) regatear; (expect) contar con
bargaining [bɑ́rgənɪŋ] N (haggling) regateo *m*; (negotiation) negociación *f*; —**ing position** posición de negociación *f*
barge [bɑrdʒ] N barcaza *f*; VI **to** — **into a room** irrumpir en un cuarto
baritone [bǽrɪton] N & ADJ barítono *m*
barium [bǽriəm] N bario *m*
bark [bɑrk] N (of a dog) ladrido *m*; (on a tree)

corteza *f*; VI/VT ladrar
barley [bɑ́rli] N cebada *f*
barn [bɑrn] N (for animals) establo *m*; (for grain) granero *m*; — **owl** lechuza *f*; —**yard** corral *m*
barnacle [bɑ́rnəkəl] N percebe *m*
barometer [bərɑ́mɪdə-] N barómetro *m*
baron [bǽrən] N barón *m*
baroque [bərók] ADJ & N barroco *m*
barracks [bǽrəks] N cuartel *m*
barracuda [bærəkúɒə] N barracuda *f*
barrage [bərɑ́ʒ] N (of artillery fire) barrera de fuego *f*; (of questions) lluvia *f*, aluvión *m*
barrel [bǽrəl] N barril *m*, tonel *m*; (gun) cañón *m*, caño *m*; **he's a** — **of laughs** es un payaso; **he is scraping the bottom of the** — está desesperado; VI **to** — **along** ir disparado
barren [bǽrən] ADJ (land) árido, yermo; (female) estéril
barrette [bərét] N broche *m*
barricade [bærɪkéd] N barricada *f*; VT cerrar con barricadas; VI atrincherarse
barrier [bǽriə-] N barrera *f*; — **reef** barrera de coral *f*
barrio [bɑ́rio] N barrio hispano *m*
barter [bɑ́rɒə-] VI hacer trueque; VT trocar; N trueque *m*
bartering [bɑ́rɒə-ɪŋ] N trueque *m*
basal cell carcinoma [bésəłsɛłkɑrsɪnómə] N carcinoma de célula basal *m*
basalt [bésɔlt] N basalto *m*
base [bes] N base *f*; —**ball** béisbol *m*; —**ball player** beisbolista *m*, pelotero -ra *mf*; —**board** zócalo *m*; ADJ bajo, vil; (metal) de baja ley; — **font** tipo de letra por omisión *m*; —**line** línea de fondo *f*; — **on balls** base por bolas *f*; — **pay** salario base *m*; —**s loaded** bases llenas *f pl*; — **steal** robo de base *m*; VI/VT basar, fundamentar; **to be** —**d on** fundamentarse en; **the general is** —**d in Berlin** el general está estacionado en Berlín
baseless [béslɪs] ADJ sin fundamento
basement [bésmənt] N sótano *m*
baseness [bésnɪs] N bajeza *f*, vileza *f*
bash [bǽʃ] VT golpear; N (party) fiesta *f*
bashful [bǽʃfəl] ADJ tímido, vergonzoso
bashfulness [bǽʃfəlnɪs] N timidez *f*
basic [bésɪk] ADJ básico
basin [bésɪn] N (bowl) palangana *f*, jofaina *f*; (of a fountain) pilón *m*; (geographical formation) cuenca *f*; (pond) estanque *m*
basis [bésɪs] N fundamento *m*, base *f*; **on the** — **of** en base a, con base en; **on a regular** — regularmente
bask [bǽsk] VI (in the sun) asolearse; (in praise) deleitarse
basket [bǽskɪt] N canasta *f*, cesta *f*, cesto *m*; (in basketball) canasta *f*; —**ball** (game) baloncesto *m*, básquetbol *m*, básquet *m*; (ball) balón de baloncesto *m*; — **case** (crazy person)

chiflado -da *mf*; (helpless person) caso perdido *m*; **to make a** — (in basketball) encestar

basketful [bǽskɪtfʌɫ] N (contents of a basket) canasto *m*; (large amount) montón *m*

basketry [bǽskɪtri] N cestería *f*

Basque [bæsk] ADJ & N (person) vasco -ca *mf*; (language) vascuence *m*, vasco *m*, euskera *m*

bass¹ [bes] N (voice, bass guitar) bajo *m*; (double bass) contrabajo *m*; — **clef** clave de fa *f*; — **drum** bombo *m*; — **horn** tuba *f*

bass² [bæs] (marine fish) lubina *f*; (freshwater fish) perca *f*

bassist [bésɪst] N bajista *mf*

bassoon [bæsún] N fagot *m*

bastard [bǽstɚd] N & ADJ (illegitimate) bastardo -da *mf*; N (mean person) *offensive* hijo de puta *m*, cabrón *m*

baste [best] VT (fabric) hilvanar; (meat) rociar

bat [bæt] N (baseball, cricket) bate *m*; (animal) murciélago *m*; VT golpear; **he is at** — está al bate; **it was his first at-** — fue su primer turno; VI (baseball) batear; **not to** — **an eye** no pestañear

batch [bætʃ] N (of cookies) hornada *f*; (of cement, files) tanda *f*; (of data) colección *f*

bath [bæθ] N baño *m*; —**robe** bata [de baño] *f*; *Sp* albornoz *m*; —**room** (in a house) baño *m*, cuarto de baño *m*; (public) *Sp* aseo *m*; *Am* servicio *m*, baño *m*; —**tub** bañera *f*

bathe [beð] VI/VT bañar[se]; **bathing suit** traje de baño *m*

bather [béðɚ] N bañista *mf*

baton [bətán] N batuta *f*

battalion [bətǽljən] N batallón *m*

batter [bǽɚ] N (in baking) pasta *f*, masa *f*; (in baseball) bateador -ora *mf*; —**'s box** caja de bateo *f*; VT golpear

battery [bǽɚi] N (of car, artillery, in baseball) batería *f*; (of electronic devices) pila *f*; (of tests) serie *f*; (assault) asalto *m*

batting [bǽɪŋ] N bateo *m*; — **average** porcentaje de bateo *m*

battle [bǽɾɫ] N batalla *f*; —**ax[e]** (weapon) hacha de guerra *f*; (woman) *pej* sargenta *f*; — **cry** grito de guerra *m*; —**field** campo de batalla *m*; —**ship** acorazado *m*; VI batallar; **to** — **cancer** luchar contra el cáncer

bawl [bɔɫ] VI berrear; **to** — **somebody out** echarle la bronca a uno

bay [be] N (body of water) bahía *f*; (howl) aullido *m*; — **leaf** hoja de laurel *f*; — **window** ventana saliente *f*; **to hold at** — tener a raya; ADJ bayo; VI aullar

bayonet [beənét] N bayoneta *f*

bazaar [bəzár] N (market place) bazar *m*; (benefit) kermés *f*

bazooka [bəzúkə] N bazuca *f*

be [bi] VI ser, estar; **I am from Uruguay** soy de Uruguay; **there were four of us** éramos cuatro; **he is a doctor** es médico; **it's her** es ella; **sugar is sweet** el azúcar es dulce; **London is in England** Londres está en Inglaterra; **this water is cold** esta agua está fría; **the windows were open** las ventanas estaban abiertas; **there is a problem** hay un problema; **to** — **cold/warm/hungry/ right / in a hurry** tener frío/calor/hambre/ razón/prisa; **to be cold/hot/windy** hacer frío/calor/viento

beach [bitʃ] N playa *f*; —**comber** vagabundo -da *mf*; —**head** cabeza de playa *f*; VT varar, encallar

beacon [bíkən] N faro *m*

bead [bid] N (of glass) cuenta *f*; (of sweat) gota *f*, perla *f*; **to get a** — **on somebody** apuntarle a alguien; VT (string) enhebrar/ensartar cuentas; (decorate) adornar con cuentas

beagle [bígəɫ] N beagle *m*

beak [bik] N pico *m*

beaker [bíkɚ] N vaso de precipitados *m*

beam [bim] N (of light) rayo *m*, haz *m*; (of a building) viga *f*; (of a ship) manga *f*; (of a scale) brazo *m*; **broad in the** — ancho de caderas; VI/VT (light, radio) emitir; (smile) estar radiante

bean [bin] N judía *f*, habichuela *f*; *Sp* alubia *f*; *Am* frijol *m*, *Am* poroto *m*; **Lima** — haba *f*; —**stalk** tallo de habas / frijol *m*; **Jack and the** —**stalk** Juanito y las habichuelas; **I don't know** —**s about that** no sé ni papa / ni jota de eso

bear [bɛr] N oso *m*; — **hug** abrazo fuerte *m*; — **market** mercado bajista *m*; VT (hold up, tolerate) soportar, aguantar; (suffer) sobrellevar; (have a child) dar a luz; (produce young) parir; (produce fruit) producir; **to** — **down** (mash) apretar; (push) pujar; **to** — **a grudge** guardar rencor; **to** — **in mind** tener en cuenta; **to** — **oneself with dignity** portarse con dignidad; **to** — **out** confirmar; **to** — **testimony** dar testimonio; **to** — **interest** devengar interés; **to** — **gifts** traer regalos; **to** — **a resemblance** parecerse; **to** — **the cost of something** asumir el costo de algo; **it doesn't** — **repeating** no merece repetirse

bearable [bérəbəɫ] ADJ llevadero, soportable

beard [bird] N (on a man) barba *f*; (of wheat) aristas *f pl*

bearded [bírdɪd] ADJ barbado, barbudo

bearer [bérɚ] N portador -ora *mf*

bearing [bériŋ] N porte *m*; **to lose one's** —**s** perder el rumbo, desorientarse; **it has no** — **on our situation** no tiene relación con nuestra situación

bearish [bériʃ] ADJ (of bears) osuno; (of stock market) bajista

beast [bist] N bestia *f*
beat [bit] VT (wings, eggs) batir; (a person) golpear; (a drum) tocar; (an opponent) vencer; (tempo) marcar; VI (heart) latir; (drum) sonar; **to — around the bush** andarse por las ramas; **to — off** (repulse) rechazar; (masturbate) *vulg* hacerse una paja; **to — up** dar una paliza; **—s me!** ¡ni idea! N (blow) golpe *m*; (drum) toque *m*; (heart) latido *m*; (tempo) compás *m*; (policeman's territory) ronda *f*; ADJ cansado
beaten [bítn̩] ADJ (mixed) batido; (defeated) vencido; **— path** camino trillado *m*
beaten [bítn̩] *see* beat
beater [bíDɚ] N batidor *m*
beating [bíDɪŋ] N (whipping) paliza *f*; (pulsation) latido *m*
beau [bo] N pretendiente *m*
beautiful [bjúɒfəł] ADJ hermoso; **— people** jet set *m*
beautify [bjúɒfaɪ] VT embellecer, hermosear
beauty [bjúDi] N belleza *f*, hermosura *f*; (woman) beldad *f*; **— contest/pageant** concurso/ certamen de belleza *m*; **— parlor** salón de belleza *m*
beaver [bívɚ] N (animal) castor *m*; (vagina) *vulg* chichi *m*, conejo *m*
became [bikém] *see* become
because [bikɔ́z] CONJ porque; **— of** por, a causa de, debido a
beckon [békən] VT llamar por señas
become [bikʌ́m] VT (turn into) convertirse en; **the water became ice** el agua se convirtió en hielo; **he became a doctor** llegó a ser médico; (suit) sentar bien; **that suit —s you** ese traje te luce bien; VI (change emotional or physical condition) ponerse; **she became ill** se puso enferma; (undergo a drastic change) volverse; **he became crazy** se volvió loco; **to — angry** enojarse; **to — frightened** asustarse; **to — old** envejecer; **what has — of him?** ¿qué ha sido de él?
becoming [bikʌ́mɪŋ] ADJ (appropriate) propio; **that dress is — to you** te sienta bien ese vestido
bed [bɛd] N (furniture) cama *f*; *lit* lecho *m*; (of a river) cauce *m*; (of the sea) fondo *m*; (in a garden) cuadro *m*; **—bug** chinche *mf*; **—clothes** ropa de cama *f*; **—pan** cuña *f*, chata *f*; **—ridden** postrado en cama; **—rest** reposo *m*; **—rock** lecho de roca *m*; **—room** alcoba *f*, dormitorio *m*; *Mex* recámara *f*; **at the —side** al lado de la cama; **—side table** mesita de noche *f*; **—side manner** manera de tratar a los pacientes *f*; **—sore** llaga *f*; **—spread** colcha *f*; **—spring** resorte del colchón *m*; **—time** hora de dormir *f*; **—wetting** enuresis nocturna *f*; **to go to —** acostarse; **to put to —** acostar

bedding [béDɪŋ] N ropa de cama *f*
bee [bi] N (insect) abeja *f*; (social gathering) tertulia *f*; **to have a — in one's bonnet** tener una idea metida en la cabeza; **—hive** colmena *f*; **— sting** picadura de abeja *f*
beech [bitʃ] N haya *f*; **—nut** hayuco *m*
beef [bif] N (meat) carne de vaca/res *f*; (complaint) queja *f*; **— jerky** cecina *f*; **—steak** bistec *m*; VI quejarse; **to — up** reforzar
been [bɪn] *see* be
beep [bip] N pitazo *m*; VI/VT (alarm) sonar; (horn) tocar
beeper [bípɚ] N buscapersonas *m sg*
beer [bir] N cerveza *f*
beet [bit] N remolacha *f*
beetle [bídł] N escarabajo *m*
befall [bifɔ́ł] VT acontecerle a
befallen [bifɔ́lən] *see* befall
befell [bifɛ́ł] *see* befall
befit [bifít] VT convenir
before [bifɔ́r] ADV (temporal) antes, con anterioridad; (spatial) delante; PREP (temporal) antes de; (spatial) delante de; *lit* ante; CONJ antes [de] que, antes de; **— beginning** antes de que comiences, antes de comenzar; **—-tax earnings** ganancias pre-impositivas *f pl*
beforehand [bifɔ́rhænd] ADV de antemano, con anterioridad
befriend [bifrénd] VT hacerse amigo de
beg [bɛg] VI (ask for alms) mendigar, pedir limosna; VI/VT (implore) rogar; **to — for mercy** pedir misericordia; **she —ged me to do it** me rogó que lo hiciera; **to — the question** dar por sentado lo mismo que se arguye
began [bigǽn] *see* begin
begat [bigǽt] *see* beget
beget [bigɛ́t] VT engendrar
beggar [bégɚ] N mendigo -ga *mf*
begin [bigín] VI/VT comenzar, empezar; **the ten dollars won't — to cover the expense** los diez dólares ni siquiera cubren los gastos
beginner [bigínɚ] N principiante *mf*
beginning [bigínɪŋ] N principio *m*; (temporal only) comienzo *m*; **— with** comenzando con/ por; **at the —** al/por el principio
begotten [bigátn̩] *see* beget
begrudge [bigrʌ́ʤ] VT aceptar de mala gana
begun [bigʌ́n] *see* begin
behalf [bihǽf] PREP LOC **on — of** (in place of) por, en nombre de, de parte de; (in favor of) a favor de
behave [bihév] VI portarse, comportarse; **— yourself!** ¡pórtate bien!
behavior [bihévjɚ] N comportamiento *m*, conducta *f*
behavioral [bihévjərəł] ADJ conductual, relativo

a la conducta / al comportamiento
behead [bɪhéd] VT decapitar, descabezar
beheld [bɪhéɫd] *see* behold
behind [bɪháɪnd] ADV detrás; (in payments, schedule) atrasado; **he fell — his competitors** quedó a la zaga de sus competidores; **an hour** — una hora de retraso; **from** — desde atrás; **to fall** — atrasarse; **to leave something** — dejar atrás algo; PREP detrás de, tras; **we're all — you** todos te apoyamos; **who's — this evil plot?** ¿quién está detrás de este plan macabro? — **one's back** a espaldas de uno; N trasero *m*
behold [bɪhóɫd] VT contemplar; — **the future king!** ¡he aquí el futuro rey!
behoove [bɪhúv] VI **it behooves [one]** le corresponde [a uno]
beige [beʒ] ADJ & N beige *m*
being [bíɪŋ] N ser *m*; **for the time** — por ahora
Belarus [bɛlərús] N Bielorrusia *f*
belated [bɪléDɪd] ADJ atrasado, tardío
belch [bɛɫtʃ] VI eructar, repetir; N eructo *m*
belfry [béɫfri] N campanario *m*
Belgian [béɫdʒən] ADJ & N belga *mf*
Belgium [béɫdʒəm] N Bélgica *f*
belief [bɪlíf] N creencia *f*; (strong opinion) convicción *f*
believable [bɪlívəbəɫ] ADJ creíble
believe [bɪlív] VI/VT creer
believer [bɪlívɚ] N creyente *mf*; (proponent) partidario -ria *mf*
belittle [bɪlíɾɫ] VT (a person) menospreciar, disminuir; (a situation) minimizar
belittling [bɪlíɾɫɪŋ] N menosprecio *m*, disminución *f*
Belize [bəlíz] N Belice *m*
Belizean [bəlízɪən] ADJ & N beliceño -ña *mf*
bell [bɛɫ] N campana *f*; (small) campanilla *f*; —**boy/hop** botones *m sg*; — **curve** curva de campana *f*; —**flower** campanilla *f*, campánula *f*; — **jar** campana de cristal *f*; — **pepper** pimiento *m*, morrón *m*; — **tower** campanario *m*; **with all the —s and whistles** con todos los accesorios
bellicose [béɫɪkos] ADJ belicoso
belligerent [bəlídʒɚənt] ADJ & N beligerante *mf*
bellow [bélo] VI/VT bramar, berrear; N bramido *m*; —**s** fuelle *m*
belly [béli] N barriga *f*, vientre *m*, panza *f*; —**ache** dolor de barriga *m*; — **button** ombligo *m*; — **dance** danza del vientre *f*; — **laugh** carcajada *f*
belong [bɪlɔ́ŋ] VI (ownership) pertenecer; **this car —s to me** este coche me pertenece; (correspondence) corresponder; **this key —s to this door** esta llave corresponde a esta puerta; (placement) ir; **this —s on the shelf** esto va en el estante
belongings [bɪlɔ́ŋɪŋz] N pertenencias *f pl*

beloved [bɪlávɪd] ADJ querido; N amado -da *mf*
below [bɪló] ADV abajo; **five — [zero]** cinco bajo cero; PREP bajo, debajo de, abajo de
belt [bɛɫt] N (for the waist) cinturón *m*, cinto *m*; (for a machine) correa *f*; (region) zona *f*; — **line** cintura *f*; VT pegar; **to — out a song** cantar una canción a voz en cuello
bemoan [bɪmón] VT lamentarse de, quejarse de
bench [bɛntʃ] N banco *m*; (without a back) banqueta *f*; (in sports) banco *m*, banquillo *m*; (in court) estrado *m*; —**mark** (upper limit) cota *f*; (parameter) punto de referencia *m*; — **price** precio de referencia *m*; **opinion of the** — opinión del tribunal *f*
bend [bɛnd] VI/VT (make curved) doblar[se]; (force) someter; **to — over** inclinarse; **to — over backward** desvivirse; **to — the rules** hacer una excepción; N (road) curva *f*, recodo *m*; —**s** enfermedad de los buzos *f*
bending [béndɪŋ] N doblado *m*
beneath [bɪníθ] ADV abajo; PREP debajo de, bajo; (in rank) inferior a; — **contempt** totalmente despreciable; **that's — me** no es digno de mí
benediction [bɛnɪdíkʃən] N bendición *f*
benefactor [bénəfæktɚ] N benefactor -ora *mf*; *lit* bienhechor -ora *mf*
beneficent [bənéfɪsənt] ADJ benéfico
beneficial [bɛnəfíʃəɫ] ADJ beneficioso
beneficiary [bɛnəfíʃɪɛri] N beneficiario -ria *mf*
benefit [bénəfɪt] N beneficio *m*, provecho *m*; — **performance** función de beneficencia *f*; VI/VT beneficiar[se], sacar provecho
benevolence [bənévələns] N benevolencia *f*
benevolent [bənévələnt] ADJ benévolo
benign [bɪnáɪn] ADJ benigno
Benin [bɛnín] N Benín *m*
Beninese [bɛnɪníz] ADJ & N beninés -esa *mf*
bent [bɛnt] N inclinación *f*; **to be — on** estar resuelto a
bent [bɛnt] *see* bend
benzine [bénzin] N bencina *f*
bequeath [bɪkwíð] VT legar, heredar
bequest [bɪkwést] N legado *m*
berate [bɪrét] VT reprender
bereaved [bɪrívd] ADJ de luto
beret [bəré] N boina *f*
berry [béri] N baya *f*
berserk [bɚrzɚ́k] ADJ fuera de sí; **he went —** se puso hecho una fiera, se enfureció
berth [bɚθ] N litera *f*; **to give a wide — to** mantener una distancia prudencial de
beseech [bɪsítʃ] VT suplicar, rogar
beset [bɪsét] VT (attack) acosar; (surround) rodear
beside [bɪsáɪd] PREP al lado de; **sit down — me** siéntate a mi lado; **to be — oneself** estar fuera de sí; **that is — the point** eso no viene al caso; ADV al lado
besides [bɪsáɪdz] ADV además; **they have a**

table but not much — tienen una mesa pero poca cosa más; PREP además de, aparte de

besiege [bɪsíʤ] VT (lay siege) sitiar, cercar; (importune) importunar, asediar

best [bɛst] ADJ mejor; — **-case scenario** la mejor situación; — **man** padrino de boda *m*; — **seller** bestseller *m*; **she's the** — ella es la mejor; ADV mejor; **at** — a lo más, en el mejor de los casos; N **the** — **is still to come** lo mejor está por venir; **to do one's** — hacer lo mejor posible; **to get the** — **of a person** ganarle a una persona; **to make the** — **of** sacar el mejor partido de; VT vencer

bestial [béstʃəł] ADJ bestial

bestow [bɪstó] VT conferir; **to** — **gifts upon** dar regalos a

bet [bɛt] N apuesta *f*; VI/VT apostar; **to** — **on** apostar por

beta [béDə] N — **blocker** betabloqueador *m*, betabloqueante *m*; — **test** prueba beta *f*; — **version** versión beta *f*

betray [bɪtré] VT (a person) traicionar; (a secret) revelar; (a feeling) traslucir, delatar; **to** — **one's ignorance** hacer patente su ignorancia

betrayal [bɪtréəł] N traición *f*

betrayer [bɪtréə-] N traidor -ra *mf*

betrothal [bɪtróðəł] N esponsales *f pl*

better [béDə-] ADJ mejor; — **half** media naranja *f*; **the** — **part of a year** la mayor parte de un año; ADV mejor; **he lives** — **than a mile away** vive a más de una milla; **so much the** — tanto mejor; —**-off** en mejor posición económica; **to be** — **off** estar mejor así; **to change for the** — cambiar para bien; **to get** — mejorar[se], aliviarse; VT mejorar; **to** — **oneself** mejorarse, mejorar de situación; N **the** — **of the two** el/la mejor de los dos

better, bettor [béDə-] N apostador -ra *mf*

between [bɪtwín] PREP entre; ADV en medio

bevel [bévəł] N bisel *m*; VT biselar

beverage [bévrɪʤ] N bebida *f*

bevy [bévi] N (of birds, people) bandada *f*; (of deer) manada *f*

beware [bɪwér] VI cuidarse [de]; — **of the dog** cuidado con el perro

bewilder [bɪwíłdə-] VT dejar perplejo, aturdir; **to be —ed** estar perplejo

bewilderment [bɪwíłdə-mənt] N perplejidad *f*, aturdimiento *m*

bewitch [bɪwítʃ] VT hechizar, embrujar

beyond [bɪjánd] ADV más allá; PREP más allá de; — **my reach** fuera de mi alcance; N **the great** — el más allá

Bhutan [butǽn] N Bután *m*

Bhutanese [butṇíz] ADJ & N butanés -esa *mf*

biannual [baɪǽnjuəł] ADJ bianual, semestral, semianual

bias [báɪəs] N (prejudice) prejuicio *m*; (in fabric) sesgo *m*; ADJ sesgado, oblicuo; VT predisponer; —**ed** parcial

bib [bɪb] N babero *m*; (of an apron) pechera *f*

Bible [báɪbəł] N Biblia *f*

biblical [bíblɪkəł] ADJ bíblico

bibliography [bɪbliágrəfi] N bibliografía *f*

bicarbonate [baɪkárbənɪt] N bicarbonato *m*

bicep, biceps [báɪsɛp[s]] N bíceps *m sg*

bicker [bíkə-] VI reñir

bicuspid [baɪkáspɪd] ADJ bicúspide

bicycle [báɪsɪkəł] N bicicleta *f*; VI andar en bicicleta

bid [bɪd] N (in an auction, contest) licitación *f*, puja *f*; (in card games) apuesta *f*; (attempt) tentativa *f*; VI/VT (offer) pujar; (command) mandar; (invite) rogar; (enter a bid in cards) apostar; **to** — **good-bye** despedirse; **to** — **up** pujar el precio

bidden [bídṇ] *see* bid

bidding [bídɪŋ] N (in auction) puja *f*; **at someone's** — por orden de alguien; **to do someone's** — cumplir con los deseos de alguien

bide [baɪd] VI/VT **to** — **one's time** esperar una oportunidad

biennium [baɪéniəm] N bienio *m*

bifurcate [báɪfə-ket] VI/VT bifurcar[se]

big [bɪg] ADJ grande; — **Bang Theory** Teoría del Big Bang *f*; — **brother** hermano mayor *m*; — **bucks** mucha plata *f*; — **business** el gran capital *m*; — **deal** asunto importante *m*; — **deal!** ¡no es para tanto! — **Dipper** Osa Mayor *f*; — **enchilada** *fam* mandamás *m*, *fam* pez gordo *m*; —**-headed** cabezón, cabezudo; —**-hearted** magnánimo; — **house** *fam* gayola *f*; — **kahuna** *fam* mandamás *m*, *fam* pez gordo *m*; — **name** personalidad prominente *f*; — **picture** panorama general *m*; — **shot** *fam* pez gordo *m*; — **sister** hermana mayor *f*; —**-ticket** caro; —**wig** *fam* pez gordo *m*; — **with child** embarazada; **jazz was** — **in the 1920s** el jazz era popular en los años veinte; **she's a** — **deal** es una persona importante; ADV **she wants to go** —**time** se muere por ir; **to talk** — jactarse, fanfarronear; *Am* lucirse; **to go over** — tener éxito; **to be** — **on** ser entusiasta de

bigamy [bígəmi] N bigamia *f*

bigot [bígət] N intolerante *mf*

bigotry [bígətri] N intolerancia *f*

bike [baɪk] N (bicycle) bici *f*; (motorcycle) moto *f*

biker [báɪkə-] N (bicyclist) ciclista *mf*; (motorcyclist) motociclista *mf*

bikini [bɪkíni] N bikini *m*

bilateral [baɪlǽDə-əł] ADJ bilateral

bile [baɪł] N (secretion) bilis *f*; (ill temper) mal genio *m*; — **duct** conducto biliar *m*

bilingual [baɪlíŋgwəł] ADJ & N bilingüe *mf*

bilingualism [baɪlíŋgwəlɪzəm] N bilingüismo *m*

bill [bɪł] N (statement) factura*f*; (in a restaurant) cuenta*f*; (poster) cartel *m*; (bank note) billete *m*; (for movies, theater) programa *m*; (of a bird) pico *m*; (legislative) proyecto de ley *m*; —**board** cartelera*f*; —**fold** cartera*f*, billetera*f*; — **of exchange** letra de cambio*f*; — **of lading** conocimiento de embarque *m*; — **of rights** declaración de derechos*f*; — **of sale** escritura de venta*f*; VT cobrar, mandar la factura a

billable [bíləbəł] ADJ facturable

billiards [bíljə-dz] N billar *m*

billing [bílɪŋ] N (theater) orden de importancia en espectáculos *m*; (business) facturación*f*; — **cycle** ciclo de facturación *m*

billion [bíljən] NUM mil millones *m pl*

billow [bílo] N (of smoke) nube*f*; (of water) ola*f*; VI ondular, hacer olas

bimbo [bímbo] N gachí*f*; *pej* putilla*f*, *pej* putón *m*

bimonthly [baɪmánθli] ADV bimestral

bin [bɪn] N (for clothes, food) cajón *m*, recipiente *m*; (on an airplane) portaequipajes *m sg*; (for coal) carbonera*f*; (for grain) granero *m*

binary [báɪneri] ADJ binario; — **star** estrella binaria*f*

bind [baɪnd] VI/VT (unite) unir; (connect) ligar; (tie) atar; (put a cover on a book) encuadernar; (press tightly) apretar; (oblige by contract) obligar

binding [báɪndɪŋ] N (of a book) encuadernación *f*; (on a rug) ribete *m*; ADJ obligatorio

binge [bɪndʒ] N (alcoholic) juerga*f*, parranda*f*; (food) comilona*f*; VI (on alcohol) emborracharse; (on food) atiborrarse

bingo [bíŋgo] N bingo *m*

binoculars [bənákjələ-z] N gemelos *m pl*, prismáticos *m pl*

binomial [baɪnómiəł] N binomio *m*; ADJ binomial

biochemistry [baɪokémɪstri] N bioquímica*f*

biodegradable [baɪodɪgrédəbəł] ADJ biodegradable

bioengineering [baɪoɛndʒənírɪŋ] N bioingeniería*f*

biofeedback [baɪofídbæk] N biofeedback *m*, retroalimentación biológica*f*

biography [baɪágrəfi] N biografía*f*

biological [baɪɑláʤɪkəł] ADJ biológico

biologist [baɪáləʤɪst] N biólogo -ga *mf*

biology [baɪáləʤi] N biología*f*

biopsy [báɪɑpsi] N biopsia*f*

biorhythm [báɪorɪðəm] N biorritmo *m*

biotechnology [baɪotɛknáləʤi] N biotecnología *f*

bipartisan [baɪpárDɪzən] ADJ bipartidista

bipolar [baɪpólə-] ADJ bipolar; — **disorder** trastorno bipolar *m*

birch [bə-tʃ] N abedul *m*

bird [bə-d] N ave*f*; (small) pájaro *m*; — **of prey** ave de rapiña*f*; — **seed** alpiste *m*; **odd** — persona peculiar*f*

birth [bə-θ] N (act of being born) nacimiento *m*; (act of giving birth) parto *m*; (lineage) linaje *m*; (origin) origen *m*; — **canal** canal de parto *m*; — **certificate** certificado de nacimiento *m*, fe/acta de nacimiento*f*; — **control** (policy) control de la natalidad *m*; (devices) anticonceptivos *m pl*; —**day** cumpleaños *m sg*; **in his / her** —**day suit** como Dios lo/la trajo al mundo; —**mark** antojo *m*, marca de nacimiento*f*; —**place** lugar de nacimiento *m*; —**rate** natalidad*f*, tasa de natalidad*f*; —**right** derechos de nacimiento *m pl*; (of oldest child) primogenitura*f*; **to give** — dar a luz, parir, alumbrar; **by** — de nacimiento

biscuit [bískɪt] N panecillo *m*

bisect [báɪsɛkt] VT bisecar

bisexual [baɪsékʃuəł] ADJ bisexual

bishop [bíʃəp] N obispo *m*; (in chess) alfil *m*

bison [báɪsən] N bisonte *m*, búfalo *m*

bit [bɪt] N (small piece) pedacito *m*, trocito *m*; (some) poquito *m*; (of a bridle) bocado *m*, freno *m*; (of a drill) broca*f*, barrena*f*; (computer) bit *m*; **I don't care a** — no me importa en absoluto

bit [bɪt] *see* bite

bitch [bɪtʃ] N (dog) perra*f*; (woman) *offensive* hija de puta*f*, cabrona*f*; (situation) plomazo *m*, *Sp vulg* coñazo *m*; VI quejarse

bite [baɪt] VI/VT morder; (be duped) dejarse engañar; (insect, fish, snake) picar; **to** — **off** arrancar de un mordisco; N (act, wound) mordedura*f*, dentellada*f*; (morsel, small meal) bocado *m*, bocadito *m*; (of an insect) picadura*f*, roncha*f*

bitten [bítn] *see* bite

bitter [bíDə-] ADJ (taste) amargo; (cold) glacial; (enemy) acérrimo; (person) resentido; —**sweet** dulceamargo, agridulce; **to fight to the** — **end** luchar hasta morir; N —**s** cerveza amarga*f*

bitterness [bíDə-nɪs] N (taste) amargor *m*; (feelings) amargura*f*; (anger) rencor *m*, resentimiento *m*

biweekly [baɪwíkli] ADV (every two weeks) quincenal; (twice a week) bisemanal

bizarre [bɪzár] ADJ (event) extraño; (appearance) estrafalario

blab [blæb] VI parlotear; VT descubrir el pastel

black [blæk] ADJ (color, ethnicity) negro; (night) oscuro; —**-and-blue** lleno de moretones, amoratado; N negro -a *mf*; — **bean** frijol negro *m*; —**berry** zarzamora*f*, mora*f*; —**bird** mirlo *m*; —**board** pizarrón *m*, pizarra *f*; — **death** peste negra*f*; — **eye** ojo amoratado/morado *m*; —**head** espinilla*f*; —

hole agujero negro *m*; —**jack** (weapon) cachiporra *f*; (card game) black-jack *m*, veintiuno *m*; —**list** lista negra *f*; — **magic** magia negra *f*; —**mail** chantaje *m*; — **mark** mancha *f*; — **market** mercado negro *m*; —**out** apagón *m*; — **pepper** pimienta negra *f*; — **pudding** morcilla *f*; — **sheep** oveja negra *f*; —**smith** herrero *m*; —**smith's shop** herrería *f*, forja *f*; —**top** asfalto *m*; — **widow spider** viuda negra *f*; **to put down in** — **and white** poner por escrito; VI **to** — **out** (faint) desmayarse, perder el conocimiento; VT **to** —**mail** chantajear

blacken [blǽkən] VT ennegrecer, negrear; VI (sky) oscurecerse

blackness [blǽknɪs] N negrura *f*

bladder [blǽDɚ] N vejiga *f*

blade [bled] N (of a knife) hoja *f*; (of grass) brizna *f*; (of an oar) pala *f*, paleta *f*; (of a propeller) aspa *f*

blame [blem] VT culpar, echar la culpa a, achacar la culpa a; **to be to** — tener la culpa; N (responsibility) culpa *f*; (reproof) reproche *m*

blameless [blémlɪs] ADJ intachable

blanch [blæntʃ] VI palidecer; VT (whiten) blanquear; (scald) escaldar

bland [blænd] ADJ insulso

blank [blæŋk] ADJ (not written on) en blanco; (not recorded on) virgen; (unadorned, expressionless) vacío; (confused) desconcertado; — **cartridge** cartucho de fogueo *m*; — **check** cheque en blanco *m*; — **verse** verso blanco *m*; N (place to be filled in on a form) espacio [en blanco] *m*; (gap) vacío *m*; VI **to** — **out** quedarse en blanco

blanket [blǽŋkɪt] N manta *f*, frazada *f*; *Am* cobija *f*; ADJ global; VT cubrir

blare [blɛr] VI hacer un ruido estruendoso; N estruendo *m*; (of a trumpet) toque *m*

blaspheme [blæsfím] VI/VT blasfemar [contra]

blasphemy [blǽsfəmi] N blasfemia *f*

blast [blæst] N (of wind) ráfaga *f*; (of criticism) lluvia *f*; (of a trumpet) trompetazo *m*; (explosive charge) carga *f*; (explosion) explosión *f*; — **furnace** alto horno *m*; —**off** despegue *m*; **we had a** — lo pasamos bomba; **at full** — a todo volumen; VI/VT (blow a horn) pitar, tocar; (shatter) volar; (criticize) criticar duramente; (blow hard) azotar; **to** — **off** despegar

blatant [blétn̩t] ADJ descarado

blaze [blez] N (flame) llamarada *f*; (fire) incendio *m*; (glow) resplandor *m*; (mark) señal *f*; — **of anger** arranque de ira *m*; VI (burn) arder; (shine) resplandecer; **to** — **a trail** marcar una senda

blazer [blézɚ] N blazer *m*, saco *m*

bleach [blitʃ] VI/VT (intentional) blanquear[se]; (accidental) desteñir[se]; N blanqueador *m*; *Sp*

lejía *f*

bleachers [blítʃɚz] N gradas *f pl*

bleak [blik] ADJ (terrain) yermo, desolado; (winter) crudo; (wind) helado; (future) negro

bleary [blíri] ADJ nublado

bleat [blit] N balido *m*; VI balar

bled [blɛd] *see* bleed

bleed [blid] VI (lose blood) sangrar; (run, as in colors) correrse, desteñir[se]; **my heart** —**s for the poor** los pobres me dan lástima; VT (let blood) desangrar; (extort) extorsionar; (clean brakes) purgar

blemish [blémɪʃ] N mancha *f*, tacha *f*; VT manchar

blend [blɛnd] VI/VT (tea, paint) mezclar, entremezclar; (sea and sky) fundirse; (voices) armonizar; N mezcla *f*

blender [blɛ́ndɚ] N licuadora *f*

bless [blɛs] VT bendecir; INTERJ — **you!** ¡salud! ¡Jesús!

blessed[1] [blɛ́sɪd] ADJ (beatified) beato; (happy) bienaventurado, feliz; — **event** feliz acontecimiento *m*; **the whole** — **day** todo el santo día; **not a** — **drop of rain** ni una bendita gota de agua

blessed[2] [blɛst] ADJ — **with** dotado de

blessing [blɛ́sɪŋ] N bendición *f*; **to say the** — dar gracias

blew [blu] *see* blow

blight [blaɪt] N (plant disease) quemadura *f*, añublo *m*; (scourge) lacra *f*; VT (cause to wither) marchitar; (ruin) arruinar

blimp [blɪmp] N zepelín *m*

blind [blaɪnd] ADJ ciego; — **alley** callejón sin salida *m*; — **date** cita a ciegas *f*; —**fold** venda para los ojos *f*; **to** —**fold** vendar los ojos a; — **man's bluff** juego de la gallina ciega *m*; — **spot** ángulo muerto *m*; **to fly** — volar a ciegas; **to go** — quedarse ciego; N (shade) persiana *f*; (hunter's hiding place) escondite *m*; VT (make blind) cegar; (darken) oscurecer

blinder [bláɪndɚ] N anteojera *f*

blindly [bláɪndli] ADV a ciegas

blindness [bláɪndnɪs] N ceguera *f*

blink [blɪŋk] VI/VT (move eyelids) pestañear, parpadear; (go on and off, as of a light) parpadear; (ignore) pasar por alto; (flee a challenge) rajarse; N parpadeo *m*, pestañeo *m*; **on the** — averiado

blinker [blíŋkɚ] N intermitente *m*

blinking [blíŋkɪŋ] N parpadeo *m*

blip [blɪp] N (on radar) punto *m*; (moment) bache *m*

bliss [blɪs] N dicha *f*, felicidad absoluta *f*

blister [blístɚ] N ampolla *f*; (small) vejiga *f*; VT sacar ampollas; VI ampollarse

blitz [blɪts] N ataque relámpago *m*

blizzard [blízɚd] N ventisca *f*

bloat [blot] VI hinchar[se], abotagar[se]

bloated [blóʊɪd] ADJ hinchado, inflado
blob [blɑb] N pedazo de algo sin forma *m*
block [blɑk] N (piece of stone, cement) bloque *m*;
(piece of wood) trozo de madera *m*; (toy) cubo
m; (in sports) bloqueo *m*; (in basketball) tapón
m; (length from one street to the next) cuadra
f; (square block) manzana *f*; (obstacle)
obstáculo *m*; (group of tickets) sección *f*;
—**buster** éxito de taquilla *m*; —**head** tarugo
-ga *mf*, alcornoque *m*; VT (obstruct, also in
sports) bloquear, tapar; (in basketball)
taponar; (stop a pass) parar; **to — out** (an
essay) esbozar, bosquejar; (the sun) ocultar
blockade [blɑkéd] N bloqueo *m*; VT bloquear
blockage [blɑ́kɪʤ] N obstrucción *f*
blocking [blɑ́kɪŋ] N bloqueo *m*
blog [blɑg] N blog *m*; VI bloguear; —**ging**
bloqueo *m*
blogger [blɑ́gɚ] N bloguero -ra *mf*
blond [blɑnd] ADJ & N rubio -a *mf*
blood [blʌd] N sangre *f*; —**bank** banco de sangre
m; —**bath** carnicería *f*, baño de sangre *m*; —
count recuento sanguíneo *m*; — **group**
grupo sanguíneo *m*; —**hound** sabueso *m*; —
plasma plasma sanguíneo *m*; — **poisoning**
septicemia *f*; — **pressure** presión arterial *f*;
— **relative** pariente consanguíneo *mf*;
—**shed** derramamiento de sangre *m*; —**shot**
inyectado de sangre; — **thirsty** sanguinario,
sangriento; — **type** grupo sanguíneo *m*; —
vessel vaso sanguíneo *m*; **in cold —** a sangre
fría
bloody [blʌ́ɪ] ADJ (violent) sangriento;
(smeared) ensangrentado
bloom [blum] N (flower) flor *f*; (flowering)
floración *f*; (youthfulness) lozanía *f*; (flush)
rubor *m*; **in —** en flor; VI florecer
blooming [blúmɪŋ] ADJ (flowering) floreciente;
(thriving) lozano
blooper [blúpɚ] N perla *f*
blossom [blɑ́səm] N (flower) flor *f*; VI florecer
blot [blɑt] N (on paper) mancha *f*, borrón *m*; (on
honor) tacha *f*; VI/VT manchar[se],
emborronar[se]; **to — out** (obscure) borrar,
tachar
blotch [blɑtʃ] VT borronear, manchar, cubrir con
manchas; N mancha *f*, borrón *m*
blouse [blaʊs] N blusa *f*
blow [blo] VI (wind) soplar; (leaf) volar; (siren)
sonar; (horse) resoplar; VT (play a horn)
sonar; **to — a fuse** quemar un fusible; **to —
away** (amaze) dejar atónito; (carry away on
the wind) llevarse el viento; **to — down** tirar
abajo; **to —-dry** secar con secador; **to — off**
(ignore) ignorar; **to — one's nose** sonarse las
narices / la nariz; **to — on the soup** soplar la
sopa; **to — one's brains out** levantarse la
tapa de los sesos; **to — out** reventar[se]; **to —
over** (knock down) derribar; (dissipate)

disiparse; **to — up** (a balloon) inflar, hinchar;
(a bridge) volar; **this party —s** esta fiesta es
pésima; N (stroke, shock) golpe *m*; (wind)
tempestad *f*; (breath) soplo *m*; — **job** *vulg*
mamada *f*; —**out** (tire failure) reventón *m*;
(party) fiestón *m*; —**pipe** cerbatana *f*;
—**torch** soplete *m*; —**up** (fight) pelea *f*, riña *f*;
(photo) ampliación *f*; **to come to —s** irse a
las manos
blower [blóɚ] N (artisan) soplador *m*; (machine)
aventadora *f*
blown [blon] *see* blow
blue [blu] ADJ azul; (sad) triste, melancólico;
(from cold) amoratado; N azul *m*; —**bell**
campanilla *f*; —**berry** arándano *m*; —**bird**
pájaro azul *m*; —**blood** sangre azul *f*; — **book**
lista de precios de mercado *f*; —-**chip** de
primera línea; —-**collar** de clase obrera;
—**jay** arrendajo *m*; — **jeans** vaqueros *m pl*;
—**print** (of a building) cianotipo *m*; (of a
project) plan *m*, trazado *m*; —-**ribbon**
distinguido; — **whale** ballena azul *f*; **light**
[azul] celeste *m*; **the —s** (sadness) melancolía
f, murria *f*; (genre of music) blues *m pl*; VI
ponerse azul, azulear; VT azular, teñir de
azul; **to —print** trazar
bluff [blʌf] N (cliff) acantilado *m*, risco *m*; (false
boast) bluff *m*; (in poker) farol *m*; VT hacer un
bluff; **to call a —** poner en evidencia
bluffer [blʌ́fɚ] N bluff *m*
bluing [blúɪŋ] N añil *m*
bluish [blúɪʃ] ADJ azulado
blunder [blʌ́ndɚ] N disparate *m*, patochada *f*; VI
meter la pata; **to — upon/into** tropezar con
blunt [blʌnt] ADJ (not sharp) romo; (rounded)
contundente; (frank) directo, franco; VT
despuntar
blur [blɝ] VT (to obscure) emborronar,
desvanecer; (to make vision blurry) nublar; VI
empañarse, nublarse; N [indistinct sight]
mancha *f*; **it's a — in my mind** sólo tengo
un recuerdo vago de eso
blurred [blɝd] ADJ borroso
blurry [blɝ́i] ADJ borroso
blurt [blɝt] VT **to — [out]** espetar
blush [blʌʃ] VI sonrojarse, ponerse colorado,
ruborizarse; N (act of blushing) sonrojo *m*;
(effect of blushing) rubor *m*; **at first — a**
primera vista
bluster [blʌ́stɚ] VI (blow hard) soplar fuerte,
rugir; (boast) fanfarronear; N (sound of wind)
ventarrón *m*; (attitude) fanfarronería *f*
blustering [blʌ́stəɪŋ] ADJ fanfarrón,
jactancioso; — **wind** ventarrón *m*
BM [**bowel movement**] [bíém] N defecación *f*
boa constrictor [bóəkənstríktɚ] N boa *f*
boar [bɔr] N jabalí *m*
board [bɔrd] N (wood) tabla *f*, listón *m*; (for a
game) tablero *m*; (meals) pensión *f*; (for

bulletins) cartelera f; — **of directors** junta directiva f; **—ing school** pensionado m, internado m; **—inghouse** pensión f; — **of trustees** patronato m; **—room** sala de directorio f; **on** — a bordo; **to go by the** — irse por la borda; VI (lodge) alojarse; **to** — **up** tapiar, cerrar con tablas; VT (boat, plane, train) abordar; (provide lodging) alojar

boarder [bɔ́rDɚ] N pensionista mf

boast [bost] N alarde m; VI jactarse, vanagloriarse, blasonar; VT **the town —s two new schools** el pueblo ostenta dos escuelas nuevas

boastful [bóstfəł] ADJ jactancioso, vanaglorioso

boastfulness [bóstfəłnɪs] N jactancia f, vanagloria f

boat [bot] N (any water vessel) embarcación f; (open and small) bote m, lancha f; (closed, larger) barco m; **—house** cobertizo para botes m; **—man** barquero m, botero m

boating [bóDɪŋ] N navegación f; **to go** — navegar

bob [bab] N (horsetail) cola cortada f; (of the head) sacudida f; (haircut) melena corta f; (of a pendulum) pesa f, plomada f; **—tail** rabón m; VI sacudirse; (a ship) cabecear; VT **to** — **one's hair** cortarse el pelo en melena

bobbin [bábɪn] N carrete m, bobina f

bobcat [bábkæt] N lince rojo m

bode [bod] VI **that doesn't** — **well** eso no augura nada bueno

bodice [bádɪs] N corpiño m

bodily [bádl̩i] ADJ corporal; — **harm** daño físico m

body [báDi] N (of a person, animal, wine, fabric) cuerpo m; (torso) tronco m; (corpse) cuerpo m, cadáver m; (of a text, army, etc.) parte principal f; (of water) masa f; (of a car) carrocería f; (of an airplane) fuselaje m; — **armor** armadura corporal f, armadura de cuerpo f; — **bag** bolsa para cadáveres f; —- **building** culturismo m; — **count** número de muertos m; **—guard** guardaespaldas m sg; — **language** lenguaje corporal m; — **temperature** temperatura f; — **shop** taller de carrocería m; VT **to —search** cachear

bog [bag] N pantano m; VI hundir[se]; **to get —ged down** atascarse

bogey [bógi] N (golf) bogey m

bogeyman [búgimæn] N coco m; RP cuco m

bogus [bógəs] ADJ falso, fraudulento; — **company** compañía fantasma f

Bohemian [bohímiən] ADJ & N bohemio -a mf

boil [bɔɪl] VI/VT (water) hervir; (eggs) cocer; (ocean) bullir; (angry person) echar chispas; **to** — **down to** reducirse a; **to** — **over** derramarse; N (inflammation) forúnculo m, divieso m; (act of boiling) hervor m; **—ing point** punto de ebullición m; **to come to a**

— soltar/romper el hervor

boiler [bɔ́ɪlɚ] N caldera f

boisterous [bɔ́ɪstɚəs] ADJ bullicioso

bold [bołd] ADJ (not fearful) atrevido, osado; (unconventional) audaz; (visually striking) llamativo; **—-faced** descarado; **—face type** negrita f, negrilla m

boldness [bółdnɪs] N (courage) atrevimiento m, osadía f; (unconventional attitude) audacia f

Bolivia [bəlíviə] N Bolivia f

Bolivian [bəlívian] ADJ & N boliviano -na mf

bolster [bółstɚ] N cojín cilíndrico m; VT reforzar; **to** — **someone's courage** alentar a alguien

bolt [bołt] N (door lock) pestillo m, cerrojo m; (crossbar) aldaba f; (pin) perno m, tornillo grande m; (of cloth) rollo m; **it came as a** — **from the blue** cayó como bomba; VT (fasten) atornillar; (lock door) cerrar con tranca, atrancar; (devour) engullir; (break with) romper con; VI echarse a correr

bomb [bam] N bomba f; **—shell** bomba f; — **shelter** refugio antiaéreo m; VT (attack with bombs) bombardear; VI (fail) fracasar

bombard [bambárd] VT bombardear

bombardier [bambɚdír] N bombardero -ra mf

bombardment [bambárdmənt] N bombardeo m

bombastic [bambǽstɪk] ADJ grandilocuente, ampuloso

bomber [bámɚ] N bombardero m, avión de bombardeo m

bombing [bámɪŋ] N (from airplanes) bombardeo m; (terrorist) atentado m

bona fide [bónəfaɪd] ADJ genuino; — **offer** oferta seria f

bonbon [bánban] N caramelo m; (chocolate) bombón m

bond [band] N (tie) lazo m; (fetter) cadenas f pl; (financial instrument) bono m, obligación f; (adhesion) adherencia f; (chemical) enlace m; VI/VT (stick to) adherirse; (connect) establecer vínculos

bondage [bándɪdʒ] N (slavery) servidumbre f, esclavitud f; (sexual practice) prácticas sadomasoquistas f pl

bonded [bándɪd] ADJ afianzado

bonding [bándɪŋ] N (mother-child) lazos afectivos m pl; (male) compenetración f

bondsman [bándzmən] N fiador m

bone [bon] N hueso m; (of fish) espina f; — **china** porcelana fina f; — **graft** injerto óseo m; **—head** estúpido -da mf; — **marrow** médula ósea f; **—yard** cementerio m; — **of contention** manzana de la discordia f; **to make no —s about it** no andarse con rodeos; VT deshuesar; (fish) quitar las espinas; **to** — **up on something** estudiar algo; (have intercourse) Sp vulg follar; Am vulg coger, culear

bonfire [bánfaɪr] N hoguera f, fogata f

bonnet [bánɪt] N gorro m

bonus [bónəs] N (extra salary) gratificación f, prima f; (at Christmas) aguinaldo m

bony [bóni] ADJ (with large bones) huesudo; (made of bones) óseo

boo [bu] VI/VT abuchear, rechiflar; INTERJ ¡bu! N rechifla f, abucheo m

boob [bub] N fam teta f; Am fam chiche m; Mex fam chichi f; RP fam lola f; — **tube** fam caja boba f

boo-boo [búbu] N (minor injury) lastimadura f; Sp fam pupa f; Am nana f; **to make a** — meter la pata

booby [búbi] N (fool) bobo -a mf; (bird) bobo m; — **hatch** fam loquería f; — **prize** premio al peor competidor m; — **trap** trampa explosiva f

booger [búgɚ] N moco [seco] m

book [bʊk] N libro m; —**binding** encuadernación f; —**case** estante m, estantería f, biblioteca f; —**end** sujetalibros m sg; —**keeper** tenedor -ra de libros mf; Sp contable mf; —**keeping** teneduría de libros f, contabilidad f; —**mark** marcador de libros m; —**mobile** biblioteca móvil f; — **review** reseña f; —**seller** librero -ra mf; —**shelf** estante m; —**store** librería f; — **value** valor contable m; **by the** — siguiendo las reglas; **on the** —**s** registrado en los libros; **to keep** —**s** llevar los libros; VT (reserve) reservar; (hire) contratar; (record charges against) fichar

bookish [búkɪʃ] ADJ (person) estudioso; (allusion) libresco

booklet [búklɪt] N cartilla f

boom [bum] VI (resound) resonar; (prosper) prosperar; N (noise) explosión f; (increase) auge m

boon [bun] N (blessing) bendición f; (favor) favor m

boondocks [búndɑks] ADV LOC [out] **in the** — fam en los quintos infiernos, en el quinto pino

boondoggle [búndɑgəl] N despilfarro m

boor [bur] N patán -ana mf

boorish [búrɪʃ] ADJ grosero, zafio

boost [bust] VT (to shove) empujar [desde abajo o detrás]; (to promote) estimular, impulsar; N (shove) empujón [desde abajo] m; (aid) estímulo m, impulso m; — **in prices** alza de precios f

booster [bústɚ] N (person) animador -ra mf; (rocket) acelerador m; (electronic device) amplificador m; (vaccination) refuerzo m

boot [but] N (shoe) bota f; (trunk of a car) cajuela f; (clamp for cars) cepo m; —**black** limpiabotas m sg; — **disk** disco de iniciación m; —**legger** contrabandista de licores m;

—**licker** vulg lameculos mf; —**able diskette** disquete de iniciación f; **to give the** — poner de patitas en la calle; **to** — por añadidura; VT dar una patada a; **to** — **[out]** echar a patadas; **to** — **up** (a computer) iniciar

booth [buθ] N (telephone) cabina f; (sales) puesto m; (ticket) taquilla f

booty [búɖi] N (loot) botín m; (buttocks) trasero m

booze [buz] N fam bebercio m, bebida alcohólica f

borax [bóræks] N bórax m

border [bórdɚ] N (line between countries) frontera f; (edge, brink) borde m; (bed of flowers) ariete m; (design) ribete m; — **control** control fronterizo m; — **patrol officer** carabinero -ra mf; ADJ —**line** (on a border) fronterizo; (not up to standards) dudoso; VI/VT (make a design) ribetear; **to** — **on** colindar con; **it** —**s on madness** raya en la locura

bordering [bórdəɾɪŋ] ADJ limítrofe

bore [bor] N (hole) agujero m; (of a gun, cylinder) calibre m; (uninteresting person) aburrido -da mf, pesado -da mf; (uninteresting thing) lata f; VT (make a hole) taladrar, horadar; (fail to interest) aburrir

bore [bor] see bear

bored [bord] ADJ aburrido; **I'm** — estoy aburrido

boredom [bórdəm] N aburrimiento m, tedio m

boric acid [bórɪk æsɪd] N ácido bórico m

boring [bórɪŋ] ADJ aburrido; **he's** — es aburrido

born [bɔrn] ADJ nacido; **he's a** — **dancer** es un bailarín nato; **she's a** — **liar** es una mentirosa de nacimiento; **to be** — nacer

borne [bɔrn] see bear

boron [bóɾɑn] N boro m

borrow [báɾo] VT pedir prestado; **I** —**ed money from Fred** le pedí dinero prestado a Fred; **may I** — **your car?** ¿me prestas tu coche? **I** —**ed these books from the library** saqué estos libros de la biblioteca

borrower [báɾoɚ] N (of money) prestatario -ria mf; (of library books) usuario -ria mf

Bosnia and Herzegovina [bázniənhɚtsəgəvínə] N Bosnia-Herzegovina f

Bosnian [bázniən] ADJ & N bosnio -nia mf

bosom [búzəm] N pecho m, seno m; **in the** — **of the family** en el seno de la familia; — **buddy** amigo íntimo m

boss [bɔs] N jefe -fa mf; (on a plantation) mayoral m, capataz m; (political) dirigente m; (mafia) capo m; VT **to** — **around** mandonear

bossy [bósi] ADJ mandón

botanical [bətǽnɪkəl] ADJ botánico

botany [bátn̩i] N botánica f

botch [bátʃ] VT chapucear, estropear; N chapucería f, chapuza f

both [boθ] ADJ & PRON ambos, los dos

bother [báðɚ] VT molestar, fastidiar; VI

molestarse, tomarse la molestia; N molestia *f*
bothersome [báðɚsəm] ADJ (activity) molesto,
enojoso; (person) enfadoso, molesto
botox [bótaks] N bótox *m*
Botswana [batswánə] N Botsuana *f*
bottle [bádl] N botella *f*; (for medicine, perfume)
frasco *m*; —**neck** atascadero *m*,
embotellamiento *m*; — **top** chapa de botella *f*;
VT embotellar; **to** — **up** atascar, embotellar
bottom [bápəm] N (of a hole) fondo *m*; (of a pile,
page, bed) pie *m*; (lower part) base *f*, parte de
abajo *f*; (buttocks) trasero *m*; **to be at the** —
of the class ser el último de la clase; **to hit**
— tocar fondo; **who is at the** — **of all this?**
¿quién está detrás de todo esto? ADJ de abajo;
— **line** (business) balance final *m*; (essential
element) lo esencial; VI **to** — **out** tocar fondo
bottomless [bápəmlɪs] ADJ sin fondo; —
supply recursos ilimitados *m pl*; —
accusation acusación infundada *f*; **he's a** —
pit es un barril sin fondo
botulism [bátʃəlɪzəm] N botulismo *m*
boudoir [búdwar] N tocador *m*
bough [baʊ] N rama *f*
bought [bɔt] *see* buy
bouillon [búljan] N caldo *m*
boulder [bółdɚ] N peña *f*, pedrusco *m*
boulevard [búləvard] N bulevar *m*
bounce [baʊns] N (of a ball) bote *m*, rebote *m*;
(vitality) vitalidad *f*; VT echar, botar; **to** — **a**
check rebotar un cheque; VI rebotar; **to** —
back recuperarse
bouncer [baʊnsɚ] N gorila *m*
bound [baʊnd] N (jump) salto *m*; —**s** límite *m*,
confín *m*; ADJ (tied up) atado; (confined)
confinado; (obliged) obligado; (as a book)
encuadernado; **to be** — **for** ir rumbo a; **to be**
— **up in one's work** estar absorto en su
trabajo; **it is** — **to happen** es seguro que
pasará; **I am** — **to do it** estoy resuelto a
hacerlo; VI (jump) saltar; (be contiguous)
lindar
bound [baʊnd] *see* bind
boundary [báʊndri] N (of a country, city) límite
m, término *m*; (of a property) linde *mf*,
lindero *m*
boundless [báʊndlɪs] ADJ ilimitado, sin límites
bountiful [báʊntəfəl] ADJ abundante
bounty [báʊnti] N (abundance) abundancia *f*;
(reward) recompensa *f*
bouquet [buké] N (of flowers, large) ramo *m*; (of
flowers, small) ramillete *m*; (of wine) aroma
m, bouquet *m*
bourgeois [burʒwá] ADJ & N burgués -sa *mf*
bourgeoisie [burʒwazí] N burguesía *f*
bout [baʊt] N [sports] encuentro *m*; **a** — **of flu**
una gripe
boutique [butík] N boutique *f*
bovine [bóvaɪn] ADJ vacuno

bow[1] [baʊ] N (gesture) reverencia *f*; (prow) proa
f; VI (bend at the waist) hacer una reverencia;
(yield) someterse; **to** — **out** retirarse; VT
inclinar
bow[2] [bo] N (for arrows, violin) arco *m*; (curve)
curva *f*; (decoration) moño *m*; —**knot** lazada
f; —**-string** cuerda de arco *f*; ADJ —**-legged**
patizambo; VI/VT (bend) arquear[se]; (play a
violin with a bow) tocar con arco
bowel [báʊəl] N —**s** intestinos *m pl*; —**s of the**
earth entrañas de la tierra *f pl*; —
movement evacuación del vientre *f*
bower [báʊɚ] N enramada *f*
bowl [boł] N (container) bol *m*, tazón *m*; (dish)
plato hondo *m*; (depression) cuenco *m*; (of a
toilet) taza *f*; (of a pipe) cazoleta *f*; VT **to** —
over apabullar, deslumbrar
bowling [bólɪŋ] N boliche *m*, bowling *m*; **let's**
go — vamos al boliche; —**alley** boliche *m*,
bolera *f*
box [baks] N caja *f*; (for jewelry) estuche *m*; (in
the theater) palco de teatro *m*; (for the jury)
tribuna *f*; (on a page) cuadro *m*; (in soccer)
área de penales *f*; — **car** vagón de carga *m*; —
office taquilla *f*; — **seat** asiento de palco *m*;
VT (put in a box) meter en una caja; (hit)
abofetear; (engage in sport) boxear
boxer [báksɚ] N (fighter) boxeador -ra *mf*,
pugilista *mf*; (breed of dog) bóxer *m*; —
shorts calzoncillo[s] *m*
boxing [báksɪŋ] N boxeo *m*, pugilato *m*; — **glove**
guante de boxeo *m*; — **ring** ring *m*,
cuadrilátero *m*
boy [bɔɪ] N (baby) niño *m*; (young man)
muchacho *m*, chico *m*; — **scout** boy scout *m*;
—**friend** novio *m*
boycott [bɔ́ɪkat] VT boicotear; N boicoteo *m*,
boicot *m*
boyhood [bɔ́ɪhʊd] N niñez *f*, juventud *f*
boyish [bɔ́ɪʃ] ADJ de muchacho
brace [bres] N (in construction) tirante *m*; (pair)
par *m*; (printed character) corchete *m*; (of a
carpenter) berbiquí *m*; —**s** (for teeth) aparato
ortodóntico *m*; (for a leg) aparato ortopédico
m; VT (against a shock) agarrarse; (support)
asegurar
bracelet [bréslɪt] N brazalete *m*, pulsera *f*
bracket [brǽkɪt] N (support) soporte *m*, sostén
m; (typographic sign) paréntesis recto *m*,
corchete *m*; (division) banda *f*; VT (fix with
brackets) fijar con soportes; (write in
brackets) colocar entre paréntesis rectos;
(associate) agrupar
brag [brǽg] VI jactarse [de], hacer alarde [de]
braggart [brǽgɚt] ADJ & N fanfarrón -na *mf*
braid [bred] N trenza *f*; VT trenzar
brain [bren] N cerebro *m*; (food) seso *m*; **she**
blew out his —**s** le levantó la tapa de los
sesos; **he's short on** —**s** es corto de

inteligencia; **he is the —s in this operation** él es el cerebro en esta operación; **to rack one's —s** devanarse los sesos, romperse la cabeza; — **death** muerte cerebral *f*; — **drain** fuga de cerebros *f*; — **scan** tomografía cerebral *f*; — **trust** grupo de expertos *m*; — **stem** tronco del encéfalo *m*; —**storming** lluvia de ideas *f*; — **tumor** tumor cerebral *m*; VT **to — someone** romperle la crisma a alguien; **to —wash** lavarle el cerebro a; ADJ **—-dead** clínicamente muerto, en estado vegetativo

brainy [bréni] ADJ sesudo

brake [brek] N freno *m*; — **drum** tambor del freno *m*; — **fluid** líquido para frenos *m*; —**man** guardafrenos *m sg*; — **shoe** zapata *f*; **to apply the —s** frenar; VI/VT frenar

bramble [brǽmbəł] N zarza *f*

bran [bræn] N salvado *m*; (for birds) afrecho *m*

branch [bræntʃ] N (of a plant, of a family) rama *f*; (of a train track) ramal *m*; (of antlers) brazo *m*; (of a science) ramo *m*; (of a business) sucursal *f*; (of the armed forces) arma *f*; (in a computer program) bifurcación *f*; (of a river) tributario *m*; VI/VT ramificar[se]

brand [brænd] N (make, mark) marca *f*; (of humor, etc.) tipo *m*; (mark of disgrace) estigma *m*; — **awareness** conciencia de marca *f*; — **loyalty** lealtad de marca *f*; — **name** marca *f*; ADJ **—-new** flamante, recién comprado; VT (burn) herrar, marcar; (stigmatize) estigmatizar; **to — as** tildar de, tachar de

brandish [brǽndɪʃ] VT blandir, esgrimir

brandy [brǽndi] N (fine) brandy *m*; (cheap) aguardiente *m*

brash [bræʃ] ADJ (impudent) descarado; (impetuous) impetuoso

brass [bræs] N (metal) latón *m*; (attitude) descaro *m*; (high-ranking officers) la plana mayor; — **instrument** instrumento de metal *m*; **to get down to — tacks** ir al grano; ADJ de latón

brassiere [brəzír] N sostén *m*

brat [bræt] N mocoso -sa *mf*

bravado [brəváðo] N alarde *m*

brave [brev] ADJ valiente, gallardo; N guerrero indio *m*; VT desafiar

bravery [brévəri] N valentía *f*, gallardía *f*

brawl [brɔl] N reyerta *f*, riña *f*, pelotera *f*; VI reñir

bray [bre] N rebuzno *m*; VI rebuznar

brazen [brézən] ADJ (impudent) descarado; (made of brass) de latón

brazier [bréʒɚ] N brasero *m*

Brazil [brəzíł] N Brasil *m*

Brazilian [brəzíljən] ADJ & N brasileño -ña *mf*, brasilero -ra *mf*

breach [britʃ] N (opening) brecha *f*; (infraction) infracción *f*; (severance) ruptura *f*; — **of**

contract incumplimiento de contrato *m*; — **of faith** abuso de confianza *m*; VT (make an opening) abrir una brecha en; (violate a law) violar, infringir

bread [brɛd] N pan *m*; —**basket** panera *f*; — **box** panera *f*; —**winner** sostén de la familia *m*; ADJ **—-and-butter** básico; VT empanar

breadth [brɛdθ] N anchura *f*, ancho *m*; (size) extensión *f*; (perspective) amplitud *f*

break [brek] VI (fracture) romperse; (pause) parar; VT (a record) batir; (a code) descifrar; (a law) violar; (news) dar, divulgar; (a bone) fracturar; (a horse) domar, desbravar; (a habit) quitar[se]; (a contract, promise) romper; (one's spirit) quebrar, doblegar; (one's heart) desgarrar; (cause to go bankrupt) arruinar; **to — a ten-dollar bill** conseguir cambio para un billete de diez dólares; **to — away** escaparse; **to — down** (a person) descomponerse; (a car) averiarse; (resistance) vencer; (continuity) interrumpir; **to — even** quedar a mano; **to — into** violentar; **to — loose** liberarse; **to — out** (war) estallar; (one's face) brotarse; (from prison) escaparse; **to — up** (into pieces) quebrarse; (a relationship) romper con; N (weather) cambio *m*; (from work) descanso *m*; (with tradition) quiebre *m*, rompimiento *m*; (of a bone) fractura *f*; (from prison) fuga *f*; (opportunity) oportunidad *f*; **—-in** hurto con escalo *m*; —**down** (analysis) análisis *m*; (automotive) avería *f*; (nervous) colapso *m*; —**down of charges** desglose de cargos *m*; —**even point** umbral de rentabilidad *m*; — **point** (in tennis) bola de break *f*, bola de ruptura *f*; —**through** adelanto *m*; (military) penetración *f*; —**water** rompeolas *m sg*; **give me a —!** ¡déjame en paz! **lucky —** golpe de suerte *m*

breakable [brékəbəł] ADJ quebradizo, rompible

breaker [brékɚ] N rompiente *f*

breakfast [brékfəst] N desayuno *m*; VI desayunar

breast [brɛst] N (of a woman) seno *m*, pecho *m*; *fam* teta *f*; (of a bird) pechuga *f*; —**bone** esternón *m*; — **cancer** cáncer de mama *m*; **—-feeding** lactancia materna *f*; —**stroke** (estilo de natación) pecho *m*; VI/VT **to —-feed** amamantar, dar de mamar

breath [brɛθ] N aliento *m*; *lit* hálito *m*; (current of air) soplo *m*; **in the same —** al mismo tiempo; **out of —** sin aliento; **to catch one's —** recobrar el aliento; **to hold one's —** aguantar la respiración; **to take a —** inhalar; **to take a deep —** respirar hondo; **under one's —** entre dientes, por lo bajo; ADJ —**taking** impresionante

breathe [brið] VI/VT respirar; **to — in** inspirar, aspirar; **to — into** infundir; **to — out** exhalar, espirar; **he did not — a word** no

dijo palabra
breathing [bríðɪŋ] N respiración f
breathless [brέθlɪs] ADJ sin aliento
breathlessness [brέθlɪsnɪs] N falta de aire f
bred [brεd] see breed
breed [brid] VT (mate) criar; (bring up) educar;
(give rise to) engendrar; VI reproducirse,
multiplicarse; N (species) raza f; (type) clase f
breeder [brídɚ] N (person who breeds) criador
-ora mf; (animal used for breeding) [animal]
reproductor m
breeding [brídɪŋ] N (of animals) cría f; (of
people) educación f, modales m pl
breeze [briz] N brisa f
breezy [brízi] ADJ (windy) ventoso; (jaunty)
ameno
brevity [brέvɪDi] N brevedad f
brew [bru] VT (coffee) hacer; (mischief)
fomentar, tramar; (beer) fabricar; VI (storm)
armarse una tormenta; **let the tea** — deja
reposar el té; N (mixture) mezcla f; (beer)
cerveza f
brewery [brúəri] N cervecera f, fábrica de
cerveza f
briar [bráɚ] N zarza f
bribe [braɪb] N soborno m, cohecho m; Mex
mordida f; VT sobornar
bribery [bráɪbəri] N soborno m
brick [brɪk] N ladrillo m; —**bat** (piece of brick)
pedazo de ladrillo m; (insult) insulto m;
—**layer** albañil m; —**laying** albañilería f; VT
(adorn with bricks) revestir de ladrillo; (pave
with bricks) enladrillar
bridal [bráɪdl] ADJ nupcial; — **dress** vestido de
novia m
bride [braɪd] N novia f; —**groom** novio m;
—**smaid** dama de honor f
bridge [brɪʤ] N puente m; (of the nose) caballete
m; (card game) bridge m; VT (a river) tender
un puente sobre; (a gap) llenar, salvar
bridle [bráɪdl] N (harness) brida f; (restraint)
freno m; VT (put on a bridle) poner una brida;
(restrain) frenar; VI (be insulted) ofenderse
brief [brif] ADJ (short) breve, escueto; (concise)
conciso, escueto; (curt) seco; N sumario m,
resumen m; (report) expediente m; —**case**
portafolio[s] m sg, maletín m; —**s** calzoncillos
m pl; **in** — en suma; VT informar
briefing [brífɪŋ] N reunión para dar
instrucciones f
brigade [brɪgéd] N brigada f
bright [braɪt] ADJ (shining) brillante; (full of
light) iluminado; (smart) inteligente;
(promising) venturoso, prometedor; (radiant)
radiante; (colorful) subido
brighten [bráɪtn̩] VT (a room) iluminar; VI **to** —
up (person) animar[se]; (sky) despejarse
brightness [bráɪtnɪs] N (light) claridad f;
(cheerfulness) viveza f; (intelligence)

inteligencia f
brilliance [bríljəns] N (of hair, of a historical
period) brillantez f; (of intellect) genio m
brilliant [bríljənt] ADJ (shining) brillante;
(intelligent) genial; (splendid) espléndido; N
brillante m, diamante m
brim [brɪm] N borde m; (of a hat) ala f; **to fill to
the** — llenar hasta el borde; **to be filled to
the** — estar de bote en bote; VI **to** — **over**
rebosar; **to be** —**ming with** estar rebosante
de
brine [braɪn] N salmuera f
bring [brɪŋ] VT traer; (cause) ocasionar, causar;
to — **about** producir, ocasionar; **to** — **down**
(kill) bajar; (depress) deprimir; **to** — **forth**
(give birth) dar a luz; (produce) producir; **to**
— **to a stop** parar; **to** — **a session to a
close** clausurar una sesión; **to** — **together**
reunir, juntar; **to** — **oneself to do
something** poder hacer algo; **to** — **a good
price** redituar una buena ganancia; **to** — **up**
(raise children) criar, educar; (mention)
mencionar
brink [brɪŋk] N borde m; **on the** — **of** al borde
de
brisk [brɪsk] ADJ (walk) rápido; (weather) fresco;
(trading) activo
bristle [brɪsl̩] N cerda f; VI erizar[se]; **to** — **with**
estar erizado de
bristly [brísli] ADJ (with bristles) erizado,
cerdoso; (irascible) irascible
Britain [brítn̩] N Gran Bretaña f
British [brídɪʃ] ADJ británico
brittle [brídl] ADJ quebradizo, frágil
brittleness [brídl̩nɪs] N fragilidad f
broach [brotʃ] VT sacar a colación
broad [brɔd] ADJ (wide) ancho; (vast) vasto;
(ample) amplio; —**band** banda ancha f;
—**cast** emisión f; (on TV) transmisión por
televisión f; —**cast station** emisora f; —
hint insinuación clara f; — **jump** salto de
longitud m; —-**minded** tolerante; —**side**
andanada f; — **spectrum antibiotic**
antibiótico de amplio espectro m; **in** —
daylight en pleno día; N pej tipa f; VT **to**
—**cast** (communicate electronically)
transmitir, emitir, radiar
broadcasting [brɔ́dkæstɪŋ] N (radio)
radiodifusión f; (TV) transmisión por
televisión f
brocade [brokéd] N brocado m
broccoli [brákəli] N brócoli m, brécol m
brochure [broʃúr] N folleto m
broil [brɔɪl] VI/VT asar[se] [a la parrilla]
broiler [brɔ́ɪlɚ] N (oven) parrilla f; (chicken)
pollo [para asar] m
broke [brok] ADJ **to be** — estar limpio, estar
pelado; **to go** — irse a la quiebra
broke [brok] see break

broken [brókən] ADJ (fragmented) roto, quebrado; (tamed) domado; (not functioning) descompuesto; (not continuous) interrumpido; —-**down** averiado, descompuesto; — **English** inglés chapurrado/chapurreado m; —**hearted** deshecho, con el corazón destrozado

broken [brókən] see break

broker [brókə·] N (intermediary) agente mf; (stock salesperson) corredor -ora de bolsa mf

brokerage [brókə·ɪʤ] N correduría f

bromide [brómaɪd] N bromuro m

bromine [brómin] N bromo m

bronchial [bráŋkiəł] ADJ bronquial; — **tube** bronquio m

bronchitis [braŋkáɪdɪs] N bronquitis f

bronco [bráŋko] N caballo no domado m

bronze [branz] N bronce m; VT broncear

brooch [brutʃ] N broche m, prendedor m

brood [brud] N pollada f, nidada f; VI/VT empollar; **to** — **over** rumiar

brook [brʊk] N riachuelo m, cañada f; VT tolerar

broom [brum] N (tool) escoba f; (plant) retama f; —**stick** palo de escoba m

broth [brɔθ] N caldo m

brothel [bráθəł] N burdel m

brother [bráðə·] N hermano m; —-**in-law** cuñado m; **oh** —! ¡caray!

brotherhood [bráðə·hʊd] N hermandad f

brotherly [bráðə·li] ADJ fraternal

brought [brɔt] see bring

brow [braʊ] N (eyebrow) ceja f; (ridge of eye) arco superciliar m; (forehead) frente f

brown [braʊn] ADJ (skin) moreno; (eyes, shoes, clothes) café, marrón; (hair) castaño; (dun) pardo; (tanned) bronceado; — **bear** oso pardo m; —-**noser** vulg lameculos mf sg, adulón -ona mf; — **rice** arroz integral m; — **sugar** azúcar moreno -na mf; VI/VT (food) dorar[se]; N (color) café m, castaño m, moreno m, pardo m; VI **to** —-**nose** vulg lamer culos

brownie [bráuni] N bizcocho de chocolate m; — **points** méritos m pl

browse [braʊz] VT (a book) hojear; VI (grass) pacer, pastar; (Internet) navegar

browser [bráuzə·] N navegador m

browsing [bráuzɪŋ] N navegación f

bruise [bruz] N (on skin) moretón m, cardenal m, contusión f; (on fruit) magulladura f, cardenal m; VI/VT magullar[se], machucar[se]

brunch [brʌntʃ] N brunch m, desayuno tardío m

Brunei [brunái] N Brunéi m

Bruneian [brunáiən] ADJ & N bruneano -na mf

brunette, brunet [brunét] ADJ & N moreno -na mf, morocho -cha mf; Cuba trigueño -ña mf

brunt [brʌnt] N impacto m

brush [brʌʃ] N (for teeth, clothes) cepillo m; (for paint, shaving) brocha f; (artist's) pincel m; (vegetation) maleza f; (contact) roce m; —-**off**

despedida brusca f; —**wood** (dead) broza f; (live) maleza f; VT (clean with a brush) cepillar; (touch lightly) rozar; **to** — **aside** echar a un lado; **to** — **up on** repasar; **to** — **off** (clean) quitar con cepillo; (reject) despedir bruscamente a alguien

brusque [brʌsk] ADJ brusco

Brussels sprouts [brásəłspraʊts] N coles de Bruselas f pl, repollitos de Bruselas m pl

brutal [brúdł] ADJ brutal

brutality [brutǽlɪDi] N brutalidad f

brute [brut] N (animal) bestia f; (person) bruto -ta mf; ADJ bruto

bubble [bábł] N burbuja f; (in soap) pompa f; (in boiling water) borbollón m; (illusion) encanto m; — **bath** baño de burbujas m; —**gum** chicle de globo m; —-**jet printer** impresora de burbuja f; VI (make bubbles) borbotar, borbollar; (boil) bullir, hervir; **to** — **over with joy** rebosar de alegría

bubonic plague [bubánɪkplég] N plaga bubónica f

buck [bʌk] N (deer) gamo m; (male of other animals) macho m; (leap of horse) respingo m; — **private** soldado raso m; —**shot** posta f, perdigón m; —**skin** gamuza f; —**wheat** trigo sarraceno m; **to pass the** — echarle el muerto a uno; ADJ —**toothed** de dientes salidos; VI (horse) respingar, corcovear; **to** — **a trend** oponerse; **to** — **up** cobrar ánimo

bucket [bákɪt] N cubo m, balde m; (of a loader) cuchara f; — **seat** asiento delantero individual m

buckle [bákəł] N (clasp) hebilla f; (kink in a board) torcedura f; VT (to clasp) abrocharse; (to bend) torcerse, pandearse; **to** — **down** esforzarse; **to** — **up** abrocharse

bud [bʌd] N botón m, retoño m; VI (make buds) echar retoños

Buddhism [búdɪzəm] N budismo m

Buddhist [búdɪst] ADJ & N budista mf

buddy [bádi] N camarada mf

budge [bʌʤ] VI moverse

budget [báʤɪt] N presupuesto m; VT (money) presupuestar; (time, personal resources) administrar; — **cycle** ciclo presupuestario m; — **deficit** déficit presupuestario m

budgetary [báʤɪtɛri] ADJ presupuestario

budgeting [báʤɪdɪŋ] N presupuestación f

buff [bʌf] N (leather) gamuza f; (tan color) color beige m; (wheel for polishing) pulidor m; (devotee) aficionado m; **in the** — en cueros; ADJ (beige) de color beige; (muscular) musculoso; VT pulir

buffalo [báfəlo] N bisonte m, búfalo m; — **wings** alitas f pl

buffer [báfə·] N (in a computer) memoria intermedia f; (shock absorber) amortiguador m; (polishing device) pulidor -ra mf; — **zone**

zona tampón f
buffet¹ [báfɪt] N (blow) golpe m, puñetazo m;
(shock) azote m; VT (hit) golpear; (hit
repeatedly) azotar
buffet² [bəfé] N (cabinet) aparador m; (meal)
buffet m
buffoon [bəfún] N payaso -a mf, bufón -ona mf
bug [bʌg] N bicho m; (disease-causing) microbio
m, virus m; (for eavesdropping) micrófono
oculto m; (in a computer program) fallo m,
bicho m; VT (bother) molestar; (install
microphones) colocar micrófonos ocultos;
his eyes —ged out se le saltaron los ojos
buggy [bági] N (cart) calesa f; (baby carriage)
cochecillo m
bugle [bjúgəɫ] N clarín m; VI tocar el clarín
build [bɪɫd] VT (construct) construir, edificar;
(manufacture) fabricar; **to — into**
incorporar; **to — up** (make stronger)
fortalecer; (accumulate) acumular; (enhance)
desarrollar; (urbanize) urbanizar; N **—-up** (of
military forces) concentración f; (of
substance) acumulación f; (of anticipation)
aumento m; N (of human body) complexión f
builder [bíɫdə˞] N contratista mf, constructor
-ora mf
building [bíɫdɪŋ] N (thing built) edificio m; (act
of building) construcción f, edificación f;
(unit in a housing complex) bloque m; **—
block** (solid mass) bloque [de construcción]
m; (toy) cubo m; (essential element) elemento
fundamental m
built [bɪɫt] ADJ **—-in** (furniture appliance)
empotrado; (feature) incorporado; **—-in
part** parte integrante f; **—-to-order** hecho a
pedido, **—-up** urbanizado
built [bɪɫt] see build
bulb [bʌɫb] N (plant) bulbo m; (light) bombilla f;
Am foco m
bulbous [báɫbəs] ADJ bulboso
Bulgaria [bʌɫgériə] N Bulgaria f
Bulgarian [bʌɫgériən] ADJ & N búlgaro -ra mf
bulge [bʌɫʤ] N bulto m, protuberancia f; VI
abultar, hincharse
bulgy [báɫʤi] ADJ abultado
bulimia [bjulímiə] N bulimia f
bulk [bʌɫk] N (mass) cantidad f, volumen m;
(greater part) mayor parte f; **— storage**
almacenamiento masivo m; **in — a** granel; VI
to — up echar músculos
bulky [báɫki] ADJ voluminoso
bull [bʊɫ] N toro m; **—dog** buldog m; **—dozer**
bulldozer m; **—fight** corrida de toros f;
—fighter torero m; **—fighting**
tauromaquia f; **—frog** rana grande f; **—
market** mercado alcista m; **—pen** (baseball)
zona de calentamiento f; **—shit** disparates m
pl, mentiras f pl; **that's —shit** y una polla
[como una olla]; **—'s eye** diana f; **to hit the**

—'s-eye dar en el blanco; ADJ **—headed**
terco, obstinado
bullet [búlɪt] N bala f; ADJ **—proof** antibalas inv,
antibalístico
bulletin [búlɪtn̩] N boletín m; **— board** tablero
m, cartelera f
bullion [búljən] N oro en lingotes m
bully [búli] N matón -ona mf, bravucón -ona mf;
VT intimidar
bulwark [búɫwə˞k] N baluarte m
bum [bʌm] N (lazy person) holgazán -ana mf;
(hobo) vagabundo -da mf; (sports fan)
fanático -ca mf; ADJ (accusation) falso; (knee)
vulg jodido; VI **to — around** holgazanear; VT
to — something from someone
gorronearle algo a alguien
bumblebee [bámbəɫbi] N abejorro m, abejón m
bummer [bámə˞] N vulg cagada f
bump [bʌmp] VT chocar; **to — along** ir dando
tumbos; **to — off** despachar; **to — into**
toparse con; N (blow) choque m, trastazo m;
(lump) protuberancia f; (lump on a person)
chichón m
bumper [bámpə˞] N parachoques m sg, tope m;
— car coche de choque m, autito chocador m;
— crop cosecha abundante f; **—-to-—
traffic** caravana de autos f; **— sticker**
autoadhesivo m
bumpy [bámpi] ADJ bacheado, lleno de baches
bun [bʌn] N (bread) bollo m; (in hair) moño m;
—s fam nalgas f pl
bunch [bʌntʃ] N (of things) manojo m; (of
people) montón m, grupo m; (of grapes,
bananas) racimo m; (of flowers) ramillete m;
VI/VT juntar[se], agrupar[se]
bundle [bándl] N (of things) paquete m, fardo m,
envoltorio m; (of clothes) lío m, atado m; (of
belongings) hato m, petate m; (of firewood)
haz m; VT (tie together) liar, atar; **to — up**
abrigarse; **to — off** despachar
bungalow [báŋgəlo] N bungaló m
bungee jumping [bánʤiʤámpɪŋ] N bungee m,
puénting m
bungle [báŋgəɫ] VT estropear; VI chapucear
bunion [bánjən] N juanete m
bunk [bʌŋk] N (place to sleep) litera f; (nonsense)
tonterías f pl; **— bed** litera f; VI dormir en una
litera
bunker [báŋkə˞] N búnker m
bunny [báni] N conejito m
bunt [bʌnt] N (baseball) toque de pelota m; VT
tocar la pelota
buoy [búi] N boya f; VI boyar; **to — up** mantener
a flote, animar
buoyant [bɔ́iənt] ADJ (floating) boyante,
flotante; (optimistic) optimista
burden [bɝ́dn̩] N (load) carga f; (responsibility)
peso m; **— of proof** peso de la prueba m; VT
(heavily) recargar; (oppressively) agobiar

burdensome [bɝ́dṇsəm] ADJ agobiante, gravoso

bureau [bjúro] N (government department) oficina f, agencia f; (chest of drawers) cómoda f

bureaucracy [bjʊrákrəsi] N burocracia f

bureaucrat [bjúrəkræt] N burócrata mf

burglar [bɝ́glə] N ladrón -ona mf; — **alarm** alarma antirrobo f; — **proof** a prueba de robos

burglary [bɝ́gləri] N robo con allanamiento m

burial [bériəl] N entierro m, enterramiento m; — **ground** enterramiento m; — **place** lugar de sepultura m

Burkina Faso [bəkínəfáso] N Burkina Faso m

burlap [bɝ́læp] N arpillera f

burlesque [bəlésk] ADJ burlesco; N espectáculo de variedades m

burly [bɝ́li] ADJ corpulento

Burma [bə́mə] N Birmania f

Burmese [bəmíz] ADJ & N birmano -na mf

burn [bɝn] VI/VT quemar[se], abrasar[se]; (a house) incendiar[se]; (a CD) quemar; (food) quemar[se], requemar[se]; **he got —ed in the transaction** lo estafaron en el negocio; **the bulb is still —ing** la bombilla sigue prendida; **the iodine —ed his skin** el yodo le quemó la piel; VI (with heat, passion) arder, abrasar; **my skin —s** me arde la piel; **he's —ing with desire** arde en deseos; **to — down** incendiarse; **to — off** (fog) disiparse; **to — out** (bulb) fundirse; (worker) agotarse; **to — up** quemarse completamente; N quemadura f; **—out** surmenage m

burner [bɝ́nə] N (person or thing that burns something) quemador -ra mf; (on stove) hornilla f; **Bunsen —** mechero Bunsen m

burning [bɝ́nɪŋ] ADJ (desire) ardiente, abrasador; (question) urgente; N (caused by acid) ardor m; (caused by fire) quemadura f

burnish [bɝ́nɪʃ] VT bruñir

burnt [bɝnt] see burn

burp [bɝp] N eructo m; VI eructar, repetir

burr, bur [bɝ] N abrojo m

burrow [bɝ́o] N madriguera f; VI (dig) hacer madrigueras; (live) vivir en una madriguera

bursitis [bəsáɪDɪs] N bursitis f

burst [bɝst] VI reventar[se]; **to — into a room** irrumpir en un cuarto; **to — into tears** romper en llanto; **to — out** salir disparado; **to — with laughter** estallar/reventar de risa; N (of activity) explosión f; (of laughter) carcajada f; (of machine-gun fire) ráfaga f; (of speed) aceleración f

Burundi [bʊrúndi] N Burundi m

Burundian [bʊrúndiən] ADJ & N burundés -esa mf

bury [béri] VT (body, treasure) enterrar; (body) sepultar; **to be buried in thought** estar absorto/meditabundo

bus [bʌs] N autobús m, ómnibus m; Mex camión m; RP colectivo m; Chile micro m; Cuba guagua f; (in a computer) bus m; VT transportar en autobús

bush [bʊʃ] N (plant) arbusto m, mata f; (region) matorral m; **to beat around the —** andarse por las ramas

bushed [bʊʃt] ADJ fatigado

bushel [búʃəl] N fanega f

bushing [búʃɪŋ] N buje m, cojinete m

bushy [búʃi] ADJ (whiskers) espeso; (plants) poblado de arbustos

business [bíznɪs] N (trade, store) negocio m; (occupation) ocupación f; (commercial activity) comercio m; — **acumen** buen sentido para los negocios m; — **agreement** convenio comercial m; — **card** tarjeta comercial f; — **day** día hábil m; — **group** grupo empresarial m; — **hours** horas hábiles f pl, horario de atención al público m; — **is booming** el negocio florece; **—like** (efficient) eficiente; (cold) impersonal; **—man** hombre de negocios m, negociante m; — **suit** traje m; — **transaction** negocio m, transacción comercial f; **—woman** mujer de negocios f, negociante f; **I'm tired of the whole —** este asunto me tiene harto; **I mean —** hablo en serio; **to do — with** comerciar con; **he has no — doing it** no tiene derecho a hacerlo; **it's none of your —** no es asunto tuyo; **mind your own —** no te metas en lo que no te importa

bust [bʌst] N (statue, body part) busto m; VI/VT (burst, hit, break) reventar; (force into bankruptcy) hacer quebrar; (lower in rank) degradar

bustle [bʌ́səl] N (noise) bullicio m; (movement) ajetreo m, tráfago m; VI (move busily) ajetrear[se]; (be crowded) bullir

busy [bízi] ADJ ocupado, atareado; (overdecorated) recargado; **—body** entrometido -da mf; — **signal** señal de ocupado f; VI **to — oneself** ocuparse

but [bʌt] CONJ (on the contrary) pero; (excepting) sino; PREP menos; **any day — today** cualquier día menos hoy; **he's nothing — trouble** sólo da problemas; ADV — **for you** si no fuera por ti

butane [bjúten] N butano m

butch [bʊtʃ] ADJ (of a woman) marimacha, camionera; (of a man) machote

butcher [bútʃə] N carnicero -ra mf; **—'s shop** carnicería f; VT (cattle) matar; (people) masacrar; (performance) estropear

butchery [bútʃəri] N carnicería f

butler [bátlə] N mayordomo m

butt [bʌt] N (of body) fam culo m; (of a rifle) culata f; (of a cigarette) colilla f; (blow with head) topetazo m, cabezada f, cabezazo m; **the**

— **of ridicule** el blanco de las burlas; VT embestir, topar; **to — in** entrometerse; **to — into a conversation** meter baza; Am meter la cuchara

butter [bÁDɚ] N mantequilla f; **—cup** botón de oro m; — **dish** mantequera f; **—fingers** manos de mantequilla mf sg; **—milk** suero de leche m; **—scotch** dulce de azúcar y mantequilla m; VT (bread) untar con mantequilla; (a cakepan) enmantecar

butterfly [bÁDɚflaɪ] N mariposa f; — **stroke** estilo mariposa m

buttery [bÁDɚi] ADJ mantecoso

buttocks [bÁDəks] N nalgas f pl, asentaderas f pl, cachas f pl

button [bÁtn̩] N botón m; **—hole** ojal m; VI/VT abotonar[se]; VI **to —hole** hacer ojales; VT **to —hole someone** detener a alguien

buttress [bÁtrɪs] N apoyo m, sostén m; (of a building) contrafuerte m; VT apoyar, reforzar

buxom [bÁksəm] ADJ (full-bosomed) pechugona; (fat and cheerful) frescachona, jamona

buy [baɪ] VT comprar; **to — on credit** comprar a crédito; **to — in installments** comprar a plazos; **to — off** sobornar; **to — out** comprar la parte de; **to — up** acaparar; **I don't — that** no me lo trago; N (purchase) compra f; (bargain) ganga f

buyer [báɪɚ] N comprador -ra mf

buying [báɪɪŋ] N — **frenzy** frenesí de compras m; — **habits** hábitos de compras m pl

buzz [bʌz] N zumbido m; (feeling of intoxication) borrachera f; (phone call) telefonazo m; **—word** palabra de moda f; — **saw** sierra circular f; VI (insect, ears) zumbar; (group) murmurar; VT hacer zumbar; **to — the bell** tocar el timbre; **to give someone a —** pegarle/echarle un telefonazo a alguien; **to — off** largarse; — **off!** ¡no jodas!

buzzard [bÁzɚd] N buitre m

buzzer [bÁzɚ] N timbre m, chicharra f

by [baɪ] PREP por; — **and** — a la larga; — **chance** por casualidad; — **dint of** a fuerza de; — **far** con mucho; — **night** de noche; — **the way** a propósito; — **the liter** por litro; — **this time tomorrow** mañana a esta hora; — **two o'clock** para las dos; **we drove — the church** pasamos por la iglesia; **a 4 — 3 room** un cuarto de 4 por 3; **multiply 2 — 2** multiplica 2 por 2; **we live — the church** vivimos al lado de la iglesia; **she had a son — him** tuvo un hijo con él; **piece — piece** pedazo a/por pedazo; ADV **the factory is close —** la fábrica está cerca; **the bus drove —** pasó el autobús

bye-bye [báɪbáɪ] INTERJ ¡adiós! ¡chaucito!

bygones [báɪgɔnz] N **let — be —** lo pasado pisado

bylaw [báɪlɔ] N estatuto m

by-line [báɪlaɪn] N pie de autor m

bypass [báɪpæs] VT evitar; N desvío m; — **operation** bypass m

by-product [báɪprɑDəkt] N subproducto m; (chemical) derivado m

bystander [báɪstændɚ] N persona presente f

byte [baɪt] N byte m, octeto m

Cc

cab [kæb] N (of a truck) cabina f; (taxi) taxi m; — **driver** taxista mf

cabaret [kæbəré] N cabaret m

cabbage [kæbɪʤ] N col f, repollo m, berza f

cabin [kæbɪn] N (hut) cabaña f; (in an airplane) cabina f; (in a ship) camarote m

cabinet [kæbnɪt] N (for dishes) armario m; (for medicines) botiquín m; (for display) vitrina f; (of ministers) gabinete m; **—level appointment** nombramiento ministerial m; **—maker** ebanista mf

cable [kébəl] N cable m; (on ships) amarra f; (telegram) telegrama m; — **car** funicular m, teleférico m; — **television** televisión por cable f, cablevisión f; VI/VT telegrafiar

caboose [kəbús] N furgón de cola m

cache [kæʃ] N (of weapons) alijo m; (in a computer) caché m; — **memory** memoria de caché f

cachet [kæʃé] N caché m

cackle [kǽkəl] VI (hen) cacarear; (people) parlotear; N (hen) cacareo m; (people) parloteo m

cacophony [kəkáfəni] N cacofonía f

cactus [kǽktəs] N cacto m, cactus m

cad [kæd] N pej canalla mf

cadaver [kədǽvɚ] N cadáver m

caddie [kǽDi] N caddy m, caddie m

cadence [kédn̩s] N cadencia f

cadet [kədét] N cadete mf

cadmium [kǽdmiəm] N cadmio m

café [kæfé] N (coffee only) café m; (coffee and food) cafetería f

cafeteria [kæfɪtíriə] N cafetería f

caffeine [kæfín] N cafeína f

cage [keʤ] N jaula f; VT enjaular

cahoots [kəhúts] ADV LOC **in —** arreglados

cajole [kəʤól] VI/VT engatusar, persuadir con halagos

cake [kek] N pastel m, torta f; (sponge) bizcocho m; (soap) pastilla f; **a piece of —** pan comido; **to take the —** ser el colmo; VI/VT apelmazar[se]

calamine [kǽləmaɪn] N calamina f

calamity [kəlǽmɪDi] N calamidad f

calcium [kǽlsiəm] N calcio *m*
calculate [kǽlkjəlet] VI/VT calcular; **his actions were —d to fool us** con sus acciones trataba de engañarnos
calculating [kǽlkjəleDɪŋ] ADJ calculador
calculation [kælkjəléʃən] N cálculo *m*
calculator [kǽlkjəleDɚ] calculadora *f*
calculus [kǽlkjələs] N cálculo *m*
calendar [kǽlɪndɚ] N calendario *m*; **— year** año civil *m*
calf [kæf] N (of leg) pantorrilla *f*, canilla *f*; (animal) ternero -ra *mf*, becerro -rra *mf*; **— skin** piel de becerro *f*
caliber [kǽləbɚ] N calibre *m*
calibrate [kǽləbret] VT calibrar, graduar
calico [kǽlɪko] N calicó *m*
caliper [kǽləpɚ] N (on brakes) calibrador *m*; (for measuring) calibre *m*
call [kɔl] VT (summon, by telephone, a name, a strike) llamar; (cry out) gritar; (a meeting) convocar; **she —ed me a liar** me llamó mentiroso; **— me back** llámame tú, devuélveme la llamada; VI/VT (birds) reclamar; **to — roll** pasar lista; VI (call out) gritar; **to — a meeting to order** abrir la sesión; **to — at a port** hacer escala en un puerto; **to — for** pedir; **to — off** cancelar; **to — on** (visit) visitar; (depend on) acudir a; **to — together** convocar; **to — up** llamar por teléfono; N (by telephone) llamada *f*; (summons) llamamiento *m*, llamado *m*; (to the ministry) vocación *f*; (for conference papers) convocatoria *f*; (device for calling birds) reclamo *m*; **— girl** prostituta de cita *f*; **to be on —** estar de guardia; **there's no — for panic** no hay motivo de alarma; **it's your —** tú decides; **within —** al alcance de la voz
caller [kɔ́lɚ] N visita *f*, visitante *mf*; (by telephone) persona que llama *f*; **— ID** identificador de llamadas *m*
calligraphy [kəlígrəfi] N caligrafía *f*
calling [kɔ́lɪŋ] N vocación *f*
callous [kǽləs] ADJ (having calluses) calloso; (insensitive) insensible
callus [kǽləs] N callo *m*
calm [kɑm] ADJ tranquilo, reposado, calmo; N calma *f*, tranquilidad *f*, sosiego *m*; VT calmar, tranquilizar, sosegar; **to — down** calmar[se]
calmness [kɑ́mnɪs] N calma *f*, tranquilidad *f*
calorie [kǽləri] N caloría *f*
calumny [kǽləmni] N calumnia *f*
cam [kæm] N leva *f*
Cambodia [kæmbódiə] N Camboya *f*
Cambodian [kæmbódiən] ADJ & N camboyano -na *mf*
camcorder [kǽmkɔrdɚ] N videocámara *f*
came [kem] *see* come
camel [kǽməl] N camello *m*

cameo [kǽmio] N camafeo *m*; **— appearance** actuación especial *f*
camera [kǽmrə] N cámara *f*, cámara fotográfica *f*; **—man** cámara *m*, camarógrafo *m*; **—ready copy** texto listo para cámara *f*; **—woman** cámara *f*, camarógrafa *f*
Cameroon [kæmərún] N Camerún *m*
Cameroonian [kæmərúniən] ADJ & N camerunés -esa *mf*
camouflage [kǽməflɑʒ] N camuflaje *m*; VT camuflar
camp [kæmp] N (campsite) campamento *m*; (faction) bando *m*; **—fire** fogata *f*, hoguera *f*; **—ground** campamento *m*, cámping *m*; **—site** campamento *m*; VI/VT acampar
campaign [kæmpén] N campaña *f*; VI hacer campaña
camper [kǽmpɚ] N acampante *mf*, campista *mf*
camphor [kǽmfɚ] N alcanfor *m*
camping [kǽmpɪŋ] N cámping *m*, acampada *f*; **let's go —** vamos de camping / de acampada
campus [kǽmpəs] N campus *m*
can [kæn] N lata *f*, bote *m*; **— of worms** caja de Pandora *f*; **— opener** abrelatas *m sg*; VT enlatar; V AUX **— you come tomorrow?** ¿puedes venir mañana? **— you see me?** ¿me ves? **I — ride a bicycle** sé andar en bicicleta; **a —-do attitude** un espíritu emprendedor
Canada [kǽnəDə] N Canadá *m*
Canadian [kənédiən] ADJ & N canadiense *mf*
canal [kənǽl] N canal *m*
canary [kənéri] N canario *m*; **Canary Islands** Islas Canarias *f pl*
Canary Islands [kənériáɪlənz] N Islas Canarias *f pl*
cancel [kǽnsəl] VT cancelar; (a stamp) matasellar; (an order) anular
cancellation [kænsəléʃən] N (of a flight, performance) cancelación *f*; (of an order) anulación *f*
cancer [kǽnsɚ] N cáncer *m*; **— patient** canceroso -sa *mf*; ADJ **—-causing** cancerígeno
cancerous [kǽnsɚəs] ADJ canceroso
candelabrum, candelabra [kændəlábrəm -brə] N candelabro *m*
candid [kǽndɪd] ADJ franco, sincero
candidacy [kǽndɪDəsi] N candidatura *f*
candidate [kǽndɪDɪt] N (for office) candidato -ta *mf*; (for a job) aspirante *mf*, postulante *mf*
candle [kǽndl] N vela *f*, candela *f*; (on the altar) cirio *m*; **—stick** candelero *m*
candor [kǽndɚ] N franqueza *f*
candy [kǽndi] N dulce *m*, caramelo *m*, confite *m*; (with chocolate) bombón *m*; **— store** bombonería *f*; VT confitar, acaramelar; (nuts) garapiñar; VI (syrup) cristalizarse
cane [ken] N (sugar) caña *f*; (walking) bastón *m*; **— chair** silla de mimbre *f*

canine [kénaɪn] ADJ canino, perruno; N (dog) can *m*, perro *m*; (tooth) canino *m*
canister [kǽnɪstɚ] N lata *f*
canker [kǽŋkɚ] N úlcera *f*
cannery [kǽnəri] N fábrica de conservas *f*
cannibal [kǽnəbəɬ] N caníbal *m*
cannon [kǽnən] N cañón *m*; — **fodder** carne de cañón *f*
canny [kǽni] ADJ sagaz, astuto
canoe [kənú] N canoa *f*
canon [kǽnən] N (rule, melody, body of works) canon *m*; (priest) canónigo *m*
canopy [kǽnəpi] N (of a bed) dosel *m*; (of a building) toldo *m*
cantaloupe [kǽntḷop] N melón *m*
canteen [kæntín] N (snack bar) cantina *f*; (container) cantimplora *f*
canvas [kǽnvəs] N (fabric) lona *f*; (for painting) lienzo *m*
canvass [kǽnvəs] VI/VT (poll) encuestar; (solicit votes) solicitar votos en; (solicit sales) buscar pedidos comerciales en; N solicitud *f*
canyon [kǽnjən] N cañón *m*
cap [kæp] N (head covering without visor) gorro *m*; (head covering with visor) gorra *f*; (of a bottle) tapa *f*; (of a pen) capucha *f*, contera *f*; (limit) tope *m*; (for capgun) fulminante *m*, pistón *m*; VT (to cover, put a cap on) tapar; (to complete) rematar; (to limit) limitar
capability [kepəbíliɒi] N capacidad *f*
capable [képəbəɬ] ADJ capaz
capacious [kəpéʃəs] ADJ amplio
capacity [kəpǽsɪɒi] N capacidad *f*
cape [kep] N (clothing) capa *f*; (promontory) cabo *m*
caper [képɚ] N (skipping) cabriola *f*; (prank) treta *f*, triquiñuela *f*; (crime) delito *m*; (food) alcaparra *f*; VI retozar
Cape Verde [kepvɝ́d] N Cabo Verde *m*
Cape Verdean [kepvɝ́ɒiən] ADJ & N caboverdiano -na *mf*
capillary [kǽpəlɛri] N & ADJ [vaso] capilar *m*
capital [kǽpɪdḷ] N (city) capital *f*; (wealth) capital *m*; (of a column) capitel *m*; (letter) mayúscula *f*; **to make — of** sacar partido de, aprovecharse de; ADJ (city) capital; (financial) de capital; — **gains** ganancias en bienes de capital *f pl*; — **investment** inversión de capital *f*; — **punishment** pena de muerte *f*
capitalism [kǽpɪdḷɪzəm] N capitalismo *m*
capitalist [kǽpɪdḷɪst] N capitalista *mf*
capitalistic [kǽpɪdḷístɪk] ADJ capitalista
capitalization [kǽpɪdḷɪzéʃən] N capitalización *f*
capitalize [kǽpɪdḷaɪz] VT (finance) capitalizar; (write) escribir con mayúscula; **to — on** sacar provecho de
capitol [kǽpɪdḷ] N capitolio *m*
capitulate [kəpítʃələt] VI capitular
cappuccino [kæpətʃíno] N capuchino *m*

caprice [kəprís] N capricho *m*
capricious [kəpríʃəs] ADJ caprichoso
capsize [kǽpsaɪz] VI/VT volcar[se]
capsule [kǽpsəɬ] N cápsula *f*
captain [kǽptɪn] N capitán *m*; VT capitanear
caption [kǽpʃən] N (with illustration) pie *m*; (subtitle) subtítulo *m*
captivate [kǽptəvet] VT cautivar
captive [kǽptɪv] ADJ & N cautivo -va *mf*; — **animals** animales en cautiverio *m pl*
captivity [kæptíviɒi] N cautiverio *m*
captor [kǽptɚ] N captor -ra *mf*
capture [kǽptʃɚ] VT (apprehend, record data) capturar; (give expression to) plasmar; (attract) cautivar; (conquer) tomar; N captura *f*
car [kɑr] N (automobile) coche *m*, automóvil *m*; Am carro *m*, auto *m*; (railroad) vagón *m*, coche *m*; (elevator) cabina *f*; Am elevador *m*; — **bomb** coche bomba *m*; —**fare** pasaje *m*; —**jacking** secuestro de vehículo *m*; —**load** carga de un coche *f*; —**port** cochera *f*; — **wash** túnel de lavado *m*; ADJ —**sick** mareado; **to get —sick** marearse en el coche
caramel [kǽrəməɬ] N caramelo *m*
carat [kǽrət] N quilate *m*
caravan [kǽrəvæn] N caravana *f*
carbohydrate [kɑrbəháɪdret] N carbohidrato *m*, hidrato de carbono *m*
carbon [kɑrbən] N carbono *m*; — **copy** copia en papel carbón *f*; — **dioxide** dióxido de carbono *m*; — **monoxide** monóxido de carbono *m*; — **paper** papel carbón *m*
carburetor [kɑrbəreɒɚ] N carburador *m*
carcass [kɑrkəs] N (of an animal) cuerpo muerto *m*; (of a ship) casco *m*
carcinogen [kɑrsínədʒən] N cancerígeno *m*, carcinógeno *m*
carcinoma [kɑrsənómə] N carcinoma *m*
card [kɑrd] N (piece of stiff paper) tarjeta *f*; (for games) naipe *m*, carta *f*; (for boxing events) programa *m*; (for textiles) carda *f*; (witty person) gracioso -sa *mf*; (in a computer) tarjeta *f*, placa *f*; —**board** (thick) cartón *m*; (thin) cartulina *f*; — **reader** lector de tarjetas *m*; — **sharp** fullero -ra *mf*; **pack of —s** baraja *f*; **to play —s** jugar a la baraja, jugar a los naipes; **he's holding all the —s** tiene todas las ventajas; VT (comb) cardar; (ask for identification) pedir identificación
cardiac [kɑ́rɒiæk] ADJ cardiaco, cardíaco
cardinal [kɑ́rɒnəɬ] ADJ (number, main) cardinal; (colored red) rojo, bermellón; N (bishop, bird) cardenal *m*
cardioangiogram [kɑrɒioǽndʒiəgræm] N cardioangiograma *m*
cardiogram [kɑ́rɒiogræm] N cardiograma *m*
cardiologist [kɑrɒiálədʒɪst] N cardiólogo -ga *mf*
cardiology [kɑrɒiálədʒi] N cardiología *f*

cardiopulmonary [kɑrDiopúłmənɛri] ADJ cardiopulmonar; — **bypass** puente cardiopulmonar *m*
cardiovascular [kɑrDiováskjələ-] ADJ cardiovascular
care [kɛr] N (worry) preocupación *f*; (attention) cuidado *m*, atención *f*, tiento *m*; (extreme attention) esmero *m*, primor *m*; —**giver** cuidador -ra de enfermos *mf*; —**taker** (of a house) casero -ra *mf*; **to be under the** — **of** estar al cuidado de; **to take** — **of** cuidar de, atender; ADJ —**free** despreocupado; VI (be concerned) importarle a uno; **to** — **about** interesarle a uno, importarle a uno; **to** — **for** (look after) cuidar de; (love) tenerle cariño a; **to** — **to** tener ganas de; **I couldn't** — **less** me importa un rábano; **what does he** —? ¿a él qué le importa? **would you** — **for a drink?** ¿te puedo ofrecer algo?
careen [kərín] VI ladearse a toda velocidad
career [kərír] N carrera *f*, trayectoria *f*
careful [kérfəł] ADJ (cautious) cuidadoso, cauteloso; (painstaking) esmerado; **to be** — tener cuidado
carefully [kérfəli] ADV (safely) con cuidado; (painstakingly) esmeradamente
carefulness [kérfəłnɪs] N cuidado *m*
careless [kérlɪs] ADJ descuidado
caress [kərés] N caricia *f*; VT acariciar
cargo [kárgo] N cargamento *m*
Caribbean [kærəbíən] N Caribe *m*; ADJ caribeño
caricature [kérɪkətʃə-] N caricatura *f*; VT caricaturizar
caries [kériz] N caries *f*
carnage [kárnɪdʒ] N carnicería *f*
carnal [kárnl] ADJ carnal
carnation [karnéʃən] N (flower) clavel *m*; (color) rosado *m*
carnival [kárnəvəł] N carnaval *m*; (traveling) feria *f*
carnivorous [karnívə-əs] ADJ carnívoro, carnicero
carol [kérəl] N villancico *m*; VI cantar villancicos
carom [kérəm] N carambola *f*; VI rebotar
carotid artery [kərɑDɪdárDəri] N [arteria] carótida *f*
carouse [kəráuz] VI andar de parranda
carp [karp] N carpa *f*; VI (complain) quejarse
carpenter [kárpəntə-] N carpintero -ra *mf*
carpentry [kárpəntri] N carpintería *f*
carpet [kárpɪt] N alfombra *f*; —**bagger** político -ca oportunista *mf*; VT alfombrar
carriage [kérɪdʒ] N (wheeled vehicle) carruaje *m*, coche *m*; (posture) porte *m*
carrier [kériə-] N (one who carries) portador -ra *mf*; (postal worker) cartero -ra *mf*; (transport company) mensajería *f*
carrion [kériən] N carroña *f*
carrot [kérət] N zanahoria *f*

carry [kéri] VT llevar; **do you** — **Italian wine?** ¿venden vino italiano? **the bill carried** se aprobó el proyecto de ley; **you** — **yourself well** te comportas bien; **he can't** — **a tune** no puede seguir una tonada; **this suitcase will** — **a lot** esta maleta es espaciosa; **to** — **away** llevarse; **he got carried away** se le fue la mano; **to** — **on** continuar; **to** — **out** (complete) llevar a cabo, ejecutar; (take out) sacar; N —**-on** maleta de mano *f*
cart [kart] N (also golf) carro *m*; VT acarrear
cartilage [kárdlɪdʒ] N cartílago *m*
carton [kártn] N caja de cartón *f*
cartoon [kartún] N (drawing) caricatura *f*; (strip) tira cómica *f*; (film) dibujo animado *m*
cartoonist [kartúnɪst] N caricaturista *mf*
cartridge [kártrɪdʒ] N cartucho *m*; — **belt** cartuchera *f*, canana *f*
carve [karv] VI/VT (a piece of wood) tallar; (a turkey) trinchar; **to** — **out a career** labrarse una carrera
carving [kárvɪŋ] N (action) tallado *m*; (figure) talla *f*; — **knife** trinchante *m*
cascade [kæskéd] N cascada *f*
case [kes] N caso *m*; (box) caja *f*; (of a pillow) funda *f*; — **history** historia clínica *f*; **in** — **[that]** en caso de [que]; **in** — **it rains** por si llueve; **in any** — en todo caso; **just in** — por si acaso; **get off my** —! ¡déjame en paz! — **-sensitive** sensible a la diferencia entre mayúsculas y minúsculas
cash [kæʃ] N efectivo *m*; — **advance** anticipo en efectivo *m*; — **and carry** al contado y sin entrega a domicilio; — **flow** corriente en efectivo *f*; — **on delivery** entrega contra reembolso *f*; — **payment** pago en efectivo *m*; — **register** caja registradora *f*; **to pay** — pagar al contado; VT cobrar
cashew [kéʃu] N marañón *m*, castaña de cajú *f*, *Sp* anacardo *m*
cashier [kæʃír] N cajero -ra *mf*; —**'s check** cheque de caja *m*
casino [kəsíno] N casino *m*
cask [kæsk] N tonel grande *m*
casket [késkɪt] N ataúd *m*
casserole [késərołl] N (container) cazuela *f*; (food) guiso *m*
cassette [kəsét] N cassette *mf*, casete *mf*
cast [kæst] VT (throw) tirar, echar; (form an object) moldear, vaciar; (give out dramatic roles) repartir papeles; **to** — **a ballot** votar; **to** — **about** buscar; **to** — **a glance** echar un vistazo; **to** — **aside** desechar; **to** — **doubt** poner en duda; **to** — **light on** aclarar; **to** — **lots** echar suertes; **to** — **off** (a ship) soltar amarras; (something rejected) deshacerse de; **to** — **out** exiliar; **to be** — **down** estar abatido; N (form) molde *m*; (in theater) reparto *m*, elenco *m*; (for broken bones) yeso;

to put in a — enyesar; — **iron** hierro fundido *m*

castanet [kǽstənεt] N castañuela *f*

caste [kæst] N casta *f*

castigate [kǽstɪget] VT (criticize) criticar, reprender; (punish) castigar

Castile [kæstíł] N Castilla *f*

Castilian [kæstíljən] N & ADJ castellano -na *mf*; — **speaker** castellanohablante *mf*; ADJ — **speaking** castellanohablante

casting [kǽstɪŋ] N (throwing) tiro *m*; (piece of metal) pieza fundida *f*; (selection of actors) cásting *m*

castle [kǽsəł] N castillo *m*; (chess piece) torre *f*, roque *m*

castor oil [kǽstəɔɪł] N aceite de ricino *m*

castrate [kǽstret] VT castrar; (animals) capar

casual [kǽʒuəł] ADJ (informal) informal; (offhand) al pasar

casualty [kǽʒuəłti] N (of war) baja *f*; (in an accident) víctima *f*

cat [kæt] N (domestic) gato -ta *mf*; (others) felino *m*; —'**s meow** súmmum *m*; —**fish** siluro *m*; —**house** burdel *m*

Catalan [kǽdḷæn] ADJ & N catalán -ana *mf*; (language) catalán *m*

catalog, catalogue [kǽdḷɔg] N catálogo *m*; VT catalogar

Catalonia [kædḷóniə] N Cataluña *f*

Catalonian [kædḷóniən] ADJ catalán

catalyst [kǽdḷɪst] N catalizador *m*

cataract [kǽdərækt] N catarata *f*

catastrophe [kətǽstrəfi] N catástrofe *f*

catatonia [kædətóniə] N catatonia *f*

catch [kætʃ] VT (a criminal, ball) atrapar; *Sp, Cuba* coger; (a fish) pescar, capturar; (someone in an act) pillar; (a bus) agarrar; (what someone said) comprender, agarrar; **to** — **a glimpse of** vislumbrar; **to** — **cold** resfriarse; **to** — **fire** prenderse fuego; **to** — **on** (understand) caer en cuenta; (become popular) ponerse de moda; **to** — **oneself** contenerse; **to** — **one's eye** llamarle a uno la atención; **to** — **sight of** avistar; **to** — **unawares** sorprender; **to** — **up** (with a person) alcanzar; (on work) ponerse al día, actualizarse; VI (get entangled) enredarse; (snap into place) agarrar; N (act of catching prey, quantity caught) captura *f*, redada *f*, pesca *f*; (prey) presa *f*; (device) pestillo *m*; (act of catching a ball) atrapada *f*; —**phrase** eslogan *m*; — **twenty-two** paradoja *f*; **he is a good** — es un buen partido; **to play** — jugar a la pelota; **what's the** —? ¿cuál es la treta?

catcher [kǽtʃə] N (baseball) receptor -ora *mf*

catching [kǽtʃɪŋ] ADJ contagioso

catchy [kǽtʃi] ADJ pegadizo

catechism [kǽdɪkɪzəm] N catecismo *m*

category [kǽdɪgɔri] N categoría *f*

cater [kédə] VI/VT abastecer de alimentos [banquetes, fiestas, etc.]; **to** — **to** atender a

caterpillar [kǽdəpɪlə] N (insect) oruga *f*; (tractor) tractor oruga *m*, caterpillar *m*

cathedral [kəθídrəł] N catedral *f*

catheter [kǽθɪdə] N catéter *m*, sonda *f*

catheterization [kæθədəɪzéʃən] N cateterización *f*

catheterize [kǽθədəaɪz] VT cateterizar

cathode [kǽθod] N cátodo *m*; — **rays** rayos catódicos *m pl*

Catholic [kǽθlɪk] N & ADJ católico -ca *mf*

Catholicism [kəθálɪsɪzəm] N catolicismo *m*

CAT [computerized axial tomography] scan [kǽtskæn] N TAC *f*

catsup [kǽtʃəp] N cátsup *m*, ketchup *m*, salsa de tomate *f*

cattle [kǽdḷ] N ganado [vacuno] *m*; —**breeding** ganadería *f*; —**man** ganadero *m*; — **rustler** cuatrero *m*; — **rustling** abigeato *m*

catty [kǽdi] ADJ malicioso

caught [kɔt] *see* catch

cauliflower [kɔ́lɪflaʊə] N coliflor *f*

cause [kɔz] N causa *f*, causante *f*; — **for celebration** motivo de celebración *m*; **the democratic** — la causa democrática *f*; — **without** — sin motivo; VT (make happen) causar, ocasionar; (motivate) motivar; **to** — **to flee** hacer huir; **the heat** —**d her to faint** el calor la hizo desmayar

caustic [kɔ́stɪk] ADJ cáustico

cauterize [kɔ́dəraɪz] VT cauterizar

caution [kɔ́ʃən] N (prudence) cautela *f*, recato *m*; (warning) advertencia *f*; —! ¡cuidado! ¡atención! VT advertir; **to** — **against** desaconsejar

cautious [kɔ́ʃəs] ADJ cauto, cauteloso, precavido

cava [kávə] N (wine) cava *f*

cavalier [kævəlír] N caballero *m*, galán *m*; ADJ (disdainful) desdeñoso; (overly casual) displicente

cavalry [kǽvəłri] N caballería *f*

cave [kev] N cueva *f*, caverna *f*; —**man** hombre de las cavernas *m*; VI **to** — **in** (yield) ceder; (collapse) derrumbarse, desplomarse

cavern [kǽvən] N caverna *f*, gruta *f*

cavity [kǽvɪdi] N cavidad *f*; (in a tooth) caries *f*; (nasal) fosa *f*

cavort [kəvɔ́rt] VI cabriolar, retozar

caw [kɔ] N graznido *m*; VI graznar

CD [compact disc] [sídí] N CD *m*, disco compacto *m*; — **player** reproductor de discos compactos *m*; —-**ROM** CD-ROM *m*

cease [sis] VI cesar; VT interrumpir; N —-**fire** alto el fuego *m*; *Am* cese el fuego *m*

ceaseless [síslɪs] ADJ incesante

cedar [sídə] N cedro *m*

cede [sid] VT ceder

ceiling [síliŋ] N techo *m*, cielo raso *m*; (cap) tope *m*; (sky) altura máxima *f*
celebrate [sélǝbret] VI/VT celebrar, festejar
celebrated [sélǝbreDɪd] ADJ célebre
celebration [sɛlǝbréʃǝn] N (action) celebración *f*, festejo *m*; (festivities) fiesta *f*
celebratory [sǝlébrǝtori] ADJ festivo
celebrity [sǝlébrɪDi] N celebridad *f*
celery [sélǝri] N apio *m*
celestial [sǝléstʃǝł] ADJ celeste; (heavenly) celestial; — **body** astro *m*
celibate [sélǝbɪt] ADJ célibe
cell [sɛł] N (room) celda *f*; (structural) célula *f*; — **biology** citología *f*
cellar [sélǝ˞] N sótano *m*; (for wine) bodega *f*, cava *f*
cello [tʃélo] N violonchelo *m*
cellophane [sélǝfen] N celofán *m*
cellular [séljǝlǝ˞] ADJ celular; — **phone** celular *m*; *Sp* móvil *m*
cellulite [séljǝlaɪt] N celulitis *f*
celluloid [séljǝlɔɪd] N celuloide *m*
cellulose [séljǝlos] N celulosa *f*
cement [sɪmént] N cemento *m*; (glue) adhesivo *m*; — **mixer** hormigonera *f*; VI/VT cementar
cemetery [sémɪtɛri] N cementerio *m*
censor [sénsǝ˞] N censor -ora *mf*; VT censurar
censorship [sénsǝ˞ʃɪp] N censura *f*
censure [sénʃǝ˞] N censura *f*; VT censurar
census [sénsǝs] N censo *m*; **to take a** — censar
cent [sɛnt] N centavo *m*, céntimo *m*
centennial [sɛnténiǝł] ADJ & N centenario *m*
center [séntǝ˞] N centro *m*; (in basketball) centro *m*, *Am* pivot *m*; — **forward** (soccer) ariete *mf*; — **of gravity** centro de gravedad *m*; VI/VT centrar[se]
centigrade [séntɪgred] ADJ centígrado
centimeter [séntǝmiDǝ˞] N centímetro *m*
centipede [séntǝpid] N ciempiés *m*
central [séntrǝł] ADJ central; (downtown) céntrico; N central de teléfonos *f*; — **heating** calefacción central *f*; — **nervous system** sistema nervioso central *m*; — **processing unit** unidad central de proceso/ procesamiento *f*
Central [séntrǝł] ADJ — **African Republic** República Centroafricana *f*; — **America** Centroamérica *f*; — **American** centroamericano
centralize [séntrǝlaɪz] VI/VT centralizar[se]; **to be/become** —**d** centralizarse
centrifugal [sɛntrífǝgǝł] ADJ centrífugo
centripetal [sɛntrípɪdl̩] ADJ centrípeto
century [séntʃǝri] N siglo *m*
CEO [**chief executive officer**] [sííó] N *Am* director -ora general *mf*, *Sp* consejero -ra, delegado -da *mf*
ceramic [sǝrǽmɪk] ADJ cerámico; N —**s** cerámica *f*

cereal [síriǝł] N (breakfast food) cereal *m*; (the grain itself) grano *m*; ADJ cereal
cerebral [sǝríbrǝł] ADJ cerebral; — **concussion** conmoción cerebral *f*; — **cortex** corteza cerebral *f*; — **embolism** embolia cerebral *f*; — **hemorrhage** hemorragia cerebral *f*; — **palsy** parálisis cerebral *f*
ceremonial [sɛrǝmóniǝł] ADJ & N ceremonial *m*
ceremonious [sɛrǝmóniǝs] ADJ ceremonioso
ceremony [sérǝmoni] N ceremonia *f*
certain [sɝ́tn̩] ADJ seguro; — **people** determinadas personas *f pl*; — **rules are inviolable** ciertas/determinadas reglas son inviolables; **death and taxes are** — lo único seguro son los impuestos y la muerte; **he's** — **to come** seguro que viene; **it is** — **that it rained** seguro que llovió
certainly [sɝ́tn̩li] ADV seguramente, sin duda; **she** — **gets her way** no cabe duda de que se sale con la suya; INTERJ ¡cómo no!
certainty [sɝ́tn̩ti] N certeza *f*, certidumbre *f*
certificate [sǝtífɪkɪt] N certificado *m*; — **of baptism** fe de bautismo *f*; — **of deposit** certificado de depósito *m*
certification [sɝDǝfɪkéʃǝn] N certificación *f*
certify [sɝ́Dǝfaɪ] VT certificar; **certified check** cheque certificado *m*; **certified mail** correo certificado *m*; **certified public accountant** contador -ora público -ca *mf*
cervical [sɝ́vɪkǝł] ADJ cervical
cervix [sɝ́vɪks] N (neck) cerviz *f*; (uterine) cérvix *m*, cuello uterino *m*
cesarean section [sɪzériǝnsékʃǝn] N cesárea *f*
cessation [sɛséʃǝn] N cese *m*
cesspool [séspuł] N pozo séptico *m*, fosa séptica *f*
Chad [tʃæd] N Chad *m*
Chadian [tʃǽDiǝn] ADJ & N chadiano -na *mf*
chafe [tʃef] VI/VT rozar[se]; N rozadura *f*
chaff [tʃæf] N ahechaduras *f pl*
chagrin [ʃǝgrín] N mortificación *f*; VT mortificar
chain [tʃen] N cadena *f*; — **reaction** reacción en cadena *f*; — **saw** sierra *f*; — **smoker** persona que fuma como una chimenea *f*; — **store** tienda de cadena *f*; VI/VT encadenar[se]
chair [tʃɛr] N silla *f*; (academic) cátedra *f*; (of a meeting) presidente -ta *mf*; (of a department) jefe -fa *mf*; —**man** presidente *m*, director *m*, jefe *m*; —**manship** dirección *f*; —**person** presidente -ta *mf*, jefe -fa *mf*; —**woman** presidenta *f*, jefa *f*
chalk [tʃɔk] N (substance) caliza *f*; (piece) tiza *f*; —**board** pizarrón *m*, pizarra *f*, tablero *m*; VT marcar con tiza; **to** — **up** (attribute) atribuir; (score) marcar
chalky [tʃɔ́ki] ADJ de/con/como tiza
challenge [tʃǽlɪndʒ] N desafío *m*, reto *m*; (of a jury) recusación *f*; VT (defy) desafiar, retar; (take exception) cuestionar, disputar; (recuse) recusar; **to be vertically** —**d** ser muy bajito

chamber [tʃémbɚ] N (legislative) cámara f; (in a palace) aposento m; (of a cannon) recámara f; —**maid** camarera f, mucama f; — **music** música de cámara f; — **of commerce** cámara de comercio f; — **pot** orinal m; —**s** (of a judge) despacho m

chameleon [kəmíljən] N camaleón m

chamois [ʃǽmi] N gamuza f

champagne [ʃæmpén] N champán m, champaña mf

champion [tʃǽmpiən] N campeón -ona mf; (of a cause) defensor -ora mf, paladín m; VT defender

championship [tʃǽmpiənʃɪp] N campeonato m

chance [tʃæns] N (opportunity) oportunidad f; (probability) probabilidad f; (unpredictable element) casualidad f, azar m; **by** — por casualidad; **game of** — juego de azar m; **to take a** — correr riesgo, arriesgarse; ADJ casual; VI arriesgarse; **we —d to meet him at the bar** nos encontramos con él en el bar por casualidad

chancellor [tʃǽnsəlɚ] N (chief minister) canciller m; (of a university) rector -ora de universidad mf

chandelier [ʃændəlír] N araña de luces f

change [tʃendʒ] VT cambiar; **to** — **clothes** cambiarse de ropa; **to** — **into** transformar[se] en; **to** — **trains** cambiar de tren; N cambio m; (money returned) vuelta f; Am vuelto m; (fresh clothes) muda de ropa f; — **of heart** cambio de opinión m; — **over** (tennis) cambio de lado m; —-**up** (baseball) cambio m, cambio de velocidad m

changeable [tʃéndʒəbəl] ADJ (variable) cambiante, variable; (fickle) inconstante, tornadizo; — **silk** seda tornasolada f

channel [tʃǽnl] N canal m; (bed of stream) cauce m; VT canalizar, encauzar

chant [tʃænt] N (plain song) canto llano m; (hymn) cántico m; (repeated slogan) cantinela f; VI/VT (sing) cantar; (repeat a slogan) corear

chaos [kéas] N caos m

chaotic [keáDɪk] ADJ caótico

chap [tʃæp] VI/VT cuartear[se], agrietar[se]; —**ped lips** labios agrietados m pl; —**stick®** crema para los labios f; N (fellow) tipo m

chaparral [ʃæpərǽl] N chaparral m

chapel [tʃǽpəł] N capilla f

chaperon, chaperone [ʃǽpəron] N chaperón -ona f; VI ir de chaperón -ona

chaplain [tʃǽplɪn] N capellán m

chapter [tʃǽptɚ] N capítulo m

char [tʃɑr] VI/VT (reduce to ashes) carbonizar[se]; (scorch) chamuscar[se]

character [kǽrɪktɚ] N carácter m; (of a novel) personaje m; — **actor** actor de carácter m; **Chinese** —**s** caracteres chinos m pl; **he's quite a** — es todo un personaje; **that's out**

of — **for him** eso no es característico de él

characteristic [kærɪktərístɪk] ADJ característico; N característica f; (genetic) carácter m

characterization [kærɪktɚɪzéʃən] N caracterización f

characterize [kǽrɪktəraɪz] VT (describe) caracterizar; (attribute) calificar

charade [ʃəréd] N farsa f; —**s** charada f

charcoal [tʃárkoł] N carbón de leña m; — **drawing** dibujo al carbón m

charge [tʃɑrdʒ] VT (demand money) cobrar; (load) cargar; (buy on credit) cargar a cuenta; (attack) embestir; (in basketball) cargar; **to** — **off a loss** restar una pérdida; **to** — **someone with a task** encargarle a alguien una tarea; **to** — **with murder** acusar de homicidio; N (mission) misión f, encargo m; (accusation) cargo m, acusación f; (charge in account) cargo m, débito m; (explosives, electricity) carga f; (attack) embestida f; — **account** cuenta de crédito f; — **card** tarjeta de crédito f; **there will be a** — **for delivery** se cobra entrega a domicilio; **to be in** — **of** estar a cargo de; **under my** — a mi cargo

charger [tʃárdʒɚ] N (for a battery) cargador m; (horse) corcel m

chariot [tʃǽriət] N carro de guerra m

charisma [kərízmə] N carisma m

charitable [tʃǽrɪDəbəł] ADJ caritativo

charity [tʃǽrɪDi] N (virtue, aid to the poor) caridad f; (institution) institución benéfica f, institución de beneficencia f; **to give to** — dar dinero a las instituciones benéficas; **to live on** — vivir de la caridad

charlatan [ʃárlətən] N charlatán -ana mf

charm [tʃɑrm] N (attractiveness) encanto m, saleroso m; (trinket) dije m; (spell) sortilegio m, hechizo m; (amulet) talismán m, amuleto m; VT (delight) encantar; (influence) hechizar, subyugar

charming [tʃármɪŋ] ADJ encantador, saleroso; Sp majo

chart [tʃɑrt] N (table) tabla f; (graph) gráfica f; (marine map) carta f; (of musical hits) lista de éxitos f; VT (in a table) tabular; (in a graph) graficar; (a region) cartografiar; **to** — **a course** trazar una ruta

charter [tʃárDɚ] N (of a city) fuero m; (of an organization) estatuto m; (document granting rights) constitución f, carta f; (hire) flete m; — **flight** [vuelo] chárter m; — **member** socio -cia fundador -ora mf; VT (a corporation) aprobar los estatutos; (a flight) fletar

chase [tʃes] VT (hunt) cazar; (follow rapidly) perseguir; **to** — **after** correr tras; **to** — **away** ahuyentar; N caza f, persecución f

chasm [kǽzəm] N sima f

chassis [tʃǽsi] N chasis m, bastidor m

chaste [tʃest] ADJ casto, honesto
chastise [tʃǽstaɪz] VT (punish) castigar;
(criticize) criticar
chastisement [tʃæstáɪzmənt] N (punishment)
castigo m; (criticism) crítica f
chastity [tʃǽstɪɒi] N castidad f, honestidad f
chat [tʃæt] N charla f; Mex plática f; — **room** sala
de chat f; VI charlar; Mex platicar; VI chatear
chattel [tʃǽdl] N (movable property) bien
mueble m; (slave) esclavo -va mf
chatter [tʃǽDɚ] VI (jabber) cotorrear, parlotear;
VT (click rapidly) castañetear; N (of speech)
cotorreo m, parloteo m; (of teeth) castañeteo
m; —**box** charlatán -ana mf, cotorra f
chauffeur [ʃofɚ] N chófer m
chauvinism [ʃóvənɪzəm] N (nationalist)
chovinismo m; (sexist) machismo m
cheap [tʃip] ADJ (economical) barato; (stingy)
avaro; **life is — there** la vida no vale nada
allí; **talk is —** hablar no cuesta nada; **to feel**
— sentirse despreciable; N — **shot** golpe bajo
m; —**skate** tacaño -ña mf
cheapen [tʃípən] VI/VT (lower in price)
abaratar[se]; VT (lower in esteem)
desvalorizar
cheapness [tʃípnɪs] N (low price) baratura f;
(stinginess) avaricia f
cheat [tʃit] N tramposo -sa mf, fullero -ra mf; VT
engañar; **to — at cards** hacer trampa en/a las
cartas, trampear; **to — on a test** copiar; **to —**
on one's spouse engañar a la pareja de uno
check [tʃɛk] VT (stop) refrenar; (restrain)
reprimir; (leave luggage) facturar; (leave a
coat) dejar; (verify) comprobar, verificar; Am
chequear; Mex checar; (in chess) dar jaque; **to**
— **against** cotejar con; **to — into a hotel**
registrarse; **to — into something** averiguar
algo; **to — off** puntear; **to — out a book**
sacar [prestado] un libro; **to — up on**
controlar; **that —s out** lo hemos
comprobado; N (bank) cheque m; (means of
restraint) control m; (ticket) ficha f; (mark)
marca f; (in a restaurant) cuenta f; (in fabric)
cuadro m; (checked fabric) tela a cuadros f;
(examination) comprobación f; (in chess)
jaque m; —**book** chequera f, talonario m;
—**ing account** cuenta corriente f; — **kiting**
giro de cheques sin fondos m; —**list** lista de
control f; —**mate** jaque mate m; —**out**
counter caja f; —**point** control m, retén m;
—**room** guardarropa m; — **stub** talón m;
—**up** examen físico m
checker [tʃɛkɚ] N (on a fabric) cuadro m; (on a
checkerboard) casilla f; (game piece) ficha f;
(cashier) cajero -ra mf; (person who checks)
verificador -ora mf; —**board** tablero m; —**ed**
cloth tela a cuadros f; —**ed past** pasado
oscuro m; —**s** juego de damas m; VT
cuadricular

cheek [tʃik] N (on face) mejilla f; Am cachete m;
(impudence) descaro m; (of buttocks) nalga f;
—**bone** pómulo m
cheer [tʃir] N (shout) viva m, vítor m; (applause)
aplausos m pl; (encouragement) ánimo m;
(joy) alegría f; —**leader** animador -ora mf;
Am porrista mf; INTERJ —**s!** ¡salud! VI/VT
vitorear; **to — on** dar ánimo; **to — up**
animar[se]
cheerful [tʃírfəl] ADJ (person) risueño, alegre;
(room) alegre
cheerfulness [tʃírfəlnɪs] N alegría f
cheerless [tʃírlɪs] ADJ triste, sombrío
cheese [tʃiz] N queso m; —**burger** hamburguesa
con queso f; —**cake** tarta de queso f
cheesy [tʃízi] ADJ (of cheese) de queso; (cheap)
barato; (uncool) Sp hortera
cheetah [tʃíDə] N guepardo m
chef [ʃɛf] N chef mf
chemical [kɛ́mɪkəl] ADJ químico; —
engineering ingeniería química f; —
warfare guerra química f; N producto
químico m
chemist [kɛ́mɪst] N químico -ca f
chemistry [kɛ́mɪstri] N química f
chemotheraphy [kimoθɛ́rəpi] N quimioterapia f
cherish [tʃɛ́rɪʃ] VT apreciar; **I — the memory of**
him tengo muy buenos recuerdos de él
cherry [tʃɛ́ri] N cereza f; — **tree** cerezo m
chess [tʃɛs] N ajedrez m; —**board** tablero de
ajedrez m
chest [tʃɛst] N (body part) pecho m; (box) arca f;
— **of drawers** cómoda f
chestnut [tʃɛ́snʌt] N castaña f; — **tree** castaño
m; ADJ castaño; (horse) zaino
chew [tʃu] VT (food) masticar; (nonfood) mascar;
—**ing gum** goma de mascar f; Am chicle m;
to — a hole hacer un agujero a mordiscones;
to — out reprender; **to — over** meditar
sobre; **to — up** romper a mordiscones; N
mascada f, bocado m
chewy [tʃúi] ADJ correoso
chic [ʃik] ADJ & N chic m
chick [tʃɪk] N (young chicken) pollito m; (young
bird) pichón m; (young woman) fam chavala f,
tía f; —**pea** garbanzo m
chicken [tʃɪkɪn] N gallina f; (flesh) pollo m; —
coop gallinero m; —**-hearted** cobarde; —
pox varicela f
chicory [tʃɪ́kəri] N achicoria f
chide [tʃaɪd] VT regañar
chief [tʃif] N jefe m; (of a tribe) cacique m; — **of**
staff (military) jefe del estado mayor m; (of a
division) secretario -ria general mf; ADJ
principal; — **justice** presidente de la
Suprema Corte de los Estados Unidos m
chieftain [tʃíftən] N cacique m
chiffon [ʃɪfán] N chifón m
chigger [tʃígɚ] N nigua f

chilblain [tʃílblen] N sabañón *m*
child [tʃaɪld] N (young person) niño -ña *mf*; (offspring) hijo -ja *mf*; —**birth** parto *m*, alumbramiento *m*; —**like** infantil, aniñado; —**proof** a prueba de niños; —**'s play** cosa de niños *f*; **to be with** — estar embarazada; ADJ **of**—**bearing age** en edad de procrear
childhood [tʃáɪldhʊd] N niñez *f*, infancia *f*
childish [tʃáɪldɪʃ] ADJ infantil, pueril
childless [tʃáɪldlɪs] ADJ sin hijos
Chile [tʃíli] N Chile *m*
Chilean [tʃílián] ADJ & N chileno -na *mf*
chili, chile [tʃíli] N (pepper) chile *m*, ají *m*; (meat dish) chile con carne *m*
chill [tʃɪl] N (coldness) frío *m*; (fear, cold with shivering) escalofrío *m*; **it had a** —**ing effect on the group** le cayó al grupo como un baldazo de agua fría; VI/VT enfriar[se]; **to** — **out** tranquilizarse, relajarse
chilly [tʃíli] ADJ frío
chime [tʃaɪm] N (sound) repique *m*; (instrument) carillón *m*, carrillón *m*; VI repicar; VT tañer; **to** — **in** intervenir [en una conversación]
chimney [tʃímni] N chimenea *f*
chimpanzee [tʃɪmpænzí] N chimpancé *m*
chin [tʃɪn] N barbilla *f*, mentón *m*
china [tʃáɪná] N (material) porcelana *f*, china *f*; (dishes) vajilla de porcelana *f*, china *f*; —**ware** vajilla de porcelana *f*
China [tʃáɪná] N China *f*
Chinese [tʃaɪníz] ADJ chino; N (inhabitant of China) chino -na *mf*; (language) chino *m*
chink [tʃɪŋk] N grieta *f*
chip [tʃɪp] N (of wood) astilla *f*; (in glass) desportilladura *f*; (in gambling) ficha *f*; (in computers) chip *m*; **he's a** — **off the old block** de tal palo, tal astilla; **he has a** — **on his shoulder** guarda resentimientos; VI/VT (wood) astillar[se]; (glass, plaster) desportillarse, desconchar[se]; (paint) descascarar[se]; (in golf) chipear; **to** — **in** contribuir; **to** — **a tooth** romperse un diente
chipmunk [tʃípmʌŋk] N ardilla listada *f*
chiropractic [kaɪrəpræktɪk] ADJ quiropráctico; N quiropráctica *f*
chiropractor [káɪrəpræktɚ] N quiropráctico -ca *mf*
chirp [tʃɚp] N pío *m*, gorjeo *m*; VI/VT piar, gorjear
chisel [tʃízəl] N escoplo *m*; (for stone) cincel *m*; (for wood) formón *m*; VT cincelar; (swindle) estafar
chiseler [tʃízlɚ] N estafador -ra *mf*
chit-chat [tʃíttʃæt] N palique *m*; VI charlar
chivalrous [ʃívəlrəs] ADJ (of knights) caballeresco; (courteous to women) caballeroso
chivalry [ʃívəlri] N caballerosidad *f*
chloride [klóraɪd] N cloruro *m*

chlorine [klórin] N cloro *m*
chloroform [klórəfɔrm] N cloroformo *m*
chlorophyl, chlorophyll [klórəfɪl] N clorofila *f*
chocolate [tʃáklɪt] N chocolate *m*; (bar) chocolatina *f*; — **pot** chocolatera *f*
choice [tʃɔɪs] N (act of selecting, thing selected) selección *f*; (alternative) opción *f*; **to have no other** — no tener más remedio; ADJ selecto
choir [kwaɪr] N coro *m*
choke [tʃok] VI/VT (suffocate) ahogar[se]; (strangle) estrangular[se]; (on food) atragantarse, atorarse; (obstruct) tapar[se]; VI (in sports) bloquearse; **I'm all** —**d up** estoy muy conmovido; **to** — **back/down** contener; N (act of choking on something) atragantamiento *m*; (act of choking someone) estrangulación *f*; (device in cars) obturador *m*; (in sports) bloqueo *m*
cholera [kálɚə] N cólera *m*
choleric [kálɚɪk] ADJ colérico
cholesterol [kəléstərɔl] N colesterol *m*
choose [tʃuz] VI/VT elegir, seleccionar, escoger; **to** — **to** optar por
choosy [tʃúzi] ADJ quisquilloso
chop [tʃap] VI/VT cortar; **to** — **down** talar; **to** — **off** mochar, tronchar; **to** — **up** picar; N (act of chopping) golpe *m*; (cut of meat) chuleta *f*; —**s** morro *m*; —**stick** palillo *m*
choppy [tʃápi] ADJ picado, agitado
choral [kórəl] ADJ coral
chord [kɔrd] N (mathematical) cuerda *f*; (musical) acorde *m*; **it struck a** — **with me** me conmovió
chore [tʃɔr] N tarea *f*, faena *f*, quehacer *m*; **it's such a** — es un trabajo horrible
choreography [kɔriágrəfi] N coreografía *f*
chorus [kórəs] N coro *m*
chose [tʃoz] *see* choose
chosen [tʃózən] ADJ **my** — **profession** la profesión de mi preferencia; **the** — **one** el elegido, la elegida
chosen [tʃózən] *see* choose
christen [krísən] VT bautizar
Christendom [krísəndəm] N cristianismo *m*
christening [krísənɪŋ] N bautizo *m*, bautismo *m*
Christian [krístʃən] ADJ & N cristiano -na *mf*; — **name** nombre de pila *m*
Christianity [krɪstʃiǽnɪDi] N cristianismo *m*
Christmas [krísməs] N Navidad *f*, Pascua de Navidad *f*; — **card** tarjeta de Navidad *f*; — **Eve** Nochebuena *f*; — **gift** regalo de Navidad *m*; — **tree** árbol de Navidad *m*; ADJ navideño
chrome [krom] N cromo *m*; ADJ cromado
chromium [krómiəm] N cromo *m*
chromosome [króməsom] N cromosoma *m*
chronic [kránɪk] ADJ crónico
chronicle [kránɪkəl] N crónica *f*; VT registrar
chronicler [kránɪklɚ] N cronista *mf*
chronological [kranládʒɪkəl] ADJ cronológico

chronology [krənálədʒi] N cronología f
chronometer [krənámɪDɚ] N cronómetro m
chrysalis [krísəlɪs] N crisálida f
chrysanthemum [krɪsǽnθəməm] N
   crisantemo m
chubby [tʃʎbi] ADJ rechoncho, gordito
chuck [tʃʌk] N (cut of meat) paletilla f; VT (to
   throw) lanzar; (to discard) tirar, botar
chuckle [tʃʎkəł] N risita f; VI reírse levemente
chum [tʃʌm] N compinche mf
chunk [tʃʌŋk] N trozo m, pedazo m; **a — of cash**
   un montón de plata
church [tʃɚtʃ] N iglesia f; **—man** clérigo m
churn [tʃɚn] N mantequera f; VI/VT (make
   butter) batir; (agitate) agitar, revolver
CIA [Central Intelligence Agency] [síáɪé] N
   CIA f
cicada [sɪkéDə] N chicharra f
cider [sáɪDɚ] N (alcoholic) sidra f;
   (non-alcoholic) Am jugo de manzana m; Sp
   zumo de manzana m
cigar [sɪgár] N puro m, habano m; **— store**
   tabaquería f; **close, but no —** bien, pero te
   quedaste corto
cigarette [sɪgərét] N cigarrillo m; Sp pitillo m;
   Am cigarro m; **— case** cigarrera f; Sp pitillera
   f; **— holder** boquilla f; **— lighter**
   encendedor m
cinch [sɪntʃ] N (for a saddle) cincha f; (something
   easy) pan comido m; (favorite) favorito -ta mf;
   VT cinchar
cinder [síndɚ] N ceniza f, rescoldo m
cinema [sínəmə] N cine m
cinematography [sɪnəmətágrəfi] N
   cinematografía f
cinnamon [sínəmən] N canela f; **— tree** canelo f
cipher [sáɪfɚ] N cifra f, guarismo m; VI/VT
   cifrar[se]
circle [sɚkəł] N círculo m; (literary) ámbito m,
   círculo m; VT (draw a circle) encerrar en un
   círculo; VI (go around) dar una vuelta
circuit [sɚkɪt] N circuito m; **— board** circuito
   impreso m; **— breaker** cortacircuitos m sg
circuitry [sɚkɪtri] N circuitería f
circular [sɚkjələ] ADJ circular; **— saw** sierra
   circular f; N circular f
circulate [sɚkjəlet] VI circular; VT (distribute)
   poner en circulación
circulation [sɚkjəléʃən] N circulación f
circulatory [sɚkjələtɔri] ADJ circulatorio; **—
   system** aparato circulatorio m
circumcise [sɚkəmsaɪz] VT circuncidar
circumference [səkámfəəns] N circunferencia f
circumlocution [sɚkəmlokjúʃən] N
   circunlocución f, rodeo m
circumscribe [sɚkəmskráɪb] VT circunscribir
circumspect [sɚkəmspɛkt] ADJ circunspecto
circumstance [sɚkəmstæns] N circunstancia f;
   —s condiciones financieras f pl

circumstantial [sɚkəmstǽnʃəł] ADJ
   circunstancial; **— evidence** pruebas
   circunstanciales f pl
circumvent [sɚkəmvént] VT evitar, obviar
circus [sɚkəs] N circo m
cirrhosis [sɪrósɪs] N cirrosis f
cirrus [sírəs] N cirro m
cistern [sístɚn] N cisterna f, aljibe m
citadel [síDədəł] N ciudadela f
citation [saɪtéʃən] N (summons) citación f;
   (quote, quotation) cita f; (commendation for
   bravery) mención f
cite [saɪt] VT (quote, summon) citar; (comment
   on) mencionar
citizen [síDɪzən] N (of a nation) ciudadano -na
   mf; (of a city or region) habitante mf
citizenship [síDɪzənʃɪp] N ciudadanía f
citrus [sítrəs] ADJ & N cítrico m
city [síDi] N ciudad f; **— council** concejo m; **—
   hall** ayuntamiento m, alcaldía f; **—
   planning** urbanismo m; ADJ municipal,
   urbano
civic [sívɪk] ADJ cívico; N **—s** educación cívica f
civil [sívəł] ADJ (civilian) civil; (polite) cortés; **—
   disobedience** desobediencia civil f; **—
   engineer** ingeniero -ra civil mf; **— rights**
   derechos civiles m pl; **— service**
   administración pública f; **— war** guerra civil f
civilian [sɪvíljən] ADJ & N civil mf
civility [sɪvílɪDi] N civilidad f, cortesía f
civilization [sɪvəlɪzéʃən] N civilización f
civilize [sívəlaɪz] VT civilizar
clad [klæd] ADJ vestido
claim [klem] VT (demand) reclamar, reivindicar;
   (assert) sostener, pretender; **to — to be**
   pretender ser; **to — responsibility**
   atribuirse la responsabilidad; **to — a mine**
   denunciar una mina; N (demand)
   reclamación f, reclamo m; (assertion)
   afirmación f; (right) derecho m, título m; (on
   insurance) demanda f, denuncia f
claimant [klémənt] N demandante mf,
   reclamante mf; (to the throne) pretendiente
   mf
clairvoyant [klɛrvɔ́ɪənt] ADJ & N clarividente mf
clam [klæm] N almeja f; VI **to — up** callarse
clamber [klǽmbɚ] VI/VT (climb with effort)
   trepar con dificultad; (climb on all fours)
   subir gateando
clammy [klǽmi] ADJ frío y húmedo
clamor [klǽmɚ] N clamor m, vocerío m; VI
   clamar, vociferar
clamorous [klǽməəs] ADJ clamoroso
clamp [klæmp] N (support) grapa f; (vice)
   tornillo m; (wrap-around) abrazadera f;
   (medical) pinza f; VT sujetar; **to — down on**
   reprimir
clan [klæn] N clan m
clandestine [klændéstɪn] ADJ clandestino

clang [klæŋ] VI sonar; N sonido metálico *m*
clap [klæp] N (tap) palmada *f*; (blow) golpe seco
m; (gonorrhea) gonorrea *f*; — **of thunder**
trueno *m*; VT (on the back) palmear; (in
approval) aplaudir; (a book) cerrar de golpe
clapper [klǽpə-] N badajo *m*
clarification [klærəfɪkéʃən] N aclaración *f*
clarify [klǽrəfaɪ] VT aclarar, clarificar
clarinet [klærənét] N clarinete *m*
clarity [klǽrɪɪ] N claridad *f*
clash [klæʃ] N (noise) estruendo metálico *m*;
(collision) choque *m*; (conflict) conflicto *m*,
enfrentamiento *m*; VI/VT (collide) chocar;
(oppose, fight) enfrentarse a; (not go with) no
combinar, no pegar
clasp [klæsp] N (fastener) broche *m*, cierre *m*;
(grip) apretón *m*; VT (fasten) abrochar; (grip)
apretar; (embrace) abrazar, prender
class [klæs] N clase *f*; (graduation class)
promoción *f*, graduación *f*; **in a — by itself**
único; —**mate** compañero -ra de clase *mf*,
condiscípulo -la *mf*; —**room** salón de clase *m*,
aula *f*; — **struggle** lucha de clases *f*; VI/VT
clasificar[se]
classic [klǽsɪk] ADJ & N clásico -ca *mf*
classical [klǽsɪkəł] ADJ clásico
classicism [klǽsɪsɪzəm] N clasicismo *m*
classification [klæsəfɪkéʃən] N clasificación *f*
classify [klǽsəfaɪ] VT clasificar; **classified ad**
anuncio clasificado *m*
classy [klǽsi] ADJ elegante
clatter [klǽɪɒ-] N (noise) estrépito *m*;
(movement) traqueteo *m*; VI (make noise)
causar estrépito; (move) traquetear
clause [klɔz] N cláusula *f*
claustrophobia [klɔstrəfóbiə] N claustrofobia *f*
claustrophobic [klɔstrətobɪk] ADJ
claustrofóbico
clavicle [klǽvɪkəł] N clavícula *f*
claw [klɔ] N (of a bear) garra *f*, zarpa *f*; (of a cat)
uña *f*; (of a crab) pinza *f*; (of a hammer) orejas
f pl; VI/VT arañar; **they —ed their way**
through se abrieron paso con las uñas
clay [kle] N arcilla *f*; (for ceramics) greda *f*; (in
tennis) tierra batida *f*
clean [klin] ADJ limpio; (free from impurities,
not ornate) puro; (honorable) decente; —-
cut (person) acicalado; (concept) bien
definido; — **joke** broma inocente *f*; —-
shaven afeitado; **he has a — record** no
tiene antecedentes; **you'd better come —**
deberías confesar; VI/VT limpiar; **he —ed me**
out me limpió, me desvalijó; **to — up** (a
room) limpiar, asear; (a document) pasar en
limpio; (get rich) forrarse; N —**up** limpieza *f*
cleaner [klínə-] N limpiador -ra *mf*; —**s**
tintorería *f*
cleanliness [klénlinɪs] N limpieza *f*; (personal)
aseo *m*

cleanse [klɛnz] VT limpiar
cleanser [klénzə-] N limpiador *m*
clear [klir] ADJ claro; (skin, conscience) limpio;
(sky) despejado; (path) libre; —-**cut** (clearly
defined) bien definido; (obvious) claro; —-
headed lúcido; — **profit** ganancia neta *f*; **to**
keep — of someone evitar a alguien; **to**
pass — through pasar de lado a lado; N **to**
be in the — estar libre de culpa; VT (the
mind, confusion, voice) aclarar[se]; (a road,
one's reputation, computer screen) limpiar;
(of criminal charges) absolver; (of suspicion)
eximir; (liquid) clarificar; (a legislative bill,
plan) aprobar, obtener autorización para;
(land for farming) desmontar; (a hurdle)
salvar; (a net gain) sacar; **to — the air**
sincerarse; **to — the table** levantar la mesa;
to — up (a mystery) aclarar[se]; (the sky)
despejar[se]
clearance [klírəns] N (space) espacio libre *m*;
(vertical) margen de altura *m*; (permission)
autorización *f*; — **sale** liquidación *f*
clearing [klírɪŋ] N (terrain) claro *m*; (of checks)
compensación *f*; — **house** banco de
compensación
cleats [klits] N (projection) tacos *m pl*, tapones *m*
pl; (shoes) zapatos con tacos *m pl*
cleavage [klívɪʤ] N (cut) hendidura *f*; (in dress)
escote *m*
cleave [kliv] VT hender[se]; **to — to** adherirse a
cleaver [klívə-] N cuchilla *f*
clef [klɛf] N clave *f*
cleft [klɛft] N hendidura *f*; ADJ hendido, partido;
— **lip** labio leporino *m*; — **palate** paladar
hendido *m*
clemency [klémənsi] N clemencia *f*
clench [klɛntʃ] VT agarrar, asir; (teeth, fist)
apretar
clergy [klɝʤi] N clero *m*, clerecía *f*; —**man**
clérigo *m*, pastor *m*; —**woman** pastora *f*
clerical [klérɪkəł] ADJ (of the clergy) clerical,
eclesiástico; (of office personnel) de oficina;
— **error** error de copia *m*; — **work** trabajo
de escritorio *m*
clerk [klɝk] N (sales) dependiente -ta *mf*; (office)
empleado -da de oficina *mf*; (court)
escribiente *mf*, actuario -ria *mf*; VI trabajar
como actuario -ria
clever [klévə-] ADJ (ingenious) ingenioso; (smart)
listo, vivo; (dexterous) habilidoso
cleverness [klévə-nɪs] N (ingenuity) ingenio *m*;
(intelligence) inteligencia *f*, viveza *f*;
(dexterity) habilidad *f*
cliché [klijé] N cliché *m*, muletilla *f*; Sp tópico *m*
click [klɪk] N (sound) clic *m*, chasquido *m*; (sound
of heels) taconeo *m*; (on a computer) clic *m*,
pulsación *f*; VI chascar; (on a computer) hacer
clic, oprimir, pulsar; (heels) taconear; VT
chascar, chasquear; — **and drag** pulsar y

arrastrar
clickable image [klíkəbəɬímɪʤ] N imagen en
donde se puede pulsar *f*
client [kláɪənt] N (of professional or store)
cliente -ta *mf*; (of social service) beneficiario
-ria *mf*
clientele [klaɪəntéɬ] N clientela *f*
cliff [klɪf] N precipicio *m*, despeñadero *m*; (by the
sea) acantilado *m*
climate [kláɪmɪt] N clima *m*
climatic [klaɪmǽDɪk] ADJ climático
climax [kláɪmæks] N clímax *m*, punto
culminante *m*; VI culminar, alcanzar el
clímax
climb [klaɪm] N (ascent) subida *f*; (in alpinism)
escalada *f*; VI/VT (ascend) subir; (ascend with
effort) trepar[se] [a], encaramar[se] [a]; VT (a
mountain, wall) escalar; **to — down** bajar
climber [kláɪmə-] N (in alpinism) escalador -ora
mf; (plant) trepadora *f*
clinch [klɪntʃ] VT (resolve) rematar; (hammer
down) remachar; (hug, in boxing) trabar;
(secure) sujetar; (finalize) cerrar; N (nail)
remache *m*; (embrace) abrazo *m*; (in boxing)
clinch *m*
cling [klɪŋ] VI (to stick to) pegarse; (to hold onto)
aferrarse
clinic [klínɪk] N clínica *f*; (workshop) taller *m*
clinical [klínɪkəl] ADJ clínico; — **trial** ensayo
clínico *m*
clink [klɪŋk] N tintín *m*; VI tintinear
clip [klɪp] VT (cut) cortar; (trim) recortar; (shear)
esquilar; (shorten) acortar; (hit) tocar;
(fasten) abrochar; (attach paper) sujetar con
un clip; N (fastener) gancho *m*; (for paper) clip
m; (of cartridge) cargador *m*; (brooch) broche
m; —**board** portapapeles *m sg*
clipper [klípə-] N (shearer) esquilador -ra *mf*; —**s**
(scissors) tijeras *f pl*; (hair trimmer)
maquinilla *f*
clipping [klípɪŋ] N recorte *m*
clique [klɪk] N (political) camarilla *f*; (in school)
pandilla *f*
clitoris [klíDə-ɪs] N clítoris *m*
cloak [klok] N capa *f*; (military) capote *m*;
—**room** guardarropa *m*; VT (put a cloak on)
vestirse con una capa; (hide) encubrir
clock [klɑk] N reloj *m*; —-**making** relojería *f*; —
radio radio reloj *f*; —**work** maquinaria de
reloj *f*; **like** —**work** con precisión, sin falta;
VT **you swim and I'll** — **you** tú nadas y yo te
tomo el tiempo; **the police** —**ed him at 90
mph** la policía lo pescó haciendo noventa
millas por hora
clockwise [klákwaɪz] ADV en el sentido de las
manecillas dc rcloj
clod [klɑd] N (piece of dirt) terrón *m*, pelotón *m*;
(dolt) tonto -ta *mf*, necio -cia *mf*
clog [klɑg] VI/VT obstruir[se], tapar[se]; N (shoe)

zueco *m*; — **dance** baile zapateado *m*
cloister [klɔ́ɪstə-] N claustro *m*; (monastery)
monasterio *m*; VT enclaustrar
clone [klon] N clon *m*; VT clonar
cloning [klónɪŋ] N clonaje *m*, clonación *f*
close[1] [kloz] VI/VT cerrar[se]; VT (a hole) tapar; **to
— an account** cerrar una cuenta; **to — a
meeting** levantar una sesión; **to — down a
store** clausurar una tienda; **to — in upon**
(oppress) oprimir; (approach) cercar a uno; **to
— out** liquidar; N fin *m*; (act of closing) cierre
m; **at the** — al cierre
close[2] [klos] ADJ (near) cercano; (dense) tupido;
(intimate) íntimo, entrañable; — **attention**
mucha atención *f*; — **by** cercano, *Am* aquí
nomás; —-**fought** reñido; —-**knit** muy
unido; — **translation** traducción fiel *f*; **at** —
range de cerca; **that was a** — **call** nos
salvamos por poco; N —**up** primer plano *m*;
ADV cerca
closed [klozd] ADJ cerrado; — **circuit** circuito
cerrado *m*; —-**minded** cerrado; —
-**mindedness** cerrazón *f*
closely [klósli] ADV (examine) de cerca;
(resemble) mucho; (study) detenidamente;
(work) estrechamente
closeness [klósnɪs] N (of location) cercanía *f*; (of
friendship) intimidad *f*; (correctness)
fidelidad *f*
closer [klózə-] N (baseball) relevista de cierre *mf*,
cerrador -ora *mf*
closet [klázɪt] N ropero *m*, armario *m*; VI
enclaustrarse; ADJ a escondidas
closure [klóʒə-] N (conclusion) cierre *m*; (sense of
completeness) clausura *f*
clot [klɑt] VI/VT coagular[se]; N coágulo *m*,
cuajarón *m*
cloth [klɔθ] N tela *f*, tejido *m*; (wool) paño *m*; ADJ
de tela; — **bound** encuadernado en tela;
man of the — clérigo *m*
clothe [kloð] VT vestir; N —**s** ropa *f*; —**sline**
tendedero *m*; —**spin** pinza *f*
clothier [klóðjə-] N comerciante en ropa o paño
mf
clothing [klóðɪŋ] N ropa *f*
clotting [kláDɪŋ] N coagulación *f*
cloud [klaud] N nube *f*; —**burst** chaparrón *m*,
aguacero *m*; VT nublar, anublar; (make
indistinct, place under suspicion) enturbiar;
to — up nublarse, anublarse; **to be on —
nine** estar en el séptimo cielo; **under a** —
bajo sospecha
cloudiness [kláuDɪnɪs] N nebulosidad *f*,
nubosidad *f*
cloudless [kláudlɪs] ADJ despejado
cloudy [kláuDi] ADJ nublado; *Sp* nuboso;
(gloomy) sombrío
clout [klaut] N influencia *f*
clove [klov] N clavo *m*; — **of garlic** diente

de ajo *m*
cloven [klóvən] ADJ hendido; —**-hoofed** patihendido
clover [klóvɚ] N trébol *m*; —**leaf** trébol *m*; **to be in** — vivir en el lujo
clown [klaʊn] N payaso *m*; VI payasear, bufonear
cloy [klɔɪ] VI/VT (to satiate) hastiar; (to be too sweet for) repugnar
club [klʌb] N (society, nightclub) club *m*; (stick) porra *f*, garrote *m*; (suit of cards) basto *m*; —**foot** pie zambo *m*; —**house** casa de club *f*; VT aporrear
cluck [klʌk] VI cloquear; N cloqueo *m*
clue [klu] N pista *f*, indicio *m*; **to have no** — no tener ni noción
clueless [klúlɪs] ADJ (absent-minded) despistado; (uninformed) en ayunas
clump [klʌmp] N (of bushes) matorral *m*; (of trees) arboleda *f*; VI/VT apiñar[se]
clumsiness [klʌ́mzinɪs] N torpeza *f*
clumsy [klʌ́mzi] ADJ torpe, desmañado, chambón; *Sp* patoso
clung [klʌŋ] *see* cling
clunker [klʌ́ŋkɚ] N cacharro *m*
cluster [klʌ́stɚ] N grupo *m*; (of grapes) racimo *m*; VI/VT agrupar[se], arracimar[se]
clutch [klʌtʃ] N (in a car) embrague *m*; — **pedal** pedal del embrague *m*; **to step on the** — pisar el embrague; —**es** garras *f pl*; VT (seize) asir; (hold) apretar
clutter [klʌ́DƏ] N desparramo *m*, desorden *m*, confusión *f*; VT **books —ed her desk** tenía libros desparramados por todo el escritorio
coach [kotʃ] N (carriage) coche *m*, carruaje *m*, carroza *f*; (bus) autobús *m*; (in sports) entrenador -ra *mf*; (in soccer) técnico -ca *mf*, director -ora técnico -ca *mf*; (in air travel) clase turista *f*; (tutor) profesor -ra particular *mf*; —**man** cochero *m*; VI/VT entrenar
coagulant [koǽgjələnt] ADJ & N coagulante *m*
coagulate [koǽgjəlet] VI/VT coagular[se]
coagulation [koægjəléʃən] N coagulación *f*
coal [koɫ] N carbón *m*; — **bin** carbonera *f*; — **tar** alquitrán *m*
coalition [koəlíʃən] N coalición *f*
coarse [kɔrs] ADJ (fabric) burdo, basto; (sand) grueso; (manners, language) grosero, tosco, rudo
coarseness [kɔ́rsnɪs] N (fabric) bastedad *f*; (language, manners) tosquedad *f*, rudeza *f*; (of a joke) chocarrería *f*
coast [kost] N costa *f*; — **Guard** Guardia Costera *f*; —**line** costa *f*; ADJ & ADV —**-to-** — de costa a costa; VI (on a sled) deslizar[se]; (in a car, on a bike) tirarse por una bajada; **he —ed through medical school** la Facultad de Medicina le resultó muy fácil
coastal [kóstl] ADJ costero
coat [kot] N abrigo *m*; (of paint) capa *f*, mano *f*;

(on animals) pelaje *m*; — **of arms** escudo de armas *m*, blasón *m*; — **rack** percha *f*, perchero *m*; —**tail** faldón *m*; VT cubrir; (with paint) recubrir, dar una mano a; (with grease) engrasar; (with soap) enjabonar; (with sugar) bañar
coax [koks] VT persuadir con halagos, engatusar
coaxial cable [koǽksiəɫkébəɫ] N cable coaxial *m*
cob [kab] N mazorca *f*, panoja *f*; —**web** telaraña *f*
cobalt [kóbɔɫt] N cobalto *m*
cobbler [kábla] N (person who repairs shoes) zapatero -ra *mf*, remendón -ona *mf*; (dessert) budín de bizcocho y fruta *m*
cobblestone [kábəɫston] N adoquín *m*
cobra [kóbrə] N cobra *f*
cocaine [kokén] N cocaína *f*
coccyx [káksɪks] N cóccix *m*
cock [kak] N (rooster) gallo *m*; (male bird) macho de ave de corral *m*; (faucet) llave *f*; (gun part) martillo *m*; (penis) *vulg* polla *f*, pija *f*; —**fight** riña de gallos *f*; —**pit** (for cockfights) gallera *f*; (in an airplane) cabina *f*; —**scomb** cresta de gallo *f*; ADJ —**sure** gallito; VT (a gun) amartillar; (one's head) ladear
cock-a-doodle-doo [kákədudl̩dú] INTERJ quiquiriquí
cockatoo [kákətu] N cacatúa *f*
cocker spaniel [kákɚspǽnjəɫ] N cócker *m*
cockroach [kákrotʃ] N cucaracha *f*
cocktail [káktɛɫ] N cóctel *m*; — **party** cóctel *m*
cocky [káki] ADJ gallito, valentón
cocoa [kóko] N (powder) cacao *m*; (drink) chocolate *m*
coconut [kókənʌt] N coco *m*
cocoon [kəkún] N capullo *m*
cod [kad] N *Sp* abadejo *m*; *Am* bacalao *m*; —**-liver oil** aceite de hígado de bacalao *m*
coddle [kádl] VT mimar
code [kod] N código *m*; — **switching** alternancia de códigos *f*; VT codificar
codeine [kódin] N codeína *f*
codger [kádʒɚ] N vejete *m*, vejancón *m*
codify [kádəfaɪ] VT codificar
coding [kódɪŋ] N codificación *f*
coed [kóɛd] ADJ mixto; N alumna universitaria *f*
coefficient [koəfíʃənt] N coeficiente *m*
coerce [koɝs] VT forzar, obligar
coercion [koɝʒən] N coacción *f*
coexist [koɪgzíst] VI coexistir, convivir
coexistence [koɪgzístəns] N coexistencia *f*, convivencia *f*
coffee [kɔ́fi] N café *m*; (with a little milk) cortado *m*; — **bean** grano de café *m*; — **break** descanso para tomar el café *m*; — **bush** cafeto *m*; — **maker** máquina de café *f*, cafetera *f*; —**pot** cafetera *f*; — **shop** (for coffee) café *m*; (for coffee and light meals) cafetería *f*; — **table** mesa baja *f*
coffer [kɔ́fɚ] N cofre *m*

coffin [kɔ́fɪn] N ataúd *m*, féretro *m*

cog [kɑg] N diente *m*; —**wheel** rueda dentada *f*

cogent [kóʤənt] ADJ convincente

cognac [kónjæk] N coñac *m*

cognate [kágnet] ADJ & N cognado *m*

cognitive [kágnɪDɪv] ADJ cognitivo

cohabitate [kohǽbɪtet] VI cohabitar, convivir

cohabitation [kohæbɪtéʃən] N cohabitación *f*, convivencia *f*

coherent [kohírənt] ADJ coherente; (sticking together) cohesivo

cohesion [kohíʒən] N cohesión *f*

coiffure [kwɑfjúr] N peinado *m*

coil [kɔɪɬ] VI/VT arrollar[se], enrollar[se]; (snake) enroscar[se]; N (roll) rollo *m*; (spiral) tirabuzón *m*; (electric) bobina *f*; — **spring** muelle en espiral *m*

coin [kɔɪn] N moneda *f*; ADJ —-**operated** de monedas; VT acuñar (also words)

coinage [kɔ́ɪnɪʤ] N acuñación *f* (also of words)

coincide [koɪnsáɪd] VI coincidir

coincidence [koínsɪDəns] N coincidencia *f*, casualidad *f*

coitus [kóɪDəs] N coito *m*

coke [kok] N (coal) cok *m*, coque *m*; (cocaine) *fam* coca *f*

cola [kólə] N gaseosa *f*

colander [káləndɚ] N colador *m*

cold [kołd] ADJ frío; — **cream** cold cream *m*; — **cuts** fiambres *m pl*; — **fish** *fam* témpano *m*; — **snap** ola de frío *f*; — **sore** herpes *m sg*; — **war** guerra fría *f*; **to be** — tener frío; **to be out** — quedar seco; **it is** — **today** hace frío hoy; **he gave me the** — **shoulder** me hizo el vacío; **he quit** — **turkey** dejó de un día para otro; **he got** — **feet** se acobardó; N frío *m*; (illness) resfrío *m*, resfriado *m*, catarro *m*; **to catch a** — resfriarse

coldness [kółdnɪs] N frialdad *f*

colic [kálɪk] N cólico *m*

colicky [kálɪki] ADJ que sufre de cólico

coliseum [kɑlɪsíəm] N coliseo *m*

collaborate [kəlǽbəret] VI colaborar

collaboration [kəlæbəréʃən] N colaboración *f*

collaborator [kəlǽbəreDɚ] N colaborador -ora *mf*

collage [kəláʒ] N collage *m*

collagen [kálədʒən] N colágeno *m*

collapse [kəlǽps] VI (fold into sections) plegarse; (cave in) hundirse, derrumbarse; (fail) fracasar; (faint) desmayarse; (empty of air, decline in value) colapsar[se]; N (falling in) derrumbe *m*, derrumbamiento *m*, desplome *m*; (breakdown) colapso *m*

collar [kálɚ] N (for restraining dogs, necklace) collar *m*; (of a shirt) cuello *m*; —**bone** clavícula *f*; VT acollarar; (grab by the neck) agarrar por el cuello; **I was** —**ed by the boss** el jefe me agarró de charla

collate [kólet] VT (put in order) colacionar; (compare) cotejar

collateral [kəlǽDəɚɬ] ADJ (on the side) colateral; (auxiliary) subsidiario; N garantía subsidiaria *f*; — **damage** daño colateral *m*

colleague [kálig] N colega *mf*

collect [kəlékt] VT (gather) recoger; (build a collection) coleccionar; (receive taxes) recaudar; VI/VT (receive payment) cobrar, percibir; (assemble) reunir[se]; (accumulate) acumular[se]; **to** — **oneself** calmarse; N — **call** llamada de cobro revertido *f*, llamada por/a cobrar *f*; — **on delivery** pago contra reembolso *m*

collection [kəlékʃən] N (set of collectibles, clothes) colección *f*; (for charity) colecta *f*; (of taxes) recaudación *f*, cobranza *f*, cobro *m*; (of data, fruit) recolección *f*; (of texts) recopilación *f*; (of water) captación *f*

collective [kəléktɪv] ADJ colectivo; — **bargaining** convenio colectivo *m*; N colectivo *m*, colectividad *f*

collector [kəléktɚ] N (of taxes) recaudador -ora *mf*; (of collectibles) coleccionista *mf*; (of other things) colector -ora *mf*

college [kálɪʤ] N (institution) universidad *f*; (university division) facultad *f*; (association) colegio *m*; **let's give it the old** — **try** esforcémonos al máximo

collegial [kəlíʤəɬ] ADJ cooperador

collegiate [kəlíʤɪt] ADJ universitario

collide [kəláɪd] VI/VT chocar

collie [káli] N collie *m*

collision [kəlíʒən] N colisión *f*, choque *m*

colloid [kálɔɪd] N coloide *m*

colloquial [kəlókwiəɬ] ADJ coloquial; — **expression** frase familiar *f*

colloquium [kəlókwiəm] N coloquio *m*, jornada *f*

collusion [kəlúʒən] N confabulación *f*

cologne [kəlón] N colonia *f*

Colombia [kəlámbiə] N Colombia *f*

Colombian [kəlámbiən] ADJ & N colombiano -na *mf*

colon[1] [kólən] N (punctuation) dos puntos *m pl*; (bowels) colon *m*

colon[2] [kəlón] (currency of El Salvador and Costa Rica) colón *m*

colonel [kɚ́nɬ] N coronel *m*

colonial [kəlóniəɬ] ADJ colonial

colonist [kálənɪst] N (settler) colono *m*; (colonizer) colonizador -ra *mf*

colonization [kɑlənɪzéʃən] N colonización *f*

colonize [kálənaɪz] VT colonizar

colonoscopy [kolánəskəpi] N colonoscopia *f*

colony [káləni] N colonia *f*

color [kálɚ] N color *m*; (colorfulness) colorido *m*; — **blindness** ceguera cromática *f*; — **monitor** monitor [a] color *m*; — **scanner** escáner color *m*; **the** —**s** la bandera; **he**

showed his true —s se mostró tal cual era; **persons of —** gente de color *f*; **a — TV** un televisor en/a color; ADJ **—-blind** daltónico; **—fast** de colores firmes; VT (give color) colorear; (make colorful) dar colorido; (influence) influir; (blush) ruborizarse

colorectal cancer [kolərɛ́kt̪ḷkǽnsɚ] N cáncer de colon *m*

colored [kʌ́lɚd] ADJ coloreado; (biased) sesgado

colorful [kʌ́lɚfəɫ] ADJ (full of color) colorido; (animals, plants) pintado; (eccentric) pintoresco

coloring [kʌ́lɚɪŋ] N (tone) colorido *m*; (action) coloración *f*; (substance) colorante *m*

colorless [kʌ́lɚlɪs] ADJ (without color) incoloro; (bleached) descolorido

colossal [kəlásəɫ] ADJ colosal

colostomy [kəlástəmi] N colostomía *f*

colt [koɫt] N potro *m*

column [káləm] N columna *f*

columnist [káləmnɪst] N columnista *mf*

coma [kómə] N coma *m*

comatose [kómətos] ADJ comatoso

comb [kom] N (for hair) peine *m*; (of a rooster) cresta *f*; (for wool) carda *f*; (for horses) almohaza *f*; (of honey) panal *m*; VT (hair) peinar; (wool) cardar; (search an area) peinar, batir; **to — one's hair** peinarse

combat[1] [kámbæt] N combate *m*

combat[2] [kəmbǽt] VI/VT combatir

combatant [kəmbǽtn̩t] ADJ & N combatiente *mf*

combative [kəmbǽdɪv] ADJ combativo

combination [kɑmbənéʃən] N combinación *f*; — **lock** cerradura de combinación *f*

combine[1] [kəmbáɪn] VI/VT combinar[se]

combine[2] [kámbaɪn] N cosechadora *f*

combo [kámbo] N combo *m*

combustible [kəmbástəbəɫ] ADJ & N combustible *m*

combustion [kəmbástʃən] N combustión *f*

come [kʌm] VI (arrive) venir; (have an orgasm) *fam* venirse; *Sp fam* correrse; **an idea came to me** se me ocurrió una idea; **Christmas is coming** llega la Navidad; **milk —s from cows** la leche se saca de las vacas; **no harm will — to you** no te va a pasar nada; **the dress —s to her knees** el vestido le llega a las rodillas; **to — about** suceder; **to — across** (find) encontrar; (make an impression) parecer; **to — along** (accompany) acompañar; (appear) surgir; **how's your paper coming along?** ¿cómo va tu trabajo? **to — again** volver, volver a venir; **to — back** volver; **to make a —back** resurgir; (in sports) recuperarse; **to — down with a cold** cogerse un resfriado; **to — downstairs** bajar; **to — from** ser de; **to — in** entrar; **to — out** (of a place) salir; (reveal one's homosexuality) *Am* salir del clóset, *Sp*

salir del armario; **to — over** venir para acá; **to — to** volver en sí; **to — together** (meet) juntarse, unirse; (reach agreement) ponerse de acuerdo; **to — up** subir; **your name came up** tu nombre vino a colación; **to — up short** quedarse corto; N (semen) *vulg* leche *f*; **—back** (reply) réplica *f*; (in sports) remontada *f*, recuperación *f*

comedian [kəmíːdiən] N cómico -ca *mf*, comediante *mf*

comedy [káməɖi] N (genre) comedia *f*; (profession) humorismo *m*

comet [kámɪt] N cometa *m*

comfort [kʌ́mfɚt] VT reconfortar; N (feeling of ease) comodidad *f*, confort *m*, holgura *f*; (solace) consuelo *m*

comfortable [kʌ́mfɚ-ɖəbəɫ] ADJ cómodo, confortable; — **life** vida holgada/ desahogada *f*

comforter [kʌ́mfɚ-ɖɚ-] N edredón *m*

comic [kámɪk] ADJ cómico, chistoso, gracioso; — **book** revista de historietas *f*, cómic *m*; **—s** tiras cómicas *f pl*, historietas *f pl*; — **strip** tira cómica *f*

comical [kámɪkəɫ] ADJ cómico, gracioso

coming [kʌ́mɪŋ] N venida *f*; — **of Christ** advenimiento de Cristo *m*; — **from** proveniente de, originario de; **—s and goings** idas y venidas *f pl*; ADJ que viene, próximo

comma [kámə] N coma *f*

command [kəmǽnd] VT (order) mandar; (have authority over) comandar; **to — respect** inspirar respeto, imponerse; N (order) mandato *m*, orden *f*; (post) comandancia *f*; (dominance) dominio *m*; (on a computer) comando *m*; **key** tecla de comando *f*; **he has a good — of English** domina bien el inglés; **to be in — of** estar al mando de; **to be under the — of** estar al mando de; **at your — a** sus órdenes

commandeer [kɑməndír] VT apoderarse de; (for the military) requisar

commander [kəmǽndɚ-] N (leader) jefe -fa *mf*; (army officer) comandante *mf*; (navy officer) capitán -ana de fragata *mf*; — **in chief** comandante en jefe *mf*

commandment [kəmǽndmənt] N mandamiento *m*

commemorate [kəmɛ́mɚət] VT conmemorar

commemoration [kəmɛməréʃən] N conmemoración *f*

commence [kəmɛ́ns] VI/VT comenzar, principiar

commencement [kəmɛ́nsmənt] N (beginning) comienzo *m*; (graduation) graduación *f*, colación *f*

commend [kəmɛ́nd] VT (praise) alabar; (entrust) encomendar

commendation [kɑməndéʃən] N (praise) alabanza f; (mention) mención de honor f
commensurate [kəménsə-ɪt] ADJ proporcional, acorde
comment [kámɛnt] N comentario m; **no** — sin comentarios; VI/VT comentar
commentary [káməntɛri] N comentario m
commentator [káməntɛDə-] N (person who comments) comentador -ra mf; (talking head) comentarista mf
commerce [kámə-s] N comercio m
commercial [kəmɔ́-ʃəł] ADJ comercial; N (on radio or television) anuncio m
commercialize [kəmɔ́-ʃəlaɪz] VT comercializar
commiserate [kəmízəret] VI/VT compadecerse de
commiseration [kəmɪzəréʃən] N conmiseración f
commissary [kámɪsɛri] N economato m
commission [kəmíʃən] N (act, committee, payment) comisión f; (of a broker) corretaje m; (charge) encargo m; (mission) misión f; (title) nombramiento m; **to be in** — estar en servicio; **to be out of** — estar fuera de servicio; **to put out of** — (object) inutilizar; (person) retirar de servicio; VT (authorize) comisionar; (order) encargar; (appoint) nombrar; (get ready) poner en servicio; **—ed officer** oficial m
commissioner [kəmíʃənə-] N comisario -ria mf
commit [kəmít] VT (perpetrate) cometer; (entrust) encargar; (direct) destinar; **to — an error** cometer un error; **to — a foul** cometer/hacer falta; **to — oneself to** comprometerse a/con; **to — to an asylum** internar; **to — to memory** aprender de memoria
commitment [kəmítmənt] N compromiso m
committed [kəmíDɪd] ADJ (to a cause) comprometido
committee [kəmíDi] N comité m, comisión f
commode [kəmód] N wáter m, inodoro m
commodity [kəmáDɪti] N (product) mercancía f, artículo m, producto m; (raw material) materia prima f
common [kámən] ADJ (shared, frequent) común; (general) general; (vulgar) ordinario; (unremarkable) simple; **— cold** resfriado m; **— denominator** denominador común m; **— law** derecho consuetudinario m; **— sense** sentido común m, sensatez f; **— soldier** soldado raso m; **— stock** acciones ordinarias f pl; **—wealth** (state) estado m; (republic) república f; ADJ **—place** trivial; N **—s** (land) ejido m
commotion [kəmóʃən] N conmoción f, revuelo m
communal [kəmjúnł] ADJ comunitario
commune[1] [kəmjún] VI (communicate)

comunicarse, departir; (take communion) comulgar
commune[2] [kámjun] N comuna f
communicable [kəmjúnɪkəbəł] ADJ comunicable; (disease) transmisible
communicate [kəmjúnɪket] VI/VT comunicar[se]; (disease) transmitir[se]
communication [kəmjunɪkéʃən] N comunicación f
communicative [kəmjúnɪkəDɪv] ADJ comunicativo
communion [kəmjúnjən] N comunión f
communiqué [kəmjunɪké] N comunicado m
communism [kámjənɪzəm] N comunismo m
communist [kámjənɪst] N & ADJ comunista mf
community [kəmjúnɪDi] N comunidad f, colectividad f; **— spirit** espíritu comunitario m
commute [kəmjút] VT (reduce a sentence) conmutar; VI viajar diariamente al trabajo
commuter [kəmjúDə-] N persona que viaja diariamente al trabajo f
Comoros [káməroz] N Comoras f pl
compact[1] [kámpækt, kəmpǽkt] ADJ compacto; (dense) tupido, apretado; (concise) conciso; (make denser) tupir
compact[2] [kámpækt] N (agreement) pacto m; (case for powder) polvera f; **— disk** disco compacto m; VT compactar
compactness [kámpǽktnɪs] N densidad f; (conciseness) concisión f
companion [kəmpǽnjən] N (comrade, partner) compañero -ra mf; (caregiver) acompañante mf
companionship [kəmpǽnjənʃɪp] N compañía f
company [kámpəni] N compañía f; **to keep — with** codearse con, frecuentar
comparable [kámpə-əbəł] ADJ comparable
comparative [kəmpǽrəDɪv] ADJ comparativo
compare [kəmpér] VI/VT comparar[se]; **beyond —** incomparable, sin parangón
comparison [kəmpǽrɪsən] N comparación f; **in — with** comparado con
compartment [kəmpártmənt] N compartimiento m
compass [kámpəs] N (for drawing) compás m; (for directions) brújula f
compassion [kəmpǽʃən] N compasión f
compassionate [kəmpǽʃənɪt] ADJ compasivo
compatibility [kəmpæDəbílɪDi] N compatibilidad f
compatible [kəmpǽDəbəł] ADJ compatible (also of computers)
compatriot [kəmpétriət] N compatriota mf
compel [kəmpéł] VT (force) obligar; (demand) exigir
compelling [kəmpélɪŋ] ADJ (argument) convincente; (story) emocionante
compensate [kámpənset] VT (make up for)

compensar, resarcir; (pay) remunerar
compensation [kɑmpənséʃən] N (making up
for) compensación f; (remuneration)
remuneración f
compete [kəmpít] VI/VT competir
competence [kámpɪdəns] N competencia f
competent [kámpɪdənt] ADJ competente
competition [kɑmpɪtíʃən] N competencia f;
(sports match) competición f, contienda f
competitive [kəmpéDIDIV] ADJ competitivo; —
examination Sp oposición f; Am concurso
m; — **sports** deportes de competición m pl
competitiveness [kəmpéDItɪvnɪs] N
competitividad f
competitor [kəmpéDIDə-] N (business)
competidor -ora mf; (sports) atleta mf
compilation [kɑmpɪléʃən] N recopilación f
compile [kəmpáɪɫ] VT recopilar, compilar
compiler [kəmpáɪlə-] N compilador m; —
language lenguaje compilador m
complacency [kəmplésənsi] N confianza
infundada f
complacent [kəmplésənt] ADJ confiado
complain [kəmplén] VI quejarse
complainant [kəmplénənt] ADJ & N recurrente
mf
complaint [kəmplént] N queja f; (official)
reclamo m; (civil charge) demanda f;
(ailment) dolencia f
complement[1] [kámpləmənt] N complemento
m; (of staff) dotación f
complement[2] [kámpləmɛnt] VT complementar
complementary [kɑmpləméntri] ADJ
complementario
complete [kəmplít] ADJ completo, pleno; a —
stranger un perfecto desconocido; VT
completar; **to — a pass** completar un pase
completion [kəmplíʃən] N finalización f,
terminación f; **she brought the project to
— completó** el proyecto
complex[1] [kəmplɛ́ks] ADJ complejo
complex[2] [kámplɛks] N complejo m
complexion [kəmplɛ́kʃən] N (skin) cutis m;
(color) tez f; (perspective) cariz m
complexity [kəmplɛ́ksɪDi] N complejidad f
compliance [kəmpláɪəns] N (obedience)
conformidad f, acatamiento m; (polite
reverence) pleitesía f; **in — with** en
conformidad con
complicate [kámplɪket] VT complicar
complicated [kámplɪkeDɪd] ADJ complicado
complication [kɑmplɪkéʃən] N complicación f
complicity [kəmplísɪDi] N complicidad f
compliment [kámpləmənt] N cumplido, halago
m; (on looks) piropo m; (from a suitor)
galantería f; **to pay someone a —** hacerle un
cumplido a alguien; **to send one's —s** enviar
saludos; VI/VT elogiar, halagar
comply [kəmpláɪ] VI obedecer; **to — with**

cumplir con, acatar
component [kəmpónənt] ADJ & N componente m
compose [kəmpóz] VI/VT componer; **to —
oneself** sosegarse
composed [kəmpózd] ADJ sosegado; **to be — of**
estar compuesto de, componerse de, constar
de
composer [kəmpózə-] N compositor -ra mf
composite [kəmpázɪt] ADJ compuesto; N
amalgama f
composition [kɑmpəzíʃən] N (make-up, musical
piece) composición f; (aggregate material)
compuesto m; (school essay) composición f,
redacción f
composure [kəmpóʒə-] N compostura f
compound[1] [kámpaʊnd] ADJ & N compuesto m;
— **fracture** fractura expuesta f; — **interest**
interés compuesto m
compound[2] [kɑmpáʊnd] VT (combine)
combinar; (worsen) empeorar
comprehend [kɑmprɪhénd] VT comprender
comprehensible [kɑmprɪhénsəbəɫ] ADJ
comprensible
comprehension [kɑmprɪhénʃən] N
comprensión f
comprehensive [kɑmprɪhénsɪv] ADJ
exhaustivo; — **insurance** seguro contra
todo riesgo m
compress[1] [kəmprés] VT comprimir; —**ed disk**
disco comprimido m; —**ed file** archivo
comprimido m
compress[2] [kámprɛs] N compresa f
compression [kəmpréʃən] N compresión f
comprise [kəmpráɪz] VT comprender, incluir;
to be —d of comprender, incluir
compromise [kámprəmaɪz] N (arrangement)
arreglo por concesiones mutuas m,
compromiso m; (intermediate thing) cruce m,
término medio m; VI/VT (make agreement)
transigir; Am transar; (jeopardize)
comprometer
comptroller [kəntrólə-] N controlador -ra mf;
Am contralor -ora mf
compulsion [kəmpʌ́ɫʃən] N (impulse)
compulsión f, coacción f; (coercion) coerción f
compulsive [kəmpʌ́lsɪv] ADJ compulsivo
compulsory [kəmpʌ́ɫsəri] ADJ obligatorio,
obligado
computation [kɑmpjʊtéʃən] N cómputo m,
cálculo m
compute [kəmpjút] VI/VT computar, calcular
computer [kəmpjúDə-] N Am computadora f; Sp
ordenador m; — **engineer** ingeniero -ra en
computación mf, ingeniero -ra informático
-ca mf; — **graphics** gráficos por
computadora/ordenador m pl; — **literacy**
(process) alfabetización digital f; (result)
alfabetismo digital m; — **science** informática
f; — **virus** virus de computadora/

ordenador *m*
computerization [kəmpjuDəɪzéʃən] N *Sp*
ordenación *f, Am* computarización *f*
computerize [kəmpjúDəraɪz] VI/VT
informatizar, computarizar
computing [kəmpjúDɪŋ] N informática *f;* ADJ
informático
comrade [kámræd] N camarada *mf*
concave [kánkev] ADJ cóncavo
conceal [kənsíł] VT encubrir, ocultar, disimular
concealment [kənsíłmənt] N encubrimiento *m,*
disimulo *m*
concede [kənsíd] VI/VT (recognize) conceder,
reconocer; (allow) conceder
conceit [kənsít] N (vanity) vanidad *f;* (literary
device) concepto *m*
conceited [kənsíDɪd] ADJ engreído, presumido
conceivable [kənsívəbəł] ADJ imaginable,
concebible
conceive [kənsív] VI/VT concebir; (a plan)
concebir, idear
concentrate [kánsəntret] VI/VT concentrar[se]
concentration [kansəntréʃən] N concentración
f; — **camp** campo de concentración *m*
concept [kánsɛpt] N concepto *m*
conception [kənsɛ́pʃən] N concepción *f*
conceptual [kənsɛ́ptʃuəł] ADJ conceptual
concern [kənsɝn] VT (be of interest) concernir,
atañer; (worry) preocupar; **to — oneself
with** ocuparse de; **to whom it may —** a
quien corresponda; N (interest) interés *m;*
(matter) asunto *m;* (worry) preocupación *f;*
(company) compañía *f;* **to be of no —** no
tener consecuencia
concerned [kənsɝnd] ADJ (involved)
involucrado; (anxious) preocupado; **as far as
I am —** en lo que a mí respecta; **to be —
about** preocuparse por
concerning [kənsɝnɪŋ] PREP tocante a,
respecto a
concert[1] [kánsɝt] N concierto *m*
concert[2] [kənsɝt] VT concertar
concession [kənsɛ́ʃən] N concesión *f*
conciliate [kənsíliet] VI/VT (make compatible)
conciliar; (appease) aplacar
conciliation [kənsɪliéʃən] N conciliación *f*
concise [kənsáɪs] ADJ conciso, sucinto
conciseness [kənsáɪsnɪs] N concisión *f*
conclude [kənklúd] VI/VT concluir
conclusion [kənklúʒən] N conclusión *f*
conclusive [kənklúsɪv] ADJ concluyente
concoct [kənkákt] VT (contrive) fabricar, urdir;
(prepare by cooking) preparar
concoction [kənkákʃən] N mejunje *m*
concord [kánkɔrd] N (peace) concordia *f;*
(agreement) convenio *m,* acuerdo *m*
concrete[1] [kankrít] ADJ concreto
concrete[2] [kánkrit] N hormigón *m;* (made of
concrete) de hormigón

concubine [káŋkjəbaɪn] N concubina *f*
concur [kənkɝ] VI estar de acuerdo
concussion [kənkʌ́ʃən] N (brain injury)
conmoción cerebral *f;* (shock) concusión *f*
condemn [kəndɛ́m] VT condenar; (acquire
public ownership) expropiar; (declare unsafe)
declarar ruinoso
condemnation [kandɛmnéʃən] N condenación
f, condena *f*
condensation [kandɛnséʃən] N condensación *f;*
(of a book) compendio *m*
condense [kəndɛ́ns] VI/VT condensar[se]
condescend [kandəsénd] VI condescender a
condescension [kandəsénʃən] N
condescendencia *f*
condiment [kándəmənt] N condimento *m,*
aliño *m*
condition [kəndíʃən] N condición *f;* **he's got a
heart —** sufre del corazón, tiene una
afección cardíaca; **he's in good physical —**
está en buen estado físico; **the patient is in
critical —** el paciente está en estado crítico;
on — that a condición de que; VT (restrict on
a condition, establish a conditioned response)
condicionar; (accustom oneself)
acostumbrarse
conditional [kəndíʃənł] ADJ & N condicional *m*
conditioning [kəndíʃənɪŋ] N condicionamiento
m
condolences [kəndólənsɪz] N pésame *m,*
condolencias *f;* **to express one's —** dar las
condolencias
condom [kándəm] N condón *m,* preservativo *m*
condominium [kandəmíniəm] N condominio
m
condone [kəndón] VT tolerar
conducive [kəndúsɪv] ADJ conducente
conduct[1] [kándʌkt] N conducta *f,*
comportamiento *m*
conduct[2] [kəndʌkt] VI/VT (behave) conducirse,
comportarse; (carry out) llevar a cabo;
(direct, lead) dirigir; (serve as channel for)
conducir
conduction [kəndʌ́kʃən] N conducción *f*
conductor [kəndʌ́ktɚ] N (substance that
conducts) conductor *m;* (of an orchestra)
director -ora *mf;* (of a train) revisor -ora *mf*
conduit [kánduɪt] N conducto *m*
cone [kon] N cono *m;* (container) cucurucho *m*
confection [kənfɛ́kʃən] N (of clothes) confección
f; (of candy) confitura *f*
confectionery [kənfɛ́kʃənɛri] N confitería *f;*
(shop) dulcería *f;* (candies) dulces *m pl*
confederacy [kənfɛ́Dɚəsi] N confederación *f*
confederate[1] [kənfɛ́Dɚɪt] ADJ & N confederado
-da *mf*
confederate[2] [kənfɛ́Dɚet] VI/VT confederar[se]
confederation [kənfɛDɚréʃən] N confederación *f*
confer [kənfɝ] VT (grant) conferir, atribuir;

(consult) consultar; (negotiate) conferenciar
conference [kánfə-əns] N (consultation)
consulta f; (professional meeting) congreso
m; (legislative) asamblea general f; (sports
league) liga f; — **call** llamada en conferencia f
confess [kənfés] VI/VT confesar[se]
confession [kənféʃən] N confesión f
confessional [kənféʃənl] N confesionario m
confessor [kənfésə-] N confesor m
confidant [kánfɪdɑnt] N confidente mf
confide [kənfáɪd] VI/VT (entrust) confiar; VI (tell
secrets to) hacer confidencias a
confidence [kánfɪDəns] N confianza f;
(certainty) seguridad f; (secret
communication) confidencia f; — **game** timo
m; — **man** timador m, embaucador m; **in** —
en confianza
confident [kánfɪDənt] ADJ seguro; **he's a** —
person tiene mucha confianza
confidential [kɑnfɪdénʃəł] ADJ confidencial;
(secretary, etc.) de confianza
configuration [kənfɪgjəréʃən] N configuración f
(also for computers)
configure [kənfígjə-] VT configurar
confine[1] [kənfáɪn] VT confinar, recluir; **to** —
oneself to limitarse a
confine[2] [kánfaɪn] N confin m
confinement [kənfáɪnmənt] N confinamiento m
confirm [kənfɜ́m] VT confirmar
confirmation [kɑnfə-méʃən] N confirmación f
confiscate [kánfɪsket] VT confiscar
confiscation [kɑnfɪskéʃən] N confiscación f
conflagration [kɑnfləgréʃən] N incendio m
conflict[1] [kánflɪkt] N conflicto m, contienda f; —
of interest conflicto de intereses m
conflict[2] [kənflíkt] VI oponerse
confluence [kánfluəns] N confluencia f
conform [kənfórm] VI/VT conformar[se]
conformity [kənfórmɪDi] N (agreement)
conformidad f; (passive acquiescence)
conformismo m
confound [kənfáʊnd] VT (bewilder)
desconcertar; (confuse) confundir; — **it!** fam
¡caramba!
confront [kənfránt] VT (set face to face, fight)
confrontar; (face up to) enfrentarse a
confrontation [kɑnfrəntéʃən] N confrontación
f, enfrentamiento m
confuse [kənfjúz] VT confundir
confused [kənfjúzd] ADJ (person) confundido;
(situation) confuso; **to become** —
confundirse
confusing [kənfjúzɪŋ] ADJ confuso
confusion [kənfjúʒən] N confusión f
congeal [kəndʒíł] VI/VT cuajar[se]
congenial [kəndʒínjəł] ADJ agradable, simpático
congenital [kəndʒénɪdł] ADJ congénito
congestion [kəndʒéstʃən] N congestión f
congestive heart failure [kəndʒɛstɪv hárt feljə-]

ADJ insuficiencia cardíaca congestiva f
conglomeration [kənglɑməréʃən] N (unit)
conglomeración f; (mass) conglomerado m
Congo [káŋgo] N Congo m
Congolese [kɑŋgəlíz] ADJ & N congoleño -ña mf
congratulate [kəngrǽtʃələt] VT felicitar
congratulation [kəngrætʃəléʃən] N felicitación
f, parabién m; —**s!** ¡enhorabuena! ¡albricias!
congregate [káŋgrɪget] VI/VT congregar[se]
congregation [kɑŋgrɪgéʃən] N (worshipers)
fieles m pl, feligreses m pl; (act of
congregating, committee of cardinals)
congregación f
congress [káŋgrɪs] N (professional) congreso m;
(political) asamblea legislativa f; (US)
congreso m; —**man** (US) congresista m;
—**woman** (US) congresista f
congressional [kəngréʃənł] ADJ congresual
congruence [kəngrúəns] N congruencia f
conifer [kánəfə-] N conífera f
conjecture [kəndʒéktʃə-] N conjetura f; VI/VT
conjeturar
conjugal [kándʒəgəł] ADJ conyugal
conjugate [kándʒəget] VI/VT conjugar[se]
conjugation [kɑndʒəgéʃən] N conjugación f
conjunction [kəndʒʌ́ŋkʃən] N conjunción f
conjunctivitis [kəndʒʌ̀ŋktəváɪDɪs] N
conjuntivitis f
conjure [kándʒə-] VT invocar; **to** — **up** evocar; VI
hacer hechizos
connect [kənékt] VI/VT conectar[se], enlazar[se];
(buildings, callers) comunicar[se]; (concepts)
relacionar[se]; (pipes) acoplar[se]; —**ing rod**
biela f
connection [kənékʃən] N (act of connecting)
conexión f, vinculación f; (of telephone)
comunicación f, enganche m; (of concepts)
relación f; (of pipes) acople m; (affinity)
afinidad f; (supplier) contacto m; —**s**
contactos m pl, enchufe m
connectivity [kɑnɛktívɪDi] N conectividad f
connive [kənáɪv] VI conspirar
connoisseur [kɑnəsúr] N conocedor -ora f
connotation [kɑnətéʃən] N connotación f
conquer [káŋkə-] VT (win) conquistar;
(overcome) vencer
conqueror [káŋkərə-] N conquistador -ora mf;
(one who overcomes) vencedor -ora mf
conquest [káŋkwɛst] N conquista f
conscience [kánʃəns] N conciencia f
conscientious [kɑnʃiéntʃəs] ADJ concienzudo
conscious [kánʃəs] ADJ consciente
consciousness [kánʃəsnɪs] N conciencia f; **to**
lose — perder el conocimiento
conscript[1] [kənskrípt] VT reclutar
conscript[2] [kánskrɪpt] N recluta mf
conscription [kənskrípʃən] N reclutamiento m
consecrate [kánsɪkret] VT consagrar
consecration [kɑnsɪkréʃən] N consagración f

consecutive [kənsékjəDɪv] ADJ consecutivo
consensus [kənsénsəs] N consenso *m*
consent [kənsént] N consentimiento *m*; VI
  consentir
consequence [kánsɪkwɛns] N consecuencia *f*;
  (negative) secuela *f*
consequent [kánsɪkwənt] ADJ consiguiente,
  resultante; N (in mathematics) consecuente
  m; (in logic) consiguiente *m*
consequently [kánsɪkwəntli] ADV por
  consiguiente, en consecuencia
conservation [kansɚvéʃən] N conservación *f*,
  preservación *f*
conservatism [kənsɚ́vətɪzəm] N
  conservadurismo *m*
conservative [kənsɚ́vəDɪv] ADJ & N conservador
  -ora *mf*
conservatory [kənsɚ́vətɔri] N conservatorio *m*
conserve[1] [kənsɚ́v] VT conservar, preservar
conserve[2] [kánsɚv] N confitura *m*
consider [kənsíDɚ] VT considerar
considerable [kənsíDɚəbəł] ADJ considerable
considerate [kənsíDɚɪt] ADJ considerado
consideration [kənsɪDɚéʃən] N consideración
  f; (respect) miramiento *m*; (payment)
  remuneración *f*
considering [kənsíDɚɪŋ] PREP en vista de,
  teniendo en cuenta; **she cooks well, —** para
  ser ella, cocina bien
consign [kənsáɪn] VT consignar
consignee [kansaɪní] N consignatario -ria *mf*
consignment [kənsáɪnmənt] N consignación *f*;
  on — a/en consignación
consist [kənsíst] VI consistir [en]
consistency [kənsístənsi] N (adherence to
  principles) coherencia *f*, consecuencia *f*;
  (density) consistencia *f*
consistent [kənsístənt] ADJ (adherent to
  principles) consecuente, coherente;
  (cohering) consistente
consolation [kansəléʃən] N consuelo *m*,
  consolación *f*
console[1] [kənsół] VT consolar
console[2] [kánsoł] N consola *f*
consolidate [kənsálɪdet] VI/VT consolidar[se]
consolidation [kənsalɪdéʃən] N consolidación *f*
consonant [kánsənənt] N consonante *f*; ADJ
  consonante, conforme
consort[1] [kənsɔ́rt] VI **to — with** asociarse con
consort[2] [kánsɔrt] N consorte *mf*
consortium [kənsɔ́rʃiəm] N consorcio *m*
conspicuous [kənspíkjuəs] ADJ evidente
conspiracy [kənspírəsi] N conspiración *f*,
  conjura *f*
conspirator [kənspírəDɚ] N conspirador -ora
  mf, conjurado -da *mf*
conspire [kənspáɪr] VI conspirar, conjurar
constable [kánstəbəl] N oficial de policía *mf*;
  (keeper of fortress) condestable *m*

constancy [kánstənsi] N constancia *f*
constant [kánstənt] ADJ & N constante *f*
constellation [kanstəléʃən] N constelación *f*
consternation [kanstɚnéʃən] N consternación *f*
constipate [kánstəpet] VT estreñir
constipated [kánstəpeDɪd] ADJ estreñido
constipation [kanstəpéʃən] N estreñimiento *m*
constituent [kənstítʃuənt] ADJ componente,
  constitutivo; N (component) componente *m*;
  (voter) votante *mf*; (part of a sentence)
  constituyente *m*
constitute [kánstɪtut] VT constituir
constitution [kanstɪtúʃən] N constitución *f*
constitutional [kanstɪtúʃən] ADJ
  constitucional; N caminata *f*
constrain [kənstrén] VT constreñir, restringir
constraint [kənstrént] N constreñimiento *m*
constrict [kənstríkt] VT constreñir
constriction [kənstríkʃən] N (action)
  constricción *f*; (place) estrechamiento *m*
construct[1] [kənstrʌ́kt] VT construir
construct[2] [kánstrʌkt] N invención *f*
construction [kənstrʌ́kʃən] N construcción *f*; —
  company constructora *f*
constructive [kənstrʌ́ktɪv] ADJ constructivo
construe [kənstrú] VT interpretar
consul [kánsəl] N cónsul *mf*
consulate [kánsəlɪt] N consulado *m*
consult [kənsʌ́łt] VI/VT consultar; VI (serve as a
  consultant) asesorar
consultant [kənsʌ́łtənt] N asesor -ora *mf*
consultation [kansəłtéʃən] N consulta *f*
consultative [kənsʌ́łtəDɪv] ADJ consultivo
consulting [kənsʌ́łtɪŋ] N asesoramiento *m*,
  consultoría *f*; ADJ consultor; — **firm** firma
  consultora *f*
consumable [kənsúməbəł] ADJ — **goods** bienes
  consumibles *m pl*
consume [kənsúm] VI/VT consumir
consumer [kənsúmɚ] N consumidor -ora *mf*; —
  confidence index índice de confianza del
  consumidor *m*; — **credit** crédito al
  consumidor *m*; — **protection** protección al
  consumidor *f*
consumerism [kənsúmɚɪzəm] N
  consumismo *m*
consuming [kənsúmɪŋ] ADJ (need) imperioso;
  (drive) abrasador
consummate[1] [kánsəmet] VT consumar
consummate[2] [kánsəmɪt] ADJ consumado
consumption [kənsʌ́mpʃən] N (using up)
  consumo *m*; (wasting of the body) consunción
  f; (tuberculosis) tisis *f*
consumptive [kənsʌ́mptɪv] ADJ tísico
contact [kántækt] N contacto *m*; — **lens** lente de
  contacto *mf*; VI/VT (touch) tocar;
  (communicate with) contactar
contagion [kəntédʒən] N (spread) contagio *m*;
  (disease spread) enfermedad contagiosa *f*

contagious [kəntéʤəs] ADJ contagioso

contain [kəntén] VI/VT contener

container [kənténɚ] N recipiente *m*; (on a ship) contenedor *m*; —**ship** buque portacontenedores *m*

containerize [kənténəraɪz] VT contenedorizar

containment [kənténmɔnt] N contención *f*

contaminate [kəntǽmənet] VT contaminar

contamination [kəntæmənéʃən] N contaminación *f*

contemplate [kántəmplet] VT (observe) contemplar; (consider) considerar

contemplation [kantəmpléʃən] N (observation) contemplación *f*; (consideration) consideración *f*

contemporary [kəntémpərɛri] ADJ contemporáneo

contempt [kəntémpt] N desprecio *m*, menosprecio *m*; — **of court** desacato al tribunal *m*

contemptible [kəntémptəbəł] ADJ despreciable, rastrero

contemptuous [kəntémptʃuəs] ADJ desdeñoso

contend [kənténd] VI (struggle) contender, lidiar; (argue) disputar; VT afirmar

content¹ [kəntént] ADJ (happy) contento; (resigned) conforme; N **to one's heart's** — a discreción

content², **contents** [kántɛnt[s]] N contenido *m*

contented [kənténtɪd] ADJ contento, satisfecho

contention [kənténʃən] N (opinion) opinión *f*; **in** — (disputed) en discusión; (still eligible) con posibilidades

contentious [kənténʃəs] ADJ conflictivo

contentment [kənténtmənt] N contento *m*

contest¹ [kántɛst] N (competition) concurso *m*, certamen *m*; (struggle) contienda *f*

contest² [kəntést] VT (compete) contender; (dispute) disputar; (challenge) impugnar

contestant [kəntéstənt] N concursante *mf*, participante *mf*

context [kántɛkst] N contexto *m*

contiguous [kəntígjuəs] ADJ contiguo, pegado

continent [kántənənt] N (landmass) continente *m*; ADJ (sexually abstinent) continente; (of bodily functions) capaz de controlar los esfínteres

continental [kantənéntł] ADJ continental

contingency [kəntínʤənsi] N contingencia *f*; — **fund** fondo de contingencia *m*; — **planning** planificación para contingencias *f*

contingent [kəntínʤənt] ADJ & N contingente *m*

continual [kəntínjuəł] ADJ continuo

continuance [kəntínjuəns] N continuación *f*; (delay) aplazamiento *m*

continuation [kəntɪnjuéʃən] N continuación *f*

continue [kəntínju] VI/VT continuar

continuing [kəntínjuɪŋ] ADJ continuado; — **education** educación para adultos *f*

continuity [kantɪnúɪDi] N continuidad *f*

continuous [kəntínjuəs] ADJ (uninterrupted in time) continuo; (uninterrupted in space) ininterrumpido

contortion [kəntɔ́rʃən] N contorsión *f*

contour [kántur] N contorno *m*

contra account [kántrə əkaʊnt] N cuenta de contrapartida *f*

contraband [kántrəbænd] N contrabando *m*

contraception [kantrəsépʃən] N anticoncepción *f*

contraceptive [kantrəséptɪv] ADJ & N anticonceptivo *m*

contract¹ [kántrækt] N contrato *m*; — **killer** asesino -na a sueldo *mf*; **by** — por contrato

contract² [kəntrækt] VI/VT contraer[se]; (assign by contract) contratar; **to** — **out** subcontratar

contraction [kəntrækʃən] N contracción *f*; (in childbirth) contracción *f*, pujo *m*

contractor [kántræktɚ] N contratista *mf*

contractual agreement [kəntræktʃuəłəgrímənt] N acuerdo contractual *m*

contradict [kantrədíkt] VI/VT contradecir

contradiction [kantrədíkʃən] N contradicción *f*

contradictory [kantrədíktəri] ADJ contradictorio

contraption [kəntræpʃən] N chisme *m*, coso *m*

contrary [kántreri] ADJ contrario, opuesto; (obstinate) testarudo; N **lo contrario**; **on the** — al contrario

contrast¹ [kántræst] N contraste *m*

contrast² [kəntræst] VI/VT contrastar

contravene [kantrəvín] VT contravenir

contribute [kəntríbjut] VI contribuir; (to a newspaper) colaborar; VT contribuir con, aportar

contribution [kantrəbjúʃən] N (donation, article) contribución *f*; (scientific) aporte *m*, aportación *f*

contributor [kəntríbjəDɚ] N colaborador -ra *mf*

contrite [kəntráɪt] ADJ contrito

contrivance [kəntráɪvəns] N artefacto *m*

contrive [kəntráɪv] VI/VT ingeniar; **he** —**d to get their money** se las ingenió para sacarles el dinero

contrived [kəntráɪvd] ADJ artificioso

control [kəntrół] VI/VT controlar; N control *m*; (of a machine) mando *m*; **who's in** —? ¿quién manda? **under** — bajo control; — **freak** mandón -ona *mf*; — **key** tecla de control/mando *f*; — **panel** panel de control *m*; — **tower** torre de control *f*

controller [kəntrólɚ] N (comptroller) controlador -ora *mf*; Am contralor *m*; (device) regulador *m*

controversial [kantrəvɚ́ʃəł] ADJ controvertido

controversy [kántrəvɚsi] N controversia *f*, polémica *f*

contusion [kəntúʒən] N contusión *f*,

magulladura *f*

conundrum [kənʌ́ndrəm] N (riddle) adivinanza *f*, acertijo *m*; (mystery) enigma *m*

convalesce [kɑnvəlés] VI convalecer

convalescence [kɑnvəlésəns] N convalecencia *f*

convalescent [kɑnvəlésənt] ADJ & N convaleciente *mf*

convection [kənvékʃən] N convección *f*

convene [kənvín] VT convocar; VI reunirse

convenience [kənvínjəns] N (practicality) conveniencia *f*; (appliance) comodidad *f*; — **store** autoservicio *m*; **at your** — cuando le venga bien

convenient [kənvínjənt] ADJ conveniente, oportuno; (at hand) accesible

convent [kánvɛnt] N convento *m*

convention [kənvénʃən] N (political assembly) convención *f*; (professional assembly) congreso *m*; (pact) convenio *m*; (international agreement, acceptable usage) convención *f*

conventional [kənvénʃənl] ADJ (not original) convencional; (traditional) clásico; — **loan** préstamo convencional *m*

conventioneer [kənvɛnʃənír] N congresista *mf*

converge [kənvɝ́ʤ] VI converger

convergence [kənvɝ́ʤəns] N convergencia *f*

conversant [kənvɝ́sənt] ADJ — **with** versado en

conversation [kɑnvɚséʃən] N conversación *f*; — **piece** tema de conversación *m*

converse [kənvɝ́s] VI conversar

conversion [kənvɝ́ʒən] N conversión *f*

convert[1] [kənvɝ́t] VI/VT convertir[se]

convert[2] [kánvɝt] N converso -sa *mf*

converter [kənvɝ́Dɚ] N convertidor *m*

convertible [kənvɝ́Dəbəl] ADJ convertible; (car) descapotable; — **assets** activo convertible *m*; N (car) descapotable *m*

convex [kánvɛks] ADJ convexo

convey [kənvé] VT (carry) llevar; (transfer) transferir; (transmit) transmitir; (communicate) comunicar

conveyance [kənvéəns] N (vehicle) vehículo *m*; (transfer of property) transferencia *f*; (document) escritura de traspaso *f*

conveyer, conveyor [kənvéɚ] N transmisor -ora *mf*; — **belt** cinta transportadora *f*

convict[1] [kánvɪkt] N convicto -ta *mf*

convict[2] [kənvíkt] VI/VT declarar culpable

conviction [kənvíkʃən] N (belief) convicción *f*, convencimiento *m*; (act of convicting) declaración de culpabilidad *f*; (on one's record) condena *f*

convince [kənvíns] VT convencer

convincing [kənvínsɪŋ] ADJ convincente, contundente

convocation [kɑnvəkéʃən] N (act) convocación *f*; (group of people) asamblea *f*

convoke [kənvók] VT convocar

convoluted [kɑnvəlúDɪd] ADJ retorcido

convoy [kánvɔɪ] N convoy *m*; VT convoyar

convulse [kənvʌ́ls] VI/VT convulsionar[se]

convulsion [kənvʌ́lʃən] N convulsión *f*

coo [ku] VI arrullar; N arrullo *m*

cook [kʊk] N cocinero -ra *mf*; —**book** libro de cocina *m*; VT cocinar, guisar; **to** — **the books** falsificar los libros de contabilidad; **to** — **up a plan** urdir un plan; **her** —**ing is outstanding** cocina muy bien; **now we're** —**ing!** ahora sí

cookery [kúkəri] N cocina *f*

cookie [kúki] N (sweet food) galletita dulce *f*; (computer record) archivo cookie *m*

cool [kuł] ADJ (not hot) fresco; (indifferent) frío, indiferente; (calm) tranquilo; (good) excelente; *Carib* chévere; *RP* macanudo; *Sp* guay; *Sp vulg* cojonudo; **that's not** — eso no se hace; —**ing-off period** tregua *f*; N (cold) fresco *m*; (composure) tranquilidad *f*; VT (make cooler) enfriar; (air condition) refrigerar; **to** — **off** (get cold) enfriarse; (get cooler) refrescar[se]; (calm down) calmarse

coolant [kúlənt] N refrigerante *m*

cooler [kúlɚ] N (room) cámara frigorífica *f*; (container) nevera portátil *f*

coolness [kúłnɪs] N (cold weather) fresco *m*, frescor *m*; (indifference) frialdad *f*, indiferencia *f*

coon [kun] N (raccoon) mapache *m*; **a** —**'s age** una eternidad

co-op [kóap] N cooperativa *f*

coop [kup] N jaula *f*; (for chickens) gallinero *m*; VT enjaular; **to** — **up** encerrar

cooperate [koápəret] VI cooperar

cooperation [koɑpəréʃən] N cooperación *f*

cooperative [koápəəDɪv] ADJ (helpful) cooperativo; (relative to a cooperative) cooperativista; N cooperativa *f*

coordinate[1] [koɔ́rdn̩ɪt] ADJ coordinado; N coordenada *f*; —**s** (clothes) conjunto *m*

coordinate[2] [koɔ́rdn̩et] VI/VT coordinar

coordinating [koɔ́rdn̩eDɪŋ] ADJ coordinador

coordination [koɔrdn̩éʃən] N coordinación *f*

coordinator [koɔ́rdn̩eDɚ] N coordinador -ora *mf*

cop [kap] N *fam* poli *mf*, polizonte *m*; VI **to** — **out** zafarse

copayment [kópemənt] N copago *m*

cope [kop] VI **to** — **with** arreglárselas con; **I cannot** — **with this** no puedo con esto

copious [kópiəs] ADJ copioso

copper [kápɚ] N cobre *m*; (cop) *fam* poli *mf*; ADJ de cobre

copulate [kápjəlet] VI copular

copulation [kɑpjəléʃən] N copulación *f*

copy [kápi] N (reproduction) copia *f*; (specimen, example) ejemplar *m*; (news story) texto *m*; —**cat** copión -ona *mf*; — **machine** copiadora *f*; — **protection** protección contra copias *f*; —**right** copyright *m*, derechos de autor *m pl*;

this material is —righted reservados todos los derechos; VT copiar; **to —right** registrar los derechos

coquette [kokét] N coqueta f

coral [kɔ́rəł] N coral m; ADJ (related to coral) coralino; (made of coral) de coral; **— reef** arrecife de coral m

cord [kɔrd] N (thread) cuerda f; (for shoes) cordón m; (firewood measure) medida de leña f; **—s** pantalones de pana m pl

cordial [kɔ́rdʒəł] ADJ cordial; N licor m

cordless [kɔ́rdlɪs] ADJ inalámbrico

corduroy [kɔ́rDərɔɪ] N pana f; **—s** pantalones de pana m pl

core [kor] N (of fruit) corazón m; (of a problem) meollo m; (of a magnet, reactor) núcleo m; **— business** negocio principal m; **— inflation** inflación básica f; VT despepitar

cork [kɔrk] N (woody material) corcho m; (stopper, buoy) tapón m; **—screw** sacacorchos m sg, tirabuzón m; **— tree** alcornoque m; VT tapar con un corcho

corn [kɔrn] N (plant) maíz m; (painful growth) callo m; **—bread** pan de maíz m; **—cob** mazorca f; Sp zuro m; **— on the cob** choclo m; Mex elote m; **—ed beef** corned beef m; **—field** maizal m; Mex milpa f; **—flakes** copos de maíz m pl; **—meal** harina de maíz f; **—starch** Maicena™ f

corner [kɔ́rnə-] N (angle) ángulo m; (of a space) rincón m; (of two streets) esquina f; **—back** (football) esquinero m; **— kick** (soccer) saque/tiro de esquina m, córner m; **—stone** piedra angular f; **— table** mesa rinconera f; VT (trap) arrinconar, acorralar; (monopolize) monopolizar; VI doblar, Sp girar; **— the market** acaparar el mercado

cornered [kɔ́rnə-d] ADJ (animal) acorralado; (person) arrinconado

cornet [kɔrnét] N corneta f

cornice [kɔ́rnɪs] N cornisa f

corny [kɔ́rni] ADJ sensiblero; (joke) viejo

corollary [kɔ́rəleri] N corolario m

coronary [kɔ́rənɛri] ADJ coronario; **— bypass** puente cardiopulmonar m; **— care unit** unidad de cuidado coronario f; **— failure** insuficiencia coronaria f; **— thrombosis** trombosis coronaria f

coronation [kɔrənéʃən] N coronación f

coroner [kɔ́rənə-] N médico -ca forense mf

corporal [kɔ́rpəəł] ADJ corporal; N (rank) cabo m

corporate [kɔ́rpə-ɪt] ADJ corporativo; **— backing** patrocinio empresarial m; **— officers** ejecutivos -vas de empresa mf pl

corporation [kɔrpəréʃən] N sociedad anónima f

corps [kor] N cuerpo m

corpse [kɔrps] N cadáver m

corpulent [kɔ́rpjələnt] ADJ corpulento

corpus [kɔ́rpəs] N corpus m

corpuscle [kɔ́rpʌsəł] N corpúsculo m; (of blood) glóbulo m

corral [kərǽł] N corral m; VT acorralar

correct [kərékt] VT corregir; ADJ correcto; **that is** — es cierto

correction [kərékʃən] N corrección f; (for glasses) graduación f

correctness [kəréktnɪs] N corrección f

corrector [kərékta-] N corrector -ora mf

correlate[1] [kɔ́rəlet] VI/VT correlacionar

correlate[2] [kɔ́rəlɪt] N correlato m

correlation [kɔrəléʃən] N correlación f

correspond [kɔrɪspánd] VI (be in agreement) corresponder, responder; (exchange letters) cartearse, escribirse

correspondence [kɔrɪspándəns] N correspondencia f

correspondent [kɔrɪspándənt] ADJ correspondiente; N (writer of letters) correspondiente mf; (news gatherer) corresponsal mf, enviado -da mf

corresponding [kɔrɪspándɪŋ] ADJ correspondiente; (secretary) encargado de la correspondencia

corridor [kɔ́rɪdɔr] N corredor m, pasillo m

corroborate [kərábəret] VT corroborar

corrode [kəród] VI/VT corroer[se]

corrosion [kəróʒən] N corrosión f

corrupt [kərápt] ADJ (dishonest) corrupto; (rotten) corrompido; **to become —** corromperse; VT corromper, viciar; **—ed file** archivo corrupto m

corruption [kərápʃən] N corrupción f

corset [kɔ́rsɪt] N corsé m

cortex [kɔ́rteks] N córtex m, corteza cerebral f

corticosteriod [kɔrDɪkostérɔɪd] N corticoesterolide m

cortisone [kɔ́rDɪzon] N cortisona f

cosigner [kósaɪnə-] N cosignatario -ria mf

cosmetic [kazmɛ́Dɪk] ADJ & N cosmético m; **— surgery** cirugía estética f

cosmic [kázmɪk] ADJ cósmico

cosmology [kazmáləʤi] N cosmología f

cosmonaut [kázmənɔt] N cosmonauta mf

cosmopolitan [kazməpálɪtn̩] ADJ cosmopolita

cosmos [kázmos] N cosmos m

cost [kɔst] N costo m; Sp coste m; **—s** (in court) costas f pl; **at** — al coste/costo; **at all —s** a toda costa; **— of living** costo/coste de vida m; **to sell at** — vender al costo / al coste; VT costar; **how much does this —?** ¿cuánto vale/cuesta esto? ADJ **—-benefit analysis** análisis costo-beneficio m; **— effective** económico

costar [kóstar] N coprotagonista mf, oponente mf

Costa Rica [kóstəríkə] N Costa Rica f

Costa Rican [kóstəríkən] ADJ & N costarricense mf, costarriqueño -ña mf

costly [kɔ́stli] ADJ costoso, caro

costume [kástum] N (style of clothing) vestimenta *f*; (in the theater) vestuario *m*; (disguise) disfraz *m*; — **jewelry** bisutería *f*

cot [kɑt] N catre *m*

cottage [kɑ́DIʤ] N (small house) casita *f*; (vacation house) cabaña *f*, chalé *m*; — **cheese** requesón *m*

cotter pin [kɑ́Də-pIn] N chaveta *f*

cotton [kɑtṇ] N algodón *m*; — **candy** algodón de azúcar *m*; — **gin** desmontadora de algodón *f*; —**seed** semilla de algodón *f*; —**wood** álamo [de Virginia] *m*

couch [kaUtʃ] N sofá *m*; (psychiatrist's) diván *m*; — **potato** telebobo -ba *mf*; VT expresar

cougar [kúgə-] N puma *f*

cough [kɔf] VI toser; **to** — **up** (spit) expectorar; (hand over) soltar, largar; N tos *f*; — **drop** pastilla para la tos *f*; — **syrup** jarabe para la tos *m*

could [kUd] V AUX I — **do it if I wanted** podría hacerlo si quisiera; — **you arrive early?** ¿podrías llegar temprano? — **I leave early?** ¿puedo salir temprano? **you** — **be right** quizá tengas razón

council [káUnsəɫ] N (religious) concilio *m*; (advisory) consejo *m*, junta *f*; (provincial) diputación *f*; (municipal) concejo *m*; —**man** concejal *m*; —**woman** concejal *f*, concejala *f*

councilor [káUnsələ-] N concejal *mf*

counsel [káUnsəɫ] N (advice) consejo *m*; (lawyer) abogado -da *mf*; VI/VT (give advice) aconsejar

counseling [káUnsəlIŋ] N (academic) asesoramiento *m*, orientación *f*; (psychological, marriage) terapia *f*

counselor [káUnsələ-] N consejero -ra *mf*; (lawyer) abogado -da *mf*

count [kaUnt] VI/VT contar; **to** — **in** incluir; **to** — **on** contar con; **to** — **oneself lucky** considerarse dichoso; **to** — **out** excluir; N (reckoning) cuenta *f*; (charge) cargo *m*; (noble) conde *m*; (in baseball) conteo *m*; —**down** cuenta regresiva *f*

countenance [káUntṇəns] N (expression) semblante *m*; (face) cara *f*; VT (tolerate) tolerar; (approve) aprobar

counter [káUntə-] N (in a kitchen) *Sp* encimera *f*; *Am* mostrador *m*; (in a store) mostrador *m*; (in a bar) barra *f*; (in board games) tablero *m*; (counting device) contador *m*; **over the** — sin receta; ADJ contrario, opuesto; ADV — **to** contra; **to run** — **to** ser contrario a; VT (an argument) retrucar (a blow), devolver; VI/VT (reply) replicar

counteract [kaUntə-ǽkt] VT contrarrestar

counterattack [káUntə-ɔtæk] N contraataque *m*; VI/VT contraatacar

counterbalance[1] [kaUntə-bǽləns] VI/VT contrapesar

counterbalance[2] [káUntə-bæləns] N contrapeso *m*

counterclockwise [kaUntə-klákwaIz] ADV en el sentido opuesto al de las manecillas del reloj

counterculture [káUntə-kʌɫtʃə-] N contracultura *f*

counterespionage [kaUntə-éspiənɑʒ] N contraespionaje *m*

counterexample [káUntə-Igzæmpəɫ] N contraejemplo *m*

counterfeit [káUntə-fIt] N falsificación *f*; ADJ falso; — **money** moneda falsa *f*; VT falsificar

countermand[1] [kaUntə-mǽnd] VT contramandar

countermand[2] [káUntə-mænd] N contraorden *f*

countermeasure [káUntə-mɛʒə-] N contramedida *f*

counteroffer [káUntə-ɔfə-] N contraoferta *f*

counterpart [káUntə-pɑrt] N homólogo -ga *mf*

counterproductive [kaUntə-prədʌ́ktIv] ADJ contraproducente

counterrevolution [kaUntə-rɛvəlúʃən] N contrarrevolución *f*

countersign [káUntə-saIn] N contraseña *f*; VT refrendar

countess [káUntIs] N condesa *f*

countless [káUntlIs] ADJ incontables, innumerables

country [kántri] N (nation) país *m*; (territory) territorio *m*; (homeland) patria *f*; (rural area) campo *m*; ADJ (of the countryside) rural; (uncouth) rústico; — **club** club campestre *m*; — **code** código de país *m*; —**man** compatriota *m*; — **music** música country *f*; — **of origin** país de origen *m*; —**side** (rural area) campo *m*; (scenery) paisaje *m*; —**woman** compatriota *f*

county [káUnti] N condado *m*; — **fair** feria [de ganado] *f*; — **seat** capital de condado *f*

coup [ku] N (success) golpe maestro *m*; (putsch) golpe de estado *m*; — **d'état** golpe de estado *m*

coupe [kup] N cupé *m*

couple [kápəɫ] N (of times, of forces, of people) par *m*; (romantic) pareja *f*; VI/VT (pair up) formar parejas; VT (connect) acoplar; VI (copulate) copular

couplet [káplIt] N pareado *m*

coupling [káplIŋ] N (mechanical action) acoplamiento *m*, enganche *m*; (device) acople *m*, enganche *m*; (mating) cópula *f*

coupon [kjúpɑn] N cupón *m*

courage [kɝ́Iʤ] N valentía *f*, valor *m*, coraje *m*

courageous [kəréʤəs] ADJ valiente

courier [kúriə-] N mensajero -ra *mf*

course [kɔrs] N (of a river, of study, of a disease) curso *m*; (of a road, route) trayecto *m*; (of a ship, plane) derrotero *m*; (progression of time) marcha *f*; (dish) plato *m*; — **of action**

línea de conducta f, proceder m; **in the — of a year** en el transcurso de un año; **in due —** a la larga; INTERJ **of —** claro, por supuesto, naturalmente; VI correr, fluir
court [kɔrt] N (courtyard) patio m; (atrium) patio interior m; (in sports) cancha f, pista f; (in a city) plazuela f, plazoleta f; (lower tribunal) juzgado m; (higher tribunal) tribunal m; (session) audiencia f; (royal residence, retinue) corte f; **—-martial** consejo de guerra m; **— of law** tribunal de justicia m; **— order** orden judicial f; **— reporter** estenotipista mf; **— room** tribunal m; **—yard** patio m; **to settle out of —** llegar a un arreglo extrajudicial; **to pay — to** cortejar; VT cortejar, galantear; **to — danger** tentar a la suerte; **to —-martial** someter a consejo de guerra; VI estar de novios
courteous [kɝˈdiəs] ADJ cortés
courtesy [kɝˈdisi] N (attitude) cortesía f; (act) fineza f, atención f
courtier [kɔrˈdiɚ] N (member of the court) cortesano -na mf; (sycophant) adulador -ora mf
courtship [kɔrtʃip] N cortejo m
cousin [kázən] N primo -ma mf; **first —** primo -ma hermano -na mf
cove [kov] N ensenada f
covenant [kávənənt] N pacto m; (religious) alianza f
cover [kávɚ] VI/VT cubrir, recubrir; (with lid, screen) tapar; (replace) sustituir; (include, deal with) comprender; (traverse) recorrer; (sing) hacer una versión; **—ed losses** pérdidas cubiertas f pl; **to — one's ass** cuidarse la retaguardia; **to — up** (wrap up) tapar bien; (hide) ocultar; N (lid) tapa f; (book) cubierta f, tapa f; (blanket) manta f; (for appliances, furniture) funda f; (front for activity) tapadera f, pantalla f; (shelter) resguardo m, abrigo m; **—all** mono m; **— charge** entrada f; **— girl** modelo de portada f; **— letter** carta con anexos f, carta de remisión f; **—-up** encubrimiento m; **to send under separate —** enviar por separado; **to take —** resguardarse; **under —** de incógnito; **under — of dark** bajo el manto de la noche
coverage [kávɚɪdʒ] N cobertura f; **— level** nivel de cobertura m
covert [kovɚt] ADJ encubierto
covet [kávɪt] VT (desire wrongfully) codiciar; (want) ansiar
covetous [kávɪdəs] ADJ codicioso
cow [kaU] N (bovine female) vaca f; (female of other animals) hembra f; **—bell** cencerro m, esquila f; **—boy** vaquero m; **—hide** cuero de vaca m, vaqueta f; **—lick** remolino m; **—pox** vacuna f; **—shed** vaquería f, vaqueriza f; **to have a —** tener una pataleta; VT intimidar

coward [káUəd] N cobarde mf
cowardice [káUəˌdɪs] N cobardía f
cowardly [káUəˌdli] ADJ cobarde
cower [káUɚ] VI achicarse
cowl [kaUł] N capucha f
coy [kɔɪ] ADJ (coquettish) remilgado; (evasive) esquivo
coyote [kaɪóDi, káɪot] N coyote m
cozy [kózi] ADJ (warm) acogedor; (beneficial) conveniente; VI **to — up to** adular
CPA [certified public accountant] [sípíé] N contador -ora público -ca con licencia mf
CPI [consumer price index] [sípíáɪ] N índice de precios al consumidor m
CPR [cardiopulmonary resuscitation] [sípíár] N reanimación cardiopulmonar f
CPU [central processing unit] [sípíjú] N UCP f
crab [kræb] N cangrejo m; (mechanism) carro corredizo m; (grouch) cascarrabias mf sg; **— apple** manzana silvestre f; **—s** (parasites) ladillas f pl; VI (fish) pescar cangrejos; (complain) quejarse
crack [kræk] VI (single fissure) rajarse; (multiple fissures) resquebrajarse, agrietarse; (psychological breakdown) sufrir un ataque de nervios; (of voice) quebrarse; VT (knuckles) hacer un chasquido con, chascar, chasquear; (nuts) cascar; (jokes) contar; (a prisoner) quebrar; (a case) resolver; (a code) descifrar; (a door) entreabrir; **to — down on** reprimir; **that —s me up** eso me hace desternillar de risa; N (fissure) rajadura f, grieta f, resquebrajadura f; (sound) chasquido m; (joke) pulla f, chanza f; (of the butt) vulg raja f; **— cocaine** crack m; **—down** represión f; **—house** fumadero m; **— pot** excéntrico -ca mf; **at the — of dawn** al romper el alba; **I'd like a — at the championship** me gustaría poder participar en el campeonato
cracked [krækt] ADJ rajado, quebrado; (crazy) chiflado; **it's not all it's — up to be** no es para tanto
cracker [krǽkɚ] N galleta f
crackle [krǽkəł] N (of paper) crujido m; (of fire) crepitación f; VI crujir, crepitar
cradle [krédł] N cuna f
craft [kræft] N (skill) destreza f; (cunning) astucia f; (occupation) arte m, oficio m; (boat) embarcación f; **—sman** artesano m; **—swoman** artesana f; VT fabricar
crafty [krǽfti] ADJ astuto, taimado
crag [kræg] N risco m, peñasco m, peñón m
craggy [krǽgi] ADJ peñascoso
cram [kræm] VT (pack in) embutir; VI (study intensely) memorizar; Sp empollar; **the bar was —med with people** el bar estaba atestado
cramp [kræmp] N (spasm) calambre m; (staple) grapa f; VI/VT (to suffer a spasm)

acalambrar[se]; VT (to staple) engrapar; **you're —ing my style** me estorbas
cranberry [krǽnbɛri] N arándano rojo *m*
crane [kren] N (bird) grulla *f*; (machine) grúa *f*; VT **to — one's neck** estirar el cuello
cranium [kréniəm] N cráneo *m*
crank [kræŋk] N (mechanism) manivela *f*; (grouch) cascarrabias *mf sg*; (overzealous advocate) fanático -ca *mf*; **—case** cárter superior del aceite *m*; **—shaft** cigüeñal *m*; VI/VT arrancar con manivela
cranky [krǽŋki] ADJ (irritable) irritable; (eccentric) excéntrico
cranny [krǽni] N (crevice) rendija *f*; (corner) recoveco *m*
crap [kræp] N (excrement) *vulg* mierda *f*; (nonsense) estupideces *f pl*; **to take a —** *vulg* cagar; **—s** dados *m pl*; VI *vulg* cagar
crappy [krǽpi] ADJ *vulg* de porquería
crash [kræʃ] VI (collide) estrellarse; (market) quebrar; (stay overnight with someone) quedarse a dormir; (hang up, as with a computer) bloquearse, caerse; (sleep) dormir; VT **to — a party** colarse en una fiesta; N (noise) estallido *m*; (collision) choque *m*; (financial collapse) quiebra *f*, colapso *m*; (computer failure) bloqueo *m*, caída *f*; **— landing** aterrizaje forzoso *m*
crass [kræs] ADJ craso
crate [kret] N cajón *m*, guacal *m*; VT poner en cajones
crater [kréɖɚ] N cráter *m*
cravat [krəvǽt] N corbata *f*
crave [krev] VT anhelar; **I — chocolate** me muero por un chocolate
craving [krévɪŋ] N antojo *m*
crawl [krɔł] VI (on hands and knees) gatear; (on the belly) arrastrarse, reptar; (proceed slowly) avanzar a paso de tortuga; **to be —ing with** hormiguear de; N (swimming stroke) crol *m*; **traffic is going at a —** el tráfico va a paso de tortuga
crayon [kréan] N lápiz de color *m*, Crayola™ *f*
craze [krez] N (fad) moda pasajera *f*; VI/VT enloquecer[se]
craziness [krézɪnɪs] N locura *f*, chifladura *f*
crazy [krézi] ADJ & N loco -ca *mf*; **I'm — about you** estoy loco por ti; **that's —!** ¡qué locura! **to go —** volverse loco, enloquecerse
creak [krik] N (of wooden floor) crujido *m*; (of a hinge) rechinamiento *m*; VI (a wooden floor) crujir; (a hinge) rechinar
cream [krim] N (milk product) crema *f*; *Sp* nata *f*; (medicament) crema *f*; **— cheese** queso de untar *m*, queso crema *m*; **— of tomato soup** sopa crema de tomate *f*; **the — of the crop** la flor y nata; VT (decream) desnatar; (butter, sugar) batir; (vegetables) preparar con salsa blanca; (defeat) aplastar

creamy [krími] ADJ cremoso
crease [kris] N (in trousers) raya *f*, repliegue *m*; (wrinkle) arruga *f*; VT (trousers) planchar la raya; (wrinkle) arrugar
create [kriét] VI/VT crear
creation [kriéʃən] N creación *f*
creationism [kriéʃənɪzəm] N creacionismo *m*
creative [kriéɖɪv] ADJ creativo
creativity [kriətívɪɖi] N creatividad *f*
creator [kriéɖɚ] N creador -ra *mf*
creature [krítʃɚ] N (being) ser *m*; (animal) animal *m*; **a — of your imagination** un producto de tu imaginación
credence [krídn̩s] N crédito *m*
credentials [krɪdéntʃəłz] N credenciales *f pl*
credibility [krɛdɪbílɪɖi] N credibilidad *f*
credible [krɛ́ɖəbəł] ADJ creíble
credit [krɛ́ɖɪt] N crédito *m*; (commendation) reconocimiento *m*; **— approval** aprobación de crédito *f*; **— card** tarjeta de crédito *f*; **— counseling** asesoramiento de crédito *m*; **— line** línea de crédito *f*; **— history** historial de crédito *m*; **— rating** calificación crediticia *f*; **— report** informe de crédito *m*; **—s** créditos *m pl*; **— underwriters** aseguradores de crédito *m pl*; **— union** banco cooperativo *m*; **on —** a crédito; **to give — to** (believe) dar crédito; (ascribe) acreditar; ADJ **—worthy** solvente; VT (believe) creer; (enter as credit) acreditar; (attribute) atribuir; **— an account** abonar/acreditar a una cuenta
creditor [krɛ́ɖɪɖɚ] N acreedor -ora *mf*
credulous [krɛ́dʒələs] ADJ crédulo
creed [krid] N credo *m*
creek [krik] N arroyo *m*, quebrada *f*
creep [krip] VI (crawl on belly) arrastrarse; (crawl on all fours) gatear; (grow upward) trepar; (go slowly) andar a paso de tortuga; **to — up on** acercarse furtivamente a; N (obnoxious person) *pej* persona repulsiva *f*, sinvergüenza *mf*; **that gives me the —s** eso me da asco; *Sp* eso me da grima
creeper [krípɚ] N enredadera *f*, planta trepadora *f*
creepy [krípi] ADJ repulsivo
cremate [krímet] VT cremar
Creole [kríoł] ADJ & N criollo -lla *mf*
creosote [kríəsot] N creosota *f*
crepe [krep] N (fabric) crespón *m*; (band of fabric) crespón negro *m*
crept [krɛpt] *see* creep
crescent [krɛ́sənt] N media luna *f*; ADJ creciente
crest [krɛst] N (of a wave, rooster) cresta *f*; (of feathers) penacho *m*, copete *m*; (of mountain) cima *f*, cumbre *f*; (of heraldic arms) timbre *m*; **—fallen** alicaído, cabizbajo; VI **the river —ed at two meters above flood level** el río creció hasta dos metros por encima de lo normal

crevice [krévɪs] N grieta *f*

crew [kru] N (for ships, etc.) tripulación *f*; (of workers) cuadrilla *f*; — **member** tripulante *mf*

crib [krɪb] N (bed) cuna *f*; (manger) pesebre *m*; (bin for grain) granero *m*; (cheat notes) hoja para copiar *f*; — **death** síndrome de muerte súbita infantil *m*; VI copiar

cricket [kríkɪt] N (insect) grillo *m*; (game) críquet *m*

crime [kraɪm] N (illegal act) delito *m*; (act of violence against people) crimen *m*; (criminal activity) delincuencia *f*, criminalidad *f*

criminal [krímǝnǝł] ADJ & N delincuente *mf*, malhechor -ora *mf*; (perpetrator of violent crimes) criminal *mf*; — **record** antecedentes delictivos *m pl*

crimp [krɪmp] VT rizar; N rizo *m*

crimson [krímzǝn] ADJ & N carmesí *m*, carmín *m*

cringe [krɪndʒ] VI **it makes me** — me da vergüenza ajena

cripple [krípǝł] N *offensive* tullido -da *mf*; (in the legs) *pey* cojo -ja *mf*; (in the arms) *offensive* manco -ca *mf*; VT tullir

crisis [kráɪsɪs] N crisis *f*

crisp [krɪsp] ADJ (apple, bacon) crocante, crujiente; (weather) fresco y despejado; (hair) crespo; VI/VT volver crujiente

crispy [kríspi] ADJ crocante, crujiente

criterion [kraɪtíriǝn] N criterio *m*

critic [krídɪk] N crítico -ca *mf*

critical [krídɪkǝł] ADJ crítico; — **stage** punto culminante *m*

criticism [krídɪsɪzǝm] N crítica *f*

criticize [krídɪsaɪz] VT criticar

croak [krok] VI (make the sound of a frog) croar; (make the sound of a crow) graznar, (die) *fam* espichar; N (sound made by frogs) canto de rana *m*; (sound made by crows) graznido *m*

Croatia [kroéʃǝ] N Croacia *f*

Croatian [kroéʃǝn] ADJ & N croata *mf*

crochet [kroʃé] N ganchillo *m*, croché *m*, crochet *m*; — **hook** aguja de croché *f*; VI hacer ganchillo, hacer croché

crock [krak] N (pot) vasija *f*; (lies) pamplinas *f pl*

crockery [krákǝri] N loza *f*

crocodile [krákǝdaɪł] N cocodrilo *m*

croissant [krǝsánt] N cruasán *m*, croissant *m*

crony [króni] N compinche *mf*, compadre *m*, comadre *f*

cronyism [króniɪzǝm] N amiguismo *m*

crook [krʊk] N (criminal) delincuente *mf*; (curve) curva *f*; (hook) gancho *m*; (staff) cayado *m*

crooked [krúkɪd] ADJ (bent) torcido; *Am* chueco; (dishonest) deshonesto

crop [krap] N (harvest) cosecha *f*; (group of contemporaries) promoción *f*; (of a bird) buche *m*; (horse whip) fusta *f*; — **rotation** rotación de cultivos *f*; VT (graze) pastar, pacer; (trim) recortar; **to** — **up** surgir

croquet [kroké] N cróquet *m*

cross [krɔs] N (symbol) cruz *f*; (street intersection) cruce *m*; (soccer) pase cruzado *m*; (act of mixing) cruzamiento *m*; (in boxing) cruzado *m*; —**bar** (soccer) travesaño *m*, larguero *m*; (in gymnastics) barra *f*; (in high jump) listón *m*; (of a door) tranca *f*; —**-check** verificación *f*; —**court shot** golpe cruzado *m*; —**-dresser** travesti *mf*, travestí *mf*; —**-fertilization** fecundación cruzada *f*; —**piece** cruceta *f*; —**-reference** referencia cruzada *f*; —**road** encrucijada *f*; — **section** corte transversal *m*; —**walk** cruce peatonal *m*, cebra *f*; —**word puzzle** crucigrama *m*; **to bear one's** — cargar la cruz; VI/VT (intersect, form a cross, breed, meet) cruzar[se]; (make sign of the cross) santiguarse; **to** —**-check** verificar; **to** —**-dress** transvestir[se]; VT (betray) traicionar; (move to other side) cruzar; **to** — **examine** interrogar; **to** — **out** tachar; **to** — **over** (change allegiance) cambiar de bando; (go to the other side) traspasar; **to** —**-reference** hacer una referencia cruzada; **you've** —**ed the line** te pasaste de la raya; ADJ (transverse) transversal; (angry) enojado; —**-country** a campo traviesa; —**-cultural** transcultural; —**-eyed** bizco; **to be** —**-eyed** bizquear

crossing [krɔ́sɪŋ] N (street or railroad intersection, pedestrian path) cruce *m*; (hybridization, act of mixing) cruzamiento *m*; (of ocean) travesía *f*; (of a border) paso *m*; (of a river) vado *m*

crotch [krɑtʃ] N entrepierna *f*

crotchety [krátʃɪdi] ADJ cascarrabias *inv*

crouch [kraʊtʃ] VI (stoop) agacharse; (prepare to spring) agazaparse

croup [krup] N tos *f*, croup *m*

crow [kro] N (bird) cuervo *m*; (sound of rooster) canto del gallo *m*; —**bar** alzaprima *f*; —**'s-foot** pata de gallo *f*; **to eat** — comerse sus propias palabras; VI cantar; (gloat, brag) jactarse

crowd [kraʊd] N (group of people) muchedumbre *f*, gentío *m*, aglomeración *f*; (at a performance) público *m*; (clique) pandilla *f*; VI (push forward) agolparse; VI/VT (gather in large numbers) apiñar[se], amontonar[se], aglomerar[se]; (gather in a confined space) hacinar[se]

crowded [kráʊdɪd] ADJ **it is** — **in here** hay demasiada gente aquí; **the restaurant is** — el restaurante está lleno

crown [kraʊn] N corona *f*; (of head) coronilla *f*, crisma *f*; (of a hat) copa *f*; — **jewels** joyas de la corona *f pl*; VT coronar; (hit on head) dar un coscorrón

crucial [krúʃǝł] ADJ (element) fundamental;

(moment) crucial
crucible [krúsəbəɫ] N crisol *m*
crucifix [krúsəfɪks] N crucifijo *m*
crucify [krúsəfaɪ] VT crucificar
crud [krʌd] N (filth) mugre *f*; (worthless thing, sickness, despicable person) *fam* porquería *f*
crude [krud] ADJ (vulgar, unpolished) basto, tosco; — **oil** petróleo crudo *m*
cruel [krúəɫ] ADJ cruel
cruelty [krúəɫti] N crueldad *f*
cruise [kruz] VI (take a cruise) tomar un crucero; (patrol) patrullar; (seek sexual partners) salir a buscar plan; — **control** control de crucero *m*; **cruising speed** velocidad de crucero *f*; N crucero *m*; — **missile** misil crucero *m*
cruiser [krúzɚ] N crucero *m*
crumb [krʌm] N (small) miga *f*, migaja *f*; (large) mendrugo *m*; VT (break into crumbs) desmigajar; (remove crumbs) sacar las migas
crumble [krʌmbəɫ] VI/VT (bread) desmigajar[se]; (clods of dirt) desmenuzar[se]; (house) desmoronar[se]
crummy [krʌmi] ADJ (place) *fam* de mala muerte; (object) *fam* de porquería; (show) flojo
crumple [krʌmpəɫ] VI/VT (crush) arrugar[se]; VI (collapse) aplastarse
crunch [krʌntʃ] VI/VT (eat noisily) mascar; N (sound) crujido *m*; (shortage) crisis *f*; —**es** abdominales *m pl*
crunchy [krʌntʃi] ADJ crocante, crujiente
crusade [kruséd] N cruzada *f*; VI (engage in a campaign) hacer una campaña
crusader [kruséDɚ] N cruzado -da *mf*; **a — for human rights** un paladín de los derechos humanos
crush [krʌʃ] VI/VT aplastar, machacar; (stone) demoler; N (act of crushing) aplastamiento *m*; (crowd) tumulto *m*; (infatuation) enamoramiento *m*; —**ing victory** victoria contundente *f*
crust [krʌst] N (of bread, earth) corteza *f*; (of bread) costra *f*; (of pie) tapa *f*
crusty [krʌsti] ADJ (with a crust) costroso; (grouchy) irascible
crutch [krʌtʃ] N muleta *f*
cry [kraɪ] N (shout) grito *m*; (weeping) llanto *m*; (call of a bird) reclamo *m*; —**baby** llorón -ona *mf*; **a far — from** muy distante de, muy lejos de; VI (shout) gritar; (weep) llorar; **to — over spilt milk** hacer como la lechera; **to — for attention** reclamar atención; **to — out for help** pedir socorro; **to — out** vocear
cryogenic [kraɪədʒénɪk] ADJ criogénico
crystal [krístl] N cristal *m*; — **ball** bola de cristal *f*; — **clear** cristalino
crystalline [krístlɪn] ADJ cristalino
crystallize [krístlaɪz] VI/VT cristalizar[se]
cub [kʌb] N (lion) cachorro *m*; (bear) osezno *m*;

(whale) ballenato *m*; (wolf) lobato *m*, lobezno *m*; — **reporter** reportero -ra novato -ta *mf*
Cuba [kjúbə] N Cuba *f*
Cuban [kjúbən] ADJ & N cubano -na *mf*
cubbyhole [kʌ́bihoɫ] N casilla *f*
cube [kjúb] N cubo *m*; — **root** raíz cúbica *f*; VT (cut) cortar en cubos; (raise to the third power) elevar al cubo
cubic [kjúbɪk] ADJ cúbico
cubicle [kjúbɪkəɫ] N cubículo *m*
cubism [kjúbɪzəm] N cubismo *m*
cuckold [kʌ́kəɫd] N cornudo *m*, cabrón *m*; VT poner los cuernos a
cuckoo [kúku] N cuclillo *m*, cuco *m*; — **clock** reloj de cucú *m*; ADJ & N chiflado -da *mf*; INTERJ cucú
cucumber [kjúkʌmbɚ] N pepino *m*
cud [kʌd] N **to chew the** — rumiar
cuddle [kʌ́dl] VI/VT hacer[se] mimos; N mimo *m*
cuddly [kʌ́dli] ADJ mimoso
cudgel [kʌ́dʒəl] N porra *f*; VT aporrear
cue [kju] N (in theater) pie *m*; (psychological stimulus) estímulo *m*; — **ball** bola blanca *f*; — **stick** taco de billar *m*; VT dar pie, dar la señal
cuff [kʌf] N (of sleeve, glove) puño *m*; (of pants) bajo *m*; (blow) bofetada *f*; **hand—s** esposas *f pl*; VT (in making pants) hacer los bajos; (put on handcuffs) esposar; (hit) abofetear
cuisine [kwɪzín] N cocina *f*
cul-de-sac [kʌ́ldəsæk] N callejón sin salida *m*
culinary [kjúlənɛri, kʌ́lənɛri] ADJ culinario
cull [kʌɫ] VT (choose) seleccionar, entresacar; (collect) recoger
culminate [kʌ́lmənet] VI/VT culminar
culmination [kʌ̀lmənéʃən] N culminación *f*
culprit [kʌ́lprɪt] N culpable *mf*
cult [kʌɫt] N (sect) secta religiosa *f*; (worship) culto *m*
cultivable [kʌ́ltəvəbəɫ] ADJ cultivable
cultivate [kʌ́ltəvet] VT cultivar
cultivated [kʌ́ltəveDɪd] ADJ (land) cultivado; (plant) de cultivo; (person) culto
cultivation [kʌ̀ltəvéʃən] N (tillage) cultivo *m*; (education) cultura *f*
cultivator [kʌ́ltəveDɚ] N (person) cultivador -ora *mf*; (implement) cultivadora *f*
cultural [kʌ́ltʃɚəɫ] ADJ cultural
culture [kʌ́ltʃɚ] N cultura *f*; (microorganisms) cultivo *m*; — **shock** choque cultural *m*; VT (microorganisms) cultivar
cultured [kʌ́ltʃɚd] ADJ (person) culto; (pearl) cultivado, de cultivo
cumbersome [kʌ́mbɚsəm] ADJ (bulky) voluminoso; (unwieldy) incómodo
cumulative [kjúmjələDɪv] ADJ acumulativo
cumulus [kjúmjələs] N cúmulo *m*
cunnilingus [kʌnɪlíŋgəs] N cunilinguo *m*
cunning [kʌ́nɪŋ] ADJ (sly) astuto, zorro; N astucia *f*, maña *f*

cunt [kʌnt] N *Sp vulg* coño *m*; *Mex vulg* chocho *m*; *RP vulg* concha *f*

cup [kʌp] N (with handle) taza *f*, pocillo *m*; (without handle) vaso *m*; (measure) taza *f*; (trophy, brassiere part) copa *f*; —**board** armario *m*, aparador *m*

cur [kɜ˞] N (dog) perro *m*; (villain) *pej* villano -na *mf*

curable [kjúrəbəɫ] ADJ curable

curator [kjúreDɚ] N conservador -ora *mf*

curb [kɜ˞b] N (of a street) *Sp* bordillo *m*; *Mex* borde *m*; *RP* cordón *m*; (of a well) brocal *m*; (restraint) freno *m*, restricción *f*; VT (emotions) refrenar; (spending) limitar

curd [kɜ˞d] N cuajada *f*; VI/VT cuajar[se], coagular[se]

curdle [kɜ˞dl] VI/VT cuajar[se], coagular[se]; **my blood** —**d** se me heló la sangre

cure [kjur] N (healing, preserving meat) cura *f*, curación *f*; (method) tratamiento *m*; VI/VT curar[se]; —**-all** sanalotodo *m*

curfew [kɜ˞fju] N toque de queda *m*, queda *f*

curio [kjúrio] N curiosidad *f*

curiosity [kjuriásıDi] N curiosidad *f*

curious [kjúriəs] ADJ curioso

curl [kɜ˞l] VI/VT (form ringlets) rizar[se], ensortijar[se]; (coil) enroscar[se]; (smoke) alzarse en espirales; **to** — **up** ovillar[se]; N (of hair) rizo *m*, bucle *m*; (of smoke) espiral *f*

curler [kɜ˞lɚ] N *Sp* rulo *m*; *Mex* tubo *m*; *RP* rulero *m*

curly [kɜ˞li] ADJ rizado

currant [kɜ˞ənt] N (fruit) grosella *f*; (tree) grosellero *m*

currency [kɜ˞ənsi] N (money) moneda *f*, divisa *f*; (acceptance) aceptación *f*; — **exchange** mercado de divisas *m*; — **unit** unidad monetaria *f*

current [kɜ˞ənt] ADJ (commonly used) corriente; (prevalent) actual; **the** — **issue of a magazine** el último número de una revista; — **year** año en curso *m*; N (of river, electricity, air) corriente *f*

currently [kɜ˞əntli] ADV actualmente

curriculum [kəríkjələm] N plan de estudios *m*, currículo *m*

curry [kɜ˞ri] N curry *m*

curse [kɜ˞s] N (ill wish) maldición *f*; (swear word) palabrota *f*; VI/VT (wish ill) maldecir; (swear) decir palabrotas

cursive [kɜ˞sıv] ADJ cursivo; N cursiva *f*

cursor [kɜ˞sɚ] N cursor *m*

curt [kɜ˞t] ADJ (abrupt) seco, brusco; (brief) breve

curtail [kətéɫ] VT restringir, cercenar

curtain [kɜ˞tn] N cortina *f*; (theater) telón *m*; VT ponerle cortinas a

curvature [kɜ˞vətʃur] N curvatura *f*; (of the spine) desviación *f*

curve [kɜ˞v] N (also in baseball) curva *f*; **he**

threw me a — me agarró desprevenido; VI/ VT encorvar[se]; (road) torcer[se], desviar[se]

curved [kɜ˞vd] ADJ curvo

cushion [kúʃən] N (pad) almohadilla *f*; (emergency resources, pad of air) colchón *m*; (pillow) almohadón *m*; (decorative pillow) cojín *m*; VT (put pads) poner almohadones; (soften a blow) amortiguar

cuspid [kʌspɪd] N colmillo *m*

cuss [kʌs] VI decir palabrotas; N —**word** *fam* palabrota *f*; **strange old** — *fam* bicho raro *m*

custard [kʌstɚd] N flan *m*, natilla[s] *f sg or pl*

custodian [kʌstóDiən] N (caretaker) cuidador -ora *mf*; (guardian) custodio -dia *mf*

custody [kʌstədi] N custodia *f*; **to take into** — detener

custom [kʌstəm] N costumbre *f*, uso *m*; —**s** (government department) aduana *f*; (taxes) derechos de aduana *m pl*; —[**s**]**house** aduana *f*; ADJ —**-built** construido por encargo; —**made** hecho a medida

customary [kʌstəmeri] ADJ acostumbrado

customer [kʌstəmɚ] N cliente -ta *mf*; — **base** clientela *f*; — **care** atención al cliente *f*; — **rights** derechos del cliente *m pl*; ADJ —**oriented** orientado al cliente

customize [kʌstəmaɪz] VT adaptar por encargo

cut [kʌt] VI/VT cortar; (shorten) acortar; (harvest) talar; (lower) rebajar; —! ¡corte[n]! **to** — **a deal** llegar a un arreglo; **to** — **across** (take a shortcut) cortar por; (transcend) trascender; **to** — **and paste** cortar y pegar; **to** — **back** reducir; **to** — **class** faltar a clase; **to** — **costs** reducir costos; **to** — **down on** reducir; **to** — **in** (interrupt) interrumpir; (in traffic) atravesarse; **to** — **prices** bajar los precios; **may I** — **in?** ¿me permite? **to** — **off** (interrupt) interrumpir; (intercept) interceptar; **to** — **out** omitir; **to be** — **out for** estar hecho para; **to** — **up** (divide) trozar; (misbehave) portarse mal; N corte *m*; (in salary) recorte *m*, reducción *f*; (of prices) rebaja *f*; (of a suit) hechura *f*, corte *m*; (insult) desaire *f*; —**back** recorte *m*; — **glass** cristal labrado *m*; —**off date** fecha límite *f*; ADJ —**-and-dried** predeterminado; —**-rate** de rebajas; —**throat** despiadado

cutaneous [kjuténiəs] ADJ cutáneo

cute [kjut] ADJ mono, rico; **to act** — ser afectado, ser melindroso

cuticle [kjúDɪkəɫ] N cutícula *f*

cutlery [kʌtləri] N (knives, knife store) cuchillería *f*; (eating utensils) cubiertos *m pl*

cutlet [kʌtlɪt] N filete *m*

cutter [kʌDɚ] N (person) cortador -ora *mf*; (device) cortadora *f*; (sleigh) trineo *m*; **Coast Guard** — guardacostas *m sg*

cutting [kʌDɪŋ] ADJ (sharp) cortante; (cold) penetrante; (sarcastic) mordaz, sarcástico; —

board tabla de cortar *f*; — **edge** filo *m*; —-
edge technology tecnología de punta *f*; N
(action) cortado *m*
CV [curriculum vitae] [síví] N currículo *m*,
currículum vitae *m*
cyanide [sáɪənaɪd] N cianuro *m*
cybercafe [saɪbə-kafé] N cibercafé *m*
cybernetics [saɪbə-néDɪks] N cibernética *f*
cyberpunk [sáɪbə-pʌnk] N ciberpunk *m*
cyberspace [sáɪbə-spes] N ciberespacio *m*
cyborg [sáɪbɔrg] N cyborg *m*
cycle [sáɪkəł] N ciclo *m*
cyclical [síklɪkəł] ADJ cíclico
cyclone [sáɪklon] N ciclón *m*
cyclotron [sáɪklətran] N ciclotrón *m*
cylinder [sílɪndə-] N cilindro *m*; (of a gun)
tambor *m*; — **head** culata *f*
cylindrical [sɪlíndrɪkəł] ADJ cilíndrico
cymbal [símbəł] N címbalo *m*, platillo *m*
cynic [sínɪk] N cínico -ca *mf*
cynical [sínɪkəł] ADJ cínico
cynicism [sínɪsɪzəm] N cinismo *m*
cypress [sáɪprɪs] N ciprés *m*
Cypriot, Cypriote [sípriət] ADJ & N chipriota *mf*
Cyprus [sáɪprəs] N Chipre *m*
cyst [sɪst] N quiste *m*
cystic [sístɪk] ADJ cístico; — **fibrosis** fibrosis
cística *f*
cytology [saɪtáɫədʒi] N citología *f*
czar [zɑr] N zar *m*
Czech [tʃɛk] ADJ & N checo -ca *mf*; — **Republic**
República Checa *f*

Dd

dab [dæb] VT (pat) dar toques; (apply) aplicar con
golpecitos; N toque *m*
dabble [dǽbəł] VI (splash) chapotear; (be
interested superficially) ser aficionado a
dachshund [dáksənd] N perro salchicha *m*
dad [dæd] N papá *m*
daddy [dǽDi] N papaíto *m*, papito *m*, papacito *m*
daffodil [dǽfədɪł] N narciso *m*
dagger [dǽgə-] N daga *f*, puñal *m*
dahlia [dǽljə] N dalia *f*
daily [déli] ADJ diario; — **planner** agenda *f*; —
wage jornal *m*, salario *m*; N (newspaper)
diario *m*
dainty [dénti] ADJ (delicate) delicado, exquisito;
(finicky) remilgado
dairy [déri] N (milk) lechería *f*; (cheese) quesería
f; ADJ (industry) lechero; (product) lácteo; N
producto lácteo *m*
daisy [dézi] N margarita *f*; **to be pushing up
daisies** *fam* estar criando malvas
dale [deł] N valle *m*

dally [dǽli] VI (flirt) coquetear; (risk danger)
jugar con fuego; (waste time) remolonear
dam [dæm] N presa *f*, represa *f*; VT represar
damage [dǽmɪdʒ] N daño *m*, destrozo *m*; —
control control de daños *m*; —**s** daños y
perjuicios *m pl*; **to pay —s** indemnizar *m*;
VI/VT dañar[se]
damaging [dǽmɪdʒɪŋ] ADJ perjudicial
dame [dem] N (noblewoman) dama *f*; (woman)
pej tipa *f*
damn [dæm] VT condenar; **it's not worth a —**
no vale un comino; INTERJ *vulg* ¡maldito sea!
damnation [dæmnéʃən] N condenación *f*,
perdición *f*
damned [dæmd] ADJ condenado
damp [dæmp] ADJ húmedo; N humedad *f*; VT
(wet) humedecer; (deaden) amortiguar;
(extinguish) apagar
dampen [dǽmpən] VT (wet) humedecer;
(deaden) amortiguar; (depress) deprimir
dampness [dǽmpnɪs] N humedad *f*
damsel [dǽmzəł] N damisela *f*
dance [dæns] N (act of dancing, party, activity)
baile *m*; (artistic activity, animal courtship
movements) danza *f*; — **music** música
bailable *f*; VI/VT (at a party) bailar; (in ballet,
of animals) danzar; **she —d her way to
stardom** llegó al estrellato bailando
dancer [dǽnsə-] N bailarín -ina *mf*, danzante *mf*
dancercise [dǽnsə-saɪz] N baile aeróbico *m*
dandelion [dǽndlaɪən] N diente de león *m*
dandruff [dǽndrəf] N caspa *f*
dandy [dǽndi] N dandi *m*, señorito *m*; ADJ
estupendo
Dane [den] N danés -esa *mf*
danger [déndʒə-] N peligro *m*
dangerous [déndʒə-əs] ADJ peligroso
dangle [dǽŋgəł] VI/VT (hang) colgar; (sway)
bambolear[se]; **her legs were dangling off
the bench** sus piernas pendían del banco
Danish [dénɪʃ] ADJ danés; N bollo dulce *m*
dapple, dappled [dǽpəl[d]] ADJ pinto, moteado
dare [dɛr] VI/VT (be brave) atreverse [a], osar;
(challenge) desafiar; **how — you?** ¿cómo te
atreves? N desafío *m*; —**devil** temerario -ria
mf
daring [dérɪŋ] N atrevimiento *m*, osadía *f*; ADJ
atrevido, osado, arriesgado
dark [dɑrk] ADJ (in color) oscuro; (of hair)
moreno, morocho, trigueño; (gloomy)
sombrío, tenebroso; (evil, ignorant) oscuro;
(shameful) turbio; — **Ages** [Alta] Edad Media
f; —**room** cuarto oscuro *m*; —**-skinned**
moreno; N oscuridad *f*; **after —** después de
que oscurece
darken [dárkən] VI/VT oscurecer
darkness [dárknɪs] N (complete) oscuridad *f*,
tinieblas *f pl*; (partial) penumbra *f*
darling [dárlɪŋ] ADJ & N amado -da *mf*, querido

-da *mf*; **my** — vida mía, amor mío

darn [dɑrn] VT zurcir, remendar; **—ing needle** aguja de zurcir *f*; N zurcido *m*; **it is not worth a** — no vale un comino; INTERJ ¡caramba! ¡caracoles!

dart [dɑrt] N (missile) dardo *m*; (tuck) pinza *f*; (swift movement) movimiento rápido *m*; **—board** diana *f*; **to play —s** jugar a los dardos; VI disparar; **to — out** salir disparado

dash [dæʃ] VI/VT (of waves, porcelain) estrellar[se]; VT (plans) frustrar; VI (hopes) desplomarse; **to — by** pasar corriendo; **to — off/out** salir disparado; **to — off a letter** escribir de prisa una carta; N (line) raya *f*; (run) corrida *f*; (race) carrera *f*; (small amount) pizca *f*; (splash) salpicadura *f*; **the one-hundred-meter** — la carrera de los cien metros llanos/planos; **—board** tablero *m*, salpicadero *m*

data [déɖə, dǽɖə] N datos *m pl*; **—base** base de datos *f*; **—bank** banco de datos *m*; **— encryption** cifrado de datos *m*; **— file** archivo de datos *m*; **— input** entrada de datos *f*; **— management** gestión de datos *f*; **— processing** procesamiento de datos *m*, fichero de datos *m*; **— recovery** recuperación de datos *f*; **— storage** almacenamiento de datos *m*

date [det] N (time) fecha *f*; (appointment) cita *f*; (person) acompañante *mf*; (fruit) dátil *m*; **— due** fecha de vencimiento *f*; **out of** — anticuado; **to** — hasta ahora; **up to** — al día; VI (be dated) estar fechado; (go out socially) salir; VT (write the date) fechar; (show to be old-fashioned) delatar la edad; (go out socially) salir con; **to — from** datar de, remontarse a

dated [déɖɪd] ADJ (having a date) fechado; (old-fashioned) anticuado

daub [dɔb] VT (smear) embarrar, embadurnar; (apply unskillfully) pintarrajear

daughter [dɔ́ɖə-] N hija *f*; **—-in-law** nuera *f*

daunt [dɔnt] VT (intimidate) intimidar; (dishearten) desanimar

dauntless [dɔ́ntlɪs] ADJ intrépido

davenport [dǽvənpɔrt] N sofá grande *m*

dawn [dɔn] N alba *f*, amanecer *m*, aurora *f*; **the — of civilization** los albores de la civilización; VI amanecer, aclarar; **it just —ed on me that** caí en [la] cuenta de que

day [de] N día *m*; **— after tomorrow** pasado mañana *m*; **— before yesterday** anteayer *m*; **—break** amanecer *m*; **at —break** al amanecer; **—care** guardería *f*; **—dream** fantasía *f*; **— laborer** jornalero -ra *mf*; **—light** luz del día *f*; **—light saving time** adelanto de la hora en verano *m*; **—time** día *m*; **—time activity** actividad diurna *f*; **—-to-day** día a día; **by** — de día; **by the** — por día;

eight-hour — jornada de ocho horas *f*; **in my** — en mis tiempos; **in the old —s** antaño; **make my** — dame el gusto; **New Year's** — Año Nuevo *m*; ADJ diurno; VI **to —dream** soñar despierto

daze [dez] VT aturdir; N **to be in a** — estar aturdido

dazzle [dǽzəl] VI/VT deslumbrar

deacidify [diəsídɪfaɪ] VT neutralizar la acidez

deacon [díkən] N diácono *m*

deactivate [diǽktɪvet] VI/VT desactivar

deactivation [diæktɪvéʃən] N desactivación *f*

dead [dɛd] ADJ muerto; **he's a — duck** está muerto; **—-end job** puesto sin perspectivas *m*; **— sure** completamente seguro; **— tired** muerto de cansancio; N **— air** aire viciado *m*; **—beat** moroso -sa *mf*; **—bolt** pestillo *m*; **— end** callejón sin salida *m*; **— letter** letra muerta *f*; **—line** fecha límite *f*; **— link** enlace muerto *m*; **—lock** punto muerto *m*; **—pan** de palo; **— ringer** fiel retrato *m*; **—wood** (person) persona inútil *f*; (thing) cosa inútil *f*; **the —** los muertos; **in the — of the night** en el silencio de la noche; **in the — of winter** en pleno invierno; VI **to —lock** trancarse

deaden [dédn̩] VT amortiguar

deadly [dédli] ADJ (enemy) mortal; (poison) letal; (weapon) mortífero; ADV mortalmente; **— dull** sumamente aburrido

deaf [dɛf] ADJ sordo; **—-mute** ADJ & N sordomudo -da *mf*

deafen [défən] VT (make deaf) ensordecer; (deaden) amortiguar

deafening [défənɪŋ] ADJ ensordecedor, atronador

deafness [défnɪs] N sordera *f*

deal [dil] VT (cards) dar, repartir; (drugs) vender; (a blow) dar, asestar; **to — in** comerciar en; **biology —s with the study of life** la biología se ocupa del estudio de la vida; **I have to — with all kinds of people** tengo que vérmelas con todo tipo de gente; N (business transaction) trato *m*, negocio *m*; (shady transaction) componenda *f*; (act of dealing cards) reparto *m*; **a great — of** una gran cantidad de; **it's a** — ¡trato hecho! **I got a raw** — me clavaron

dealer [dílə-] N (in cars, antiques) comerciante *mf*; (in drugs, arms) traficante *mf*; (of cards) el/la que reparte *mf*

dealership [dílə-ʃɪp] N concesionario *m*

dealings [dílɪŋz] N trato *m*, relaciones *f pl*; (business) negocios *m pl*

dealt [dɛłt] *see* deal

dean [din] N (of university, professional group) decano -na *mf*; (in church) deán *m*

dear [dir] ADJ (beloved) querido; (expensive) caro; (cherished) apreciado; **— Sir/Madam**

Estimado señor / Estimada señora; **my —est wish** mi deseo más ferviente; N **he's such a —!** ¡es un amor! **my —** querido mío *m* / querida mía *f*; ADV caro; **that cost me —** eso me costó caro; **— me!** ¡Dios mío! **oh —!** ¡Dios mío!

dearth [dɜ˞θ] N escasez *f*

death [dɛθ] N muerte *f*; **—bed** lecho de muerte *m*; **— benefits** beneficios por fallecimiento *m*; **— certificate** partida de defunción *f*; **— penalty** pena de muerte *f*; **— rate** tasa de mortalidad *f*; **— row** pabellón de los condenados a muerte *m*; **he's on — row** está condenado a muerte; **— squad** escuadrón de la muerte *m*; **— toll** mortandad *f*; **—trap** trampa mortal *f*; **— wish** instinto suicida *m*; **to put to —** ejecutar; **we have discussed this to —** hemos discutido esto hasta el hartazgo; **I'm sick to — of this job** estoy harto de este trabajo

debacle [dɪbákəɫ] N debacle *f*

debase [dɪbés] VT degradar, envilecer

debatable [dɪbéɒəbəɫ] ADJ discutible

debate [dɪbét] N debate *m*; VI/VT (discuss) debatir, discutir; (weigh a decision) considerar

debilitate [dɪbílɪtet] VT debilitar

debilitating [dɪbílɪteDɪŋ] ADJ debilitante

debit [débɪt] N débito *m*, adeudo *m*; (column in an account) debe *m*; (total sum owed) pasivo *m*; **— card** tarjeta de débito *f*; VT adeudar; **to — an account** adeudar una cuenta

debriefing [dibrífɪŋ] N informe *m*

debris [dəbrí] N (ruins) escombros *m pl*; (detritus) detritus *m* [*pl*]

debt [dɛt] N deuda *f*; **— relief** alivio de la deuda *m*; **bad —** cuenta incobrable *f*; **to get into —** endeudarse; ADJ **—-ridden** sobreendeudado

debtor [débɚ] N deudor -ora *mf*

debug [dibág] VT depurar

debugger [dibágɚ] N depurador *m*

debugging [dibágɪŋ] N depuración *f*

debunk [dibáŋk] VT (ideas, beliefs) desacreditar; (myths) desmitificar

debut [debjú] N (of a play or film) estreno *m*; (in society) presentación en sociedad *f*; **to make a —** (an actor) debutar; (in society) presentarse en sociedad; VI/VT (a film) estrenar[se]; (a product) lanzar[se] al mercado

decade [déked] N década *f*, decenio *m*

decadence [dékəɒəns] N decadencia *f*

decadent [dékəɒənt] ADJ decadente

decaffeinated [dɪkǽfɪneDɪd] ADJ descafeinado

decal [díkæɫ] N calcomanía *f*, autoadhesivo *m*

decalcification [dikælsɪfɪkéʃən] N descalcificación *f*

decanter [dɪkǽntɚ] N garrafa *f*

decapitate [dɪkǽpɪtet] VT decapitar

decathlon [dɪkǽθlɑn] N decatlón *m*

decay [dɪké] VI/VT (biological matter) descomponer[se]; (teeth) cariar[se]; VI (health) deteriorarse; (radioactive matter) desintegrarse; N (moral) decadencia *f*; (biological) descomposición *f*; (nuclear) desintegración *f*; (tooth) caries *f*

decayed [dɪkéd] ADJ (flesh) putrefacto; (tooth) cariado

decease [dɪsís] N muerte *f*, fallecimiento *m*; VI morir, fallecer

deceased [dɪsíst] ADJ & N difunto -ta *mf*

deceit [dɪsít] N engaño *m*, trampa *f*

deceitful [dɪsítfəɫ] ADJ tramposo, engañoso

deceive [dɪsív] VI/VT engañar

decelerate [diséləret] VI desacelerar

December [dɪsémbɚ] N diciembre *m*

decency [dísənsi] N decencia *f*

decent [dísənt] ADJ decente

decentralization [disɛntrəlɪzéʃən] N descentralización *f*

deception [dɪsépʃən] N engaño *m*

deceptive [dɪséptɪv] ADJ engañoso; **— practice** práctica comercial desleal *f*

decibel [désəbəɫ] N decibelio *m*

decide [dɪsáɪd] VT (make a decision) decidir; (award victory) fallar; **what —d you to come?** ¿qué te motivó a venir?

decided [dɪsáɪdɪd] ADJ (resolute) decidido; (clear) claro

deciduous [dɪsídʒuəs] ADJ deciduo, caduco; **— tooth** diente de la primera dentición *m*

decimal [désəməɫ] ADJ decimal

decimate [désəmet] VT diezmar

decipher [dɪsáɪfɚ] VT descifrar

decision [dɪsíʒən] N decisión *f*; (in court) fallo *m*

decisive [dɪsáɪsɪv] ADJ decisivo

deck [dɛk] N (of a boat) cubierta *f*; (of a house) terraza *f*; (of playing cards) baraja *f*; **hit the —!** ¡cuerpo a tierra! VT (knock down) tumbar; (decorate) decorar; **to — oneself out** emperifollarse

declaration [dɛkləréʃən] N declaración *f*, pronunciamiento *m*

declare [dɪklér] VI/VT declarar, afirmar

decline [dɪkláɪn] N (deterioration) decadencia *f*; (slope) declive *m*; (reduction in prices) baja *f*; VI/VT declinar; (an offer) rechazar; **to — to do something** negarse a hacer algo

decode [dikód] VT descodificar

decompose [dikəmpóz] VI/VT descomponer[se]

decompress [dikəmprés] VT descomprimir

decongest [dikəndʒést] VT descongestionar

decongestant [dikəndʒéstənt] N descongestionante *m*

decontaminate [dikəntǽmɪnet] VT descontaminar

decontamination [dikəntæmɪnéʃən] N descontaminación *f*

decorate [dékəret] VT decorar; (award medals)

condecorar
decoration [dɛkəréʃən] N (embellishment)
  adorno *m*; (interior decorating) decoración *f*;
  (medal of honor) condecoración *f*
decorative [dékəəDIv] ADJ decorativo
decorous [dékəəs] ADJ decoroso
decorum [dɪkɔ́rəm] N decoro *m*
decoy [díkɔI] N (artifact) señuelo *m*, reclamo *m*;
  (live animal or person) cimbel *m*; VT atraer
  con señuelo/cimbel
decrease[1] [díkris] N disminución *f*, merma *f*
decrease[2] [dɪkrís] VI/VT disminuir, mermar
decree [dɪkrí] N decreto *m*; VI/VT decretar
decrepit [dɪkrépɪt] ADJ decrépito
decrepitude [dɪkrépɪtud] N decrepitud *f*
decry [dɪkráI] VT condenar
decrypt [dikrípt] VT descifrar
decryption [dikrípʃən] N descifrado *m*,
  descodificación *f*
dedicate [déDIket] VI/VT dedicar[se]; VT (a
  highway) inaugurar
dedication [deDIkéʃən] N (act of dedicating)
  dedicación *f*; (in a book) dedicatoria *f*; (of a
  highway, etc.) inauguración *f*
deduce [dɪdús] VT deducir
deduct [dɪdʌ́kt] VT deducir
deductible [dɪdʌ́ktəbəł] ADJ deducible,
  desgravable; N deducible *m*
deduction [dɪdʌ́kʃən] N deducción *f*
deed [did] N (action) acción *f*; (exploit) hazaña *f*;
  (certificate of ownership) escritura *f*
deem [dim] VT considerar
deep [dip] ADJ (extending down) hondo,
  profundo; (dark) oscuro; (of a voice) grave; —
  in debt cargado de deudas; — **in thought**
  absorto; —**-sea** de altura; **he's got —**
  pockets es un ricachón; **he went off the —**
  end with his hobby se le fue la mano con el
  pasatiempo; **she went — into the woods**
  se adentró en el bosque; **ten meters —** de
  diez metros de profundidad; N — **freeze**
  congelador *m*; **the —** el piélago, el abismo;
  ADV **to dive —** bucear en las profundidades;
  VT **to —-six** hacer desaparecer
deepen [dípən] VI/VT ahondar, profundizar
deer [dir] N ciervo *m*, venado *m*; —**skin** gamuza *f*
deface [dɪfés] VT (disfigure) desfigurar; (smear
  with paint) pintarrajear; (mutilate) mutilar
defame [dɪfém] VT difamar
default [dɪfɔ́łt] N (negligence) negligencia *f*;
  (failure to pay) incumplimiento *m*; (failure to
  appear in court) rebeldía *f*; (computer setting)
  opción por defecto *f*; **in —** en mora; **by —** por
  defecto, por omisión; (in sports) por
  abandono de los contrincantes; VI (on a loan)
  incumplir, no pagar; (in a sports match) no
  comparecer
defeat [dɪfít] VT vencer, derrotar; N derrota *f*
defecate [défIket] VI defecar, evacuar

defect[1] [dífɛkt] N defecto *m*
defect[2] [dɪfɛ́kt] VI desertar
defection [dɪfɛ́kʃən] N defección *f*
defective [dɪfɛ́ktIv] ADJ defectuoso
defend [dɪfénd] VI/VT defender
defendant [dɪféndənt] N (criminal) acusado -da
  mf, reo -a *mf*; (civil) demandado -da *mf*
defender [dɪféndə-] N defensor -ora *mf*; (sports)
  defensa *mf*
defense [dɪféns] N defensa *f*
defenseless [dɪfénslɪs] ADJ indefenso
defensible [dɪfénsəbəł] ADJ defendible
defensive [dɪfénsIv] ADJ defensivo; —
  medicine medicina defensiva *f*; N **on the —**
  a la defensiva
defer [dɪfɝ] VT (a meeting) diferir, posponer; (a
  payment) prorrogar; (an appointment)
  dilatar; (from military service) eximir; **to —**
  to another's opinion remitirse a la opinión
  de otro
deference [défəəns] N deferencia *f*
deferral [dɪfɝ́əł] N aplazamiento *m*
defiance [dɪfáIəns] N (challenge) desafío *m*;
  (resistance to authority) rebeldía *f*; **in — of** en
  abierta oposición a
defiant [dɪfáIənt] ADJ desafiante
defibrillate [difíbrəlet] VT desfibrilar
defibrillation [difIbrIléʃən] N desfibrilación *f*
defibrillator [difíbrIleDə-] N desfibrilador *m*
deficiency [dɪfíʃənsi] N deficiencia *f*
deficient [dɪfíʃənt] ADJ deficiente
deficit [défIsIt] N déficit *m*; — **spending** gastos
  deficitarios *m pl*
defile [dɪfáIł] VT (violate) mancillar; (desecrate)
  profanar; (to make dirty) ensuciar
define [dɪfáIn] VI/VT definir
defining [dɪfáInIŋ] ADJ decisivo
definite [défənIt] ADJ (clearly defined) definido,
  determinado; (certain) seguro; **she was — in**
  her demands ella fue terminante es sus
  exigencias; — **article** artículo definido *m*
definitely [défənItli] ADV sin duda,
  definitivamente
definition [defəníʃən] N definición *f*
definitive [dɪfínIDIv] ADJ (final) definitivo;
  (authoritative) de mayor autoridad
deflate [dɪflét] VI/VT desinflar[se]
deflation [dɪfléʃən] N deflación *f*
deflect [dɪflɛ́kt] VI/VT desviar[se]
deforestation [difɔrIstéʃən] N deforestación *f*
deform [dɪfɔ́rm] VI/VT deformar[se]
deformed [dɪfɔ́rmd] ADJ deforme
deformity [dɪfɔ́rmIDi] N (body part) deformidad
  f; (act or result of deforming) deformación *f*
defraud [dɪfrɔ́d] VT defraudar
defray [dɪfré] VT sufragar, costear
defrost [difrɔ́st] VI/VT descongelar[se]
deft [dɛft] ADJ diestro, habilidoso
defunct [dɪfʌ́ŋkt] ADJ caduco; **the Whig party**

is now — el partido de los whigs se disolvió
defuse [difjúz] VT (bomb) desactivar; (situation) distender
defy [dɪfáɪ] VT (challenge) desafiar; (resist) resistir
degenerate[1] [dɪʤénə-ɪt] ADJ & N degenerado -da *mf*
degenerate[2] [dɪʤénəret] VI degenerar[se]
degenerative [dɪʤénə-ətɪv] ADJ degenerativo; **— joint disease** artrosis *f*, enfermedad degenerativa articular *f*
degradation [dɛgrədéʃən] N degradación *f*
degrade [dɪgréd] VI/VT degradar[se]
degree [dɪgrí] N (stage) grado *m*; (academic) título *m*; **by —s** gradualmente; **to a** — hasta cierto punto; **to get a** — graduarse
dehumanize [dihjúmənaɪz] VI/VT deshumanizar
dehumidifier [dihjumíDɪfaɪə-] N deshumidificador *m*
dehydrate [diháɪdret] VI/VT deshidratar[se]
deign [den] VI dignarse
deity [díɪDi] N deidad *f*
déjà vu [deʒavú] N deja vu *m*
dejected [dɪʤéktɪd] ADJ abatido, desconsolado
dejection [dɪʤékʃən] N abatimiento *m*, desconsuelo *m*
delay [dɪlé] N demora *f*, retraso *m*; VT demorar, retrasar; VI demorar, retrasarse
delectable [dɪléktəbəł] ADJ delicioso; N delicia *f*
delegate[1] [délɪgɪt] N delegado -da *mf*
delegate[2] [délɪget] VT delegar
delegation [dɛlɪgéʃən] N delegación *f*, representación *f*
delete [dɪlít] VT (omit) suprimir; (cross out) tachar; **— key** tecla de borrado *f*
deleterious [dɛlɪtíriəs] ADJ nocivo
deletion [dɪlíʃən] N supresión *f*
deliberate[1] [dɪlíbə-ɪt] ADJ (intentional) deliberado; (careful) cuidadoso
deliberate[2] [dɪlíbəret] VI/VT deliberar
deliberately [dɪlíbə-ɪtli] ADV a propósito, deliberadamente
deliberation [dɪlɪbəréʃən] N deliberación *f*
delicacy [délɪkəsi] N (fineness, precision, sensitivity) delicadeza *f*; (food) manjar *m*, delicatessen *f pl*, gollería *f*; (breakability) fragilidad *f*
delicate [délɪkɪt] ADJ delicado, tenue; (breakable) frágil; (acute) fino
delicatessen [dɛlɪkətésən] N (store) tienda de fiambres *f*, charcutería *f*; *RP* rotisería *f*; (foods) delicatessen *f pl*
delicious [dɪlíʃəs] ADJ delicioso, rico
delight [dɪláɪt] N (pleasure) deleite *m*, regalo *m*; (source of pleasure) delicia *f*; VI/VT deleitar[se]
delighted [dɪláɪDɪd] ADJ encantado; **to be — to** alegrarse de; **I'm — to meet you** me alegro de conocerla; **I'd be — to dance with you**

me encantaría bailar contigo
delightful [dɪláɪtfəł] ADJ encantador
delimit [dɪlímɪt] VT delimitar
delineate [dɪlíniet] VT delinear
delinquent [dɪlíŋkwənt] ADJ & N (debtor) moroso -sa *mf*; (wrongdoer) delincuente *mf*; (juvenile) delincuente juvenil *mf*
delirious [dɪlíriəs] ADJ (hysterical) delirante; (happy) contentísimo; **to be** — delirar
delirium [dɪlíriəm] N delirio *m*
deliver [dɪlívə-] VT (hand over) entregar; (hand out) repartir; (liberate) liberar; (pronounce a speech) pronunciar; (administer a blow) dar; (have a baby) dar a luz; (assist a birth) atender en un parto; **to — the goods** cumplir con lo prometido
deliverance [dɪlívə-əns] N liberación *f*
delivery [dɪlívəri] N (handing out) entrega *f*, expedición *f*; (things to be delivered) pedido *m*; (birth) parto *m*; (speaking) ejecución *f*, expresión oral *f*; **on** — a la entrega; — **service** servicio de entrega *m*; — **truck** camión de reparto *m*; **to take** — aceptar entrega
dell [dɛł] N hondonada *f*
deltoids [déłtɔɪdz] N deltoides *m sg*
delude [dɪlúd] VT engañar
deluge [déljuʤ] N diluvio *m*; VT abrumar
delusion [dɪlúʒən] N (act of deluding, state of being deluded) engaño *m*; **—s of grandeur** delirios de grandeza *m pl*
deluxe [dɪlʌ́ks] ADJ de lujo
demagogue, demagog [déməgɑg] N demagogo -ga *mf*
demand [dɪmǽnd] VT (ask for) exigir; (require) requerir, exigir; N exigencia *f*, reivindicación *f*; **on** — por demanda
demanding [dɪmǽndɪŋ] ADJ exigente
demarcate [dɪmárket] VT demarcar
demean [dɪmín] VT menospreciar
demeanor [dɪmínə-] N conducta *f*, comportamiento *m*
demented [dɪméntɪd] ADJ demente
dementia [dɪménʃə] N demencia *f*
demijohn [démiʤɑn] N damajuana *f*
demise [dɪmáɪz] N fallecimiento *m*, desaparición *f*
demo [démo] N demostración *f*
demobilize [dimóbəlaɪz] VT desmovilizar
democracy [dɪmákrəsi] N democracia *f*
democrat [déməkræt] N demócrata *mf*
democratic [dɛməkrǽDɪk] ADJ democrático
democratization [dɪmɑkrəDɪzéʃən] N democratización *f*
demographics [dɛməgrǽfɪks] N demografía *f*
demolish [dɪmálɪʃ] VT demoler, derrumbar
demon [dímən] N demonio *m*
demonstrate [démənstret] VT (prove) demostrar; (show a product) hacer una

demostración; VI manifestar

demonstration [dɛmənstréʃən] N (proof, exhibition) demostración *f*; (protest) manifestación *f*, concentración *f*

demonstrative [dɪmánstrəDɪv] ADJ demostrativo

demonstrator [démənstreDə⋅] N manifestante *mf*

demoralize [dɪmɔ́rəlaɪz] VT desmoralizar

demote [dɪmót] VT degradar, bajar de categoría

den [dɛn] N (of an animal) guarida *f*; (room in a house) cuarto de estar *m*; (cave) cueva *f*; — **of iniquity** antro de perdición *m*

dengue fever [déŋgi fívə⋅] N dengue *m*

denial [dɪnáɪəł] N (assertion that an allegation is false) desmentido *m*; (refusal to approve) denegación *f*, negativa *f*; (refusal to recognize) negación *f*; **he is in** — no lo quiere aceptar

denigrate [dénɪgret] VT denigrar

denim [dénɪm] N tela de vaquero *f*

Denmark [dénmɑrk] N Dinamarca *f*

denomination [dɪnɑmənéʃən] N (name, monetary value) denominación *f*; (sect) secta religiosa *f*

denominator [dɪnámɪneDə⋅] N denominador *m*

denotation [dinotéʃən] N denotación *f*

denote [dɪnót] VT denotar

denounce [dɪnáʊns] VT denunciar

dense [dɛns] ADJ (compacted) denso, tupido, cerrado; (stupid) *fam* burro, duro de entendederas

density [dénsɪDi] N densidad *f*

dent [dɛnt] N abolladura *f*; **to make a** — **in a task** hacer mella en una tarea; VI/VT abollar[se]

dental [dént̪ł] ADJ dental; — **care** cuidado dental *m*; — **floss** hilo dental *m*; — **hygienist** higienista dental *mf*; — **implant** implante dental *m*; — **plaque** placa dental *f*; — **school** facultad de odontología *f*

dentifrice [déntəfrɪs] N dentífrico *m*, pasta dental *f*

dentist [déntɪst] N dentista *mf*

dentistry [déntɪstri] N odontología *f*

dentures [déntʃə⋅z] N dientes postizos *m pl*

denunciation [dɪnʌnsiéʃən] N denuncia *f*, acusación *f*

deny [dɪnáɪ] VT (state that something is false) negar, desmentir; (refuse to approve) rechazar; **to** — **oneself** abstenerse

deodorant [dióDə⋅ənt] N desodorante *m*

deodorize [dióDəraɪz] VT desodorizar

deoxidize [diáksɪdaɪz] VT desoxidar

depart [dɪpárt] VI (leave) salir, partir; (deviate) desviarse, apartarse; (die) fallecer, dejar de existir

departed [dɪpárDɪd] ADJ & N difunto -ta *mf*

department [dɪpártmənt] N (of company,

school, country) departamento *m*; (of government) ministerio *m*; (of a store) sección *f*; (of knowledge, expertise) especialidad *f*; — **head** jefe -fa de departamento *mf*; — **store** gran almacén *m*

departure [dɪpártʃə⋅] N (scheduled) salida *f*; (not scheduled) partida *f*; (deviation) desviación *f*

depend [dɪpénd] VI depender; **to** — **on** (rely on) contar con; (be conditioned by) depender de; —**ing on the number of guests** dependiendo de la cantidad de invitados

dependable [dɪpéndəbəł] ADJ confiable, fiable

dependence [dɪpéndəns] N dependencia *f*

dependency [dɪpéndənsi] N dependencia *f*

dependent [dɪpéndənt] ADJ dependiente; **success is** — **on perseverance** el éxito depende de la perseverancia; N familiar a cargo *mf*

depict [dɪpíkt] VT (verbally) describir; (visually) representar

depilate [dépələt] VT depilar[se]

depilatory [dɪpílətɔri] ADJ & N depilatorio *m*

deplane [dɪplén] VI desembarcar

deplete [dɪplít] VT agotar

depletion [dɪplíʃən] N agotamiento *m*

deplorable [dɪplɔ́rəbəł] ADJ deplorable

deplore [dɪplɔ́r] VT deplorar

deploy [dɪplɔ́ɪ] VT desplegar

deport [dɪpɔ́rt] VT deportar; VI comportarse

deportment [dɪpɔ́rtmənt] N comportamiento *m*, conducta *f*

depose [dɪpóz] VT (overthrow) deponer, derrocar; (testify) declarar; (take testimony) tomar declaración

deposit [dɪpázɪt] VT (add to an account) depositar; *Sp* ingresar; (place) colocar; N (amount added to an account) depósito *m*; *Sp* ingreso *m*; (of a mineral) yacimiento *m*; (earnest money) señal *f*, anticipo *m*; — **slip** hoja de depósito *f*

deposition [dɛpəzíʃən] N (removal from office) deposición *f*; (testimony) declaración *f*

depositor [dɪpázɪDə⋅] N depositante *mf*

depot [dípo] N (of trains) estación *f*; (of buses) terminal *mf*; (for storage) almacén *m*, depósito *m*; (for military training) cuartel *m*

depraved [dɪprévd] ADJ depravado

deprecate [déprɪket] VT despreciar

depreciate [dɪpríʃiet] VT (currency) depreciar[se]; (goods) desvalorizar[se], amortizar[se]

depreciation [dɪpriʃiéʃən] N (of currency) depreciación *f*; (of goods) amortización *f*

depress [dɪprés] VT deprimir

depressed [dɪprést] ADJ deprimido

depressing [dɪprésɪŋ] ADJ deprimente

depression [dɪpréʃən] N depresión *f*

deprive [dɪpráɪv] VT privar

depth [dɛpθ] N (of hole, feeling) profundidad *f*,

hondura *f*; (of the voice) gravedad *f*; **in the
—s** en las profundidades; **in —** a fondo;
what is the — of that bookshelf? ¿cuánto
miden estos estantes de fondo? **he has sunk
to such —s** ha caído muy bajo; **in the — of
the night** bien entrada la noche; **in the —
of winter** en lo más crudo del invierno

deputation [dɛpjətéʃən] N delegación *f*

deputy [dépjəpi] N (elected official) diputado -da
mf; (substitute) suplente *mf*

derail [dirét] VI/VT descarrilar[se]

deranged [dıréndʒd] ADJ trastornado, demente

derby [dɜ́ɾbi] N (hat) sombrero hongo *m*; (race)
derby *m*

deregulate [dirégjələt] VT desregular

derelict [déɾəlıkt] ADJ (deserted) abandonado;
(negligent) negligente; N (ship) buque
abandonado *m*; (person) vagabundo -da *mf*

dereliction [dɛɾəlíkʃən] N **— of duties**
abandono de funciones *m*

deride [diráıd] VT escarnecer, ridiculizar

derision [diríʒən] N escarnio *m*

derivation [dɛɾəvéʃən] N derivación *f*

derivative [diríʋəpıv] ADJ & N derivado *m*

derive [diráıv] VI/VT derivar[se]; **to — pleasure
from** disfrutar de

dermabrasion [dɜ́ɾməbreʒən] N abrasión
cutánea *f*, dermabrasión *f*

dermatologist [dɜ́ɾmətáləʤıst] N dermatólogo
-ga *mf*

dermatology [dɜ́ɾmətáləʤi] N dermatología *f*

derogatory [dirágətɔri] ADJ despectivo

derrick [déɾık] N torre de perforación *f*

descend [dısénd] VI/VT descender; **—ing sort**
clasificación descendiente *f*; **to — upon** caer
sobre

descendant [dıséndənt] ADJ & N descendiente
mf

descent [dısént] N (act of descending, decline)
descenso *m*; (slope) bajada *f*; (lineage)
descendencia *f*

describe [dıskráıb] VT describir

description [dıskrípʃən] N descripción *f*,
caracterización *f*; **of all —s** de todas clases

descriptive [dıskríptıv] ADJ descriptivo

desecrate [désıkret] VT profanar

desecration [dɛsıkréʃən] N profanación *f*

desegregate [diségrıget] VI/VT eliminar la
segregación racial

deselect [disılékt] VT anular [una selección
previa]

desensitize [disénsıtaız] VT insensibilizar

desert[1] [dézəɾt] ADJ (barren, empty) desierto; (of
the desert) desértico; N desierto *m*

desert[2] [dızɜ́ɾt] VI/VT (a person, place)
abandonar; (military service) desertar

deserter [dızɜ́ɾpəɾ] N desertor -ora *mf*

desertion [dızɜ́ɾʃən] N (of a person or place)
abandono *m*; (from the military) deserción *f*

deserve [dızɜ́ɾv] VT merecer

deserving [dızɜ́ɾvıŋ] ADJ merecedor

desiccate [désıket] VI/VT desecar[se]

design [dızáın] VI/VT (prepare a sketch of)
diseñar, trazar; (plan) planear, idear; N
(model, pattern) diseño *m*; (sketch) esbozo *m*;
he has —s on her le ha echado el ojo

designate [dézıgnet] VT designar, denominar;
—d hitter bateador -ora designado -da *mf*

designation [dɛzıgnéʃən] N denominación *f*,
designación *f*

designer [dızáınəɾ] N diseñador -ora *mf*; **—
drugs** drogas de diseño *f pl*

desirability [dızaırəbílıpi] N deseabilidad *f*,
conveniencia *f*

desirable [dızáırəbəł] ADJ deseable

desire [dızáır] VT desear; **I — your
cooperation** requiero tu cooperación; N
deseo *m*

desirous [dızáırəs] ADJ deseoso

desist [dısíst] VI desistir

desk [dɛsk] N escritorio *m*; (school) pupitre *m*;
—top computer *Am* computadora de
escritorio *f*, *Sp* ordenador de sobremesa *m*;
—top publishing edición de sobremesa *f*,
autoedición *f*

desolate[1] [désəlıt] ADJ (barren) desolado

desolate[2] [désəlet] VT desolar, asolar

desolation [dɛsəléʃən] N desolación *f*,
asolamiento *m*

despair [dıspéɾ] N desesperanza *f*; VI
desesperarse, perder la esperanza

despairing [dıspéɾıŋ] ADJ de desesperación

desperate [déspəɾıt] ADJ desesperado

desperately [déspəɾıtli] ADV desesperadamente;
— ill gravemente enfermo; **he's — looking
for funds** está desesperado buscando
financiación

desperation [dɛspəɾéʃən] N desesperación *f*

despicable [dıspíkəbəł] ADJ despreciable,
deleznable

despise [dıspáız] VT despreciar, menospreciar

despite [dıspáıt] N despecho *m*; PREP a pesar de

despoil [dıspɔ́ıł] VT despojar

despondency [dıspándənsi] N abatimiento *m*,
desaliento *m*

despondent [dıspándənt] ADJ abatido,
desalentado

despot [déspət] N déspota *mf*

despotic [dıspápık] ADJ despótico

despotism [déspətızəm] N despotismo *m*

dessert [dızɜ́ɾt] N postre *m*

destabilize [distébələız] VT desestabilizar

destination [dɛstənéʃən] N destino *m*

destine [déstın] VT destinar; **she's —d for
greatness** promete grandes cosas

destiny [déstəni] N destino *m*

destitute [déstıtut] ADJ menesteroso, indigente;
— of falto de, desprovisto de

destroy [dɪstrɔ́ɪ] VT (demolish) destruir, deshacer; (kill an animal) sacrificar; (ruin a reputation) arruinar

destroyer [dɪstrɔ́ɪɚ] N (person who destroys) destructor -ora *mf*; (ship) destructor *m*

destructible [dɪstrʌ́ktəbəł] ADJ destructible

destruction [dɪstrʌ́kʃən] N (act of demolishing) destrucción *f*; (act of killing) matanza *f*; (act of ruining a reputation) ruina *f*

destructive [dɪstrʌ́ktɪv] ADJ destructivo, destructor

detach [dɪtǽtʃ] VT separar, desprender; (troops) destacar

detachment [dɪtǽtʃmənt] N (physical) separación *f*; (emotional) desapego *m*; (of troops) destacamento *m*; (of the retina) desprendimiento *m*

detail[1] [díteł] N detalle *m*, pormenor *m*; (military) destacamento *m*; **to go into —** detallar, pormenorizar

detail[2] [dɪtéł] VT detallar, pormenorizar; (assign duties) destacar

detain [dɪtén] VT detener

detect [dɪtékt] VT detectar

detection [dɪtékʃən] N detección *f*

detective [dɪtéktɪv] N detective *mf*; **— novel** novela policial *f*

detector [dɪtéktɚ] N detector *m*

detention [dɪténʃən] N (in jail) detención *f*; (in school) castigo *m*

deter [dɪtɚ́] VT (dissuade) disuadir; (prevent) prevenir

detergent [dɪtɚ́dʒənt] N detergente *m*

deteriorate [dɪtíriəret] VI deteriorar[se]

deterioration [dɪtiriəréʃən] N deterioro *m*

determination [dɪtɚmənéʃən] N (act of determining) determinación *f*; (resolution) resolución *f*; (persistence) tesón *m*, perseverancia *f*

determine [dɪtɚ́mɪn] VT determinar; **to — to do something** decidirse a hacer algo

determined [dɪtɚ́mɪnd] ADJ (resolute) decidido, resuelto; (persistent) tesonero

determiner [dɪtɚ́rmɪnɚ] N (grammatical) determinante *m*

determining [dɪtɚ́rmɪnɪŋ] ADJ determinante

detest [dɪtést] VT detestar, abominar de

detestable [dɪtéstəbəł] ADJ detestable

dethrone [diθrón] VT destronar

detonate [détṇet] VI/VT detonar

detonation [dɛtṇéʃən] N detonación *f*

detour [dítur] N desvío *m*; VI/VT desviar[se]

detoxification [ditɑksəfɪkéʃən] N destoxificación *f*

detract [dɪtrǽkt] VT distraer; VI **to — from** disminuir

detrimental [dɛtrəméntḷ] ADJ perjudicial

deuce [dus] N (in tennis) deuce *m*, cuarenta iguales

devaluation [divæljuéʃən] N devaluación *f*

devastate [dévəstet] VT devastar, asolar

devastating [dévəsteDɪŋ] ADJ devastador

develop [dɪvéləp] VI/VT (mature, elaborate) desarrollar[se]; (build houses on) construir, edificar; (treat film) revelar; **she —ed an allergy** le vino una alergia; **—ing country** país en desarrollo *m*

developer [dɪvéləpɚ] N (of computer programs) desarrollador -ora *mf*; (of real estate) promotor -ora *mf*; **a late —** persona de maduración tardía *f*

development [dɪvéləpmənt] N (evolution) desarrollo *m*; (buildings) urbanización *f*, colonia *f*; (of a photograph) revelado *m*

developmental [dɪveləpméntḷ] ADJ relativo al desarrollo

deviate [díviet] VI/VT desviar[se]

deviation [diviéʃən] N desviación *f*

device [dɪváɪs] N (gadget) dispositivo *m*; (literary convention) recurso *m*; (emblem) divisa *f*; **they left me to my own —s** me dejaron que me las arreglara sola

devil [dévəł] N diablo *m*; **lucky —!** ¡suertudo! **what the — are you saying?** ¿qué diablos dices? **—'s advocate** abogado del diablo *m*

devilish [dévəlɪʃ] ADJ (evil) diabólico; (extreme) endiablado, endemoniado

deviltry [dévəltri] N (mischief) diablura *f*; (witchcraft) brujería *f*

devious [díviəs] ADJ (roundabout) sinuoso, tortuoso; (crafty) taimado, retorcido

devise [dɪváɪz] VT idear, urdir

devoid [dɪvɔ́ɪd] ADJ **— of** falto de, desprovisto de

devolution [devəlúʃən] N devolución *f*

devote [dɪvót] VT dedicar; (consecrate) consagrar

devoted [dɪvóDɪd] ADJ (friend) leal; (parent) dedicado; (worshiper) devoto

devotion [dɪvóʃən] N devoción *f*

devour [dɪváʊr] VT devorar

devout [dɪváʊt] ADJ devoto

dew [du] N rocío *m*; **—drop** gota de rocío *f*; **—point** punto de condensación *m*

dexterity [dɛkstéɾɪDi] N destreza *f*

dextrose [dékstros] N dextrosa *f*

diabetes [daɪəbídɪz] N diabetes *f*

diabolic [daɪəbálɪk] ADJ diabólico

diacritic [daɪəkrídɪk] ADJ & N diacrítico *m*

diagnose [daɪəgnós] VT diagnosticar

diagnosis [daɪəgnósɪs] N diagnóstico *m*, diagnosis *f*

diagnostic [daɪəgnástɪk] ADJ diagnóstico

diagonal [daɪǽgənḷ] ADJ & N diagonal *f*

diagram [dáɪəgræm] N diagrama *m*

dial [dáɪəł] N (of a watch, clock) esfera *f*; (of radio) dial *m*; **— tone** *Sp* señal de marcar *f*; *Am* tono de discar *m*; VI/VT (a telephone number) *Sp* marcar; *Am* discar

dialect [dáɪəlɛkt] N dialecto *m*

dialectic [daɪəléktɪk] ADJ dialéctico; N dialéctica *f*
dialectology [daɪəlɛktáləʤi] N dialectología *f*
dialogue, dialog [dáɪəlɑg] N diálogo *m*; VI dialogar
dialysis [daɪǽlɪsɪs] N diálisis *f*
diameter [daɪǽmɪDə⋅] N diámetro *m*
diamond [dáɪəmənd] N (stone) diamante *m*; (shape) rombo *m*
diaper [dáɪpə⋅] N pañal *m*; VT poner pañales
diaphragm [dáɪəfræm] N diafragma *m*
diarrhea [daɪəríə] N diarrea *f*
diary [dáɪəri] N diario *m*
diastolic [daɪəstálɪk] ADJ diastólico
diatribe [dáɪətraɪb] N diatriba *f*
dice [daɪs] N PL dados *m pl*; VT cortar en cubos; **no —!** (impossibility) no hay forma, *Am* ¡ni modo! (refusal) de ninguna manera
dichotomy [daɪkáDəmi] N dicotomía *f*
dick [dɪk] N (penis) *vulg* polla *f*, pija *f*, verga *f*, rabo *m*; (detective) sabueso -sa *mf*; **—head** *offensive* capullo *m*; VI **to — somebody around** fastidiar a alguien
dicker [díkə⋅] VI regatear
dictate [díktet] VI/VT dictar; N dictado *m*, precepto *m*
dictation [dɪktéʃən] N dictado *m*; **to take —** escribir al dictado
dictator [díkteDə⋅] N dictador -ora *mf*
dictatorship [dɪktéDə⋅ʃɪp] N dictadura *f*
diction [díkʃən] N dicción *f*
dictionary [díkʃənɛri] N diccionario *m*
did [dɪd] *see* do
didactic [daɪdǽktɪk] ADJ didáctico
die [daɪ] VI morir[se]; **to — down/away** disminuir; **to — off** irse muriendo; **to — out** morirse, extinguirse; **my car —d** se me murió el coche; N (game piece) dado *m*; (press) molde *m*; (stamp) cuño *m*, troquel *m*; **—hard** intransigente *mf*
diesel [dízəł] N diesel *m*; **— engine** motor diesel *m*
diet [dáɪɪt] N (food) dieta *f*; (controlled intake of food) dieta *f*, régimen *m*; **to be/go on a —** estar a dieta/régimen; **to put on a —** poner a dieta; VI estar a dieta, hacer dieta
dietary [dáɪɪtɛri] ADJ dietético
dietitian [daɪɪtíʃən] N dietista *mf*
differ [dífə⋅] VI diferir; **to — with** disentir, no estar de acuerdo con; **to — from** ser diferente de
difference [dífə⋅əns] N diferencia *f*; **it makes no —** no importa, da igual
different [dífə⋅ənt] ADJ diferente, distinto
differential [dɪfə⋅rénʃəł] ADJ & N (difference, car part) diferencial *m*; **— equation** diferencial *f*
differentiate [dɪfə⋅rénʃiet] VI/VT diferenciar[se], distinguir[se]
differentiation [dɪfə⋅rɛnʃiéʃən] N diferenciación *f*
differently [dífə⋅əntli] ADV de manera

diferente; **they act —** no se comportan igual
difficult [dífɪkəłt] ADJ difícil
difficulty [dífɪkʌłti] N dificultad *f*; **with —** con dificultad, difícilmente
diffident [dífɪDənt] ADJ tímido
diffuse¹ [dɪfjúz] VI/VT difundir
diffuse² [dɪfjús] ADJ difuso
diffusion [dɪfjúʒən] N difusión *f*
dig [dɪg] VI/VT cavar; (by machine) excavar; (superficially) escarbar; **to — in the files** escarbar en los archivos; **to — under** socavar; **to — up** desenterrar; **he dug his heels into the ground** clavó los talones en el suelo; **I — your new shoes** están muy buenos tus zapatos nuevos; N (archaeological site) excavación *f*; (sarcastic remark) pulla *f*; **a — in the ribs** un codazo
digest¹ [dɪʤést] VI/VT digerir
digest² [dáɪʤest] N (summary) compendio *m*; (legal) digesto *m*
digestible [dɪʤéstəbəł] ADJ digerible, digestible
digestion [dɪʤéstʃən] N digestión *f*
digestive [dɪʤéstɪv] ADJ digestivo
digit [díʤɪt] N dígito *m*
digital [díʤɪdł] ADJ digital; **— camera** cámara digital *f*; **— computer** *Am* computadora digital *f*, *Sp* ordenador digital *m*; **— photography** fotografía digital *f*
digitalize [díʤɪdłaɪz] VT digitalizar
digitize [díʤɪtaɪz] VT digitalizar
dignified [dígnəfaɪd] ADJ digno
dignitary [dígnɪtɛri] N dignatario -ria *mf*
dignity [dígnɪDi] N dignidad *f*
digress [dɪgrés] VI divagar
digression [dɪgréʃən] N digresión *f*
dike [daɪk] N dique *m*
dilapidated [dɪlǽpɪdeDɪd] ADJ (machine) destartalado; (furniture) desvencijado; (house) derruido, venido abajo
dilate [dáɪlet] VI/VT dilatar[se]
dilation [daɪléʃən] N dilatación *f*
dilemma [dɪlémə] N dilema *m*
dilettante [dílɪtɑnt] N diletante *mf*
diligence [díləʤəns] N diligencia *f*
diligent [díləʤənt] ADJ diligente, hacendoso
dill [dɪł] N eneldo *m*; **— pickle** pepinillo en vinagre con eneldo *m*
dilute [dɪlút] VI/VT diluir[se]; ADJ diluido
dim [dɪm] ADJ (light) tenue; (outline) difuso; (room) oscuro, en penumbras; (person) *fam* de pocas luces; **—wit** *fam* tonto, bobo; VI/VT (make less bright) atenuar; VT (switch to low beam) bajar
dimension [dɪménʃən] N dimensión *f*
diminish [dɪmínɪʃ] VI/VT disminuir, menguar; **the law of —ing returns** la ley de los

rendimientos decrecientes
diminution [dɪmənúʃən] N disminución f,
mengua f
diminutive [dɪmínjətɪv] ADJ diminuto; N
diminutivo m
dimmer [dímɚ] N regulador de voltaje m
dimness [dímnɪs] N oscuridad f, penumbra f
dimple [dímpəł] N hoyuelo m; VT formar
hoyuelos
din [dɪn] N estruendo m, estrépito m
dine [daɪn] VI cenar; **to — out** cenar afuera
diner [dáɪnɚ] N (restaurant) cafetería f; (on a
train) coche comedor m; (person) comensal
mf
ding-a-ling [díŋəlɪŋ] N (silly person) ganso -sa
mf; (eccentric person) excéntrico -ca mf;
(sound) tilín m
dingy [díndʒi] ADJ deslucido
dining [dáɪnɪŋ] ADJ **— car** coche comedor m; **—
room** comedor m
dinner [dínɚ] N (main meal) comida f; (at
midday) almuerzo m; (in the evening) cena f;
— jacket smoking m; **—time** hora de la
comida f
dinosaur [dáɪnəsɔr] N dinosaurio m
dint [dɪnt] ADV LOC **by — of** a fuerza de
dip [dɪp] VT (make wet) mojar; (scoop) sacar;
(immerse) sumergir; (immerse in insecticide)
bañar; (immerse in sauce, coffee) pringar,
mojar; VI (sun) hundirse; (stocks) bajar;
(road) hacer una bajada; (airplane) descender
súbitamente; N (act of wetting) mojada f;
(portion of ice-cream) bola f, cucharada f;
(sauce) mojo m; (reduction in sales)
disminución f; (low place in a road) declive m;
(low place in the land) hondonada f; (swim)
baño m; (airplane maneuver) descenso rápido
m; (irritating person) pej pesado -da mf
diphtheria [dɪpθíriə] N difteria f
diphthong [dípθɔŋ] N diptongo m
diploma [dɪplómə] N diploma m
diplomacy [dɪplómə si] N diplomacia f
diplomat [dípləmæt] N diplomático -ca mf
diplomatic [dɪpləmǽDɪk] ADJ diplomático
dipper [dípɚ] N cucharón m, cazo m
dire [daɪr] ADJ terrible, espantoso; **— need**
necesidad acuciante f; **— predictions**
predicciones funestas f pl; **— situation**
situación extrema f
direct [dɪrɛ́kt] ADJ directo; **— current** corriente
continua f; **— object** complemento directo
m; **— quotation** cita textual f; ADV directo,
directamente; VI/VT dirigir; **he —ed me to
leave** me mandó irme
direction [dɪrɛ́kʃən] N dirección f; **—s**
indicaciones f pl; **I'm thinking in that —**
me inclino por eso
directive [dɪrɛ́ktɪv] ADJ directivo; N directiva f
director [dɪrɛ́ktɚ] N (theater, movies) director

-ra mf; (film, TV) realizador -ora mf
directory [dɪrɛ́ktəri] N directorio m
dirigible [dərídʒəbəł] ADJ & N dirigible m
dirt [dɚt] N (filth) suciedad f; (foul substance)
mugre f; (vile person) offensive mierda f;
(earth) tierra f; **—bag** offensive porquería f;
I've got some — on him le conozco los
trapos sucios; ADJ **— cheap** baratísimo; **—-
poor** pobrísimo
dirty [dɚ́Di] ADJ sucio, mugriento; **— joke** chiste
verde m; **— look** mirada asesina f; **— money**
dinero sucio m; **— shame** pena horrible f; **—
trick** trampa f; **— word** palabrota f; Sp taco
m; **— work** trabajo sucio m; VI/VT ensuciar;
ADV **to talk —** decir cosas obscenas
disability [dɪsəbílIDi] N incapacidad f,
discapacidad f, minusvalía f; **— insurance**
seguro de discapacidad m
disable [dɪsébəł] VT (person) incapacitar;
(device) desactivar
disabled [dɪsébəłd] ADJ discapacitado,
minusválido
disabuse [dɪsəbjúz] VT desengañar
disadvantage [dɪsɪdvǽntɪdʒ] N desventaja f; **to
be at a —** estar en desventaja
disadvantaged [dɪsɪdvǽntɪdʒd] ADJ carenciado
disagree [dɪsəgrí] VI (differ in opinion) disentir,
no estar de acuerdo; (differ) diferir; **pizza —s
with me** no me cae bien la pizza
disagreeable [dɪsəgríəbəł] ADJ desagradable
disagreement [dɪsəgrímənt] N (lack of
agreement, argument) desacuerdo m;
(discrepancy) discrepancia f
disallow [dɪsəláu] VT desaprobar; (in sports)
anular
disappear [dɪsəpír] VI desaparecer
disappearance [dɪsəpírəns] N desaparición f
disappoint [dɪsəpɔ́ɪnt] VI/VT decepcionar,
desilusionar; **to be —ed** estar desilusionado
disappointing [dɪsəpɔ́ɪntɪŋ] ADJ decepcionante
disappointment [dɪsəpɔ́ɪntmənt] N decepción
f, desilusión f
disapproval [dɪsəprúvəł] N desaprobación f
disapprove [dɪsəprúv] VI/VT desaprobar
disarm [dɪsárm] VI/VT desarmar[se]
disarmament [dɪsárməmənt] N desarme m
disarray [dɪsəré] VT desordenar; N confusión f,
desorden m; **in —** en desorden
disaster [dɪzǽstɚ] N desastre m
disastrous [dɪzǽstrəs] ADJ desastroso
disavow [dɪsəváu] VT negar
disband [dɪsbǽnd] VT disolver; VI desbandarse
disbelief [dɪsbɪlíf] N incredulidad f
disbelieve [dɪsbɪlív] VI/VT descreer de
disburse [dɪsbɚ́s] VT desembolsar
disbursement [dɪsbɚ́smənt] N desembolso m
discard[1] [dɪskárd] VT (a card) descartar;
(garbage) desechar
discard[2] [dískɑrd] N (card) descarte m; (garbage)

desecho *m*

discern [dɪsɚ́n] VT (distinguish mentally) discernir; (perceive) percibir

discernment [dɪsɚ́nmənt] N discernimiento *m*

discharge[1] [dɪstʃárdʒ] VI/VT (battery, load, firearm) descargar[se]; (obligation) cumplir; (prisoner) poner en libertad, soltar; (odor) despedir; (soldier) dar de baja; (patient) dar de alta; (a debt) pagar; (pus) supurar

discharge[2] [dístʃardʒ] N (of a battery, load, firearm) descarga*f*; (of an obligation) cumplimiento *m*; (of a prisoner) puesta en libertad *f*; (of an odor) emisión *f*; (of a soldier) baja *f*; (of a patient) alta *f*; (of a debt) pago *m*; (of oil) pérdida *f*; (of pus) supuración *f*; (uterine, vaginal) flujo *m*; (from a job) despido *m*

disciple [dɪsáɪpəl] N discípulo -la *mf*

discipline [dísəplɪn] N disciplina *f*; VT disciplinar

disclaimer [dɪsklémɚ] N descargo de responsabilidad *m*

disclose [dɪsklóz] VT revelar

disco [dísko] N discoteca *f*

discolor [dɪskʌ́lɚ] VI/VT decolorar[se]

discomfort [dɪskʌ́mfɚt] N malestar *m*

disconcert [dɪskənsɚ́t] VT desconcertar

disconnect [dɪskənékt] VI/VT desconectar; N desconexión *f*

disconnected [dɪskənéktɪd] ADJ (broken) desconectado; (incoherent) inconexo

disconsolate [dɪskánsəlɪt] ADJ desconsolado

discontent [dɪskəntént] N descontento *m*

discontinue [dɪskəntínju] VT suspender, interrumpir

discontinuous [dɪskəntínjuəs] ADJ discontinuo

discord [dískɔrd] N (lack of concord) discordia *f*, desavenencia *f*; (dissonance) disonancia *f*, discordancia *f*

discotheque [dískotek] N discoteca *f*

discount [dískaʊnt] VT (deduct from a charge, take into account in advance) descontar; (sell at a reduced price) rebajar; (disregard) ignorar; N descuento *m*; **at a** — con descuento, con rebaja

discourage [dɪskɚ́ɪdʒ] VT desanimar, desalentar; **to — from** disuadir de

discouragement [dɪskɚ́ɪdʒmənt] N desánimo *m*, desaliento *m*

discourse[1] [dískɔrs] N (conversation, talk) discurso *m*; (treatise) disertación *f*

discourse[2] [dɪskórs] VI (talk) discurrir; (treat a subject) disertar

discourteous [dɪskɚ́ɪdiəs] ADJ descortés

discourtesy [dɪskɚ́ɪdɪsi] N descortesía *f*

discover [dɪskʌ́vɚ] VT descubrir

discoverer [dɪskʌ́vərɚ] N descubridor -ora *mf*

discovery [dɪskʌ́vəri] N descubrimiento *m*

discredit [dɪskrédɪt] VT (injure the reputation

of) desacreditar; (give no credence to) no creer; N descrédito *m*

discreet [dɪskrít] ADJ discreto

discrepancy [dɪskrépənsi] N discrepancia *f*

discrete [dɪskrít] ADJ (separate) separado; (en matemáticas) discreto

discretion [dɪskréʃən] N discreción *f*; **at your own** — a discreción; **at the judge's** — al arbitrio del juez

discretionary [dɪskréʃənɛri] ADJ discrecional; **— income** ingresos discrecionales *m pl*

discriminate [dɪskrímənet] VI/VT distinguir; **to — against** discriminar a

discrimination [dɪskrɪmɪnéʃən] N discriminación *f*

discuss [dɪskʌ́s] VT discutir

discussion [dɪskʌ́ʃən] N discusión *f*

disdain [dɪsdén] N desdén *m*, desprecio *m*; VT (treat with contempt) desdeñar; (think unworthy of a response) no dignarse a

disdainful [dɪsdénfəl] ADJ desdeñoso

disease [dɪzíz] N enfermedad *f*

diseased [dɪzízd] ADJ enfermo

disembark [dɪsɪmbárk] VI/VT desembarcar

disenfranchise [dɪsɪnfrǽntʃaɪz] VT (politician) proscribir; (minorities) privar de derechos, desheredar

disengage [dɪsɪngédʒ] VI/VT (a clutch) soltar[se]; (from a situation) distanciar[se]

disentangle [dɪsɪntǽŋgəl] VI/VT desenredar[se], desenmarañar[se]

disfavor [dɪsfévɚ] VT mirar con malos ojos; N **to fall into** — (a person) caer en desgracia; (a fashion) caer en desuso

disfigure [dɪsfígjɚ] VT desfigurar

disgrace [dɪsgrés] N (dishonor) deshonra *f*; (shame) vergüenza *f*; **to fall into** — caer en desgracia; VT deshonrar

disgraceful [dɪsgrésfəl] ADJ vergonzoso

disgruntled [dɪsgrʌ́ntḷd] ADJ descontento, resentido

disguise [dɪsgáɪz] VT disfrazar[se]; N disfraz *m*

disgust [dɪsgʌ́st] VT (repel) asquear, repugnar; (displease) disgustar; N asco *m*, repugnancia *f*

disgusted [dɪsgʌ́stɪd] ADJ asqueado, repugnado

disgusting [dɪsgʌ́stɪŋ] ADJ asqueroso, repugnante

dish [dɪʃ] N (plate, food, quantity) plato *m*; (serving container) fuente *f*; (attractive person) *fam* bombón *m*; —**es** vajilla *f*; —**cloth/towel** paño de cocina *m*, repasador *m*; —**washer** lavaplatos *m sg*, lavavajillas *m sg*; —**water** agua de fregar *f*; VI/VT (serve food) servir; **to — out** repartir

dishearten [dɪshártṇ] VT desanimar, descorazonar, desalentar

disheartening [dɪshártṇɪŋ] ADJ descorazonador, desalentador

dishevel [dɪʃévəl] VT desgreñar

disheveled [dɪʃévəld] ADJ (hair) desgreñado, revuelto; (clothes) desaliñado
dishonest [dɪsánɪst] ADJ deshonesto
dishonesty [dɪsánɪsti] N deshonestidad f
dishonor [dɪsánɚ] N deshonra f; VT deshonrar; (a check) no pagar
dishonorable [dɪsánɚəbəl] ADJ deshonroso
disillusion [dɪsɪlúʒən] N desilusión f, desencanto m; VT desilusionar, desencantar
disinfect [dɪsɪnfékt] VT desinfectar
disinfectant [dɪsɪnféktənt] N desinfectante m
disinfection [dɪsɪnfékʃən] N desinfección f
disinfestation [dɪsɪnfestéʃən] N desinfestación f
disinformation [dɪsɪnfɚméʃən] N desinformación f
disinherit [dɪsɪnhérɪt] VT desheredar
disintegrate [dɪsíntɪgret] VI/VT desintegrar[se]
disintegration [dɪsɪntɪgréʃən] N desintegración f
disinterested [dɪsíntrɪstɪd] ADJ desinteresado
disjointed [dɪsʤóɪntɪd] ADJ desarticulado
disk, disc [dɪsk] N disco m; (game piece) tejo m; (in a computer) disco m, disquete m; **— brake** freno de disco m; **— capacity** capacidad de almacenamiento de disco f; **— drive** disquetera f; **— jockey** pinchadiscos mf sg
diskette [dɪskét] N disquete m; **— drive** unidad de disquete f
dislike [dɪsláɪk] N aversión f, tirria f; VT **I — parties** no me gustan las fiestas
dislocate [dɪslóket] VT dislocar, descoyuntar
dislocation [dɪslokéʃən] N dislocación f, luxación f
dislodge [dɪsláʤ] VT (force out) desatascar; (displace) desprender
disloyal [dɪslóɪəl] ADJ desleal
dismal [dízməl] ADJ pésimo; **a — failure** un fracaso rotundo
dismantle [dɪsmæntl] VT (a factory) desmantelar; (a car, watch) desmontar
dismay [dɪsmé] VT (disappoint) consternar; (daunt) desalentar; (alarm) alarmar; N (disappointment) consternación f; (loss of courage) desaliento m; (alarm) alarma f
dismember [dɪsmémbɚ] VT desmembrar
dismiss [dɪsmís] VT (fire a private employee) despedir; (fire a public employee) destituir, cesar; (reject a possibility) desechar, descartar; (discharge from military service) dar de baja; (reject a claim) desestimar; (ignore a person) ningunear; **class —ed!** ¡pueden retirarse!
dismissal [dɪsmísəl] N (firing) destitución f, despido m; (of a possibility) rechazo m; (from military service) baja f; (of a claim) desestimación f; (of a person) ninguneo m
dismount [dɪsmáʊnt] VI (get off a horse) desmontarse, apearse; (take apart) desarmar; N bajada f

disobedience [dɪsəbíɒɪəns] N desobediencia f
disobedient [dɪsəbíɒɪənt] ADJ desobediente
disobey [dɪsəbé] VI/VT desobedecer
disorder [dɪsórɒɚ] N (confusion) desorden m; (public disturbance) desorden público m; (illness) trastorno m, desarreglo m
disorderly [dɪsórɒɚli] ADJ (untidy) desordenado; (unruly) revoltoso; **— conduct** alteración del orden público f
disorganization [dɪsɔrgənɪzéʃən] N desorganización f
disorganized [dɪsórgənaɪzd] ADJ desorganizado
disown [dɪsón] VT repudiar
disparage [dɪspǽrɪʤ] VT denigrar
disparate [díspɚɪt] ADJ dispar
dispassionate [dɪspǽʃənɪt] ADJ desapasionado
dispatch [dɪspǽtʃ] VT despachar; N (sending off) envío m; (putting to death) ejecución f; (news story, official communication) despacho m; (promptness) prontitud f
dispel [dɪspél] VT disipar
dispensable [dɪspénsəbəl] ADJ prescindible
dispensary [dɪspénsəri] N dispensario m
dispensation [dɪspɛnséʃən] N (relaxation of law) dispensa f; (act of handing out) dispensación f
dispense [dɪspéns] VT (goods) dispensar; (justice) administrar; **to — from an obligation** eximir de una obligación; **to — with** prescindir de
dispersal [dɪspɚ́səl] N dispersión f
disperse [dɪspɚ́s] VI/VT dispersar[se]; ADJ disperso
dispersed [dɪspɚ́st] ADJ disperso
displace [dɪsplés] VT (evict) desalojar; (take up space, remove from office) desplazar; **—d person** (domestic) desplazado -da mf, (foreign) expatriado -da mf
displacement [dɪsplésmənt] N (of refugees, of a ship) desplazamiento m; (of an engine) cilindrada f
display [dɪsplé] VT (exhibit) exhibir, exponer; (unfold) desplegar; (flaunt) ostentar; (show on a computer screen) visualizar; N (of wares, etc.) exhibición f, despliegue m; (advertisement) cartel m; (flaunting) ostentación f; (computer screen) pantalla f, visualizador m, display m
displease [dɪsplíz] VT contrariar, desagradar, descontentar; VI molestar
displeasure [dɪspléʒɚ] N disgusto m, desagrado m
disposable [dɪspózəbəl] ADJ **— income** ingresos disponibles m pl
disposal [dɪspózəl] N (arrangement) disposición f; (elimination) eliminación f
dispose [dɪspóz] VT (give inclination) predisponer; (set in order, make ready) disponer; **to — of** descartar, eliminar

disposition [dɪspəzíʃən] N (attitude) temperamento *m*; (inclination) inclinación *f*, tendencia *f*; (arrangement, disposal) disposición *f*

dispossess [dɪspəzés] VT desposeer

disproportionate [dɪsprəpɔ́rʃənɪt] ADJ desproporcionado

disprove [dɪsprúv] VT refutar

dispute [dɪspjút] N disputa *f*; VT discutir, impugnar

disqualify [dɪskwáləfaɪ] VT (deprive of rights) inhabilitar; (exclude from a sport event) descalificar

disregard [dɪsrɪgárd] VT hacer caso omiso de, ignorar; N (neglect) descuido *m*; (disrespect) falta de respeto *f*

disrepair [dɪsrɪpér] N mal estado *m*; **in —** deteriorado

disreputable [dɪsrépjəDəbəł] ADJ (of bad reputation) de mala reputación; (shabby) de mala muerte

disrespect [dɪsrɪspékt] N desacato *m*, falta de respeto *f*; VT faltar el respeto

disrespectful [dɪsrɪspéktfəł] ADJ irrespetuoso

disrobe [dɪsrób] VI/VT desvestir[se]

disrupt [dɪsrápt] VT (cause disorder) trastornar, trastocar; (interrupt) interrumpir

dissatisfied [dɪssǽDɪsfaɪd] ADJ insatisfecho, disconforme

dissatisfy [dɪssǽDɪsfaɪ] VT no satisfacer

dissect [daɪsékt] VT (cut apart) disecar; (analyze argument) analizar minuciosamente

dissemble [dɪsémbəł] VI/VT (hide) disimular; (feign) fingir

disseminate [dɪsɛ́mənet] VT (spread out) diseminar, propagar; (publicize) divulgar

dissemination [dɪsɛmənéʃən] N (spreading out) diseminación *f*; (publicizing) divulgación *f*

dissension [dɪsénʃən] N disensión *f*, disenso *m*

dissent [dɪsént] VI disentir; N disenso *m*

dissertation [dɪsɚtéʃən] N (formal discourse) disertación *f*; (doctoral treatise) tesis de doctorado *f*

dissident [dísɪDənt] N disidente *mf*

dissimilar [dɪssímələ˞] ADJ diferente

dissimulation [dɪsɪmjəléʃən] N disimulo *m*

dissipate [dísəpet] VI/VT disipar[se]

dissipation [dɪsəpéʃən] N disipación *f*

dissolute [dísəlut] ADJ disoluto, vicioso

dissolution [dɪsəlúʃən] N disolución *f*

dissolve [dɪzáłv] VI/VT disolver[se]

dissuade [dɪswéd] VT disuadir

distance [dístəns] N distancia *f*, recorrido *m*; **— learning** educación a distancia *f*; **in the —** a lo lejos, en la lejanía; VT distanciarse de, distanciar

distant [dístənt] ADJ (far away, aloof) distante; (remote) lejano, remoto; **to be — from** distar de

distaste [dɪstést] N aversión *f*

distasteful [dɪstéstfəł] ADJ desagradable

distemper [dɪstémpə˞] N moquillo *m*

distend [dɪsténd] VI/VT distender[se]

distill [dɪstíł] VI/VT destilar[se]

distillation [dɪstəléʃən] N destilación *f*

distillery [dɪstíləri] N destilería *f*

distinct [dɪstíŋkt] ADJ (different) distinto; (clear) bien delineado, neto

distinction [dɪstíŋkʃən] N (honor) distinción *f*; (differentiation) distinción *f*, diferenciación *f*; **he passed with —** aprobó con sobresaliente

distinctive [dɪstíŋktɪv] ADJ distintivo

distinguish [dɪstíŋgwɪʃ] VI/VT distinguir

distinguished [dɪstíŋgwɪʃt] ADJ distinguido

distinguishing [dɪstíŋgwɪʃɪŋ] ADJ distintivo

distort [dɪstɔ́rt] VT (an object) deformar; (reports, sound) distorsionar

distortion [dɪstɔ́rʃən] N (object) deformación *f*; (image, sound) distorsión *f*; (of a statement) tergiversación *f*

distract [dɪstrǽkt] VT distraer, entretener

distracted [dɪstrǽktɪd] ADJ distraído, disperso

distraction [dɪstrǽkʃən] N distracción *f*; **to drive to —** volver loco

distraught [dɪstrɔ́t] ADJ angustiado

distress [dɪstrés] N (anxiety) angustia *f*; (pain) dolor *m*, congoja *f*; **to be in —** (a person) estar en apuros; (a ship, plane) estar en peligro; VT (cause anxiety) angustiar, atribular; (cause pain) acongojar, afligir

distressing [dɪstrésɪŋ] ADJ inquietante

distribute [dɪstríbjut] VT distribuir, repartir

distribution [dɪstrəbjúʃən] N distribución *f*, reparto *m*

distributor [dɪstríbjəDə˞] N distribuidor *m*

district [dístrɪkt] N distrito *m*, comarca *f*; **— attorney** fiscal de distrito *mf*

District of Columbia [dístrɪktəvkəlʌ́mbiə] N Distrito de Columbia *m*

distrust [dɪstrást] N desconfianza *f*; VT desconfiar de

distrustful [dɪstrástfəł] ADJ desconfiado

disturb [dɪstɝ́b] VI/VT (interrupt, interfere, perplex) perturbar; (trouble) turbar, perturbar, trastornar; (mess up) desarreglar; **do not —** se ruega no molestar

disturbance [dɪstɝ́bəns] N disturbio *m*; (weather) perturbación *f*

disuse [dɪsjús] N desuso *m*; **to fall into —** caer en desuso

ditch [dɪtʃ] N (trench) zanja *f*; (roadside) cuneta *f*; (for irrigation) acequia *f*; VT (make ditches) abrir zanjas; (get rid of) deshacerse de; (crash-land an airplane on water) hacer un amarizaje

dither [díðə˞] VI (hesitate) titubear; N **it threw her into a —** se puso muy nerviosa

ditsy [dítsi] ADJ atolondrado, cabeza de chorlito

ditto [díĐo] PRON & ADV ídem
diuretic [daɪəréĐɪk] ADJ & N diurético *m*
diurnal [daɪɨ́nl] ADJ diurno
divan [dɪvǽn] N diván *m*, canapé *m*
dive [daɪv] VI (into water) zambullirse, chapuzar, *Am* tirarse un clavado; (into an activity) zambullirse; (with scuba equipment) bucear; (airplane) bajar en picado -da; (submarine) sumergirse; N (of a person) zambullida *f*, chapuz *m*; (of an airplane) picado -da *mf*; (cheap bar) antro *m*
diver [dáɪvɚ] N saltador -ora *mf*; (high-dive) clavadista *mf*; (scuba) buzo *mf*
diverge [dɪvɨ́ʤ] VI (branch off, differ in opinion) divergir; VI/VT (deviate) desviar
divergence [dɪvɨ́ʤəns] N (separation, difference in opinion) divergencia *f*; (deviation) desviación *f*
diverse [dɪvɨ́s] ADJ (of various kinds) diverso; (different) diferente
diversify [dɪvɨ́səfaɪ] VI/VT diversificar[se]
diversion [dɪvɨ́ʒən] N (entertainment) entretenimiento *m*; (distraction) distracción *f*; (military) diversión *f*; (turning aside) desvío *m*, desviación *f*
diversity [dɪvɨ́sIDi] N diversidad *f*
divert [dɪvɨ́t] VI/VT (turn aside) desviar, distraer; (distract) entretener
diverticulitis [dɪvɚtɪkjəláɪDɪs] N diverticulitis *f*
divest [dɪvést] VT (strip) despojar; (get rid of) deshacerse de
divide [dɪváɪd] VI/VT dividir[se]; (classify) clasificar[se]; N línea divisoria *f*
dividend [dívɪdɛnd] N dividendo *m*
divine [dɪváɪn] ADJ divino; VI/VT adivinar
divinity [dɪvínɪDi] N (godhead, state or quality of being divine) divinidad *f*; (theology) teología *f*
division [dɪvíʒən] N división *f*
divorce [dɪvɔ́rs] N divorcio *m*; VI/VT divorciar[se]
divot [dívət] N (golf) chuleta *f*
divulge [dɪvʌ́lʤ] VT divulgar, publicar
dizziness [dízinɪs] N mareo *m*
dizzy [dízi] ADJ (person) mareado; (height) vertigoso; (speed) vertiginoso; **— spell** vahido *m*
DJ [**disc jockey**] [díʤe] N pinchadiscos *mf sg*
Djibouti [ʤɪbúti] N Yibuti *m*
Djiboutian [jɪbúDiən] ADJ & N yibutiano -na *mf*
DNA [**deoxyribonucleic acid**] [díéné] N ADN *m*
do [du] VI/VT hacer; **to — away with** eliminar; **to — one's hair** arreglarse el pelo; **to — the dishes** lavar los platos; **to — drugs** tomar drogas; **to — in** matar; **to — time** cumplir una condena; **to — well** prosperar; **to — without** prescindir de; **we were —ing 100 kph** íbamos a cien kph; **to have nothing to — with** no tener nada que ver con; **that will — basta**; **that won't —** eso no sirve; **I'm**

—ing well estoy bien; **I did him last night** *fam* me lo tiré anoche; **this will have to —** habrá que conformarse con esto; **—-it-yourself** hágalo usted mismo; V AUX **I feel as you —** pienso igual que tú; **how — you —?** ¿cómo estás? **— you hear me?** ¿me oyes? **yes, I —** sí; **— come again** vuelve por favor; N (hairstyle) peinado *m*; (party) fiesta *f*
DOA [**dead on arrival**] [díóé] ADJ muerto -ta antes de ingresar al hospital
docile [dásəl] ADJ dócil
dock [dɑk] N (pier) muelle *m*; (for landing) desembarcadero *m*, atracadero *m*; (water between piers) dique *m*, dársena *f*; **— worker** trabajador -ora portuario -ria *mf*; **dry —** dique seco *m*; VI/VT (a boat) atracar; (a space ship) acoplar[se]; (wages) descontar
doctor [dáktɚ] N (physician) médico -ca *mf*; (PhD, scholar) doctor -ora *mf*; (expert) especialista *mf*; VT (treat) atender; (cure) curar; (restore) restaurar; (counterfeit) alterar; **I —ed up this recipe** le hice unos retoques a esta receta
doctorate [dáktɚɪt] N doctorado *m*
doctrine [dáktrɪn] N doctrina *f*
document[1] [dákjəmənt] N documento *m*
document[2] [dákjəmɛnt] VT documentar
documentary [dɑkjəméntəri] N documental *m*
documentation [dɑkjəmɪntéʃən] N documentación *f*
dodder [dáDɚ] VI (stumble along) tambalearse, titubear; (shake) temblequear
dodge [dɑʤ] VT esquivar, sortear; VI (be evasive) dar rodeos; (move sideways) apartarse, echarse a un lado; N evasiva *f*
doe [do] N cierva *f*; (female of various animals) hembra *f*
dog [dɔg] N perro *m*, perra *f*; **—catcher** perrero -ra *mf*; **— collar** collar de perro *m*; **—fight** (dogs) pelea de perros *f*; (aircraft) combate aéreo *m*; (people) reyerta *f*; **—house** casilla de perro *f*; *Sp* caseta *f*; **to be in the —house** haber caído en desgracia, estar en capilla; **— paddle** natación estilo perrito *m*; **—sled** trineo para perros *m*; **— tag** placa de identificación *f*; **—wood** cornejo *m*; **to go to the —s** venirse abajo; ADJ **—-eared** sobado, muy gastado; **—gone** maldito; VT (follow) seguir la pista de; (harass) hostigar; **to —-paddle** nadar estilo perrito
doggy [dógi] N perrito -ta *mf*; **— bag** bolsa para las sobras *f*
dogma [dógmə] N dogma *m*
dogmatic [dɔgmǽDɪk] ADJ dogmático
doily [dóɪli] N mantelito *m*
doings [dúɪŋz] N actividades *f pl*
dole [doł] N (alms) limosna *f*; **to be on the —** estar cobrando el seguro de desempleo/paro; **to — out** repartir

doleful [dólfəł] ADJ apesadumbrado, triste

doll [dɑł] N (toy) muñeco -ca *mf*; (attractive female) muñeca *f*; —**house** casa de muñecas *f*; VI **to get** —**ed up** emperifollarse, empaquetarse

dollar [dálɚ] N dólar *m*; — **diplomacy** diplomacia del dólar *f*; — **sign** signo del dólar *m*

dolly [dáli] N (doll) muñeca *f*; (cart) carretilla *f*

dolphin [dółfɪn] N (mammal) delfín *m*; (fish) dorado *m*

dolt [dołt] N zopenco -ca *mf*

domain [domén] N dominio *m*

dome [dom] N (roof) cúpula *f*, domo *m*; (head) coco *m*, pelada *f*

domestic [dəméstɪk] ADJ (appliance, pet, chore) doméstico; (devoted to homemaking) hogareño; (home-loving) casero; (of a country) interno, nacional; — **violence** violencia doméstica *f*; N doméstico -ca *mf*

domesticate [dəméstɪket] VI/VT (animals) domesticar; (plants) aclimatar

domicile [dáməsaɪł] N domicilio *m*

dominant [dámənənt] ADJ dominante

dominate [dámənet] VI/VT dominar; VI señorear

domination [dɑmənéʃən] N (act of dominating) dominación *f*; (rule) dominio *m*

domineer [dɑmənír] VI/VT dominar, mandonear

domineering [dɑmənírɪŋ] ADJ tiránico, mandón

Dominica [dəmínɪkə] N Dominica *f*

Dominican [dəmínɪkən] ADJ & N (of Dominica) dominiqués -esa *mf*; (of the Dominican Republic) dominicano -na *mf*

Dominican Republic [dəmínɪkənrɪpábłɪk] N República Dominicana *f*

dominion [dəmínjən] N dominio *m*, señorío *m*

domino [dáməno] N (game, costume) dominó *m*; (piece) ficha *f*

don [dɑn] N (title, form of address, mafia boss) don *m*; (lecturer) profesor -ora universitario -ria *mf*; VT ponerse, vestirse

donate [dónet] VI/VT donar

donation [donéʃən] N donación *f*

done [dʌn] *see* do

done [dʌn] ADJ terminado, acabado; **when you are** — cuando termines; **to be all** — **in** estar muerto de cansancio; **the meat is well** — está bien asada la carne; **that sort of thing just isn't** — eso no se hace

donkey [dáŋki] N burro *m*, asno *m*, borrico *m*

donor [dónɚ] N donante *mf*, donador -ora *mf*

doodad [dúdæd] N (trinket) chuchería *f*; (device) chisme *m*, coso *m*

doohickey [dúhɪki] N chisme *m*, coso *m*

doom [dum] N perdición *f*; —**sday** día del juicio final *m*; VT condenar; **to be** —**ed to failure** estar condenado al fracaso

door [dɔr] N puerta *f*; —**bell** timbre *m*; —**keeper** portero -ra *mf*; —**knob** pomo *m*; —**man** portero *m*; —**mat** felpudo *m*; —**step** umbral *m*; —**way** puerta *f*, portal *m*; **I showed him the** — lo eché; ADJ —**-to-** — de puerta a puerta

dopamine [dópəmin] N dopamina *f*

dope [dop] N (narcotic) droga *f*; (stimulant) estimulante *m*; (information) chismes *m pl*; (moron) *fam* zopenco; VT dopar; **to** — **oneself up** medicarse en exceso

dork [dɔrk] N *fam* idiota *mf*, tarambana *mf*

dorky [dɔrki] ADJ **that's a** — **dress** *fam* pareces una tonta con ese vestido

dormant [dɔrmənt] ADJ latente

dormitory [dɔrmɪtɔri] N residencia estudiantil *f*

DOS [**Disk Operating System**] [dɑs] N DOS *m*

dose [dos] N dosis *f*; VT dosificar

dossier [dósie] N expediente *m*

dot [dɑt] N punto *m*; (on a tie) pinta *f*; —**-com** punto com; —**matrix printer** impresora de matriz de puntos *f*; —**ted eighth note** corchea con puntillo *f*; **on the** — en punto; VT marcar con puntos

dotage [dóDɪʤ] N chochez *f*, chochera *f*; **to be in one's** — chochear, estar chocho

dote [dot] VI **to** — **on** estar chocho con

double [dʌbəł] ADJ doble; — **agent** doble agente *mf*; —**-barreled** de doble caño; — **bass** contrabajo *m*; — **bed** cama doble *f*; —**-blind test** prueba de doble incógnita *f*; — **bind** dilema *m*; — **boiler** baño de María *m*; —**-breasted** cruzado; — **chin** papada *f*; — **cross** traición *f*; — **click** doble pulsación *f*; — **dealing** duplicidad *f*; — **entry** entrada por partida doble *f*; — **fault** doble falta *f*; — **indemnity** doble indemnización *f*; — **play** doble matanza *f*; — **sided** de dos caras; — **shift** turno doble *m*; — **standard** trato discriminatorio *m*; — **vision** doble visión *f*; **to do a** — **take** quedar atónito; ADV **to sleep** — dormir de a dos; N (in baseball) doble *m*, doblete *m*; (in tennis) —**s** dobles *m pl*, juego de dobles *m*; VI/VT duplicar[se]; (an effort) redoblar[se]; (fold, be twice as old, challenge a bid) doblar[se]; **to** — **up** (bend over) doblarse; (crowd) amontonarse; **to** —**-check** verificar; **to** —**-click** pulsar dos veces; **to** —**-cross** traicionar; **to** —**-date** salir dos parejas juntas; **to** —**-talk** salirse con evasivas; **this sofa** —**s as a bed** este sofá sirve también de cama

doubt [daʊt] VI/VT dudar; (not trust) desconfiar; N duda *f*; **beyond a** — indudablemente; **in** — en duda; **no** —! ¡sin duda!

doubtful [dáʊtfəł] ADJ dudoso

doubtless [dáʊtlɪs] ADV (certainly) sin duda; (probably) probablemente

douche [duʃ] N ducha vaginal *f*; **—bag** *offensive* porquería *f*

dough [do] N pasta *f*, masa *f*; (money) pasta *f*, mosca *f*; **—nut** rosquilla *f*; *Mex* dona *f*; *Sp* donut *m*

douse [daʊs] VI/VT empapar; (a flame) apagar [con agua]

dove [dʌv] N paloma *f*

dove [dov] *see* dive

dowdy [dáʊdi] ADJ (article of clothing) pasado de moda; (person) sin gracia

dowel [dáʊəł] N clavija *f*

down [daʊn] ADV abajo; **— and dirty** sucio; **— and out** tirado; **to be — with** estar de acuerdo con; **to come — with a cold** caer con gripe, *Sp* cogerse un resfriado; **to fall —** caerse; **to get — to work** aplicarse al trabajo; **to go/come —** bajar; **to lie —** acostarse, echarse; **to put someone —** denigrar a alguien; **to turn — the volume** bajar el volumen; **to water — a drink** rebajar una bebida con agua; **to write —** anotar; **two blocks —** dos calles más abajo; **slow —!** ¡anda más despacio! **the wind died —** amainó el viento; **one — and two to go** hicimos uno y nos quedan dos por hacer; **prices are —** han bajado los precios; **the system is —** se cayó el sistema; **they're — on me** están mal conmigo; PREP **— the street** calle abajo; ADJ (depressed) abatido; N (turn for the worse) revés *m*; (feathers) plumón *m*; VT (knock, shoot) derribar; (drink quickly) despachar de un solo trago; (defeat) vencer; (football play) oportunidad *f*

downcast [dáʊnkæst] ADJ abatido, cabizbajo

downfall [dáʊnfɔł] N ruina *f*

downgrade [dáʊngred] N declive *m*, pendiente *f*; VT quitarle importancia a

downhill[1] [dáʊnhíł] ADV cuesta abajo; **his health is going —** su salud se deteriora

downhill[2] [dáʊnhił] ADJ **a — slope** una pendiente; N bajada contra-reloj *f*

download [dáʊnlod] VT descargar; N descarga *f*

down payment [dáʊnpémənt] N entrega inicial *f*, entrada *f*

downplay [dáʊnple] VT quitar la importancia a

downpour [dáʊnpɔr] N aguacero *m*

downright [dáʊnraɪt] ADJ absoluto; **— foolishness** reverenda tontería *f*; **he was — angry** echaba chispas

downshift [dáʊnʃɪft] VI rebajar [el cambio]

downside [dáʊnsaɪd] N inconveniente *m*

downsize [dáʊnsaɪz] VI (personnel) hacer reducción; VT (an object or organization) reducir el tamaño de; (one's lifestyle) simplificar *f*; **he got —d** perdió el trabajo cuando hicieron reducción de personal

downstairs[1] [dáʊnstérz] ADV abajo; (in the apartment one floor lower) en el piso de abajo

downstairs[2] [dáʊnstɛrz] ADJ de abajo; N planta baja *f*

downstream [dáʊnstrím] ADV río abajo

downtime [dáʊntaɪm] N (of a machine) tiempo de inactividad *m*; (of a person) horas de ocio *f* pl

down-to-earth [dáʊntəɣθ] ADJ sensato, práctico

downtown [dáʊntáʊn] ADV (toward) al centro; (in) en el centro; ADJ del centro, céntrico; N centro *m*

downturn [dáʊntɜn] N tendencia a la baja *f*

down under [dáʊnʌndɚ] ADV en/a Australia

downward [dáʊnwɚd] ADJ descendente; **— mobility** descenso social *m*; **—s** hacia abajo

downwind [dáʊnwínd] ADV en la dirección del viento

downy [dáʊni] ADJ sedoso, suave

dowry [dáʊri] N dote *f*

doze [doz] VI dormitar; N siesta *f*

dozen [dʌzən] N docena *f*

drab [dræb] ADJ triste; N pardo *m*

draft [dræft] N (of air) corriente *f*; (drink) trago *m*; (bank) giro *m*; (outline) esbozo *m*; (military) conscripción *f*, quinta *f*; (of a ship) calado *m*; **— beer** cerveza de barril *f*; **— horse** caballo de tiro *m*; **—sman** dibujante *m*; VT (to sketch) esbozar; (to compose) redactar; (to select for military service) conscribir

drag [dræg] VI/VT (haul slowly) arrastrar[se]; (search a body of water) dragar; **don't — me into this** no me metas en esto; **to — and-drop/release** arrastrar y soltar; **to — on and on** eternizarse; **to — out** estirar; N (dredge) draga *f*; (boring person) pesado -da *mf*; (hassle) lata *f*; (counterforce) resistencia *f*, (on a cigarette) pitada *f*; **— race** carrera de dragsters *f*; **— strip** pista de dragsters *f*; **in —** vestido de mujer

dragon [drǽgən] N dragón *m*; **—fly** libélula *f*

drain [dren] N (channel) desagüe *m*, sumidero *m*; (depletion of resources) sangría *f*, fuga *f*; **—pipe** desaguadero *m*, desagüe *m*; **to go down the —** irse por la borda; VI/VT (empty a sink) desagotar[se], desaguar[se]; (exhaust) agotar[se]; VT (wetlands) drenar, sanear; VI (a battery) descargarse

drainage [drénɪʤ] N (act of draining) desagüe *m*, drenaje *m*; (system for draining) drenaje *m*; **— pipe** tubo de desagüe *m*

drake [drek] N pato [macho] *m*

drama [drámə] N drama *m*

dramatic [drəmǽdɪk] ADJ dramático

dramatically [drəmǽdɪkli] ADV (changing) de forma fundamental, fundamentalmente; (presenting) de manera dramática/teatral

dramatist [drámətɪst] N dramaturgo -ga *mf*

dramatize [drámətaɪz] VI/VT dramatizar

drank [dræŋk] *see* drink
drape [drep] VI (hang in folds) colgar, drapear; VT (cover) cubrir; N cortina *f*
drapery [drépəri] N cortinado *m*, colgadura *f*
drastic [dræstɪk] ADJ drástico
draw [drɔ] VT (a picture) dibujar; (lines, shapes) trazar; (a cart) tirar de; (a curtain) correr; (cards, blood, water, conclusion, strength) sacar; (a crowd) atraer; (comparison, distinction) hacer; (a sword) desenvainar; VI (of a boat) tener calado; (of a fireplace) tirar; (in sports, have the same score) empatar; (receive money) cobrar; (withdraw money) retirar, sacar; **to — aside** apartar[se]; **to — away** separar[se]; **to — a breath** aspirar, tomar aliento; **to — a blank** quedarse en blanco; **to — in** involucrar; **to — lots/ straws** echar a la suerte, sortear; **to — near** acercarse; **to — off** irse, retirarse; **to — on** (be based on) basarse en; (have recourse to) recurrir a; **to — out** (remove) sacar; (prolong) alargar, prolongar; **to — up** (approach) acercar[se]; (write) redactar; (shrink) encoger; N (in sports, tie game) empate *m*; (lot) número sorteado *m*; (attraction) atracción *f*; **—back** inconveniente *m*; **—bridge** puente levadizo *m*
drawer [drɔɚ] N cajón *m*; (small) gaveta *f*; **—s** calzones *m pl*
drawing [drɔ́ɪŋ] N (picture) dibujo *m*; (raffle) sorteo *m*; **— room** sala [de recibo] *f*
drawn [drɔn] ADJ demacrado; **—-out** interminable
drawn [drɔn] *see* draw
dread [drɛd] N pavor *m*, terror *m*, espanto *m*; VT **I — going to the dentist** me aterra ir al dentista
dreadful [drédfəl] ADJ horrendo, espantoso, temible
dream [drim] N sueño *m* (also aspiration); (reverie) ensueño *m*, ensoñación *f*; (fancy) ilusión *f*; **—land** tierra del ensueño *f*; **— team** equipo de estrellas *m*; **— world** mundo de ensueño *m*; VI/VT soñar; **to — of** soñar con; **I wouldn't — of stealing** no se me ocurriría robar; **to — that** soñar que; **to — up** imaginar; ADJ **a — holiday** unas vacaciones perfectas
dreamer [drímɚ] N (impractical person) soñador -ora *mf*; (visionary) visionario -ria *mf*
dreamt [drɛmt] *see* dream
dreary [dríri] ADJ sombrío, deprimente
dredge [drɛdʒ] N draga *f*; VT (a river) dragar; (facts) desenterrar, sacar a luz
dregs [drɛgz] N heces *f pl*, poso *m*; **— of society** escoria de la sociedad *f*
drench [drɛntʃ] VT empapar, calar; **—ed in blood** bañado en sangre

dress [drɛs] N (article of clothing for women) vestido *m*; (attire) ropa *f*; (formal) traje de etiqueta *m*, ropa de etiqueta *f*; (costume) vestimenta *f*; **—maker** modista *mf*; **— rehearsal** ensayo general *m*; **— shirt** camisa para traje *f*; **what's the — code?** ¿cómo hay que ir vestido? VI/VT vestir; VT (store window) arreglar; (slaughtered animals) limpiar; (salad) aderezar; (hides) adobar; (a wound) vendar; **to — down** (scold) regañar; (wear casual clothes) ponerse ropa informal; **to — up** (wear fine clothes) vestirse de gala; (make more appealing) embellecer
dresser [drésɚ] N cómoda *f*; **she is a good —** se viste con elegancia
dressing [drésɪŋ] N (act, result) vestir *m*; (for salad) aderezo *m*; (for fowl) relleno *m*; (for wounds) gasa *f*, vendaje *m*; **—-down** regaño *m*; **— gown** bata *f*; **— room** (in a theater) camerino *m*; (in a store) probador *m*; **— table** tocador *m*
drew [dru] *see* draw
dribble [dríbəl] VI (trickle) gotear; (drool) babear; VT (a ball) driblar, regatear; (liquid) rociar; N (trickle) goteo *m*; (small quantity) chorrito *m*; (of a ball) drible *m*, regate *m*
dried [draɪd] ADJ seco; **— fig** higo paso/seco *m*; **—-up** (without water) seco; (wizened) arrugado
drift [drɪft] N (direction) deriva *f*; (current) corriente *f*; (meaning) sentido *m*, tenor *m*; (pile) montón *m*, acumulación *f*; **—wood** madera flotante *f*; **do you get my —?** ¿me captas la onda? VI (float) flotar; (be adrift) ir a la deriva; (wander) errar; **he —ed off** se durmió; VI/VT (deviate) desviar[se]; (accumulate) amontonar[se], acumular[se]
drifter [dríftɚ] N (wanderer) vagabundo -da *mf*; (of a worker) itinerante *mf*
drill [drɪl] N (tool) taladro *m*; (dental) fresa *f*; (training) ejercicios *m pl*; (procedure) procedimiento *m*; (rehearsal) simulacro *m*; (cloth) dril *m*; VI/VT (make a hole) taladrar, perforar, barrenar; (train) entrenar[se], adiestrar[se]; VI (train) hacer ejercicios; (practice) practicar; VT hacer practicar
drink [drɪŋk] VI/VT (person) beber; (animal) abrevar; (absorb, take in) absorber; **to — up** apurar el trago; **to — to someone's health** brindar por alguien; N bebida *f* (also alcoholic); (a measure of beverage) trago *m*
drinkable [dríŋkəbəl] ADJ potable
drinking [dríŋkɪŋ] ADJ **— water** agua potable *f*; **he has a — problem** tiene problemas con el alcohol
drip [drɪp] N goteo *m*; (a bore) plasta *mf*; VI gotear
drive [draɪv] VI/VT (a car) conducir, manejar; (an

animal) arrear; VI (go in a vehicle) ir en coche; VT (move forth) impulsar, impeler; (convey) llevar [en coche]; (force) forzar; (a nail) clavar; (a ball) tirar, golpear; **to — a hard bargain** regatear mucho; **to — away** ahuyentar; **to — someone mad** volver loco a alguien; **what are you driving at?** ¿qué quieres decir con eso? N (ride) paseo [en coche] *m*; (of an animal) arreo *m*; (urge) impulso *m*; (of a computer) unidad *f*; (military offensive) ofensiva *f*; (road) carretera *f*; (driveway) camino *m*; (campaign) campaña *f*; (energy) empuje *m*; (propulsion system) propulsión *f*; (of a ball) tiro *m*; (in tennis and golf) drive *m*; **—-by shooting** tiroteo desde un coche *m*; **—-in** drive-in *m*, establecimiento en que el cliente es atendido en el coche *m*; **—-in movie theater** autocine *m*; **—way** camino de entrada *m*, entrada de coches *f*; **front wheel —** tracción delantera *f*

drivel [drívəł] N (saliva) baba *f*; (idiocy) tontería *f*; VI babearse

driveling [drívəlɪŋ] ADJ baboso; **he's a — idiot** es un oligofrénico

driven [drívən] *see* drive

driver [dráɪvɚ] N (chauffeur) chofer *mf*, conductor -ra *mf*; (of animals) arriero -ra *mf*; (golf club) driver *m*; (in a computer) controlador *m*

driving [dráɪvɪŋ] ADJ **— force** impulso *m*; **— rain** lluvia torrencial *f*; **— school** autoescuela *f*

drizzle [drízəł] VI llovizar; N llovizna *f*

drone [dron] N (male bee, idler) zángano *m*; (remote-controlled vehicle) vehículo teledirigido *f*; (drudge) esclavo *m*; (sound) zumbido *m*; VI/VT (make a sound) zumbar; (talk) hablar monótonamente

drool [druł] N baba *f*; VI babearse

droop [drup] VI (sag) colgarse; (flag) languidecer; (wither) marchitarse; **his shoulders —** tiene los hombros caídos; **—ing ears** orejas gachas *f pl*

drop [drɑp] N (liquid quantity) gota *f*; (descent) caída *f*; (incline) declive *m*; (in value) baja *f*; (in prices) caída *f*; (lozenge) pastilla *f*; (of mail, etc.) buzón *m*, punto de recolección *m*; (of supplies) lanzamiento *m*; **—out** (student) desetor -ora escolar *mf*; (marginalized person) marginado -da *mf*; **— shot** dejada de volea *f*; VI caer; (let fall) dejar caer, descargar; (in golf) dropar; **to — a line** mandar unas líneas; **to — from sight** desaparecer; **to — in** caer de sorpresa; **to — out** (sports) retirarse; (school) abandonar; **why don't you — by?** ¿por qué no pasas por aquí? VI/VT (a course) abandonar; (a curtain) bajar; ADJ **—-dead beautiful** hermosísima

dropper [drápɚ] N gotero *m*

drought [draʊt] N sequía *f*

drove [drov] N tropel *m*

drove [drov] *see* drive

drown [draʊn] VI/VT ahogar[se]

drowning [dráʊnɪŋ] N ahogamiento *m*

drowse [draʊz] VI (be half-asleep) dormitar; (feel drowsy) estar amodorrado

drowsiness [dráʊzɪnɪs] N modorra *f*, somnolencia *f*

drowsy [dráʊzi] ADJ amodorrado, somnoliento; **to become —** amodorrarse

drudge [drʌdʒ] N esclavo del trabajo *m*, fregona *f*; VI trabajar como un esclavo

drug [drʌg] N (chemical substance, narcotic) droga *f*; (medicine) medicamento *m*; **—ged** drogado, endrogado; **— abuse** abuso de drogas *m*; **— addict** drogadicto -ta *mf*; **—store** (drugs) farmacia *f*; (non-drug items) droguería *f*; perfumería *f*; **— trafficker** narcotraficante *mf*; VT (stupefy with drugs) drogar; (mix with a drug) adulterar con droga

druggist [drʌ́gɪst] N farmacéutico -ca *mf*, droguero -ra *mf*

drum [drʌm] N (musical instrument) tambor *m*; (of ear) tímpano *m*; (receptacle for storing liquids) barril *m*; **—head** parche *m*; **—stick** (music) palillo de tambor *m*; (fowl) pata *f*; VI (play a drum) tocar el tambor; (beat rhythmically) tamborilear; **to — out** expulsar; **to — up** fomentar; **I'm trying to — this idea into his head** le estoy repitiendo esta idea con insistencia

drummer [drʌ́mɚ] N (classical) tambor *m*; (folk) tamborilero -ra *mf*; (rock & roll) baterista *mf*

drunk [drʌŋk] ADJ & N borracho -cha *mf; fam* mamado -da *mf*; **to get —** emborracharse

drunk [drʌŋk] *see* drink

drunkard [drʌ́ŋkɚd] N borracho -cha *mf*, borrachín -ina *mf*

drunken [drʌ́ŋkən] ADJ borracho, embriagado

drunkenness [drʌ́ŋkənnɪs] N borrachera *f*, embriaguez *f*

dry [draɪ] ADJ seco; (sober) sobrio; (topic, book) árido, aburrido; **— land** tierra firme *f*; **— cleaner** (business) tintorería *f*; (owner of business) tintorero -ra *mf*; **— cleaning** limpieza en seco *f*; **— county** condado seco *m*; **— wit** humor agudo *m*; **— goods** géneros *m pl*; **— measure** medida para áridos *f*; **— run** prueba *f*; **— ice** hielo seco *m*; **— dock** dique seco *m*, varadero *m*; VI/VT (wet clothes) secar[se]; (leather) resecar[se]; **to — up** secarse, resecarse; **to — out** desintoxicar[se]

dryer [dráɪɚ] N (hair) secador *m*; (clothes) secadora *f*

dryness [dráɪnɪs] N (skin) sequedad *f*; (land, lecture) aridez *f*

dual [dúəł] ADJ (function) doble; (ownership) compartido

dub [dʌb] VT (translate a film) doblar; (give a nickname) apodar

dubious [dúbiəs] ADJ dudoso

duchess [dʌ́tʃɪs] N duquesa f

duck [dʌk] N (bird) pato m; (downward dodge) agachada f; VI/VT (plunge under water) hundir[se]; (bend down) agachar[se]; VT (avoid) esquivar

duckling [dʌ́klɪŋ] N patito m

duct [dʌkt] N conducto m; — **tape** cinta aislante f

ductile [dʌ́ktl̩] ADJ dúctil

dud [dʌd] N (disappointing thing) chasco m; (useless person) inútil m; (unexploded bomb) bomba que no estalla f; —**s** (clothes) ropa f, fam trapos m pl; (belongings) pertenencias f pl

dude [dud] N (dandy) chulo m; (fellow) tipo m

due [du] ADJ (payable) pagadero; (immediately owed) vencido; (fitting, rightful) debido; (adequate) suficiente; — **date** fecha de vencimiento f; — **diligence** diligencia debida f; **in** — **time/course** a su debido tiempo; **the train is** — **at two o'clock** se supone que el tren llega a las dos; ADV — **east** hacia el este; N (punishment) merecido m; **give Mary her**—; **she's honest** tienes que reconocer que María es honrada; —**s** cuotas f pl

duel [dúəł] N duelo m; VI/VT batirse en/a duelo [con alguien]

duet [duét] N (played) dúo m; (sung) dueto m

dug [dʌg] see dig

dugout [dʌ́gaʊt] N (canoe) piragua f; (underground refuge) trinchera f

DUI [driving under the influence] [díjúái] N delito de conducir en estado de ebriedad m

duke [duk] N duque m; **to put up one's** —**s** levantar los puños; VT **to** — **it out** arreglarlo con los puños

dukedom [dúkdəm] N ducado m

dull [dʌl] ADJ (lackluster) opaco; (listless, muted) apagado; (boring) aburrido, soso, desanimado; (blunt) romo, desafilado; (sluggish, stupid) lento; (pain) sordo; VI/VT (a knife) desafilar[se]; (color) opacar[se]; (sound, impact) amortiguar[se]; (pain) aliviar[se]; (senses) embotar[se], entorpecer[se]

duly [dúli] ADV debidamente

dumb [dʌm] ADJ (mute) mudo; (dull) tonto; —**bell** (handweight) mancuerna f; (stupid person) bobo -ba mf; —**founded** patitieso, atónito; VT **to** — **down** simplificar demasiado

dumbness [dʌ́mnɪs] N (muteness) mudez f; (foolishness) estupidez f

dummy [dʌ́mi] N (figure) muñeco m; (fool) tonto -ta mf; offensive pendejo -ja mf; (front) hombre de paja m; ADJ (fake) falso; **a** — **president** un títere

dump [dʌmp] VT (unload) descargar; (empty)

botar; (transfer computer data) vaciar; (dismiss) echar, despedir; (discard waste) tirar la basura, descargar desechos; (flood a market) hacer dumping; (abandon) plantar; **to** — **on** (criticize) criticar; (unload problems) descargarse; N (place for waste) vertedero m, basural m, basurero m; (of weapons) depósito m; (act of discarding) vertido m; (act or effect of defecating) vulg cagada f; —**truck** camión volteador m, volquete m, Am volqueta f; **to be in the** —**s** estar deprimido, estar depre; **to take a** — vulg cagar

dumping [dʌ́mpɪŋ] N vertido m

dunce [dʌns] N burro -rra mf, tonto -ta de capirote mf

dune [dun] N duna f, médano m

dung [dʌŋ] N boñiga f, bosta f; —**hill** estercolero m

dungeon [dʌ́ndʒən] N mazmorra f

dunk [dʌŋk] VT (a donut) remojar; (a basketball) volcar, enterrar; (a person) sumergir

duodenum [duədínəm] N duodeno m

dupe [dup] N (gullible person) ingenuo -nua mf, inocente mf; Sp primo -ma mf; (manipulated person) títere m; VT embaucar

duplex [dúplɛks] N & ADJ dúplex m

duplicate[1] [dúplɪkɪt] ADJ & N duplicado m; **in** — por duplicado

duplicate[2] [dúplɪket] VT duplicar[se]

duplicity [duplísɪDi] N duplicidad f

durability [dʊrəbílɪDi] N durabilidad f

durable [dʊ́rəbəł] ADJ (long-lasting) duradero; (serviceable) sufrido

duration [dʊréʃən] N duración f

duress [dʊrés] N coacción f

during [dʊ́rɪŋ] PREP durante

dusk [dʌsk] N atardecer m, anochecer m; **at** — al atardecer

dusky [dʌ́ski] ADJ (dark) oscuro; (gloomy) sombrío

dust [dʌst] N polvo m; —**pan** pala f; **to bite the** — (die) fam espichar; (lose) morder el polvo de la derrota; **cloud of** — polvareda f; VI/VT (remove dust) quitar/sacudir el polvo [a]; VT (sprinkle with powder) espolvorear; VI (become dusty) empolvarse; **to** — **off** desempolvar

duster [dʌ́stɚ] N plumero m

dusty [dʌ́sti] ADJ polvoriento

Dutch [dʌtʃ] ADJ & N holandés -esa mf; (language) holandés m; **to go** — pagar a escote

Dutchman [dʌ́tʃmən] N holandés m

duty [dúDi] N deber m, obligación f; (tax on imports) derechos aduaneros m pl; (any tax) impuesto m; **to be on** — estar de guardia; **to be off** — no estar de guardia; ADJ —**-free** libre de impuestos

DVD [digital versatile disc] [dívidí] N DVD m

dwarf [dwɔrf] ADJ & N enano -na *mf*; VT hacer parecer pequeño

dwarfism [dwɔrfɪzəm] N enanismo *m*

dwell [dwɛl] VI morar, habitar; **to — on a subject** dilatarse en un asunto

dweller [dwɛlɚ] N habitante *mf*, morador -ora *mf*

dwelling [dwɛlɪŋ] N vivienda *f*, domicilio *m*

dwelt [dwɛlt] *see* dwell

DWI [**driving while intoxicated**] [dídʌ́bəljuáɪ] N delito de conducir en estado de ebriedad *m*

dwindle [dwíndḷ] VI/VT menguar, mermar

dye [daɪ] N tinte *m*, tintura *f*; VT teñir

dying [dáɪɪŋ] ADJ moribundo

dyke [daɪk] N *offensive* tortillera *f*

dynamic [daɪnǽmɪk] ADJ dinámico; N dinámica *f*

dynamite [dáɪnəmaɪt] N dinamita *f*; VT dinamitar; ADJ fabuloso

dynamo [dáɪnəmo] N dínamo *m*

dynasty [dáɪnəsti] N dinastía *f*

dysentery [dísənteri] N disentería *f*

dysfunction [dɪsfʌ́ŋkʃən] N disfunción *f*

dyslexia [dɪsléksiə] N dislexia *f*

Ee

each [itʃ] ADJ cada; **— person** cada persona; PRON cada uno; **— receives a prize** cada uno recibe un premio; **they looked at — other** se miraron el uno al otro

eager [ígɚ] ADJ (enthusiastic) ansioso; (avid) ávido

eagerness [ígɚnɪs] N (enthusiasm) ansia *f*, afán *m*; (strong desire) avidez *f*

eagle [ígəl] N águila *f*; **—-eye** ojo de lince *m*

eaglet [íglɪt] N aguilucho *m*

ear [ir] N (outer organ) oreja *f*; (inner organ, sense of hearing, musical aptitude) oído *m*; (of corn) mazorca *f*; *Am* elote *m*; **—ache** dolor de oídos *m*; **—drops** gotas para los oídos *f pl*; **—drum** tímpano *m*; **—lobe** lóbulo de la oreja *m*; **— muff** orejera *f*; **—phone** audífono *m*, auricular *m*; **—plug** tapón del oído *m*; **—ring** pendiente *m*, zarcillo *m*, arete *m*; **by —** de oído; **within —shot** al alcance del oído; **he has the — of the governor** el gobernador le presta mucha atención; VT **to —mark** asignar

earful [írfʊl] N **I got an —** (scolding) me echó un rapapolvo; (gossip) me dio la lata

early [ɚ́li] ADJ temprano; **— detection** diagnóstico precoz *m*; **— man** hombre primitivo *m*; **— retirement** jubilación anticipada *f*; **— riser/bird** madrugador -ora

mf, mañanero -ra *mf*; **the — bird gets the worm** al que madruga, Dios lo ayuda

earn [ɚn] VI/VT (money, admiration, etc.) ganar; (salary) cobrar, ganar; (interest) devengar; **—ed run** carrera limpia *f*; **—ed run average** promedio de carreras limpias permitidas *m*; **to — a living** ganarse la vida

earnest [ɚ́nɪst] ADJ (sincere) serio, formal; (grave) grave; **in —** en serio; **— money** señal *f*; *Mex* enganche *m*

earnestness [ɚ́nɪstnɪs] N (sincerity) seriedad *f*, formalidad *f*; (gravity) gravedad *f*; **in all —** con toda sinceridad

earnings [ɚ́nɪŋz] N (of a person) ingresos *m pl*; (of a business) ganancias *f pl*

earth [ɚθ] N tierra *f*; **—mover** excavadora *f*; **—quake** terremoto *m*, temblor de tierra *m*; **—worm** lombriz *f*; **the —** la Tierra; ADJ **—shaking** revolucionario

earthen [ɚ́θən] ADJ (wall) de tierra; (pot) de barro; **—ware** vajilla de barro *f*, cerámica *f*

earthly [ɚ́θli] ADJ terrenal; **— possessions** bienes terrenales *m pl*; **to be of no — use** no servir para nada

earthy [ɚ́θi] ADJ natural; (person) campechano; (sense of humor, joke) basto; **— smell** olor a tierra *m*

ease [iz] N (facility) facilidad *f*; (unaffectedness) soltura *f*, desparpajo *m*; (comfort) comodidad *f*; (lack of worry) tranquilidad *f*; (fullness of a garment) holgura *f*; **at —** (military) en descanso; (comfortable) tranquilo, a gusto; **a life of —** una vida desahogada; **ill at —** incómodo; VT (make easier) facilitar; VI/VT (relieve pain) aliviar[se]; (release from tension) aflojar[se]; (relieve anxiety) tranquilizar[se]; **to — up** aflojar

easel [ízəl] N caballete *m*

east [ist] N este *m*, oriente *m*; ADJ del este, oriental; ADV **— of here** al este [de aquí]; **to go —** ir al / hacia el este; **back —** en el este

Easter [ístɚ] N Pascua *f*; **— egg** huevo de Pascua *m*; **— Sunday** Domingo de Pascua *m*

eastern [ístən] ADJ oriental, del este

eastward [ístwəd] ADV & ADJ hacia el este

easy [ízi] ADJ (simple) fácil, sencillo; (compliant) fácil; (comfortable) cómodo; (informal) desenvuelto; (unworried) tranquilo; **— chair** poltrona *f*; **—-going** calmoso; **— terms** facilidades de pago *f pl*; **— does it** despacito; **take it —** cálmate; **he's on — street** vive en la abundancia; **within — reach** al alcance de la mano; ADV **go — on me** sea bueno

eat [it] VI/VT comer[se]; VT (costs) absorber; **to — away** corroer, comer; **to — breakfast** desayunar[se]; **to — dinner** (midday) comer; (evening) cenar; **to — lunch** comer, almorzar; **to — one's heart out** morirse de envidia; **to — one's words** tragarse las palabras; **to— supper** cenar; **to— up** comerse todo; **what's —ing you?** ¿qué bicho te picó?

eaten [ítṇ] *see* eat

eating [íDɪŋ] N (act) comer *m*; (food) comida *f*; — **disorder** trastorno de la alimentación *m*; — **utensils** cubiertos *m pl*; — **apples** manzanas para comer *f pl*

eaves [ivz] N PL alero *m*; **to —drop** escuchar furtivamente

e-banking [íbæŋkɪŋ] N banca electrónica *f*

ebb [ɛb] N (flowing back) reflujo *m*; (decay) decadencia *f*; — **tide** reflujo *m*; **to be at a low** — estar en un punto bajo; VI (tide) bajar; (energy) decaer

ebony [ébəni] N ébano *m*

e-book [íbʊk] N libro electrónico *m*

e-business [íbɪznɪs] N comercio electrónico *m*

eccentric [ɛkséntrɪk] ADJ & N excéntrico -ca *mf*

ecclesiastic [ɪklizíæstɪk] ADJ & N eclesiástico *m*

echelon [éʃəlɑn] N (military formation) escalón *m*; (rank) nivel *m*, estrato *m*

echo [ɛ́ko] N eco *m*; VI hacer eco; **the gym —ed with laughter** el gimnasio resonó de risas; VT repetir

echocardiogram [ɛkokárDiəgræm] N ecocardiograma *m*

eclectic [ɪkléktɪk] ADJ ecléctico

eclipse [ɪklíps] N eclipse *m*; VT eclipsar

eco-friendly [ikofréndli] ADJ ecológico

ecological [ikəláʤɪkəɫ] ADJ ecológico

ecology [ɪkáɫəʤi] N ecología *f*

e-commerce [íkámɚs] N comercio electrónico *m*

economic [ɛkənámɪk] ADJ económico; N —**s** economía *f*

economical [ɛkənámɪkəɫ] ADJ económico

economist [ɪkánəmɪst] N economista *mf*

economize [ɪkánəmaɪz] VI economizar

economy [ɪkánəmi] N economía *f* (also thrift); ADJ — **car** coche económico *m*; — **class** clase turista *f*

ecosystem [íkosɪstəm] N ecosistema *m*

ecstasy [ɛ́kstəsi] N éxtasis *m* (also drug)

Ecuador [ɛ́kwədɔr] N Ecuador *m*

Ecuadorian [ɛkwədɔ́riən] ADJ & N ecuatoriano -na *mf*

ecumenical [ɛkjəménɪkəɫ] ADJ ecuménico

eczema [ɛ́gzəmə] N eccema *m*

eddy [éDi] N remolino *m*; VI arremolinarse

edge [ɛʤ] N borde *m*, canto *m*; (of a knife) filo *m*; (of a block) arista *f*; **to be on** — estar nervioso; **her voice has an — to it** tiene la voz penetrante; **a competitive** — una ventaja sobre la competencia; VT (make an edge) hacerle el borde; (sharpen) afilar; (move sideways) meterse de costado; **to — out** ganar por un pelito; **to — up** aproximarse; ADV —**wise** de costado

edgy [éʤi] ADJ nervioso

edible [éDəbəɫ] ADJ & N comestible *m*

edict [íDɪkt] N edicto *m*, bando *m*

edifice [éDəfɪs] N edificio *m*

edify [éDəfaɪ] VT edificar

edit [éDɪt] VT (revise, correct) corregir; (serve as editor) editar; (revise a film) montar; **to — out** eliminar; N corrección *f*

edition [ɪdíʃən] N edición *f*

editor [éDɪtɚ] N (director of a publication) redactor -ora *mf*; (compiler, radio or film worker) editor -ora *mf*; (proofreader) corrector -ora *mf*

editorial [ɛDɪtɔ́riəɫ] ADJ editorial; N editorial *f*

editorialize [ɛDɪtɔ́riəlaɪz] VI editorializar

educate [éʤəket] VT educar

education [ɛʤəkéʃən] N educación *f*, enseñanza *f*; (academic subject) pedagogía *f*; **school of** — escuela normal *f*

educational [ɛʤəkéʃənɫ] ADJ educativo

educator [éʤəkeDɚ] N educador -ora *mf*

EEG [electroencephalogram] [íiʤí] N electroencefalograma *m*

eel [iɫ] N anguila *f*

eerie [íri] ADJ misterioso

effect [ɪfékt] N efecto *m*; **to go into** — entrar en vigencia, ponerse en operación; **in** — vigente, operativo; **I wrote a letter to that** — escribí una carta en ese sentido; **personal** —**s** efectos personales *m pl*; VT efectuar

effective [ɪféktɪv] ADJ efectivo, eficaz; (a law) vigente; — **date** fecha de vigencia *f*

effectively [ɪféktɪvli] ADV (well) eficazmente; (in fact) de hecho, en efecto

effectiveness [ɪféktɪvnɪs] N efectividad *f*, eficacia *f*

effectual [ɪféktʃuəɫ] ADJ eficaz

effeminate [ɪfémənɪt] ADJ afeminado

efficacy [éfɪkəsi] N eficacia *f*

efficiency [ɪfíʃənsi] N eficiencia *f*; — **apartment** estudio *m*

efficient [ɪfíʃənt] ADJ eficiente; (motor) económico

effigy [éfəʤi] N efigie *f*; **to burn in** — quemar en efigie

effort [éfɚt] N (exertion) esfuerzo *m*; (work of art) obra *f*; (campaign) campaña *f*

effrontery [ɪfrántəri] N descaro *m*

effusive [ɪfjúsɪv] ADJ efusivo

egg [ɛg] N huevo *m*; (female gamete) óvulo *m*; (fellow) tipo *m*; —**beater** batidor de huevos *m*; —**head** empollón -na *mf*; —**nog** rompopo *m*, rompope *m*, ponche de huevo *m*; —**plant** berenjena *f*; —**shell** cáscara de huevo *f*; — **white** clara de huevo *f*; — **yolk** yema de huevo *f*; **to have — on one's face** estar avergonzado, quedar mal; **to lay an —** (of a hen) poner un huevo; (fail) fracasar; **to walk on —shells** ir pisando huevos; ADJ —**shaped** ovoide; VT **to — on** incitar

ego [ígo] N (self) yo *m*, ego *m*; (vanity) ego *m*; (self-esteem) amor propio *m*; **winning the prize was an — trip for him** ganar el premio le aceitó el ego
egocentric [igoséntrɪk] ADJ egocéntrico
egotism [ígətɪzəm] N egotismo *m*
Egypt [ídʒɪpt] N Egipto *m*
Egyptian [ɪdʒípʃən] ADJ & N egipcio -cia *mf*
eight [et] NUM ocho; **— hundred** ochocientos
eighteen [ettín] NUM dieciocho
eighth [etθ] ADJ, N & ADV octavo *m*; **— note** corchea *f*
eighty [éɒi] NUM ochenta
either [íðɚ] ADJ & PRON **— will do** cualquiera de los dos está bien; **choose — suit** elige uno de los dos trajes; **choose —** elige uno [u otro] de los dos; **there were flowers on — side of the road** había flores a ambos lados de la carretera; ADV **if you don't, I won't —** si tú no lo haces, yo tampoco; **I'll go — by bus or by car** voy [o] en autobús o en auto
ejaculate [ɪdʒækjəlet] VI/VT eyacular; (exclaim) exclamar
eject [ɪdʒékt] VT (throw out) echar, expulsar; VI/VT (throw from a plane) eyectar[se]
ejection [ɪdʒékʃən] N expulsión *f*
EKG [electrocardiogam] [íkédʒí] N electrocardiograma *m*
elaborate¹ [ɪlǽbɚɪt] ADJ (ornate) elaborado; (detailed) detallado
elaborate² [ɪlǽbəret] VI/VT (create) elaborar; (develop) desarrollar
elapse [ɪlǽps] VI transcurrir, pasar
elastic [ɪlǽstɪk] ADJ elástico; N elástico *m*; (rubber band) goma elástica *f*
elasticity [ɪlæstísɪɒi] N elasticidad *f*
elated [ɪléɒɪd] ADJ eufórico
elbow [éɫbo] N codo *m*; VI/VT codear, dar codazos; **to — one's way through** abrirse paso a codazos
elder [éɫdɚ] ADJ (older) mayor; N (older person) mayor *mf*; (old person) anciano -na *mf*; (in a church) miembro del consejo de una iglesia *m*; **our —s** nuestros mayores *m pl*
elderly [éɫdɚli] ADJ anciano
e-learning [ílɚnɪŋ] N educación en línea *f*
elect [ɪlékt] ADJ (elected) electo; (chosen by God) elegido; VI/VT elegir
election [ɪlékʃən] N elección *f*
elector [ɪléktɚ] N elector -ora *mf*
electoral [ɪléktɚəɫ] ADJ electoral
electric [ɪléktrɪk] ADJ eléctrico; (exciting) electrizante; (excited) electrizado; **— chair** silla eléctrica *f*; **— eel** anguila eléctrica *f*; **— eye** célula fotoeléctrica *f*; **— meter** contador eléctrico *m*; **— storm** tormenta eléctrica *f*
electrical [ɪléktrɪkəɫ] ADJ eléctrico; **— engineer** ingeniero -ra electricista *mf*; **— engineering** ingeniería eléctrica *f*; **— tape** cinta aislante *f*

electrician [ɪlɛktríʃən] N electricista *mf*
electricity [ɪlɛktrísɪɒi] N electricidad *f*
electrify [ɪléktrəfaɪ] VT (apply electricity) electrificar; (thrill) electrizar
electrocardiogram [ɪlɛktrokárɒiəgræm] N electrocardiograma *m*
electrocute [ɪléktrəkjut] VT electrocutar
electrode [ɪléktrod] N electrodo *m*
electroencephalogram [ɪlɛktroɛnséfələgræm] N electroencefalograma *m*
electrolysis [ɪlɛktrálɪsɪs] N electrólisis *f*
electromagnet [ɪlɛktromǽgnɪt] N electroimán *m*
electromagnetic [ɪlɛktromægnéɒɪk] ADJ electromagnético
electron [ɪléktrɑn] N electrón *m*; **— microscope** microscopio electrónico *m*
electronic [ɪlɛktránɪk] ADJ electrónico; **— banking** banca electrónica *f*; **— mail** correo electrónico *m*; **—s** electrónica *f*; **— signature** firma electrónica *f*
elegance [élɪgəns] N elegancia *f*, gallardía *f*
elegant [élɪgənt] ADJ elegante, gallardo; (gift) de lujo
element [éləmənt] N elemento *m*; (component part) componente *m*, pieza *f*; (for heating) resistencia *f*; **the —s** los elementos
elemental [ɛləméntl] ADJ elemental; **— forces** fuerzas de la naturaleza *f pl*
elementary [ɛləméntri] ADJ elemental; **— school** escuela primaria *f*
elephant [éləfənt] N elefante -ta *mf*
elevate [éləvet] VT elevar
elevation [ɛləvéʃən] N (action of elevating, elevated place) elevación *f*; (altitude) altura *f*
elevator [éləveɒɚ] N ascensor *m*; *Am* elevador *m*; (for grain) elevador *m*
eleven [ɪlévən] NUM once
elf [ɛlf] N elfo *m*; (mischievous person) pillo -lla *mf*
elicit [ɪlísɪt] VT provocar; **to — admiration** despertar admiración
eligibility [ɛlɪdʒəbílɪɒi] N elegibilidad *f*
eligible [élɪdʒəbəɫ] ADJ elegible; **an — bachelor** un buen partido; **you are — for a scholarship** tienes derecho a solicitar una beca
eliminate [ɪlímənet] VT eliminar
elimination [ɪlɪmənéʃən] N eliminación *f*
elite [ɪlít] N elite *f*, élite *f*
elitist [ɪlíɒɪst] ADJ & N elitista *mf*
elk [ɛlk] N alce *m*
elliptical [ɪlíptɪkəɫ] ADJ elíptico
elm [ɛlm] N olmo *m*
elongate [ɪlɔ́ŋget] VI/VT alargar[se]
elope [ɪlóp] VI fugarse para casarse a escondidas
eloquence [éləkwəns] N elocuencia *f*
eloquent [éləkwənt] ADJ elocuente
El Salvador [ɛɫsǽɫvədɔr] N El Salvador *m*

else [ɛls] ADJ & ADV **who — was there?** ¿quién más estaba? **someone —'s son** el hijo de otro; **somebody —** [algún] otro; **or —** si no; **leave town or —** vete del pueblo o sufre las consecuencias / o verás lo que es bueno; **nobody —** nadie más; **nothing —** nada más; **how —?** ¿de qué otra forma? ADV **—where** (location) en otra parte / en otro lado; (movement) a otra parte / a otro sitio

elucidate [ɪlúsɪdet] VI/VT elucidar, dilucidar, esclarecer

elucidation [ɪlusɪdéʃən] N elucidación f, dilucidación f

elude [ɪlúd] VT eludir

elusive [ɪlúsɪv] ADJ (slippery) escurridizo; (evasive) esquivo; (difficult to understand) difícil de entender

emaciated [ɪméʃieDɪd] ADJ escuálido, descarnado

e-mail [ímeł] N correo electrónico m; — **address** dirección de correo electrónico f

emanate [émənet] VI/VT emanar

emanation [emənéʃən] N emanación f

emancipate [ɪmǽnsəpet] VT emancipar

emancipation [ɪmǽnsəpéʃən] N emancipación f

emasculate [ɪmǽskjəlet] VT castrar; (remove testicles) castrar, emascular

embalm [ɪmbám] VT (the body of a deceased person) preparar; (a mummy) embalsamar

embalming [ɪmbámɪŋ] N preparación del cuerpo f

embankment [ɪmbǽŋkmənt] N terraplén m

embargo [ɪmbárgo] N embargo m; VT imponer un embargo a/contra

embark [ɪmbárk] VI/VT embarcar[se]

embarrass [ɪmbǽrəs] VT (cause shame) hacerle pasar vergüenza a; (cause discomfit, financial difficulties) poner en aprietos; **—ed** avergonzado, en aprietos; **I'm —ed about my teeth** me dan vergüenza mis dientes; **I'm —ed to tell you** me da vergüenza decírtelo

embarrassing [ɪmbǽrəsɪŋ] ADJ (shameful) vergonzoso, penoso; (hindering) embarazoso

embarrassment [ɪmbǽrəsmənt] N (shame) vergüenza f, bochorno m, pena f; (act of embarrassing) vergüenza f; (financial difficulty) aprieto m; **he's an — to the company** hace quedar mal a la compañía; **we have an — of riches** nadamos en la abundancia

embassy [émbəsi] N embajada f

embattled [ɪmbǽdld̩] ADJ hostigado, agobiado

embed [ɪmbéd] VT incrustar

embedded [ɪmbéDɪd] ADJ incrustado

embellish [ɪmbélɪʃ] VT adornar, ornamentar

ember [émbɚ] N ascua f, brasa f

embezzle [ɪmbézəł] VT desfalcar, malversar

embezzlement [ɪmbézəłmənt] N desfalco m,

peculado m, malversación f

embitter [ɪmbíDɚ] VT amargar

emblem [émbləm] N emblema m, divisa f

embody [ɪmbáDi] VT (personify) personificar; (to provide with a body) encarnar

embolism [émbəlɪzəm] N embolia f

embrace [ɪmbrés] VI/VT (hug, adopt) abrazar[se]; (include) abarcar; N abrazo m

embroider [ɪmbrɔ́ɪDɚ] VI/VT bordar, recamar

embroidery [ɪmbrɔ́ɪDəri] N bordado m

embroil [ɪmbrɔ́ɪł] VT (involve in a conflict) meter en un lío; (throw into confusion) embrollar

embryo [émbrio] N embrión m

embryonic [embriánɪk] ADJ embriónico, embrionario

emerald [émɚəłd] N esmeralda f

emerge [ɪmɝ́ʤ] VI (come into view) emerger; (arise, as a question, problem) surgir

emergency [ɪmɝ́ʤənsi] N emergencia f; — **brake** freno de emergencia m; — **exit** salida de emergencia f; — **room** urgencias f pl

emergent [ɪmɝ́ʤənt] ADJ emergente

emerging [ɪmɝ́ʤɪŋ] ADJ emergente

emigrant [émɪgrənt] ADJ & N emigrante mf

emigrate [émɪgret] VI emigrar

emigration [emɪgréʃən] N emigración f

eminence [émənəns] N eminencia f

eminent [émənənt] ADJ eminente

emissary [émɪseri] N emisario -ria mf

emission [ɪmíʃən] N emisión f

emit [ɪmít] VT (light, sound) emitir; (smells) despedir; (sparks) echar

emoticon [ɪmóDɪkɑn] N emoticón m, emoticono m

emotion [ɪmóʃən] N emoción f

emotional [ɪmóʃən̩l] ADJ (of the emotions) emocional; (arousing or expressing emotions) emotivo; (easily moved) sensible

empathy [émpəθi] N empatía f

emperor [émpərɚ] N emperador m; — **penguin** pingüino emperador m

emphasis [émfəsɪs] N énfasis m, hincapié m

emphasize [émfəsaɪz] VT enfatizar, hacer hincapié en, subrayar

emphatic [ɪmfǽDɪk] ADJ enfático

emphysema [emfɪsímə] N enfisema m

empire [émpaɪr] N imperio m

empirical [empírɪkəł] ADJ empírico

employ [ɪmplɔ́ɪ] VT emplear; (hire) emplear, ocupar; N empleo m; **to be in someone's —** trabajar a las órdenes de alguien

employee [ɪmplɔɪí] N empleado -da mf

employer [ɪmplɔ́ɪɚ] N patrón -na mf; **—s'** patronal

employment [ɪmplɔ́ɪmənt] N empleo m; (occupation) ocupación f; — **bureau** agencia de empleo f; — **opportunities** oportunidades laborales f pl; **place of —**

lugar de trabajo *m*

empower [ɪmpáʊɚ] VT (authorize) autorizar; (give strength) potenciar

empress [émprɪs] N emperatriz *f*

emptiness [émptɪnɪs] N vacío *m*

empty [émpti] ADJ (devoid of content) vacío; (devoid of activity) desocupado; —**-handed** con las manos vacías; VI/VT vaciar[se], volcar[se]; (flow into) desembocar; N **to run on** — (of a car, person) quedarse sin combustible

emulate [émjəlet] VT emular (also computer term)

enable [ɪnébəl] VT permitir

enact [ɪnǽkt] VT (a law) promulgar; (a role) desempeñar

enamel [ɪnǽməl] N esmalte *m*; VT esmaltar

enamor [ɪnǽmɚ] VT enamorar; **to be —ed of** estar enamorado de

encamp [ɪnkǽmp] VI acampar

encephalitis [ɪnsefəláɪdɪs] N encefalitis *f*

enchant [ɪntʃǽnt] VT (bewitch) hechizar; (delight) encantar

enchanting [ɪntʃǽntɪŋ] ADJ encantador

enchantment [ɪntʃǽntmənt] N encantamiento *m*, encanto *m*, hechicería *f*

encircle [ɪnsɚ́kəl] VT cercar, ceñir

enclave [ánklev] N enclave *m*

enclose [ɪnklóz] VT (confine someone or something) encerrar; (fence in) cercar; (put in the same envelope) adjuntar, anexar

enclosure [ɪnklóʒɚ] N (wall or fence) cerca *f*; (enclosed area) cercado *m*, recinto *m*; (enclosed document) documento adjunto *m*; (act of enclosing) encierro *m*

encode [ɪŋkód] VT codificar

encoding [ɪŋkódɪŋ] N codificación *f*

encompass [ɪnkámpəs] VT (include) abarcar, englobar; (surround) circundar

encore [ánkɔr] N bis *m*; INTERJ ¡otra!

encounter [ɪnkáʊntɚ] VI/VT encontrar[se]; **they —ed the enemy army** se enfrentaron con el ejército enemigo; N (meeting, athletic event) encuentro *m*; (battle) enfrentamiento *m*

encourage [ɪnkɚ́ɪdʒ] VT (inspire with confidence) alentar, animar; (promote) fomentar, estimular

encouragement [ɪnkɚ́ɪdʒmənt] N (inspiration) aliento *m*, ánimo *m*; (promotion) estímulo *m*, fomento *m*

encouraging [ɪŋkɚ́ədʒɪŋ] ADJ alentador

encroach [ɪnkrótʃ] VT **to — upon** (liberties) cercenar; (territory) usurpar; (time) quitar

encrypt [ɪnkrípt] VT codificar, cifrar

encryption [ɪŋkrípʃən] N cifrado *m*

encumber [ɪnkámbɚ] VT (block) impedir; (burden) agobiar; (charge an account) gravar

encumbrance [ɪŋkámbrəns] N gravamen *m*

encyclopedia [ɪnsaɪkləpídiə] N enciclopedia *f*

end [ɛnd] N (temporal) fin *m*, término *m*; (limit, boundary) final *m*, extremo *m*; (tip) cabo *m*; (aim) fin *m*; (in football) exterior *m*; — **key** tecla [de] fin *f*; —**-of-life care** cuidado terminal *m*; — **table** mesa pequeña *f*; — **zone** zona de ensayo *f*, zona de anotación *f*; **at the** — **of the movie** al final de la película; **the north** — **of town** el barrio norte; **no** — **of things** un sinfín de cosas; **at the** — **of the day** al fin y al cabo; **on** — de punta; **for days on** — día tras día; **to put an** — **to** poner fin a; VI/VT terminar; (a street) morir; **he** —**ed his life** puso fin a su vida; **a prayer** —**s the class** la clase termina con una oración; **a war to** — **all wars** una guerra que supera a todas las anteriores; ADV — **to** — uno tras otro

endanger [ɪndéndʒɚ] VT poner en peligro; —**ed species** especie en peligro de extinción *f*

endear [ɪndír] VI **to** — **oneself** congraciarse; **his humor** —**ed him to her** se ganó la simpatía de ella gracias a su humor

endearing [ɪndírɪŋ] ADJ entrañable

endeavor [ɪndévɚ] VT (try) tratar de, intentar, procurar; VI (strive) esforzarse por; N esfuerzo *m*

endemic [ɪndémɪk] ADJ endémico

ending [éndɪŋ] N final *m*; (of a story) desenlace *m*; (derivational, inflectional) terminación *f*; (inflectional) desinencia *f*

endless [éndlɪs] ADJ (having no end) interminable; (continuous) sin fin; (infinite) eterno

endocrine [éndəkrɪn] ADJ endocrino

endocrinology [endəkrɪnálədʒi] N endocrinología *f*

endoderm [éndodɚm] N endodermo *m*

endorphin [ɪndɔ́rfɪn] N endorfina *f*

endorse [ɪndɔ́rs] VT (sign a check) endosar; (support) respaldar; (authorize a document) refrendar, visar

endorsement [ɪndɔ́rsmənt] N (signature) endoso *m*; (backing) respaldo *m*; (authorization) refrendo *m*

endorser [ɪndɔ́rsɚ] N (check signer) endosante *mf*; (supporter) partidario -ria *mf*; (authorizer) refrendario -ria *mf*

endow [ɪndáʊ] VT (grant funds) hacer un legado; (furnish powers) dotar

endowment [ɪndáʊmənt] N (funds granted) legado *m*, dotación *f*; (power) dote *f*; — **annuity** anualidad dotal *f*; — **fund** fondo de un legado *m*

endurance [ɪndúrəns] N (stamina) resistencia *f*; (ability to bear pain) aguante *m*

endure [ɪndúr, ɪndjúr] VT (undergo) sobrellevar, soportar, pasar; VI (live on) durar; (bear up) aguantar

enema [énəmə] N enema *m*, lavativa *f*

enemy [ɛ́nəmi] N enemigo -ga *mf*
energetic [ɛnəʤɛ́DIk] ADJ enérgico
energy [ɛ́nəʤi] N energía *f*; — **policy** política energética *f*
enervate [ɛ́nəvet] VT enervar, debilitar
enforce [ɪnfɔ́rs] VT hacer cumplir
enforcement [ɪnfɔ́rsmənt] N **the sheriff is responsible for the** — **of the law** el alguacil es responsable de hacer cumplir la ley
engage [ɪngéʤ] VT (hire) contratar; (attract) captar, atraer; (interlock) engranar; **to** — **the brake** poner el freno; **to** — **someone in conversation** trabar conversación con alguien; **to** — **in battle** trabar batalla; **to be** —**d in something** estar ocupado en algo; **to be** —**d to be married** estar comprometido [para casarse], estar prometido
engaged [ɪngéʤd] ADJ comprometido
engagement [ɪngéʤmənt] N (commitment) compromiso *m*; (betrothal) compromiso *m*, noviazgo *m*; (employment) empleo *m*; (battle) batalla *f*; (gear interlocking) engranaje *m*
engender [ɪnʤɛ́ndə] VT engendrar
engine [ɛ́nʤɪn] N (machine) máquina *f*; (in a vehicle) motor *m*; (locomotive) locomotora *f*; — **block** bloque del motor *m*
engineer [ɛnʤənír] N ingeniero -ra *mf*; (of locomotive) maquinista *mf*; VT (create) idear; (plot) maquinar
engineering [ɛnʤəníriŋ] N ingeniería *f*
English [íŋglɪʃ] ADJ inglés; N (spin) efecto *m*; **the** — los ingleses; —**man,** —**woman** inglés -esa *mf*
engrave [ɪngrév] VI/VT grabar
engraver [ɪngrévə] N grabador -ora *mf*
engraving [ɪngréviŋ] N grabado *m*
engross [ɪngrós] VT absorber
engrossed [ɪngróst] ADJ absorto
engulf [ɪngʌ́lf] VT (swallow) tragar; (overwhelm) abrumar
enhance [ɪnhǽns] VT (intensify) realzar; (improve) mejorar
enigma [ɪnígmə] N enigma *m*
enjoin [ɪnʤɔ́ɪn] VT instar; **to** — **from** prohibir
enjoy [ɪnʤɔ́ɪ] VI/VT (take pleasure) disfrutar [de], gozar [de]; (benefit from) gozar [de]; —! ¡que lo disfrutes! **to** — **oneself** divertirse; **to** — **the use of** usufructuar
enjoyable [ɪnʤɔ́ɪəbəl] ADJ (pleasant) agradable, gozoso; (fun) ameno
enjoyment [ɪnʤɔ́ɪmənt] N (act of enjoying) goce *m*, disfrute *m*; (right of use) usufructo *m*; (pleasure) placer *m*, gozo *m*
enlarge [ɪnlárʤ] VI/VT agrandar[se]; VT (blow up a photo) ampliar; VI **to** — **upon** explayarse sobre, extenderse sobre
enlargement [ɪnlárʤmənt] N (photo, building) ampliación *f*; (act of enlarging) agrandamiento *m*; (temporary swelling)

dilatación *f*
enlighten [ɪnláItn̩] VT (morally) iluminar; (intellectually) explicar, ilustrar
enlightenment [ɪnláItn̩mənt] N (moral) iluminación *f*; (intellectual) explicación *f*; **the** — la Ilustración
enlist [ɪnlíst] VI/VT (for the army) alistar[se]; (for a campaign) conseguir el apoyo de
enlistment [ɪnlístmənt] N alistamiento *m*
enliven [ɪnláɪvən] VT animar, avivar
enmity [ɛ́nmɪDi] N enemistad *f*
ennoble [ɪnnóbəl] VT ennoblecer
enormous [ɪnɔ́rməs] ADJ enorme, descomunal
enough [ɪnʌ́f] ADJ suficiente; ADV **he's tall** — tiene altura suficiente; N lo suficiente; **we have** — **to live comfortably** tenemos lo suficiente como para vivir cómodamente; **that is** — con eso basta; **more than** — bastante; INTERJ ¡basta!
enrage [ɪnréʤ] VT enfurecer
enrapture [ɪnrǽptʃə] VT embelesar
enrich [ɪnrítʃ] VT enriquecer
enrichment [ɪnrítʃmənt] N enriquecimiento *m*
enroll [ɪnró̵l] VI/VT matricular[se], inscribir[se]
enrollment [ɪnró̵lmənt] N matrícula *f*, inscripción *f*; **what is your** —? ¿cuántos alumnos tienes matriculados?
ensemble [ɑnsámbəl] N conjunto *m*
ensign [ɛ́nsɪn] N (naval rank) alférez de fragata *mf*; (flag) enseña *f*; (badge) insignia *f*
enslave [ɪnslév] VT esclavizar
ensnare [ɪnsnér] VT atrapar, coger en una trampa
ensue [ɪnsú] VI (follow) ocurrir después, suceder; (result from) resultar; **the ensuing events** los sucesos subsiguientes
ensure [ɪnʃúr] VT asegurar
entail [ɪntél] VT implicar, conllevar
entangle [ɪntǽŋgəl] VT enredar
enter [ɛ́ntə] VT (go in) entrar en/a; (join) ingresar en/a; (write) escribir; (put data in a computer) dar entrada a; (put data in account books) asentar; (start negotiations) iniciar; VI/VT (register for a competition) inscribir[se]; VI salir / entrar a escena; **to** — **into** (make an agreement) concertar; (form part of) figurar en
enterprise [ɛ́ntəpraɪz] N empresa *f*
enterprising [ɛ́ntəpraɪzɪŋ] ADJ emprendedor
entertain [ɛntətén] VI/VT (amuse) divertir, recrear; (host) invitar; **we** — **a lot** tenemos invitados muy a menudo; (consider) contemplar; (harbor) abrigar
entertainer [ɛntəténə] N artista *mf*
entertaining [ɛntəténɪŋ] ADJ (fun) divertido; (serving as pastime) entretenido; (pleasant) ameno
entertainment [ɛntəténmənt] N (source of fun) diversión *f*; (pastime) entretenimiento *m*; (of

guests) agasajo *m*
enthrall [ɪnθrɔ́ɫ] VT (captivate) cautivar, hechizar; (make a slave of) esclavizar
enthusiasm [ɪnθúziæzəm] N entusiasmo *m*
enthusiast [ɪnθúziɪst] N entusiasta *mf*
enthusiastic [ɪnθuziǽstɪk] ADJ entusiasta; **I'm very — about the trip** estoy muy entusiasmado con el viaje
entice [ɪntáɪs] VI/VT (attract) atraer; (lure) tentar; (seduce) seducir
entire [ɪntáɪr] ADJ (unbroken) entero; (complete) completo; **the — crew** toda la tripulación, la tripulación entera
entirety [ɪntáɪrɪḒi] N totalidad *f*
entitle [ɪntáɪdl] VT (give a title) titular, intitular; (give a right) dar derecho
entitlement [ɪntáɪdl̩mənt] N derecho *m*
entity [éntɪḒi] N (institution) entidad *f*; (being) ente *m*, ser *m*
entomology [ɛntəmáləʤi] N entomología *f*
entourage [ántUraʤ] N séquito *m*, cortejo *m*
entrails [éntrelz] N entrañas *f pl*
entrance[1] [éntrəns] N (act, point of entering) entrada *f*; (permission to enter) ingreso *m*; — **examination** examen de ingreso *m*
entrance[2] [ɪntrǽns] VT embelesar
entrant [éntrənt] N participante *mf*; —**s in the law profession** abogados recién recibidos *m pl*
entrap [ɪntrǽp] VT (ensnare) coger con una trampa; (deceive) embaucar
entreaty [ɪntríḒi] N súplica *f*, ruego *m*
entrench [ɪntréntʃ] VI (establish) afianzar[se]; (dig trenches) atrincherar; **a deeply —ed habit** un hábito muy arraigado
entrepreneur [antrəprənúr] N empresario -ria *mf*
entrepreneurship [antrəprənúrʃɪp] N espíritu emprendedor *m*
entropy [éntrəpi] N entropía *f*
entrust [ɪntrást] VT confiar, encomendar
entry [éntri] N (act, point of entry) entrada *f*; (permission to enter) ingreso *m*; (record) anotación *f*; (contestant) participante *mf*; (dictionary definition) entrada *f*, artículo *m*; (computer) entrada *f*; (in bookkeeping) asiento *m*; **double — accounting** contabilidad por partida doble *f*; ADJ —**level** que no requiere experiencia
enumerate [ɪnúmərət] VT enumerar
enunciate [ɪnánsiet] VI/VT (pronounce) articular; (state a theory) enunciar; (proclaim) proclamar
envelop [ɪnvéləp] VT envolver
envelope [énvəlop] N sobre *m*
enviable [énviəbəl] ADJ envidiable
envious [énviəs] ADJ envidioso
environment [ɪnváɪə-nmənt] N ambiente *m*, medio ambiente *m*; (biological) medio

ambiente *m*, ecología *f*; (in computers) entorno *m*; ADJ ambiental; (biological) medioambiental, ecológico
environmental [ɪnvaɪə-nméntl] ADJ ambiental; (biological) medioambiental, ecológico; — **impact study** estudio del impacto ambiental *m*
environmentalist [ɪnvaɪə-néntl̩ɪst] N ecologista *mf*
envisage [ɪnvízɪʤ] VT anticipar, prever
envision [ɪnvíʒən] VT imaginar
envoy [ánvɔɪ] N enviado -da *mf*
envy [énvi] N envidia *f*; VI/VT envidiar
enzyme [énzaɪm] N enzima *f*
ephemeral [ɪfémə-əɫ] ADJ efímero
epic [épɪk] ADJ épico; N (poem) epopeya *f*; (genre) épica *f*
epicenter [épɪsɛntə-] N epicentro *m*
epidemic [ɛpɪdémɪk] ADJ epidémico; N epidemia *f*
epidermis [ɛpɪdə́-mɪs] N epidermis *f*
epiglottis [épɪglaḒɪs] N epiglotis *f*
epilepsy [épələpsi] N epilepsia *f*
epileptic [ɛpəléptɪk] ADJ epiléptico
epilogue, epilog [épələɔg] N epílogo *m*
epiphany [ɪpífəni] N epifanía *f*
episode [épɪsod] N episodio *m*
episodic [ɛpɪsádɪk] ADJ (sporadic) episódico; (serial) en episodios
epitaph [épɪtæf] N epitafio *m*
epitome [ɪpíḒəmi] N epítome *m*
epoch [épək] N época *f*; —**-making** trascendental
Epsom salt [épsəmsɔ́ɫt] N sal de Epsom *f*
equal [íkwəɫ] ADJ igual; — **rights** igualdad de derechos *f*; **an — contest** una competición pareja; **to be — to a task** ser capaz de cumplir una tarea; N igual *m*; — **sign** signo de igual *m*; VT igualar
equality [ɪkwálɪḒi] N igualdad *f*
equalize [íkwəlaɪz] VT igualar; (electronically) ecualizar
equalizer [íkwəlaɪzə-] N (in soccer) gol del empate *m*
equally [íkwəli] ADV igualmente
equate [ɪkwét] VT equiparar
equation [ɪkwéʒən] N ecuación *f*
equator [ɪkwéḒə-] N ecuador *m*
Equatorial Guinea [ɛkwətɔ́riəlgíni] N Guinea Ecuatorial *f*
equidistant [ikwɪdístənt] ADJ equidistante
equilibrium [ikwəlíbriəm] N equilibrio *m*
equine [íkwaɪn] ADJ & N equino *m*
equinox [íkwənaks] N equinoccio *m*
equip [ɪkwíp] VT equipar
equipment [ɪkwípmənt] N (supplies) equipo *m*; (act of equipping) equipamiento *m*
equitable [ékwɪḒəbəl] ADJ equitativo, justo
equity [ékwɪḒi] N equidad *f*, valor libre de

hipoteca de una propiedad *m*; **equities** acciones *f pl*
equivalent [ɪkwívələnt] ADJ & N equivalente *m*
equivocal [ɪkwívəkəł] ADJ equívoco
era [írə] N era *f*
eradicate [ɪrǽDɪket] VT (extirpate) erradicar; (pull up by roots) arrancar
eradication [ɪrǽDɪkéʃən] N erradicación *f*
erase [ɪrés] VI/VT borrar[se]
eraser [ɪrésɚ] N (pencil) goma de borrar *f*; (blackboard) borrador *m*
erasure [ɪréʃɚ] N (act of erasing) borrado *m*; (smudge) borrón *m*
erect [ɪrékt] ADJ (of an organ) erecto; (of the body) erguido; VT erigir
erectile [ɪréktaɪł] ADJ eréctil
erection [ɪrékʃən] N erección *f*
ergonomic [ɝgənámɪk] ADJ ergonómico
ergonomics [ɝgənámɪks] N ergonomía *f*
Eritrea [ɛrɪtríə] N Eritrea *f*
Eritrean [ɛrɪtríən] ADJ & N eritreo -a *mf*
ermine [ɝ́mɪn] N armiño *m*
erode [ɪród] VI/VT erosionar[se]
erogenous [ɪrádʒənəs] ADJ erógeno
erosion [ɪróʒən] N erosión *f*
erotic [ɪrádɪk] ADJ erótico
eroticism [ɪrádɪsɪzəm] N erotismo *m*
err [ɛr] VI errar
errand [érənd] N mandado *m*, recado *m*; — **boy** mandadero *m*
errant [érənt] ADJ errante
erratic [ɪrǽDɪk] ADJ (unpredictable) irregular, errático; (eccentric) excéntrico; (wandering) errante
erroneous [ɪróniəs] ADJ erróneo, errado
error [érɚ] N (also in baseball) error *m*; **to be in** — estar errado; — **message** mensaje de error *m*
erudite [érjədaɪt] ADJ erudito
erudition [ɛrjədíʃən] N erudición *f*
erupt [ɪrápt] VI (volcano) hacer erupción; (angry person) estallar; (pimples) salir
eruption [ɪrápʃən] N erupción *f*
escalate [éskəlet] VI (prices) aumentar; (violence) intensificarse, aumentar
escalator [éskəleDɚ] N escalera mecánica *f*
escapade [éskəped] N (adventure) aventura *f*; (prank) travesura *f*
escape [ɪskép] N (of gas) escape *m*; (from reality) escape *m*, evasión *f*; (of prisoners) fuga *f*, evasión *f*; (means of escaping) escapatoria *f*; — **key** tecla de escape *f*; VI escapar[se], evadirse; VT (elude) eludir; **his name** —**s me** no me acuerdo de su nombre
escort[1] [éskɔrt] N (people who accompany) escolta *mf*; (male companion) acompañante *m*; (paid female companion) señorita de compañía *f*
escort[2] [ɪskɔ́rt] VT (protect) escoltar;

(accompany) acompañar
escrow [éskro] N — **account** cuenta de depósito en garantía *f*; ADV LOC **in** — en custodia
escudo [ɪskúdo] N escudo *m*
Eskimo [éskəmo] N esquimal *mf*
esophagus [ɪsáfəgəs] N esófago *m*
esoteric [ɛsətérɪk] ADJ esotérico
especial [ɪspéʃəł] ADJ especial
especially [ɪspéʃəli] ADV (above all) especialmente; (mainly) sobre todo; **he's** — **tired today** hoy está más cansado que de costumbre
espionage [éspiənaʒ] N espionaje *m*
esplanade [ésplənad] N explanada *f*
espouse [ɪspáʊz] VT defender, abrazar
essay[1] [ése] N ensayo *m*
essay[2] [ɛsé] VT ensayar
essence [ésəns] N esencia *f*; **time is of the** — el tiempo apremia
essential [ɪsénʃəł] ADJ esencial
establish [ɪstǽblɪʃ] VT (cause to be accepted, prove the validity of) establecer; (found) fundar
establishment [ɪstǽblɪʃmənt] N (action or fact) establecimiento *m*, conformación *f*; (authority) establishment *m*; (of a custom, system) implantación *f*; (of a regime) instauración *f*
estate [ɪstét] N (piece of land) hacienda *f*; (possessions) bienes *m pl*; (property) propiedades *f pl*; (of a deceased person) testamentaria *f*; — **tax** impuesto de sucesión *m*
esteem [ɪstím] VT (regard highly) estimar; (consider) considerar; N estima *f*
estimate[1] [éstəmet] VT estimar, evaluar; VI hacer una estimación
estimate[2] [éstəmɪt] N (calculation) estimación *f*; (approximate charge) presupuesto *m*
estimation [ɛstəméʃən] N (opinion) juicio *m*; (esteem) estima *f*; (estimate) estimación *f*; **in my** — a mi juicio
Estonia [ɛstóniə] N Estonia *f*
Estonian [ɛstóniən] ADJ & N estonio -nia *mf*
estrange [ɪstréndʒ] VT (alienate) enajenar; **to become —d** separarse
estrogen [éstrədʒən] N estrógeno *m*
estuary [éstʃueri] N estuario *m*
et cetera, etc. [ɛtsétrə] ADV etcétera, etc.
etch [ɛtʃ] VI/VT (engrave) grabar; (outline) perfilar[se]
etching [étʃɪŋ] N grabado *m*
eternal [ɪtɝ́nł] ADJ eterno
eternity [ɪtɝ́nɪDi] N eternidad *f*
ethanol [éθənoł] N etanol *m*
ether [íθɚ] N éter *m*
ethernet [íθɚnɛt] N ethernet *m*
ethical [éθɪkəł] ADJ ético
ethics [éθɪks] N ética *f*

Ethiopia [iθiópiə] N Etiopía f
Ethiopian [iθiópiən] ADJ & N etíope mf
ethnic [éθnɪk] ADJ étnico; (dances, clothes) tradicional; — **Chinese** de ascendencia china; — **cleansing** limpieza étnica f
ethnicity [ɛθnísɪDi] N etnicidad f; (group) grupo étnico m
ethnography [ɛθnágrəfi] N etnografía f
ethnology [ɛθnáləʤi] N etnología f
ethyl alcohol [éθəlǽlkəhɑɫ] N alcohol etílico m
etiquette [édɪkɪt] N etiqueta f
etymology [ɛDəmáləʤi] N etimología f
EU [European Union] [íjú] N UE f
eucalyptus [jukəlíptəs] N eucalipto m
eulogy [júləʤi] N (praise) elogio m; (at a funeral) panegírico m
eunuch [júnək] N eunuco m
euphemism [júfəmɪzəm] N eufemismo m
euphoria [jufɔ́riə] N euforia f
euro [júro] N euro m
Europe [júrəp] N Europa f
European [jurəpíən] ADJ & N europeo -a mf; — **Union** Unión Europea f; — **Union budget** presupuesto comunitario m
Eustachian tube [justéʃən] N trompa de Eustaquio f
euthanasia [juθənéʒə] N eutanasia f
evacuate [ɪvǽkjuet] VI/VT (remove due to danger, defecate) evacuar; (empty a building) desalojar
evade [ɪvéd] VT (taxes, responsibilities) evadir, burlar; (questions) eludir
evaluate [ɪvǽljuet] VT (assess) evaluar; (appraise) avaluar, tasar
evaluation [ɪvæljuéʃən] N evaluación f
evangelical [ivænʤélɪkəl] ADJ evangélico
evaporate [ɪvǽpəret] VI/VT evaporar[se]; VI (vanish) esfumarse
evaporation [ɪvæpəréʃən] N evaporación f
evasion [ɪvéʒən] N (escape) evasión f; (subterfuge) evasiva f
evasive [ɪvésɪv] ADJ evasivo
eve [iv] N (day before) víspera f; (evening) atardecer m; **on the — of** en vísperas de
even [ívən] ADJ (flat) plano, llano; (smooth) liso; (parallel) paralelo; (without fluctuation) parejo; (equal) igual; (divisible by two) par; (placid) tranquilo; —**handed** imparcial; —-**tempered** apacible; **an — dozen** una docena exacta; **to be — with someone** estar a mano con alguien; **to get — with someone** desquitarse de alguien; ADV (still, yet) aun; (for extreme case) hasta, inclusive, incluso; — **if/though** aun cuando; — **my mother went** hasta mi madre fue; — **so** aun así; **it's — more expensive** es aun más caro; **not** — ni siquiera; VI/VT (make a surface even) nivelar[se]; (make accounts even) emparejar

evening [ívnɪŋ] N tarde f; (dusk) atardecer m; — **gown** vestido de fiesta m, vestido de noche m; — **party** velada f; — **star** lucero de la tarde m; **good** —! ¡buenas noches!
event [ɪvént] N (happening) hecho m, evento m; (of importance) acontecimiento m, suceso m; **in any** — en todo caso; **in the — of** en caso de
eventful [ɪvéntfəɫ] ADJ agitado, movido
eventual [ɪvéntʃuəɫ] ADJ (later) posterior; (final) final
eventuality [ɪventʃuǽlɪDi] N eventualidad f
eventually [ɪvéntʃuəli] ADV a la larga
ever [évə-] ADV alguna vez; —**more** para siempre; — **since** desde entonces; **have you — studied French?** ¿alguna vez has estudiado francés? **how did you — do this?** ¿cómo pudiste hacer esto? **for — and** — por/para siempre jamás; **hardly** — casi nunca; **if** — si alguna vez; **more than** — más que nunca; **the best friend I — had** el mejor amigo que he tenido jamás; **for —more** para/por siempre jamás; ADJ —**green** [planta] perenne f; —**lasting** eterno
every [évri] ADJ (each) cada; — **child is different** cada niño es diferente; (all) todo[s]; — **once in a while** de vez en cuando; — **other day** cada dos días, un día sí y otro no; —**where** (location) por/en todas partes; (direction) a todas partes; **we go — Friday** vamos todos los viernes; PRON —**body** todos -das mf pl, todo el mundo m; — **day** todos los días; —**one** todos -das mf pl, todo el mundo m; —**thing** todo; **you are —thing to me** eres todo para mí; ADJ —**day** (of clothes) de diario, de todos los días; (of occurrences) cotidiano
evict [ɪvíkt] VT desalojar
evidence [évɪDəns] N evidencia f; (data in court) prueba f; **to be in** — ser evidente; VI/VT evidenciar[se], demostrar[se]
evident [évɪDənt] ADJ evidente
evil [ívəɫ] ADJ (wicked) malo, malvado; (harmful) maligno; N (force of nature) mal m; (human wickedness) maldad f; —**doer** malhechor -ora mf; — **eye** mal de ojo m; **the lesser of two** —**s** el mal menor
evocation [ɛvəkéʃən] N evocación f
evoke [ɪvók] VT (call up) evocar; (elicit) provocar
evolution [ɛvəlúʃən] N evolución f
evolutionary [ɛvəlúʃənɛri] ADJ evolutivo
evolve [ɪvɑ́ɫv] VI/VT desarrollar[se]; VI evolucionar
ewe [ju] N oveja f
ex [ɛks] N ex mf
exacerbate [ɪgzǽsə-bet] VI/VT exacerbar
exact [ɪgzǽkt] ADJ exacto; VT exigir
exacting [ɪgzǽktɪŋ] ADJ exigente
exactly [ɪgzǽktli] ADV exactamente,

precisamente; **he's not — a genius** no es un genio ni mucho menos / no es ningún genio que digamos; **they arrived — at three** llegaron exactamente a las tres
exaggerate [ɪgzǽdʒəret] VT exagerar
exalt [ɪgzɔ́łt] VT exaltar
exam [ɪgzǽm] N examen *m*
examination [ɪgzæmənéʃən] N examen *m* (also medical)
examine [ɪgzǽmɪn] VT (inspect) examinar; (analyze) analizar
example [ɪgzǽmpəł] N ejemplo *m*
exasperate [ɪgzǽspəret] VT exasperar
excavate [ékskəvet] VT excavar
excavator [ékskəveDɚ] N (person) excavador -ora *mf*; (machine) excavadora *f*
exceed [ɪksíd] VT (go beyond) exceder, rebasar; (be superior to) superar, sobrepasar
exceeding [ɪksíDɪŋ] N superación *f*
exceedingly [ɪksíDɪŋli] ADV sumamente, extremadamente
excel [ɪksél] VI sobresalir, lucirse, descollar
excellence [éksələns] N excelencia *f*
excellent [éksələnt] ADJ excelente
except [ɪksépt] PREP excepto, menos; **all the students — Pam** todos los estudiantes menos Pam; CONJ excepto, salvo; **the cars are identical — that one is older** los coches son idénticos salvo que uno es más viejo; **we would go to the beach, — for the inclement weather** iríamos a la playa si no fuera por el mal tiempo; VT exceptuar
excepting [ɪkséptɪŋ] PREP exceptuando
exception [ɪksépʃən] N excepción *f*; **with the — of** con/a excepción de; **to take — (object)** objetar; (resent) ofenderse
exceptional [ɪksépʃənl̩] ADJ (unusual) excepcional; (gifted) superdotado; (handicapped) con necesidades especiales
excerpt[1] [éksɚpt] N fragmento *m*
excerpt[2] [éksɚpt, ɪksɚ́pt] VT seleccionar fragmentos
excess [ékses] N exceso *m*, hartazgo *m*; — **baggage** exceso de equipaje *m*; — **profits tax** impuesto sobre ganancias excesivas *m*; — **weight** exceso de peso *m*; **in — of twenty pounds** más de veinte libras; **to drink to —** beber en exceso
excessive [ɪksésɪv] ADJ excesivo, desmedido
exchange [ɪkstʃéndʒ] VT (replace with something similar) cambiar; (give mutually) intercambiar; (trade political prisoners, books, CDs) canjear; (barter) permutar; **to — greetings** saludarse; N (replacement) cambio *m*; (interchange) intercambio *m*; (barter) permuta *f*; (of prisoners, books) canje *m*; (for stock trading) bolsa *f*; (for commodity trading) lonja *f*; (telephone) central de teléfonos *f*; — **student** estudiante de

intercambio *mf*; **rate of —** tipo de cambio *m*, tasa de cambio *f*
excise [éksaɪz] N impuesto sobre bienes de consumo *m*
excite [ɪksáɪt] VT (agitate, arouse) excitar, alborotar; (enthuse) entusiasmar
excited [ɪksáɪDɪd] ADJ (agitated, aroused) excitado; (enthusiastic) entusiasmado, ilusionado; **to get — (aroused)** excitarse; (enthused) entusiasmarse
excitement [ɪksáɪtmənt] N (arousal) excitación *f*; (enthusiasm) entusiasmo *m*
exciting [ɪksáɪDɪŋ] ADJ (stimulating) excitante; (thrilling) emocionante, apasionante
exclaim [ɪksklém] VI exclamar
exclamation [ekskləméʃən] N exclamación *f*; — **point** signo de admiración *m*
exclude [ɪksklúd] VT excluir
exclusion [ɪksklúʒən] N exclusión *f*
exclusive [ɪksklúsɪv] ADJ exclusivo; — **of** sin incluir
excommunicate [ekskəmjúnɪket] VT excomulgar
excrement [ékskrəmənt] N excremento *m*
excrescence [ɪkskrésəns] N excrecencia *f*
excrete [ɪkskrít] VI/VT excretar
excretion [ɪkskríʃən] N excreción *f*
excruciating [ɪkskrúʃieDɪŋ] ADJ insoportable, atroz
excursion [ɪkskɚ́ʒən] N excursión *f*
excusable [ɪkskjúzəbəł] ADJ excusable, disculpable
excuse[1] [ɪkskjúz] VT (release from a duty, seek exemption) excusar, eximir; (forgive) disculpar, perdonar; — **me!** (forgive me) disculpe; (let me pass) con permiso; (excuse me?) ¿cómo? ¿perdón? *Mex* ¿mande?
excuse[2] [ɪkskjús] N excusa *f*, disculpa *f*; **it's a poor — for a car** no merece llamarse un coche
executable [egzəkjúDəbəł] ADJ ejecutable
execute [éksɪkjut] VT ejecutar (also computer term); (by firing squad) fusilar
execution [eksɪkjúʃən] N ejecución *f*; (by firing squad) fusilamiento *m*; — **wall** paredón *m*
executioner [eksɪkjúʃənɚ] N verdugo *mf*
executive [ɪgzékjəDɪv] ADJ ejecutivo; N (person) ejecutivo -va *mf*; (branch of government) poder ejecutivo *m*
executor [ɪgzékjəDɚ] N albacea *mf*
exemplary [ɪgzémpləri] ADJ ejemplar
exemplify [ɪgzémpləfaɪ] VT ejemplificar
exempt [ɪgzémpt] VT eximir, dispensar; ADJ exento, libre
exemption [ɪgzémpʃən] N exención *f*, franquicia *f*
exercise [éksɚsaɪz] N ejercicio *m*; —**s** ceremonia *f*; VT ejercer; VI hacer ejercicio; — **electrocardiogram** prueba de esfuerzo

máximo *f*; **to be —d about something**
estar disgustado por algo
exert [ɪgzэ́t] VT ejercer; **to — oneself**
esforzarse, empeñarse
exertion [ɪgzэ́ʃən] N (use of powers, faculties)
ejercicio *m*; (vigorous action) esfuerzo *m*,
empeño *m*
exfoliation [ɪksfoliéʃən] N exfoliación *f*
exhale [ɛkshéɫ] VT exhalar; VI espirar
exhaust [ɪgzɔ́st] VT agotar, desmadejar; (a
topic) tratar exhaustivamente; N (from a car)
escape *m*
exhausted [ɪgzɔ́stɪd] ADJ rendido, agotado
exhausting [ɪgzɔ́stɪŋ] ADJ agotador
exhaustion [ɪgzɔ́stʃən] N (act or process of
exhausting) agotamiento *m*; (weakness,
tiredness) fatiga *f*
exhaustive [ɪgzɔ́stɪv] ADJ exhaustivo
exhibit [ɪgzíbɪt] VI/VT (manifest) exhibir; (put
on view) exponer; N exposición *f*
exhibition [ɛksəbíʃən] N (manifestation, show
of skills) exhibición *f*; (public display of
objects) exposición *f*
exhibitionism [ɛksɪbíʃənɪzəm] N
exhibicionismo *m*
exhilarated [ɪgzílərɛDɪd] ADJ exultante
exhort [ɪgzɔ́rt] VT exhortar
exhumation [ɛgzjuméʃən] N exhumación *f*
exile [égzaɪɫ] N exilio *m*, destierro *m*; (person
exiled) exiliado -da *mf*, desterrado -da *mf*; VT
exiliar
exist [ɪgzíst] VI existir
existence [ɪgzístəns] N existencia *f*
existential [ɛgzɪsténʃəɫ] ADJ existencial
existing [ɪgzístɪŋ] ADJ existente
exit [égzɪt] N salida *f*; VI/VT salir [de]; (theater)
hacer mutis; **— interview** entrevista de
salida *f*; **— strategy** estrategia de salida *f*; VI
salir; **he —ed the building** salió del edificio
exodus [éksəDəs] N éxodo *m*
exonerate [ɪgzánəret] VT exonerar
exorbitant [ɪgzɔ́rbɪDənt] ADJ exorbitante
exorcise [éksɔrsaɪz] VT exorcisar
exorcism [éksɔrsɪzəm] N exorcismo *m*
exotic [ɪgzáDɪk] ADJ exótico
expand [ɪkspǽnd] VI/VT expandir[se],
ampliar[se]; (an equation, an idea)
desarrollar[se]; (through heat) dilatar[se];
—ed memory memoria expandida *f*
expanse [ɪkspǽns] N extensión *f*
expansion [ɪkspǽnʃən] N expansión *f*; (of an
equation, of an idea) desarrollo *m*; (through
heat) dilatación *f*; **— slot** ranura para
accesorios *f*
expansive [ɪkspǽnsɪv] ADJ expansivo
expatriate[1] [ɛkspétriet] VI/VT expatriar[se]
expatriate[2] [ɛkspétriɪt] N expatriado -da *mf*
expect [ɪkspékt] VT esperar; **we — guests**
esperamos visita[s]; **I — you to be on time**

cuento con que vengas puntualmente; **I'm
—ed to work fifty hours a week** tengo
que trabajar cincuenta horas por semana; **I —
you're tired** estarás cansado; **she's —ing**
está embarazada/encinta
expectation [ɛkspɛktéʃən] N (anticipation)
expectación *f*; (expected thing) expectativa *f*;
he has great —s tiene grandes expectativas
expectorant [ɪkspéktə·ənt] ADJ & N expectorante
m
expectorate [ɪkspéktəret] VI/VT expectorar
expedient [ɪkspíDiənt] ADJ conveniente,
expeditivo
expedite [ékspɪdaɪt] VT (facilitate) agilizar; (deal
with promptly) despachar
expedition [ɛkspɪdíʃən] N expedición *f*
expeditionary [ɛkspɪdíʃənɛri] ADJ
expedicionario
expel [ɪkspéɫ] VT (discharge) expeler; (throw out)
expulsar
expend [ɪkspénd] VT gastar, agotar
expenditure [ɪkspéndɪtʃэ·] N gasto *m*
expense [ɪkspéns] N gasto *m*; **— account** cuenta
de gastos *f*; **they had fun at my —** se
divirtieron a mi costa
expensive [ɪkspénsɪv] ADJ caro
experience [ɪkspíriəns] N experiencia *f*; VT
experimentar; **—d** experimentado
experiment [ɪkspérəmənt] N experimento *m*; VI
experimentar
experimental [ɪkspɛrəméntḷ] ADJ experimental
experimentation [ɪkspɛrɪməntéʃən] N
experimentación *f*
expert [ékspэ·t] N experto -ta *mf*; ADJ experto,
idóneo, perito; **— system** sistema experto *m*
expertise [ɛkspэ·tíz] N pericia *f*
expiration [ɛkspəréʃən] N (of a contract)
vencimiento *m*, caducidad *f*; (breathing out)
espiración *f*
expire [ɪkspáɪr] VI (die, terminate) expirar;
(breathe out) espirar; (lapse) vencer, caducar
explain [ɪksplén] VT explicar; **he tried to —
away his absence** trató de justificar su
ausencia
explainable [ɪksplénəbəɫ] ADJ explicable
explanation [ɛksplənéʃən] N explicación *f*
explanatory [ɪksplǽnətɔri] ADJ explicativo
expletive [éksplɪDɪv] N palabrota *f*
explicable [ɪksplíkəbəɫ] ADJ explicable
explicit [ɪksplísɪt] ADJ explícito
explode [ɪksplód] VI/VT estallar, hacer
explosión, explotar; VT (a theory) hacer
añicos; VI (population) dispararse
exploit[1] [éksplɔɪt] N hazaña *f*, proeza *f*
exploit[2] [ɪksplɔ́ɪt] VT explotar
exploitation [ɛksplɔɪtéʃən] N explotación *f*
exploration [ɛkspləréʃən] N exploración *f*
exploratory [ɪksplɔ́rətɔri] ADJ exploratorio
explore [ɪksplɔ́r] VI/VT explorar; (a topic) bucear

explorer [ɪksplɔ́rə-] N explorador -ora *mf*
explosion [ɪksplóʒən] N explosión *f*, estallido *m*
explosive [ɪksplósɪv] ADJ & N explosivo *m*
exponent [ɪkspónənt] N exponente *m*
export[1] [ɪkspɔ́rt] VI/VT exportar
export[2] [ékspɔrt] N exportación *f*
exportation [ɛkspɔrtéʃən] N exportación *f*
exporter [ɪkspɔ́rɒə-] N exportador -ora *mf*
exporting [ɪkspɔ́rɒɪŋ] N exportación *f*; — **firm** empresa exportadora *f*
expose [ɪkspóz] VT (to lay open to danger, exhibit, subject to light) exponer; (to make known) revelar; (to unmask) desenmascarar
exposition [ɛkspəzíʃən] N exposición *f*
exposure [ɪkspóʒə-] N (to danger, to light, act of exposing) exposición *f*; (disclosure) revelación *f*; **to die of** — morir de frío
expound [ɪkspáʊnd] VI/VT exponer, explicar
express [ɪksprés] VT expresar; (send by mail) enviar por correo expreso; (squeeze out) exprimir; ADJ (clearly indicated) expreso; — **delivery** envío rápido *m*; — **train** tren expreso *m*; ADV por expreso; N (train) expreso *m*
expression [ɪkspréʃən] N expresión *f*
expressive [ɪksprésɪv] ADJ expresivo
expressiveness [ɪksprésɪvnɪs] N expresividad *f*
expropriate [ɛksprópriet] VT expropiar
expulsion [ɪkspʌ́lʃən] N expulsión *f*
exquisite [ɛkskwízɪt] ADJ exquisito, primoroso; (pain) penetrante
extant [ékstənt] ADJ existente
extemporaneous [ɪkstɛmpəréniəs] ADJ improvisado
extend [ɪksténd] VI/VT extender[se]; (a street) ampliar[se]; **he —ed his hand to her** le tendió la mano
extended [ɪksténdɪd] ADJ (extensive) extenso; (prolonged) prolongado; (folded out) extendido; — **coverage** cobertura extendida *f*; — **care facility** centro de atención médica prolongada *m*
extension [ɪksténʃən] N extensión *f* (also phone line); (of a deadline) prórroga *f*; (addition) anexo *m*, ampliación *f*; — **cord** extensión *f*
extensive [ɪksténsɪv] ADJ extenso; (agriculture) extensivo
extent [ɪkstént] N extensión *f*; **to a great** — en alto grado; **to such an** — **that** a tal grado que; **to the** — **that you are able** en la medida en que seas capaz; **to a certain** — hasta cierto punto
extenuate [ɪksténjuet] VT atenuar
exterior [ɪkstíriə-] ADJ & N exterior *m*
exterminate [ɪkstá-mənet] VT exterminar
extermination [ɪkstə-mənéʃən] N exterminio *m*, exterminación *f*
external [ɪkstá-nl] ADJ externo; (concerned with foreign countries) exterior

extinct [ɪkstíŋkt] ADJ extinto
extinguish [ɪkstíŋgwɪʃ] VT apagar, extinguir
extol [ɪkstól] VT ensalzar, enaltecer
extort [ɪkstɔ́rt] VT extorsionar
extortion [ɪkstɔ́rʃən] N extorsión *f*
extra [ékstrə] ADJ de más, adicional; **make some** — **cakes** haz unos pasteles de más / adicionales / extras; N extra *m* (including newspaper, actor); ADV extra; extrasensorial; (soccer) — **time** tiempo suplementario *m*, tiempo de descuento *m*; ADJ —**marital** extramarital; —**ordinary** extraordinario; —**sensory** extrasensorial
extract[1] [ékstrækt] N (something extracted) extracto *m*; (passage from a book) fragmento *m*
extract[2] [ɪkstrǽkt] VT extraer; (a secret) sonsacar
extraction [ɪkstrǽkʃən] N extracción *f*
extradite [ékstrədaɪt] VT extraditar
extradition [ɛkstrədíʃən] N extradición *f*
extraneous [ɪkstréniəs] ADJ superfluo
extrapolate [ɪkstrǽpəlet] VI/VT extrapolar
extravagance [ɪkstrǽvəgəns] N (unnecessary expense) despilfarro *m*, derroche *m*; (excess) exceso *m*; (oddity) extravagancia *f*
extravagant [ɪkstrǽvəgənt] ADJ (shopper) gastador, derrochador; (price) exorbitante; (praise, demand) excesivo
extreme [ɪkstrím] ADJ & N extremo *m*; **to go to** —**s** exagerar, llegar a extremos; **to the** — extremadamente, sumamente
extremely [ɪkstrímli] ADV extremadamente, sumamente; **it's** — **cold** hace un frío que pela; **she's** — **intelligent** es inteligentísima
extremity [ɪkstrémɪɒi] N extremidad *f*
extricate [ékstrɪket] VT sacar; VI **to** — **oneself from** conseguir salir de
extrovert [ékstrəvɜt] N extrovertido -da *mf*
extroverted [ékstrəvɜ-ɒɪd] ADJ extrovertido
exuberant [ɪgzúbə-ənt] ADJ exuberante
exude [ɪgzúd] VI/VT (liquid) exudar; (cheerfulness, confidence) emanar
exult [ɪgzʌ́lt] VI exultar
eye [aɪ] N ojo *m* (also of hurricane, needle, tools); (look) mirada *f*; —**ball** globo ocular *m*; —**brow** ceja *f*; — **chart** cartilla de examen de vista *f*; — **contact** contacto visual *m*; —**dropper** cuentagotas *m sg*; — **drops** colirio *m*, gotas oftálmicas *f pl*; —**glass** (of a telescope, microscope) ocular *m*; —**glasses** anteojos *m pl*, lentes *m pl*; — **injury** lesión ocular *f*; —**lash** pestaña *f*; —**lid** párpado *m*; —**liner** delineador *m*; —-**opener** revelación *f*; —**piece** ocular *m*; —**sight** vista *f*; —**sore** monstruosidad *f*; — **shadow** sombra para ojos *f*; — **socket** órbita *f*; — **strain** vista cansada *f*; —**tooth** colmillo *m*; —**witness** testigo ocular *mf*; **my —s are bad** tengo mala vista; **in the twinkling of an** — en un

abrir y cerrar de ojos; **her dress caught his
— su vestido le llamó la atención; to keep an
— on** cuidar, vigilar; **to see — to —** estar de
acuerdo; **in the —s of the law** ante la ley; **to
give someone the —** hacerle ojito a
alguien; **to have —s for someone** estar
prendado de alguien; **to keep one's — open**
tener cuidado; VT mirar
eyeful [áɪfʊł] N **we got an —** vimos más que
suficiente
e-zine [ízin] N revista electrónica*f*

Ff

fable [fébəł] N fábula*f*
fabric [fǽbrɪk] N tela*f*, tejido *m*; (wool) paño *m*;
(of society) estructura*f*; **— softener**
suavizante *m*
fabricate [fǽbrɪket] VT (goods) fabricar; (a story)
inventar
fabulous [fǽbjələs] ADJ fabuloso
facade [fəsád] N fachada*f*
face [fes] N (of head, coin, cube, facial
expression) cara*f*; (of a building) frente *m*; (of
a watch) esfera*f*; (of the Earth) faz*f*; **—cloth**
toalla para la cara*f*; **—lift** lifting *m*; **— value**
valor nominal *m*; **about —!** ¡media vuelta!
left —! ¡a la izquierda! **on the — of it**
aparentemente; **she put on a brave —** se
comportó con entereza; **to make —s** hacer
muecas; **to lose —** quedar mal; **to save —**
quedar bien; **to show one's —** aparecerse;
ADJ **—-to-—** cara a cara; ADV **in the — of**
ante, frente a; VT (stand opposite to) encarar;
(meet defiantly) enfrentar, enfrentarse con,
afrontar; (look forward) mirar a/hacia; (to
have the front toward) dar a/hacia; (to put on
facing) ribetear; **to — down** intimidar; **to —
the music** dar la cara; **to — with marble**
revestir de mármol
faceless [féslɪs] ADJ (anonymous) anónimo;
(without a face) sin cara
facet [fǽsɪt] N faceta*f*
facetious [fəsíʃəs] ADJ gracioso
facial [féʃəł] ADJ facial; N limpieza de cutis*f*
facilitate [fəsílɪtet] VT facilitar
facility [fəsílɪɒi] N (skill) facilidad*f*; **facilities**
(of a building) instalaciones*f pl*; (restroom)
aseo *m*, servicio *m*
fact [fækt] N hecho *m*; **hard —s** datos concretos
m pl; **is that a —!** ¡no me digas! **as a matter
of —** de hecho; **in —** de hecho; **it's a — of
life** así son las cosas
faction [fǽkʃən] N facción*f*
factor [fǽktɚ] N factor *m*; VT descomponer en

factores; VI **to — in** tener en cuenta
factory [fǽktəri] N fábrica*f*
factual [fǽktʃuəł] ADJ (of facts) fáctico; (based on
facts) objetivo; **— error** error de hecho *m*
faculty [fǽkəłti] N (ability) facultad*f*; (in a
college) profesorado *m*, cuerpo docente *m*,
claustro *m*
fad [fæd] N moda pasajera*f*
fade [fed] VI/VT (cloth) decolorar[se],
desteñir[se]; (color) deslavar[se]; VI (strength)
disminuir; (lights) apagarse; (feelings, colors)
desvanecerse
fag [fæg] N *offensive* marica *m*, maricón *m*
faggot [fǽgət] N (male homosexual) *offensive*
marica *m*, maricón *m*; (bundle) haz *m*
fail [feł] VI (faculties, organs, machinery,
structure) fallar; (experiment, plan) fracasar,
frustrarse; (health) decaer; (business)
quebrar, hacer bancarrota; VI/VT (exam,
student) suspender, reprobar; **he —ed to
remember their anniversary** no se
acordó de su aniversario; **don't — to come**
no dejes de venir; **without —** sin falta
failure [féljɚ] N (of a plan, a person) fracaso *m*;
(of organs) insuficiencia*f*; (of faculties)
deterioro *m*; (of machinery) falla*f*, Sp fallo *m*
(of business), quiebra*f*, bancarrota*f*; (in an
exam) suspenso *m*; (to keep a promise, to
reach a goal) incumplimiento *m*; **her — to
respond puzzled me** su falta de respuesta
me confundió
faint [fent] ADJ (sound) débil; (light) tenue;
(image) vago; **to feel —** sentirse mareado;
—-hearted timorato, cobarde; N desmayo
m, desfallecimiento *m*; VI desmayarse,
desfallecer
faintness [féntnɪs] N (of sound) debilidad*f*; (of
light) tenuidad*f*; (of an image) vaguedad*f*
fair [fer] ADJ (just) justo; (by the rules) limpio;
(large) considerable; (of weather) bueno; (of
sky) despejado; (of wind) propicio; (of
complexion) blanco; **— market price** precio
justo en el mercado *m*; **— play** juego limpio
m; **— chance of success** buena probabilidad
de éxito*f*; **the — sex** el sexo bello; **that's
not —!** ¡no vale! ¡no es justo! ADV **to play —**
jugar limpio; N feria*f*; **—ground** real de la
feria *m*; **—way** calle*f*, fairway *m*
fairly [férli] ADV (justly) justamente;
(moderately) medianamente; **— difficult**
bastante difícil
fairness [férnɪs] N (justice) justicia*f*; (whiteness)
blancura*f*
fairy [féri] N hada*f*; (male homosexual) *offensive*
maricón *m*; **— godmother** hada madrina*f*;
—land país de las hadas *m*; **— tale** cuento de
hadas *m*
faith [feθ] N fe*f*; (fidelity) fidelidad*f*; **— healing**
curanderismo *m*; **in good —** de buena fe; **to**

have — in someone tener confianza en alguien; **to keep —** cumplir con la palabra
faithful [féθfəł] ADJ fiel
faithfulness [féθfəłnıs] N fidelidad *f*
faithless [féθlıs] ADJ (disloyal) desleal, falso; (lacking in faith, fidelity) infiel
fake [fek] N (object) objeto falso *m*; (person who fakes) farsante *mf*; ADJ falso; **— pearls** perlas de fantasía *f pl*; N (in sports) amague *m*, finta *f*; VT (render false, counterfeit) falsificar; **to — a foul** tirarse; VI/VT (feign) fingir
falcon [fǽłkən] N halcón *m*
Falkland Islands [fɔ́kləndáıləndz] N Islas Malvinas *f pl*
fall [fɔ́ł] VI (drop) caer[se]; (slope downward) bajar; (be assigned to) tocar a, recaer sobre; **to — asleep** dormirse; **to — back** retroceder; **to — back on** recurrir a; **to — behind** atrasarse, retrasarse; **to — down** (drop) caerse; (fail) fallar; **to — in with** asociarse con; **to — in love** enamorarse; **to — off** disminuir; **to — out with** reñir con; **to — through** quedar en la nada; **he —s for blondes** se enamora de las rubias; **you — for it** te dejas engañar; N (drop) caída *f*; (of a terrain) declive *m*; (season) otoño *m*; **— guy** cabeza de turco *mf*; **—ing out** desavenencia *f*, pique *m*; **—ing star** estrella fugaz *f*; **—s** catarata *f*, salto de agua *m*
fallacious [fəléʃəs] ADJ falaz
fallacy [fǽləsi] N (false notion) falacia *f*; (false argument) sofisma *m*
fallen [fɔ́lən] *see* fall
fallible [fǽləbəł] ADJ falible
Fallopian tubes [fəlópiəntúbz] ADJ trompas de Falopio *f pl*
fallout [fɔ́laut] N (particle-settling) precipitación radiactiva *f*; (consequences) repercusiones *f pl*
fallow [fǽlo] ADJ baldío, en barbecho; N barbecho *m*; VT dejar en barbecho
false [fɔ́łs] ADJ falso; **to bear — witness** jurar en falso; **— advertising** publicidad engañosa *f*; **— alarm** falsa alarma *f*; **— arrest** detención ilegal *f*; **— pretense** estafa *f*; **— start** salida en falso *f*; **— step** paso en falso *m*; **— teeth** dentadura postiza *f*
falsehood [fɔ́łshud] N falsedad *f*, mentira *f*
falseness [fɔ́łsnıs] N falsedad *f*
falsify [fɔ́łsəfaı] VT falsificar, falsear
falter [fɔ́łtɚ] VI (hesitate) vacilar, entrecortarse; (stutter) titubear
fame [fem] N fama *f*
famed [femd] ADJ afamado
familiar [fəmíljɚ] ADJ (generally known) familiar, conocido; (informal) familiar; (too friendly) confianzudo; (closely personal) íntimo; **to be — with a subject** conocer bien un tema
familiarity [fəmıljǽrıDi] N familiaridad *f*

family [fǽmli] N familia *f*; **— doctor** médico general *m*; **— jewels** *vulg* cojones *m pl*; **— man** hombre de familia *m*; **— name** apellido *m*; **— planning** planificación familiar *f*; **— practice** medicina familiar *f*; **— room** cuarto de estar *m*; **— tree** árbol genealógico *m*; **— values** valores tradicionales *m pl*
famine [fǽmın] N (lack of food) hambruna *f*, hambre *f*; (scarcity) escasez *f*
famished [fǽmıʃt] ADJ hambriento, muerto de hambre; **to be —** morirse de hambre
famous [féməs] ADJ famoso
fan [fæn] N (handheld) abanico *m*; (electrical) ventilador *m*; (for cleaning grain) aventadora *f*; (of sports) aficionado -da *mf*, hincha *mf*; (of a person) admirador -ora *mf*; **— belt** correa del ventilador *f*; **— mail** correo de admiradores *m*; VT (blow air) abanicar; (enliven) avivar; **to — out** abrirse en abanico
fanatic [fənǽDık] ADJ & N fanático -ca *mf*
fanaticism [fənǽDısızəm] N fanatismo *m*
fanciful [fǽnsıfəł] ADJ (whimsical) caprichoso; (imaginary) imaginario; (given to fantasy) fantasioso
fancy [fǽnsi] N fantasía *f*; (whim) capricho *m*; **to strike one's —** gustarle a alguien; **to take a — to** aficionarse a; **he took a — to his teacher** se enamoró de su maestra; ADJ (luxurious) de lujo; (elaborate) elaborado; (strange) estrafalario; **— free** despreocupado; **— work** bordado fino *m*; VT imaginar[se]; **he fancies himself an artist** se cree artista; **just — the idea!** ¡figúrate!
fanfare [fǽnfɛr] N fanfarria *f*; **with great —** con bombo y platillo
fang [fæŋ] N colmillo *m*
fantasize [fǽntəsaız] VI fantasear
fantastic [fæntǽstık] ADJ fantástico
fantasy [fǽntəsi] N fantasía *f*
FAQ [frequently asked questions] [fæk] N preguntas frecuentes *f pl*
far [far] ADV lejos; **— and away** sin duda; **— and wide** por todas partes; **— away/off** lejos, lejano; **— be it from me to complain** no es mi intención quejarme; **— more money** mucho más dinero; **— off we could see land** a lo lejos divisábamos tierra; **as — as I know** que yo sepa; **as — as I'm concerned** en lo que a mí respecta; **by —** con mucho; **how — do I need to walk?** ¿cuánto tengo que caminar? **how — is the church?** ¿a cuánto queda la iglesia? **so —** hasta ahora; **we talked — into the night** hablamos hasta entrada la noche; **we traveled as — as Chicago** viajamos hasta Chicago; ADJ lejano; **—fetched** (implausible) inverosímil, peregrino; (forced) traído por los cabellos; **—-flung** remoto; **—-off** distante; **—-out** radical, poco convencional; **—-**

reaching de gran alcance; **—sighted** (with defective vision) présbita, hipermétrope; (seeing the future) con visión de futuro; **the — corner** la esquina de más allá; **it is a — cry from what you said** dista mucho de lo que dijiste

farce [fɑrs] N farsa *f*

fare [fɛr] N (ticket) billete *m*; (ticket price) pasaje *m*; (price of transport) tarifa *f*; (food) comida *f*; (taxi patron) pasajero -ra *mf*; **—well** despedida *f*; **to bid —well to** despedirse de; **—well!** ¡adiós! VI I **—d well in the course** me fue bien en el curso

farm [fɑrm] N (large) hacienda *f*; (small) granja *f*; **—hand** labrador -ora *mf*, peón *m*; **—house** alquería *f*, caserío *m*; **—land** tierra de cultivo *f*; **— produce** productos agrícolas *m pl*; **—yard** (enclosed) corral *m*; (open) patio *m*; VI/VT cultivar; **to — out** (lease) dar en arriendo; (distribute) repartir; (subcontract) subcontratar

farmer [fɑ́rmə] N agricultor -ora *mf*; (small) granjero -ra *mf*; (large) hacendado -da *mf*

farming [fɑ́rmɪŋ] N agricultura *f*; ADJ agrícola *mf*

fart [fɑrt] N *vulg* pedo *m*; **old — fam, pej** viejo pesado *m*; VI *vulg* tirar[se] pedos; **to — around** *vulg* rascarse el culo

farther [fɑ́rðə] ADV más lejos; **it's an even — distance** es una distancia mayor todavía; **the concept was extended —** el concepto se extendió más; **— on** más adelante; ADJ más lejano

farthest [fɑ́rðɪst] ADJ el más lejano; ADV lo más lejos

fascinate [fǽsənɛt] VI/VT fascinar, alucinar

fascinating [fǽsənɛDɪŋ] ADJ fascinante

fascination [fæsənéʃən] N fascinación *f*

fascism [fǽʃɪzəm] N fascismo *m*

fascist [fǽʃɪst] N fascista *mf*

fashion [fǽʃən] N (style) moda *f*; (way) manera *f*, modo *m*; **— plate** figurín *m*; **after a —** más o menos; **to be in —** estar de moda; VT hacer; (with metal) forjar; (with putty) moldear; (character) formar

fashionable [fǽʃənəbəl] ADJ de moda

fast [fæst] ADJ (quick) rápido, veloz; (ahead, of a watch) adelantado; (firm, permanent) firme; (closed) atrancado; (loyal) fiel; (dissolute) disipado; **—ball** recta *f*; **— break** contraataque *m*; **— food** comida rápida *f*; **life in the — lane** vida loca *f*; **— money** dinero mal habido *m*; **— woman** mujer ligera de cascos *f*; ADV (quickly) rápido, rápidamente; (firmly) firmemente; **— asleep** profundamente dormido; N ayuno *m*; VI ayunar; VI/VT **to —-forward** avanzar

fasten [fǽsən] VT (with buckles, buttons, hooks) abrochar[se], prender; (with ribbon, thread)

atar; (door) atrancar

fastener [fǽsənə] N cierre *m*

fastidious [fæstídiəs] ADJ (hard to please) maniático; (painstaking) minucioso

fasting [fǽstɪŋ] N ayuno *m*

fat [fæt] ADJ gordo; **— cat** pez gordo *m*; **— cell** célula adiposa *f*; **— chance** ¡ni soñar! **—head** idiota *mf*; **— job** trabajo lucrativo *m*; **— profits** pingües ganancias *f pl*; **to get —** engordar; N (oily substance) grasa *f*; (animal tissue) gordura *f*, sebo *m*; **the — of the land** la abundancia de la tierra

fatal [fédl] ADJ letal

fatality [fətǽlɪDi] N víctima fatal *f*; **— rate** índice de mortalidad *m*

fate [fet] N (lot) destino *m*, fatalidad *f*, hado *m*; (outcome) suerte *f*; VT destinar

father [fɑ́ðə] N padre *m*; **— figure** figura paterna *f*; **—-in-law** suegro *m*; **—land** patria *f*; VT engendrar

fatherhood [fɑ́ðəhʊd] N paternidad *f*

fatherly [fɑ́ðəli] ADV paternal

fathom [fǽðəm] N braza *f*; VT (measure) sondear; (understand) comprender

fatigue [fətíg] N fatiga *f*; **—s** ropa de faena *f*; VI/VT fatigar[se], rendir[se]

fatness [fǽtnɪs] N gordura *f*

fatso [fǽtso] N *pej* gordinflón *m*, tonel *m*

fatten [fǽtn̩] VT engordar, cebar

fatty [fǽDi] ADJ adiposo, graso; **— acids** ácidos grasos *m pl*; N (insult for fat people) *pej* gordo -da *mf*

faucet [fɔ́sɪt] N grifo *m*, llave *f*

fault [fɔlt] N (defect, misdeed) falta *f*; (responsibility) culpa *f*; (geological) falla *f*; **—finder** criticón -ona *mf*; **no-—** sin culpa; **careful to a —** demasiado cuidadoso; **to be at —** ser culpable; **to find — with** criticar a

faultless [fɔ́ltlɪs] ADJ perfecto

faulty [fɔ́lti] ADJ defectuoso; (grammar) vicioso

fauna [fɔ́nə] N fauna *f*

faux pas [fopá] N gaffe *f*, metedura de pata *f*

favor [févə] N (kind act, goodwill) favor *m*, gracia *f*; (popularity) popularidad *f*; (party gift) sorpresa *f*; VT (give help, show preference) favorecer; (foster) propiciar; (approve of) estar a favor de; **they are —ed to win** son los favoritos; **she —s her mother** se parece a su madre; **he's out of —** ha caído en desgracia

favorable [févəəbəl] ADJ favorable

favorite [févəɪt] ADJ & N preferido -da *mf*, favorito -ta *mf*, predilecto -ta *mf*

favoritism [févəɪtɪzəm] N favoritismo *m*

fawn [fɔn] N cervatillo *m*; VI **to — over** adular

fax [fæks] N fax *m*, facsímil *m*; VT faxear, enviar por fax

FBI [Federal Bureau of Investigation] [éfbíáí] N FBI *m*

fear [fir] N miedo *m*, temor *m*; — **of God** temor de Dios *m*; VI/VT (be afraid of) temer, tenerle miedo a; (suspect) temerse; **to — for** temer por

fearful [fírfəł] ADJ (causing fear) terrible, espantoso; (showing fear) temeroso, miedoso, medroso

fearless [fírlɪs] ADJ intrépido

fearlessness [fírlɪsnɪs] N intrepidez *f*

feasible [fízəbəł] ADJ factible

feast [fist] N (party, religious celebration) fiesta *f*; (abundant meal) festín *m*, banquete *m*; VI **to — on** darse un festín de; **to — one's eyes on** deleitarse la vista con

feat [fit] N (heroic act) hazaña *f*; (achievement) logro *m*

feather [féðɚ] N pluma *f*; **a — in one's cap** un triunfo personal; **—weight** peso pluma *m*; **birds of a — flock together** Dios los cría y ellos se juntan; VI/VT (grow feathers, cover with feathers) emplumar; (change blade angle) poner horizontal

feature [fítʃɚ] N (characteristic) aspecto *m*, característica *f*; (newspaper article) reportaje *m*; (facial) facción *f*, fisonomía *f*, rasgo *m*; — **article** artículo principal *m*; — **film** largometraje *m*; VT (give prominence to) destacar; (depict) mostrar; **this film —s John Smith** esta película cuenta con la actuación de John Smith; — **that!** ¡imagínate! VI figurar

February [fébjuɛri] N febrero *m*

fecal [fíkəł] ADJ fecal

feces [físiz] N PL heces *f pl*

fed [fɛd] *see* feed

federal [fédɚəł] ADJ federal

federation [fɛdɚéʃən] N federación *f*

fee [fi] N (professional) honorarios *m pl*; (artist) cachet *m*; (admission) derecho de admisión *m*; **—s** (university) matrícula *f*

feeble [fíbəł] ADJ (person) débil, endeble; (sound, light) tenue; **—-minded** (retarded) *pej* retrasado; (stupid) tonto

feed [fid] VI/VT (supply with food, materials) alimentar[se]; (prompt lines) apuntar; (broadcast) transmitir; **he —s sugar cubes to his horse** le da terrones de azúcar a su caballo; **I fed him a lie** le dije una mentira; **to be fed up** estar harto, estar hasta la coronilla; VI **to — into** desembocar en; N (fodder) pienso *m*, cebo *m*; (transmission) transmisión *f*; **—back** (electronic, mechanical) retroalimentación *f*; (critical) respuesta *f*, reacción *f*

feeding [fídɪŋ] N alimentación *f*; **—ing frenzy** (of the press) escándalo periodístico *m*; (of sharks, etc.) carnicería *f*; — **tube** sonda de alimentación *f*

feel [fił] VI/VT (perceive, experience) sentir[se];

(examine with the hands) palpar, manosear; (suffer) sufrir; (have an opinion) creer; VI (grope, check out) tantear; (seem) parecer; **to — one's way** tantear el camino, andar a tientas; **I — for you** te compadezco; **to — up/off** toquetear, manosear; **it —s soft** está suave al tacto; **I — like a coffee** tengo ganas de tomar un café; **to — up to something** sentirse capaz de algo; N (feeling) sensación *f*; (sense) tacto *m*; (ability) don *m*; (groping) manoseo *m*, toqueteo *m*

feeler [fílɚ] N (of insects) antena *f*; (of snails) cuerno *m*; (person who feels) persona emotiva *f*; **to put out —s** tantear el terreno

feeling [fílɪŋ] N (sense of touch) tacto *m*; (instance of physical perception) sensación *f*; (emotion) sentimiento *m*; (opinion) opinión *f*; (compassion) compasión *f*; **a — of sadness** un sentimiento de tristeza; **with —** con sentimiento; **to hurt someone's —s** herirle los sentimientos a alguien; ADJ sensible

feign [fen] VI/VT fingir, simular, aparentar

feisty [fáɪsti] ADJ (aggressive) pugnaz, belicoso; (energetic) vivaz

feline [fílaɪn] ADJ felino

fell [fɛł] VT (an animal) derribar; (a tree) talar; N (pelt) piel de animal *f*; **in one — swoop** de un golpe

fell [fɛł] *see* fall

fellatio [fəléʃio] N felación *f*

fellow [félo] N (member) miembro *m*; (scholar) becario -ria *mf*; (man or boy) tipo *m*; — **citizen** conciudadano -na *mf*; — **man** prójimo *m*; — **student** compañero -ra de clase *mf*

fellowship [féloʃɪp] N (friendly relations) amistad *f*; (community of interest) confraternidad *f*; (scholarship) beca *f*

felony [féləni] N delito grave *m*

felt [fɛłt] N fieltro *m*; ADJ de fieltro

felt [fɛłt] *see* feel

female [fímeł] N (animal) hembra *f*; (person) mujer *f*; ADJ (animal, fastener) hembra; (person) femenino

feminine [fémənɪn] ADJ femenino

femininity [femənínɪti] N feminidad *f*

feminism [fémənɪzəm] N feminismo *m*

feminist [fémɪnɪst] ADJ & N feminista *mf*

femur [fímɚ] N fémur *m*

fence [fɛns] N (barrier) cerca *f*, cerco *m*, valla *f*; (person who deals in stolen goods) *Am* reducidor -ora *mf*, *Sp* perista *mf*; (store for stolen goods) tienda de artículos robados *f*; **to be sitting on the —** estar indeciso; VT (enclose) cercar, vallar; **to — in** cercar; **to — off** dividir con una cerca; VI (sport) practicar esgrima

fencing [fénsɪŋ] N (dealing in stolen goods) tráfico en artículos robados *m*; (barrier) cerca *f*; (construction of barrier) cerco *m*; (sport) esgrima *f*

fender [féndə-] N guardabarro[s] *m sg*, guardafango *m*; — **bender** choquecito *m*

ferment¹ [fɜ-mɛnt] N fermento *m*

ferment² [fə-mént] VI/VT fermentar[se]

fermentation [fɜ-mɛntéʃən] N fermentación *f*

fern [fɜ-n] N helecho *m*

ferocious [fəróʃəs] ADJ feroz, fiero

ferocity [fərásɪDi] N ferocidad *f*, fiereza *f*

ferret [férɪt] N hurón *m*; VI **to — out** hurgar

Ferris wheel [férɪshwił] N rueda gigante *f*

ferry [féri] N ferry *m*, transbordador *m*; — **boat** ferry *m*; VT transportar de una orilla a otra; VI viajar en ferry

fertile [fɜ-dl] ADJ fértil, fecundo

fertility [fə-tílɪDi] N fertilidad *f*

fertilization [fɜ-dlɪzéʃən] N fertilización *f*, fecundación *f*

fertilize [fɜ-dlaɪz] VT fertilizar; (female, egg) fecundar; (land) abonar

fertilizer [fɜ-dlaɪzə-] N fertilizante *m*, abono *m*

fervent [fɜ-vənt] ADJ ferviente

fervor [fɜ-və-] N fervor *m*

fester [féstə-] VI (form pus) supurar; (rankle) enconarse

festival [féstəvəł] N festival *m*

festive [féstɪv] ADJ festivo

festivity [festívɪDi] N festividad *f*

fetal [fídl] ADJ fetal; — **position** posición fetal *f*; — **monitoring** monitorización fetal *f*

fetch [fetʃ] VT *Sp* ir a por; *Am* ir a buscar; **the ring —ed a fancy price** nos dieron una buena suma por el anillo; VI/VT (dog) buscar

fetching [fétʃɪŋ] ADJ atractivo

fetish [féDɪʃ] N fetiche *m*

fetter [féDɵ] N grillete *m*; VT engrillar

fetus [fíDəs] N feto *m*

feud [fjud] N enemistad hereditaria *f*; VI pelear

feudal [fjúdl] ADJ feudal

fever [fívə-] N fiebre *f*, calentura *f*; — **blister** herpes febril *m*; — **pitch** punto álgido *m*

feverish [fívə-ɪʃ] ADJ (related to fever) febril; (having a fever) afiebrado, destemplado

few [fju] ADJ & PRON pocos; — **er than expected** menos de los que se esperaba; **a —** unos pocos, algunos; **the —** una minoría

fiancé [fiɑnsé] N novio *m*, prometido *m*; —**e** novia *f*, prometida *f*

fiasco [fiǽsko] N fiasco *m*

fib [fɪb] N mentirilla *f*; VI decir mentirillas

fiber [fáɪbə-] N (textile) fibra *f*; (animal, vegetable) hebra *f*; —**-optic** de fibra óptica; —**glass** fibra de vidrio *f*

fibrous [fáɪbrəs] ADJ fibroso

fickle [fíkəł] ADJ veleidoso, mudable

fiction [fíkʃən] N ficción *f*

fictional [fíkʃən] ADJ novelesco

fictitious [fɪktíʃəs] ADJ ficticio

fiddle [fídl] N violín *m*; VI (play the violin) tocar el violín; **to — around** perder el tiempo; **to — with** juguetear con; **they like to — with the computer** siempre juguetean con la computadora

fidelity [fɪdélɪDi] N fidelidad *f*; **high —** alta fidelidad *f*

fidget [fídʒɪt] VI estar inquieto; **stop —ing!** ¡deja de moverte!

fiduciary [fɪdúʃieri] ADJ & N fiduciario -ria *mf*

field [fíłd] N (land, computers, heraldry, optics) campo *m*; (in sports) campo *m*; *Am* cancha *f*; (of oil) yacimiento *m*; (group of competitors) participantes *mf pl*; (of knowledge) campo *m*, terreno *m*; — **artillery** artillería de campaña *f*; — **day** (day for outdoor activity) día de campo *m*; (for military maneuvers) día de maniobras *m*; (unrestrained enjoyment) festín *m*; — **glasses** binoculares *m pl*; — **goal** gol de campo *m*; — **mouse** ratón de campo *m*; — **trip** (in school) paseo escolar *m*; (in science) viaje de estudio *m*; —**work** trabajo de campo *m*; VT (a baseball) atrapar, fildear; (questions) contestar

fielding [fíłdɪŋ] N (of questions) contestación *f*; (of baseballs) fildeo *m*

fiend [find] N (devil) demonio *m*, diablo *m*; (fanatic) fanático -ca *mf*

fierce [firs] ADJ (animals) feroz, fiero; (illness) espantoso; (storms, etc.) furioso, espantoso; (competition, debate) intenso, encarnizado; (look) torvo

fierceness [fírsnɪs] N ferocidad *f*, bravura *f*

fiery [fáɪəri] ADJ (passionate) fogoso; (hot, causing burning sensation) ardiente

fife [faɪf] N pífano *m*

fifteen [fɪftíɪn] NUM quince

fifth [fɪfθ] ADJ & N quinto *m*; (measure of liquor) tres cuartos de un litro *m pl*

fifty [fífti] NUM cincuenta; ADV **to go —** ir a medias; ADJ **a —-— chance** un cincuenta por ciento de probabilidades

fig [fɪg] N higo *m*; — **leaf** hoja de higuera *f*; — **tree** higuera *f*; **it's not worth a —** no vale ni un pepino/pito

fight [faɪt] N (combat) lucha *f*, combate *m*; **the — against AIDS** la lucha contra el SIDA; (argument) pelea *f*, riña *f*; VI/VT (combat) luchar [con], pelear [con]; VI (argue) pelear, reñir; **to — a duel** batirse a duelo; **to — back** (to hold back) contener; (resist) resistir; **to — it out** arreglarlo a los golpes; **to — off** rechazar; **to — one's way through** abrirse camino a la fuerza

fighter [fáɪDə-] N (boxer) boxeador -ora *mf*; (someone who fights) luchador -ora *mf*; (dog, cock) animal de pelea/riña *m*; — **airplane** avión caza *m*

fighting [fáɪDɪŋ] N (fight) lucha *f*; ADJ

combativo; — **chance** posibilidad remota f;
— **words** palabras incendiarias f pl
figurative [fígjə-əDIv] ADJ (art) figurativo;
(language) figurado
figure [fígjə-] N (number, amount) cifra f; (form,
bodily shape, representation, dance move,
syllogism) figura f; (character) personaje m;
—**head** figurón de proa m; — **of speech**
figura retórica f; —**s** (written symbols)
números m pl; — **skating** patinaje artístico
m; **to cut a poor** — dar una mala impresión;
VI (appear) figurar; VI/VT (think)
imaginar[se], figurar[se]; **to** — **in** tener en
cuenta; **to** — **on** contar con; **to** — **out** (solve)
resolver; (calculate) calcular; **it** —**s**! no me
extraña, era de esperar; VT calcular
Fijian [fídʒiən] N fijiano -na mf
Fiji Islands [fídʒiáiləndz] N Islas Fiji f pl
filament [fíləmənt] N filamento m
file [faɪł] N (documents) archivo m; (for
computers) archivo m, fichero m; (official
report) expediente m, legajo m; (line) fila f;
(tool) lima f; — **compression** compresión
de archivos f; — **format** formato de archivo/
fichero m; —**name** nombre de archivo m; —
server servidor m; **on** — archivado; **filing**
cabinet fichero m, archivador m; VT (papers)
archivar; (news story) entregar; (tax return,
claim, etc.) presentar; **to** — **a suit** entablar
una demanda, querellarse; VI (for a job)
presentarse; (walk in a line) desfilar; VI/VT
(smooth) limar
filial [fíliəł] ADJ filial
filiation [filiéʃən] N filiación f
filibuster [fíləbʌstə-] VI/VT practicar
obstrucción parlamentaria; N filibusterismo
m, obstrucción f
filigree [fíligri] N filigrana f
fill [fíł] VI/VT (glass, container) llenar[se]; (a hole,
a pastry, land) rellenar; **the smell** —**ed the**
room la habitación se llenó del olor; **the**
airline —**ed the position** la compañía
aérea llenó el cargo; **the new employee**
—**ed the vacancy** el nuevo empleado ocupó
el cargo vacante; VT (a tooth) empastar;
(prescription, order) despachar; (a need)
satisfacer; VI (sails) hinchar; **to** — **out** llenar;
to — **in** (inform) informar; (fill out a form)
llenar; (replace) sustituir; **to** — **up** llenarse
hasta el tope
fillet[1] [fɪlé] N filete m; VT filetear
fillet[2] [fílɪt] N cinta f
filling [fílɪŋ] N (act) rellenado m; (filler) relleno
m; (of a tooth) empaste m; — **station**
estación de servicio f, gasolinera f
filly [fíli] N potranca f
film [fíłm] N (video) película f, filme m;
(celluloid) película f, cinta f; (thin coating)
película f; — **industry** industria

cinematográfica f; —**maker** cineasta mf;
VI/VT filmar, cinematografiar
filming [fíłmɪŋ] N filmación f
filter [fíłtə-] N filtro m; VI/VT filtrar[se]
filtering [fíłtə-ɪŋ] N filtración f
filth [fíłθ] N (dirt, despicable person) mugre f,
suciedad f; (moral impurity) porquería f;
(vulgar material) obscenidades f pl
filthiness [fíłθinɪs] N suciedad f
filthy [fíłθi] ADJ (dirty) cochino, mugriento;
(vile) puerco, cochino; Sp guarro; (obscene)
obsceno; — **rich** riquísimo
filtration [fíłtréʃən] N filtración f
fin [fín] N aleta f
final [fáɪnł] ADJ (result, conclusion) final; (last)
último; (conclusive) definitivo; — **score**
resultado final m; — **stretch** recta final f; N
(in sports) final f; (exam) examen final m
finalist [fáɪnłɪst] N finalista mf
finalize [fáɪnłaɪz] VT completar, ultimar
finally [fáɪnłi] ADV (at last) finalmente, por fin;
(lastly) finalmente, por último
finance [fáɪnæns] N finanza f; —**s** finanzas f pl;
VI/VT (to fund) financiar; (to purchase on
credit) comprar financiado
financial [fɪnǽnʃəł] ADJ financiero; —
disclosure divulgación financiera f
financier [fɪnænsír] N financiero -ra mf
financing [fáɪnænsɪŋ] N financiamiento m; Am
financiación f
find [faɪnd] VT hallar, encontrar; (discover)
descubrir; (determine innocence or guilt)
declarar; VI (determine officially) fallar; **to** —
fault with criticar a, censurar a; **to** — **out**
(discover) descubrir; (verify) averiguar; N
hallazgo m
finding [fáɪndɪŋ] N fallo m; —**s** resultados m pl
fine [faɪn] ADJ (wine, sand, hair, precious metal)
fino; (thread) delgado; (cloth) delicado;
(artist, athlete) consumado; (manners)
refinado; (good-looking person) atractivo,
guapo; (weather) bueno; (distinction) sutil; —
arts bellas artes f pl; — **print** letra pequeña f,
letra chica f; **I'm** — estoy bien; **to feel** —
sentirse muy bien de salud; **to have a** —
time pasarlo bien; N multa f; VT multar; **to**
—**-tune** (a receiver) sintonizar; (an engine)
ajustar; (a plan) afinar
finery [fáɪnəri] N galas f pl
finesse [fɪnés] N (subtlety) sutileza f; (tact)
diplomacia f; VI usar artimañas; VT conseguir
por artimañas
finger [fíŋgə-] N dedo m; — **food** canapé m,
aperitivo m; —**nail** uña f; —**print** huella
dactilar/digital f; —**tip** punta del dedo f; **at**
one's —**tips** al alcance de la mano; **little** —
dedo meñique m; **middle** — dedo del
corazón m; **to give someone the** — hacerle
un gesto obsceno a alguien; **I'll keep my** —**s**

crossed cruzo los dedos; **to wrap someone around one's** — meterse a alguien en el bolsillo; **I can't put my** — **on it** no sabría decir lo que es; VT (play a guitar) tañer; (squeal on) delatar

finicky [fíniki] ADJ melindroso, dengoso

finish [fíniʃ] VI/VT (end) terminar[se], finalizar[se]; VT (polish) pulir; (varnish) barnizar; (kill) liquidar; **to** — **off** acabar con, rematar; **to** — **up** terminar; N (ending) final *m*; (decisive end) fin *m*; (polish, treatment) acabado *m*; (varnish) barniz *m*; (coat of paint) última mano *f*; — **line** meta *f*; **with a rough** — sin pulir

finished [fíniʃt] ADJ (doomed) acabado; (polished) pulido

finite [fáinait] ADJ finito

Finland [fínlənd] N finlandia *f*

Finn [fin] N finlandés -esa *mf*, finés -esa *mf*

Finnish [fíniʃ] ADJ finlandés, finés

fir [fɝ] N abeto *m*

fire [fair] N (flame) fuego *m*; (conflagration) incendio *m*; (passion) ardor *m*; (for cigarettes, hearths) lumbre *f*; — **alarm** alarma contra incendios *f*; —**cracker** triquitraque *m*; — **drill** simulacro de incendio *m*; — **department** cuerpo de bomberos *m*; — **engine** coche de bomberos *m*, autobomba *f*; — **escape** escalera de incendios *f*; — **extinguisher** extinguidor [de incendios] *m*, extintor *m*; — **fighter** bombero -ra *mf*; —**fly** luciérnaga *f*; — **hydrant** boca de incendio *f*; — **insurance** seguro contra incendios *m*; —**man** (who extinguishes) bombero *m*; (who stokes) fogonero *m*; —**place** hogar *m*, chimenea *f*; —**proof** ininflamable, a prueba de incendio; — **sale** venta de liquidación *f*; —**side** hogar *m*; — **station** estación de bomberos *f*; — **trap** edificio sin medios de escape en caso de incendio *m*; —**wall** cortafuegos *m sg*; —**wood** leña *f*; —**works** fuegos artificiales *m pl*; **when he finds out, there will be** —**works** cuando se entere, se va a armar la gorda; **to be on** — estar quemándose; **to catch** — incendiarse, prenderse fuego; **to set** — **to** prender fuego a, incendiar; **under** — bajo fuego; **to play with** — jugar con fuego; **firing pin** percutor *m*; **firing squad** pelotón de fusilamiento *m*; VT (pottery) cocer; (an employee) despedir; (a projectile) lanzar; **to** —**proof** hacer incombustible, ignifugar; VI/VT (a gun) disparar; VI **to** — **up** entusiasmar; **to** — **off** (gun) disparar; (letter) despachar

firm [fɝm] ADJ (solid, unwavering) firme; (fixed) fijo; (not fluctuating, as prices) estable; VI/VT **to** — **up** (finalize) concretar; (harden) endurecer; N firma *f*; —**ware** programas almacenados en circuitos integrados *m pl*

firmly [fɝmli] ADV con firmeza, firmemente

firmness [fɝmnis] N firmeza *f*

first [fɝst] ADJ primero; — **aid** primeros auxilios *m pl*; — **base** primera base *f*, inicial *f*; — **baseman** primera base *mf*, inicialista *mf*; **to get to** — **base** comenzar con éxito; —**born** primogénito -ta *mf*; — **chapter** capítulo primero *m*, primer capítulo *m*; — **class** primera clase *f*; —**-class** de primera clase; — **cousin** primo hermano; —**-degree** (burn) de primer grado; (murder) en primer grado; — **floor** (ground floor) planta baja *f*; **for the** — **time** por primera vez; — **half** primer tiempo *m*; —**hand** de primera mano; — **lady** primera dama *f*; — **name** nombre de pila *m*; — **person** primera persona *f*; —**-rate** de primera clase; ADV (before anything else) primero; **I'd die** — antes la muerte; **at** — al principio; — **off** al principio; N (first in series) primero -ra *mf*; (low gear) primera *f*

fiscal [fískəɫ] ADJ fiscal; — **period** año fiscal *m*

fish [fiʃ] N (in water) pez *m*; (out of water) pescado *m*; — **farm** piscifactoría *f*; —**hook** anzuelo *m*; — **market** pescadería *f*; — **story** patraña *f*; **like a** — **out of water** como sapo de otro pozo; **neither** — **nor fowl** ni chicha ni limonada; **I have other** — **to fry** tengo otras cosas mejores que hacer; VI/VT pescar; **to** — **out** sacar, rebuscar; **to** — **for compliments** buscar cumplidos; **to** —**tail** colear

fisherman [fíʃəmən] N pescador *m*

fishery [fíʃəri] N (for breeding) piscifactoría *f*; (for fishing) pesquería *f*; (industry) industria pesquera *f*

fishing [fíʃiŋ] N pesca *f*; — **pole/rod** caña de pescar *f*; — **tackle** aparejos de pescar *m pl*; **to go** — ir de pesca

fishy [fíʃi] ADJ (of smell, taste) a pescado; (suspicious) sospechoso

fissure [fíʃə] N fisura *f*

fist [fist] N puño *m*; —**fight** pelea a puñetazos *f*

fistula [fístʃələ] N fístula *f*

fit [fit] ADJ (suited) apto; (healthy) en buen estado físico; **are you** — **for driving?** ¿estás en condiciones de manejar? ADV **he didn't see** — **to greet her** no se dignó a saludarla; N (process of fitting) prueba *f*; (mechanical union) encaje *m*; (attack of a disease) ataque *m*; (sudden outburst) rapto *m*; (of anger, coughing) acceso *m*; **to throw a** — tener una pataleta; **by** —**s and starts** a trompicones; **that suit is a good** — ese traje le queda bien; VT (be suitable for) adecuarse a; (be in agreement with) cuadrar con, ajustarse a; (measure for clothes) tomarle las medidas a; (make suitable) capacitar, preparar; **to** — **in with** acomodarse a; **I tried to** — **you in** traté de incluirte; VI (conform to contours of a person) quedarle bien a alguien; (conform to the contours of a mechanism) encajar

fitness [fítnɪs] N (suitability) aptitud *f*; (health) buen estado físico *m*

fitting [fíDɪŋ] ADJ apropiado; N ajuste *m*; (trying on) prueba *f*

five [faɪv] NUM cinco; — **hundred** quinientos

fix [fɪks] VT (repair, arrange) arreglar; (place permanently, determine) fijar; (prepare food) preparar; **to** — **up** arreglar, aviar; **to get an animal** —**ed** castrar a un animal; **I was** —**ing to call** estaba a punto de llamar; **I'll** — **you!** ¡ya te arreglo! N (predicament) apuro *m*, aprieto *m*; (temporary repair) arreglo provisorio *m*; (narcotic injection) chute *m*; **to get a** — **on** localizar

fixed [fɪkst] ADJ (stationary) fijo; (arranged in advance) arreglado; — **term** a plazo fijo; —- **rate mortgage** hipoteca de tasa fija *f*

fixture [fíkstʃɚ] N (bath, kitchen component) instalaciones *f pl*; **she's a permanent** — **in this office** está siempre en la oficina

fizzle [fízəł] VI (fail) fracasar; **to** — **[out]** (make a noise) apagarse chisporroteando; (interest) esfumarse

flabby [flǽbi] ADJ flácido/fláccido

flaccid [flǽsɪd] ADJ flácido/fláccido

flag [flæg] N (also in golf) bandera *f*; —**pole** mástil *m*; —**staff** mástil *m*; —**stone** losa *f*, baldosa *f*; VT (adorn with flags) embanderar; (mark with flags) marcar con banderas; (for attention) marcar, identificar; **to** — **[down]** hacer parar; VI (diminish) menguar

flagrant [flégrənt] ADV flagrante

flair [flɛr] N (aptitude) aptitud *f*, facilidad *f*; (style) estilo *m*

flak [flæk] N (antiartillery fire) fuego antiaéreo *m*; (criticism) crítica *f*

flake [flek] N (snow) copo *m*; (small thin piece) escama *f*; (eccentric person) chiflado -da *mf*; VI descascararse

flamboyant [flæmbóɪənt] ADJ (clothes) llamativo; (behavior) extravagante

flame [flem] N llama *f*; — **thrower** lanzallamas *m sg*; **old** — viejo amor *m*; VI llamear, flamear, encenderse

flaming [flémɪŋ] ADJ (emitting flames) llameante; (like a flame) flamígero; (ardent) ardiente; — **red** rojo encendido

flammable [flǽməbəł] ADJ inflamable

flank [flæŋk] N (of a bastion or army) flanco *m*; (of an animal) ijar *m*; VT flanquear

flannel [flǽnl̩] N franela *f*, lanilla *f*

flap [flæp] VI (wings) aletear; (flag) flamear; VT (wings) batir; (arms) sacudir; N (of a jacket, pocket) cartera *f*; (of a saddle, table) hoja *f*; (of an airplane) alerón *m*; (action of flapping) aleteo *m*

flare [flɛr] VI (burn unsteadily) llamear; (become

wider) ensancharse; **to** — **up** (fire) avivarse; (activity, illness) recrudecer; VT (a skirt) levantar; (a flame) avivar; (a pipe) abocinar; (signal by flare) señalar con bengala; N (flaring light, burst of flame) llamarada *f*; (signal light) bengala *f*; (sudden emotional outburst) arranque *m*; (outward curvature) vuelo *m*; —**up** recrudecimiento *m*

flash [flæʃ] N (of light) destello *m*, ráfaga *f*; (of explosion) fogonazo *m*; (news, camera, vision, computer memory) flash *m*; —**back** flashback *m*, escena retrospectiva *f*; —**bulb** flash *m*; —**flood** riada *f*; —**light** linterna *f*; — **of hope** rayo de esperanza *m*; — **of lightning** relampagueo *m*, rayo *m*; **in a** — en un instante; VI/VT (shine) destellar [sobre]; (expose oneself) exhibir[se]; VI (gleam) relucir, fulgurar, relampaguear; (appear) aparecer; VT (display) ostentar; **to** — **by** pasar como un relámpago

flashing [flǽʃɪŋ] ADJ destellante

flashy [flǽʃi] ADJ (colorful) llamativo; (ostentatious) ostentoso; (tasteless) chillón, de mal gusto

flask [flæsk] N (glass container) frasco *m*; (in a laboratory) matraz *m*, redoma *f*; (for alcoholic beverages) petaca *f*

flat [flæt] ADJ (surface) plano; (land) llano; (skin) liso; (spatial orientation) horizontal, acostado; (city) arrasado, aplastado; (shoes, nose) chato; (tire) desinflado, pinchado; (color) apagado; (beer, tonic water) sin gas; (mood) soso; (paint) mate; (denial) terminante; (photo) sin contraste; (pitch) demasiado grave; (musical note) bemol; —**footed** con pie plano; — **rate** tarifa fija *f*; — **tax** impuesto de tasa única *m*; **trading was** — hubo poco movimiento bursátil; **to be** — **broke** estar completamente pelado; **to fall** — (of a body) caer de plano/redondo; (of a joke) caer mal; (of a plan) fracasar; N (shoe) zapato sin tacón *m*; (flat tire) desinflado *m*, pinchadura *f*, pinchazo *m*; (wooden box) caja para plantas *f*; (musical note) bemol *m*; —**iron** plancha *f*; ADV —-**out** (directly) absolutamente; (at full speed) a toda velocidad; **in two minutes** — en dos minutos exactos

flatten [flǽtn̩] VI/VT (make flat) achatar[se], aplanar[se]; VT (knock down) tumbar, voltear; (raze) arrasar

flatter [flǽDɚ] VI/VT (manipulate) lisonjear, adular; (praise) halagar; **this picture** —**s you** esta foto te favorece; **I was** —**ed by his attentions** me halagaron sus atenciones

flatterer [flǽDərɚ] N lisonjero -ra *mf*, adulador -ora *mf*

flattering [flǽDɚɪŋ] ADJ (comment) lisonjero, halagüeño; (person) adulón

flattery [fléeDəri] N lisonja f, adulación f, halago m
flatulence [flǽtʃələns] N flatulencia f
flaunt [flɔnt] VI/VT ostentar, lucir[se]
flavor [flévə-] N (taste, quality) sabor m; (flavoring) condimento m; VT sazonar
flavorless [flévə-lɪs] ADJ insípido
flaw [flɔ] N (in character, in construction) defecto m; (in an argument) falla f
flawless [flɔ́lɪs] ADJ (logic) impecable; (behavior) intachable, irreprochable; (appearance) perfecto
flax [flæks] N lino m
flea [fli] N pulga f; — **collar** collar antipulgas m; — **market** Sp rastro m; Am mercado de [las] pulgas m
fled [flɛd] see flee
flee [fli] VI huir; VT huir de
fleece [flis] N vellón m; VT (shear) trasquilar, esquilar; (defraud) estafar; (in card games) pelar, desplumar
fleet [flit] N (of boats, buses) flota f; (of cars) parque m; ADJ veloz
fleeting [flíDɪŋ] ADJ fugaz, efímero, pasajero
flemish [flémɪʃ] ADJ & N flamenco ca m f
flesh [flɛʃ] N carne f; (of a fruit) pulpa f; — **and blood** carne y hueso; **of my own — and blood** de mi propia sangre; **in the —** en persona; VI/VT **to — out** (a character) dar cuerpo a; (an argument) desarrollar
fleshy [fléʃi] ADJ (succulent) carnoso; (fat) metido en carnes
flew [flu] see fly
flexibility [flɛksəbílɪDi] N flexibilidad f
flexible [fléksəbəł] ADJ flexible
flicker [flíkə-] VI (stars) titilar; (candle) parpadear; N (of light) parpadeo m, titilación f; (of hope) rayo m
flier [fláɪə-] N (one who flies) volador -ora m f; (aviator) aviador -ora m f; (leaflet) volante m
flight [flaɪt] N (act of flying, trip) vuelo m; (trajectory) trayectoria f; (flock of birds) bandada f; (group of military aircraft) escuadrilla f; (escape) fuga f, huida f; — **attendant** auxiliar de vuelo m f; — **plan** plan de vuelo m; — **school** escuela de aviación f; — **recorder** caja negra f; — **simulator** simulador de vuelo m, registrador de vuelo m; **a — of fancy** una fantasía; — **of stairs** tramo de escalera m; **to put to —** poner en fuga; **to take —** darse a la fuga
flimsy [flímzi] ADJ (structure, argument) endeble; (excuse) flojo, pobre
flinch [flɪntʃ] VI pestañear
fling [flɪŋ] VT arrojar, lanzar; **she flung herself at the attacker** se le tiró arriba al atacante; **he flung himself into his work** se dedicó de lleno a su trabajo; **he flung**

open the door abrió la puerta de golpe; N (act of flinging) lanzamiento m; (sexual affair) aventura f
flint [flɪnt] N pedernal m
flip [flɪp] VT (a coin) tirar; (a switch on) levantar; (a switch off) bajar; (a pancake) dar vuelta; VI (go head over heels) dar una voltereta; (get excited, go crazy) volverse loco; **to — through** hojear; — **-flop** (reversal of opinion) giro de 180 grados m; (backward somersault) voltereta para atrás f; (slipper) chancleta f; — **side** la otra cara de la moneda
flippant [flípənt] ADJ (frivolous) frívolo, displicente; (impudent) impertinente
flipper [flípə-] N aleta f
flirt [flɜ-t] VI coquetear; N coqueto -ta m f
flirtation [flɜ-téʃən] N coquetería f, coqueteo m
flit [flɪt] VI revolotear; **a smile —s across her face** una sonrisa le cruza la cara
float [flot] VI (rest on water, air, fluctuate freely) flotar; (in soup) sobrenadar; (drift) errar, ir a la deriva; **she —ed down the stairs** se deslizó por la escalera; VT (set afloat) poner a flote; (start a company, scheme) lanzar; (issue shares) emitir; (let fluctuate) dejar flotar; (try out an idea) proponer; N (thing that floats) flotador m; (on a line) corcho m, boya f; (in a parade) carro alegórico m, carroza f; (with soda) gaseosa con helado f
flock [flɑk] N (birds, children) bandada f; (sheep) rebaño m; (worshipers) grey f; (people) muchedumbre f; VI acudir en masa, afluir; **to — around someone** rodear a alguien; **to — together** andar juntos
flog [flɑg] VT azotar
flood [flʌd] N inundación f; (of tides) creciente f; —**gate** (of a dam) compuerta f; (of a canal lock) esclusa f; — **insurance** seguro contra inundaciones m; —**light** reflector m; — **of tears** torrente de lágrimas m; **the —** el Diluvio Universal; VI/VT inundar[se], anegar[se]; (car) ahogar[se], emborrachar[se]
floor [flɔr] N (surface of a room, vehicle) suelo m, piso m; (story) piso m; (of sea) fondo m; (for dancing) pista f; (minimum level) mínimo m; **to have the —** tener la palabra; VT (knock down) tumbar, derribar; (stun, surprise) asombrar; — **it!** ¡acelera! Sp ¡mete caña!
flooring [flɔ́rɪŋ] N revestimiento m
flop [flɑp] VI (flail) zarandearse; (fish) dar coletazos; (drop) dejarse caer; (fail) fracasar; **to — down** dejarse caer, desplomarse; **to — over** voltear[se] flojamente; N (failure) fracaso m; (sound) ruido sordo m
floppy [flápi] ADJ caído; — **disk** disquete m, floppy m
flora [flɔ́rə] N flora f
florist [flɔ́rɪst] N florista m f; —**'s shop** florería f
floss [flɔs] N (silk fibers) seda floja f; (for

embroidery) hilo de seda *m*; (dental) hilo
dental *m*; VI/VT pasar hilo dental [por]
flounder [fláʊndɚ] VI (in mud, etc.) andar/
moverse con dificultades; (for an answer)
quedarse sin saber qué decir, perder pie; N
platija *f*
flour [flaʊr] N harina *f*
flourish [flɝɪʃ] VI (prosper) florecer, prosperar;
VT (brandish) blandir; N (ornament, florid
language, brandishing) floreo *m*; (of music)
floritura *f*; (of a signature) rúbrica *f*; **in full**
— en plena eclosión
flow [flo] VI (run) fluir, correr; (issue forth)
surgir, brotar; (come and go) circular; (fall
loosely) caer; (abound) abundar; (rise) crecer;
to — into desembocar en, afluir a; N (of
liquid) flujo *m*; (of electricity) corriente *f*; (of
traffic, blood, air) circulación *f*; **—chart**
diagrama de flujo *m*, organigrama *m*; **— of
words** torrente de palabras *m*
flower [fláʊɚ] N flor *f*; (paragon) flor y nata *f*; **in
— en flor; — bed** *Mex*, *Sp* arriate *m*; *RP*
cantero *m*; **—pot** maceta *f*, tiesto *m*; **— vase**
florero *m*; VI florecer
flowery [fláʊɚi] ADJ (of a garden, language)
florido; (of a pattern) floreado; (of a
fragrance) floral
flowing [flóɪŋ] ADJ (liquid) fluyente; (clothing)
suelto
flown [flon] *see* fly
flu [flu] N gripe *f*, *Am* gripa *f*
fluctuate [flʌ́ktʃuet] VI fluctuar
fluctuation [flʌktʃuéʃən] N fluctuación *f*
fluency [flúənsi] N fluidez *f*
fluent [flúənt] ADJ fluido; **he is — in French**
habla francés con fluidez/soltura
fluff [flʌf] VT mullir; (blunder) pifiar; N pelusa *f*;
(blunder) pifia *f*; **this book is pure —** este
libro es insustancial
fluffy [flʌ́fi] ADJ (airy) mullido; (covered with
fluff) peludo
fluid [flúɪd] ADJ & N fluido *m*, líquido *m*; **—
ounce** onza líquida [29.42 mililiters] *f*; **—
retention** retención de líquido *f*
fluke [fluk] N (of whale) aleta *f*; (chance) chiripa
f; **by a —** por chiripa
flung [flʌŋ] *see* fling
flunk [flʌŋk] VI/VT *Am* reprobar, *Sp* suspender;
VI **to — out** *Am* salir reprobado, *Sp* salir
suspendido
flunky [flʌ́ŋki] N (lackey, servant) lacayo *m*;
(yes-man) adulón *m*
fluorescent [flʊrésənt] ADJ fluorescente; **—
light** tubo fluorescente *m*
fluoride [flɔ́raɪd] N (chemical) fluoruro *m*;
(dental aid) flúor *m*
fluorine [flɔ́rin] N flúor *m*
flurry [flɝi] N (of snow) nevisca *f*; (of activity)
frenesí *m*

flush [flʌʃ] N (rosy glow, heat) rubor *m*; (of
anger) arranque *m*; (of youth, color)
resplandor *m*; (of embarrassment) sonrojo *m*;
(in poker) color *m*; **did you hear the — of
the toilet?** ¿oíste el sonido de la cisterna?
ADJ (well supplied, rich) forrado; (ruddy,
reddish) rubicundo; (full) rebosante; **— with**
a[l] ras de; **— against** pegado a; VI/VT (make
or turn red) sonrojar[se], ruborizar[se];
(activate toilet) tirar la cadena; (rinse) baldear
fluster [flʌ́stɚ] VI/VT agitar[se], poner[se]
nervioso
flute [flut] N (musical instrument) flauta *f*; (of a
column) estría *f*; VT estriar
flutter [flʌ́dɚ] VI (wings) aletear; (butterfly)
revolotear; (flag) tremolar; (heart) palpitar;
VT (agitate) agitar; N (of wings) aleteo *m*; (of
excitement) agitación *f*; (of a fly) tremolar *m*;
(of the heart) palpitación *f*
flux [flʌks] N flujo *m*; **a state of —** un estado de
cambio continuo
fly [flaɪ] VI (through air) volar; (from danger)
huir; (flag) ondear; (kite) remontar; VT
(aircraft) pilotar; (air cargo) transportar en
avión; **to — away** volarse; **to — into a rage**
montar en cólera; **to — off the handle**
perder los estribos; **to — open [shut]** abrirse
[cerrarse] de un golpe; **to — out of a room**
salir disparado de un cuarto; **that idea
won't —** esa idea no va a ser aceptada; **he
flew the coop** se escapó; N (insect) mosca *f*;
(over a zipper) bragueta *f*; **— ball** (in baseball)
volea *f*, bombo *m*, elevado *m*, palomita *f*;
—catcher papamoscas *m sg*; **—swatter**
matamoscas *m sg*; **—wheel** volante *m*; **on
the —** al vuelo
flying [fláɪɪŋ] ADJ (passing through the air)
volador; (fluttering) ondeante; **with —
colors** con distinción; **— saucer** platillo
volador *m*; N **I hate —** no me gusta viajar en
avión
foam [fom] N (suds, padding) espuma *f*; **—
rubber** goma espuma *f*; VI hacer espuma; **to
— at the mouth** echar espuma por la boca
focus [fókəs] N foco *m*; VI/VT (bring into or be in
focus) enfocar[se]; (concentrate) centrarse; **to
— on** fijarse en
fodder [fádɚ] N forraje *m*
foe [fo] N enemigo -ga *mf*
fog [fɑg] N niebla *f*; **to be in a —** estar
confundido; **—horn** sirena de niebla *f*; VI/VT
(confuse) ofuscar; (spray with insecticide)
fumigar; (become faded) velar[se]; **to — up**
(window) empañar[se]; (one's sight)
nublar[se]; **the airport was —ged in** el
aeropuerto estaba cerrado por niebla
foggy [fági] ADJ (weather) brumoso, nebuloso;
(window) empañado; (confused) confuso;
(blurred, as a photograph) borroso

foil [fɔɪł] N (any metal) hoja de metal f; (aluminum) papel de aluminio m; (on mirrors) azogue m; (rapier) florete m; (thing contrasted) contraste m; VT frustrar

fold [fołd] VI/VT (sheets) doblar[se]; (paper, folding chairs) plegar[se]; (wings, flag) replegar[se]; (in cards) abandonar; (close a business) cerrar[se]; (end a performance) bajar de cartel; **to — one's arms** cruzarse de brazos; N (pleat, hollow) pliegue m; (crease) doblez m; (enclosure) redil m, aprisco m; (sheep) rebaño m; (congregation) grey f; **to rejoin the —** volver al redil; **three—** tres veces

folder [fółdɚ] N (file) carpeta f; (instrument for folding) plegadera f

folding [fółdɪŋ] ADJ plegadizo, plegable; — **chair** silla plegadiza f; — **screen** biombo m; N doblado m

foliage [fóliɪʤ] N follaje m, fronda f, ramaje m

folic acid [fólɪkæsɪd] N ácido fólico m

folio [fólio] N (page) folio m; (book) libro en folio m

folk [fok] N (people) gente f; (nation) pueblo m; ADJ popular; — **dance** baile folclórico/folklórico m; —**lore** folclore/folklore m; (traditional stories) leyendas tradicionales f pl; — **medicine** medicina tradicional f; — **music** música folclórica/folklórica f; — **song** canción tradicional f; — **tale** cuento folclórico/folklórico m; **old —s** los viejos; —**s** (relatives) parientes m pl; fam (parents) padres m pl, viejos m pl

folkloric [foklórɪk] ADJ folclórico/folklórico

follicle [fálɪkəł] N folículo m

folliculitis [fəlɪkjəláɪdɪs] N foliculitis f

follow [fálo] VI/VT seguir; VI (be a consequence) seguirse; (come next) ir a continuación; **to — suit** seguir el ejemplo, secundar; **to — through** llevar a cabo; **to — up [on]** (pursue) obtener más detalles [sobre]; (develop) desarrollar; N —**through** (in sports) acompañamiento m, continuación f; —**-up** seguimiento m

follower [fáloɚ] N seguidor -ora mf

following [fáloɪŋ] N seguidores -oras mf pl; **the — lo siguiente; ADJ siguiente

foment [fomént] VT fomentar

fond [fand] ADJ **I'm — of cats** soy amigo de los gatos, me encantan los gatos; **I'm — of Chinese food** me gusta la comida china; **I'm — of John** le tengo cariño a Juan; — **hopes** ilusión f; **to become — of** encariñarse de

fondle [fándl] VI/VT (touch affectionately) acariciar; (grope) manosear, sobar

fondness [fándnɪs] N (affection) cariño m, afecto m; (liking or weakness) afición f

font [fant] N (of water) pila f; (of characters) tipo de letra m

food [fud] N comida f, alimento m; — **chain** cadena alimenticia f; — **poisoning** intoxicación por alimentos f; — **stamps** cupones para alimentos m pl; —**stuff** producto alimenticio m; — **for thought** algo para reflexionar

fool [fuł] N (foolish person) tonto -ta mf, bobo -ba mf, necio -cia mf; (jester) bufón m; —**proof** (plan) infalible, a prueba de fallos; (device) a prueba de tontos; **to make a — of** hacer quedar como un tonto; **to play the —** hacer el tonto; **I'm a card-playing —** soy loco por los naipes; VI bromear; **to — around** tontear; VT engañar

foolish [fúlɪʃ] ADJ tonto, necio

foolishness [fúlɪʃnɪs] N tontería f, bobería f, sandez f

foot [fʊt] N pie m; (of an animal) pata f; —**-and-mouth disease** fiebre aftosa f; —**ball** (American) fútbol americano m; (soccer) fútbol m; (ball) balón [de fútbol] m, pelota [de fútbol] f; — **fault** falta de pie f; —**hill** pie de la montaña m; —**hold** punto de apoyo m; —**lights** candilejas f pl; —**man** lacayo m; —**note** nota al pie de página f, llamada f; —**path** senda f; —**print** huella f, pisada f; —**race** carrera a pie f; — **soldier** soldado de infantería m; —**step** pisada f, paso m; —**print** huella f, pisada f; —**stool** taburete m; —**wear** calzado m; —**work** (in sports) juego de piernas m; **to follow in the —steps of** seguir los pasos de; **he has a —hold in the computer business** ha logrado establecerse en el negocio de la informática; **it'll take some pretty fancy —work to get out of this** va a ser difícil zafarse de esto; **on —** a pie; **to put one's — in it** meter la pata; VI **to — it** andar a pie; VT **to — the bill** pagar la cuenta

footing [fúdɪŋ] N (basis) base f; (foothold) punto de apoyo m; **to be on a friendly — with** tener relaciones amistosas con; **to lose one's —** perder pie

for [fɔr] PREP para, por; **this gift is — John** este regalo es para John; **we're headed — the beach** vamos para la playa; **this is a device — sorting letters** este es un aparato para clasificar cartas; **they gave me enough food — three people** me dieron comida [como] para tres personas; **she's studying — the bar** está estudiando para el examen de abogacía; **the party is planned — Saturday** la fiesta está organizada para el sábado; **he has a good eye — talent** tiene buen ojo para descubrir talento; **he works — IBM** trabaja para IBM; **smoking is bad — your health** fumar es perjudicial para la salud; **he's mature — his age** es maduro para su edad; **I've come — the money** he

venido por el dinero; **she asked — you**
preguntó por ti; **I walk to work — the
exercise** voy al trabajo andando por el
ejercicio; **we went to Spain — a month**
fuimos a España por un mes; **she did it —
the first time** lo hizo por primera vez; **my
wife signed — me** mi esposa firmó por mí;
mothers feel love — their children las
madres sienten amor por sus hijos; **they
fired him — arriving late** lo echaron por
llegar tarde; **run — your life!** ¡corre por tu
vida! **she took me — a fool** me tomó por
tonto; **thanks — the help** gracias por la
ayuda; **I paid ten dollars — the book**
pagué diez dólares por el libro; **I'm — gun
control** estoy por el control de armas; **— all
her intelligence** a pesar de su inteligencia;
that's not — you to decide a ti no te toca
decidir esto; **as — him** en cuanto a él; **it's
time — me to go** es hora de que me vaya; **to
know — a fact** saber a ciencia cierta; CONJ
porque, pues; **I wish to eat, — I'm hungry**
quiero comer, pues tengo hambre
forage [fɔ́rɪʤ] N (feed) forraje *m*; (searching)
recolección *f*; VI (gather food) forrajear; VT
(feed) dar forraje a; (collect) recolectar
foray [fɔ́re] N incursión *f*, correría *f*; VI (explore)
incursionar; (maraud) saquear
forbade [fɔrbéd] *see* forbid
forbear [fɔrbér] VT abstenerse de; VI contenerse
forbid [fəbíd] VT prohibir
forbidden [fəbídn̩] ADJ prohibido
forbidden [fɔrbídn̩] *see* forbid
forbidding [fəbídɪŋ] ADJ (strict) severo;
(daunting) imponente
force [fɔrs] N fuerza *f*; **— out** (baseball) out
forzado *m*; **in —** (effective) en vigor, vigente;
(in large numbers) en masa; **armed —s**
fuerzas armadas *f pl*; VT (oblige, compel)
obligar; (rape, break open) forzar; **she —d a
laugh** soltó una risa forzada; **to — upon**
imponer; **to — one's way** abrirse paso a la
fuerza; **to — out** (from a place) echar a la
fuerza; (in baseball) forzar out
forced [fɔrst] ADJ forzado, obligado; (of a
landing) forzoso; **— page break** salto de
página forzado *m*
forceful [fɔ́rsfəl] ADJ (of personality) fuerte; (of
arguments) convincente, contundente; (of
behavior) enérgico
forceps [fɔ́rsəps] N (in obstetrics) fórceps *m*; (in
dentistry) tenazas *f pl*, gatillo *m*
forcible [fɔ́rsəbəl] ADJ (done by force) forzoso;
(effective) convincente; **— entry**
allanamiento de morada *m*
ford [fɔrd] N vado *m*; VT vadear
fore [fɔr] ADJ delantero; (of a ship) de proa; N **to
come to the —** ponerse en evidencia; INTERJ
(in golf) ¡cuidado!

forearm [fɔ́rɑrm] N antebrazo *m*
forebear [fɔ́rbɛr] N antepasado -da *mf*
forebode [fɔrbód] VT (foretell) presagiar; (have a
presentiment) presentir
foreboding [fɔrbódɪŋ] N (omen) presagio *m*;
(presentiment) presentimiento *m*
forecast [fɔ́rkæst] N pronóstico *m*; VI/VT
pronosticar
foreclose [fɔrklóz] VI ejecutar una hipoteca
foreclosure [fɔrklóʒɚ] N ejecución *f*
forefather [fɔ́rfɑðɚ] N antepasado *m*
forefront [fɔ́rfrʌnt] ADV LOC **at the —** a la
cabeza, a la vanguardia
forego, forgo [fɔrgó] VT abstenerse de
foregone [fɔ́rgɔn] ADJ **it's a — conclusion** eso
es de cajón
foreground [fɔ́rgraʊnd] N primer plano *m*
forehand [fɔ́rhænd] N (in tennis) derecha *f*,
golpe de derecha *m*
forehead [fɔ́rɪd] N frente *f*
foreign [fɔ́rɪn] ADJ (from another country)
extranjero; (not local) foráneo; (alien) ajeno;
— affairs relaciones exteriores *f pl*; **— aid**
ayuda exterior *f*; **— body** cuerpo extraño *m*;
—-born nacido en el extranjero; **—
currency** divisa *f*; **— debt** deuda exterior *f*;
— exchange cambio de divisas *m*; **—
exchange system** sistema cambiario *m*; **—
matter** materia extraña *f*; **— policy** política
exterior *f*; **— trade** comercio exterior *m*
foreigner [fɔ́rənɚ] N extranjero -ra *mf*
foreman [fɔ́rmən] N (in a factory) capataz *m*,
sobrestante *m*; (of a jury) presidente *m*
foremost [fɔ́rmost] ADJ principal, preeminente
forensic [fərénzɪk] ADJ forense
forerunner [fɔ́rrʌnɚ] N (precursor) precursor
-ora *mf*; (omen) presagio *m*; (harbinger)
mensajero -ra *mf*
foresaw [fɔrsɔ́] *see* foresee
foresee [fɔrsí] VT prever, prevenir
foreseeable [fɔrsíəbəl] ADJ previsible
foreseen [fɔrsín] *see* foresee
foresight [fɔ́rsaɪt] N previsión *f*
foreskin [fɔ́rskɪn] N prepucio *m*
forest [fɔ́rɪst] N (temperate) bosque *m*; (tropical)
selva *f*; **— fire** incendio forestal *m*; **— ranger**
guardabosque[s] *m sg*
forestall [fɔrstɔ́ł] VT bloquear
forester [fɔ́rɪstɚ] N (forest ranger)
guardabosque[s] *m sg*
forestry [fɔ́rɪstri] N silvicultura *f*; **— division**
división forestal *f*
foretell [fɔrtéł] VT predecir, vaticinar
foretold [fɔrtółd] *see* foretell
forever [fɔrévɚ] ADV para siempre; **I'm —
having to pick up after him** siempre
tengo que estar juntando sus cosas; **we can't
go on like this —** no podemos seguir así por
toda la vida

foreword [fɔ́rwɚd] N prólogo *m*

forfeit [fɔ́rfɪt] VT perder; N (fine) multa *f*; (loss) pérdida *f*

forfeiture [fɔ́rfɪtʃɚ] N confiscación *f*, pérdida *f*

forgave [fɔrgév] *see* forgive

forge [fɔrdʒ] N fragua *f*, forja *f*; VT (plans) fraguar; (metal, agreement) forjar, fraguar; VI/VT (signature, legal document) falsificar; **to — ahead** abrirse paso

forgery [fɔ́rdʒəri] N falsificación *f*

forget [fɚgét] VI/VT olvidar, olvidarse de; **I forgot my keys** se me olvidaron las llaves; **to — oneself** meter la pata; N **—-me-not** nomeolvides *mf*

forgetful [fɚgétfəł] ADJ olvidadizo; **— of** negligente de

forgetfulness [fɚgétfəłnɪs] N falta de memoria *f*

forgive [fɚgív] VI/VT perdonar; (a debt) perdonar, disculpar

forgiven [fɚgívən] *see* forgive

forgiveness [fɚgívnɪs] N perdón *m*

forgiving [fɚgívɪŋ] ADJ clemente

forgo [fɔrgó] *see* forego

forgot [fɔrgát] *see* forget

forgotten [fɔrgátṇ] *see* forget

fork [fɔrk] N (for eating) tenedor *m*; (for hay) horca *f*, trinche *m*; (for tuning) diapasón *m*; (in a road) bifurcación *f*; **—lift** montacargas de horquilla *m sg*; VI bifurcarse; **to — over** soltar

forlorn [fɔrlɔ́rn] ADJ desamparado, abandonado

form [fɔrm] N forma *f*; (type) modalidad *f*; (physical condition) condiciones físicas *f pl*; (document to be filled in) formulario *m*; VI/VT formar[se]

formal [fɔ́rməł] ADJ formal; **— attire** ropa de etiqueta *f*; **— dance** baile de etiqueta *m*

formaldehyde [fɔrmǽłdɪhaɪd] N formaldehído *m*

formality [fɔrmǽłɪDi] N (conventionality) formalidad *f*; (rigidity) formalismo *m*; (legal step) trámite *m*

format [fɔ́rmæt] N formato *m*; VT formatear

formation [fɔrméʃən] N formación *f*

formative [fɔ́rməDɪv] ADJ formativo

formatting [fɔ́rmæDɪŋ] N formateo *m*

former [fɔ́rmɚ] ADJ **the — capital** la antigua capital; **my — husband** mi ex-marido; **the — president** el ex-presidente; **in — times** antiguamente; PRON aquel [aquella, etc.], ese [esa, etc.]

formerly [fɔ́rmɚli] ADV antes, anteriormente

formidable [fɔ́rmɪDəbəł] ADJ formidable

formula [fɔ́rmjələ] N fórmula *f*, formulación *f*; (for babies) preparado para biberón *m*

formulate [fɔ́rmjəlet] VT formular

formulation [fɔrmjəléʃən] N formulación *f*

fornicate [fɔ́rnɪket] VI fornicar

forsake [fɔrsék] VT abandonar, desamparar

forsaken [fɔrsékən] *see* forsake

forsook [fɔrsúk] *see* forsake

fort [fɔrt] N fuerte *m*, fortaleza *f*; **to hold [down] the —** quedar de guardián

forth [fɔrθ] ADV (time) en adelante; (space) hacia adelante; **to go —** irse; **and so —** etcétera, y así sucesivamente

forthcoming [fɔrθkámɪŋ] ADJ (approaching) venidero, próximo; (available) disponible; (frank, friendly) abierto; (soon to be published) de próxima aparición

forthright [fɔ́rθraɪt] ADJ directo

forthwith [fɔrθwíθ] ADV en seguida, al punto

fortification [fɔrDəfɪkéʃən] N fortificación *f*

fortify [fɔ́rDəfaɪ] VT (building, body) fortificar; (food) enriquecer; (hair, mind) fortalecer; (argument) reforzar

fortitude [fɔ́rDɪtud] N fortaleza *f*, entereza *f*

fortress [fɔ́rtrɪs] N fortaleza *f*

fortuitous [fɔrtúɪDəs] ADJ (coincidental) fortuito; (lucky) afortunado

fortunate [fɔ́rtʃənɪt] ADJ afortunado

fortunately [fɔ́rtʃənɪtli] ADV afortunadamente

fortune [fɔ́rtʃən] N fortuna *f*; **— teller** adivino -na *mf*; **it cost me a —** me costó un dineral; **to tell someone's —** decirle la buenaventura a alguien

forty [fɔ́rDi] NUM cuarenta; **— love** (in tennis) quince a nada

forum [fɔ́rəm] N foro *m*

forward [fɔ́rwɚd] ADJ (toward the front) hacia adelante; (leading, in the front) delantero; (pushy) descarado; ADV adelante, en adelante; **to bring —** presentar; VT reexpedir; N (in sports) delantero -ra *mf*; (in basketball) alero -ra *mf*

fossil [fásəł] N fósil *m*; (old fogey) carcamal *m*, carca *mf*; **— fuel** combustible fósil *m*

foster [fɔ́stɚ] VT (promote) fomentar, promover; (bring up) criar; **— family** familia de acogida *f*

fought [fɔt] *see* fight

foul [faʊł] ADJ (dirty, illicit) sucio; (disgusting) asqueroso; (of a smell) fétido; (of weather) inclemente; (of winds) adverso; (morally offensive) vil; (of air) viciado; **—mouthed** mal hablado; **the police suspect — play** la policía sospecha que fue un crimen; N (in sports) falta *f*, faul *m*; **—-up** desastre *m*; VT (make dirty) ensuciar; (pollute) viciar; (tarnish) manchar; VI cometer una falta; **to — up** estropear

found [faʊnd] VT (establish) fundar; (build) cimentar

found [faʊnd] *see* find

foundation [faʊndéʃən] N (establishment, institution) fundación *f*; (of a building) cimiento *m*; (of an argument) fundamento *m*; (cosmetic) base *f*

founder [fáʊndɚ] N (establisher) fundador -ora *mf*; (smith) fundidor -ora *mf*; VI (sink) zozobrar, irse a pique; (fail) fracasar

foundry [fáʊndri] N fundición *f*

fountain [fáʊntn̩] N fuente *f*; — **pen** pluma fuente *f*

four [fɔr] NUM cuatro; — **hundred** cuatrocientos; —**score** ochenta; N —**-eyes** *fam* cuatro ojos *mf sg*; —**-letter word** palabrota *f*; —**some** grupo de cuatro *m*

fourteen [fɔrtín] NUM catorce

fourth [fɔrθ] ADJ cuarto; N cuarta parte *f*; **the Fourth of July** el cuatro de julio

fowl [faʊł] N (domestic) ave de corral *m*; (wild) ave *m*

fox [faks] N zorro *m*, zorra *f*; (crafty person) persona astuta *f*; (attractive person) guapetón -ona *mf*; —**hole** madriguera *f*; (military) trinchera *f*

foxy [fáksi] ADJ (crafty) zorro; (attractive) sexy

foyer [fɔ́ɪɚ] N vestíbulo *m*

fraction [frǽkʃən] N fracción *f*, quebrado *m*

fracture [frǽktʃɚ] N fractura *f*; VI/VT fracturar[se]

fragile [frǽdʒəł] ADJ frágil

fragment¹ [frǽgmənt] N fragmento *m*

fragment² [frǽgmɛ́nt] VI/VT fragmentar[se]

fragmentation [frǽgməntéʃən] N fragmentación *f*

fragrance [frégrəns] N fragancia *f*

fragrant [frégrənt] ADJ fragante

frail [freł] ADJ frágil, débil

frailty [fréłti] N fragilidad *f*, debilidad *f*

frame [frem] N (of a building, airplane, furniture) armazón *m*; (of eyeglasses) montura *f*, armadura *f*; (of a car) chasis *m*; (of a person's body) estatura *f*; (of a picture, door) marco *m*; (for embroidery) bastidor *m*; (on a strip of film) imagen *f*; — **of mind** disposición *f*; —**work** (of a house, structure) armazón *m*; (of reference) marco *m*, esquema *m*; VT (a document) forjar; (a question, plan) formular; (a picture) enmarcar; (a person) tenderle una trampa

franc [fræŋk] N franco *m*

France [fræns] N Francia *f*

franchise [frǽntʃaɪz] N (license) concesión *f*, franquicia *f*; (voting privilege) derecho al voto *m*; VT conceder en franquicia, dar la concesión para

frank [fræŋk] ADJ franco, abierto; VT franquear; N salchicha alemana *f*

frankfurter [frǽŋkfɚdɚ] N salchicha alemana *f*

frankness [frǽŋknɪs] N franqueza *f*

frantic [frǽntɪk] ADJ (wild) frenético; (desperate) desesperado

fraternal [frətɚ́nł] ADJ fraternal, fraterno

fraternity [frətɚ́nɪDi] N (relationship) fraternidad *f*, confraternidad *f*; (student association) asociación estudiantil *f*

fraternize [frǽDɚnaɪz] VI confraternizar, fraternizar

fraud [frɔd] N (deceit) fraude *m*; (impostor) farsante *mf*, impostor -ora *mf*

fraudulent [frɔ́dʒələnt] ADJ (of a business, etc.) fraudulento; (of a person) engañoso

fray [fre] N (fight) reyerta *f*, riña *f*; (harsh debate) refriega *f*; VI/VT (rub, wear out) desgastar[se], deshilachar[se]; (strain) crispar[se]

freak [frik] N (anomaly) anomalía *f*; (monster) monstruo *m*, anormal *mf*; (enthusiast) fanático -ca *mf*; (pervert) pervertido -da *mf*; ADJ (unusual) insólito; VI chiflar, flipar; **to — out** chiflar[se], flipar[se]

freakish [fríkɪʃ] ADJ insólito

freckle [frékəł] N peca *f*; VI/VT cubrir[se] de pecas

freckled [frékəłd] ADJ pecoso

free [fri] ADJ (having liberty, unrestricted, loose, uncombined chemically, independent) libre; (unobstructed, unoccupied) libre, despejado; (without charge) gratis, gratuito; (generous) generoso; (unstinted) sin límites, descontrolado; (frank) franco, abierto; — **and clear** libre de gravámenes; — **and easy** despreocupado; — **delivery** entrega gratuita *f*; — **enterprise** empresa libre *f*; — **fall** caída libre *f*; —**-for-all** rifirrafe *m*; — **kick** tiro libre *m*; —**lance** freelance *m*; — **lunch/ride** algo gratis *m*; — **market** mercado libre *m*; — **radical** radical libre *m*; — **speech** libertad de expresión *f*; — **spirit** espíritu fuerte *m*; —**style** estilo libre *m*, crol *m*; —**thinker** libre pensador -ora *mf*; — **throw** tiro libre *m*; — **trade** libre comercio *m*; — **verse** verso libre *m*; —**way** autopista *f*, autovía *f*; — **will** libre albedrío *m*; **to give someone a — hand** dar rienda suelta a alguien; **to set — poner en libertad; sugar-—** sin azúcar; ADV libremente; — **lance** por cuenta propia; **for — gratis; VT (liberate) liberar; (deliver, rid) librar; (untie a knot) desenredar; (drain) desatascar; **to —load** gorronear; **to — up** (time) dejar libre

freebie [fríbi] N yapa *f*

freedom [fríDəm] N libertad *f*; — **of speech** libertad de expresión *f*; **we all want — from fear** todos queremos vivir libres de miedo; **I want — from having to go to work every day** no quiero tener que ir a trabajar todos los días

freeze [friz] VI/VT (food, water) congelar[se]; (accounts) bloquear[se], congelar[se]; **to —-dry** liofilizar; **he froze to death** murió congelado; **my computer froze up** se me colgó la computadora / el ordenador; VI (of temperature) helar; N (action or state of being frozen) congelación *f*; (cold snap) helada *f*

freezer [fríizɚ] N congelador *m*

freezing [fríziŋ] ADJ helado; — **cold** frío glacial *m*; — **point** punto de congelación *m*

freight [fret] N (load) carga *f*; (charge) flete *m*, porte *m*; — **train** tren de carga *m*, tren de mercancías *m*

freighter [frédэ] N buque de carga *m*

French [frɛntʃ] ADJ francés; — **dressing** salsa francesa *f*; — **fries** *Am* papas fritas *f pl*; *Sp* patatas fritas *f pl*; — **horn** corno francés *m*; — **kiss** beso francés *m*; —**man** francés *m*; —**woman** francesa *f*; N (language) francés; **the** — los franceses

frenzy [frénzi] N frenesí *m*; **he worked himself into a** — se puso histérico

frequency [fríkwənsi] N frecuencia *f*

frequent [fríkwənt] ADJ frecuente; VT frecuentar

frequently [fríkwəntli] ADV con frecuencia, a menudo; — **asked questions** preguntas frecuentes *f pl*

fresh [frɛʃ] ADJ (pure, cool, not stale, not frozen, not tired) fresco; (new) nuevo; (bold) impertinente, atrevido; (healthy) lozano; — **paint** pintura fresca *f*; — **water** agua dulce *f*; ADV — **out of school** recién salido de la escuela; **we're** — **out of ideas** se nos acabaron las ideas

freshen [fréʃən] VI/VT refrescar[se]; **to** — **up** arreglarse, lavarse

freshman [fréʃmən] N (student) estudiante de primer año *mf*; (novice) novato -ta *mf*

freshness [fréʃnɪs] N (of food, of temperature) frescor *m*, frescura *f*; (of skin, flowers, youth) lozanía *f*; (of an idea) originalidad *f*; (impudence) descaro *m*

fret [frɛt] VI/VT (worry) preocupar[se]; (irritate) irritar[se]; N traste *m*

fretful [frétfəł] ADJ ansioso, inquieto

friar [fráɪɚ] N fraile *m*

friction [fríkʃən] N fricción *f*, rozamiento *m*

Friday [fráɪde] N viernes *m*

fried [fraɪd] ADJ frito

friend [frɛnd] N amigo -ga *mf*

friendliness [fréndlinɪs] N afabilidad *f*, simpatía *f*

friendly [fréndli] ADJ amistoso, simpático, amigable; — **advice** consejo de amigo *m*; **user-** — fácil de usar

friendship [fréndʃɪp] N amistad *f*

frigate [frígɪt] N fragata *f*

fright [fraɪt] N (fear) espanto *m*, susto *m*; (grotesque thing or person) espantajo *m*, esperpento *m*; **to take** — asustarse

frighten [fráɪtn̩] VI/VT espantar[se], asustar[se]; **to** — **away** ahuyentar, espantar

frightened [fráɪtn̩d] ADJ asustado, espantado; **to get** — espantarse

frightful [fráɪtfəł] ADJ espantoso, pavoroso; **we had a** — **time** lo pasamos horrible; **he's a** — **flatterer** es un adulón espantoso

frigid [frídʒɪd] ADJ (of weather) gélido; (of sexual response) frígida; (of personal relations) frío

frigidity [frɪdʒídɪDi] N frigidez *f*

frill [frɪɫ] N (trimming) volante *m*; (something superfluous) adorno *m*; **no-** —**s** sin lujos

fringe [frɪndʒ] N (of a rug) fleco *m*, orla *f*; (of a city) periferia *f*; (of a political party) extremo *m*; (of society) margen *m*; — **benefits** prestaciones *f pl*, complementos *m pl*; VT orlar, poner un fleco

Frisbee® [frízbi] N disco volador *m*

frisk [frɪsk] VI/VT (frolic) retozar, triscar; (search) cachear

frisky [fríski] ADJ retozón

fritter [fríDɚ] VI/VT desmenuzar[se]; VI irse gastando de poco a poco; **to** — **away** malgastar; N buñuelo *m*, churro *m*

frivolity [frɪválɪDi] N frivolidad *f*

frivolous [frívələs] ADJ frívolo

fro [fro] ADV **to and** — de aquí para allá

frock [frɑk] N (dress) vestido *m*; (habit) hábito *m*

frog [frɑg] N (animal) rana *f*; (fastener) alamar *m*; (of a hoof) ranilla *f*; (French person) *pej* franchute -ta *mf*; **to have a** — **in one's throat** tener gallos en la garganta; —**man** hombre rana *m*

frolic [frálɪk] N retozo *m*; VI retozar

from [frɑm, frəm] PREP desde, de, por; — **here to there** desde aquí hasta allá; — **two to four** de las dos a las cuatro; — **what I can tell** por lo que yo veo; **four hours** — **now** de aquí a cuatro horas, dentro de cuatro horas; **different** — **the other one** diferente del otro; **to come** — **Minnesota** ser de Minesota; **death** — **starvation** muerte por inanición *f*

front [frʌnt] N frente *m*; (cover for illegal activity) pantalla *f*; —-**runner** favorito -ta *mf*; —-**wheel drive** tracción delantera *f*; **in** — **of** en frente de, delante de; ADJ delantero; VI/VT (face) dar a; (cover up) servir de pantalla

frontal [frʌ́ntł] ADJ frontal

frontier [frʌntír] N frontera *f*; ADJ fronterizo; — **spirit** espíritu pionero *m*; — **town** pueblo fronterizo *m*

frost [frɔst] N helada *f*, escarcha *f*; VI/VT helar, escarchar; VT (a cake) bañar; (glass) esmerilar; (hair) hacer rayitos/reflejos; —**bite** necrosis por congelación *f*

frosting [frɔ́stɪŋ] N (of a cake) baño *m*; (for glass) esmerilado *m*; (of hair) rayos *m pl*, reflejos *m pl*

frosty [frɔ́sti] ADJ (cold, unfriendly) helado; (covered with frost) escarchado

froth [frɔθ] N espuma *f*; VI echar espuma; VT batir

frown [fraʊn] VI fruncir el ceño; **to** — **on** desaprobar; N ceño *m*

froze [froz] *see* freeze

frozen [frózən] ADJ congelado
frozen [frózən] *see* freeze
fructose [frúktos] N fructosa *f*
frugal [frúgəł] ADJ (economical) económico, ahorrativo; (meager) frugal
fruit [frut] N (food) fruta *f*; (plant part, product of labor) fruto *m*; (male homosexual) *offensive* maricón *m*; —**cake** (food) torta de frutas secas *f*; (crazy person) *fam* chiflado -da *mf*
fruitful [frútfəł] ADJ fructífero
fruitless [frútlɪs] ADJ infructuoso
frumpy [frʌ́mpi] ADJ matrona
frustrate [frʌ́stret] VT frustrar; **to get —d** frustrar[se]
frustration [frʌstréʃən] N frustración *f*
fry [fraɪ] VI/VT (cook, also execute by electrocution) freír[se]; —**ing pan** sartén *f*; N (fried potato) papa/patata frita *f*; (gathering with fried food) fiesta con comida frita *f*; (young fish) alevín *m*; **small** — gente menuda *f*
fuck [fʌk] VI/VT (have intercourse) *Sp vulg* follar; *Am vulg* coger, culear; (treat harshly) *vulg* joder; INTERJ **to — around** (be idle) *vulg* rascarse las bolas; (be promiscuous) *vulg* coger/follar con todo el mundo; **to — up** *vulg* cagar, joder; **to be —ed up** (mentally ill, in trouble) *vulg* estar jodido; (under the influence) estar colocado; (confused) estar confundido; N (sexual act) *fam* polvo *m*; —**up** *offensive* pendejo -ja *mf*; **he's a good** — *vulg* folla/coge muy bien; **what the — do you want?** *vulg* ¿qué carajo quieres? ¿qué demonios quieres? —! *vulg* ¡mierda! ¡coño! — **off!** *vulg* ¡vete a la mierda! — **you!** *vulg* ¡vete a la mierda!
fucker [fʌ́kɚ] N (person who fucks) *vulg* follador -ora *mf*; (annoying person) *offensive* hijo -ja de puta *mf*
fucking [fʌ́kɪŋ] ADJ *vulg* jodido, de mierda, *Mex* pinche; **the whole — day** *fam* todo el maldito día
fudge [fʌʤ] N turrón blando de chocolate *m*; VI (cheat) hacer trampa; (avoid an issue) dar rodeos
fuel [fjúəł] N (combustible) combustible *m*, carburante *m*; (topic) tema *m*; — **injection** inyección *f*; — **oil** fuel *m*; VT (a vehicle) llenar el tanque, cargar de combustible; (fire, debate) avivar
fugitive [fjúʤɪdɪv] ADJ (fleeing) fugitivo; (transitory) fugaz; N fugitivo -va *mf*, prófugo -ga *mf*
fulfill [fʊłfíł] VT (promise, order) cumplir; (need) satisfacer; **she doesn't feel —ed** no se siente realizada
fulfillment [fʊłfíłmənt] N (of a promise, order) cumplimiento *m*; (of a need) satisfacción *f*; (of a person) realización *f*; (of a dream) culminación *f*
full [fʊł] ADJ (completely filled) lleno; (complete) completo; (a dress) amplio; (a person's figure) relleno; (sated) harto; —**blooded** de raza; —**blown** (of disease) declarado; (complete) auténtico; —**bodied** con cuerpo; —**fledged** verdadero; —**grown** adulto; — **house** full *m*; —**length** (movie) de largometraje; (mirror) de cuerpo entero; — **moon** luna llena *f*; — **name** nombre completo *m*; —**scale** (model) de tamaño natural; (war) total; (investigation) exhaustivo; —**service** de servicio completo; —**size** (bed) de matrimonio; (model) de tamaño natural; —**term** a término; — **time** tiempo completo *m*, de tiempo completo; **to pay in** — pagar el total de la deuda; ADV **you know — well** sabes perfectamente; **it hit him — in the chest** le pegó en pleno pecho
fully [fʊ́li] ADV (entirely) completamente, plenamente; (at least) al menos
fumble [fʌ́mbəł] N pérdida de balón *f*; VI (search for) buscar a tientas; (move clumsily) andar a tientas; (blunder) meter la pata; (football) perder el balón; **he —d his way into the living room** entró a tientas a la sala
fume [fjum] VI (be angry) rabiar; (emit vapors, smoke) emitir humo; N —**s** gases *m pl*, vapores *m pl*, tufo *m*
fumigate [fjúmɪget] VT fumigar
fun [fʌn] N diversión *f*; **for —** por gusto; **to make — of** burlarse de; **to have —** divertirse; ADJ divertido
function [fʌ́ŋkʃən] N función *f*; — **key** tecla de función *f*; VI (work) funcionar; (serve) oficiar
functional [fʌ́ŋkʃənł] ADJ funcional
fund [fʌnd] N (of money) fondo *m*; (of knowledge) acervo *m*; —**raising** recaudación de fondos *f*; VT financiar
fundamental [fʌndəméntł] ADJ fundamental; N fundamento *m*
fundamentalism [fʌndəméntłɪzəm] N fundamentalismo *m*
fundamentally [fʌndəméntłi] ADV fundamentalmente
funding [fʌ́ndɪŋ] N financiamiento *m*, financiación *f*
funeral [fjúnəəł] N funeral *m*, entierro *m*, exequias *f pl*; — **director** director -ora de pompas fúnebres *mf*; — **home** casa de pompas fúnebres *f*, funeraria *f*; — **service** funeral *m*; **it's your** — te estás cavando tu propia tumba; ADJ (march, procession) fúnebre; (pyre) funerario; (expenses) de entierro
funereal [fjuníriəł] ADJ lúgubre
fungible [fʌ́nʤɪbəł] ADJ fungible
fungicide [fʌ́nʤɪsaɪd] N fungicida *m*
fungus [fʌ́ŋgəs] N hongo *m*

funky [fʌ́ŋki] ADJ (of music) funky; (strange) estrafalario, raro; (smelly) hediondo

funnel [fʌ́nl] N (for liquids) embudo *m*; (in a chimney) humero *m*; VT canalizar, encauzar

funny [fʌ́ni] ADJ (amusing) cómico, chistoso, gracioso; (strange) raro; — **farm** *fam* loquero *m*, loquería *f*; **that's not** — eso no tiene gracia; **don't get** — **with me** no te pases de listo; N **funnies** historietas *f pl*, tiras cómicas *f pl*; ADV raro

fur [fɝ] N (hair) pelo *m*; (coat) pelaje *m*; (hide) piel *f*; — **store** peletería *f*; VT forrar de piel

furious [fjúriəs] ADJ (person) furioso, sañudo, rabioso; (fight, storm) feroz; (activity) febril

furlough [fɝ́lo] N licencia *f*, permiso *m*; VT dar licencia

furnace [fɝ́nɪs] N (for heating) caldera *f*; (in industry) horno *m*

furnish [fɝ́nɪʃ] VT (put in furniture) amueblar; (equip) equipar; (provide) proporcionar, suministrar, facilitar

furniture [fɝ́nɪtʃɚ] N muebles *m pl*, mobiliario *m*; — **store** mueblería *f*

furrow [fɝ́o] N surco *m*; VT (soil) arar; (face) fruncir

furry [fɝ́i] ADJ peludo

further [fɝ́ðɚ] ADV **we want to go** — queremos ir más lejos; **I refuse to discuss this** — me niego a seguir discutiendo esto; (additionally) [lo que] es más; ADJ (more distant) más lejano; (additional) adicional; VT (promote) promover; ADV —**more** además

furthest [fɝ́ðɪst] ADJ [el] más lejano, [el] más remoto; ADV más lejos

furtive [fɝ́DIV] ADJ (stealthy) furtivo; (shifty) sospechoso

fury [fjúri] N furia *f*, furor *m*, saña *f*

fuse [fjuz] N (in an explosive) mecha *f*; (in a circuit) fusible *m*; **he has a short** — tiene pocas pulgas; **he blew a** — estalló; VT (to join) fusionar; VI/VT (to merge) fusionar[se]; (to blend metals) fundir[se]

fuselage [fjúsəlaʒ] N fuselaje *m*

fusion [fjúʒən] N fusión *f*

fuss [fʌs] N (bustle) alboroto *m*, bulla *f*; (uproar) escándalo *m*; (argument) discusión *f*; VI (worry about trifles) preocuparse por naderías; (complain) quejarse

fussiness [fʌ́sɪnɪs] N remilgo *m*, ñoñería *f*

fussy [fʌ́si] ADJ (particular) quisquilloso, remilgado; (whiny) quejica, cargoso

futile [fjúdl] ADJ inútil

futility [fjutílɪDi] N inutilidad *f*

future [fjútʃɚ] N futuro *m*, porvenir *m*; —**s** futuros *m pl*; ADJ futuro

fuzz [fʌz] N (fluff) pelusa *f*; (fine hair) vello fino *m*; (on the lip) bozo *m*

fuzzy [fʌ́zi] ADJ (fluffy) cubierto de pelusa; (hairy) velloso; (blurred) borroso; (muddled) confuso

FYI [**for your information**] [ɛ́fwáɪáɪ] ADV para su información

Gg

gab [gæb] VI parlotear, charlar; N parloteo *m*, charla *f*; **gift of** — labia *f*, facundia *f*

gable [gébəl] N hastial *m*; — **roof** tejado de dos aguas *m*; — **window** buhardilla *f*

Gabon, Gabun [gəbón] N Gabón *m*

Gabonese [gæbəníz] ADJ & N gabonés -esa *mf*

gad [gæd] VI **to** — **about** callejear

gadget [gǽdʒɪt] N coso *m*, chisme *m*

gaffe [gæf] N gaffe *f*, metedura de pata *f*

gag [gæg] VT (stop up mouth, silence) amordazar; (cause to choke) dar arcadas; VI tener arcadas; N (thing stuffed into mouth) mordaza *f*; (joke) gag *m*, burla *f*; — **order** orden de supresión de la libertad de expresión *f*

gaiety [géIDi] N alegría *f*; **gaieties** festejos *m pl*

gain [gen] VT ganar; VI **to** — **on** irse acercando a; VI/VT (watch) adelantar; N (profit, act of gaining) ganancia *f*; (in weight) aumento *m*

gainful [génfəl] ADJ remunerado

gait [get] N marcha *f*, paso *m*

galaxy [gǽləksi] N galaxia *f*

gale [gel] N ventarrón *m*, vendaval *m*; —**-force winds** vientos huracanados *m pl*; — **of laughter** risotada *f*

Galicia [gəlíʃə] N Galicia *f*

Galician [gəlíʃən] ADJ & N gallego -ga *mf*

gall [gɔl] N (bile, bitterness) hiel *f*; (impudence) morro *m*; (of a plant) agalla *f*; — **bladder** vesícula [biliar] *f*; —**nut** agalla *f*; —**stone** cálculo biliar *m*; VT (irritate) irritar

gallant[1] [gǽlənt] ADJ (brave) valiente; (attentive to women) galante

gallant[2] [gəlánt] N galán *m*

gallantry [gǽləntri] N (courage) valentía *f*, bizarría *f*; (chivalrous attention) galantería *f*

gallery [gǽləri] N (art, shopping) galería *f*; (theater) paraíso *m*, gallinero *m*; (golf) público *m*

galley [gǽli] N (kitchen) cocina *f*; (boat) galera *f*; — **proof** galerada *f*

gallium [gǽliəm] N galio *m*

gallon [gǽlən] N galón [3.7853 liters] *m*

gallop [gǽləp] VI galopar; N galope *m*

gallows [gǽloz] N horca *f*, cadalso *m*

galore [gəlór] ADV en abundancia

galoshes [gəláʃɪz] N chanclos *m pl*

galvanize [gǽlvənaɪz] VT (metals) galvanizar; (a crowd) electrizar

Gambia [gǽmbiə] N Gambia *f*

Gambian [gǽmbiən] ADJ & N gambiano -na *mf*
gamble [gǽmbəł] VI jugar; VT jugarse; **I'll — my whole fortune on this venture** voy a jugarme todo en este negocio; **to — away** perder en el juego; N (risk) riesgo *m*; (bet) apuesta *f*
gambler [gǽmblɚ] N apostador -ora *mf*, tahúr *m*
gambling [gǽmblɪŋ] N juego [de apuestas] *m*
game [gem] N juego *m*; (match of chess, etc.) partida *f*; (sports match) partido *m*; (wild animals and their meat) caza *f*; — **console** consola de juegos *f*; — **plan** (deporte) plan de juego *m*; (negocios) estrategia *f*; — **point** punto de juego *m*; — **room** sala recreativa *f*; — **show** programa concurso *m*; **to be fair —** ser blanco legítimo; ADJ **I'm — for some tennis** me apunto para jugar al tenis; **he has a — knee** tiene la rodilla lisiada
gamut [gǽmət] N gama *f*
gander [gǽndɚ] N ganso [macho] *m*; **to take a — at** echarle un vistazo a
gang [gæŋ] N (of youths, thieves, etc.) pandilla *f*, gavilla *f*, banda *f*; (group of friends) grupo *m*; —**plank** pasarela *f*; —**way** (passage way) pasillo *m*; (on a ship) pasamano *m*; —**way!** ¡abran cancha! VI **to — up on** conspirar contra, conspirar en masa
gangrene [gǽŋgrin] N gangrena *f*; VI/VT gangrenar[se]
gangster [gǽŋstɚ] N gángster *m*, maleante *m*
gap [gæp] N (breach) brecha *f*, hueco *m*; (of memory) laguna *f*; (of time) intervalo *m*; **she has a — between her teeth** tiene los dientes separados; VT espaciar [correctamente]
gape [gep] VI mirar boquiabierto
garage [gəráʒ] N (for parking) garaje *m*; (for repairing) taller mecánico *m*; — **sale** venta de garaje *f*; VT estacionar en un garaje
garb [gɑrb] N vestimenta *f*, atavío *m*; VT vestir, ataviar
garbage [gárbɪdʒ] N basura *f*; — **can** bote de basura *m*; — **disposal unit** trituradora *f*; —**man** basurero *m*; — **truck** camión de la basura *m*; **what a load of —!** ¡qué montón de mentiras!
garden [gárdn̩] N jardín *m*; — **of Eden** jardín del Edén *m*; VI cultivar un jardín
gardener [gárdnɚ] N jardinero -ra *mf*
gargle [gárgəł] VI hacer gárgaras; VT hacer gárgaras con; N (liquid) gargarismo *m*; (sound) gárgara *f*
garland [gárlənd] N guirnalda *f*
garlic [gárlɪk] N ajo *m*
garment [gármənt] N prenda *f*
garner [gárnɚ] VT cosechar
garnet [gárnɪt] N granate *m*
garnish [gárnɪʃ] VT (decorate) decorar; (decorate food) aderezar, guarnecer; (withhold wages) retener; N (decoration) adorno *m*,

decoración *f*
garret [gǽrɪt] N desván *m*, buhardilla *f*
garrison [gǽrɪsən] N guarnición *f*; VT guarnecer
garrulous [gǽrələs] ADJ locuaz, gárrulo
garter [gárDɚ] N liga *f*; — **belt** liguero *m*, portaligas *m sg*; — **snake** culebra de jaretas *f*; VT sujetar con ligas
gas [gæs] N (vapor) gas *m*; (fuel) gasolina *f*; (flatulence) gases *m pl*; — **chamber** cámara de gas *f*; — **mask** máscara de gas *f*; — **pedal** acelerador *m*; — **station** gasolinera *f*; **to step on the —** acelerar; **we had a —** lo pasamos bomba; VT asfixiar con gas, matar en la cámara de gas; **to — up** llenar el tanque
gaseous [gǽʃəs] ADJ gaseoso
gash [gæʃ] N tajo *m*; VT hacer un tajo en
gasket [gǽskɪt] N junta [de culata] *f*
gasoline [gǽsəlin] N gasolina *f*, nafta *f*
gasp [gæsp] N (cry) grito sofocado *m*; (pant) jadeo *m*, boqueada *f*; VI (cry out) dar un grito sofocado; (in surprise) quedar boquiabierto; (for breath) jadear, boquear
gastric [gǽstrɪk] ADJ gástrico; — **ulcer** úlcera gástrica *f*
gastritis [gæstráɪDɪs] N gastritis *f*
gastroenteritis [gæstroɛntəráɪDɪs] N gastroenteritis *f*
gastrointestinal [gæstroɪntɛstínl̩] ADJ gastrointestinal; — **tract** tubo digestivo *m*
gastronomy [gæstránəmi] N gastronomía *f*
gate [get] N (to a garden) portón *m*; (to a city) puerta *f*; (at an airport) puerta de embarque *f*; —**way** (entrance, access) puerta [de entrada] *f*; (in computers) portal *m*
gather [gǽðɚ] VT (bring together) reunir, allegar; (pick) recolectar; (deduce) deducir, colegir; (sew) fruncir; VI (come together) reunirse; (collect) juntarse; (contract into folds) fruncirse; **to — dust** juntar polvo/tierra; **to — speed** acelerar; N frunce *m*
gathering [gǽðɚɪŋ] N (meeting) asamblea *f*; (social) tertulia *f*; (assemblage of people) concurrencia *f*, reunión *f*; (act of gathering fruit, etc.) recolección *f*
gaudy [gɔ́di] ADJ (of bright color) chillón; (ostentatious) llamativo
gauge [gedʒ] VT (measure) medir; (estimate) estimar; (calibrate) calibrar; N (measurement standard) medida *f*; (caliber) calibre *m*; (measuring device) medidor *m*; (track width) entrevía *f*
gaunt [gɔnt] ADJ demacrado
gauntlet [gɔ́ntlɪt] N (glove) guante *m*; (mailed glove) guantelete *m*; **to throw down the —** retar, desafiar; **to run the —** sufrir acosos
gauze [gɔz] N gasa *f*
gave [gev] *see* give
gavel [gǽvəł] N martillo *m*
gawk [gɔk] VT mirar boquiabierto

gawky [gɔ́ki] ADJ torpe, desgarbado
gay [ge] ADJ (happy) alegre, festivo; (homosexual) gay, homosexual; N *fam* gay *m*, homosexual *m*
gaze [gez] VI mirar fijamente, contemplar; N mirada fija *f*
gazelle [gəzɛ́ł] N gacela *f*
gazette [gəzɛ́t] N gaceta *f*
gear [gir] N (equipment) equipo *m*; (cog) rueda dentada *f*; (assembly of cogs) engranaje *m*; (transmission speed) marcha *f*, cambio *m*; (personal property) pertenencias *f pl*; —**box** caja de cambios *f*; —**shift lever** palanca de cambios *f*; **to be in** — estar engranado; **to change** —**s** cambiar de marcha, poner el cambio; **to put into** — engranar; **to put out of** — desengranar; VI **to** — **up** prepararse
gearing [gírɪŋ] N engranaje *m*
gecko [gɛ́ko] N geco *m*
geek [gik] N persona que tiene exagerada pasión por la informática *f*
Geiger counter [gáɪɡɚkáʊntɚ] N contador Geiger *m*
gel [ʤɛł] VI/VT cuajar[se]
gelatin [ʤɛ́lətṇ] N gelatina *f*
gem [ʤɛɪn] N (precious stone) gema *f*; (valuable person) joya *f*; —**stone** piedra preciosa *f*
gender [ʤɛ́ndɚ] N género *m*; — **discrimination** discriminación de género *f*; — **gap** diferencias entre los sexos *f pl*; —-**specific** propio de un solo sexo
gene [ʤin] N gen *m*; — **marker** marcador genético *m*; N — **pool** conjunto de genes de una población *m*; — **splicing** empalme genético *m*; — **therapy** terapia genética *f*
genealogy [ʤiniálədʒi] N genealogía *f*
general [ʤɛ́nəəł] ADJ & N general *mf*; **in** — por lo general; — **practitioner** médico -ca general *mf*
generality [ʤɛnərǽlɪDi] N generalidad *f*
generalization [ʤɛnəəlɪzéʃən] N generalización *f*
generalize [ʤɛ́nəəlaɪz] VI/VT generalizar
generally [ʤɛ́nəəli] ADV generalmente
generate [ʤɛ́nəret] VT generar
generation [ʤɛnəréʃən] N generación *f*; — **gap** brecha generacional *f*, abismo generacional *m*
generator [ʤɛ́nəreDɚ] N generador *m*
generic [ʤənɛ́rɪk] ADJ genérico; — **brand** marca genérica *f*
generosity [ʤɛnərásɪDi] N generosidad *f*, largueza *f*
generous [ʤɛ́nəəs] ADJ generoso
genetic [ʤənɛ́Dɪk] ADJ genético; — **code** código genético *m*; — **engineering** ingeniería genética *f*; — **fingerprinting** identificación genética *f*; — **marker** marcador genético *m*; N —**s** genética *f*
genetically [ʤənɛ́Dɪkli] ADV — **modified**

transgénico
genial [ʤínjəł] ADJ afable, de buen genio
genital [ʤɛ́nɪdḷ] ADJ genital; — **herpes** herpes genital *m*; — **wart** verruga genital *f*; N —**s** genitales *m pl*, sexo *m*
genius [ʤínjəs] N genio *m*
genocide [ʤɛ́nəsaɪd] N genocidio *m*
genome [ʤínom] N genoma *m*
genre [ʒánrə] N género *m*
genteel [ʤɛntíł] ADJ refinado
gentile [ʤɛ́ntaɪł] ADJ & N gentil *mf*
gentle [ʤɛ́ntl] ADJ (kindly) amable; (mild, slow, gradual) suave; (tame) manso
gentleman [ʤɛ́ntḷmən] N caballero *m*
gentlemanly [ʤɛ́ntḷmənli] ADJ caballeroso
gentleness [ʤɛ́ntḷnɪs] N (kindness) amabilidad *f*; (mildness) suavidad *f*; (tameness) mansedumbre *f*
gently [ʤɛ́ntli] ADV (smoothly) suavemente; (tactfully) con mucho tacto
genuine [ʤɛ́njuɪn] ADJ genuino
genus [ʤínəs] N género *m*
geocentric [ʤiosɛ́ntrɪk] ADJ geocéntrico
geographical [ʤiəgrǽfɪkəl] ADJ geográfico
geography [ʤiágrəfi] N geografía *f*
geological [ʤiəládʒɪkəl] ADJ geológico
geology [ʤiálədʒi] N geología *f*
geometric [ʤiəmétrɪk] ADJ geométrico
geometry [ʤiámɪtri] N geometría *f*
geophysics [ʤiofízɪks] N geofísica *f*
geopolitical [ʤiopəlíDɪkəl] ADJ geopolítico
Georgia [ʤɔ́rʤə] N Georgia *f*
Georgian [ʤɔ́rʤən] ADJ & N georgiano -na *mf*
geostationary [ʤiostéʃəneri] ADJ geoestacionario
geothermal [ʤioθɚməl] ADJ geotérmico
geranium [ʤəréniəm] N geranio *m*
geriatric [ʤɛriǽtrɪk] ADJ geriátrico; N —**s** geriatría *f*
germ [ʤɚm] N (microorganism) microbio *m*, germen *m*; (bud, embryo, rudiment) germen *m*; — **warfare** guerra biológica *f*
German [ʤɚmən] ADJ & N alemán -na *mf*; — **measles** rubeola, rubéola *f*; — **shepherd** pastor alemán *m*
germane [ʤɚmén] ADJ pertinente, relacionado
Germanic [ʤɚmǽnɪk] ADJ germánico -ca *m*
Germany [ʤɚməni] N Alemania *f*
germinate [ʤɚmənet] VI germinar; VT hacer germinar
gerund [ʤɛ́rənd] N gerundio *m*
gestate [ʤɛ́stet] VI/VT gestar[se]
gestation [ʤɛstéʃən] N gestación *f*
gesticulate [ʤɛstíkjəlet] VI gesticular
gesture [ʤɛ́stʃɚ] N gesto *m*, ademán *m*; (token) muestra *f*; VI gesticular
gesundheit [gəzúnthaɪt] INTERJ (after a sneeze) ¡salud! *Sp* ¡Jesús!
get [gɛt] VT (receive, earn) recibir; (obtain)

obtener; (reach by phone) comunicarse con; (hear, understand) entender; (seize) agarrar; *Sp* coger; (prevail) conseguir, lograr; (affect) afectar; (catch disease) pescar; *Sp* coger; **to — across** comunicar; **to — ahead** prosperar; **to — along [with]** llevarse bien [con]; **to — angry** enojarse; **to — around** (skirt) esquivar, evitar; (go out) salir mucho; **to — away** escapar[se]; **to — away with** quedar impune; **to — back** (return) volver; (recover something) recuperar; **to — back at** vengarse de; **to be —ting on in years** ponerse viejo; **to — by** (go past) pasar; (survive) ir tirando; **to — dark** oscurecer; **to — down** (lower oneself) bajar; (depress) deprimir; (swallow) tragar; **to — down to business / brass tacks** ir al grano; **to — going** ponerse en marcha; **to — in** (enter) entrar; (arrive) llegar; (a vehicle) subir a; **to — it** captar, entender; **to — married** casarse; **to — nowhere** no llegar a ningún lado; **to — off** (dismount, get down) bajar; (not receive punishment) salir impune; (leave work) salir; **to — off on** enloquecerse por; **to — off someone's back** dejar de fastidiar; **to — old** envejecer; **to — on** montarse a; **to — out** (take out) sacar; (exit) salir; **to — over** (recuperate) recuperarse, sobreponerse a; (forgive) olvidar; **to — ready** preparar[se]; **to — rich** enriquecerse; **to — rid of** deshacerse de; **to — sick** enfermarse; **to — somewhere** tener resultado; **to — through** (survive an ordeal) sobrevivir; (reach by phone, be understood) comunicarse; (complete) lograr terminar; **to — to someone** afectar a alguien; **to — together** reunirse; **to — up** (arise) levantarse; (prepare) montar; **I got him to do it** conseguí/logré que lo hiciera; **I have got to do it** tengo que hacerlo; **we got our house painted** nos pintaron la casa; **he got a year in jail** le dieron un año de cárcel; **we — to stay up late in summer** en el verano nos dejan quedarnos despiertos hasta tarde; **that —s my goat** eso me fastidia; N **—away** (escape) escape *m*; (vacation) escapada *f*; **—-together** reunión *f*; **—up** disfraz *m*, atuendo *m*; **from the —-go** desde el principio

geyser [gáɪzɚ] N géiser *m*

Ghana [gánə] N Ghana *f*

Ghanaian [gániən] ADJ & N ghanés -esa *mf*

ghastly [gǽstli] ADJ (horrible) horrendo, espantoso; (cadaverous) cadavérico

ghetto [gέDo] N gueto *m*

ghost [gost] N fantasma *m*; **— town** pueblo fantasma *m*; **—writer** colaborador -ora anónimo -ma *mf*; **not a — of a chance** ni la menor posibilidad

ghostly [góstli] ADJ fantasmagórico

ghoul [guɫ] N fantasma *m*

giant [ʤáɪənt] N & ADJ gigante -ta *mf*

gibberish [ʤíbɚɪʃ] N jerigonza *f*

gibbon [gíbən] N gibón *m*

Gibraltar [ʤɪbrɔ́ɫtɚ] N Gibraltar *m*

Gibraltarian [ʤɪbrɔ́ɫtériən] ADJ & N gibraltareño -ña *mf*

giddy [gíDi] ADJ (dizzy) mareado; (of heights) vertigoso; (of speed) vertiginoso

gift [gɪft] N (thing given, act of giving) regalo *m*, presente *m*; (special ability) don *m*; **— certificate** vale por un regalo *m*; **— tax** impuesto sobre las donaciones *m*; **—-wrap** envolver para regalo; VT regalar

gifted [gíftɪd] ADJ (artist) talentoso; (child) superdotado

gigabyte [gígəbaɪt] N gigabyte *m*

gigahertz [gígəhɚts] N gigahercio *m*

gigantic [ʤaɪgǽntɪk] ADJ gigantesco, gigante

giggle [gígəɫ] VI reír tontamente; N risita tonta *f*

gild [gɪɫd] VT dorar

gill [gɪɫ] N agalla *f*

gilt [gɪɫt] ADJ & N dorado *m*

gimmick [gímɪk] N treta *f*, estratagema *f*

gin [ʤɪn] N (liquor) ginebra *f*; **— rummy** gin rummy *m*

ginger [ʤínʤɚ] N jengibre *m*; **— ale** ginger ale *m*; **—bread** pan de jengibre *m*

gingham [gíŋəm] N guingán *m*

gingivitis [ʤɪnʤəváɪdɪs] N gingivitis *f*

giraffe [ʤərǽf] N jirafa *f*

gird [gɚd] VT ceñir; **to — oneself** prepararse

girder [gɚ́Dɚ] N viga *f*

girdle [gɚ́dɫ] N faja *f*; VT rodear

girl [gɚ́ɫ] N (female child) niña *f*; (young female) muchacha *f*, joven *f*, chica *f*; (servant) muchacha *f*, chacha *f*; **—friend** novia *f*

girlhood [gɚ́ɫhʊd] N niñez *f*

girlish [gɚ́ɫɪʃ] ADJ de niña

girth [gɚθ] N (of things) circunferencia *f*; (of persons) contorno *m*; (of horses) cincha *f*; VT cinchar

gist [ʤɪst] N esencia *f*, lo esencial

GI [gastrointestinal] tract [ʤíáɪ] N tubo digestivo *m*

give [gɪv] VT dar; (a gift) regalar; (a party) organizar; (a name) poner; (a donation) donar; **I don't — a hoot** me importa un comino; VI dar; (yield) ceder; (break) romperse; **to — away** (a gift) regalar, donar; (the bride) entregar; (a secret) revelar; **to — back** devolver; **to — in** (acknowledge defeat) rendirse; **to — off** emitir, despedir, desprender; **to — out** (announce) anunciar; (distribute) repartir; (become exhausted) rendirse; (run out) acabarse; **to — over** entregar; **to — up** (surrender) darse por vencido; (stop) dejar [de]; **we'll work on this two years, — or take a month** vamos a trabajar en esto dos años, un mes más, un mes menos; N elasticidad *f*; — **and take** toma y daca *m*

given [gívən] ADJ (stated, fixed) dado; (bestowed) regalado; — **name** nombre de pila *m*; — **that she's not here** dado que ella no está; — **to** propenso a; N premisa *f*

given [gívən] *see* give

giver [gívə-] N dador -ora *mf*, donador -ora *mf*

gizmo [gízmo] N coso *m*, chisme *m*

glacial [gléʃəł] ADJ glacial

glacier [gléʃə-] N glaciar *m*

glad [glæd] ADJ contento; **I'm — to see you** me alegro de verte; **I'd be — to help** sería un placer ayudarte

gladden [glǽdn̩] VT alegrar, regocijar, alborozar

gladiator [glǽDieDə-] N gladiador *m*

glamorous [glǽmə-əs] ADJ glamoroso, encantador

glamour [glǽmə-] N (charm) glamour *f*, encanto *m*; (excitement) atractivo *m*

glance [glæns] VI echar un vistazo; **to — off** rebotar con efecto; N (look) vistazo *m*; (bounce) rebote oblicuo *m*

gland [glænd] N glándula *f*

glandular [glǽnʤələ-] ADJ glandular

glare [glɛr] N (bright light) relumbre *m*; (stare) mirada furiosa *f*; VI (shine) relumbrar; (stare fiercely) lanzar una mirada hostil

glaring [glérɪŋ] ADJ (blinding) deslumbrante; (obvious) evidente; (hostile) hostil

glass [glæs] N (substance) vidrio *m*; (window pane) vidrio *m*, cristal *m*; (tumbler) vaso [de vidrio] *m*; (mirror) espejo *m*; (glassware) cristalería *f*; (magnifier) lupa *f*; —**blowing** soplado de vidrio *m*; — **ceiling** techo de cristal *m*; — **cutter** cortavidrio *m*; —**es** anteojos *m pl*, lentes *m pl*, gafas *f pl*; — **eye** ojo de vidrio *m*; —**maker** vidriero -ra *mf*; —**ware** cristalería *f*

glassy [glǽsi] ADJ vidrioso

glaucoma [glɔkómə] N glaucoma *m*

glaze [glez] VT (windows) poner vidrios a; (ceramics) vidriar; (food) glasear; (wood) barnizar; VI vidriarse; N (pottery) vidriado *m*, barniz *m*; (food) glaseado *m*

glazier [gléʒə-] N vidriero -ra *mf*

gleam [glim] N reflejo *m*, brillo *m*; **a — of hope** un rayo de esperanza; VI brillar, relucir

glean [glin] VT (grain) espigar; (information) extraer, deducir

glee [gli] N regocijo *m*, júbilo *m*; — **club** coro *m*

glib [glɪb] ADJ (fluent) de mucha labia; (superficial) simplista, superficial

glide [glaɪd] VI (slide) deslizarse; (fly) planear; N (sliding movement) deslizamiento *m*; (flight) planeo *m*

glider [gláɪDə-] N planeador *m*

glimmer [glímə-] N luz trémula *f*; **a — of hope**

un destello de esperanza; **the — of an idea** el atisbo de una idea; VI guiñar, emitir una luz trémula

glimpse [glɪmps] N (look) ojeada *f*, vistazo *m*; (hint) atisbo *m*; VT ojear

glint [glɪnt] N destello *m*; VI destellar

glisten [glísən] VI brillar, relucir

glitch [glɪtʃ] N fallo *m*, problema técnico *m*

glitter [glíDə-] VI destellar; N (light) destello *m*; (showiness) brillo *m*; (sparkling powder) brillantina *f*

gloat [glot] VI regodearse; N regodeo *m*

glob [glab] N pegote *m*

global [glóbəł] ADJ global, mundial; — **backup** respaldo global *m*; — **positioning system** sistema mundial de posicionamiento *m*; — **warming** calentamiento global *m*

globalization [globəlɪzéʃən] N globalización *f*

globe [glob] N globo *m*; (map of the Earth) globo terráqueo *m*

globule [glábjuł] N glóbulo *m*

globulin [glábjəlɪn] N globulina *f*

gloom [glum] N (darkness) oscuridad *f*; (melancholy) melancolía *f*, tristeza *f*

gloomy [glúmi] ADJ (dark, depressing) sombrío, lúgubre, tenebroso; (melancholic) melancólico, deprimido

glorify [glórəfaɪ] VT glorificar

glorious [glórias] ADJ (wonderful) magnífico, excelente; (related to glory) glorioso

glory [glóri] N gloria *f*; VI **to — in** regocijarse con

gloss [glɔs] N (shine, cosmetic) brillo *m*; (marginal note) glosa *f*; (in a dictionary) acepción *f*; VT (polish) lustrar, dar brillo a; (explain) glosar; **to — over** disfrazar, encubrir

glossary [glásari] N glosario *m*

glossy [glósi] ADJ lustroso; (paper) glaseado

glottal [gladł] ADJ (cancer) glótico; (phonetic) glotal

glottis [gládɪs] N glotis *f*

glove [glʌv] N guante *m*; (baseball) guante *m*, manopla *f*; — **compartment** guantera *f*

glow [glo] N incandescencia *f*; (of cheeks) rubor *m*; (of emotion) calor *m*; VI resplandecer; (of metal) estar al rojo vivo; (of cheeks) ruborizarse; **to — with health** estar rebosante de salud; —**worm** luciérnaga *f*

glowing [glóɪŋ] ADJ (with light) incandescente; (colors) vivo; (with health) rebosante; (report) favorable

glucose [glúkos] N glucosa *f*

glue [glu] N cola *f*, pegamento *m*; VT (put glue on) engomar; (stick together) pegar; (stick wood together) encolar; **she's —d to the television** está pegada al televisor

glum [glʌm] ADJ tristón

glut [glʌt] VI/VT (with food) hartar[se]; VT (with products) saturar; N superabundancia *f*

gluten [glútn̩] N gluten *m*
glutton [glʌ́tn̩] N glotón -ona *mf*
gluttonous [glʌ́tn̩əs] ADJ glotón
gluttony [glʌ́tn̩i] N glotonería *f*, gula *f*
glycerin [glísɚɪn] N glicerina *f*
gnarled [nɑrɫd] ADJ (knotty) nudoso, sarmentoso; (twisted) retorcido
gnash [næʃ] VI/VT rechinar
gnat [næt] N jején *m*
gnaw [nɔ] VI/VT (bite, corrode) roer; (torment) remorder; **to — a hole** hacer un agujero a mordiscos
GNP [gross national product] [ʤíénpí] N PNB *m*
gnu [nu] N ñu *m*
go [go] VI (move) ir; (function) andar, marchar; **—ing price** precio vigente *m*; **to — against** oponerse a; **to — ahead** seguir adelante; **to — all out** dar todo de sí; **to — along** conformarse; **to — around** (circumvent) dar la vuelta a; (circulate) circular; (be sufficient) alcanzar; **to — around with** andar con; **to — away** irse; **to — back** volver; **to — back on one's word** faltar a la palabra; **to — beyond** traspasar; **to — by** (pass) pasar; (be guided by) guiarse por; **to — by another name** usar otro nombre; **to — crazy** enloquecerse; **to — down** (descend) bajar; (fall) caer, estrellarse; (lose) perder; (be accepted) gustar; **to — down on** practicar sexo oral a; **to — for it** atreverse; **— for it!** ¡adelante! ¡atrévete! **to — in with** participar; **to — it alone** tirarse solo; **to — off** (explode) estallar; (happen) suceder; (leave) irse; **to — off on** regañar; **to — on** (happen) pasar; (continue) seguir; **to — out** (extinguish) apagarse; (socialize) salir; **to — over** (review) repasar, revisar; (read) leer; (cross) cruzar; **to — through** (suffer) sufrir; (examine) examinar; (be approved) ser aprobado; (spend) gastar; **to — through with** llevar a cabo; **to — to sleep** dormirse; **to — under** (go bankrupt) quebrar; (sink) hundirse; **to — up** (building) levantarse; (prices) subir; **pizza to —** pizza para llevar; **to let —** soltar[se]; **the car went for a good price** el coche se vendió a un buen precio; **he's smart, as dogs —** para ser perro, es inteligente; **that old couch has got to —** hay que deshacerse de ese sofá viejo; **cows — "moo"** las vacas hacen "mu"; **they — straight for the pizza** se van derechito a la pizza; **she's —ing to buy a house** va a comprar una casa; **anything —es** todo vale; **what I say —es** lo que yo digo, vale; **don't — to any trouble** no te molestes; **— figure!** ¡vaya a saber uno! **I've got to — [to the bathroom]** tengo que ir [al baño]; N (energy) energía *f*; (attempt) intento *m*; —-

ahead visto bueno *m*; **—-between** intermediario -ria *mf*; **—-cart** kart *m*; **in one — de una vez**; **on the —** a las corridas; **at the first —** de primera; **they made a — of it** tuvieron éxito; **it's a —** ¡trato hecho! **from the word —** desde el vamos
goad [god] N aguijada *f*; VT aguijonear
goal [goɫ] N (objective) meta *f*; (score) gol *m*; **— area** área de penales *f*; **—keeper** portero -ra *mf*, arquero -ra *mf*; **— kick** saque de meta *m*, saque de puerta *m*; **— line** línea de meta *f*; **— post** palo *m*, poste *m*
goalie [góli] N guardameta *mf*
goat [got] N cabra *f*; **—herd** cabrero -ra *mf*; **he gets my —** me saca de quicio
goatee [gotí] N perilla *f*
gobble [gábəɫ] VI/VT (devour) engullir; VI (turkey) gluglutear; **to — up** engullir
gobbledygook [gábəɫdiguk] N jerigonza *f*
gobbler [gáblɚ] N pavo *m*
goblet [gáblɪt] N copa *f*
goblin [gáblɪn] N duende *m*
god, God [gɑd] N dios *m*, Dios *m*; **— bless you!** (blessing) ¡que Dios te bendiga! (after a sneeze) ¡salud! ¡Jesús! **—child** ahijado -da *mf*; **—damned** *vulg* maldito; **—father** padrino *m*; **—forsaken** de mala muerte; **—-given** divino; **—mother** madrina *f*; **—send** bendición *f*; **— willing** si Dios quiere; **by —** por Dios; **my —!** ¡Dios mío!
goddess [gádɪs] N diosa *f*
godless [gádlɪs] ADJ impío
godly [gádli] ADJ piadoso
goggles [gágəɫz] N gafas protectoras *f pl*, antiparras *f pl*
going [góɪŋ] ADJ que marcha bien; **—s-on** tejemanejes *m pl*
goiter [góɪDɚ] N bocio *m*
gold [goɫd] N oro *m*; **— bullion** oro en lingotes *m*; **— digger** mujer cazafortunas *f*; **—finch** jilguero *m*; **—fish** pez dorado *m*; **— medal** medalla de oro *f*; **—smith** orfebre *m*; **a heart of —** un corazón de oro
golden [góɫdən] ADJ (made of gold) de oro, áureo; (of gold color) dorado; **— eagle** águila dorada *f*; **— parachute** paracaídas dorado *m sg*; **— retriever** golden retriever *m*; **— rule** regla de oro *f*
golf [gaɫf] N golf *m*; **— bag** bolsa de golf *f*; **— ball** pelota de golf *f*; **— cart** coche/cochecito de golf *m*; **— club** (stick) palo de golf *m*; (place) club de golf *m*; **— course** campo de golf *m*
gonad [gónæd] N gónada *f*
gondola [gándələ] N (boat, basket under a balloon) góndola *f*; (cable car) cabina *f*
gone [gɔn] ADJ **my computer is —** desapareció mi computadora; **the candy is all —** se acabaron los dulces

gone [gɔn] *see* go
gong [gɑŋ] N batintín *m*, gong *m*
gonorrhea [gɑnəríə] N gonorrea *f*
good [gʊd] ADJ bueno; (valid) válido; — **faith**
buena fe *f*; —**-for-nothing** inútil,
zanguango; — **for two burritos** vale por
dos burritos; —**-looking** guapo, apuesto; —
natured apacible, bonachón, de buen genio;
—**will** buena voluntad *f*; **for** — para siempre;
a — **hour** una hora larga; **a** — **many**
muchos; **to have a** — **time** divertirse; **to**
make — cumplir; **to smell** — oler bien; N
(moral act, benefit) bien *m*; **for your own** —
por tu propio bien; INTERJ ¡bien! —
afternoon buenas tardes; —**bye** adiós; —
day buenos días; — **evening** buenas noches;
— **morning** buenos días; — **night** buenas
noches; N —**s** mercancías *f pl*; —**s and**
services bienes y servicios *m pl*; **to deliver**
the —**s** cumplir lo prometido
goodly [gʊ́dli] ADJ (considerable) considerable;
(of fine appearance) de buen aspecto
goodness [gʊ́dnɪs] N bondad *f*; (of food) calidad
f; INTERJ ¡Dios mío!
goody [gʊ́Di] N golosina *f*; —-— santurrón -ona
mf; INTERJ ¡qué bien!
goof [guf] VI pifiar; **to** — **off** perder el tiempo; **to**
— **up** pifiarla; N pifia *f*
goofy [gʊ́fi] ADJ (person) bobalicón; (idea) tonto
goose [gus] N (bird, fool) ganso -sa *mf*; —**berry**
(berry) grosella espinosa *f*; (bush) grosellero
m; —**bumps** carne de gallina *f*; — **egg** cero
m; VT **to** — **someone** sorprender a alguien
tocándole entre las nalgas
GOP [Grand Old Party] [dʒíópí] N Partido
Republicano *m*
gopher [gófɚ] N ardilla de tierra *f*
gore [gɔr] N sangre derramada *f*; VT cornear
gorge [gɔrdʒ] N (body part) garganta *f*; (ravine)
garganta *f*, tajo *m*; VI **to** — **one's self [on]**
atracarse [de], darse un atracón [de]
gorgeous [gɔ́rdʒəs] ADJ (woman, outfit)
precioso; (weather) espléndido
gorilla [gərílə] N gorila *mf*; (thug) matón *m*
gory [góri] ADJ (of a battle) sangriento; (of a
surface) ensangrentado
gospel [gáspəł] N evangelio *m*; (music) gospel *m*;
— **truth** pura verdad *f*
gossip [gásəp] N (rumor) chismorreo *m*,
murmuración *f*, habladurías *f pl*; (person)
chismoso -sa *mf*; (woman) comadre *f*; **a piece**
of — un chisme *m*; VI chismear, murmurar
gossipy [gásəpi] ADJ chismoso, lenguaraz
got [gɑt] *see* get
Gothic [gáθɪk] ADJ gótico; N (language) gótico *m*,
godo *m*; (style) estilo gótico *m*
gotten [gɑtn̩] *see* get
gouge [gaʊdʒ] N gubia *f*; VT (scoop) sacar con
gubia; (overcharge) cobrar de más; **to** —

someone's eyes out arrancarle los ojos a
alguien
gourd [gɔrd] N calabaza *f*
gourmet [gɔrmé] N & ADJ gourmet *mf*; —
cheese queso fino *m*
gout [gaʊt] N gota *f*
govern [gÁvɚn] VI/VT gobernar, regir; VT (in
grammar) regir
governability [gÁvɚnəbílɪDi] N gobernabilidad *f*
governess [gÁvɚnɪs] N institutriz *f*
governing [gÁvɚnɪŋ] N gobernación *f*; —
principle principio rector *m*
government [gÁvɚnmənt] N gobierno *m*; (in
grammar) rección *f*; — **agency** agencia
gubernamental *f*; —**-backed** respaldado por
el gobierno
governmental [gÁvɚnmɛ́ntl̩] ADJ
gubernamental, gubernativo
governor [gÁvɚnɚ] N (leader) gobernador -ora
mf; (of an engine) regulador *m*
gown [gaʊn] N (woman's dress) vestido *m*; (for
sleeping) camisón *m*; (in hospital) bata *f*; (for
graduation) toga *f*
grab [græb] VT agarrar, prender; **how does**
that idea — **you?** ¿qué te parece esa idea? VI
to — **at** tratar de agarrar; N agarrón *m*; **up**
for —**s** a la rebatiña
grace [gres] N gracia *f*; (of movement) garbo *m*;
(of expression) donaire *m*; **to say** — dar la
oración; **to be in the good** —**s of someone**
gozar del favor de alguien, disfrutar de la
gracia de alguien; VT (adorn) adornar;
(honor) honrar, agraciar
graceful [grésfəł] ADJ (of movement) grácil,
garboso; (of behavior) donoso
gracefulness [grésfəłnɪs] N gracia *f*, donaire *m*
gracious [gréʃəs] ADJ (kind) gentil, cortés;
(elegant) elegante; (merciful) misericordioso;
—! ¡válgame Dios!
graciousness [gréʃəsnɪs] N gentileza *f*
gradation [gredéʃən] N gradación *f*
grade [gred] N (rank) grado *m*; (category) calidad
f; (year in school) año *m*, curso *m*; (marks)
nota *f*, calificación *f*; (slope) declive *m*; **to**
make the — alcanzar el nivel deseado; —
point average promedio de notas *m*; VT
(classify) clasificar; (assign grades) calificar,
corregir; (level) nivelar
gradual [grædʒuəł] ADJ gradual
graduate[1] [grǽdʒuɪt] N (advanced student)
estudiante de posgrado *mf*; (degree-holder)
graduado -da *mf*, egresado -da *mf*; ADJ
de posgrado; — **school** programa de
posgrado *m*
graduate[2] [grǽdʒuet] VI graduarse, titularse; VT
(confer a degree) dar un diploma a; (mark a
scale) graduar
graduation [grædʒuéʃən] N graduación *f*
graffiti [grəfíDi] N grafiti *m*, pintada *f*

graft [græft] N (of plant, tissue) injerto *m*; (corruption) concusión *f*, corrupción *f*; VI/VT injertar[se]

grain [gren] N (cereal, seed) grano *m*, mies *f*; (photographic texture) grano *m*; (of gold) pepita *f*; (of wood, meat, stone) veta *f*; (texture) textura *f*; (small amount) pizca *f*; **against the** — a/al redopelo, a contrapelo

gram [græm] N gramo *m*

grammar [grǽmɚ] N gramática *f*

grammatical [grəmǽDɪkəl] ADJ gramatical

granary [grénəri] N granero *m*, troje *m*

grand [grænd] ADJ (splendid) grandioso, espléndido; (lofty) elevado; (impressive) impresionante; —**child** nieto -ta *mf*; —**children** nietos *m pl*; —**daughter** nieta *f*; —**father** abuelo *m*; —**fathered** eximido por la cláusula del abuelo; — **jury** jurado de acusación *m*; —**mother** abuela *f*; —**ma** abuelita *f*; —**pa** abuelito *m*; —**parent** abuelo *m*; —**parents** abuelos *m pl*; — **piano** piano de cola *m*; —**son** nieto *m*; —**stand** tribuna *f*; **a** — **old man** un gran señor; **the** — **total** el total

grandeur [grǽndʒɚ] N grandiosidad *f*

grandiose [grǽndios] ADJ (complex) complejo; (of speech) grandilocuente, rimbombante; (imposing) grandioso

granite [grǽnɪt] N granito *m*

grant [grænt] VT (give) conceder, otorgar, dispensar; (accept) admitir; (transfer) ceder; **to take for** —**ed** (an assumption) dar por sentado; (a person) no valorar; N (something granted) concesión *f*; (act of granting) concesión *f*, otorgamiento *m*; (subsidy, e.g., for scientists) subvención *f*

granular [grǽnjələ] ADJ granuloso

granulate [grǽnjələt] VI/VT granular[se]

grape [grep] N uva *f*; —**fruit** pomelo *m*, toronja *f*; —**vine** vid *f*; (ornamental) parra *f*; **I heard it through the** —**vine** me lo contó un pajarito

graph [græf] N (curve) gráfica *f*; — **paper** papel cuadriculado *m*; VT grafiar

graphic [grǽfɪk] ADJ gráfico; — **design** diseño gráfico *m*; N gráfico *m*; —**s** gráfica *f*; —**s card** tarjeta gráfica *f*

graphite [grǽfaɪt] N grafito *m*

grapple [grǽpəl] VI/VT (hold) aferrar; (struggle) luchar, lidiar

grasp [græsp] VT (seize) agarrar, asir, aferrar; (understand) comprender; VI **to** — **at/for** tratar de agarrar; N (hold) agarre *m*, asidero *m*; (comprehension) comprensión *f*; **within one's** — al alcance; **to have a good** — **of a subject** dominar una materia

grass [græs] N (plant) hierba *f*; (lawn) césped *m*; (pasture) pasto *m*; (in tennis) césped *m*, hierba *f*; (marijuana) marihuana *f*, maría *f*;

—**hopper** saltamontes *m sg*, saltón *m*; —**land** pradera *f*, pastizal *m*; — **roots** las bases *f pl*

grassy [grǽsi] ADJ herboso

grate [gret] N (of a fireplace) parrilla *f*; (partition, guard) reja *f*, verja *f*; VT (install a grate) enrejar; (mince) rallar; (rub teeth together) crujir, rechinar; VI **to** — **on** rechinar

grateful [grétfəl] ADJ agradecido

grater [grépɚ] N rallador *m*

gratification [græDəfɪkéʃən] N gratificación *f*

gratify [grǽDəfaɪ] VT complacer, gratificar

grating [gréDɪŋ] N reja *f*, enrejado *m*, rejilla *f*; ADJ (discordant) rechinante; (irritating) irritante

gratitude [grǽDɪtud] N gratitud *f*

gratuitous [grətúɪDəs] ADJ gratuito

gratuity [grətúɪDi] N propina *f*

grave [grev] ADJ grave; N fosa *f*, sepultura *f*; —**digger** sepulturero *m*; —**stone** lápida *f*; —**yard** cementerio *m*; —**yard shift** turno de la noche *m*; **to have one foot in the** — *fam* estar por reventar

gravel [grǽvəl] N grava *f*; VT cubrir con grava

gravitation [grævɪtéʃən] N gravitación *f*

gravitational [grævɪtéʃənl] ADJ gravitatorio

gravity [grǽvɪDi] N gravedad *f* (also seriousness)

gravy [grévi] N jugo de carne *m*; **the rest is** — el resto es fácil

gray [gre] ADJ gris; (hair) canoso; (horse) rucio; — **area** zona gris *f*; —-**haired** cano, canoso; — **matter** materia gris *f*; N gris *m*; VI/VT agrisar; (hair) encanecer

grayish [gréɪʃ] ADJ grisáceo

graze [grez] VI/VT (feed) pacer, pastar, apacentar; (brush) rozar; N roce *m*

grease [gris] N grasa *f*; VT engrasar; **to** — **someone's palm** untarle la mano a alguien, engrasar a alguien

greasy [grísi, grízi] ADJ (covered with grease) grasiento; (impregnated with grease) grasoso; (hair) graso

great [gret] ADJ (large, numerous) grande; (good, excellent, considerable) gran; —-**aunt** tía abuela *f*; —-**grandchild** bisnieto -ta *mf*; —-**grandfather** bisabuelo *m*; —-**grandmother** bisabuela *f*; —-**grandchild** tataranieto -ta *mf*; **a** — **tree blocked the path** un árbol grande bloqueaba el camino; **she's a** — **friend es** una gran amiga; **a** — **while** un largo rato; **she's** — **at tennis** juega muy bien al tenis; **a** — **deal of** mucho; ADV muy bien, excelente; **she did** — le fue muy bien; N **the** —**s** los/las grandes *mf*; **they occur in** —**er numbers** son más numerosos; **he's the** —**est** es el mejor; INTERJ ¡qué bien!

greatly [grétli] ADV **it's** — **improved** lo han mejorado mucho / está mucho mejor; **we're**

— **interested** estamos muy interesados

greatness [grétnɪs] N grandeza f

Greece [gris] N Grecia f

greed [grid] N codicia f

greedy [grídi] ADJ (covetous) codicioso; (voracious) voraz; (eager) ávido

Greek [grik] ADJ & N griego -ga mf; **that's — to me** para mí es chino

green [grin] ADJ (green in color, verdant, unripe, inexperienced, nauseated, environmentally conscious) verde; **—back** dólar m; **— bean** Sp judía verde f; Mex ejote m; RP chaucha f; Carib habichuela; **— card** tarjeta verde f; **—horn** novato -ta mf; **—house** invernadero m; **—house effect** efecto invernadero m; **— light** luz verde f; **— pepper** pimiento verde m; N (color) verde m; (lawn) césped m; (pasture) prado m; (in golf) green m; (commons) ejido m; **—s** verduras de hoja verde f pl

greenish [gríniʃ] ADJ verdoso

greenness [grínnɪs] N verdor m

greet [grit] VT (say hello) saludar; (welcome) dar la bienvenida; (receive) recibir

greeting [grídɪŋ] N saludo m; **— card** tarjeta de felicitación f; **—s!** ¡saludos!

gregarious [grɪgériəs] ADJ (person) sociable; (animal) gregario

gremlin [grémlɪn] N duende m

Grenada [grənéɒə] N Granada f

grenade [grənéd] N granada f

Grenadian [grənéɒiən] ADJ & N granadino -na mf

grew [gru] see grow

greyhound [gréhaʊnd] N galgo m

griddle [grídl] N plancha f

gridlock [grídlɑk] N paralización f; VI paralizarse

grief [grif] N congoja f, pesar m, pesadumbre f; **to come to —** sufrir una desgracia; **to give someone —** meterse con alguien, jorobar a alguien; **good —!** ¡caramba! ADJ **—-stricken** acongojado, desconsolado

grievance [grívəns] N (complaint) queja f; (cause for complaint) motivo de queja m

grieve [griv] VI estar de duelo; **to — for/over** llorar, lamentar [la muerte de alguien]; **he's grieving over the loss of his dog** lamenta la muerte de su perro; VT **that —s me** eso me apena

grieved [grivd] ADJ apenado

grievous [grívəs] ADJ (painful) doloroso, penoso; (atrocious) grave, atroz; (sorrowful) dolido

grill [grɪl] N (metal grid, restaurant fixture) parrilla f; (food) parrillada f; VI/VT asar a la parrilla; (interrogate) interrogar

grille [grɪl] N parrilla f

grim [grɪm] ADJ (news, situation) desalentador;

(war) cruento; (joke) macabro

grimace [grímɪs] N mueca f, mohín m; VI hacer muecas

grime [graɪm] N mugre f, suciedad f

grimy [gráɪmi] ADJ mugriento, sucio; **to make — percudir**; **to get —** percudirse

grin [grɪn] VI sonreír; N sonrisa f; **wipe that — off your face** deja de reírte

grind [graɪnd] VI/VT (mill finely) moler; (mill coarsely) triturar; (make shiny) pulir; (rub harshly) rechinar; (study hard) estudiar mucho; Sp empollar; **to — to a halt** pararse con un chirrido; N (drudgery) trabajo pesado m; (overzealous student) empollón -ona mf; **—stone** muela f; **the daily —** la lucha diaria; **to keep one's nose to the —stone** matarse trabajando/estudiando

grinder [gráɪndɚ] N (for coffee, pepper) molinillo m; (for meat) picadora f; (for sharpening tools) afilador m

grip [grɪp] N (hold) agarre m; (control) control m; (handle) mango m; (on a baseball bat, golf club) agarre m, empuñadura f; **he had a firm — on the tool** tenía bien agarrada la herramienta; **get a — on yourself** contrólate, cálmate; VT (seize) agarrar, asir; (take hold, interest) atrapar

gripe [graɪp] VI quejarse, rezongar, renegar; N queja f

grisly [grízli] ADJ cruento, espantoso

gristle [grísəl] N cartílago m

grit [grɪt] N (sand) arena f; (pluck) firmeza f, fam cojones m pl; **—s** sémola de maíz f; VT **to — one's teeth** apretar los dientes

gritty [grídi] ADJ (sandy) arenoso; (plucky) resuelto, fam cojonudo

grizzly [grízli] ADJ (grayish) grisáceo; **— bear** oso pardo m

groan [gron] N quejido m, gemido m; VI quejarse, gemir; (creak) crujir

grocer [grósɚ] N tendero -ra mf; Mex abarrotero -ra mf; Carib bodeguero -ra mf; RP almacenero -ra mf

grocery [grósɚi] N tienda de comestibles f; Mex tienda de abarrotes f; Carib bodega f; RP almacén m; **groceries** comestibles m pl

groin [grɔɪn] N ingle f

groom [grum] N (in a wedding) novio m; (in a stable) mozo de cuadra m, caballerizo m; VT (a horse) almohazar; (prepare for a position) preparar; **to — oneself** arreglarse; **well-—ed** bien arreglado

groove [gruv] N (narrow cut) estría f, ranura f; (on a record, road) surco m; (routine) rutina f; VT estriar, acanalar

grope [grop] VI (feel one's way) andar a tientas; (search) buscar a tientas; VT manosear, toquetear; N manoseo m, toqueteo m

gross [gros] ADJ (before deductions) bruto;

(flagrant) flagrante; (indecent) grosero; (overall) general; (disgusting) asqueroso; — **domestic product** producto interno bruto *m*; — **income** ingreso bruto *m*; — **pay** salario bruto *m*; N gruesa*f*; VT recaudar en bruto; **to — out** dar asco, asquear

grotesque [grotésk] ADJ grotesco

grotto [grádo] N gruta*f*

grouch [grautʃ] N cascarrabias *mf sg*, refunfuñón -ona *mf*, rezongón -ona *mf*; VI refunfuñar

grouchy [gráutʃi] ADJ cascarrabias, refunfuñón

ground [graUnd] N (land, electrical cable) tierra *f*; (soil) suelo *m*; (basis) fundamento *m*; — **ball** (in baseball) roletazo *m*; — **floor** planta baja*f*; —**hog** marmota*f*; —**s** (reason) motivo *m*; (dregs) borra*f*, poso *m*; (tract of land) terreno *m*; **to gain/lose** — ganar/perder terreno; **to stand one's** — ponerse firme; **from the — up** de piso a techo; VT (a wire) conectar a tierra; (a ship) hacer encallar; (punish) poner en penitencia; **the 747 was —ed** se prohibió volar en el 747

ground [graUnd] *see* grind

groundless [gráUndlɪs] ADJ infundado

group [grup] N grupo *m*; — **discount** descuento por grupo *m*; — **therapy** terapia de grupo*f*; VI/VT agrupar[se]

grouper [grúpə˞] N mero *m*

groupie [grúpi] N admiradora*f*

grouping [grúpɪŋ] N agrupamiento *m*

grove [grov] N arboleda*f*, plantío *m*; **orange** — naranjal *m*

grovel [grávəł] VI arrastrarse, humillarse

grow [gro] VI (naturally increase in size) crecer; (increase) aumentar, acrecentarse; (expand) desarrollarse; VT (crops) cultivar; (beard) dejarse crecer; **to — old** envejecer; **to — up** madurar; **Thai food —s on you** la comida tailandesa acaba gustándote

growing [gróɪŋ] N cultivo *m*; — **pains** (physical symptom) dolores del crecimiento *m pl*; (troubles) dificultades iniciales*f pl*; **he's a — boy** es un muchacho en crecimiento

growl [graUł] VI gruñir; (of thunder) retumbar; (of stomach) rugir; N gruñido *m*

grown [gron] ADJ adulto; — **man** hombre hecho y derecho *m*; N —**-up** adulto *m*; ADJ —- **up** para adultos

grown [gron] *see* grow

growth [groθ] N (increase in size) crecimiento *m*; (increase in number) aumento *m*, acrecentamiento *m*; (tumor) bulto *m*; (expansion) desarrollo *m*; — **hormone** hormona del crecimiento*f*; **a — industry** una industria en expansión

grudge [grʌdʒ] N resentimiento *m*

grueling [grúlɪŋ] ADJ arduo

gruesome [grúsəm] ADJ cruento, truculento

gruff [grʌf] ADJ (manner) bronco; (voice) ronco

grumble [grʌ́mbəł] VI/VT refunfuñar, rezongar; N refunfuño *m*, gruñido *m*

grumpy [grʌ́mpi] ADJ refunfuñón, gruñón, rezongón

grunt [grʌnt] VI/VT gruñir; N gruñido *m*

guarantee [gærəntí] N (promise, pledge) garantía*f*; (guaranty) fianza*f*; VT (promise, pledge) garantizar; (warrant) dar fianza, avalar; —**d loan** préstamo garantizado *m*

guarantor [gærəntɔr] N fiador -ora *mf*

guaranty [gærənti] N (guarantee) garantía*f*; (thing taken as security) fianza*f*; (guarantor) fiador -ora *mf*

guard [gard] VT custodiar; (watch over) vigilar; (protect) proteger; VI **to — against** guardarse de; N (person that guards) guardia *mf*, guarda *mf*; (of a machine) dispositivo protector *m*; **to be on** — estar alerta / estar en guardia; — **dog** perro guardián *m*; —**rail** baranda*f*, pasamano *m*

guardian [gárdiən] N guardián -ana *mf*; (legal) tutor -ora *mf*; — **angel** ángel de la guarda *m*

guardianship [gárdiənʃɪp] N tutela*f*

Guatemala [gwɑdəmálə] N Guatemala*f*

Guatemalan [gwɑdəmálən] ADJ & N guatemalteco -ca *mf*

guava [gwávə] N guayaba*f*

guerrilla [gərílə] N — **army** guerrilla*f*

guess [gɛs] VT (hazard, conjecture) adivinar; (suppose) suponer; N (conjecture) conjetura*f*; (supposition) suposición*f*; **I'll give you three —es** te doy tres oportunidades para adivinar

guest [gɛst] N (to a party, function) invitado -da *mf*; (at a restaurant) cliente *mf*; (overnight) huésped *mf*

guffaw [gəfɔ́] N carcajada*f*, risotada*f*

guidance [gáɪdns] N (act of guiding) dirección*f*; (counsel) orientación*f*; (in a missile) teledirección*f*

guide [gaɪd] VT (serve as a guide) guiar; (direct the course of) dirigir; (counsel) orientar; —**d missile** misil guiado *m*; N (person) guía *mf*; (publication, mechanism) guía*f*; —**book** guía *f*; — **dog** perro guía *m*; —**lines** directivas*f pl*, pautas*f pl*, directrices*f pl*

guild [gɪłd] N gremio *m*, corporación*f*

guile [gaɪł] N astucia*f*

guilt [gɪłt] N culpa*f*; — **trip** manipulación por acusaciones falsas*f*

guiltless [gíłtlɪs] ADJ inocente

guilty [gíłti] ADJ culpable; **we find the defendant not —** hallamos al acusado inocente

Guinea [gíni] N Guinea*f*; — **pig** conejillo de Indias *m*; —-**Bissau** Guinea-Bissau*f*

Guinean [gíniən] ADJ & N guineano -na *mf*

guise [gaɪz] ADV LOC **under the — of** so/bajo pretexto de; **in the — of** a manera de

guitar [gɪtár] N guitarra *f*
gulf [gʌlf] N (body of water) golfo *m*; (abyss, gap) abismo *m*; — **Stream** Corriente del Golfo *f*
gull [gʌl] N (bird) gaviota *f*; (dupe) crédulo -la *mf*; *Sp* primo -ma *mf*
gullet [gálɪt] N gaznate *m*
gullible [gáləbəł] ADJ crédulo, ingenuo
gully [gáli] N barranco *m*, barranca *f*; (gutter) alcantarilla *f*
gulp [gʌłp] VT tragar saliva; N trago *m*
gum [gʌm] N goma *f*; (for chewing) chicle *m*; —**s** encías *f pl*; VT **to — up** (ruin) jorobar; (stick) pegotear
gumption [gámpʃən] N (initiative) iniciativa *f*, arranque *m*; (courage) agallas *f pl*
gun [gʌn] N (firearm) arma de fuego *f*; (revolver) revólver *m*; (rifle) rifle *m*; (shotgun) escopeta *f*; (cannon) cañón *m*; (for painting, nailing) pistola *f*; VT (an engine) acelerar; —**boat** cañonero *m*; —**fire** tiroteo *m*; —**man** pistolero *m*; —**powder** pólvora *f*; —**shot** disparo *m*; —**shot wound** herida de bala *f*; **at —point** a mano armada; **to stick to one's —s** mantenerse firme; **don't jump the —** no te precipites; **to be under the —** estar bajo mucha presión; VT **to — down** matar a tiros; **to — for** andar a la caza de
gung-ho [gáŋhó] ADJ fanático, entusiasta
gunner [gánɚ] N (shooting artillery) artillero -ra *mf*; (shooting a machine gun) ametrallador -ora *mf*
gurgle [gɚgəł] VI (water) borbotar; (baby) gorjear; N (of water) borboteo *m*; (of a baby) gorjeo *m*
gush [gʌʃ] VI (liquids) chorrear, brotar; (talk effusively) hablar con efusividad
gust [gʌst] N ráfaga *f*; — **of wind** racha/ráfaga de viento *f*, ventolera *f*; VI soplar en ráfagas
gusto [gásto] N (pleasure) placer *m*; (enthusiasm) entusiasmo *m*
gut [gʌt] N tripa *f*; (belly) barriga *f*; — **feeling** corazonada *f*; —**s** (intestines) entrañas *f pl*; (courage) *fam* cojones *m pl*; VT (eviscerate) destripar; (destroy the insides of) destrozar el interior de; (strip) desarmar
gutsy [gátsi] ADJ *fam* cojonudo
gutter [gádɚ] N (in the street) alcantarilla *f*; (on the roof) canaleta *f*, desagüe *m*; (squalor) miseria *f*
guy [gaɪ] N (man) tipo *m*; *Sp* tío *m*; **you —s** ustedes; *Sp* vosotros/vosotras; — **wire** cable *m*
Guyana [gaɪánə] N Guyana *f*
Guyanese [gaɪəníz] ADJ & N guyanés -esa *mf*
gym [ʤɪm] N gimnasio *m*
gymnasium [ʤɪmnéziəm] N gimnasio *m*
gymnastics [ʤɪmnǽstɪks] N gimnasia *f*
gynecologist [gaɪnəkáləʤɪst] N ginecólogo -ga *mf*

gynecology [gaɪnəkáləʤi] N ginecología *f*
gyp [ʤɪp] VT estafar, timar; N estafa *f*, timo *m*
gypsum [ʤípsəm] N yeso *m*
gypsy [ʤípsi] N & ADJ gitano -na *mf*
gyrate [ʤáɪret] VI girar
gyroscope [ʤáɪrəskop] N giroscopio *m*

Hh

habit [hǽbɪt] N (custom) hábito *m*, costumbre *f*; (clerical dress) hábito *m*; (vice) vicio *m*; —**forming** adictivo
habitat [hǽbɪtæt] N hábitat *m*
habitual [həbítʃuəł] ADJ habitual
hack [hæk] N (cut) tajo *m*, machetazo *m*; (cough) tos seca *f*; (horse for hire) caballo de alquiler *m*; (nag) jamelgo *m*; (writer) escritor -ora mercenario -ria *mf*; —**saw** sierra para metales *f*; VI/VT tajar, cortar a machetazos; VI toser con tos seca
hacker [hǽkɚ] N pirata informático -ca *mf*
had [hæd] *see* have
hag [hæg] N (witch) bruja *f*; (ugly old woman) vieja fea *f*
haggard [hǽgɚd] ADJ demacrado
haggle [hǽgəł] VI regatear
hail [heł] N (precipitation) granizo *m*; (greeting) saludo *m*; (shout) llamada *f*; — **Mary** Ave María *f*; —**storm** granizada *f*; VI (precipitate) granizar; VT (greet) saludar; (call out) llamar; (acclaim) aclamar; **to — from** ser oriundo de
hair [hɛr] N pelo *m*; (of the head only) cabello *m*; (of the body only) vello *m*; (on plants) pelusa *f*; —**brush** cepillo para el cabello *m*; —**cut** corte de pelo *m*; **to get a —cut** cortarse el pelo; —**do** peinado *m*; —**dresser** peluquero -ra *mf*, peinador -ora *mf*; — **follicle** folículo capilar *m*; —**line** nacimiento del pelo *f*; —**line fracture** fractura fina *f*; —**piece** postizo *m*; —**pin** horquilla *f*; —**raising** horripilante, espeluznante; —**spray** fijador *m*
hairless [hérlɪs] ADJ (deprived of hair) pelado; (growing no hair) lampiño
hairy [héri] ADJ (including head) peludo; (body only) velludo
Haiti [hédi] N Haití *m*
Haitian [héʃən] ADJ & N haitiano -na *mf*
hake [hek] N merluza *f*
half [hæf] N mitad *f*; — **an apple** media manzana *f*; ADJ medio; —**baked** (not fully cooked) a medio cocer; (not fully developed) mal concebido; —**breed** mestizo -za *mf*; — **brother** medio hermano *m*; —**cocked** mal preparado; **he went off —-cocked** actuó

precipitadamente; —-**cooked** a medio cocer; —-**dozen** media docena*f*; —**hearted** desganado; —-**hour** media hora*f*; —-**life** vida media*f*; —-**moon** media luna*f*; — **note** blanca*f*; —-**open** entreabierto, entornado; — **past one** la una y media; —**time** medio tiempo *m*, descanso *m*; —-**truth** verdad a medias*f*; — **volley** media volea*f*; —**way** a medio camino; —**way house** casa de rehabilitación*f*; —**way measures** medidas parciales*f pl*; —**way point** punto medio *m*; —-**wit** *pej* imbécil *mf*, papamoscas *mf*; at —-**mast** a media asta; **to do something** —**way** hacer algo a medias; **to go halves** ir a medias

halibut [hǽləbət] N hipogloso *m*

halitosis [hælɪtósɪs] N halitosis*f*

hall [hɔl] N (corridor) corredor *m*, pasillo *m*; (large room) salón *m*, sala*f*; (building) edificio *m*; —**mark** distintivo *m*; —**way** (corridor) corredor *m*, pasillo *m*; (entrance) zaguán *m*, vestíbulo *m*

Halloween [hæləwín] N víspera del día de Todos los Santos*f*, noche de brujas*f*

hallucinate [həlúsənet] VI alucinar

hallucination [həlusənéʃən] N alucinación*f*

hallucinogen [həlúsənədʒən] N alucinógeno *m*

halo [hélo] N halo *m*, aureola*f*

halogen [hǽlədʒən] ADJ halógeno

halt [hɔlt] N **to come to a** — detenerse; VI/VT parar, detener[se]; —! ¡alto!

halter [hɔ́ltɚ] N cabestro *m*

halting [hɔ́ltɪŋ] ADJ vacilante

halve [hæv] VT partir por la mitad

ham [hæm] N (meat) jamón *m*; (attention getter) payaso *m*; —**string** (human) ligamento de la corva *m*; (horse) tendón del jarrete *m*; **to** — **it up** sobreactuar, exagerar

hamburger [hǽmbɚgɚ] N (meat) carne picada de vaca/res*f*; (sandwich, patty) hamburguesa*f*

hamlet [hǽmlɪt] N aldea*f*, poblado *m*, caserío *m*

hammer [hǽmɚ] N martillo *m*; VI/VT martillar, amartillar; **to** — **out** (an agreement) forjar; (differences) negociar

hammock [hǽmək] N hamaca*f*

hamper [hǽmpɚ] N canasto *m*, cesto *m*; VT impedir, embarazar

hamster [hǽmstɚ] N hámster *m*

hand [hænd] N mano*f*; (of a clock) aguja*f*, manecilla*f*; (farm helper) peón *m*; —**bag** (purse) bolsa*f*, cartera*f*; (valise) maletín *m*; —**ball** (American game) pelota*f*, frontón *m*; (European game) balonmano *m*; (in soccer) mano*f*; —**bill** volante *m*; —**cuffs** esposas*f pl*; — **grenade** granada de mano*f*, bomba de piña*f*; —**gun** revólver *m*; — **in** — [cogidos] de la mano; —**kerchief** pañuelo *m*; —**out** (notes) repartido *m*, ejemplario *m*; (alms)

limosna*f*; —**saw** serrucho *m*; —**shake** apretón de manos *m*; —**stand** pino *m*, paro de manos *m*; —**work** trabajo manual *m*; —**writing** letra*f*; **at** — (within reach) al alcance; (about to happen) cerca; **in** — (under control) bajo control; (available) disponible, en mano; **on** — disponible, a mano; **on the other** — en cambio, por otra parte; **to have one's** —**s full** estar ocupadísimo; ADJ —**held** de mano; —**made** hecho a mano; —-**picked** cuidadosamente seleccionado; —**s-on** práctico; VT entregar, dar; **to** —**cuff** esposar; **to** — **down** (a thing) pasar; (a judgment) pronunciar; **to** — **in** entregar; **to** — **over** entregar

handful [hǽndfʊl] N manojo *m*, puñado *m*

handicap [hǽndikæp] N (physical disability) impedimento *m*, minusvalía*f*; (mental disability) retardo *m*; (disadvantage) desventaja*f*; (in golf) hándicap *m*; — **race** carrera de hándicap*f*; VT (hinder) perjudicar, handicapar; (injure) lisiar; **physically** —**ped** minusválido físico

handiwork [hǽndiwɚk] N labor*f*

handle [hǽndl] N (straight) mango *m*; (curved) asa*f*; (of a drawer) manija*f*; (of a knife) empuñadura*f*, puño *m*; —**bar** manubrio *m*; VT (manage) manejar; (touch) manipular, tocar; (deal in) comerciar en; **the car** —**s easily** el coche tiene buena maniobrabilidad

handling [hǽndlɪŋ] N (dealing) manejo *m*; (touching) manipulación*f*; (charge) porte *m*; (of a car) maniobrabilidad*f*; — **charges** cargos de tramitación *m pl*

handsome [hǽnsəm] ADJ guapo, bien parecido; **a** — **sum** una suma considerable

handy [hǽndi] ADJ (near) a [la] mano; (practical) práctico; (skillful) hábil, diestro; N —**man** hombre habilidoso *m*

hang [hæŋ] VI/VT colgar, suspender; VT (door) colocar; (one's head) inclinar; (a condemned person) ahorcar; VI pender; — **in there!** ¡ánimo! **to** — **around** quedarse por ahí, rondar; **to** — **on** (hold tight) agarrarse bien; (persevere) aguantar; (wait) esperar; **to** — **out** (be outside) estar fuera; (socialize with) andar [con]; **to** — **over** sobresalir; **to** — **paper on a wall** empapelar una pared; **to** — **up** colgar; **sentenced to** — condenado a la horca; N caída*f*; — **glider** ala delta*f*; —**man** verdugo *m*; —**nail** padrastro *m*, uña encarnada*f*, uñero *m*; —**out** sitio frecuentado *m*; —**over** resaca*f*; —-**up** complejo *m*; **to get the** — **of something** agarrarle la onda a algo

hangar [hǽŋɚ] N hangar *m*

hanger [hǽŋɚ] N colgadero *m*; (for clothes) percha*f*

hanging [hǽŋɪŋ] N muerte en la horca*f*; —**s**

colgaduras *f pl*, tapiz *m*; ADJ colgante
hanky-panky [hǽŋkipǽŋki] N (deceit)
tejemaneje *m*; (illicit sexual activity)
aventuras *f pl*
haphazard [hæphǽzəd] ADV a la buena de Dios;
ADJ irregular
happen [hǽpən] VI suceder, pasar, acontecer; **I
— to know** da la casualidad de que sé; **to —
to pass by** acertar a pasar; **to — upon**
encontrarse con, toparse con
happening [hǽpənɪŋ] N acontecimiento *m*,
suceso *m*
happily [hǽpɪli] ADV (in a state of happiness)
felizmente; (luckily) afortunadamente; **they
lived — ever after** vivieron felices y
comieron perdices
happiness [hǽpinɪs] N felicidad *f*, dicha *f*
happy [hǽpi] ADJ (satisfied) feliz, dichoso;
(pleased) contento; (lucky) afortunado; —
ending final feliz *m*; **to be — to** hacer algo
de buena gana
harangue [hərǽŋ] N arenga *f*; VT arengar
harass [hərǽs] VT acosar, hostigar
harassment [hərǽsmənt] N acoso *m*,
hostigamiento *m*
harbor [hárbə] N (for ships) puerto *m*; (refuge)
refugio *m*; — **authority** autoridad portuaria;
VT (refugees, criminals, suspicions) albergar;
(hopes) abrigar
hard [hɑrd] ADJ (firm) duro; (erect) tieso;
(difficult) difícil; (arduous) arduo; **to play
—ball** ser despiadado; —**-boiled egg** huevo
duro *m*; — **cash** dinero contante y sonante *m*;
— **coal** antracita *f*; — **copy** copia en papel *f*,
copia impresa *f*; — **core** núcleo resistente *m*;
—**-core** (pornography) duro; (politics)
radical; — **disk** disco duro *m*; — **disk drive**
unidad de disco duro *f*; — **feelings**
resentimiento *m*; — **hat** casco *m*; —**headed**
testarudo; —**hearted** duro de corazón; —
liquor bebida alcohólica fuerte *f*; — **luck**
mala suerte *f*; — **of hearing** medio sordo; —
-on erección *f*; **he had a —-on** la tenía dura;
— **page break** salto de página forzado *m*; —
palate paladar óseo *m*; —**-pressed** en
aprietos; — **return** salto de línea forzado *m*;
—**ware** (metal articles) ferretería *f*;
(computer) hardware *m*; —**ware store**
ferretería *f*; —**wood** madera noble *f*; —
water agua dura *f*; — **winter** invierno crudo
m; —**-wired** programado; —**-working**
trabajador; ADV (fall, push) con fuerza; (work)
duro, con ahínco
harden [hárdn̩] VI/VT (make or become hard)
endurecer[se]; (make or become experienced)
curtir[se]
hardening [hárdn̩ɪŋ] N endurecimiento *m*
hardly [hárdli] ADV (scarcely) apenas,
difícilmente; (at all) en absoluto; — **anyone**

casi nadie; — **surprising** nada sorprendente
hardness [hárdnɪs] N dureza *f*
hardship [hárdʃɪp] N penuria *f*, penalidad *f*
hardy [hárdi] ADJ robusto
hare [hɛr] N liebre *f*; —**brained** descabellado;
—**lip** labio leporino *m*; —**lipped** con labio
leporino, labihendido
harem [hérəm] N harén *m*
harm [hɑrm] N daño *m*, mal *m*, perjuicio *m*; VT
(object) dañar; (person) hacer daño; (chances)
perjudicar
harmful [hármfəl] ADJ perjudicial, dañino,
nocivo
harmless [hármlɪs] ADJ inocuo, inofensivo
harmonic [hɑrmánɪk] ADJ & N armónico *m*
harmonious [hɑrmóniəs] ADJ armonioso
harmonize [hármənaɪz] VI/VT armonizar
harmony [hárməni] N armonía *f*
harness [hárnɪs] N arnés *m*, jaez *m*, guarnición *f*;
VT (put on a harness) enjaezar; (utilize)
aprovechar
harp [hɑrp] N arpa *f*; VI (play the harp) tocar el
arpa; (insist) machacar; **to — on** insistir sobre
harpoon [hɑrpún] N arpón *m*; VT arponear
harpsichord [hárpsɪkɔrd] N clavicémbalo *m*
harrowing [hǽroɪŋ] ADJ angustioso; —
adventure aventura espeluznante *f*
harry [hǽri] VT acosar, hostigar
harsh [hɑrʃ] ADJ (words) duro; (surface) áspero;
(character, discipline) severo, férreo; (winter)
crudo, riguroso
harshness [hárʃnɪs] N (of words) dureza *f*; (of a
surface) aspereza *f*; (of character, discipline)
severidad *f*; (of a winter) rigor *m*
harvest [hárvɪst] N cosecha *f*; (of sugar) zafra *f*;
VT cosechar
has [hæz] *see* have
hash [hæʃ] N guisado *m*, picadillo *m*
hashish [hæʃíʃ] N hachís *m*
hassle [hǽsəl] N rollo *m*, lío *m*; VT jorobar
haste [hest] N prisa *f*; **in —** de prisa; **to make —**
darse prisa, apresurarse; *Am* apurarse
hasten [hésən] VI apresurarse; *Am* apurarse; VT
acelerar, adelantar
hasty [hésti] ADJ apresurado, precipitado,
presuroso; *Am* apurado; **to be —** precipitarse,
apresurarse
hat [hæt] N sombrero *m*
hatch [hætʃ] VI/VT (chicks) empollar; (plot,
scheme) fraguar, maquinar; N (chicks) nidada
f; (opening) escotilla *f*; — **way** escotilla *f*
hatchet [hætʃɪt] N hacha *f*; — **job** crítica feroz *f*;
— **man** sicario *m*; **to bury the —** hacer las
paces
hate [het] N odio *m*; VI/VT odiar; **I — to admit it**
me molesta admitirlo; **I — eating leftovers**
detesto comer restos
hateful [hétfəl] ADJ odioso, aborrecible
hatred [hétrɪd] N odio *m*

haughtiness [hɔ́dɪnɪs] N altivez f, altanería f, soberbia f

haughty [hɔ́di] ADJ altivo, altanero, soberbio

haul [hɔl] VT (transport) transportar; (drag) arrastrar; (pull) jalar [de], tirar [de]; N (quantity transported) carga f; (tug) tirón m; (catch of fish) redada f; (stolen goods) botín m; **long** — distancia larga f

haunch [hɔ́ntʃ] N anca f

haunt [hɔnt] VI/VT (frequent) frecuentar, rondar; (enchant) embrujar; **that idea —s me** me obsesiona esa idea; **—ed house** casa embrujada f; N (of animals, criminals) guarida f; (of people socializing) sitio frecuentado m

have [hæv] V AUX haber; VT tener; **to — to** tener que; **to — a baby** dar a luz; **to — a look at** echar una mirada a; **to — a suit made** mandarse hacer un traje; **— him come later** dile que venga más tarde; **what did she — on?** ¿qué tenía puesto? **we've been had** nos estafaron

haven [hévən] N abrigo m, refugio m

havoc [hǽvək] N estrago m; **to wreak —** hacer estragos

hawk [hɔk] N gavilán m; VT pregonar

hay [he] N heno m; **— fever** alergia al polen f; **— loft** henil m; **—seed** paleto -ta mf; **—stack** almiar m; **to look for a needle in a —stack** buscar una aguja en un pajar

hazard [hǽzɚd] N (chance) azar m; (danger) peligro m; VT arriesgar, aventurar

hazardous [hǽzɚDəs] ADJ peligroso; **— substance** sustancia peligrosa f

haze [hez] N neblina f, calina f; VT atormentar [como parte de un rito de iniciación]

hazel [hézəl] N avellano m; **—nut** avellana f; ADJ de avellano

hazy [hézi] ADJ (weather) brumoso; (idea) confuso, vago

HDL [high density lipoprotein] [étʃdíél] N LAD f

he [hi] PRON él; **—-goat** macho cabrío m; **— who** el que, quien

head [hɛd] N (of body) cabeza f; (of bed) cabecera f; (chief) jefe -fa mf; **—ache** dolor de cabeza m; **— coach** entrenador -ora en jefe mf; **— cold** resfrío m; **—count** recuento de personas m; **—dress** tocado m, adorno para la cabeza m; **—gear** (hat) sombrero m; (helmet) casco m; (for a horse) cabezada f; **—hunter** cazatalentos mf sg; **—land** cabo m, promontorio m; **—light** faro delantero m; **—line** titular m; **—long** (head first) de cabeza; (hastily) precipitadamente; **— of hair** cabellera f; **— of state** mandatario -ria mf; **—phone** audífono m, auricular m; **—quarters** (military) cuartel general m; (police) jefatura f; (corporation) oficina

central f; **—rest** reposacabezas m sg; **—set** auriculares m pl; **—s or tails** cara o cruz; **I can't make —s or tails of it** esto no tiene ni pies ni cabeza; **— start** ventaja f; **—stone** lápida f; **—strong** testarudo; **—way** avance m; **—word** voz f; **to make —way** avanzar, progresar; **it went to his —** se le fue a la cabeza; **to be out of one's —** desvariar; **to come to a —** (a crisis) precipitarse; (an abscess) supurar; **to keep one's —** mantener la calma; VT (lead) encabezar; (steer) dirigir; (in soccer) cabecear; VI dirigirse; **to — up** liderar; **to — off** atajar; ADV **—-on** de frente, frontal

header [hédɚ] N (in soccer) cabezazo m, pase de cabeza m; (in text) cabecera f, encabezado m

heading [hédɪŋ] N encabezamiento m

heal [hil] VT curar; VI (get well) sanar, curarse; (form a scar) cicatrizarse

health [hɛlθ] N salud f; **— care** asistencia médica f; **— care system** sistema de asistencia de salud m; **— care provider** profesional de la salud mf; **— food** comida macrobiótica f; **— insurance** seguro de salud m

healthful [hélθfəl] ADJ saludable, sano

healthy [hélθi] ADJ sano, saludable

heap [hip] N montón m, pila f; VT amontonar, apilar; VI **to — up** amontonarse

hear [hir] VI/VT (perceive) oír; VT (listen) escuchar; **to — about/of someone/something** oír hablar de alguien/algo; **to — from someone** tener noticias de alguien; **I won't — of your leaving** no quiero saber de que te vayas

heard [hɝd] see hear

hearer [hírɚ] N oyente mf

hearing [hírɪŋ] N (sense) oído m; (trial) audiencia f; **within —** al alcance del oído; **— aid** audífono m; ADJ **—-impaired** sordo

hearsay [hírse] N testimonio de oídas m; **by —** de oídas

hearse [hɝs] N coche fúnebre m, carroza f

heart [hart] N (organ) corazón m; (spirit) ánimo m; **—ache** angustia f; **— attack** ataque cardíaco m; **—beat** latido m; **I would do it in a —beat** lo haría sin pestañear; **—burn** acidez de estómago f; **— disease** enfermedad coronaria f; **— murmur** soplo cardíaco m; **at —** en realidad, en el fondo; **from the bottom of one's —** de corazón, con toda el alma; **to learn by —** aprender de memoria; **to take —** cobrar ánimo; **to take to —** tomar a pecho; ADJ **—broken** inconsolable; **—felt** sincero, sentido; **my —felt sympathy** mi más sentido pésame; **—-warming** reconfortante

hearten [hártn̩] VT animar

hearth [harθ] N hogar m

heartless [hártlɪs] ADJ despiadado, desalmado

hearty [hárɒi] ADJ (cordial) cordial; (strong) fuerte; — **appetite** apetito saludable *m*; **a — laugh** una risa desbordante; — **meal** una comida abundante

heat [hit] N (warmth) calor *m*; (passion) ardor *m*; (estrus) celo *m*; (source of heat) calefacción *f*; (preliminary race) eliminatoria *f*; — **exchange** equilibrio térmico *m*; —**stroke** insolación *f*; VI/VT calentar[se]; **to — up** acalorarse

heater [híɒɚ] N calentador *m*

heating [híɒɪŋ] N calefacción *f*; — **pad** almohadilla eléctrica *f*

heave [hiv] VT (raise) levantar; (throw) arrojar, lanzar; (sigh) exhalar; (pull) jalar; VI (pant) jadear; (vomit) hacer arcadas; N (throw) lanzamiento *m*; (pull) tirón *m*

heaven [hévən] N cielo *m*

heavenly [hévənli] ADJ celestial; — **bodies** cuerpos celestes *m pl*; **it was** — estuvo divino

heavily [hévəli] ADV (fall) pesadamente; (drink) mucho; **he's breathing** — está jadeando; **he's — indebted** está muy endeudado / tiene muchas deudas

heaviness [hévɪnɪs] N pesadez *f*

heavy [hévi] ADJ (weighty) pesado; (thick) grueso, pesado; (dense) denso; (oppressive) opresivo; — **artillery** artillería pesada *f*; — **breathing** jadeos *m pl*; —**-duty** de servicio pesado; —**-handed** severo, autoritario; **with a — heart** abatido; — **rain** lluvia fuerte *f*; — **schedule** agenda cargada *f*; —**weight** peso pesado *m*; N villano -na *mf*

Hebrew [híbru] N & ADJ hebreo -a *mf*; (language) hebreo *m*

heck [hɛk] INTERJ ¡caramba! **what the — are you doing?** ¿qué demonios haces? **that was a — of a good game** fue un partidazo

hectare [hɛ́ktɛr] N hectárea *f*

hectic [hɛ́ktɪk] ADJ febril, agitado

hedge [hɛdʒ] N (row of bushes) seto *m*; (precaution) precaución *f*; — **fund** fondo especulativo *m*; —**hog** erizo *m*; VI/VT (a bet) cubrir[se]; VT (a question) evadir

hedonism [hídn̩ɪzəm] N hedonismo *m*

heebie-jeebies [híbidʒíbiz] N **it gives me the** — me pone los pelos de punta

heed [hid] VT atender; N atención *f*, cuidado *m*; **to pay** — **to** prestar atención a

heel [hił] N (of foot or sock) talón *m*; (of shoe) tacón *m*; **to kick up one's —s** tirar la chancleta, soltarse el pelo; VT poner tacón a; VI/VT seguir de cerca

hegemony [hɪdʒémәni] N hegemonía *f*

heifer [héfɚ] N novilla *f*, vaquilla *f*

height [haɪt] N (of a building, mountain) altura *f*; (of a person) estatura *f*; (utmost point) colmo *m*

heighten [háɪtn̩] VI/VT (increase) aumentar[se]; (intensify) realzar

Heimlich maneuver [háɪmlɪkmənúvɚ] N maniobra de Heimlich *f*

heinous [hénəs] ADJ aborrecible

heir [ɛr] N heredero -ra *mf*; — **apparent** presunto heredero *m*, presunta heredera *f*; —**s and assigns** herederos y cesionarios *m pl*

heiress [érɪs] N heredera *f*

held [hɛłd] *see* hold

helicopter [hélɪkaptɚ] N helicóptero *m*

helium [híliəm] N helio *m*

helix [hílɪks] N hélice *f*

hell [hɛł] N infierno *m*; —**-raiser** camorrista *mf*

hello [hɛló] INTERJ ¡hola! (on the telephone) hola; *Sp* diga; *Mex* bueno

helm [hɛłm] N timón *m*

helmet [hɛłmɪt] N (for bikes, etc.) casco *m*; (armor) yelmo *m*

help [hɛłp] N (aid) ayuda *f*; (rescue) auxilio *m*; (remedy) remedio *m*; (employee) empleado -da *mf*; — **desk** servicio de ayuda al usuario *m*; INTERJ ¡auxilio! ¡socorro! VI/VT (aid) ayudar, asistir; (rescue) auxiliar, socorrer; — **yourself** sírvete; **he cannot — it** no puede evitarlo; **he cannot — but come** no puede menos que venir; **may I — you?** ¿en qué le puedo servir?

helper [hɛłpɚ] N ayudante *mf*, asistente *mf*

helpful [hɛłpfәł] ADJ (useful) útil; (willing to help) servicial

helping [hɛłpɪŋ] N porción *f*

helpless [hɛłplɪs] ADJ desamparado, desvalido

helplessness [hɛłplɪsnɪs] N desamparo *m*, desvalimiento *m*

hem [hɛm] N dobladillo *m*, *Am* ruedo *m*; VT hacer dobladillos en, orillar; **to — in** arrinconar; **to — and haw** vacilar

hematoma [himətómə] N hematoma *m*

hemisphere [hémɪsfir] N hemisferio *m*

hemlock [hémlak] N cicuta *f*

hemoglobin [híməglobɪn] N hemoglobina *f*

hemophilia [himəfíliə] N hemofilia *f*

hemorrhage [hémərɪdʒ] N hemorragia *f*

hemorrhoids [hémərɔɪdz] N hemorroides *f pl*

hemp [hɛmp] N cáñamo *m*

hen [hɛn] N (chicken) gallina *f*; (female bird) ave hembra *f*; ADJ —**pecked** dominado por su mujer

hence [hɛns] ADV de ahí; —**forth** de aquí en adelante, de hoy en adelante; **a week** — de aquí a una semana

hepatitis [hɛpətáɪDɪs] N hepatitis *f*

her [hɚ] PRON **I see** — la veo; **I talk to** — le hablo [a ella]; **I went with** — fui con ella; POSS ADJ **this is** — **dog** este es su perro, este es el perro de ella

herald [hérəld] N heraldo *m*; VT anunciar, proclamar

herb [ɚb] N hierba *f*

herbal [ɜ́·bəł] ADJ de hierbas; **— tea** tisana *f*
herbicide [hɜ́·bɪsaɪd] N herbicida *m*
herbivore [hɜ́·bəvɔr] N herbívoro *m*
herbivorous [hɜ·bívərəs] ADJ herbívoro
herd [hɜ·d] N (of animals) manada *f*; (of goats) hato *m*; (of sheep) rebaño *m*; (of horses, donkeys) recua *f*; **the common —** el populacho, la chusma; **—sman** pastor *m*; VT arrear; VI ir en manada
here [hir] ADV aquí, acá; **— it is** aquí está; **—after** en adelante; **the —after** el más allá; **—by** (in writing) por la presente; **I —by pronounce you husband and wife** los declaro marido y mujer; **—in** en el presente; **—'s to you!** ¡a tu salud! **—tofore** hasta ahora; **—with** (hereby) por la presente; (attached) adjunto; **come —!** ¡ven acá! **the — and now** el presente; **that is neither — nor there** eso no viene al caso
hereditary [hərépɪteri] ADJ hereditario
heredity [hərépɪti] N herencia *f*
heresy [hérɪsi] N herejía *f*
heretic [hérɪtɪk] N hereje *mf*
heritage [hérɪtɪʤ] N herencia *f*, patrimonio *m*
hermaphrodite [hə·mǽfrədaɪt] N hermafrodita *mf*
hermetic [hɜ·médɪk] ADJ hermético
hermit [hɜ́·mɪt] N ermitaño -ña *mf*; **— crab** ermitaño *m*
hernia [hɜ́·niə] N hernia *f*; **—ted** herniado; **—ted disk** hernia de disco *f*
hero [híro] N (brave man) héroe *m*; (main character) protagonista *mf*
heroic [hɪróɪk] ADJ heroico
heroin [héroɪn] N heroína *f*
heroine [héroɪn] N heroína *f*
heroism [héroɪzəm] N heroísmo *m*
heron [hérən] N garza *f*
herpes [hɜ́·piz] N herpes *m*
herring [hérɪŋ] N arenque *m*
hers [hɜ·z] PRON **this book is —** este libro es suyo / de ella; **these things are —** estas cosas son suyas; **— is bigger** el suyo / la suya es más grande; **a friend of —** un amigo suyo / de ella
herself [hɜ·séłf] PRON ella misma; **she's not — today** hoy no es la misma de siempre; **she was sitting by —** estaba sentada sola; **she — did it** lo hizo sola, lo hizo ella misma; **she talks to —** ella habla para sí, habla consigo misma; **she looked at — in the mirror** se miró en el espejo; **she bought — a house** se compró una casa
hesitant [hézɪtənt] ADJ vacilante
hesitate [hézɪtet] VI (pause) vacilar; (stutter) titubear; (doubt) dudar
hesitating [hézɪteDɪŋ] ADJ vacilante
hesitation [hɛzɪtéʃən] N (pause) vacilación *f*; (stammer) titubeo *m*; (doubt) duda *f*

heterogeneous [hɛDə·əʤíniəs] ADJ heterogéneo
heterosexual [hɛDərosékʃuəł] ADJ heterosexual
hexagon [héksəgan] N hexágono *m*
hey [he] INTERJ ¡oiga!
heyday [héde] N auge *m*
hi [haɪ] INTERJ hola; **say — to your sister for me** dale recuerdos a tu hermana de mi parte
hiatus [haɪéDəs] N hiato *m*
hibernate [háɪbə·net] VI hibernar
hiccup, hiccough [híkʌp] N hipo *m*; VI hipar, tener hipo
hick [hɪk] N & ADJ paleto -ta *mf*
hickory [híkəri] N nogal americano *m*
hid, hidden [hɪd, hídn̩] *see* hide
hidden [hídn̩] ADJ (out of sight) oculto; (illegal) clandestino; **— agenda** intereses ocultos *m pl*
hide [haɪd] VI/VT ocultar[se], esconder[se]; **— and seek** escondite *m*, escondidas *f pl*; **—out** escondite *m*; N cuero *m*, piel *f*, pellejo *m*
hideous [hídiəs] ADJ horrendo, espantoso
hierarchy [háɪərarki] N jerarquía *f*
hieroglyphic [haɪrəglífɪk] ADJ & N jeroglífico *m*
high [haɪ] ADJ alto; (intoxicated) ebrio; (on drugs) volado; **— altitude sickness** enfermedad de altura *f*; **— and dry** (ship) en seco; (person) colgado; **— blood pressure** hipertensión *f*; **—brow** culto; **—-class** de clase; **— contrast** alto contraste *m*; **— definition television** televisión de alta definición *f*; **— density** alta densidad *f*; **—er-up** superior; **—er education** educación superior *f*; **— explosive** explosivo de alta potencia *m*; **— fever** fiebre elevada *f*; **— fidelity** alta fidelidad *f*; **— finance** finanzas *f pl*; **—-grade** de calidad superior; **—-handed** arbitrario; **— jump** salto alto *m*; **—lands** tierras altas *f pl*; **—-level** de alto nivel; **—light** lo más destacado; **—lighting** (on a computer) selección de texto *f*; **—lights** (in hair) claritos *m pl*, mechas *f pl*; **—- minded** idealista; **—-octane gasoline** súper *m*; **—-pitched** agudo; **— point** culminación *f*; **—-powered** de alta potencia; **—-pressure** estresante, intenso; **—-priced** caro; **—-quality** de alta calidad; **—-return** de alta rentabilidad; **—-rise** de muchos pisos; **—-risk** de alto riesgo; **—-risk behavior** conducta de alto riesgo *f*; **—-risk patient** paciente con alto riesgo *mf*; **— school** escuela secundaria *f*, colegio *m*; *Sp* instituto *m*; **— seas** alta mar *f*; **—-sounding** altisonante; **—-speed** de alta velocidad; **— spirits** buen ánimo *m*; **—-strung** nervioso; **—-tech** alta tecnología *f*; **— temperature** temperatura máxima *f*; **— tide** pleamar *f*; **—way** carretera *f*, ruta *f*; **— wind** ventarrón *m*; **in — gear** a toda marcha; **two feet —** dos pies de altura; **it is — time that** ya era hora de que; **to look**

— **and low** buscar por todas partes; N flash
m, subida *f*; VT **to —light** (emphasize)
destacar, resaltar
highly [háɪli] ADV — **amusing** sumamente
divertido; — **paid** muy bien pagado; —
qualified altamente cualificado; **he spoke**
— **of her** habló muy bien de ella
highness [háɪnɪs] N alteza *f*
hijack [háɪʤæk] VT secuestrar [un vehículo]
hike [haɪk] N caminata *f*; **take a —!** ¡ve a freír
espárragos! VI salir a caminar
hilarious [hɪlériəs] ADJ graciosísimo, para
morirse de risa
hill [hɪl] N (elevated area) colina *f*, cerro *m*; (pile)
montón *m*; **—billy** paleto -ta *mf*; **—side**
ladera *f*; **—top** cumbre *f*, cima *f*
hillock [hílək] N otero *m*
hilly [híli] ADJ accidentado
hilt [hɪlt] N empuñadura *f*; **to the** — al máximo
him [hɪm] PRON **I see** — lo veo; *Sp* le veo; **I talk**
to — le hablo; **I went with** — fui con él
himself [hɪmsɛ́lf] PRON él mismo; **he — wrote**
the letter él mismo escribió la carta; **he's**
not — today hoy no es el mismo de siempre;
he was sitting by — estaba sentado solo;
he talks to — él habla para sí, habla consigo
mismo; **he looked at — in the mirror** se
miró en el espejo; **he bought — a house** se
compró una casa
hind [haɪnd] ADJ trasero; **—most** último; **in**
—sight a posteriori; N cierva *f*
hinder [híndɚ] VT impedir, entorpecer, estorbar
Hindi [híndi] N hindi *m*
hindrance [híndrəns] N obstáculo *m*,
impedimento *m*, traba *f*
Hindu [híndu] ADJ & N hindú *mf*
hinge [hɪnʤ] N gozne *m*, quicio *m*; VT engoznar,
poner goznes; VI **to — on** depender de
hint [hɪnt] N (clue) indirecta *f*, pista *f*; (trace) dejo
m; **to take the** — darse por enterado; VT
insinuar
hip [hɪp] N cadera *f*; — **replacement**
(operation) sustitución protésica de la cadera
f; (prosthesis) prótesis de cadera *f*
Hippocratic oath [hɪpəkrǽDɪkóθ] N juramento
hipocrático *m*
hippopotamus [hɪpəpáDəməs] N hipopótamo *m*
hire [haɪr] VT (engage for work) contratar; VI/VT
(rent) alquilar[se]; — **and fire** contratar y
despedir; **to — out** dar en alquiler, alquilar;
N (engagement) contratación *f*; (employee)
nuevo -va empleado -da *mf*; (rent) alquiler *m*
his [hɪz] POSS ADJ **this is — dog** este es su
perro / el perro de él; PRON **these things**
are — estas cosas son suyas; — **is right here**
el suyo / la suya está aquí; **a friend of** — un
amigo suyo / una amiga suya
Hispanic [hɪspǽnɪk] ADJ hispánico, hispano; N
hispano -na *mf*

hiss [hɪs] VI sisear; (to boo) silbar; N siseo *m*
histamine [hístəmin] N histamina *f*
historian [hɪstɔ́riən] N historiador -ra *mf*
historic [hɪstɔ́rɪk] ADJ histórico
historical [hɪstɔ́rɪkəl] ADJ histórico
history [hístəri] N historia *f*
histrionics [hɪstriánɪks] N histrionismo *m*
hit [hɪt] VT (a target) dar en; (a car) chocar con; (a
key) pulsar, tocar; (a baseball) batear; **to** — **a**
homerun batear un jonrón, pegar un
cuadrangular; **to** — **it off** llevarse bien desde
el principio; **to** — **the mark** acertar, dar en
el blanco; **to** — **upon an idea** dar con una
idea; **to** — **on a person** tratar de ligar con
alguien; N (blow) golpe *m*; (success) éxito *m*;
(dose) dosis *f*; **that was a** — **with me** me
encantó; **—man** sicario *m*; **—s** (on a website)
visitas *f pl*; ADJ — **-and-run** que se da a la fuga
después de atropellar a alguien; — **-or-miss**
al azar
hitch [hɪtʃ] VT atar, amarrar; (pants) levantar;
(yoke) uncir, enganchar; **to get —ed** casarse;
to —hike *Sp* hacer autostop; *Am* hacer dedo;
N (knot) nudo *m*; (difficulty) dificultad *f*;
(period) período *m*
hither [híðɚ] ADV acá; — **and thither** acá y
allá; **—to** hasta ahora
HIV [human immunodeficiency virus]
[étʃaɪví] N VIH *m*
hive [haɪv] N (shelter for bees) colmena *f*; (colony
of bees) enjambre *m*; **—s** urticaria *f*
HMO [health maintenance organization]
[étʃémó] N organización de mantenimiento de
salud *f*
hoard [hɔrd] N reserva *f*; VI/VT acaparar
hoarse [hɔrs] ADJ ronco; (like alcoholics)
aguardentoso
hoarseness [hɔ́rsnɪs] N ronquera *f*
hoax [hoks] N engaño *m*
hobble [hábəl] VI (limp) cojear; VT (tie to impede
walking) manear; (hinder) trabar; N cojera *f*;
(rope) traba *f*, manea *f*
hobby [hábi] N hobby *m*
hobo [hóbo] N vagabundo *m*
hockey [háki] N hockey *m*
hodgepodge [háʤpaʤ] N mezcolanza *f*,
batiburrillo *m*
hoe [ho] N azada *f*, azadón *m*; VI/VT limpiar con
azadón
hog [hɑg] N puerco *m*, cerdo *m*, marrano *m*; *Am*
chancho *m*; **—wash** pamplinas *f pl*; **to live**
high on the — vivir en la abundancia; VT
acaparar, adueñarse de
hoist [hɔɪst] VT izar; N torno *m*, guinche *m*
hokey [hóki] ADJ sensiblero
hold [hold] VT (bear) llevar, sujetar; (contain)
contener; (detain) detener; (decide legally,
sustain a note) sostener; (opine) opinar; **to** —
back detener; **to — down** sujetar; **to** —

forth perorar; **to — hands** tomarse de la mano; **to — in place** sujetar; **to — a meeting** celebrar una reunión; **to —** someone responsible hacerle a uno responsable; **to — someone to his word** obligar a uno a cumplir con su palabra; **to — oneself erect** ponerse derecho; **to — one's own** defenderse; **to — one's tongue** callarse, morderse la lengua; **— the pickles on that burger!** una hamburguesa sin pepinillos, por favor; VI (remain fast) aguantar, resistir; (occupy a position) ocupar; (be valid) ser válido; **to — off** mantener[se] a distancia; **to — off doing something** abstenerse de hacer algo; **to — liable** responsabilizar; **to — on** (not let go) agarrar[se], sujetar[se]; (stop) esperar; (persist) persistir; **to — out** aguantar; **to — still** quedarse/estarse quieto; **to — tight** agarrarse; **to — to one's promise** cumplir con la palabra; **to — up** (raise) alzar; (detain) detener; (rob) atracar, asaltar; (persevere) aguantar; **how much does it — ?** ¿Qué capacidad tiene? N (grip) agarro m; (thing to grasp) asidero m; (dominion) dominio m; (wrestling move) llave f; (in music) calderón m; (of a ship) bodega f; **—up** golpe m, atraco m; **to get — of** agarrar; **to take — of** Sp coger, agarrar; **to have a good — on something** agarrarse bien de algo

holder [hółdɚ] N (person) tenedor -ora mf, poseedor -ora mf; (device) receptáculo m

holding [hółdɪŋ] N propiedad f; **— company** holding m; **—s** (financial) valores en cartera m pl; (of a library) fondos m pl

hole [hoł] N agujero m; (in a wall) boquete m; (of an animal) madriguera f; (in the ground, in golf) hoyo m; **to be in a —** hallarse/estar en un apuro/aprieto; **—in-one** hoyo en uno m

holiday [hálɪde] N día de fiesta m; **—s** vacaciones f pl

holiness [hólɪnɪs] N santidad f

holistic [holístɪk] ADJ holístico

Holland [hálənd] N Holanda f

hollow [hálo] ADJ (empty) hueco; (concave) cóncavo; (sunken) hundido; (insincere) falso; N (cavity) hueco m, concavidad f; (valley) hondonada f, hondo m; VT **to — out** ahuecar, vaciar

holly [háli] N acebo m

holocaust [háləkɔst] N holocausto m

holster [hółstɚ] N pistolera f, funda de pistola f

holy [hóli] ADJ santo, sagrado; **— Bible** Santa Biblia f; **— cow/Moses/mackerel!** ¡que increíble! Sp ¡jobar! **— Ghost** Espíritu Santo m; **— Spirit** Espíritu Santo m; **— war** guerra santa f; **— water** agua bendita f

homage [hámɪʤ] N homenaje m; **to pay —** rendir homenaje, honrar

home [hom] N casa f, hogar m; (for old people, orphans) asilo m, hogar m; **—boy** amigo del barrio m; **— economics** economía doméstica f; **— delivery** entrega a domicilio f; **— equity loan** préstamo garantizado por el valor residual de la vivienda m; **— game** partido en casa m; **—land** patria f; **—less** sin techo; **— office** (headquarters) oficina central f; (at home) oficina en el hogar f; **—owner** propietario -ria de vivienda mf; **—owners' association** asociación de propietarios de vivienda f; **— page** página de inicio f; **— plate** goma f, plato m; **— rule** autonomía f; **— run** jonrón m, cuadrangular m; **at —** en casa; **to be —sick** echar de menos / extrañar [a la familia]; **—sickness** morriña f, añoranza f; **— stretch** último trecho m; **—work** tarea domiciliaria f, deber m; **—** doméstico; ADV (direction) a casa; (location) en casa; **to strike —** dar en el blanco; ADJ **—made** casero

homely [hómli] ADJ (ugly) feo; (familiar) familiar, doméstico

homeopathic [homiopǽθɪk] ADJ homeopático

homeopathy [homiápəθi] N homeopatía f

homestead [hómstɛd] N heredad f, casa de la familia f

homeward [hómwɚd] ADV a casa; **— bound** camino a casa

homicide [hámɪsaɪd] N homicidio m

homogeneous [homəʤínɪəs] ADJ homogéneo

homogenize [həmáʤənaɪz] VT homogeneizar

homonym [hámənɪm] N homónimo m

homophobia [homəfóbiə] N homofobia f

homophobic [homəfóbɪk] ADJ homofóbico

homosexual [homosékʃuəl] ADJ & N homosexual mf

Honduran [handúrən] ADJ & N hondureño -ña mf

Honduras [handúrəs] N Honduras f

hone [hon] VT afilar; **to — one's skills** desarrollar las destrezas; N piedra de afilar f

honest [ánɪst] ADJ honrado, honesto; **I'll be — with you** voy a ser franco contigo; **—!** ¡de veras!

honesty [ánɪsti] N (integrity) honradez f, honestidad f; (sincerity) franqueza f

honey [háni] N (sweet substance) miel f; (endearment) querido -da mf; **—bee** abeja f; **—comb** panal m; **—suckle** madreselva f

honeymoon [hánimun] N luna de miel f; VI pasar la luna de miel

honk [haŋk] N (of a car) bocinazo m, pitazo m; (of a goose) graznido m; VI/VT (car) tocar la bocina; VI (goose) graznar

honor [ánɚ] N (respect, privilege) honor m; (good reputation) honra f; **with —s** con honores; **your —** su señoría; VT (revere) honrar; (accept invitation, check) aceptar; **to**

— **a promise** cumplir [con] una promesa
honorable [ánəˑəbəɫ] ADJ honorable
honorary [ánəɾeri] ADJ honorario
hood [hʊd] N (of a coat) capucha f, caperuza f; (of a car) capó m; Am tapa f; VT encapuchar
hoodlum [húdləm] N maleante mf, gamberro -rra mf
hoof [hʊf] N casco m, pezuña f; VI **to — it** ir andando
hook [hʊk] N (for lifting) gancho m, garfio m; (for fishing) anzuelo m; — **and eye** alamar m, macho y hembra m; **by — or by crook** por las buenas o por las malas; —**up** conexión f, enganche m; VT (snag) enganchar; (a dress) abrochar; **to — up** conectar, enganchar
hooked [hʊkt] ADJ (shaped like a hook) ganchudo; (addicted) enganchado
hooker [húkəˑ] N prostituta f; pej tía f, puta f
hooky [húki] N **to play** — hacer novillos
hooligan [húlɪgən] N Sp gamberro -rra mf, Am patotero -ra mf
hoop [hup] N (also in basketball) aro m
hoot [hut] VI/VT (of owl) ulular; (in derision) abuchear; N (of an owl) ululato m; (cry of derision) abucheo m; **I don't give a** — no me importa un comino; **it's a** — es para morirse de risa
hop [hɑp] VI saltar, brincar; **to — on** subirse a montar; N (short jump) saltito m, brinco m; (dance) bailongo m; —**s** lúpulo m
hope [hop] N esperanza f; VI/VT esperar; **to — for** esperar; **to — against** — esperar lo imposible
hopeful [hópfəɫ] ADJ (having hopes) esperanzado; (giving hopes) esperanzador, alentador
hopefully [hópfəli] ADV — **she'll come** ojalá [que] venga
hopeless [hóplɪs] ADJ (without hope) desesperanzado; (with no solution) irremediable; (unattainable) inalcanzable; — **cause** causa perdida f; **it is** — no tiene remedio; **the new secretary is — with numbers** el nuevo secretario es un desastre con los números
hopelessness [hóplɪsnɪs] N desesperanza f
horde [hɔrd] N (of people) horda f; (of animals) plaga f
horizon [həráɪzən] N horizonte m
horizontal [hɔrɪzántl̩] ADJ horizontal
hormone [hɔ́rmon] N hormona f; — **therapy** terapia hormonal f
horn [hɔrn] N (of an animal, substance) cuerno m, asta f; (of an automobile) bocina f, claxon m; (musical) corno m, trompa f; — **of plenty** cuerno de la abundancia m; **to toot one's own** — darse autobombo; VI **to — in** entrometerse
hornet [hɔ́rnɪt] N avispón m; —**'s nest**

avispero m
horny [hɔ́rni] ADJ (with hard skin) calloso; (sexually excited) Sp fam cachondo; Am fam caliente
horoscope [hɔ́rəskop] N horóscopo m
horrendous [hɔréndəs] ADJ horrendo
horrible [hɔ́rəbəɫ] ADJ horrible
horrid [hɔ́rɪd] ADJ horrendo
horrify [hɔ́rəfaɪ] VT horrorizar
horror [hɔ́rəˑ] N horror m
hors d'oeuvre [ɔrdɔ́ˑv] N entremés m
horse [hɔrs] N caballo m; —**back** lomo de caballo m; **to ride — back** montar a caballo, cabalgar; —**fly** tábano m; —**laugh** carcajada f; —**man** jinete m; —**manship** equitación f; —**play** payasadas f pl; —**power** caballo de fuerza m; — **race** carrera de caballos f; —**radish** rábano picante m; — **sense** sentido común m; —**shoe** herradura f; **hold your** —**s!** ¡para el carro! VI **to — around** payasear
horticulture [hɔ́rdɪkʌɫtʃəˑ] N horticultura f
hose [hoz] N (for legs) medias f pl; (for liquids) manguera f, manga f
hosiery [hóʒəri] N (stockings) medias f pl; (shop for stockings) calcetería f
hospice [háspɪs] N (inn) hospicio m; (hospital) hospital para enfermos terminales m
hospitable [haspíꟾəbəɫ] ADJ hospitalario, acogedor
hospital [háspɪdl̩] N hospital m
hospitality [haspɪtǽlɪDi] N hospitalidad f
hospitalize [háspɪdl̩aɪz] VT internar
host [host] N (also computer) anfitrión m; (in a home or hotel, for a parasite) huésped m; (on television) presentador -ora mf; (army) hueste f; (multitude) multitud f, cúmulo m; (wafer) hostia f
hostage [hástɪdʒ] N rehén mf
hostel [hástl̩] N hostal m
hostelry [hástl̩ri] N hostería f
hostess [hóstɪs] N anfitriona f
hostile [hástl̩] ADJ hostil; — **takeover** compra hostil f
hostility [hastílɪDi] N hostilidad f
hot [hɑt] ADJ (at high temperature) caliente; (sweltering) caluroso; (spicy) picante; (sexy) bueno; (sexually aroused) Sp cachondo; Am caliente; (stolen) robado; (recent) de último momento; (popular) popular; — **and heavy** apasionado, apasionadamente; —**bed** semillero m; — **dog** perro caliente m; —**headed** impetuoso, exaltado; —**house** invernadero m; — **potato** patata caliente f; — **seat** situación embarazosa f; —**shot** estrella f; —**tub** jacuzzi m; **it is — today** hace calor hoy; — **under the collar** enojado; VT **to — -wire** hacerle un puente a
hotel [hotéɫ] N hotel m; —**keeper** hotelero -ra mf

hound [haʊnd] N perro de caza *m*, sabueso *m*; VT acosar, perseguir

hour [aʊr] N hora *f*; — **hand** horario *m*; **his finest** — su mejor momento *m*

hourly [áʊrli] ADV (on the hour) cada hora; (by the hour) por horas; — **wages** salario por hora *m*

house[1] [haʊs] N (residence) casa *f*; (legislature) cámara legislativa *f*; — **arrest** detención domiciliaria *f*; —**boat** casa flotante *f*; —**cleaning** limpieza de la casa *f*; —**hold** casa *f*, familia *f*; —**keeper** (in a house) ama de llaves *f*; (in a home) encargado -da de limpieza *mf*; —**keeping** mantenimiento del hogar *m*; —**top** techo *m*, tejado *m*; —**wife** ama de casa *f*; —**work** trabajo de casa *m*, quehaceres domésticos *m pl*; **in-** — interno; **on the** — la casa paga; **to keep** — cuidar la casa; —**hold expenses** gastos del hogar *m pl*; —-**to-** — puerta a puerta

house[2] [haʊz] VI/VT alojar

housing [háʊzɪŋ] N (place to live) vivienda *f*; (protective covering) caja *f*

hovel [hávəl] N (hut) choza *f*, cabaña *f*, tugurio *m*; (open shed) cobertizo *m*

hover [hávɚ] VI (bird) cernerse; (hang in air) estar suspendido; (linger) rondar; —**craft** aerodeslizador *m*

how [haʊ] ADV cómo; — **about your mom?** ¿y tu mamá? — **beautiful!** ¡qué hermoso! — **come?** ¿por qué? — **early [late, soon]?** ¿cuándo? ¿a qué hora? — **far is it?** ¿a qué distancia está? ¿cuánto dista de aquí? — **long?** ¿cuánto tiempo? — **many?** ¿cuántos? — **much is it?** ¿cuánto vale? — **old are you?** ¿cuántos años tienes? **no matter** — **much it rains** por mucho que llueva; **he knows** — **difficult it is** él sabe lo difícil que es

however [haʊévɚ] CONJ sin embargo, no obstante; ADV — **you want it** como quieras; — **difficult it may be** por muy difícil que sea; — **much it rains** por mucho que llueva

howl [haʊł] VI aullar; (wind) ulular; (with laughter) reír a carcajadas; N aullido *m*, alarido *m*

HQ [headquarters] [étʃkjú] N oficina central *f*, sede central *f*

HR [human resources] [étʃár] N recursos humanos *m pl*

HTML [HyperText Markup Language] [étʃtiéméł] N HTML *m*

hub [hʌb] N (center of wheel) cubo *m*; (center of activity) núcleo *m*; —**cap** tapacubos *m sg*

hubbub [hábʌb] N alboroto *m*, barullo *m*

huckster [hákstɚ] N (peddler) vendedor ambulante *m*; (promoter) mercachifle *m*

huddle [hádl̩] VI/VT (form a group) apiñar[se]; (curl up) acurrucar[se]; (consult)

conferenciar; N tropel *m*; (group meeting for consultation) reunión *f*; **to be in a** — estar agrupados; **to get in a** — agruparse

hue [hju] N matiz *m*

huff [hʌf] N **to get into a** — enojarse; VI **to** — **and puff** resoplar

hug [hʌg] VI/VT abrazar[se]; **to** — **the coast** costear; N abrazo *m*

huge [hjudʒ] ADJ enorme, fiero

hull [hʌl] N (of a ship, airplane) casco *m*; (of beans, peas) vaina *f*; (of fruits, nuts) cáscara *f*; VT (beans, peas) desvainar; (nuts) cascar

hum [hʌm] VI/VT (person) tararear; (insect, machine) zumbar; (place of activity) hervir; **to** — **to sleep** arrullar; N (of voice) tarareo *m*; (of insect, machine) zumbido *m*

human [hjúmən] ADJ & N humano *m*; — **being** ser humano *m*; — **immunodeficiency virus** virus de inmunodeficiencia humana *m*

humane [hjumén] ADJ humano, humanitario

humanism [hjúmənɪzəm] N humanismo *m*

humanitarian [hjumænɪtériən] ADJ humanitario

humanity [hjumǽnɪDi] N humanidad *f*; **humanities** humanidades *f pl*

humble [hámbəł] ADJ humilde; VT humillar

humid [hjúmɪd] ADJ húmedo

humidify [hjumíDəfaɪ] VT humidificar

humidity [hjumíDɪDi] N humedad *f*

humiliate [hjumíliet] VT humillar, vejar

humiliation [hjumɪliéʃən] N humillación *f*

humility [hjumílɪDi] N humildad *f*

hummingbird [hámɪŋbɚd] N colibrí *m*

humor [hjúmɚ] N humor *m*, humorismo *m*; **out of** — de mal humor, malhumorado; VT complacer a

humorous [hjúmɚəs] ADJ gracioso, chistoso

hump [hʌmp] N joroba *f*, giba *f*, corcova *f*; **we're over the** — ya pasamos lo peor; —**back** jorobado -da *mf*; —**back whale** ballena jorobada *f*, yubarta *f*; VI/VT (have sex with) *Sp vulg* follar; *Am* coger, culear

hunch [hʌntʃ] N presentimiento *m*, corazonada *f*; —**back** (person) jorobado -da *mf*; (hump) corcova *f*; VI encorvar

hundred [hándrɪd] NUM cien[to]; **a** — **people** cien personas; **a** — **and fifty people** ciento cincuenta personas; N cien/ciento *m*; —**s** centenares *m pl*, cientos *m pl*

hundredth [hándrɪdθ] ADJ centésimo

hung [hʌŋ] *see* hang 'ahorcar'

Hungarian [hʌŋgériən] ADJ & N húngaro -ra *mf*

Hungary [háŋgəri] N Hungría *f*

hunger [háŋgɚ] N hambre *f*; VI pasar hambre; **to** — **for** ansiar, anhelar

hungry [háŋgri] ADJ hambriento; **to be** — tener hambre; **to go** — pasar hambre

hunk [hʌŋk] N pedazo *m*, cacho *m*; **he's a real** — es un cacho de hombre, es un papacito

hunt [hʌnt] VI/VT (seek prey) cazar; **to — down** dar caza a; **to — for** buscar; N (activity of hunting) caza *f*; (instance of hunting) cacería *f*; (search) búsqueda *f*

hunter [hántɚ] N (who captures game) cazador -ora *mf*; (seeker) buscador -ora *mf*; (dog) perro de caza *m*

hunting [hántɪŋ] N caza *f*; **— knife** cuchillo de caza *m*

huntsman [hántsmən] N cazador *m*

hurdle [hɝdl] N (impediment) obstáculo *m*; (in races) valla *f*; VT saltar

hurl [hɝl] VI/VT arrojar, lanzar, precipitar

hurrah [hərá] INTERJ ¡hurra!

hurricane [hɝɪken] N huracán *m*

hurried [hɝid] ADJ apresurado; *Am* apurado

hurry [hɝi] VI darse prisa, apresurarse; *Am* apurarse; **to — in [out]** entrar [salir] de prisa; **to — up** apresurar[se], dar[se] prisa; *Am* apurar[se]; VT apresurar; *Am* apurar; N prisa *f*; *Am* apuro *m*; **to be in a —** tener prisa; *Am* estar apurado

hurt [hɝt] VI/VT (to injure) lastimar[se], hacer[se] daño; (damage) dañar[se]; (harm) perjudicar[se]; **to — someone's feelings** lastimar/herir a alguien; VI (suffer pain) doler; **my tooth —s** me duele la muela / el diente; N (damage) daño *m*; (wound) herida *f*, lastimadura *f*; ADJ (physically) lastimado, herido; (emotionally) herido; **to get —** lastimarse

hurtful [hɝtfəl] ADJ hiriente

husband [házbənd] N marido *m*, esposo *m*; VT administrar

hush [hʌʃ] VI/VT aquietar[se], callar[se]; —! ¡chitón! ¡silencio! **to — up a scandal** encubrir un escándalo; N silencio *m*; **he gave her — money** compró su silencio

husk [hʌsk] N (shell) cáscara *f*; (pod) vaina *f*; (of corn) *Am* chala *f*; *Sp* farfolla *f*; VT (corn) quitar la chala/farfolla a; (beans, peas) desvainar

husky [háski] ADJ (build) ronco; (strong) recio; N (breed of dog) husky *m*, perro esquimal *m*

hustle [hásəl] VI (work energetically) afanarse; (swindle) estafar; VT (hurry along) empujar; N (bustle) ajetreo *m*; (scheme) timo *m*; **— and bustle** ajetreo *m*, trajín *m*

hut [hʌt] N choza *f*, cabaña *f*

hyacinth [háɪəsɪnθ] N jacinto *m*

hybrid [háɪbrɪd] ADJ híbrido

hybridization [haɪbrɪdɪzéʃən] N hibridación *f*

hydrate [háɪdret] N hidrato *m*; VI/VT hidratar[se]

hydraulic [haɪdrɔ́lɪk] ADJ hidráulico

hydrocarbon [háɪdrəkɑrbən] N hidrocarburo *m*

hydroelectric [haɪdroɪléktrɪk] ADJ hidroeléctrico

hydrogen [háɪdrədʒən] N hidrógeno *m*; **— bomb** bomba de hidrógeno *f*; **— peroxide** peróxido de hidrógeno *m*, agua oxigenada *f*

hydrophobia [haɪdrəfóbiə] N hidrofobia *f*

hydroplane [háɪdrəplen] N hidroavión *m*

hyena [haɪínə] N hiena *f*

hygiene [háɪdʒin] N higiene *f*

hygienic [haɪdʒénɪk] ADJ higiénico

hygienist [haɪdʒínɪst] N higienista *mf*

hymen [háɪmən] N himen *m*

hymn [hɪm] N himno *m*

hype [haɪp] N exageración *f*; VT promocionar [exageradamente]

hyper [háɪpɚ] ADJ hiperactivo

hyperactive [haɪpɚǽktɪv] ADJ hiperactivo

hyperbaric chamber [haɪpɚbǽrɪk tʃémbɚ] N cámara hiperbárica *f*

hyperdocument [haɪpɚdákjəmənt] N hiperdocumento *m*

hyperlink [háɪpɚlɪŋk] N hiperenlace *m*, hipervínculo *m*

hypermedia [haɪpɚmídiə] N hipermedia *m*

hypersensitive [haɪpɚsénsɪdɪv] ADJ hipersensible

hypertension [haɪpɚténʃən] N hipertensión *f*, presión arterial alta *f*

hyperventilate [haɪpɚvéntlet] VI hiperventilar

hyphen [háɪfən] N guión *m*

hypnosis [hɪpnósɪs] N hipnosis *f*

hypnotherapy [hɪpnoθérəpi] N hipnoterapia *f*

hypnotize [hípnətaɪz] VT hipnotizar

hypoallergenic [haɪpoælədʒénɪk] ADJ hipoalérgico

hypochondriac [haɪpokándriæk] N hipocondríaco *mf*, hipocondriaco *mf*

hypocrisy [hɪpákrɪsi] N hipocresía *f*

hypocrite [hípəkrɪt] N hipócrita *mf*

hypocritical [hɪpəkrídɪkəl] ADJ hipócrita, doblado

hypodermic needle [haɪpədɝmɪk nídl] N aguja hipodérmica *f*

hypoglycemia [haɪpoglaɪsímiə] N hipoglucemia *f*

hypothesis [haɪpáθɪsɪs] N hipótesis *f*

hypothyroidism [haɪpoθáɪrɔɪdɪzəm] N hipotiroidismo *m*

hysterectomy [hɪstəréktəmi] N histerectomía *f*

hysterical [hɪstérɪkəl] ADJ (out of control) histérico; (funny) desternillante

Ii

I [aɪ] PRON yo

I-beam [áɪbim] N viga doble *f*

Iberian [aɪbíriən] ADJ ibérico

Ibero-American [aɪbiroəmérɪkən] ADJ iberoamericano -na

ibuprofen [aɪbjuprófɪn] N ibuprofeno *m*

ice [aɪs] N hielo *m*; — **age** periodo glaciar *m*; —**berg** iceberg *m*; —**box** nevera *f*; refrigerador *m*; — **cream** helado *m*; — **cream cone** cucurucho de helado *m*; —-**cream parlor** heladería *f*; — **hockey** hockey sobre hielo *m*; — **skates** patines de cuchilla *m pl*; — **water** agua helada *f*; **to break the** — romper el hielo; **on** — en suspenso; VI/VT (freeze) helar[se]; (cover with ice) cubrir[se] de hielo; VT (cover with icing) bañar; (insure a deal) cerrar; **to** —-**skate** patinar sobre hielo; —**d tea** té helado *m*

Iceland [áɪslənd] N Islandia *f*

Icelander [áɪsləndɚ] N islandés -esa *mf*

Icelandic [aɪslǽndɪk] ADJ islandés

icicle [áɪsɪkəł] N carámbano *m*

icing [áɪsɪŋ] N (frosting) baño *m*; (formation of ice) formación de hielo *f*

icon [áɪkɑn] N icono *m*, ícono *m* (also computer term)

ICU [intensive care unit] [áɪsíjú] N unidad de cuidados intensivos *f*

icy [áɪsi] ADJ helado

ID [identification card] [áɪdí] N tarjeta de identidad *m*

idea [aɪdíə] N idea *f*

ideal [aɪdíəł] N ideal *m*; ADJ ideal, idóneo

idealism [aɪdíəlɪzəm] N idealismo *m*

idealist [aɪdíəlɪst] N idealista *mf*

idealistic [aɪdiəlístɪk] ADJ idealista

identical [aɪdéntɪkəł] ADJ idéntico; — **twins** gemelos *m pl*, gemelas *f pl*

identification [aɪdɛntəfɪkéʃən] N identificación *f*; — **card** tarjeta de identidad *m*, cédula de identidad *f*

identify [aɪdéntəfaɪ] VI/VT identificar[se]

identity [aɪdéntɪDi] N identidad *f*; — **theft** robo de identidad *m*

ideological [aɪdiəládʒɪkəł] ADJ ideológico

ideology [aɪdiálədʒi] N ideología *f*

idiocy [ídiəsi] N idiotez *f*

idiom [ídiəm] N modismo *m*

idiosyncrasy [ɪDiosínkrəsi] N idiosincrasia *f*

idiot [ídiət] N idiota *mf*, gilipollas *mf sg*

idiotic [ɪDiáDIk] ADJ idiota

idle [áɪdl] ADJ (not active) ocioso; (lazy) perezoso, holgazán; (of a machine, worker) parado; (of an engine) en ralentí; (meaningless) vacío; VI (person) holgazanear; (motor) girar en vacío; VT (cause to be idle) dejar parado/desocupado

idleness [áɪdl̩nɪs] N (inactivity) ociosidad *f*, ocio *m*, holganza *f*; (sloth) pereza *f*

idler [áɪdlɚ] N holgazán -ana *mf*, zanguango -ga *mf*

idol [áɪdl̩] N ídolo *m*

idolatry [aɪdáłətri] N idolatría *f*

idolize [áɪdlaɪz] VT idolatrar

idyll [áɪdl̩] N idilio *m*

if [ɪf] CONJ si; — **I were you** en tu lugar / yo que

tú; — **only I had known** de haber sabido / ojalá hubiera sabido; **he's tall,** — **a bit stooped** es alto, aunque un poco encorvado; N —**s** condiciones *f pl*; **no** —**s, ands, or buts** no hay pero que valga

igloo [íglu] N iglú *m*

ignite [ɪgnáɪt] VI/VT encender[se], prender fuego [a]

ignition [ɪgníʃən] N ignición *f*, encendido *m*; — **switch** llave de contacto *f*

ignoble [ɪgnóbəł] ADJ innoble

ignorance [ígnərəns] N ignorancia *f*

ignorant [ígnərənt] ADJ ignorante

ignore [ɪgnór] VT ignorar

ilk [ɪłk] N ralea *f*, calaña *f*

ill [ɪł] ADJ enfermo, malo; — **fortune** mala suerte *f*; — **nature** mal genio *m*, mala índole *f*; — **repute** mala fama *f*; — **will** mala voluntad *f*; N (sickness) enfermedad *f*; (calamity) calamidad *f*; ADJ —**advised** imprudente; — **at ease** incómodo; —-**bred** maleducado; —-**fated** fatídico, funesto, desastrado; —-**gotten** mal adquirido; —-**humored** malhumorado; —-**mannered** maleducado, grosero; —-**natured** de mal genio; ADV **we can** — **afford to stop now** no podemos darnos el lujo de detenernos ahora

illegal [ɪlígəł] ADJ ilegal

illegitimate [ɪlɪdʒídəmɪt] ADJ ilegítimo

illicit [ɪlísɪt] ADJ ilícito

illiteracy [ɪlíDərəsi] N analfabetismo *m*

illiterate [ɪlíDərɪt] ADJ & N analfabeto -ta *mf*

illness [íłnɪs] N enfermedad *f*

illuminate [ɪlúmənet] VI/VT iluminar[se]

illumination [ɪlumənéʃən] N iluminación *f*

illusion [ɪlúʒən] N ilusión *f*

illusory [ɪlúzəri] ADJ ilusorio

illustrate [íləstret] VI/VT ilustrar

illustration [ɪləstréʃən] N ilustración *f*, estampa *f*

illustrator [íləstreDɚ] N ilustrador -ra *mf*, dibujante *mf*

illustrious [ɪlʌ́striəs] ADJ ilustre, eximio

image [ímɪdʒ] N imagen *f*

imagery [ímɪdʒri] N conjunto de imágenes *m*

imaginary [ɪmǽdʒənɛri] ADJ imaginario, fabuloso

imagination [ɪmædʒənéʃən] N imaginación *f*, fantasía *f*

imaginative [ɪmǽdʒənəDɪv] ADJ imaginativo, fantasioso

imagine [ɪmǽdʒɪn] VI/VT imaginar[se]; — **that!** ¡figúrate!

imbalance [ɪmbǽləns] N desequilibrio *m*

imbecile [ímbəsəł] N imbécil *mf*

imbibe [ɪmbáɪb] VI/VT beber

imbue [ɪmbjú] VT imbuir, infundir

IMF [International Monetary Fund] [áɪéméf] N FMI *m*

imitate [ímɪtet] VT imitar
imitation [ɪmɪtéʃən] N imitación *f*; — **leather** imitación de cuero *f*
imitator [ímɪteDɚ] N imitador -ora *mf*
immaculate [ɪmǽkjəlɪt] ADJ inmaculado
immaterial [ɪmətíriəł] ADJ inmaterial; **it is — to me** me es indiferente
immature [ɪmətʃúr] ADJ inmaduro
immediate [ɪmíDiɪt] ADJ inmediato
immediately [ɪmíDiɪtli] ADV inmediatamente, enseguida
immense [ɪméns] ADJ inmenso
immensity [ɪménsɪDi] N inmensidad *f*
immerse [ɪmɚs] VT (submerge) sumergir; (absorb) sumir
immersed [ɪmɚst] ADJ inmerso
immigrant [ímɪgrənt] ADJ & N inmigrante *mf*
immigrate [ímɪgret] VI inmigrar
immigration [ɪmɪgréʃən] N inmigración *f*
imminent [ímənənt] ADJ inminente
immobile [ɪmóbəł] ADJ inmóvil
immobilize [ɪmóbəlaɪz] VT inmovilizar
immodest [ɪmáDɪst] ADJ inmodesto
immodesty [ɪmáDɪsti] N inmodestia *f*
immoral [ɪmɔ́rəł] ADJ inmoral
immorality [ɪmɔrǽlɪDi] N inmoralidad *f*
immortal [ɪmɔ́rdl̩] ADJ & N inmortal *mf*
immortality [ɪmɔrtǽlɪDi] N inmortalidad *f*
immovable [ɪmúvəbəł] ADJ inamovible
immune [ɪmjún] ADJ inmune; — **system** sistema inmune *m*
immunity [ɪmjúnɪDi] N inmunidad *f*
immunodeficiency [ɪmjənodɪfíʃənsi] N inmunodeficiencia *f*
immutable [ɪmjúDəbəł] ADJ inmutable
impact [ímpækt] N impacto *m*; VI/VT repercutir [sobre]; **—ed molar** muela impactada *f*
impair [ɪmpér] VT dañar, deteriorar, menoscabar; **—ed** con las facultades disminuidas
impairment [ɪmpérmənt] N daño *m*, deterioro *m*, menoscabo *m*
impala [ɪmpálə] N impala *m*
impale [ɪmpéł] VT empalar
impart [ɪmpárt] VT (bestow knowledge) impartir; (reveal) revelar
impartial [ɪmpárʃəł] ADJ imparcial
impartiality [ɪmpɑrʃiǽlɪDi] N imparcialidad *f*
impasse [ímpæs] N impasse *m*
impassioned [ɪmpǽʃənd] ADJ apasionado
impassive [ɪmpǽsɪv] ADJ impasible
impatience [ɪmpéʃəns] N impaciencia *f*
impatient [ɪmpéʃənt] ADJ impaciente
impeach [ɪmpítʃ] VT acusar formalmente; **to — a person's honor** poner en tela de juicio el honor de uno
impeachment [ɪmpítʃmənt] N impeachment *m*
impede [ɪmpíd] VT obstaculizar, estorbar, trabar
impediment [ɪmpéDəmənt] N impedimento *m*,

obstáculo *m*; (of speech) defecto *m*
impel [ɪmpéł] VT impeler
impending [ɪmpéndɪŋ] ADJ inminente
impenetrable [ɪmpénɪtrəbəł] ADJ impenetrable
imperative [ɪmpérəDɪv] ADJ (like a command) imperativo; (necessary) imperioso; N (command, grammatical mood) imperativo *m*; (obligation) obligación *f*
imperceptible [ɪmpɚséptəbəł] ADJ imperceptible
imperfect [ɪmpɚfɪkt] ADJ & N imperfecto *m*
imperial [ɪmpíriəł] ADJ imperial
imperialism [ɪmpíriəlɪzəm] N imperialismo *m*
imperil [ɪmpérəł] VT poner en peligro
imperious [ɪmpíriəs] ADJ imperioso
impersonal [ɪmpɚsən̩ł] ADJ impersonal
impersonate [ɪmpɚsənet] VT (assume traits of) hacerse pasar por; (mimic) imitar
impersonator [ɪmpɚsəneDɚ] N imitador -ora *mf*
impertinence [ɪmpɚtn̩əns] N impertinencia *f*
impertinent [ɪmpɚtn̩ənt] ADJ impertinente
impervious [ɪmpɚviəs] ADJ impermeable; (to reason) refractario
impetigo [ɪmpɪtáɪgo] N impétigo *m*
impetuous [ɪmpétʃuəs] ADJ impetuoso
impetus [ímpəDəs] N ímpetu *m*, empuje *m*
impious [ímpiəs] ADJ impío
implacable [ɪmplǽkəbəł] ADJ implacable
implant¹ [ɪmplǽnt] VT implantar
implant² [ínplænt] N implante *m*
implantation [ɪmplæntéʃən] N implantación *f*
implement¹ [ímpləmənt] N implemento *m*, utensilio *m*
implement² [ímpləmɛnt] VT implementar, instrumentar
implementation [ɪmpləmɪntéʃən] N implementación *f*
implicate [ímplɪket] VT implicar, involucrar
implication [ɪmplɪkéʃən] N implicación *f*; **by —** implícitamente
implicit [ɪmplísɪt] ADJ implícito
implore [ɪmplɔ́r] VI/VT implorar
imply [ɪmpláɪ] VT dar a entender
impolite [ɪmpəláɪt] ADJ descortés
import¹ [ɪmpɔ́rt] VT (bring in) importar
import² [ímpɔrt] N (act of importing, thing imported) importación *f*; (significance) significado *m*; **—-export company** compañía de importación y exportación *f*
importance [ɪmpɔ́rtn̩s] N importancia *f*, relevancia *f*
important [ɪmpɔ́rtn̩t] ADJ importante, relevante
impose [ɪmpóz] VT imponer; **to — [upon]** abusar [de]
imposing [ɪmpózɪŋ] ADJ imponente, impresionante
imposition [ɪmpəzíʃən] N (act of imposing,

burden) imposición f; (abuse) abuso m
impossibility [ɪmpɑsəbílɪɒi] N imposibilidad f
impossible [ɪmpásəbəł] ADJ (not possible)
imposible; (unbearable) insoportable; **to
make** — imposibilitar
impostor [ɪmpástə-] N impostor -ora mf
impotence [ímpətəns] N impotencia f
impotent [ímpətənt] ADJ impotente
impoverish [ɪmpávə-ɪʃ] VT empobrecer
impregnate [ɪmprégnet] VT (cause to be
permeated) impregnar; (make pregnant)
fecundar, preñar
impress [ɪmprés] VT (make a mark by pressing)
estampar; VI/VT (affect deeply) impresionar
impression [ɪmpréʃən] N impresión f; (feeling)
impresión f, sensación f
impressive [ɪmprésɪv] ADJ impresionante
imprint[1] [ímprɪnt] N (indentation) impresión f,
marca f; (printer's mark) pie de imprenta m
imprint[2] [ɪmprínt] VT (impress on) imprimir;
(fix firmly in mind) grabar
imprison [ɪmprízən] VT (in jail) encarcelar;
(anywhere) apresar
imprisonment [ɪmprízənmənt] N
encarcelamiento m
improbable [ɪmprábəbəł] ADJ improbable
impromptu [ɪmprámptu] ADJ improvisado; **he
gave the speech** — improvisó el discurso; N
impromptu m
improper [ɪmprápə-] ADJ indecoroso,
inconveniente
improve [ɪmprúv] VI/VT mejorar[se]; **to** —
upon mejorar
improvement [ɪmprúvmənt] N (of a plan)
mejora f; (in health) mejoría f
improvisation [ɪmprɑvɪzéʃən] N improvisación f
improvise [ímprəvaɪz] VI/VT improvisar
imprudent [ɪmprúdn̩t] ADJ imprudente,
desatinado
impudence [ímpjədəns] N impertinencia f,
descaro m, desparpajo m
impudent [ímpjədənt] ADJ impertinente,
descarado
impulse [ímpʌls] N impulso m; **to act on** —
obrar impulsivamente
impulsive [ɪmpʌ́łsɪv] ADJ impulsivo
impunity [ɪmpjúnɪɒi] N impunidad f
impure [ɪmpjúr] ADJ impuro
impurity [ɪmpjúrɪɒi] N impureza f
in [ɪn] PREP en; (in tennis) buena, dentro; —
London en Londres; — **haste** de prisa; —
the morning por/en la mañana; — **writing**
por escrito; **she was walking** — **the street**
andaba por la calle; **to arrive** — **London**
llegar a Londres; **the books** — **the box** los
libros de la caja; **at two** — **the morning** a
las dos de la mañana; **dressed** — **white**
vestido de blanco; **the tallest** — **his class** el
más alto de su clase; **to come** — **a week**

venir dentro de una semana; ADV adentro,
dentro; **is she** — **or out?** ¿está adentro o
afuera? **to be all** — estar rendido; **to be** —
with someone estar bien con alguien; **to
come** — entrar; **to have it** — **for someone**
tenerle ojeriza a una persona; **to put** —
meter; **the doctor is** — el doctor está; **hats
are** — los sombreros están de moda; —**field**
cuadro interior m; N —**patient** paciente
internado -da mf; —**patient care**
internación f; —**seam** entrepierna f; —**step**
empeine m; ADJ **the** — **place to eat** el
restaurante de moda; **an** — **joke** una broma
para un grupo selecto
inability [ɪnəbílɪɒi] N inhabilidad f,
incapacidad f
inaccessible [ɪnæksésəbəł] ADJ inaccesible,
inasequible
inaccurate [ɪnǽkjə-ɪt] ADJ (not precise)
inexacto, impreciso; (wrong) incorrecto
inactive [ɪnǽktɪv] ADJ inactivo
inactivity [ɪnæktívɪɒi] N inactividad f
inadequate [ɪnǽdɪkwɪt] ADJ (insufficient)
insuficiente; (unacceptable) inaceptable
inadmissible [ɪnədmísəbəł] ADJ inadmisible
inadvertent [ɪnədvə́-tn̩t] ADJ (unintentional)
involuntario; (careless) descuidado,
negligente
inadvisable [ɪnədváɪzəbəł] ADJ desaconsejable
inane [ɪnén] ADJ necio
inanimate [ɪnǽnəmɪt] ADJ inanimado
inasmuch as [ɪnəzmátʃæz] CONJ puesto que
inattentive [ɪnətɛ́ntɪv] ADJ desatento
inaudible [ɪnɔ́ɒəbəł] ADJ inaudible
inaugurate [ɪnɔ́gjəret] VT (initiate) inaugurar;
(induct into office) investir de un cargo
inauguration [ɪnɔgjəréʃən] N (initiation)
inauguración f; (induction) investidura f
inboard [ínbɔrd] ADJ dentro del casco
inborn [ɪnbɔ́rn] ADJ innato
Inca [íŋkə] ADJ & N inca mf
incandescence [ɪŋkændésəns] N
incandescencia f
incandescent [ɪnkændésənt] ADJ incandescente
incantation [ɪnkæntéʃən] N conjuro m
incapable [ɪnképəbəł] ADJ incapaz
incapacitate [ɪnkəpǽsɪtet] VT incapacitar
incarcerate [ɪnkársəret] VT encarcelar
incarnation [ɪnkarnéʃən] N encarnación f
incendiary [ɪnséndiɛri] ADJ & N incendiario -ria
mf; — **bomb** bomba incendiaria f
incense[1] [ínsɛns] N incienso m
incense[2] [ɪnséns] VT encolerizar
incentive [ɪnséntɪv] N incentivo m, acicate m
inception [ɪnsépʃən] N comienzo m
incessant [ɪnsésənt] ADJ incesante
incest [ínsɛst] N incesto m
incestuous [ɪnséstʃuəs] ADJ incestuoso
inch [ɪntʃ] N pulgada [2.54 centímetros] f; **to be**

within an — of estar a un punto de; VI avanzar poco a poco

incidence [ínsɪdəns] N incidencia *f*

incident [ínsɪdənt] N incidente *m*, lance *m*; (crime, accident) suceso *m*

incidental [ɪnsɪdéntl] ADJ (happening in accordance with) accesorio; **— music** música incidental *f*; N **—s** gastos menores *m pl*

incidentally [ɪnsɪdéntli] ADV a propósito

incinerate [ɪnsínəret] VT incinerar

incipient [ɪnsípiənt] ADJ incipiente, naciente

incision [ɪnsíʒən] N incisión *f*

incisive [ɪnsáɪsɪv] ADJ incisivo

incisor [ɪnsáɪzɚ] N (tooth) incisivo *m*

incite [ɪnsáɪt] VT incitar

inclement [ɪnklémənt] ADJ inclemente

inclination [ɪnklənéʃən] N (slope) inclinación *f*; (tendency) afición *f*, inclinación *f*

incline¹ [ɪnkláɪn] VI/VT inclinar[se]

incline² [ínklaɪn] N declive *m*, pendiente *f*

include [ɪnklúd] VT incluir

including [ɪŋklúDɪŋ] ADJ **it costs a thousand dollars, not — air travel** cuesta mil dólares, sin incluir el vuelo; **that whole week, — Saturday** toda esa semana, incluyendo el sábado / el sábado inclusive; **— you, there are four of us** incluyéndote a ti, somos cuatro

inclusion [ɪŋklúʒən] N (acceptance) inclusión *f*; (addition) incorporación *f*

inclusive [ɪnklúsɪv] ADJ inclusivo; **from Monday to Friday —** de lunes a viernes inclusive

incoherent [ɪnkohírɔnt] ADJ incoherente

income [ínkʌm] N *Sp* renta *f*; *Am* ingreso *m*; **— tax** *Sp* impuesto sobre la renta *m*; *Am* impuesto sobre ingresos *m*; **— tax return** declaración de impuestos sobre la renta / los ingresos *f*

incoming [ínkʌmɪŋ] ADJ entrante

incomparable [ɪnkámpəəbəl] ADJ incomparable, sin parangón

incompatible [ɪnkəmpǽDəbəl] ADJ incompatible

incompetent [ɪnkámpɪtənt] ADJ incompetente

incomplete [ɪnkəmplít] ADJ incompleto

incomprehensible [ɪnkɑmprɪhénsəbəl] ADJ incomprensible

inconceivable [ɪnkənsívəbəl] ADJ inconcebible

inconclusive [ɪnkənklúsɪv] ADJ no concluyente

inconsiderate [ɪnkənsíDɚɪt] ADJ desconsiderado

inconsistency [ɪnkənsístənsi] N (condition) inconsecuencia *f*; (instance) incoherencia *f*

inconsistent [ɪnkənsístənt] ADJ inconsecuente

inconspicuous [ɪnkənspíkjuəs] ADJ poco llamativo; **to be —** pasar inadvertido

inconstancy [ɪnkánstənsi] N inconstancia *f*

inconstant [ɪnkánstənt] ADJ inconstante

incontinent [ɪnkántənənt] ADJ incontinente

incontrovertible [ɪnkɑntrəvɚ́Dəbəl] ADJ incontrovertible

inconvenience [ɪnkənvínjəns] N (state of being inconvenient) inconveniencia *f*; (thing that is inconvenient) molestia *f*, inconveniente *m*; VT incomodar, molestar

inconvenient [ɪnkənvínjənt] ADJ (bothersome) incómodo; (untimely) inoportuno

incorporate [ɪnkɔ́rpəret] VI/VT (include) incorporar[se]; (form a corporation) constituir[se] en sociedad

incorporation [ɪŋkɔrpəréʃən] N (inclusion) incorporación *f*; (integration) integración *f*

incorrect [ɪnkərékt] ADJ incorrecto

incorrigible [ɪnkɔ́rɪdʒəbəl] ADJ incorregible

increase¹ [ɪnkrís] VI/VT aumentar[se], incrementar[se]

increase² [ínkris] N aumento *m*, incremento *m*

increasingly [ɪnkrísɪŋli] ADV cada vez más

incredible [ɪnkréDəbəl] ADJ increíble

incredulous [ɪnkrédʒələs] ADJ incrédulo

increment [ínkrəmənt] N incremento *m*

incriminate [ɪnkrímənet] VT incriminar

incubator [íŋkjəbeDɚ] N incubadora *f*

inculcate [ɪnkʌ́łket] VT inculcar

incumbent [ɪnkʌ́mbənt] ADJ **a duty — upon me** un deber que me incumbe; N titular *m*

incur [ɪnkɚ́] VT (an expense) incurrir en; (a debt) contraer

incurable [ɪŋkjúrəbəl] ADJ incurable

indebted [ɪndéDɪd] ADJ endeudado, en deuda

indebtedness [ɪndéDɪdnɪs] N endeudamiento *m*, adeudo *m*

indecency [ɪndísənsi] N indecencia *f*

indecent [ɪndísənt] ADJ indecente; **— exposure** delito de exhibicionismo *m*

indecision [ɪndɪsíʒən] N indecisión *f*

indeed [ɪndíd] ADV de verdad; INTERJ (ironically) ¡no me digas! (sincerely) ¡tienes razón! ¡efectivamente!

indefensible [ɪndɪfénsəbəl] ADJ indefendible

indefinite [ɪndéfənɪt] ADJ indefinido

indelible [ɪndéləbəl] ADJ indeleble

indelicate [ɪndélɪkɪt] ADJ (tactless) indelicado; (offensive) indecoroso

indemnify [ɪndémnəfaɪ] VT indemnizar

indemnity [ɪndémnɪDi] N indemnización *f*

indent [ɪndént] VI/VT sangrar

indentation [ɪndentéʃən] N (notch) muesca *f*; (blank space) sangría *f*

independence [ɪndɪpéndəns] N independencia *f*

independent [ɪndɪpéndənt] ADJ independiente, autónomo

indestructible [ɪndɪstrʌ́ktəbəl] ADJ indestructible

indeterminate [ɪndɪtɚ́mənɪt] ADJ indeterminado

index [índɛks] N índice *m*; **— card** ficha *f*; **—**

finger índice *m*; VT (incorporate into an index) poner en el índice; (make the index) poner/hacer un índice; (adjust wages) indexar
indexing [índɛksɪŋ] N indexación *f*
India [índiə] N India *f*
Indian [índiən] ADJ & N indio -a *mf*; — **Ocean** Océano Indico *m*
indicate [índɪket] VT indicar
indication [ɪndɪkéʃən] N indicación *f*
indicative [ɪndíkəDɪv] ADJ & N indicativo *m*
indicator [índɪkeDə-] N indicador *m*
indict [ɪndáɪt] VT acusar
indictment [ɪndáɪtmənt] N acusación *f*
indifference [ɪndífrəns] N indiferencia *f*
indifferent [ɪndífrənt] ADJ indiferente
indigenous [ɪndíʤənəs] ADJ (person) indígena; (plant, animal) autóctono
indigent [índɪʤənt] ADJ & N indigente *mf*
indigestion [ɪndɪʤéstʃən] N indigestión *f*
indignant [ɪndígnənt] ADJ indignado
indignation [ɪndɪgnéʃən] N indignación *f*
indignity [ɪndígnɪDi] N ultraje *m*, afrenta *f*
indigo [índɪgo] N índigo *m*, añil *m*; — **blue** azul añil *m*
indirect [ɪndɪrékt] ADJ indirecto; — **object** complemento/objeto indirecto *m*
indiscreet [ɪndɪskrít] ADJ indiscreto
indiscretion [ɪndɪskréʃən] N indiscreción *f*
indispensable [ɪndɪspénsəbəł] ADJ indispensable, imprescindible
indispose [ɪndɪspóz] VT indisponer
indisposed [ɪndɪspózd] ADJ indispuesto; **to become** — indisponerse
indistinct [ɪndɪstíŋkt] ADJ indistinto
individual [ɪndəvíʤuəł] ADJ individual; N individuo *m*, persona *f*; *pej* sujeto *m*, individuo *m*
individualism [ɪndəvíʤuəlɪzəm] N individualismo *m*
individualist [ɪndəvíʤuəlɪst] N individualista *mf*
individuality [ɪndəvɪʤuǽlɪDi] N individualidad *f*
indivisible [ɪndəvízəbəł] ADJ indivisible
indoctrinate [ɪndáktrɪnet] VT adoctrinar
indolence [índələns] N indolencia *f*, desidia *f*
indolent [índələnt] ADJ indolente, haragán
indomitable [ɪndámɪDəbəł] ADJ indomable
Indonesia [ɪndəníʒə] N Indonesia *f*
Indonesian [ɪndəníʒən] ADJ & N indonesio -sia *mf*
indoor [índɔr] ADJ interior
indoors [ɪndɔ́rz] ADV dentro; **to go** — entrar, ir para adentro
induce [ɪndús] VT inducir
inducement [ɪndúsmənt] N aliciente *m*, incentivo *m*
induct [ɪndʌkt] VT (initiate) admitir, iniciar; (draft) reclutar

induction [ɪndʌ́kʃən] N (philosophical, electrical) inducción *f*; (into an organization) admisión *f*, iniciación *f*
indulge [ɪndʌ́łʤ] VT mimar, consentir; VI **to** — **in** darse a, entregarse a; **to** — **oneself** [**in**] darse el gusto [de]
indulgence [ɪndʌ́łʤəns] N (act or state of indulging, religious) indulgencia *f*; (thing indulged in) exceso *m*, lujo *m*
indulgent [ɪndʌ́łʤənt] ADJ indulgente; (toward a child) complaciente
industrial [ɪndʌ́striəł] ADJ industrial
industrialist [ɪndʌ́striəlɪst] N industrial *mf*
industrialization [ɪndʌstriəlɪzéʃən] N industrialización *f*
industrious [ɪndʌ́striəs] ADJ (student) aplicado, diligente; (worker) industrioso
industry [índəstri] N (manufacturing) industria *f*; (hard work) diligencia *f*; — **standards** normas industriales *f pl*
inebriated [ɪníbrieDɪd] ADJ ebrio
inedible [ɪnéDəbəł] ADJ incomestible, incomible
ineffable [ɪnéfəbəł] ADJ inefable
ineffective [ɪnɪféktɪv] ADJ ineficaz, ineficiente
ineffectual [ɪnɪféktʃuəł] ADJ ineficaz
inefficient [ɪnɪfíʃənt] ADJ ineficiente
ineligible [ɪnélɪʤəbəł] ADJ inelegible
inept [ɪnépt] ADJ inepto
inequality [ɪnɪkwálɪDi] N desigualdad *f*
inert [ɪnɜ́t] ADJ inerte
inertia [ɪnɜ́ʃə] N inercia *f*
inescapable [ɪnɪsképəbəł] ADJ inevitable, ineludible
inestimable [ɪnéstəməbəł] ADJ inestimable
inevitable [ɪnévɪDəbəł] ADJ inevitable
inexcusable [ɪnɪkskjúzəbəł] ADJ inexcusable
inexhaustible [ɪnɪgzóstəbəł] ADJ inagotable
inexorable [ɪnéksə-əbəł] ADJ inexorable
inexpensive [ɪnɪkspénsɪv] ADJ económico, barato
inexperienced [ɪnɪkspíriənst] ADJ no experimentado, inexperto
inexplicable [ɪnɪksplíkəbəł] ADJ inexplicable
infallible [ɪnfǽləbəł] ADJ infalible
infamous [ínfəməs] ADJ infame, de mala fama
infamy [ínfəmi] N infamia *f*
infancy [ínfənsi] N primera infancia *f*
infant [ínfənt] N bebé *mf*
infantile [ínfəntaɪł] ADJ infantil
infantry [ínfəntri] N infantería *f*; —**man** infante *m*
infatuated [ɪnfǽtʃueDɪd] ADJ enamorado
infect [ɪnfékt] VT (cause disease) infectar; (spread a mood) contagiar
infection [ɪnfékʃən] N infección *f*
infectious [ɪnfékʃəs] ADJ (disease) infeccioso, contagioso; (mood) contagioso
infer [ɪnfɜ́] VT inferir, deducir
inference [ínfə-əns] N inferencia *f*, deducción *f*

inferior [ɪnfíriəʳ] ADJ inferior
inferiority [ɪnfiriɔ́rɪDi] N inferioridad f; —
   complex complejo de inferioridad m
infernal [ɪnfɝ́nl] ADJ infernal
inferno [ɪnfɝ́no] N (fire) incendio m; (hot place)
   infierno m
infertility [ɪnfəʳtílɪDi] N infertilidad f
infest [ɪnfést] VT infestar, plagar
infestation [ɪnfɛstéʃən] N infestación f
infiltrate [ɪnfíltret] VI/VT infiltrar[se]; **to — an**
   organization infiltrarse en una
   organización
infinite [ínfənɪt] ADJ & N infinito m
infinitive [ɪnfínɪDɪv] ADJ & N infinitivo m
infinity [ɪnfínɪDi] N (large number) infinidad f;
   (space) infinito m
infirm [ɪnfɝ́m] ADJ enfermizo, achacoso
infirmary [ɪnfɝ́məri] N enfermería f
infirmity [ɪnfɝ́mɪDi] N enfermedad f, achaque m
inflame [ɪnflém] VT (with infection)
   inflamar[se]; (with passion) enardecer[se];
   (with fire) encender[se]
inflammation [ɪnfləméʃən] N inflamación f
inflate [ɪnflét] VI/VT (fill with air) inflar[se],
   hincharse; (exaggerate) exagerar
inflation [ɪnfléʃən] N (rise in prices) inflación f;
   (introduction of air) inflado m
inflexible [ɪnfléksəbəl] ADJ inflexible
inflict [ɪnflíkt] VT (impose on) infligir; **to — a**
   blow asestar un golpe
influence [ínfluəns] N influencia f, influjo m; VT
   influir en/sobre, incidir en; **— peddling**
   tráfico de influencias m
influential [ɪnfluénʃəl] ADJ influyente
influenza [ɪnfluénzə] N gripe f
influx [ínflʌks] N (of fluid, goods) entrada f; (of
   people) afluencia f
infomercial [ínfomɝ́ʃəl] N infomercial m,
   publirreportaje m
inform [ɪnfɔ́rm] VI/VT (give knowledge)
   informar[se]; VT (inspire) inspirar; **to —**
   against/on delatar a, denunciar a
informal [ɪnfɔ́rməl] ADJ informal
informant [ɪnfɔ́rmənt] N informante mf
information [ɪnfəʳméʃən] N (news, data, details,
   act of informing) información f; (details)
   informes m pl; **— superhighway** autopista
   de la información f
informative [ɪnfɔ́rməDɪv] ADJ informativo
informer [ɪnfɔ́rməʳ] N informante mf, delator
   -ora mf, pej soplón -ona mf
infotainment [ɪnfoténmənt] N entretenimiento
   informativo m
infraction [ɪnfrǽkʃən] N infracción f
infrared [ɪnfrəréd] ADJ & N infrarrojo m
infrastructure [ínfrəstrʌktʃəʳ] N
   infraestructura f
infringe [ɪnfrínʤ] VT infringir; VI **to — upon**
   violar

infringement [ɪnfrínʤmənt] N infracción f,
   violación f
infuriate [ɪnfjúriet] VT enfurecer, sublevar
infuse [ɪnfjúz] VT infundir
ingenious [ɪnʤínjəs] ADJ ingenioso
ingenuity [ɪnʤənúɪDi] N ingenio m, inventiva f
ingenuous [ɪnʤénjuəs] ADJ ingenuo f
ingenuousness [ɪnʤénjuəsnɪs] N ingenuidad f
ingest [ɪnʤést] VI/VT ingerir
ingrate [íngret] N ingrato -ta mf
ingratitude [ɪngrǽDɪtud] N ingratitud f
ingredient [ɪngrídiənt] N ingrediente m
ingrown [íngron] ADJ encarnado
inhabit [ɪnhǽbɪt] VT habitar
inhabitant [ɪnhǽbɪtənt] N habitante mf
inhale [ɪnhél] VI/VT inhalar, aspirar
inherent [ɪnhérənt] ADJ inherente
inherit [ɪnhérɪt] VI/VT heredar
inheritance [ɪnhérɪDəns] N herencia f; **— tax**
   impuesto a la herencia m
inherited [ɪnhérɪDɪd] ADJ patrimonial
inhibit [ɪnhíbɪt] VT inhibir, cohibir
inhibiting [ɪnhíbɪDɪŋ] ADJ inhibidor
inhibition [ɪnɪbíʃən] N inhibición f, cohibición f
inhibitor [ɪnhíbɪDəʳ] N inhibidor m
inhospitable [ɪnhaspíDəbəl] ADJ (person)
   inhospitalario; (place) inhóspito
inhuman [ɪnhjúmən] ADJ inhumano
inimitable [ɪnímɪDəbəl] ADJ inimitable
initial [ɪníʃəl] ADJ & N inicial f; VT firmar las
   iniciales
initialize [ɪníʃəlaɪz] VT inicializar
initially [ɪníʃəli] ADV al comienzo, inicialmente
initiate [ɪníʃiet] VT iniciar
initiative [ɪníʃəDɪv] N iniciativa f
inject [ɪnʤékt] VI/VT inyectar[se], pinchar[se]
injection [ɪnʤékʃən] N inyección f
injunction [ɪnʤʌ́ŋkʃən] N mandato judicial m,
   orden judicial f
injure [índʒəʳ] VI/VT herir[se]; (sports)
   lesionar[se]
injurious [ɪnʤúriəs] ADJ (harmful) perjudicial;
   (defamatory) injurioso
injury [índʒəri] N herida f, lesión f; **— time**
   (soccer) descuento m
injustice [ɪnʤʌ́stɪs] N injusticia f
ink [ɪŋk] N tinta f; VT (mark with ink) entintar;
   (sign) firmar; **— cartridge** cartucho de tinta
   m; **-jet printer** impresora de inyección de
   tinta f; **—pad** almohadilla f; **—well** tintero m
inkling [íŋklɪŋ] N idea f
inlaid [ínled] ADJ incrustado; **— work**
   incrustación f
inland [ínlənd] ADJ interior; ADV tierra adentro
inlay¹ [ɪnlé] VT incrustar
inlay² [ínle] N incrustación f
inmate [ínmet] N (in a prison) preso -sa mf,
   recluso -sa mf; (in an asylum) internado -da
   mf; (in a hospital) paciente mf

inn [ɪn] N posada f, fonda f; —**keeper** posadero -ra mf, fondista mf

innate [ɪnét] ADJ innato

inner [ínɚ] ADJ (inside) interior; (intimate) íntimo; — **city** zona céntrica empobrecida f; — **ear** oído interno m; —**most** más recóndito; — **tube** cámara f

inning [ínɪŋ] N entrada f

innocence [ínəsəns] N (absence of guilt) inocencia f; (naiveté) candidez f, candor m

innocent [ínəsənt] ADJ & N inocente mf

innocuous [ɪnákjuəs] ADJ innocuo, inocuo

innovate [ínəvet] VI innovar

innovating [ínəveDɪŋ] ADJ innovador, renovador

innovation [ɪnəvéʃən] N innovación f

innovative [ínəveDɪV] ADJ innovador

innovator [ínəveDɚ] N innovador -ora mf

innuendo [ɪnjuéndo] N insinuación f

innumerable [ɪnúmɚəbəł] ADJ innumerables

inoculate [ɪnákjəlet] VI/VT inocular[se]

inoffensive [ɪnəfénsɪv] ADJ inofensivo

inoperable [ɪnápɚəbəł] ADJ inoperable

inopportune [ɪnɑpɚtún] ADJ inoportuno

inordinate [ɪnɔ́rdn̩ɪt] ADJ desmesurado

inorganic [ɪnɔrgǽnɪk] ADJ inorgánico; — **chemistry** química inorgánica f

input [ínpʊt] N (electric, computer) entrada f; (opinion) opinión f; VT ingresar/entrar datos

inquire [ɪŋkwáɪr] VI/VT inquirir, preguntar; **to** — **about/after** preguntar por; **to** — **into** indagar, investigar

inquiry [íŋkwəri] N (scientific) investigación f; (police) pesquisa f; **we made inquiries about hotels** hicimos averiguaciones acerca de hoteles

inquisition [ɪŋkwɪzíʃən] N inquisición f

inquisitive [ɪnkwízɪDɪv] ADJ (curious) inquisitivo, curioso; (asking many questions) preguntón

insane [ɪnsén] ADJ demente, loco; — **asylum** manicomio m

insanity [ɪnsǽnɪDi] N locura f, demencia f

insatiable [ɪnséʃəbəł] ADJ insaciable

inscribe [ɪnskráɪb] VT (mark) inscribir; (engrave) grabar; (dedicate) dedicar

inscription [ɪnskrípʃən] N (marks, engraving) inscripción f; (dedication) dedicatoria f

inscrutable [ɪnskrúDəbəł] ADJ inescrutable

insect [ínsɛkt] N insecto m

insecticide [ɪnséktɪsaɪd] N insecticida m

insectivorous [ɪnsɛktívɚəs] ADJ insectívoro

insecure [ɪnsɪkjúr] ADJ inseguro

insecurity [ɪnsɪkjúrɪDi] N inseguridad f

insemination [ɪnsɛmɪnéʃən] N inseminación f

insensible [ɪnsénsəbəł] ADJ insensible

insensitive [ɪnsénsɪDɪv] ADJ insensible

inseparable [ɪnsépɚəbəł] ADJ inseparable

insert¹ [ɪnsɚt] VT insertar, introducir; (into a

text) intercalar

insert² [ínsɚt] N encarte m

insertion [ɪnsɚ́ʃən] N inserción f; (into a text) intercalación f

inside¹ [ɪnsáɪd] PREP dentro de; ADV dentro, adentro

inside² [ínsaɪd] N interior m; — **job** delito cometido por un empleado m; —**s** entrañas f pl; — **track** pista interior f; **to turn** — **out** volver del revés; **he passed me on the** — me pasó por la derecha; ADJ (interior) interior

insider [ɪnsáɪDɚ] N privilegiado -da mf; — **trading** abuso de información privilegiada m

insidious [ɪnsíDiəs] ADJ insidioso

insight [ínsaɪt] N (intuition) perspicacia f; (discernment) discernimiento m

insignia [ɪnsígniə] N insignia f

insignificant [ɪnsɪgnífɪkənt] ADJ insignificante, menudo, nimio

insincere [ɪnsɪnsír] ADJ insincero

insinuate [ɪnsínjuet] VT insinuar

insinuation [ɪnsɪnjuéʃən] N insinuación f

insipid [ɪnsípɪd] ADJ insípido, soso

insist [ɪnsíst] VI/VT insistir; **to** — **on** insistir en

insistence [ɪnsístəns] N insistencia f

insistent [ɪnsístənt] ADJ insistente

insole [ínsoł] N plantilla f

insolence [ínsələns] N insolencia f

insolent [ínsələnt] ADJ insolente, atrevido

insoluble [ɪnsáljəbəł] ADJ insoluble

insolvent [ɪnsáłvənt] ADJ insolvente

insomnia [ɪnsámniə] N insomnio m

inspect [ɪnspékt] VT inspeccionar; **to** — **the troops** pasar revista a la tropa, revistar a la tropa

inspection [ɪnspékʃən] N inspección f; (of troops) revista f

inspector [ɪnspéktɚ] N inspector -ora mf

inspiration [ɪnspəréʃən] N inspiración f

inspire [ɪnspáɪr] VI/VT inspirar

instability [ɪnstəbílɪDi] N inestabilidad f

install [ɪnstɔ́ł] VT instalar; N — **program** programa instalador m

installation [ɪnstəléʃən] N instalación f

installment [ɪnstɔ́łmənt] N (payment of debt) cuota f; (of a book) entrega f, fascículo m; **to pay in** —**s** pagar a plazos

instance [ínstəns] N ejemplo m; **for** — por ejemplo; **court of first** — tribunal de primera instancia m

instant [ínstənt] N instante m; **this** — ahora mismo; ADJ inmediato; — **coffee** café instantáneo m; — **messaging** mensajería instantánea f

instantaneous [ɪnstənténiəs] ADJ instantáneo

instead [ɪnstéd] ADV — **of** en lugar de, en vez de; **she didn't want a desk, so she ordered a chair** — no quería un escritorio, así que pidió

una silla en su lugar
instigate [ínstɪget] VT instigar
instigator [ínstɪgeДə-] N (of a crime) instigador
-ora *mf*; (of an event) causante *mf*
instill [ɪnstíł] VT inculcar
instinct [ínstɪŋkt] N instinto *m*
instinctive [ɪnstíŋktɪv] ADJ instintivo
institute [ínstɪtut] N instituto *m*; VT instituir
institution [ɪnstɪtúʃən] N institución *f*
institutional [ɪnstɪtúʃənəł] ADJ institucional
instruct [ɪnstrʌ́kt] VT (teach) instruir;
(command, advise) dar instrucciones;
(command) mandar
instruction [ɪnstrʌ́kʃən] N instrucción *f*; —**s**
(orders) órdenes *f pl*; (information)
instrucciones *f pl*, indicaciones *f pl*
instructive [ɪnstrʌ́ktɪv] ADJ instructivo
instructor [ɪnstrʌ́ktə-] N (of skills) instructor
-ora *mf*; (of knowledge) profesor -ora *mf*
instrument [ínstrəmənt] N instrumento *m*; —
panel salpicadero *m*, tablero *m*
instrumental [ɪnstrəméntł] ADJ instrumental;
to be — in ser fundamental para
insubordinate [ɪnsəbórdṇɪt] ADJ insubordinado
insufferable [ɪnsʌ́fə-əbəł] ADJ insufrible
insufficiency [ɪnsəfíʃənsi] N insuficiencia *f*
insufficient [ɪnsəfíʃənt] ADJ insuficiente
insulate [ínsəlet] VT aislar
insulation [ɪnsəléʃən] N aislamiento *m*
insulator [ínsəleДə-] N (material) aislante *m*;
(device) aislador *m*
insulin [ínsəlɪn] N insulina *f*; — **shock** choque
insulínico *m*
insult[1] [ɪnsʌ́łt] VT insultar, injuriar
insult[2] [ínsʌłt] N insulto *m*, injuria *f*
insulting [ɪnsʌ́łtɪŋ] ADJ insultante, injurioso
insuperable [ɪnsúpə-əbəł] ADJ insuperable
insurable [ɪnʃúrəbəł] ADJ asegurable
insurance [ɪnʃúrəns] N seguro *m*; — **agent**
agente de seguros *mf*; — **company** compañía
de seguros *f*; — **policy** póliza de seguro *f*
insure [ɪnʃúr] VI/VT asegurar[se]
insurgent [ɪnsɔ́ʤənt] N alzado -da *mf*
insurmountable [ɪnsə-máUntəbəł] ADJ
insuperable
insurrection [ɪnsərékʃən] N insurrección *f*
intact [ɪntǽkt] ADJ intacto
intangible [ɪntǽnʤəbəł] ADJ intangible
integer [íntɪʤə-] N [número] entero *m*
integral [íntɪgrəł] ADJ (complete) integral;
(forming part of) integrante; — **calculus**
cálculo integral *m*; N integral *f*
integrate [íntɪgret] VT integrar; VI integrarse a
integration [ɪntɪgréʃən] N integración *f*
integrity [ɪntégrɪDi] N integridad *f*
intellect [íntḷɛkt] N intelecto *m*
intellectual [ɪntḷɛktʃuəł] ADJ & N intelectual *mf*
intelligence [ɪntéłɪʤəns] N inteligencia *f* (also
· secret information); — **quotient** coeficiente

intelectual / de inteligencia *m*
intelligent [ɪntéłɪʤənt] ADJ inteligente
intelligible [ɪntéłɪʤəbəł] ADJ inteligible
intend [ɪnténd] VT pensar; **to — to do**
something pensar hacer algo; **a book —ed**
for children un libro destinado/dirigido a
los niños
intense [ɪnténs] ADJ intenso
intensify [ɪnténsɪfaɪ] VI/VT intensificar[se]
intensity [ɪnténsɪDi] N intensidad *f*
intensive [ɪnténsɪv] ADJ intensivo; — **care unit**
sala de cuidados intensivos *f*
intent [ɪntént] N intención *f*, propósito *m*; **to/**
for all — s and purposes en la práctica; ADJ
atento; — **on** resuelto a
intention [ɪnténʃən] N intención *f*
intentional [ɪnténʃənəł] ADJ intencional; —
base on balls base por bolas intencional *f*
intentionally [ɪnténʃənəli] ADV a propósito
inter [ɪntɔ́-] VT sepultar
interact [ɪntə-ǽkt] VI interactuar
interaction [ɪntə-ǽkʃən] N interacción *f*
interactive [ɪntə-ǽktɪv] ADJ interactivo
intercede [ɪntə-síd] VI interceder
intercept [ɪntə-sépt] VT interceptar
interception [ɪntə-sépʃən] N interceptación *f*
intercession [ɪntə-séʃən] N intercesión *f*
interchange[1] [íntə-tʃenʤ] N cambio *m*; (on
road) enlace *m*; *Sp* intercambiador *m*
interchange[2] [ɪntə-tʃénʤ] VI/VT cambiar,
intercambiar
intercourse [íntə-kɔrs] N (sexual) relación
sexual *f*; (social) comunicación *f*, trato *m*
interest [íntrɪst] N interés *m*; (financial) interés
m, rédito *m*; (share in a business)
participación *f*; — -**bearing** que devenga
intereses; — -**free** libre de intereses, sin
intereses; — **rate** tasa de interés *f*; **mining**
—**s** los negocios mineros; VT interesar; **may I**
— **you in a cookie?** ¿te puedo ofrecer una
galleta?
interested [íntrɪstɪd] ADJ interesado; — **party**
parte interesada *f*; **to be/become — in**
interesarse en/por
interesting [íntrɪstɪŋ] ADJ interesante
interface [íntə-fes] N interface *mf*, interfaz *f*
interfere [ɪntə-fír] VI interferir; (meddle)
entrometerse; **to — with** interferir en
interference [ɪntə-fírəns] N interferencia *f*,
injerencia *f*
interferon [ɪntə-fírɑn] N interferón *m*
interim [íntə-ɪm] N ínterin *m*; ADJ (person)
interino; (decision) provisional
interior [ɪntíriə-] ADJ & N interior *m*; —
decoration decoración de interiores *f*; —
design diseño de interiores *m*
interjection [ɪntə-ʤékʃən] N interjección *f*,
exclamación *f*
interlace [ɪntə-lés] VI/VT entrelazar[se]

interlinear [ɪntərlíniə·] ADJ interlineal
interlock [ɪntə·lák] VI/VT (gears) engranar[se]; (branches, etc.) entrelazar[se]; N interlock m
interlocking [ɪntə·lákɪŋ] ADJ (gears) engranado; (branches) entrelazado
interlude [íntə·lud] N (interval) intervalo m; (musical) interludio m; (theatrical) entremés m
intermediary [ɪntə·mídiɛri] ADJ intermediario
intermediate [ɪntə·mídiɪt] ADJ intermedio
interment [ɪntɜ·mənt] N entierro m
interminable [ɪntɜ·mənəbəl] ADJ interminable
intermingle [ɪntə·míŋgəl] VI/VT entremezclar[se]
intermission [ɪntə·míʃən] N entreacto m, intervalo m
intermittent [ɪntə·mítn̩t] ADJ intermitente
intern [íntɜ·n] VT internar, confinar; N (prisoner, doctor) interno -na mf
internal [ɪntɜ·nl̩] ADJ interno, interior; — **combustion engine** motor de combustión interna m; — **hard disk** disco duro interno m; — **revenue** rentas internas f pl; — **Revenue Service** Hacienda f
internalize [ɪntɜ·nəlaɪz] VT interiorizar, internalizar
international [ɪntə·næʃənl̩] ADJ internacional; — **law** derecho internacional m
Internet [ínta·nɛt] N internet m, red f, web f; — **access** acceso a internet m; — **access provider** proveedor de acceso a internet m; — **banking** banca por internet f; — **community** comunidad internauta f; — **user** internauta mf
internist [ɪntɜ·nɪst] N internista mf
internship [íntə·nʃɪp] N (medical) internado m; (student) práctica f
interpersonal [ɪntə·pɜ·sənl̩] ADJ interpersonal
interpose [ɪntə·póz] VI/VT interponer[se]
interpret [ɪntɜ·prɪt] VI/VT interpretar
interpretation [ɪntɜ·prɪtéʃən] N interpretación f
interpreter [ɪntɜ·prɪDə·] N intérprete mf
interracial [ɪntə·réʃəl] ADJ interracial
interrelated [ɪntə·rɪléDɪd] ADJ interrelacionado
interrogate [ɪntérəget] VI/VT interrogar
interrogation [ɪntɛrəgéʃən] N interrogación f, interrogatorio m
interrogative [ɪntərágəDɪv] ADJ interrogativo; N palabra/oración interrogativa f
interrupt [ɪntərʌ́pt] VI/VT interrumpir
interruption [ɪntərʌ́pʃən] N interrupción f
intersect [ɪntə·sɛ́kt] VI/VT (math) intersecar[se]; (road) cruzar[se]
intersection [ínta·sɛkʃən] N (math) intersección f; (street) cruce m, intersección f
intersperse [ɪntə·spɜ́·s] VT (scatter) esparcir; (intermingle) entremezclar, entreverar; (spice up) salpicar
interstate [ínta·stet] ADJ interestatal; —

highway autopista interestatal f
interstellar [ɪntə·stélə·] ADJ interestelar
interstice [ɪntɜ́·stɪs] N intersticio m
intertwine [ɪntə·twáɪn] VI/VT entrelazar[se]
interval [íntə·vəl] N intervalo m
intervene [ɪntə·vín] VI intervenir; (mediate) interponerse, mediar
intervening [ɪntə·vínɪŋ] ADJ interventor
intervention [ɪntə·vénʃən] N intervención f; (mediation) mediación f
interview [ínta·vju] N entrevista f; (for entertainment) Sp interviú f; VT entrevistar; VI entrevistarse
intestinal [ɪntéstənl̩] ADJ intestinal; — **flora** flora intestinal f; — **obstruction** obstrucción intestinal f
intestine [ɪntéstɪn] ADJ & N intestino m; **small** — intestino delgado m; **large** — intestino grueso m
intimacy [íntəməsi] N intimidad f
intimate[1] [íntəmɪt] ADJ íntimo, entrañable; (knowledge) profundo
intimate[2] [íntəmet] VT insinuar, dar a entender
intimation [ɪntəméʃən] N insinuación f
intimidate [ɪntímɪdet] VT intimidar, acobardar
into [íntu] PREP **she came — the room** entró en/a la habitación; **he put it — the box** lo metió en la caja; **he translated it —German** lo tradujo al alemán; **he ran — a tree** chocó contra un árbol; **it fell —oblivion** cayó en el olvido; **he went —medicine** entró a medicina; **I'm really —pop music** me ha dado por la música pop
intolerable [ɪntálə·əbəl] ADJ intolerable
intolerance [ɪntálə·əns] N intolerancia f
intolerant [ɪntálə·ənt] ADJ intolerante
intonation [ɪntənéʃən] N entonación f
intoxicate [ɪntáksɪket] VI/VT embriagar (also exhilarate); (poison) intoxicar
intoxication [ɪntaksɪkéʃən] N (drunkenness) embriaguez f; (poisoning) intoxicación f
intransigent [ɪntrǽnzɪdʒənt] ADJ intransigente
intransitive [ɪntrǽnzɪDɪv] ADJ intransitivo
intrauterine device [ɪntrəjúDə·ɪndɪváɪs] N dispositivo intrauterino m
intravenous [ɪntrəvínəs] ADJ intravenoso; — **feeding** alimentación intravenosa f
intrepid [ɪntrépɪd] ADJ intrépido
intricate [íntrɪkɪt] ADJ intrincado
intrigue[1] [ɪntríg] VI/VT intrigar
intrigue[2] [íntrig] N intriga f
intrinsic [ɪntrínzɪk] ADJ intrínseco
introduce [ɪntrədús] VT (put in, bring) introducir; (make acquainted) presentar
introduction [ɪntrədʌ́kʃən] N (of a book) introducción f; (of a custom or system) introducción f, implantación f; (to a person) presentación f
introspection [ɪntrəspékʃən] N introspección f

introvert [íntrəvɜˈt] N introvertido -da *mf*
introverted [íntrəvɜˈDɪd] ADJ introvertido
intrude [ɪntrúd] VI/VT interrumpir; (penetrate, of rock) penetrar
intruder [ɪntrúDə·] N intruso -sa *mf*
intrusion [ɪntrúʒən] N (interruption) interrupción *f*; (penetration) intrusión *f*
intrusive [ɪntrúsɪv] ADJ (rock) intrusivo; (people) entrometido
intubation [ɪntjubéʃən] N intubación *f*
intuition [ɪntuíʃən] N intuición *f*
intuitive [ɪntúɪDɪv] ADJ intuitivo
inundate [ínəndet] VT inundar
invade [ɪnvéd] VI/VT invadir
invader [ɪnvéDə·] N invasor -ora *mf*
invalid[1] [ɪnvəlɪd] ADJ & N (infirm) inválido -da *mf*
invalid[2] [ɪnvǽlɪd] ADJ (not valid) nulo
invaluable [ɪnvǽljuəbəl] ADJ invalorable, inestimable
invariable [ɪnvériəbəl] ADJ invariable
invariably [ɪnvériəbli] ADV siempre
invasion [ɪnvéʒən] N invasión *f*
invasive [ɪnvésɪv] ADJ invasivo
invent [ɪnvént] VT inventar
invention [ɪnvénʃən] N (act of inventing, thing invented) invención *f*, invento *m*; (falsehood) invención *f*
inventive [ɪnvéntɪv] ADJ inventivo
inventor [ɪnvéntə·] N inventor -ora *mf*
inventory [ínvəntɔri] N inventario *m*; VT inventariar
inverse [ɪnvɜˈs] ADJ & N inverso *m*
inversion [ɪnvɜˈʒən] N inversión *f*
invert [ɪnvɜˈt] VT invertir
invest [ɪnvést] VI/VT (money) invertir; (a rank upon someone) investir
investigate [ɪnvéstɪget] VI/VT investigar, indagar
investigation [ɪnvestɪɡéʃən] N investigación *f*
investigator [ɪnvéstɪɡeDə·] N investigador -ora *mf*
investment [ɪnvéstmənt] N (of money) inversión *f*; (of rank) investidura *f*; — **broker** corredor -ora de bolsa *mf*
investor [ɪnvéstə·] N inversionista *mf*, inversor -ora *mf*
invigorate [ɪnvíɡəret] VT vigorizar
invincible [ɪnvínsəbəl] ADJ invencible
invisible [ɪnvízəbəl] ADJ invisible
invitation [ɪnvɪtéʃən] N invitación *f*
invite[1] [ɪnváɪt] VI/VT invitar; **to — trouble** buscarse problemas
invite[2] [ínvaɪt] N *fam* invitación *f*
inviting [ɪnváɪDɪŋ] ADJ atractivo, seductor
in vitro fertilization [ɪnvítrofɜˈdl̩ɪzéʃən] N fertilización in vitro *f*
invocation [ɪnvəkéʃən] N invocación *f*
invoice [ínvɔɪs] N factura *f*; VT facturar

invoke [ɪnvók] VT invocar
involuntary [ɪnválənteri] ADJ involuntario
involve [ɪnvάlv] VT (take, last) suponer; **how much time will this —?** ¿cuánto tiempo supone esto?; (consist of, entail) consistir en, involucrar; **what does your work —?** ¿en qué consiste tu trabajo?; (be in question) ser cuestión de; **national security is —d!** ¡es una cuestión de seguridad nacional!; (implicate) implicar; **they tried to — her** trataron de implicarla; (wrapped up in) estar metido; **he's very —d in the family business** está muy metido en el negocio familiar; (have a liaison) enredarse; **she got —d with a married man** se enredó con un hombre casado
involved [ɪnvάlvd] ADJ complicado, enrevesado
involvement [ɪnvάlvmənt] N (in a crime) implicación *f*; (in a project) participación *f*; (with a person) relación *f*
inward [ínwə·d] ADV hacia dentro; ADJ interior
iodide [áɪədaɪd] N yoduro *m*
iodine [áɪədaɪn] N yodo *m*
ion [áɪɑn] N ión *m*
ionize [áɪənaɪz] VT ionizar
ipecac syrup [ípɪkæksírəp] N jarabe de ipecacuana *m*
IPO [initial public offering] [áɪpíó] N oferta pública inicial *f*
IQ [intelligence quotient] [áɪkjú] N coeficiente de inteligencia *m*
Iran [ɪrán] N Irán *m*
Iranian [ɪréniən] ADJ & N iraní *mf*
Iraq [ɪrǽk] N Irak *m*
Iraqi [ɪrǽki] ADJ & N iraquí *mf*
irascible [ɪrǽsəbəl] ADJ irascible
irate [aɪrét] ADJ airado
ire [aɪr] N ira *f*
Ireland [áɪrlənd] N Irlanda *f*
iridescent [ɪrɪdésənt] ADJ iridiscente, tornasolado
iridium [ɪríDiəm] N iridio *m*
iris [áɪrɪs] N (part of eye) iris *m*; (plant, flower) lirio *m*; (rainbow) arco iris *m*
Irish [áɪrɪʃ] ADJ irlandés; N (language) irlandés *m*; **the —** los irlandeses
irk [ɜˈk] VT fastidiar; **—ed** fastidiado
irksome [ɜˈksəm] ADJ engorroso, molesto
iron [áɪə·n] N (element, golf club) hierro *m*; (appliance) plancha *f*; **in —s** en grilletes; **— deficiency anemia** anemia por deficiencia de hierro *f*; **—work** herrajes *m pl*; **—works** fundición *f*; ADJ férreo, de hierro; VI/VT planchar; **to — out a difficulty** allanar una dificultad
ironic [aɪránɪk] ADJ irónico
ironing [áɪə·nɪŋ] N planchado *m*
irony [áɪrəni] N ironía *f*; (mockery) ironía *f*, sorna *f*

irradiate [ɪréɒiet] VT irradiar
irrational [ɪrǽʃənl] ADJ irracional
irrefutable [ɪrɪfjúɒəbəl] ADJ irrefutable
irregular [ɪrégjələ] ADJ irregular
irregularity [ɪrɛgjəlǽrɪɒi] N irregularidad f
irrelevant [ɪrélɒvənt] ADJ no pertinente; **your age is** — tu edad no viene al caso
irreparable [ɪrépə-əbəl] ADJ irreparable
irreplaceable [ɪrɪplésəbəl] ADJ irreemplazable
irreproachable [ɪrɪprótʃəbəl] ADJ irreprochable
irresistible [ɪrɪzístəbəl] ADJ irresistible
irresponsibility [ɪrɪspɑnsəbílɪɒi] N irresponsabilidad f
irresponsible [ɪrɪspánsəbəl] ADJ irresponsable
irretrievable [ɪrɪtrívəbəl] ADJ irrecuperable
irreverent [ɪrévə-ənt] ADJ irreverente
irreversible [ɪrɪvɝsəbəl] ADJ irreversible
irrevocable [ɪrévəkəbəl] ADJ irrevocable
irrigate [ɪ́rɪget] VI/VT (a garden) irrigar, regar; (the eyes) irrigar
irrigation [ɪrɪgéʃən] N riego m, irrigación f; — **ditch** acequia f
irritable [ɪ́rɪɒəbəl] ADJ irritable, colérico
irritate [ɪ́rɪtet] VT irritar
irritating [ɪ́rɪteɒɪŋ] ADJ irritante
irritation [ɪrɪtéʃən] N irritación f
IRS [Internal Revenue Service] [áɪárés] N Hacienda f
is [ɪz] see be
Islam [ízlɑm] N islamismo m, islam m
Islamic [ɪzlámɪk] ADJ islámico
island [áɪlənd] N isla f
islander [áɪləndə] N isleño -ña mf
isle [aɪl] N isla f
isobar [áɪsəbɑr] N isobara f
isolate [áɪsəlet] VT aislar
isolation [aɪsəléʃən] N aislamiento m, marginación f
isolationism [aɪsəléʃənɪzəm] N aislacionismo m
isometric [aɪsəmétrɪk] ADJ isométrico
isotope [áɪsətop] N isótopo m, isotopo m
Israel [ízriəl] N Israel m
Israeli [ɪzréli] ADJ & N israelí mf
issue [íʃu] N (of printed matter) tirada f; (of stock, bonds) emisión f; (copy of a magazine) número m, entrega f; (of a fluid) flujo m; (problem) problema m, tema m; (progeny) descendencia f; **he's got —s** es muy acomplejado; **to take — with** discrepar de; VT (written material) publicar; (a decree) promulgar; (a permit, document) expedir; (shares) emitir; (to flow) brotar; (to come out of) salir de; (to descend from) descender de
isthmus [ísməs] N istmo m
it [ɪt] PRON — **all started yesterday** todo empezó ayer; — **is necessary** es necesario; — **is raining** llueve, está lloviendo; — **is said that** se dice que; — **is two o'clock** son las dos; — **was broken** estaba roto; **who is**

—? ¿quién es? **if — weren't five o'clock** si no fueran las cinco; **I saw —** lo/la vi; **he talked about —** habló de eso; **what time is —**? ¿qué hora es? **how is — going?** ¿qué tal? **I don't get —** no entiendo; **you're —**! ¡tú la quedas! / ¡tú la traes!
IT [information technology] [áɪtí] N informática f
Italian [ɪtǽljən] ADJ & N italiano -na mf
italic [ɪtǽlɪk] ADJ itálico; N —**s** letra bastardilla/ cursiva f
italicize [ɪtǽlɪsaɪz] VT poner en bastardilla/ cursiva
Italy [ɪ́dli] N Italia f
itch [ɪtʃ] VI/VT picar; **to be —ing to** tener ganas de; N (sensation) comezón f, picazón f; (longing) ansia f
itching [ítʃɪŋ] N comezón f, picazón f
itchy [ítʃi] ADJ que pica; **it feels —** me pica
item [áɪɒəm] N (piece of news) artículo m; (topic of gossip) tema de conversación m; (unit) ítem m; (couple) pareja f
itemize [áɪɒəmaɪz] VT (list) enumerar; (break down) desglosar; —**d invoice** factura detallada f
itinerant [aɪtínə-ənt] ADJ itinerante, ambulante
itinerary [aɪtínə-eri] N (schedule) itinerario m; (guidebook) guía de viajeros f
its [ɪts] POSS ADJ su/sus, de él, de ella, de ello
itself [ɪtséɫf] PRON **this story wrote —** esta historia se escribió sola; **the bike was standing by —** la bici estaba parada sola; **the dog bit —** el perro se mordió [a sí mismo]; **the fox found — a hole** la zorra se encontró una guarida
IUD [intrauterine device] [áɪjúdí] N DIU m
IV [intravenous] [áɪví] ADJ intravenoso
Ivorian [aɪvórian] ADJ & N marfileño -ña mf
ivory [áɪvri] N marfil m; — **tower** torre de marfil f
Ivory Coast [áɪvrikóst] N Costa de Marfil f
ivy [áɪvi] N hiedra f

Jj

jab [dʒæb] VI/VT (hit) golpear; (hit with elbow) codear; N (blow) golpe m; (blow with elbow) codazo m; (in boxing) jab m, puñetazo directo m
jabber [dʒǽbə] VI (unintelligibly) farfullar; (incessantly) charlotear; N (unintelligible) farfulla f; charloteo m
jack [dʒæk] N (tool) gato m; (card) sota f; (plug-in) hembra f, toma f; (flag) bandera de proa f; —**ass** asno m, burro m (also person);

—hammer martillo neumático *m*; **—knife** navaja *f*; **— of all trades** hombre orquesta *m*; **—pot** premio gordo *m*; **—rabbit** liebre americana *f*; **you don't know —** no sabes ni un comino; VI/VT **to — off** *vulg* hacer[se] una paja; VT **to — up** (a car) alzar con gato; (prices) subir

jackal [dʒǽkəl] N chacal *m*

jacket [dʒǽkɪt] N (clothing) chaqueta *f*; (of a book) forro *m*; (of a potato) piel *f*

jade [dʒed] N jade *m*

jaded [dʒédɪd] ADJ (disenchanted) de vuelta; (sated) hastiado

jagged [dʒǽgɪd] ADJ recortado, desigual

jaguar [dʒǽgwɑr] N jaguar *m*

jail [dʒel] N cárcel *f*; **—break** fuga *f*; VT encarcelar

jailer [dʒélɚ] N carcelero -ra *mf*

jalopy [dʒəlápi] N cacharro *m*

jam [dʒæm] VT (stuff) embutir; (block) atestar; (immobilize) trabar; (make unworkable) obstruir, atascar, atorar; (stop radio signals) interferir; VI (become stuck or unworkable) atascarse; (crowd in) apiñarse; **to — on the brakes** frenar de golpe; **to — one's fingers** pillarse los dedos; N (jelly) mermelada *f*, dulce *m*; (difficult situation) aprieto *m*; (traffic) embotellamiento *m*; **— session** jam *m*

Jamaica [dʒəmékə] N Jamaica *f*

Jamaican [dʒəmékən] ADJ & N jamaicano -na *mf*, jamaiquino -na *mf*

janitor [dʒǽnɪDɚ] N conserje *m*

January [dʒǽnjuɛri] N enero *m*

Japan [dʒəpǽn] N Japón *m*

Japanese [dʒæpəníz] ADJ & N japonés -esa *mf*

jar [dʒɑr] VI/VT (shake) sacudir[se]; (clash) chocar; **to — one's nerves** ponerle a uno los nervios de punta; N (container) tarro *m*, frasco *m*, pote *m*; (large earthen container) tinaja *f*; (collision) choque *m*; (shake) sacudida *f*

jargon [dʒárgən] N jerga *f*

jasmine [dʒǽzmɪn] N jazmín *m*

jasper [dʒǽspɚ] N jaspe *m*

jaundice [dʒóndɪs] N ictericia *f*

jaundiced [dʒóndɪst] ADJ ictérico

jaunt [dʒɔnt] N excursión *f*; VI pasear

javelin [dʒǽvlɪn] N jabalina *f*

jaw [dʒɔ] N (of animal) quijada *f*; (of human) mandíbula *f*; (of mammals) fauces *f pl*; **—bone** mandíbula *f*, maxilar *m*

jay [dʒe] N arrendajo *m*

jazz [dʒæz] N jazz *m*; VI **to — up** animar

jealous [dʒéləs] ADJ (possessive) celoso; (envious) envidioso; (protective) protector

jealousy [dʒéləsi] N celos *m pl*

jeans [dʒinz] N jeans *m pl*, vaqueros *m pl*

jeer [dʒir] VI/VT (mock) mofarse [de], burlarse [de]; (boo) abuchear, befar; N (act of mockery) mofa *f*, burla *f*; (boos) abucheo *m*, befa *f*

jelly [dʒéli] N jalea *f*; **—fish** medusa *f*

jeopardize [dʒépɚdaɪz] VT comprometer, poner en peligro

jeopardy [dʒépɚdi] ADV LOC **in —** en peligro

jerk [dʒɚk] N (quick pull) tirón *m*; (muscular contraction) espasmo *m*; (idiot) *pej* pelmazo *m*; VI/VT tironear; **to — around** manipular, *vulg* joder; **to — off** *vulg* hacerse una paja

jerky [dʒɚki] ADJ espasmódico; N tasajo *m*

jersey [dʒɚzi] N jersey *m*

jest [dʒɛst] N broma *f*, chanza *f*; **in —** en broma; VI bromear

jester [dʒɛstɚ] N bufón *m*

Jesuit [dʒézuɪt] N jesuita *m*

jet [dʒet] N (stream) chorro *m*; (spout) surtidor *m*; (stone) azabache *m*; **— [air]plane** avión a reacción *m*; **— engine** motor a reacción *m*; **— lag** jet lag *m*; **—liner** avión a reacción de pasajero *m*; **— propulsion** propulsión a chorro *f*; **— set** jet *m*, jet-set *m*; **— stream** (of air) corriente en chorro *f*; (of a jet) chorro *m*; ADJ **-black** negro como el azabache; VI (stream out) salir a chorros; (travel) volar en avión a reacción; VT (spew out) lanzar a chorros; (transport) transportar en avión a reacción

jettison [dʒéDɪsən] VT echar por la borda

Jew [dʒu] N judío -a *mf*

jewel [dʒúəl] N (ornament, prized person) joya *f*, alhaja *f*; (stone) gema *f*; (watch jewel) rubí *m*; **— box** joyero *m*

jeweler [dʒúəlɚ] N joyero -ra *mf*; **—'s shop** joyería *f*

jewelry [dʒúəlri] N joyas *f pl*, alhajas *f pl*; **— box** alhajero *m*; **— store** joyería *f*

Jewish [dʒúɪʃ] ADJ judío

jitty [dʒɪti] ADV LOC **in a —** en un santiamén

jig [dʒɪg] N (dance) giga *f*; **—saw** sierra de vaivén *f*; **—saw puzzle** rompecabezas *m sg*; VI (dance) bailotear

jiggle [dʒígəl] VI/VT zangolotear[se], zarandear[se]; N zangoloteo *m*, zarandeo *m*

jilt [dʒɪlt] VT dejar plantado

jingle [dʒíŋgəl] VI tintinear; VT agitar; N retintín *m*; (short song) jingle *m*

jinx [dʒɪŋks] N persona que trae mala suerte *f*; VT traer mala suerte

job [dʒab] N (task) tarea *f*; (position) trabajo *m*, empleo *m*; (theft) golpe *m*; **to be out of a —** estar sin trabajo; *Sp* estar en [el] paro; **by the —** a destajo; **to do a good —** hacer buen trabajo; VI trabajar a destajo; **on-the-— training** capacitación en el lugar de trabajo *f*

jobber [dʒábɚ] N (day-worker) trabajador -ora a destajo *mf*; (wholesaler) vendedor -ora mayorista *mf*

jobless [dʒáblɪs] ADJ sin trabajo; *Sp* en paro

jock [dʒak] N deportista *mf*; **— [strap]**

suspensorio *m*
jockey [dʒáki] N jockey *m*; VI **to — for position** disputarse la posición
jocular [dʒákjələ·] ADJ jocoso
jog [dʒag] VI (run) correr, trotar; VT (refresh) refrescar; N trote *m*; **to go for a —** salir a correr
jogging [dʒágɪŋ] N jogging *m*, footing *m*
john [dʒan] N (urinal) *fam* meadero *m*; (customer of a prostitute) *fam* putañero *m*
join [dʒɔɪn] VI/VT juntar[se]; (pipes) acoplar[se], unir[se]; (bones) articular[se]; (a club) asociarse [a]; (the navy, etc.) alistarse [en]
joint [dʒɔɪnt] N (point of contact) juntura *f*, junta *f*; (connection between bones) articulación *f*, coyuntura *f*; (nodule on a plant) nudo *m*; (marijuana cigarette) porro *m*; (dive, bar) antro *m*; **out of —** descoyuntado; ADJ (shared) común; **— account** cuenta conjunta *f*; **— action** acción colectiva *f*; **— custody** custodia compartida *f*; **— owner** copropietario -ria *mf*; **— session** sesión plena *f*; **— venture** joint venture *m*
jointly [dʒɔɪntli] ADV conjuntamente
joke [dʒok] N broma *f*, chiste *m*; VI bromear
joker [dʒókə·] N (person who jokes) bromista *mf*, guasón -ona *mf*; (card) comodín *m*
jokingly [dʒókɪŋli] ADV en broma
jolly [dʒáli] ADJ jovial
jolt [dʒoɫt] N sacudida *f*; VT sacudir; **to — along** avanzar a los tumbos
Jordan [dʒɔrdn̩] N Jordania *f*
Jordanian [dʒɔrdéniən] ADJ & N jordano -na *mf*
jostle [dʒásəɫ] VI/VT codear[se], dar empujones [a]; N empujón *m*
jot [dʒat] VT **to — down** apuntar; N pizca *f*
journal [dʒɜ́nl̩] N (diary) diario *m*; (periodical) revista *f*; (logbook) cuaderno de bitácora *m*
journalism [dʒɜ́nəlɪzəm] N periodismo *m*
journalist [dʒɜ́nəlɪst] N periodista *mf*
journalistic [dʒɜnəlístɪk] ADJ periodístico
journey [dʒɜ́ni] N viaje *m*; VI viajar
joust [dʒaʊst] N justa *f*
jowl [dʒáʊɫ] N carrillo *m*, moflete *m*
joy [dʒɔɪ] N (delight) alegría *f*, regocijo *m*, alborozo *m*; (source of delight) deleite *m*; **—ride** paseo en coche robado *m*; **—stick** joystick *m*, palanca de mando *f*
joyful [dʒɔ́ɪfəɫ] ADJ alborozado
joyous [dʒɔ́ɪəs] ADJ jubiloso, alegre
jubilant [dʒúbələnt] ADJ jubiloso
jubilee [dʒubəlí] N jubileo *m*
Judaism [dʒúⁿⁱɪzəm] N judaísmo *m*
judge [dʒʌdʒ] N juez -eza *mf*; (in tennis) juez -eza de silla *mf*; **to be a good — of character** saber juzgar a la gente; VI/VT juzgar; (estimate) calcular
judgment [dʒʌ́dʒmənt] N juicio *m*; (in court) fallo *m*; **— day** día del juicio final *m*

judicial [dʒudíʃəɫ] ADJ judicial
judicious [dʒudíʃəs] ADJ juicioso, sensato
judo [dʒúⁿo] N judo *m*, yudo *m*
jug [dʒag] N (pitcher) jarro *m*, jarra *f*; (storage jar) pote *m*; **—s** *vulg* tetas *f pl*
juggle [dʒʌ́gəɫ] VI/VT hacer juegos malabares [con], hacer malabarismo [con]; **to — the accounts** manipular las cuentas
juggler [dʒʌ́glə·] N malabarista *mf*
jugular [dʒʌ́gjələ·] N yugular *f*
juice [dʒus] N jugo *m*; (fruit only) *Sp* zumo *m*
juicer [dʒúsə·] N exprimidor *m*
juicy [dʒúsi] ADJ jugoso; **a — story** un cuento sabroso
juke [dʒuk] N (in sports) amague *m*, finta *f*; **—box** juke-box *m*
July [dʒulái] N julio *m*
jumble [dʒʌ́mbəɫ] VI/VT revolver[se] *m*; N revoltijo *m*
jumbo [dʒʌ́mbo] ADJ jumbo, gigantesco; **— jet** jumbo *m*
jump [dʒʌmp] VI (spring) saltar; (increase, as temperature, prices) dar un salto; VT (capture in checkers) comer; (ride a horse over barrier) hacer saltar; (mug) asaltar; (cross a river, mountains, etc.) salvar; **to — at** abalanzarse sobre; **to — over** saltar; **to —-start** hacer un puente; **to — the track** descarrilarse; **to — to conclusions** hacer deducciones precipitadas; N salto *m*; (in prices) subida repentina *f*; **—rope** cuerda de saltar *f*; **— shot** tiro en suspensión *m*; **—suit** mono *m*
jumper [dʒʌ́mpə·] N (person who jumps) saltador -ora *mf*; (dress) jumper *m*; *Sp* pichi *m*; **— cable** puente *m*
jumpy [dʒʌ́mpi] ADJ nervioso, asustadizo
junction [dʒʌ́ŋkʃən] N (act or state of joining) unión *f*; (joining of two rivers) confluencia *f*; (of two railways) empalme *m*, entronque *m*; (of roads) cruce *m*
juncture [dʒʌ́ŋktʃə·] N (point where joined) juntura *f*; **at this —** en esta coyuntura
June [dʒun] N junio *m*
jungle [dʒʌ́ŋgəɫ] N selva *f*, jungla *f*; **the law of the —** la ley de la selva
junior [dʒúnjə·] ADJ (younger) menor; (more recent) más nuevo, de menos antigüedad; **— college** institución para los dos primeros años de la licenciatura *f*; **John Smith Jr.** John Smith, hijo; N estudiante del tercer año *mf*
juniper [dʒúnəpə·] N enebro *m*
junk [dʒʌŋk] N (useless articles) trastos viejos *m pl*; (metal) chatarra *f*; (Chinese boat) junco *m*; **— dealer** chatarrero -ra *mf*; **— food** comida basura *f*, porquerías *f pl*; **— mail** publicidad por correo *f*; **— e-mail** correo electrónico basura *m*; **—yard** chatarrería *f*; VT desechar, echar a la basura

junkie [ʤʌ́ŋki] N *fam* drogata *mf*, drogota *mf*
jurisdiction [ʤʊrɪsdík∫ən] N jurisdicción *f*
jurisprudence [ʤʊrɪsprúdn̩s] N jurisprudencia *f*
juror [ʤúrə-] N miembro de un jurado *m*, jurado -da *mf*
jury [ʤúri] N jurado *m*; — **box** banco de jurado *m*; VT **to** —-**rig** chapucear
just [ʤʌst] ADJ justo; ADV (exactly) exactamente, precisamente; (only) solo; — **like that** *Am* así nomás; **he** — **left** acaba de salir; **she is** — **a little girl** no es más que una niña; **you'll** — **have to wait** tendrás que esperar; — **barely** apenas; **the meeting is** — **starting** la reunión apenas comienza; **that is** — **what I wanted to talk to you about** precisamente de eso te quería hablar
justice [ʤʌ́stɪs] N (fairness) justicia *f*; (judge) juez -eza *mf*; **to bring to** — enjuiciar; **the painting doesn't do him** — el retrato no le favorece
justification [ʤʌstəfɪké∫ən] N justificación *f*
justify [ʤʌ́stəfaɪ] VT justificar
jut [ʤʌt] VI sobresalir, proyectarse
juvenile [ʤúvənaɪɫ] ADJ juvenil; — **delinquent** delincuente juvenil *mf*
juxtapose [ʤʌ́kstəpoz] VT yuxtaponer

Kk

kangaroo [kæŋgərú] N canguro *m*
karat, carat [kǽrət] N quilate *m*
kayak [káɪæk] N kayak *m*
Kazak, Kazakh [kəzǽk] ADJ & N kazako -ka *mf*
Kazakhstan [kəzákstɑn] N Kazajstán *m*
keel [kiɫ] N quilla *f*; VI/VT volcar[se]; **to** — **over** (ship) volcar[se]; (person) caer de cabeza, desplomarse
keen [kin] ADJ (edge) afilado; (perception) fino; (mind) agudo, penetrante
keenness [kínnɪs] N (of a blade) lo afilado; (of perception) fineza *f*; (of mind) agudeza *f*
keep [kip] VI (continue) seguir; (not spoil) aguantar; VT (retain) guardar; (maintain) mantener; (employ) tener; (look after) cuidar; **to** — **a diary** llevar un diario; **to** — **a secret** guardar un secreto; **to** — **at it** persistir; **to** — **away** mantener[se] alejado; **to** — **back** (stay away) tener a raya; (restrain) contener; **to** — **bad company** andar en mala compañía; **to** — **from** (prevent) impedir; (protect) proteger contra; **to** — **[on] talking** seguir hablando; **to** — **the door open** mantener la puerta abierta; **to** — **off the grass** no pisar el césped; **to** — **up** (perform as well) seguir el tren; (stay informed) mantener al tanto; **to**

— **one's hands off** no tocar; **to** — **someone posted** mantener al corriente a alguien; **to** — **quiet** estarse callado; **to** — **to the right** mantenerse a la derecha; **to** — **track of** (do accounts) llevar la cuenta de; (consider) no perder de vista; **to** — **watch** vigilar; **he** —**s a maid** tiene una criada; **she kept me on the phone** me [re]tuvo en el teléfono; N **for** —**s** (forever) para siempre; (for real) en serio; —**sake** recuerdo *m*
keeper [kípə-] N (of people) guardián *m*; (of things) custodio *m*
keeping [kípɪŋ] N custodia *f*; **in** — **with** en armonía con
keg [kɛg] N barril *m*
Kegel exercises [kégəɫ ɛksə-saɪzɪz] N ejercicios de Kegel *m pl*
kennel [kénl̩] N residencia de perros *f*
Kenya [kénjə] N Kenia *f*
Kenyan [kénjən] ADJ & N keniata *mf*
kept [kɛpt] *see* keep
kernel [kə́-nl̩] N (seed) semilla *f*, grano *m*; (essence) meollo *m*
kerosene [kérəsin] N queroseno *m*
kestrel [késtrəɫ] N cernícalo *m*
ketchup [két∫əp] N salsa de tomate *f*, cátsup *m*
kettle [kédl̩] N caldera *f*, hervidor *m*; (for tea) tetera *f*; —**drum** tímpano *m*, timbal *m*; **that's another** — **of fish** es harina de otro costal
key [ki] N (for locks) llave *f*; (secret, book of answers) clave *f*; (for winding) clavija *f*; (on keyboard) tecla *f*; (island) cayo *m*; (music) clave *f*; —**board** teclado *m*; —**hole** ojo de la cerradura *m*; — **indicator** indicador clave *m*; —**note** tónica *f*; —**note address** discurso de apertura *m*; —**pad** teclado numérico *m*; —**ring** llavero *m*; — **signature** armadura *f*; —**stone** piedra angular *f*; —**stroke** pulsación [de la tecla] *f*; —**word** palabra clave *f*; —**word search** búsqueda por palabra clave *f*; **to sing on** — cantar a tono; ADJ clave; VT (scratch) rayar; **to be** —**ed up** estar sobreexcitado
kg [kíləgræm] *see* kilogram
khaki [kǽki] N kaki *m*, caqui *m*
kick [kɪk] VI/VT (person) patear; (horse) dar coces [a], cocear; VI (gun) dar un culatazo, retroceder; **to** — **around** (discuss) discutir; (to mistreat) dar por la cabeza; **to** — **at** dar patadas; **to** — **out** echar a patadas; **to** —**start** arrancar; **to** — **the bucket** estirar la pata; **to** — **up a lot of dust** levantar una polvareda; **to** — **a habit** dejar un vicio; N (by a person) patada *f*, puntapié *m*; (by a soccer player) patada *f*; (of a horse) coz *f*; *Am* patada *f*; (of a gun) culatazo *m*; (in the air) pataleo *m*; **this whisky has a** — este whisky es fuerte; **I get a** — **out of swimming** me encanta nadar;

—**back** comisión ilegal *f; Mex* mordida *f;*
—**off** (football) saque de inicio *m;* (soccer)
saque inicial *m;* —**stand** soporte *m*
kid [kɪd] N (young goat) cabrito *m,* chivo *m;*
(leather) cabritilla *f;* (child) niño -ña *mf;*
(young person) chico -ca *mf;* — **stuff** juego de
niños *m;* VI bromear, embromar, tomar el
pelo
kidnap [kídnæp] VT secuestrar, raptar
kidnapper [kídnæpə-] N secuestrador -ora *mf*
kidnapping [kídnæpɪŋ] N secuestro *m,* rapto *m*
kidney [kídni] N riñón *m;* — **bean** judía *f;* —
failure insuficiencia renal *f;* — **stone**
cálculo renal *m*
kill [kɪɫ] VI/VT matar; (drink completely)
terminar; (turn off) apagar; **that comedian**
—**s me** ese cómico me mata de risa; N (animal
killed) caza *f;* (slaughter) matanza *f;* —**joy**
aguafiestas *mf sg*
killer [kílə-] N asesino -na *mf;* — **bee** abeja
asesina *f;* — **whale** orca *f;* **a** — **game** un
partidazo
killing [kílɪŋ] N (slaughter) matanza *f;* (murder)
asesinato *m;* (animal killed) caza *f;* **to make a**
— llenarse de oro
kilo [kílo] N kilo *m,* quilo *m*
kilobyte [kíləbaɪt] N kilobyte *m*
kilogram [kíləgræm] N kilogramo *m*
kilometer [kɪlámɪdə-] N kilómetro *m*
kilowatt [kíləwɑt] N kilovatio *m;* —-**hour**
kilovatio-hora *f*
kin [kɪn] N parentela *f,* parientes *m pl;* —**sman**
pariente *m;* —**swoman** parienta *f;* **next of**
— deudos *m pl*
kind [kaɪnd] ADJ (benevolent) bondadoso,
bueno; (words) amable; **to be** — **to animals**
ser cariñoso con los animales; —**hearted** de
buen corazón; — **of tired** algo cansado; N
clase *f,* tipo *m,* género *m;* **to pay in** —
(without money) pagar en especie; (retaliate)
pagar con la misma moneda
kindergarten [kíndə-gɑrtn̩] N jardín infantil /
de niños *m; Sp* parvulario *m*
kindle [kíndl] VT (fire) prender; (interest)
despertar, provocar; VI encenderse
kindling [kíndlɪŋ] N leña ligera *f,* astillas *f pl*
kindly [káɪndli] ADJ bondadoso, bueno; ADV
(with kindness) amablemente; (please) por
favor; **we thank you** — le agradecemos
mucho; **not to take** — **to criticism** no
aceptar de buen grado las críticas
kindness [káɪndnɪs] N (state) bondad *f,*
amabilidad *f;* (act) favor *m*
kindred [kíndrɪd] ADJ emparentado; — **spirits**
espíritus afines *m pl,* almas gemelas *f pl*
kinesiology [kəniziáləʤi] N quinesiología *f*
kinesthesia [kɪnɪsθíʒə] N cinestesia *f*
king [kɪŋ] N rey *m* (also in chess, cards); (in
checkers) dama *f;* —**fisher** martín pescador

m; —**pin** (in a mechanism) pivote central *m;*
(in bowling) bolo central *m;* (person) figura
central *f;* ADJ —-**sized** extra grande
kingdom [kíŋdəm] N reino *m*
kingly [kíŋli] ADJ real
kink [kɪŋk] N (bend) doblez *m;* (pain) tortícolis *f*
kinky [kɪŋki] ADJ crespo; (sex) pervertido, *Sp*
morboso
kinship [kínʃɪp] N (family connection)
parentesco *m;* (likeness) afinidad *f*
kiosk [kíɑsk] N quiosco *m*
Kiribati [kirəbádi] N Kiribati *m*
kiss [kɪs] VI/VT besar[se]; N beso *m*
kit [kɪt] N (of tools) caja *f;* (of first aid) botiquín
m; (of sewing notions) costurero *m*
kitchen [kítʃɪn] N cocina *f;* —**ware** utensilios de
cocina *m pl*
kite [kaɪt] N (toy) cometa *f;* (bird) milano *m*
kitten [kítn̩] N gatito *m*
kitty [kídi] N (young cat) gatito *m,* minino *m;*
(petty cash) caja chica *f,* fondo *m*
kleptomania [klɛptəméniə] N cleptomanía *f*
kleptomaniac [klɛptəméniæk] N cleptómano
-na *mf*
knack [næk] N buena mano *f,* maña *f;* **once you**
get the — una vez que le agarras la vuelta/
onda
knapsack [næpsæk] N mochila *f*
knave [nev] N pícaro *m;* (in cards) sota *f*
knead [nid] VT amasar, sobar
knee [ni] N rodilla *f;* —**cap** rótula *f;* —-**deep**
hasta las rodillas; —-**jerk liberal** liberal
fanático *m;* —-**jerk reaction** reacción
visceral *f;* VT dar un rodillazo
kneel [niɫ] VI arrodillarse
knell [nɛl] N doble *m;* VI doblar
knelt [nɛɫt] *see* kneel
knew [nu] *see* know
knickknack [níknæk] N chuchería *f,* baratija *f*
knife [naɪf] N cuchillo *m;* (big) cuchilla *f;*
(folding) navaja *f;* (for carving) trinchante *m;*
VT acuchillar; **at** —**point** a punta de cuchillo
knight [naɪt] N caballero *m;* (in chess) caballo *m;*
— **errant** caballero andante *m;* VT armar
caballero
knighthood [náɪthʊd] N (all knights) caballería
f; (title) orden de la caballería *f*
knit [nɪt] VI/VT tejer; **to** — **one's brow** fruncir el
entrecejo / el ceño
knitting [nídɪŋ] N tejido *m;* — **needle** aguja de
punto *f*
knob [nɑb] N (on a door) pomo *m,* perilla *f,*
tirador *m;* (protuberance) protuberancia *f*
knock [nɑk] VI (hit) golpear; (precombust)
golpetear; (call at the door) llamar, tocar; VT
(criticize) criticar; **to** — **a hole in the wall**
hacer un agujero en la pared a golpes; **to** —
down derribar, echar abajo, tumbar; **to** —
off (stop working) terminar; (reduce) rebajar;

(make fall) tirar; (kill) liquidar; — **it off!**
¡basta! **to — into** golpearse contra; **to — out**
noquear; **to — over** voltear, revolcar; **to —
up** *vulg* preñar; N (pounding) golpe *m*, toque
m; (criticism) crítica*f*; (in a motor) golpeteo
m; —**out** (boxing) nocaut *m*; (attractive
person) bomba*f*; ADJ —-**kneed** patizambo,
zambo
knocker [nákɚ] N (handle on door) llamador *m*,
aldaba*f*; (breast) *vulg* teta*f*
knoll [noł] N morro *m*, loma*f*
knot [nɑt] N nudo *m* (also in wood, unit of
speed); (of people) grupo *m*; (swelling)
chichón *m*; VI/VT anudar[se]
knotty [nádi] ADJ (full of knots) nudoso;
(difficult) dificultoso, enredado
know [no] VI/VT (to have knowledge of, to know
how to) saber; VT (to be acquainted with, have
sexual intercourse with) conocer; (to
recognize) reconocer; (distinguish)
distinguir; **to — how to swim** saber nadar;
to — of estar enterado de; N **to be in the —**
estar al tanto; —-**how** pericia*f*; —-**it-all**
sabelotodo *mf*
knowing [nóɪŋ] ADJ (complicitous) cómplice;
(astute) astuto
knowingly [nóɪŋli] ADV a sabiendas
knowledge [nálɪdʒ] N (awareness) conocimiento
m; (information known) saber *m*,
conocimientos *m pl*; **not to my —** no que yo
sepa
known [non] ADJ **little —** poco conocido; **well
—** bien conocido; **he's — for his cooking** se
le conoce por su cocina; **the truth wasn't —
until last year** no se supo la verdad hasta el
año pasado
known [non] *see* know
knuckle [nákəł] N nudillo *m*; —**ball** bola de
nudillos*f*; —**head** tarambana *mf*; VI **to —
down** arremangarse, aplicarse con empeño;
to — under someterse
Korea [kɔría] Corea*f*
Korean [kɔríən] ADJ & N coreano -na *mf*
kosher [kóʃɚ] ADJ kosher
Kuwait [kuwét] N Kuwait *m*
Kuwaiti [kuwédi] ADJ & N kuwaití *mf*
Kyrgyzstan [kírgistɑn] N Kirguistán *m*

Ll

lab [læb] *see* laboratory
label [lébəł] N (sticker) etiqueta*f*, rótulo *m*;
(characterization) calificativo *m*; (brand)
marca*f*; (of recording companies) sello *m*; VT
etiquetar, rotular
labial [lébiəł] ADJ labial

labium [lébiəm] N labio *m*
labor [lébɚ] N trabajo *m*, labor*f*; (body of
workers) mano de obra*f*; (working class) clase
obrera*f*; (uterine contractions) trabajo de
parto *m*; —-**intensive** que requiere mucha
mano de obra; — **pains** dolores de parto *m pl*;
— **union** sindicato *m*; **to be in** — estar de
parto; ADJ laboral; VI (work) trabajar;
(dedicate oneself) afanarse; **to — under a
disadvantage** sufrir una desventaja
laboratory [lǽbrətɔri] N laboratorio *m*
laborer [lébərɚ] N jornalero -ra *mf*; (unskilled)
peón -ona *mf*
laborious [ləbóriəs] ADJ (industrious) laborioso;
(difficult) trabajoso
labrador [lǽbrədɔr] N (dog) labrador *m*
labyrinth [lǽbərɪnθ] N laberinto *m*
lace [les] N (cloth) encaje *m*; (cord) cordón *m*; VT
(to adorn with lace) bordar con encaje; (to
insert laces into) poner cordones a; (to spike)
echar alcohol; VI atarse
lack [læk] N falta*f*, carencia*f*; VI/VT carecer de,
faltarle a uno; **he —s courage** le falta
valentía; —**luster** mediocre
lackey [lǽki] N lacayo *m*
lacking [lǽkɪŋ] ADJ (deficient) deficiente; **good
bars are — in this town** faltan buenos
bares en este pueblo; — **in** falto de, carente de
laconic [ləkánɪk] ADJ lacónico
lacquer [lǽkɚ] N laca*f*; VT lacar, laquear
lactation [læktéʃən] N lactancia*f*
lactic acid [lǽktɪkǽsɪd] N ácido láctico *m*
lactose [lǽktos] N lactosa*f*; — **intolerance**
intolerancia a la lactosa*f*
ladder [lǽDɚ] N escalera*f*
laden [lédn] ADJ cargado
ladle [lédl] N cucharón *m*, cazo *m*; VT servir con
cucharón
lady [lépi] N señora*f*, dama*f*; —**bug** mariquita*f*;
—**like** muy fina; —**love** amada*f*; **ladies'
room** *Sp* aseo de damas *m*, *Am* servicio de
damas *m*
lag [læg] VI (fall behind) quedarse atrás,
rezagarse; (flag) disminuir; N retardo *m*,
retraso *m*
lagoon [ləgún] N laguna*f*
laid [led] *see* lay
laid-back [ledbǽk] ADJ apacible, tranquilo
lain [len] *see* lie 'estar situado'
lair [lɛr] N guarida*f*
lake [lek] N lago *m*
lamb [læm] N cordero *m*; (yearling) borrego *m*
lame [lem] ADJ cojo; *Am* rengo; —**brained**
idiota; — **duck** funcionario -ria cesante *mf*;
— **excuse** pretexto tonto *m*; VT dejar cojo
lament [ləmént] N lamento *m*; VI lamentar[se];
VT llorar
lamentable [ləméntəbəł] ADJ lamentable
lamentation [læməntéʃən] N lamentación*f*,

lamento *m*
laminate [lǽmənet] VT laminar
lamp [læmp] N lámpara *f*; (on a street) farol *m*; **—post** farol *m*; **—shade** pantalla *f*
LAN [**local area network**] [læn] N red [de área] local *f*
lance [læns] N lanza *f*; (lancet) lanceta *f*; VT lancear; (a wound) abrir con una lanceta
lancet [lǽnsɪt] N lanceta *f*
land [lænd] N tierra *f*; (lot) terreno *m*; (country) país *m*, tierra *f*; **—fill** vertedero *m*; **— grant university** universidad con terrenos concedidos por el estado *f*; **—lady** casera *f*, propietaria *f*; **—lord** casero *m*, propietario *m*; **—mark** (marker) hito *m*, mojón *m*; (historical) hito *m*; **— mine** mina *f*; **—owner** hacendado -da *mf*; **—scape** (terrain) paisaje *m*; (in printing) orientación horizontal *f*; **—scape architecture** paisajismo *m*; **—slide** (mass of land) derrumbe *m*, desprendimiento *m*; (election) victoria aplastante *f*; **— use** ordenamiento territorial *m*; VI/VT (a ship) atracar; (an airplane) aterrizar; **you'll — in jail** terminarás en la cárcel; VT (a fish) *Sp* coger; *Am* pescar; (a job) conseguir
landing [lǽndɪŋ] N (of a ship) desembarco *m*; (of cargo) desembarque *m*; (of an airplane) aterrizaje *m*; (place) desembarcadero *m*; (on stairs) descansillo *m*; **— field** campo de aterrizaje *m*; **— gear** tren de aterrizaje *m*; **— strip** pista de aterrizaje *f*
lane [len] N (country road) sendero *m*; (road division) carril *m*; (for ships) ruta *f*
language [lǽŋgwɪdʒ] N lengua *f*, idioma *m*; (faculty of speech, computer code) lenguaje *m*
languid [lǽŋgwɪd] ADJ lánguido
languish [lǽŋgwɪʃ] VI languidecer
languor [lǽŋgɚ] N languidez *f*
lanky [lǽŋki] ADJ larguirucho, zancudo
lanolin [lǽnəlɪn] N lanolina *f*
lantern [lǽntɚn] N farol *m*; (of a lighthouse) faro *m*, linterna *f*
Laos [léas] N Laos *m*
Laotian [leóʃən] ADJ & N laosiano -na *mf*
lap [læp] N (part of body) regazo *m*; (part of a race) vuelta *f*; **—dog** perro faldero *m*; **—top computer** *Am* computadora portátil *f*, *Sp* ordenador portátil *m*; **to live in the — of luxury** vivir en la abundancia; VI/VT lamer
lapel [ləpɛ́l] N solapa *f*
lapidary [lǽpɪdɛri] ADJ & N lapidario -ria *mf*
lapse [læps] N (period of time) lapso *m*; (linguistic error) lapsus *m*; (defect in memory) fallo *m*; (fall) caída *f*; (termination) caducidad *f*; VI (fall) caer; (decline) decaer; (end) caducar, vencer
larceny [lársəni] N latrocinio *m*, hurto *m*
lard [lɑrd] N manteca *f*; VT enmantecar; (with

bacon) mechar
large [lɑrdʒ] ADJ grande; **—-scale** a gran escala; **a — company** una gran compañía / una compañía grande; **at —** (not in jail) suelto, libre; N tamaño grande *m*
largely [lárdʒli] ADV (in the greatest number) en su mayoría; (to the greatest degree) en gran parte
lariat [lǽriət] N reata *f*
lark [lɑrk] N (bird) alondra *f*; (bit of fun) diversión *f*; **to go on a —** ir de jarana
larva [lárvə] N larva *f*
laryngeal [ləríndʒəl] ADJ laríngeo; **— angina** angina laríngea *f*
laryngitis [lærəndʒáɪdɪs] N laringitis *f*
larynx [lǽrɪŋks] N laringe *f*
lascivious [ləsíviəs] ADJ lascivo
laser [lézɚ] N láser *m*; **— beam** rayo láser *m*; **— printer** impresora láser *f*
lash [læʃ] N (blow with a whip, tail, etc.) azote *m*, latigazo *m*; (blow of waves) embate *m*; (part of eye) pestaña *f*; VT (whip) azotar; (tie) amarrar; **to — out at** fustigar
lasso [lǽso] N lazo *m*, reata *f*; VT lazar; *Am* enlazar
last [læst] ADJ (in a series) último; (definitive) final; **—-ditch** desesperado; **— minute** de último momento; **— name** apellido *m*; **— night** anoche; **— rites** extrema unción *f*, viático *m*; **— straw** colmo *m*; **— word** última palabra *f*; **— year** el año pasado; **next to the —** penúltimo; ADV último; **to arrive —** ser el último en llegar; **when — seen** cuando se lo vio por última vez; **at —** finalmente; N el último; (of a shoe) horma *f*; VI durar; (live on) perdurar
lasting [lǽstɪŋ] ADJ duradero, perdurable
lastly [lǽstli] ADV por último
latch [lætʃ] N pestillo *m*, picaporte *m*, cierre *m*; VI cerrar con el pestillo; **to — on** agarrarse de; **to — onto** pegarse a
late [let] ADJ (tardy) tardío; (hour) avanzada; (recent) reciente, último; (recently deceased) finado; **— afternoon** atardecer *m*; **— comer** rezagado -da *mf*; **— fee** recargo por mora *m*; ADV tarde; **— in the night** a una hora avanzada de la noche; **— into the night** hasta cualquier hora de la noche; **— in the week** a finales de la semana; **it is —** ya es tarde; **of —** últimamente; **to be —** llegar tarde; **to work —** trabajar hasta tarde; **the train was ten minutes —** el tren llegó con diez minutos de retraso
lately [létli] ADV últimamente
lateness [létnɪs] N tardanza *f*
latent [létn̩t] ADJ latente
later [létɚ] ADJ posterior; ADV más tarde, con posterioridad; **see you —** hasta luego; **— on** más tarde

lateral [lǽDə-əł] ADJ lateral
latest [léDɪst] ADJ último; **the — fashion** la última moda; **the — news** las últimas novedades; N **at the —** a más tardar
latex [léteks] N látex *m*
lathe [leð] N torno *m*
lather [lǽðə-] N (foam) espuma *f*; (sweat) sudor *m*; **he got into a —** se puso histérico; VT enjabonar; VI hacer espuma
Latin [lǽtn̩] ADJ latino; — **America** América Latina *f*, Latinoamérica *f*; — **American** latinoamericano -na *mf*; N (language) latín *m*
latitude [lǽDɪtud] N latitud *f*; (freedom) flexibilidad *f*
latrine [lətrín] N letrina *f*
latter [lǽDə-] ADJ último; **in the — days of the Roman Republic** en los últimos días de la República Romana; **toward the — part of the week** a finales de la semana; **the —** este *m*, esta *f*
lattice [lǽDɪs] N enrejado *m*, entramado *m*; (of a window) celosía *f*
Latvia [lǽtviə] N Letonia *f*
Latvian [lǽtviən] ADJ & N letón -ona *mf*
laud [lɔd] VT loar
laudable [lɔ́Dəbəł] ADJ laudable, loable
laugh [læf] VI reír[se]; **to — at** reírse de; **to — loudly** reírse a carcajadas; **to — up/in one's sleeve** reírse para sus adentros; **she —ed in his face** se rió en su cara; N risa *f*; **we did it for —s** lo hicimos por diversión
laughable [lǽfəbəł] ADJ risible
laughingstock [lǽfɪŋstɑk] N hazmerreír *m*
laughter [lǽftə-] N risa *f*
launch [lɔntʃ] VT (a boat) botar; (a rocket, new product) lanzar; (software) iniciar; **to — forth/out** lanzarse; N lancha *f*; (act of launching a boat) botadura *f*; (act of launching a rocket) lanzamiento *m*
launder [lɔ́ndə-] VI/VT (clothes) lavar; (money) blanquear, lavar; (wash and iron clothes) lavar y planchar
Laundromat™ [lɔ́ndrəmæt] N lavadero automático *m*
laundry [lɔ́ndri] N (business establishment) lavandería *f*, lavadero *m*; (room in house) cuarto de lavado *m*, lavadero *m*; (clothes to be washed) ropa sucia *f*; (washed clothes) ropa limpia *f*
laurel [lɔ́rəł] N laurel *m* (also honor); **to rest on one's —s** dormirse sobre los laureles
lava [lávə] N lava *f*
lavatory [lǽvətɔri] N (basin) lavabo *m*; (bathroom) baño *m*, retrete *m*
lavender [lǽvəndə-] N espliego *m*, lavanda *f*; ADJ lavanda
lavish [lǽvɪʃ] ADJ (generous) pródigo, espléndido; (abundant) abundante, copioso; VT prodigar; **to — praise upon** colmar de alabanzas a

law [lɔ] N ley *f*; (discipline) derecho *m*, jurisprudencia *f*; (police) policía *f*; — **and order** orden público *m*; —**breaker** infractor -ora *mf*, transgresor -ora *mf*; —**maker** legislador -ora *mf*; — **of diminishing returns** ley de [los] rendimientos decrecientes *f*; — **student** estudiante de derecho *mf*; —**suit** pleito *m*, litigio *m*; **to practice —** ejercer la abogacía; **to take the — into one's hands** hacer justicia por mano propia; ADJ —**-abiding** respetuoso de las leyes
lawful [lɔ́fəł] ADJ (in accordance with the law) legal; (allowed by law) lícito; (recognized by law) legítimo
lawless [lɔ́lɪs] ADJ (anarchic) anárquico; (illegal) ilegal
lawn [lɔn] N césped *m*, grama *f*; — **mower** cortadora de césped *f*
lawyer [lɔ́jə-] N abogado -da *mf*
lax [læks] ADJ laxo
laxative [lǽksəDɪv] ADJ & N laxante *m*, purgante *m*
laxity [lǽksɪDi] N flojedad *f*, laxitud *f*
lay [le] VT colocar; (eggs) poner; (a cable) tender; (to have sexual intercourse with) *fam* tirarse a; **to — aside** (abandon) dejar de lado; (save) guardar; **to — a wager** apostar; **to — bare** poner al descubierto; **to — bricks** poner ladrillos; **to — down arms** rendir las armas; **to — down the law** imponerse; **to — hold of** asir, agarrar; **to — into** atacar; **to — off a workman** despedir temporalmente a un obrero; **to — one's head on a pillow** recostar la cabeza sobre una almohada; **to — open** exponer; **to — out a plan** trazar un plan; **to — up** almacenar; **to be laid up** estar en cama; **to — waste to** asolar; N situación *f*, orientación *f*; **she's an easy —** *fam* es una mujer fácil; —**man** (nonexpert) lego *m*; (clergy) laico *m*; —**off** despido temporal de un empleado *m*; —**out** diseño/trazado de página *m*; ADJ lego, laico
lay [le] *see* **lie** 'estar situado'
layer [léə-] N capa *f*; (geological) estrato *m*; (hen) gallina ponedora *f*; — **cake** tarta de capas *f*
laziness [lézɪnɪs] N pereza *f*, holgazanería *f*, flojera *f*
lazy [lézi] ADJ perezoso, holgazán, flojo
LBO [**leveraged buyout**] [ɛ́łbíó] N compra apalancada *f*
LDL [**low density lipoprotein**] [ɛ́łdíɛ́ł] N LBD *f*
lead¹ [lɛd] N (metal) plomo *m*; (graphite) mina *f*; — **poisoning** intoxicación con plomo *f*
lead² [lid] VT (guide) guiar; (guide a horse) llevar de la rienda; (induce, take) llevar, inducir; (be in charge, be first) encabezar, liderar; (direct) dirigir; (be superior to) estar a la cabeza de; **to**

— **a life of ease** llevar una vida fácil; **to** — **the way** mostrar el camino; VI (provide passage to, result in) llevar a; (be first) estar a la cabeza; **to** — **astray** llevar por mal camino; N (first position) delantera f, primer lugar m; (clue) indicio m; (most important role) papel principal m, liderazgo m; —**off** comienzo; — **story** noticia principal f; **to take the** — (in sports) ponerse por delante en el marcador

leaden [lédn̩] ADJ (of lead) de plomo; (color) plomizo; (oppressive, slow) pesado

leader [líDɚ] N (in politics) líder mf, caudillo m; (in a race) líder mf; (in music) director -ora mf; (as a guide) guía mf

leadership [líDɚʃɪp] N dirección f, liderazgo m

leading [líDɪŋ] ADJ (most important) principal; (arriving first) delantero; — **indicators** indicadores anticipados m pl; — **man** actor principal m

leaf [lif] N hoja f; VI echar hojas; **to** — **through a book** hojear un libro

leafless [líflɪs] ADJ sin hojas, deshojado

leaflet [líflɪt] N (small leaf) folíolo m; (printed matter) volante m; (folded printed matter) pliego m

leafy [lífi] ADJ (with foliage) frondoso; (in the form of leaves) de hoja

league [lig] N (alliance) liga f; (unit of distance) legua f; VI/VT aliar[se]

leak [lik] N (in a roof) gotera f; (in a boat, bucket, etc.) agujero m; (of information) filtración f; (of gas, steam, electricity) escape m, fuga f; VI (roof) gotear[se]; (boat) hacer agua; (gas) salirse, escaparse; (information) filtrarse; VT revelar información interna confidencial

leaky [líki] ADJ (roof) que tiene goteras; (boat) que hace agua; (gas, electricity) que pierde

lean [lin] VI/VT (incline) inclinar[se]; (support) apoyar[se], reclinar[se], recostar[se]; **to** — **on** presionar; ADJ magro; — **year** mal año m

leap [lip] VI/VT saltar; **to** — **at a chance** aprovechar una oportunidad; **to** — **to mind** ocurrírsele a uno; N salto m; —**frog** pídola f; — **year** año bisiesto m

leapt [lɛpt] see leap

learn [lɝn] VI/VT aprender; (find out) enterarse de

learned [lɝnɪd] ADJ erudito, letrado

learner [lɝnɚ] N estudiante mf; (driver) aprendiz -iza mf

learning [lɝnɪŋ] N (result) erudición f, saber m; (process) aprendizaje m; — **disability** problema de aprendizaje m

learnt [lɝnt] see learn

lease [lis] N (action) arrendamiento m; (contract) contrato de arrendamiento m; (period) período de arrendamiento m; **for** — se arrienda; **to have a new** — **on life** nacer de nuevo; VI/VT arrendar

leash [liʃ] N traílla f, correa f

least [list] ADJ **he doesn't have the** — **chance** no tiene la más mínima posibilidad; **the** — **amount of money** la menor cantidad de dinero; — **common denominator** mínimo común denominador m; ADV menos; **the** — **important** el/la menos importante; **at** — al menos, por lo menos; N **I received the** — **of anyone** yo fui el que recibió menos de todos

leather [léðɚ] N cuero m; ADJ de cuero; — **strap** correa f

leave [liv] VT (a person, thing) dejar; (a place) salir de, irse de; VI salir, partir; **to** — **off** (stop) parar de; (omit) omitir; **to** — **out** omitir; **I have two books left** me quedan dos libros; N permiso m; **to be on** — estar de licencia; — **of absence** licencia f; **to take** — **of** despedirse de

leaven [lévən] N levadura f; VT leudar

leavings [lívɪŋz] N (leftovers) sobras f pl; (refuse) desperdicios m pl

Lebanese [lɛbəníz] ADJ & N libanés -esa mf

Lebanon [lébənɑn] N Líbano m

lecherous [létʃɚəs] ADJ lujurioso

lecture [léktʃɚ] N (presentation) conferencia f, disertación f; (sermon) sermón m; (long-winded speech) perorata f; VI (present) dar una conferencia, disertar; VT (scold) sermonear

lecturer [léktʃərɚ] N conferenciante mf; (academic rank) profesor -ora mf

led [lɛd] see lead

LED [light-emitting diode] [ɛ́lidí] N LED m

ledge [lɛdʒ] N cornisa f

ledger [lédʒɚ] N libro mayor m

leech [litʃ] N sanguijuela f

leer [lir] VT (sideways) mirar de soslayo; (lecherously) mirar con lujuria; N (sideways) mirada de soslayo f; (lecherous) mirada lujuriosa f

leeway [líwe] N margen de maniobra m; (of a ship) deriva f

left [lɛft] ADJ izquierdo; —**-click** presionar el botón izquierdo del ratón; —**-handed** zurdo; —**-handed compliment** alabanza irónica f; —**-handed tool** herramienta para zurdos f; — **justification** alineación a la izquierda f; —**-wing** de izquierdas; N izquierda f; **at / on/to/toward the** — a/hacia la izquierda; **to make a** — doblar/girar a la izquierda

left [lɛft] see leave

leftist [léftɪst] N & ADJ izquierdista mf

leg [lɛg] N (human) pierna f; (animal, furniture) pata f; (wading bird) zanca f; (of a journey) etapa f; **to be on one's last** —**s** estar en las últimas; **to pull someone's** — tomarle el pelo a alguien; **to stretch one's** —**s** estirar las piernas

legacy [légəsi] N legado *m*
legal [lígəł] ADJ (in accordance with the law) legal; (permitted by law) lícito; (recognized by law) legítimo; (having to do with the law) jurídico; — **age** mayoría de edad *f*; — **code** ordenamiento *m*; — **fees** honorarios del abogado *m pl*; — **holiday** día feriado *m*; — **procedure** procedimiento jurídico *m*; — **tender** moneda de curso legal *f*
legality [lɪgǽlɪDi] N legalidad *f*
legalization [ligəlɪzéʃən] N legalización *f*
legalize [lígəlaɪz] VT legalizar
legation [lɪgéʃən] N legación *f*
legend [lédʒənd] N leyenda *f* (also inscription); (of a map) clave *f*
legendary [lédʒəndɛri] ADJ legendario
leggings [légɪŋz] N (ankle to knee) polainas *f pl*; (trousers) leggings *m pl*
legible [lédʒəbəł] ADJ legible
legion [lídʒən] N legión *f*
legionnaire [lidʒənér] N legionario *m*; —'**s disease** enfermedad del legionario *f*, legionelosis *f*
legislate [lédʒɪslet] VI/VT legislar
legislation [lɛdʒɪsléʃən] N legislación *f*
legislative [lédʒɪsleDɪv] ADJ legislativo
legislator [lédʒɪsleDɚ] N legislador -ora *mf*
legislature [lédʒɪsletʃɚ] N legislatura *f*
legitimacy [ləXdʒídəməsi] N legitimidad *f*
legitimate [lɪdʒídəmɪt] ADJ legítimo
legitimize [lədʒídəmaɪz] VT legitimar
legume [légjum] N legumbre *f*
leisure [líʒɚ] N ocio *m*, holgura *f*; — **activities** actividades recreativas *f pl*; — **hours** horas de ocio *f pl*, tiempo libre *m*; **to be at** — estar desocupado; **do it at your** — hazlo cuando te convenga
leisurely [líʒɚli] ADJ lento, deliberado; ADV sin prisa
lemon [lémən] N limón *m*; ADJ de limón; — **tree** limonero *m*
lemonade [lɛmənéd] N limonada *f*
lend [lɛnd] VI/VT prestar; **to** — **a hand** dar una mano
lender [léndɚ] N (person who lends) prestador -ora *mf*; (professional) prestamista *mf*
length [lɛŋkθ] N (of an object, road) largo *m*, largura *f*, longitud *f*; (of a movie) duración *f*; (of a book) extensión *f*; **at** — (in detail) pormenorizadamente; (finally) finalmente; **by two** —**s** por dos cuerpos; **two meters in** — dos metros de largo; **to go to any** —**s** hacer lo imposible
lengthen [léŋkθən] VI/VT alargar[se]
lengthwise [léŋkθwaɪz] ADV & ADJ a lo largo
lengthy [léŋkθi] ADJ largo, prolongado
lenient [líniənt] ADJ indulgente
lens [lɛnz] N lente *m*; (of the eye) cristalino *m*
Lent [lɛnt] N Cuaresma *f*

lent [lɛnt] *see* lend
lentil [léntł] N lenteja *f*
Leon [león] N León *m*
Leonese [liəníz] ADJ leonés
leopard [lépɚd] N leopardo *m*
leprosy [léprəsi] N lepra *f*
lesbian [lézbiən] ADJ lesbiano; N lesbiana *f*
lesion [líʒən] N lesión *f*
Lesotho [ləsóto] N Lesoto *m*
less [lɛs] ADJ, ADV & PREP menos; **I have** — **than you do** tengo menos que tú; — **and** — cada vez menos
lessen [lésən] VI/VT disminuir, aminorar
lessening [lésənɪŋ] N disminución *f*
lesser [lésɚ] ADJ menor
lesson [lésən] N lección *f*
lest [lɛst] CONJ no sea que; — **you should think I'm teasing** para que no vayas a creer que estoy bromeando
let [lɛt] VT (permit) dejar, permitir; (rent) alquilar; — **him come** que venga; —'**s do it** hagámoslo; **to** — **be** dejar en paz; **to** — **down** (lower) bajar; (disappoint) decepcionar; **to** — **go** soltar; **to** — **in** dejar entrar; **to** — **know** hacer saber; **to** — **off** (not punish) dejar ir; (allow to get off) dejar bajar; **to** — **through** dejar pasar; **to** — **up** (permit to stand) dejar incorporarse; (cease) disminuir; N (in tennis) repetición *f*; —**down** desilusión *f*; —**up** tregua *f*
lethal [líθəł] ADJ letal
lethargic [ləθárdʒɪk] ADJ aletargado, letárgico
lethargy [léθɚdʒi] N letargo *m*; **to fall into a** — aletargarse
letter [léDɚ] N (of alphabet) letra *f*; (missive) carta *f*; — **carrier** cartero -ra *mf*; —**head** membrete *m*; —**head paper** papel membretado *m*; —-**spacing** espacio entre caracteres *m*; —**s** letras *f pl*; **the** — **of the law** la letra de la ley *f*; **to the** — al pie de la letra; VT grabar
lettuce [léDɪs] N lechuga *f*
leukemia [lukímiə] N leucemia *f*
levee [lévi] N dique *m*
level [lévəł] ADJ llano, plano; —-**headed** sensato; — **playing field** terreno de juego parejo *m*; — **with** a nivel de; **a** — **tablespoon** una cucharada al ras; N nivel *m* (also tool); **on the** — en serio; VT (make level) nivelar, igualar; (to demolish) arrasar, allanar; (to knock down a person) tumbar; (to aim criticism) dirigir; (to aim a gun) apuntar; **to** — **off** quedar paralelo al suelo; **to** — **with** hablar en serio con/a
lever [lévɚ] N palanca *f*
leverage [lévɚɪdʒ] N (influence) palanca *f*; (physical, financial) apalancamiento *m*
levity [lévɪDi] N ligereza *f*
levy [lévi] N (of taxes) recaudación *f*; (of troops)

lew–lig 460

leva *f*; VT (taxes) recaudar; (troops) reclutar, hacer una leva de
lewd [lud] ADJ lascivo
lewdness [lúdnɪs] N lascivia *f*
lexical [léksɪkəl] ADJ léxico
lexicography [lɛksɪkágrəfi] N lexicografía *f*
lexicon [léksɪkɑn] N léxico *m*
liability [laɪəbílɪDi] N (disadvantage) desventaja *f*; (debit) pasivo *m*; (debts) deudas *f pl*; (responsibility) responsabilidad legal *f*; — **insurance** seguro contra daños a terceros *m*; **liabilities** obligaciones *f pl*
liable [láɪəbəl] ADJ responsable; — **to** propenso a; **she's — to get angry** es probable que se enoje
liaison [liézɑn] N (connection) enlace *m*; (illicit love affair) aventura *f*
liar [láɪɚ] N mentiroso -sa *mf*, embustero -ra *mf*
libel [láɪbəl] N libelo *m*, difamación *f*; VT difamar
liberal [líbɚəl] ADJ & N liberal *mf*
liberalism [líbɚəlɪzəm] N liberalismo *m*
liberality [lɪbɚǽlɪDi] N (generosity) liberalidad *f*; (tolerance) tolerancia *f*
liberalization [lɪbɚəlɪzéʃən] N liberalización *f*
liberalize [líbɚəlaɪz] VI/VT liberalizar[se]
liberate [líbɚet] VT (give freedom to) libertar, liberar; (release from obligation) librar; (give off) desprender
liberation [lɪbɚéʃən] N liberación *f*
liberator [líbɚeDɚ] N libertador -ora *mf*
Liberia [laɪbíriə] N Liberia *f*
Liberian [laɪbíriən] ADJ & N liberiano -na *mf*
libertine [líbɚtin] ADJ & N libertino -na *mf*, calavera *m*
liberty [líbɚDi] N libertad *f*; **at —** autorizado
libidinous [lɪbídnəs] ADJ libidinoso
libido [lɪbíDo] N libido *f*
librarian [laɪbrériən] N bibliotecario -ria *mf*
library [láɪbreri] N biblioteca *f*
libretto [lɪbréDo] N libreto *m*
Libya [líbjə] N Libia *f*
Libyan [líbjən] ADJ & N libio -bia *mf*
license [láɪsəns] N (permission) permiso *m*; (driver's permit, poetic freedom) licencia *f*; — **plate** placa *f*, matrícula *f*; VT (issue license to) otorgar una licencia; (give permission) autorizar
licensing authority [láɪsənsɪŋ əθɔ́rɪDi] N autoridad para otorgar licencias *f*
licentious [laɪsénʃəs] ADJ licencioso
lick [lɪk] VT (touch with tongue) lamer (also waves); (thrash) dar una paliza; (defeat) derrotar; N lamida *f*, lengüetazo *m*; (blow) golpe *m*; **not to do a — of work** no mover un dedo
lickety-split [lɪkɪDisplít] ADV en un santiamén
licking [líkɪŋ] N paliza *f*
licorice [líkɚɪʃ] N regaliz *m*
lid [lɪd] N (of a container) tapadera *f*, tapa *f*; (of

eye) párpado *m*; (on prices) tope *m*
lie [laɪ] N (falsehood) mentira *f*, embuste *m*; (orientation of an object) orientación *f*; — **detector** detector de mentiras *m*; **to give the — to** desmentir; VI mentir; **to — one's way out of a situation** salirse de una situación a mentiras; (be buried) yacer; (to be on a flat surface) estar; (to be situated) estar situado; (be horizontal) tumbarse, acostarse; **he's lying in bed** está acostado en la cama; **to — back** recostarse; **to — down** acostarse, tumbarse; **to — in wait** acechar
Liechtenstein [líktənstaɪn] N Liechtenstein *m*
Liechtensteiner [líktənstaɪnɚ] N liechtensteiniano -na *mf*
lien [lin] N gravamen *m*, carga *f*
lieu [lu] ADV LOC **in — of** en vez de
lieutenant [luténənt] N teniente *mf*; — **colonel** teniente coronel *mf*; — **governor** vicegobernador -ora *mf*
life [laɪf] N vida *f*; —**-and-death** de vida o muerte; —**boat** bote de salvamento *m*; — **cycle** ciclo vital *m*; — **expectancy** expectativa de vida *f*; —**guard** salvavidas *mf sg*; — **imprisonment** prisión perpetua *f*; — **insurance** seguro de vida *m*; — **jacket** salvavidas *m sg*; — **of the party** alma de la fiesta *f*; — **preserver** salvavidas *m sg*; — **raft** balsa salvavidas *f*; — **savings** ahorros de toda la vida *m pl*; —**span** duración de la vida *f*; —**style** estilo de vida *m*; —**-support system** (in space) equipo de vida *m*; (in a hospital) máquina corazón-pulmón *f*; —**time** vida *f*; ADJ (relative to life) vital; (for duration of life) vitalicio; ADJ —**like** natural, que parece vivo; —**long** de toda la vida; —**-sized** de tamaño natural
lifeless [láɪflɪs] ADJ (without living things) sin vida; (dead) muerto, sin vida; (fainted) desfallecido; (without liveliness) sin animación
lifer [láɪfɚ] N (prisoner) condenado -da a cadena perpetua *mf*; (soldier) militar de carrera *m*
lift [lɪft] VT (hoist) levantar; (steal) robar; (plagiarize) copiar; VI (disperse) disiparse; (go up) elevarse; N (upward force) empuje *m*; (feeling) mejoría de ánimo *f*; (device for lifting) montacargas *m sg*; **to give someone a —** llevar en coche; *Mex* dar un aventón; —**off** despegue *m*
ligament [lígəmənt] N ligamento *m*
ligature [lígətʃɚ] N ligadura *f*
light [laɪt] N (luminescence) luz *f*; (device) luz *f*, lámpara *f*; (for traffic) semáforo *m*; (perspective) perspectiva *f*; (for cigarettes) fuego *m*; —**-emitting diode** diodo electroluminiscente *m*; —**house** faro *m*; —**-year** año luz *m*; ADJ (well-lighted) claro; (of little weight) ligero, leve; (of clothes) fresco;

Am liviano; — **blue** azul claro *m*; —**-headed** mareado; —**hearted** alegre; — **rain** lluvia fina *f*; —**-skinned** de tez blanca; — **touch** mano delicada *f*; —**weight** de peso ligero; **to make** — **of** restar importancia a; VI/VT (turn on, ignite) encender[se], prender[se]; (provide light, brighten) iluminar[se]; (land on) posarse en; **to** — **up** (cigarette) prender, encender; (face) iluminarse; **to** — **upon** caer sobre

lighten [láɪtn̩] VI/VT (make / become lighter) aligerar[se], alivianar[se]; (brighten) iluminar[se]; — **up!** ¡no tomes las cosas a la tremenda!

lighter [láɪɖɚ] N encendedor *m*

lighting [láɪDɪŋ] N iluminación *f*; (in the street) alumbrado *m*

lightly [láɪtli] ADV (toast) ligeramente; (touch) levemente, suavemente; **I don't take your criticism** — no tomo tus críticas a la ligera

lightness [láɪtnɪs] N (little weight) ligereza *f*, levedad *f*; (brightness) claridad *f*

lightning [láɪtnɪŋ] N relámpago *m*; — **bug** luciérnaga *f*; — **rod** pararrayos *m sg*; **it happened at** — **speed** pasó como rayo; VI relampaguear

likable [láɪkəbəł] ADJ agradable, simpático

like [laɪk] ADV & PREP como; **to feel** — **going** tener ganas de ir; **to look** — **someone** parecerse a alguien; **it looks** — **rain** parece que va a llover; ADJ semejante, parecido; **in** — **manner** del mismo modo; —**-minded** del mismo parecer; N —**s** gustos *m pl*, preferencias *f pl*; VT gustarle a uno; **he** —**s dogs** le gustan los perros; **do whatever you** — haz lo que quieras; CONJ **he talked** — **he was crazy** hablaba como si estuviera loco; **she came** — **you predicted she would** vino, tal como tú pronosticaste; **I'm** —, **"you're crazy"** yo pensé/dije, "estás loco"; INTERJ **he was,** —, **way too old** era como que demasiado viejo

likelihood [láɪklihʊd] N probabilidad *f*; **in all** — **he came** lo más probable es que haya venido

likely [láɪkli] ADJ (probable) probable; (believable) creíble; (promising) prometedor; **John is** — **to win** es probable que gane Juan; ADV probablemente

liken [láɪkən] VT comparar

likeness [láɪknɪs] N (similarity) parecido *m*; (portrait) retrato *m*

likewise [láɪkwaɪz] ADV (the same thing) lo mismo; **we did** — hicimos lo mismo; (similarly) asimismo; (also) también

liking [láɪkɪŋ] N preferencia *f*, gusto *m*

lilac [láɪlək] N lila *f*; ADJ lila

lily [lɪ́li] N lirio *m*, azucena *f*; ADJ —**-white** (very white) blanquísimo; (pure) puro; (for whites only) exclusivamente para blancos

limb [lɪm] N (branch) rama *f*; (appendage) miembro *m*

limber [lɪ́mbɚ] ADJ flexible; VT hacer flexible; VI **to** — **up** estirarse

lime [laɪm] N (mineral) cal *f*; (fruit, color) lima *f*; —**light** candilejas *f pl*; **in the** —**light** en el candelero; —**stone** piedra caliza *f*; — **tree** limero *m*

limit [lɪ́mɪt] N límite *m*; **to the** — al máximo; VT limitar

limitation [lɪmɪtéʃən] N limitación *f*

limitless [lɪ́mɪtlɪs] ADJ ilimitado

limousine [lɪ́məzin] N limusina *f*

limp [lɪmp] N cojera *f*, renguera *f*; VI cojear, renguear, renquear; ADJ (body) flácido; (plants) mustio

limpid [lɪ́mpɪd] ADJ límpido

line [laɪn] N (bus route, telephone connection) línea *f*; (of words) renglón *m*, línea *f*; (row) raya *f*, hilera *f*; (cord) cuerda *f*; (persons waiting) cola *f*, fila *f*; (business) ramo *m*; (wrinkle) arruga *f*; (boundary) límite *m*; — **drive** (baseball) línea *f*; — **of credit** línea de crédito *f*; — **of scrimmage** línea de golpeo *f*; —**s** (in a play) parte *f*; —**sman** juez -eza de línea *mf*; —**up** hilera de personas *f*; (sports) alineación *f*; **drop me a** — escríbeme unas líneas; **out of** — irrespetuoso; **to get in** — hacer cola; VI/VT (border) alinear, bordear; (put in a lining) forrar; **to** — **up** alinear[se]; ADJ **off-** — fuera de línea; **on-** — en línea

lineage [lɪ́niidʒ] N linaje *m*, estirpe *f*

linear [lɪ́niɚ] ADJ lineal

lined [laɪnd] ADJ (with lines) rayado; (with a lining) forrado

linen [lɪ́nɪn] N (fabric) lino *m*; (bedclothes) ropa blanca *f*

liner [láɪnɚ] N (ocean) transatlántico *m*; (air) avión comercial *m*; (eye) delineador *m*

linger [lɪ́ŋɡɚ] VI (stay) quedarse, demorarse; (persist) persistir; (saunter) rezagarse; (contemplate) detenerse; (delay death) aguantar

lingerie [lɑnʒəré] N lencería *f*

linguist [lɪ́ŋɡwɪst] N lingüista *mf*

linguistics [lɪŋɡwɪ́stɪks] N lingüística *f*

liniment [lɪ́nəmənt] N linimento *m*

lining [láɪnɪŋ] N forro *m*; **every cloud has a silver** — no hay mal que por bien no venga

link [lɪŋk] N (of a chain) eslabón *m*; (bond, tie) vínculo *m*; (rail, radio connection) enlace *m*; (computer) enlace *m*, vínculo *m*; VI/VT enlazar[se], conectar[se]; (on a computer) vincular

linnet [lɪ́nɪt] N pardillo *m*

linoleum [lɪnóliəm] N linóleo *m*

linseed [lɪ́nsid] N linaza *f*; — **oil** aceite de linaza *m*

lint [lɪnt] N pelusa *f*

lion [láɪən] N león m; —**'s share** la parte del león
lioness [láɪənɪs] N leona f
lip [lɪp] N labio m; (of a pitcher) borde m; — **balm** crema para labios f; —**stick** lápiz de labios m, carmín m; **don't give me no** —! no me contestes; VI **to** —**read** leer los labios
liposuction [láɪpɔsʌkʃən] N liposucción f
liqueur [lɪkɟ] N licor m
liquid [líkwɪd] ADJ líquido; — **assets** activo líquido m; — **measure** medida para líquidos f; N líquido m
liquidate [líkwɪdet] VI/VT liquidar
liquidation [lɪkwɪdéʃən] N liquidación f
liquidity [lɪkwídɪDi] N liquidez f
liquor [líkɚ] N bebida espirituosa f
lira [lírə] N lira f
lisp [lɪsp] N ceceo m; VI cecear
list [lɪst] N (series of items) lista f; (of a ship) escora f; — **price** precio de lista m; — **server** servidor de lista m; VT (make a list) hacer una lista de; VI (lean) escorar; **this chair** —**s for two hundred dollars** esta silla está a doscientos dólares
listen [lísən] VI/VT (hear) escuchar, oír; (heed) escuchar, prestar atención; **to** — **in** (on radio) sintonizar; (eavesdrop) escuchar a hurtadillas
listener [lísənɚ] N oyente mf; **radio** — radioescucha mf, oyente mf
listing [lístɪŋ] N listado m
listless [lístlɪs] ADJ lánguido
lit [lɪt] ADJ (provided with light) iluminado; (tipsy) alegre, alumbrado
lit [lɪt] see **light**
literacy [líDɚəsi] N (action of making literate) alfabetización f; (rate) alfabetismo m
literal [líDɚəl] ADJ literal
literary [líDɚɛri] ADJ literario
literate [líDɚɪt] ADJ (who can read and write) alfabeto; (erudite) erudito, letrado; **he's barely** — apenas sabe leer y escribir
literature [líDɚətʃɚ] N literatura f; (handbills) impresos m pl, folletos m pl; **the scientific** — la literatura científica
lithium [líθiəm] N litio m; —**-ion battery** batería de iones de litio f
Lithuania [lɪθuéniə] N Lituania f
Lithuanian [lɪθuéniən] ADJ & N lituano -na mf
litigant [líDɪgənt] N litigante mf
litigation [lɪDɪgéʃən] N litigio m, pleito m
litter [líDɚ] N (young animals) camada f, cría f; (stretcher) camilla f; (straw) cama de paja para animales f; (trash) basura f; (for cats) arena higiénica f; VI/VT (dirty) ensuciar; (strew) esparcir; VI (give birth) parir
little [líDl] ADJ (small) pequeño, chico; (not much) poco; — **brother** hermano menor m, hermanito m; — **finger** [dedo] meñique m; — **pig** puerquito m; **a** — **coffee** un poco de café; **a** — **while** un ratito, un poco; ADV & N poco;

— **by** — poco a poco
livable [lívəbəl] ADJ funcional
live[1] [lɪv] VI/VT vivir; **to** — **together** convivir; **to** — **up to** cumplir; **to** — **it up** tirar la casa por la ventana; **long** — **the king!** ¡viva el rey! ADJ **all the** —**long day** todo el santo día
live[2] [laɪv] ADJ vivo; (ammunition) cargado; — **coal** ascua encendida f; — **oak** roble de Virginia m; —**stock** ganado m, ganadería f; — **wire** (electric) cable cargado m; (person) persona vivaz f; **before a** — **audience** en vivo; —**-in** con cama; ADV en vivo y en directo
livelihood [láɪvlihʊd] N sustento m
liveliness [láɪvlinɪs] N viveza f, animación f
lively [láɪvli] ADJ (party) animado; (person) vivaz, avispado; ADV con animación
liver [lívɚ] N hígado m
livid [lívɪd] ADJ (pallid, bluish) lívido; (angry) furibundo
living [lívɪŋ] N (life) vida f; — **expenses** gastos de subsistencia m pl; — **room** sala f, living m; — **together** cohabitación f; — **wage** salario de subsistencia m; — **will** documento de instrucciones previas m, documento de voluntad anticipada m; **to earn/make a** — ganarse la vida; **the** — los vivos; ADJ vivo, viviente
lizard [lízɚd] N lagartija f
llama [lámə] N llama f
load [lod] N (supported mass) carga f; (weight) peso m; (ship cargo) cargamento m; **no-** — **fund** fondo sin comisión de entrada m; —**s of** montones de; VI/VT cargar; **to** — **down** colmar; **to** — **oneself down** agobiarse
loaf [lof] N hogaza de pan f, pan m; VI holgar, holgazanear, haraganear
loafer [lófɚ] N (idler) holgazán -ana mf, haragán -ana mf, gandul -la mf; (shoe) mocasín m
loan [lon] N préstamo m; (to a government) empréstito m; — **application** solicitud de préstamo f; — **guarantee** garantía de préstamo f; — **officer** funcionario -ria de préstamos m; — **shark** usurero -ra mf; —**word** préstamo m; VI/VT prestar
loath [loθ] ADJ renuente; **to be** — **to** ser renuente a
loathe [loð] VT aborrecer
loathsome [lóðsəm] ADJ repugnante, abominable
lob [lɑb] VT tirar por lo alto; N (tennis) globo m
lobby [lábi] N (vestibule) vestíbulo m; (special interest) grupo de presión m, lobby m; VI/VT (influence) presionar
lobbyist [lábiɪst] N representante de un grupo de presión mf
lobe [lob] N lóbulo m
lobotomy [ləbáDəmi] N lobotomía f
lobster [lábstɚ] N langosta f

local [lókəł] ADJ local; — **bus** (computer) vía de transmisión local *f*; — **printer** impresora local *f*; — **train** tren de cercanías *m*
localize [lókəlaɪz] VT localizar
locate [lóket] VI/VT (establish in a place) situar, ubicar; (find) localizar; VI (settle) radicarse, establecerse
location [lokéʃən] N (position) ubicación *f*, emplazamiento *m*; (finding) localización *f*; **on** — en exteriores
lock [lɑk] N (door) cerradura *f*; (canal) esclusa *f*; (firearms, wrestling) llave *f*; (of hair) mecha *f*, mechón *m*; —**jaw** tétanos *m sg*; —**out** cierre patronal *m*; —**smith** cerrajero -ra *mf*; **to have a — on the award** tener asegurado el premio; VI/VT cerrar con llave; (make immovable) trabar[se]; **to — in** encerrar; **to — out** dejar afuera; **to — up** (door) cerrar con llave; (animal) encerrar; (prisoner) encarcelar; (valuables) poner bajo llave
locker [lákə-] N (for athletic equipment) casillero *m*; (for frozen food) cámara frigorífica *f*; — **room** vestuario *m*
locket [lákɪt] N relicario *m*, guardapelo *m*
locomotive [lokəmóDɪv] N locomotora *f*
locust [lókəst] N langosta *f*; — **tree** algarrobo *m*
lodge [lɑdʒ] N (of fraternal organization) logia *f*; (cabin) cabaña *f*; (hotel) posada *f*, mesón *m*; VI/VT alojar[se], hospedar[se]; **to — a complaint** presentar una queja
lodger [lɑ́dʒə-] N inquilino -na *mf*
lodging [lɑ́dʒɪŋ] N alojamiento *m*, hospedaje *m*, albergue *m*
loft [lɔft] N (attic) desván *m*; (for choir) coro *m*; (for hay) pajar *m*; VT tirar por lo alto
lofty [lɔ́fti] ADJ elevado, encumbrado
log [lɑg] N (wood) leño *m*, madero *m*, rollizo *m*; (ship record) cuaderno de bitácora *m*; (record of activity) diario *m*; (on a computer) registro *m*; — **cabin** cabaña de troncos *f*; VI/VT (cut trees) cortar; —**in name** nombre de acceso *m*; VT (write down) anotar; **to — in** ingresar al sistema; **to — off/out** finalizar una sesión; VT registrar una acción
logarithm [lágərɪðəm] N logaritmo *m*
logic [lɑ́dʒɪk] N lógica *f*; — **board** placa lógica *f*
logical [lɑ́dʒɪkəł] ADJ lógico
logically [lɑ́dʒɪkli] ADV lógicamente
logistics [lədʒístɪks] N logística *f*
loin [lɔɪn] N ijada *f*; (in animals) ijar *m*; (cut of meat) lomo *m*; —**s** entrañas *f pl*
loiter [lɔ́ɪDə-] VI (idly) holgazanear; (with ill intent) merodear; **to — behind** rezagarse
loll [lɑł] VI arrellanarse
lollipop [lálɪpɑp] N *Sp* pirulí *m*; *Mex* paleta *f*; *RP* chupetín *m*
lone [lon] ADJ (solitary) solitario; (only) único
loneliness [lónlinɪs] N soledad *f*
lonely [lónli] ADJ solo

lonesome [lónsəm] ADJ solo
long [lɔŋ] ADJ largo; **a — way from home** lejos de casa; **to work — hours** trabajar muchas horas; — **distance** de larga distancia; — **division** división de más de una cifra *f*; —**hand** letra manuscrita *f*; — **johns** calzoncillos largos *m pl*; — **jump** salto largo *m*; —**-lasting** duradero, perdurable; —**-lived** (batteries) duradero; (people) longevo; —**-range** (missiles) de largo alcance; (plans) a largo plazo; —**shoreman** estibador *m*; —**-suffering** sufrido; —**-term** a largo plazo; —**-term care** atención médica a largo plazo *f*; —**time friend** viejo amigo; — **underwear** calzoncillo largo *m*; —**-winded** verborrágico, palabrero; **it's a — shot** es muy improbable; ADV mucho, mucho tiempo; — **ago** hace mucho tiempo; — **before** mucho antes; — **live . . . !** ¡viva . . . ! **all winter** — todo el invierno; **how — did he stay?** ¿cuánto tiempo se quedó? **not for** — no por mucho tiempo; **so** — ! ¡hasta luego! **to be — in coming** tardar en venir; **three meters** — tres metros de largo; **will you be** —**?** ¿tardarás mucho? **the whole day** — todo el santo día; VI **to — for** anhelar
longer [lɔ́ŋgə-] ADJ más largo; ADV más; **no** — ya no; **how much** —**?** ¿hasta cuándo?
longevity [lɑndʒévɪDi] N longevidad *f*
longing [lɔ́ŋɪŋ] N anhelo *m*; ADJ anhelante
longitude [lɑ́ndʒɪtud] N longitud *f*
look [lʊk] VI (see) mirar; (seem) parecer; **it —s good on you** te queda bien, te luce; **to — after** atender, cuidar; **to — alike** parecerse; **to — down on someone** despreciar a alguien; **to — for** (search for) buscar; (anticipate) esperar; **I — forward to it** lo espero con ansia, me da mucha ilusión; **to — into** investigar; **she —s her age** aparenta la edad que tiene; **to — out on** dar a, tener vista a; **to — out of** asomarse a; — **out!** ¡cuidado! **to — over** dar un vistazo a; **to — up** (upward) levantar la vista; (in a directory) buscar; **to — up to** admirar; N (gaze) mirada *f*; (examination) vistazo *m*; —**-alike** doble *mf*; —**out** (person) vigía *mf*; (place) mirador *m*, vigía *f*; **to be on the** —**out** estar alerta; —**s** aspecto *m*, pinta *f*; **good** —**s** belleza *f*
looking glass [lʊ́kɪŋglæs] N espejo *m*
loom [lum] N telar *m*; VI (appear indistinctly) dibujarse; (threaten) cernerse
loon [lún] N (bird) somorgujo *m*; (person) chiflado -da *mf*
loony [lúni] ADJ chiflado
loop [lup] N (for fastening) presilla *f*; (in a rope) lazo *m*; (of a flight) rizo *m*; (electric) circuito cerrado *m*; (computer programming, ice-skating) bucle *m*; —**hole** escapatoria *f*; **in the** — al corriente, al tanto de lo que pasa; VI

(make a loop) hacer un lazo; (curve around) serpentear; (loop the loop) rizar el rizo; VT enlazar

loose [lus] ADJ (free) suelto; (not tight) flojo; (approximate) libre; (unfettered) desatado; (immoral) disoluto; (promiscuous) fácil; — **cannon** mono con una metralleta *m*; — **change** suelto *m*, cambio *m*; — **end** cabo suelto *m*; —-**fitting** holgado; —-**jointed** de articulaciones flexibles; —-**leaf** [de] hojas sueltas; **to let** — soltar; VT desatar, soltar

loosen [lúsən] VI/VT (untie) soltar[se], desatar; (make/become less tight/dense/strict) aflojar[se]

looseness [lúsnɪs] N (of skin) flojedad *f*; (of morals) relajamiento *m*; (of clothing) holgura *f*; (of soil) friabilidad *f*; (of translation) lo libre

loot [lut] N botín *m*; VI/VT saquear

lop [lɑp] VT (cut) cortar; (eliminate) eliminar; VI caer[se]; ADJ —**sided** (leaning to one side) ladeado; (unbalanced) desequilibrado; (listing) escorado

lope [lop] VI correr a pasos largos

loquacious [lokwéʃəs] ADJ locuaz

loquat [lókwɑt] N níspero *m*

lord [lɔrd] N señor *m*; (God) Señor *m*; (British title) lord *m*; —**'s Prayer** Padrenuestro *m*; **my** —! ¡Dios mío! VI **to** — **it over someone** tratarle a alguien con arrogancia

lordly [lɔ́rdli] ADJ (kingly) señorial; (haughty) altivo

lordship [lɔ́rdʃɪp] N (title) señoría *f*; (power) señorío *m*

lore [lɔr] N saber *m*

lose [luz] VI/VT perder; (a pursuer) dejar atrás; **to** — **sight of** perder de vista; **to** — **oneself in thought** ensimismarse

loser [lúzɚ] N perdedor -ora *mf*

loss [lɔs] N (destruction) pérdida *f*; (misplacement) pérdida *f*, extravío *m*; (sports) derrota *f*; **to be at a** — no saber qué hacer; **to sell at a** — vender con pérdida; —**es** bajas *f pl*

lost [lɔst] ADJ perdido; — **cause** caso perdido *m*; — **in thought** absorto; **to get** — perderse, extraviarse

lost [lɔst] *see* lose

lot [lɑt] N (parcel) lote *m*; (fate) suerte *f*, destino *m*; (piece of land) solar *m*, terreno *m*; **the** — todo; **a** — **of /** —**s of** mucho[s]; **a** — **of money** mucho dinero; **by** — al azar; **to draw** —**s** echar suertes; **to fall to one's** — caerle en suerte a uno; ADV **a** — **better** mucho mejor

lotion [lóʃən] N loción *f*

lottery [lɑ́Dəri] N lotería *f*

loud [laud] ADJ (noisy) ruidoso; (strong) fuerte; (ostentatious) chillón; —**speaker** altavoz *m*, altoparlante *m*; —**mouth** bocazas *mf sg*; ADV fuerte, alto

Lou Gehrig's disease [lugɛ́rɪgz dɪzíz] N enfermedad de Lou Gehrig *f*

lounge [laundʒ] VI repantigarse, arrellanarse; N (waiting room) sala de espera *f*; (room in bar) salón *m*; (divan) diván *m*; — **chair** diván *m*

louse [laus] N piojo *m*

lousy [láuzi] ADJ (infested with lice) piojoso; (contemptible) despreciable; (poorly done) pésimo

lout [laut] N bruto *m*

lovable [lʌ́vəbəł] ADJ adorable

love [lʌv] N (affection) amor *m*; (fondness) afición *f*; (in tennis) nada *f*; — **affair** aventura *f*, amorío *m*; — **at first sight** amor a primera vista *m*, flechazo *m*; — **life** vida sentimental *f*; — **seat** confidente *m*; **books were her great** — los libros fueron su gran pasión; **to be in** — estar enamorado; **to fall in** — **with** enamorarse de; **to make** — **to** hacerle el amor a; VI/VT amar, querer; **I** — **to eat apples** me encanta comer manzanas

loveliness [lʌ́vlinɪs] N (beauty) hermosura *f*; (charm) encanto *m*

lovely [lʌ́vli] ADJ (beautiful) hermoso; (charming) encantador; (pleasant) ameno

lover [lʌ́vɚ] N (sexually involved) amante *mf*; (in love) enamorado -da *mf*, amante *mf*; (interested in) aficionado -da *mf*

loving [lʌ́vɪŋ] ADJ cariñoso, afectuoso

low [lo] ADJ (not high) bajo; (base) vil; (humble) humilde; (downcast) abatido; (deep in pitch) grave; — **beam** luces cortas *f pl*; —**brow** poco culto; —-**budget** de bajo presupuesto; —-**cal** de bajas calorías; —-**cost** de bajo precio; —**down** verdad *f*; —-**end** de baja calidad; — **gear** primera marcha *f*; —-**grade** (inferior) inferior; (low) bajo; —-**income** de bajos ingresos; —-**key** tranquilo; —**land** tierra baja *f*; —-**level** de bajo nivel; —**life** canalla *f*; — **quality** baja calidad *f*; —-**tech** sencillo; — **tide** bajamar *f*, marea baja *f*; **dress with a** — **neck** vestido escotado *m*; **to be** — **on something** estar escaso de algo; **to be in** — **spirits** estar abatido/desanimado; ADV bajo; **to buy** — comprar barato; N (sound of a cow) mugido *m*; VI mugir

lower [lóɚ] VI/VT bajar; (prices) rebajar; (flag, sail) arriar; ADJ más bajo, inferior; —**case** minúscula *f*; — **house** cámara de diputados *f*

lowliness [lólinɪs] N humildad *f*

lowly [lóli] ADJ humilde

loyal [lɔ́ɪəł] ADJ leal

loyalty [lɔ́ɪəłti] N lealtad *f*

LSD [**lysergic acid diethylamide**] [ɛ́łɛsdí] N LSD *m*

lubricant [lúbrɪkənt] ADJ & N lubricante *m*

lubricate [lúbrɪket] VI/VT lubricar

lucid [lúsɪd] ADJ lúcido

lucidity [lusíDIDi] N lucidez *f*

luck [lʌk] N suerte f; **in —** de suerte; **to be out of —** estar de mala suerte; VI **to — into** conseguir por un golpe de suerte; **to — out** tener suerte

luckily [lʌkəli] ADV afortunadamente

lucky [lʌki] ADJ afortunado; **— charm** amuleto de la suerte m; **to be —** tener suerte

lucrative [lúkrəDIV] ADJ lucrativo

ludicrous [lúDIkrəs] ADJ ridículo

lug [lʌg] VT acarrear

luggage [lʌgɪdʒ] N equipaje m; **— rack** rejilla f

lukewarm [lúkwɔrm] ADJ (not warm or cold) tibio; (indifferent) indiferente

lull [lʌl] VT (put to sleep) arrullar; VI/VT (soothe) calmar[se]; N (calm) calma f, tregua f; (sound) arrullo m

lullaby [lʌləbaɪ] N canción de cuna f, nana f

lumbago [lʌmbégo] N lumbago m

lumbar [lʌmbɑr] ADJ lumbar

lumber [lʌmbɚ] N madera f; **—jack** leñador m; **—man** maderero m; **— mill** aserradero m; **—yard** almacén de maderas m; VI/VT (cut trees) talar; (move heavily) moverse pesadamente; (make a low noise) tronar

luminous [lúmiənəs] ADJ luminoso

lump [lʌmp] N (in breast) bulto m; (in sauce) grumo m; (in throat) nudo m; (of coal) trozo m; (of food) plasta f; (on head) chichón m; (of sugar) terrón m; **to take one's —s** recibir palos; **— sum** pago global m; VT juntar; VI agrumarse

lumpectomy [lʌmpéktəmi] N tumorectomía f

lumpy [lʌmpi] ADJ grumoso

lunar [lúnɚ] ADJ lunar; **— eclipse** eclipse lunar m

lunatic [lúnətɪk] ADJ & N lunático -ca mf, loco -ca mf; **— fringe** extremistas mf pl

lunch [lʌntʃ] N comida f, almuerzo m; **—time** hora de comer/almorzar f; **out to —** (having lunch) almorzando; (crazy) en la luna; VI comer, almorzar

lung [lʌŋ] N pulmón m

lunge [lʌndʒ] N arremetida f; VI arremeter, abalanzarse; **to — at** arremeter contra, abalanzarse sobre

lupus [lúpəs] N lupus m

lurch [lɝtʃ] N tambaleo m; **to give a —** tambalearse; **to leave someone in the —** dejar a alguien en la estacada; VI tambalearse, dar quinquinazos

lure [lʊr] N (thing that attracts) atractivo m, gancho m; (in hunting) señuelo m; (in fishing) cebo m; VT atraer, seducir

lurid [lúrɪd] ADJ (gruesome) sangriento; (shocking) escabroso

lurk [lɝk] VI (lie in wait) estar en acecho, acechar; (move furtively) moverse furtivamente

luscious [lʌʃəs] ADJ (delicious) exquisito, delicioso; (sexy) voluptuoso

lust [lʌst] N (sexual desire) lujuria f, lascivia f; (craving) deseo m, ansia f; VI desear; **to — after** codiciar

luster [lʌstɚ] N lustre m, brillo m

lustful [lʌstfəl] ADJ lujurioso

lusty [lʌsti] ADJ (robust) robusto; (full of lust) lujurioso

Luxembourg [lʌksəmbɝg] N Luxemburgo m

Luxembourger [lʌksəmbɝgɚ] N luxemburgués -esa mf

Luxembourgian [lʌksəmbɝgiən] ADJ luxemburgués

luxurious [lʌgʒúriəs] ADJ (characterized by luxury) lujoso; (luxuriant) exuberante

luxury [lʌgʒəri] N lujo m; **— tax** impuesto suntuario m; ADJ de lujo

lye [laɪ] N lejía f

lying [láiɪŋ] ADJ mentiroso

Lyme disease [láɪm dɪziz] N enfermedad de Lyme f

lymph [lɪmf] N linfa f; **— node** nodo linfático m

lymphocyte [lɪmfəsaɪt] N linfocito m

lymphoma [lɪmfómə] N linfoma m

lynch [lɪntʃ] VT linchar

lynx [lɪŋks] N lince m

lyre [laɪr] N lira f

lyric [lírɪk] N poema lírico m; **— poetry** lírica f; **—s** letra f; ADJ lírico

lyrical [lírɪkəl] ADJ lírico

lyricism [lírɪsɪzəm] N lirismo m

Mm

ma'am |mæm| N señora f

Macao [məkáu] N Macao m

macaroni [mækəróni] N macarrones m pl

Macedonia [mæsɪdóniə] N Macedonia f

Macedonian [mæsɪdóniən] ADJ & N macedonio -nia mf

machine [məʃín] N máquina f; (of government) maquinaria f, aparato m; **— gun** (not portable) ametralladora f; (portable) metralleta f; **— language** lenguaje de máquina m, lenguaje máquina m; ADJ **—-made** hecho a máquina; VT trabajar a máquina

machinery [məʃínəri] N maquinaria f

machinist [məʃínɪst] N maquinista mf, operario -ria mf

mackerel [mækɚəl] N caballa f

macro [mækro] N serie de instrucciones f

mad [mæd] ADJ (crazy) loco; (angry) rabioso, enojado; (hydrophobic) rabioso; **— cow disease** encefalopatía espongiforme bovina f, enfermedad de las vacas locas f; **—man**

loco *m*; **to be — about someone** estar loco por alguien; **to drive —** enloquecer, volver loco; **to get —** enojarse; **to go —** volverse loco, enloquecerse; **like —** como loco

Madagascan [mædəgǽskən] ADJ & N malgache *mf*

Madagascar [mædəgǽskɑr] N Madagascar *m*

madam [mǽɒəm] N (title) señora *f*; (of a brothel) madama *f*

maddening [mǽdnɪŋ] ADJ enloquecedor

made [med] ADJ **—-to-measure** hecho a la medida; **—-to-order** hecho por encargo; **—-up** (invented) inventado, falso; (wearing makeup) maquillado; **to be — of** ser de; **to have something —** mandar hacer algo; **I'm a — man** estoy hecho; **to have it —** estar hecho

made [med] *see* make

madness [mǽdnɪs] N (insanity) locura *f*; (anger) rabia *f*

Mafia [máfiə] N mafia *f*

mafioso [mɑfióso] N mafioso *m*

magazine [mǽgəzin] N (publication) revista *f*; (room for ammunition) polvorín *m*; (part of gun) cargador *m*

magic [mǽdʒɪk] N magia *f*; ADJ mágico; **— bullet** panacea *f*; **— wand** varita mágica *f*

magical [mǽdʒɪkəł] ADJ mágico

magician [mədʒíʃən] N (person adept at magic) mágico -ca *mf*; (person adept at finances) mago -ga *mf*

magistrate [mǽdʒɪstret] N magistrado -da *mf*

magma [mǽgmə] N magma *m*

magnanimous [mægnǽnəməs] ADJ magnánimo

magnate [mǽgnet] N magnate *m*

magnesia [mægnízə] N magnesia *f*

magnesium [mægníziəm] N magnesio *m*

magnet [mǽgnɪt] N imán *m*

magnetic [mægnéɒɪk] ADJ magnético; **— pole** polo magnético *m*; **— resonance imaging** imagen por resonancia magnética *f*; **— tape** cinta magnetofónica *f*

magnetism [mǽgnɪtɪzəm] N magnetismo *m*

magnetize [mǽgnɪtaɪz] VT magnetizar, imantar

magnificence [mægnífɪsəns] N magnificencia *f*

magnificent [mægnífɪsənt] ADJ magnífico

magnify [mǽgnɪfaɪ] VT (to make larger) aumentar; (to make louder) amplificar; (to exaggerate) exagerar, magnificar

magnitude [mǽgnɪtud] N magnitud *f*

magnolia [mægnóljə] N (flower) magnolia *f*; (tree) magnolio *m*

magpie [mǽgpaɪ] N urraca *f* (also hoarder)

mahogany [məhágəni] N caoba *f*

maid [med] N criada *f*, sirvienta *f*; (in hotel) camarera *f*; **— of honor** dama de honor *f*

maiden [médṇ] N *lit* doncella *f*, virgen *f*; **— voyage** primer viaje *m*; **— name** nombre de

soltera *m*

mail [meł] N correo *m*; (electronic) mensaje *m*; (of metal) malla *f*; **—bag** cartera *f*; **—box** buzón *m*; **—man** cartero *m*; **— order** pedido por correo *m*; **— order business** negocio de ventas por correo *m*; VT echar al correo; **—ing list** lista de correo *f*

maim [mem] VT mutilar

main [men] ADJ principal; **— office** oficina central *f*; N (pipe) cañería principal *f*; (sea) alta mar *f*; **—frame** *Sp* ordenador central *m*, *Am* computadora central *f*; **—land** continente *m*; **—spring** muelle real *m*; **—stream** tendencia mayoritaria *f*; **—stream engineering** ingeniería conforme a la corriente dominante *f*; **—stay** pilar *m*, puntal *m*; **— street** calle principal *f*

mainly [ménli] ADV principalmente, fundamentalmente

maintain [mentén] VT (repair, support) mantener; (assert) afirmar

maintenance [méntnəns] N (repairs) mantenimiento *m*; (monetary support) manutención *f*; **— cost** costo de mantenimiento *m*

maize [mez] N maíz *m*

majestic [mədʒéstɪk] ADJ majestuoso

majesty [mǽdʒɪsti] N majestad *f*; **Your —** Su Majestad

major [médʒɚ] ADJ (greater) mayor, más grande; (large) grande; **— key** mayor *m*; N (military rank) comandante *m*; (field of study) especialidad *f*, carrera *f*; **— league** liga mayor *f*; VI especializarse

majority [mədʒɔ́rɪɒi] N (greater number) mayoría *f*; (age) mayoría de edad *f*; **— ownership** propiedad mayoritaria *f*; **the —** el grueso

make [mek] VT (do) hacer; (create) fabricar; (cause) causar; (earn) ganar; (a speech) pronunciar; **to — a clean breast of** sacarse del pecho; **to — a decision** tomar una decisión; **to — a living** ganarse la vida; **to — a train** llegar a tiempo para tomar un tren; **to — a turn** girar, doblar; **to — away with** fugarse con; **to — believe** hacer de cuenta que; **to — out** (see) vislumbrar, divisar; (read) descifrar; (kiss) *Sp* morrear; *Am* besuquearse; **to — possible** posibilitar; **to — too much of** exagerar; **to — up** (a story) inventar; (after a quarrel) hacer las paces; (a loss) recuperar; (one's face) maquillarse; (one's mind) decidirse; **to — up for** compensar; **two plus two —s four** dos y dos son cuatro; **what do you — of that?** ¿cómo interpretas eso? **I'll — it up to you** te voy a compensar por eso; **you'll — a good teacher** vas a ser un buen profesor; N (brand) marca *f*; **—-up** (composition)

composición *f*; (character) carácter *m*;
(cosmetics) maquillaje *m*; ADJ **—shift**
provisional
maker [mékɚ] N (creator) creador -ora *mf*,
hacedor -ora *mf*; (manufacturer) fabricante *m*
makings [mékɪŋz] N (potential) potencial *m*;
(ingredients) ingredientes *m pl*
maladjusted [mælədʒʌ́stɪd] ADJ inadaptado
malady [mǽlədi] N mal *m*
malaise [məléz] N malestar *m*
malaria [məlériə] N malaria *f*, paludismo *m*
Malawi [məláwi] N Malawi *m*
Malawian [məláwiən] ADJ & N malawiano -na
mf
Malaysia [məléʒə] N Malasia *f*
Malaysian [məléʒən] ADJ & N malasio -sia *mf*
malcontent [mǽlkəntɛnt] ADJ & N descontento
-ta *mf*
Maldives [mɔ́ldaɪvz] N Maldivas *f pl*
Maldivian [mɔldíviən] ADJ & N maldivo -va *mf*
male [meł] ADJ (animal, plant) macho; (person)
varón; (trait) masculino; N (animal, plant)
macho *m*; (person) varón *m*
malevolent [məlévələnt] ADJ malévolo
malformation [mælfɔrméʃən] N malformación *f*
malfunction [mælfʌ́ŋkʃən] N funcionamiento
defectuoso *m*; VI funcionar mal
Mali [máli] N Malí *m*
Malian [máliən] ADJ & N malí *mf*
malice [mǽlɪs] N malicia *f*; **with —**
aforethought con premeditación y alevosía
malicious [məlíʃəs] ADJ malicioso
malign [məláɪn] VT calumniar, difamar
malignancy [məlígnənsi] N (quality)
malignidad *f*; (tumor) tumor maligno *m*
malignant [məlígnənt] ADJ maligno
mall [mɔł] N (closed street) paseo *m*; (enclosed
shopping area) galería *f*, centro comercial *m*
mallet [mǽlɪt] N mazo *m*
malnourished [mælnɚ́rɪʃt] ADJ desnutrido
malnutrition [mælnutríʃən] N desnutrición *f*
malpractice [mælprǽktɪs] N negligencia *f*, mala
práctica *f*
malt [mɔłt] N malta *f*; **—ed milk** leche
malteada *f*
Malta [mɔ́łtə] N Malta *f*
Maltese [mɔłtíz] ADJ & N maltés -esa *mf*
mama, mamma [mámə] N mamá *f*; **—'s boy**
nene de mamá *m*
mammal [mǽməł] N mamífero *m*
mammary [mǽməri] ADJ mamario
mammography [mæmágrəfi] N mamografía *f*
mammoth [mǽməθ] ADJ enorme; N mamut *m*
man [mæn] N hombre *m*; (servant) criado *m*; (in
games) pieza *f*, ficha *f*; **— and wife** marido y
mujer; **—hunt** persecución *f*; **—kind**
humanidad *f*; **—-of-war** (ship) buque de
guerra *m*; (jellyfish) medusa *f*; **—power** (for
work) mano de obra *f*; **—slaughter**

(accidental) homicidio culposo *m*, homicidio
involuntario *m*; (unpremeditated) homicidio
sin premeditación *m*; **—-to-— defense**
defensa al hombre *f*, defensa de asignación *f*,
defensa individual *f*; **every — for himself**
cada cual para sí; **to a —** unánimamente; ADJ
—-eating que come carne humana; **—-
made** (fiber) sintético; (lake) artificial;
INTERJ ¡hombre! VT (a fort) guarnecer; (a
ship) tripular; **to —handle** violentar
manage [mǽnɪdʒ] VT (succeed in) conseguir,
lograr; (direct) dirigir, administrar,
gestionar; (maneuver) manejar; VI **to —
without help** arreglárselas sin ayuda
manageable [mǽnɪdʒəbəł] ADJ manejable;
(hair) dócil
managed [mǽnɪdʒd] ADJ **— care** plan de salud
administrado *m*; **— funds** fondos
administrados *m pl*
management [mǽnɪdʒmənt] N (act of
managing) dirección *f*, gestión *f*; (persons
controlling a business) gerencia *f*, patronal *f*,
gestión *f*; (area of study) empresariales *f pl*
manager [mǽnɪdʒɚ] N (of a store) gerente -ta
mf; (of a company) director -ora *mf*
mandate [mǽndet] N mandato *m*; VT decretar
mandatory [mǽndətɔri] ADJ obligatorio
mandolin [mǽndəlɪn] N mandolina *f*
mane [men] N (of a lion) melena *f*; (of a horse)
crin *f*
maneuver [mənúvɚ] N maniobra *f*; VI/VT
maniobrar
manganese [mǽŋgəniz] N manganeso *m*
mange [mendʒ] N sarna *f*, roña *f*
manger [méndʒɚ] N pesebre *m*
mangle [mǽŋgəł] VT (mutilate) magullar,
mutilar; (ruin) estropear
mango [mǽŋgo] N mango *m*
mangrove [mǽŋgrov] N mangle *m*
mangy [méndʒi] ADJ sarnoso
manhood [mǽnhʊd] N virilidad *f*; (male
genitals) miembro viril *m*; (men collectively)
hombres *m pl*; (adult age) edad adulta *f*
mania [méniə] N manía *f*
maniac [méniæk] N maníaco -ca *mf*, maniaco -ca
mf
maniacal [mənáɪəkəł] ADJ maníaco
manic-depressive [mǽnɪkdɪprésɪv] ADJ
maniaco-depresivo
manicure [mǽnɪkjʊr] N manicura *f*; VT
manicurar
manifest [mǽnəfɛst] ADJ manifiesto; N (list of
cargo) manifiesto *m*, hoja de ruta *f*; VT (show)
manifestar, poner de manifiesto; (express)
declarar
manifestation [mænəfɛstéʃən] N
manifestación *f*
manifesto [mænɪfésto] N manifiesto *m*
manifold [mǽnəfołd] ADJ diverso; N (on a

motor) colector *m*
manila [mənílə] N abacá *m*; — **envelope** sobre
manila *m*
manioc [mǽniak] N mandioca*f*, yuca*f*
manipulate [mənípjəlet] VT manipular
manipulation [mənɪpjəléʃən] N manipulación*f*
manlike [mǽnlaɪk] ADJ (manly) varonil;
(mannish) hombruna; (resembling a human)
de hombre
manliness [mǽnlinɪs] N virilidad*f*
manly [mǽnli] ADJ varonil, viril
manner [mǽnə-] N (way) manera*f*, modo *m*,
forma*f*; (type) tipo *m*; (outward bearing) aire
m, ademán *m*, porte *m*; —**s** modales *m pl*,
crianza*f*; **in the** — **of** a la manera de
mannerism [mǽnərɪzəm] N peculiaridad*f*
mannish [mǽnɪʃ] ADJ hombruno, varonil
manor [mǽnə-] N feudo *m*, solar *m*; — **house**
casa solariega*f*
mansion [mǽnʃən] N mansión*f*
mantel [mǽntl̩] N repisa de chimenea*f*
mantle [mǽntl̩] N manto *m*
mantra [mǽntrə] N mantra*f*
manual [mǽnjuəl̩] ADJ & N manual *m*; — **labor**
trabajo manual *m*
manufacture [mænjəfǽktʃə-] VT fabricar,
manufacturar; (clothes, shoes) confeccionar;
N fabricación*f*, manufactura*f*; (of clothes,
shoes) confección*f*
manufacturer [mænjəfǽktʃərə-] N fabricante
m; —**'s suggested retail price** precio
sugerido por el fabricante *m*
manufacturing [mænjəfǽktʃə-ɪŋ] N fabricación
f, manufactura*f*; ADJ fabril, manufacturero;
— **empire** imperio industrial *m*
manure [mənúr] N estiércol *m*; VT estercolar,
abonar
manuscript [mǽnjəskrɪpt] ADJ & N
manuscrito *m*
many [méni] ADJ muchos; — **apples** muchas
manzanas; — **came** vinieron muchos; — **a
time** muchas veces; **a great** — muchísimos;
as — **as** tantos como; **as** — **as five** hasta
cinco; **how** —? ¿cuántos? **three books too**
— tres libros de más; **too** — demasiados
map [mæp] N (geographical) mapa *m*; (of streets)
plano *m*; VT trazar un mapa de; **to** — **out**
planear
maple [mépəl̩] N *Sp* arce *m*; *Am* maple *m*; —
syrup miel de arce/maple*f*
mar [mɑr] VT estropear
marathon [mǽrəθɑn] N maratón *mf*
marble [mɑ́rbəl̩] N mármol *m*; (toy) canica*f*,
bola*f*; **to play** —**s** jugar a las canicas; ADJ de
mármol, marmóreo
march [mɑrtʃ] N marcha*f*; VI marchar; (leave)
marcharse; **to** — **in** entrar; **to** — **out**
marcharse; VT hacer marchar
March [mɑrtʃ] N marzo *m*

mare [mɛr] N yegua*f*
margarine [mɑ́rdʒə-ɪn] N margarina*f*
margin [mɑ́rdʒɪn] N margen *m*; — **of error**
margen de error *m*; — **of safety** margen de
seguridad *m*; **on** — comprado en cuenta de
margen
marginal [mɑ́rdʒənl̩] ADJ marginal
marginalization [mɑrdʒənl̩ɪzéʃən] N
marginación*f*
marginalize [mɑ́rdʒənl̩aɪz] VT marginar
marigold [mǽrɪgol̩d] N caléndula*f*, maravilla*f*
marijuana, marihuana [mærəwánə] N
marihuana*f*, mariguana*f*
marinate [mǽrənet] VT marinar
marine [mərín] ADJ (of the sea) marino;
(maritime) marítimo; — **corps** infantería de
marina*f*; N soldado de infantería de marina *m*
marionette [mæriənét] N marioneta*f*
marital [mǽrɪdl̩] ADJ conyugal, matrimonial; —
status estado civil *m*
maritime [mǽrɪtaɪm] ADJ marítimo
mark [mɑrk] N marca*f*, seña*f*; (token) señal*f*;
(indication) seña*f*; (grade) nota*f*, calificación
f; (former German currency) marco *m*;
—**down** rebaja de precio*f*; —**sman** tirador
m; **he's a good** —**sman** tiene muy buena
puntería / muy buen tino; —**up** (amount
above wholesale price) margen de ganancia
m; **the halfway** — el punto medio, la mitad;
to hit the — dar en el blanco; **on your** —,
get set, go! ¡en sus marcas, listos y ya! ¡en
sus marcas, listos, fuera! **to make one's** —
distinguirse; **to miss the** — errar el tiro;
easy — blanco fácil *m*; VT (write on) marcar;
(indicate) señalar; (observe) observar, notar;
(grade) calificar; —**ed for greatness**
destinado a la grandeza; — **my words!** ¡ya
verás! **to** — **down prices** rebajar los precios;
to — **off** acotar, deslindar; **to** — **up prices**
subir los precios
marker [mɑ́rkə-] N marcador *m*
market [mɑ́rkɪt] N mercado *m*; — **analysis**
análisis de mercado *m*; —**place** mercado *m*;
— **price** precio de mercado *m*; — **share**
sector del mercado *m*; **I'm in the** — **for** estoy
buscando; VT comercializar, mercadear
marketable [mɑ́rkɪɒbəl̩] ADJ vendible
marketing [mɑ́rkɪɒɪŋ] N (field of study)
mercadotecnia*f*, marketing *m*; (selling)
comercialización*f*
marmalade [mɑ́rməled] N mermelada de
naranja*f*
maroon [mərún] ADJ & N bordó/bordeaux *m*; VT
abandonar
marquis [mɑrkí] N marqués *m*
marquise [mɑrkíz] N marquesa*f*
marriage [mǽrɪdʒ] N matrimonio *m*;
(combination) combinación*f*; — **license**
licencia de matrimonio*f*

marriageable [mǽrɪʤəbəl] ADJ casadero
married [mǽrid] ADJ (united in marriage)
casado; (relation to marriage) conyugal; —
couple matrimonio *m*; **to get** — casarse
marrow [mǽro] N (in the bones) médula *f*;
(food) tuétano *m*; (essential part) meollo *m*
marry [mǽri] VT (to marry off) casar; (to get
married) casarse con; VI casarse
marsh [marʃ] N pantano *m*, ciénaga *f*
marshal [márʃəl] N (military) mariscal *m*;
(police chief) alguacil *m*; (of a parade) maestro
de ceremonia *m*; VT (facts, forces) reunir;
(troops) formar
Marshallese [marʃəlíz] ADJ & N marshalés -esa
mf
Marshall Islands [márʃəláɪləndz] N Islas
Marshall *f pl*
marshmallow [márʃmɛlo] N malvavisco *m*
marshy [márʃi] ADJ pantanoso, cenagoso
martial [márʃəl] ADJ marcial; — **arts** artes
marciales *f pl*; — **law** ley marcial *f*
martin [mártn̩] N avión *m*
martini [martíni] N martini *m*
martyr [márɽɚ] N mártir *m*; VT martirizar
martyrdom [márɽɚdəm] N martirio *m*
marvel [márvəl] N maravilla *f*; VI maravillarse
marvelous [márvələs] ADJ maravilloso
Marxism [márksɪzəm] N marxismo *m*
mascara [mæskǽrə] N rímel *m*
mascot [mǽskat] N mascota *f*
masculine [mǽskjəlɪn] ADJ masculino
mash [mæʃ] VT aplastar, pisar; —**ed potatoes**
puré de papas/patatas *m*; N (pulpy mass) puré
m; (food for livestock) afrecho *m*; (malt) malta
remojada *f*
mask [mæsk] N máscara *f*, careta *f*; VT
enmascarar; —**ed ball** baile de máscaras *m*
masochism [mǽsəkɪzəm] N masoquismo *m*
mason [mésən] N (builder) albañil *m*;
(Freemason) masón *m*
masonry [mésənri] N (bricklaying) albañilería *f*;
(fraternal order) masonería *f*
masquerade [mæskəréd] N mascarada *f*; VI **to**
— **as** hacerse pasar por
mass [mæs] N masa *f*; (in church) misa *f*; —
communication comunicación de masas *f*;
— **marketing** comercialización masiva *f*; —
media medios de comunicación [de masas] *m*
pl; — **production** fabricación en masa *f*; —
storage almacenamiento masivo *m*; —
transit transporte público *m*; —
unemployment desempleo/paro masivo *m*;
the —**es** las masas *f pl*; VI/VT juntar[se] en
masa; (troops) concentrar[se]
massacre [mǽsəkɚ] N masacre *m*; VT masacrar
massage [məsáʒ] N masaje *m*; — **parlor** salón
de masajes *m*; VT (give a massage) masajear;
(change data) manipular
masseur [məsɚ́] N masajista *m*

masseuse [məsús] N masajista *f*
massive [mǽsɪv] ADJ (severe) masivo; (solid)
macizo; (large) enorme
mast [mæst] N mástil *m*, árbol *m*
mastectomy [mæstéktəmi] N mastectomía *f*
master [mǽstɚ] N (person in control) amo -a *mf*,
señor -ora *mf*; (owner of slave or animal) amo
-a *mf*; (best representative, skilled laborer)
maestro *m*; (young boy) señorito *m*; (tape or
disk) original *m*; —**'s degree** maestría *f*; ADJ
(dominant) dominante; — **bedroom**
dormitorio principal *m*; — **key** llave maestra
f; —**mind** cerebro *m*; —**piece** obra maestra
f; VT dominar; **to** —**mind** planificar y dirigir
masterful [mǽstɚfəl] ADJ magistral
masterly [mǽstɚli] ADJ magistral
mastery [mǽstəri] N dominio *m*
mastiff [mǽstɪf] N mastín *m*, alano *m*
masturbate [mǽstɚbet] VI/VT masturbar[se]
mat [mæt] N (floor covering) estera *f*; (for wiping
feet) felpudo *m*; (in gymnastics) colchoneta *f*;
(of hair) maraña *f*; VI enmarañarse
match [mætʃ] N (pair) pareja *f*; (chess game)
partida *f*; (tennis, golf game) partido *m*;
(boxing encounter) combate *m*; (device for
fire) fósforo *m*, cerilla *f*; —**ball** bola de
partido *f*; —**box** cajita de fósforos *f*; —**maker**
casamentero -ra *mf*; —**point** punto de
partido *m*; **he has no** — no tiene igual; **he is
a good** — es un buen partido; **the hat and
coat are a good** — el abrigo y el sombrero
hacen juego; VI/VT hacer juego [con]; VI (to
correspond) estar de acuerdo; **the colors
don't** — los colores no combinan; VT (equal)
igualar; (come to correspond) poner de
acuerdo; (form pairs) parear
matching [mǽtʃɪŋ] ADJ emparejados; — **colors**
colores que combinan *m pl*; — **pair** pareja *f*;
— **shoes** zapatos del mismo par *m pl*
matchless [mǽtʃlɪs] ADJ sin par
mate [met] N (one of a pair) pareja *f*; (friend)
compañero -ra *mf*; (on a ship) oficial *m*; (in
chess) mate *m*; VI/VT aparear[se]
material [mətíriəl] ADJ (made of matter)
material; (pertinent) pertinente; N
(substance) material *m*; (fabric) tejido *m*,
género *m*
materialism [mətíriəlɪzəm] N materialismo *m*
materialize [mətíriəlaɪz] VI/VT materializar[se],
plasmarse
maternal [mətɚ́nl̩] ADJ (motherly) maternal;
(on mother's side of family) materno
maternity [mətɚ́nɪDi] N maternidad *f*; — **leave**
licencia por maternidad *f*
math [mæθ] N matemática[s] *f* [*pl*]
mathematical [mæθəmǽDɪkəl] ADJ
matemático
mathematician [mæθəmətíʃən] N matemático
-ca *mf*

mathematics [mæθəmǽDɪks] N matemática[s] f
[pl]
matinee [mætṇé] N matiné f
mating [méDɪŋ] N (copulation) cópula f;
(reproduction) reproducción f
matriarch [métriɑrk] N matriarca f
matriculate [mətríkjələt] VI/VT matricular[se]
matriculation [mətrɪkjəléʃən] N matriculación
f, matrícula f
matrilineal [mætrəlíniəl] ADJ matrilineal
matrimony [mætrəmoni] N matrimonio m
matrix [métrɪks] N matriz f
matron [métrən] N (married woman or widow)
matrona f; (in a hospital) jefa de enfermeras f
matter [mæDɚ] N (substance, pus) materia f;
(affair) asunto m; (printed) impreso m;
(reading) material de lectura m; — **for**
complaint motivo de queja m; **a — of two**
minutes cosa de dos minutos f; **as a — of**
fact de hecho, precisamente; **it is of no —**
no tiene importancia; **no — what you say**
no importa lo que digas; **as a — of course**
por rutina; **what is the —?** ¿qué pasa? VI
importar; **it doesn't —** no importa
mattress [mætrɪs] N colchón m
maturation [mætʃəréʃən] N maduración f
mature [mətʃúr] ADJ maduro; **a — note** un
pagaré vencido/pagadero m; **for —**
audiences para adultos; VI/VT madurar[se];
(a savings bond) vencer[se]
maturing [mətʃúrɪŋ] N maduración f
maturity [mətúrɪDi] N madurez f; (of a debt)
vencimiento m
maul [mɔl] VT atacar, herir gravemente
Mauritania [mɔrɪténiə] N Mauritania f
Mauritanian [mɔrɪténiən] ADJ & N mauritano
-na mf
Mauritian [mɔríʃən] ADJ & N mauriciano -na mf
Mauritius [mɔríʃəs] N Mauricio m
maverick [mǽvɚɪk] N cimarrón m; (person)
inconformista mf, cimarrón -ona mf
maxim [mǽksɪm] N máxima f, sentencia f
maximize [mǽksəmaɪz] VT maximizar
maximum [mǽksəməm] ADJ & N máximo m
may [me] V AUX **— I sit down?** ¿puedo
sentarme? **— you have a merry**
Christmas que pases una feliz Navidad; **it**
— be that puede ser que; **it — rain** puede
[ser] que llueva, tal vez llueva; **she — have**
been late puede [ser] que haya llegado tarde;
be that as it — sea como fuere
May [me] N mayo m; **— Day** primero de mayo m;
—pole mayo m
Maya [máɪə] N & ADJ maya mf
Mayan [máɪən] N & ADJ maya mf
maybe [mébi] ADV quizá[s], tal vez
mayonnaise [méənez] N mayonesa f,
mahonesa f
mayor [méɚ] N alcalde m

mayoralty [méɚəlti] N alcaldía f
maze [mez] N laberinto m
MBA [master of business administration]
[émbíé] N máster en administración de
empresas m, maestría en administración de
empresas f
MD [medicinae doctor] [émdí] N doctor -ora
en medicina mf
me [mi] PRON **she sees —** me ve; **he talks to —**
me habla; **he comes with —** viene conmigo;
he did it for — lo hizo para mí
meadow [méDo] N pradera f, prado m; **—lark**
alondra f
meager [mígɚ] ADJ escaso, exiguo
meal [mil] N (repast) comida f; (flour) harina f;
—time hora de comer f
mean [min] ADJ (unkind) cruel; (petty) vil;
(humble) humilde; (stingy) mezquino;
(difficult) de mal genio; (middle) medio; —-
spirited mezquino; **I make a — lasagna**
me sale muy rica la lasagna; N (average)
media f, promedio m; **—s** medios m pl; **the**
ends justify the —s el fin justifica los
medios; **a man of —s** un hombre adinerado;
by —s of por medio de; **—s of transport**
medios de transporte m pl; **—s test** prueba de
ingresos f; **by all —s** (of course) por
supuesto; (using all resources) por todos los
medios; **by no —s** de ningún modo; VT
(intend) querer, tener intenciones de;
(signify) querer decir, significar; **he —s well**
tiene buenas intenciones; **winning —s**
everything to them lo que más les importa
es ganar; **they are meant for each other**
son el uno para el otro
meander [miǽndɚ] VI (be winding) serpentear;
(to wander) vagar
meaning [mínɪŋ] N (sense) significado m,
sentido m; (purpose) sentido m; ADJ **well-—**
bien intencionado
meaningful [mínɪŋfəl] ADJ (result, event)
significativo, trascendente; (sentence)
coherente
meaningless [mínɪŋlɪs] ADJ sin sentido
meanness [mínnɪs] N (cruelty) crueldad f;
(pettiness) mezquindad f
meant [mɛnt] see mean
meantime [míntaɪm] ADV LOC **in the —**
mientras tanto
meanwhile [mínhwaɪl] ADV mientras tanto
measles [mízəlz] N sarampión m
measurable [méʒɚəbəl] ADJ medible,
mensurable
measure [méʒɚ] N (dimension) medida f;
(criterion) criterio m; (in musical bar) compás
m; (bill) proyecto de ley m; **beyond —**
sobremanera; **dry —** medida de áridos f; **in**
large — en gran parte; **—s** medidas f pl;
VI/VT medir; **to — up** compararse con;

measuring tape cinta de medir*f*, metro *m*
measured [mέʒəd] ADJ (rhythmical) acompasado; (moderate) moderado, mesurado
measurement [mέʒə-mənt] N (act of measuring) medición *f*; (dimension) medida *f*, dimensión *f*
meat [mit] N carne *f*; (essential point) meollo *m*; **—ball** albóndiga *f*; **—loaf** pan/pastel de carne *m*
meaty [míᴅi] ADJ (with meat) con mucha carne; (substantial) sustancioso
mechanic [mɪkǽnɪk] ADJ & N mecánico *m*; N **—s** mecánica *f*
mechanical [mɪkǽnɪkəł] ADJ mecánico
mechanism [mέkənɪzəm] N mecanismo *m*
medal [mέdl̩] N medalla *f*; VI ganar una medalla
meddle [mέdl̩] VI entrometerse, inmiscuirse
meddler [mέdlə-] N entrometido -da *mf*
meddlesome [mέdl̩səm] ADJ entrometido
media [míᴅiə] N (communication) medios *m pl*, media *m pl*, medios de comunicación masiva *m pl*; (cables) cables del ordenador/ de la computadora *m pl*
median [míᴅiən] ADJ mediano; N (middle value, line) mediana *f*
mediate [mípiet] VI/VT mediar
mediation [miᴅiéʃən] N mediación *f*
mediator [míᴅieᴅə-] N mediador -ora *mf*
medical [mέᴅɪkəł] ADJ médico; **— chart** hoja clínica *f*; **— exam** examen médico *m*; **— examiner** médico -ca forense *mf*; **— history** historia clínica *f*; **— record** expediente médico *m*; **— school** facultad de medicina *f*
medicate [mέᴅɪket] VT medicar
medication [mεᴅɪkéʃən] N medicación *f*
medicine [mέᴅɪsɪn] N (profession) medicina *f*; (drug) medicamento *m*, fármaco *m*; **— ball** balón medicinal *m*; **— cabinet** botiquín *m*; **— man** curandero *m*
medieval [mɪdívəł] ADJ medieval
mediocre [miᴅióka-] ADJ mediocre
mediocrity [miᴅiákrɪᴅi] N mediocridad *f*
meditate [mέᴅɪtet] VI meditar
meditation [mεᴅɪtéʃən] N meditación *f*, recogimiento *m*
Mediterranean [mεᴅɪtərénian] ADJ mediterráneo
medium [míᴅiəm] N (substance, agency) medio *m*; (person who contacts spirits) médium *mf*; **— of exchange** medio de cambio *m*; ADJ mediano; ADV término medio
medley [mέdli] N (music) popurrí *m*; (mixture) mezcla *f*
meek [mik] ADJ manso
meekness [míknɪs] N mansedumbre *f*
meet [mit] VT (encounter) encontrarse con; (make acquaintance) conocer; (face in

conflict) enfrentar; (satisfy) satisfacer; (pay) pagar; **to — a deadline** cumplir el plazo; **to — expenses** sufragar los gastos; **to — halfway** partir la diferencia; **to — a train** esperar un tren; **I will — you at the station** nos encontramos/vemos en la estación; **have you met my brother?** ¿conoces a mi hermano? **we were met with disapproval** se nos recibió con desaprobación; VI (encounter) encontrarse; (make acquaintance) conocerse; (have a meeting) reunirse; (cross) cruzarse; **to — in battle** trabar batalla; **to — with** (intentional) reunirse con; (unintentional) tropezar con; N encuentro deportivo *m*, competición *f*
meeting [míᴅɪŋ] N reunión *f*, junta *f*; (political) mitin *m*; (crossing of roads) cruce *m*
megabyte [mέgəbaɪt] N megabyte *m*
megahertz [mέgəhз-tz] N megahertz *m*, megahercio *m*
megalomania [mεgəlomέniə] N megalomanía *f*
megaphone [mέgəfon] N megáfono *m*, bocina *f*
melancholy [mέlənkɑli] N melancolía *f*; ADJ melancólico
melanoma [mεlənómə] N melanoma *m*
meld [mεłd] VT fusionar
melee [méle] N reyerta *f*, tumulto *m*
mellow [mέlo] ADJ (soft) dulce, suave; (gentle) tranquilo; VI/VT suavizar[se]
melodic [məlɑ́ᴅɪk] ADJ melódico
melodious [məlóᴅiəs] ADJ melodioso, melódico
melodrama [mέlodrɑmə] N melodrama *m*
melody [mέləᴅi] N melodía *f*
melon [mέlən] N melón *m*
melt [mεłt] VI/VT (liquefy) derretir[se]; (dissolve) disolver[se]; **—ing pot** crisol *m*; N **—down** (fusion) catástrofe por fusión nuclear incontrolada *f*; (any developing disaster) catástrofe *f*
member [mέmbə-] N miembro *m* (also body part)
membership [mέmbə-ʃɪp] N (number) número de miembros/socios *m*; (state) calidad de miembro/socio *f*
membrane [mέmbren] N membrana *f*
memento [məmέnto] N recuerdo *m*
memoir [mέmwɑr] N memoria *f*; **—s** memorias *f pl*, autobiografía *f*
memorable [mέmə-əbəł] ADJ memorable
memorandum [mεmərǽndəm] N memorándum *m*
memorial [məmɔ́riəł] N (monument) monumento conmemorativo *m*; (petition) memorial *m*; ADJ conmemorativo
memorize [mέməraɪz] VI/VT memorizar
memory [mέməri] N (faculty) memoria *f*; (recollection) recuerdo *m*; **— cache** caché de memoria *f*; **— map** mapa de memoria *m*
menace [mέnɪs] N amenaza *f*; VI/VT amenazar

mend [mɛnd] VT remendar; **to — matters** enmendar la situación; **to — one's ways** enmendarse, reformarse; VI (sick person) mejorarse; (bones) soldarse; N remiendo *m*; **to be on the —** ir mejorando

menial [míniəł] ADJ (lowly) bajo; (job) servil; N criado -da *mf*

meningitis [mɛnɪndʒaɪDɪs] N meningitis *f*

menopause [ménəpɔz] N menopausia *f*

menstruate [ménstruet] VI menstruar

menstruation [mɛnstruéʃən] N menstruación *f*

mental [méntl] ADJ mental; (insane) *fam* chiflado; **— health** salud mental *f*; **— illness** enfermedad mental *f*; **— retardation** retraso mental *m*

mentality [mentǽlɪDi] N mentalidad *f*

mention [ménʃən] VT mencionar; **don't — it** no hay de qué; N mención *f*

mentor [méntɔr] N mentor -ora *mf*

menu [ménju] N (list of dishes) carta *f*, menú *m*; (computer) menú *m*; **— bar** (computer) barra de menú *f*

meow [mjaU] INTERJ miau

mercantile [mɝkəntił] ADJ mercantil

mercenary [mɝsənɛri] ADJ mercenario

merchandise[1] [mɝtʃəndaɪs] N mercancía *f*, mercadería *f*

merchandise[2] [mɝtʃəndaɪz] VT comercializar

merchandising [mɝtʃəndaɪzɪŋ] N mercadeo *m*, comercialización *f*

merchant [mɝtʃənt] N (trader) comerciante *m*, mercader *m*; ADJ mercante; **— marine** marina mercante *f*

merciful [mɝsɪfəł] ADJ misericordioso

merciless [mɝsɪlɪs] ADJ despiadado

mercury [mɝkjəri] N mercurio *m*; (on a mirror) azogue *m*

mercy [mɝsi] N (compassion) misericordia *f*, clemencia *f*, piedad *f*; **to be at the — of** estar a merced de; **— killing** eutanasia *f*

mere [mir] ADJ mero, simple; **a — trifle** una nonada

merely [mírli] ADV (only) solo, solamente; (simply) simplemente

merge [mɝdʒ] VI/VT (forces) unir[se]; (colors) fundir[se]; (companies) fusionar[se]; (data files) fusionar; N fusión *f*

merger [mɝdʒɚ] N fusión *f*; **—s and acquisitions** fusiones y adquisiciones *f pl*

meridian [mərídiən] ADJ & N meridiano *m*

merit [mérɪt] N mérito *m*; **— pay** paga por mérito *f*; **— raise** aumento por mérito *m*; VT merecer

meritorious [mɛrɪtóriəs] ADJ meritorio

mermaid [mɝmed] N sirena *f*

merriment [mérɪmənt] N alegría *f*, algazara *f*

merry [méri] ADJ alegre; **—-go-round** tiovivo *m*; **—maker** fiestero -ra *mf*, juerguista *mf*; **—making** fiesta *f*, juerga *f*; **to make —** divertirse; INTERJ **— Christmas** Feliz Navidad *f*, Felices Pascuas

mesa [mésə] N mesa *f*

mesh [mɛʃ] N (of metal) malla *f*; (of fiber) red *f*; (of gears) engranaje *m*; VI engranar

mesmerize [mézməraɪz] VI/VT hipnotizar

mess [mɛs] N (state of confusion) desorden *m*, desarreglo *m*; (disorderly person) desordenado -da *mf*, mugriento -ta *mf*; (confused person) desastre *m*; (difficult situation) lío *m*, jaleo *m*; (food for soldiers) rancho *m*; (cafeteria) cantina *f*; **— hall** cantina *f*; **— of fish** plato de pescado *m*; **to make a — of** (a room) ensuciar, desordenar; (a project) estropear; VI/VT **to — around** (waste time) perder el tiempo; (philander) correr detrás de las mujeres; **to — up** (a room) alborotar, desordenar; (clothes, hair) desarreglar; (a project) estropear; (make a muddle of) *vulg* cagarla; **to — with** meterse con

message [mésɪdʒ] N mensaje *m*, recado *m*; **I get the —** ya caí en cuenta

messenger [mésəndʒɚ] N mensajero -ra *mf*

messy [mési] ADJ (chaotic) desordenado; (embarrassing) embarazoso

met [mɛt] *see* meet

metabolic [mɛDəbálɪk] ADJ metabólico

metabolism [mətǽbəlɪzəm] N metabolismo *m*

metal [médl̩] N metal *m*; **— detector** detector de metales *m*; ADJ de metal, metálico

metallic [mətǽlɪk] ADJ metálico

metallurgy [médl̩ɚdʒi] N metalurgia *f*

metamorphosis [mɛDəmórfəsɪs] N metamorfosis *f*

metaphor [méDəfɔr] N metáfora *f*

metaphysical [mɛDəfízɪkəł] ADJ metafísico

metaphysics [mɛDəfízɪks] N metafísica *f*

metastasis [mətǽstəsɪs] N metástasis *f*

metastasize [mətǽstəsaɪz] VI metastatizar

meteor [míDiɔr] N meteoro *m*; **— shower** lluvia de meteoritos *f*

meteorite [míDiəraɪt] N meteorito *m*

meteorological [miDiɚəládʒɪkəł] ADJ meteorológico

meteorology [miDiɚálədʒi] N meteorología *f*

meter [míDɚ] N (unit of length) metro *m*; (measuring device) contador *m*, medidor *m*

methane [méθen] N metano *m*

method [méθəd] N método *m*

methodical [məθádɪkəł] ADJ metódico

methodology [mɛθədálədʒi] N metodología *f*

meticulous [mətíkjələs] ADJ detallista

metric [métrɪk] ADJ métrico

metro [métro] N metro *m*

metronome [métrənom] N metrónomo *m*

metropolis [mətrápəlɪs] N metrópoli *f*, urbe *f*

metropolitan [mɛtrəpálɪDən] ADJ metropolitano

mettle [médl] N temple *m*, valor *m*
mew [mju] N maullido *m*; VI maullar
Mexican [méksɪkən] ADJ & N mexicano -na *mf*
Mexico [méksɪko] N México *m*
mezzanine [mézənin] N entrepiso *m*, entresuelo *m*
mickey mouse [míkimáʊs] ADJ poco serio, informal
microbe [máɪkrob] N microbio *m*
microbiology [maɪkrobaɪáləʤi] N microbiología *f*
microcomputer [maɪkrokəmpjúDə-] N *Am* microcomputadora *f*; *Sp* microordenador *m*
microeconomics [maɪkroɛkənámɪks] N microeconomía *f*
microfiche [máɪkrofiʃ] N microficha *f*
microfilm [máɪkrofɪlm] N microfilme *m*
micromanage [maɪkromǽnɪʤ] VI/VT administrar con excesivo control
micron [máɪkrɑn] N micrón *m*, micrómetro *m*
Micronesia [maɪkroníʒə] N Micronesia *f*
Micronesian [maɪkrəníʒən] ADJ & N micronesio -sia *mf*
microorganism [maɪkroɔ́rgənɪzəm] N microorganismo *m*
microphone [máɪkrəfon] N micrófono *m*
microprocessor [maɪkroprásesə-] N microprocesador *m*
microscope [máɪkrəskop] N microscopio *m*
microscopic [maɪkrəskápɪk] ADJ microscópico
microsurgery [maɪkrosɝ́ʤəri] N microcirujía *f*
microwave [máɪkrowev] N microonda *f*; — **oven** [horno] microondas *m sg*
mid [mɪd] ADJ medio; —**air** en el aire; —**day** [del] mediodía *m*; —**field player** (soccer) centrocampista *m*; —**life** madurez *f*; —**life crisis** crisis de la edad madura *f*; —**night** [de] medianoche *f*; —**shipman** guardiamarina *m*; **in** —**stream** (of a river) en medio del río; (of a task) en plena actividad; —**summer** pleno verano *m*; —**term examination** examen a mitad del curso *m*; —**way** a medio camino, a mitad del camino; —**wife** partera *f*, comadre *f*
middle [mídl] ADJ (average) medio, mediano; (intermediate) intermedio; (central) central; —**-aged** de mediana edad; — **Ages** Edad Media *f*; — **class** clase media *f*, burguesía *f*; —**-class neighborhood** barrio de clase media; — **ear** oído medio *m*; — **finger** dedo mayor *m*, dedo del corazón *m*; —**man** intermediario *m*, revendedor *m*; — **management** administración intermedia *f*; — **name** segundo nombre *m*; —**-of-the-road** moderado; —**-sized** [de] tamaño mediano; N medio *m*; (waist) cintura *f*; **in the** — **of** en el medio de; **I'm in the** — **of something** estoy ocupado haciendo algo; **toward the** — **of the month** a mediados del mes

midget [mídʒɪt] N enano -na *mf*
MIDI [**musical instrument digital interface**] [míDi] N interfaz digital de instrumentos musicales *f*
midst [mɪdst] ADV LOC medio *m*, centro *m*; **in the** — **of** en medio de, entre; **in our** — entre nosotros
mien [min] N porte *m*
might [maɪt] V AUX **it** — **be that** podría ser que; **he said it** — **rain tomorrow** dijo que tal vez lloviera mañana; **she** — **have been late** puede ser que haya llegado tarde; N poder *m*, poderío *m*
mighty [máɪDi] ADJ (strong) poderoso, potente; (large) imponente; ADV muy
migraine [máɪgren] N migraña *f*, jaqueca *f*
migrant [máɪgrənt] ADJ migratorio, migrante; N trabajador -ora itinerante *mf*, bracero -ra *mf*
migrate [máɪgret] VI (also computers) migrar
migration [maɪgréʃən] N migración *f*
migratory [máɪgrətɔri] ADJ migratorio
mild [maɪld] ADJ (gentle) suave; (moderate) moderado; (not serious) leve
mildew [mílldu] N moho *m*
mildness [máɪldnɪs] N (gentleness) suavidad *f*; (lack of gravity) levedad *f*
mile [maɪl] N milla *f*; —**stone** hito *m*
mileage [máɪlɪʤ] N (distance, odometer reading) millaje *m*, kilometraje *m*; **this car gets good** — este coche es económico; **what kind of** — **are you getting?** ¿cuántos kilómetros por litro hace tu coche?
milieu [mɪljú] N ambiente *m*
militance [mílɪtəns] N militancia *f*
militancy [mílɪtənsi] N militancia *f*
militant [mílɪtənt] ADJ & N (fanatic) militante *mf*; (combatant) combatiente *mf*
military [mílɪteri] ADJ militar; N **the** — (armed forces) el ejército; (military personnel) los militares
militia [məlíʃə] N milicia *f*
milk [mɪlk] N leche *f*; — **chocolate** chocolate con leche *m*; —**maid** lechera *f*; —**man** lechero *m*; — **shake** batido *m*; VT ordeñar; (exploit) exprimir; **he's** —**ing it for all it's worth** le está sacando todo el jugo
milky [mílki] ADJ (consistency) lechoso; (product) lácteo; — **Way** Vía Láctea *f*
mill [mɪl] N (building) molino *m*; (factory) fábrica *f*; (for sugar) trapiche *m*, ingenio *m*; (rotating tool) fresa *f*; (small grinder) molinillo *m*; —**stone** muela de molino *f*; **a** —**stone around your neck** una piedra al cuello; VT (grind grain) moler; (cut wood) aserrar; (cut grooves on coins) acordonar; (machine) fresar; **to** — **around** dar vueltas
millennium [məlíniəm] N milenio *m*
miller [mílə-] N (person who mills) molinero -ra

mf; (machine for milling) fresadora *f*; (moth) mariposa nocturna *f*

milligram [mílɪgræm] N miligramo *m*

milliliter [mílǝliDǝ·] N mililitro *m*

millimeter [mílǝmiDǝ·] N milímetro *m*

milliner [mílǝnǝ·] N sombrerero -ra *mf*

millinery [mílǝnɛri] N (shop) sombrerería *f*; (hats) sombreros de señora *m pl*

million [míljǝn] N millón *m*; **a—dollars** un millón de dólares

millionaire [mɪljǝnér] N millonario -ria *mf*

millionth [míljǝnθ] ADJ & N millonésimo *m*

mime [maɪm] N (actor) mimo *m*; (technique, performance) pantomima *f*; VI hacer la mímica

mimic [mímɪk] VT imitar, remedar; N mono -na *mf*, remedador -ora *mf*

mince [mɪns] VT picar, desmenuzar; **not to— words** no tener pelos en la lengua; **—meat** picadillo *m*; **I'm going to make —meat of you** te voy a hacer picadillo

mind [maɪnd] N (thinking process) mente *f*; (person of intellect) inteligencia *f*; (opinion) parecer *m*, opinión *f*; **— games** manipulación psicológica *f*; **— over matter** el espíritu sobre la materia; **—-set** actitud *f*, forma de pensar *f*; **to be out of one's—** estar loco; **to bear in —** tener en cuenta; **to change one's—** cambiar de parecer/ opinión; **to give someone a piece of one's — cantarle** a alguien las cuarenta; **I have a — to** me dan ganas de; **to make up one's —** decidirse; **to my —** a mi modo de ver; **to speak one's — freely** hablar con toda franqueza; **what do you have in —?** ¿qué tienes en mente? **to call to —** recordar; **to keep one's — on one's work** concentrarse en el trabajo; ADJ **—-altering** alucinógeno; VT (take care of) cuidar; (pay attention to) atender a; (obey) obedecer; **I don't —** no tengo inconveniente en ello; **— what you say** cuidado con lo que dices; **to — one's own business** no meterse en lo ajeno

mindful [máɪndfǝɫ] ADJ atento

mine [maɪn] PRON **this book is —** este libro es mío; **these things are —** estas cosas son mías; **— is bigger** el mío / la mía es más grande; **a friend of —** un amigo mío / una amiga mía; N mina *f* (also explosive device); **—field** campo minado *m*; **— sweeper** dragaminas *m sg*, barreminas *m sg*; VT (plant explosives) minar; (dig out minerals) extraer; (exploit an area for minerals) explotar; VI (lay mines) sembrar minas; (dig a mine) cavar una mina; **to — for** extraer

miner [máɪnǝ·] N minero -ra *mf*

mineral [mínǝ·ǝɫ] ADJ & N mineral *m*; **— rights** derechos mineros *m pl*; **— water** agua mineral *f*

mingle [míŋgǝɫ] VI mezclarse; (sounds) confundirse; VT mezclar

miniature [míniǝtʃǝ·] N miniatura *f*; ADJ en miniatura

minicomputer [mɪnikǝmpjúDǝ·] N *Am* minicomputadora *f*; *Sp* miniordenador *m*

minimal [mínǝmǝɫ] ADJ mínimo

minimize [mínǝmaɪz] VT minimizar

minimum [mínǝmǝm] ADJ & N mínimo *m*; **— wage** salario mínimo *m*

mining [máɪnɪŋ] N (exploitation of mines) minería *f*; (act of mining) minado *m*; ADJ minero; **open —** minería a cielo abierto *f*

miniskirt [mínɪskɚt] N minifalda *f*

minister [mínɪstǝ·] N (official) ministro -tra *mf*; (pastor) pastor -ora *mf*, clérigo *m*; VI **to — to** atender a

ministerial [mɪnɪstíriǝɫ] ADJ ministerial

ministry [mínɪstri] N (government agency) ministerio *m*; (functions of pastor) clerecía *f*

minivan [mínivæn] N camioneta *f*

mink [mɪŋk] N visón *m*

minnow [míno] N pececillo *m*

minor [máɪnǝ·] ADJ (smaller) menor, más pequeño; (of secondary importance) menor; **— key** tono menor *m*; **— league** liga menor *f*; N (young person) menor de edad *mf*; (musical interval) tono menor *m*; (subfield) asignatura secundaria *f*; VI tener como segunda especialización

minority [mǝnɔ́rɪDi] N (smaller part or group) minoría *f*; (state of being underage) minoridad *f*; (member of a minority) miembro de una minoría *m*; ADJ minoritario; **— partner** socio -cia minoritario -ria *mf*

mint [mɪnt] N (flavor) menta *f*, hierbabuena *f*; (candy) pastilla de menta *f*; (money) casa de la moneda *f*; VT acuñar

minus [máɪnǝs] PREP **seven — four** siete menos cuatro; **we came — my brother** vinimos sin mi hermano; N signo de menos *m*; ADJ negativo

minuscule [mínǝskjuɫ] ADJ minúsculo

minute[1] [mínɪt] N minuto *m*; **— hand** minutero *m*; **—s** actas *f pl*

minute[2] [maɪnút] ADJ (small) diminuto; (detailed) detallado, minucioso

miracle [mírǝkǝɫ] N milagro *m*

miraculous [mɪrǽkjǝlǝs] ADJ milagroso

mirage [mɪráʒ] N espejismo *m*

mire [maɪr] N (mud) cieno *m*, fango *m*; (muddy place) ciénaga *f*; VI/VT (bog down) atascar[se] en el fango; (be or get covered with mud) enlodar[se]

mirror [mírǝ·] N espejo *m*; (large) luna *f*; **— image** imagen especular *f*; VT reflejar

mirth [mɝθ] N risa *f*, hilaridad *f*

mirthful [mɝ́θfǝɫ] ADJ risueño

miry [máɪri] ADJ cenagoso, fangoso

misanthropy [mɪsǽnθrəpi] N misantropía f
misappropriation [mɪsəproprié∫ən] N
malversación f
misbehave [mɪsbɪhév] VI portarse mal
miscalculate [mɪskǽɫkjəlet] VI/VT (in math)
calcular mal; (in situations) equivocarse
miscarriage [mískæɪ ʤ] N aborto espontáneo
m, malparto m; — **of justice** injusticia f
miscarry [mɪskǽri] VI (abort) abortar
espontáneamente; (fail) malograrse,
frustrarse
miscellaneous [mɪsəléniəs] ADJ diverso; (texts)
misceláneo; — **expenses** gastos varios mf
mischief [míst∫ɪf] N travesura f, diablura f,
picardía f; (serious prank) barrabasada f,
bellaquería f; **this will come to** — va a
suceder una desgracia
mischievous [míst∫əvəs] ADJ travieso, pícaro
misconception [mɪskənsép∫ən] N concepto
erróneo m
misconduct[1] [mɪskándʌkt] N (bad behavior)
mala conducta f; (malfeasance) mala
administración f
misconduct[2] [mɪskəndʌkt] VT administrar mal;
to — oneself portarse mal
miscue [mɪskjú] N pifia f; VI/VT pifiar
misdeed [mɪsdíd] N fechoría f
misdemeanor [mɪsdɪmínɚ] N delito menor m
miser [máɪzɚ] N avaro -ra mf, tacaño -ña mf
miserable [mízɚəbəɫ] ADJ infeliz, desdichado; **a**
— **day** un día asqueroso; **a — failure** un
fracaso rotundo
miserly [máɪzɚli] ADJ avariento, tacaño
misery [mízəri] N (wretchedness) desgracia f;
(poverty) miseria f; (unhappiness)
infelicidad f
misfit [mísfɪt] N inadaptado -da mf
misfortune [mɪsfɔ́rt∫ən] N desgracia f, desdicha
f, desventura f
misgivings [mɪsgívɪŋz] N aprensión f, recelo m
misguided [mɪsgáɪdɪd] ADJ mal aconsejado,
poco feliz
mishap [míshæp] N contratiempo m, percance m
misinform [mɪsɪnfɔ́rm] VT desinformar, dar
información errónea
misjudge [mɪsʤʌ́ʤ] VT juzgar mal
mislay [mɪslé] VT (keys, etc.) extraviar, perder;
(a document) traspapelar; (lay wrong) colocar
mal
mislead [mɪslíd] VT (in the wrong direction)
guiar por mal camino; (into error) engañar,
confundir
misleading [mɪslídɪŋ] ADJ engañoso
mismanage [mɪsmǽnɪʤ] VT administrar mal
misogyny [mɪsáʤəni] N misoginia f
misplace [mɪsplés] VT (lose keys, etc.) extraviar;
(lose a document) traspapelar; (place wrong)
colocar mal; **she** — **d her trust** confió en la
persona equivocada

misprint [mísprɪnt] N errata f, error de
imprenta m
misrepresent [mɪsrɛprɪzént] VT distorsionar,
tergiversar
misrepresentation [mɪsrɛprɪzɛnté∫ən] N
distorsión f, tergiversación f
miss [mɪs] VI (fail to hit) errar; (misfire) fallar; VT
(fail to hit) errar, no acertar; (fail to be on
time for) perder; (fail to attend) faltar a; (feel
absence of) echar de menos; Am extrañar; **he
just** — **ed being killed** por poco se mata; N
(of a target) tiro errado m; (in a motor) falla f;
(from class) falta f; (young woman) señorita f;
— **Smith** la señorita Smith
misshapen [mɪs∫épən] ADJ deforme
missile [mísəɫ] N (projectile) proyectil m;
(guided weapon) misil m
missing [mísɪŋ] ADJ (not present) ausente; (lost)
perdido; — **link** eslabón perdido m; **one
book is** — falta un libro
mission [mí∫ən] N misión f; — **statement**
declaración de la misión f
missionary [mí∫əneri] ADJ & N misionero -ra mf;
— **position** posición del misionero f
misspell [mɪsspéɫ] VT (written) escribir mal;
(oral) deletrear mal
misstatement [mɪsstétmənt] N declaración
errónea/falsa f
misstep [místep] N paso en falso m
mist [mɪst] N (of water droplets) neblina f,
bruma f; (of perfume) rocío m; VI lloviznar;
VT rociar
mistake [mɪsték] N error m, equivocación f;
(orthographical) falta f; **to make a** —
equivocarse; VI/VT equivocar[se]; **I** — **my
sister for my mother** confundo a mi
hermana con mi madre
mistaken [mɪstékən] ADJ equivocado; **to be** —
estar equivocado, equivocarse; **unless I'm** —
si no me equivoco
mistaken [mɪstékən] see mistake
mister [místɚ] N señor m
mistletoe [mísəɫto] N muérdago m
mistook [mɪstúk] see mistake
mistreat [mɪstrít] VT maltratar
mistreatment [mɪstrítmənt] N maltrato m
mistress [místrɪs] N (of a household) señora f;
(employing servants, animal owner) ama f;
(lover) amante f
mistrial [místraɪɫ] N proceso viciado de
nulidad m
mistrust [mɪstrʌ́st] N desconfianza f; VT
desconfiar de
mistrustful [mɪstrʌ́stfəɫ] ADJ desconfiado,
receloso
misty [místi] ADJ (foggy) neblinoso, brumoso;
(in tears) nublado; (blurry) empañado
misunderstand [mɪsʌndɚstǽnd] VT
comprender mal, malinterpretar

misunderstanding [mɪsʌndəˈstændɪŋ] N (confusion) malentendido *m*; (failure to understand) equivocación *f*, mala inteligencia *f*; (argument) desavenencia *f*

misuse[1] [mɪsjús] N (of drugs) abuso *m*; (of a word) mal uso *m*; (of funds) malversación *f*

misuse[2] [mɪsjúz] VT (drugs) abusar de; (a friend) maltratar; (a word) emplear mal; (funds) malversar

mite [maɪt] N ácaro *m*; ADV **a — greedy** un poquito codicioso

mitigate [mɪ́dɪget] VT mitigar

mitochondria [maɪdokándriə] N mitocondria *f*

mitten [mɪ́tn̩] N manopla *f*

mix [mɪks] VI/VT mezclar[se]; **to — up** confundir; N mezcla *f*; (for baking) preparado *m*; **—-up** (confusion) confusión *f*; (fight) pelea *f*

mixed [mɪkst] ADJ mixto; **— bag** grupo heterogéneo *m*; **— doubles** dobles mixtos *m pl*; **— drink** cóctel *m*; **—-up** confundido

mixer [mɪ́ksə-] N (appliance) batidora *f*; (party) fiesta *f*; (soda) refresco *m*; (sound technician) mezclador -ora *mf*; (sound device) mezcladora *f*

mixture [mɪ́kstʃə-] N mezcla *f*

moan [mon] N quejido *m*, gemido *m*; VI gemir, quejarse; VI/VT lamentar

moat [mot] N foso *m*

mob [mɑb] N (disorderly crowd) tumulto *m*, turba *f*; (crowd) muchedumbre *f*, populacho *m*; (mafia) mafia *f*; VT (attack) asaltar; (crowd) atestar

mobile [móbəl] ADJ móvil; (personnel) que tiene movilidad; **— home** casa prefabricada *f*; **— Internet** internet móvil *m*; **— phone** [teléfono] móvil *m*, [teléfono] celular *m*

mobility [mobɪ́lɪdi] N movilidad *f*

mobilization [mobəlɪzéʃən] N movilización *f*

mobilize [móbəlaɪz] VI/VT movilizar[se]

moccasin [mákəsɪn] N mocasín *m* (also snake)

mock [mɑk] VI (ridicule) burlar[se]; VT (imitate) remedar; ADJ de práctica; **— battle** simulacro de batalla *m*; N **—-up** maqueta *f*, modelo *m*

mockery [mákəri] N (ridicule) burla *f*; (imitation) remedo *m*; (travesty) farsa *f*

mockingbird [mákɪŋbɜ-d] N sinsonte *m*

mode [mod] N modo *m*; **— of delivery** modo de entrega *m*; **— of payment** forma de pago *f*

model [mádl] N (guide) modelo *m*; (person) modelo *mf*, maniquí *mf*; ADJ modelo, ejemplar; **— school** escuela modelo *f*; VI/VT modelar; (display clothes) lucir

modem [módəm] N módem *m*

moderate[1] [mádə-ɪt] ADJ (not excessive) moderado, mesurado; (person) comedido; (weather) templado; (price) módico; N moderado -da *mf*

moderate[2] [mádəret] VI/VT moderar[se] (also preside at meetings)

moderation [madəréʃən] N moderación *f*, mesura *f*

modern [mádə-n] ADJ moderno; **— age** modernidad *f*

modernism [mádə-nɪzəm] N modernismo *m*

modernity [mədɜ́-nɪdi] N modernismo *m*

modernization [madə-nɪzéʃən] N modernización *f*

modernize [mádə-naɪz] VI/VT modernizar[se], innovar

modernness [mádə-nnɪs] N modernismo *m*

modest [mádɪst] ADJ (humble) modesto; (chaste) recatado, honesto

modesty [mádɪsti] N (humility) modestia *f*; (chastity) recato *m*, pudor *m*, honestidad *f*

modification [madəfɪkéʃən] N modificación *f*

modify [mádəfaɪ] VT modificar

modulate [mádʒəlet] VI/VT modular[se]

modulation [madʒəléʃən] N modulación *f*

module [mádʒul] N módulo *m*

mohair [móhɛr] N mohair *m*

moist [mɔɪst] ADJ húmedo

moisten [mɔ́ɪsən] VI/VT humedecer[se]

moisture [mɔ́ɪstʃə-] N humedad *f*

moisturizer [mɔ́ɪstʃəráɪzə-] N [crema] hidrante/ humectante *f*

molar [mólə-] ADJ molar; N muela *f*, molar *m*

molasses [məlǽsɪz] N melaza *f*

mold [moɫd] N (form) molde *m*; (fungi) moho *m*; (mettle) temple *m*; VT (shape) moldear, plasmar; (adapt) amoldar; (fuse) fundir; VI/VT (become moldy) enmohecer[se]

molder [móɫdə-] VI/VT descomponerse; (paper) enmohecerse

molding [móɫdɪŋ] N (adornment) moldura *f*; (action of molding) moldeado *m*

Moldova [mɔɫdóvə] N Moldavia *f*

Moldovan [mɔɫdóvən] ADJ & N moldavo -va *mf*

moldy [móɫdi] ADJ mohoso

mole [moɫ] N (blemish) lunar *m*; (animal, spy) topo *m*; (breakwater) rompeolas *m sg*

molecular [məlékjələ-] ADJ molecular

molecule [málɪkjuɫ] N molécula *f*

molest [məlést] VT abusar sexualmente de

mollify [máləfaɪ] VT apaciguar, aplacar

mollusk [máləsk] N molusco *m*

molt [moɫt] VI (birds) mudar la pluma; (snakes) mudar la piel; N muda *f*

molten [móɫtn̩] ADJ fundido

molybdenum [məlíbdənəm] N molibdeno *m*

mom [mɑm] N mamá *f*; **— and pop store** tienda familiar *f*

moment [mómənt] N momento *m*; **being a parent has its —s** ser padre/madre tiene sus momentos de recompensa

momentary [mómənteri] ADJ momentáneo

momentous [moméntəs] ADJ importante,

trascendental
momentum [moméntəm] N (in physics) momento *m*; (in politics, sports) empuje *m*
mommy [mámi] N mami *f*
Monaco [mánəko] N Mónaco *m*
monarch [mánɑrk] N monarca *mf*
monarchical [mənárkɪkəl] ADJ monárquico
monarchist [mánəˌkɪst] N monárquico -ca *mf*
monarchy [mánəˌki] N monarquía *f*
monastery [mánəsteri] N monasterio *m*
Monday [mánde] N lunes *m*
Monegasque [manɪgásk] ADJ & N monegasco -ca *mf*
monetary [mánɪteri] ADJ monetario
money [máni] N dinero *m*; —-**back guarantee** garantía de devolución de dinero *f*; — **belt** faltriquera en forma de cinturón *f*; — **changer** cambista *mf*; — **laundering** lavado de dinero *m*; — **machine** cajero automático *m*; — **market** mercado de valores *m*; — **market account** cuenta de mercado monetario *f*; — **order** giro postal *m*; **to get one's** —'**s worth** sacar jugo al dinero; ADJ —-**grubbing** codicioso; —-**making** lucrativo, rentable
moneyed [mánid] ADJ adinerado
Mongolia [maŋgóliə] N Mongolia *f*
Mongolian [maŋgóliən] ADJ & N mongol -ola *mf*
mongoloid [máŋgələɔɪd] ADJ mongoloide
mongoose [máŋgus] N mangosta *f*
mongrel [máŋgrəl] ADJ & N mestizo *m*
monitor [mánɪtə-] N monitor *m*; (in a school) celador -ora *mf*; — **lizard** varano *m*; VT monitorear
monitoring [mánɪtə-ɪŋ] N monitoreo *m*, monitorización *f*
monk [mʌŋk] N monje *m*, religioso *m*
monkey [máŋki] N mono *m*, mico *m*; — **bars** jaula de los monos *f*; — **business** (mischief) picardía *f*; (trickery) chanchullo *m*; — **wrench** llave inglesa *f*; **to have a** — **on one's back** estar adicto; VI **to** — **around** bobear, payasear; **to** — **with** bobear con
monogamy [mənágəmi] N monogamia *f*
monologue, monolog [mánəbg] N monólogo *m*
mononucleosis [manonukliósɪs] N mononucleosis *f*
monopolize [mənápələaɪz] VT monopolizar
monopoly [mənápəli] N monopolio *m*
monotonous [mənátṇəs] ADJ monótono
monotony [mənátṇi] N monotonía *f*
monsignor [mansínjə-] N monseñor *m*
monster [mánstə-] N monstruo *m*; ADJ enorme, monstruo *inv*
monstrosity [manstrásɪDi] N monstruosidad *f*
monstrous [mánstrəs] ADJ monstruoso
month [mʌnθ] N mes *m*
monthly [mánθli] ADJ mensual; — **installment** mensualidad *f*; N publicación

mensual *f*, mensuario *m*; ADV mensualmente
monument [mánjəmənt] N monumento *m*
monumental [manjəméntl] ADJ monumental
moo [mu] N mugido *m*; VI mugir
mooch [mutʃ] VI/VT gorronear; N pedigüeño -ña *mf*
mood [mud] N (emotional state) humor *m*, vena *f*, ánimo *m*; (grammatical category) modo *m*; **to be in a good** — estar de buen humor; **to be in the** — **to** tener ganas de
moody [múDi] ADJ (sullen) malhumorado; (changing) voluble
moon [mun] N luna *f*; —**beam** rayo de luna *m*; —**light** claro de la luna *m*, luz de la luna *f*; —**lighting** pluriempleo *m*; —**shine** bebida alcohólica destilada sin licencia *f*; **once in a blue** — de Pascuas a Ramos; VT *fam* mostrarle el culo [a alguien]
moor [mʊr] VI/VT amarrar; N páramo *m*
Moor [mʊr] N moro -ra *mf*
Moorish [múrɪʃ] ADJ morisco, moro
moose [mus] N alce *m*
moot [mut] ADJ **it became a** — **point** dejó de tener importancia
mop [mɑp] N (for floors) *Sp* fregona *f*, *Sp* mopa *f*; *Mex* trapeador *m*; (for dust) plumero *m*; (of hair) greña *f*; —-**up** (of an enemy) limpieza *f*; (of a task) remate *m*; VI/VT pasar la mopa [sobre]; *Am* trapear; VT **to** — **one's brow** enjugarse la frente; **to** — **up** (a spill) limpiar; (an enemy) acabar con; (a task) rematar
mope [mop] VI andar abatido
moped [móped] N ciclomotor *m*, scooter *m*
moral [mórəl] ADJ moral; N moraleja *f*; —**s** moral *f*
morale [mərǽl] N moral *f*
moralist [mórəlɪst] N moralista *mf*
morality [mórǽlɪDi] N moralidad *f*
moralize [mórəlaɪz] VI/VT moralizar
morbid [mórbɪd] ADJ mórbido, morboso
morbidity [mɔrbíDɪDi] N (predisposition to illness) morbilidad *f*; (producing illness) morbosidad *f*
more [mɔr] ADJ & ADV más; — **and** — cada vez más; — **or less** más o menos; **there is no** — no hay más; —**over** además
morgue [mɔrg] N depósito de cadáveres *m*, morgue *f*
moribund [mórəbʌnd] ADJ moribundo
morning [mórnɪŋ] N mañana *f*; — **glory** dondiego de día *m*; — **sickness** náuseas *f pl*; — **star** lucero del alba *m*; **good** —! ¡buenos días! **tomorrow** — mañana por la mañana; ADJ de la mañana, matutino
Moroccan [mərákən] ADJ & N marroquí *mf*
Morocco [məráko] N Marruecos *m*
moron [móran] N imbécil *m*
morphine [mórfin] N morfina *f*
morsel [mórsəl] N bocado *m*

mortal [mɔ́rdl] ADJ & N mortal *mf*; — **sin** pecado mortal *m*
mortality [mɔrtǽlɪDi] N (rate) mortalidad *f*; (toll) mortandad *f*
mortar [mɔ́rDɚ] N (for pounding) mortero *m* (also ballistics); (for bricks) argamasa *f*, mezcla *f*; —**board** birrete *m*
mortgage [mɔ́rgɪʤ] N hipoteca *f*; VT hipotecar; ADJ hipotecario; —**-backed securities** valores respaldados por hipoteca *m pl*
mortgagor [mɔ́rgɪʤɚ] N deudor -ora hipotecario -ria *mf*
mortification [mɔ́rDəfɪkéʃən] N mortificación *f*
mortify [mɔ́rDəfaɪ] VI/VT mortificar[se]
mortuary [mɔ́rtʃuɛri] N mortuorio *m*
mosaic [mozéɪk] N mosaico *m*
Moslem [mázləm] ADJ & N musulmán -ana *mf*
mosque [mɔsk] N mezquita *f*
mosquito [məskíDo] N mosquito *m*; — **net** mosquitero *m*
moss [mɔs] N musgo *m*
mossy [mɔ́si] ADJ musgoso
most [most] ADJ — **children are good** la mayoría de los niños son buenos; — **people** la mayoría de la gente; **the** — **money** más dinero *m*; **the** — **votes** el mayor número de votos; **for the** — **part** generalmente; PRON **the** — **that I can do** lo más que puedo hacer; **we ate the** — comimos más que nadie; — **of the guests are here** ha llegado la mayoría de los invitados; ADV **the** — **ambitious** el más ambicioso; **a** — **pleasant day** un día de lo más agradable
mostly [móstli] ADV generalmente
motel [motɛ́ł] N motel *m*
moth [mɔθ] N (pest) polilla *f*; (nocturnal insect) mariposa nocturna *f*; —**ball** bolita de naftalina *f*; —**-eaten** apolillado
mother [mʌ́ðɚ] N madre *f*; —**board** placa madre *f*; — **country** madre patria *f*; —**fucker** *offensive* hijo de puta *m*; —**-in-law** suegra *f*; —**-of-pearl** madreperla *f*; — **tongue** lengua materna *f*; VT mimar a, cuidar de/a
motherhood [mʌ́ðɚhʊd] N maternidad *f*
motherly [mʌ́ðɚli] ADJ maternal
motif [motíf] N motivo *m*
motion [móʃən] N (movement) movimiento *m*; (signal) ademán *m*; (proposal) moción *f*; — **picture** película de cine *f*; —**-picture industry** industria cinematográfica *f*; — **sickness** mareo *m*; VI/VT hacer un ademán
motionless [móʃənlɪs] ADJ inmóvil
motivate [móDəvet] VT motivar
motivation [moDəvéʃən] N motivación *f*
motive [móDɪv] N motivo *m*; ADJ motriz
motley [mátli] ADJ abigarrado
motor [móDɚ] N motor *m*; —**bike** motocicleta pequeña *f*; —**boat** lancha a motor *f*; —**cycle**

motorcycle *f*; —**cyclist** motociclista *mf*; — **home** casa rodante *f*, caravana *f*; — **scooter** scooter *m*; — **vehicle** vehículo motorizado *m*; VI pasear en coche
motorist [móDɚɪst] N automovilista *mf*
motto [máDo] N lema *f*
mound [maʊnd] N montículo *m*; **burial** — túmulo *m*; — **of laundry** pila de ropa *f*
mount [maʊnt] VI/VT (get on) montar; VI (increase) subir; VT (assemble) armar; N (mountain) monte *m*; (getting on a horse) montar *f*; (animal for riding) montura *f*
mountain [maʊntṇ] N montaña *f*; — **bike** bicicleta de montaña *f*; — **climber** alpinista *mf*; — **climbing** alpinismo *m*, montañismo *m*; — **goat** cabra montés *f*; — **lion** puma *f*, gato montés *m*; — **range** (large) cordillera *f*; (small) sierra *f*; —**side** ladera [de una montaña] *f*; —**top** cumbre [de una montaña] *f*; ADJ (animal, person) montañés; (thing) de montaña
mountaineer [maʊntṇír] N alpinista *mf*
mountainous [maʊntṇəs] ADJ montañoso
mourn [mɔrn] VI estar de duelo/luto; VT llorar; **to** — **for** llorar a
mourner [mɔ́rnɚ] N doliente *mf*
mournful [mɔ́rnfəł] ADJ lúgubre, triste
mourning [mɔ́rnɪŋ] N luto *m*, duelo *m*; **to be in** — estar de luto/duelo; ADJ de luto
mouse [maʊs] N ratón *m* (also computer); — **pad** alfombrilla [de ratón] *f*; — **port** puerto de ratón *m*; —**trap** ratonera *f*
mouth[1] [maʊθ] N boca *f*; (of a cave) abertura *f*; (of a river) desembocadura *f*; —**piece** (part of a trumpet) boquilla *f*; (spokesman) portavoz *mf*; —**-to-mouth resuscitation** respiración boca a boca *f*; —**wash** enjuague bucal *m*; ADJ —**-watering** delicioso
mouth[2] [maʊð] VT articular silenciosamente una palabra; VI **to** — **off** contestar
mouthful [maʊθfʊł] N (of food) bocado *m*; (of liquid) bocanada *f*, buche *m*
movable [múvəbəł] ADJ movible, móvil
move [muv] VT (change position) mover[se] (also board games); (change residence) mudar[se] de casa; (sell) venderse; **to** — **away** (distance oneself) apartarse; (change residence) irse; **to** — **forward** avanzar; **to** — **on** seguir adelante; **to** — **out** mudarse de casa; VT (propose) proponer; (affect emotionally) conmover; N (act of changing position) movimiento *m*; (change of residence) mudanza *f*; (action toward a goal) paso *m*; (play, in games) jugada *f*; **get a** — **on there!** ¡date prisa! **he made the first** — dio el primer paso
movement [múvmənt] N (motion, part of a watch) movimiento *m*; (of troops) desplazamiento *m*; **to have a bowel** —

mover el vientre
mover [múvɚ] N compañía de mudanzas ƒ; —**s
and shakers** la plana mayor
movie [múvi] N película ƒ, filme *m*; —**s** cine *m*;
—**making** cinematografía ƒ
moving [múvɪŋ] ADJ (target) móvil; (car) en
movimiento; (company) de mudanzas; (story)
conmovedor; — **picture** película ƒ; — **van**
camión de mudanzas *m*
mow [mo] VT cortar; (harvest) segar
mower [móɚ] N (for lawns) cortadora de
céspedes ƒ, cortacésped *m*; (farm implement)
segadora ƒ; (farmworker) segador -ora *mf*
mown [mon] *see* mow
Mozambican [mozæmbíkən] ADJ & N
mozambiqueño -ña *mf*
Mozambique [mozæmbík] N Mozambique *m*
Mozarabic [mozǽrəbɪk] ADJ mozárabe
Mr. [místɚ] N Sr. *m*
MRI [**magnetic resonance imaging**] [émáráí]
N IRM ƒ
Mrs. [mísɪz] N Sra. ƒ
Ms. [mɪz] N Sra. ƒ
much [mʌtʃ] ADJ & ADV mucho; — **the same**
casi lo mismo; — **like the others** muy
parecido a los demás; **as** — **as** tanto como;
how — ? ¿cuánto? **too** — demasiado; **very** —
muchísimo; **to make** — **of** dar mucha
importancia a; — **as I'd like, I won't do it**
aunque me gustaría, no lo voy a hacer; **that's
not** — **of a book** ese libro no es gran cosa;
she cried so — lloró tanto; **they need
water,** — **as they need sun** necesitan agua,
del mismo modo que necesitan sol
muck [mʌk] N (manure) estiércol *m*; (mire) cieno
m, lodo *m*; (filth) porquería ƒ; **to** — **up** *vulg*
cagarla
mucous [mjúkəs] ADJ mucoso
mucus [mjúkəs] N mucosidad ƒ
mud [mʌd] N lodo *m*, barro *m*; —**slinging**
difamación ƒ
muddle [mʌdl] VT (confuse) confundir; (make
turbid) enturbiar; VI **to** — **along** ir tirando;
to — **through** salir del paso; N (confusion)
confusión ƒ; (confused situation) embrollo *m*
muddy [mʌdi] ADJ (path) lodoso, barroso;
(shoes) embarrado; (vague) confuso; VT
(cover with mud) enlodar, embarrar; (make
unclear) enturbiar
muff [mʌf] N manguito *m*; VT estropear
muffin [mʌfɪn] N mollete *m*
muffle [mʌfəl] VT amortiguar
muffler [mʌflɚ] N (scarf) bufanda ƒ; (exhaust
device) silenciador *m*
mug [mʌg] N (ceramic) tazón *m*; (glass) jarra ƒ;
(face) jeta ƒ; VT atracar
mugger [mʌgɚ] N asaltante *mf*; atracador -ora
mf
muggy [mʌgi] ADJ bochornoso

mulatto [muláDo] ADJ & N mulato -ta *mf*
mulberry [mʌlbɛri] N mora ƒ; — **tree** moral *m*
mule [mjul] N mulo -la *mf* (also in drug
trafficking)
mull [mʌl] VI/VT rumiar
multicultural [mʌltikʌltʃəɚl] ADJ
multicultural
multilateral [mʌltilǽDəɚl] ADJ multilateral
multimedia [mʌltimíDiə] N & ADJ INV
multimedia *m*
multiple [mʌltəpəl] N múltiplo *m*; ADJ múltiple;
—**-choice** de opción múltiple; —
personality disorder trastorno de
personalidad múltiple *m*; — **sclerosis**
esclerosis múltiple ƒ
multiplication [mʌltəplɪkéʃən] N
multiplicación ƒ; — **sign** signo de
multiplicación *m*; — **table** tabla de
multiplicar ƒ
multiplicity [mʌltəplísɪDi] N multiplicidad ƒ
multiply [mʌltəplaɪ] VI/VT multiplicar[se]
multiscreen [mʌltiskrin] ADJ multipantalla
multitasking [mʌltitæskɪŋ] N multitarea ƒ
multitude [mʌltitud] N multitud ƒ
multiuser [mʌltijúzɚ] N multiusuario -ria *mf*
multi-year [mʌltijír] ADJ multianual
mum [mʌm] ADJ callado; **to keep** — callarse la
boca
mumble [mʌmbəl] VI/VT mascullar; N
refunfuño *m*
mumbo jumbo [mʌmbodʒʌmbo] N jerigonza ƒ
mummy [mʌmi] N momia ƒ
mumps [mʌmps] N paperas ƒ *pl*
munch [mʌntʃ] VT mascar
mundane [mʌndén] ADJ mundano
municipal [mjunísəpəl] ADJ municipal; —
council concejo *m*
municipality [mjunɪsəpǽlɪDi] N municipio *m*,
municipalidad *m*
munition [mjuníʃən] N munición ƒ
mural [mjúrəl] ADJ & N mural *m*
murder [mɝDɚ] N asesinato *m*, homicidio *m*; **to
get away with** — salirse con la suya; **that
exam was** — ese examen fue matador; VI/VT
asesinar
murderer [mɝDərɚ] N asesino *mf*, homicida *mf*
murderous [mɝDəɚs] ADJ asesino, homicida
murky [mɝki] ADJ (of water, matter) turbio; (of
sky) oscuro
murmur [mɝmɚ] N (noise) murmullo *m*,
susurro *m*; (complaint) queja ƒ; VI/VT (make
noise) murmurar, susurrar; (complain)
quejarse
muscle [mʌsəl] N músculo *m*; — **relaxant**
relajante muscular *m*; — **strain** distensión
muscular ƒ; — **tone** tonicidad muscular ƒ,
tono muscular *m*
muscular [mʌskjələɚ] ADJ (relative to muscles)
muscular; (endowed with muscles)

musculoso; — **dystrophy** distrofia
muscular*f*
muse [mjuz] VI meditar; VT cavilar; N musa*f*
museum [mjuzíəm] N museo *m*
mushroom [mÁʃrum] N seta*f*, hongo *m*,
champiñón *m*
mushy [mÁʃi] ADJ (soft) fofo; (sentimental)
sensiblero
music [mjúzɪk] N música*f*; — **stand** atril *m*; —
video *Am* video musical *m*; *Sp* vídeo
musical *m*
musical [mjúzɪkəl] ADJ (pertaining to music)
musical; (fond of music) aficionado a la
música, melómano; — **comedy** comedia
musical*f*
musician [mjuzíʃən] N músico -ca *mf*
muskrat [mÁskræt] N ratón almizclero *m*
Muslim [mÁzləm] ADJ & N musulmán -ana *mf*
muslin [mÁzlɪn] N muselina*f*
muss [mʌs] VT revolver, alborotar; N revoltijo *m*
mussel [mÁsəl] N mejillón *m*
must [mʌst] V AUX **you — arrive before nine**
debes llegar antes de las nueve; **you really —
eat at that restaurant** tienes que comer en
ese restaurante; **you — be his son** debes
[de] / has de ser su hijo; **they — have seen
me** deben [de] haberme visto
mustache, moustache [mÁstæʃ] N bigote *m*;
(large) mostacho *m*
mustard [mÁstɚd] N mostaza*f*; — **gas** gas
mostaza *m*
muster [mÁstɚ] VT (troops) formar; (courage)
juntar, reunir; VI (assemble for inspection)
formar; (come together) reunirse; **to — out**
dar de baja; **to — up one's courage** juntar
valor; N revista*f*; **to pass —** ser aceptable
musty [mÁsti] ADJ (stale smelling) con olor a
encierro/humedad; (antiquated) anticuado
mutant [mjútn̩t] ADJ & N mutante *mf*
mutation [mjutéʃən] N mutación*f*
mute [mjut] ADJ mudo; N (mute person) mudo
-da *mf*; (for musical instruments) sordina*f*
mutilate [mjúdlet] VT mutilar
mutiny [mjútṇi] N motín *m*; VI amotinarse
mutter [mÁDɚ] VI/VT refunfuñar, musitar; N
refunfuño *m*
mutton [mÁtṇ] N carne de cordero*f*
mutual [mjútʃuəl] ADJ mutuo; — **fund** fondo
mutuo/mutual *m*
muzzle [mÁzəl] N (snout) hocico *m*;
(mouthguard) bozal *m*; (gun opening) boca*f*;
VT (a dog) abozalar, poner bozal a; (critics)
amordazar, silenciar
my [maɪ] POSS ADJ mi; **these are — friends**
estos son mis amigos; **oh —!** ¡Dios mío! —
foot! ¡ni lo pienses!
Myanmar [mjɑnmár] N Myanmar *m*
myocardial infarction [maɪokárDiəl ɪnfárkʃən]
N infarto del miocardio *m*

myopia [maɪópiə] N miopía*f*
myriad [mírɪəd] N miríada*f*, sinfín *m*; —
problems un sinfín de problemas
myrtle [mɝ́dl] N mirto *m*, arrayán *m*
myself [maɪsɛ́lf] PRON **I — wrote the letters**
yo mismo escribí las cartas; **I'm not — today**
hoy no soy la misma de siempre; **I was
sitting by —** estaba sentado solo; **I talk to
—** hablo solo; **I looked at — in the mirror**
me miré en el espejo; **I bought — a house**
me compré una casa
mysterious [mɪstíriəs] ADJ misterioso
mystery [místəri] N misterio *m*
mystic [místɪk] ADJ & N místico -ca *mf*
mystical [místɪkəl] ADJ místico
myth [mɪθ] N mito *m*
mythic [míθɪk] ADJ mítico
mythical [míθɪkəl] ADJ mítico
mythological [mɪθəládʒɪkəl] ADJ mitológico
mythology [mɪθálədʒi] N mitología*f*

Nn

nab [næb] VT pescar; *Sp* coger
nag [næg] N (horse) jaca*f*, rocín *m*, penco *m*;
(complainer) quejica *mf*; VI/VT regañar,
criticar
nail [nel] N (for wood) clavo *m*; (of finger, toe)
uña*f*; —**-biter** situación angustiante*f*; —
file lima*f*; — **polish** esmalte para uñas *m*; **to
hit the — on the head** dar en el clavo; VT
(fasten) clavar; (nab) pescar; *Sp* coger
naive [nɑív] ADJ ingenuo, cándido, bonachón
naiveté [nɑivté] N ingenuidad*f*
naked [nékɪd] ADJ desnudo
nakedness [nékɪdnɪs] N desnudez*f*
name [nem] N nombre *m*; —**-brand** marca
comercial*f*; —**plate** placa*f*; —**sake** tocayo
m; —**tag** etiqueta de identificación*f*; — **of
the game** lo esencial *m*; **to call someone
—s** motejar a alguien; **to make a — for
oneself** hacerse un nombre; **what is your
—?** ¿cómo te llamas? VT nombrar; — **your
price** haz una oferta
nameless [némlɪs] ADJ anónimo
namely [némli] ADV a saber, en concreto
Namibia [nəmíbiə] N Namibia*f*
Namibian [nəmíbiən] ADJ & N namibio -bia *mf*
nanny [nǽni] N niñera*f*
nanosecond [nǽnosɛkənd] N nanosegundo *m*
nanotechnology [nǽnotɛknálədʒi] N
nanotecnología*f*
nap [næp] N (sleep) siesta*f*; (fibers) pelo *m*; **to
take a —** echar/dormir una siesta; VI echar/
dormir una siesta

napalm [népɑɫm] N napalm *m*
nape [nep] N nuca *f*
napkin [nǽpkɪn] N servilleta *f*
narcissism [nɑ́rsɪsɪzəm] N narcisismo *m*
narcissus [nɑrsísəs] N narciso *m*
narcolepsy [nɑ́rkələpsi] N narcolepsia *f*
narcotic [nɑrkɑ́DIk] ADJ & N narcótico *m*, estupefaciente *m*
narcotrafficking [nɑrkotrǽfIkɪŋ] N narcotráfico *m*
narrate [nǽret] VI/VT narrar
narration [næréʃən] N narración *f*
narrative [nǽrəDIv] ADJ narrativo; N narrativa *f*
narrator [nǽreDɚ] N narrador -ora *mf*
narrow [nǽro] ADJ (of little width) estrecho, angosto; (limited in scope) limitado; (intolerant) intolerante; **to have a — escape** salvarse por poco; **— gauge** de vía angosta/estrecha; **—-minded** intolerante; N **—s** desfiladero *m*, estrecho *m*, angostura *f*; VI/VT angostar[se], estrechar[se]; **to — down** reducir
narrowness [nǽronIs] N (quality of being narrow) estrechez *f*, angostura *f*
nasal [nézəɫ] ADJ nasal
nastiness [nǽstinIs] N (filth) suciedad *f*; (stinkiness) asquerosidad *f*; (rudeness, obscenity) grosería *f*
nasturtium [nəstɝ́ʃəm] N capuchina *f*
nasty [nǽsti] ADJ (mess) sucio; (smell) asqueroso; (comment) hiriente; (accident) feo; (word) grosero; (disposition) malo
natal [nédɫ] ADJ natal
nation [néʃən] N nación *f*; ADJ **—wide** a escala nacional
national [nǽʃənɫ] ADJ nacional; **— park** parque nacional *m*; **— team** seleccionado nacional *m*; N ciudadano -na *mf*, nacional *mf*
nationalism [nǽʃənəlIzəm] N nacionalismo *m*
nationalist [nǽʃənəlIst] N & ADJ nacionalista MF
nationality [næʃənǽlIDi] N nacionalidad *f*; **adjective of —** gentilicio *m*
nationalize [nǽʃənəlaIz] VT nacionalizar
native [néDIv] ADJ nativo; **— language** lengua nativa *f*; **— plants** flora nativa *f*; **my — Italy** mi Italia natal *f*; (innate) innato; N (person born in a place) natural *m*; (member of a tribal group) indígena *mf*, nativo -va *mf*; **he's a — of Italy** es oriundo de Italia
nativity [nətívIDi] N nacimiento *m*; **— scene** pesebre *m*; **the —** la Natividad
NATO [North Atlantic Treaty Organization] [néDo] N OTAN *f*
natural [nǽtʃəɫ] ADJ natural; (inborn) innato; **— childbirth** parto natural *m*; **— gas** gas natural *m*; **— resources** recursos naturales *m pl*; **— selection** selección natural *f*; N (musical sign) becuadro *m*; **he is a — for that job** tiene aptitud natural para ese puesto

naturalist [nǽtʃəəlIst] N naturalista *mf*
naturalization [nǽtʃəəlIzéʃən] N naturalización *f*
naturalize [nǽtʃəəlaIz] VI/VT naturalizar[se]
naturally [nǽtʃəəli] ADV (of course) naturalmente; **I have — curly hair** tengo rizos naturales
naturalness [nǽtʃəəɫnIs] N naturalidad *f*
nature [nétʃɚ] N naturaleza *f*; (disposition) genio *m*, natural *m*
naught [nɔt] N (zero) cero *m*; (nothing) nada *f*
naughtiness [nɔ́DinIs] N travesuras *f pl*
naughty [nɔ́Di] ADJ (child) travieso, pícaro, pillo; **— word** picardía *f*
Nauru [nɑúru] N Nauru *m*
Nauruan [nɑúruən] ADJ & N nauruano -na *mf*
nausea [nɔ́ziə] N náuseas *f pl*, mareo *m*
nauseate [nɔ́ziet] VT dar náuseas; **to be —d** tener náuseas
nauseating [nɔ́zieDIŋ] ADJ nauseabundo, nauseoso
nauseous [nɔ́ʃəs] ADJ (feeling nausea) mareado, nauseoso; (causing nausea) nauseabundo, nauseoso
nautical [nɔ́DIkəɫ] ADJ náutico
naval [névəɫ] ADJ naval; **— officer** oficial de marina *m*
Navarrese [nævəríz] ADJ & N navarro -rra *mf*
nave [nev] N nave *f*
navel [névəɫ] N ombligo *m*; **— orange** naranja de ombligo *f*
navigable [nǽvigəbəɫ] ADJ navegable
navigate [nǽviget] VI/VT navegar
navigation [nævigéʃən] N navegación *f*; (science) náutica *f*
navigator [nǽvigeDɚ] N navegante *mf*
navy [névi] N marina [de guerra] *f*, armada *f*; **— bean** judía blanca *f*; **— blue** azul marino *m*
nay [ne] N (refusal) no *m*; (negative vote) voto negativo *m*
Nazi [nɑ́tsi] N nazi *mf*
near [nir] ADV cerca; **— at hand** cerca, a la mano; **to come/go/draw —** acercarse; PREP cerca de; **— the end of the month** hacia fines del mes; **to be — death** estar a punto de morir; ADJ cercano, próximo; **— East** Cercano Oriente *m*, Oriente Próximo *m*; **—sighted** miope; **I had a — miss** por poco me sucede un accidente; VI/VT acercarse [a]
nearby [nírbái] ADV cerca; ADJ cercano, próximo
nearly [nírli] ADV casi, cerca de; **I — did it** casi lo hago
nearness [nírnIs] N cercanía *f*, proximidad *f*
neat [nit] ADJ (clean) limpio, pulcro; (ordered) ordenado; (cool) bueno
neatness [nítnIs] N (cleanness) limpieza *f*, pulcritud *f*; (order) orden *m*
nebulous [nébjələs] ADJ nebuloso
nebulousness [nébjələsnIs] N nubosidad *f*

necessary [nésısɛri] ADJ (needed) necesario; (involuntary) forzoso

necessitate [nəsésıtet] VT requerir

necessity [nəsésıDi] N necesidad *f*; **out of** — por necesidad

neck [nɛk] N (of a human) cuello *m*; (of an animal) pescuezo *m*; (of clothes) escote *m*; (throat) garganta *f*; — **and** — parejos; —**lace** collar *m*; —**line** escote *m*; — **of land** istmo *m*; —**tie** corbata *f*

necrology [nəkráləʤi] N necrología *f*

necrosis [nəkrósıs] N necrosis *f*

nectar [néktə] N néctar *m*

nectarine [nɛktərín] N nectarina *f*

need [nid] N (lack) necesidad *f*; (poverty) carencia *f*; **in** — en aprietos; **if** — **be** en caso de necesidad; VT necesitar, precisar; **you** — **to come at four** tienes que venir a las cuatro

needle [nídl] N aguja *f*; —**point** bordado *m*; —**work** (embroidery) bordado *m*; (sewing) costura *f*; VT pinchar

needless [nídlıs] ADJ innecesario; — **to say** huelga decir

needy [níDi] ADJ necesitado, menesteroso

ne'er-do-well [nérduwɛł] N inútil *mf*

negate [nıgét] VT negar

negation [nıgéʃən] N negación *f*

negative [négəDıv] ADJ negativo; **the search proved** — la búsqueda no dio resultado; N negativa *f*; (photographic) negativo *m*; **this plan has one** — este plan tiene una contra; INTERJ ¡negativo!

neglect [nıglékt] VT (fail to heed) postergar; (fail to care for) descuidar; (fail to carry out) desatender; **you're** —**ing your friends** tienes abandonados a tus amigos; **to** — **to** olvidarse de; N negligencia *f*, descuido *m*

neglectful [nıgléktfəł] ADJ negligente, descuidado

negligence [néglıʤəns] N negligencia *f*

negligent [néglıʤənt] ADJ negligente, descuidado

negligible [néglıʤəbəł] ADJ despreciable, minúsculo

negotiate [nıgóʃiet] VI/VT (a contract) negociar, gestionar; (an obstacle) salvar

negotiating [nıgóʃieDıŋ] ADJ negociador

negotiation [nıgoʃiéʃən] N negociación *f*, gestión *f*

negotiator [nıgóʃieDə] N negociador -ora *mf*

Negro [nígro] ADJ & N negro -gra *mf*

neigh [ne] N relincho *m*; VI relinchar

neighbor [nébə] N (person who lives near) vecino -na *mf*; (fellow human) prójimo -ma *mf*; ADJ vecino; VI **to** — **with** lindar con

neighborhood [nébəhud] N vecindario *m*, barrio *m*; **in the** — **of a hundred dollars** alrededor de cien dólares

neighboring [nébərıŋ] ADJ vecino, colindante

neither [níðə] PRON ninguno de los dos, ni [el] uno ni [el] otro; — **of the two** ninguno de los dos; ADJ ninguno de los dos; — **one of us** ninguno de nosotros dos; CONJ ni; — **hot nor cold** ni caliente ni frío; — **will I** yo tampoco

nemesis [némısıs] N némesis *f*

neologism [niáləʤızəm] N neologismo *m*

neon [nían] N neón *m*

neonatal [nionédl] ADJ neonatal

Nepal [nəpół] N Nepal *m*

Nepali [nəpóli] ADJ & N nepalés -esa *mf*, nepalí *mf*

nephew [néfju] N sobrino *m*

nephritis [nəfráıDıs] N nefritis *f*

nepotism [népətızəm] N nepotismo *m*

nerd [nɝd] N (technological adept) persona aficionada a las computadoras / los ordenadores *f*; (socially inept person) persona socialmente inepta *f*

nerve [nɝv] N (anatomy) nervio *m*; (courage) valor *m*; (impertinence) descaro *m*, morro *m*; — **cell** neurona *f*; — **gas** gas nervioso *m*; —**[w]racking** angustiante; **he gets on my** —**s** me saca de quicio

nervous [nɝvəs] ADJ nervioso; — **breakdown** ataque de nervios *m*

nervousness [nɝvəsnıs] N nerviosismo *m*

nest [nɛst] N nido *m*; (brood) nidada *f*; — **egg** ahorros *m pl*; — **of thieves** guarida de ladrones *f*; VI/VT anidar; (fit together) encajarse

nestle [nésəł] VI acurrucarse; VT apoyar, recostar

net [nɛt] N (fishing, network, tennis) red *f*; (in hair) redecilla *f*; —**work** red *f*; —**working** (social) relaciones profesionales *f pl*; (computer) diseño de redes y comunicaciones *m*; VT (catch a fish) pescar con red; (cover with a net) cubrir con una red; (catch a criminal) atrapar; (hit the tennis net) dar en la red; (make money after expenses) producir/ganar neto; ADJ neto; — **price** precio neto *m*; — **profit** ganancia neta *f*; — **assets** activo neto *m*; — **income** ingreso neto *m*; — **worth** patrimonio neto *m*

Netherlander [néðələndə] N holandés -esa *mf*

Netherlands [néðələndz] N Países Bajos *m pl*

nettle [nédl] N ortiga *f*

neural [núrəł] ADJ neural

neuralgia [núrǽłʤə] N neuralgia *f*

neurasthenia [núrəsθíniə] N neurastenia *f*

neurologist [núrálədʒıst] N neurólogo -ga *mf*

neuron [núran] N neurona *f*

neurosis [núrósıs] N neurosis *f*

neurosurgeon [núrosɝʤən] N neurocirujano -na *mf*

neurosurgery [núrosɝʤəri] N neurocirugía *f*

neurotic [núráDık] ADJ & N neurótico -ca *mf*

neurotransmitter [núrotrǽnzmıDə] N neurotransmisor *m*

neuter [núDə] ADJ neutro; VT castrar

neutral [nútrəł] ADJ neutral, imparcial; (of colors) neutro; N punto muerto *m*

neutrality [nutrǽlɪDi] N neutralidad *f*

neutralize [nútrəlaɪz] VI/VT neutralizar[se]

neutron [nútrɑn] N neutrón *m*; — **bomb** bomba de neutrones *f*

never [névə-] ADV nunca, jamás; — **mind** no te preocupes; **this will** — **do** esto no va a funcionar; —-**ending** interminable

nevertheless [nɛvə-ðəlés] ADV & CONJ sin embargo, no obstante

new [nu] ADJ (not old) nuevo; (fresh) otro; **a** — **sheet of paper** otra hoja de papel; — **age** [music] [música] nueva era *f*; —**born baby** recién nacido -da *mf*; —**comer** recién llegado -da *mf*; —**fangled** moderno, recién inventado; —**found** nuevo; — **year** año nuevo *m*; — **Year's Eve** fin de año *m*; *Sp* nochevieja *f*

newly [núli] ADV recientemente; — **arrived** recién llegado; —**wed** recién casado

newness [núnɪs] N novedad *f*

news [nuz] N (item) noticias *f pl*; (latest gossip) novedades *f pl*; (newspaper) periódico *m*; **it is** — **to me** recién me entero; — **broadcast/ bulletin** noticiero *m*, noticiario *m*; —**cast** noticiero *m*, noticiario *m*, informativo *m*; — **clipping** recorte de diario *m*; —**letter** boletín informativo *m*; —**paper** periódico *m*, diario *m*; —**print** papel de periódico *m*; —**room** sala de redacción *f*; —**stand** quiosco *m*; **piece of** — noticia *f*; ADJ —**worthy** de interés periodístico

newt [nut] N tritón *m*

New Zealand [nuzílənd] N Nueva Zelanda *f*

New Zealander [nuzíləndə-] N neozelandés -esa *mf*

next [nɛkst] ADJ (future) próximo, entrante; (following) siguiente; (contiguous) contiguo, de al lado; —-**door** de al lado; **who's** —? ¿quién sigue? ADV después, luego; — **best** segundo en calidad; **when** — **we meet** cuando nos volvamos a ver; PREP — **of kin** familiares *m pl*; — **to** junto a, al lado de

nibble [níbəł] VI/VT (bite) mordiscar, mordisquear; (eat) picotear; (of fish) picar; N (bite) mordisco *m*; (act of nibbling) mordisqueo *m*

Nicaragua [nɪkərágwə] N Nicaragua *f*

Nicaraguan [nɪkərágwən] ADJ & N nicaragüense *mf*

nice [naɪs] ADJ (kind) amable, simpático; (agreeable) *Am* lindo, *Sp* majo; **it's** — **and hot** está bien calentito

nicety [náɪsɪDi] N (subtlety) sutileza *f*; (detail) detalle *m*

niche [nɪtʃ] N (also environmental) nicho *m*; — **marketing** mercadeo de nicho *m*; **I've found my** — he encontrado mi lugar

nick [nɪk] N (chip) muesca *f*; (cut) corte *m*; **in the** — **of time** justo a tiempo; VT (chip) hacer muescas; (cut) cortar; —**name** apodo *m*, mote *m*, sobrenombre *m*; **to** —**name** apodar

nickel [níkəł] N (metal) níquel *m*; (coin) moneda de cinco centavos *f*; —-**plated** niquelado

nicotine [níkətin] N nicotina *f*

niece [nis] N sobrina *f*

Niger [náɪdʒə-] N Níger *m*

Nigeria [naɪdʒíriə] N Nigeria *f*

Nigerian [naɪdʒíriən] ADJ & N nigeriano -na *mf*

Nigerien [naɪdʒíriɛn] ADJ & N nigerino -na *mf*

niggardly [nígə-dli] ADJ mezquino

nigger [nígə-] N *highly offensive* negro -gra de mierda *mf*

night [naɪt] N noche *f*; ADJ nocturno, de noche; —**club** club nocturno *m*; —**fall** anochecer *m*, atardecer *m*; —**gown** camisón *m*; —**life** vida nocturna *f*; *Sp* marcha *f*; —**light** lamparilla *f*; —**mare** pesadilla *f*; — **owl** trasnochador -ora *mf*; — **shift** turno de la noche *m*; —**stand** veladora *f*, mesilla de noche *f*; —**time** noche *f*; — **watchman** celador *m*

nightingale [náɪtŋɡeł] N ruiseñor *m*

nightly [náɪtli] ADV todas las noches; ADJ nocturno

nihilism [náɪəlɪzəm] N nihilismo *m*

nil [nɪł] ADJ nulo

nimble [nímbəł] ADJ ágil

nincompoop [níŋkəmpup] N *fam* tarambana *mf*, bobalicón -ona *mf*

nine [naɪn] NUM nueve; — **hundred** novecientos

nineteen [naɪntín] NUM diecinueve

ninety [náɪnti] NUM noventa

ninth [náɪnθ] ADJ & N noveno *m*

nip [nɪp] VT (pinch) pellizcar; (bite) mordiscar, mordisquear, (cause frostbite) helar; **to** — **in the bud** cortar de raíz; **to** — **off** despuntar; VI (drink in sips) dar sorbitos; N (pinch) pellizco *m*; (bite) mordisco *m*; (sip) traguito *m*, sorbito *m*; (cold) frío *m*; **it's going to be** — **and tuck** va a ser muy reñido

nipple [nípəł] N (on female breast) pezón *m*; (on male breast) tetilla *f*; (on bottle) tetina *f*

nitpick [nítpɪk] VI criticar detalles insignificantes

nitrate [náɪtret] N nitrato *m*

nitric acid [náɪtrɪkǽsɪd] N ácido nítrico *m*

nitrogen [náɪtrədʒən] N nitrógeno *m*

nitroglycerin [naɪtroglísə-ɪn] N nitroglicerina *f*

nitty-gritty [nídigríɾi] N **to get down to the** — ir al grano

no [no] ADV no; — **longer** ya no; — **man's land** tierra de nadie *f*; — **matter how much** por mucho que; — **one** ninguno, nadie; — **smoking** se prohíbe fumar; —**where** (location) en ninguna parte / ningún lado; (direction) a ninguna parte / ningún lado; **he**

was a —-**show** no se presentó; **a** —-**win situation** una situación insoluble; **there is** — **more** no hay más; ADJ ningun[o]; **I have** — **friends** no tengo amigos; **it's a** —-**brainer** la respuesta es obvia; — **friend of mine will go hungry** ningún amigo mío pasará hambre; **of** — **use** inútil; N (refusal) no *m*; (negative vote) voto negativo *m*; ADJ —-**frills** básico, sin lujos

nobility [nobílɪɒi] N nobleza *f*, hidalguía *f*

noble [nóbəł] ADJ & N noble *mf*; —**man** hidalgo *m*

nobody [nóbaɒi] PRON nadie, ninguno; N don nadie, pelagatos *mf sg*

nocturnal [naktɜ-nł] ADJ nocturno

nod [nɑd] VI/VT (signal affirmation) asentir con la cabeza; VI (doze) cabecear, dar cabezadas; **to** — **off** dormirse; N (as signal) inclinación de cabeza *f*, saludo con la cabeza *m*; (from sleepiness) cabezada *f*

node [nod] N (of cells) nódulo *m*; (in plants) nudo *m*; (in physics) nodo *m*

noise [nɔɪz] N ruido *m*; — **pollution** contaminación sonora *f*; VI **it is being** —**d about that** corre el rumor que

noiseless [nɔ́ɪzlɪs] ADJ silencioso

noisy [nɔ́ɪzi] ADJ ruidoso

nomad [nómæd] N nómada *mf*

nomenclature [nómɪnkletʃɚ] N nomenclatura *f*

nominal [námənł] ADJ nominal

nominate [námənet] VT nominar

nomination [namənéʃən] N nominación *f*

nominee [naməní] N candidato -ta *mf*

nonchalant [nanʃəlánt] ADJ despreocupado

noncollectible [nankəléktəbəł] ADJ incobrable

noncommercial [nankəmɜ́-ʃəł] ADJ no comercial

noncommissioned officer [nankəmíʃənd ɔ́fɪsɚ] N suboficial *m*

nonconforming [nankənfɔ́rmɪŋ] ADJ no conforme

nonconformist [nankənfɔ́rmɪst] ADJ & N incomformista *mf*

none [nʌn] PRON ninguno; **I want** — **of that** no me quiero meter en eso; **that is** — **of your business** no es asunto tuyo; ADV — **too soon** al último momento; —**theless** sin embargo

nonentity [nanéntɪɒi] N nulidad *f*

nonessential [nanɪsénʃəł] ADJ no esencial

nonexistent [nanɪgzístənt] ADJ inexistente

nonfiction [nanfíkʃən] N no ficción *f*

nongovernmental [nangʌvɚnméntł] ADJ no gubernamental

nonnegotiable [nannɪgóʃəbəł] ADJ no negociable

nonpartisan [nanpárɒɪzən] ADJ (neutral) imparcial; (not affiliated) sin afiliación política

nonperformance [nanpɚfɔ́rmɚns] N incumplimiento *m*

nonproductive [nanprədʌ́ktɪv] ADJ improductivo

nonprofit [nanpráfɪt] ADJ sin fines de lucro; N organización sin fines de lucro *f*

nonrefundable [nanrɪfʌ́ndəbəł] ADJ no reembolsable

nonresident [nanrézɪdənt] ADJ & N no residente *mf*

nonsense [nánsɛns] N tonterías *f pl*, monsergas *f pl*, estupideces *f pl*; **to talk** — decir barbaridades/disparates

nonstop [nánstáp] ADJ sin escala, directo; ADV sin parar

nontaxable [nantǽksəbəł] ADJ no tributable

nonvoting [nanvóɒɪŋ] ADJ sin derecho a voto

noodle [núdł] N fideo *m*, tallarín *m*

nook [nʊk] N rincón *m*

noon [nun] N mediodía *m*; — **hour** mediodía *m*, hora de comer; —**time** mediodía *m*

noose [nus] N soga *f*, lazo *m*; **with a** — **around his neck** con la soga al cuello; VT (catch with a rope) enlazar; (make a loop in) hacer un lazo corredizo en

nope [nop] ADV no

nor [nɔr] CONJ ni; **we have neither eggs** — **flour** no tenemos ni huevos ni harina

Nordic [nɔ́rdɪk] ADJ nórdico

norm [nɔrm] N norma *f*, normativa *f*

normal [nɔ́rməł] ADJ normal; (perpendicular) normal; **to return to** — volver a la normalidad; (perpendicular line) línea perpendicular *f*

normalcy [nɔ́rməłsi] N normalidad *f*

normality [nɔrmǽlɪɒi] N normalidad *f*

normalize [nɔ́rməlaɪz] VI/VT normalizar[se]

normally [nɔ́rməli] ADV (in a normal way) de manera normal, con toda normalidad *f*; (usually) normalmente

north [nɔrθ] N norte *m*; —**east** noreste, hacia el noreste; —**west** noroeste *m*, hacia el noroeste; ADJ (in the north) norte, norteño; (from the north) del norte; — **America** América del Norte *f*; — **American** norteamericano -na *mf*; —**eastern** del noreste; — **Korea** Corea del Norte *f*; — **Korean** norcoreano -na; — **Pole** Polo Norte *m*; — **wind** cierzo *m*, viento norte *m*; **the** — **entrance** la entrada norte; ADV al norte, hacia el norte

northern [nɔ́rðɚn] ADJ del norte; (from the north) norteño; (in the north) septentrional; — **lights** aurora boreal *f*

northerner [nɔ́rðɚnɚ] N norteño -ña *mf*

northward [nɔ́rθwɚd] ADV hacia el norte

Norway [nɔ́rwe] N Noruega *f*

Norwegian [nɔrwíʤən] ADJ & N noruego -ga *mf*

nose [noz] N nariz *f*; (of an airplane) morro *m*; (of

an animal) hocico *m*; (perspicacity) olfato *m*; —**bleed** hemorragia nasal*f*; —**dive** caída en picado*f*; — **job** rinoplastia*f*; **keep your — clean** no te metas en líos; **on the —** exactamente; **to pick one's —** hurgarse las narices; VI/VT (move forward) entrar de punta; (muzzle) hocicar; **to — around** husmear

nostalgia [nɑstǽłdʒə] N nostalgia*f*

nostalgic [nɑstǽłdʒɪk] ADJ nostálgico

nostrils [nɑ́strəłz] N narices*f pl*, ventanillas de la nariz*f pl*

nosy, nosey [nózi] ADJ entrometido

not [nɑt] ADV no; **I'm — your friend** no soy tu amigo; — **at all** (no way) de ningún modo; (you're welcome) de nada; — **at all sure** nada seguro; — **even a word** ni una palabra

notable [nóɾəbəł] ADJ notable, destacable

notably [nóɾəbli] ADV notablemente

notarize [nóɾəraɪz] VT notariar

notary [nóɾəri] N notario -ria *mf*; — **public** notario -ria público -ca *mf*

notation [notéʃən] N (system of signs) notación *f*; (act of writing) anotación*f*; (short note) anotación*f*, apunte *m*

notch [nɑtʃ] N (nick) muesca*f*, mella*f*; (degree) grado *m*; **a — above the rest** mejor que los demás; VT hacer una muesca; **he —ed another win** se anotó otra victoria

note [not] N (written) nota*f*, anotación*f*; (musical) nota*f*; (touch) toque *m*; (financial) pagaré *m*; (currency) billete *m*; —**book** cuaderno *m*; (small) libreta*f*; —**s** apuntes *m pl*; **of —** de renombre / de nota; **to take — of** notar; ADJ —**worthy** notable; VT (notice) notar; (write down) anotar, apuntar

noted [nóɾɪd] ADJ célebre

nothing [nʌ́θɪŋ] PRON nada; (score) cero, nada; N (insignificant person) don nadie *m*; (insignificant thing) nadería*f*; — **to it** no tiene ciencia; ADV **it was — like that** no fue así para nada; **we did it for —** (free) lo hicimos gratis; (fruitlessly) lo hicimos en balde

notice [nóɾɪs] N (information) aviso *m*; (warning) advertencia*f*; (attention) atención *f*; **a week's —** una semana de plazo; **to give — renunciar; to take —** hacer caso; VT (perceive) notar, advertir, percatarse [de]; (pay attention to) fijarse [en], reparar [en]

noticeable [nóɾɪsəbəł] ADJ perceptible, apreciable

noticeably [nóɾɪsəbli] ADV notablemente

notification [noɾəfɪkéʃən] N notificación*f*

notify [nóɾəfaɪ] VT notificar

notion [nóʃən] N noción*f*, idea*f*; (whim) capricho *m*; —**s** mercería*f*

notorious [notɔ́riəs] ADJ de mala fama; **he's a — liar** tiene fama de mentiroso

nougat [núgət] N turrón *m*

noun [naUn] N sustantivo *m*

nourish [nɜ́ɪʃ] VT (a person) nutrir, alimentar; (a hope) abrigar

nourishing [nɜ́ɪʃɪŋ] ADJ nutritivo

nourishment [nɜ́ɪʃmənt] N (food) alimento *m*; (act of nourishing) alimentación*f*

novel [návəł] N novela*f*; ADJ novedoso

novelist [návəlɪst] N novelista *mf*

novelty [návəłti] N novedad*f*; **the — soon wore off** se pasó la novedad; **novelties** chucherías*f pl*

November [novémbə] N noviembre *m*

novice [návɪs] N novato -ta *mf*, pipiolo -la *mf*; (religious) novicio -cia *mf*

novocaine [nóvəken] N novocaína*f*

now [naU] ADV ahora; — **and then** de vez en cuando; — **that** ahora que; **he left just —** salió hace poco, recién salió; —, —, **calm down!** bueno, bueno, ¡cálmate!

nowadays [náUədez] ADV hoy [en] día

noxious [nákʃəs] ADJ nocivo

nuance [núɑns] N matiz *m*

nuclear [núkliə] ADJ nuclear; — **energy** energía nuclear*f*; — **family** familia nuclear *f*; — **fission** fisión nuclear*f*; — **fusion** fusión nuclear*f*; — **physics** física nuclear*f*; — **weapon** arma nuclear*f*

nucleus [núkliəs] N núcleo *m*

nude [nud] ADJ & N desnudo *m*

nudge [nʌdʒ] VI/VT codear; N golpe suave con el codo *m*

nugget [nʌ́gɪt] N (of gold) pepita*f*; (of chicken) pedacito *m*; (of wisdom) perla*f*

nuisance [núsəns] N molestia*f*; Sp pesadez*f*; (legal) perjuicio *m*; **you're such a —!** ¡qué pesado eres tú! — **tax** impuesto de consumo *m*

nuke [nuk] N arma nuclear*f*; VT (bomb) bombardear con armas nucleares; (cook) calentar en microondas

null [nʌł] ADJ nulo; — **and void** nulo

nullify [nʌ́ləfaɪ] VT anular

numb [nʌm] ADJ entumecido; **to get —** entumecerse; VT entumecer

number [nʌ́mbə] N número *m*; — **one** uno mismo *m*; —-**crunching** procesamiento de datos numéricos complejos *m*; VI (total) ascender a; **I — him among my friends** lo cuento entre mis amigos; VT numerar

numberless [nʌ́mbəlɪs] ADJ sin número

numbskull, numskull [nʌ́mskʌł] N zopenco -ca *mf*

numeral [núməəł] N número *m*; ADJ numeral

numerical [numérɪkəł] ADJ numérico

numerous [núməəs] ADJ numeroso

nun [nʌn] N monja*f*, religiosa*f*

nuptial [nʌ́pʃəł] ADJ nupcial; N —**s** nupcias*f pl*

nurse [nɜs] N (for the sick) enfermero -ra *mf*;

(for children) niñera *f*; VT (give milk) amamantar, lactar; (tend to a sick person) cuidar; **to — a grudge** guardar rencor; **to — a cup of coffee** tomar una taza de café a sorbitos; **to — a cold** cuidarse durante un resfrío; VI (drink milk) mamar

nursery [nɚ́sri] N (children's room) cuarto para niños *m*; (day-care center) guardería *f*; (place for growing plants) almáciga *f*, vivero *m*, plantel *m*; — **rhyme** canción infantil *f*, ronda *f*; — **school** preescolar *m*; *Sp* parvulario *m*; *Am* jardín infantil *m*

nursing [nɚ́sɪŋ] N (profession) enfermería *f*; (care) cuidado *m*; — **home** (for old people) hogar de ancianos *m*; (for sick people) casa de salud *f*

nurture [nɚ́tʃɚ] VT (rear) criar; (feed) nutrir, alimentar; (encourage) fomentar; N (rearing) crianza *f*; (feeding) alimentación *f*

nut [nʌt] N (fruit) fruto seco *m*; (device) tuerca *f*; (person) excéntrico -ca *mf*; —**cracker** cascanueces *m sg*; —**meg** nuez moscada *f*; —**s** *vulg* cojones *m pl*; ADJ crazy; —**s and bolts** los fundamentos; —**shell** cáscara de fruto seco *f*; **in a —shell** en pocas palabras

nutrient [nútriənt] N nutriente *m*

nutrition [nutríʃən] N nutrición *f*, alimentación *f*

nutritious [nutríʃəs] ADJ nutritivo, alimenticio

nylon [náilɑn] N nilón *m*, nailon *m*

Oo

oak [ok] N roble *m*, encina *f*; — **grove** robledal *m*

oar [ɔr] N remo *m*; VI/VT remar, bogar; —**lock** tolete *m*

OAS [Organization of American States] [óés] N OEA *f*

oasis [oésɪs] N oasis *m*

oat [ot] N avena *f*; —**meal** (flour) harina de avena *f*; (breakfast food) gachas de avena *f pl*; —**s** avena *f*

oath [oθ] N (pledge) juramento *m*; (curse) maldición *f*; (swear word) palabrota *f*, taco *m*; **to take an —** prestar juramento

obedience [obíDiəns] N obediencia *f*

obedient [obíDiənt] ADJ obediente

obese [obís] ADJ obeso

obesity [obísiDi] N obesidad *f*

obey [obé] VI/VT obedecer

obituary [obítʃueri] N nota necrológica *f*, obituario *m*

object[1] [ábdʒɪkt] N objeto *m*; (of a verb) complemento *m*

object[2] [əbdʒékt] VI/VT objetar

objection [əbdʒékʃən] N objeción *f*

objectionable [əbdʒékʃənəbəł] ADJ objetable

objective [əbdʒéktɪv] ADJ objetivo; N objetivo *m*, finalidad *f*

objectivity [abdʒektívɪDi] N objetividad *f*

obligate [ábliget] VT obligar

obligated [ábligeDɪd] ADJ obligado, comprometido

obligation [abligéʃən] N obligación *f*; **under no — to buy** sin compromiso de compra

obligatory [əblígətɔri] ADJ obligatorio, obligado

oblige [əbláɪdʒ] VT (make obliged) obligar; VI/VT (do a favor for) complacer; VI (obey an order) obedecer; **much —d!** ¡muchas gracias! ¡muy agradecido!

obliging [əbláɪdʒɪŋ] ADJ complaciente; *Am* comedido

oblique [oblík] ADJ oblicuo

obliterate [əblíDəret] VT (blot out) tachar; (destroy) arrasar, destruir

oblivion [əblíviən] N olvido *m*

oblivious [əblíviəs] ADJ inconsciente; — **to the danger** ajeno al peligro

obnoxious [əbnákʃəs] ADJ (remark, behavior) ofensivo; (person) odioso

oboe [óbo] N oboe *m*

obscene [əbsín] ADJ obsceno; **his salary is —** lo que gana es escandaloso

obscenity [əbsénɪDi] N obscenidad *f*

obscure [əbskjúr] ADJ oscuro; VT oscurecer

obscurity [əbskjúrɪDi] N oscuridad *f*

obsequious [əbsíkwiəs] ADJ obsequioso

observance [əbzɚ́vəns] N observancia *f*

observant [əbzɚ́vənt] ADJ observador

observation [abzɚvéʃən] N observación *f*

observatory [əbzɚ́vətɔri] N observatorio *m*

observe [əbzɚ́v] VT observar; (holidays, rituals) guardar

observer [əbzɚ́vɚ] N observador -ora *mf*; (of elections) interventor -ora *mf*

obsess [əbsés] VI/VT obsesionar[se]; **he's —ing over it** está obsesionado con eso

obsession [əbséʃən] N obsesión *f*

obsessive-compulsive [əbsésɪvkəmpʌ́łsɪv] ADJ obsesivo-compulsivo

obsolescence [absəlésəns] N desuso *m*

obsolete [absəlít] ADJ anticuado, desusado

obstacle [ábstəkəł] N obstáculo *m*

obstetrician [abstətríʃən] N obstetra *mf*

obstetrics [abstétrɪks] N obstetricia *f*

obstinacy [ábstənəsi] N obstinación *f*, terquedad *f*, porfía *f*

obstinate [ábstənɪt] ADJ obstinado, terco, recalcitrante; **to be —** obstinarse

obstruct [əbstrʌ́kt] VI/VT obstruir; (traffic) atascar, obstruir

obstruction [əbstrʌ́kʃən] N obstrucción *f*

obtain [əbtén] VT obtener, procurar; VI prevalecer

obtainable [əbténəbəł] ADJ conseguible

obviate [ábviet] VT obviar
obvious [ábviəs] ADJ obvio, evidente
obviously [ábviəsli] ADV & INTERJ
evidentemente, obviamente
occasion [əkéʒən] N (moment) ocasión f;
(chance) oportunidad f, ocasión f; (cause)
motivo m; (event) acontecimiento m, ocasión
f; VT ocasionar
occasional [əkéʒənl] ADJ ocasional
occasionally [əkéʒənli] ADV de vez en cuando,
ocasionalmente
occidental [aksIdéntl] ADJ & N occidental mf
occlusion [əklúʒən] N obstrucción f, oclusión f
occult [əkʌ́lt] ADJ oculto; N ocultismo m, ciencias
ocultas f pl; VT ocultar
occupancy [ákjəpənsi] N ocupación f; — **rate**
tasa de ocupación f
occupant [ákjəpənt] N ocupante mf
occupation [akjəpéʃən] N ocupación f
occupational [akjəpéʃənl] ADJ ocupacional; —
hazard/risk riesgo ocupacional m; —
therapy laborterapia f, terapia ocupacional f
occupy [ákjəpaI] VI/VT ocupar
occur [əkɚ́] VI ocurrir, suceder; **it —red to me**
se me ocurrió
occurrence [əkɚ́əns] N suceso m,
acontecimiento m
ocean [óʃən] N océano m
oceanic [oʃiǽnIk] ADJ oceánico
oceanography [oʃənágrəfi] N oceanografía f
ocelot [ásələt] N ocelote m
o'clock [əklák] ADV **it is one** — es la una; **it is
two** — son las dos
octagon [áktəgɑn] N octágono m, octógono m
octane [ákten] N octano m
octave [áktIv] N octava f
October [aktóbɚ] N octubre m
octopus [áktəpəs] N pulpo m
oculist [ákjəlIst] N oculista mf
OD [overdose] [ódí] N sobredosis f; VI tomar una
sobredosis
odd [ɑd] ADJ (unusual) extraño; (not even) impar,
non; —**ball** excéntrico -ca mf; — **change**
suelto m, cambio m; — **job** trabajo ocasional
m; — **shoe** zapato sin compañero m; ADV
thirty-— treinta y tantos
oddity [áDIti] N rareza f; (person) excéntrico -ca
mf
odds [adz] N (probabilities) probabilidades f pl; —
and ends cachivaches m pl; **the — are
against me** llevo las de perder; **to be at** —
estar en desacuerdo; ADJ —**-on favorite**
favorito m
ode [od] N oda f
odious [óDiəs] ADJ odioso
odor [óDɚ] N olor m; (bad) hedor m
odorless [óDɚlIs] ADJ inodoro
odorous [óDɚəs] ADJ oloroso
of [ɑv] PREP de; — **course** por supuesto, desde

luego; **a quarter — five** las cinco menos
cuarto; **doctor — medicine** doctor -ora en
medicina mf; **the smell — paint** el olor a
pintura; **a friend — mine** un amigo mío
off [ɔf] ADV — **and on** de vez en cuando; — **the
record** extraoficialmente; **ten cents** —
rebaja de diez centavos f; **ten miles** — a diez
millas de distancia; **to take a day** — tomarse
un día libre; ADJ — **chance** posibilidad
remota f; —**-color** verde; — **season**
temporada baja f; — **year** de producción
decreciente; **our deal is** — se canceló
nuestro plan; **prices are** — los precios han
caído; **you're — by a mile** estás
equivocadísimo; **he's a little** — está
tocadito; **with his hat** — sin el sombrero;
the electricity is — está apagada la
electricidad; **to be — to war** haberse ido a la
guerra; **to be well** — tener mucho dinero;
PREP — **course** fuera de curso; **he drove** —
the road se salió de la carretera; **I bought it
— a gypsy** se lo compré a un gitano; **he's** —
playing golf se fue a jugar al golf; VT
liquidar
off-duty [ɔ́fdúDi] ADJ **to be** — no estar de turno
offend [əfénd] VI/VT (insult) ofender, afrentar;
(affect disagreeably) desagradar
offender [əféndɚ] N delincuente mf
offense¹ [əféns] N (sin, insult) ofensa f;
(misdemeanor) delito m; **no — was meant**
no te lo tomes a mal
offense² [áfens] (in sports) ofensiva f
offensive [əfénsIv] ADJ ofensivo; — **line** línea
ofensiva f; — **series** serie ofensiva f, ataque
m; N ofensiva f
offer [ɔ́fɚ] VT ofrecer; **to** — **to** ofrecerse a; N
oferta f; **make an** — hacer una oferta
offering [ɔ́fɚIŋ] N (thing given in worship)
ofrenda f; (thing presented for sale) oferta f;
(action of offering) ofrecimiento m
offhand [ɔ́fhǽnd] ADV **he remarked** —
mencionó al descuido; ADJ **an — remark** un
comentario descuidado
office [ɔ́fIs] N (function) cargo m, función f;
(place) oficina f, despacho m; (headquarters)
oficinas f pl; — **boy** mandadero de oficina m;
— **building** edificio para oficinas m; —
suite (furniture) juego ofimático m; (rooms)
suite f; (software) paquete de programas de
productividad m; **through the —s of** por la
intervención de
officer [ɔ́fIsɚ] N (military) oficial m; (police)
agente de policía mf; (of an organization)
directivo -va mf
official [əfíʃəl] ADJ oficial; N funcionario -ria mf
officiate [əfíʃiet] VI oficiar; (in sports) arbitrar
officious [əfíʃəs] ADJ oficioso
off-key [ɔ́fkí] ADJ desafinado
off-limits [ɔ́flímIts] ADJ vedado, de acceso

prohibido
off-line [ɔ́fláɪn] ADV fuera de línea
off-season [ɔ́fsizən] N temporada baja *f*; ADJ de temporada baja
offset[1] [ɔ́fsɛt] N offset *m*
offset[2] [ɔ́fsɛt, ɔfsét] VT compensar
offshore [ɔ́fʃɔ́r] ADJ & ADV cerca de la costa; — **account** cuenta en un paraíso fiscal *f*; — **drilling** explotación petrolífera en el fondo del mar *f*
offside [ɔ́fsáɪd] ADV fuera de juego
offspring [ɔ́fsprɪŋ] N prole *m*
offstage [ɔ́fstédʒ] ADV & ADJ entre bastidores, fuera de escena
off-the-record [ɔ́fθərékə·d] ADJ oficioso
often [ɔ́fən] ADV a menudo; **how**—? ¿con qué frecuencia? ¿cada cuánto?
ogre [ógə·] N ogro *m*
oh [o] INTERJ — **no!** ¡ay no! — **really?** ¿de veras? — **well** está bien, vale; — **yeah?** (not true) ¡qué va! (really?) ¿de veras?
ohm [om] N ohmio *m*
oil [ɔɪɬ] N (for cars, cooking) aceite *m*; (crude) petróleo *m*; —**can** alcuza *f*, aceitera *f*; —**cloth** hule *m*, tela de hule *f*; — **factory** aceitera *f*; — **field** campo petrolífero *m*; — **industry** industria petrolera *f*; — **lamp** quinqué *m*; — **painting** pintura al óleo *f*, óleo *m*; — **pan** cárter *m*; — **pipeline** oleoducto *m*; — **rig** plataforma petrolífera *f*; — **slick** mancha de petróleo *f*; — **spill** vertido de petróleo *m*; — **tanker** barco petrolero *m*; — **well** pozo de petróleo *m*; ADJ —**-bearing** petrolífero; —**-exporting** exportador de petróleo; —**-producing** petrolífero; VT (apply oil) aceitar; (bribe) untar
oily [ɔ́ɪli] ADJ (food) aceitoso; (liquid) oleoso; (hair) graso; (person) untuoso
oink [ɔɪŋk] VI gruñir; N gruñido *m*
ointment [ɔ́ɪntmənt] N ungüento *m*
OK/okay [oké] ADJ bueno; **he's an— guy** es un buen tipo; **his work is just—** su trabajo no es nada del otro mundo; ADV bien; **it's—** (fine) está bien; (adequate) es regular; N **to give one's—** dar el visto bueno; VT dar el visto bueno, aprobar; INTERJ bien, *Sp* vale
okra [ókrə] N quingombó *m*
old [oɬd] ADJ viejo; (objects only) antiguo; (wine) añejo; — **age** vejez *f*, ancianidad *f*; —**-boy network** red favoritista entre hombres *f*; —**-fashioned** (unfashionable) pasado de moda; (antiquated) anticuado; (morally prudish) chapado a la antigua; — **fogey** carcamal *m*, carca *m*; — **hat** pasado de moda; — **maid** solterona *f*; —**-time** antiguo, viejo; —**-timer** (longtime member) miembro de la vieja guardia *m*; (oldster) viejo *m*; — **wives' tale** superstición *f*; — **world** viejo mundo *m*; **days of—** antaño; **how— are you?**

¿cuántos años tienes? — **man** (husband) marido *m*; (father) *fam* viejo *m*; **I'm not— enough to drive** soy muy joven para conducir; **to be an— hand at** ser ducho en
olden [óɬdn̩] ADJ **in— days** antaño
oldie [óɬdi] N viejo éxito *m*
oleander [óliændə·] N adelfa *f*
olfactory [ɔɬfǽktəri] ADJ olfatorio
olive [áliv] N (tree) olivo *m*; (fruit) aceituna *f*, oliva *f*; — **branch** ramo de olivo *m*; — **grove** olivar *m*; — **oil** aceite de oliva *m*; — **wood** madera de olivo *m*; ADJ verde oliva
Olympiad [olímpiæd] N Olimpiada *f*, Olimpíada *f*
Olympic [olímpɪk] ADJ olímpico; — **Games** Olimpiadas *f pl*, Olimpíadas *f pl*, Juegos Olímpicos *m pl*
Oman [omán] N Omán *m*
Omani [ománi] ADJ & N omaní *mf*
omelet [ámlɪt] N tortilla francesa *f*
omen [ómən] N agüero *m*, presagio *m*
ominous [ámənəs] ADJ (threatening) amenazador; (like an omen) agorero
omission [omíʃən] N omisión *f*
omit [omít] VT omitir
omnipotence [amnípətəns] N omnipotencia *f*
omnipotent [amnípətənt] ADJ omnipotente
omniscience [amníʃəns] N omnisciencia *f*
omniscient [amníʃənt] ADJ omnisciente
omnivorous [amnívə·əs] ADJ omnívoro
on [an] PREP en, sobre, encima de; — **the table** en / sobre / encima de la mesa; — **all sides** por todos lados; — **arriving** al llegar; —**-board** a bordo; — **call** de guardia; — **credit** al fiado; — **drugs** drogado; — **horseback** a caballo; — **Monday** el lunes; — **purpose** a propósito; —**-screen** en la pantalla; — **the house** la casa paga; — **time** a tiempo; **a book— stamps** un libro sobre sellos; **do you have any cigarettes— you?** ¿tienes cigarros? **drunk— beer** borracho de cerveza; **to talk— the phone** hablar por teléfono; ADJ —**line** en línea; —**line banking** banca en línea *f*; —**line** ayuda en línea *f*; ADV — **and**— dale que dale; **his hat is—** lleva puesto el sombrero; **the light is—** está encendida la luz; **there's a war—** estamos en guerra; **you're—** (broadcasting) estás en el aire; (acceptance) te acepto la propuesta
once [wʌns] ADV (in the past, a single time) una vez; (if ever) si alguna vez; — **and for all** una vez por todas, definitivamente; — **in a while** de vez en cuando; — **upon a time** érase una vez; **at—** de inmediato, enseguida; **just this—** sólo por esta vez; **cousin— removed** primo -ma segundo -da *mf*; CONJ una vez que, cuando; N una vez; —**-over** vistazo *m*
oncology [ankálədʒi] N oncología *f*

one [wʌn] NUM uno; — **book** un libro; — **hundred** cien; — **hundred and one** ciento uno; — **thousand** mil; —-**armed** manco; —-**armed bandit** tragaperras *mf sg*; —- **eyed** tuerto; — **John Smith** un tal John Smith; —-**man band** hombre orquesta *m*; —-**night stand** aventura sexual de una noche *f*, *Sp* flete *m*; — **on** — mano a mano; —-**sided fight** pelea desigual *f*; —- **upmanship** competitividad *f*; —-**way street** calle de sentido único *f*; **his** — **chance** su única oportunidad; **the** — **and only** el único; **this is** — **smart dog** es un perro muy listo; N & PRON uno *m*; — **at a time** de a uno; — **by** — uno por uno; **love** — **another** amaos los unos a los otros; **the** — **who** el/la que; **the green** — el verde; **this** — este/esta

oneself [wʌnsélf] PRON **to be** — ser uno mismo; **to sit by** — estar sentado solo; **to talk to** — hablar para sí; **to look at** — **in the mirror** mirarse en el espejo; **to buy** — **a house** comprarse una casa

ongoing [ángoɪŋ] ADJ continuo

onion [ʌ́njən] N cebolla *f*; — **patch** cebollar *m*

onlooker [ánlʊkɚ] N espectador -ora *mf*, mirón -ona *mf*

only [ónli] ADJ único; ADV solo, solamente; **I** — **just caught the train** por poco pierdo el tren; CONJ solo que, pero

onomatopoeia [ɑnəmɑɒəpíə] N onomatopeya *f*

onset [ánsɛt] N comienzo *m*

on-side kick [ónsaɪd kík] N patada lateral *f*

onto [ántu] PREP en, sobre, encima de; **she got** — **the plane late** subió tarde al avión; **he dropped it** — **the table** lo dejó caer en la mesa; **I'm** — **your plot** conozco tu plan

onward [ánwɚd] ADV hacia adelante

onyx [ániks] N ónix *m*

oops [ʊps] INTERJ ¡huy!

ooze [uz] VI/VT rezumar[se]; N cieno *m*

opal [ópəl] N ópalo *m*

opaque [opék] ADJ opaco

OPEC [Organization of Petroleum Exporting Countries] [ópɛk] N OPEP *f*

open [ópən] VI/VT abrir[se]; **to** — **into** comunicarse con; **to** — **one's way** abrirse paso; **to** — **onto** dar a; **to** — **up** abrirse; ADJ abierto; — **and shut** claro, evidente; — **code** código abierto *m*; — **door policy** política de acceso libre *f*; —-**ended** sin restricciones; —- **heart surgery** cirugía de corazón abierto *f*; —-**minded** de amplias miras; —-**mouthed** boquiabierto; — **question** cuestión discutible *f*; — **season** temporada de caza *f*; — **source software** software de fuente abierta *m*; — **to criticism** expuesto a la crítica; N (outdoors) aire libre *m*; (tournament) abierto *m*

opener [ópənɚ] N abridor *m*; (in sports) primer partido *m*; **for** —**s** para empezar

opening [ópənɪŋ] N (open space) abertura *f*; (act of making or becoming open, ceremony) apertura *f*; (beginning) comienzo *m*; (clearing) claro *m*; (vacancy) vacante *m*, apertura *f*; (pretext) oportunidad *f*; — **bid** oferta de apertura *f*; — **ceremony** ceremonia de apertura *f*; — **night** estreno *m*; **at the** — a/en la apertura

openness [ópənnɪs] N franqueza *f*, transparencia *f*, apertura *f*

opera [ápərə] N ópera *f*; — **glasses** gemelos *m pl*; — **house** ópera *f*

operable [ápəɹəbəl] ADJ operable

operate [ápəɹet] VI (function) funcionar; (intervene surgically) operar; **to** — **on a person** operar a una persona; VT (run a machine) manejar; (administrate) dirigir; (make function) accionar

operating [ápəɹeDɪŋ] N — **costs** costos de operación *m pl*; — **room** sala de operaciones *f*, quirófano *m*; — **system** sistema operativo *m*

operation [apəɹéʃən] N (surgical intervention, mission, math function) operación *f*; (function) funcionamiento *m*; (use of a machine) manejo *m*; **to be in** — (law) estar vigente; (machine) estar funcionando

operative [ápəɹeDɪv] ADJ (law) vigente; (contract provision) pertinente; (word) clave, operativo; N (machine worker) operario -ria *mf*; (spy) agente *mf*

operator [ápəɹeDɚ] N (telephone, math) operador -ora *mf*; (machine) operario -ria *mf*; (stock) especulador -ora *mf*; **he's a smooth** — es un astuto

ophthalmologist [afθəlmálədʒɪst] N oftalmólogo -ga *mf*

opiate [ópiət] N opiáceo *m*

opinion [əpínjən] N opinión *f*

opium [ópiəm] N opio *m*

opossum [əpásəm] N zarigüeya *f*

opponent [əpónənt] N opositor -ora *mf*, contrincante *mf*, adversario -ria *mf*, oponente *mf*

opportune [apɚtún] ADJ oportuno

opportunistic [apɚtunístɪk] ADJ oportunista, aprovechado

opportunity [apɚtúnɪDi] N oportunidad *f*, ocasión *f*

oppose [əpóz] VI/VT oponer[se]

opposing [əpózɪŋ] ADJ opuesto, contrario; — **thumb** pulgar oponible *m*

opposite [ápəzɪt] ADJ (contrary) opuesto, contrario; — **to** frente a; PREP frente a, en frente de; N contrario *m*, opuesto *m*; ADV en frente

opposition [apəzíʃən] N oposición *f*; **they met**

with little — encontraron poca resistencia
oppress [əprés] VT oprimir
oppression [əpréʃən] N opresión f
oppressive [əprésIv] ADJ (regime) opresivo; (heat) bochornoso, sofocante
oppressor [əprésə-] N opresor -ora mf
optic [áptIk] ADJ óptico; N **-s** óptica f
optical [áptIkəl] ADJ óptico; — **character recognition** sistema de reconocimiento óptico de caracteres m; — **fiber** fibra óptica f; — **illusion** ilusión óptica f; — **resolution** resolución óptica f
optician [aptíʃən] N óptico -ca mf
optimal [áptəməl] ADJ óptimo
optimism [áptəmIzəm] N optimismo m
optimist [áptəmIst] N optimista mf
optimistic [aptəmístIk] ADJ optimista
optimize [áptəmaIz] VT optimizar
option [ápʃən] N opción f (also financial); (feature) extra m; **to leave one's —s open** no descartar posibilidades
optional [ápʃənl] ADJ opcional, optativo
optometrist [aptámItrIst] N optometrista mf
optometry [aptámItri] N optometría f
opulence [ápjələns] N opulencia f
opulent [ápjələnt] ADJ opulento
or [ɔr] CONJ o; **seven — eight** siete u ocho
OR [operating room] [óár] N quirófano m, sala de operaciones f
oracle [ɔ́rəkəl] N oráculo m
oral [ɔ́rəl] ADJ oral; (hygiene) bucal
orange [ɔ́rIndʒ] N naranja f; — **blossom** azahar m; — **grove** naranjal m; — **tree** naranjo m; ADJ & N anaranjado m
orangutan [ərǽŋətæn] N orangután m
orator [ɔ́rədə-] N orador -ora mf
oratory [ɔ́rətɔri] N (skill in speaking) oratoria f; (place for prayer) oratorio m
orbit [ɔ́rbIt] N órbita f; VI/VT orbitar
orbital [ɔ́rbIdl] ADJ orbital
orbiter [ɔ́rbIDə-] N orbitador m
orchard [ɔ́rtʃə-d] N huerto m; (large) huerta f
orchestra [ɔ́rkIstrə] N orquesta f
orchestrate [ɔ́rkIstret] VT orquestar
orchid [ɔ́rkId] N orquídea f
ordain [ɔrdén] VT (as minister) ordenar; (with an edict) decretar
ordeal [ɔrdíl] N suplicio m, tortura f; — **by fire** ordalía de fuego f
order [ɔ́rdə-] N (command) orden f, mandato m; (request, commission) pedido m; (sequence, obedience to law) orden m; **holy —s** órdenes sagradas f pl; **an apology is in —** corresponde una disculpa; **in — to** para; **in working —** en buen estado; **in — that** para que, a fin de que; **on —** encargado; **out of —** no funciona; **to put in —** ordenar; VI/VT (command, arrange) ordenar, mandar; (place an order) pedir

ordering [ɔ́rdə-Iŋ] N (putting in order) ordenación f, ordenamiento m
orderly [ɔ́rdə-li] ADJ ordenado; N (military) ordenanza m; (hospital) camillero m
ordinal [ɔ́rdnəl] ADJ ordinal
ordinance [ɔ́rdnəns] N ordenanza f
ordinary [ɔ́rdnɛri] ADJ común, corriente, ordinario; **do it the — way** hazlo de la forma habitual
ordination [ɔrdnéʃən] N ordenación f
ore [ɔr] N mineral m
oregano [ərégəno] N orégano m
organ [ɔ́rgən] N órgano m (also musical instrument)
organic [ɔrgǽnIk] ADJ orgánico; — **chemistry** química orgánica f
organism [ɔ́rgənIzəm] N organismo m
organist [ɔ́rgənIst] N organista mf
organization [ɔrgənIzéʃən] N organización f, planificación f
organizational [ɔrgənIzéʃənl] ADJ organizativo; — **chart** organigrama m
organize [ɔ́rgənaIz] VI/VT organizar[se]
organized [ɔ́rgənaIzd] ADJ organizado
organizer [ɔ́rgənaIzə-] N organizador -ora mf
organizing [ɔ́rgənaIzIŋ] ADJ organizativo
orgasm [ɔ́rgæzəm] N orgasmo m
orgy [ɔ́rdʒi] N orgía f
orient[1] [ɔ́rIɛnt] N oriente m
orient[2] [ɔ́rIɛnt] VT orientar
oriental [ɔriɛ́ntl] ADJ & N oriental mf
orientate [ɔ́rIɛntet] VT orientar
orientation [ɔriɛntéʃən] N (guidance) orientación f; (tendency, leaning) tendencia f
orifice [ɔ́rəfIs] N orificio m
origin [ɔ́rədʒIn] N origen m, procedencia f; (of a river) naciente f, nacimiento m
original [ərídʒənl] ADJ original, originario; N original m
originality [ərIdʒənǽlIDi] N originalidad f
originate [ərídʒənet] VI/VT originar[se]
oriole [ɔ́rioł] N oropéndola f
Orlon™ [ɔ́rlɑn] N orlón m
ornament[1] [ɔ́rnəmənt] N adorno m, ornamento m
ornament[2] [ɔ́rnəmɛnt] VT adornar, ornamentar
ornamental [ɔrnəméntl] ADJ ornamental
ornamentation [ɔrnəmIntéʃən] N ornamentación f
ornate [ɔrnét] ADJ adornado en exceso; — **style** estilo rebuscado m
ornithology [ɔrnəθálədʒi] N ornitología f
orphan [ɔ́rfən] ADJ & N huérfano -na mf; VT dejar huérfano a
orphanage [ɔ́rfənIdʒ] N orfanato m, hospicio m
orthodontics [ɔrθədántIks] N ortodoncia f
orthodox [ɔ́rθədaks] ADJ ortodoxo
orthography [ɔrθágrəfi] N ortografía f
oscillate [ásəlet] VI oscilar; VT hacer oscilar

oscillation [asəléʃən] N oscilación *f*
osmosis [azmósɪs] N ósmosis *f*
osprey [áspre] N águila pescadora *f*
ossify [ásəfaɪ] VI osificarse
ostensible [asténsəbəł] ADJ supuesto
ostentation [astɪntéʃən] N ostentación *f*
ostentatious [astɪntéʃəs] ADJ ostentoso
osteoarthritis [astioɑrθráɪdɪs] N osteoartritis *f*
osteoporosis [astiopərósɪs] N osteoporosis *f*
ostracize [ástrəsaɪz] VT aislar
ostrich [ástrɪtʃ] N avestruz *m*
OTC [over-the-counter] [ótísí] ADJ extrabursátil
other [ʌ́ðɚ] ADJ, PRON, & N otro -tra *mf*; — **than Bob** salvo Bob; **every** — **day** cada dos días, un día sí y otro no; —**wise** de otro modo; —**worldly** fantástico
otter [ádɚ] N nutria *f*
ouch [autʃ] INTERJ ¡ay!
ought [ɔt] V AUX **you** — **to sit down** deberías sentarte; **we** — **to get up early** deberíamos levantarnos más temprano
ounce [auns] N onza *f*
our [aur] POSS ADJ nuestro
ours [aurz] ADJ nuestro; **this book is** — este libro es nuestro; **these things are** — estas cosas son nuestras; PRON el nuestro / la nuestra; — **is bigger** el nuestro / la nuestra es más grande; **a friend of** — un amigo nuestro
ourselves [aursélvz] PRON **we made the cake** — nosotros mismos hicimos la torta; **we were sitting by** — estábamos sentados solos; **we look at** — **in the mirror** nos miramos en el espejo; **we bought** — **a house** nos compramos una casa
oust [aust] VT echar, expulsar
out [aut] ADV (outside) fuera; ADJ (turned off, extinguished) apagado; (tennis) fuera; (baseball) out; — **-of-date** pasado de moda, anticuado; N (way out) escape *m*; (baseball) out *m*; PREP **she ran** — **the door** salió corriendo por la puerta; **they locked me** — me dejaron fuera; — **-and-** — **criminal** criminal empedernido *m*; — **-and-** — **refusal** una negativa rotunda; — **of bounds** (golf) fuera de límites; — **of commission/ order** fuera de servicio; — **of fashion** pasado de moda; — **of fear** por miedo; **he's really** — **of it** está ido, está despistado; — **of joint** dislocado; — **of money** sin dinero; — **of print/stock** agotado; — **of touch with** desconectado de; — **of tune** desentonado; — **of work** desempleado; — **to lunch** *fam* chiflado; **made** — **of** hecho de; **miniskirts are on the way** — las minifaldas se están dejando de usar; **I had it** — **with him** me peleé con él; **you were** — no estabas; **before the week is** — antes de que termine la

semana; **the book is just** — acaba de publicarse el libro; **the secret is** — se ha divulgado el secreto; **we had some, but now we're** — teníamos, pero se nos acabó; **I'm** — **$10** perdí $10; INTERJ ¡fuera! VT (expel) expulsar; (expose) descubrir; VI **the truth will** — se descubrirá la verdad
outage [áudɪdʒ] N apagón *m*
outbreak [áutbrek] N (of pimples) erupción *f*; (of war) comienzo *m*; (of disease) brote *m*
outburst [áutbɜ˞st] N (emotional) arrebato *m*; (of tears) ataque *m*; (of violence) motín *m*, explosión *f*
outcast [áutkæst] ADJ & N marginado -da *mf*
outcome [áutkʌm] N resultado *m*, desenlace *m*
outcry [áutkraɪ] N clamor *m*, protesta *f*
outdated [autdédɪd] ADJ anticuado
outdo [autdú] VT superar
outdoor [áutdɔr] ADJ al aire libre; — **advertising** publicidad exterior *f*
outdoors [autdɔ́rz] ADV al aire libre, afuera
outer [áudɚ] ADJ exterior; — **ear** oído externo *m*; — **space** espacio exterior *m*
outfield [áutfiłd] N jardín *m*
outfielder [áutfiłdɚ] N jardinero -ra *mf*
outfit [áutfɪt] N (gear) equipo *m*; (clothes) conjunto *m*; (soldiers) unidad *f*; VI/VT equipar, habilitar
outfox [autfáks] VT ser más listo que
outgoing[1] [áutgoɪŋ] ADJ (leaving) saliente
outgoing[2] [autgóɪŋ] ADJ (extrovert) extrovertido
outgrow [autgró] VT **she will** — **her clothes** la ropa le quedará pequeña; **she will** — **her epilepsy** la epilepsia se le irá con la edad
outing [áudɪŋ] N excursión *f*, paseo *m*
outlandish [autlǽndɪʃ] ADJ estrafalario
outlast [autlǽst] VT (last longer than) durar más que; (live longer than) sobrevivir a
outlaw [áutlɔ] N bandido -da *mf*, forajido -da *mf*; VT prohibir
outlay[1] [áutle] N gasto *m*, desembolso *m*
outlay[2] [autlé] VT gastar, desembolsar
outlet [áutlɪt] N (exit) salida *f*; (stream) desagüe *m*, emisario *m*; (store) tienda *f*; (electric connection) toma de corriente *f*; **she needs an** — **for her talent** necesita canalizar su talento
outline [áutlaɪn] N (abstract) bosquejo *m*, esbozo *m*, trazado *m*; (boundary) contorno *m*; VT (summarize) bosquejar, esbozar; (draw) delinear; (plan) trazar
outlook [áutluk] N perspectiva *f*, panorama *m*
outlying [áutlaɪɪŋ] ADJ (marginal) periférico; (distant) remoto
outpatient [áutpeʃənt] N paciente ambulatorio -ria *mf*, paciente externo -na *mf*
output [áutput] N (production) rendimiento *m*; (computer information) salida *f*; — **device** dispositivo de salida *m*

outrage [áutredʒ] N (offense) ultraje *m*, agravio *m*, atropello *m*; (indignation) indignación *f*; VT (offend) ultrajar, agraviar; (enrage) indignar

outrageous [autrédʒəs] ADJ (offensive) ultrajante; (exorbitant) exorbitante; (extravagant) extravagante

outreach[1] [áutritʃ] N extensión *f*

outreach[2] [autrítʃ] VT exceder

outright[1] [autráit] ADV completamente; **he bought it** — lo compró al contado; **he rejected it** — lo rechazó categóricamente

outright[2] [áutrait] ADJ — **denial** negativa rotunda *f*; — **lie** mentira descarada *f*

outset [áutset] N comienzo *m*, principio *m*

outshine [autʃáin] VT eclipsar

outside[1] [autsáid] ADV fuera, afuera; PREP fuera de

outside[2] [áutsaid] ADJ (external) exterior; (foreign) foráneo; N exterior *m*; — **chance** posibilidad remota *f*; — **interference** interferencia externa *f*; **in a week, at the** — en una semana, a lo sumo; **to close on the** — cerrar por fuera

outsider [autsáidə] N forastero -ra *mf*

outskirts [áutskəts] N alrededores *m pl*, afueras *f pl*

outsourcing [áutsɔrsiŋ] N contratación externa *f*

outspoken [autspókən] ADJ franco

outstanding [autstǽndiŋ] ADJ (excellent) sobresaliente, destacado; (pending) pendiente

outstretched [autstrétʃt] ADJ extendido

outward [áutwəd] ADJ exterior, externo; — **appearances** apariencias *f pl*; ADV hacia fuera; — **bound** que sale

outweigh [autwé] VT (weigh more) pesar más que; (be more important) sobreponerse a, valer más que

outwit [autwít] VT ser más listo que

oval [óvəł] ADJ oval, ovalado; N óvalo *m*

ovarian [ovériən] ADJ ovárico

ovary [óvəri] N ovario *m*

ovation [ovéʃən] N ovación *f*

oven [ávən] N horno *m*

over [óvə] PREP — **here** acá; — **in Japan** allá en Japón; — **many years** durante muchos años; — **the counter** (medicine) sin receta; (stocks) extrabursátil; — **the sea** al otro lado del mar; — **the hill** viejo; — **there** allá; **an umbrella** — **his head** un paraguas sobre la cabeza; **I heard it** — **the radio** lo oí por la radio; **he jumped** — **the fence** saltó por encima de la cerca; **he is** — **her in the hierarchy** él está por encima de ella en la jerarquía; **not** — **one year** no más de un año; **he hit him** — **the head with a rock** le golpeó en la cabeza con una piedra; **all** — **the city** por toda la ciudad; **I'm** — **it** (recovered)

me he recuperado; (no longer interested) ya no me interesa; ADV — **again** de nuevo, otra vez; — **against** en contraste con; — **and** — una y otra vez; —**generous** demasiado generoso; **do it** — hazlo de nuevo, hazlo otra vez; **the world** — por todo el mundo; **it is** — **with** se acabó; INTERJ — **and out** cambio y fuera

overachiever [ovəətʃívə] N (bookish) empollón -ona *mf*; (successful) persona muy exitosa *f*

overactive [ovəǽktiv] ADJ hiperactivo, demasiado activo

overall [óvəɔł] ADJ global, total; N —**s** mono *m*, overol *m*

overbearing [ovəbériŋ] ADJ mandón -ona, dominante

overboard [óvəbɔrd] ADV (into the water) al agua; **she went** — **on her project** se le fue la mano con su proyecto

overcast [óvəkæst] ADJ nublado, encapotado; **to become** — nublarse, encapotarse

overcharge[1] [ovətʃárdʒ] VI/VT cobrar demasiado, cobrar de más

overcharge[2] [óvətʃardʒ] N cobro excesivo *m*

overcoat [óvəkot] N sobretodo *m*, gabán *m*

overcome [ovəkám] VI/VT (to get the better of) superar; (to overwhelm) embargar; **to be** — **by weariness** estar agobiado

overcompensate [ovəkámpinset] VI sobrecompensar

overcorrection [ovəkərékʃən] N sobrecorrección *f*

overdose [óvədos] N sobredosis *f*; VI tomar una sobredosis

overdraft [óvədræft] N sobregiro *m*, descubierto *m*

overdraw [ovədró] VI/VT sobregirar[se]

overdrawn [ovədrón] ADJ en descubierto, sobregirado

overdrive [óvədraiv] N superdirecta *f*

overdue [ovədú] ADJ (borrowed item) atrasado; (bill) vencido

overeat [ovəít] VI comer en exceso

overestimate [ovəéstimet] VT sobreestimar

overexcite [ovəriksáit] VT sobreexcitar

overextended [ovəiksténdid] ADJ sobreextendido

overflow[1] [ovəfló] VI desbordar, rebosar

overflow[2] [óvəflo] N desborde *m*

overgrown [ovəgrón] ADJ cubierto, crecido; — **boy** muchacho demasiado crecido para su edad *m*

overhang[1] [ovəhǽŋ] VI (jut) proyectarse; (hang over) estar suspendido

overhang[2] [óvəhæŋ] N saliente *m*

overhaul[1] [óvəhɔł] VT revisar

overhaul[2] [óvəhɔł] N revisión *f*

overhead[1] [óvəhɛd] N gastos generales *m pl*; ADJ elevado; — **projector** retroproyector *m*

overhead² [ovəhéd] ADV en lo alto
overhear [ovəhír] VT oír por casualidad
overjoyed [ovədʒɔ́ɪd] ADJ rebosante de alegría
overkill [óvəkɪɫ] N exageración f
overland [óvəlænd] ADV & ADJ por tierra
overlap¹ [ovəlǽp] VI/VT solapar[se], superponer[se]
overlap² [óvəlæp] N traslapo m
overlay¹ [ovəlé] VT cubrir; (with gold, etc.) incrustar
overlay² [óvəle] N cubierta f; (with metal, wood) revestimiento m, chapa f
overload¹ [ovəlód] VT sobrecargar, recargar, saturar
overload² [óvəlod] N sobrecarga f
overlook¹ [ovəlúk] VT (fail to mention) pasar por alto, omitir; (pardon) perdonar; (look from above) mirar desde arriba; (afford a view of) dar a, tener vista a
overlook² [óvəluk] N mirador m
overly [óvəli] ADV excesivamente
overnight¹ [óvənaɪt] ADJ — **delivery** entrega al otro día f; — **guest** invitado -da a dormir mf
overnight² [ovənáɪt] ADV **he succeeded** — tuvo éxito de la noche a la mañana
overpass [óvəpæs] N paso elevado m
overpower [ovəpáuə] VT abrumar
overpowering [ovəpáuəɪŋ] ADJ abrumador
overpriced [ovəpráɪst] ADJ demasiado caro
overproduction [ovəprədʌ́kʃən] N superproducción f
overqualified [ovəkwálɔfaɪd] ADJ sobrecalificado
overreach [ovərítʃ] VI **to** — **oneself** abarcar demasiado
overreact [ovəriǽkt] VI reaccionar exageradamente
override [ovəráɪd] VT anular
overrule [ovərúɫ] VT anular
overrun¹ [ovərʌ́n] VT (overflow) desbordar; (exceed) exceder; (invade) infestar
overrun² [óvərʌn] N exceso de costos m
overseas [ovəsíz] ADV (beyond the sea) en ultramar; (abroad) en el extranjero
oversee [ovəsí] VI (workers) dirigir, supervisar; (accounts) fiscalizar
overseer [óvəsir] N capataz -za mf, supervisor -ora mf
overshadow [ovəʃǽdo] VT eclipsar, opacar
overshoe [óvəʃu] N chanclo m
oversight [óvəsaɪt] N (mistake) descuido m; (act of overseeing workers) supervisión f; (act of overseeing accounts) fiscalización f
overstep [ovəstép] VT excederse en
overstrike [óvəstraɪk] VT imprimir un carácter directamente encima de otro
overt [ovə́t] ADJ evidente
overtake [ovəték] VT (pass someone) pasar, rebasar; (befall) abatirse sobre

overtax [ovətǽks] VT (tax too much) gravar excesivamente; (demand too much) exigir demasiado
overthrow¹ [ovəθró] VT derrocar, derribar
overthrow² [óvəθro] N derrocamiento m
overtime [óvətaɪm] N (in a game) prórroga f, tiempo suplementario m; (at work) horas extras f pl; **to work** — hacer horas extras
overture [óvətʃə] N (musical composition) obertura f; (initial move) propuesta f
overturn [ovətə́n] VI/VT volcar[se]; VT (a decision) anular; (a government) derrocar
overview [óvəvju] N vista global f, panorama m
overweight¹ [ovəwét] ADJ **he's** — pesa demasiado
overweight² [óvəwet] N sobrepeso m
overwhelm [ovəhwéɫm] VT abrumar, agobiar
overwhelming [ovəhwéɫmɪŋ] ADJ (responsibility, task) abrumador, agobiante; (victory) arrollador
overwork¹ [ovəwə́k] VI trabajar demasiado; VT hacer trabajar demasiado
overwork² [óvəwə̄k] N exceso de trabajo m
overwrite mode [óvəraɪtmod] VT modo de reescritura m
ovulate [ávjəlet] VI ovular
ovulation [avjəléʃən] N ovulación f
owe [o] VI/VT deber; (a sum) adeudar, deber
owing [óɪŋ] ADJ debido; — **to** debido a
owl [auɫ] N lechuza f, búho m
own [on] ADJ & PRON propio; — **goal** autogol m, gol en contra m; **a house of his** — una casa suya; **to be on one's** — ser independiente; **to come into one's** — conseguir lo que uno se merece; **to hold one's** — mantenerse firme; VT poseer; **to** — **up [to]** confesar
owner [ónə] N dueño -ña mf, propietario -ria mf; — **financing** financiamiento por el propietario m
ownership [ónəʃɪp] N propiedad f
ox [aks] N buey m
oxidation [aksɪdéʃən] N oxidación f
oxidize [áksɪdaɪz] VI/VT oxidar[se]
oxygen [áksɪdʒən] N oxígeno m; — **tent** cámara de oxígeno f
oyster [ɔ́ɪstə] N ostra f; (large) ostión m
ozone [ózon] N ozono m; — **layer** capa de ozono f

Pp

pace [pes] N paso m; —**maker** marcapasos m sg; VT (traverse) ir y venir por; (set the tempo) marcar al paso; (measure) medir a pasos
pacific [pəsífɪk] ADJ pacífico; — **Ocean** Océano

Pacífico *m*
pacification [pæsɪfɪkéʃən] N pacificación *f*
pacifier [pǽsəfaɪɚ] N chupete *m*
pacifism [pǽsəfɪzəm] N pacifismo *m*
pacify [pǽsəfaɪ] VT (a country) pacificar; (a person) apaciguar
pack [pæk] N (of wolves) manada *f*; (of dogs) jauría *f*; (of cigarettes) cajilla *f*, cajetilla *f*; (of cloth) compresa *f*; (of cards) baraja *f*; (of cyclists) pelotón *m*; — **animal** acémila *f*, bestia de carga *f*; —**rat** rata urraca *f*; (person who saves everything) urraca *f*; **a** — **of lies** una sarta de mentiras *f*; VT empacar, empaquetar; (carry a gun) portar; (crowd) atestar; (load) cargar; **to** — **off** despachar; **to** — **one's bags** hacer las maletas
package [pǽkɪʤ] N paquete *m* (also organized vacation); — **deal** (agreement) acuerdo global *m*; (tourism, travel) paquete turístico *m*; VT (gift) empaquetar; (food) envasar
packaging [pǽkɪʤɪŋ] N embalaje *m*, empaque *m*
packer [pǽkɚ] N empacador -ora *mf*, embalador -ora *mf*
packet [pǽkɪt] N paquete *m*
packing [pǽkɪŋ] N embalaje *m*
pact [pækt] N pacto *m*
pad [pæd] N (cushion) almohadilla *f* (also for ink); (block of paper) bloc *m*; (for aircraft) pista *f*; (for spacecraft) plataforma de lanzamiento *f*; VT (stuff with padding) acolchar; (add to dishonestly) rellenar
padding [pǽDɪŋ] N relleno *m*; (cotton) guata *f*; (of a speech) ripio *m*
paddle [pǽdl] N (for rowing) pala *f*, remo *m*; (for mixing, beating, ping-pong) paleta *f*; — **wheel** rueda de paleta *f*; VI (row) remar; VT hacer avanzar remando; (hit) dar una paletada
paddock [pǽDək] N (field) prado *m*; (enclosure at racetrack) paddock *m*
padlock [pǽdlɑk] N candado *m*; VT cerrar con candado
pagan [pégən] ADJ & N pagano -na *mf*
paganism [pégənɪzəm] N paganismo *m*
page [peʤ] N (sheet) hoja *f*, página *f*; (boy servant) paje *m*; (hotel employee) botones *m sg*; — **break** salto de página *m*; VT (number pages) paginar; (call) llamar por altavoz; *Mex* vocear; **to** — **through** hojear
pageant [pǽʤənt] N (parade) desfile *m*; (show) espectáculo *m*
pager [péʤɚ] N buscapersonas *m sg*
paid [ped] ADJ pagado; —**up** liberado, totalmente pagado, pago
paid [ped] *see* pay
pail [peł] N balde *m*, cubeta *f*
pain [pen] N dolor *m*; (suffering) sufrimiento *m*; —**killer** analgésico *m*; **on** — **of** so pena de; **to take** —**s** esmerarse; **he's a** — es un

chinche; ADJ —**staking** esmerado; VT (physical) doler; (mental) apenar
painful [pénfəł] ADJ (hurting) doloroso; (distressing) penoso; (difficult) arduo
painless [pénlɪs] ADJ sin dolor, indoloro
paint [pent] N (substance) pintura *f*; (spotted horse) pinto *m*; —**brush** (for art) pincel *m*; (for a house) brocha *f*; VI/VT pintar; **to** — **the town red** irse de juerga
painter [péntɚ] N pintor -ora *mf*
painting [péntɪŋ] N pintura *f*
pair [pɛr] N par *m*; (married couple) pareja *f*; **a** — **of scissors** unas tijeras, una tijera; VI/VT aparear[se], emparejar[se]; **to** — **off** aparearse
pajamas [pəʤáməz] N pijama/piyama *mf*
Pakistan [pǽkɪstæn] N Paquistán *m*
Pakistani [pækɪstǽni] ADJ & N paquistano -na *mf*
pal [pæł] N compañero -ra *mf*, compadre *m*, comadre *f*
palace [pǽlɪs] N palacio *m*
palate [pǽlɪt] N paladar *m*
palatial [pəléʃəł] ADJ suntuoso
Palau [pɑláu] N Paláu *m*
pale [peł] ADJ pálido, macilento; N **beyond the** — inaceptable; VI palidecer
paleness [pélnɪs] N palidez *f*
paleontology [peliəntáləʤi] N paleontología *f*
Palestine [pǽlɪstaɪn] N Palestina *f*
Palestinian [pælɪstíniən] ADJ palestino; N palestino -na *mf*
palette [pǽlɪt] N paleta *f*
palisade [pælɪséd] N empalizada *f*; —**s** acantilados *m pl*
pall [pɔł] VT (cover with a cloth) cubrir con un paño mortuorio; (satiate) hartar; VI (tire) cansar; N paño mortuorio *m*; —**bearer** portador del féretro *m*; **to cast a** — **on** empañar
palliative [pǽliəDɪv] N paliativo *m*
pallid [pǽlɪd] ADJ pálido
pallor [pǽlɚ] N palidez *f*
palm [pɑm] N (part of hand) palma *f*; (tree) palmera *f*, palma *f*; — **Sunday** Domingo de Ramos *m*; —**top computer** *Am* computadora de mano *f*, *Sp* ordenador de mano *m*; VT (hide in palm) escamotear; **to** — **something off on someone** encajar algo a alguien
palpable [pǽłpəbəł] ADJ (perceptible) palpable; (tangible) tangible
palpitate [pǽłpɪtet] VI palpitar
palpitation [pæłpɪtéʃən] N palpitación *f*
palsy [pɔ́łzi] N parálisis *f*
paltry [pɔ́łtri] ADJ miserable, despreciable
pamper [pǽmpɚ] VT mimar, consentir
pamphlet [pǽmflɪt] N (informative) folleto *m*; (political) panfleto *m*
pan [pæn] N (for boiling) cazuela *f*, cacerola *f*,

cazo *m*; (for frying) sartén *f*; (for baking) molde *m*; —**handle** mango de sartén *m*; —**handler** pordiosero -ra *mf*; VT criticar duramente; VI **to** — **for gold** extraer oro; **to** — **out** dar buen resultado; **to** —**handle** mendigar, pordiosear

panacea [pænəsíə] N panacea *f*

Panama [pǽnəmɑ] N Panamá *f*

Panamanian [pænəméniən] ADJ & N panameño -ña *mf*

Pan-American [pænəmérɪkən] ADJ panamericano

pancake [pǽnkek] N panqueque *m*; **flat as a** — chato como una tabla

pancreas [pǽnkriəs] N páncreas *m*

panda [pǽndə] N panda *m*

pandemic [pændémɪk] ADJ pandémico *m*; N pandemia *f*

pander [pǽndɚ] VI consentir

panderer [pǽndərɚ] N proxeneta *mf*

pane [pen] N vidrio *m*, cristal *m*

panel [pǽnl̩] N (wall) revestimiento *m*; (group of experts) panel *m*; (of instruments) tablero *m*; VT revestir con paneles

paneling [pǽnl̩ɪŋ] N (wall) panel *m*

pang [pæŋ] N (sharp pain, hunger) punzada *f*; (anguish) remordimientos *m pl*

panic [pǽnɪk] ADJ & N pánico *m*; ADJ — - **stricken** sobrecogido de pánico

panorama [pænərǽmə] N panorama *m*

panoramic [pænərǽmɪk] ADJ panorámico

pansy [pǽnzi] N (flower) pensamiento *m*; (sissy) *offensive* marica *m*

pant [pænt] VI jadear

panther [pǽnθɚ] N pantera *f*

panties [pǽntiz] N *Sp* bragas *f pl*; *Mex* pantaletas *f pl*; *RP* bombacha *f*

pantomime [pǽntəmaɪm] N pantomima *f*

pantry [pǽntri] N despensa *f*, alacena *f*

pants [pænts] N pantalones *m pl*, pantalón *m*

pantyhose [pǽntihoz] N panty *m*

papa [pápə] N papá *m*

papacy [pépəsi] N papado *m*

papal [pépəl] ADJ papal

papaya [pəpáɪə] N papaya *f*; *Cuba* fruta bomba *f*

paper [pépɚ] N (material) papel *m*; (newspaper) periódico *m*; (assignment) trabajo *m*; (oral contribution) comunicación *f*; (written contribution) artículo *m*; —**back** libro en rústica *m*; — **clip** clip *m*, sujetapapeles *m sg*; — **cutter** guillotina *f*; — **feeder** alimentador de hojas *m*; — **money** papel moneda *m*; —**s** papeles *m pl*; — **shredder** trituradora *f*; —**weight** pisapapeles *m sg*; —**work** (forms) papeleo *m*; (procedures) trámites *m pl*; **on** — por escrito; VI/VT empapelar

paprika [pæpríka] N pimentón *m*, páprika *f*

pap smear [pǽp smir] N citología *f*

Papua New Guinea [pǽpjuənugíni] N Papúa

Nueva Guinea *f*

Papua New Guinean [pǽpjuənugíniən] ADJ & N papú *mf*

par [pɑr] N (financial) paridad *f*; (in golf) par *m*; — **value** valor nominal *m*; **at** — a la par; **below** — bajo par; **to be on a** — **with** estar en pie de igualdad con; **to feel above** — sentirse mejor que lo normal; VT hacer el par

parachute [pǽrəʃut] N paracaídas *m sg*

parachuting [pǽrəʃudɪŋ] N paracaidismo *m*

parachutist [pǽrəʃudɪst] N paracaidista *mf*

parade [pəréd] N (procession) desfile *m*; (military review) parada *f*; — **ground** campo de maniobras *m*; VI desfilar; VT hacer ostentación de

paradigm [pǽrədaɪm] N paradigma *m*

paradise [pǽrədaɪs] N paraíso *m*

paradox [pǽrədɑks] N paradoja *f*

paradoxical [pærədáksɪkəl] ADJ paradójico

paraffin [pǽrəfɪn] N parafina *f*

paragraph [pǽrəgræf] N párrafo *m*; VT dividir en párrafos

Paraguay [pǽrəgwaɪ] N Paraguay *m*

Paraguayan [pærəgwáɪən] ADJ & N paraguayo -ya *mf*

parakeet [pǽrəkit] N perico *m*, periquito *m*

parallel [pǽrəlɛl] ADJ & N paralelo *m*; (geometry) paralela *f*; — **port** puerto paralelo *m*; VT (run equidistant from) correr paralelo a; (compare) comparar

paralysis [pərǽləsɪs] N (of the body) parálisis *f*; (of a transportation system) paralización *f*

paralytic [pærəlídɪk] ADJ paralítico -ca

paralyze [pǽrəlaɪz] VT paralizar

paramedic [pærəmédɪk] ADJ & N paramédico -ca *mf*

parameter [pərǽmɪdɚ] N parámetro *m*

paramilitary [pærəmílɪteri] ADJ & N paramilitar *mf*

paramount [pǽrəmaʊnt] ADJ supremo, sumo

paranoia [pærənɔ́ɪə] N paranoia *f*

paranoid [pǽrənɔɪd] ADJ & N paranoico -ca *mf*; — **delusion** delirio paranoico *m*

paranormal [pærənɔ́rməl] ADJ paranormal

paraphernalia [pærəfənéljə] N parafernalia *f*

paraphrase [pǽrəfrez] N paráfrasis *f*; VI/VT parafrasear

paraplegic [pærəplídʒɪk] ADJ N parapléjico -ca *mf*

parapsychology [pærəsaɪkálədʒi] N parapsicología *f*

parasite [pǽrəsaɪt] N parásito *m*

parasitic [pærəsídɪk] ADJ parasítico; — **disease** enfermedad parasitaria *f*

parasol [pǽrəsɔl] N parasol *m*, sombrilla *f*

paratroops [pǽrətrups] N tropas paracaidistas *f pl*

parcel [pársəl] N (package) paquete *m*; (lot) partida *f*; (land) parcela *f*; — **post** paquete postal *m*; VT (land) parcelar; **to — out** repartir

parch [pɑrtʃ] VT secar; **I'm —ed** estoy muerto de sed

parchment [pártʃmənt] N pergamino *m*

pardon [párdn̩] N perdón *m*, gracia *f*; (legal) indulto *m*; **I beg your —** perdone; VT perdonar, disculpar; (legally) indultar

pare [pɛr] VT mondar, pelar; **to — down expenditures** reducir gastos

parent [pérənt] N padre *m*, madre *f*; **— directory** directorio padre *m*; **—s** padres *m pl*

parental [pəréntl] ADJ parental; **— control** control paternal *m*

parenthesis [pərénθəsɪs] N paréntesis *m*

parenting [pérəntɪŋ] N **— guide** guía para padres *f*; **— skill** habilidad para educar a los hijos *f*; **good —** buena crianza de los hijos *f*

pariah [pəráɪə] N paria *mf*

parish [pǽrɪʃ] N parroquia *f*; **— priest** [cura] párroco *m*

parishioner [pəríʃənɚ] N feligrés -esa *mf*, parroquiano -na *mf*

parity [pǽrɪDi] N paridad *f*

park [pɑrk] N parque *m*; (for baseball) estadio de béisbol *m*; VI/VT estacionar, aparcar

parking [párkɪŋ] N estacionamiento *m*, aparcamiento *m*; **— lot** estacionamiento *m*, aparcamiento *m*; **— place** lugar de estacionamiento/aparcamiento *m*

Parkinson's disease [párkɪnsənzdɪzíz] N enfermedad de Parkinson *f*

parlance [párləns] N habla *f*

parley [párli] N (peace negotiation) parlamento *m*; (discussion) discusión *f*; VI parlamentar

parliament [párləmənt] N parlamento *m*

parliamentary [pɑrləméntri] ADJ parlamentario

parlor [párlɚ] N sala *f*, salón *m*; **— game** juego de salón *m*; **beauty —** salón de belleza *m*

parochial [pərókiəl] ADJ (of a parish) parroquial; (provincial) pueblerino

parody [pǽrəDi] N parodia *f*; VT parodiar

parole [pərół] N libertad condicional *f*; VT poner en libertad condicional

parrot [pǽrət] N loro *m*, papagayo *m*; VT repetir como loro

parry [pǽri] VT (a blow) parar; (a remark) eludir; N parada *f*

parse [pɑrs] VT analizar

parser [pársɚ] N analizador *m*

parsing [pársɪŋ] N análisis *m*

parsley [pársli] N perejil *m*

parsnip [pársnɪp] N chirivía *f*

parson [pársən] N pastor -ora *mf*

part [pɑrt] N (component) parte *f*; (role) papel *m*; (in hair) raya *f*; **— and parcel** parte esencial *f*; **— time** tiempo parcial *m*; **in foreign — s**

en el extranjero; **spare —s** piezas de repuesto *f pl*, repuestos *m pl*; ADJ **—-time** a tiempo parcial; VI/VT (cut into parts) partir[se]; (divide into parts) dividir[se]; (separate, leave) separar[se]; **to — company** separarse; **to — one's hair** hacerse la raya; **to — with** desprenderse de

partake [pɑrték] VI **to — in** participar; **to — of** (share) compartir; (eat) comer

partial [párʃəl] ADJ parcial

participant [pɑrtísəpənt] ADJ & N participante *mf*, partícipe *mf*

participate [pɑrtísəpet] VI participar

participation [pɑrtɪsəpéʃən] N participación *f*

participle [párDɪsɪpəl] N participio *m*

particle [párDɪkəl] N partícula *f*; **— board** aglomerado *m*

particular [pɚtíkjələ] ADJ particular; (fussy) quisquilloso; N **in —** en particular; **—s** particulares *m pl*

parting [párDɪŋ] N (farewell) despedida *f*; (separation) separación *f*; **— of the ways** encrucijada *f*

partisan [párDɪzən] N (supporter) partidario -ria *mf*, partidista *mf*; (guerrilla) partisano -na *mf*; ADJ (of supporters) partidario, partidista; (of guerrillas) de partisanos

partition [pɑrtíʃən] N (distribution) reparto *m*; (division) división *f*, partición *f*; (wall) tabique *m*, mampara *f*; VT (distribute) repartir; (divide) dividir; (divide with a wall) tabicar

partly [pártli] ADV en parte

partner [pártnɚ] N (in business) socio -cia *mf*; (in an activity) compañero -ra *mf*; (in dancing, sports, marriage) pareja *f*

partnership [pártnɚʃɪp] N (business) sociedad *f*; (relationship) asociación *f*

partridge [pártrɪdʒ] N perdiz *f*

party [párDi] N (get-together) fiesta *f*; (political group) partido *m*; (group of people) partida *f*; (litigant) parte *f*; **— of four** mesa para cuatro *f*; **— animal** fiestero -ra *mf*, parrandero -ra *mf*; VI ir de juerga

pass [pæs] VI (to go by) pasar; **to — a kidney stone** expulsar un cálculo renal; **to — away** fallecer; **to — for** pasar por; **to — in review** pasar revista; **to — on** (die) fallecer; (approve) aceptar; (refuse) no querer; **to — out** desmayarse; **to — over** pasar por alto; **to — up an opportunity** dejar pasar una oportunidad; VT (a ball) pasar; (a law) aprobar; (an exam, test) aprobar; **to — judgment** juzgar; **to — oneself off as** hacerse pasar por; **— me the salt** pásame la sal, alcánzame la sal; N (road through mountains) paso *m*; (motion, permission) pase *m*; (for transportation) abono *m*; (over a surface) pasada *f*; (on an exam) aprobación *f*; (of a ball) pase *m*; **—key** llave maestra *f*;

—**port** pasaporte *m*; —**word** contraseña *f*, clave de seguridad *f*; —**word protected** protegido por contraseña; **he made a — at her** trató de ligar con ella

passable [pǽsəbəł] ADJ (penetrable) transitable; (mediocre) pasable

passage [pǽsɪʤ] N (fare, musical or textual phrase, alley) pasaje *m*; (passing of time) paso *m*, transcurso *m*; (hallway in a house) pasillo *m*; (secret pathway) pasadizo *m*; (crossing) travesía *f*; (approval of a bill) aprobación *f*; —**way** (corridor) corredor *m*, pasillo *m*; (alley) pasaje *m*

passenger [pǽsənʤɚ] N pasajero -ra *mf*

passerby [pǽsɚbaɪ] N transeúnte *mf*, viandante *mf*

passing [pǽsɪŋ] N fallecimiento *m*; ADJ **each — day** cada día que pasa; — **grade** nota de aprobado *f*; — **fancy** capricho pasajero *m*; — **mention** mención al pasar *f*; — **shot** pasante *m*

passion [pǽʃən] N pasión *f*

passionate [pǽʃənɪt] ADJ apasionado

passive [pǽsɪv] ADJ pasivo; N pasiva *f*

past [pæst] ADJ pasado; — **due** en mora, vencido; — **participle** participio pasado *m*; — **perfect** pluscuamperfecto *m*; — **peformance** rendimiento previo *m*; — **precedents** precedentes anteriores *m pl*; — **tense** tiempo pretérito *m*; **the — president** el expresidente; PREP — **hope** más allá de toda esperanza; — **noon** después de mediodía; **the house — the store** la casa pasando la tienda; **we went — the tower** pasamos al lado de la torre; **half — two** las dos y media; **a woman — forty** una mujer de más de cuarenta años; ADV **for some time —** desde hace algún tiempo; **they drove —** pasaron en coche; N (time) pasado *m*; (tense) pretérito *m*

pasta [pástə] N pasta *f*

paste [pest] N (soft material, puree) pasta *f*; (glue) engrudo *m*; —**board** cartón *m*; VT pegar

pastel [pæstéł] ADJ & N pastel *m*

pasteurize [pǽstʃəraɪz] VT pasterizar/pasteurizar

pastime [pǽstaɪm] N pasatiempo *m*

pastor [pǽstɚ] N pastor -ora *mf*

pastoral [pǽstəəł] ADJ (literary) pastoril; (ecclesiastical) pastoral; N pastoral *f*; (literary work) égloga *f*

pastry [pǽstri] N (in general) pastelería *f*; (specific) pastel *m*; — **cook** pastelero -ra *mf*, repostero -ra *mf*; — **shop** pastelería *f*, repostería *f*

pasture [pǽstʃɚ] N (grassland) prado *m*; (grass) pasto *m*; (for horses) potrero *m*; VI/VT pastar, pacer, apacentar

pasty [pésti] ADJ pastoso

pat [pæt] ADJ banal; **down —** al dedillo; **to stand —** mantenerse firme; VI/VT dar palmaditas [a]; N palmadita *f*; N — **of butter** porción de mantequilla *f*

patch [pætʃ] N (piece of cloth to repair clothes) remiendo *m*, parche *m* (also for eye, computer); (spot or area, as of ice) tramo [con hielo] *m*; (plot) parcela *f*; VT (repair) remendar; **to — up a quarrel** hacer las paces

patent [pǽtnt] ADJ (evident) patente; (protected by patent) patentado; — **leather** charol *m*; N patente *f*; — **pending** patente en trámite; VT patentar

paternal [pətɚnl] ADJ (fatherly) paternal; (of the father's lineage) paterno

paternity [pətɚnɪDi] N paternidad *f*; — **test** prueba de paternidad *f*

path [pæθ] N (walkway) senda *f*, sendero *m*; (on a computer) ruta *f*; (of a projectile, storm) trayectoria *f*; —**way** senda *f*, sendero *m*

pathetic [pəθέDɪk] ADJ (moving) patético; (contemptible) lamentable

pathogen [pǽθəʤən] N patógeno *m*

pathology [pæθáləʤi] N patología *f*

pathos [péθɑs] N patetismo *m*

patience [péʃəns] N paciencia *f*

patient [péʃənt] ADJ & N paciente *mf*

patiently [péʃəntli] ADJ con paciencia

patriarch [pétriark] N patriarca *m*

patriarchal [petriárkəł] ADJ patriarcal

patrimonial [pætrɪmóniəł] ADJ patrimonial

patrimony [pǽtrəmoni] N patrimonio *m*

patriot [pétriət] N patriota *mf*

patriotic [petriáDɪk] ADJ patriótico

patriotism [pétriətɪzəm] N patriotismo *m*

patrol [pətrół] VI/VT patrullar, rondar; N patrulla *f*, ronda *f*; — **car** patrullero *m*; —**man** patrullero *m*

patron [pétrən] N (customer) cliente -ta *mf*; (benefactor) benefactor -ora *mf*, mecenas *mf*; (saint) patrono *m*

patronage [pétrənɪʤ] N (support of an artist) mecenazgo *m*; (clientele) clientela *f*; (political) clientelismo *m*; **we appreciate your —** agradecemos su preferencia

patronize [pétrənaɪz] VT (be condescending) tratar con condescendencia; (do business with) frecuentar

patter [pǽDɚ] VI (strike lightly) golpetear; (chatter) parlotear; N (small blows) golpeteo *m*; (chatter) parloteo *m*

pattern [pǽDɚn] N (for sewing) molde *m*; (for drawing) plantilla *f*; (of behavior) patrón *m*; VI/VT **to — something after** modelar algo a imitación de, basarse en el modelo de; **to — oneself after** seguir el ejemplo de

paucity [pósɪDi] N escasez *f*

paunch [pɔntʃ] N panza *f*, barriga *f*

pause [pɔz] N pausa*f*; VI (while talking) hacer pausa; (while moving) detenerse

pave [pev] VT (with asphalt) pavimentar; (with bricks) enladrillar; (with flagstones) enlosar; **to — the way for** preparar el camino para

pavement [pévmənt] N (roadway) calzada*f*; (of asphalt) pavimento *m*; (of bricks) enladrillado *m*; (of flagstones) enlosado *m*

pavilion [pəvíljən] N pabellón *m*

paw [pɔ] N pata*f*; (with claws) garra*f*; VT (touch with paw) tocar con la pata; (touch with claws) dar zarpazos; (grope) manosear

pawn [pɔn] N (object left in deposit) prenda*f*; (chess piece) peón *m*; (puppet) títere *m*; **—broker** prestamista *mf*; **—shop** casa de empeños*f*, monte de piedad *m*; **in —** en prenda; VT empeñar, dejar en prenda

pay [pe] VT (remit) pagar; VI (be profitable) ser provechoso, convenir; (be worthwhile) valer la pena; **to — attention** prestar atención, fijarse en; **to — back** (return) restituir; (retaliate) vengarse; **to — a compliment** hacer un cumplido; **to — homage** rendir homenaje; **to — one's respects** saludar; **to — off a debt** cancelar una deuda, amortizar una deuda; **to — out** desembolsar, pagar; **to — a visit** hacer una visita; **to — through the nose** pagar demasiado; **I will — for your meal** te pago la comida; N (payment) pago *m*; (wages) paga*f*, salario *m*; **—back** (payment) restitución*f*; (revenge) venganza*f*; **—check** cheque del sueldo *m*; **— cut** recorte salarial *m*; **—day** día de pago *m*; **— freeze** congelación salarial*f*; **—load** carga útil*f*; **—off** (pay) pago *m*; (reward) recompensa*f*; (bribe) soborno *m*; **— phone** teléfono público *m*; **— raise** aumento salarial / de sueldo *m*; **—roll** nómina*f*, planilla*f*; **— scale** escala salarial*f*; **to hit —dirt** encontrar una mina de oro

payable [péəbəl] ADJ pagadero

payee [peí] N tenedor -ora *mf*, beneficiario -ria *mf*

payment [pémənt] N pago *m*, abono *m*; **— in full** liquidación*f*; **car —s** cuotas del coche*f* *pl*

payola [peólə] N soborno *m*

PC [písí] N (personal computer) PC *m*; (political correctness) lo políticamente correcto; ADJ (politically correct) políticamente correcto

pea [pi] N guisante *m*; *Am* arveja*f*; **—nut** *Sp* cacahuete *m*; *Mex* cacahuate *m*; *Am* maní *m*; **—nut butter** *Sp* crema de cacahuete*f*; *Mex* crema de cacahuate*f*; *Am* manteca/ mantequilla de maní *f*

peace [pis] N paz*f*; **— officer** oficial de policía *m*; **— of mind** serenidad*f*; **at —** en paz; **to keep the —** mantener el orden público; **to hold one's —** callar

peaceful [písfəl] ADJ pacífico, tranquilo

peach [pitʃ] N durazno *m*; *Sp* melocotón *m*; (nice thing or person) delicia*f*, monada*f*; **— tree** durazno *m*, duraznero *m*, *Sp* melocotonero *m*

peacock [píkɑk] N pavo real *m*, pavón *m*

peak [pik] N (of a mountain) pico *m*, cumbre*f*; (of production, of one's abilities) punto máximo *m*; (of one's career) punto culminante *m*; **— load** carga máxima*f*; **— season** temporada alta*f*; **— time** hora punta*f*

peal [pil] N (of bells) repique *m*; (of laughter) carcajada*f*; VI/VT repicar

pear [pɛr] N pera*f*; **— tree** peral *m*

pearl [pɝl] N perla*f*; **— necklace** collar de perlas *m*

pearly [pɝli] ADJ (color) nacarado, perlado; (with pearls) perlado; **the — gates** las puertas del cielo

peasant [pézənt] ADJ & N campesino -na *mf*

peat [pit] N turba*f*

pebble [pébəl] N guijarro *m*, piedrecilla*f*; (smooth) canto *m*

pecan [pɪkán] N pacana*f*

peccary [pékəri] N pecarí/pécari *m*

peck [pɛk] VI/VT (strike with beak) picar; (eat bit by bit) picotear; (kiss) dar un besito; **—ing order** jerarquía*f*; **to — a hole** agujerear a picotazos; N (quick stroke) picotazo *m*; (kiss) besito *m*; (measure) medida de áridos [9 litros] *f*; **you're in a — of trouble** estás metido en un lío

pectoral [péktəɹəl] ADJ & N pectoral *m*

peculiar [pɪkjúljɚ] ADJ peculiar, particular

peculiarity [pɪkjuljǽɾɪDi] N peculiaridad*f*

pedagogical [pɛDəgádʒɪkəl] ADJ pedagógico

pedagogue [péDəgɑg] N pedagogo -ga *mf*

pedagogy [péDəgɑdʒi] N pedagogía*f*

pedal [pédl] N pedal *m*; VI/VT pedalear

pedant [pédn̩t] N pedante *mf*

pedantic [pədǽntɪk] ADJ pedante

peddle [pédl] VI/VT ir vendiendo de puerta en puerta; **to — gossip** repartir chismes

peddler [pédlɚ] N buhonero -ra *mf*, mercachifle *m*

pederast [péDəræst] N pederasta *m*

pederasty [péDəræsti] N pederastia*f*

pedestal [péDɪstl̩] N pedestal *m*

pedestrian [pədéstriən] N peatón -ona *mf*; ADJ pedestre

pediatrician [piDiətríʃən] N pediatra *mf*

pediatrics [piDIǽtrɪks] N pediatría*f*

pedigree [péDəgri] N (of persons) linaje *m*; (of animals) pedigrí *m*

pedophile [péDəfaɪl] N pedófilo -la *mf*

pedophilia [peDəfíliə] N pedofilia*f*

pee [pi] VI *fam* mear, hacer pipí; N *fam* pipí *m*

peek [pik] VI atisbar; N atisbo *m*

peel [pil] VI/VT (fruit, tree) pelar[se], descortezar[se]; (paint) descascarar[se]; **to**

keep one's eyes —ed mantener los ojos abiertos; N cáscara *f*

peeler [pílɚ] N pelador *m*

peep [pip] VI/VT (begin to appear) asomar[se]; VI (make sound of chicks) piar; **to — at** atisbar; N (look) atisbo *m*; (sound of chicks) pío *m*; **—hole** mirilla *f*; **— show** espectáculo de striptease *m*

peer [pir] N par *m* (also nobleman); **— group** grupo paritario *m*; VI (look attentively) escudriñar; (peep out) asomar

peerless [pírlɪs] ADJ incomparable, sin par

peeve [piv] VT irritar; **to get —d** ponerse de mal humor; N cosa que irrita *f*

peevish [pívɪʃ] ADJ malhumorado

peg [pɛg] N percha *f*; (on violin) clavija *f*; **to take a person down a —** bajarle los humos a alguien; VT (fix with pegs) clavar, clavetear; (set a price) fijar

pejorative [pɪdʒɔ́rədɪv] ADJ peyorativo, despectivo

pelican [pélɪkən] N pelícano *m*

pellet [pélɪt] N (ball) bola *f*, bolita *f*; (shot) perdigón *m*

pell-mell [pélmél] ADJ confuso, tumultuoso; ADV a troche y moche

pelt [pɛlt] N piel *f*, pellejo *m*; VI/VT acribillar; **to — with stones** apedrear

pelvis [pélvɪs] N pelvis *f*

pen [pɛn] N (fountain) pluma *f*; (ballpoint) bolígrafo *m*; (for pigs) pocilga *f*; (for sheep) redil *m*; (for cows) corral *m*; **— holder** mango de pluma *m*, portaplumas *m sg*; **— name** seudónimo *m*; VT (write) escribir; (shut in) acorralar, encerrar; **— computer** *Am* bolígrafo-computadora portátil *f*, *Sp* bolígrafo-ordenador portátil *m*

penal [pínl] ADJ penal

penalize [pénəlaɪz] VT penar; (in sports) penalizar

penalty [pénlti] N (punishment) pena *f*, castigo *m*; (forfeiture) multa *f*; (in sports) penalidad *f*, infracción *f*; **— area** (in soccer) área de penales *f*; **— kick** (in soccer) tiro de penalidad *f*, penalti *m*; **— shootout** (in soccer) definición por penales *f*; **— stroke** (in golf) golpe de penalidad *m*

penance [pénəns] N penitencia *f*

pencil [pénsəl] N (writing instrument) lápiz *m*; (beam of light) haz *m*; **— sharpener** sacapuntas *m sg*

pendant [péndənt] ADJ pendiente

pendent [péndənt] N colgante *m*; ADJ pendiente

pending [péndɪŋ] ADJ pendiente; PREP **— his arrival** hasta que llegue, mientras no llegue

pendulum [péndʒələm] N péndulo *m*

penetrate [pénɪtret] VT penetrar

penetrating [pénɪtreDɪŋ] ADJ penetrante

penetration [pɛnɪtréʃən] N penetración *f*

penguin [péŋgwɪn] N pingüino *m*

penicillin [pɛnɪsílɪn] N penicilina *f*

peninsula [pənínsələ] N península *f*

penis [pínɪs] N pene *m*

penitent [pénɪtənt] ADJ & N penitente *mf*

penitentiary [pɛnɪténʃəri] N penitenciaría *f*, penal *m*

penmanship [pénmənʃɪp] N escritura *f*, caligrafía *f*

pennant [pénənt] N banderín *m*, gallardete *m*

penniless [pénɪlɪs] ADJ pobre, sin dinero

penny [péni] N centavo *m*; **—-pincher** tacaño -ña *mf*; **to cost a pretty —** costar un dineral

pension [pénʃən] N (paid to a worker) jubilación *f*; (paid to a worker's survivors) pensión *f*; **— fund** caja de jubilaciones *f*; VT jubilar, pensionar

pensioner [pénʃənɚ] N pensionista *mf*

pensive [pénsɪv] ADJ pensativo

pent [pɛnt] ADJ encerrado; **—-up** acumulado

pentagon [péntəgən] N pentágono *m*

penthouse [pénthaʊs] N penthouse *m*

penultimate [pɪnʌ́ltəmɪt] ADJ penúltimo

people [pípəl] N gente *f*; (national group) pueblo *m*; VT poblar

pep [pɛp] N energía *f*; VI **to — up** animar

pepper [pépɚ] N (black) pimienta *f*; (green) pimiento *m*; (plant, shaker) pimentero *m*; **—mint** menta *f*; VT pimentar; **to — with bullets** acribillar a balazos

peptic ulcer [péptɪk ʌ́lsɚ] N úlcera péptica *f*

per [pɚ] PREP (for each) por; (according to) según; **— capita** per capita; **—cent** por ciento; **— diem** *Am* viático *m*, *Sp* dieta *f*

percale [pɚkél] N percal *m*

perceive [pɚsív] VT percibir

percentage [pɚséntɪdʒ] N porcentaje *m*

percentile [pɚséntaɪl] N percentil *m*

perceptible [pɚséptəbəl] ADJ perceptible

perception [pɚsépʃən] N percepción *f*

perceptive [pɚséptɪv] ADJ (pertaining to perception) perceptivo; (having keen perception) perspicaz

perch [pɚtʃ] N (rod for birds) percha *f*; (type of fish) perca *f*; VT (alight) posarse; VI/VT (set) encaramar[se]

percolate [pɚ́kəlet] VI/VT filtrar[se]

percussion [pɚkʌ́ʃən] N percusión *f*

perdition [pɚdíʃən] N perdición *f*

perennial [pərénɪəl] ADJ perenne; **— plant** planta perenne *f*

perfect[1] [pɚ́fɪkt] ADJ perfecto; **a — stranger** un completo desconocido

perfect[2] [pɚfékt] VT perfeccionar

perfection [pɚfékʃən] N perfección *f*

perfectionist [pɚfékʃənɪst] N perfeccionista *mf*

perfectly [pɚ́fɪktli] ADV (completely) totalmente; (without error) a la perfección, perfectamente; **stand — still** no te muevas

perforate [pɝ́fəret] VI/VT perforar[se]; VT calar
perforation [pɝfəréʃən] N perforación f
perform [pɚfɔ́rm] VT (a task) ejecutar, realizar; (a rite, ceremony) celebrar; (a contract) cumplir; (a play) representar; VI (give a performance) actuar; (play music) interpretar; (function) funcionar; (do well) rendir; **to— simultaneously** simultanear
performance [pɚfɔ́rməns] N (of a task) ejecución f; (of a ceremony) celebración f; (of a contract) cumplimiento m; (of a device) desempeño m, rendimiento m; (of a play) representación f; (of an actor) actuación f; (of music) interpretación f; **— review** evaluación del rendimiento f
performer [pɚfɔ́rmɚ] N (drama) artista mf, actor m, actriz f; (music) artista mf, intérprete mf
perfume[1] [pɝ́fjum] N perfume m
perfume[2] [pɚfjúm] VT perfumar
perfumery [pɚfjúməri] N (store) perfumería f; (collection) perfumes m pl
perhaps [pɚhǽps] ADV tal vez, quizá[s], acaso
peril [pérəł] N peligro m
perilous [pérələs] ADJ peligroso
perimeter [pərímɪDɚ] N perímetro m
period [pírɪəd] N período m; (historical) época f; (punctuation) punto m; (menstruation) período m, regla f; **you can't go, —!** no puedes ir, y sanseacabó; **within a — of ten days** en el término de diez días
periodic [pɪriádɪk] ADJ periódico; **— table** tabla periódica f
periodical [pɪriádɪkəł] ADJ periódico; N revista f
peripheral [pərífɚəł] ADJ & N periférico m; **— vision** visión periférica f
periphery [pərífɚi] N periferia f
periscope [pérɪskop] N periscopio m
perish [périʃ] VI perecer
perishable [périʃəbəł] ADJ perecedero
peritonitis [pɛrɪtnáɪDɪs] N peritonitis f
perjure [pɝ́dʒɚ] VI **to— oneself** perjurarse, jurar en falso
perjury [pɝ́dʒəri] N perjurio m
perks [pɝks] N beneficios adicionales m pl
permanence [pɝ́mənəns] N permanencia f
permanent [pɝ́mənənt] ADJ permanente; (of a position) titular
permeable [pɝ́miəbəł] ADJ permeable
permeate [pɝ́miet] VI/VT permear
permissible [pɚmísəbəł] ADJ permisible, lícito
permission [pɚmíʃən] N permiso m
permissive [pɚmísɪv] ADJ permisivo
permit[1] [pɚmít] VI/VT (allow) permitir; (make possible) posibilitar
permit[2] [pɝ́mɪt] N permiso m
permutation [pɝmjutéʃən] N permutación f
pernicious [pɚníʃəs] ADJ pernicioso
peroxide [pəráksaɪd] N peróxido m

perpendicular [pɝpɪndíkjələ] ADJ & N perpendicular f
perpetrate [pɝ́pɪtret] VT perpetrar
perpetual [pɚpétʃuəł] ADJ perpetuo
perpetuate [pɚpétʃuet] VT perpetuar
perplex [pɚpléks] VT confundir, dejar perplejo; **—ed** perplejo
perplexity [pɚpléksɪDi] N perplejidad f
persecute [pɝ́sɪkjut] VT perseguir
persecution [pɝsɪkjúʃən] N persecución f
persecutor [pɝ́sɪkjuDɚ] N perseguidor -ora mf
perseverance [pɝsəvírəns] N perseverancia f
persevere [pɝsəvír] VI perseverar, persistir
Persia [pɝ́ʒə] N Persia f
Persian [pɝ́ʒən] ADJ & N persa mf
persist [pɚsíst] VI (continue, endure) persistir; (to be insistent) insistir
persistence [pɚsístəns] N (endurance) persistencia f; (insistence) insistencia f
persistent [pɚsístənt] ADJ (lasting) persistente; (insisting) insistente, machacón
person [pɝ́sən] N persona f
personable [pɝ́sənəbəł] ADJ agradable
personage [pɝ́sənɪdʒ] N personaje m
personal [pɝ́sənł] ADJ personal; **— computer** Sp ordenador personal m; Am computadora personal f; **— effects** efectos personales m pl; **— foul** falta personal f; **— identification number** número de identificación personal m; **— pronoun** pronombre personal m; **— property** bienes muebles m pl; **to make a — appearance** presentarse en persona
personality [pɝsənǽlɪDi] N personalidad f; **— disorder** trastorno de la personalidad m
personally [pɝ́sənəli] ADV personalmente; **don't take it—** no lo tomes a pecho / a mal
personify [pɚsánəfaɪ] VT personificar
personnel [pɝsənéł] N personal m
perspective [pɚspéktɪv] N perspectiva f
perspicacious [pɝspɪkéʃəs] ADJ perspicaz
perspiration [pɝspəréʃən] N transpiración f
perspire [pɚspáɪr] VI transpirar
persuade [pɚswéd] VT persuadir, convencer
persuasion [pɚswéʒən] N persuasión f; (belief) convicción f
persuasive [pɚswésɪv] ADJ persuasivo, convincente
pert [pɝt] ADJ (insolent) insolente; (lively) vivaz
pertain [pɚtén] VI atañer, corresponder
pertinent [pɝ́tnənt] ADJ pertinente
perturb [pɚtɝ́b] VT perturbar
Peru [pərú] N Perú m
perusal [pərúzəł] N lectura f
peruse [pərúz] VT (read carefully) leer con cuidado; (read carelessly) hojear
Peruvian [pərúviən] ADJ & N peruano -na mf
pervade [pɚvéd] VT difundirse por
perverse [pɚvɝ́s] ADJ perverso
perversion [pɚvɝ́ʒən] N perversión f

perversity [pəvɜ́sɪDi] N perversidad *f*
pervert[1] [pəvɜ́t] VT pervertir; (misconstrue)
  desvirtuar
pervert[2] [pɜ́vɜt] N pervertido -da *mf*
peso [péso] N peso *m*
pessimism [pésəmɪzəm] N pesimismo *m*
pessimist [pésəmɪst] N pesimista *mf*
pest [pɛst] N (insect, disease) peste *f*, plaga *f*;
  (person) pesado -da *mf*
pester [péstə] VT molestar
pesticide [péstɪsaɪd] N pesticida *m*
pestilence [péstələns] N pestilencia *f*
pet [pɛt] N (animal) mascota *f*; (favorite) favorito
  -ta *mf*, preferido -da *mf*; ADJ predilecto; —
  name apodo cariñoso *m*; VT (caress)
  acariciar; (pat) dar palmaditas a
petal [pédl] N pétalo *m*
petition [pətíʃən] N petición *f*, solicitud *f*; VI/VT
  peticionar, solicitar
petrify [pétrəfaɪ] VI/VT petrificar[se]
petroleum [pətróliəm] N petróleo *m*; —
  products productos petrolíferos *m pl*; —
  jelly vaselina *f*
petticoat [péDikot] N enaguas *f pl*
petty [péDi] ADJ (trivial) trivial; (mean)
  mezquino; — **cash** caja chica *f*; — **larceny**
  ratería *f*; — **officer** suboficial de marina *m*
petunia [pɪtúnjə] N petunia *f*
pew [pju] N banco *m* / banca *f* de iglesia
pewter [pjúdə] N peltre *m*
peyote [peóDi] N peyote *m*
phallus [fǽləs] N falo *m*
phantom [fǽntəm] N fantasma *m*
pharmaceutical [fɑrməsúDikəl] ADJ
  farmacéutico; N producto farmacéutico *m*,
  fármaco *m*
pharmacist [fɑ́rməsɪst] N farmacéutico -ca *mf*
pharmacology [fɑrməkúlədʒi] N farmacología *f*
pharmacy [fɑ́rməsi] N farmacia *f*
pharynx [fǽrɪŋks] N faringe *f*
phase [fez] N fase *f*; VI **to — out** retirar por
  etapas; **to — in** incorporar paulatinamente
pheasant [fézənt] N faisán *m*
phenomenon [fɪnámənan] N fenómeno *m*
philanthropy [fɪlǽnθrəpi] N filantropía *f*
philharmonic [fɪlhɑrmánɪk] ADJ filarmónico;
  N filarmónica *f*
Philippine [fíləpin] ADJ & N filipino -na *mf*
Philippines [fíləpinz] N filipinas *f pl*
philosopher [fɪlásəfə] N filósofo -fa *mf*
philosophical [fɪləsáfɪkəl] ADJ filosófico
philosophy [fɪlásəfi] N filosofía *f*
phishing [fíʃɪŋ] N phishing *m*
phlegm [flɛm] N flema *f*
phobia [fóbiə] N fobia *f*
phone [fon] N teléfono *m*; — **card** tarjeta
  telefónica *f*; VI/VT telefonear
phonetic [fənéDɪk] ADJ fonético
phonetics [fənéDɪks] N fonética *f*

phonograph [fónəgræf] N fonógrafo *m*
phonology [fənálədʒi] N fonología *f*
phony [fóni] ADJ falso
phosphate [fásfet] N fosfato *m*
phosphorus [fásfəəs] N fósforo *m*
photo [fóDo] N foto *f*; — **finish** final muy
  reñido *m*
photocopier [fóDəkɑpiə] N fotocopiadora *f*
photocopy [fóDəkɑpi] N fotocopia *f*; VI/VT
  fotocopiar
photoelectric [foDoɪléktrɪk] ADJ fotoeléctrico
photogenic [foDədʒénɪk] ADJ fotogénico
photograph [fóDəgræf] N fotografía *f*; VT
  fotografiar
photographer [fətágrəfə] N fotógrafo -fa *mf*
photography [fətágrəfi] N fotografía *f*
photon [fótɑn] N fotón *m*
photosynthesis [foDosínθəsɪs] N fotosíntesis *f*
phrase [frez] N frase *f*; VI/VT expresar; (musical)
  frasear
phylum [fáɪləm] N filo *m*
physical [fízɪkəl] ADJ físico; — **education**
  educación física *f*; — **geography** geografía
  física *f*; — **science** ciencia física *f*; —
  therapy fisioterapia *f*
physician [fɪzíʃən] N médico -ca *mf*; —'**s**
  assistant ayudante médico -ca sanitario -ria
  mf
physicist [fízɪsɪst] N físico -ca *mf*
physics [fízɪks] N física *f*
physiological [fɪziəládʒɪkəl] ADJ fisiológico
physiology [fɪziálədʒi] N fisiología *f*
physique [fɪzík] N físico *m*
pianist [piǽnɪst] N pianista *mf*
piano [piǽno] N piano *m*; — **bench** banqueta de
  piano *f*; — **hammer** martinete *m*; — **player**
  pianista *mf*; — **stool** taburete de piano *m*
picaresque [pɪkərésk] ADJ picaresco
piccolo [píkəlo] N flautín *m*, pícolo *m*
pick [pɪk] VT (choose) escoger, elegir; (gather
  flowers) juntar; (play a guitar) puntear; (clean
  teeth) mondarse; (eat with the bill) picotear;
  (provoke a fight) armar, entablar; VI picar; **to**
  — **at** picotear; **to** — **apart** criticar; **to** — **a**
  lock violar una cerradura con ganzúa; **to** —
  on meterse con; **to** — **out** (choose) escoger;
  (distinguish) distinguir; **to** — **pockets**
  ratear; **to** — **up** (gather) recoger; (lift)
  levantar; (learn) aprender; (order) ordenar;
  (improve) mejorar; (contact in hope of sex)
  ligar con; **to** — **up speed** acelerar la marcha;
  N (tool) pico *m*; (of a guitar) púa *f*; (act of
  selecting) selección *f*; (thing or person
  selected) elección *f*; (the best) lo selecto, lo
  mejor; —**ax**[e] zapapico *m*; —**lock** ganzúa *f*;
  —**pocket** ratero -ra *mf*, carterista *mf*; —**up**
  (taking on freight) recolección *f*;
  (improvement in business) recuperación *f*;
  (casual sexual acquaintance) ligue *m*, plan *m*;

(acceleration) aceleración *f;* —**up truck** camioneta *f;* ADJ —**-proof** a prueba de ladrones
picket [píkɪt] N piquete *m* (also union worker); — **fence** cerca de piquetes *f;* VT (fence) vallar; (block with workers) bloquear, *Am* piquetear
pickle [píkəł] N pepinillo en vinagre *m,* curtido *m;* **to be in a** — hallarse en un aprieto; VT encurtir, escabechar; —**d fish** pescado al/en escabeche *m,* pescado adobado *m*
picnic [píknɪk] N picnic *m;* — **area** merendero *m;* VI hacer un picnic
pictorial [pɪktóriəł] ADJ pictórico
picture [píktʃɚ] N (image) imagen *f;* (drawing) dibujo *m;* (photo) fotografía *f;* (situation) panorama *m;* (movie) película *f;* — **frame** marco *m;* — **gallery** galería de pinturas *f;* — **tube** tubo de imagen *m;* **she is the** — **of unhappiness** es la imagen de la infelicidad; VT (describe) describir; (imagine) imaginar
picturesque [pɪktʃərésk] ADJ pintoresco
pie [paɪ] N pastel *m,* tarta *f;* — **chart** diagrama de pastel *m;* — **graph** gráfica de pastel *f;* — **in the sky** castillos en el aire *m pl;* **it's as easy as** — es pan comido
piece [pis] N (of music, in a board game, of furniture) pieza *f;* (of wood, rock, pie) pedazo *m,* trozo *m;* —**meal** por partes; — **of advice** consejo *m;* — **of cake** pan comido *m;* — **of land** parcela *f,* terreno *m;* — **of one's mind** regaño *m;* — **of news** noticia *f;* — **of shit** *vulg* mierda *f;* —**work** trabajo a destajo *m;* **to go to** —**s** descomponerse; VI **to** — **together** (assemble) armar; (make sense of) atar cabos
pier [pir] N muelle *m,* embarcadero *m;* (breakwater) rompeolas *m sg*
pierce [pirs] VI/VT (make a hole in) agujerear, perforar; (penetrate) penetrar; (cause a sharp pain) punzar
piercing [pírsɪŋ] ADJ (glance, sound) penetrante; (pain) punzante; N perforación *f*
piety [páɪɪɒi] N piedad *f*
pig [pɪg] N puerco *m,* cerdo *m,* cochino *m; Sp* guarro *m;* —**-headed** testarudo, cabezón; —**-iron** hierro en lingotes *m;* — **Latin** jerigonza *f;* —**pen** pocilga *f;* —**tail** coleta *f*
pigeon [píʤən] N paloma *f;* (young) pichón *m;* —**hole** casilla *f;* — **loft** palomar *m;* VT **to** —**hole** encasillar
piggy [pígi] N cerdito *m;* —**bank** alcancía *f; Sp* hucha *f;* ADV —**back** a hombros, a cuestas
pigment [pígmənt] N pigmento *m*
pike [paɪk] N (weapon) pica *f;* (fish) lucio *m*
pile [paɪł] N (ordered stack) pila *f;* (chaotic group) montón *m,* amontonamiento *m;* (surface of a carpet) pelo *m;* (post) pilote *m;* — **driver** martinete *m;* —**s** almorranas *f pl;* —**-up** accidente múltiple *m;* VI/VT apilar[se], amontonar[se]

pilfer [píłfɚ] VI/VT ratear, sisar
pilferage [píłfɚɪʤ] N ratería *f*
pilgrim [píłgrəm] N peregrino -na *mf,* romero -ra *mf*
pilgrimage [píłgrəmɪʤ] N peregrinación *f,* romería *f*
pill [pɪł] N píldora *f,* pastilla *f;* (naughty child) pesado -da *mf*
pillage [pílɪʤ] N pillaje *m,* saqueo *m,* rapiña *f;* VI/VT pillar, saquear
pillar [pílɚ] N pilar *m,* columna *f*
pillow [pílo] N almohada *f;* —**case** funda *f*
pilot [páɪlət] N piloto *mf* (also test, light); (of a boat) timonel *m,* piloto *mf;* VT pilotar, comandar
pimp [pɪmp] N proxeneta *mf,* rufián *m*
pimple [pímpəł] N grano *m,* barro *m*
pin [pɪn] N (sewing implement) alfiler *m;* (ornament) prendedor *m;* (rod) pasador *m,* perno *m;* (bowling) bolo *m;* (electric) pata *f,* clavija *f;* —**cushion** alfiletero *m;* —**wheel** molinete *m,* remolino *m;* **to be on** —**s and needles** estar en ascuas; VT (affix with pins) prender; (in wrestling) inmovilizar; **to** — **someone down** (hold down) inmovilizar; (force to act) hacer que concrete detalles; **to** — **one's hopes on** poner sus esperanzas en; **to** —**point** localizar con precisión; **to** — **up** sujetar con alfileres
PIN [personal identification number] [pɪn] N PIN *m*
pincers [pínsɚz] N (of lobsters) pinzas *f pl;* (tool) tenazas *f pl*
pinch [pɪntʃ] VT (squeeze with fingers) pellizcar; (squeeze tightly, hamper) apretar; (steal) birlar; (arrest) prender; VI (be too tight) apretar; (economize) economizar; —**ed nerve** nervio pellizcado *m,* nervio pinzado *m;* N (act of pinching) pellizco *m;* (small amount) pizca *f;* (trying circumstances) aprieto *m,* apuro *m;* — **hitter** bateador -ora emergente *m;* — **runner** corredor emergente
pine [paɪn] N pino *m;* —**apple** piña *f,* ananá[s] *m;* — **cone** piña *f;* — **grove** pinar *m;* — **nut** piñón *m;* VI **to** — **away** languidecer; **to** — **for** anhelar, suspirar por
pingpong [píŋpɑŋ] N ping-pong *m,* tenis de mesa *m*
pinion [pínjən] N piñón *m*
pink [pɪŋk] N rosado *m,* rosa *m;* —**eye** conjuntivitis *f;* — **slip** notificación de despido *f;* **in the** — rebosante de salud; ADJ rosado, rosa
pinnacle [pínəkəł] N pináculo *m*
pint [paɪnt] N pinta *f;* ADJ —**-sized** diminuto
pinto bean [píntobin] N judía pinta *f*
pioneer [paɪənír] N pionero -ra *mf;* VI ser el primero en hacer algo; VT promover

pious [páɪəs] ADJ (religious) pío, piadoso; (hypocritical) beato

pipe [paɪp] N (for smoking) pipa f; (for water) tubo m, caño m; (of an organ) tubo m; (flute) caramillo m, flauta f; — **dream** ilusiones f pl; —**line** (for oil) oleoducto m; (for gas) gasoducto m; (for water) tubería f; **in the** —**line** en trámite; — **wrench** llave inglesa f; VT (convey water) conducir por cañerías; (make music) tocar la flauta; VI chillar; **to** — **down** callarse

piping [páɪpɪŋ] N (many pipes) cañería f, tubería f; (border on clothes) ribete m; (sound of pipes) sonido de la gaita/flauta m; ADJ — **hot** hirviendo

pipsqueak [pípskwik] N chisgarabís m, mequetrefe m

piracy [páɪrəsi] N piratería f

pirate [páɪrɪt] N pirata mf; VT piratear

piss [pɪs] VI/VT fam mear; **to** — **off** enfadar

pistol [pístl] N pistola f, revólver m; VT **to** — - **whip** dar culatazos

piston [pístn̩] N pistón m, émbolo m; — **ring** segmento de compresión m; — **rod** eje del pistón m

pit [pɪt] N (hole) hoyo m, pozo m; (in a garage, theater) foso m; (trap) trampa f; (seed) hueso m; (part of a racetrack) box m, paddock m; (part of the stomach) boca f; —**fall** (trap) trampa f; (difficulty) dificultad f; **this is the** —**s** esto es lo peor; VI/VT (make holes) picarse; VT **to** — **against** oponer, enfrentar

pitch [pɪtʃ] VT (throw) tirar, lanzar; (try to sell) pregonar; **to** — **a tent** armar una tienda; VI (plane, ship) cabecear; **to** — **in** colaborar; N (throw) tiro m, lanzamiento m; (in music) tono m; (in printing) espaciado m; (slope) grado de inclinación m; (tar) brea f, pez f; **dark** oscuro como boca del lobo; —**fork** horca f, horquilla f

pitcher [pítʃɚ] N (vessel) cántaro m, jarro m, jarra f; (in baseball) lanzador -ora mf; —**'s mound** montículo m

pith [pɪθ] N (in plants, feathers) médula f; (essence) meollo m

pithy [píθi] ADJ sustancial

pitiful [pídɪfəl] ADJ (deserving pity) lastimoso; (deserving contempt) despreciable

pitiless [pídɪlɪs] ADJ despiadado

pituitary [pɪtúɪteri] ADJ pituitario; — **gland** glándula pituitaria f

pity [pídi] N compasión f, lástima f; **what a** —! ¡qué lástima! VT compadecerse [de]

pivot [pívət] N pivote m; VI pivotar

pixel [píksəł] N píxel m

pizza [pítsə] N pizza f

placard [plǽkɚd] N cartel m

placate [pléket] VT apaciguar

place [ples] N (site) lugar m, sitio m; (position)

puesto m; — **mat** mantel individual m; — **of birth** lugar de nacimiento m; — **of business** oficina f; — **of worship** templo m; — **setting** cubierto para una persona m; **in** — **of** en lugar de; **it is not my** — **to do it** no me corresponde a mí hacerlo; VT (put) colocar; (identify) situar, ubicar; **to** — **an order** hacer un pedido; **to** — **an ad** poner un anuncio; VI (in sports) clasificarse

placebo [pləsíbo] N placebo m

placement [plésmənt] N (in levels, categories) colocación f, posicionamiento m; (in space) emplazamiento m

placenta [pləséntə] N placenta f

placid [plǽsɪd] ADJ plácido

plagiarism [pléʤərɪzəm] N plagio m

plague [pleg] N plaga f, peste f; VT atormentar, apestar

plaid [plæd] N tela escocesa f

plain [plen] ADJ (without embellishment) sencillo, llano; (clear) claro; (downright, unadulterated) puro; (ordinary) común; (unattractive) poco atractivo; **in** — **sight** en plena vista; —**clothesman** policía en traje de civil m; —-**Jane** sencillo; ADV completamente; N llano m, llanura f

plaintiff [pléntɪf] N demandante mf, querellante mf

plan [plæn] N plan m; (drawing, sketch, map, outline) plano m; VI/VT planear, planificar; (diagram) hacer el plano de; —**ned parenthood** planificación familiar f

plane [plen] N (airplane) avión m; (surface) plano m; (tool) cepillo m; — **tree** plátano m; ADJ plano; — **geometry** geometría plana f; VI (glide, hover) planear; VT (smooth) cepillar, planear

planet [plǽnɪt] N planeta m

planetarium [plænɪtériəm] N planetario m

plank [plæŋk] N (board) tabla f, tablón m; (tenet) principio m, base f; VT entarimar

plankton [plǽŋktən] N plancton m

planning [plǽnɪŋ] N planeamiento m, planificación f

plant [plænt] N (vegetation) planta f; (industrial installation) fábrica f, planta f; (mole, spy) topo m; VT (plants) plantar; (ideas) sembrar; (a spy, evidence) colocar

plantain [plǽnten] N plátano m

plantation [plæntéʃən] N plantación f

plaque [plæk] N placa f; (on teeth) sarro m, placa f

plasma [plǽzmə] N plasma m, gas ionizado m

plaster [plǽstɚ] N (substance) yeso m; (preparation applied to body) emplasto m; — **of Paris** yeso m; VT (cover with plaster) revocar; (apply a preparation) enyesar; (cover with posters) cubrir, empapelar; (defeat) aplastar; **to** — **down one's hair** achatarse el pelo; **to get** —**ed** emborracharse

plastic [plǽstɪk] ADJ plástico; — **surgery** cirugía plástica/estética f
plate [plet] N (for food) plato m; (for collections) bandeja f; (metal) plancha f, lámina f; (license) placa f; — **glass** vidrio cilindrado m; — **tectonics** tectónica de placas f; VT (apply metal covering) chapar, enchapar; (apply armor) blindar
plateau [plætó] N meseta f, macizo m
platform [plǽtfɔrm] N plataforma f (also in politics, computers); (railway) andén m; (mobile) tarima f, tinglado m
platinum [plǽtnəm] N platino m
platitude [plǽdɪtud] N lugar común m, perogrullada f
platter [plǽDɚ] N fuente f
plausible [plɔ́zəbəł] ADJ plausible
play [ple] VT (game) jugar; (an opponent) jugar contra; (an instrument) tocar; (a drama) representar; (a role) desempeñar; (bet on) apostar; **to — a joke** gastar una broma; **to — cards** jugar a los naipes; **to — havoc** hacer estragos; **to — tennis** jugar al tenis; **to — the fool** hacerse el tonto; VI (divert oneself, gamble) jugar; (kid) bromear; (make music) tocar; **to — along** seguir la corriente; **to — down** minimizar; **to be all — ed out** estar agotado; N (recreational activity, looseness) juego m; (instance of playing) jugada f; (theater work) obra de teatro f; — **on words** juego de palabras m; —**boy** playboy m; —**ground** recreo m, patio m; —**ing card** naipe m; —**mate** compañero -ra de juego mf; —**off [game]** [partido de] desempate m; **the** —**offs** las eliminatorias f pl; —**thing** juguete m
player [pléɚ] N (one who plays, gambler) jugador -ora mf; (musician) músico -ca mf; (influential person) persona influyente f; (womanizer) mujeriego m; (actor) actor m, actriz f; (participant) participante mf; — **piano** pianola f
playful [pléfəł] ADJ juguetón
playwright [pléraɪt] N dramaturgo -ga mf
plea [pli] N (entreaty) súplica f, ruego m; (allegation) alegato m; **to enter a — of guilty** declararse culpable
plead [plid] VI/VT (entreat) suplicar, rogar; (defend) abogar, defender; **to — guilty** declararse culpable
pleasant [plézənt] ADJ agradable, grato, placentero
pleasantry [plézəntri] N cortesía f
please [pliz] ADV por favor; VI/VT agradar, complacer; **as you —** como quieras; **to be** —**d to** tener el gusto de, tener gusto en; **to be** —**d with** estar satisfecho con
pleasing [plízɪŋ] ADJ agradable
pleasure [pléʒɚ] N placer m, gusto m, agrado m;

— **trip** viaje de placer m
pleat [plit] N pliegue m, tabla f; (wide) tabla f; VT plisar; (wide) tablear
pled [plɛd] see plead
pledge [plɛdʒ] N (promise) promesa f; (security deposit) prenda f; (in a fraternity) miembro provisorio m; **as a — of** en prenda de; VI/VT (promise) prometer; VT (give as a deposit) empeñar; **to — one's word** dar la palabra; **to — to secrecy** exigir promesa de discreción
plenary [plénəri] ADJ & N plenario m
plentiful [pléntɪfəł] ADJ abundante, copioso
plenty [plénti] N abundancia f; — **of time** suficiente tiempo m; **that's —** con eso basta
pliable [pláɪəbəł] ADJ (flexible) flexible; (docile) dócil
pliant [pláɪənt] ADJ (flexible) flexible; (docile) dócil
pliers [pláɪɚz] N alicates m pl, tenazas f pl
plight [plaɪt] N aprieto m
plod [plɑd] VI (walk) caminar trabajosamente; (work) trabajar laboriosamente
plop [plɑp] VI hacer plaf; VT dejar caer; N plaf m
plot [plɑt] N (storyline) trama f, argumento m; (conspiracy) complot m, conspiración f; (land) parcela f, era f; (floor plan) plano m; VI/VT (plan secretly) tramar, conspirar, maquinar; VT (make a graph) hacer un gráfico; **to — a course** trazar un curso
plotter [plɑ́dɚ] N (one who plots) conspirador -ora mf; (device) trazador de gráficos m
plover [plóvɚ] N chorlito m
plow [plaʊ] N arado m; —**share** reja de arado f; VI/VT arar; (uncultivated area) roturar; **to — through** abrirse paso
plowing [pláʊɪŋ] N labranza f
pluck [plʌk] VT (a feather, flower) arrancar; (bird) desplumar; (guitar) puntear, pulsar; **to — out/off** desprender; **to — up courage** animarse, cobrar ánimo; N (act of plucking) tirón m; (courage) valor m
plug [plʌg] N (stopper) tapón m; (horse) pej penco m; (electric) enchufe m; (advertisement) mención favorable f; (tobacco) rollo m; —-**in** (electrical) enchufe m; (computer accessory) plug-in m; VT (close) tapar; (advertise) hacer una mención favorable de; VI **to — along** no parar; **to — in** enchufar; **to — up** tapar
plum [plʌm] N (fruit) ciruela f; — **tree** ciruelo m; **that job is a real —** ese trabajo es estupendo
plumage [plúmɪdʒ] N plumaje m
plumb [plʌm] N (lead weight) plomada f; — **bob** plomada f; **to be out of —** no estar a plomo; ADJ (perpendicular) a plomo; ADV (in a vertical direction) a plomo; (completely) completamente; VT (measure depth) sondear; (test for verticality) aplomar; (examine) examinar
plumber [plʌ́mɚ] N plomero -ra mf; Sp

fontanero -ra *mf*
plumbing [plʌ́mɪŋ] N (work and trade) plomería *f*; *Sp* fontanería *f*; (system of pipes) cañerías *f* *pl*
plume [plum] N penacho *m*; VT adornar con plumas
plummet [plʌ́mɪt] VI precipitarse; N plomada *f*
plump [plʌmp] ADJ rechoncho, regordete, rollizo; VI/VT **to — down** dejar[se] caer
plunder [plʌ́ndɚ] N (act of plundering) pillaje *m*, saqueo *m*; (loot) botín *m*; VI/VT pillar, saquear
plunge [plʌndʒ] VI/VT (into water) zambullir[se], sumergir[se]; (into something solid) hundir[se]; VI (fall) precipitarse; (slope downward) bajar repentinamente; **to — headlong** echarse de cabeza; N zambullida *f*; (rush) salto *m*
plunger [plʌ́ndʒɚ] N (for a toilet) desatascador *m*; (of a pump) émbolo *m*
pluperfect [plupɚ́fɪkt] N pluscuamperfecto *m*
plural [plúrəł] ADJ & N plural *m*
plurality [plʊrǽlɪDi] N pluralidad *f*
plus [plʌs] PREP más; N (advantage) ventaja *f*; **two — three** dos más tres *m*; **on the — side** en el lado positivo; **— sign** signo de más *m*
plush [plʌʃ] N felpa *f*; ADJ (fabric) afelpado; (hotel) lujoso
plutonium [plutóniəm] N plutonio *m*
ply [plaɪ] VT (use) manejar; (assail with questions) acosar; (navigate a body of water) surcar; VI (travel regularly) recorrer con regularidad; (work steadily) aplicarse; **to — a trade** ejercer un oficio; N (layer of cloth, rubber) capa *f*; (layer of plywood) chapa *f*; **—wood** madera compensada *f*, contrachapado *m*
pneumatic [numǽDɪk] ADJ neumático
pneumonia [numónjə] N pulmonía *f*
poach [potʃ] VT (eggs) escalfar; VI/VT (game) cazar furtivamente
pocket [pákɪt] N (in clothes) bolsillo *m*; (vein of ore) filón *m*; (on a pool table) tronera *f*; (of air) bache *m*; (of poverty) bolsa *f*; **—book** cartera *f*, *Sp* bolso *m*; **— book** libro de bolsillo *m*; **—knife** navaja *f*; **— of resistance** foco de resistencia *m*; VT meterse en el bolsillo; (appropriate) embolsar; (knock in a billiard ball) meter en la tronera
pod [pɑd] N (seed vessel) vaina *f*; (herd of cetaceans) manada *f*
podiatrist [pədáɪətrɪst] N podólogo -ga *mf*
podiatry [pədáɪətri] N podiatría *f*
podium [pódiəm] N podio *m*
poem [póəm] N poema *m*, poesía *f*
poet [póɪt] N poeta *mf*
poetic [poéDɪk] ADJ poético; **— justice** justicia divina *f*; N **—s** poética *f*
poetry [póɪtri] N poesía *f*
poignant [póɪnjənt] ADJ conmovedor
poinsettia [pɔɪnséDə] N flor de Pascua *f*

point [pɔɪnt] N (place) punto *m*; (score, in sports) punto *m*, anotación *f*; (sharp end) punta *f*; **— after touchdown** punto extra *m*; **— guard** (basketball) base *mf*, conductor -ora *mf*, guardia *mf*; **— of origin** punto de origen *m*; **— of view** punto de vista *m*; **it is not to the — no viene al caso; I don't see the —** no le veo el sentido; **on the — of** a punto de; ADV **—-blank** a quemarropa; VT (direct finger at) apuntar con, señalar con; (indicate) señalar; **to — at** (with finger) señalar; (with a gun) apuntar hacia; **to — out** señalar, indicar; **to — up** enfatizar
pointed [pɔ́ɪntɪd] ADJ (having a point) puntiagudo; (piercing) agudo; **— arch** arco ojival *m*
pointer [pɔ́ɪntɚ] N (stick) puntero *m*; (on a scale) indicador *m*; (dog) perro de muestra *m*; (advice) consejo *m*
pointless [pɔ́ɪntlɪs] ADJ inútil
poise [pɔɪz] N (balance, steadiness) equilibrio *m*; (dignified bearing) aplomo *m*; **to be —d to** estar listo para; VI/VT equilibrar[se]
poison [pɔ́ɪzən] N veneno *m*, ponzoña *f*; **— ivy** hiedra venenosa *f*; VT envenenar, emponzoñar
poisoning [pɔ́ɪzənɪŋ] N (accidental) intoxicación *f*; (intentional) envenenamiento *m*
poisonous [pɔ́ɪzənəs] ADJ venenoso, ponzoñoso
poke [pok] VT (jab) clavar, pinchar; (stir a fire) atizar; (thrust out, as one's head) asomar; **— out an eye** sacar un ojo; VI **to — along** andar perezosamente; **to — around** husmear; **to — fun at** burlarse de; **to — into** meterse en; **to — out** (project) sobresalir; N pinchazo *m*
Poland [pólənd] N Polonia *f*
polar [pólɚ] ADJ polar; **— bear** oso polar *m*
polarity [pəlǽrɪDi] N polaridad *f*
polarization [polɚɪzéʃən] N polarización *f*
polarize [pólaraɪz] VI/VT polarizar[se]
pole [poł] N (long piece of wood, metal) poste *m*; (for a flag) asta *f*; (for vaulting) pértiga *f*, garrocha *f*; (earth's axis) polo *m*; (for skiing) bastón *m*; **— vault** salto con pértiga *m*
Pole [poł] N polaco -ca *mf*
polemic [pəlémɪk] ADJ polémico *m*; N polémica *f*
police [pəlís] N policía *f*; **— car** patrullero *m*; **— dog** perro policía *m*; **— force** cuerpo de policía *m*; **—man** policía *m*; **— officer** oficial de policía *mf*, *Am* carabinero -ra *mf*; **— operation** *Am* operativo policial *m*; **— report** parte policial *m*; **— state** estado policíaco *m*; **— station** comisaría de policía *f*; **—woman** policía *f*; VT patrullar
policy [pálɪsi] N (procedure) política *f*; (for insurance) póliza *f*
polio [pólio] N polio *f*
Polish [pólɪʃ] ADJ & N polaco -ca *mf*

polish [páliʃ] N (sheen) lustre *m*, refinamiento *m*; (refinement) urbanidad *f*, cultura *f*; (substance for furniture) cera *f*; (substance for shoes) betún *m*; VT (a speech) pulir; (a metal) sacar brillo; (a car) encerar; (shoes) lustrar, embetunar; **to — off** despachar; **to — up** (metal) sacar brillo; (speech) pulir

polite [pəláɪt] ADJ cortés

politeness [pəláɪtnɪs] N cortesía *f*

politic [pálɪtɪk] ADJ diplomático, político

political [pəlíDɪkəɫ] ADJ político; **— prisoner** preso -sa político -ca *mf*; **— science** ciencias políticas *f pl*

politically correct [pəlíDɪklikɔrékt] ADJ políticamente correcto

politician [palɪtíʃən] N político -ca *mf*

politics [pálɪtɪks] N política *f*

polka [pólkə] N polca *f*; **— dot** lunar *m*

poll [poɫ] N (survey) encuesta *f*; **—s** (elections) comicios *m pl*; (voting place) urna *f*; VT (survey) encuestar; (receive votes) obtener; (record vote of) registrar

pollen [pálən] N polen *m*

pollinate [pálənet] VT polinizar

pollute [pəlút] VI/VT contaminar

pollution [pəlúʃən] N contaminación *f*

polo [pólo] N polo *m*

polyester [paliéstə-] N poliéster *m*

polygamy [pəlígəmi] N poligamia *f*

polyglot [páliglat] ADJ & N políglota *mf*

polygraph [páligræf] N polígrafo *m*

polymer [páləmə-] N polímero *m*

polyp [pálɪp] N pólipo *m*

polyunsaturated [paliʌnsǽtʃəreDɪd] ADJ poliinsaturado

polyurethane [palijúrəθen] N poliuretano *m*

pomegranate [pámɪgrænɪt] N granada *f*; **— tree** granado *m*

pomp [pamp] N pompa *f*, boato *m*, aparato *m*

pompous [pámpəs] ADJ pomposo, aparatoso

pond [pand] N (natural) charca *f*; (artificial) estanque *m*; (for irrigation) balsa *f*

ponder [pándə-] VI meditar; VT considerar

ponderous [pándə-əs] ADJ enorme

pontoon [pantún] N (on a bridge) pontón *m*; (on an airplane) flotador *m*

pony [póni] N póney *m*; **—tail** colita *f*, cola de caballo *f*; VI **to — up** soltar

Ponzi scheme [pánzi skím] N timo en pirámide *m pl*

poodle [púdl̩] N caniche *m*

pool [puɫ] N (puddle of water, blood, etc.) charco *m*; (swimming place) piscina *f*, *Mex* alberca *f*; (association of competitors) pool *m*; (game) pool *m*, billar *m*; (bets) pozo *m*; **— table** billar *m*; **— hall** billar *m*; VI acumularse; VT combinar fondos

poop [pup] N (part of ship) popa *f*; (excrement) *fam* caca *f*; VI *fam* hacer caca

poor [pʊr] ADJ (lacking money) pobre; (deficient) malo; **I'm a — cook** no sé cocinar; **—house** asilo para los pobres *m*; **— little thing** pobrecito -ta *mf*; N **the —** los pobres

pop [pap] VI (balloon) reventar, estallar; (eyes, cork) saltar; **to — in** entrar de paso; VT (make explode) hacer reventar; (take out cork) hacer saltar; (put) meter; (take, as pills) tomar; **to — a question** espetar una pregunta; **to — corn** hacer palomitas; N estallido *m*, detonación *f*; **—corn** palomitas *f pl*; **— music** música popular *f*; **— quiz** prueba sorpresa *f*; **— of a cork** taponazo *m*; **—-up menu** menú emergente *m*

pope [pop] N papa *m*

poplar [páplə-] N álamo *m*, chopo *m*; **— grove** alameda *f*

poppy [pápi] N amapola *f*

popular [pápjələ-] ADJ popular; **he's very — with the ladies** tiene mucho éxito con las mujeres

popularity [papjəlǽrɪDi] N popularidad *f*

populate [pápjəlet] VT poblar

population [papjəléʃən] N población *f*

populous [pápjələs] ADJ populoso

porcelain [pɔ́rsəlɪn] N porcelana *f*

porch [pɔrtʃ] N porche *m*

porcupine [pɔ́rkjəpaɪn] N puercoespín *m*

pore [pɔr] N poro *m*; VI **to — over a book** estudiar detenidamente un libro

pork [pɔrk] N carne de cerdo *f*; **— chop** chuleta de cerdo *f*

porn [pɔrn] N porno *m*

pornography [pɔrnágrəfi] N pornografía *f*

porous [pɔ́rəs] ADJ poroso

porpoise [pɔ́rpəs] N marsopa *f*

port [pɔrt] N (harbor, computer) puerto *m*; (wine) oporto *m*; (left side of ship) babor *m*; **— city** ciudad portuaria *f*; **—hole** ojo de buey *m*; **— of entry** puerto de entrada *m*

portable [pɔ́rDəbəl] ADJ portátil

portal [pɔ́rdl̩] N portal *m* (also of Internet)

portent [pɔ́rtent] N (omen) presagio *m*, agüero *m*; (marvel, prodigy) portento *m*

portentous [pɔrténtəs] ADJ (ominous) de mal agüero; (prodigious) portentoso

porter [pɔ́rDə-] N mozo -za *mf*

portfolio [pɔrtfólio] N cartera *f*

portion [pɔ́rʃən] N porción *f*; VI **to — out** repartir

portly [pɔ́rtli] ADJ grueso

portrait [pɔ́rtrɪt] N (likeness) retrato *m*; (printing orientation) orientación vertical *f*

portray [pɔrtré] VT (draw, describe) retratar; (in a drama) representar

portrayal [pɔrtréəl] N (portrait) retrato *m*; (act of portraying) representación *f*, caracterización *f*

Portugal [pɔ́rtʃəgəl] N Portugal *m*

Portuguese [pórtʃəgiz] ADJ & N portugués -esa mf
pose [poz] N (posture) pose f, postura f; (affected attitude) afectación f; VI (sit as a model) posar; (act affectedly) afectar una actitud; VT (to make sit as model) hacer posar; (to present) plantear; **to — as** hacerse pasar por
position [pəzíʃən] N (place) posición f; (job) puesto m, colocación f; (political stance) posicionamiento m; VI situar, colocar; **to — oneself** posicionarse
positive [pázɪDɪv] ADJ positivo; **— proof** prueba certera f; **I am —** estoy seguro
possess [pəzés] VT poseer
possessed [pəzést] ADJ (by a spirit) poseído; (by an idea) obsesionado
possession [pəzéʃən] N posesión f; **to take —** tomar posesión
possessive [pəzésɪv] ADJ & N posesivo m
possessor [pəzésə-] N poseedor -ora f
possibility [pasəbílɪDi] N posibilidad f
possible [pásəbəl] ADJ posible, eventual
post [post] N (pole) poste m; (position) puesto m; (mail) correo m; **—card** tarjeta postal f; **—haste** a la brevedad; **—man** cartero m; **—mark** matasellos m; **—master** director de correos m; **— office** oficina de correos f, casa de correos f; **—-office box** apartado postal m; ADJ **— paid** porte pagado; VT (affix) fijar; (announce) anunciar; (list) poner en lista; (place) apostar, situar; (mail) echar al correo; **kccp me —ed** mantenme al tanto
postage [póstɪʤ] N franqueo m; **— meter** franqueadora f; **— stamp** Sp sello m; Am estampilla f; Mex timbre m
postal [póstl] ADJ postal; **to go —** perpetrar un ataque homicida, volverse loco
postdate [posdét] VT posfechar
poster [póstə-] N cartel m, póster m, afiche m; **— child** modelo perfecto m
posterior [pɑstíriə-] ADJ posterior; N trasero m
posterity [pastérɪDi] N posteridad f
postgraduate [postgrǽʤuɪt] ADJ de posgrado; N posgrado -da mf
posthumous [pástʃəməs] ADJ póstumo
postnasal [postnézəł] ADJ postnasal
postnatal [postnédl] ADJ posparto; **— care** cuidado posparto m inv
postpartum [postpárɖəm] ADJ posparto m
postpone [postpón] VT posponer, aplazar
postponement [postpónmənt] N aplazamiento m
postscript [póstskrɪpt] N posdata f
postulate[1] [pástʃəlet] VT postular
postulate[2] [pástʃəlɪt] N postulado m
posture [pástʃə-] N (carriage, attitude) postura f; (affectation) afectación f; VI darse aires
postwar period [póstwár píriəd] N posguerra f
posy [pózi] N ramillete m

pot [pɑt] N (vessel) olla f, marmita f; (marijuana) marihuana f; (hashish) fam chocolate m; **—hole** bache m; ADJ **—-bellied** panzudo, barrigón
potable [póɖəbəł] ADJ potable
potassium [pətǽsiəm] N potasio m
potato [pətéɖo] N Sp patata f; Am papa f; **— chip** patata/papa frita [a la inglesa] f, chip m
potency [pótnsi] N potencia f
potent [pótnt] ADJ potente
potentate [pótntet] N potentado -da mf
potential [pəténʃəł] ADJ & N potencial m
potion [póʃən] N poción f
potter [páɖə-] N alfarero -ra mf
pottery [páɖəri] N (craft, shop) alfarería f; (objects) cerámica f, objetos de alfarería m pl
pouch [pautʃ] N bolsa f; (for mail) valija f; (for tobacco) petaca f
poultry [półtri] N aves de corral f pl
pounce [pauns] VI saltar; **to — upon/on** abalanzarse sobre; **to — on an opportunity** no dejar pasar una oportunidad; N salto m
pound [paund] N (unit of weight, British currency) libra f; (place for stray dogs) perrera f; VT (on a door) golpear; (seeds) machacar; (a military target) bombardear; VI (beat) latir con fuerza
pour [pɔr] VT verter; VI (leave en masse) salir en tropel; (rain) llover a cántaros; **to — out one's feelings** desahogarse
pout [paut] VI hacer pucheros; N puchero m
poverty [pávə-Di] N pobreza f, penuria f; ADJ **—-stricken** indigente
powder [páuɖə-] N polvo m; (for the face) polvos m pl; (for guns) pólvora f; **— compact** polvera f; **— puff** borla f; **to take a —** poner pies en polvorosa; VI/VT (use powder) empolvar[se]; (pulverize) pulverizar[se]
power [páuə-] N (control, military might) poder m, poderío m; (in physics, in math) potencia f; (physical strength) fuerza f; (energy) energía f; **— of attorney** poder m; **— plant** central eléctrica f; **—-save mode** modo de ahorro de energía m; **— steering** dirección asistida f; **— supply** suministro de energía m; **— surge** sobrecarga de voltaje f; **in —** oficialista; **legislative —s** atribuciones legislativas f pl; VI **—ed by gas** movido por gas; **to — down** apagar; **to — on/up** encender
powerful [páuə-fəł] ADJ poderoso, potente
powerless [páuə-lɪs] ADJ impotente
PR [public relations] [piár] N relaciones públicas f pl
practical [prǽktɪkəł] ADJ práctico; **— joke** broma pesada f, chasco m; **— nurse** enfermero -ra sin título mf
practically [prǽktɪkli] ADV prácticamente
practice [prǽktɪs] N (repeated exercise) práctica f; (habit) costumbre f; (doctor's office)

consultorio *m*; (lawyer's office) bufete *m*;
VI/VT practicar; VT (a profession) ejercer; **in**
— en la práctica, prácticamente
practiced [prǽktɪst] ADJ experto, perito
practitioner [præktíʃənɚ] N practicante *mf*;
general — médico -ca general *mf*
pragmatic [prægmǽDɪk] ADJ pragmático
prairie [préri] N pradera*f*, llanura*f*
praise [prez] N alabanza*f*, elogio *m*; VT alabar,
elogiar; —**worthy** loable, encomiable
prance [præns] VI cabriolar, hacer cabriolas; N
cabriola*f*
prank [præŋk] N travesura*f*, chasco *m*; **to play**
—**s** hacer travesuras
prawn [prɔn] N langostino *m*; *Sp* gamba
pequeña*f*
pray [pre] VI/VT (religious) rezar, orar; (beg)
rogar, suplicar
prayer [prɛr] N (devout petition to God) oración
f, rezo *m*; (entreaty) ruego *m*, súplica*f*
praying mantis [préɪŋmǽntɪs] N mantis
religiosa*f*
preach [pritʃ] VI/VT predicar; (moralize)
sermonear
preacher [prítʃɚ] N predicador -ora *mf*
preamble [príæmbəl] N preámbulo *m*
preapproved [priəprúvd] ADJ preaprobado
precancerous [prikǽnsəəs] ADJ precanceroso
precarious [prikériəs] ADJ precario
precaution [prikɔ́ʃən] N precaución*f*
precautionary [prikɔ́ʃəneri] ADJ preventivo
precede [prisíd] VI/VT preceder
precedence [présɪDəns] N precedencia*f*,
prioridad*f*
preceding [prisíDɪŋ] ADJ precedente, anterior
precept [prísɛpt] N precepto *m*
precinct [prísɪŋkt] N distrito *m*; (police station)
comisaría*f*; —**s** límites *m pl*
precious [préʃəs] ADJ precioso; (overly refined)
preciosista; — **little** muy poco; — **metal**
metal precioso *m*; — **stone** piedra preciosa*f*
precipice [présəpɪs] N precipicio *m*,
derrumbadero *m*
precipitate[1] [prisípɪtet] VI/VT precipitar[se]
precipitate[2] [prisípɪtɪt] ADJ & N precipitado *m*
precipitation [prisipɪtéʃən] N precipitación*f*
precipitous [prisípɪDəs] ADJ (steep) escarpado;
(hasty) precipitado
precise [prisáɪs] ADJ preciso, exacto
precisely [prisáɪsli] ADV & INT precisamente,
exactamente
precision [prisíʒən] N precisión*f*, exactitud*f*;
(of expression) propiedad*f*
preclude [priklúd] VT excluir; **that doesn't** —
our considering your application esto
no obsta para que tengamos en cuenta su
solicitud
precocious [prikóʃəs] ADJ precoz
precursor [prikɔ́ɚsɚ] N precursor *m*

predator [prɛ́Dətɚ] N depredador *m*
predatory [prɛ́Dətɔri] ADJ (animal) depredador;
(persona) rapaz
predecessor [prɛ́DɪsɛSɚ] N predecesor -ora *mf*,
antecesor -ora *mf*
predestine [pridéstɪn] VT predestinar
predetermined [priditɚmɪnd] ADJ
predeterminado
predicament [prɪdíkəmənt] N aprieto *m*
predicate[1] [prɛ́Dɪkɪt] ADJ & N predicado *m*
predicate[2] [prɛ́Dɪket] VT basar
predict [prɪdíkt] VT predecir
prediction [prɪdíkʃən] N predicción*f*, vaticinio *m*
predilection [prɛdlékʃən] N predilección*f*
predispose [pridɪspóz] VI/VT predisponer
predisposition [pridɪspəzíʃən] N
predisposición*f*
predominance [prɪdámənəns] N predominio *m*
predominant [prɪdámənənt] ADJ
predominante
predominate [prɪdámənet] VI/VT predominar,
preponderar
preeclampsia [priiklǽmpsiə] N preeclampsia*f*
preexisting [priigzístɪŋ] ADJ preexistente
preface [préfɪs] N prefacio *m*, prólogo *m*; VT
hacer una introducción; (a book) prologar
prefer [prɪfɚ] VT preferir; **to** — **a claim**
presentar una demanda
preferable [préfɚəbəl] ADJ preferible
preference [préfɚəns] N preferencia*f*
preferential [prefɚénʃəl] ADJ preferente
preferred [prɪfɚd] ADJ preferido; — **stocks**
acciones preferentes*f pl*
prefix [prífɪks] N prefijo *m*; VT poner un prefijo
pregnancy [prégnənsi] N embarazo *m*; (of
an animal) preñez*f*; — **test** prueba de
embarazo*f*
pregnant [prégnənt] ADJ (person) embarazada,
encinta; (animal) preñada; (full of meaning,
rain) preñado, cargado
prehensile [prihénsəl] ADJ prensil
prehistoric [prihistɔ́rɪk] ADJ prehistórico
prejudge [priʤʌ́ʤ] VT prejuzgar
prejudice [préʤəDɪs] N (bias) prejuicio *m*;
(harm) perjuicio *m*; VT (cause bias against)
predisponer en contra; (harm) perjudicar
preliminary [prɪlímənɛri] ADJ & N preliminar *m*
prelude [prélud] N preludio *m*; VI/VT preludiar
premarital [primǽrɪdl̩] ADJ prematrimonial
premature [primətʃúr] ADJ prematuro; —
birth parto prematuro *m*
premeditated [primɛ́DɪteDɪd] ADJ premeditado
premenstrual [priménstruəl] ADJ
premenstrual
premier [prɪmír] N primer ministro *m*; primera
ministra*f*; ADJ principal
premiere [prɪmír] N estreno *m*, première*f*
premise [prémɪs] N premisa*f*; —**s** local *m*
premium [prímiəm] N (bonus) premio *m*;

(insurance) prima *f*; (surcharge) recargo *m*; **at a** — muy escaso; ADJ superior

premonition [prɛməníʃən] N premonición *f*

prenatal [prinédl̩] ADJ prenatal; — **care** atención prenatal *f*, cuidado prenatal *m*

prenuptial [prinʌ́pʃəl̩] ADJ prenupcial; — **agreement** capitulaciones matrimoniales *f pl*

preoccupy [priʌ́kjəpaɪ] VT absorber

preowned [priónd] ADJ de segunda mano

prepacked [pripǽkt] ADJ preempacado

prepaid [pripéd] ADJ pagado de antemano; **to send** — enviar porte pagado

preparation [prɛpəréʃən] N (act of preparing) preparación *f*; (substance) preparado *m*; (for a trip) preparativos *m pl*

preparatory [prépəətɔri] ADJ preparatorio, preparativo

prepare [pripér] VI/VT preparar[se]

preponderance [pripʌ́ndəəns] N preponderancia *f*

preponderant [pripʌ́ndəənt] ADJ preponderante

preposition [prɛpəzíʃən] N preposición *f*

preposterous [pripʌ́stəəs] ADJ absurdo

prerecorded [prirɪkɔ́rdɪd] ADJ pregrabado

prerequisite [prirékwəzɪt] N prerequisito *m*

prerogative [prɪrágəDɪv] N prerrogativa *f*

prescribe [prɪskráɪb] VT (order) prescribir; (medicine) recetar

prescription [prɪskrípʃən] N (order) prescripción *f*; (of medicine) receta *f*

presence [prézəns] N presencia *f*; — **of mind** aplomo *m*, presencia de ánimo *f*

present¹ [prézənt] N (time) presente *m*; (gift) regalo *m*, presente *m*; **at** — ahora; **for the** — por ahora; ADJ (at a place) presente; (at this time) actual; — **company excepted** con perdón de los presentes; — **participle** gerundio *m*; — **perfect** pretérito perfecto *m*; —**-day** actual

present² [prɪzént] VT presentar, entregar

presentable [prɪzéntəbəl̩] ADJ presentable

presentation [prɛzəntéʃən] N (act of presenting) presentación *f*, entrega *f*; (speech) ponencia *f*; (exposition) planteamiento *m*

presentiment [prɪzéntəmənt] N presentimiento *m*

presently [prézəntli] ADV (soon) pronto; (now) actualmente

preservation [prɛzəvéʃən] N preservación *f*, conservación *f*

preservative [prɪzə́vəDɪv] N conservante *m*

preserve [prɪzə́v] VI/VT (protect) preservar; (keep food fresh) conservar; N (for game) coto *m*; (for animals) reserva *f*; —**s** mermelada *f*, dulce *m*

preset [prisét] ADJ preestablecido

preside [prɪzáɪd] VI presidir; **to** — **over a** meeting presidir una reunión

presidency [prézɪDənsi] N presidencia *f*

president [prézɪDənt] N presidente -ta *mf*

presidential [prɛzɪdénʃəl̩] ADJ presidencial

press [prɛs] VI/VT (bear down, squeeze) apretar, oprimir; (a computer key) oprimir, presionar; (iron) planchar; (force) presionar; (extract juice) prensar; (put under pressure) apremiar; **to** — **on** avanzar; **to** — **one's point** insistir en un argumento; **to** — **through** abrirse paso; N (newspapers) prensa *f*; (printing machine) imprenta *f*; (crowding) empuje *m*; — **conference** conferencia de prensa *f*; — **corps** cuerpo de prensa *m*; — **release** comunicado de prensa *m*

pressing [présɪŋ] ADJ apremiante, urgente

pressure [préʃə] N presión *f*; — **cooker** olla a presión *f*; — **gauge** manómetro *m*; — **group** grupo de presión *m*; VT apremiar, presionar

prestige [prestíʒ] N prestigio *m*

prestigious [prestídʒəs] ADJ prestigioso

presumably [prizúməbli] ADV — **he is already prepared** es de suponer que ya esté preparado

presume [prizúm] VI (be presumptuous) presumir; VT (suppose) suponer; (dare) atreverse a

presumption [prizʌ́mpʃən] N presunción *f*

presumptuous [prizʌ́mptʃuəs] ADJ presuntuoso, presumido

presuppose [prisəpóz] VT presuponer

pretax [pritǽks] ADJ antes de impuestos

preteen [pritín] ADJ & N preadolescente *mf*

pretend [priténd] VI/VT (make believe) hacer de cuenta que; (feign) fingir; VT (claim) pretender; **to** — **to the throne** pretender el trono

pretense [prítens] N (faked action or belief) engaño *m*; (false show) apariencia *f*; **under** — **of** so pretexto de

pretension [priténʃən] N pretensión *f*; (pretext) pretexto *m*

pretentious [priténʃəs] ADJ (full of pretension) pretencioso; (showy) ostentoso

pretext [prítɛkst] N pretexto *m*

pretrial [pritráɪl̩] ADJ anterior al juicio

pretty [prídi] ADJ bonito; (human only) *Sp* guapo; ADV bastante; — **well** bastante bien, francamente bien; VI/VT **to** — **up** embellecer

prevail [privél̩] VI (win) prevalecer; (be widespread, dominant) preponderar, imperar; **to** — **on/upon** persuadir

prevailing [privélɪŋ] ADJ (opinion) predominante; (feeling) reinante, imperante; — **winds** vientos predominantes

prevalent [prévələnt] ADJ prevaleciente, preponderante

prevent [privént] VT (keep from occurring) prevenir; VI/VT (impede) impedir

prevention [prɪvénʃən] N prevención f; (of a disease) prevención f, profilaxis f
preventive [prɪvéntɪv] ADJ preventivo, cautelar
preview [prívju] N preestreno m
previewing [prívjuwɪŋ] N previsualización f
previous [prívɪəs] ADJ previo, anterior
previously [prívɪəsli] ADV previamente, anteriormente
prey [pre] N (animal) presa f; VI **to — on** (animals) alimentarse de; (people) explotar; **it —s upon my mind** me tiene preocupado
price [praɪs] N precio m; **at any** — a toda costa; **— control** control de precios m; **— fixing** fijación de precios f; **— index** índice de precios m; **— tag** etiqueta de precio f; VT (set price) poner precio a; (ask price) averiguar el precio de
priceless [práɪslɪs] ADJ (without price) invalorable; (amusing) divertidísimo
pricey [práɪsi] ADJ caro
pricing [práɪsɪŋ] N fijación de precios f
prick [prɪk] N (puncture) pinchazo m; (sharp point) púa f; (penis) vulg pija f; (creep) offensive hijo de puta m; VI/VT pinchar, punzar; **to — up one's ears** parar las orejas
prickly [príkli] ADJ espinoso; **— heat** sarpullido causado por el calor m; **— pear** tuna f, nopal m
pride [praɪd] N orgullo m; (excessive) soberbia f; VI **to — oneself on** enorgullecerse de
priest [prist] N sacerdote m; (Catholic only) cura m
priesthood [prísthʊd] N sacerdocio m
prim [prɪm] ADJ remilgado
primarily [praɪmérɪli] ADV principalmente, más que nada
primary [práɪmɛri] N elección primaria f; ADJ primario; (main) fundamental, principal; **— care** atención primaria f; **— colors** colores primarios m pl; **— election** elección primaria f; **— school** escuela primaria f
primate [práɪmet] N primate m
prime [praɪm] ADJ (principal) fundamental; (of a number) primo; (select) de primera; **— minister** primer ministro m, primera ministra f; N (number) número primo m; **to be in one's** — estar en la flor de la edad, estar en la plenitud de la vida; **— rate** tasa prima f; VT preparar; (a pump) cebar
primer¹ [prímɚ] N (first book) manual elemental m
primer² [práɪmɚ] N (pump part) cebador m
primitive [prímɪdɪv] ADJ & N primitivo -va mf
prince [prɪns] N príncipe m
princely [prínsli] ADJ noble, principesco; **a — sum** una suma muy grande
princess [prínsɛs] N princesa f
principal [prínsəpəl] ADJ principal; N (money invested) capital m; (giver of power of

attorney) poderdante mf, mandante mf; (head of a school) director -ora mf
principle [prínsəpəl] N principio m
print [prɪnt] VI/VT imprimir; (write in block letters) escribir en letra de molde; **to — out** imprimir; N (type) letra de imprenta f; (of art) lámina f; (of photographs) copia f; (of finger) huella digital f; (on cloth) estampado m; **—out** versión impresa f; **in** — publicado, en venta; **out of** — agotado
printer [príntɚ] N (person) impresor -ora mf, gráfico -ca mf; (machine) impresora f; **— driver** controlador de impresora m; **— feeder** alimentador de impresora m
printing [príntɪŋ] N (art, trade) imprenta f; (process) impresión f, tipografía f; (block letters) letra de molde f, letra de imprenta f; **— press** imprenta f; **this book is in its second** — este libro está en su segunda tirada
prior [práɪɚ] ADJ previo; **— to** anterior a
priority [praɪórɪDi] N prioridad f; **having** — prioritario
prism [prízəm] N prisma m
prison [prízən] N prisión f, cárcel f, presidio m
prisoner [prízənɚ] N (captive) prisionero -ra mf; (in jail) preso -sa mf, presidiario -ria mf; **— of war** prisionero -ra de guerra mf
pristine [prɪstín] ADJ (immaculate) puro; (perfect) perfecto
privacy [práɪvəsi] N privacidad f; **— statement** declaración sobre la privacidad f
private [práɪvɪt] ADJ (not public) privado; (individual) particular; **— enterprise** empresa privada f; **— eye** detective privado -da mf; **— parts** partes pudendas f pl; **— property** propiedad privada f; **—s** partes pudendas f pl; **— school** escuela privada f; **— sector** sector privado m; **a — citizen** un particular; **in** — en privado; N soldado raso m
privation [praɪvéʃən] N privación f
privatization [praɪvəDɪzéʃən] N privatización f
privatize [práɪvətaɪz] VT privatizar
privilege [prívəlɪʤ] N privilegio m
privileged [prívəlɪʤd] ADJ privilegiado
privy [prívi] ADJ **to be — to** estar enterado de; N retrete m
prize [praɪz] N (reward) premio m; (booty) botín m; **— fight** pelea de boxeo profesional f; **— fighter** boxeador -ora mf, pugilista mf; VT apreciar
pro [pro] N profesional mf
probability [prɑbəbílɪDi] N probabilidad f
probable [prábəbəl] ADJ probable
probate [próbet] N legalización de una validación testamentaria f
probation [probéʃən] N libertad condicional f
probationary [probéʃənɛri] ADJ probatorio; **— period** período de prueba m
probe [prob] VI/VT (explore with a probe)

sondear; (examine) examinar; N sonda f (also
in space); (investigation) indagación f
problem [prábləm] N problema m; **—s**
problemática f
procedure [prəsídʒə-] N procedimiento m;
(legal) trámite m
proceed [prəsíd] VI (originate) proceder;
(continue) proseguir, continuar; **to —
against** demandar a; **to — to** proceder a
proceeds [prósidz] N ganancia f, lo recaudado
proceedings [prəsíDIŋz] N (events)
acontecimientos m pl; (record of a conference)
actas f pl, memoria f; (legal action)
procedimiento m
process [práses] N proceso m; **in the — of** en
vías de
processing [prásesIŋ] N (of applications)
tramitación f; (of data, substances)
procesamiento m; **— power** potencia
procesadora f
procession [prəséʃən] N procesión f
processor [prásesə-] N procesador m
pro-choice [protʃóIs] ADJ pro-elección
proclaim [prəklém] VT proclamar
proclamation [prakləméʃən] N proclamación f,
proclama f
procrastinate [prəkrǽstənet] VI/VT dejar para
último momento
procreate [prókriet] VI/VT procrear, engendrar
proctology [praktáləʤi] N proctología f
procure [prəkjúr] VT procurar, obtener; VI ser
proxeneta
prod [prad] VT aguijonear; **they —ded me into
going / to go** insistieron en que fuera
prodigal [práDIgəł] ADJ & N pródigo -ga mf
prodigious [prədíʤəs] ADJ prodigioso
prodigy [práDəʤi] N prodigio m
produce[1] [pródus] N (vegetables) verduras f pl,
hortalizas f pl
produce[2] [prədús] VI/VT producir; VT (present)
presentar
producer [prədúsə-] N productor -ora mf; (of a
movie) realizador -ora mf
product [práDəkt] N producto m
production [prədʌ́kʃən] N producción f; (TV,
radio) producción f, realización f;
(exaggerated situation) teatro m
productive [prədʌ́ktIv] ADJ productivo
productivity [praDəktíviDi] N productividad f
profane [profén] ADJ profano; (vulgar) grosero;
VT profanar
profanity [prəfǽnIDi] N groserías f pl,
palabrotas f pl
profess [prəfés] VI (publicly accept, take vows)
profesar; VT (state) afirmar; (claim) pretender
profession [prəféʃən] N profesión f
professional [prəféʃənł] ADJ & N profesional mf
professor [prəfésə-] N profesor -ora
universitario -ria mf; (full) catedrático -ca mf

proffer [práfə-] VT ofrecer; N oferta f
proficiency [prəfíʃənsi] N competencia f
proficient [prəfíʃənt] ADJ competente
profile [prófaIł] N (contour) perfil m; **a high- —
case** un caso muy sonado
profit [práfIt] N (gain) ganancia f; **— and loss**
ganancias y pérdidas f pl; **— margin** margen
de ganancia m; **— sharing** participación en
las ganancias de una empresa f; **at a —** con
ganancia; **to turn a —** dar ganancia; **not for
—** sin fines de lucro; VI salir ganando; **to —
from** (benefit) aprovechar, sacar provecho
de; (use to get an advantage) aprovecharse de;
VT servir
profitability [prafIDəbílIDi] N rentabilidad f
profitable [práfIDəbəł] ADJ (beneficial)
provechoso; (lucrative) lucrativo, rentable
profound [prəfáUnd] ADJ profundo
profundity [prəfʌ́ndIDi] N profundidad f
profuse [prəfjús] ADJ profuso, pródigo
progesterone [proʤéstərən] N progesterona f
prognosis [pragnósIs] N pronóstico m
program [prógræm] N programa m; VI/VT
programar
programmable [progrǽməbəł] ADJ
programable
programmer [prógræmə-] N programador -ora
mf
programming [prógræmIŋ] N programación f;
— language lenguaje de programación m
progress[1] [prágrɛs] N progreso m
progress[2] [prəgrés] VI progresar
progression [prəgréʃən] N progresión f
progressive [prəgrésIv] ADJ (advancing)
progresivo; ADJ & N (liberal) progresista mf,
progresivo -va mf
prohibit [prohíbIt] VT prohibir, vedar
prohibition [proəbíʃən] N prohibición f
project[1] [práʤɛkt] N proyecto m
project[2] [prəʤékt] VI/VT (plan) proyectar[se]; VI
(jut out) sobresalir
projectile [prəʤéktaIł] N proyectil m; ADJ
arrojadizo
projection [prəʤékʃən] N (plan) proyección f;
(jut) saliente f
projector [prəʤéktə-] N proyector m
proletariat [prolItériət] N proletariado m
pro-life [prólaIf] ADJ antiaborto
proliferation [prəlIfəréʃən] N proliferación f
prolific [prəlífIk] ADJ prolífico
prologue [prólɔg] N prólogo m
prolong [prəlɔ́ŋ] VT prolongar
prolongation [prolɔŋgéʃən] N prolongación f
promenade [pramənéd] N paseo m; (dance)
baile m; VI/VT pasear[se]
prominent [prámənənt] ADJ prominente
promiscuous [prəmískjuəs] ADJ promiscuo,
liviano
promise [prámIs] N promesa f; **he showed —**

prometía mucho; VI/VT prometer
promising [prámɪsɪŋ] ADJ prometedor
promissory [prámɪsɔri] ADJ promisorio; —
note pagaré m
promontory [prámǝntɔri] N promontorio m
promote [prǝmót] VT (foster) promover,
fomentar; (advance in rank) ascender; (in
school) pasar de año, promover; (advertise)
promocionar
promoter [prǝmóDɚ] N (fomenter) propulsor
-ora mf; (organizer) promotor -ora mf
promotion [prǝmóʃǝn] N (act of promoting)
promoción f; (advance in rank) ascenso m
promotional [prǝmóʃǝnl] ADJ promocional
prompt [prɑmpt] ADJ (quick) rápido; (punctual)
puntual; VT (cause) inducir; (in theater)
apuntar; **to give someone a** — apuntarle a
alguien
promptly [prámptli] ADV (soon) pronto;
(punctually) puntualmente
promulgate [prámǝɫget] VT promulgar
prone [pron] ADJ (disposed) propenso, proclive;
(face down) boca abajo; (prostrate) postrado
prong [prɔŋ] N púa f, diente m
pronoun [prónaʊn] N pronombre m
pronounce [prǝnáʊns] VT (enunciate)
pronunciar; (declare) declarar
pronounced [prǝnáʊnst] ADJ pronunciado
pronouncement [prǝnáʊnsmǝnt] N
pronunciamiento m
pronunciation [prǝnʌnsiéʃǝn] N pronunciación
f
proof [pruf] N (evidence, test, trial printing)
prueba f; (of alcohol) graduación f, grado m;
— **of purchase** comprobante de compra m;
—**reader** corrector -ora de pruebas mf,
revisor -ora de pruebas mf; **fifty** —
veinticinco por ciento de graduación
alcohólica; **fire**— a prueba de incendios;
water— impermeable; **bullet**— a prueba de
balas
prop [prɑp] N (pole) puntal m; (in theater)
accesorio m; (propeller) hélice f; (support)
sostén m, apoyo m; (of a plant) tutor m; VT **to**
— **against** apoyar en, sostener en; **to** — **up**
apuntalar, sostener
propaganda [prɑpǝgǽndǝ] N propaganda f
propagate [prápǝget] VI/VT propagar[se]
propagation [prɑpǝgéʃen] N propagación f
propane [própen] N propano m
propel [prǝpéɫ] VT propulsar, impulsar
propeller [prǝpélɚ] N hélice f
propensity [prǝpénsɪDi] N propensión f
proper [prápɚ] ADJ (appropriate) apropiado;
(decorous) decoroso; (genuine) como Dios
manda; (correct) correcto; (in math,
grammar) propio; **to be** — **to** ser propio de
properly [prápɚli] ADV (appropriately)
apropiadamente; (correctly) correctamente;

(decorously) decorosamente
property [prápɚDi] N (characteristic) propiedad
f; (real estate) propiedad f, finca f; (assets)
bienes m pl; — **damage** daños materiales m pl
prophecy [práfisi] N profecía f
prophesy [práfisaɪ] VI/VT profetizar
prophet [práfit] N profeta -tisa mf
prophetic [prǝféDɪk] ADJ profético
propitious [prǝpíʃǝs] ADJ propicio
proponent [prǝpónǝnt] N (person who
proposes) proponente mf; (adherent)
defensor -ora mf
proportion [prǝpɔrʃǝn] N proporción f; **out of**
— desproporcionado; VT proporcionar; **well**
—**ed** bien proporcionado
proportional [prǝpɔrʃǝnl] ADJ proporcional
proportionate [prǝpɔrʃǝnɪt] ADJ proporcional
proposal [prǝpózǝɫ] N (suggestion) propuesta f;
(of marriage, dishonest) proposición f
propose [prǝpóz] VI/VT (suggest) proponer; VI
(ask in marriage) declararse, hacer una
propuesta de matrimonio; **to** — **to do
something** proponerse hacer algo
proposition [prɑpǝzíʃǝn] N proposición f; VT
hacer proposiciones deshonestas
proprietor [prǝpráɪɪDɚ] N propietario -ria mf
propriety [prǝpráɪɪDi] N decoro m
propulsion [prǝpʌ́ɫʃǝn] N propulsión f
prorate [prorét] VT prorratear
prosaic [prozéɪk] ADJ prosaico
prose [proz] N prosa f
prosecute [prásɪkjut] VI/VT (take to court)
procesar, enjuiciar; VT (pursue) llevar
adelante
prosecution [prasɪkjúʃǝn] N (act of prosecuting)
procesamiento m; (officials who prosecute)
ministerio público m, fiscalía f
prosecutor [prásɪkjuDɚ] N fiscal mf
proselytize [prásǝlɪtaɪz] VT convertir; VI buscar
ganar prosélitos
prospect [práspɛkt] N (outlook, possibility)
perspectiva f, expectativa f; (candidate)
candidato -ta mf; (possible client) posible
cliente -ta mf; VT prospectar; VI **to** — **for**
buscar
prospective [prǝspéktɪv] ADJ posible, potencial
prospector [práspɛktɚ] N prospector -ora mf
prosper [práspɚ] VI prosperar
prosperity [praspérɪDi] N prosperidad f,
bonanza f
prosperous [práspǝrǝs] ADJ próspero
prostate [prástet] N próstata f; — **gland**
próstata f
prosthesis [prasθísɪs] N prótesis f
prostitute [prástɪtut] N prostituto -ta mf; VT
prostituir
prostitution [prastɪtúʃǝn] N prostitución f
prostrate [prástret] VT postrar; ADJ (lying flat,
overcome) postrado; (lying face down) boca

abajo
protagonist [protǽgənɪst] N protagonista *mf*
protect [prətékt] VI/VT proteger, amparar
protection [prətékʃen] N protección *f*
protectionist [prətékʃənɪst] ADJ & N
proteccionista *mf*
protective [prətéktɪv] ADJ protector
protector [prətéktɚ] N protector -ora *mf*
protectorate [prətéktərɪt] N protectorado *m*
protégé, protégée [próDəʒe] N protegido -da
mf
protein [prótin] N proteína *f*
protest[1] [prótɛst] N protesta *f*, reclamación *f*
protest[2] [prətést] VI/VT protestar, reclamar
Protestant [práDɪstənt] ADJ & N protestante *mf*
protestation [protɛstéʃən] N declaración *f*
protocol [próDəkɔɫ] N protocolo *m*
proton [prótɑn] N protón *m*
protoplasm [próDəplæzəm] N protoplasma *m*
prototype [próDətaɪp] N prototipo *m*
protozoan [proDəzóən] N protozoario *m*
protract [protrǽkt] VT prolongar
protrude [protrúd] VI sobresalir, proyectarse
protuberance [prətúbərəns] N protuberancia *f*
proud [praUd] ADJ orgulloso; (haughty)
soberbio; **to be — of** enorgullecerse de,
ufanarse de
prove [pruv] VT (demonstrate, verify) probar,
demostrar; VI resultar; **events have —d me
right** los hechos me han dado la razón
proverb [právɚb] N proverbio *m*, refrán *m*
provide [prəváɪd] VT (furnish) proveer,
proporcionar; (supply) abastecer, aportar;
(stipulate) estipular, prevenir; VI **to — for**
(support) mantener; (stipulate) estipular; **to
— with** proveer de, proporcionar; CONJ **—d
[that]** con tal [de] que, siempre que
providence [právɪDəns] N providencia *f*
provider [prəváɪDɚ] N (supplier) proveedor -ora
mf; (breadwinner) sostén *m*
province [právɪns] N (area) provincia *f*;
(competence) competencia *f*
provincial [prəvínʃəɫ] ADJ (of a province)
provincial; (rustic) provinciano, pueblerino;
N provinciano -na *mf*
provision [prəvíʒən] N (act of providing, thing
provided) provisión *f*, suministro *m*,
prestación *f*; (precaution) medida *f*,
precaución *f*; (clause) estipulación *f*,
prevención *f*; **—s** provisiones *f pl*, víveres *m
pl*, bastimentos *m pl*, suministros *m*
provisional [prəvíʒənɫ] ADJ provisional
proviso [prəváɪzo] N condición *f*, estipulación *f*
provocation [provəkéʃən] N provocación *f*
provoke [prəvók] VT provocar
provost [próvost] N vicerrector -ora *mf*
prow [praU] N proa *f*
prowess [práUɪs] N valentía *f*
prowl [praUɫ] VI/VT rondar en acecho

proximity [prɑksímɪDi] N proximidad *f*
proxy [práksi] N (person) apoderado -da *mf*;
(power of attorney) poder *m*; **by —** por poder
prude [prud] N mojigato -ta *mf*, gazmoño -ña *mf*
prudence [prúdns] N prudencia *f*
prudent [prúdnt] ADJ prudente
prudery [prúdəri] N mojigatería *f*, gazmoñería *f*
prudish [prúDɪʃ] ADJ mojigato, gazmoño
prune [prun] N ciruela pasa *f*; VI/VT podar
pry [praɪ] VT curiosear; **to — into** entrometerse;
to — open abrir por la fuerza; **to — a secret
out** extraer/arrancar un secreto
pseudonym [súdnɪm] N pseudónimo/
seudónimo *m*
psoriasis [səráɪəsɪs] N psoriasis/soriasis *f*
psych [saɪk] VT **to — out** intimidar
psicológicamente
psychedelic [saɪkɪdélɪk] ADJ psicodélico/
sicodélico
psychiatrist [saɪkáɪətrɪst] N psiquiatra/siquiatra
mf
psychiatry [saɪkáɪətri] N psiquiatría/siquiatría *f*
psychic [sáɪkɪk] ADJ psíquico/síquico; N médium
mf, psíquico -ca / síquico -ca *mf*
psychoanalysis [saɪkoǽnəlaɪz] N psicoanálisis/
sicoanálisis *m*
psychological [saɪkəládʒɪkəɫ] ADJ psicológico/
sicológico
psychologist [saɪkáləɖʒɪst] N psicólogo -ga /
sicólogo -ga *mf*
psychology [saɪkáləɖʒi] N psicología/sicología *f*
psychopath [sáɪkəpæθ] N psicópata/sicópata *mf*
psychosis [saɪkósɪs] N psicosis/sicosis *f*
psychosomatic [saɪkosəmǽDɪk] ADJ
psicosomático/sicosomático
psychotherapy [saɪkoθérəpi] N psicoterapia/
sicoterapia *f*
psychotic [saɪkáDɪk] ADJ psicótico/sicótico
puberty [pjúbɚDi] N pubertad *f*
pubic [pjúbɪk] ADJ púbico; **— hair** pelo púbico
m, *vulg* pendejo *m*
public [páblɪk] ADJ público; **— domain** dominio
público *m*; **— health** salud pública *f*; **—
relations** relaciones públicas *f pl*; **— school**
escuela pública *f*; **— service** servicio público
m; **to go —** proceder a la venta pública de
acciones, salir a bolsa; N público *m*
publication [pʌblɪkéʃən] N publicación *f*
publicity [pʌblísɪDi] N publicidad *f*, propaganda
f; **— campaign** campaña publicitaria *f*
publicize [páblɪsaɪz] VT promocionar
publish [páblɪʃ] VI/VT publicar, editar; **—ing
house** [casa] editorial *f*
publisher [páblɪʃɚ] N editor -ora *mf*
puck [pʌk] N puck *m*
pucker [pákɚ] VI/VT fruncir[se]; N frunce *m*
pudding [púDɪŋ] N budín *m*, pudín *m*
puddle [pádɫ] N charco *m*
pudendum [pjudéndəm] N partes pudendas *f pl*

Puerto Rican [pɔrɒəríkən] ADJ & N
puertorriqueño -ña *mf*
Puerto Rico [pɔrɒəríko] N Puerto Rico *m*
puff [pʌf] N (air) resoplido *m*, soplo *m*; (smoke)
bocanada *f*; (on a cigarette) pitada *f*, chupada
f; (of a sleeve) bullón *m*; — **pastry** masa de
hojaldre *f*; VI (blow) resoplar; (breathe hard)
jadear; (smoke a cigarette) echar bocanadas;
to — up hincharse; **to — up with pride**
henchirse de orgullo
pug [pʌg] N dogo *m*; — **nose** nariz chata *f*
puke [pjuk] VI/VT vomitar, lanzar; N vómito *m*
pull [pʊl] VI/VT (tug) tirar, jalar; (extract)
arrancar, extraer; (stretch) estirar; (injure)
desgarrar; **to — apart** destrozar; **to — down**
(demolish) demoler; (earn) sacar; **to — for**
hinchar por; **to — off** conseguir; **to —**
oneself together calmarse; **to — over**
parar; **to — up** parar; **to — through**
salvarse; **to — strings** mover palancas; **to —**
out (leave a place) salir; (back out) retirarse;
the train —ed into the station el tren
entró a la estación; N (act of pulling) tirón *m*;
(force) fuerza *f*; (influence) influencia *f*;
(injury) desgarro *m*; —**-down menu** menú
abatible *m*
pullet [púlɪt] N polla *f*
pulley [púli] N polea *f*, carrucha *f*
pulmonary [púlmənɛri] ADJ pulmonar
pulp [pʌlp] N (of paper, wood, fruit) pulpa *f*; (of
grape, sugarcane, olive, etc.) bagazo *m*
pulpit [púlpɪt] N púlpito *m*
pulsar [púlsɑr] N púlsar *m*
pulsate [púlset] VI latir
pulse [pʌls] N pulso *m*; (single pulsation, act of
pulsing) pulsación *f*
pulverize [púlvəraɪz] VT pulverizar[se]
puma [pjúmə] N puma *f*
pumice [púmɪs] N piedra pómez *f*
pump [pʌmp] N bomba *f*; (shoe) zapatilla *f*,
zapato escotado *m*; (for gasoline) surtidor *m*;
VI/VT bombear; (inflate) inflar; **to —**
someone for information sonsacar
[información] a alguien
pumpkin [púmpkɪn] N calabaza *f*
pun [pʌn] N juego de palabras *m*, retruécano *m*;
VI hacer juegos de palabras
punch [pʌntʃ] N (blow) puñetazo *m*; (drink)
ponche *m*; (drill) sacabocados *m sg*; (force)
fuerza *f*, empuje *m*; — **bowl** ponchera *f*; —
line remate de un chiste *m*; VI/VT (hit) dar un
puñetazo; VT (drive cattle) arriar; (make a
hole) agujerear; **to — in/out** marcar tarjeta
punctual [púŋktʃuəl] ADJ puntual
punctuality [pʌŋktʃuǽlɪɒi] N puntualidad *f*
punctuate [púŋktʃuet] VI/VT puntuar;
(interrupt) interrumpir; (accentuate) salpicar
punctuation [pʌŋktʃuéʃən] N puntuación *f*
puncture [púŋktʃɚ] VI/VT pinchar[se]; *Mex*

ponchar[se]; —**d tire** neumático pinchado *m*;
N (action of perforating) perforación *f*; (hole)
pinchazo *m*; — **wound** herida perforada *f*
pundit [púndɪt] N experto -ta *mf*
pungent [púndʒənt] ADJ (acrid) acre; (sarcastic)
mordaz
punish [púnɪʃ] VT castigar, penar
punishment [púnɪʃmənt] N castigo *m*
punitive [pjúnɪɒɪv] ADJ punitivo; — **damages**
daños punitivos *m pl*
punk [pʌŋk] N (inexperienced boy) mocoso *m*;
(hoodlum) gamberro *m*; (rock) punk *m*;
(punker) punkero -ra *mf*
punt [pʌnt] N (kick) patada de despeje *f*; (boat)
balsa *f*; VI/VT despejar; VI andar en balsa
punter [púntɚ] N despejador *m*
puny [pjúni] ADJ endeble
pupil [pjúpəl] N (student) escolar *mf*; (part of
eye) pupila *f*, niña *f*
puppet [púpɪt] N títere *m*, monigote *m*; — **show**
teatro de títeres *m*
puppy [púpi] N cachorro *m*
purchase [pɚ́tʃəs] VI/VT comprar, adquirir; N
compra *f*; (hold) asidero *m*; — **order** orden
de compra *f*; — **price** precio de compra *m*
purchaser [pɚ́tʃəsɚ] N comprador *mf*
purchasing [pɚ́tʃəsɪŋ] N compra *f*; — **agent**
agente de compras *mf*; — **power** poder
adquisitivo *m*
pure [pjʊr] ADJ puro; ADJ & N —**bred**
purasangre *m*
puree [pjuré] N puré *m*
purgative [pɚ́gəɒɪv] ADJ & N purgante *m*
purgatory [pɚ́gətɔri] N purgatorio *m*
purge [pɚʤ] VI/VT purgar[se]; N purga *f*
purify [pjúrəfaɪ] VI/VT purificar[se], depurar[se]
purist [pjúrɪst] N purista *mf*
puritanical [pjurɪtǽnɪkəl] ADJ puritano
purity [pjúrɪɒi] N pureza *f*
purple [pɚ́pəl] N morado *m*, púrpura *f*; ADJ
morado, púrpura
purport[1] [pɚ́pɔrt] N (meaning) significado *m*;
(purpose) propósito *m*
purport[2] [pɚpórt] VT pretender
purpose [pɚ́pəs] N propósito *m*, objetivo *m*; **on**
— adrede, a propósito
purr [pɚ] N ronroneo *m* (also motors); VI
ronronear
purse [pɚs] N bolso *m*, cartera *f*; VT **to — one's**
lips fruncir los labios
pursuant [pɚsúənt] ADV LOC — **to** conforme a,
de acuerdo con
pursue [pɚsú] VT (follow) perseguir; (strive)
dedicarse a; (continue) continuar con;
(practice a profession) ejercer
pursuer [pɚsúɚ] N perseguidor -ora *mf*
pursuit [pɚsút] N (chase) persecución *f*,
seguimiento *m*, acoso *m*; (striving for)
búsqueda *f*; (pastime) pasatiempo *m*;

(practice) ejercicio *m*; **in — of** (chasing)
detrás de; (striving for) en busca de
pus [pʌs] N pus *m*
push [pʊʃ] VI/VT (shove) empujar; VT (pressure)
presionar, promover; (sell drugs) camellear;
to — a button apretar un botón; VI (in
childbirth) pujar; **to — aside/away** apartar;
to — forward abrirse paso, avanzar; **to —
open** abrir de un empujón; **to — through**
hacer pasar; N empujón *m*; (military) ofensiva
f; **—-up** lagartija *f*; ADJ **—-button** de
botones
pusher [pʊʃɚ] N camello *mf*
pushy [pʊʃi] ADJ insistente
pussy [pʊsi] N (cat) minino *m*, gatito *m*; (female
genitalia) *vulg* coño *m*; Am *vulg* concha *f*; —
willow sauce *m*
put [pʊt] VT poner, colocar; **to — a question**
plantear una pregunta; **to — across**
expresar; **to — away** guardar; **to — down**
(write down) apuntar; (suppress) sofocar;
(attribute) atribuir; (humiliate) humillar;
(make a down payment) hacer un depósito; (a
pet) sacrificar; **to — into** meter; **to — into
words** expresar, decir; **to — in writing**
poner por escrito; **to — off** (postpone)
aplazar, posponer; (perturb) desagradar;
(dissuade) disuadir; **to — on** ponerse; **to —
on airs** darse tono; **to — on weight**
engordar; **to — out** (extinguish) apagar,
extinguir; (annoy) molestar; **to — the
blame** echar la culpa; **to — to sea** echar al
mar; **to — to sleep** sacrificar; **to — up**
(construct) levantar; (lodge) alojar; **to — up
for sale** poner a la venta; **to — up with**
aguantar; **I felt —-upon** sentí que se habían
aprovechado de mí; N **— option** opción de
venta *f*; **—-down** insulto *m*
putrid [pjútrɪd] ADJ putrefacto
putt [pʌt] VI/VT potear; N pat
putter [pʌdɚ] VI entretenerse; N (golf) putter *m*
putty [pʌdi] N masilla *f*; VT rellenar con masilla
puzzle [pázəl] N (jigsaw) rompecabezas *m sg*;
(riddle) acertijo *m*; (problem) enigma *m*;
(crossword) crucigrama *m*; VT dejar perplejo,
desconcertar; VI **to — out** desentrañar; **to —
over** meditar sobre; **to be —d** estar perplejo
pygmy [pígmi] N pigmeo -a *mf*
pylon [páɪlɑn] N pilón *m*
pyramid [pírəmɪd] N pirámide *f*
pyromania [paɪroméniə] N piromanía *f*
pyromaniac [paɪroméniæk] N pirómano -na *mf*
pyrotechnics [paɪrətékniks] N pirotecnia *f*
python [páɪθɑn] N pitón *mf*

Qq

Qatar [kətár] N Qatar *m*
Qatari [kətári] ADJ & N catarí *mf*
quack [kwæk] N (sound of duck) graznido *m*;
(charlatan) matasanos *mf*, charlatán -ana *mf*;
ADJ charlatán; VI graznar
quadrilateral [kwɑdrəlǽɖəɬ] ADJ & N
cuadrilátero *m*
quadriplegic [kwɑdrəplíʤɪk] ADJ & N
tetraplégico -ca *mf*
quadruped [kwádrəpɛd] ADJ & N cuadrúpedo *m*
quadruplet [kwɑdrúplɪt] N cuatrillizo -za *mf*
quagmire [kwǽgmaɪr] N (bog) cenagal *m*,
atascadero *m*; (crisis) atolladero *m*,
atascadero *m*
quail [kweł] N codorniz *f*
quaint [kwent] ADJ pintoresco
quake [kwek] N (instance of quaking) temblor *m*;
(earthquake) terremoto *m*; VI temblar
qualification [kwɑləfɪkéʃən] N (for a race)
clasificación *f*; (requirement) requisito *m*;
without — sin reservas
qualify [kwáləfaɪ] VT (characterize) calificar;
(moderate) moderar; (provide with
credentials) capacitar; VI (for a race)
clasificarse; (for a position) estar capacitado
qualifying [kwáləfaɪɪŋ] ADJ calificativo
qualitative [kwálɪteɖɪv] ADJ cualitativo
quality [kwálɪɖi] N (characteristic) cualidad *f*;
(excellence) calidad *f*; **— control** control de
calidad *m*
qualm [kwɔm] N escrúpulo *m*
quantify [kwántəfaɪ] VT cuantificar
quantitative [kwántɪteɖɪv] ADJ cuantitativo
quantity [kwántɪɖi] N cantidad *f*
quantum mechanics [kwántəmməkæniks] N
mecánica cuántica *f*
quarantine [kwɔrəntin] N cuarentena *f*; VT
poner en cuarentena
quarrel [kwɔrəɬ] N riña *f*, rencilla *f*; VI reñir,
pelear
quarrelsome [kwɔrəɬsəm] ADJ pendenciero
quarry [kwɔri] N (stone) cantera *f*; (game) presa
f; VT explotar
quart [kwɔrt] N cuarto de galón [0.9463 litros] *m*
quarter [kwɔrɖɚ] N (one-fourth) cuarto *m*,
cuarta parte *f*; (coin) moneda de 25 centavos *f*;
(of a sporting match) tiempo *m*; (of a calendar
or school year) trimestre *m*; (district) barrio
m; **—back** mariscal de campo *m*; **—master
general** intendente *mf*; **— note** negra *f*; **—s**
alojamiento *m*; **from all —s** de todas partes;
to give no — to the enemy no dar cuartel al
enemigo; ADJ cuarto; VT (divide) cuartear,

dividir en cuartos; (execute) descuartizar; (lodge troops) acuartelar, acantonar

quarterly [kwɔ́rᴅə-li] ADV trimestralmente; ADJ trimestral; N publicación trimestral f

quartet [kwɔrtét] N cuarteto m

quartz [kwɔrts] N cuarzo m

quasar [kwézɑr] N cuásar m, quásar m

quash [kwɑʃ] VT (a rebellion) sofocar; (a decision) anular

quaver [kwévə-] VI temblar; N temblor m; (in music) trémolo m

queasy [kwízi] ADJ nauseoso

queen [kwin] N reina f; (effeminate male homosexual) *offensive* loca f; *offensive* reinona f

queer [kwir] ADJ (strange) raro; (eccentric) excéntrico; (homosexual) *offensive* maricón; **to feel —** sentirse raro; N (homosexual) *offensive* marica m, maricón m; VT comprometer

quell [kwɛł] VT (suppress) reprimir, sofocar; (calm) calmar

quench [kwɛntʃ] VT (flames, thirst) apagar; (passions) aplacar, apagar

query [kwíri] N (question) pregunta f; (question mark) signo de interrogación m; (doubt) duda f; VT (ask) preguntar; (question) expresar dudas; (mark with a question mark) marcar con signo de interrogación

quest [kwɛst] N búsqueda f

question [kwéstʃən] N (thing asked) pregunta f; (issue) cuestión f; **— mark** signo de interrogación m; **beyond —** fuera de duda; **that is out of the —** ¡ni pensarlo! VT (ask) preguntar; (interrogate) interrogar; (call into doubt) dudar, cuestionar

questionable [kwéstʃənəbəł] ADJ (doubtful) cuestionable, discutible; (morally dubious) equívoco

questioner [kwéstʃənə-] N interrogador -ora mf

questioning [kwéstʃənɪŋ] N interrogatorio m; ADJ (asking) interrogador; (doubting) cuestionador

questionnaire [kwɛstʃənér] N cuestionario m

queue [kju] N cola f, fila f; VT poner en la cola

quibble [kwíbəł] VI (split hairs) sutilizar; (evade) evadir; (argue) andar en dimes y diretes; N (hairsplitting) sutileza f; (evasion) evasiva f

quiche [kiʃ] N quiche f

quick [kwɪk] ADJ rápido, pronto; **—-tempered** irascible, geniudo; **—-witted** agudo; ADV rápido; N (flesh under nails) carne viva f; (the living) los vivos; **to cut to the —** herir en lo vivo; **—sand** arena movediza f; **—silver** mercurio m, azogue m

quicken [kwíkən] VI/VT (speed up) acelerar[se], aligerar[se]; (liven) avivar[se]

quickly [kwíkli] ADV rápido, deprisa, de prisa

quickness [kwíknɪs] N (speed) rapidez f; (of wit)

agudeza f

quiet [kwáɪt] ADJ (not noisy) silencioso; (not talking) callado; (restrained) tranquilo; (peaceful, still) reposado; **be —!** ¡silencio! ¡cállate! N (freedom from noise) silencio m; (tranquillity) tranquilidad f, sosiego m; VT (make quiet) acallar; (make tranquil) sosegar, tranquilizar, serenar; VI **to — down** calmarse

quietly [kwáɪtli] ADV (talk) en voz baja; (walk) silenciosamente; **they — went about buying up shares** fueron comprando acciones sin llamar la atención

quill [kwɪł] N (feather) pluma f; (hollow base of feather) cañón m; (spine on a porcupine) púa f

quilt [kwɪłt] N colcha de retazos f; VI/VT hacer una colcha de retazos

quinine [kwáɪnaɪn] N quinina f

quip [kwɪp] N ocurrencia f; VI decir ocurrencias

quirk [kwɝk] N excentricidad f

quit [kwɪt] VT (a competition) abandonar; (a place) irse de, salir de; (a job) dejar; (a computer program) salir; **to call it —s** abandonar; **to — smoking** dejar de fumar; VI (withdraw) abandonar; (stop) parar; (resign) renunciar

quite [kwaɪt] ADV (very) bastante; (entirely) del todo, enteramente; **— a person** una persona admirable f; **— a lot** bastante; **it's — the fashion** está muy de moda

quiver [kwívə-] VI temblar; N (shake) temblor m; (sheath for arrows) carcaj m, aljaba f

quiz [kwɪz] N (test) prueba f; (show) concurso m; VI (give a quiz) examinar, poner una prueba; (interrogate) interrogar

quota [kwóᴅə] N cuota f

quotation [kwotéʃən] N cita f; (of a price) cotización f; **— marks** comillas f pl

quote [kwot] VI/VT (words) citar; (prices) cotizar; **to — from** citar a; N (of words) cita f; (of a price) cotización f; **in —s** entre comillas

quotient [kwóʃənt] N cociente m

Rr

R & D [research and development] [árṇdí] N ID mf

rabbi [rǽbaɪ] N rabino m

rabbit [rǽbɪt] N conejo m

rabble [rǽbəł] N chusma f, plebe f, gentuza f

rabid [rǽbɪd] ADJ rabioso

rabies [rébiz] N rabia f

raccoon [rækún] N mapache m

race [res] N (lineage) raza f; (competition) carrera f; **—horse** caballo de carreras m; **—track** (for runners) pista f; (for horses) hipódromo *m*; VI (participate in competition) correr, competir en una carrera; (hurry) ir corriendo; (of heart) latir rápido; (of a motor) acelerar; VT (a horse) hacer correr; (an engine) acelerar; **I'll— you** te echo una carrera

racer [résə-] N corredor -ora *mf*; (horse) caballo de carreras *m*

racial [réʃəł] ADJ racial

racism [résɪzəm] N racismo *m*

rack [ræk] N (for clothes) perchero *m*; (for luggage) baca *f*; (for spices) especiero *m*; (for towels) toallero *m*; (for torture) potro de tormento *m*; (breasts) *fam* tetamen *m*; — **and pinion** cremallera *f* y piñón *m*; VT **to be —ed with pain** estar transido de dolor; **to — one's brain** devanarse los sesos; **to — up** acumular

racket [rǽkɪt] N (sports) raqueta *f*; (noise of an impact) estrépito *m*, estruendo *m*; (noise of voices and movement) barahúnda *f*, batahola *f*; (swindle) estafa *f*; (extortion) extorsión *f*

racketeer [rækɪtír] N (swindler) trapacero -ra *mf*, estafador -ora *mf*; (extortionist) extorsionista *mf*; VI (swindle) estafar; (extort) extorsionar

radar [réDɑr] N radar *m*

radial [réDiəł] ADJ radial

radiance [réDiəns] N resplandor *m*, fulgor *m*

radiant [réDiənt] ADJ radiante, resplandeciente

radiate [réDiet] VI/VT irradiar, radiar

radiation [reDiéʃən] N radiación *f*; — **sickness** enfermedad por radiación *f*; — **therapy** radioterapia *f*

radiator [réDieDə-] N radiador *m*

radical [rǽDikəł] ADJ & N radical *mf*

radicalism [rǽDikəlɪzəm] N radicalismo *m*

radio [réDio] N (device, system of communication) radio *f*; — **announcer** locutor -ora *mf*; — **listener** radioescucha *mf*; — **station** radiodifusora *f*; — **telescope** radiotelescopio *m*; — **transmitter** radiotransmisor *m*; **by —** por radio; ADJ **—active** radiactivo, radioactivo; VT (broadcast) transmitir por radio; VI/VT (call) llamar por radio

radiologist [reDiáləʤɪst] N radiólogo -ga *mf*

radiology [reDiáləʤi] N radiología *f*

radish [rǽDiʃ] N rábano *m*

radium [réDiəm] N radio *m*

radius [réDiəs] N radio *m*

radon [rédɑn] N radón *m*

raffle [rǽfəł] N rifa *f*, sorteo *m*; VI rifar, sortear

raft [ræft] N balsa *f*

rafter [rǽftə-] N viga *f*

rag [ræg] N (piece of cloth) trapo *m*, guiñapo *m*; (on clothes) harapo *m*, andrajo *m*; — **doll** muñeca de trapo *f*

rage [reʤ] N ira *f*, rabia *f*, cólera *f*; **to be all the — estar de moda**; VI enfurecerse; **to — with**

anger bramar de ira

ragged [rǽgɪd] ADJ (ill-clothed) andrajoso, harapiento, desharrapado; (voice) ronco, roto; (on an edge) irregular, desigual; **to be on the — edge** estar al borde

raid [red] N (military) incursión *f*; (by police) allanamiento *m*, redada *f*; (by air) bombardeo aéreo *m*; VI/VT hacer una incursión; VT (attack) atacar; (rob) asaltar; (carry out a police operation on) allanar

raider [réDə-] N empresa tiburón *f*

rail [reł] N (of a railroad track) riel *m*, carril *m*; (on a balcony) baranda *f*, barandilla *f*; — **fence** barrera *f*; —**road** ferrocarril *m*; —**road company** empresa ferroviaria *f*; —**road crossing** cruce de ferrocarril *m*; —**road employee** ferroviario -ria *mf*; —**way** ferrocarril *m*; **by —** por ferrocarril; VT **to —road** (goods) transportar por ferrocarril; (laws) hacer aprobar apresuradamente; (a person) condenar injustamente

railing [rélɪŋ] N (barrier) baranda *f*; (on a bridge) pretil *m*; (on a stairway) pasamano *m*

rain [ren] N lluvia *f*; —**bow** arco iris *m*; —**coat** impermeable *m*; —**drop** gota de lluvia *f*; —**fall** precipitación *f*; — **forest** selva tropical *f*; — **gauge** pluviómetro *f*; —**storm** temporal de lluvia *f*; — **water** agua llovediza *f*; VI/VT llover; — **or shine** llueva o truene; **to — cats and dogs** llover a cántaros

rainy [réni] ADJ lluvioso

raise [rez] VI/VT (voice, hand, a house, spirits) levantar[se]; VT (an alarm) dar; (funds) recaudar, captar; (a salary) aumentar; (a flag) izar; (crops) cultivar; (animals, children) criar; (money) recabar, recaudar; **to — a question** plantear una pregunta; **to — a racket** armar un alboroto; N aumento *m*

raisin [rézɪn] N pasa [de uva] *f*

rake [rek] N rastrillo *m*; VI/VT rastrillar; **to — in money** amasar dinero

rally [rǽli] VI/VT (reorganize troops) reunir[se], juntar[se]; (inspire) reanimar; VI (demonstrate) concentrarse; (recuperate) recuperarse; (reinvigorate) recobrar ánimo; (rise in value) repuntar; (in tennis) pelotear; **to — around someone** apoyar a alguien; N (demonstration) concentración *f*; (recovery) recuperación *f*; (rise in prices) subida *f*; (in tennis) peloteo *m*

RAM [random-access memory] [ræm] N RAM *m*

ram [ræm] N (male sheep) carnero *m*; (tool for battering) ariete *m*; (part of a ship) espolón *m*; VT chocar contra; **to — a boat** embestir un buque con el espolón

ramble [rǽmbəł] VI vagar; **to — on** divagar; N paseo *m*

ramp [ræmp] N rampa f
rampage [rǽmpeʤ] N **to go on a** — andar destrozando todo; VI andar destrozando todo
rampant [rǽmpənt] ADJ desenfrenado
ran [ræn] see run
ranch [ræntʃ] N hacienda f; Mex rancho m
rancid [rǽnsɪd] ADJ rancio
rancor [rǽŋkɚ] N rencor m
random [rǽndəm] ADJ aleatorio, azaroso; **at** — al azar; — **access memory** memoria de acceso directo f
randomize [rǽndəmaɪz] VT aleatorizar
rang [ræŋ] see ring
range [rénʤ] N (of types) gama f; (of a gun) alcance m; (of variation) fluctuación f; (of mountains) cadena f; (for shooting) campo de tiro m; (of an aircraft) autonomía f; (grazing place) campo abierto m; (stove) cocina f; estufa f; — **finder** telémetro m; — **of vision** alcance visual m; VT (align) alinear; (of a gun) tener alcance; VI (vary) oscilar; (be found in an area) extenderse; **his children** — **in age between 2 and 10** sus hijos van en edad entre 2 y 10
ranger [rénʤɚ] N (in a park) guardabosque[s] mf; (soldier) guardia de asalto m
rank [ræŋk] N (in a hierarchy) rango m, grado m; (line) fila f; — **and file** (of an army) tropa f sg; **the** —**s** (soldiers) la tropa; (union members) bases f pl; **a sculptor of the first** — un escultor de primer orden; VT (arrange) poner en orden de importancia; VI (rate) figurar; **to** — **high** tener alto rango; **to** — **second** estar clasificado en el segundo lugar; ADJ (smelly) hediondo; (growing vigorously) exuberante
ranking [rǽŋkɪŋ] N ránking m
ransack [rǽnsæk] VT saquear, desvalijar
ransom [rǽnsəm] N rescate m; VT rescatar
rant [rænt] VI/VT despotricar
rap [ræp] VI/VT (strike) golpear; (chat) charlar; VI (in music) rapear, cantar rap; N (blow) golpe m; (accusation) cargo m; **to take the** — ser el cabeza de turco; — **music** música rap f
rapacious [rəpéʃəs] ADJ rapaz
rape [rep] N (violation) violación f; (statutory) estupro m; (plant) colza f; (grape pulp) orujo m; VT violar
rapid [rǽpɪd] ADJ rápido; N —**s** rápidos m pl
rapidity [rəpídɪti] N rapidez f
rapport [rəpɔ́r] N relación f
rapt [ræpt] ADJ extasiado
rapture [rǽptʃɚ] N éxtasis m, embeleso m; **to go into a** — arrobarse
rare [rɛr] ADJ (infrequent) raro, poco frecuente, extraño; (of gas, earth) raro; (thin, of air) enrarecido; (excellent) excepcional; (not well cooked) crudo; — **earths** tierras raras f pl
rarely [rérli] ADV raramente, raras veces
rarity [rérɪdi] N rareza f; (of air)

enrarecimiento m
rascal [rǽskəł] N bribón m, bellaco m, pícaro m; Sp golfo m; **you little** —! ¡bandido! ¡sinvergüenza!
rash [ræʃ] ADJ (thoughtless) precipitado, temerario; N (on skin) sarpullido m
raspberry [rǽzbɛri] N frambuesa f; — **bush** frambueso m
raspy [rǽspi] ADJ ronco, áspero
rat [ræt] N rata f; **I smell a** — aquí hay gato encerrado; VT (one's hair) cardar; VI **to** — **on** delatar
ratchet [rǽtʃɪt] N trinquete m
rate [ret] N (charge) tarifa f; (unit charge for insurance) prima f; (pace) paso m, ritmo m; — **of exchange** tipo de cambio m; — **of interest** tasa de interés f; **at any** — en todo caso; **at this** — a este ritmo; **at the** — **of** a razón de; VT (estimate) valorar, estimar; (esteem) considerar; **he** —**s as the best** se le considera como el mejor; **he** —**s high** se le tiene en alta estima
rather [rǽðɚ] ADV (somewhat) bastante; (more precisely) más bien; — **than** en vez de; **I would** — **die than** antes la muerte que; **I would** — **not go** prefiero no ir
ratification [rædɪfɪkéʃən] N ratificación f
ratify [rǽdəfaɪ] VT ratificar
rating [rédɪŋ] N (act of adjudging) calificación f; (for credit) clasificación f; (TV quotient) rating televisivo m, índice de audiencia m
ratio [réʃio] N razón f, proporción f
ration [rǽʃən] N ración f; VT racionar
rational [rǽʃənł] ADJ racional
rationale [ræʃənǽł] N motivo m
rationalize [rǽʃənḷaɪz] VI/VT racionalizar
rationing [rǽʃənɪŋ] N racionamiento m
rattle [rǽdł] VI (bang) golpetear; (move noisily) traquetear; **to** — **on** parlotear; VT hacer sonar, sacudir; **to** — **off** recitar; N (banging) golpeteo m; (movement) traqueteo m; (toy) sonaja f, sonajero m; (of a rattlesnake) cascabel m; (of death) estertor m; —**snake** víbora de cascabel f
raucous [rókəs] ADJ (loud) estridente; (rowdy) escandaloso
ravage [rǽvɪʤ] VI/VT asolar, arruinar; N estrago m
rave [rev] VI (rant) desvariar, delirar; VI/VT (roar) bramar; **to** — **about** deshacerse en elogios; N (theater review) crítica muy favorable f
raven [révən] N cuervo m; ADJ azabache
ravenous [rǽvənəs] ADJ voraz, famélico; **to be** — tener un hambre canina
ravine [rəvín] N quebrada f, barranco m, cañada f
raving [révɪŋ] ADJ delirante; (extraordinary) extraordinario; — **mad** loco de remate; N desvarío m
ravish [rǽvɪʃ] VT (kidnap) raptar, secuestrar;

(rape) violar
raw [rɔ] ADJ (uncooked, unprocessed, damp and cold) crudo; (of vegetables) fresco, crudo; (unadorned) descarnado; — **flesh** carne viva *f*; — **material** materia prima *f*; — **sugar** azúcar bruto *m*; N —**hide** cuero crudo *m*
ray [re] N (beam) rayo *m*; (stingray) raya *f*
rayon [réɑn] N rayón *m*
raze [rez] VT arrasar, asolar
razor [rézɚ] N (device with blade) maquinilla de afeitar *f*, rasuradora *f*; (barber's tool) navaja *f*; (electric) rasuradora electrica *f*; — **blade** hoja de afeitar *f*; **safety** — navaja de seguridad *f*
reach [ritʃ] VI/VT (extend) alcanzar; **to** — **for** tratar de agarrar; *Sp* tratar de coger; **to** — **into** meter la mano en; VT (arrive at) llegar a; (contact) ponerse en contacto con; **to** — **out one's hand** alargar la mano; N alcance *m*; **beyond his** — fuera de su alcance; **within his** — a su alcance; **far** —**es** zona remota *f*
react [riǽkt] VI reaccionar
reaction [riǽkʃən] N reacción *f*
reactionary [riǽkʃənɛri] ADJ & N reaccionario -ria *mf*
reactor [riǽktɚ] N reactor *m*
read [rid] VI/VT leer; VT (interpret) interpretar; (give as a reading, indicate) decir, indicar, marcar; **it** —**s easily** es fácil de leer; N lectura *f*; — **protect** protección contra lectura *f*; —/**write file** archivo de lectura/escritura *m*
readable [rídəbəl] ADJ (legible) legible; (nice to read) ameno
reader [rídɚ] N (person who reads) lector -ora *mf*; (schoolbook) libro de lectura *m*, cartilla *f*; (anthology) antología *f*
readership [rídɚʃɪp] N lectores *m pl*
readily [rédli] ADV fácilmente
readiness [rédinis] N estado de preparación *m*; (willingness) buena disposición *f*; **to be in** — estar preparado, estar listo
reading [rídɪŋ] N lectura *f*; (interpretation) interpretación *f*; — **room** sala de lectura *f*
readjust [riədʒʌ́st] VI/VT (improve fit) reajustar; (acclimate) readaptar
readjustment [riədʒʌ́stmənt] N (fitting) reajuste *m*; (acclimation) readaptación *f*
ready [rédi] ADJ (prepared) listo, preparado, pronto; (willing) dispuesto; (available) disponible; (quick) rápido; —-**made** de confección
reaffirm [riəfɚ́m] VT reafirmar
reagent [riédʒənt] ADJ & N reactivo *m*
real [ril] ADJ real, verdadero; — **estate** bienes raíces *m pl*, bienes inmuebles *m pl*; — **time** tiempo real *m*
realism [ríəlizəm] N realismo *m*
realist [ríəlist] N realista *mf*
realistic [riəlístik] ADJ realista

reality [riǽlidi] N realidad *f*; — **check** ajuste de perspectiva *m*
realization [riəlizéʃən] N (making real) realización *f*; (understanding) comprensión *f*
realize [ríəlaiz] VT (achieve) realizar; (comprehend) darse cuenta [de], comprobar, percatarse [de]
really [rili] ADV (extremely) realmente; (truly) verdaderamente; (as question) ¿de veras? ¿verdad? **he's not** — **a lawyer** en realidad, no es abogado / no es abogado de verdad; **it's** — **hot in Seville** hace mucho calor en Sevilla; **she's a** — **good colleague** es una colega superbuena / es una buenísima colega
realm [rɛlm] N (kingdom) reino *m*; (domain) terreno *m*, esfera *f*
realtor™ [ríɫtɚ] N agente inmobiliario -ria *mf*
reap [rip] VI/VT (cut with sickle) segar; (harvest) cosechar; **to** — **a benefit** obtener beneficio, sacar provecho
reaper [rípɚ] N (person) segador -ora *mf*; (machine) segadora *f*; (death) la Parca, la Muerte
reappear [riəpír] VI reaparecer
rear [rir] ADJ trasero, posterior; —**guard** retaguardia *f*; N (space at the back) parte de atrás *f*, fondo *m*; (backside) trasero *m*, posaderas *f pl*; — **end** trasero *m*; —**view mirror** espejo retrovisor *m*; VT (raise) criar; VI (rise on back legs) encabritarse, empinarse
reason [rízən] N (faculty) razón *f*; (cause) motivo *m*, razón *f*; **by** — **of** por causa de; **it stands to** — es lógico; VT razonar; **to** — **out** resolver por medio de la razón; **to** — **with** hacer entrar en razón
reasonable [rízənəbəl] ADJ razonable; (in price) módico, moderado
reasoning [rízonɪŋ] N razonamiento *m*, raciocinio *m*; ADJ racional
reassert [riəsɚ́t] VT reafirmar
reassure [riəʃúr] VT tranquilizar
rebate [ríbet] N reembolso *m*, reintegro *m*; VT reembolsar, reintegrar
rebel[1] [rébəl] ADJ & N rebelde *mf*, insurrecto -ta *mf*
rebel[2] [ribéɫ] VI rebelarse
rebellion [ribéljən] N rebelión *f*
rebellious [ribéljəs] ADJ rebelde, insurrecto
rebelliousness [ribéljəsnis] N rebeldía *f*
reboot [ribút] VT reiniciar
rebound[1] [ribáund] VI (bounce) rebotar; (catch a rebound) rebotear; (recover) recuperarse
rebound[2] [ríbaund] N (bounce) rebote *m*; (recovery) recuperación *f*; **on the** — de rebote
rebuff [ribʌ́f] N desaire *m*, repulsa *f*; VT desairar, rechazar
rebuild [ribíɫd] VI/VT reconstruir, reedificar; (car engine) reacondicionar

rebuke [rɪbjúk] VT reprender, reprochar; N reproche *m*, reprimenda *f*

recall[1] [rɪkɔ́l] VT (remember) recordar; (call back) retirar; (remove from office) destituir

recall[2] [ríkɔl] N (memory) memoria *f*; (of a diplomat, product) retirada *f*; (from office) destitución *f*

recapitulate [rikəpítʃəlet] VI/VT recapitular

recast [rikǽst] VT refundir

recede [rɪsíd] VI retroceder; (of hairline) tener entradas

receipt [rɪsít] N recibo *m*; **upon — of** al recibo de; **—s** entradas *f pl*, ingresos *m pl*

receivable [rɪsívəbəl] ADJ a cobrar

receive [rɪsív] VI/VT recibir; (suggestions) acoger, recibir; (a broadcast) captar, recibir

receiver [rɪsívɚ] N recibidor -ora *mf*; (of a telephone) auricular *m*; (of a television or radio, in football) receptor *m*; (in tennis) restador -ora *mf*; (of a bankrupt business) síndico *m*

recent [rísənt] ADJ reciente

receptacle [rɪséptəkəl] N receptáculo *m*

reception [rɪsépʃən] N (hotel, social event, TV) recepción *f*; (act of receiving) recibimiento *m*, acogida *f*; **— room** recibidor *m*

recess [ríses] N (niche) nicho *m*; (pause) descanso *m*; (playtime) recreo *m*; **in the —es of** en lo más recóndito de; VI/VT (a meeting) interrumpir; VT (a wall) hacer un nicho en

recession [rɪséʃən] N (act of receding) retroceso *m*; (economic) recesión *f*

recessive gene [rɪsésɪvdʒín] N gen recesivo *m*

recidivism [rɪsídɪvɪzəm] N reincidencia *f*

recipe [résəpi] N receta *f*

recipient [rɪsípiənt] N destinatario -ria *mf*

reciprocal [rɪsíprəkəl] ADJ recíproco

reciprocate [rɪsíprəket] VI/VT corresponder [a], *Am* reciprocar

recital [rɪsáidl̩] N recital *m*

recitation [rɛsɪtéʃən] N recitación *f*

recite [rɪsáit] VI/VT recitar

reckless [réklɪs] ADJ (driver) temerario, imprudente; (speed) desenfrenado

recklessness [réklɪsnɪs] N temeridad *f*, imprudencia *f*

reckon [rékən] VI/VT (calculate) calcular; (consider) considerar; (think) suponer

reckoning [rékənɪŋ] N (computation) cálculo *m*; (settlement of accounts) ajuste de cuentas *m*; **the day of —** el día del juicio *m*

reclaim [rɪklém] VT (win back, recover) recuperar; (make land usable) ganar, sanear

recline [rɪkláin] VI/VT reclinar[se], recostar[se]

recluse [réklus] ADJ & N solitario -ria *mf*, ermitaño -ña *mf*

recognition [rɛkəgníʃən] N reconocimiento *m*

recognizable [rɛkəgnáizəbəl] ADJ reconocible

recognize [rékəgnaiz] VT reconocer

recoil[1] [rɪkɔ́il] VI (firearm) dar un culatazo; (move back) retroceder

recoil[2] [ríkɔil] N (of a gun) culatazo *m*; (move back) retroceso *m*

recollect [rɛkəlékt] VI/VT recordar

recollection [rɛkəlékʃən] N recuerdo *m*

recommend [rɛkəménd] VI/VT recomendar

recommendation [rɛkəmɛndéʃən] N recomendación *f*

recompense [rékəmpɛns] VI/VT recompensar; N recompensa *f*

reconcile [rékənsail] VT (persons) reconciliar; (statements) conciliar; **to — oneself to** resignarse a, conformarse con

reconciliation [rɛkənsɪliéʃən] N reconciliación *f*

reconnoiter [rikənɔ́idɚ] VT reconocer; VI hacer un reconocimiento

reconsider [rikənsídɚ] VI/VT reconsiderar

reconstruct [rikənstrÁkt] VT reconstruir

reconstruction [rikənstrÁkʃən] N reconstrucción *f*

record[1] [rékɚd] N (account) registro *m*, asiento *m*; (account of a meeting) acta *f*; (of criminal acts) antecedentes *m pl*; (of past activities) historial *m*, hoja de servicios *f*; (phonographic) disco *m*; (best performance) récord *m*, plusmarca *f*; **— player** tocadiscos *m sg*; **off the —** extraoficialmente

record[2] [rɪkɔ́rd] VI/VT (write down) registrar, apuntar; (cut a recording) grabar

recorder [rɪkɔ́rdɚ] N (archivist) archivero -ra *mf*; (sound device) grabadora *f*; (musical instrument) flauta dulce *f*

recording [rɪkɔ́rdɪŋ] N grabación *f*; **— company** grabadora *f*

recount[1] [rɪkáunt] VT (tell) narrar, relatar

recount[2] [ríkaunt] VT (count again) contar

recoup [rɪkúp] VI/VT recuperar

recourse [ríkɔrs] N recurso *m*; **to have — to** recurrir a

recover [rɪkÁvɚ] VI/VT recobrar[se], recuperar[se]; VI (lost health) restablecerse; VT (lost time, property) recuperar; (damages) obtener indemnización

recovery [rɪkÁveri] N (from an illness) recuperación *f*; (of investments) amortización *f*; (through a lawsuit) indemnización *f*; **— room** sala de recuperación *f*

recreation [rɛkriéʃən] N recreación *f*, recreo *m*, esparcimiento *m*

recreational [rɛkriéʃənəl] ADJ recreativo, de recreo; **— drug** droga de recreo *f*; **— vehicle** caravana *f*

recriminate [rɪkrímənet] VI/VT recriminar

recruit [rɪkrút] N recluta *mf*; VI/VT reclutar

recruitment [rɪkrútmənt] N reclutamiento *m*, recluta *f*

rectangle [réktæŋgəl] N rectángulo *m*

rectangular [rɛktǽŋgjəlɚ] ADJ rectangular

rectify [réktəfaɪ] VT rectificar
rector [réktə-] N rector -ora *mf*
rectum [réktəm] N recto *m*
recuperate [rɪkúpəret] VI/VT recuperar[se], recobrar[se]
recur [rɪkɜ́-] VI volver a ocurrir, repetirse
recurring [rɪkɜ́ɪŋ] ADJ recurrente
recycle [risáɪkəł] VI/VT reciclar
recycling [risáɪklɪŋ] N reciclaje *m*
red [rɛd] ADJ & N rojo *m*, colorado *m*; — **blood cell** glóbulo rojo *m*; — **card** tarjeta roja *f*; — **-handed** *fam* in fraganti; —**headed** pelirrojo; —**-hot** candente, al rojo vivo; — **light** luz roja *f*; —**neck** granjero -ra blanco -ca pobre *mf*; — **pepper** pimienta de cayena *f*; — **prawn** carabinero *m*; — **snapper** pargo *m*; — **tape** trámites *m pl*; — **wine** vino tinto *m*; —**wood** secoya/secuoya *f*; **in the —** en números rojos; **to see —** enfurecerse
redden [rédn̩] VI/VT enrojecer, ruborizar[se]
reddish [rédɪʃ] ADJ rojizo, bermejo
redeem [rɪdím] VT (deliver from sin) redimir; (pay off a mortgage) cancelar; (buy back from pawnshop) desempeñar; (exchange) canjear; (fulfill) cumplir
redemption [rɪdémpʃən] N redención *f*; (of something pawned) desempeño *m*
redevelopment [ridɪvéləpmənt] N remodelación *f*
redness [rédnɪs] N rojez *f*; (inflammation) inflamación *f*
redress[1] [rídrɛs] N reparación *f*, desagravio *m*
redress[2] [rɪdrés] VT reparar, desagraviar
reduce [rɪdús] VI/VT reducir[se]; **she was —d to tears** se echó a llorar
reduction [rɪdákʃən] N reducción *f*
redundant [rɪdándənt] ADJ (repetitive) redundante; (superfluous) superfluo
reed [rid] N caña *f*, junco *m*, carrizo *m*; (of a musical instrument) lengüeta *f*
reef [rif] N (underwater ridge) escollo *m*; (of coral) arrecife *m*
reek [rik] VI heder, apestar; N hedor *m*
reel [rił] N carrete *m*, bobina *f*; VT (on a spool) bobinar; VI tambalearse; **to — off** recitar; **to — in a fish** sacar un pez del agua
reelect [riɪlékt] VT reelegir
reelection [riɪlékʃən] N reelección *f*
reemployment [riɪmplɔ́ɪmənt] N reinserción laboral *f*
reestablish [riɪstǽblɪʃ] VT restablecer
refer [rɪfɜ́-] VI/VT referir; (direct to a source of information) remitir; (direct to a doctor) mandar; (mention) referirse a, aludir a
referee [rɛfərí] N árbitro *m*; VT (a game) arbitrar; (a submission) hacer el referato
reference [réfərəns] N (mention) referencia *f*; — **book** libro de consulta *m*; **with — to** con respecto a, respecto de

referendum [rɛfəréndəm] N referéndum *m*
referral [rɪfɜ́-əł] N **he gave me a — to a specialist** me mandó con/a un especialista
refill[1] [rifíł] VI/VT rellenar
refill[2] [rífíł] N (for a pen) repuesto *m*; (for a lighter) carga *f*; **may I have a —?** ¿me sirve más?
refinance [rifáɪnæns] VI/VT refinanciar
refine [rɪfáɪn] VT (purify) refinar; (polish) refinar, pulir
refined [rɪfáɪnd] ADJ refinado
refinement [rɪfáɪnmənt] N (of manners) refinamiento *m*, pulimento *m*; (of oil) refinación *f*
refinery [rɪfáɪnəri] N (of oil) refinería *f*; (of sugar) ingenio *m*
reflect [rɪflékt] VI/VT (mirror) reflejar; VI (ponder) reflexionar; **to — poorly on** desacreditar
reflection [rɪflékʃən] N (image) reflejo *m*; (consideration) reflexión *f*; (unfavorable observation) tacha *f*; **on —** pensándolo bien
reflector [rɪfléktə-] N reflector *m*
reflex [rífleks] ADJ & N reflejo *m*
reflexive [rɪfléksɪv] ADJ reflexivo
reflux [rífl\ks] N reflujo *m*
reform [rɪfɔrm] VI/VT reformar[se]; N reforma *f*
reformation [rɛfə-méʃən] N reforma *f*
reformatory [rɪfɔ́rmətɔri] N reformatorio *m*
reformer [rɪfɔ́rmə-] N reformador -ora *mf*, reformista *mf*
refraction [rɪfrǽkʃən] N refracción *f*
refractory [rɪfrǽktəri] ADJ (not malleable) refractario; (rebellious) rebelde
refrain [rɪfrén] VI abstenerse; N (of a song) estribillo *m*
refresh [rɪfréʃ] VI/VT refrescar[se]; (computer screen) actualizar, refrescar
refreshing [rɪfréʃɪŋ] ADJ (drink) refrescante; (sleep) reparador; (honesty) agradable
refreshment [rɪfréʃmənt] N (drink) refresco *m*; (food) refrigerio *m*
refrigerate [rɪfrídʒəret] VT refrigerar
refrigeration [rɪfrɪdʒəréʃən] N refrigeración *f*
refrigerator [rɪfrídʒəredə-] N frigorífico *m*, nevera *f*, refrigerador *m*; RP heladera *f*
refuge [réfjudʒ] N refugio *m*; **to give — dar albergue**
refugee [rɛfjudʒí] N refugiado -da *mf*
refund[1] [rífʌnd] N reembolso *m*
refund[2] [rɪfʌnd] VT reembolsar
refurbish [rifɜ́-bɪʃ] VT restaurar
refusal [rɪfjúzəł] N negativa *f*, rechazo *m*; **first — opción *f***
refuse[1] [rɪfjúz] VI/VT (deny a request) negar[se] [a]; **to — to** rehusarse a, negarse a; VT (decline to accept) rechazar, no aceptar
refuse[2] [réfjus] N desechos *m pl*, desperdicios *m pl*

refute [rɪfjút] VT refutar, rebatir
regain [rɪgén] VT (recover) recobrar; (get back to) volver a
regal [rígəł] ADJ regio, real
regard [rɪgárd] VT (consider) considerar; (esteem) estimar; N (consideration) consideración f; (esteem) respeto m, estima f; —s recuerdos m pl, saludos m pl; **as —s** en cuanto a; **with — to** con respecto a
regarding [rɪgárDɪŋ] PREP con respecto a
regardless [rɪgárdlɪs] ADV LOC — **of** independientemente de
regenerate [rɪʤénəret] VI/VT regenerar[se]
regent [ríʤənt] N regente -ta mf
reggae [rége] N reggae m
regime [rɪʒím] N régimen m
regiment [réʤəmənt] N regimiento m
region [ríʤən] N región f
regional [ríʤənl] ADJ regional
register [réʤɪstɚ] N (recording, range of voice) registro m; (entry) asiento m; VI/VT (enter into a list) registrar[se]; (enroll) matricular[se], inscribir[se]; VT (indicate) indicar, registrar; (a letter) certificar; VI (appear) aparecer; **that didn't —** no cayó en la cuenta
registered [réʤɪstɚd] ADJ registrado; — **mail** correo certificado m; — **nurse** enfermero -ra titulado -da mf; — **trademark** marca registrada f
registrar [réʤɪstrɑr] N secretario -ria de admisiones mf
registration [reʤɪstréʃən] N (of a car) matrícula f; (of a student) inscripción f
regret [rɪgrét] VT (feel sorry) lamentar; (feel rueful) arrepentirse de; N arrepentimiento m; **to send —s** enviar sus excusas
regretful [rɪgrétfəł] ADJ lleno de remordimientos
regrettable [rɪgréDəbəł] ADJ lamentable
regroup [rigrúp] VT reagrupar; VI reorganizarse
regular [régjəlɚ] ADJ (symmetrical, uniform) regular; (normal) normal; (habitual) habitual; **a — fool** un verdadero necio; **a — guy** un buen tipo; (habitual customer) parroquiano -na mf; (soldier) soldado de línea m
regularity [regjəlǽrɪDi] N regularidad f
regulate [régjəlet] VT (control) regular; (make regular) regularizar
regulation [regjəléʃən] N (act of regulating) regulación f; —**s** reglamento m, reglamentación f
regulator [régjəleDɚ] N regulador m
regurgitate [rɪgɚ́ʤɪtet] VI/VT regurgitar
rehabilitate [rihəbílɪtet] VI/VT rehabilitar[se]
rehabilitation [riəbɪlɪtéʃən] N rehabilitación f
rehearsal [rɪhɚ́səł] N ensayo m
rehearse [rɪhɚ́s] VI/VT ensayar

reign [ren] N reino m, reinado m; VI reinar
reimburse [riɪmbɚ́s] VI/VT reembolsar
reimbursement [riɪmbɚ́smənt] N reembolso m
rein [ren] N rienda f (also control); VI **to — in** dominar, refrenar
reincarnation [riɪnkɑrnéʃən] N reencarnación f
reindeer [réndɪr] N reno m
reinforce [riɪnfɔ́rs] VT reforzar
reinforcement [riɪnfɔ́rsmənt] N refuerzo m, reforzado m
reinsertion [riɪnsɚ́ʃən] N reinserción f
reinstate [riɪnstét] VT reinstaurar
reiterate [ríɪDəret] VT reiterar
reject[1] [rɪʤékt] VT rechazar
reject[2] [ríʤekt] N (thing) cosa rechazada f, desecho m; (person) rechazado -da mf
rejoice [rɪʤɔ́ɪs] VI regocijarse
rejoicing [rɪʤɔ́ɪsɪŋ] N regocijo m
rejoin [rɪʤɔ́ɪn] VT (come again into a group) reincorporarse a; VI/VT (reunite) volver a unir[se]
rejuvenate [rɪʤúvənet] VI/VT rejuvenecer
relapse[1] [rɪlǽps] VI (into bad health) recaer; (into crime) reincidir
relapse[2] [rílæps] N (into bad health) recaída f, recidiva f; (into crime) reincidencia f
relate [rɪlét] VT (tell) relatar, narrar; (connect) relacionar; VI **to — to** relacionarse con
related [rɪléDɪd] ADJ (connected) relacionado; (kin) emparentado
relation [rɪléʃən] N (association) relación f; (act of narrating) narración f; (kinship) parentesco m; (relative) pariente -ta mf; **with — to** con respecto a
relationship [rɪléʃənʃɪp] N relación f
relative [rélədɪv] ADJ relativo; N pariente -ta mf, allegado -da mf; — **to** relativo a, referente a
relativity [relədívɪDi] N relatividad f
relax [rɪlǽks] VI/VT relajar[se], distender[se]; VT (grip) aflojar
relaxation [rilækséʃən] N (recreation) esparcimiento m, recreo m; (loosening) relajamiento m, relajación f
relay[1] [ríle] N relevo m, posta f; (electrical) relé m; — **race** carrera de relevos/postas f
relay[2] [ríle, rɪlé] VT transmitir; **to — a broadcast** transmitir un programa
release [rɪlís] VT (let go) soltar; (free prisoners) librar, poner en libertad; (energy) liberar; (news) divulgar; (discharge from hospital) dar de alta; N (liberation) liberación f; (permission) permiso m; (of film) estreno m; (of gas) escape m; (of energy) desprendimiento m
relegate [rélɪget] VT relegar
relent [rɪlént] VI aplacarse
relentless [rɪléntlɪs] ADJ implacable
relevant [réləvənt] ADJ pertinente
reliability [rɪlaɪəbílɪDi] N fiabilidad f,

confiabilidad *f*
reliable [rɪláɪəbəł] ADJ fiable, confiable; (a person) formal
reliance [rɪláɪəns] N (dependency) dependencia *f*; (trust) confianza *f*
relic [rélɪk] N reliquia *f*
relief [rɪlíf] N (ease) alivio *m*; (aid) ayuda *f*; (projection) relieve *m*; (soldier) relevo *m*; (in golf) alivio *m*; **in** — en relieve; — **map** mapa en relieve *m*
relieve [rɪlív] VT (alleviate) aliviar; (free) liberar; (replace) relevar; VI **to** — **oneself** orinar
reliever [rɪlívɚ] N (baseball) relevista *mf*
religion [rɪlíʤən] N religión *f*
religious [rɪlíʤəs] ADJ religioso
relinquish [rɪlíŋkwɪʃ] VT (give up) renunciar; (let go) soltar
relish [rélɪʃ] VT (to like the taste) saborear, paladear; (enjoy) disfrutar; N (enjoyment) gusto *m*; (condiment) condimento de pepinillos en vinagre *m*
relocate [rilóket] VI/VT trasladar[se]
reluctance [rɪláktəns] N renuencia *f*
reluctant [rɪláktənt] ADJ renuente, reacio
rely [rɪláɪ] VI **to** — **on** (trust) confiar en; (depend on) depender de
REM [rapid eye movement] [áríém] N REM *m*, MOR *m pl*
remain [rɪmén] VI (continue to be) seguir siendo; (stay) quedar[se], permanecer; (to be left) quedar, restar; (to be left over) sobrar; N —**s** restos *m pl*
remainder [rɪméndɚ] N (extra) sobrante; (other) restante
remake[1] [rimék] VT rehacer; (film) hacer de nuevo
remake[2] [rímek] N nueva versión *f*
remark [rɪmárk] VT (comment) comentar, observar; (notice) notar, observar; **to** — **on** comentar; N observación *f*, comentario *m*
remarkable [rɪmárkəbəł] ADJ notable
remedial [rɪmíɒiəł] ADJ (rehabilitative) rehabilitador; (to improve skills) de recuperación
remedy [rémɪɒi] N (solution) remedio *m*; (cure) cura *f*; VT (solve) remediar, subsanar; (heal) curar
remember [rɪmémbɚ] VI/VT recordar, acordarse [de]; — **me to him** mándale saludos míos
remind [rɪmáɪnd] VT recordar
reminder [rɪmáɪndɚ] N (of a date, deadline) recordatorio *m*; (warning) advertencia *f*
reminiscence [rɛmənísəns] N reminiscencia *f*, recuerdo *m*
remiss [rɪmís] ADJ negligente
remission [rɪmíʃən] N remisión *f*
remit [rɪmít] VI/VT remitir
remittance [rɪmítn̩s] N remesa *f*, giro *m*

remnant [rémnənt] N (remainder) resto *m*; (of fabric) retazo *m*, retal *m*; (vestige) vestigio *m*
remodel [rimádl] VI/VT remodelar
remodeling [rimádl̩ɪŋ] N remodelación *f*
remorse [rɪmɔ́rs] N remordimiento *m*
remote [rɪmót] ADJ (far away) remoto, recóndito; (aloof) distante; (in kinship) lejano; — **access** acceso remoto *m*; — **control** control remoto *m*, mando a distancia *m*; — **login** acceso remoto *m*; — **server** servidor remoto *m*
removal [rɪmúvəł] N (dismissal) deposición *f*, alejamiento *m*; (elimination) eliminación *f*; (extirpation) extirpación *f*
remove [rɪmúv] VT (an obstacle) remover; (take away, take off) quitar; (dismiss) deponer; (eliminate) eliminar; (extirpate) extirpar; **to** — **from office** separar/apartar del cargo
remunerate [rimjúnəret] VT remunerar *f*, retribuir *f*
remuneration [rɪmjunəréʃən] N remuneración *f*, retribución *f*
renaissance [rénɪsɑns] N renacimiento *m*; — **architecture** arquitectura renacentista *f*
renal [rínl] ADJ renal; — **failure** insuficiencia renal *f*
rend [rɛnd] VI/VT desgarrar[se], rajar[se]
render [réndɚ] VT (give) dar; (cause to become) dejar; (depict) representar; (translate) traducir; (give homage, account) rendir; (provide services, assistance) prestar; (melt down fat) derretir; (deliver a verdict) pronunciar; **to** — **useless** inutilizar
rendition [rɛndíʃən] N (translation) traducción *f*; (interpretation) interpretación *f*, versión *f*
renegade [rénɪged] N renegado -da *mf*
renegotiate [rinɪɡóʃiet] VI/VT renegociar
renege [rɪnɪ́ɡ] VI incumplir
renew [rɪnú] VT (vows, contract) renovar; (furniture) restaurar; (friendship, effort) reanudar; (a loan) prorrogar
renewable [rɪnúəbəł] ADJ renovable
renewal [rɪnúəł] N (of vows, contract) renovación *f*; (of furniture) restauración *f*; (of a city) remodelación *f*; (of friendship, effort) reanudación *f*; (of loan) prórroga *f*
renounce [rɪnáʊns] VT (give up) renunciar a; (repudiate) repudiar, renegar de
renovate [rénəvet] VT renovar
renown [rɪnáʊn] N renombre *m*
renowned [rɪnáʊnd] ADJ renombrado
rent [rɛnt] N (monthly payment) alquiler *m*, arrendamiento *m*; **for** — se alquila, se arrienda; (fissure) rajadura *f*, hendidura *f*; (tear) rasgadura *f*; VI/VT (lease) alquilar, arrendar
rent [rɛnt] *see* rend
rental [réntł] ADJ de alquiler; — **agreement** contrato de alquiler *m*; N alquiler *m*,

arrendamiento *m*
renter [réntɚ] N inquilino -na *mf*
renunciation [rɪnʌnsiéʃən] N renuncia *f*
reopen [riópən] VI/VT (doors) reabrir[se]; (negotiations) reanudar[se]
reorganization [riɔrgənɪzéʃən] N reorganización *f*
reorganize [riɔ́rgənaɪz] VI/VT reorganizar[se]
repaginate [ripǽdʒɪnet] VT repaginar
repair [rɪpér] VT (fix) reparar, arreglar, componer; (shoes) remendar; **to — to** acudir a; N (fixing) reparación *f*; (of shoes) remiendo *m*, compostura *f*; **in good —** en buen estado; **—man** técnico en reparaciones *m*
reparation [rɛpəréʃən] N reparación *f*, indemnización *f*
repay [rɪpé] VT (return money, favor) devolver; (pay off) pagar
repayment [rɪpémənt] N (of a sum) reembolso *m*; (of a loan) pago *m*
repeal [rɪpíl] VT derogar, revocar, abrogar; N derogación *f*, revocación *f*, abrogación *f*
repeat[1] [rɪpit] VI/VT repetir; N repetición *f*
repeat[2] [rɪpít] N repetición *f*
repeated [rɪpíDɪd] ADJ repetido
repel [rɪpɛ́l] VI/VT repeler; (an attack) rechazar
repellent [rɪpɛ́lənt] ADJ & N repelente *m*
repent [rɪpɛ́nt] VI/VT arrepentirse [de]
repentance [rɪpɛ́ntəns] N arrepentimiento *m*
repentant [rɪpɛ́ntənt] ADJ arrepentido, pesaroso
repercussion [rɛpɚkʌ́ʃən] N repercusión *f*; **to have —s** repercutir
repertoire [répɚtwɑr] N repertorio *m*
repetition [rɛpɪtíʃən] N repetición *f*
replace [rɪplés] VT (place again) volver a colocar; (substitute for) sustituir, reemplazar; (provide a substitute for) reponer
replaceable [rɪplésəbəl] ADJ reemplazable, sustituible
replacement [rɪplésmənt] N (substitute, substitution) sustituto *m*, reemplazo *m*; (making up for) reposición *f*; **— parts** piezas de repuesto *f pl*
replenish [rɪplénɪʃ] VI/VT (supply) reabastecer; (fill again) rellenar
replete [rɪplít] ADJ repleto
replica [réplɪkə] N réplica *f*
replicate [réplɪket] VT reproducir, replicar
replication [rɛplɪkéʃən] N reproducción *f*, replicación *f*
reply [rɪplái] VI replicar, contestar; N réplica *f*, contestación *f*
report [rɪpɔ́rt] VT (recount) relatar; (make a crime known, denounce) denunciar; (make an accident known) dar parte de; VI hacer un informe, informar; **to — for duty** presentarse; **to — on** hacer un informe sobre; **to — sick** dar parte de enfermo, reportarse enfermo; **it is —ed that** se dice que; N

informe *m*, comunicado *m*; (rumor) rumor *m*; (loud noise) estallido *m*; **— card** boletín de calificaciones *m*
reportedly [rɪpɔ́rDɪdli] ADV según se informa
reporter [rɪpɔ́rDɚ] N (news) reportero -ra *mf*; (sports) cronista *mf*
repose [rɪpóz] VI/VT reposar, descansar; N reposo *m*, descanso *m*
repository [rɪpázitɔri] N (object) depósito *m*; (person) depositario -ria *mf*
repossess [ripəzés] VT retomar posesión de
represent [rɛprɪzént] VT representar
representation [rɛprɪzentéʃən] N representación *f*
representative [rɛprɪzéntəDɪv] ADJ representativo; N representante *mf*
repress [rɪprés] VI/VT reprimir
repression [rɪpréʃən] N represión *f*
repressive [rɪprésɪv] ADJ represivo
reprieve [rɪprív] VT (pardon) indultar; (commute) conmutar; (delay) aplazar; N (pardon) indulto *m*; (commutation) conmutación *f*; (delay) aplazamiento *m*
reprimand [réprəmænd] N reprimenda *f*, regaño *m*; VT reprender, regañar
reprint[1] [riprínt] VI/VT reimprimir
reprint[2] [ríprɪnt] N (action, result) reimpresión *f*; (offprint) separata *f*
reprisal [rɪpráɪzəl] N represalia *f*
reproach [rɪprótʃ] VT reprochar; N reproche *m*
reproduce [riprədús] VI/VT reproducir[se]
reproduction [riprədʌ́kʃən] N reproducción *f*
reproof [rɪprúf] N reprobación *f*
reprove [rɪprúv] VT reprobar
reptile [réptaɪl] N reptil *m*
republic [rɪpʌ́blɪk] N república *f*
republican [rɪpʌ́blɪkən] ADJ & N republicano -na *mf*
repudiate [rɪpjúDiet] VT repudiar
repugnance [rɪpʌ́gnəns] N repugnancia *f*
repugnant [rɪpʌ́gnənt] ADJ repugnante
repulse [rɪpʌ́ls] VT repeler, rechazar; N repulsa *f*, rechazo *m*
repulsive [rɪpʌ́lsɪv] ADJ repulsivo
reputable [répjəDəbəl] ADJ reputado
reputation [rɛpjətéʃən] N reputación *f*, fama *f*
request [rɪkwést] N solicitud *f*, petición *f*, requerimiento *m*; **at the — of** a solicitud de, a instancias de; VT solicitar, pedir
require [rɪkwáɪr] VI/VT (need) requerir; (demand) exigir
requirement [rɪkwáɪrmənt] N (demand) requisito *m*; (need) necesidad *f*
requisite [rékwɪzɪt] ADJ requerido, necesario; N requisito *m*
requisition [rɛkwɪzíʃən] N (taking over) requisa *f*; (order) pedido *m*; VT (take over) requisar; (order) pedir
rerun [rírʌn] N refrito *m*

rescind [rɪsínd] VT rescindir
rescue [réskju] VT rescatar, salvar; N rescate *m*, salvamento *m*; **to go to the — of** acudir al socorro de, salir al quite de
research[1] [rísɚtʃ] N investigación *f*
research[2] [rísɚtʃ] VI/VT investigar
researcher [rísɚtʃɚ] N investigador -ora *mf*
resell [risél] VT revender
resemblance [rɪzémbləns] N semejanza *f*, parecido *m*
resemble [rɪzémbəl] VT semejar, asemejarse a, parecerse a
resent [rɪzént] VT resentirse de
resentful [rɪzéntfəl] ADJ resentido, rencoroso
resentment [rɪzéntmənt] N resentimiento *m*
reservation [rɛzɚvéʃən] N reserva *f*; *Am* reservación *f*; **to have one's —s** tener reservas
reserve [rɪzɚ́v] VT reservar; N reserva *f*; (shyness) pudor *m*
reserved [rɪzɚ́vd] ADJ reservado
reservoir [rézɚvwɑr] N (tank) depósito *m*, alberca *f*; (artificial lake) embalse *m*, represa *f*
reset [risét] VT (computer, machine) reiniciar; — **key** tecla de reinicio *f*
reside [rɪzáɪd] VI residir
residence [rézɪDəns] N residencia *f*
resident [rézɪDənt] ADJ & N residente *mf*; (of a neighborhood) vecino -na *mf*
residential [rɛzɪdéntʃəl] ADJ residencial
residue [rézɪdu] N residuo *m*
resign [rɪzáɪn] VI/VT renunciar [a], dimitir [de]; **to — oneself to** resignarse a
resignation [rɛzɪgnéʃən] N (act of resigning an office) renuncia *f*, dimisión *f*; (accepting attitude) resignación *f*; — **letter** carta de renuncia *f*
resilience [rɪzíljəns] N (elasticity) elasticidad *f*; (adaptability) adaptabilidad *f*
resilient [rɪzíljənt] ADJ (elastic) elástico; (adaptable) adaptable
resin [rézɪn] N resina *f*
resist [rɪzíst] VT (a temptation) resistir; VI/VT (tyranny) resistirse [a]
resistance [rɪzístəns] N resistencia *f*
resistant [rɪzístənt] ADJ resistente
resolute [rézəlut] ADJ resuelto, decidido
resolution [rɛzəlúʃən] N resolución *f*
resolve [rɪzáɫv] VI/VT resolver[se]; **to — into** convertirse en; **to — to** decidir, resolver; N resolución *f*
resonance [rézənəns] N resonancia *f*
resonate[2] [rézənet] VI/VT resonar
resort [rɪzɔ́rt] N (seaside) centro de veraneo *m*; (for skiing) estación de esquí *f*; **as a last —** como último recurso; VI **to — to** recurrir a
resound [rɪzáʊnd] VI/VT resonar; —**ing victory** victoria contundente *f*
resource [rísɔrs] N recurso *m*

resourceful [rɪzɔ́rsfəl] ADJ ingenioso
respect [rɪspékt] VT respetar; N (esteem) respeto *m*; (detail) aspecto *m*; **with — to** [con] respecto a, respecto de
respectable [rɪspéktəbəl] ADJ respetable
respectful [rɪspéktfəl] ADJ respetuoso
respective [rɪspéktɪv] ADJ respectivo
respiration [rɛspəréʃən] N respiración *f*
respiratory [réspəətɔri] ADJ respiratorio; — **failure** insuficiencia respiratoria *f*
respite [réspɪt] N (pause) respiro *f*, tregua *m*; (postponement) prórroga *f*
resplendent [rɪspléndənt] ADJ resplandeciente, refulgente
respond [rɪspánd] VI/VT responder
respondent [rɪspándənt] N (to a lawsuit) demandado -da *mf*; (to a poll) encuestado -da *mf*
response [rɪspáns] N respuesta *f*
responsibility [rɪspɑnsəbílɪDi] N responsabilidad *f*, reivindicación *f*
responsible [rɪspánsəbəl] ADJ responsable
rest [rɛst] N (repose) descanso *m*, reposo *m*; (musical) pausa *f*; (support) apoyo *m*; (remainder) resto *m*; — **home** (for convalescents) casa de reposo *f*; (for the aged) casa de ancianos *f*; — **room** servicio *m*; *Sp* aseo *m*; **an object at —** un objeto en reposo; VI/VT descansar, reposar; VT (one's gaze) posar; (against a wall) reclinar; VI (stop) parar; **to — on** depender de; **let it —** déjalo en paz
restaurant [réstərɑnt] N restaurante *m*; *Am* restorán *m*
restitution [rɛstɪtúʃən] N restitución *f*
restless [réstlɪs] ADJ (worried) inquieto; (fidgety) movedizo
restlessness [réstlɪsnɪs] N inquietud *f*, desasosiego *m*
restoration [rɛstəréʃən] N restauración *f*
restore [rɪstɔ́r] VT restaurar
restrain [rɪstrén] VT (hold back) refrenar, contener, moderar; (bring under control) reducir; —**ing order** medida cautelar *f*
restraint [rɪstrént] N (self-control) compostura *f*, moderación *f*; (device) seguro *m*; **under — bajo** control
restrict [rɪstríkt] VT restringir; (someone's liberty) coartar
restriction [rɪstríkʃən] N restricción *f*
restructuring [ristráktʃɚɪŋ] N reestructuración *f*
result [rɪzáɫt] VI resultar; **to — from** resultar de; **to — in** dar por resultado; N resultado *m*; **as a —** de resultas, como resultado
resume [rɪzúm] VI/VT (take up again) reasumir, volver a asumir; (continue) reanudar
résumé [rézume] N currículum *m*, historial personal *m*
resurrection [rɛzərékʃən] N resurrección *f*

resuscitate [rɪsÁsɪtet] VI/VT resucitar
resuscitation [rɪsʌsɪtéʃən] N resucitación f
retail [ríteɫ] N venta al por menor f; — **store** tienda minorista f; — **trade** comercio minorista m; VI/VT vender al por menor; **at —** al por menor, al menudeo
retailer [rítelɚ] N minorista mf, detallista mf
retain [rɪtén] VT (recall, confine, detain) retener; (keep) conservar, quedarse con; (hire) contratar
retainer [rɪténɚ] N (device that holds back) retén m; (payment) honorarios pagados por adelantado m pl
retaliate [rɪtǽliet] VI vengarse
retaliation [rɪtæliéʃən] N venganza f
retard [rɪtárd] VI/VT retardar
retarded [rɪtárdɪd] ADJ retrasado
retention [rɪténʃən] N retención f
reticence [rédɪsəns] N reserva f
retina [rétṇə] N retina f
retinue [rétṇu] N séquito m, comitiva f
retire [rɪtáɪr] VI/VT (stop working) retirar[se], jubilar[se]; (withdraw) retirar[se]; (go to bed) acostarse; (withdraw money, troops, machines) retirar
retiree [ritaɪrí] N jubilado -da mf
retirement [rɪtáɪrmənt] N retiro m, jubilación f; — **of debt** retiro de deuda m
retort [rɪtɔ́rt] N (reply) réplica f; (vessel) retorta f
retouch [rɪtʌ́tʃ] VT retocar; N retoque m
retrace [ritrés] VT (mental steps) repasar; (one's route) volver sobre
retract [rɪtrǽkt] VT (a statement) retractar; (claws) retraer[se]; VI desdecirse, retractarse
retreat [rɪtrít] N (place of refuge, period of meditation) retiro m, refugio m; (military) retirada f, repliegue m; (bugle call) retreta f; VI batirse en retirada, retroceder, replegarse
retrench [rɪtréntʃ] VI economizar
retrieval [rɪtrívəɫ] N recuperación f
retrieve [rɪtrív] VT (game animals) cobrar; (something lost) recuperar
retriever [rɪtrívɚ] N perro cobrador m
retro [rétro] ADJ retro
retroactive [rɛtroǽktɪv] ADJ retroactivo
retrospect [rétrəspɛkt] ADV LOC **in —** mirando para atrás
retrovirus [rétrovaɪrəs] N retrovirus m
return [rɪtɚ́n] VI (come back) volver, regresar; VT (put back) devolver, retornar; (deliver a verdict) fallar; — **to sender** devolver al remitente; N (to a place) vuelta f, regreso m; (of a thing) devolución f; (of profit) ganancia f; (on a typewriter) retorno de carro m; (on a computer) retroceso m, salto de línea m; — **address** señas del remitente f pl; — **game** revancha f; — **key** tecla de retorno f, tecla de retroceso f; — **of service** (tennis) resto m; — **ticket** billete de vuelta m; **by — mail** a

vuelta de correo; **election —s** resultados electorales m pl; **in —** a cambio; **in — for** a cambio de; **income tax —** Sp declaración de la renta f; Am declaración de impuestos f
reunification [rijunɪfɪkéʃən] N reunificación f
reunion [rijúnjən] N reunión f
reunite [rijunáɪt] VI/VT reunir[se]
rev [rɛv] VI/VT acelerar en vacío
reveal [rɪvíɫ] VT revelar
revealing [rɪvílɪŋ] ADJ revelador; (neckline) atrevido
revel [révəɫ] VI (enjoy) deleitarse, gozar; (party) parrandear; N parranda f
revelation [rɛvəléʃən] N revelación f; (book in Bible) Apocalipsis m sg
revelry [révəlri] N parranda f, jarana f
revenge [rɪvéndʒ] N venganza f, revancha f
revengeful [rɪvéndʒfəɫ] ADJ vengativo
revenue [révənu] N (of a government) rentas públicas f pl; (of a person) ingresos m pl; — **stamp** sello fiscal m
reverberate [rɪvɚ́bəret] VI reverberar; VT hacer reverberar
revere [rɪvír] VT reverenciar
reverence [révəəns] N reverencia f, veneración f; VT venerar
reverend [révəənd] ADJ & N reverendo -da mf
reverent [révəənt] ADJ reverente
reverie, revery [révəri] N ensueño m, ensoñación f
reverse [rɪvɚ́s] ADJ inverso, opuesto; **the — side** el revés; N (opposite) lo opuesto; (back of clothing, mishap) revés m; (back of a coin, medal) reverso m; (gear) marcha atrás f; (back of a piece of paper) dorso m; VI/VT invertir[se]; VT (a policy, a vehicle) dar marcha atrás; (a verdict) revocar
revert [rɪvɚ́t] VI revertir
review [rɪvjú] N (inspection of a military unit, periodical publication) revista f; (repetition of studied material) repaso m; (critique of a book, drama) reseña f, crítica f; (examination of a judicial case) revisión f; VI/VT (examine) repasar, revisar; VT (reexamine) revisar, examinar; (inspect troops) pasar revista a; (write a critique of) reseñar
revile [rɪváɪɫ] VT vilipendiar, denostar
revise [rɪváɪz] VT corregir, enmendar
revision [rɪvíʒən] N (action of revising) corrección f; (revised version) versión corregida f
revitalize [riváɪdḷaɪz] VT revitalizar
revival [rɪváɪvəɫ] N (of customs) retorno m; (of religious feeling) resurgimiento m, despertar m; (from unconsciousness) resucitación f; (of a play) reposición f, revisión f; (evangelical meeting) asamblea evangelística f
revive [rɪváɪv] VT (an unconscious person) reavivar, reanimar; (an apparently dead

person) resucitar; (an old play) reponer; (a custom) restablecer; VI revivir, reanimarse; (be reestablished) restablecerse

revocation [rɛvəkéʃən] N revocación f

revoke [rɪvók] VT revocar

revolt [rɪvóɫt] N revuelta f, sublevación f; VI rebelarse, sublevarse; **it —s me** me da asco

revolting [rɪvóɫtɪŋ] ADJ repugnante, asqueroso

revolution [rɛvəlúʃən] N revolución f

revolutionary [rɛvəlúʃɛnɛri] ADJ & N revolucionario -ria mf

revolve [rɪváɫv] VI/VT girar

revolver [rɪváɫvɚ] N revólver m

revolving credit [rɪváɫvɪŋ] N crédito rotativo m

revue [rɪvjú] N revista f

revulsion [rɪváɫʃən] N repugnancia f, asco m

reward [rɪwɔ́rd] N recompensa f; VT recompensar

rewind [riwáɪnd] VI/VT rebobinar

rewrite[1] [ríráɪt] VI/VT reescribir

rewrite[2] [ríraɪt] N corrección f

rhea [ríə] N ñandú m

rhetoric [rɛ́Dɚɪk] N retórica f

rheumatic [rumǽDɪk] ADJ reumático; **— fever** fiebre reumática f

rheumatism [rúmətɪzəm] N reumatismo m, reuma m

rheumatoid [rúmətɔɪd] ADJ reumatoide

Rh factor [árétʃfæktɚ] N factor Rh m

rhinoceros [raɪnásərəs] N rinoceronte m

rhinoplasty [ráɪnoplæsti] N rinoplastia f

rhinovirus [ráɪnováɪrəs] N rinovirus m

rhododendron [roDədéndrən] N rododendro m

rhubarb [rúbɑrb] N (vegetable) ruibarbo m; (brawl) reyerta f

rhyme [raɪm] N rima f; **without — or reason** sin ton ni son; VI/VT rimar

rhythm [ríðəm] N ritmo m

rhythmical [ríðmɪkəɫ] ADJ rítmico; (breathing) acompasado

rib [rɪb] N (of person, animal) costilla f; (of umbrella) varilla f; (in garment) canalé m, cordoncillo m; **— cage** caja torácica f; VT burlarse de

ribbon [ríbən] N (of cloth) cinta f; (of land) franja f, faja f

rice [raɪs] N arroz m; **— field** arrozal m

rich [rɪtʃ] ADJ rico; (tasty) sabroso; (buttery) mantecoso; (colorful) vivo; **— text format** formato de texto enriquecido m; N **—es** riquezas f pl

rickety [ríkɪDi] ADJ (shaky) desvencijado; (affected with rickets) raquítico

ricochet [ríkəʃe] N rebote m; VI rebotar

rid [rɪd] VT librar, desembarazar; **to get — of** librarse de, deshacerse de

ridden [rídn] see ride

riddle [rídl̩] N (puzzle) acertijo m, adivinanza f; (something puzzling) enigma m; VI hablar en

enigmas; VT acribillar, perforar; **to be —d with graft** estar plagado de corrupción

ride [raɪd] VI (on a horse) cabalgar, jinetear; (on a bicycle) montar; (in a vehicle) andar/viajar/ir en; **this car —s well** este coche anda bien; **his hopes are riding on that** tiene las esperanzas puestas en eso; **just let it —** déjalo tranquilo; VT (travel on horse, bicycle) montar; (travel on bus) andar en; (harass) hostigar; **to — away** irse; **to — by** pasar; **to — out** capear; **to — up** subirse; N (in a vehicle) paseo m, viaje m; (at an amusement park) aparato m; **to give someone a —** llevar/acercar en coche; **to go on a —** dar un paseo

rider [ráɪDɚ] N (on a horse) jinete m; (on a bicycle) ciclista mf; (on an insurance policy) cláusula añadida f; (law) anexo m

ridge [rɪdʒ] N (back of an animal) espinazo m, lomo m; (chain of hills) cadena f; (of a roof) caballete m; (of cloth) cordoncillo m

ridicule [ríDɪkjuɫ] N burla f, mofa f; VT ridiculizar, poner en ridículo

ridiculous [rɪdíkjələs] ADJ ridículo

riffraff [rífræf] N pej gentuza f, chusma f

rifle [ráɪfəɫ] N rifle m, fusil m; VT robar; **to — through** revolver

rift [rɪft] N (opening) grieta f, hendidura f; (disagreement) desavenencia f

rig [rɪg] VT (sails) aparejar, equipar; (an election) amañar; **to — up** armar; N (on a ship) aparejo m, equipo m; (apparatus) aparato m; (truck) camión m

rigging [rígɪŋ] N jarcia f

right [raɪt] ADJ (not left) derecho; (not wrong) correcto, acertado; (suitable) adecuado; **— angle** ángulo recto m; **—-hand** derecho; **— hand man** brazo derecho m; **—-handed** diestro; **— justification** alineación a la derecha f; **—-to-life** antiaborto, pro vida; **— triangle** triángulo recto m; **—-wing** derechista, de derecha; **at the — moment** en el momento justo; **the — people** la gente indicada; **to be —** tener razón; **to be all —** estar bien; **he's not in his — mind** no está en sus cabales; **to turn out —** salir bien; ADV (straight) derecho, directamente; (correctly) correctamente; (to the right) a la derecha; **— after** justo después de; **—-face** media vuelta a la derecha; **— now** ahora mismo, ahorita; **— there** allí mismo; **it is — where you left it** está exactamente donde lo dejaste; **to hit — in the eye** darle de lleno en el ojo; **— click** pulsación en el botón derecho del ratón f; N (just claim) derecho m; (moral good) bien m; (direction, political persuasion) derecha f; **— of way** prioridad f, preferencia f; **— to work** derecho al trabajo m; **make a — at the corner** gira/dobla a la derecha; **to the —**

a la derecha; **to be in the** — tener razón;
VI/VT (make upright) enderezar[se]; **to —
click** pulsar el botón derecho del ratón; VT
(correct) corregir
righteous [ráɪtʃəs] ADJ recto, justo; — **anger**
rabia justificada f
righteousness [ráɪtʃəsnɪs] N rectitud f,
superioridad moral f
rightful [ráɪtfəl] ADJ legítimo
rightist [ráɪdɪst] N derechista mf
rightly [ráɪtli] ADV con razón
rigid [ríʤɪd] ADJ rígido
rigidity [rɪʤíDɪti] N rigidez f
rigor [rígə-] N rigor m
rigorous [rígə-əs] ADJ riguroso
rim [rɪm] N (edge) borde m; (on a car) llanta f; Am
rin m; (on a bicycle) aro m; (on a plate) filete
m; (of glasses) montura f
rind [raɪnd] N (cheese) corteza f; (fruit) cáscara f
ring [rɪŋ] N (on finger, of smoke) anillo m; (for
women only) sortija f; (under the eyes) ojeras
f pl; (in the nose) argolla f; (circle) círculo m,
redondel m, ruedo m; (in a circus) pista f; (for
bullfights) plaza de toros f; (for boxing)
cuadrilátero m; (for gymnastics) anillas f pl;
(of criminals) banda f; (undertone) tono m;
(sound of telephone) timbrazo m, telefonazo
m; (sound of bells) retintín m, repique m; —
finger anular m; —**leader** cabecilla mf;
—**worm** tiña f; VT (surround) cercar; (make
doorbell sound) tocar; (make bell sound)
tañer; VI (of ears) zumbar; (make sound of a
doorbell) sonar; (make sound of a bell)
repicar, repiquetear; **to — the nose of an
animal** ponerle una argolla en la nariz a un
animal; **to — the hour** dar la hora; **to —
true** parecer verdad; **to — up the sale**
marcar la venta
ringlet [ríŋlɪt] N (curl) rizo m, bucle m, sortija f;
(small ring) sortija pequeña f
rink [rɪŋk] N pista de patinaje f
rinkydink [ríŋkidɪŋk] ADJ de pacotilla
rinse [rɪns] VI/VT enjuagar, aclarar; N enjuague
m, aclarado m
riot [ráɪət] N (uprising) motín m, tumulto m;
(excess) exceso m; **he's a —** es un cómico; VI
amotinarse
riotous [ráɪəDəs] ADJ (wanton) desenfrenado;
(funny) graciosísimo
rip [rɪp] VI/VT rasgar[se], rajar[se]; VT (something
sewn) descoser; **to — away** desprender; **to —
into** asaltar; **to — off** robar; **to — out a
seam** descoser una costura; N rasgadura f,
rajadura f; — **cord** cordón de apertura m;
—**off** robo m
ripe [raɪp] ADJ maduro; **to be — for** estar
preparado/listo para; — **old age** edad
avanzada f
ripen [ráɪpən] VI/VT madurar[se], sazonar[se]

ripeness [ráɪpnɪs] N madurez f
ripening [ráɪpənɪŋ] N maduración f
ripple [rípəl] VI/VT (water) rizar[se]; (grass)
agitar[se]; N ondulación f, rizo m
rise [raɪz] VI (go up) subir; (increase) aumentar;
(get up, stand up) levantarse; (slope up)
elevarse; (arise) surgir; (of mist) levantarse;
(of the sun, moon) salir; (of dough) crecer,
leudar; **to — up in rebellion** sublevarse,
alzarse; **to — above** superar; **to — to the
challenge** aceptar el desafío y triunfar; N (of
prices, volume) subida f, aumento m; (of an
empire, talent) surgimiento m; (slope
upward) elevación f; **to get a — out of
someone** provocar a alguien; **to give — to**
ocasionar
risen [rízən] see rise
risk [rɪsk] N riesgo m; — **factors** factores de
riesgo m pl; **at —** a riesgo; ADJ —-**free** sin
riesgo; VT arriesgar, aventurar; **to — defeat**
correr el riesgo de perder, exponerse a perder
risky [ríski] ADJ arriesgado, aventurado
risqué [rɪské] ADJ subido de tono, atrevido,
picante
Ritalin hydrochloride [rídəlɪnhaɪdrəklɔ́raɪd]
N clorhidrato de Ritalina m
rite [raɪt] N rito m
ritual [rítʃuəl] ADJ & N ritual m
ritzy [rítsi] ADJ elegante
rival [ráɪvəl] ADJ & N rival mf; VT rivalizar con,
competir con
rivalry [ráɪvəlri] N rivalidad f
river [rívə-] N río m; —**bank** orilla f, ribera f; —
transport transporte fluvial m
rivet [rívɪt] N remache m; VT (put rivets)
remachar; (fix) fijar, clavar
riveting [rívɪDɪŋ] N (action) remache m; ADJ
(fascinating) fascinante
RNA [ribonucleic acid] [áréné] N ARN m
roach [rotʃ] N cucaracha f
road [rod] N (in the country) camino m;
(highway) carretera f; **on the — to recovery**
en vías de recuperación; — **map** mapa
carretero m; — **rage** ira caminera f; —**side**
borde del camino m; —**way** camino m
roam [rom] VI/VT vagar [por], errar [por], rodar
[por]; VI vagabundear
roar [rɔr] VI/VT rugir, bramar; **to — with
laughter** reír a carcajadas; N rugido m,
bramido m; — **of laughter** risotada f,
carcajada f
roast [rost] VI/VT (meat, potatoes) asar[se];
(coffee, nuts) tostar, torrar; (criticize) criticar;
N (meat) asado m; (party) barbacoa f; — **beef**
rosbif m
rob [rɑb] VI/VT robar; **to — someone of
something** robarle algo a alguien
robber [rábə-] N ladrón -ona mf
robbery [rábəri] N robo m

robe [rob] N manto *m*, traje talar *m*, túnica *f*; (ceremonial dress) toga *f*; (bath wrap) bata *f*

robin [rábɪn] N petirrojo *m*

robot [róbɑt] N robot *m*

robotics [robáDɪks] N robótica *f*

robust [robÁst] ADJ (strong) robusto; (hearty) saludable; (solid) sólido

rock [rɑk] N roca *f*; (crag) peñasco *m*, peñón *m*; (diamond) diamante *m*; (music style) rock *m*; — **crystal** cristal de roca *m*; — **salt** sal de piedra *f*, sal gema/mineral *f*; **on the** — en las rocas; **to go on the** —s tropezar en un escollo; *Am* escollar; **to hit** —**-bottom** tocar fondo; VI/VT (move to and fro) mecer[se]; (stagger) sacudir, estremecer; **to** — **to sleep** arrullar

rocker [rákə-] N (chair) mecedora *f*; (fan or performer of rock music) roquero -ra *mf*

rocket [rákɪt] N cohete *m*

rocketry [rákɪtri] N cohetería *f*

rocking [rákɪŋ] N — **chair** mecedora *f*; — **horse** caballito de madera *m*, caballito mecedor *m*

rocky [ráki] ADJ (with rocks) rocoso; (difficult) difícil

rod [rɑd] N (stick) vara *f*, varilla *f*; (in engine) vástago *m*; (measure of length) aproximadamente 5 metros *f*

rode [rod] *see* ride

rodent [róDənt] N roedor *m*

rodeo [róDio] N rodeo *m*

rogue [rog] N pícaro -ra *mf*, bribón -ona *mf*; ADJ solitario y bravo

roguish [rógɪʃ] ADJ (rascally) pícaro, bribón; (mischievous) travieso

role [roł] N (in a drama) papel *m*, rol *m*; — **model** modelo ejemplar *m*; —**-playing** improvisación *f*

roll [roł] VI (move on wheels, rotate) rodar; (rotate one's eyes) revolear; (sway) balancearse, bambolearse; (reverberate) retumbar; (flow as waves) ondular; VT (steel) aplanar; (cigarettes) liar; (a drum) redoblar; (one's r's) pronunciar la erre; **to** — **over in the snow** revolcarse en la nieve; **to** — **up** arrollar, enrollar; **to** — **around** llegar; **to** — **back** reducir, rebajar; **to** — **by** pasar; **to** — **out** (products) lanzar; **to** — **over** (physically) volcar, darse vuelta; (investments) reinvertir; **to get** —**ing** ponerse en marcha; N (of paper, fabric, etc.) rollo *m*; (of coins) cartucho *m*; (of a ship) balanceo *m*; (of thunder) retumbo *m*; (of a drum) redoble *m*; (of members) lista *f*; (of waves) ondulación *f*; (of a typewriter) carro *m*; (of bread) bollo *m*, panecillo *m*; (of dice) tiro *m*; ADJ —**-on** de bolita

roller [rólə-] N (for painting, moving things) rodillo *m*; (hair) rulo *m*, rulero *m*; — **coaster** montaña rusa *f*; — **skate** patín de ruedas *m*

rolling [rólɪŋ] ADJ (countryside) ondulado; (wheel) rodante; — **pin** rodillo *m*, palote *m*

roly-poly [rólipóli] ADJ rechoncho

ROM [read-only memory] [rɑm] N ROM *f*, memoria de ROM *f*, memoria de sólo lectura *f*

Roman [rómən] ADJ & N romano -na *mf*; — **numeral** número romano *m*

romance [rómæns] N (love affair, story) romance *m*; (romantic atmosphere) romanticismo *m*; VT cortejar; ADJ (linguistic) romance, románico

romanesque [románésk] ADJ románico

Romania [róméniə] N Rumania *f*

Romanian [róméniən] ADJ & N rumano -na *mf*

romantic [rómæntɪk] ADJ romántico

romanticism [rómæntəsɪzəm] N romanticismo *m*

romp [rɑmp] VI (frolic) retozar, brincar; (win easily) arrasar; N (frolic) retozo *m*; (victory) victoria fácil *f*

roof [ruf] N (ceiling) techo *m*, tejado *m*; (flat roof) azotea *f*; — **of the mouth** paladar *m*; **to hit the** — poner el grito en el cielo; VT techar

rookie [rúki] N novato -ta *mf*

room [rum] N (in building) cuarto *m*; (large) sala *f*; (in a hotel) habitación *f*; (space) lugar *m*, sitio *m*; — **and board** pensión completa *f*; —**mate** compañero -ra de cuarto *mf*; — **service** servicio a la habitación *f*; **to take up** — ocupar espacio; **the whole** — **laughed** todos los presentes se rieron; VI hospedarse, alojarse

roomy [rúmi] ADJ espacioso, amplio

roost [rust] N vara *f*; VI posarse [para dormir]

rooster [rústə-] N gallo *m*

root [rut] N raíz *f*; — **canal** (part of tooth) canal radicular *m*, tratamiento de conducto *m*; — **directory** directorio de raíz *m*, directorio raíz *m*; **to take** — (a plant) echar raíces, prender; (an idea) arraigar[se]; VI (grow roots) arraigar[se], echar raíces; (dig) hozar; **to** — **for** animar; **to** — **out/up** (uproot) arrancar de raíz; (eradicate) erradicar

rope [rop] N (cord) soga *f*, cuerda *f*; (lasso) reata *f*, lazo *m*; (on a ship) cabo *m*; (thick) maroma *f*; **to be at the end of one's** — no dar más; **to know the** —s conocer el paño, sabérselas todas; VT enlazar; **to** — **off** acordonar; **to** — **someone in** agarrar a alguien

Rorschach test [rórʃɑk tɛst] N prueba de Rorschach *f*

rosary [rózəri] N rosario *m*

rose [roz] N rosa *f*; (color) rosa *m*; —**bud** capullo de rosa *m*, pimpollo de rosa *m*; —**bush** rosal *m*; ADJ —**-colored** de color rosa

rose [roz] *see* rise

rosemary [rózmɛri] N romero *m*

roseola [rozíələ] N roséola *f*

roster [rástə-] N lista *f*

rostrum [rástrəm] N tribuna f
rosy [rózi] ADJ (pink) rosado, color de rosa; (of cheeks) sonrosado; — **future** porvenir halagüeño m
rot [rɑt] VI/VT pudrir[se]; N podredumbre f
rotary [róDəri] ADJ rotatorio, rotativo
rotate [rótet] VI/VT rotar
rotation [rotéʃən] N rotación f, giro m
rotor [róDɚ] N rotor m
rotten [rátn̩] ADJ (decomposing) podrido; (stinking) hediondo; (morally corrupt) corrupto; (despicable) odioso
rotund [rotʌ́nd] ADJ rollizo
rouge [ruʒ] N colorete m
rough [rʌf] ADJ (coarse) áspero, rugoso; (violent) violento; (rude) tosco; (approximate) aproximado; (bumpy) desigual, irregular; (rugged) agreste, bronco; (stormy) picado, revuelto; — **diamond** diamante en bruto m; — **draft** borrador m; — **estimate** aproximación f; — **weather** mal tiempo m; **he had a** — **time** le fue mal; VI **to** — **it** vivir sin lujos ni comodidades
roughly [rʌ́fli] ADV (not smoothly) ásperamente; (rudely) groseramente, rudamente; (approximately) aproximadamente; **to estimate** — tantear
roughness [rʌ́fnɪs] N (lack of smoothness) aspereza f; (rudeness) rudeza f; (unevenness) desigualdad f; **the** — **of the sea** lo picado del mar
roulette [rulét] N ruleta f
round [raʊnd] ADJ redondo; — **number** número redondo m; — **trip** viaje de ida y vuelta m; N (of talks, drinks, dance) ronda f; (of cheese) rodaja f; (in cards, sports) vuelta f; (in boxing) round m, asalto m; (of golf) partido m, ronda f; (canon) canon m; — **of ammunition** carga de municiones f; — **of applause** aplauso m; —**up** (of cattle) rodeo m; (of criminals) redada f; **to make the** —**s** hacer la ronda; PREP & ADV —**about** indirecto; —-**the-clock** veinticuatro horas al día; **all year** — todo el año; **to come** — pasar; **to go** — **a corner** doblar una esquina; VT (a corner) doblar; (an edge, a number) redondear; **to** — **off/out** redondear; **to** — **up** juntar, reunir; **to** — **up cattle** juntar el ganado
roundness [ráʊndnɪs] N redondez f
rouse [raʊz] VI/VT (wake) despertar[se]; VT (instigate) incitar
rout [raʊt] N (defeat) derrota aplastante f; (flight) huida en desbandada f; VT (defeat) derrotar, destrozar; (cause to flee) poner en fuga
route [raʊt, rut] N ruta f, trayecto m, recorrido m; (of newspaper delivery) reparto m; VT dirigir
routine [rutín] N rutina f

rove [rov] VI/VT vagar [por], errar [por]
rover [róvɚ] N vagabundo -da m f
row[1] [raʊ] N (fight) riña f, pelea f, bronca f
row[2] [ro] N (line) fila f, hilera f, ringlera f; **four times in a** — cuatro veces seguidas; VI/VT (propel with oars) remar, bogar; —**boat** bote de remos m, barca f
rowdy [ráʊDi] ADJ (person) alborotador; (party) bullicioso; N camorrista m f
rower [róɚ] N remero -ra m f
royal [rɔ́ɪəl] ADJ real; — **blue** azul marino m; — **flush** escalera real f
royalty [rɔ́ɪəlti] N (group) realeza f; (person) miembro de la realeza m; **royalties** derechos m pl, regalías f pl
RSVP [**répondez s'il vous plaît**] [árésvípí] LOC S.R.C.
rub [rʌb] VI/VT (apply friction) frotar[se]; (massage) friccionar; (spread on) aplicar frotando; (make sore) rozar; **to** — **off** quitar[se] frotando; **to** — **out** borrar; **to** — **shoulders with** codearse con; **to** — **the wrong way** peinar a contrapelo; **don't** — **it in!** ¡no me lo refriegues por la cara! N (act of rubbing) fricción f; (difficulty) dificultad f; (abraded area) roce m, frote m
rubber [rʌ́bɚ] N caucho m, goma f; (condom) condón m, preservativo m; — **band** goma elástica f; —**s** chanclos m pl; — **stamp** sello de goma m; — **tree** gomero m; VT **to** —-**stamp** autorizar automáticamente
rubbing alcohol [rʌ́bɪŋ ǽɫkəhɔ̀ɫ] N alcohol para fricciones m
rubbish [rʌ́bɪʃ] N (trash) basura f; (nonsense) pamplinas f pl
rubble [rʌ́bəɫ] N (debris) escombros m pl; (stone fragments) ripios m pl, cascote m
rubella [rubélə] N rubéola/rubeola f, sarampión alemán m
rubric [rúbrɪk] N rúbrica f
ruby [rúbi] N rubí m
ruckus [rʌ́kəs] N barahúnda f, jaleo m
rudder [rʌ́Dɚ] N timón m
ruddy [rʌ́Di] ADJ rubicundo
rude [rud] ADJ (impolite) grosero; (uncouth, crude, simple) tosco; (harsh) rudo
rudeness [rúdnɪs] N (impoliteness) grosería f; (crudeness) tosquedad f; (harshness) rudeza f
rueful [rúfəɫ] ADJ (inspiring pity) triste; (repentant) arrepentido
ruffian [rʌ́fiən] N rufián m
ruffle [rʌ́fəɫ] VI/VT (gather cloth) fruncir[se]; (raise feathers) erizar[se]; (ripple water) agitar[se], rizar[se]; (muss hair) desgreñar[se]; (bother a person) molestar[se], fastidiar[se]; N (frill on clothes) volante m; (gathering in cloth) frunce m, pliegue m; (ripples in water) ondulación f, rizo m
rug [rʌg] N alfombra f; (hairpiece) peluquín m

rugby [rʌ́gbi] N rugby *m*
rugged [rʌ́gɪd] ADJ (terrain) escarpado, áspero,
fragoso; (face) recio; (manners) tosco; (way of
life) duro; (man) robusto
ruin [rúɪn] N ruina *f*; **to go to** — arruinarse,
venirse abajo; VI/VT arruinar[se],
estropear[se]; (spoil) echar[se] a perder
ruinous [rúɪnəs] ADJ ruinoso
rule [ruł] N (principle) regla *f*; (line separating
newspaper columns) filete *m*; (government)
mando *m*, gobierno *m*; —**s and regulations**
reglamentos y disposiciones administrativas
m pl; **the** — **of law** el imperio de la ley; **as a**
— **of thumb** por regla general, a ojo de buen
cubero; VI/VT (govern) reinar, gobernar;
(decree) fallar, dictaminar, sentenciar; (put
lines on paper) rayar, poner renglones; **to** —
out excluir; **to** — **over** reinar, gobernar
ruler [rúlə-] N (governor) gobernante *mf*;
(measuring instrument) regla *f*
ruling [rúlɪŋ] N (decision) fallo *m*, sentencia *f*,
dictamen *m*; (line on paper) renglón *m*; ADJ
(governing) gobernante, reinante
rum [rʌm] N ron *m*
rumba [rʌ́mbə] N rumba *m*; VI rumbear
rumble [rʌ́mbəł] VI (as thunder) retumbar; (as a
stomach) hacer ruido; (fight) pelear; N (roar)
retumbo *m*; (growl) ruido *m*; (fight) pelea *f*
ruminate [rúmənet] VI rumiar
rummage [rʌ́mɪʤ] VI/VT rebuscar, hurgar; N
cachivaches *m pl*; — **sale** venta de
beneficencia *f*
rumor [rúmə-] N rumor *m*; VT murmurar; **it is**
—**ed that** se rumorea que, corre la voz que
rump [rʌmp] N (of quadruped) anca *f*, grupa *f*;
(of bird) rabadilla *f*; (of person) trasero *m*
run [rʌn] VI (person, tears, water) correr;
(stockings, dyes) correrse; (machines)
funcionar; (faucet) chorrear; (candidate)
presentarse como candidato; (sore) supurar;
VT (a mile, a risk) correr; (one object through
another) pasar; (a business) manejar, dirigir;
(a red light) comerse; (a news story) publicar;
(a sum of money) costar; (a computer
program) ejecutar; (a fever) tener; — **along
now!** ¡vete! **to** — **across someone**
encontrarse con alguien; **to** — **after**
perseguir; **to** — **around with** andar con; **to**
— **away** fugarse, escaparse; **to** — **down**
(stop working) dejar de funcionar; (capture)
aprehender; (criticize) hablar mal de; (run
over) atropellar; (tire) cansar; **to** — **dry**
secarse; **to** — **into** (encounter) tropezarse
con, encontrarse con; (collide) chocar con; **to**
— **out** salir corriendo; **to** — **out of money**
quedarse sin dinero; **to** — **over** (spill)
derramarse; (run down) atropellar, arrollar;
(move along a surface) deslizar por; **to** —
through (stab) atravesar; (squander)

despilfarrar; **to** — **up** acumular; **the play
ran for three months** la obra estuvo en
cartel durante tres meses; **it** —**s in the
family** es un rasgo de familia; N (act of
running) carrera *f*, corrida *f*; (point in
baseball) carrera *f*, anotación *f*; (defect in
stockings) carrera *f*, corrida *f*; (routine trip)
recorrido *m*; (of newspapers) tirada *f*; (of a
play) temporada en cartel *f*; (on a bank)
pánico *m*, corrida *f*; —**away** fugitivo -va *mf*;
—**away horse** caballo desbocado *m*; —
batted in carrera impulsada *f*; — **of good
luck** racha de buena suerte *f*; — **of the mill**
del montón; —**way** (for planes) pista *f*; (for
models) pasarela *f*; **to be on the** — estar
huyendo; **in the long** — a la larga; **the** —**s**
vulg cagalera *f*; **he gave me the** —**around**
contestó con evasivas; **she gave us a**
—**down** nos hizo un resumen; ADJ —-
down desvencijado
rung [rʌŋ] N (of a chair) barrote *m*; (of a ladder)
peldaño *m*
rung [rʌŋ] *see* ring
runner [rʌ́nə-] N (one who runs) corredor -ora
mf; (on a table) tapete *m*; (on a sled) patín *m*;
(on a skate) cuchilla *f*; (on a plant) estolón *m*;
(of drugs, contraband) contrabandista *mf*; —-
up segundo -da *mf*
running [rʌ́nɪŋ] N (of a race) corrida *f*, carrera *f*;
(of a business) manejo *m*, dirección *f*; (of
water) flujo *m*; (of machines) funcionamiento
m; (of a car) rodaje *m*; **to be out of the** —
estar fuera de combate; — **board** estribo *m*;
ADJ (sore) supurante; — **water** agua
corriente *f*; **in** — **condition** en buen estado;
for ten days — durante diez días seguidos
runt [rʌnt] N (animal) animal más pequeño de la
camada *m*; (person) *pej* mequetrefe *m*
rupture [rʌ́ptʃə-] N (of relations, internal organ)
ruptura *f*; (of a tire) rotura *f*; (hernia) hernia *f*;
VI/VT romper[se], reventar[se]
rural [rúrəł] ADJ rural
rush [rʌʃ] VI/VT (hurry) apresurar[se]; *Am*
apurar[se]; VT (a parcel) llevar con prisa,
llevar rápido; (an enemy) precipitarse,
abalanzarse sobre; **to** — **by/past** pasar
corriendo; **to** — **out** salir corriendo; N (haste)
prisa *f*; *Am* apuro *m*; (attack) acometida *f*;
(hurried activity) bullicio *m*; (plant) junco *m*;
— **hour** hora punta *f*; — **of air** ráfaga *f*; — **of
people** tumulto *m*; — **of water** torrente *m*;
— **order** pedido urgente *m*
Russia [rʌ́ʃə] N Rusia *f*
Russian [rʌ́ʃən] ADJ & N ruso -sa *mf*
rust [rʌst] N (oxidation) herrumbre *f*, orín *m*;
(disease) tizón *m*; ADJ —-**colored** color
herrumbre; —-**proof** inoxidable; VI/VT
herrumbrar[se]
rustic [rʌ́stɪk] ADJ rústico; N campesino -na *mf*,

paleto -ta *mf*
rusting [rʌ́stɪŋ] N oxidación *f*
rustle [rʌ́səł] VI susurrar, crujir; VT hacer
susurrar, hacer crujir; **to — cattle** robar
ganado; N susurro *m*, crujido *m*
rusty [rʌ́sti] ADJ (oxidized) herrumbrado,
oxidado; (rust-colored) color herrumbre; (out
of practice) falto de práctica; **my German is
— se me ha olvidado el alemán**
rut [rʌt] N (furrow) surco *m*; (of a wheel) rodada
f; (routine) rutina *f*; (heat) celo *m*; **to be in a
— ser esclavo de la rutina; VI estar en celo
ruthless [rúθlɪs] ADJ despiadado
ruthlessness [rúθlɪsnɪs] N crueldad *f*
Rwanda [ruándə] N Ruanda *f*
Rwandan [ruándən] ADJ & N ruandés -esa *mf*
rye [raɪ] N centeno *m*; **— bread** pan de centeno *m*

Ss

saber [sébɚ] N sable *m*
sabotage [sǽbətɑʒ] N sabotaje *m*; VT sabotear
sac [sæk] N bolsa *f*, saco *m*
saccharine [sǽkɚɪn] ADJ empalagoso; N
sacarina *f*
sack [sæk] N (bag) saco *m*, bolso *m*; (looting)
saqueo *m*; (in football) captura *f*; **in the —** en
la cama; VT (bag) embolsar, ensacar; (loot)
saquear; (fire) despedir
sacrament [sǽkrəmənt] N sacramento *m*
sacred [sékrɪd] ADJ sagrado
sacrifice [sǽkrəfaɪs] N (also in baseball)
sacrificio *m*; **at a —** con pérdida; VT sacrificar
sacrilege [sǽkrəlɪdʒ] N sacrilegio *m*
sacrilegious [sækrəlídʒəs] ADJ sacrílego
sacrum [sékrəm] N sacro *m*
sad [sæd] ADJ triste
sadden [sǽdn̩] VI/VT entristecer[se]; VT pesar
saddle [sǽdl̩] N (for horse) silla de montar *f*,
montura *f*; (for bicycle) sillín *m*; **—bag** alforja
f; **— horse** caballo de silla *m*; **— pad** carona *f*;
— tree arzón *m*; VT ensillar; **to — up**
ensillar; **to — someone with
responsibilities** cargar a alguien de
responsabilidades
sadism [sédɪzəm] N sadismo *m*
sadistic [sədístɪk] ADJ sádico
sadness [sǽdnɪs] N tristeza *f*
sadomasochism [seɪDomǽsəkɪzəm] N
sadomasoquismo *m*
safari [səfári] N safari *m*
safe [sef] ADJ (secure) seguro, salvo;
(trustworthy) digno de confianza; (careful)
precavido, prudente; **— and sound** sano y
salvo; **— deposit box** caja de seguridad *f*;
—guard salvaguarda *f*; **—keeping** custodia

f; **— mode** modo a prueba de fallos/errores
m; **— sex** sexo seguro *m*; N caja fuerte *f*; **—
-conduct** salvoconducto *m*; ADV (in baseball)
safe; VT **to —guard** salvaguardar
safely [séfli] ADV (without danger) sin peligro;
(without incident) sin percances; **I can — say**
puedo decir con toda seguridad
safety [séfti] N seguridad *f*; **— belt** cinturón de
seguridad *m*; **— device** mecanismo de
seguridad *m*, seguro *m*; **— glass** vidrio
inastillable *m*; **— net** red *f*; **— pin**
imperdible *m*
saffron [sǽfrən] N (spice) azafrán *m*; (color)
color azafrán *m*
sag [sæg] VI/VT (wall) combar[se], pandear[se]; VI
(stock market, breast) caer; (spirits) decaer;
(rope) aflojarse; (pants) abolsarse; **his
shoulders —** tiene las espaldas caídas; N (of
a wall) pandeo *m*, comba *f*; (in prices) caída *f*
sage [sedʒ] ADJ sabio; N (wise person) sabio -bia
mf; (plant) salvia *f*
said [sed] *see* say
sail [seł] N (part of a boat) vela *f*; (trip) viaje en
barco *m*; **—boat** velero *m*; **—fish** pez vela *m*;
under full — a toda vela; **to set —** zarpar;
VI/VT (travel by boat) navegar; (set sail)
zarpar; **to — along** deslizarse, navegar; **to —
along the coast** costear; **to — through an
exam** aprobar un examen con facilidad
sailor [sélɚ] N marinero -ra *mf*
saint [sent] N santo -ta *mf*; **— John** San Juan
saintly [séntli] ADJ santo, piadoso
sake [sek] N **for the — of** por; **for my —** por mí;
for pity's — por el amor de Dios; **for
brevity's —** para ser breve; **for the — of
argument** por vía de argumento; **art for
art's —** el arte por el arte
salad [sǽləd] N ensalada *f*; **— dressing**
aderezo *m*
salamander [sǽləmændɚ] N salamandra *f*
salary [sǽləri] N sueldo *m*, retribución *f*; **—
bracket** categoría salarial *f*; **— range** escala
de sueldos *f*, escala salarial *f*
sale [seł] N (act of selling) venta *f*; (special sales
event) liquidación *f*, saldo *m*; **—s clerk**
dependiente -ta *mf*; **—s force** personal de
ventas *m*; **—sperson** dependiente -ta *mf*; **—s
tax** impuesto sobre las ventas *m*; **for —** en
venta; **on —** con rebaja, rebajado
salient [séliənt] ADJ & N saliente *m*
saline [sélin] ADJ salino; **— solution** solución
salina *f*
saliva [səláɪvə] N saliva *f*
sally [sǽli] N (sortie) salida *f*; (excursion)
excursión *f*; VI salir, hacer una salida; **to —
forth** salir
salmon [sǽmən] N salmón *m*
salmonella [sælmənélə] N salmonela *f*
salon [səlán] N salón *m*; (beauty parlor) salón de

belleza *m*, peluquería *f*
saloon [səlún] N salón *m*, taberna *f*, bar *m*
salt [sɔlt] N sal *f*; (for smelling) sales *f pl*;
—**cellar** salero *m*; — **lick** salegar *m*; — **mine**
salina *f*; —**peter** salitre *m*; —**shaker** salero
m; —**water** agua salada *f*; **old** — lobo de mar
m; **the** — **of the earth** la sal de la tierra; VT
salar; **to** — **away** ahorrar
salty [sɔ́lti] ADJ (food, water) salado; (soil, water)
salobre
salutation [sæljətéʃən] N saludo *m*
salute [səlút] N saludo *m*; (of guns) salva *f*; VI/VT
(greet) saludar; (acknowledge) reconocer
Salvadoran, Salvadorian [sælvədɔ́r[i]ən] ADJ
& N salvadoreño -ña *mf*
salvage [sǽlvɪʤ] N (recovery) salvamento *m*;
(objects recovered) objetos salvados *m pl*; VT
salvar
salvation [sælvéʃən] N salvación *f*
salve [sæv] N ungüento *m*, pomada *f*
salvo [sǽlvo] N salva *f*
same [sem] ADJ (identical) mismo; (similar)
igual; —-**day delivery** entrega el mismo día
f; —-**sex marriage** matrimonio
homosexual *m*; **it is all the** — **to me** me da
igual, me da lo mismo; **the** — **to you**
igualmente; **all the** — de todos modos
Samoa [səmóə] N Samoa *f*
Samoan [səmóən] ADJ & N samoano -na *mf*
sample [sǽmpəl] N muestra *f*; VT (try) probar;
(take samples) muestrear
sampling [sǽmplɪŋ] N muestreo *m*
sanatorium [sænətɔ́riəm] N sanatorio *m*
sanctify [sǽŋktəfaɪ] VT santificar
sanction [sǽŋkʃən] N sanción *f*; VT sancionar
sanctity [sǽŋktɪɒi] N santidad *f*
sanctuary [sǽŋktʃueri] N (church auditorium,
place of refuge) santuario *m*; (game preserve)
reserva *f*
sand [sænd] N arena *f*; —**box** arenero *m*; —
dollar erizo de mar plano *m*; —**paper** papel
de lija *m*; **to** —**paper** lijar; —**stone** arenisca
f; —**storm** tormenta de arena *f*; —**trap**
trampa de arena *f*; VT lijar, pulir
sandal [sǽndl] N sandalia *f*
sandwich [sǽndwɪtʃ] N bocadillo *m*,
emparedado *m*; VT intercalar; **to be** —**ed**
between quedar apretado entre
sandy [sǽndi] ADJ (full of sand) arenoso,
arenisco; (yellowish red) rubio
sane [sen] ADJ cuerdo
sang [sæŋ] *see* sing
sanitary [sǽnɪteri] ADJ sanitario; — **napkin**
paño higiénico *m*
sanitation [sænɪtéʃən] N (sewers) saneamiento
m; (hygiene) salubridad *f*
sanity [sǽnɪɒi] N cordura *f*
sank [sæŋk] *see* sink
San Marinese [sænmærəníz] ADJ & N

sanmarinense *mf*, sanmarinés -esa *mf*
San Marino [sænməríno] N San Marino *m*
Sanskrit [sǽnskrɪt] N sánscrito *f*
Santa Claus [sǽntəklɔz] N Papá Noel *m*, Santa
Claus *m*
São Tomean [saʊtoméən] ADJ & N santotomense
mf
São Tome and Principe [saʊtoméændprínsipe]
N Santo Tomé y Príncipe *m*
sap [sæp] N (juice) savia *f*; (fool) tonto -ta *mf*; VT
(exhaust) agotar
sapling [sǽplɪŋ] N (tree) árbol joven *m*; (person)
jovenzuelo -la *mf*
sapphire [sǽfaɪr] N zafiro *m*
sarcasm [sárkæzəm] N sarcasmo *m*,
socarronería *f*
sarcastic [sarkǽstɪk] ADJ sarcástico, socarrón
sarcoma [sarkómə] N sarcoma *m*
sarcophagus [sarkáfəgəs] N sarcófago *m*
sardine [sardín] N sardina *f*
sardonic [sardánɪk] ADJ sardónico
sash [sæʃ] N (around waist) faja *f*; (around
shoulder) banda *f*; (on window) marco *m*,
bastidor *m*
sassy [sǽsi] ADJ insolente
sat [sæt] *see* sit
satanic [sətǽnɪk] ADJ satánico
satchel [sǽtʃəl] N cartera *f*
satellite [sǽdlaɪt] N satélite *m*; — **dish** [antena]
parabólica *f*
satiate [séʃiet] VT saciar, hartar
satin [sǽtn̩] N raso *m*, satén *m*
satire [sǽtaɪr] N sátira *f*
satirical [sətírɪkəl] ADJ satírico
satirize [sǽɒəraɪz] VT satirizar
satisfaction [sædɪsfǽkʃən] N satisfacción *f*
satisfactory [sædɪsfǽktəri] ADJ satisfactorio
satisfied [sǽdɪsfaɪd] ADJ satisfecho
satisfy [sǽdɪsfaɪ] VI/VT satisfacer
saturate [sǽtʃəret] VI/VT (impregnate)
saturar[se]; (soak) empapar[se]; —**d fat** grasa
saturada *f*
Saturday [sǽɒəɒe] N sábado *m*
sauce [sɔs] N salsa *f*; —**pan** cacerola *f*; VT
aderezar con salsa
saucer [sɔ́sɚ] N platillo *m*
saucy [sɔ́si] ADJ (insolent) fresco, descarado,
insolente; (who talks back) respondón
Saudi Arabia [sɔ́ɒɪərébiə] N Arabia Saudí *f*,
Arabia Saudita *f*
Saudi Arabian [sɔ́ɒɪərébiən] ADJ & N saudí *mf*,
saudita *mf*
saunter [sɔ́ntɚ] VI pasearse, deambular
sausage [sɔ́sɪʤ] N (thick) chorizo *m*; (thin)
salchicha *f*; (cured) longaniza *f*; —-**making**
charcutería *f*
savage [sǽvɪʤ] ADJ (uncivilized) salvaje;
(furious) rabioso; (rugged) agreste; N salvaje
m; VT hacer trizas de

savagery [sǽvɪʤri] N salvajismo *m*, barbarie *f*
savannah [səvǽnə] N sabana *f*
save [sev] VT (a sinner, a person in danger) salvar; (furniture) salvaguardar, proteger; (money, time, energy) ahorrar, economizar; (data) guardar; VI (lay up money, be economical) ahorrar; (protect) salvaguardar; **to — from** librar de; **— as** (on a computer) almacenar como, guardar como; **to — one's eyes** cuidarse la vista; N (in baseball) salvado *m*; PREP salvo, menos
savings [sévɪŋz] N ahorros *m pl*; **— account** cuenta de ahorros *f*; **— bank** caja de ahorros *f*
savior [sévjɚ] N salvador -ora *mf*
savor [sévɚ] N (taste) sabor *m*; (trace) dejo *m*; VT saborear
savory [sévəri] ADJ (delicious) sabroso; (not sweet) salado
savvy [sǽvi] N astucia *f*; ADJ astuto
saw [sɔ] N sierra *f*; **—horse** caballete *m*; VI/VT aserrar[se]; **—dust** aserrín *m*, serrín *m*; **—mill** aserradero *m*
saw [sɔ] *see* see
sawn [sɔn] *see* saw
saxophone [sǽksəfon] N saxofón *m*
say [se] VT (something interesting) decir; (a prayer) rezar; VI (a clock) marcar; (a sign) rezar, decir; **—!** ¡oye! **that is to —** es decir; **— I bought it** supongamos que yo lo comprara; **it goes without —ing** huelga decir[lo]; **there's a lot to be said for** es muy recomendable; **when all is said and done** al fin y al cabo; **you can — that again** tú lo has dicho; N **the final —** la última palabra; **to have one's —** dar su opinión; ADV **you could earn, —, a million dollars** podrías ganar, pongamos, un millón de dólares
saying [séɪŋ] N dicho *m*, refrán *m*
scab [skæb] N (of a wound) costra *f*; (on plants) roña *f*; (strikebreaker) esquirol *m*, amarillo -lla *mf*; VI (wound) formar una costra; (break a strike) ser esquirol
scabby [skǽbi] ADJ (wound) costroso; (plant) roñoso
scaffold [skǽfəld] N (in construction) andamio *m*; (of a gallows) patíbulo *m*
scald [skɔld] VI/VT escaldar[se]; N escaldadura *f*
scale [skel] N (progression) escala *f*; (for weighing) balanza *f*; (heavy-duty) báscula *f*; (on fish, reptiles, human skin) escama *f*; **pair of —s** balanza *f*; VT (climb) escalar; (remove scales) escamar; VI/VT (adjust proportionately) graduar, escalar; **to — down** rebajar proporcionalmente
scallion [skǽljən] N cebollino *m*
scallop [skǽləp] N (mollusk) vieira *f*; (of beef) escalope *m*; (of fabric) festón *m*; VT festonear
scalp [skælp] N cuero cabelludo *m*; VT (to skin) arrancar la cabellera; (to resell) revender

scalpel [skǽlpəl] N bisturí *m*
scalper [skǽlpɚ] N revendedor -ora *mf*
scam [skæm] N timo *m*, estafa *f*
scamp [skæmp] N pícaro -ra *mf*, tunante -ta *mf*, pillo -lla *mf*
scamper [skǽmpɚ] VI (run) escabullirse, escaparse; (caper) cabriolar
scan [skæn] VT (horizon) escudriñar, escrutar; (brain) hacer una tomografía; (page) echar un vistazo a; (verse) escandir; (digitalize for computer) escanear; N tomografía *f*
scandal [skǽndl] N escándalo *m*
scandalize [skǽndlaɪz] VT escandalizar
scandalous [skǽndləs] ADJ escandaloso
scanner [skǽnɚ] N escáner *m*
scanning [skǽnɪŋ] N escaneado *m*
scant [skænt] ADJ escaso
scanty [skǽnti] ADJ (provisions) escaso; (skirt) muy corto; (bikini) breve
scapegoat [sképgot] N chivo expiatorio *m*, cabeza de turco *m*
scapula [skǽpjələ] N escápula *f*, omóplato *m*
scar [skar] N cicatriz *f*, lacra *f*; VT dejar una cicatriz
scarce [skers] ADJ escaso; **to be —** escasear
scarcely [skérsli] ADV (barely) apenas; **he's — a genius** no es un genio ni mucho menos
scarcity [skérsɪDi] N escasez *f*, pobreza *f*, carestía *f*
scare [sker] VI/VT espantar[se], asustar[se]; **to — away** ahuyentar; **to — up** reunir; N susto *m*, sobresalto *m*; (of war, of a heart attack) amago *m*; **—crow** espantapájaros *m sg*
scared [skerd] ADJ asustado; **I'm — of spiders** tengo miedo de las arañas / las arañas me dan miedo
scarf [skarf] N (woolen) bufanda *f*; (silk, cotton) pañuelo *m*; VI **to — up** engullir
scarlet [skárlɪt] N escarlata *m*, grana *f*; **— fever** escarlatina *f*
scary [skéri] ADJ (causing fright) de miedo; (easily frightened) asustadizo
scat [skæt] INTERJ ¡fuera!
scatter [skǽDɚ] VI/VT (seeds) esparcir[se], desparramar[se], desperdigar[se]; (crowd) dispersar[se]; **—brained** atolondrado; N **—brain** cabeza de chorlito *mf*
scattered [skǽDɚd] ADJ disperso
scavenge [skǽvɪnʤ] VT recoger, rescatar; VI hurgar
scenario [sɪnério] N guión *m*; **worst-case —** el peor de los casos
scene [sin] N escena *f*; (sphere of activity) ambiente *m*, ámbito *m*; **to make a —** montar una escena; **behind the —s** entre bastidores
scenery [sínəri] N paisaje *m*; (on a stage) decorado *m*
scenic [sínɪk] ADJ panorámico
scent [sent] N (smell) olor *m*; (fragrance)

perfume *m*; (trace) pista *f*, rastro *m*; (sense of smell) olfato *m*; VI/VT (perceive through smell) olfatear; (intuit) presentir; (give fragrance to) perfumar

schedule [skédʒʊł] N (plan) calendario *m*; (timetable) horario *m*; (appendix) apéndice *m*; (list) lista *f*; **on** — al día, a la hora prevista; **ahead of** — adelantado; VT programar, fijar

scheme [skim] N (plan) plan *m*, proyecto *m*; (plot) ardid *m*, trama *f*; (of colors) combinación *f*; VI/VT maquinar, intrigar, tramar

schemer [skímə-] N maquinador -ora *mf*, intrigante *mf*

scheming [skímɪŋ] ADJ intrigante; N maquinación *f*

schizophrenia [skɪtsəfréniə] N esquizofrenia *f*

schmuck [ʃmʌk] N *pej* pendejo -ja *mf*, *pej* gilipollas *mf sg*

scholar [skálə-] N (student) alumno -na *mf*; (fellow) becario -ria *mf*; (erudite person) erudito -ta *mf*, estudioso -sa *mf*

scholarly [skálə-li] ADJ erudito

scholarship [skálə-ʃɪp] N (erudition) erudición *f*; (award) beca *f*

school [skuł] N (primary) escuela *f*, colegio *m*; (secondary) secundaria *f*; *Sp* instituto *m*; (university) universidad *f*; (of law, etc.) facultad *f*; (of language, driving) academia *f*; (of thought) escuela *f*; (of fish) banco *m*, cardumen *m*; —**boy** escolar *m*; —**girl** escolar *f*; —**house** escuela *f*; —**master** maestro -tra *mf*; —**mate** compañero -ra de escuela *mf*; —**room** aula *f*, sala de clase *f*; —**teacher** maestro -tra *mf*; — **year** año lectivo *m*; VT instruir, entrenar

schooling [skúlɪŋ] N instrucción *f*

schooner [skúnə-] N goleta *f*

sciatic nerve [saɪǽDɪknɝv] N nervio ciático *m*

science [sáɪəns] N ciencia *f*; — **fiction** ciencia ficción *f*

scientific [saɪəntífɪk] ADJ científico; — **method** método científico *m*

scientist [sáɪəntɪst] N científico -ca *mf*

scintillate [síntļet] VI (diamonds) centellear, destellar; (stars) titilar

scissor [sízə-z] VT cortar con tijera; N —**s** tijera *f*, tijeras *f pl*; — **kick** tijera *f*, tijereta *f*

sclerosis [sklərósɪs] N esclerosis *f*

scoff [skaf] N mofa *f*, burla *f*; VI mofarse; **to** — **at** mofarse de, burlarse de

scold [skołd] VI/VT reprender, regañar, reñir; N regañón -ona *mf*

scolding [skółdɪŋ] N regaño *m*, reprimenda *f*

scoliosis [skoliósɪs] N escoliosis *f*

scoop [skup] N (ladle) cucharón *m*; (spoon for ice cream) cuchara *f*; (shovel) pala *f*; (news item) primicia *f*; VT sacar con cuchara; (report first) adelantarse a; **to** — **in a good profit** sacar buena ganancia; **to** — **out** (water) achicar; (a hole) cavar; **to** — **up** recoger

scoot [skut] VI (go fast) correr; (go away) largarse

scooter [skúDə-] N (with motor) scooter *m*; (toy) monopatín *m*, patinete *m*

scope [skop] N (range) alcance *m*, ámbito *m*; (sphere) esfera *f*; VT observar

scorch [skɔrtʃ] VI/VT chamuscar[se], quemar[se]; N chamuscadura *f*; Am quemadura *f*

score [skor] N (partial result) tanteo *m*; (total result) resultado *m*; (on a test) calificación *f*; (scratch) arañazo *m*; (twenty) veintena *f*; (of music) partitura *f*; —**board** marcador *m*; **on that** — a ese respecto; **to keep** — llevar la cuenta; **to settle old** —**s** ajustar cuentas; **what is the** —? ¿cómo va el marcador? VT (grade) calificar; (orchestrate) orquestar; (scratch) arañar; VI/VT (make points) marcar, tantear; (hook up with someone) ligar; **to** — **a goal** marcar/meter un gol

scorn [skɔrn] N desdén *m*, menosprecio *m*; VI/VT desdeñar, menospreciar

scornful [skɔrnfəł] ADJ desdeñoso

scorpion [skɔrpiən] N escorpión *m*, alacrán *m*

Scotch [skatʃ] ADJ escocés; — **whisky** whisky escocés *m*

Scotland [skátlənd] N Escocia *f*

Scotsman [skátsmən] N escocés *m*

Scotswoman [skátswʊmən] N escocesa *f*

Scottish [skáDɪʃ] ADJ escocés

scoundrel [skáʊndrəł] N bellaco *m*, infame *m*, truhán *m*

scour [skaʊr] VT (clean) fregar, restregar; (search an area) inspeccionar

scourge [skɝdʒ] N (affliction, means of affliction) azote *m*; VT azotar

scout [skaʊt] N (military) explorador -ora *mf*; (child explorer) explorador -ora *mf*, scout *mf*; (for talent) cazatalentos *mf sg*; **a good** — una buena persona; VI/VT explorar; VI **to** — **for** buscar

scowl [skaʊł] N ceño fruncido *m*; VI fruncir el ceño

scram [skræm] VI largarse

scramble [skrǽmbəł] VI (climb) subir a gatas; **to** — **for** pelearse por; **to** — **up** subir a gatas; VT (eggs) revolver; (numbers) mezclar; —**d eggs** huevos revueltos *m pl*; N (difficult climb) subida difícil *f*; (struggle for possession) arrebatiña *f*

scrap [skræp] N (fragment) fragmento *m*, pedacito *m*; (of truth) ápice *m*; (fight) riña *f*, reyerta *f*; —**book** álbum de recortes *m*; — **iron** chatarra *f*; — **paper** papel borrador *m*; —**s** sobras *f pl*, desperdicios *m pl*; VT (break apart) desguazar; (discard) desechar; VI (fight) pelearse, reñir

scrape [skrep] VI/VT (rub) raspar; (damage) arañar; **to** — **along** ir tirando, ir pasándola;

to — by arreglárselas; **to — together**
reunir; **to bow and —** ser muy servil; N (act
of scraping) raspado *m*; (injury) raspón *m*,
raspadura *f*; (sound) chirrido *m*; (fight) pelea
f; (difficult situation) aprieto *m*
scraper [skrépə-] N raspador *m*
scratch [skrætʃ] VI/VT (mark) arañar, rasguñar;
(relieve itching) rascar[se]; (cancel from a
race) retirar[se]; (cause itching) picar; VI (to
dig, as a hen) escarbar; **to — out** (words)
tachar; (eyes) sacar; N (injury) arañazo *m*,
rasguño *m*; (sound) chirrido *m*; **to start
from —** empezar de cero; **— test** examen
dérmico de alergias *m*
scrawny [skrɔ́ni] ADJ esmirriado
scream [skrim] N grito *m*, alarido *m*; **he's a —** es
un payaso; VI/VT gritar
screech [skritʃ] N (of brakes) chirrido *m*; (of
voice) chillido *m*; **— owl** lechuza *f*; VI (of
brakes) chirriar; (of voice) chillar
screen [skrin] N (movie, computer) pantalla *f*;
(divider) biombo *m*; (on window) mosquitero
m; (sifter) tamiz *m*; **— door** puerta con
mosquitero *f*; **—ing test** prueba de detección
f; **—pass** pase pantalla *m*; **—play** guión *m*; **—
saver** protector de pantalla *m*, salvapantallas
m sg; **—writer** guionista *mf*; VT (conceal)
tapar; (sift) tamizar; (project) proyectar;
(select) seleccionar
screw [skru] N (device) tornillo *m*; (one turn)
vuelta *f*; (propeller) hélice *f*; (sexual
intercourse) *fam* polvo *m*; **—driver**
destornillador *m* (also cocktail); VT (turn)
atornillar; (have intercourse) *Sp vulg* follar;
Am vulg coger, culear; **to — on** enroscar; **to
— up one's courage** cobrar ánimo; **to —
around** (waste time) perder tiempo; (be
promiscuous) ser promiscuo; **to —
something up** *vulg* chingar algo, joder algo;
I —ed up *vulg* la cagué; **to — with** *vulg*
chingar
scribble [skríbəl] VI/VT garabatear, garrapatear;
N garabato *m*
scrimp [skrɪmp] VI hacer economías
script [skrɪpt] N (writing) escritura *f*;
(screenplay) guión *m*
scripture [skrɪptʃə-] N escritura sagrada *f*
scroll [skroł] N (roll) rollo *m*; (adornment) voluta
f; VI **to — down** bajar el cursor
scrotum [skróDəm] N escroto *m*
scrub [skrʌb] VI/VT (rub) fregar, restregar; **to —
up** lavarse las manos; VT (cancel) cancelar; N
(cleaning) friega *f*, fregada *f*; (bushes) maleza
f; (rough terrain) breña *f*; **— pine** pino
achaparrado *m*; **— team** equipo suplente *m*;
—woman fregona *f*
scruple [skrúpəl] N escrúpulo *m*
scrupulous [skrúpjələs] ADJ escrupuloso
scrutinize [skrútṇaɪz] VI/VT escrutar,

escudriñar
scrutiny [skrútṇi] N escrutinio *m*, examen
minucioso *m*
scuba [skúbə] N escafandra *f*; VI **to — -dive**
bucear
scuff [skʌf] VT (shoes) rayar; (floor) marcar; N
(on shoes) raya *f*; (on floor) marca *f*
scuffle [skʌ́fəł] N refriega *f*, riña *f*; VI (fight)
pelear, reñir; (shuffle) arrastrar los pies
sculptor [skʌ́lptə-] N escultor -ora *mf*
sculpture [skʌ́lptʃə-] N escultura *f*; VI/VT
esculpir
scum [skʌm] N (in a glass) capa de suciedad *f*; (on
a pond) verdín *m*; (people) *pej* escoria *f*; (vile
person) *pej* canalla *mf*; **—bag** *pej* canalla *mf*; VI
cubrirse de espuma; VT espumar
scurrilous [skɜ́-ələs] ADJ (coarse) grosero
scurry [skɜ́-i] VI correr; **to — away/off**
escabullirse
scurvy [skɜ́-vi] N escorbuto *m*
scuttle [skʌ́dļ] VI (run) correr; **to — away/off**
escabullirse; VT (sink a ship) hundir;
(abandon a plane) abandonar
scythe [saɪð] N guadaña *f*
sea [si] N mar *mf*; **— battle** batalla naval *f*;
—board costa *f*, litoral *m*; **—coast** costa *f*,
litoral *m*; **— cow** vaca marina *f*; **— current**
corriente marina *f*; **—food** frutos del mar *m*
pl; **— green** verdemar *m*; **—gull** gaviota *f*; **—
horse** caballito de mar *m*; **— lion** léon marino *m*; **—man**
marino *m*, marinero *m*; **—plane** hidroavión
m; **—port** puerto de mar *m*; **— power**
potencia naval *f*; **—shore** costa *f*;
—sickness mareo *m*; **—side** costa *f*, litoral
m; **— turtle** tortuga marina *f*; **— urchin**
erizo de mar *m*; **—weed** alga [marina] *f*; **at —**
(on the ocean) en el mar; (confused) perdido;
by — por barco; **to put to —** hacerse a la
mar; **on the high —s** en alta mar; ADJ
marino; **—faring** marinero; **—sick**
mareado; **to get —sick** marearse; **—worthy**
marinero
seal [sił] N (stamp) sello *m*; (on a jar) precinto *m*;
(animal) foca *f*; **to set one's — to** sellar; VT
(put a seal on) sellar; (close with a seal)
precintar; **—ing wax** lacre *m*; **to — one's
fate** determinar el destino de uno; **to — off**
acordonar; **to — in** cerrar herméticamente;
to — with wax lacrar
seam [sim] N (sewing) costura *f*; (in rock) grieta *f*;
(in ore deposits) veta *f*; VT coser
seamstress [símstrɪs] N costurera *f*
seamy [sími] ADJ sórdido
sear [sir] VT chamuscar
search [sɜ-tʃ] VI/VT (an area) rastrear, requisar; (a
suitcase) registrar; (a person) cachear; **— me!**
¡a mí que me registren! ¡yo que sé! **to — for**
buscar; N (for something) búsqueda *f*; (of

baggage, ships) registro *m*; (of an area) rastreo *m*; — **and replace** buscar y reemplazar; — **engine** motor de búsqueda *m*, máquina de búsqueda *f*; — **function** función de búsqueda *f*; —**light** reflector *m*; — **warrant** orden de registro *m*; **in** — **of** en busca de

season [sízən] N (of the year) estación *f*; (period of time) temporada *f*, época *f*; (sports schedule) temporada *f*; **in** — en temporada/época; — **ticket** billete de abono *m*; **open** — temporada de caza/pesca *f*; **out of** — fuera de temporada/época; VT (to spice) sazonar, aderezar; VI (wood) secarse; **a** —**ed pilot** un piloto experimentado

seasonal [sízənəł] ADJ estacional

seasoning [sízənɪŋ] N condimento *m*, aliño *m*

seat [sit] N (furniture) asiento *m*; (of bicycle) sillín *m*; (in parliament) escaño *m*; (of government) sede *f*; (in the theater) localidad *f*; (buttocks) asentaderas *f pl*; (of clothes) fondillos *m pl*; **to take a** — sentarse, tomar asiento; — **belt** cinturón de seguridad *m*; VT (cause to sit) sentar; (accommodate with seats) tener capacidad para; (place) colocar; **to** — **oneself** sentarse

seborrhea [sebəría] N seborrea *f*

seclude [sɪklúd] VT aislar; **to** — **oneself from** recluirse de, aislarse de

secluded [sɪklúDɪd] ADJ apartado, aislado, recogido

seclusion [sɪklúʒən] N recogimiento *m*, aislamiento *m*

second [sékənd] ADJ segundo; — **base** segunda base *f*, intermedia *f*; — **baseman** segunda base *mf*, camarero -ra *mf*, intermediarista *mf*; — **child** segundón -ona *mf*; — **cousin** primo -ma segundo -da *mf*; — **fiddle** segundón -ona *mf*; — **floor** primer piso *m*; — **half** (sports) segundo tiempo *m*; —**hand** de segunda mano; — **lieutenant** subteniente *mf*; — **mortgage** segunda hipoteca *f*; — **nature** automático; —**rate** mediocre, de segunda; **to get** —**s** repetir, servirse por segunda vez; — **serve** segundo servicio *m*; **on** — **thought** pensándolo bien; N (part of a minute) segundo *m*; (helper in a duel) padrino *m*; —**s** (inferior wares) artículos de segunda *m pl*; (additional helping) segunda ración *f*; **in a** — ahorita; **may I have** —**s?** ¿puedo repetir? VT (support) secundar, apoyar; (assist in duels) apadrinar; (support a motion) apoyar; **to** —- **guess** cuestionar

secondary [sékəndɛri] ADJ secundario; — **school** escuela secundaria *f*

secondly [sékəndli] ADV en segundo lugar

secrecy [síkrɪsi] N secreto *m*

secret [síkrɪt] ADJ & N secreto *m*

secretariat [sɛkrɪtǽriət] N secretaría *f*

secretary [sékrɪtɛri] N (assistant) secretario -ria *mf*; (government) ministro -tra *mf*; (furniture) escritorio *m*

secrete [sɪkrít] VT (discharge) secretar, segregar; (hide) ocultar

secretion [sɪkríʃən] N secreción *f*

secretive [síkrɪDɪv] ADJ hermético

sect [sɛkt] N secta *f*

section [sékʃən] N (component) sección *f*; (of a chapter) apartado *m*; (of a text) trozo *m*; (of a city) sector *m*; (incision) corte *m*; (of orange) gajo *m*; VT seccionar

sector [séktə] N sector *m*

sectorial [sɛktóriəł] ADJ sectorial

secular [sékjələ] ADJ secular; N (person) seglar *mf*, lego -ga *mf*

secure [sɪkjúr] ADJ (certain, safe) seguro; (firm) firme; VT (make certain, guarantee) asegurar, afianzar; (make firm) afirmar, cimentar; (obtain) obtener; (protect) proteger; (lock) cerrar con llave; (capture) capturar; (tie) amarrar

security [sɪkjúrɪDi] N (safety, freedom from worry) seguridad *f*; (guarantee) fianza *f*, garantía *f*; (guarantor) fiador -ora *mf*; — **deposit** depósito de garantía *m*; **securities** valores *m pl*

sedan [sɪdǽn] N sedán *m*

sedate [sɪdét] ADJ sosegado, tranquilo; VT sedar

sedation [sɪdéʃən] N sedación *f*

sedative [sédətɪv] ADJ & N calmante *m*, sedante *m*

sedentary [sédn̩tɛri] ADJ sedentario

sediment [sédəmənt] N sedimento *m*; (dregs) heces *f pl*

sedition [sɪdíʃən] N sedición *f*

seduce [sɪdús] VI/VT seducir [a]

seduction [sɪdʌ́kʃən] N seducción *f*

see [si] VI/VT (perceive, find out, meet, visit) ver; (understand) entender; (make sure) fijarse, asegurarse; (date) salir con; —**ing-eye dog** perro guía *m*; **let me** — a ver; **to** — **to** encargarse de, atender; **to** — **off** despedir; **to** — **through someone** calar a alguien; **to** — **about** ocuparse de; **to** — **out** acompañar a la puerta; N sede *f*

seed [sid] N (grains) semilla *f*; (semen) simiente *f*; (in tennis) cabeza de serie *f*; **to go to** — echarse a perder; — **bed** semillero *m*; VI/VT (sow) sembrar; VT (remove seeds) despepitar, quitar las semillas; (player) clasificar; VI producir semillas

seedy [sídi] ADJ sórdido

seek [sik] VT (search for) buscar; (ask for) pedir; **to** — **after** buscar; **to** — **to** tratar de, esforzarse por

seem [sim] VI parecer; **they** — **to be here** parece que están aquí; **it** —**s to me** me parece

seemingly [símɪŋli] ADV aparentemente

seen [sin] *see* see

seep [sip] VI/VT rezumar[se]
seer [sir] N vidente *mf*
seesaw [síso] N balancín *m*, subibaja *m*; VI oscilar
seethe [sið] VI bullir, hervir; **he was seething** hervía de rabia
segment [ségmənt] N segmento *m*
segregate [ségrıget] VI/VT segregar
seismic [sáızmık] ADJ sísmico
seize [siz] VT (grab) asir, agarrar; (take possession) apoderarse de; (take advantage of) aprovecharse de; (confiscate) embargar, incautarse de, secuestrar; **to — upon** asir; VI **to — [up]** (mechanism, motor) agarrotarse; **to — upon** valerse de
seizure [síʒɚ] N (of power) toma *f*; (of property) confiscación *f*; (of drugs, guns) incautación *f*, secuestro *m*; (epileptic) ataque *m*
seldom [sέldəm] ADV rara vez, raramente
select [sılέkt] ADJ selecto; VI/VT elegir, seleccionar
selection [sılέkʃən] N selección *f*, elección *f*
selective [sılέktıv] ADJ selectivo
self [sεlf] N (ego) yo *m*; —**-assurance** desenvoltura *f*; —**-control** autocontrol *m*; —**-defense** defensa propia *f*; (juridical term) legítima defensa *f*; —**-denial** abnegación *f*; —**-determination** autodeterminación *f*; —**-discipline** autodisciplina *f*; —**-esteem** autoestima *f*; —**-government** autogobierno *m*; —**-help** autoayuda *f*; —**-image** autoimagen *f*; —**-improvement** mejora personal *f*; —**-interest** interés personal *m*; —**-made man** hombre que debe su éxito a sus propios esfuerzos *m*; —**-pity** autocompasión *f*; —**-reliance** independencia *f*, autosuficiencia *f*; —**-respect** amor propio *m*; —**-sacrifice** sacrificio *m*; —**-satisfaction** autosatisfacción *f*; **his better** — su lado bueno *m*; **his former** — lo que era antes; ADJ —**-assured** desenvuelto; —**-centered** egocéntrico; —**-composed** tranquilo; —**-confident** con confianza de sí mismo; —**-conscious** (shy) cohibido; (with complexes) acomplejado; —**-destructive** autodestructivo; —**-employed** que trabaja por cuenta propia; —**-evident** evidente; —**-explanatory** claro, fácil de entender; —**-propelled** autopropulsado; —**-righteous** que afecta superioridad moral; —**-satisfied** pagado de sí, satisfecho de sí; —**-service** autoservicio; —**-serving** interesado; —**-sufficient** autosuficiente
selfish [sέlfıʃ] ADJ egoísta
selfishness [sέlfıʃnıs] N egoísmo *m*
selfless [sέlflıs] ADJ desinteresado, generoso
sell [sεl] VI/VT vender[se]; **his books — well** se venden bien sus libros; **to be sold on** estar entusiasmado con; **to — off** liquidar; **to —**

out (dispose of) liquidar; (betray) traicionar, vender; (run out) agotarse; N —**-off** (liquidation) liquidación *f*; (decline) baja *f*; —**out** traición *f*
seller [sέlɚ] N vendedor -ora *mf*
selling [sέlıŋ] N venta *f*
semantics [sımǽntıks] N semántica *f*
semblance [sέmbləns] N apariencia *f*
semen [símın] N semen *m*
semester [səmέstɚ] N semestre *m*
semicircle [sέmısɚkəł] N semicírculo *m*
semicolon [sέmıkolən] N punto y coma *m*
semiconductor [sεmikəndʌktɚ] N semiconductor *m*
semifinal [sέmifaınł] ADJ & N semifinal *f*
seminar [sέmənɑr] N seminario *m*
seminary [sέmənεri] N seminario *m*
Semitic [səmídık] ADJ semítico
senate [sέnıt] N senado *m*
senator [sέnətɚ] N senador -ora *mf*
send [sεnd] VT enviar, mandar; **that sent chills down my spine** me dio escalofríos; **to — away** hacer salir; **to — back** devolver; **to — for** mandar buscar a; **to — in** remitir; **to — out for** encargar; **to — word** mandar decir
sender [sέndɚ] N remitente *m*
Senegal [sέnıgɔł] N Senegal *m*
Senegalese [sεnıgəlíz] ADJ & N senegalés -esa *mf*
senile [sínaıł] ADJ senil, chocho
senility [sınílıDi] N senilidad *f*, chochera *f*, chochez *f*
senior [sínjɚ] ADJ (with more seniority) más antiguo; (in school) de cuarto año; (for the elderly) para ancianos; **John Smith —** John Smith padre; N (person of higher rank) superior *mf*; (fourth-year student) estudiante de cuarto año *mf*; (elderly person) persona de la tercera edad *f*; **to be somebody's —** ser mayor que alguien; **— citizen** persona de la tercera edad *f*; **— partner** socio -cia principal *mf*
seniority [sinjɔ́rıDi] N antigüedad *f*
sensation [sεnséʃən] N sensación *f*
sensational [sεnséʃənł] ADJ sensacional
sense [sεns] N (of humor, honor, direction) sentido *m*; (of pain, insecurity) sensación *f*; (meaning) significado *m*, sentido *m*; **— of hearing** sentido del oído *m*; **— of humor** sentido del humor *m*; **— of sight** sentido de la vista *m*; **— of smell** sentido del olfato *m*; **— of taste** sentido del gusto *m*; **— of touch** sentido del tacto *m*; **to make — of something** entender algo; **in a —** en cierto sentido; **to take leave of one's —s** volverse loco; **to come to one's —s** (wake up) volver en sí; (be reasonable) recobrar el juicio; VT (perceive) percibir, sentir; (intuit) intuir
senseless [sέnslıs] ADJ (meaningless) sin

sentido; (unconscious) inconsciente
sensibility [sɛnsəbílɪDi] N sensibilidad *f*
sensible [sɛ́nsəbəł] ADJ sensato, razonable,
juicioso
sensitive [sɛ́nsɪDɪv] ADJ (to emotions) sensible;
(to stimuli) sensitivo
sensitivity [sɛnsɪtívɪDi] N sensibilidad *f*
sensitize [sɛ́nsɪtaɪz] VT sensibilizar
sensor [sɛ́nsɔr] N sensor *m*
sensory [sɛ́nsəri] ADJ sensorial; — **overload**
sobrecarga sensorial *f*
sensual [sɛ́nʃuəł] ADJ sensual
sensuality [sɛnʃuǽlɪDi] N sensualidad *f*
sensuous [sɛ́nʃuəs] ADJ sensual
sent [sɛnt] *see* send
sentence [sɛ́ntəns] N (to prison) sentencia *f*,
condena *f*; (phrase) oración *f*; VT condenar,
sentenciar
sentiment [sɛ́ntəmənt] N sentimiento *m*
sentimental [sɛntəmɛ́ntḷ] ADJ sentimental;
(excessively) sensiblero
sentimentality [sɛntəmɛntǽlɪDi] N
sentimentalismo *m*; (excessive) sensibleria *f*
sentinel [sɛ́ntṇəł] N centinela *m*
sentry [sɛ́ntri] N centinela *m*; — **box** garita *f*
separate[1] [sɛ́prɪt] ADJ (apart) separado
separate[2] [sɛ́pəret] VI/VT separar[se]
separation [sɛpəréʃən] N separación *f*
Sephardi [səfárdi] N sefardí *mf*, sefardita *mf*
September [sɛptɛ́mbɚ] N septiembre *m*,
setiembre *m*
sequel [síkwəł] N continuación *f*
sequence [síkwəns] N secuencia *f*; (of events)
serie *f*; **in** — en orden; VT secuenciar
Serb [sɚb] N (person) serbio -bia *mf*
Serbian [sɚ́biən] ADJ serbio; N (language) serbio
m; (person) serbio -bia *mf*
serenade [sɛrənéd] N serenata *f*, ronda *f*; VI/VT
dar [una] serenata [a], rondar [a]
serene [sərín] ADJ sereno
serenity [sərɛ́nɪDi] N serenidad *f*
sergeant [sárdʒənt] N sargento *m*
serial [síriəł] N (novel) novela por entregas *f*; ADJ
(published in installments) por entregas;
(murder) en serie; — **bus** bus en serie *m*; —
connector conector en serie *m*; — **killer**
asesino -na en serie *mf*; — **mouse** ratón en
serie *m*; — **number** número de serie *m*; —
port puerto serie/serial *m*; — **printer**
impresora en serie *f*
series [síriz] N serie *f*
serious [síriəs] ADJ serio; (illness) grave
seriously [síriəsli] ADV (consider) en serio;
(injure) gravemente; —, **what do you
want?** hablando en serio, ¿qué es lo que
quieres?
seriousness [síriəsnɪs] N seriedad *f*; (of an
illness) gravedad *f*
sermon [sɚ́mən] N sermón *m*

serpent [sɚ́pənt] N sierpe *f*, serpiente *f*
serrated [sɛ́rɛDɪd] ADJ serrado
serum [sírəm] N suero *m*
servant [sɚ́vənt] N sirviente -ta *mf*, criado -da *mf*
serve [sɚv] VI/VT (in a restaurant, in a store)
servir, atender; (in tennis) sacar; **to** — **a
term in prison** cumplir una condena; **to** —
a warrant entregar una orden judicial; **to** —
as servir de; **to** — **notice** advertir; **to** —
one's purpose resultarle útil a alguien; **it
—s me right** me lo merezco; N (in tennis)
saque *m*; — **and volley** saque y volea *m*
server [sɚ́vɚ] N (one who serves) servidor -ora
mf; (in a restaurant) camarero -ra *mf*; (for pie)
utensilio para servir *m*; (computer) servidor
m; (tennis player) sacador -ora *mf*
service [sɚ́vɪs] N servicio *m*; (in tennis) saque *m*,
servicio *m*; (of a warrant) entrega *f*; — **break**
rotura de servicio *f*; — **entrance** entrada de
servicio *f*; —**man** (soldier) militar *m*; (for
repairs) reparador *m*; — **station** gasolinera *f*,
estación de servicio *f*; **at your** — a su
servicio; VT (a car) revisar; (an industry)
atender, servir; (a debt) pagar; **in-** —
training capacitación para empleados; **out
of** — (broken) averiado, fuera de servicio
serviceable [sɚ́vɪsəbəł] ADJ (practical) práctico;
(durable) duradero
servile [sɚ́vaɪł] ADJ servil
servitude [sɚ́vɪtud] N servidumbre *f*
sesame [sɛ́səmi] N sésamo *m*, ajonjolí *m*
session [sɛ́ʃən] N (meeting) sesión *f*; (semester)
semestre *m*; (of Congress) período de
sesiones *m*
set [sɛt] VT (place) colocar; (fix) fijar, establecer;
(sic) azuzar; (print) componer; VI (cement)
fraguar; (jelly) cuajar; (sun) ponerse; (glue)
endurecerse; **to** — **a bone** reducir un hueso
dislocado; **to** — **a diamond** engastar un
diamante; **to** — **an example** dar ejemplo; **to**
— **a poem to music** ponerle música a un
poema; **to** — **a precedent** establecer un
precedente; **to** — **a trap** tender una trampa;
to — **a watch** poner el reloj en hora; **to** —
about disponerse a; **to** — **aside** (move an
object) apartar; (money) ahorrar; (a claim)
rechazar; (a verdict) anular; **to** — **back**
(hinder, make earlier) atrasar; (cost) costar; (a
clock) retrasar; **to** — **forth** exponer; **to** —
forth on a journey ponerse en camino; **to**
— **free** librar; **to** — **off** (make explode) hacer
estallar; (start on a journey) ponerse en
camino; (intensify) resaltar; **to** — **one's
heart on** tener la esperanza puesta en; **to** —
one's mind on resolverse a; **to** — **out for**
partir para; **to** — **out to** proponerse; **to** —
right rectificar; **to** — **the table** poner la
mesa; **to** — **up** (assemble) armar; (set a trap
for) tender; (establish) establecer; (a

computer program) instalar; **to — upon
someone** acometer a alguien; ADJ (fixed)
fijo; (ready) listo; (hard) duro; N (ensemble)
juego *m*; (group) conjunto *m*; (TV) aparato *m*;
(scenery) escenario *m*; (of tennis) set *m*,
manga *f*; **—back** revés *m*; **— of teeth**
dentadura *f*; **— point** punto de set/manga *m*;
—up (arrangement) arreglo *m*; (assembly)
montaje *m*; (installation) instalación *f*; (trap)
tongo *m*, timo *m*; **—up program** programa
de instalación *m*

setter [sɛ́Dɚ] N sétter *m*

setting [sɛ́DIŋ] N (act of putting down)
colocación *f*; (jewel) engaste *m*; (in theater)
escenario *m*; (of sun, moon) puesta *f*; (of dial)
posición *f*; **— sun** sol poniente *m*

settle [sɛ́dl̩] VT (a territory) colonizar, poblar;
(affairs) arreglar; (argument) zanjar; (lawsuit)
arreglar; (an estate) liquidar; (a bill) saldar,
solventar; (one's nerves) calmar; VI (end a
dispute) llegar a un arreglo; (take up
residence) establecerse; (alight) posarse; (sink
to bottom) depositarse; **to — down** (get
married) casarse; (mend one's ways) sentar
cabeza; (take up residence) instalarse;
(become calm) calmarse; **to — on a date**
fijar/señalar una fecha; **to — for** conformarse
con; **to — up** pagar

settlement [sɛ́dl̩mənt] N (community) colonia *f*,
población *f*; (act of establishing)
asentamiento *m*; (agreement) acuerdo *m*; (of a
lawsuit) arreglo *m*; (of a bill) pago *m*, finiquito
m; (final disposition) liquidación *f*

settler [sɛ́tlɚ] N colono -na *mf*, poblador -ora *mf*

settling [sɛ́dl̩ɪŋ] N asentamiento *m*

seven [sɛ́vən] NUM siete; **— hundred**
setecientos

seventeen [sɛvəntín] NUM diecisiete

seventh [sɛ́vənθ] ADJ séptimo

seventy [sɛ́vənti] NUM setenta

sever [sɛ́vɚ] VT (an arm) cortar; (relations)
romper

several [sɛ́vəɫ] ADJ varios

severance pay [sɛ́vɚənspe] N indemnización
por despido *f*

severe [səvír] ADJ (criticism, standards) severo;
(winter, test) duro; (storm, heat) intenso;
(illness) grave

severity [səvɛ́rIDi] N (of criticism, standards)
severidad *f*; (of water, test) dureza *f*; (of
storm, heat) intensidad *f*; (of illness)
gravedad *f*

Sevillian [səvíɫjən] ADJ & N sevillano -na; **—
dances** sevillanas *f pl*

sew [so] VI/VT coser

sewage [súɪdʒ] N aguas negras *f pl*; **— system**
alcantarillado *m*

sewer [súɚ] N alcantarilla *f*, cloaca *f*, colector *m*

sewing [sóɪŋ] N costura *f*; **— machine** máquina

de coser *f*

sewn [son] *see* sew

sex [sɛks] N sexo *m*; **— appeal** atractivo sexual
m; **— symbol** símbolo sexual *m*; **to have —**
tener relaciones [sexuales]; VT sexar

sexism [sɛ́ksIzəm] N sexismo *m*

sexist [sɛ́ksIst] ADJ & N sexista *mf*

sexton [sɛ́kstən] N sacristán *m*

sexual [sɛ́kʃuəɫ] ADJ sexual; **— assault** violación
f; **— discrimination** discriminación sexual
f; **— harassment** acoso sexual *m*; **—
intercourse/relations** relaciones sexuales
f pl; **—ly transmitted disease** enfermedad
de transmisión sexual *f*

sexuality [sɛkʃuǽlIDi] N sexualidad *f*

sexy [sɛ́ksi] ADJ sexy, morboso

Seychelles [seʃɛ́ɫ] N Seychelles *f pl*

shabby [ʃǽbi] ADJ (worn) gastado; (slovenly)
andrajoso; (tawdry) sórdido; (mean)
mezquino; **not too —** no está mal

shack [ʃæk] N casucha *f*, choza *f*

shackle [ʃǽkəɫ] N grillete *m*; **—s** cadenas *f pl*,
grillos *m pl*; VT (put in chains) engrillar;
(impede) estorbar

shad [ʃæd] N sábalo *m*

shade [ʃed] N (shadow) sombra *f*; (nuance) matiz
m; (for windows) persiana *f*; (phantom)
espectro *m*; (of a lamp) pantalla *f*; **a — longer**
un poco más largo; **in the —** a la sombra; **—s**
(sunglasses) *Am* lentes negros/oscuros *m pl*;
Sp gafas de sol *f pl*; VT (protect from sun)
sombrear, dar sombra

shadow [ʃǽdo] N (dark image, shade) sombra *f*;
(phantom) espectro *m*; **in the — of** a la
sombra de; **without a — of doubt** sin
sombra de duda; VT (darken) sombrear;
(make gloomy) ensombrecer; **to — someone**
seguirle la pista a alguien

shady [ʃɛ́Di] ADJ sombreado, umbrío; **—
character** sospechoso -sa *mf*; **— dealings**
negocios turbios *m pl*

shaft [ʃæft] N (of a mine) pozo *m*; (of a feather)
cañón *m*; (of an elevator) hueco *m*; (of an
arrow) asta *f*

shaggy [ʃǽgi] ADJ peludo, lanudo

shake [ʃek] VI (tremble) temblar; VI/VT (move
back and forth) sacudir[se]; (in order to mix)
agitar[se]; (elude) deshacerse de; **to — hands**
darse la mano; **to — one's head** menear la
cabeza; **to — with cold** tiritar; **to — with
fear** temblar de miedo; **to — off** (a cold,
disappointment, etc.) deshacerse de;
(depression) librarse de; **to — up** (a liquid)
agitar; (a person) trastornar; N (violent)
sacudida *f*; (of milk) batido *m*; **hand—**
apretón de manos *m*; **the —s** escalofríos *m pl*;
—-up reorganización *f*

shaken [ʃékən] *see* shake

shaky [ʃéki] ADJ (hand) tembloroso; (start)

vacilante

shall [ʃæl] v AUX **I — come** vendré; **— I help you?** ¿te ayudo? **thou shalt not steal** no robarás

shallow [ʃælo] ADJ (plate) llano; (water) poco profundo; (breathing) superficial; (explanation) superficial, somero

shallowness [ʃælonɪs] N (of plate) lo llano; (of water) poca profundidad ƒ; (of person) superficialidad ƒ

sham [ʃæm] N (hoax) farsa ƒ; (impostor) impostor -ora mf; **— battle** simulacro de batalla m

shambles [ʃæmbəlz] N desorden m, caos m

shame [ʃem] N (embarrassment) vergüenza ƒ; (dishonor) deshonra ƒ; (pity) lástima ƒ; **— on you!** ¡qué vergüenza! **to bring — upon** deshonrar; VT avergonzar

shameful [ʃémfəl] ADJ vergonzoso

shameless [ʃémlɪs] ADJ desvergonzado, descarado

shamelessness [ʃémlɪsnɪs] N desvergüenza ƒ

shampoo [ʃæmpú] N (product) champú m; (act of washing) lavado del cabello m; VI/VT lavar con champú

shamrock [ʃæmrɑk] N trébol m

shank [ʃæŋk] N (part of leg) canilla ƒ, espinilla ƒ; (cut of meat) pierna ƒ, pata ƒ

shanty [ʃænti] N casucha ƒ; Sp chabola ƒ; **—town** suburbio m

shape [ʃep] N (form) forma ƒ; (condition) condición ƒ; (silhouette) bulto m; **to be in bad —** andar mal; **to get in —** ponerse en forma; **to take —** configurarse; VT plasmar, dar forma a; **to — up** reformarse

shapeless [ʃéplɪs] ADJ informe

share [ʃer] N (portion) parte ƒ, porción ƒ; (stock) acción ƒ; **—cropper** aparcero m; **—holder** accionista mf; VI/VT compartir; **to — in** participar en

shark [ʃɑrk] N (fish) tiburón m; (swindler) estafador -ora mf

sharp [ʃɑrp] ADJ (blade) afilado, filoso; (needle) puntiagudo; (curve) cerrado; (contrast) marcado, nítido; (smell) acre; (wind) cortante; (pain) punzante; (remark) mordaz, agudo; (mind) perspicaz; (musical note) sostenido; (dresser) elegante; (cheese) picante; (ear) fino; **— eye** vista aguzada ƒ; **—shooter** tirador -ora de primera mf; **--tongued** mordaz; **--witted** agudo; N (in music) sostenido m

sharpen [ʃárpən] VI/VT (knife) afilar[se]; VT (pencil) sacar punta a; (skill) afinar

sharply [ʃárpli] ADV (contrast) marcadamente; (respond) bruscamente, con aspereza; (turn) bruscamente

sharpness [ʃárpnɪs] N (of a blade) lo afilado; (of a needle) lo puntiagudo; (of a curve) lo

cerrado; (of a contrast) nitidez ƒ; (of a smell) acritud ƒ; (of pain) intensidad ƒ; (of a remark) mordacidad ƒ; (of a mind) perspicacia ƒ, agudeza ƒ; (of cheese) lo picante

shatter [ʃǽDɚ] VI/VT (glass) astillar[se], hacer[se] añicos; (nerves) destrozar[se]; (health) quebrantar[se]; (hopes) frustrar

shave [ʃev] VI/VT (remove hair) afeitar[se], rasurar[se]; VT (cut thin slices) cepillar; (graze) rozar; **to — off** rapar; N afeitado m, rasurado m; **he had a close —** se salvó por poco

shaven [ʃévən] see shave

shaver [shévɚ] N afeitadora ƒ

shavings [ʃévɪŋz] N virutas ƒ pl

shawl [ʃɔl] N mantón m, chal m

she [ʃi] PRON ella; **— who** la que, quien; N —- **bear** osa ƒ

sheaf [ʃif] N (of corn) gavilla ƒ; (of arrows) haz m; (of paper) fajo m

shear [ʃir] VT esquilar, trasquilar; N **—s** (for sheep) tijeras para esquilar ƒ pl; (for plants) tijeras para podar ƒ pl; (for metal) cizallas ƒ pl; (for hair) tijeras de peluquero ƒ pl

shearing [ʃírɪŋ] N esquila ƒ, esquileo m

sheath [ʃiθ] N (of sword, peas) vaina ƒ; (of knife, umbrella) funda ƒ

sheathe [ʃið] VT (a sword) envainar; (a knife) enfundar

shed [ʃɛd] N cobertizo m, tinglado m, Am galpón m; VT (tears) derramar; (light) arrojar; (leaves) perder; (skin, hair) mudar, perder; VI (be waterproof) ser impermeable; (lose hair) pelechar; (lose leaves) deshojarse; (lose skin) mudar la piel

sheen [ʃin] N brillo m

sheep [ʃip] N oveja ƒ; **—dog** perro pastor m, ovejero m; **—skin** (hide) piel de oveja ƒ; (leather) badana ƒ; (parchment) pergamino m; (diploma) diploma m

sheepish [ʃípɪʃ] ADJ vergonzoso, tímido

sheer [ʃir] ADJ (absolute) puro, total; (fine) fino; (vertical) vertical, acantilado

sheet [ʃit] N (bedding) sábana ƒ; (of ice) capa ƒ; (of glass) lámina ƒ; (of rain) cortina ƒ; **— metal** chapa de metal ƒ; **music** música en hojas de partitura ƒ

shelf [ʃɛlf] N estante m, repisa ƒ, anaquel m; (of rock) saliente ƒ

shell [ʃɛl] N (turtles, snail) caparazón ƒ; (of mollusk) concha ƒ; (of egg, nut) cáscara ƒ; (of peas) vaina ƒ; (of a ship) casco m; (of a building) armazón m; (of artillery) proyectil m; (of a rifle) cartucho m; **—fish** mariscos m pl; VT (nuts, eggs) pelar; (peas) desgranar; (military target) bombardear

shelter [ʃéltɚ] N (refuge) refugio m, resguardo m, abrigo m; **to take —** refugiarse, guarecerse; VI/VT (take or give refuge)

refugiar[se], resguardar[se], abrigar[se]
shelve [ʃɛɫv] VT (place on a shelf) colocar en un estante; (defer) archivar
shepherd [ʃépə·d] N pastor *m*; (dog) perro pastor *m*
sherbet [ʃɔ·bɪt] N sorbete *m*
sheriff [ʃérɪf] N alguacil *m*
sherry [ʃéri] N jerez *m*
shield [ʃiɫd] N escudo *m*; VI/VT (protect) escudar[se]; VT (conceal) ocultar
shift [ʃɪft] VI/VT (gears) cambiar; **to — for oneself** arreglárselas solo; **to — the blame** echar la culpa a otro; N (of gears, of wind) cambio *m*; (dress) vestido suelto *m*; (of workers) turno *m*; — **key** tecla de [cambio a] mayúsculas *f*
shiftless [ʃíftlɪs] ADJ holgazán
shimmer [ʃímə·] VI titilar; N titileo *m*
shin [ʃɪn] N espinilla *f*, canilla *f*; VI **to — up** trepar
shine [ʃaɪn] VI brillar, relucir; VT (shoes) limpiar, lustrar; (furniture) lustrar; N brillo *m*, resplandor *m*; (of shoes) lustre *m*
shingle [ʃíŋgəɫ] N (on roof) teja *f*; (sign) chapa *f*; —**s** (skin disorder) culebrilla *f*, zona *f*; **to hang out one's** — abrir un consultorio; VT cubrir con tejas
shiny [ʃáɪni] ADJ (bright) brillante; (worn) brilloso
ship [ʃɪp] N (on water) buque *m*, navío *m*; (in air) avión *m*; —**builder** constructor -ora naval *mf*; —**mate** camarada de a bordo *mf*; —**wreck** naufragio *m*; —**yard** astillero *m*; ADJ —**shape** ordenado; VT transportar; **to — off** sacarse de encima; VI **to —wreck** naufragar
shipment [ʃípmənt] N cargamento *m*, remesa *f*
shipper [ʃípə·] N (sender) expedidor -ora *mf*; (carrier) transportista *mf*
shipping [ʃípɪŋ] N envío *m*; — **charges** gastos de envío *m pl*; — **and handling** gastos de envío *m pl*
shirk [ʃɔ·k] VT evadir, esquivar, rehuir
shirt [ʃɔ·t] N camisa *f*; **in —sleeves** en mangas de camisa; —**tail** faldón *m*
shit [ʃɪt] N (excrement) *vulg* mierda *f*; (stuff) porquerías *f pl*; **the —s** *fam* cagalera; **that's a crock of** — y una polla [como una olla]; **he doesn't know** — *vulg* no sabe un carajo; **he's on my —list** estoy enojado con él; VI/VT (defecate) *vulg* cagar; (lie to) *vulg* joder; **to — bricks** *vulg* cagarse de miedo; INTERJ *vulg* carajo; *Sp vulg* joder
shitty [ʃíbi] ADJ *vulg* de mierda
shiver [ʃívə·] VI (from cold) tiritar; (from cold, fear, etc.) temblar; N temblor *m*; —**s** escalofríos *m pl*
shoal [ʃoɫ] N (sandbank) bajío *m*, banco de arena *m*; (school of fish) banco *m*, bandada *f*

shock [ʃak] N (impact, disturbance) choque *m*; (of electricity) sacudida *f*; (of wheat) hacina *f*; (physical convulsion) shock *m*, choque *m*; — **absorber** amortiguador *m*; — **of hair** guedeja *f*; — **therapy** terapia de electroshock *f*, terapia electroconvulsiva *f*; — **troops** tropas de choque *f pl*; — **wave** onda expansiva *f*; VT (bewilder) chocar, horrorizar; (discharge electricity) dar una descarga eléctrica; (make bundles of grain) hacinar, hacer gavillas de
shocking [ʃákɪŋ] ADJ chocante, escandaloso
shod [ʃad] *see* shoe
shoddy [ʃáDi] ADJ chapucero
shoe [ʃu] N zapato *m*; (for brakes) zapata *f*; (for horses) herradura *f*; —**horn** calzador *m*; —**lace** cordón *m*; —**maker** zapatero -ra *mf*; — **polish** betún *m*; — **repairman** zapatero -ra remendón -ona *mf*; — **store** zapatería *f*; —**string** cordón *m*; **to live on a —string** vivir con poco dinero; **to tie one's —s** atarse los zapatos; VT (a person) calzar; (a horse) herrar
shone [ʃon] *see* shine
shoo-in [ʃúin] N favorito -ta *mf*
shook [ʃuk] *see* shake
shoot [ʃut] VT (wound with a bullet) pegar un tiro; (discharge a firearm) disparar; (film a movie) rodar; (hit a soccer ball) chutar; VI (discharge bullet, arrow) disparar, tirar; (be discharged) dispararse; (hunt with a gun) cazar; (germinate) brotar; (throw) lanzar; (take a photo) fotografiar; (film) filmar; (try to score, in soccer) chutar; (try to score, in basketball) tirar; **to — at** disparar a, tirar a; **to — at goal** patear al arco; **to — by** pasar rápidamente; **to — down** (plane) derribar; (argument) refutar; **to — forth** brotar; **to — up** (grow) crecer rápidamente; (damage by shooting) tirotear; (inject drugs) chutar; N (new growth) yema *f*, retoño *m*, vástago *m*; (filming) rodaje *m*
shooter [ʃúDə·] N (of guns) tirador -ora *mf*; (of balls, soccer) goleador -ora *mf*
shooting [ʃúDɪŋ] N (discharge of a gun) tiro *m*, disparo *m*; (exchange of shots) tiroteo *m*; (filming) filmación *f*; — **guard** escolta *mf*; — **match** concurso de tiro *m*; — **pain** punzada *f*; — **star** estrella fugaz *f*
shop [ʃap] N (store) tienda *f*; (artisan's place of business, carpentry course) taller *m*; (business) planta *f*; —**keeper** tendero -ra *mf*; —**lifter** ladrón -ona de tiendas *mf*; —**lifting** hurto en las tiendas *m*; — **window** escaparate *m*, vitrina *f*; **to talk** — hablar de negocios; VI ir de compras; **to — for** ir a comprar; **to —lift** hurtar [en las tiendas]
shopper [ʃápə·] N cliente -ta *mf*, comprador -ora *mf*

shopping [ʃápɪŋ] N **to go** — ir de compras; — **center** centro comercial *m*

shore [ʃɔr] N costa *f*, ribera *f*; (of a lake) orilla *f*; VT **to** — **up** apuntalar

shorn [ʃɔrn] *see* shear

short [ʃɔrt] ADJ (not long in duration) corto, breve; (not long in length) corto; (not tall) bajo; (scanty) escaso; (curt) brusco; — **circuit** cortocircuito *m*; —**comings** limitaciones *f pl*; —**cut** atajo *m*, cortada *f*; —**fall** déficit *m*, insuficiencia *f*; —**hand** taquigrafía *f*; —- **handed** escaso de personal; —-**legged** pernicorto; —**sighted** miope, corto de vista; — **stop** torpedero -ra *mf*, campocorto *mf*; — **story** cuento *m*; —**wave** onda corta *f*; **in the** — **run/haul/term** a corto plazo; **for** — para abreviar; **in** — en resumen, en suma; **in** — **order** rápidamente; **to be** — **on** estar escaso de, estar alcanzado de; **to be** — **on something** faltarle a uno algo; **to cut** — interrumpir; **I'm running** — **on sugar** se me está acabando el azúcar; ADV **to stop** — parar de repente, parar en seco; **to come up** — quedarse corto; N (circuit) cortocircuito *m*; —**s** short *m*, pantalón corto *m*; VI/VT (a circuit) cortocircuitar[se]; (change) dar de menos; **to** —**change** dar de menos; **to** — **out** fundir

shortage [ʃɔ́rDɪʤ] N escasez *f*, penuria *f*

shorten [ʃɔ́rtn̩] VI/VT acortar[se]; VT recortar

shortening [ʃɔ́rtnɪŋ] N (lard) manteca *f*; (abbreviation) acortamiento *m*

shortly [ʃɔ́rtli] ADJ (soon) en breve, pronto; (curtly) bruscamente, secamente

shortness [ʃɔ́rtnɪs] N (of length, height) cortedad *f*; (of time) brevedad *f*; (of breath) falta *f*; (of a reply) brusquedad *f*

shot [ʃɑt] N (discharge) tiro *m*, disparo *m*; (photograph) foto *f*; (pellet) perdigón *m*, plomo *m*; (ball in shot-putting) bala *f*; (injection) inyección *f*; (swallow) trago *m*; (throw) tirada *f*; (in soccer) tiro *m*, disparo *m*; —**gun** escopeta *f*; — **put** lanzamiento de bala *m*; **not by a long** — ni con mucho; **he is a good** — tiene buena puntería; **to take a** — disparar; **to take a** — **at** intentar

shot [ʃɑt] *see* shoot

should [ʃud] V AUX **I** — **think so** ya lo creo; **you** — **arrive before nine** deberías llegar antes de las nueve; **you** — **eat less** tendrías que comer menos; **you** — **have seen her** tendrías que haberla visto; **were he to come, I** — **be pleased** si viniera, me alegraría

shoulder [ʃóɫdɚ] N (of a person, coat) hombro *m*; (cut of meat) paletilla *f*; (of a road) arcén *m*; — **blade** (person) homóplato *m*; (animal) paletilla *f*; — **pad** hombrera *f*; **to turn a cold** — **to** hacerle el vacío a; **the responsibility**

is on your —**s** tú tienes la responsabilidad; VT (a load) cargar al hombro; (a task, an expense) cargar con, asumir; (a door) empujar con el hombro

shout [ʃaut] VI/VT gritar; N grito *m*

shove [ʃʌv] VI/VT empujar; **to** — **aside** echar a un lado; **to** — **off** (go away) largarse; (push off) desatracar; N empujón *m*, empellón *m*

shovel [ʃʌ́vəɫ] N pala *f*; VT echar con la pala

show [ʃo] VT (exhibit) mostrar, manifestar; (prove) demostrar; (indicate) indicar, marcar; (a film, a TV program) dar; VI (be visible) verse, asomar; (make an appearance) aparecerse; — **him in** hazle entrar; **to** —**case** presentar; **to** — **mercy** tener piedad; **to** — **off** hacer alarde, aparentar; **to** — **up** aparecer; **to** — **someone up** poner a alguien en evidencia; **to** — **the way** señalar el camino; N (exhibition) exposición *f*; (display) demostración *f*; (ostentation) ostentación *f*, alarde *m*; (performance) espectáculo *m*; (showing) función *f*; (on TV) programa *m*; (movie theater) cine *m*; — **business** farándula *f*; —**case** vitrina *f*; —**down** confrontación *f*; —-**off** fanfarrón -ona *mf*; **to go to the** — ir al cine; **for** — para impresionar

shower [ʃáuɚ] N (rain) aguacero *m*, chubasco *m*; (bath) ducha *f*; (for brides) fiesta para novias *f*; (of sparks, blows) lluvia *f*; VI (bathe) ducharse; (rain) llover; VT (with gifts) inundar; (with praise) colmar

shown [ʃon] *see* show

showy [ʃói] ADJ ostentoso; (attractive) vistoso

shrank [ʃræŋk] *see* shrink

shred [ʃred] N (of paper) tira *f*; (of evidence) pizca *f*; **to be in** —**s** estar hecho jirones; **to tear to** —**s** hacer trizas; VI/VT (documents) triturar; (vegetables) rallar

shrew [ʃru] N (animal) musaraña *f*; (woman) arpía *f*

shrewd [ʃrud] ADJ astuto, sagaz

shriek [ʃrik] VI/VT chillar; N chillido *m*

shrill [ʃrɪɫ] ADJ chillón

shrimp [ʃrɪmp] N (animal) camarón *m*; (small person) renacuajo *m*; VI pescar camarones

shrine [ʃraɪn] N (chapel) capilla *f*; (altar) altar *m*

shrink [ʃrɪŋk] VI/VT (in size) encoger; VI (in value) reducirse; **to** — **from** retroceder; N (psychiatrist) *fam* loquero -ra *mf*; —**wrap** envoltura de plástico transparente *f*

shrinkage [ʃríŋkɪʤ] N (of clothes) encogimiento *m*; (of value) reducción *f*

shrivel [ʃrívəɫ] VI/VT secar[se], marchitar[se]

shroud [ʃraud] N mortaja *f*; VT (to wrap for burial) amortajar; (to hide) cubrir

shrub [ʃrʌb] N arbusto *m*

shrug [ʃrʌg] VI encogerse de hombros; VT encogerse de; **to** — **off** minimizar, ignorar; N

encogimiento de hombros *m*
shrunk [ʃrʌŋk] *see* shrink
shrunken [ʃrʌ́ŋkən] *see* shrink
shudder [ʃʌ́Dɚ] vɪ (from cold) tiritar; (from fear) temblar, estremecerse; N temblor *m*, estremecimiento *m*
shuffle [ʃʌ́fəl] vɪ/vᴛ (cards) barajar; vᴛ (mix) mezclar; vɪ (walk) arrastrar los pies; (dance) bailar arrastrando los pies; **to — along** ir arrastrando los pies; N (of cards) barajadura *f*; (of feet) arrastrapiés *m sg*
shun [ʃʌn] vᴛ rehuir, evitar
shut [ʃʌt] vɪ/vᴛ cerrar[se]; **to — down** cerrar; **to — off** cortar; **to — out** impedir la entrada de; **to — up** (close) cerrar bien; (lock up) encerrar; (be quiet) callarse; N **—-down** cese de actividades *m*; **—-eye** sueño *m*; **—-in** enfermo -ma confinado -da a la casa *mf*
shutter [ʃʌ́Dɚ] N (of a window) postigo *m*, contraventana *f*; (of a camera) obturador *m*
shuttle [ʃʌ́dl̩] N (in loom) lanzadera *f*; (spaceship) transbordador espacial *m*; (airplane) puente aéreo *m*; (bus, train) servicio regular *m*; vɪ ir y venir; vᴛ llevar y traer
shy [ʃaɪ] ᴀᴅᴊ tímido, retraído; (wary) esquivo; (lacking) escaso; vɪ asustarse, respingar; **to — away** (start) asustarse, respingar; (avoid) esquivar
shyness [ʃáɪnɪs] N timidez *f*, retraimiento *m*
shyster [ʃáɪstɚ] N *fam* picapleitos *m sg*
sibling [síblɪŋ] N hermano *m*; hermana *f*; **— rivalry** rivalidad entre hermanos *f*
sic [sɪk] vᴛ azuzar
sick [sɪk] ᴀᴅᴊ (ill) enfermo; (deranged) enfermizo, morboso; (at heart) angustiado; **— and tired** harto; **to be — of** estar harto de; **to be — to one's stomach** tener náuseas; **to make —** (disgust) dar asco; (anger) dar rabia, enfermar; **— leave** licencia por enfermedad *f*
sicken [síkən] vɪ/vᴛ (with illness) enfermar[se], poner[se] enfermo; (with disgust) dar asco; (with anger) dar rabia, enfermar
sickening [síkənɪŋ] ᴀᴅᴊ repugnante
sickle [síkəl] N hoz *f*; **— cell anemia** anemia falciforme *f*
sickly [síkli] ᴀᴅᴊ enfermizo, enclenque
sickness [síknɪs] N enfermedad *f*
side [saɪd] N lado *m*; (of a coin, piece of paper) cara *f*; (of a person) costado *m*; (of a hill) ladera *f*; (of beef) media res *f*; (of a boat) banda *f*; (team) equipo *m*; (garnish) acompañamiento *m*; **—arm** arma de mano *f*; **—bar** ladillo *m*; **—board** aparador *m*; **—burns** patillas *f pl*; **—-glance** mirada de soslayo/reojo *f*; **—light** (illumination) luz lateral *f*; (detail) detalle incidental *m*; **—line** (in sports) banda *f*, línea de banda *f*; (in business) negocio suplementario *m*; **to sit on**

the —lines no intervenir; **—walk** acera *f*; *Carib* andén *m*; *Am* vereda *f*; *Mex* banqueta *f*; **—wall** flanco *m*; **—ways** (walk) de costado; (glance) de soslayo; **— by —** uno al lado del otro; **by his —** a su lado; **by the — of** al lado de; **on all —s** por todos lados; ᴀᴅᴊ (on the side) lateral; (secondary) secundario; vɪ **to —step** evitar, esquivar; **to —track** (a train) desviar; (attention) distraer; **to — with** ponerse del lado de
siding [sáɪDɪŋ] N revestimiento *m*
SIDS [sudden infant death syndrome] [sídz] N síndrome de muerte súbita infantil *m*
siege [sidʒ] N sitio *m*, asedio *m*, cerco *m*; **to lay — to** sitiar
Sierra Leone [siérəlión] N Sierra Leona *f*
sieve [sɪv] N tamiz *m*, cedazo *m*
sift [sɪft] vᴛ cerner, tamizar; **to — through** revisar
sigh [saɪ] vɪ suspirar; N suspiro *m*
sight [saɪt] N (sense) vista *f*; (attraction) punto de interés *m*; (ridiculous thing or person) adefesio *m*, mamarracho *m*; (on a gun) mira *f*; **—seeing** turismo *m*; **in —** a la vista; **on —** en el acto; **he is out of —** ya no se ve; **at first —** a primera vista; **to catch — of** divisar; **to lose — of** perder de vista; **you're a — for sore eyes** dichosos los ojos que te ven; vᴛ (a ship) avistar, divisar; (a gun) apuntar
sign [saɪn] N (gesture) seña *f*, señal *f*; (indication) muestra *f*, señal *f*, indicio *m*; (placard) letrero *m*; (omen) agüero *m*, presagio *m*; (astrological, mathematical) signo *m*; (on road) cartel *m*, letrero *m*; **— language** lenguaje de signos *m*; vɪ/vᴛ (write name) firmar; (signal) hacer señas [de]; vᴛ (hire) contratar; (use sign language) hablar por señas; **to — off on** aprobar; **to — over property** ceder una propiedad; **to — up** (in a club) anotarse; (in the army) alistarse
signal [sígnl̩] N señal *f*; vɪ/vᴛ señalar, hacer señas [a]; ᴀᴅᴊ notable
signature [sígnətʃɚ] N firma *f*
signer [sáɪnɚ] N firmante *mf*, signatario -ria *mf*
significance [sɪgnífɪkəns] N significación *f*
significant [sɪgnífɪkənt] ᴀᴅᴊ significativo; **my — other** mi media naranja *f*
significantly [sɪgnífɪkəntli] ᴀᴅᴠ (considerably) apreciablemente, considerablemente; **he looked at me —** me dio una mirada significativa/expresiva
signify [sígnəfaɪ] vᴛ significar
silence [sáɪləns] N silencio *m*; vᴛ (child, fears) acallar; (criticism) silenciar, enmudecer
silencer [sáɪlənsɚ] N silenciador *m*
silent [sáɪlənt] ᴀᴅᴊ (machine) silencioso; (person) callado, silencioso; **— agreement** acuerdo tácito *m*; **— film** película muda *f*
silhouette [sɪluét] N silueta *f*; vᴛ **to be —d**

against perfilarse contra
silicon [sílikɑn] N silicio *m*; — **chip** chip de
     silicio *m*
silk [sɪłk] N seda *f*; — **industry** industria sedera
     f; —**worm** gusano de seda *m*
silken [síłkən] ADJ (of silk) de seda; (like silk)
     sedoso
silky [síłki] ADJ sedoso
sill [sɪł] N alféizar *m*, antepecho *m*
silly [síli] ADJ necio, bobo, lelo
silo [sáɪlo] N silo *m*
silt [sɪłt] N cieno *m*, limo *m*
silver [sílvɚ] N (metal, color) plata *f*; (tableware)
     cubiertos de plata *m pl*; ADJ (of silver) de plata;
     (silver-colored) plateado; — **anniversary** las
     bodas de plata *f pl*; —-**plated** bañado en
     plata; —-**plating** plateado *m*; —**smith**
     platero -ra *mf*; —**ware** cubiertos de plata *m*
     pl; VT platear; (a mirror) azogar
similar [símələ] ADJ semejante, similar
similarity [sɪmələ́ɛrɪDi] N semejanza *f*,
     similitud *f*
similarly [símɪlɚli] ADV de manera similar; —,
     a mile is longer than a kilometer del
     mismo modo, una milla es más larga que un
     kilómetro; **they were — surprised**
     quedaron igualmente sorprendidos
simile [síməli] N símil *m*
simmer [símɚ] VI/VT hervir a fuego lento; **to** —
     down calmarse
simple [símpəł] ADJ (uncomplicated) simple,
     sencillo; (naive) simple; —**minded** simple,
     simplón
simpleton [símpəłtən] N simplón -ona *mf*,
     mentecato -ta *mf*
simplicity [sɪmplísɪDi] N (lack of complication)
     sencillez *f*, simplicidad *f*; (naiveté) simpleza *f*
simplify [símpləfaɪ] VI/VT simplificar
simplistic [sɪmplístɪk] ADJ simplista
simply [símpli] ADV (in a simple manner) con
     sencillez; (merely) simplemente; **it is** —
     ridiculous francamente, es ridículo
simulate [símjəlet] VI/VT simular
simulation [sɪmjəléʃən] N simulación *f*
simultaneous [saɪməłténiəs] ADJ simultáneo
sin [sɪn] N pecado *m*; VI pecar
since [sɪns] CONJ (continuously) desde que;
     (inasmuch as) puesto que, ya que; PREP
     (continuously) desde; (from a past time) a
     partir de; **we have been here — five**
     estamos aquí desde las cinco; ADV desde
     entonces; **ever** — desde entonces; **he died**
     long — murió hace mucho tiempo; **she has**
     — **agreed** después de eso consintió
sincere [sɪnsír] ADJ sincero
sincerity [sɪnsɛ́rɪDi] N sinceridad *f*
sine [saɪn] N seno
sinew [sínju] N tendón *m*
sinewy [sínjui] ADJ (full of tendons) nervudo;

(robust) membrudo; (chewy) estropajoso
sinful [sínfəł] ADJ (act) pecaminoso; (person)
     pecador
sing [sɪŋ] VI/VT cantar; N —**song** sonsonete *m*
Singapore [síŋəpɔr] N Singapur *m*
Singaporean [sɪŋəpóriən] ADJ & N singapurense
     mf
singe [sɪndʒ] VT chamuscar, socarrar; N
     chamusquina *f*, socarrina *f*
singer [síŋɚ] N cantante *mf*; intérprete *mf*
single [síŋgəł] ADJ (only one) solo, único; (for
     one person) individual; (unmarried) soltero;
     — **bed** cama de una plaza *f*; —-**entry**
     bookkeeping teneduría por partida simple
     f; —-**family home** vivienda unifamiliar *f*; —
     file fila india *f*; —-**handed** solo, sin ayuda;
     —-**minded** resuelto; —-**spacing** sencillo
     m; **every — one** cada uno; **not a — word** ni
     una sola palabra; N (bill) billete de uno *m*;
     (unmarried person) soltero -ra *mf*; (record)
     disco sencillo *m*; (in baseball) sencillo *m*; —**s**
     (in tennis) individuales *m pl*; VT **to — out**
     elegir
singular [síŋgjəlɚ] ADJ & N singular *m*
sinister [sínɪstɚ] ADJ siniestro
sink [sɪŋk] VI/VT (ship) hundir[se]; VT (money)
     invertir; (a well) cavar; (a pipeline) enterrar;
     it finally sank in finalmente nos dimos
     cuenta de eso; **to — one's teeth into** clavar
     los dientes en; **to — to one's knees** caer de
     rodillas; **sunk in thought** absorto; **my**
     heart sank se me fue el alma al piso; **the**
     sun was —ing se iba poniendo el sol; N (in
     the kitchen) fregadero *m*; (in bathroom)
     lavabo *m*; (pond for sewage) pozo negro *m*;
     —**hole** socavón *m*, sumidero *m*
sinner [sínɚ] N pecador -ora *mf*
sinuous [sínjuɔs] ADJ sinuoso
sinus [sáɪnəs] N seno *m*
sinusitis [saɪnəsáɪDɪs] N sinusitis *f*
sip [sɪp] VI/VT sorber; N sorbo *m*
siphon [sáɪfən] N sifón *m*; VI/VT (liquid) sacar
     con sifón; (money) desviar
sir [sɚ] N señor *m*
siren [sáɪrən] N sirena *f*
sirloin [sɚ́lɔɪn] N solomillo *m*
sissy [sísi] ADJ & N afeminado *m*; *offensive* marica
     m, maricón *m*
sister [sístɚ] N hermana *f*; —-**in-law** cuñada *f*;
     — **Mary** Sor María *f*
sit [sɪt] VI sentar[se]; (pose) posar; (be seated)
     estar sentado; (be located) estar situado; **to** —
     down sentarse; **to — in on a class** ir de
     oyente a una clase; **to — on** posponer; **to** —
     out a dance saltearse una pieza; **to — still**
     estarse quieto; **to — tight** mantenerse firme
     en su puesto; **to — up** incorporarse; **to — up**
     all night quedarse en vela; N —-**in** sentada *f*; —-**up** abdominal *m*

sitcom [sítkɑm] N comedia de situación *f*
site [saɪt] N (for construction) terreno *m*, solar *m*; (on the Internet) sitio *m*; — **license** licencia de sitio *f*; **on-** — **training** capacitación en el lugar de trabajo
sitter [sípɚ] N niñera *f*, *Sp* canguro *mf*
sitting [sípɪŋ] N sesión *f*; **in one** — de una sentada, de un tirón; ADJ — **duck** blanco fácil *m*; — **room** cuarto de estar *m*
situated [sítʃueɪdɪd] ADJ situado, ubicado
situation [sɪtʃuéʃən] N situación *f*
Sitz bath [síts bæθ] N baño de asiento *m*
six [sɪks] NUM seis; — **hundred** seiscientos; N — -**pack** paquete de seis *m*; — -**shooter** revólver de seis tiros *m*
sixteen [sɪkstín] NUM dieciséis
sixth [sɪksθ] ADV & N sexto *m*
sixty [síksti] NUM sesenta
size [saɪz] N tamaño *m*; (of clothing) talla *f*; VT clasificar según el tamaño; **to** — **up** juzgar
sizable, sizeable [sáɪzəbəl] ADJ de tamaño considerable
sizzle [sízəl] VI chisporrotear; N chisporroteo *m*
skate [sket] N patín *m*; —**board** monopatín *m*; VI/VT patinar
skein [sken] N madeja *f*
skeletal [skélɪdl] ADJ esquelético
skeleton [skélɪtən] N esqueleto *m*, osamenta *f*; (of a building) armazón *m*; — **key** llave maestra *f*
skeptic, sceptic [sképtɪk] N escéptico -ca *mf*
skeptical [sképtɪkəl] ADJ escéptico
skepticism [sképtɪsɪzəm] N escepticismo *m*
sketch [sketʃ] N (drawing) boceto *m*, croquis *m*; (outline) esbozo *m*, bosquejo *m*; (skit) sketch *m*; VI/VT (draw) dibujar; (outline) bosquejar
skew [skju] VT (cloth) sesgar; (data) tergiversar
skewer [skjúɚ] N brocheta *f*
ski [ski] N esquí *m*; — **jump** (sport) salto con esquís *m*; (course) pista de saltos *f*; — **lift** telesquí *m*; VI/VT esquiar [en]
skid [skɪd] N patinazo *m*; VI patinar
skiing [skíɪŋ] N esquí *m*
skill [skɪl] N destreza *f*, habilidad *f*, maña *f*
skilled [skɪld] ADJ diestro, habilidoso; — **worker** obrero -ra calificado -da *mf*
skillet [skílɪt] N sartén *f*
skillful, skilful [skílfəl] ADJ diestro, habilidoso
skim [skɪm] VT (milk) desnatar; (a broth) espumar; (pass near surface) rozar; VI/VT (read) leer por encima, repasar; **to** — **over** rozar; N — **milk** *Sp* leche desnatada *f*; *Am* leche descremada *f*
skimp [skɪmp] VI escatimar; **to** — **on** escatimar
skimpy [skímpi] ADJ (funds) escaso; (dress) corto; (bikini) pequeño
skin [skɪn] N piel *f* (also of animal, sausage, potato); (of the face) cutis *m*, tez *f*; (for carrying wine) pellejo *m*; (of boiled milk) nata

f; (of grapes) hollejo *m*; — -**deep** superficial; — -**diving** natación submarina *f*; — **flick** película pornográfica *f*; —**flint** roña *mf*; —**head** cabeza rapada *mf*; **to save one's** — salvar el pellejo; **to be saved by the** — **of one's teeth** salvarse por un pelo; VT (animal) despellejar, desollar; (fruit) pelar; (a person) quitarle a uno el dinero
skinny [skíni] ADJ flaco; **to** — -**dip** nadar desnudo
skip [skɪp] VI (jump) brincar, ir dando saltos; (omit) saltarse; (bounce) rebotar; VT (a page) saltar[se]; (class) faltar a; (a stone) hacer rebotar; **to** — **out** escaparse; N salto *m*, brinco *m*
skipper [skípɚ] N (captain) patrón -ona *mf*, capitán -ana *mf*; (jumper) saltador -ora *mf*
skirmish [skɚmɪʃ] N escaramuza *f*; VI escaramuzar
skirt [skɚt] N falda *f*; VT bordear; **to** — **an issue** evitar un tema
skit [skɪt] N sketch *m*
skull [skʌl] N cráneo *m*, calavera *f*; — **and crossbones** calavera *f*
skunk [skʌŋk] N mofeta *f*; *Am* zorrillo *m*
sky [skaɪ] N cielo *m*; — **blue** azul celeste *m*; —**diving** paracaidismo extremo *m*; — -**high** muy alto; —**lark** alondra *f*; —**light** claraboya *f*; —**line** horizonte *m*; —**scraper** rascacielos *m sg*; VI **to** —**rocket** subir vertiginosamente
slab [slæb] N (of wood) trozo *m*; (of stone) losa *f*, laja *f*; (of meat) tajada *f*
slack [slæk] ADJ (not taut) flojo; (careless) descuidado; (sluggish) lento; — **season** temporada baja *f*; **to take up the** — llenar el vacío; —**s** pantalones *m pl*; VI holgazanear; **to** — **off** holgazanear
slag [slæg] N escoria *f*
slain [slen] *see* slay
slalom [sláləm] N slalom *m*
slam [slæm] VI/VT cerrar[se] de un golpe; VI (hit) chocar; VT (throw down) hacer golpear; (criticize) criticar; **to** — **on the brakes** dar un frenazo; **to** — **the door** dar un portazo; N (blow) golpazo *m*; (criticism) crítica *f*; (of a door) portazo *m*; — -**dunk** (easy decision) éxito seguro *m*
slander [slǽndɚ] N calumnia *f*, difamación *f*; VT calumniar, difamar
slanderous [slǽndɚəs] ADJ calumnioso, difamatorio
slang [slæŋ] N (jargon) jerga *f*; (argot) argot *m*
slant [slænt] N (orientation, bias) sesgo *m*; (of a roof) inclinación *f*; VI/VT (bias) sesgar; (slope) inclinar[se], ladear[se]
slap [slæp] N (to the body) palmada *f*; (to the face) bofetada *f*, torta *f*, cachetada *f*; (with a glove) guantada *f*; — -**happy** aturdido; —**stick** de

golpe y porrazo; **a — in the face** un desaire;
a — on the wrist un tirón de orejas; **a — on
the back** una palmadita en la espalda; VT
abofetear; **to — down** reprimir
slash [slæʃ] VI/VT (cut) acuchillar; *Am* tajear; VT
(whip) azotar; (reduce) reducir, rebajar; N
(sweeping stroke, wound) cuchillada *f*, tajo *m*;
(typographical sign) barra *f*
slat [slæt] N tablilla *f*
slate [slet] N (rock, roofing) pizarra *f*; (color)
color pizarra *m*; (list of candidates) lista de
candidatos *f*; VT empizarrar; **this building
is — d for destruction** se ha programado la
demolición de este edificio
slaughter [slɔ́Dɚ] N matanza *f*; **—house**
matadero *m*; VT (animals) matar; (people,
opponents) masacrar
slave [slev] N esclavo -va *mf*; **—driver** capataz de
esclavos *m*; **— labor** (workers) mano de obra
esclava *f*; (work) trabajo de esclavos *m*; VI
trabajar como esclavo -va
slavery [slévəri] N esclavitud *f*
Slavic [slávɪk] ADJ eslavo
sleazy [slízi] ADJ (squalid) sórdido;
(contemptible) despreciable
sled [slɛd] N trineo *m*
sledgehammer [slédʒhæmɚ] N almádena *f*
sleek [slik] ADJ (hair) lustroso; (sports car)
elegante
sleep [slip] VI/VT dormir; **it —s three** tiene
espacio para que duerman tres personas; **to —
around** ser promiscuo; **to — in** dormir hasta
tarde; **to — it off** dormir la mona; **to —
something off** dormir para que desaparezca
algo; **to — over** dormir en casa ajena; **to —
together** acostarse juntos; **to — with**
acostarse con; **to — on it** consultarlo con la
almohada; N sueño *m*; **— apnea** apnea
obstructiva del sueño *f*; **— disorder**
trastorno del sueño *m*; **— mode** modo de
dormir *m*; **—walker** sonámbulo -la *mf*; **to go
to —** dormirse; **to put to —** (put to bed)
dormir a; (euthanize) sacrificar
sleeper [slípɚ] N (one who sleeps) persona que
duerme *f*; (beam) durmiente *m*; (on a train)
coche cama *m*; (unexpected success) éxito
inesperado *m*; (sofa bed) sofá-cama *m*
sleepily [slípɪli] ADV con somnolencia
sleepiness [slípinɪs] N sueño *m*, somnolencia *f*
sleeping [slípɪŋ] N sueño *m*; ADJ dormido; **—
bag** saco de dormir *m*; **— pill** píldora para
dormir *f*, somnífero *m*; **— sickness**
enfermedad del sueño *f*
sleepless [slíplɪs] ADJ (person) desvelado;
(night) en blanco
sleepy [slípi] ADJ somnoliento, adormilado; **to
be —** tener sueño
sleet [slit] N cellisca *f*; VI caer cellisca
sleeve [sliv] N manga *f*; **to have something up**

one's — tener algo en la manga
sleigh [sle] N trineo *m*; **—bell** cascabel *m*; VI
pasear en trineo
sleight of hand [sláɪD əvhǽnd] N
prestidigitación *f*
slender [sléndɚ] ADJ delgado, esbelto
slept [slɛpt] *see* sleep
sleuth [sluθ] N sabueso -sa *mf*
slew [slu] *see* slay
slice [slaɪs] N (of bread, cheese) rebanada *f*; (of
fruit) tajada *f*, raja *f*; (of meat) lonja *f*; (in
tennis) cortado *m*, golpe cortado *m*; VT cortar,
rebanar, tajar
slick [slɪk] ADJ (unctuous) untuoso; (sly) astuto;
(slippery) resbaladizo
slicker [slíkɚ] N impermeable *m*
slid [slɪd] *see* slide
slide [slaɪd] VI/VT deslizar[se]; **to — in** cerrar[se]
deslizando; **to — out** abrirse deslizando; **to
let something —** dejar pasar algo; N
deslizamiento *m*; (playground equipment)
tobogán *m*; (of a trombone) vara corredora *f*;
(photographic) diapositiva *f*; (for
microscopes) portaobjeto *m*
slight [slaɪt] N desaire *m*; VT (snub) desairar;
(neglect) descuidar; ADJ (slim) delgado;
(delicate) delicado, tenue; (small in degree)
leve, ligero
slightly [sláɪtli] ADV algo, un poco
slim [slɪm] ADJ delgado, esbelto; **a — chance**
una posibilidad remota
slime [slaɪm] N (in rivers) limo *m*, fango *m*; (of
snails) baba *f*; (despicable person) asqueroso
-sa *mf*
slimy [sláɪmi] ADJ (muddy) fangoso; (slobbery)
baboso, gomoso; (despicable) asqueroso
sling [slɪŋ] N (weapon) honda *f*; (for arm)
cabestrillo *m*; **—shot** (toy) tirachinas *m sg*,
tirador *m*; (weapon) honda *f*; VT lanzar; **to —
a rifle over one's shoulder** ponerse el rifle
en bandolera
slink [slɪŋk] VI (move furtively) andar
furtivamente; (move provocatively) caminar
provocativamente; **to — away** escurrirse
slip [slɪp] VI (slide) deslizarse; (slide accidentally)
resbalar[se]; (fail to engage) patinar;
(deteriorate) empeorar; VT (make slip) hacer
resbalar; (put) meter; **to — away** escaparse,
escabullirse; **to — by** correr; **to — in**
meter[se]; **to — one's dress on** ponerse el
vestido; **to — out** (leave) salir inadvertido;
(say inadvertently) escapársele a uno algo; **to
— up** meter la pata; **to let an opportunity
— by** dejar pasar una oportunidad; **it —ped
my mind** se me olvidó; **it —ped off** se zafó;
N (act of slipping) resbalón *m*, traspié *m*;
(mistake) equivocación *f*; (pillow cover) funda
f; (underskirt) viso *m*; (piece of paper)
papeleta *f*, tira de papel *f*; (space for boats)

embarcadero *m*; — **of the tongue** lapsus [linguae] *m*; —**knot** nudo corredizo *m*; **Freudian** — acto fallido *m*

slipper [slípɚ] N zapatilla *f*, pantufla *f*

slippery [slípəri] ADJ resbaloso, resbaladizo; (evasive) evasivo, escurridizo

slipshod [slípʃad] ADJ chapucero

slit [slɪt] VT cortar a lo largo; **to** — **someone's throat** degollar a alguien; **to** — **into strips** cortar en tiras; N raja *f*, hendidura *f*

slither [slíðɚ] VI serpentear, culebrear; N serpenteo *m*, culebreo *m*

sliver [slívɚ] N astilla *f*; VI/VT astillar[se]

slob [slab] N (unkempt) dejado -da *mf*; (uncouth) bruto -ta *mf*

slobber [slábɚ] N baba *f*; VI/VT babosear, babear[se]

slogan [slógən] N eslogan *m*, lema *m*

slop [slap] VT (splash) salpicar; (feed) dar de comer; N (pigswill) bazofia *f*; (mud) fango *m*

slope [slop] VI/VT inclinar[se]; N vertiente *f*, declive *m*, cuesta *f*, cortado *m*; (in math) pendiente *f*

sloppiness [slápinɪs] N chapucería *f*

sloppy [slápi] ADJ (muddy) fangoso; (splashed) salpicado; (slovenly) cochino; (poorly done) chapucero

slot [slat] N (for coins, letters) ranura *f*; (in a computer) bahía *f*, ranura *f*; (place in a series) casilla *f*; (job) puesto *m*; — **machine** tragamonedas *mf sg*, tragaperras *mf sg*; VT hacer una ranura

sloth [slɔθ] N (vice) pereza *f*; (animal) perezoso *m*

slouch [slaʊtʃ] N (posture) encorvamiento *m*; (inept person) torpe *mf*; (lazy person) holgazán -ana *mf*; VI/VT (crouch) andar agachado, encorvar[se]; (shuffle) andar caído de hombros

Slovakia [slovákiə] N Eslovaquia *f*

Slovakian [slovákiən] ADJ & N eslovaco -ca *mf*

Slovene [slóvin] ADJ & N esloveno -na *mf*

Slovenia [slóvíniə] N Eslovenia *f*

slovenliness [slávənlinɪs] N (of a person) desaseo *m*, desaliño *m*; (of work) descuido *m*

slovenly [slávənli] ADJ (unclean) desaseado; (unkempt) desaliñado; (poorly done) descuidado

slow [slo] ADJ (not fast) lento, tardo; (running behind) atrasado; (sluggish) lerdo, torpe, pesado; **in** — **motion** en cámara lenta; ADV lentamente, despacio; VI/VT **to** — **down/up** andar más despacio, frenar; N —**down** (in business) disminución de actividades *f*; (in labor disputes) huelga de celo *f*

slowly [slóli] ADV despacio, lento, lentamente; — **but surely** lenta pero seguramente

slowness [slónɪs] N (of speed) lentitud *f*; (of intelligence) torpeza *f*

slug [slʌg] N (bullet) bala *f*; (coin) moneda falsa *f*;

(animal) babosa *f*; (swallow) trago *m*; (blow with fist) puñetazo *m*; VT aporrear; **to** — **it out** agarrarse a puñetazos

sluggard [slʌgɚd] N holgazán -ana *mf*

sluggish [slʌgɪʃ] ADJ (slow) lento; (torpid) aletargado, torpe

sluggishness [slʌgɪʃnɪs] N torpeza *f*

sluice [slus] N (channel with a gate) esclusa *f*; (channel) canal *m*; — **gate** compuerta *f*

slum [slʌm] N barrio bajo *m*; —**s** tugurios *m pl*; —**lord** propietario de tugurio *m*; VI visitar los barrios bajos; **to** — **it** divertirse en lugares de poca categoría

slumber [slʌmbɚ] VI dormir; N sueño *m*; — **party** fiesta de niñas que se quedan a dormir *f*

slump [slʌmp] VI (a person) desplomarse; (prices, markets) bajar repentinamente; N (in prices) baja repentina *f*; (in the economy) ralentización *f*; (in sports) mala racha *f*

slung [slʌŋ] *see* sling

slunk [slʌŋk] *see* slink

slur [slɚ] VT (pronounce indistinctly) pronunciar mal; (connect notes) ligar; N (connection of notes) ligado *m*; (insult) insulto *m*

slush [slʌʃ] N (melted snow) nieve a medio derretir *f*; (sludge) nieve fangosa *f*; (mud) fango *m*; (refuse) desperdicios *m pl*; — **fund** (illicit fund) cuenta para fines ilícitos *f*; (petty cash) caja chica *f*

slut [slʌt] N (slovenly woman) *pej* puerca *f*; (loose woman) *offensive* mujerzuela *f*, puta *f*

sly [slaɪ] ADJ astuto, taimado; **on the** — a escondidas

smack [smæk] N (taste) dejo *m*; *Sp* deje *m*; (kiss) beso ruidoso *m*; (loud eating) chasquido *m*; (slap) palmada *f*, sopapo *m*; (heroin) *fam* caballo *m*; VT (kiss) dar un beso ruidoso; (eat loudly) chascar, chasquear; (slap) dar una palmada; **to** — **of** tener un dejo de

small [smɔl] ADJ (not large) pequeño, chico; (of build) menudo; (narrow) estrecho; (lowercase) minúsculo; (petty) mezquino; — **caps** versalillas *f pl*, versalitas *f pl*; — **change** cambio suelto *m*; — **fry** gente menuda *f*; — **intestine** intestino delgado *m*; —**pox** viruela *f*; — **talk** cháchara *f*; **to feel** — avergonzarse; N (size) pequeño *m*; — **of the back** baja espalda *f*

smallness [smɔlnɪs] N pequeñez *f*

smart [smart] ADJ (intelligent) listo, inteligente; (astute) astuto; (stylish) elegante; — **aleck/ alec** sabihondo -da *mf*; —**ass** *fam* sabihondo -da *mf*; — **bomb** bomba inteligente *f*; — **card** tarjeta de circuito integrado *f*, tarjeta inteligente *f*; — **money** inversión inteligente *f*; — **remark** insolencia *f*; N (pain) escozor *m*; VI picar; **I'm** —**ing from his rude remarks** todavía me duelen sus groserías

smash [smæʃ] VT (destroy) estrellar, destrozar; (a rebellion) aplastar; **to — into** estrellarse contra; N (sound) estrépito *m*; (blow) choque violento *m*; (tennis shot) remate *m*; **a — hit** un exitazo

smear [smir] VT (daub) untar; (spot, vilify) manchar; (blur) correrse; (defeat) reventar; **to — with paint** pintorrear, pintarrajear; N (stain) mancha *f*; (culture) frotis *m*; — **campaign** campaña de difamación *f*

smell [smɛł] VI/VT oler; **to — of** oler a; **that —s** huele mal, apesta; **to — up** apestar; N (odor) olor *m*; (sense) olfato *m*; — **of** olor a

smelly [sméli] ADJ hediondo, apestoso

smile [smaɪł] VI sonreír[se]; N sonrisa *f*

smiling [smáɪlɪŋ] ADJ risueño, sonriente

smirk [smɚk] N sonrisa suficiente *f*; VI sonreír con suficiencia

smith [smɪθ] N herrero -ra *mf*

smitten [smítn̩] *see* smite

smog [smɑg] N smog *m*

smoke [smok] N humo *m*; (cigarette) cigarro *m*, cigarrillo *m*; — **detector** detector de humo *m*, detector de incendios *m*; — **inhalation** inhalación de humo *f*; — **screen** cortina de humo *f*; —**stack** chimenea *f*; **to have a —** fumar; VI (put off smoke) echar humo; (go fast) volar; VT (tobacco) fumar; (ham, fish, glass) ahumar; **to — out** (drive out) ahuyentar con humo; (expose) poner al descubierto

smoker [smóka˞] N fumador -ora *mf*; (train car) vagón de fumar *m*

smoking [smókɪŋ] ADJ humeante; — **car** vagón de fumar *m*; — **gun** prueba irrefutable *f*; — **room** cuarto de fumar *m*; N (use of tobacco) tabaquismo *m*, fumar *m*

smoky [smóki] ADJ humoso

smolder, smoulder [smółdɚ] VI arder

smooth [smuð] ADJ (surface) liso; (skin) suave, terso; (tire) gastado; (sea) sereno, tranquilo; (manners) agradable, fino; (flatterer) zalamero; VT (make surface even) alisar; (make easy) allanar; **to — away** hacer desaparecer; **to — one's hair** atusarse el cabello; **to — over** limar asperezas

smoothness [smúðnɪs] N (of a surface) lisura *f*; (of skin) tersura *f*, suavidad *f*; (of sea) tranquilidad *f*; (of manners) fineza *f*; (of a flatterer) zalamería *f*

smote [smot] *see* smite

smother [smʌ́ðɚ] VT (stifle) ahogar[se], sofocar[se], asfixiar[se]; (envelop) cubrir; (overprotect) sobreproteger

smudge [smʌdʒ] N borrón *m*, mancha *f*; VI/VT borronear[se], manchar[se]

smug [smʌg] ADJ suficiente, petulante

smuggle [smʌ́gəł] VI/VT contrabandear, hacer contrabando; **to — in** entrar de contrabando; **to — out** sacar de contrabando

smuggler [smʌ́glɚ] N contrabandista *mf*

smut [smʌt] N (soot) hollín *m*; (pornography) pornografía *f*; (parasite) tizon *m*

snack [snæk] N tentempié *m*, bocadillo *m*; — **bar** cafetería *f*, tizón *m*

snafu [snæfú] N relajo *m*

snag [snæg] N (branch) gancho *m*; (in fabric) enganchón *m*; (any obstacle) pega *f*, obstáculo *m*, contrariedad *f*; **to hit a —** tropezar con un obstáculo; VI/VT enganchar[se]; VT (a ball) agarrar

snail [snełł] N caracol *m*; — **mail** correo regular *m*; —**'s pace** paso de tortuga *m*

snake [snek] N serpiente *f*; —**bite** mordedura de serpiente *f*; — **in the grass** víbora *f*; —**skin** piel de serpiente *f*; VI serpentear

snap [snæp] VI (make sound) chasquear, dar un chasquido; (lose control) estallar, perder los estribos; VT (take a photograph) sacar; VI/VT (break) quebrar[se]; **to — at** (try to bite) tirar un mordiscón; (speak harshly) ladrar; **to — one's fingers** chasquear los dedos, castañetear con los dedos; **to — out of** recuperarse de; **to — shut** cerrar[se] de golpe; **to — together** abrochar; **to — up** llevarse; N (sound) chasquido *m*; (fastener) broche *m*; (bite) tarascada *f*; **it's a —** es pan comido; — **judgment** decisión atolondrada *f*; —**dragon** dragón *m*; —**shot** instantánea, foto *f*

snappy [snǽpi] ADJ (biting) mordedor; (elegant) elegante; **make it —!** ¡date prisa!

snare [snɛr] N (trap) trampa *f*; — **drum** tambor con bordón *m*; VT atrapar

snarl [snɑrł] VI/VT (growl) regañar; (tangle) enmarañar[se], enredar[se]; N (growl) gruñido *m*; (tangle) maraña *f*, enredo *m*

snatch [snætʃ] VT (seize) arrebatar; (kidnap) secuestrar; VI **to — at** dar manotazos; N (act of snatching) arrebato *m*; (fragment) fragmento *m*

snazzy [snǽzi] ADJ llamativo

sneak [snik] VI andar furtivamente; **to — in** entrar a escondidas; **to — out** salir a hurtadillas; VT **to — something in** meter algo a escondidas; **to — something out** sacar a escondidas; **to — a cigarette** fumar a escondidas; N persona solapada *f*

sneakers [sníkɚz] N zapatillas [deportivas] *f pl*, tenis *m pl*

sneer [snir] VI (smile) sonreír con sorna; **to — at** mofarse de; N expresión de sorna *f*

sneeze [sniz] VI estornudar; **that's nothing to — at** no es nada desdeñable; N estornudo *m*

snicker [sníkɚ] VI reírse burlonamente; N risita burlona *f*

snide [snaɪd] ADJ malévolo

sniff [snɪf] VI/VT husmear, olfatear; **to — at**

husmear; (ridicule) menospreciar; N (act of
sniffing) husmeo *m*, olfateo *m*; (smell)
bocanada *f*
sniffle [snífəł] VI (with a cold) sorberse los
mocos; (when crying) gimotear; N (when
crying) gimoteo *m*; **the —s** un resfrío
snip [snɪp] VT tijeretear; **to — off** cortar de un
tijeretazo; N (act of snipping) tijeretada *f*,
tijeretazo *m*; (piece cut off) pedacito *m*,
recorte *m*; **— of conversation** retazo de
conversación *m*
sniper [snáɪpɚ] N francotirador -ora *mf*
snitch [snɪtʃ] VI (tell on) chivar, chivatar; VT
(rob) ratear; N soplón -ona *mf*, chivato -ta *mf*
snob [snɑb] N esnob *mf*
snoop [snup] VI fisgar, fisgonear; N fisgón -ona
mf
snooze [snuz] VI dormitar; N siesta *f*; **to take a
—** echar un sueñecito / un sueñito / una siesta
snore [snɔr] VI roncar; N ronquido *m*
snorkel [snɔ́rkəł] N esnórquel *m*
snort [snɔrt] VI resoplar, bufar; VI/VT (drugs)
esnifar; N resoplido *m*, bufido *m*; (drink)
trago *m*
snot [snɑt] N (mucus) *fam, vulg* moco *m*; (person)
pej mocoso -sa *mf*
snout [snaʊt] N hocico *m*, jeta *f*, morro *m*; (nose)
fam napias *f pl*
snow [sno] N nieve *f* (also cocaine, heroin);
—ball bola de nieve *f*; **—board** monopatín
de nieve *m*; **—drift** ventisquero *m*; **—fall**
nevada *f*; **—flake** copo de nieve *m*; **—man**
muñeco de nieve *m*; **—mobile** motonieve *f*;
—plow quitanieves *m sg*; **—shoe** raqueta *f*;
—storm ventisca *f*; VI nevar; **the airport
was —ed in** cerraron el aeropuerto por
nieve; **to — under** (cover in snow) cubrir de
nieve; (overwhelm) abrumar; **to —ball**
aumentar rápidamente
snowy [snói] ADJ nevado; (white) níveo
snub [snʌb] VT volverle la cara a, desairar,
despreciar; N desaire *m*, desprecio *m*; **—-
nosed** chato; *Am* ñato
snuck [snʌk] *see* sneak
snuff [snʌf] VI **to — out** apagar, extinguir; N
(tobacco product) rapé *m*; **to be up to —** dar
la talla
snug [snʌg] ADJ (tight-fitting) ajustado;
(comfortable) cómodo
so [so] ADV (in this way) así; (to this degree) tan;
(so much) tanto; **— am I** yo también; **—-
and-—** fulano [de tal]; **—-called** llamado; **—
as to** para; **— far as I know** que yo sepa; **—
many** tantos; **— much** tanto; **—-— regular;
— much the better** tanto mejor; **— that** de
modo que; **I was — a beauty queen!** ¡sí que
fui reina de belleza! **— long!** ¡hasta luego!
and — forth etcetera, y así sucesivamente; **I
believe —** creo que sí; **is that —** ? ¿en serio?

¡no me digas! **ten minutes or —** unos diez
minutos; INTERJ (upon discovering a secret)
ajajá; CONJ (in order that) de modo que;
(consequently) así que, entonces
soak [sok] VI/VT (immerse) remojar[se]; (drench)
empapar[se]; **to — through** colarse por; **to
— up** absorber, embeber; **to be —ed
through** estar empapado, estar calado hasta
los huesos; N remojón *m*
soap [sop] N jabón *m*; (television show)
telenovela *f*; **— bubble** pompa de jabón *f*; **—
dish** jabonera *f*; VT enjabonar
soapy [sópi] ADJ jabonoso
soar [sɔr] VI/VT (airplane) elevar[se]; (kite)
remontar[se]; (hopes) aumentar[se]; (prices)
disparar[se]; (glider) planear[se]; VI (bird)
volar
sob [sɑb] VI sollozar, hipar; N sollozo *m*, hipo *m*
SOB [son of a bitch] [ésóbí] N *offensive* hijo de
puta *m*, *offensive* hijo de perra *m*
sober [sóbɚ] ADJ (not drunk) sobrio; (temperate)
moderado; (serious, subdued) serio, sobrio;
VI **to — up** (get over drunkenness)
despejarse; (become more serious) sentar
cabeza
sobriety [səbráɪIDi] N (not being drunk)
sobriedad *f*; (moderation) moderación *f*;
(seriousness) seriedad *f*
soccer [sákɚ] N fútbol *m*, balompié *m*; **— ball**
esférico *m*; **— field** campo de juego *m*, cancha
f; **— player** futbolista *mf*; **— World Cup**
Campeonato Mundial de Fútbol *m*
sociable [sóʃəbəł] ADJ sociable
social [sóʃəł] ADJ (of society) social; (friendly)
sociable; **— climber** arribista *mf*; **— science**
ciencias sociales *f pl*; **— security** seguridad
social *f*; **— welfare** asistencia social *f*; **—
work** asistencia social *f*; N reunión social *f*
socialism [sóʃəlɪzəm] N socialismo *m*
socialist [sóʃəlɪst] ADJ & N socialista *mf*
socialize [sóʃəlaɪz] VT socializar; VI salir, tener
trato social
society [səsáɪIDi] N sociedad *f*; (companionship)
compañía *f*
socioeconomic [sosioɛkənámɪk] ADJ
socioeconómico
sociology [sosiálədʒi] N sociología *f*
sociopath [sósiəpæθ] N sociópata *mf*
sock [sak] N (garment) calcetín *m*; (blow)
puñetazo *m*, zumbido *m*; VT pegar, zumbar;
to — away ahorrar
socket [sákɪt] N (of eye) cuenca *f*; (electrical
outlet) enchufe *m*; (for bulb) portalámparas *m
sg*, casquillo *m*
sod [sad] N (lawn) césped *m*; (piece) tepe *m*; VT
cubrir de césped
soda [sóDə] N (drink) gaseosa *f*; (sodium
hydroxide) soda *f*, sosa *f*; **— fountain** bar de
bebidas sin alcohol *m*; **— pop** gaseosa *f*; —

water agua con gas *f*
sodium [sóɒiəm] N sodio *m*
sodomy [sáɒəmi] N sodomía *f*
sofa [sófə] N sofá *m*; — **bed** sofá-cama *m*
soft [sɔft] ADJ (butter, bed, water, penalty) blando; (life) fácil, cómodo; (hair, skin) suave; (light) tenue; —**ball** softball *m*; —-**boiled eggs** huevos pasados por agua *m pl*; — **coal** carbón bituminoso *m*; — **drink** gaseosa *f*; — **page break** salto de página suave/automático *m*; — **palate** velo del paladar *m*; — **return** salto de línea suave *m*; —**ware** software *m*
soften [sɔ́fən] VI/VT (butter) ablandar[se]; (skin) suavizar[se]; VT (a blow) amortiguar; (voice) bajar
softly [sɔ́ftli] ADV (talk) en voz baja; (walk) sin hacer ruido
softness [sɔ́ftnɪs] N (of butter) blandura *f*; (of hair, skin) suavidad *f*; (of light) tenuidad *f*
soggy [sági] ADJ (clothes) empapado; (day) húmedo
soil [sɔɪɬ] N suelo *m*, tierra *f*; VI/VT ensuciar[se], manchar[se]
solace [sálɪs] N consuelo *m*; VT consolar
solar [sólɚ] ADJ solar; — **eclipse** eclipse de sol *m*; — **energy** energía solar *f*; — **plexus** plexo solar *m*; — **system** sistema solar *m*
sold [soɬd] *see* sell
solder [sáɒɚ] VI/VT soldar[se]; N soldadura *f*; —**ing iron** soldador *m*
soldier [sóɬʤɚ] N (of low rank) soldado *m*; (of any rank) militar *m*
sole [soɬ] ADJ solo, único; N (of a foot) planta *f*; (of a shoe) suela *f*; (fish) lenguado *m*
solely [sóɬli] ADV solamente; **you are — responsible** eres el único responsable
solemn [sáləm] ADJ solemne
solemnity [səlémnɪɒi] N solemnidad *f*
solenoid [sólənɔɪd] N solenoide *m*
solicit [səlísɪt] VT (aid) pedir; (a prostitute) ofrecerse; VI (sell) vender, ofrecer productos
solicitor [səlísɪɒɚ] N abogado *m*; — **general** subsecretario -ria de justicia *mf*
solicitous [səlísɪɒəs] ADJ solícito
solid [sálɪd] ADJ (firm) sólido; (dense) denso; — **blue** azul liso *m*; — **geometry** geometría del espacio *f*; — **gold** oro puro *m*; — **line** línea continua *f*; —-**state** de estado sólido; **for one — hour** por una hora entera; N sólido *m*
solidarity [salɪdǽrɪɒi] N solidaridad *f*
solidify [səlídəfaɪ] VI/VT solidificar[se]
solidity [səlídɪɒi] N solidez *f*
solitary [sálɪteri] ADJ solitario; **to be in — confinement** estar incomunicado
solitude [sálɪtud] N soledad *f*
solo [sólo] N (in music) solo *m*
soloist [sóloɪst] N solista *mf*
Solomon Islander [sáləmənáɪləndɚ] N

salomonense *mf*
Solomon Islands [sáləmənáɪləndz] N Islas Salomón *f pl*
solstice [sóɬstɪs] N solsticio *m*
soluble [sáljəbəɬ] ADJ soluble
solution [səlúʃən] N solución *f*
solve [sɑɬv] VT resolver, solucionar
solvent [sáɬvənt] N solvente *m*, disolvente *m*
Somalia [somáljə] N Somalia *f*
Somalian [somáljən] ADJ & N somalí *mf*
somber [sámbɚ] ADJ sombrío
some [sʌm] ADJ algún, alguno; **I worked for — time** trabajé por un rato; **that is — dog!** ¡menudo perro! PRON algunos; **and then —** y más todavía; ADV — **twenty people** unas veinte personas; **I like it —** me gusta un poco
somebody [sámbɑɒi] PRON alguien
someday [sámde] ADV algún día
somehow [sámhaʊ] ADV de alguna manera; — **or other** de alguna manera u otra
someone [sámwʌn] PRON alguien, alguno
somersault [sámɚsɔɬt] N (on ground) voltereta *f*; (in air) salto mortal *m*; VI (on ground) dar una voltereta; (in air) dar un salto mortal
something [sámθɪŋ] PRON algo *m*; — **else** otra cosa; **thirty—** (age) treinta y tantos; (person) treintañero -ra *mf*
sometime [sámtaɪm] ADV algún día, en algún momento; —**s** a veces, de vez en cuando
somewhat [sámhwɑt] ADV algo
somewhere [sámhwɛr] ADV en alguna parte; — **else** en alguna otra parte
son [sʌn] N hijo *m*; —-**in-law** yerno *m*; — **of a bitch** *offensive* hijo de puta *m*; — **of a gun** *fam* hijo de su madre *m*
sonar [sónɑr] N sonar *m*
song [sɔŋ] N canción *f*; (of a bird) canto *m*; — **and dance** cuento chino *m*; —**writer** compositor -ora *mf*; —**bird** ave canora *f*, pájaro cantor *m*; **to buy something for a —** comprar algo muy barato
sonic barrier [sánɪkbǽriɚ] N barrera del sonido *f*
sonnet [sánɪt] N soneto *m*
sonority [sənɔ́rɪɒi] N sonoridad *f*
sonorous [sánɚəs] ADJ sonoro
soon [sun] ADV pronto; — **after nine** poco después de las nueve; **as — as** tan pronto como, en cuanto; **see you —** hasta pronto; **how — do you want it?** ¿para cuándo lo necesitas? **he arrived —er** llegó antes; —**er or later** tarde o temprano; **I'd —er stay here** prefiero quedarme aquí
soot [sut] N hollín *m*, tizne *m*
soothe [suð] VT calmar, aliviar
soothsayer [súθseɚ] N agorero -ra *mf*
sooty [súɒi] ADJ tiznado
sop [sɑp] VT empapar; **to — up** absorber; **to be —ping wet** estar empapado; N —**s** sopas *f pl*
sophisticated [səfístɪkeɒɪd] ADJ sofisticado

sophomore [sáfəmɔr] N estudiante de segundo año *mf*

soprano [səprǽno] N soprano *m*

sorcerer [sɔ́rsərə-] N brujo *m*, hechicero *m*

sorceress [sɔ́rsə-ɪs] N hechicera *f*

sordid [sɔ́rDɪd] ADJ sórdido, escabroso

sore [sɔr] ADJ (painful) dolorido, doloroso; (grieved) dolorido; (angry) enojado; —**head** cascarrabias *mf*; **my arm is** — me duele el brazo; **to have a** — **throat** tener dolor de garganta; N llaga *f*, úlcera *f*

soreness [sɔ́rnɪs] N dolor *m*

sorority [sərɔ́rɪDi] N asociación femenina de estudiantes *f*

sorrow [sáro] N (sadness) pena *f*, pesar *m*, pesadumbre *f*; (cause of sadness) disgusto *m*

sorrowful [sárəfəɫ] ADJ triste, pesaroso

sorry [sári] ADJ **I am** — lo siento; **I am** — **about that** lo lamento; **I am** — **for her** la compadezco; —**?** ¿Cómo? **a** — **SOB** *pej* un desgraciado; **you'll be** — te arrepentirás; **he was in** — **shape** estaba en un estado lamentable

sort [sɔrt] N clase *f*, tipo *m*; — **of tired** algo cansado; **all** —**s of** toda clase de; **out of** —**s** (depressed) de mal humor; (ill) indispuesto; — **key** tecla de ordenación *f*; — **order** orden de clasificación *m*; VT (classify) clasificar; (put in order) ordenar; **to** — **out** separar, apartar; **to** — **out a problem** resolver un problema

SOS [ésoés] N SOS *m*

sought [sɔt] *see* seek

soul [soɫ] N alma *f*; — **music** música soul *f*; **not a** — nadie, ni un alma; **the** — **of tact** la imagen del tacto

sound [saʊnd] N sonido *m*; (inlet) brazo de mar *m*; — **barrier** barrera del sonido *f*; — **card** tarjeta de sonido *f*; —**proof** a prueba de sonido; —**track** banda sonora *f*; — **wave** onda sonora *f*; ADJ (healthy) sano; (sane) cuerdo; (well founded) bien fundado, lógico; — **advice** buen consejo *m*; — **sleep** sueño profundo *m*; **a** — **beating** una buena paliza; **of** — **mind** en su sano juicio; **safe and** — sano y salvo; VI sonar; VT (an alarm) tocar; (a channel) sondar; (opinion) sondear; **to** — **out** tantear, sondear

soup [sup] N sopa *f*; — **dish** plato sopero *m*; —**spoon** cuchara sopera *f*; — **tureen** sopera *f*

sour [saʊr] ADJ (acidic) agrio, ácido; (peevish) agrio, avinagrado; **to go** — (milk) cortarse, agriarse; (a relationship) estropearse; — **cream** *Sp* nata agria *f*; *Am* crema agria *f*; — **milk** leche cortada *f*; —**puss** cascarrabias *mf*, avinagrado -da *mf*; VI/VT agriar[se], avinagrar[se]; (milk) cortar[se]

source [sɔrs] N fuente *f*, origen *m*; — **code** código fuente *m*

sourness [sáʊrnɪs] N acidez *f*

souse [saʊs] VI/VT (plunge) zambullir[se]; (soak) empapar[se]; N borracho -cha *mf*, esponja *f*

south [saʊθ] N sur *m*, mediodía *f*; ADJ meridional, sureño; — **Africa** Sudáfrica *f*; — **African** sudafricano -na *mf*; — **America** América del Sur *f*, Sudamérica *f*; — **American** sudamericano -na *mf*; —**bound** con rumbo al sur; —**east** sureste, sudeste; —**eastern** sureste, sudeste; — **Korea** Corea del Sur *f*; — **Korean** surcoreano -na *mf*; —**paw** zurdo -da *mf*; — **pole** polo sur *m*; —**west** sudoeste, suroeste; —**western** sudoeste, suroeste; ADV hacia el sur

southern [sʌ́ðə-n] ADJ meridional, sureño

southerner [sʌ́ðə-nə-] N sureño -ña *mf*, meridional *mf*, habitante del sur *mf*

southward [sáʊθwə-d] ADV hacia el sur, rumbo al sur

souvenir [suvənír] N recuerdo *m*

sovereign [sávə-ɪn] ADJ & N soberano -na *mf*

sovereignty [sávə-ɪnti] N soberanía *f*

sow¹ [saʊ] N puerca *f*

sow² [so] VI/VT sembrar

sown [son] *see* sow²

soy [sɔi] N *Sp* soja *f*; *Am* soya *f*; —**bean** *Sp* semilla de soja *f*; *Am* semilla de soya *f*; — **sauce** *Sp* salsa de soja *f*; *Am* salsa de soya *f*

spa [spɑ] N balneario *m*

space [spes] N espacio *m*; —**-age** de la era espacial; —**bar** barra espaciadora *f*; —**craft** nave espacial *f*; —**ship** nave espacial *f*; — **shuttle** transbordador espacial *m*; — **station** estación espacial *f*; — **suit** traje espacial *m*; VT espaciar; **to** — **out** distraerse

spacious [spéʃəs] ADJ espacioso, amplio

spade [sped] N (shovel) pala *f*; (in cards) pica *f*; **to call a** — **a** — al pan, pan y al vino, vino

Spain [spen] N España *f*

spam [spæm] N correo electrónico basura *m*, spam *m*

span [spæn] N (of hand) palmo *m*; (of time) espacio *m*; (of attention) lapso *m*, período *m*; (of bridge) tramo *m*; (of wing) envergadura *f*; (of life) duración *f*; VT (time) abarcar; (a river) atravesar, salvar

Spaniard [spǽnjə-d] N español -ola *mf*

Spanish [spǽnɪʃ] ADJ (of Spain) español; (Spanish-speaking) hispano; N (language) español *m*; — **America** Hispanoamérica *f*

spank [spæŋk] VT dar nalgadas; N palmada *f*, nalgada *f*

spanking [spǽŋkɪŋ] N zurra en las nalgas *f*; ADJ — **new** flamante

spare [spɛr] VT (embarrassment) ahorrar, evitar; (money) prestar; (an enemy) perdonar la vida a; (a worker) prescindir de; — **me!** ¡ten piedad de mí! **to** — **no expense** no escatimar gastos; **to have time to** — tener tiempo de sobra; ADJ (austere) austero; (extra) de sobra, de más; — **cash** dinero disponible *m*; — **parts** repuestos *m pl*; — **time** tiempo libre *m*; N (part) repuesto *m*; (tire) neumático de repuesto *m*

spark [spɑrk] N chispa *f*; — **plug** bujía *f*; VI chispear, echar chispas; VT (a riot) desencadenar; (interest, criticism) provocar

sparkle [spárkəł] VI (diamond) centellear; (sparkler) chispear; (eyes) brillar; N (flashing) brillo *m*, centelleo *m*; (spirit) viveza *f*, animación *f*

sparkling [spárklɪŋ] ADJ (diamond) centelleante; (eyes) brillante; — **water** agua con gas *f*; — **wine** vino espumoso *m*

sparrow [spǽro] N gorrión *m*

sparse [spɑrs] ADJ escaso; (hair) ralo

spasm [spǽzəm] N espasmo *m*

spasmodic [spæzmáDɪk] ADJ espasmódico

spastic [spǽstɪk] ADJ espástico

spat [spæt] N riña *f*

spat [spæt] *see* spit

spatial [spéʃəł] ADJ espacial

spatter [spǽDɚ] VI/VT salpicar; N salpicadura *f*

spatula [spǽtʃələ] N espátula *f*

spawn [spɔn] VI desovar; VT engendrar; N (of fish) huevas *f pl*; (of frogs) huevos *m pl*

spay [spe] VT esterilizar, castrar

speak [spik] VI hablar; VT (a language) hablar; (the truth) decir; (one's lines) recitar, decir; **so to** — por decirlo así, valga la expresión; **to** — **for** hablar en nombre de / a favor de; **to** — **one's mind** hablar sin rodeos; **to** — **out against** denunciar; **to** — **out for** defender; **to** — **up** hablar fuerte

speaker [spíkɚ] N orador -ora *mf*; (at a conference) conferenciante *mf*; (of a language) hablante *mf*; — **of the House** presidente -ta de la cámara de representantes *mf*; —**phone** teléfono con parlante *m*

spear [spir] N (weapon) lanza *f*; (for fishing) arpón *m*; (sprout) brote *m*; VT (a person, animal) alancear, herir con lanza; (a fish) arponear

spearmint [spírmɪnt] N mentaverde *f*

special [spéʃəł] ADJ especial; — **delivery** entrega inmediata *f*; — **education** educación especial *f*; — **effects** efectos especiales *m pl*; — **interest [group]** grupo de presión *m*; N (sale item) especialidad *f*; (TV program) especial *m*

specialist [spéʃəlɪst] N especialista *mf*

specialization [spɛʃəlɪzéʃən] N especialización *f*, especialidad *f*

specialize [spéʃəlaɪz] VI/VT especializar[se]

specially [spéʃəli] ADV especialmente, específicamente

specialty [spéʃəłti] N especialidad *f*

species [spíʃiz] N especie *f*

specific [spɪsífɪk] ADJ específico, determinado; — **gravity** peso específico *m*; N —**s** detalles *m pl*

specifically [spɪsífɪkli] ADV concretamente, específicamente

specify [spésəfaɪ] VI/VT especificar

specimen [spésəmən] N (representative) espécimen *m*, ejemplar *m*; (sample) muestra *f*

speck [spɛk] N (small dot) mota *f*, manchita *f*; (small amount) pizca *f*

speckle [spékəł] N manchita *f*, mota *f*; VT salpicar, motear; —**d** moteado

spectacle [spéktəkəł] N espectáculo *m*; —**s** gafas *f pl*, anteojos *m pl*; **to make a** — **of oneself** dar un espectáculo, ponerse en ridículo

spectacular [spɛktǽkjəlɚ] ADJ espectacular

spectator [spékteDɚ] N espectador -ora *mf*

spectrum [spéktrəm] N espectro *m*

speculate [spékjəlet] VI/VT especular

speculation [spɛkjəléʃən] N especulación *f*

speculative [spékjələDɪv] ADJ especulativo

speculator [spékjələDɚ] N especulador -ora *mf*

sped [spɛd] *see* speed

speech [spitʃ] N (faculty of speaking) habla *f*; (formal) discurso *m*; (in a play) parlamento *m*; — **defect** defecto de pronunciación *m*; — **recognition** reconocimiento de habla *m*; — **synthesis** síntesis de habla *m*; **to make a** — pronunciar un discurso

speechless [spítʃlɪs] ADJ (dumb) mudo; (astonished) estupefacto

speed [spid] N (rapidity) velocidad *f*, rapidez *f*; (gear) velocidad *f*; (amphetamine) anfeta *f*; — **limit** límite de velocidad *m*; **at full** — a toda velocidad; VI (break speed limit) ir con exceso de velocidad; **to** — **by** pasar a toda velocidad; **to** — **off/away** irse a toda velocidad; **to** — **up** (a car, work) acelerar; (a delivery) hacer llegar a toda velocidad

speedometer [spɪdámɪDɚ] N velocímetro *m*

speedy [spíDi] ADJ veloz, rápido

spell [spɛł] N (charm) hechizo *m*, sortilegio *m*, conjuro *m*; (period) temporada *f*; (sickness) ataque *m*; **to put under a** — hechizar; ADJ —**bound** hechizado; VT (spoken) deletrear; (written) escribir; (represent) significar, representar; **to** —-**check** comprobar la ortografía; **I** —**ed it out for him** se lo dije con todas las letras

spelling [spélɪŋ] N ortografía *f*; — **bee** concurso de ortografía *m*

spend [spɛnd] VT (money) gastar; (time) pasar; —**thrift** derrochador -ora *mf*, gastador -ora *mf*, pródigo -ga *mf*

spending [spéndɪŋ] N gastos *m pl*; — **cut** recorte de gastos *m*; **to go on a** — **spree** salir a gastar dinero a lo loco

spent [spɛnt] *see* spend

sperm [spɝm] N esperma *mf*, semen *m*; — **bank**

banco de semen/esperma *m*; — **whale** cachalote *m*

spermicide [spɜ́·məsaɪd] N espermicida *m*

sphere [sfɪr] N esfera *f*; — **of influence** esfera de influencia *f*

spherical [sférɪkəł] ADJ esférico

sphincter [sfíŋktə·] N esfínter *m*

spice [spaɪs] N especia *f*; VT condimentar; **to —** **up** dar sal

spiciness [spáɪsɪnɪs] N lo picante

spick and span [spíkənspǽn] ADJ impecable

spicy [spáɪsi] ADJ picante

spider [spáɪDə·] N araña *f*; — **monkey** mono araña *m*; **—'s web** telaraña *f*

spigot [spígət] N grifo *m*, espita *f*

spike [spaɪk] N (sprout) espiga *f*; (sharp object) púa *f*, pincho *m*; (on shoes) clavo *m*; **—s** zapatillas con clavos *f pl*; VT (impale) clavar; (add alcohol to) echar alcohol a; (hit a volleyball) picar

spill [spɪł] VI/VT volcar[se], derramar[se], verter[se]; VT (a rider) hacer caer; **to — the** **beans** descubrir el pastel; VI **to — over** (a liquid) desbordarse; (a conflict) extenderse; N (of water) derrame *m*; (of blood) derramamiento *m*; (fall) caída *f*

spilt [spɪłt] *see* spill

spin [spɪn] VT (wool) hilar; (a top, one's partner) hacer girar; VI dar vueltas, girar; **to — yarns** contar cuentos; N (turning) giro *m*, vuelta *f*; (of an airplane) barrena *f*; (political) sesgo *m*; **to take a —** dar una vuelta

spinach [spínɪtʃ] N espinaca *f*

spinal [spáɪnł] ADJ espinal, vertebral; — **column** columna vertebral *f*, espina dorsal *f*; — **cord** médula espinal *f*

spindle [spíndł] N (for weaving) huso *m*; (on machines) eje *m*

spine [spaɪn] N espina *f*, espinazo *m*

spinning [spínɪŋ] N (action) hilado *m*; (art) hilandería *f*; — **machine** máquina de hilar *f*; — **mill** hilandería *f*; — **top** trompo *m*, peonza *f*; — **wheel** rueca *f*

spinster [spínstə·] N solterona *f*

spiral [spáɪrəł] ADJ & N espiral *m*; — **notebook** cuaderno de espiral *m*; — **staircase** escalera de caracol *f*

spire [spaɪr] N aguja *f*, chapitel *m*

spirit [spírɪt] N (ghost) espíritu *m*; (animation) ánimo *m*, brío *m*; (alcohol) alcohol *m*; **low** **—s** abatimiento *m*; **to be in good —s** estar de buen humor; VT **to — away** llevar como por arte de magia

spirited [spírɪDɪd] ADJ fogoso, brioso

spiritual [spírɪtʃuəł] ADJ & N espiritual *m*

spirituality [spɪrɪtʃuǽlɪDi] N espiritualidad *f*

spit [spɪt] VI/VT escupir; N (saliva) escupitajo *m*; (for roasting) asador *m*, espeto *m*, espetón *m*; (of sand) banco *m*

spite [spaɪt] N despecho *m*, inquina *f*; **in — of** a pesar de; **out of —** por despecho; VT contrariar

spiteful [spáɪtfəł] ADJ malicioso

splash [splæʃ] VI/VT salpicar; VI chapotear, chapalear; N salpicadura *f*, chapoteo *m*; **to** **make a —** hacer olas

splatter [splǽDə·] VI/VT salpicar; N salpicadura *f*

spleen [splin] N bazo *m*; (ill humor) mal humor *m*

splendid [spléndɪd] ADJ espléndido

splendor [spléndə·] N esplendor *m*

splice [splaɪs] VT (tape, genes) empalmar, unir; N empalme *m*, unión *f*

splint [splɪnt] N tablilla *f*; VT entablillar

splinter [splíntə·] N astilla *f*; VI/VT astillar[se]

split [splɪt] VI/VT (stone, wood) hender[se], rajar[se]; (candy bar) partir[se], dividir[se]; **to** **— hairs** hilar fino; **to — one's sides with** **laughter** desternillarse de risa; **to — the** **difference** partir la diferencia; ADJ (wood) partido, hendido; (a group) dividido; **— -** **level** en desnivel; — **personality** doble personalidad *f*; — **screen** pantalla dividida *f*; — **second** fracción de segundo *f*; N hendidura *f*, grieta *f*; (in a group) escisión *f*, división *f*

spoil [spɔɪł] VI (milk) cortar[se]; (food) echarse a perder; VT (vacation, performance) estropear, arruinar; (plans) desbaratar; (enjoyment) aguar; (child) malcriar, mimar demasiado; N **—s** botín *m*

spoiler [spɔ́ɪlə·] N alerón *m*

spoke [spok] N rayo *m*

spoke [spok] *see* speak

spoken [spókən] *see* speak

spokesperson [spókspɜ·sən] N portavoz *mf*, vocero -ra *mf*

sponge [spʌndʒ] N (animal, utensil) esponja *f*; (parasite) gorrón -ona *mf*; — **bath** baño de esponja *m*; — **cake** *Am* bizcochuelo *m*; *Sp* bizcocho *m*; VI **to — off** (clean) quitar con esponja; (take advantage of) gorronear; **to —** **up** absorber con una esponja

sponger [spándʒə·] N gorrón -ona *mf*, parásito *m*

spongy [spándʒi] ADJ esponjoso, esponjado

sponsor [spánsə·] N (of the arts) mecenas *mf*; (of sports, TV program) patrocinador -ora *mf*; (of a bill) proponente *mf*; VT (a child) apadrinar; (arts, sports, TV show) patrocinar; (bill) proponer

sponsorship [spánsə·ʃɪp] N patrocinio *m*

spontaneity [spɑntənéɪDi] N espontaneidad *f*

spontaneous [spɑnténiəs] ADJ espontáneo; — **abortion** aborto espontáneo *m*

spook [spuk] N (ghost) espectro *m*; (spy) espía *mf*

spool [spuł] N carrete *m*, carretel *m*; VT (wool) devanar; (tape) enrollar

spoon [spun] N cuchara *f*; VT cucharear, poner

con una cuchara; **to —-feed** dar de comer en
la boca
spoonful [spúnfʊɫ] N cucharada *f*
spore [spɔr] N espora *f*
sport [spɔrt] N deporte *m*; **to be a good —** tener
espíritu deportivo; **— utility vehicle**
vehículo utilitario deportivo *m*; **—s car** coche
deportivo *m*; **—s jacket** saco de sport *m*,
americana *f*; **—sman** (hunter) cazador *m*; (in
sports) hombre de espíritu deportivo *m*;
—smanship espíritu deportivo *m*,
deportividad *f*; **—swriter** cronista deportivo
-va *mf*; ADJ deportivo; VT lucir
sporty [spɔ́rDi] ADJ deportivo
spot [spɑt] N (stain) mancha *f*, mota *f*; (blemish)
espinilla *f*; (insect bite) roncha *f*; (place) lugar
m, paraje *m*; (difficult situation) aprieto *m*; **on
the —** en el acto; **—-check** inspección al azar
f; **—light** (in theater) foco *m*; (outdoors)
reflector *m*; **to be in the —light** ser el
centro de atención; **— remover**
quitamanchas *m sg*; VI/VT (stain) manchar,
ensuciar; VT (see in the distance) divisar;
(notice) notar; (give advantage) dar como
ventaja
spotless [spátlɪs] ADJ inmaculado
spotted [spáDɪd] ADJ manchado, moteado
spouse [spaʊs] N cónyuge *mf*; **— abuse** abuso
conyugal *m*
spout [spaʊt] VT (throw) arrojar chorros de;
(talk) soltar tonterías; VI (flow out) salir a
chorros; (talk) perorar; N (of a fountain) caño
m; (of a gutter) canalón *m*; (of a teapot) pico *m*
sprain [spren] VT torcerse; N torcedura *f*
sprang [spræŋ] *see* spring
sprawl [sprɔɫ] VI (spread limbs) despatarrarse;
(extend) extenderse; (fall) tumbarse; N
postura despatarrada *f*
spray [spre] VI/VT rociar[se]; N (of liquid) rociada
f; (foam) espuma *f*; (of flowers) ramillete *m*;
— can aerosol *m*; **— paint** pintura en
aerosol *f*
spread [sprɛd] VI/VT (arms, newspaper)
extender[se]; (butter) untar[se]; (map)
desdoblar[se]; (legs) abrir[se]; (seeds)
esparcir[se]; (news) difundir[se],
diseminar[se]; (odor) difundir[se],
expandirse; (rumor) propalar; (panic)
sembrar; VT (panic, news) sembrar; N (of
ideas) difusión *f*; (of opinion) diseminación *f*;
(of disease) propagación *f*; (of nuclear
weapons) proliferación *f*; (for a bed)
cubrecama *m*; (for bread) pasta *f*; (of food)
festín *m*; (ranch) hacienda *f*; **—sheet** (paper)
planilla de cálculo *f*; (program) planilla
electrónica *f*
spree [spri] N parranda *f*, farra *f*; **to go on a —** ir
de parranda/farra; **to go on a shopping —**
gastar dinero desenfrenadamente

spring [sprɪŋ] VI saltar; **to — at** abalanzarse
sobre; **to — from** nacer de; **to — open**
abrir[se] de golpe; **to — to mind** venir a la
mente; **to — up** surgir; VT **to — a leak** (boat)
hacer agua; (pipe) comenzar a gotear; **to —
news** dar una noticia de sopetón; N (season)
primavera *f*; (coil) muelle *m*, resorte *m*;
(elasticity) elasticidad *f*; (jump) salto *m*;
(water) manantial *m*, fuente *f*; **—board**
trampolín *m*; **— fever** fiebre de primavera *f*;
— mattress colchón de muelles *m*; **—time**
primavera *f*; **— water** agua de manantial *f*;
he's no — chicken no se cuece en el primer
hervor
sprinkle [sprɪ́ŋkəɫ] VT (with sugar) espolvorear;
(with droplets) salpicar, rociar; (rain) gotear,
chispear
sprint [sprɪnt] VI (run) echarse una carrera; (run
a competitive race) [e]sprintar; N (run)
corrida corta *f*; (race) [e]sprint *m*
sprocket [sprákɪt] N piñón *m*, rueda dentada *f*
sprout [spraʊt] VI (leaf) brotar, salir; (plants)
retoñar; (seeds) germinar; (houses) surgir; VT
echar; **he —ed horns** le salieron cuernos; N
retoño *m*, brote *m*, renuevo *m*
spruce [sprus] N picea *f*; VI **to — up** arreglarse
sprung [sprʌŋ] *see* spring
spun [spʌn] *see* spin
spunk [spʌŋk] N agallas *f pl*, *vulg* cojones *m pl*
spur [spɝ] N (on stirrups) espuela *f*; (stimulus)
aguijón *m*; (of a rooster) espolón *m*; (of a
mountain) estribación *f*; (of a railroad track)
ramal *m*; **on the — of the moment**
espontáneamente; VT espolear; **to — on**
animar
spurious [spjúriəs] ADJ espurio
spurn [spɝn] VT rechazar, desdeñar
spurt [spɝt] VI salir a chorros; N (of water)
chorro *m*; (of a runner) esfuerzo repentino *m*;
in —s por rachas
sputter [spʌ́Dɚ] VI (fire) chisporrotear; (person)
refunfuñar; N (fire) chisporroteo *m*
sputum [spjúbəm] N esputo *m*
spy [spaɪ] N espía *mf*; **—glass** catalejo *m*; VI
espiar; **to — on** espiar
squabble [skwábəɫ] VI reñir; N reyerta *f*
squad [skwɑd] N (of police) patrulla *f*; (for
execution) pelotón *m*; (of athletes) equipo *m*;
(for guarding) retén *m*; **— car** [coche]
patrullero *m*
squadron [skwádrən] N (in navy) escuadra *f*; (in
army) escuadrón *m*
squalid [skwálɪd] ADJ escuálido
squall [skwɔɫ] N (rain) chubasco *m*, borrasca *f*;
(sound) berrido *m*; VI berrear
squalor [skwálɚ] N miscria *f*, escualidez *f*
squander [skwándɚ] VT despilfarrar, derrochar,
disipar
squanderer [skwándərɚ] N derrochador -ora *mf*

square [skwɛr] N (shape) cuadrado *m*; (on a pattern) cuadro *m*; (plaza) plaza *f*, *Mex* zócalo *m*; (tool in carpentry) escuadra *f*; (on chessboard) casilla *f*; — **brackets** corchetes *m pl*; — **dance** cuadrilla *f*; — **knot** nudo de rizo *m*; — **meal** comida completa *f*; — **root** raíz cuadrada *f*; **he is a** — es muy conservador; VT (make square) cuadrar; (draw squares on) cuadricular; (multiply by itself) elevar al cuadrado; **to** — **one's shoulders** erguirse; ADJ (in shape) cuadrado; (at ninety degrees) en ángulo recto; (tied) empatado; (frank) franco; **to be** — **with someone** estar a mano con alguien; ADV **right** — **between the eyes** justo entre los ojos

squash [skwɑʃ] N (gourd) calabaza *f*; (sport) squash *m*; VT (smash) aplastar, despachurrar

squat [skwɑt] VI (sit low) acuclillarse; (occupy) ocupar sin autorización; ADJ (sitting low) acuclillado; (thickset) rechoncho, achaparrado; N (nothing) nada; **he doesn't know** — no sabe un comino; **in a** — en cuclillas

squawk [skwɔk] VI (of chickens) cacarear; (complain) quejarse; N (of chickens) cacareo *m*; (complaint) quejido *m*

squeak [skwik] VI (door) rechinar, chirriar; (shoe) rechinar; (mouse) chillar; N (of door) rechinamiento *m*, chirrido *m*; (of shoe) rechinamiento *m*; (of mouse) chillido *m*

squeaky [skwíki] ADJ (door) chirriante; (shoes) rechinante

squeal [skwił] VI chillar; (complain) protestar; (snitch) chivatar, delatar; N chillido *m*

squeamish [skwímɪʃ] ADJ delicado

squeegee [skwíʤi] N escurridor de goma *m*, limpiavidrios *m sg*

squeeze [skwiz] VT apretar; (press very hard) estrujar; (an orange) estrujar, exprimir; (hug) abrazar; **to** — **into** meter[se] con dificultad en, encajar[se] en; **to** — **out** (an orange) exprimir; (a towel) escurrir; **to** — **through a crowd** abrirse paso entre la multitud; N (of hands) apretón *m*; (excessive squeeze) estrujón *m*; (hug) abrazo *m*; (lack) restricción *f*

squelch [skwɛłtʃ] VT (revolt) aplastar, sofocar; (criticism) acallar

squid [skwɪd] N calamar *m*

squint [skwɪnt] VI (partially close eyes) entrecerrar los ojos; (look askance) mirar de soslayo; N (look with partially closed eyes) mirada con los ojos entrecerrados *f*; (side glance) mirada de soslayo *f*

squirm [skwɝm] VI retorcerse; **to** — **out of a difficulty** zafarse de un aprieto

squirrel [skwɝ́əł] N ardilla *f*

squirt [skwɝt] VT echar un chisguete en; VI salir a chorritos; N chisguete *m*, chorrito *m*; —

gun pistola lanzaagua *f*, pistola de agua *f*

Sri Lanka [srilɑ́ŋkə] N Sri Lanka *f*

Sri Lankan [srilɑ́ŋkən] ADJ & N cingalés -esa *mf*

stab [stæb] VI/VT apuñalar, acuchillar; **to** — **at** tirar puñaladas a; N (with a dagger) puñalada *f*; (with a knife) cuchillada *f*; (with a pocketknife) navajazo *m*; (of pain) punzada *f*, pinchazo *m*; **to take a** — **at** intentar; — **wound** cuchillada *f*

stability [stəbíliDi] N estabilidad *f*

stabilization [stebəlizéʃən] N estabilización *f*

stable [stébəł] ADJ estable; N establo *m*, cuadra *f*; (for horses only) caballeriza *f*; VT poner en el establo

stack [stæk] N (ordered) pila *f*; (chaotic) montón *m*; (of a chimney) chimenea *f*; (in a library) estantería *f*; VT amontonar, apilar

stadium [stédiəm] N estadio *m*

staff [stæf] N (stick) cayado *m*; (of a flag) asta *f*; (personnel) personal *m*, plantel *m*; (of music) pentagrama *m*; — **of life** pan de cada día *m*; — **officer** oficial de estado mayor *m*; **editorial** — redacción *f*; **teaching** — cuerpo docente *m*; VT contratar personal para

stag [stæg] N (deer) venado *m*, ciervo *m*; (other animals) macho *m*; — **beetle** ciervo volante *m*; — **party** fiesta para hombres *f*

stage [steʤ] N (showplace) escenario *m*; (for popular entertainment) tablado *m*; (theater) teatro *m*, las tablas *f pl*; (period) etapa *f*, estadio *m*; (distance) etapa *f*; —**coach** diligencia *f*; — **fright** miedo al escenario *m*, fiebre de candilejas *f*; —**hand** tramoyista *mf*; **by** —**s** por etapas; VT (a play) poner en escena; (an attack) organizar

stagger [stǽgɚ] VI (totter) tambalearse, dar tumbos; VT (hit hard) hacer tambalear; (overwhelm) dejar azorado; (alternate) escalonar; N tambaleo *m*

stagnant [stǽgnənt] ADJ estancado

stagnate [stǽgnet] VI estancarse

stagnation [stægnéʃən] N estancamiento *m*

staid [sted] ADJ envarado

stain [sten] N (spot) mancha *f*; (color) tinte *m*, tintura *f*; VI/VT (spot) manchar[se]; (color) teñir[se]; —**ed-glass window** vitral *m*

stainless [sténlɪs] ADJ sin mancha; — **steel** acero inoxidable *m*

stair [stɛr] N peldaño *m*, escalón *m*; —**case** escalera *f*; —**s** escalera *f*; —**way** escalera *f*

stake [stek] N (pole) estaca *f*; (investment) interés *m*; (bet) apuesta *f*; **at** — en juego; **to die at the** — morir en la hoguera; VT estacar; **to** — **out** vigilar

stalactite [stəlǽktaɪt] N estalactita *f*

stalagmite [stəlǽgmaɪt] N estalagmita *f*

stale [steł] ADJ (bread) duro; (air) viciado; (joke) viejo; —**mate** punto muerto *m*

stalk [stɔk] N tallo *m*; VT acechar

stall [stɔł] N (at a market) puesto *m*; (at a fair) caseta *f*, barraca *f*; (in a stable) compartimiento *m*; VI (airplane) entrar en pérdida; (talks) llegar a un punto muerto; (motor) pararse; **he is —ing** está arrastrando los pies; VT (airplane) hacer entrar en pérdida; (talks) paralizar; (motor) parar

stallion [stǽljən] N semental *m*

stamina [stǽmənə] N resistencia *f*, aguante *m*

stammer [stǽmɚ] VI balbucear; N balbuceo *m*

stamp [stæmp] VT (a letter) sellar; *Mex* timbrar; *Am* estampillar; (an official document) sellar, timbrar; (a coin) acuñar; VI (with foot) pisotear, patalear; (with hoof) piafar; **to — out** eliminar; N (on a letter) *Sp* sello *m*; *Mex* timbre *m*; *Am* estampilla *f*; (on an official document) sello *m*, timbre *m*; (instrument, character) sello *m*; (on the ground) pisotón *m*; (sound) paso *m*; **— tax** timbre *m*

stampede [stæmpíd] N estampida *f*; VI huir en estampida; VT hacer huir en estampida

stance [stæns] N posición *f*, postura *f*; (political) posicionamiento *m*

stanch, staunch [stɔntʃ] VT restañar; ADJ (strong) firme; (loyal) fiel

stand [stænd] VI (take a standing position) ponerse de pie, levantarse; *Am* parar[se]; (to be in a standing position) estar de pie; *Am* estar parado; (stop) detenerse; (withstand, tolerate) aguantar, tolerar, soportar; (remain valid) mantenerse; **to — aside** apartarse; **to — back** retroceder; **to — behind someone** respaldar a alguien; **to — by** (be uninvolved) mantenerse al margen; (be alert) estar alerta; (support) respaldar; **to — for** (denote) significar; (tolerate) tolerar; **to — one's ground** mantenerse firme; **to — out** destacarse, sobresalir; **to — up for** defender; **it —s to reason** es razonable; **it —s one meter tall** mide un metro de alto; **to — a chance of** tener posibilidad de; **where do you — on this issue?** ¿qué opinas al respecto? N (at a market) puesto *m*; (at a fair) caseta *f*; (of trees) bosque *m*; (opinion) posición *f*; (for music) atril *m*; (for taxis) parada *f*; **—by** recurso viejo *m*; **—by passenger** pasajero -ra en la lista de espera *mf*; **—off** empate *m*; **—point** punto de vista *m*; **to come to a —still** pararse; **to be at a —still** estar parado; ADJ **—alone** autónomo

standard [stǽndɚd] N (of behavior) norma *f*; (of living, performance) nivel *m*; (of weights) patrón *m*; (banner) estandarte *m*; **gold —** patrón oro *m*; **—bearer** portaestandarte *mf*; **— deviation** desviación estándar *f*; **— of living** nivel de vida *m*; **— time** hora oficial *f*; **to be up to —** satisfacer los requisitos; ADJ (normal) normal; (standardized) estándar

standardization [stændɚDizéʃən] N

estandarización *f*

standardize [stǽndɚdaɪz] VT estandarizar, uniformar

standby [stǽndbaɪ] ADV **we're flying —** estamos volando standby

standing [stǽndɪŋ] N (position) posición *f*; (rank) rango *m*; (reputation) reputación *f*; ADJ (not seated) derecho, en pie; (permanent) permanente; (stagnant) estancado; **— order** pedido fijo *m*; **— ovation** ovación de pie *f*

stank [stæŋk] *see* stink

stanza [stǽnzə] N estrofa *f*

staple [stépəł] N (for paper) grapa *f*; (main product) producto principal *m*; (food) alimento básico *m*; ADJ (principal) principal; (basic) básico; VT engrapar

stapler [stéplɚ] N grapadora *f*

star [stɑr] N estrella *f* (also actor); (asterisk) asterisco *m*; **— attraction** atracción principal *f*; **—fish** estrella de mar *f*; **—light** luz de las estrellas *f*; **—-spangled** salpicado de estrellas; **a — student** un[a] estudiante sobresaliente; VT (act in) protagonizar; (put asterisk on) marcar con asterisco; (cover with stars) estrellar

starboard [stárbɚd] N estribor *m*; ADV a estribor

starch [stɑrtʃ] N almidón *m* (also food); VT almidonar

stardom [stárDəm] N estrellato *m*

stare [ster] VI/VT mirar fijamente; N mirada fija *f*

stark [stɑrk] ADJ (landscape) yermo; (truth) descarnado, desnudo; (contrast) marcado; ADV **— naked** en cueros; **— raving mad** loco de remate

starling [stárlɪŋ] N estornino *m*

starry [stári] ADJ estrellado

start [stɑrt] VI/VT (begin) comenzar, empezar; (a car) poner[se] en marcha, arrancar; VT (a fire) provocar; VI (jump) sobresaltarse; **to — off/ out/up** empezar; **don't get him —ed** no le des cuerda; N (beginning) comienzo *m*, principio *m*; (of a race) salida *f*; (nervous jump) sobresalto *m*; (nervous jump of a horse) respingo *m*; **—-up** compañía recién establecida *f*; **—-up funds** capital inicial *m*; **— button** botón de inicio *m*; **— menu** menú de inicio *m*

starter [stárDɚ] N (on an automobile) arranque *m*; (for a race) juez de salida *mf*; **for —s** para empezar

startle [stárdl] VI/VT asustar[se], sobresaltar[se]

startling [stárdlɪŋ] ADJ asombroso, sorprendente

starvation [stɑrvéʃən] N inanición *f*

starve [stɑrv] VI/VT hambrear; VI morirse de hambre; VT matar de hambre; (for affection) privar de cariño

starving [stárvɪŋ] ADJ hambriento, muerto de

hambre
stash [stæʃ] VI **to — away** ir ahorrando; N alijo *m*
state [stet] N estado *m*; **— of the art** con los
   últimos avances; **—room** (on a ship)
   camarote *m*; (on a train) compartimiento *m*;
   —-run company compañía estatal *f*;
   —sman estadista *m*; **—swoman** estadista *f*;
   VT (declare) declarar, aseverar, manifestar;
   (describe) exponer
stately [stétli] ADJ majestuoso, imponente
statement [stétmənt] N (declaration)
   declaración *f*, aseveración *f*; (bill) estado de
   cuentas *m*
static [stǽDɪk] ADJ estático; N interferencia *f*; **—
   electricity** electricidad estática *f*; **don't
   give me any —** no me compliques la vida
station [stéʃən] N estación *f*; (on the radio)
   emisora *f*; (on television) canal *m*; (social
   rank) condición *f*; **— wagon** camioneta *f*; VT
   (a sentry) apostar; (troops) estacionar
stationary [stéʃənɛri] ADJ (not moving)
   estacionario; (stopped) detenido; (fixed) fijo
stationery [stéʃənɛri] N (material) artículos de
   papelería *m pl*; (paper) papel de carta *m*
statistical [stətístɪkəł] ADJ estadístico
statistics [stətístɪks] N (science) estadística *f*;
   (data) estadísticas *f pl*
statue [stǽtʃu] N estatua *f*
stature [stǽtʃɚ] N (physical) estatura *f*; (moral)
   talla *f*
status [stǽDəs] N (prestige, rank) status *m*;
   (legal, financial) situación *f*; (marital) estado
   m; **— bar** (computer) barra de estado *f*; **—
   symbol** símbolo de status *m*
statute [stǽtʃut] N (bylaw) estatuto *m*; (law) ley *f*;
   — of limitations ley de prescripción *f*
statutory [stǽtʃətɔri] ADJ estatutario; **— rape**
   estupro *m*
stave [stev] N (of a barrel) duela *f*; VI **to — off**
   evitar
stay [ste] VI (remain) quedarse, permanecer; **to
   — away** mantenerse alejado; **to — in**
   quedarse en casa; **to — out of trouble** no
   meterse en líos; **to — up** quedarse levantado;
   VT **to — an execution** aplazar una
   ejecución; N (time spent) estancia *f*, estadía *f*,
   permanencia *f*; (support) sostén *m*, soporte *m*
STD [sexually transmitted disease] [éstídí]
   N ETS *f*
stead [stɛd] N **in her —** en su lugar; **to stand
   one in good —** ser de provecho para uno
steadfast [stédfæst] ADJ fijo, firme
steadiness [stéDɪnɪs] N (firmness) firmeza *f*; (of
   the hand) pulso *m*; (constancy) constancia *f*;
   (continuity) continuidad *f*
steady [stéDi] ADJ (not shaky) firme; (constant)
   constante; (continuous) continuo; **—
   boyfriend** novio formal *m*; **— customer**
   cliente -ta asiduo -dua *mf*; **— income** ingreso

fijo *m*; VI/VT (an object) asegurar; (nerves)
   calmar
steak [stek] N bistec *m*, churrasco *m*
steal [stił] VT (a thing, a base) robar, hurtar; (a
   girlfriend) soplar; VI **to — away/out**
   escabullirse, escaparse; N (bargain) ganga *f*
stealth [stɛłθ] N sigilo *m*; **by —** furtivamente
stealthy [stɛłθi] ADJ furtivo
steam [stim] N (evaporated water) vapor *m*;
   (arising from an object) vaho *m*; **— engine**
   máquina de vapor *f*; **— roller** apisonadora *f*,
   aplanadora *f*; **— ship** [buque de] vapor *m*; **—
   shovel** excavadora *f*; VT (cook) cocer al
   vapor; VI (give off steam) echar vapor; **to get
   —ed up** (angry) indignarse; (covered with
   vapor) empañarse
steamer [stímɚ] N buque de vapor *m*
steed [stid] N corcel *m*
steel [stił] N acero *m*; **— blue** azul acero *m*; **—
   industry** siderurgia *f*; **— mill** acería *f*; **—
   wool** lana de acero *f*; VT acerar; **to —
   oneself** prepararse
steep [stip] ADJ (hill) empinado, escarpado,
   acantilado; (decline) marcado; (price)
   excesivo; VT (tea) infusionar; VI (tea) estar en
   infusión, infusionarse
steeple [stípəł] N (spire) aguja *f*, chapitel *m*; (bell
   tower) campanario *m*
steer [stir] N (young bovine) novillo *m*; (grown
   bovine) buey *m*; VI/VT (a car) conducir,
   manejar; (a ship) gobernar, timonear; VI
   (turn) girar, doblar; **to — clear of** evitar; **to
   — a conversation** desviar una
   conversación; **the car —s easily** el coche es
   fácil de conducir; **—ing** dirección *f*; **—ing
   wheel** volante *m*
stellar [stélɚ] ADJ estelar
stem [stɛm] N (of a plant) tallo *m*; (of a leaf)
   pedúnculo *m*, rabo *m*; (of a glass) pie *m*; (of a
   pipe) cañón *m*; **— cell** célula estaminal/
   embrional *f*; VT detener, contener, estancar;
   to — from provenir de
stench [stɛntʃ] N hedor *m*, hediondez *f*, tufo *m*
stencil [sténsəł] N plantilla *f*, matriz *f*
stenographer [stənágrəfɚ] N taquígrafo -fa *mf*
step [stɛp] N (in walking, dancing) paso *m*; (on
   stairs) peldaño *m*, escalón *m*; (in music) tono
   m; **— by —** paso a paso; **—ladder** escalera *f*;
   to take —s (walk) dar pasos; VI dar un paso;
   — this way pase por aquí; **to — aside**
   hacerse a un lado; **to — back** retroceder; **to
   — down** (descend) bajar; (resign) renunciar;
   to — off bajar; **to — off a distance** medir a
   pasos una distancia; **to — on** pisar, pisotear;
   to — on the gas pisar el acelerador; **to —
   out** salir; (act) tomar medidas; **to — up**
   subir; **in — with the music** al compás de la
   música
stepbrother [stépbrʌðɚ] N hermanastro *m*

stepdaughter [stépdɔDə-] N hijastra f
stepfather [stépfaðə-] N padrastro m
stepmother [stépmʌðə-] N madrastra f
steppe [stɛp] N estepa f
stepsister [stépsɪstə-] N hermanastra f
stepson [stépsʌn] N hijastro m
stereo [stério] ADJ & N estéreo m
stereotype [stériətaɪp] N estereotipo m
sterile [stérəł] ADJ estéril
sterility [stərílɪDi] N esterilidad f
sterilize [stérəlaɪz] VT esterilizar
stern [stɜ-n] ADJ austero, severo, adusto; N (of a ship) popa f
sternum [stɜ́-nəm] N esternón m
steroid [stérɔɪd] N esteroide m
stethoscope [stéθəskop] N estetoscopio m
stew [stu] VI/VT (cook) estofar[se], guisar[se]; VI (worry) preocuparse; N estofado m, guiso m; **to be in a —** estar preocupado
steward [stúə-d] N (manager) administrador m; (on a ship) camarero m; (on an airplane) auxiliar de vuelo m
stewardess [stúə-DIs] N (on a ship) camarera f; (on an airplane) auxiliar de vuelo f, azafata f
stick [stɪk] N (of wood) palo m, vara f; (of firewood) raja f; (of dynamite) cartucho m; **— shift** palanca de cambios f; **—-up** atraco m, asalto m; VI/VT (adhere) pegar[se], adherir[se]; VT (place) poner, meter; (stab) clavar, pinchar; VI (become jammed) atascarse; **—'em up!** ¡arriba las manos! **to — out** salir, sobresalir; **to — out one's head** asomar la cabeza; **to — out one's tongue** sacar la lengua; **to — to a job** persistir en una tarea; **to — up** (point up) estar parado de punta; **to — up for** defender; **to — someone up** asaltar/atracar a alguien
sticker [stíkə-] N (thistle) abrojo m; (adhesive) etiqueta adhesiva f
sticky [stíki] ADJ pegajoso
stiff [stɪf] ADJ (leather, cardboard) tieso, duro; (drink) fuerte, cargado; (shirt) almidonado; (back) entumecido; (test) difícil; (breeze) fuerte; (personality) envarado; (climb) arduo; (price) alto; **to get —** entumecerse; N (cadaver) fam fiambre m
stiffen [stífən] VI/VT (leather) endurecer[se]; (back) entumecer[se]; (shirt) almidonar[se]; **to — up** agarrotar[se]
stiffness [stífnɪs] N (of leather) dureza f, tiesura f; (of one's back) entumecimiento m; (of one's personality) envaramiento m; (of resistance) firmeza f
stifle [stáɪfəł] VI/VT ahogar[se], sofocar[se]; **to — a yawn** contener un bostezo
stigma [stígmə] N estigma m
stigmatize [stígmətaɪz] VI/VT estigmatizar
still [stɪł] ADJ (not moving) quieto; (quiet) silencioso; **—born** nacido muerto; **— life**

naturaleza muerta f; VT acallar; ADV todavía, aún; **he's — here** todavía está [aquí]; CONJ de todos modos, en todo caso; **—, it's a good buy** en todo caso, es una ganga; N (for distilling) alambique m; (quiet) silencio m
stillness [stíłnɪs] N (not moving) quietud f; (silence) silencio m
stilt [stɪłt] N (for walking) zanco m; (support) pilote m
stilted [stíłtɪd] ADJ (personality) envarado; (style) afectado
stimulant [stímjələnt] ADJ & N estimulante m
stimulate [stímjələet] VT estimular
stimulation [stɪmjəléʃən] N estimulación f
stimulus [stímjələs] N estímulo m
sting [stɪŋ] VI/VT (insects, thorns) picar; (insects) aguijonear; VT (shampoo) hacer picar; (rain) azotar; (cheat) timar; N (pain) picadura f; (stinger) aguijón m; (confidence game) golpe m; **— of remorse** punzada de remordimiento f; **—ray** manta raya f
stinger [stíŋə-] N aguijón m
stinginess [stíndʒinɪs] N tacañería f, mezquindad f
stingy [stíndʒi] ADJ mezquino, tacaño
stink [stɪŋk] VI (smell bad) heder, apestar; **to — of** heder a; **to — up** dar mal olor a; **your performance —s** tu actuación es un desastre; N hedor m
stipend [stáɪpɪnd] N (fellowship) beca f; (salary) estipendio m
stipulate [stípjələt] VT estipular
stipulation [stɪpjəléʃən] N estipulación f
stir [stɜ-] VI (move) bullir, rebullir; (awaken) despertar; VT (mix) revolver; (move emotionally) conmover; (stoke) atizar; **to — up** (trouble) provocar, suscitar; (an old grudge) remover; **to —-fry** saltear; N **—-crazy** claustrofóbico; **to give something a — revolver algo; **to cause a —** causar revuelo
stirring [stɜ́-ɪŋ] ADJ (moving) conmovedor
stirrup [stɜ́-rəp] N estribo m
stitch [stɪtʃ] N (in sewing) puntada f; (on a wound) punto m; **to be in —es** desternillarse de risa; VI/VT coser
St. Kitts and Nevis [sentkítsənnívɪs] N San Cristóbal y Nieves m
St. Lucia [sentlúʃə] N Santa Lucía f
St. Lucian [sentlúʃən] ADJ & N santalucense mf
stock [stɑk] N (selection) surtido m; (reserves) existencias f pl; (livestock) ganado m; (lineage) estirpe f; (shares) acciones f pl, valores m pl; (in grafting) patrón m; (broth) caldo m; **—broker** corredor -ora de bolsa mf, bolsista mf; **— company** sociedad anónima f; **— exchange** bolsa de valores f; **—holder** accionista mf; **— market** mercado de valores m, bolsa de valores f; **— market trends** tendencias bursátiles f pl; **— options**

opciones *f pl;* —**pile** acopio *m;* —**room** depósito *m;* — **size** tamaño ordinario *m;* —**yard** corral *m;* **in** — en existencia; **out of** — agotado; VT (sell) vender; (fill shelves) abastecer; **to** — **up on** surtirse de, acumular; **to** —**pile** acopiar; ADJ (trite) trillado

stockade [stɑkéd] N (fence) estacada *f,* empalizada *f;* (prison) prisión militar *f*

stocking [stákɪŋ] N (hose) media *f;* (sock) calcetín *m*

stocky [stáki] ADJ robusto

stoic [stóɪk] ADJ & N estoico -ca *mf*

stoke [stok] VT (fire) atizar; (engine) alimentar

stole [stol] (fur) estola *f*

stole [stol] *see* steal

stolen [stólən] *see* steal

stomach [stʌ́mək] N (organ) estómago *m;* (belly) panza *f,* barriga *f;* **he has a big** — es barrigón; **to lie on one's** — estar panza abajo; VT (tolerate) aguantar

stomp [stɑmp] VI pisar fuerte; VT (crush) pisotear; (defeat) aplastar

stone [ston] N (rock, gem) piedra *f;* (in fruit) hueso *m;* (in kidneys) cálculo *m;* **within a** —**'s throw** a tiro de piedra; — **Age** Edad de Piedra *f;* ADJ —**-deaf** sordo como una tapia; VT (a person) lapidar; (a fruit) deshuesar; **to** —**wall** bloquear, ignorar; **to get** —**d** (get high) *fam* volarse; *Sp fam* colocarse

stony [stóni] ADJ (made of stone) pétreo; (driveway) pedregoso; (silence) sepulcral

stood [stʊd] *see* stand

stool [stuɬ] N (furniture) taburete *m,* banqueta *f;* (excrement) materia fecal *f;* — **pigeon** soplón -ona *mf,* chivato -ta *mf*

stoop [stup] VI (bend over) agacharse; (have bad posture) encorvarse; **to** — to rebajarse a; N (posture) encorvamiento *m;* (porch) entrada *f,* porche *m;* **to walk with a** — andar encorvado; ADJ —**-shouldered** encorvado, cargado de espaldas

stop [stɑp] VI (halt) parar, detenerse; (malfunction) parar[se]; VT (halt) parar, detener; (cancel) cancelar; (suspend) suspender; (plug) tapar; **to at nothing** no tener escrúpulos; **to** — **by/in** visitar; **to** — **from** impedir; **to** — **over at** hacer escala en; **to** — **short** parar en seco; **to** — **up** tapar, atascar; **it** —**ped raining** paró/dejó de llover; N parada *f,* detención *f;* (on organ) registro *m;* —**gap** arreglo provisorio *m;* —**light** semáforo *m;* —**over** escala *f;* — **sign** *Sp* stop *m; Am* señal de pare *f; Mex* alto *m;* —**volley** (tennis) dejada de volea *f;* —**watch** cronómetro *m;* **to bring to a** — parar; **to make a** — parar

stoppage [stápɪʤ] N interrupción *f;* (strike) huelga *f*

stopper [stápɚ] N tapón *m*

storage [stɔ́rɪʤ] N almacenaje *m,* almacenamiento *m;* (of electronic data) almacenamiento *m;* — **battery** acumulador *m;* — **device** dispositivo de almacenamiento *m;* **to keep in** — almacenar

store [stɔr] N (shop) tienda *f,* almacén *m;* (supply) reserva *f,* provisión *f;* —**house** (warehouse) almacén *m,* depósito *m;* (source) mina *f,* fuente *f;* —**keeper** tendero -ra *mf,* almacenista *mf;* —**room** almacén *m,* depósito *m;* **what is in** — **for us?** ¿qué nos espera? VT (commercial goods) almacenar; (personal effects) guardar; **to** — **up** acumular

stork [stɔrk] N cigüeña *f*

storm [stɔrm] N (on land) tormenta *f;* (at sea) tempestad *f,* temporal *m;* (of protest) ola *f;* — **troops** tropas de asalto *f pl;* VT (attack) tomar por asalto; VI **to** — **in/out** entrar/salir en tromba

stormy [stɔ́rmi] ADJ tormentoso, tempestuoso

story [stɔ́ri] N (tale) cuento *m,* historia *f;* (newspaper article) artículo *m;* (lie) mentira *f;* (information) información *f;* (plot) argumento *m,* trama *f;* (floor) piso *m*

stout [staʊt] ADJ (fat) corpulento; (robust) robusto, fornido; (strong) fuerte; (courageous) valiente

stove [stov] N (for heating) estufa *f;* (for cooking) cocina *f;* estufa *f*

stow [sto] VT (keep) guardar; (hide) esconder; (put in cargo hold) estibar; **to** — **away on a ship** viajar de polizón

stowaway [stóəwe] N polizón -ona *mf*

straddle [strǽdl̩] VI/VT estar a horcajadas; VT (a fence) ponerse a horcajadas; (one's legs) abrir; (not take sides) no comprometerse

strafe [stref] VT ametrallar

straggle [strǽgəɬ] VI **to** — **along/behind** rezagarse; **to** — **in** entrar de a pocos

straight [stret] ADJ (not curved) recto; (not tilted) derecho; (in succession) seguido; (hair) lacio, liso; (teeth) parejo; (frank) franco; (heterosexual) heterosexual; — **A's** sobresaliente en todo; —**edge** regla *f;* — **face** cara seria *f;* — **flush** escalera de color *f;* ADJ —**forward** (honest) honesto; (simple) sencillo, campechano; (clear) claro; ADV — **ahead** todo derecho, todo recto; **for two hours** — dos horas seguidas; **to come** — **home** volver derecho a casa; **to leave** — **after lunch** irse justo después de comer; **to set a person** — aclararle algo a alguien; **tell me** — dímelo francamente; **he can't think** — no puede pensar con claridad; N (of a racetrack) recta *f*

straighten [strétn̩] VI/VT enderezar[se]; (situation) arreglar[se]; VT (hair) alisar, *RP* laciar; **to** — **out a child** enderezar a un niño

straightness [strétnɪs] N derechura *f*

strain [stren] VI (pull) tironear; (try hard) esforzarse; VT (exhaust) agotar; (hurt voice) forzar; (injure a joint) torcer; (injure a muscle) sufrir un tirón en; (hurt a relationship) crear una tirantez en; VI/VT (filter) colar[se]; N (effort) esfuerzo m; (injury) torcedura f; (pressure) presión f; (trouble in a relationship) tirantez f; (lineage) cepa f

strainer [strénæ] N colador m

strait [stret] N estrecho m; **in dire —s** en aprietos; **—jacket** camisa de fuerza f, chaleco de fuerza m; ADJ **—laced** puritano

strand [strænd] VI/VT (a ship) encallar, varar; VT (a person) dejar plantado; **to be —ed** (boat) estar encallado; (person) quedar plantado; N (beach) costa f, playa f; (of rope) ramal m; (of thread) hebra f; (of hair) mechón m

strange [strendʒ] ADJ (bizarre) extraño, raro; (unknown) desconocido

strangeness [stréndʒnɪs] N (unusualness) lo extraño, rareza f; (unexpectedness) lo inesperado

stranger [stréndʒæ] N (unknown person) extraño -ña mf, desconocido -da mf; (outsider) forastero -ra mf; **to be no — to something** tener experiencia con algo

strangle [strǽŋɡəł] VI/VT estrangular[se]; VT (creativity) coartar; N **—hold** (in wrestling) llave al cuello f; (in markets) monopolio m

strap [stræp] N (leather band) correa f, tira f; (on a dress) tirante m; VT atar con correa; **to — in** amarrar[se], abrochar[se]

stratagem [strǽDədʒəm] N estratagema f

strategic [strətídʒɪk] ADJ estratégico

strategy [strǽDədʒi] N estrategia f

stratosphere [strǽDəsfir] N estratosfera f

stratum [strǽDəm] N estrato m

straw [strɔ] N paja f (also for drinking); **—berry** fresa f; **— man** testaferro m; **— vote** votación de prueba f; ADJ **—-colored** pajizo

stray [stre] VI (deviate, digress) desviarse; (get lost) perderse; (wander) vagar; (sin) descarriarse, perderse; ADJ extraviado, perdido; N perro/gato mostrenco m

streak [strik] N (line) raya f; (vein) vena f; (of luck) racha f; (of light) rayo m; VI (run naked) correr desnudo; (get discolored) aclararse

stream [strim] N (jet) chorro m; (river) río m; (brook) arroyo m; ADJ **—lined** (vehículo) aerodinámico; (business) racionalizado; VI (water) correr, fluir; (blood) derramar; **to — out** brotar, manar; **to — in** entrar a raudales

streaming [strímɪŋ] N corriente f, flujo m; **— audio** flujo continuo de datos de audio m; **— video** flujo continuo de datos de vídeo m

street [strit] N calle f; **—car** tranvía f; **—lamp** farol m, poste de alumbrado m; **— sweeper** barrendero -ra mf; **—walker** prostituta f

strength [streŋθ] N fuerza f; (spiritual) firmeza f;

on the — of en base a

strengthen [stréŋθən] VI/VT fortalecer[se], reforzar[se]

strengthening [stréŋθənɪŋ] N fortalecimiento m

strenuous [strénjuəs] ADJ arduo

strep throat [strépθrót] N infección por estreptococo f

stress [strɛs] N (tension) tensión f; (strain) estrés m; (pressure) esfuerzo m; (emphasis) énfasis m; (accent) acento m; **— test** prueba de esfuerzo f; VT (emphasize) enfatizar; (accentuate) acentuar; (exert force) someter a un esfuerzo; (put under pressure) estresar; **to — out** estresarse

stressful [strésfəl] ADJ estresante

stretch [strɛtʃ] VI/VT (make or become longer) estirar[se], alargar[se]; (extend) extender[se]; (exaggerate) exagerar; **to — oneself** estirarse, desperezarse; **to — out** (lengthen) extender[se]; (lie) tumbarse, tenderse; N (act of stretching) desperezo m; (segment of road) trecho m, tramo m; (period of time) período m; (exaggeration) exageración f; **— mark** estría f

stretcher [strétʃæ] N camilla f

strew [stru] VT esparcir

strewn [strun] *see* strew

stricken [stríkən] ADJ (with disease) aquejado; (by a flood) afectado; (with fear) aterrado

stricken [stríkən] *see* strike

strict [strɪkt] ADJ estricto; **in — confidence** en absoluta confianza

stridden [strídn̩] *see* stride

stride [straɪd] VI caminar a paso largo, dar zancadas; N (gait) paso m; (long step) zancada f, tranco m

strident [stráɪDənt] ADJ estridente

strife [straɪf] N conflictos m pl

strike [straɪk] VI/VT (hit) golpear, pegar; (stop work) hacer huelga [contra]; VT (find oil, etc.) dar con, encontrar; (occur to) ocurrírsele a uno; (cross out) tachar; (mark by chimes) dar; (light a match, etc.) encender; (make a coin) acuñar; **to — a compromise/deal** llegar a un acuerdo; **to — one's fancy** antojársele a uno; **to — out** (cross out) tachar; (set forth) encaminarse; (fail) fracasar; (in baseball) poncharse; **to — someone out** ponchar a alguien; **to — up a conversation** entablar conversación; **to — up a friendship** trabar amistad; **how does she — you?** ¿qué tal te parece? N (work stoppage) huelga f; (attack) ataque m; (finding of oil) descubrimiento m; (in baseball) strike m; **—breaker** esquirol m, rompehuelgas m sg; **—out** ponchado m, ponche m; **—through** tachado m; **— zone** zona de strike f; **called —** strike cantado m

striker [stráɪkæ] N (person on strike) huelguista mf; (of a bell) badajo m; (in soccer) artillero

-ra *mf*
striking [stráɪkɪŋ] ADJ (unusual, conspicuous) notable; (attractive) llamativo; (on strike) en huelga
string [strɪŋ] N (cord) cuerda *f*, cordel *m*; (of pearls, lies) sarta *f*; (of questions) serie *f*; (of data) secuencia *f*; (of beans) fibra *f*; (of garlic, peppers) ristra *f*; — **bean** habichuela *f*, judía verde *f*; —**s** (in an orchestra) cuerdas *f* pl; (on a tennis racket) cordaje *m*, encordado *m*; **no** —**s attached** sin condiciones; VT (beads) ensartar; (a musical instrument) encordar; **to** — **along** tener en ascuas; **to** — **out** extender[se], prolongar[se]; **to** — **up** colgar, ahorcar; **to be strung out** estar muy tenso
stringent [stríndʒənt] ADJ (law, need) riguroso; (time limit) estrecho, ajustado
strip [strɪp] VI/VT (make/get naked) desnudar[se]; VT (remove bark) descortezar; (remove leaves) deshojar; (remove sheets) deshacer; (remove varnish) quitar el barniz; (damage gears) estropear el engranaje; **to** — **search** registrar al desnudo; **to** —**-mine** explotar a cielo abierto; N (of a thing) tira *f*; (of land) faja *f*; — **mall** centro comercial *m*; — **search** registro al desnudo *m*; —**tease** strip-tease *m*
stripe [straɪp] N (band) raya *f*, lista *f*, banda *f*; (military insignia) galón *m*; (type) tipo *m*
striped [straɪpt, stráɪpɪd] ADJ listado, rayado
stripper [strɪpɚ] N striptisero -ra *mf*
strive [straɪv] VI esforzarse por, luchar por
striven [strívən] see strive
strode [strod] see stride
stroke [strok] N (in golf, tennis, of luck, of genius) golpe *m*; (cerebral hemorrhage) derrame cerebral *m*; (movement in swimming) brazada *f*; (style in swimming) estilo *m*; (of a piston) carrera *f*; (of a painter's brush) pincelada *f*, trazo *m*; (of lightning) rayo *m*; **at the** — **of ten** al dar las diez; VT (pet) acariciar; (praise) halagar
stroll [strol] VI dar un paseo, pasearse; N paseo *m*, caminata *f*
stroller [strólɚ] N cochecito de bebé *m*
strong [strɔŋ] ADJ fuerte; (husky) recio; (eyesight, probability) bueno; (protest) enérgico; (views, faith, support) firme; (features, resemblance) marcado; (argument) sólido; —**hold** (fortress) fortaleza *f*; (center of activity) baluarte *m*; —**-willed** (resolute) resuelto, decidido; (stubborn) terco; ADV **to be going** — seguir activo; VT **to** —**-arm** intimidar
strongly [strɔ́ŋli] ADV (argue, object) enérgicamente; (pull) con fuerza
strove [strov] see strive
struck [strʌk] see strike
structural [strʌ́ktʃərəl] ADJ estructural

structure [strʌ́ktʃɚ] N (the way parts are arranged) estructura *f*; (thing constructed) construcción *f*; VT estructurar
structuring [strʌ́ktʃəɪŋ] N estructuración *f*
struggle [strʌ́gəl] VI (with difficulties) luchar, bregar; (with an assailant) forcejear; **she** —**s in math** la pasa mal en matemáticas; N lucha *f*; (of ideas) pugna *f*, lucha *f*; (fight) contienda *f*, forcejeo *m*; **it's a** — da mucho trabajo
strung [strʌŋ] see string
strut [strʌt] VI pavonearse; N pavoneo *m*; (support) tirante *m*, puntal *m*; (shock absorber) amortiguador *m*
strychnine [stríknaɪn] N estricnina *f*
stub [stʌb] N talón *m*; VT **to** — **one's toe** dar[se] un tropezón, reventarse el dedo
stubble [stʌ́bəl] N (of a crop) rastrojo *m*; (of a beard) barba de unos días *f*
stubborn [stʌ́bən] ADJ terco, testarudo
stubbornness [stʌ́bənnɪs] N terquedad *f*, testarudez *f*
stucco [stʌ́ko] N estuco *m*; VT estucar
stuck [stʌk] ADJ (unable to move) atascado; (adhering) pegado; **to be** — **on someone** estar loco por alguien; —**-up** estirado, presumido
stuck [stʌk] see stick
stud [stʌd] N (knob) tachuela *f*, tachón *m*; (earring) arete *m*; (cufflink) gemelo *m*; (on shirtfront) botón *m*; (horse, man) semental *m*; (horse) garañón *m*; VT tachonar
student [stúdn̩t] N alumno -na *mf*; (secondary, university) estudiante *mf*; — **body** alumnado *m*; ADJ estudiantil
studio [stúDio] N estudio *m*, taller *m*; — **apartment** estudio *m*
studious [stúDiəs] ADJ estudioso
study [stʌ́Di] N estudio *m*; VT estudiar
stuff [stʌf] N (material) materia *f*, material *m*; (things) trastos *m* pl, bártulos *m* pl; (cloth) paño *m*, tela *f*; (affair) cosa *f*; (junk) cachivaches *m* pl; VT (mattress) rellenar; (dead animal) embalsamar, disecar; **to** — **into** meter en; **I'm** —**ed** estoy lleno
stuffing [stʌ́fɪŋ] N relleno *m*
stuffy [stʌ́fi] ADJ (person) envarado; (air) viciado; (nose) tapado
stumble [stʌ́mbəl] VI (trip) tropezar, trastabillar, dar un traspié; (stutter) balbucear; **to** — **out** salir a tropezones; **to** — **upon** tropezar con; **stumbling block** obstáculo *m*; N tropezón *m*, tropiezo *m*, traspié *m*
stump [stʌmp] N (of a tree) tocón *m*, cepa *f*; (of a tooth) raigón *m*; (of a limb) muñón *m*; **to be on the** — hacer una campaña electoral; VT (baffle) dejar perplejo; (remove stumps) arrancar los tocones de; **to** — **the country** recorrer el país haciendo campaña

stun [stʌn] VT (shock, surprise) dejar atónito, pasmar; (render unconscious) dejar sin sentido; — **gun** pistola tranquilizante *f*

stung [stʌŋ] *see* sting

stunk [stʌŋk] *see* stink

stunning [stʌnɪŋ] ADJ (shocking) pasmoso; (beautiful) elegante, bellísimo

stunt [stʌnt] VT (stop growth) atrofiar; (do acrobatic tricks) hacer acrobacia; N (feat) acrobacia *f*; (for publicity) maniobra *f*; —**man** doble *m*; —**woman** doble *f*; **to pull a** — hacerse el listo

stupefy [stúpəfaɪ] VT (make lethargic) atontar, embrutecer; (astonish) dejar estupefacto, alelar

stupendous [stupéndəs] ADJ estupendo

stupid [stúpɪd] ADJ tonto, estúpido, majadero

stupidity [stupídɪDi] N tontería *f*, estupidez *f*, majadería *f*

stupor [stúpɚ] N estupor *m*

sturdy [stɝDi] ADJ (person) fornido, fuerte; (construction) sólido, robusto

stutter [stʌDɚ] VI tartamudear, tartajear; VT decir tartamudeando; N (act of stuttering) tartamudeo *m*; (speech defect) tartamudez *f*

stutterer [stʌDərɚ] N tartamudo -da *mf*

stuttering [stʌDərɪŋ] ADJ tartamudo; N (act of stuttering) tartamudeo *m*; (speech defect) tartamudez *f*

St. Vincent and the Grenadines [sentvínsəntənðəgrénədinz] N San Vicente y las Granadinas *m*

sty [staɪ] N (for pigs) pocilga *f*; (in eye) orzuelo *m*

style [staɪɫ] N estilo *m*; (type) modelo *m*; — **sheet** página de estilo *f*; **out of** — fuera de moda; **like it's going out of** — como loco; VT (a book) intitular; (hair) peinar; **he —s himself Professor Smith** se hace llamar Profesor Smith

stylish [stáɪlɪʃ] ADJ elegante, de moda

stylistic [staɪlístɪk] ADJ estilístico

stylistics [staɪlístɪks] N estilística *f*

stymie, stymy [stáɪmi] VT obstaculizar

Styrofoam™ [stáɪrəfom] N poliestireno *m*

suave [swɑv] ADJ urbano, educado

subcommittee [sʌ́bkəmɪDi] N subcomité *m*

subconscious [sʌbkánʃəs] ADJ subconsciente

subcontract [sʌbkántrækt] VT subcontratar

subdivide [sʌbdɪváɪd] VT subdividir

subdivision [sʌ́bdɪvɪʒən] N subdivisión *f*; (of land) parcelación *f*

subdue [səbdú] VT (overcome, vanquish) sojuzgar, someter, rendir; (repress) reprimir; (attenuate) atenuar

subdued [səbdúd] ADJ (atmosphere) tranquilo; (mood) deprimido; (lighting, color) tenue

subject¹ [sʌ́bdʒɪkt] N (of a king) súbdito -ta *mf*; (of a sentence, in an experiment) sujeto *m*; (in school) asignatura *f*, materia *f*; — **matter**

tema *m*; ADV LOC — **to** (changes, laws, conditions) sujeto a; (depression, earthquakes) propenso a

subject² [səbdʒékt] VT someter

subjection [səbdʒékʃən] N sometimiento *m*

subjective [səbdʒéktɪv] ADJ subjetivo

subjectivity [sʌbdʒɛktívɪDi] N subjetividad *f*

subjugate [sʌ́bdʒəget] VT sojuzgar, avasallar

subjunctive [səbdʒʌ́ŋktɪv] ADJ & N subjuntivo *m*

sublet [sʌ́blét] VI/VT subarrendar

sublime [səbláɪm] ADJ sublime

submarine [sʌbmərín, sʌ́bmərin] ADJ submarino; N submarino *m*

submerge [səbmɝdʒ] VI/VT sumergir[se]

submerged [səbmɝdʒd] ADJ inmerso, sumergido

submission [səbmíʃən] N (humility) sumisión *f*; (subjugation) sometimiento *m*, sumisión *f*; (sending) entrega *f*, envío *m*

submissive [səbmísɪv] ADJ sumiso

submit [səbmít] VI/VT someter[se]; (to a judge) elevar[se]; **to** — **a report** presentar un informe

subordinate¹ [səbɔ́rdṇɪt] ADJ & N subordinado -da *mf*, subalterno -na *mf*

subordinate² [səbɔ́rdṇet] VT subordinar

subpar [sʌ́bpár] ADJ inferior

subpoena [səpínə] N citación *f*, orden de comparecencia *f*

subroutine [sʌ́brutin] N subrutina *f*

subscribe [səbskráɪb] VI (underwrite, sign) suscribir; (receive a magazine) abonarse, suscribirse; (agree with) adherirse a

subscriber [səbskráɪbɚ] N (to shares) suscriptor -ora *mf*; (to services) abonado -da *mf*; (to a magazine) suscriptor -ora *mf*, abonado -da *mf*; (to an idea) partidario -ria *mf*

subscript [sʌ́bskrɪpt] N subíndice *m*

subscription [səbskrípʃən] N suscripción *f*, abono *m*

subsequent [sʌ́bsɪkwənt] ADJ subsiguiente

subsequently [sʌ́bsɪkwəntli] N posteriormente, con posterioridad *f*

subservient [səbsɝviənt] ADJ servil

subside [səbsáɪd] VI (sediment) hundirse; (water level) bajar; (volcano, storm, anger) calmarse, aquietarse

subsidiary [səbsídiɛri] ADJ subsidiario; N sucursal *f*, filial *f*

subsidize [sʌ́bsɪdaɪz] VT subvencionar, subsidiar

subsidy [sʌ́bsɪDi] N subvención *f*, subsidio *m*

substance [sʌ́bstəns] N sustancia *f*; — **abuse** abuso de sustancias *m*

substandard [sʌbstǽndɚd] ADJ de calidad inferior

substantial [səbstǽnʃəɫ] ADJ (changes) sustancial; (food, lecture) sustancioso; (furniture) sólido; (amount) considerable, importante; **to be in** — **agreement** estar

básicamente de acuerdo
substantiate [səbstǽnʃiet] VT (verify) verificar;
(prove) probar
substantive [sʌ́bstəntɪv] ADJ & N sustantivo *m*
substitute [sʌ́bstɪtut] VT sustituir, reemplazar; I
—**d water for milk** usé agua en vez de
leche, sustituí/reemplacé la leche por agua; VI
John —d for Mary Juan sustituyó/
reemplazó a María; N (one who substitutes)
sustituto *m*, reemplazo *m*; (teacher, athlete)
suplente *mf*; (thing) sucedáneo *m*
substitution [sʌbstɪtúʃən] N sustitución *f*; **the**
— of water for milk la sustitución de leche
por agua
subterfuge [sʌ́btɚfjuʤ] N subterfugio *m*
subterranean [sʌbtəréniən] ADJ subterráneo
subtitle [sʌ́btaɪdl̩] N subtítulo *m*
subtle [sʌ́dl̩] ADJ sutil
subtlety [sʌ́dl̩ti] N sutileza *f*
subtotal [sʌ́btodl̩] N subtotal *m*
subtract [səbtrǽkt] VT (deduct) restar; (take
away) sustraer
subtraction [səbtrǽkʃən] N sustracción *f*, resta *f*
suburb [sʌ́bɝb] N barrio residencial periférico *m*
suburban [səbɝ́bən] ADJ (residential)
residencial; (on the outskirts) periférico
subversive [səbvɝ́sɪv] ADJ subversivo
subway [sʌ́bwe] N metropolitano *m*, metro *m*,
subterráneo *m*
succeed [səksíd] VI (be successful) tener éxito;
(manage) lograr; **to — to** heredar; VT (follow)
suceder a
success [səksés] N éxito *m*
successful [səksésfəl] ADJ (person) exitoso;
(effort) productivo, satisfactorio; **to be —**
tener éxito
succession [səkséʃən] N sucesión *f*
successive [səksésɪv] ADJ sucesivo
successor [səksésɚ] N sucesor -ora *mf*
succinct [səksíŋkt] ADJ sucinto, escueto
succor [sʌ́kɚ] N socorro *m*; VT socorrer
succumb [səkʌ́m] VI sucumbir
such [sʌtʃ] ADJ tal; **— as** tal como; **at — and — a**
place en tal o cual lugar; **he's — an idiot!**
¡es tan idiota! **in — a case** en tal caso / en
semejante caso; **there's no — thing** eso no
existe; PRON **hobbies, pastimes, and —**
hobbies, pasatiempos y cosas por el estilo; **a**
car — as yours un coche como el tuyo; ADV
— nice neighbors vecinos tan simpáticos
suck [sʌk] VI/VT chupar; (suckle) mamar;
(vacuum, pump) aspirar; (perform fellatio)
vulg mamarla; **to be —ed into** ser arrastrado
a; VI **this book —s!** *vulg* ¡este libro es una
cagada! **to — in air** aspirar; **to — up to**
someone *vulg* lamerle el culo a alguien; N
chupada *f*; (sexual) *vulg* mamada *f*
sucker [sʌ́kɚ] N (gullible person) primo -ma *mf*;
(lollipop) *Sp* pirulí *m*; *Mex* paleta *f*; *RP*

chupetín *m*
sucrose [súkros] N sacarosa *f*
suction [sʌ́kʃən] N succión *f*, aspiración *f*
Sudan [sudǽn] N Sudán *m*
Sudanese [sudníz] ADJ & N sudanés -esa *mf*
sudden [sʌ́dn̩] ADJ súbito, repentino, brusco; —
death (also in sports) muerte súbita *f*; —
infant death syndrome síndrome de
muerte infantil súbita *m*; **all of a —** de
repente, de improviso
suddenly [sʌ́dn̩li] ADV de repente,
repentinamente
suddenness [sʌ́dn̩nɪs] N brusquedad *f*, lo
repentino
suds [sʌdz] N espuma *f*
sue [su] VI/VT demandar, poner pleito; **to — for**
pedir, suplicar; **to — for damages**
demandar por daños y perjuicios
suede [swed] N gamuza *f*, ante *m*
suffer [sʌ́fɚ] VI/VT (feel pain) sufrir, padecer; VT
(tolerate) tolerar
sufferer [sʌ́fərɚ] N paciente *mf*
suffering [sʌ́fəɪŋ] N sufrimiento *m*,
padecimiento *m*
suffice [səfáɪs] VI/VT bastar, ser suficiente
sufficient [səfíʃənt] ADJ suficiente, bastante
suffix [sʌ́fɪks] N sufijo *m*
suffocate [sʌ́fəket] VI/VT ahogar[se], sofocar[se];
(to die, kill) asfixiar[se]
suffocation [sʌfəkéʃən] N ahogo *m*, sofoco *m*
suffrage [sʌ́frɪʤ] N sufragio *m*
sugar [ʃúgɚ] N azúcar *mf*; (endearment) cariño
m; **— cane** caña de azúcar *f*; VT azucarar; **to**
— the pill dorar la píldora
suggest [səgʤést] VT (propose) sugerir;
(hint) insinuar; **—ed retail price** precio
sugerido *m*
suggestion [səgʤéstʃən] N (proposal)
sugerencia *f*; (in hypnosis) sugestión *f*
suggestive [səgʤéstɪv] ADJ insinuante; **to be —**
of evocar
suicide [súɪsaɪd] N (act) suicidio *m*; (person)
suicida *mf*; **to commit —** suicidarse
suit [sut] N (clothes) traje *m*; (in cards) palo *m*,
color *m*; (lawsuit) demanda *f*, pleito *m*,
querella *f*; **—case** maleta *f*, valija *f*; VT (adapt)
adaptar, ajustar; (satisfy) satisfacer; (look
good) quedarle bien a, sentarle bien a; (be
convenient, appropriate) convenir, venir
bien; **— yourself** haz lo que te parezca
suitable [súdəbəl] ADJ (appropriate) apropiado;
(apt) apto
suitably [súdəbli] ADV como corresponde
suite [swit] N (series) serie *f*; (series of rooms,
musical composition) suite *f*; (furniture)
juego *m*; (software) paquete de programas de
productividad *m*
suitor [súɪʌɚ] N pretendiente *m*, galán *m*
sulfate, sulphate [sʌ́lfet] N sulfato *m*

sulfide, sulphide [sʌ́lfaɪd] N sulfuro *m*
sulfur, sulphur [sʌ́lfɚ] N azufre *m*
sulfuric, sulphuric [sʌlfjúrɪk] ADJ sulfúrico
sulk [sʌlk] VI enfurruñarse; N **to be in a** — estar enfurruñado
sulky [sʌ́lki] ADJ malhumorado, enfurruñado
sullen [sʌ́lən] ADJ hosco, huraño
sully [sʌ́li] VT mancillar, ensuciar
sultry [sʌ́ltri] ADJ (hot) bochornoso, sofocante; (sensual) sensual
sum [sʌm] N suma *f*; **in** — en resumen; VI **to** — **up** resumir, recapitular
summarize [sʌ́məraɪz] VI/VT resumir
summary [sʌ́məri] N resumen *m*; ADJ sumario
summer [sʌ́mɚ] N verano *m*, *lit* estío *m*; — **resort** balneario *m*, lugar de veraneo *m*; — **school** cursos de verano *m pl*; —**time** verano *m*; VI veranear
summit [sʌ́mɪt] N cumbre *f*, cima *f*
summon [sʌ́mən] VT (a witness) citar; (an employee, the police) llamar; N —**s** citación judicial *f*
sumptuous [sʌ́mptʃuəs] ADJ suntuoso
sun [sʌn] N sol *m*; **to** —**bathe** tomar el sol; —**beam** rayo de sol *m*; —**block** protector solar *m*; —**burn** quemadura de sol *f*; —**dial** reloj de sol *m*; —**down** puesta de[l] sol *f*; —**flower** girasol *m*; —**glasses** gafas de sol *f pl*, anteojos de sol *m pl*; — **lamp** lámpara solar *f*; —**light** luz del sol *f*; —**rise** salida de[l] sol *f*, amanecer *m*; —**screen** protector solar *m*; —**set** puesta de[l] sol *f*; —**shine** luz [del sol] *f*; —**spot** mancha solar *f*; —**stroke** insolación *f*; —**tan** bronceado *m*; —**up** salida del sol *f*; VI **to** — **oneself** tomar el sol; **to** —**burn** quemar[se] al sol
Sunday [sʌ́nde] N domingo *m*; — **school** escuela dominical *f*
sundry [sʌ́ndri] ADJ diversos
sung [sʌŋ] *see* sing
sunk [sʌŋk] *see* sink
sunny [sʌ́ni] ADJ (day, patio) soleado; (disposition) alegre
super [súpɚ] N (of a building) conserje *m*, portero -ra *mf*; ADJ (wonderful) súper, bárbaro
superb [supɚ́b] ADJ excelente
supercharger [súpɚtʃɑrdʒɚ] N sobrealimentador *m*
supercomputer [súpɚkəmpjuDɚ] N *Am* supercomputadora *f*; *Sp* superordenador *m*
superego [supɚ́go] N superego *m*, superyó *m*
superficial [supɚfíʃəl] ADJ superficial
superfluous [supɚ́fluəs] ADJ superfluo
superhuman [supɚhjúmən] ADJ sobrehumano
superimpose [supɚɪmpóz] VT superponer, sobreponer
superintendent [supɚɪnténdənt] N (of work) superintendente *mf*, supervisor -ora *mf*; (of

building) conserje *mf*, portero -ra *mf*
superior [supíriɚ] ADJ & N superior *mf*
superiority [supiriórɪDi] N superioridad *f*
superlative [supɚ́ləDɪv] ADJ & N superlativo *m*
supermarket [súpɚmɑrkɪt] N supermercado *m*, súper *m*
supernatural [supɚnǽtʃɚəl] ADJ sobrenatural
superpower [súpɚpaʊɚ] N superpotencia *f*
superscript [súpɚskrɪpt] N superíndice *m*
supersede [supɚsíd] VT reemplazar
supersonic [supɚsánɪk] ADJ supersónico
superstar [súpɚstar] N superestrella *f*
superstition [supɚstíʃən] N superstición *f*
superstitious [supɚstíʃəs] ADJ supersticioso
superstore [súpɚstɔr] N hipermercado *m*
supervise [súpɚvaɪz] VI/VT supervisar, fiscalizar
supervision [supɚvíʒən] N supervisión *f*, fiscalización *f*
supervisor [súpɚvaɪzɚ] N supervisor -ora *mf*
supine [súpaɪn] ADJ supino
supper [sʌ́pɚ] N cena *f*
supplant [səplǽnt] VT suplantar
supple [sʌ́pəl] ADJ (flexible) flexible, elástico; (agile) ágil, grácil
supplement[1] [sʌ́pləmənt] N (of a newspaper) suplemento *m*; (of a book) apéndice *m*; (of one's diet) complemento *m*
supplement[2] [sʌ́pləmɛnt] VT complementar, suplementar
supplemental [sʌpləméntəl] ADJ suplementario
supplier [səpláɪɚ] N abastecedor -ora *mf*, proveedor -ora *mf*
supply [səplái] VT abastecer, suministrar; N (act of supplying) abastecimiento *m*; — **and demand** oferta y demanda *f*; **in short** — escaso; **supplies** suministros *m pl*, provisiones *f pl*; **office supplies** artículos de oficina *m pl*; **military supplies** pertrechos *m pl*
support [səpórt] VT (keep from falling) sostener, soportar; (encourage) apoyar; (facilitate) potenciar; (corroborate) corroborar; (help with computers) soportar; **to be** —**ed by** fundamentarse en/sobre; N (of a structure) sostén *m*, soporte *m*; (of a family) sustento *m*; (of a candidate, idea) apoyo *m*; (of a theory) respaldo *m*; (for a computer) soporte *m*; — **group** grupo de apoyo *m*
supporter [səpórDɚ] N partidario -ria *mf*, simpatizante *mf*; (in sports) hincha *mf*
supportive [səpórDɪv] ADJ solidario; **you've always been very** — **of us** siempre nos has apoyado
suppose [səpóz] VT suponer; **we are** —**d to go** tenemos que ir
supposedly [səpózɪdli] ADV supuestamente
supposition [sʌpəzíʃən] N suposición *f*, supuesto *m*

suppository [səpázɪtɔri] N supositorio *m*
suppress [səprés] VT (repress) reprimir; (eliminate) suprimir; (a revolt) sofocar
suppression [səpréʃən] N (repression) represión *f*; (elimination) supresión*f*; (of a revolt) sofocación*f*
supremacy [suprémǝsi] N supremacía*f*
supreme [suprím] ADJ supremo
surcharge [sɚˈtʃardʒ] N recargo *m*, prima*f*
sure [ʃur] ADJ seguro; (judgment) certero; (hand) firme; **to make — of** asegurarse de; ADV **he — drinks a lot** es una esponja; **may I sit here? —!** ¿me puedo sentar? ¡cómo no!
surely [ʃúrli] ADV seguramente, ciertamente; — **you jest** no hablarás en serio; **he will — come** seguramente vendrá
surf [sɚf] N (breaking waves) rompientes *mf pl*; (foam) espuma*f*; (undertow) resaca*f*; **—board** tabla de surf*f*; VI/VT (on water) hacer surfing [en], surfear; (on the Internet) navegar, surfear
surface [sɚ̍fɪs] N superficie*f*; (of a solid) cara*f*; VI (come to top) emerger; (turn up) salir a la luz; VT (a submarine) sacar a la superficie; (a road) revestir
surfeit [sɚ̍fɪt] N (excess) exceso *m*; (feeling of fullness) hartazgo *m*; VI/VT hartar[se]
surfing [sɚ̍fɪŋ] N (on water) surfing *m*; (on the Internet) navegación*f*
surge [sɚdʒ] N (of people, disgust) oleada*f*; (of waves) oleaje *m*; (of electricity) sobrecarga de voltaje*f*; — **protector** protector contra sobrecargas de voltaje *m*; VI (people) precipitarse; (current) subir
surgeon [sɚ̍dʒən] N cirujano -na *mf*
surgery [sɚ̍dʒəri] N cirujía*f*; (room) quirófano *m*
surgical [sɚ̍dʒɪkəl] ADJ quirúrgico; — **dressing** vendaje quirúrgico *m*; — **instruments** instrumentos quirúrgicos *m pl*
Suriname, Surinam [súrɪnɑm] N Surinam *m*
Surinamese [surɪnɑmíz] ADJ & N surinamés -esa *mf*
surly [sɚ̍li] ADJ malhumorado, hosco, arisco
surmise [səmáɪz] VT conjeturar, suponer; N conjetura*f*, suposición*f*
surmount [səmáʊnt] VT superar
surname [sɚ̍nem] N apellido *m*
surpass [səpǽs] VT superar, sobrepujar
surpassing [səpǽsɪŋ] N superación*f*
surplus [sɚ̍plʌs] N excedente *m*, sobrante *m*, sobra*f*; (of funds) superávit *m*
surprise [səpráɪz] N sorpresa*f*; VT sorprender
surprising [səpráɪzɪŋ] ADJ sorprendente
surprisingly [səpráɪzɪŋli] ADV sorprendentemente; **not** — como era de esperar
surreal [səríəl] ADJ surrealista
surrealism [səríəlɪzəm] N surrealismo *m*
surrealist [səríəlɪst] N surrealista *mf*

surrealistic [səriəlístɪk] ADJ surrealista
surrender [səréndɚ] VI (accept defeat) rendir[se], darse por vencido; (give oneself up) entregarse; VT entregar; N rendición*f*
surreptitious [sɚəptíʃəs] ADJ subrepticio
surrogate [sɚ̍əgɪt] ADJ sustituto; — **mother** madre de alquiler*f*
surround [səráʊnd] VT rodear, circundar; (a city) sitiar
surrounding [səráʊndɪŋ] ADJ circundante; N **—s** alrededores *m pl*, inmediaciones*f pl*, entorno *m*
surtax [sɚ̍tæks] N sobretasa*f*
surveillance [səvéləns] N vigilancia*f*
survey[1] [səvé] VT (evaluate) evaluar; (measure) medir; (contemplate) contemplar; (poll) encuestar
survey[2] [sɚ̍ve] N (inspection) reconocimiento *m*, inspección*f*; (measure) medición*f*; (overview) panorama *m*; (poll) encuesta*f*, sondeo *m*; — **course** curso general *m*
surveyor [səvéɚ] N agrimensor -ora *mf*
survival [səváɪvəl] N supervivencia*f*, sobrevivencia*f*; (subsistence) subsistencia*f*; **the — of the fittest** la supervivencia del más apto
survive [səváɪv] VI/VT sobrevivir (also live longer than); (subsist) subsistir
surviving [səváɪvɪŋ] ADJ superviviente
survivor [səváɪvɚ] N sobreviviente *mf*, superviviente *mf*
susceptible [səséptəbəl] ADJ susceptible; **to be — of proof** poderse demostrar; **to be — to pneumonia** ser propenso a la pulmonía
suspect[1] [sáspɛkt] N sospechoso -sa *mf*
suspect[2] [səspékt] VT sospechar, recelar
suspend [səspénd] VT suspender
suspenders [səspéndɚz] N tirantes *m pl*
suspense [səspéns] N (uncertainty) incertidumbre*f*; (in movie) suspenso *m*; Sp suspense *m*; **to keep in** — mantener en suspenso, tener en vilo
suspension [səspénʃən] N suspensión*f*; (of a ban) levantamiento *m*; — **bridge** puente colgante *m*
suspicion [səspíʃən] N sospecha*f*
suspicious [səspíʃəs] ADJ (causing suspicion) sospechoso; (experiencing suspicion) suspicaz, desconfiado
sustain [səstén] VT (weight) sostener, sustentar; (pretense, effort) mantener; (an injury) sufrir; (an objection) admitir; (a musical note) sostener
sustainable [səsténəbəl] ADJ sostenible, sustentable
sustenance [sástənəns] N sustento *m*, alimento *m*
suture [sútʃɚ] N sutura*f*
swab [swab] N bola de algodón*f*, RP hisopo *m*; VT

pasar un hisopo sobre

swagger [swǽgɚ] VI (walk) pavonearse, contonearse; (boast) fanfarronear; N (walk) pavoneo *m*, contoneo *m*; (bluster) fanfarronería *f*

swallow [swálo] N (drink) trago *m*; (bird) golondrina *f*; VI/VT tragar; **to — up** consumir

swallowing [swáloɪŋ] N deglución *f*

swam [swæm] *see* swim

swamp [swɑmp] N pantano *m*, ciénaga *f*; **—land** cenagal *m*; VI/VT (flood) inundar[se]; (overwhelm) abrumar[se], agobiar[se]

swampy [swámpi] ADJ pantanoso, cenagoso

swan [swɑn] N cisne *m*; **— dive** salto del ángel *m*; **— song** canto de cisne *m*

swap [swɑp] VT cambiar, canjear; N cambio *m*, canje *m*

swarm [swɔrm] N enjambre *m*; VI (of bees) salir en enjambre; (of people, tourists) pulular, hormiguear; **to be —ing with** ser un hervidero de, abundar en

swarthy [swórði] ADJ trigueño, moreno

swat [swɑt] VT (a person) pegar; (flies) aplastar; **to — at** manotear; N manotazo *m*

sway [swe] VI/VT (move to and fro) balancear[se], bambolear[se]; (move hips) menear[se]; (influence) influir [en]; N (movement) balanceo *m*, vaivén *m*, bamboleo *m*; (influence) influencia *f*; **to hold — over** dominar

Swazi [swázi] N suazi *mf*

Swaziland [swázilænd] N Suazilandia *f*

swear [swɛr] VI/VT (vow) jurar; (use profanity) decir palabrotas; *Sp* soltar tacos; **to — in** (give oath) juramentar; (take oath) prestar juramento; **she —s by canned peaches** para ella no hay nada como los duraznos enlatados; **to — off** renunciar a; **to — to** jurar por

sweat [swɛt] VI (perspire) sudar; (ooze) exudar, sudar; (worry) preocuparse; N sudor *m*; **— glands** glándulas sudoríparas *f pl*; **—shirt** sudadera *f*; **—suit** equipo deportivo *m*; *Sp* chándal *m*; **no —** no hay problema

sweater [swɛ́Dɚ] N suéter *m*, jersey *m*

sweating [swɛ́Dɪŋ] N sudor *m*, sudoración *f*, transpiración *f*

sweaty [swɛ́Di] ADJ sudoroso, sudado

Swede [swid] N sueco -ca *mf*

Sweden [swídn̩] N Suecia *f*

Swedish [swídɪʃ] ADJ sueco

sweep [swip] VI/VT (clean with broom, scan) barrer; (dredge) dragar; VT (touch) rozar; (search) rastrear; VI (spread) extenderse; **to — away** llevar, arrastrar; **to — down upon** caer sobre, asolar; **to — off** limpiar; **to — into** (enter majestically) entrar majestuosamente; (enter quickly) entrar rápidamente; **to — up** recoger; N (cleaning)

barrida *f*; (extension) extensión *f*; (movement) barrido *m*; (search) rastreo *m*

sweeper [swípɚ] N (for cleaning) barredora *f*; (in soccer) líbero *m*

sweeping [swípɪŋ] ADJ (statement) [demasiado] general; (victory) aplastante

sweet [swit] ADJ (in flavor, personality) dulce; (in smell) bueno, fragante; **—-and-sour** agridulce; **—heart** querido -da *mf*; **— pea** *Sp* guisante de olor *m*; **— potato** batata *f*, boniato *m*; *Mex* camote *m*; **to have a — tooth** ser goloso; N dulce *m*, golosina *f*; **my — mi vida, mi alma; VT to —-talk** halagar

sweeten [swítn̩] VI/VT (a food) endulzar[se]; (an experience) dulcificar[se]

sweetener [swítn̩ɚ] N endulzante *m*, edulcorante *m*

sweetness [swítnɪs] N (of personality) dulzura *f*; (of taste) dulzor *m*

swell [swɛɫ] VI/VT (limbs, with pride) hinchar[se], henchir[se]; VI (river) crecer; (population) crecer, engrosar[se]; VT (make grow) hacer crecer, hacer aumentar, engrosar; N (of ocean) oleaje *m*; ADJ regio, bárbaro

swelling [swɛ́lɪŋ] N hinchazón *f*

swelter [swɛ́ɫtɚ] VI sofocarse de calor

swept [swɛpt] *see* sweep

swerve [swɝv] VI/VT (in a car) virar; (from a goal) desviar[se]; N viraje *m*

swift [swɪft] ADJ ligero, veloz, raudo; N vencejo *m*

swiftness [swɪ́ftnɪs] N velocidad *f*, rapidez *f*

swim [swɪm] VI/VT nadar; (float) flotar; **to — across** atravesar nadando; **my head is —ming** me da vueltas la cabeza; **I love —ming** me encanta nadar; N *Mex* alberca *f*; **—suit** traje de baño *m*; **to take a — ir a nadar, dar una nadada

swimmer [swɪ́mɚ] N nadador -ora *mf*; **—'s ear** otitis externa *f*

swimming [swɪ́mɪŋ] N natación *f*; **— pool** piscina *f*

swindle [swɪ́ndɫ] VT estafar; N estafa *f*, trapacería *f*

swine [swaɪn] N puerco *m*, cerdo *m*; (person) *offensive* puerco -ca *mf*, sinvergüenza *mf*

swing [swɪŋ] VI/VT (on a swing) columpiar[se]; (move to and fro) balancear[se], bambolear[se]; (baseball, golf) dar un swing [con]; VI (change) virar; **to — and miss** abanicar; **to — around** dar vueltas; **to — open** abrirse; VT (make turn) hacer girar; (influence) influir sobre; **to — a deal** concretar un negocio; **I can't — a new car** no me puedo dar el lujo de comprar un auto nuevo; N (playground toy) columpio *m*; (oscillation) balanceo *m*, vaivén *m*, bamboleo *m*; (in golf, baseball, music) swing *m*;

(change) cambio *m*; — **and a miss** abanico *m*; **in full** — en su apogeo; **to get into the — of things** agarrarle la onda a algo, cogerle el tranquillo a algo

swipe [swaɪp] VT (steal) afanar, sisar; (slide) deslizar; **to — a card** pasar una tarjeta por un lector; N (insult) insulto *m*; **to take a — at someone** (physical) tirarle un manotazo a alguien; (verbal) insultar

swirl [swɜɫ] VI/VT arremolinar[se]; (dancers) girar; N remolino *m*; (smoke) espiral *f*

Swiss [swɪs] ADJ & N suizo -za *mf*; — **cheese** queso suizo *m*

switch [swɪtʃ] N (change) cambio *m*; (electrical) interruptor *m*, llave *f*; (stick for whipping) varilla *f*; (on railways) agujas *f pl*; —**blade** navaja automática *f*; —**board** centralita *f*; —**man** guardagujas *m sg*; —**-hitter** (in baseball) bateador -ora ambidiestro *mf*; (bisexual) bisexual *mf*; VI/VT cambiar [de]; (train cars) desviar; **to — off** (current) cortar; (light, TV) apagar; **to — on** encender, prender

Switzerland [swítsələnd] N Suiza *f*

swivel [swívəɫ] N pivote *m*; — **chair** silla giratoria *f*

swollen [swólən] ADJ hinchado

swollen [swólən] *see* swell

swoon [swun] VI desvanecerse, desmayarse; **to — over someone** morirse por alguien; N vahído *m*

swoop [swup] VI **to — down upon** abalanzarse sobre; N descenso súbito *m*; **at one fell —** de un tirón

sword [sɔrd] N espada *f*; —**fish** pez espada *m*

swore [swɔr] *see* swear

sworn [swɔrn] *see* swear

swum [swʌm] *see* swim

swung [swʌŋ] *see* swing

sycamore [síkəmɔr] N sicomoro *m*

syllable [síləbəɫ] N sílaba *f*

syllabus [síləbəs] N programa [de estudios] *m*

syllogism [sílədʒɪzəm] N silogismo *m*

symbiosis [sɪmbiósɪs] N simbiosis *f*

symbol [símbəɫ] N símbolo *m*

symbolic [sɪmbálɪk] ADJ simbólico

symbolism [símbəlɪzəm] N simbolismo *m*

symbolize [símbəlaɪz] VT simbolizar

symmetrical [sɪmétrɪkəɫ] ADJ simétrico

symmetry [símɪtri] N simetría *f*

sympathetic [sɪmpəθédɪk] ADJ (compassionate) compasivo; (understanding) comprensivo, solidario; (favoring) favorable; (nervous system) simpático

sympathize [símpəθaɪz] VI (be compassionate) compadecer[se]; (be understanding) comprender; (be in favor) favorecer; **to — with** estar a favor de

sympathizer [símpəθaɪzə] N simpatizante *mf*

sympathizing [símpəθaɪzɪŋ] ADJ simpatizante

sympathy [símpəθi] N (compassion) compasión *f*; (understanding) comprensión *f*; (condolence) condolencia *f*, pésame *m*; **to extend one's** — dar el pésame

symphony [símfəni] N sinfonía *f*; — **orchestra** orquesta sinfónica *f*

symposium [sɪmpóziəm] N simposio *m*

symptom [símptəm] N síntoma *m*

synagogue [sínəgɑg] N sinagoga *f*

synchronize [síŋkrənaɪz] VI/VT sincronizar[se]

synchronous [síŋkrənəs] ADJ sincrónico

syndicate[1] [síndɪkɪt] N sindicato *m*

syndicate[2] [síndɪket] VI/VT (form a syndicate) sindicar[se]; VT (sell rights) vender los derechos de

syndrome [síndrom] N síndrome *m*

synergy [sínədʒi] N sinergia *f*

synonym [sínənɪm] N sinónimo *m*

synonymous [sɪnánəməs] ADJ sinónimo

synopsis [sɪnápsɪs] N sinopsis *f*

syntax [síntæks] N sintaxis *f*

synthesis [sínθəsɪs] N síntesis *f*

synthesize [sínθəsaɪz] VI/VT sintetizar

synthesizer [sínθəsaɪzə] N sintetizador *m*

synthetic [sɪnθédɪk] ADJ sintético

syphilis [sífəlɪs] N sífilis *f*

Syria [síriə] N Siria *f*

Syrian [síriən] ADJ & N sirio -ria *mf*

syringe [səríndʒ] N jeringa *f*

syrup [sírəp] N (food) almíbar *m*, jarabe *m*; (medicine) jarabe *m*

system [sístəm] N sistema *m*; — **crashes** caídas del sistema *f pl*

systematic [sɪstəmǽdɪk] ADJ sistemático

systematize [sístəmətaɪz] VI/VT sistematizar

systemic [sɪstémɪk] ADJ sistémico

systolic [sɪstálɪk] ADJ sistólico

Tt

tab [tæb] N (on a keyboard) tabulador *m*; (on index cards) pestaña *f*, ceja *f*; (bill) cuenta *f*; — **key** tecla de tabulación *f*; VI tabular

table [tébəɫ] N (furniture) mesa *f*; (list) tabla *f*; — **lamp** lámpara de mesa *f*; — **of contents** tabla de contenido *f*, índice *m*; **at** — a la mesa; VT posponer indefinidamente, dar carpetazo a; —**cloth** mantel *m*; —**spoon** (spoon) cuchara grande *f*; (measurement) cucharada *f*; —**spoonful** cucharada *f*; — **tennis** tenis de mesa *m*; —**ware** vajilla *f*, servicio de mesa *m*

tablet [tǽblɪt] N (pill) pastilla *f*, tableta *f*; (paper) bloc *m*; (stone) tabla *f*, lápida *f*; (portable writing surface) tablilla *f*

tabloid [tǽblɔɪd] N (paper size) tabloide *m*; (type of press) prensa amarilla/sensacionalista *f*
taboo [tæbú] N tabú *m*
tabulate [tǽbjəlet] VT tabular
tachometer [tækámɪdɚ] N tacómetro *m*
tacit [tǽsɪt] ADJ tácito
taciturn [tǽsɪtɚn] ADJ taciturno
tack [tæk] N (nail) tachuela *f*; (stitch) hilván *m*; (heading of a boat) rumbo *m*; (course of action) táctica *f*; (equipment for a horse) arreos *m pl*; VT (to nail) clavar con tachuelas; (to stitch) hilvanar; **to — on** agregar; VI virar, cambiar de rumbo
tackle [tǽkəɫ] N (for fishing, hoisting) aparejo *m*; (in rugby, football) placaje *m*, parada *f*; (person) atajador *m*; VT (a problem) enfrentar, abordar; (a task) emprender; (a horse) poner arreos; VI/VT (rugby, American football) placar, atajar
tacky [tǽki] ADJ (in bad taste) de mal gusto, chabacano; *Sp* hortera; (sticky) pegajoso
tact [tækt] N tacto *m*
tactful [tǽktfəɫ] ADJ que tiene tacto
tactics [tǽktɪks] N táctica *f*
tactile [tǽktɫ] ADJ táctil
tactless [tǽktlɪs] ADJ falto de tacto
tag [tæg] N (label) etiqueta *f*; (question) coletilla *f*; (nickname) apodo *m*; **to play** — jugar al pillapilla; VT etiquetar; (in the game of tag) pillar; **to — along** acompañar
tail [teɫ] N cola *f*, rabo *m*; (of a shirt) faldón *m*; (pursuer) perseguidor -ora *mf*; (buttocks) *vulg* culo *m*; **—bone** rabadilla *f*; **— end** (of a concert) final *m*; (of a procession) cola *f*; **—light** luz trasera *f*; **—pipe** tubo de escape *m*; **—s** (of a coin) cruz *f*; (of a tuxedo) frac *m*; **—spin** barrena *f*; **to —gate** seguir demasiado de cerca [a otro coche]
tailor [télɚ] N sastre *m*; **— shop** sastrería *f*; VT hacer a medida; (adapt) adaptar
taint [tent] N (stain) mancha *f*; (contamination) contaminación *f*; VI/VT (stain) manchar[se]; (contaminate) contaminar[se]
Taiwan [taɪwán] N Taiwán *m*
Taiwanese [taɪwaníz] ADJ & N taiwanés -esa *mf*
Tajik [tɑdʒík] ADJ & N tayiko -ka *mf*
Tajikistan [tɑdʒíkɪstæn] N Tayikistán *m*
take [tek] VT (a load) llevar; (someone else's property) robar, llevarse; (one number from another) restar; (prisoner, medicine, measures, a course) tomar; (one of a set) elegir, coger; (a bribe) aceptar; (a prize) recibir; (advice) seguir; (a walk) dar; (a vacation) irse; (a trip) hacer; (a piece of news) recibir; (a photo) sacar; **to — a bath** bañarse; **to — after** parecerse a; **to — a look at** echar un vistazo a; **to — a notion to** ocurrírsele a uno; **to — apart** desarmar, desmontar; **to — aside** apartar; **to — away** (carry away)

llevarse; (steal) sustraer; **to — back** devolver; **to — back one's words** retractarse; **to — by surprise** tomar desprevenido; **to — care of** (a person) cuidar de; (a matter) atender a; **to — charge of** encargarse de; **to — down in writing** anotar, apuntar; **to — effect** entrar en vigencia; **to — exercise** hacer ejercicio; **to — in** (include) incluir; (observe) observar; (deceive) embaucar; (provide shelter for) albergar; (make smaller) tomar, achicar; **to — leave** despedirse; **to — off** (remove) quitar[se]; (conduct) llevar; (discount) rebajar; (start flight) despegar; **to — offense** ofenderse; **to — office** asumir un cargo; **to — on** (accept) asumir; (hire) tomar, contratar; (acquire) adquirir; **to — out** (withdraw) sacar; (carry out [food], take on a date) llevar; (discount) adquirir; **to — over** hacerse cargo [de]; **to — place** tener lugar; **to — revenge** vengarse; **to — stock** hacer un balance; **to — stock in** tener confianza en; **to — the floor** tomar la palabra; **to — to heart** tomar a pecho; **to — to one's heels** poner pies en polvorosa; **to — to task** reprender, regañar; **to — up a matter** tratar un asunto; **to — up again** retomar; **to — up space** ocupar espacio; **I — it that** supongo que; **it —s ten minutes** lleva diez minutos; **the vaccination didn't —** la vacuna no prendió; N (profits) ingresos *m pl*; (of fish) pesca *f*, captura *f*; (of a film production) toma *f*; (opinion) opinión *f*; (approach) enfoque *m*; **—off** (of an airplane) despegue *m*; (parody) parodia *f*; **—over** (of a government) toma de poder *f*; (of a company) adquisición *f*
taken [tékən] *see* take
talcum [tǽɫkəm] N talco *m*; **— powder** polvo de talco *m*
tale [teɫ] N (story) cuento *m*, relato *m*; (lie) mentira *f*
talent [tǽlənt] N talento *m*
talented [tǽləntɪd] ADJ talentoso
talk [tɔk] VI/VT hablar; (chat) charlar; VT (nonsense) decir; (a language) hablar; (politics) hablar de; **to — back** contestar con impertinencia; **to — down to** hablar con arrogancia a; **to — someone into something** convencer a alguien para que haga algo; **to — out of** disuadir de; **to — over** discutir; **to — up** alabar, hacer propaganda; N (formal speech) charla *f*; (gossip) habladurías *f pl*; (lingo) habla *f*; **— of the town** la comidilla del pueblo *f*; **— show** programa de entrevistas *m*
talkative [tɔ́kədɪv] ADJ hablador, parlanchín, charlatán
tall [tɔl] ADJ alto; **— order** misión imposible *f*; **— tale** cuento chino *m*, patraña *f*; **six feet —** de seis pies de altura; **how — are you?** ¿cuánto

mides?

tallow [tǽlo] N sebo *m*

tally [tǽli] N (account) cuenta *f*; VT llevar la cuenta; **to — up** sumar; **to — with** concordar con

tambourine [tæmbərín] N pandereta *f*

tame [tem] ADJ (docile) manso, dócil; (domesticated) domesticado; (dull) aburrido; VT (make docile) amansar, domar; (domesticate) domesticar

tamper [tǽmpɚ] VI **to — with** (a jury) sobornar; (a lock) intentar forzar; (a document) alterar, amañar; ADJ **-proof** a prueba de alteración

tampon [tǽmpɑn] N tampón *m*

tan [tæn] VI/VT (cure) curtir[se]; (darken skin) broncear[se], tostar[se]; VT (cure) adobar; (spank) zurrar; N color tostado *m*; (of skin) bronceado *m*; ADJ (car) color tostado; (skin) bronceado, tostado

tandem [tǽndəm] N tándem *m*; **in — with** en colaboración con

tangent [tǽndʒənt] ADJ & N tangente *f*; **to go off on a —** salirse por la tangente

tangerine [tǽndʒərín] N mandarina *f*; *Am* tangerina *f*

tangible [tǽndʒəbəl] ADJ tangible

tangle [tǽŋgəl] VI/VT enredar[se], enmarañar[se]; N enredo *m*, maraña *f*; (in hair) nudo *m*, enredijo *m*

tank [tæŋk] N tanque *m* (also military), depósito *m*; VT guardar en un tanque; VI **to — up** (with gasoline) llenar el tanque; (with alcohol) emborracharse

tannery [tǽnəri] N curtiduría *f*, tenería *f*; *Am* curtiembre *f*

tantalize [tǽntl̩aɪz] VT atormentar con tentaciones

tantamount [tǽntəmaʊnt] ADJ **to be — to** equivaler a

tantrum [tǽntrəm] N berrinche *m*, perrera *f*, rabieta *f*

Tanzania [tænzəníə] N Tanzania *f*

Tanzanian [tænzéniən] ADJ & N tanzano -na *mf*

tap [tæp] N golpecito *m*; (repeated) golpeteo *m*; (with the hand) palmadita *f*; (faucet) llave *f*; *Sp* grifo *m*; **— dance** claqué *m*; **— water** agua de llave *f*; VI/VT (once) tocar; (repeatedly) golpetear; (with fingers) tamborilear; (utilize) explotar; (draw off liquid) extraer; **to — a tree** sangrar un árbol; **to — a telephone** intervenir un teléfono

tape [tep] N (adhesive, magnetic) cinta *f*; **— measure** cinta métrica *f*; **— recorder** grabadora *f*, grabador *m*; **— recording** grabación *f*; **—worm** lombriz *f*, solitaria *f*; VT (affix) atar con cinta; VI/VT (record) grabar; **to —-record** grabar

taper [tépɚ] N (diminished size) estrechamiento *m*; (candle) vela *f*, candela *f*; VI/VT afinar[se];

to — off (become smaller) afinar[se]; (diminish) ir disminuyendo

tapestry [tǽpɪstri] N (wall hanging) tapiz *m*; (art, industry) tapicería *f*

tapioca [tæpiókə] N tapioca *f*

tapir [tépər] N tapir *m*

tar [tɑr] N alquitrán *m*, brea *f*; VT alquitranar; **to — and feather** emplumar

tarantula [tərǽntʃələ] N tarántula *f*

tardy [tárDi] ADJ **to be —** llegar tarde

target [tárgɪt] N blanco *m*; **— practice** tiro al blanco *m*

tariff [tǽrɪf] N tarifa *f*, arancel *m*

tarnish [tárnɪʃ] VI/VT (metal) deslustrar[se], empañar; (reputation) manchar[se]

tart [tɑrt] ADJ (fruit) agrio, ácido; (remark) mordaz; N (pie) tarta *f*; (woman) *pej* fulana *f*

tartar [tárDɚ] N (in wine) tártaro *m*; (on teeth) sarro *m*; **— sauce** salsa tártara *f*

task [tæsk] N tarea *f*, labor *f*; **— bar** barra de tareas *f*; **— force** fuerza de tarea *f*; **—master** tirano -na *mf*; **to take to —** reprender, regañar

tassel [tǽsəl] N borla *f*

taste [test] VT (perceive) sentir el gusto/sabor de; (try) probar; (try wine) catar; VI **to — of onion** saber a cebolla; **it —s sour** tiene un sabor agrio; N (sense, aesthetic judgment) gusto *m*; (flavor) sabor *m*; (small amount of food) bocadito *m*; (small amount of drink) sorbo *m*; **— bud** papila gustativa *f*

tasteless [téstlɪs] ADJ (with no taste) soso, desabrido; (in bad taste) de mal gusto

tasty [tésti] ADJ sabroso

tatter [tǽDɚ] N andrajo *m*, harapo *m*, pingajo *m*

tattered [tǽDɚd] ADJ harapiento, andrajoso

tattle [tǽdl] VI acusar; **to — on** acusar a; N **—tale** acusetas *mf sg*

tattoo [tætú] N tatuaje *m*; VI/VT tatuar[se]

taught [tɔt] *see* teach

taunt [tɔnt] VT provocar, burlarse de; N provocación *f*, pulla *f*

taut [tɔt] ADJ tenso, tirante

tavern [tǽvɚn] N taberna *f*, cantina *f*

tawdry [tɔ́dri] ADJ (affair) sórdido; (outfit) charro

tax [tæks] N impuesto *m*, contribución *f*, gravamen *m*; (burden) carga *f*; VT (a product) gravar; (a person) cobrarle impuestos a; (patience, resources) poner a prueba; **— attorney/lawyer** abogado -da tributarista *mf*; **— code** código impositivo *m*; **—- deductible** desgravable; **— deduction** deducción impositiva *f*; **— evasion** evasión de impuestos *f*; **—payer** contribuyente *mf*; **— return** declaración de impuestos *f*; **— shelter** abrigo impositivo *m*, refugio fiscal *m*; **— withholding** retención impositiva *f*; ADJ **—-exempt** no gravable, exento de

impuestos; —**-free** libre de impuestos
taxable [tǽksəbəł] ADJ imponible, tributable
taxation [tækséʃən] N (result of taxing)
impuestos *m pl*; (act of taxing) imposición de
contribuciones *f*
taxi [tǽksi] N taxi *m*; VI ir en taxi; (an airplane)
rodar por la pista; —**cab** taxi *m*
taxidermy [tǽksɪdɝmi] N taxidermia *f*
taxonomy [tæksánəmi] N taxonomía *f*
tea [ti] N té *m*; — **bag** bolsita de té *f*; —**cup** taza
de té *f*; —**kettle/pot** tetera *f*; — **party** té *m*;
—**spoon** (spoon) cucharita *f*, cucharilla *f*;
(measurement) cucharadita *f*; —**spoonful**
cucharadita *f*; —**time** hora del té *f*
teach [titʃ] VI/VT enseñar; **to — a class** dar clase
teacher [títʃɚ] N (primary school) maestro -tra
mf; (secondary school) profesor -ora *mf*; —**s
college** [escuela] normal *f*
teaching [títʃɪŋ] N enseñanza *f*; —**s** enseñanzas *f*
pl; — **activities** actividades pedagógicas *f pl*;
— **profession** magisterio *m*
team [tim] N equipo *m*; (of yoked animals) yunta
de bueyes *f*; (of horses) tiro *m*, enganche *m*;
—**mate** compañero -ra de equipo *mf*; VI **to —
up** unirse, formar un equipo
teamster [tímstɚ] N transportista *mf*,
camionero -ra *mf*
tear¹ [tir] N lágrima *f*; —**drop** lágrima *f*; — **gas**
gas lacrimógeno *m*; **to burst into —s**
romper a llorar
tear² [tɛr] VI/VT (rip) rasgar[se]; (rip a hole)
hacer[se] un siete; VT **to — along** ir a toda
velocidad; **to — apart** (rip up) romper,
destrozar; (separate) separar; **to — away**
apartar[se]; **to — down** (a building) demoler,
derribar; (a machine) desarmar, desmontar;
(a person) denigrar; **to — one's hair**
arrancarse los cabellos; N desgarrón *m*,
desgarradura *f*, rasgón *m*
tearful [tírfəł] ADJ (look) lloroso; (farewell) triste
tease [tiz] VT (make fun of a person) molestar,
fastidiar; (tantalize sexually) provocar; (comb
wool, hair) cardar; **to — out** sacar; N
provocadora *f*
teat [tit] N teta *f*
techie [tɛ́ki] N *fam* experto -ta en computación
mf
technical [tɛ́knɪkəł] ADJ técnico; — **support**
soporte técnico *m*
technician [tɛkníʃən] N técnico -ca *mf*, perito -ta
mf
technique [tɛkník] N técnica *f*
technological [tɛknəládʒɪkəł] ADJ tecnológico
technology [tɛknálədʒi] N tecnología *f*, técnica *f*
tectonics [tɛktánɪks] N tectónica *f*
tedious [tíɖiəs] ADJ tedioso, aburrido
tedium [tíɖiəm] N hastío *m*
tee [ti] N (T-shirt) camiseta *f*; (golf ball support)
tee *m*; (start of hole in golf) punto de salida *m*

teem [tim] VI **to — with** abundar en, estar lleno
de
teen [tin] *see* teenager
teenager [tíneɖʒɚ] N adolescente *mf*
teens [tinz] N (teenage years) adolescencia *f*;
(numbers 13–19) números de trece a
diecinueve *m pl*
teethe [tið] VI **the baby is teething** al bebé le
están saliendo los dientes
teetotaler [títóɖlɚ] N abstemio -mia *mf*
telecast [tɛ́ləkæst] N teledifusión *f*
telecommunication [tɛlɪkəmjunɪkéʃən] N
telecomunicación *f*; —**s** telecomunicaciones *f*
pl
telecommuting [tɛlɪkəmjúɖɪŋ] N teletrabajo *m*
teleconference [tɛ́lɪkɑnfɚəns] N
teleconferencia *f*
telegram [tɛ́ləgræm] N telegrama *m*
telegraph [tɛ́ləgræf] N telégrafo *m*; VI/VT
telegrafiar
telegraphic [tɛləgrǽfɪk] ADJ telegráfico
telemarketing [tɛləmárkɪɖɪŋ] N telemercadeo
m, telemarketing *m*
telepathy [təlépəθi] N telepatía *f*
telephone [tɛ́ləfon] N teléfono *m*; — **book** guía
telefónica *f*; — **booth** cabina telefónica *f*; —
number número telefónico *m*; — **operator**
telefonista *mf*; — **receiver** auricular *m*, tubo
de teléfono *m*; VI/VT telefonear, llamar por
teléfono
telescope [tɛ́lɪskop] N telescopio *m*; VI plegarse
televisable [tɛləváɪzəbəł] ADJ televisivo
televise [tɛ́ləvaɪz] VT televisar
television [tɛ́ləvɪʒən] N (medium) televisión *f*;
(device) televisor *m*; — **program** programa
televisivo *mf*; — **viewer** televidente *mf*
tell [tɛł] VI/VT (the truth) decir; (a story) contar;
to — apart distinguir; **to — on someone**
acusar a alguien; **to — someone off** regañar
a alguien; **to — time** decir la hora; **I can't —
if he's old or young** no sé si es viejo o joven;
his age is beginning to — se le comienza a
notar la edad; ADJ **a —tale sign** una señal
reveladora; **he is a —tale** es un acusica
teller [tɛ́lɚ] N (narrator) narrador -ora *mf*; (in a
bank) cajero -ra *mf*
temerity [təmérɪɖi] N temeridad *f*
temp [tɛmp] N empleado -da temporal *mf*
temper [tɛ́mpɚ] N (hardness) temple *m*; (bad
humor) mal genio *m*; **to keep one's —**
mantener la calma; **to lose one's —** perder
los estribos, encolerizarse; VT templar
temperament [tɛ́mpɚəmənt] N temperamento
m, genio *m*, talante *m*
temperance [tɛ́mpɚəns] N (moderation)
templanza *f*, temperancia *f*; (abstinence from
alcohol) abstinencia de bebidas alcohólicas *f*
temperate [tɛ́mpɚɪt] ADJ (weather) templado;
(opinions, habits) moderado

temperature [témpərətʃur] N temperatura f; **to have a —** tener fiebre

tempest [témpɪst] N tempestad f

tempestuous [tɛmpéstʃuəs] ADJ tempestuoso

template [témplɪt] N plantilla f

temple [témpəł] N (church) templo m; (side of the forehead) sien f

temporal [témpəəł] ADJ temporal

temporary [témpərɛri] ADJ temporal, eventual

tempt [tɛmpt] VT tentar

temptation [tɛmptéʃən] N tentación f

tempting [témptɪŋ] ADJ tentador

ten [tɛn] NUM diez; N **—s of candidates** decenas de candidatos f pl

tenacious [tənéʃəs] ADJ tenaz

tenacity [tənǽsɪdi] N tenacidad f

tenant [ténənt] N inquilino -na mf, arrendatario -ria mf

tend [tɛnd] VT (care for) cuidar; **to — to** (take care of) ocuparse de; (lean toward) tender, inclinarse

tendency [téndənsi] N tendencia f

tender [téndə] ADJ tierno; (painful) sensible; N (offer) oferta f; (legal currency) curso legal m; (person who tends) cuidador -ora mf, vigilante mf; VT presentar, ofrecer

tenderness [téndə-nɪs] N (of feeling) ternura f; (of meat) terneza f, ternura f; (sensitivity to pain) sensibilidad f

tendinitis [tɛndənáɪdɪs] N tendinitis f

tendon [téndən] N tendón m

tendril [téndrəł] N zarcillo m

tenement [ténəmənt] N casa de vecindad f

tenet [ténɪt] N principio m

tennis [ténɪs] N tenis m; **— court** cancha de tenis f, pista de tenis f; **— elbow** codo de tenista m; **— player** tenista mf; **— shoes** tenis m pl

tenor [ténə] N tenor m

tense [tɛns] ADJ tenso; N (grammatical) tiempo m

tension [ténʃən] N (stress) tensión f; (tautness) tirantez f

tent [tɛnt] N (camping) tienda de campaña f; (circus) carpa f; VI acampar

tentacle [téntəkəł] N tentáculo m

tentative [téntəDɪv] ADJ tentativo

tenth [tɛnθ] ADJ & N décimo m

tenuous [ténjuəs] ADJ (light, color, cloth) tenue; (peace) frágil

tenure [ténjə] N (of professorship) titularidad f; (of an office) ocupación f

tepid [tépɪd] ADJ tibio

terabyte [térəbaɪt] N terabyte m

term [tɜm] N (word, mathematical expression) término m; (period) período m; (time in office) mandato m; (semester) semestre m; (trimester) trimestre m; (set date for payment) plazo m; **— life insurance** seguro de vida a término m; **— paper** trabajo final m; **—s** condiciones f pl; **at —** a término; **to be**

on good —s estar en buenas relaciones; **not to be on speaking —s** no hablarse; **to come to —s** aceptar; VT denominar

terminal [tɜmənł] ADJ terminal; N (of airport, computer) terminal mf; (electric) terminal m

terminate [tɜmənet] VI/VT terminar[se]

termination [tɜmənéʃən] N terminación f; (of an employee) despido m

terminology [tɜmənáləʤi] N terminología f

termite [tɜmaɪt] N termita f

terrace [térɪs] N terraza f, escalón m; VT poner terrazas en, escalonar

terrain [tərén] N terreno m

terrestrial [təréstriəł] ADJ terrestre

terrible [térəbəł] ADJ terrible, tremendo

terrier [tériə] N terrier m

terrific [tərífɪk] ADJ estupendo

terrify [térəfaɪ] VT aterrar, aterrorizar, espeluznar

territory [térɪtɔri] N territorio m

terror [térə] N terror m

terrorism [térə-ɪzəm] N terrorismo m

terrorist [térə-ɪst] N terrorista mf

terrorize [térə-aɪz] VT aterrorizar

terse [tɜs] ADJ lacónico

test [tɛst] N (trial, experiment) prueba f; (of intelligence, multiple choice) test m; (examination) examen m, prueba f; **— market** mercado de prueba m; **— pilot** piloto de pruebas m; **— tube** tubo de ensayo m, probeta f; **—-tube baby** bebé de probeta m; **to undergo a —** someterse a una prueba; **to take a —** dar un examen; **to give a —** poner un examen; **to put to the —** poner a prueba; VT (put to the test) probar, poner a prueba; (give an exam) poner una prueba, examinar; **—ing** pruebas f pl; **to —-drive** probar; VI **girls — better than boys** en los exámenes salen mejor las niñas que los niños

testament [téstəmənt] N testamento m; (testimony) testimonio m

testicle [téstɪkəł] N testículo m

testify [téstəfaɪ] VI (serve as witness) testificar; (confirm) dar fe

testimony [téstəmoni] N testimonio m

testosterone [tɛstástəron] N testosterona f

tetanus [tétnəs] N tétano[s] m

tetracycline [tɛtrəsáɪklin] N tetraciclina f

Teutonic [tutánɪk] ADJ teutónico

text [tɛkst] N texto m; **—book** libro de texto m; **— editor** editor de texto[s] m; **— message** mensaje de texto m; VT enviar mensajes de texto, RP textear

textile [tékstaɪł] ADJ textil; N textil m, tejido m; **— mill** fábrica de tejidos f

texture [tékstʃə] N textura f

Thai [taɪ] ADJ & N (person) tailandés -esa mf; (language) tailandés m

Thailand [táɪlænd] N Tailandia f

than [ðæn] CONJ que; **I have more — you** tengo más que tú; **more — once** más de una vez

thank [θæŋk] VT dar las gracias, agradecer; **to have oneself to — for** tener la culpa de; INTERJ **— heaven!** ¡gracias a Dios! **— you** gracias; **—-you letter** carta de agradecimiento *f*; N **—s** gracias *f pl*

thankful [θǽŋkfəɫ] ADJ agradecido

thankfulness [θǽŋkfəɫnɪs] N gratitud *f*, agradecimiento *m*

thankless [θǽŋklɪs] ADJ ingrato

thanksgiving [θæŋksgívɪŋ] N acción de gracias *f*; **— Day** día de acción de gracias *m*

that [ðæt] ADJ (something nearer the speaker) ese, esa; (something more remote from speaker) aquel, aquella; **— dog** ese/aquel perro *m*; **— one** (nearer) ese, esa; DEMON PRON (nearer to speaker) ese, esa; (more remote from speaker) aquel, aquella; (neuter) eso, aquello; **— is my daughter** esa/aquella es mi hija; **— was a nightmare** eso/aquello fue una pesadilla; REL PRON que; **the bike — disappeared** la bici que desapareció; **the pen — I was writing with** la lapicera con la que / la cual escribía; **— is** es decir; CONJ que; **she said — she would come** dijo que vendría; ADV tan; **it's not — far** no queda tan lejos; **— much** tanto; **she was — tall** era así de alta

thatch [θætʃ] N paja *f*; *Am* quincha *f*; VT techar con paja; *Am* quinchar; **—ed roof** techo de paja *m*; *Am* techo de quincha *m*

thaw [θɔ] VI/VT (food) descongelar[se]; (ice and snow) derretir[se]; (relations, refrigerator) deshelar[se]; N deshielo *m*

the [ðə, ði] DEF ART (singular) el *m*, la *f*; **— boy** el chico *m*; (plural) los *m*, las *f*; **— girls** las chicas *f pl*; **— good thing about that** lo bueno de eso; ADV **— more I work, — less I accomplish** cuanto más trabajo, menos consigo

theater, theatre [θíəDɚ] N teatro *m*

theatrical [θiǽtrɪkəɫ] ADJ teatral

theft [θɛft] N hurto *m*, robo *m*

their [ðɛr] POSS ADJ **this is — dog** este es su perro, este es el perro de ellos

theirs [ðɛrz] PRON **this book is —** este libro es suyo, este libro es de ellos/ellas; **these things are —** estas cosas son suyas / de ellos / de ellas; **— is bigger** el suyo / la suya / el de ellos / la de ellos es más grande; **a friend of —** un amigo suyo, un amigo de ellos

them [ðɛm] PRON los *m pl*, las *f pl*; **I see —** los/las veo; **I talk to —** les hablo a ellos; **I went with —** fui con ellos/ellas

thematic [θɪmǽDɪk] ADJ temático

theme [θim] N (topic) tema *m*; (essay) ensayo *m*, redacción *f*; **— park** parque temático *m*; **—**

song tema *m*

themselves [ðɛmsɛ́ɫvz] PRON **they — built their house** ellos mismos se construyeron la casa; **they are not — today** hoy no son los mismos de siempre; **they were sitting by —** estaban sentados solos; **they looked at — in the mirror** se miraron en el espejo; **they talk to —** hablan solos; **they bought — a yacht** se compraron un yate

then [ðɛn] ADV (at that time) entonces, en aquel tiempo; **it was cheaper —** era más barato en aquel tiempo; (after) luego, después; **from — on** a partir de entonces; **now and — de vez** en cuando; **until —** hasta entonces; **I ate, — I paid** comí, luego pagué; **now —** ahora bien; **are you sorry —?** ¿estás arrepentido pues? ADJ entonces; **the — president** el entonces presidente; CONJ entonces; **if not, — you should stay** si no, entonces deberías quedarte

theologian [θiəlódʒən] N teólogo -ga *mf*

theological [θiəládʒɪkəɫ] ADJ teológico

theology [θiálədʒi] N teología *f*

theoretical [θiərɛ́Dɪkəɫ] ADJ teórico

theory [θíəri] N teoría *f*; **in —** en teoría

therapeutic [θɛrəpjúDɪk] ADJ terapéutico

therapist [θɛ́rəpɪst] N terapeuta *mf*; (psychologist) psicólogo -ga *mf*

therapy [θɛ́rəpi] N terapia *f*

there [ðɛr] ADV ahí; *Am* allí; (more remote) allá; *Sp* allí; **—abouts** por ahí, más o menos; **—after** (later) después; (always subsequently) de allí en adelante; **—by** así, de ese modo; **— ensued a war** a continuación hubo una guerra; **—fore** por consiguiente, por lo tanto; **—in** en eso, allí; **— is/are** hay; **— goes the bus** ahí va el autobús; **— —** bueno, bueno; **—of** de eso; **—on** (on that) encima; (later) luego, después; **—upon** (after) luego, después; (for this reason) por consiguiente; (upon that) encima; **—with** (with that) con eso; (after that) luego, en seguida; **who's —?** ¿quién es? **is Mary —?** ¿está María? **we got — at 5** llegamos a las 5

thermal [θɚ́məɫ] ADJ termal; **— energy** energía térmica *f*

thermal [θɚ́məɫ] ADJ térmico

thermodynamic [θɚmodaɪnǽmɪk] ADJ termodinámico

thermometer [θɚmámɪDɚ] N termómetro *m*

thermonuclear [θɚmonúkliɚ] ADJ termonuclear

thermos [θɚ́məs] N termo *m*

thermostat [θɚ́məstæt] N termostato *m*

thesaurus [θɪsɔ́rəs] N (synonym dictionary) diccionario de sinónimos *m*; (large dictionary) diccionario *m*

these [ðiz] ADJ & PRON estos, estas

thesis [θísɪs] N tesis *f*

they [ðe] PRON ellos, ellas

thick [θɪk] ADJ (slice) grueso; (fog, soup) espeso; (accent) marcado; (wit) torpe; **one inch —** una pulgada de espeso; **— as thieves** como carne y uña; ADJ **—headed** estúpido; **—set** grueso; **—-skinned** insensible; N **the — of the fight** lo más reñido de la pelea; **through — and thin** pase lo que pase

thicken [θíkən] VI/VT espesar[se], trabar[se]; **the plot —s** la trama se complica

thicket [θíkɪt] N soto m, matorral m, boscaje m

thickness [θíknɪs] N (of paper, wood) espesor m, grosor m; (of soup) lo espeso; (of lips) lo grueso; (of a beard) lo tupido; (of hair) lo abundante

thief [θif] N ladrón -ona mf

thieve [θiv] VI/VT hurtar, robar

thigh [θaɪ] N muslo m

thimble [θímbəl] N dedal m

thin [θɪn] ADJ (ice, wire) delgado, fino; (person) flaco; (vegetation, beard, hair) ralo; (voice) tenue, fino; (air) enrarecido; (excuse) débil; (soup) aguado; VI/VT (paint, soup, sauce) diluir; (hair) entresacar; **to — out** (hair) ralear; (crowd) dispersarse

thing [θɪŋ] N cosa f; **there's no such —** eso no existe; **that is the — to do** eso es lo que hay que hacer; **the — about Mary** lo que pasa con María

thingamajig [θíŋəmədʒɪg] N chisme m, coso m

think [θɪŋk] VI/VT (reason) pensar, razonar; (believe) creer, opinar; **to — about** pensar en; **to — back** recordar; **to — it over/ through** pensarlo bien, reflexionar sobre; **I'm —ing of you** pienso en ti; **what do you — of Mary?** ¿qué piensas de María? **I thought of a plan** se me ocurrió un plan; **to — up an excuse** inventar/elucubrar una excusa; **I don't — so** no creo; **who does he — he is?** ¿quién se cree que es? **to — well of** tener buena opinión de; **she —s nothing of spending $1000** no le importa nada gastar $1000

thinking [θíŋkɪŋ] N **current —** la opinión actual f; **to my way of —** a mi parecer; ADJ pensante

thinner [θínɚ] N disolvente m

thinness [θínnɪs] N (of ice, person) delgadez f, flacura f; (of hair) escasez f; (of air) enrarecimiento m; (of soup) fluidez f

third [θɚd] ADJ tercer[o]; **— base** tercera base f, antesala f; **— baseman** tercero m, antesalista m; **— chapter** capítulo tercero m, tercer capítulo m; **— person** tercera persona f; **—-rate** de poca categoría; **— World** Tercer Mundo m; ADV tercero; N tercio m; (gear, musical interval) tercera f; **the — of March** el tres de marzo

thirst [θɚst] N sed f; VI tener sed; **to — for** tener

sed de, estar sediento de

thirsty [θɚ́sti] ADJ sediento; **to be —** tener sed

thirteen [θɚtín] NUM trece

thirty [θɚ́Di] NUM treinta; ADJ & N **—something** treintañero -ra mf

this [ðɪs] ADJ & PRON este m, esta f, esto (neuter); **— dog** este perro; **— is a disaster** esto es un desastre

thistle [θísəl] N cardo m

thong [θɔŋ] N (strip of leather) correa f; (garment) tanga mf; (shoe) chancleta f

thorax [θɔ́ræks] N tórax m

thorn [θɔrn] N (sharp growth) espina f; (plant) espino m

thorny [θɔ́rni] ADJ espinoso, escabroso

thorough [θɚ́o] ADJ (exhaustive) exhaustivo, minucioso, detenido; (conscientious) concienzudo; **—bred** ADJ de pura sangre; N purasangre m

those [ðoz] ADJ & PRON (nearer) esos m, esas f; PRON (more remote) aquellos m, aquellas f; **— of you** los de vosotros/ustedes; **— that/who** los/las que

though [ðo] CONJ aunque; **as —** como si; ADV sin embargo

thought [θɔt] N (act, product of thinking) pensamiento m; (idea) idea f; (opinion) opinión f; (concern) consideración f; **to be lost in —** estar abstraído; **to give it no —** no darle importancia; **the very —** la mera idea; **at the — of** ante la idea de; **on second —** pensándolo bien; **my —s are with you** te acompaño en el sentimiento

thought [θɔt] see think

thoughtful [θɔ́tfəl] ADJ (considerate) considerado, atento; (well thought out) bien pensado; (reflective) pensativo, reflexivo

thoughtfulness [θɔ́tfəlnɪs] N consideración f

thoughtless [θɔ́tlɪs] ADJ (inconsiderate) desconsiderado; (careless) descuidado; (not reflective) irreflexivo

thoughtlessness [θɔ́tlɪsnɪs] N (lack of consideration) desconsideración f; (carelessness) descuido m; (lack of reflection) falta de reflexión f

thousand [θáʊzənd] NUM mil

thrash [θræʃ] VI/VT (whip, defeat) zurrar, vapulear, apalear; (thresh) trillar, desgranar; **to — around** revolverse, agitarse; **to — out a matter** ventilar un asunto

thread [θrɛd] N (in fabric) hilo m; (on a screw) rosca f; ADJ **—bare** raído; VT (a needle) enhebrar; (beads) ensartar; (a screw) enroscar; **to — one's way** abrirse paso

threat [θrɛt] N amenaza f

threaten [θrétṇ] VI/VT amenazar

threatening [θrétṇɪŋ] ADJ amenazador, amenazante

three [θri] NUM tres; **— hundred** trescientos;

ADJ —-**dimensional** tridimensional; —-
point basket triple *m*; —-**point play**
jugada de tres puntos *f*
thresh [θreʃ] VT trillar
threshold [θréʃhołd] N umbral *m*
threw [θru] *see* throw
thrift [θrɪft] N economía *f*
thrifty [θrɪ́fti] ADJ económico, ahorrativo
thrill [θrɪł] VI/VT emocionar[se], ilusionar[se]; N
emoción *f*, ilusión *f*
thrive [θraɪv] VI (person, economy) prosperar,
florecer; (plants) crecer mucho
throat [θrot] N garganta *f*
throb [θrɑb] VI latir, palpitar; N latido *m*,
palpitación *f*
throes [θroz] ADV LOC **in the — of war** en plena
guerra; **in the — of death** agonizando
throne [θron] N trono *m*
throng [θrɔŋ] N muchedumbre *f*, turbamulta *f*;
VI apiñarse, llegar en tropel
throttle [θrádł] N (of a motor) válvula
reguladora / de aceleración *f*, regulador *m*; (of
a motorcycle) puño giratorio del gas *m*; VT
ahogar, estrangular
through [θru] PREP por, a través de; (as
intermediary) por medio de; **Monday —
Friday** de lunes a viernes; **all — the night**
toda la noche; ADV (completely) de un lado a
otro; (from beginning to end) de principio a
fin, de cabo a rabo; **loyal — and —** leal a toda
prueba; **he's an aristocrat — and —** es un
aristócrata de pura cepa; **to carry —** llevar a
cabo; ADJ (ticket, train) directo; **to be —** (with
a task) haber terminado; (in a profession)
estar acabado; **we're —!** (with a boyfriend)
¡se acabó entre nosotros!
throughout [θruáʊt] PREP (all through) por
todo; (during) a lo largo de, durante; ADV
(duration) de principio a fin; (space) por todas
partes
throw [θro] VI/VT (a ball) tirar, lanzar; (a light,
voice) arrojar; (a switch) conectar; (a pot on a
wheel) modelar; (a punch) lanzar; (a wrestler)
tumbar; (a game for a bribe) dejarse perder; (a
rider) desmontar; (a party) dar, organizar;
that really threw me eso me confundió; **to
— away** (dispose of) tirar, arrojar; (squander)
malgastar; **to — down** tirar al suelo; **to — in**
añadir; **to — into gear** engranar; **to — in
the clutch** embragar; **to — out** (garbage)
tirar, arrojar; (unruly guest) echar; **to — up**
vomitar, devolver; N (act or instance of
throwing) tiro *m*; (of dice) tirada *f*; (shawl)
chal *m*; (blanket) manta *f*; —-**in** (soccer)
saque de banda *m*; ADJ —**away** desechable
thrown [θron] *see* throw
thrush [θrʌʃ] N tordo *m*, zorzal *m*
thrust [θrʌst] VT (stab) clavar; (shove) empujar;
to — oneself upon meterse en; **to — a task**

upon someone imponerle una tarea a
alguien; **to — aside** echar a un lado; VI (push)
dar un empujón; (stab at) lanzar una
estocada; (push through) empujar para pasar;
N (stab) estocada *f*; (force of a jet engine)
empuje *m*; (shove) empujón *m*; (military
assault) arremetida *f*, acometida *f*
thud [θʌd] N golpe sordo *m*; VI caer con un golpe
sordo
thug [θʌg] N matón *m*
thumb [θʌm] N pulgar *m*; —**tack** chinche *f*,
tachuela *f*; **under the — of** bajo la bota de;
VT hojear; **to give a —s up** aprobar
thump [θʌmp] N golpe sordo *m*; VI hacer un
ruido sordo
thunder [θʌ́ndɚ] N trueno *m*; —**bolt** rayo *m*;
—**head** nubarrón *m*; —**storm** tormenta
eléctrica *f*, tronada *f*; VI tronar
thunderous [θʌ́ndɚəs] ADJ atronador,
estruendoso
Thursday [θɚ́zde] N jueves *m*
thus [ðʌs] ADV así; — **far** (space) hasta aquí;
(time) hasta ahora
thwart [θwɔrt] VT frustrar
thyme [taɪm] N tomillo *m*
thyroid [θáɪrɔɪd] N tiroides *m sg*
Tibet [tɪbét] N Tíbet *m*
Tibetan [tɪbétn̩] ADJ & N tibetano -na *mf*
tic [tɪk] N tic *m*, manía *f*
tick [tɪk] N (sound of a clock) tic tac *m*; (cover of a
pillow) funda *f*; (checkmark) marca *f*; (insect)
garrapata *f*; VI hacer tic tac; **to — off** (check
off) marcar; (anger) enojar
ticket [tɪ́kɪt] N billete *m*; *Am* boleto *m*; (slate of
candidates) candidatura *f*; (summons) multa
f; (tag) etiqueta *f*; — **office** taquilla *f*; VT (give
passage) vender billetes; (give summons)
multar
tickle [tɪ́kəł] VT (poke) cosquillear, hacer
cosquillas; (amuse) dar ilusión; VI picar; N
picazón *f*, cosquilleo *m*
ticklish [tɪ́klɪʃ] ADJ (prone to tickling)
cosquilloso; (delicate) delicado
tidal [táɪdł] ADJ — **wave** (tsunami) tsunami *m*,
maremoto *m*; (large wave) marejada *f*
tidbit [tɪ́dbɪt] N (snack) golosina *f*; (gossip)
chisme jugoso *m*
tide [taɪd] N marea *f*; (of opinion) corriente *f*;
—**water** (water) agua de marea *f*; (land)
marisma *f*; VT **to — over** cubrir
tidy [táɪdi] ADJ (orderly) ordenado *f*; (large)
considerable; VI/VT arreglar; **to — oneself
up** arreglarse
tie [taɪ] VI (fasten) atarse; (make same score)
empatar; VT (fasten) atar; (make a knot) hacer
un nudo en; (make same score as) empatar
con; **to — a record** empatar una marca; **to —
down** atar; **to — in** cuadrar; **to — one on**
emborracharse; **to — tight** atar fuerte; **to —**

up (bind) atar; (hinder) bloquear; (occupy) ocupar; (moor a ship) amarrar; N (cord) cuerda f; (relations) lazo m, vínculo m; (cravat) corbata f; (railway) durmiente m, traviesa f; (score) empate m; —-**break** (in sports) desempate m; (in tennis) muerte súbita f

tier [tir] N nivel m

tiger [táɪgɚ] N tigre m

tight [taɪt] ADJ (knot, nut) apretado, ajustado; (clothes) ceñido, ajustado; (control) firme, estricto; (race) reñido; (stingy) tacaño, mezquino; (drunk) borracho; — **end** (football) receptor cerrado m; —-**fisted** agarrado; —**rope** cuerda floja f; —**wad** tacaño -ña mf; **to be in a — spot** estar en un aprieto; ADV bien, herméticamente; **to hold on** — agarrarse bien

tighten [táɪtn̩] VI/VT (knot, nut, belt) apretar[se]; (control) estrechar[se]

tightness [táɪtnɪs] N (narrowness) estrechez f; (stinginess) tacañería f

tilde [tɪ́ɫdə] N tilde f

tile [taɪɫ] N (on a roof) teja f; (on a floor) baldosa f; (on a wall) azulejo m; — **roof** tejado m; VT (roof) tejar; (floor) embaldosar; (wall) azulejar

till [tɪɫ] PREP hasta; CONJ hasta que; VI/VT (plow) labrar, arar; N (cash drawer) caja f

tilt [tɪɫt] VI/VT ladear[se], inclinar[se]; N (act or instance of tilting) ladeo m, inclinación f; (incline) declive m; (joust) justa f; **at full** — a toda velocidad

timber [tɪ́mbɚ] N (cut wood) madera [de construcción] f; (trees) árboles para madera m pl; (beam) viga f; —**line** límite de la vegetación arbórea m; — **wolf** lobo gris m

timbre [tɪ́mbɚ] N timbre m

time [taɪm] N (past, present, future) tiempo m; (on the clock) hora f; (occasion) vez f; (period) período m, momento m, época f; —-**and-a-half pay** paga de tiempo y medio f; — **bomb** bomba de tiempo f; — **frame** plazo aproximado de tiempo m; —**keeper** cronometrador -ora mf; — **limit** límite de tiempo m; — **out** descanso m; —**piece** reloj m; —**share** tiempo compartido m; — **signature** compás m; —**table** horario m; — **zone** huso horario m; **at —s** a veces; **at the same** — a la vez, al mismo tiempo; **at this** — en este momento; **behind** — atrasado; **lunch**— hora del almuerzo f; **from — to** — de vez en cuando; **for the — being** por el momento; **in** — a tiempo; **in no** — en seguida; **it's about** — ya era hora; **on** — puntual; **to buy on** — comprar a plazo; **after** — una vez tras otra; **to do** — cumplir una condena; **to have a good** — divertirse; **what — is it?** ¿qué hora es? VT (a race)

cronometrar; (a test) fijar la duración de; (one's arrival) fijar la hora de; **to — an attack well** atacar en el momento oportuno

timeless [táɪmlɪs] ADJ eterno

timely [táɪmli] ADJ oportuno

timer [táɪmɚ] N (person) cronometrador -ora mf; (device) reloj m

timid [tɪ́mɪd] ADJ tímido, apocado

timidity [tɪmɪ́DɪDi] N timidez f, apocamiento m

timing [táɪmɪŋ] N (measurement) cronometraje m; (synchronization) sincronización f; **that was good** — lo hiciste en el momento oportuno

timorous [tɪ́mɚəs] ADJ timorato

tin [tɪn] N (metal) estaño m; (tin plate) hojalata f; — **can** lata f; —**foil** papel de estaño m, papel de aluminio m; VT estañar

tincture [tɪ́ŋktʃɚ] N tintura f

tinder [tɪ́ndɚ] N yesca f

tinge [tɪndʒ] VT (tint) teñir; (affect slightly) matizar; N (of color) tinte m, matiz m; (of taste) dejo m; (of irony) matiz m

tingle [tɪ́ŋgəɫ] VI sentir hormigueo, hormiguear; **to — with excitement** estremecerse de entusiasmo; N hormigueo m

tinker [tɪ́ŋkɚ] VI ocuparse, entretenerse; **to — with** hacer ajustes

tinkle [tɪ́ŋkəɫ] VT (ring lightly) tintinear; (urinate) fam hacer pipí; N tintineo m

tinnitus [tɪnáɪDəs] N tinitus m

tinsel [tɪ́nsəɫ] N (Christmas trim) espumillón m, guirnalda f; (tawdry decoration) oropel m

tint [tɪnt] N (hue) matiz m; (for hair) tinte m, tintura f; (for glass) coloreado m; VT (hair) teñir; (glasses) colorear

tiny [táɪni] ADJ diminuto, chiquito

tip [tɪp] N (point) punta f; (gratuity) propina f; (piece of advice) consejo m; VI/VT (tilt) inclinar[se], ladear[se]; (give a gratuity) dar propina [a]; **to — a person off** advertir a alguien; **to — one's hat** sacarse/quitarse el sombrero; **to — over** volcar[se]

tipsy [tɪ́psi] ADJ alegre

tiptoe [tɪ́pto] N punta del pie f; **on —s** de puntillas; VI andar de puntillas

tirade [táɪred] N diatriba f

tire [taɪr] N neumático m; Mex llanta f; Am goma f; VI/VT cansar[se], fatigar[se]; **to — out** cansar, fatigar

tired [taɪrd] ADJ cansado, fatigado; — **out** agotado; **I'm — of your complaining** estoy harto de tus quejas

tireless [táɪrlɪs] ADJ incansable

tiresome [táɪrsəm] ADJ aburrido, pesado, plasta

tissue [tɪ́ʃu] N (cell aggregate) tejido m; (handkerchief) pañuelo de papel m; — **paper** papel tisú m

tit [tɪt] N (bird) paro m; (breast) vulg teta f

titanic [taɪtǽnɪk] ADJ titánico

titanium [taɪténiəm] N titanio *m*
tithe [taɪð] N diezmo *m*; VI pagar el diezmo
titillate [tídlet] VT (sexually) excitar; (interest) despertar interés
title [táɪdl] N título *m*; (of a painting) rótulo *m*; — **deed** título de propiedad *m*; — **page** portada *f*
TNT [tiéntí] N TNT *m*
to [tu] PREP **I gave it — you** te lo di a ti; **to count — ten** contar hasta diez; **I called — find out** llamé para averiguar; — **my surprise** para mi sorpresa; **a quarter — five** las cinco menos cuarto; **bills — be paid** cuentas por pagar; **things — do** cosas que hacer; **frightened — death** muerto de susto; **from house — house** de casa en casa; ADV — **and fro** de acá para allá; **to come —** volver en sí
toad [tod] N sapo *m*; —**stool** seta *f*, hongo no comestible *m*
toast [tost] VI/VT (brown) tostar[se]; VT (congratulate) brindar por; N (bread) tostada *f*; (congratulation) brindis *m*
toaster [tóstɚ] N tostadora *f*; — **oven** horno tostador *m*
tobacco [təbǽko] N tabaco *m*
today [tədé] ADV hoy; (nowadays) hoy día
toddler [tódlɚ] N niño pequeño *m*, niña pequeña *f*
toe [to] N dedo del pie *m*; (of shoe, sock) punta *f*; —**nail** uña del dedo del pie *f*; VT (touch with toe) tocar con el dedo del pie; **to — the line** hacer buena letra, entrar en vereda
together [təgéðɚ] ADV (in union) juntos; (at the same time) al mismo tiempo; — **with** junto con; **all** — todos juntos
Togo [tógo] N Togo *m*
Togolese [togəlíz] ADJ & N togolés -esa *mf*
toil [tɔɪl] VI trabajar, esforzarse, bregar; N trabajo *m*, esfuerzo *m*
toilet [tɔ́ɪlɪt] N (bowl) inodoro *m*; (lavatory) aseo *m*, lavabo *m*; — **paper** papel higiénico *m*; ADJ —**-trained** que ya no usa pañales
token [tókən] N (symbol) señal *f*; (keepsake) recuerdo *m*; (coinlike metal piece) ficha *f*; — **payment** pago nominal *m*; **as a — of friendship** en prenda de amistad
told [told] *see* tell
tolerance [tálɚəns] N tolerancia *f*
tolerant [tálɚənt] ADJ tolerante
tolerate [tálɚet] VT tolerar
toll [tol] N (of bells) tañido *m*; (payment) peaje *m*; (charges) tarifa *f*; (of victims) balance *m*; — **bridge** puente de peaje *m*; — **road** carretera de peaje *f*; ADJ —**-free** libre de cargos; VI/VT tañer [a muerto]
tomato [təmédo] N tomate *m*
tomb [tum] N tumba *f*, sepulcro *m*, sepultura *f*; —**stone** lápida *f*

tomboy [támbɔɪ] N marimacho *m*
tomcat [támkæt] N gato macho *m*
tomorrow [təmɔ́ro] ADV & N mañana *f*; — **morning** mañana por la mañana *f*
ton [tʌn] N tonelada *f*
tone [ton] N (pitch) tono *m*; (of a voice, instrument) sonoridad *f*; (of a speech) tono *m*, tónica *f*; VI **to — down** moderar, matizar
toner [tónɚ] N tóner *m*; — **cartridge** cartucho de tóner *m*
Tonga [táŋgə] N Tonga *m*
Tongan [táŋgən] ADJ & N tongano -na *mf*
tongs [tɔŋz] N tenazas *f pl*
tongue [tʌŋ] N (body part, language, of a flame) lengua *f*; (of a shoe) lengüeta *f*; — **depressor** depresor de lengua *m*; — **in cheek** irónicamente; — **twister** trabalenguas *m sg*; **on the tip of my** — en la punta de la lengua; **to hold one's** — callarse la boca; VI tocar con la lengua; **to** —**-lash** reprender; **to be —-tied** tener trabada la lengua
tonic [tánɪk] ADJ tónico; N (medicine) tónico *m*; (water, key note) tónica *f*; — **water** agua tónica *f*
tonight [tənáɪt] ADV esta noche
tonsil [tánsəl] N amígdala *f*
tonsillitis [tɑnsəláɪdɪs] N amigdalitis *f*, anginas *f pl*
too [tu] ADV (in addition) también; (excessively) demasiado; — **bad!** ¡qué lástima! — **many** demasiados; — **much** demasiado
took [tʊk] *see* take
tool [tuł] N herramienta *f*; —**bar** barra de herramientas *f*; —**box/kit** caja de herramientas *f*; —**shed** cobertizo para herramientas *m*
toot [tut] VI/VT (horn) sonar; (whistle) pitar; (trumpet) tocar; **to — one's own horn** darse autobombo; N (of horn, trumpet) toque *m*; (of horn) bocinazo *m*; (of whistle) pitido *m*
tooth [tuθ] N (front) diente *m*; (back) muela *f*; —**ache** dolor de muelas *m*; —**brush** cepillo de dientes *m*; — **decay** caries [dental] *f sg*; — **fairy** ratoncito Pérez *m*; — **mark** dentellada *f*; —**paste** pasta dental *f*, pasta dentífrica *f*; —**pick** mondadientes *m sg*, palillo de dientes *m*; **to fight — and nail** luchar a brazo partido; **to have a sweet** — ser goloso
toothed [tuθt] ADJ dentado
toothless [túθlɪs] ADJ desdentado
top [tɑp] N (of a mountain) cumbre *f*, cima *f*; (of a page) parte superior *f*; (of a jar) tapa *f*; (of a table) superficie *f*; (of a tree) copa *f*; (toy) trompo *m*, peonza *f*; (blouse) blusa *f*; —**coat** abrigo *m*; — **dollar** precio exorbitante *m*; — **hat** sombrero de copa *m*; —**spin** liftado *m*; **at — speed** a velocidad máxima; **to be — dog** ir a la cabeza; **to be at the — of the class** ser el

mejor de la clase; **at the — of one's voice** a voz en cuello; **filled up to the —** lleno hasta el tope; **from — to bottom** de arriba abajo; **on — of** encima de; ADJ (officer, floor) superior; (shelf, step) más alto; **—-flight** de primera; **—-heavy** desbalanceado; **—most** superior; **—-rated** de la más alta categoría; **—-secret** altamente confidencial; **—-notch** de primera; VT (a tree) desmochar; (a list) encabezar; (a performance) superar; (a level) exceder; **to — off** (an action) rematar; (a tank) llenar hasta el tope; **that —s everything!** ¡eso es el colmo!

topaz [tópæz] N topacio m

topic [tápɪk] N tema m, materia f, Am tópico m

topical [tápɪkəɫ] ADJ (of medicine) tópico; (current) de actualidad

topless [táplɪs] ADJ topless; **— swimsuit** monokini m

topple [tápəɫ] VT (knock over) derribar; (overthrow) derrocar; VI (fall) volcarse; (lose power) caer; **to — over** volcarse

topsy-turvy [tápsɪtɚ́vi] ADJ & ADV patas arriba

torch [tɔrtʃ] N antorcha f

tore [tɔr] see tear

torment¹ [tɔ́rmɛnt] N tormento m

torment² [tɔrmɛ́nt] VT atormentar, martirizar

torn [tɔrn] see tear²

tornado [tɔrnéɒo] N tornado m

torpedo [tɔrpíɒo] N torpedo m; **— boat** torpedero m; VT torpedear

torpid [tɔ́rpɪd] ADJ torpe

torpor [tɔ́rpɚ] N letargo m, torpor m

torque [tɔrk] N par de torsión m

torrent [tɔ́rənt] N torrente m

torrential [tɔrénʃəɫ] ADJ torrencial

torrid [tɔ́rɪd] ADJ tórrido

torsion [tɔ́rʃən] N torsión f

torso [tɔ́rso] N torso m, tronco m

tortoise [tɔ́rɒɪs] N tortuga f

tortuous [tɔ́rtʃuəs] ADJ tortuoso

torture [tɔ́rtʃɚ] N tortura f; VT torturar

torturous [tɔ́rtʃɚəs] ADJ torturante, torturador

toss [tɔs] VT (a ball, coin) tirar; (one's head) echar; (a salad) revolver; **to — aside** echar a un lado; VI (waves) cabecear; (a person in bed) dar vueltas; N (of coin, ball) tiro m; (of head) sacudida f

total [tódɫ] ADJ & N total m; **— amount** importe total m, montante m; **— loss** pérdidas totales f pl

totalitarian [totælɪtériən] ADJ totalitario

totter [tádɚ] VI tambalear[se], titubear

touch [tʌtʃ] VI/VT (have physical contact with) tocar; (move deeply) conmover, enternecer; (compare with) compararse con, igualar; (affect) afectar; **to — down** aterrizar; **to — off** provocar; **to — up** retocar; **to — upon** mencionar; N (contact) contacto m, roce m,

toque m; (sense) tacto m; (knack) mano f; (slight amount) poquito m; ; **—down** anotación f; **—down pass** envío de anotación m, pase de anotación m; **— screen** pantalla táctil f; **—-sensitive display** pantalla táctil f; **—stone** piedra de toque f; **a woman's** — un toque femenino; **finishing** — toque final m; **to keep in** — mantenerse en contacto; ADJ **—-and-go** precario; **—-tone** de botones

touching [tʌ́tʃɪŋ] ADJ conmovedor

touchy [tʌ́tʃi] ADJ hipersensible

tough [tʌf] ADJ (leather) fuerte, resistente; (fighter) duro, fuerte; (steak) duro, correoso; (situation) difícil; (neighborhood) bravo

toughen [tʌ́fən] VI/VT (leather) curtir[se]; (meat) endurecer[se]; (person) endurecerse

toughness [tʌ́fnɪs] N (of leather) resistencia f; (of a fighter, steak) dureza f; (of a situation) dificultad f; (of a neighborhood) lo bravo

toupee [tupé] N peluquín m

tour [tur] N (professional, artistic) gira f; (touristic) tour m, excursión f; (of a building) visita f; VI/VT (artistic, political) hacer una gira [por]; (touristic) hacer un tour

tourism [túrɪzəm] N turismo m

tourist [túrɪst] N turista mf; **— attraction** atracción turística f; **— class** clase turista/ turística f

tournament [tɚ́nəmənt] N torneo m

tourniquet [tɚ́nɪkɪt] N torniquete m

tow [to] VT remolcar; N (pull) remolque m; (fiber) estopa f; **—rope** cuerda de remolque f; — **truck** remolque m, grúa f, Am guinche m; **in — a cuestas

toward, towards [təwɔ́rd[z]] PREP (in the direction of) hacia; (for) para; **— four o'clock** a eso de las cuatro; **to feel angry —** estar enojado con

towel [táuəɫ] N toalla f

tower [táuɚ] N torre f; **— model** Am computadora torre f, Sp ordenador torre m; VI **to — over** elevarse sobre, dominar

towering [táuɚɪŋ] ADJ (tall) elevado, muy alto; (excessive) desmedido

town [taun] N (large) ciudad f; (small) pueblo m, localidad f; (downtown) centro m; **— hall** ayuntamiento m; **out of —** de viaje

toxic [táksɪk] ADJ tóxico; **— shock syndrome** síndrome de choque tóxico m

toxin [táksɪn] N toxina f

toy [tɔɪ] N juguete m; **— poodle** caniche enano m; VI **to — with** (fiddle with) juguetear con; (consider) considerar

trace [tres] N (path, mark, footprint) huella f; (mark) rastro m, traza f; (vestige) vestigio m; VT (a plan) trazar; (history) examinar; (an image) calcar; (a criminal) rastrear

trachea [trékiə] N tráquea f

tracheotomy [trekiáDəmi] N traqueotomía f
track [træk] N (of a heel, animal) huella f; (of a
wheel) rodada f; (for racing) pista f; (path)
senda f, sendero m; (of a railroad) vía f; (on a
record) surco m; (on a CD) tema m, pista f; (of
study) orientación f; — **and field** atletismo
m; — **meet** encuentro de atletismo m; —
record trayectoria f; **to be off the** — estar
descarrilado; **to keep** — **of** seguir el hilo de;
VI/VT (a criminal) rastrear, seguir la pista de;
(an aircraft, a student, progress) seguir; VI
(wheels) estar alineado; (stylus) seguir los
surcos; **to** — **down** perseguir; **to** — **in mud**
traer lodo en los pies
tract [trækt] N (of land) terreno m; (political)
octavilla f; (digestive) tubo m
traction [trǽkʃən] N tracción f
tractor [trǽktɚ] N tractor m; —-**trailer**
tractocamión m
trade [tred] N (buying and selling) comercio m,
trato m; (industry) industria f; (swap) canje m,
cambio m; (manual labor) oficio m;
(profession) profesión f; (people in a business)
gremio m; —-**in** entrega como parte de pago
f; —-**off** compensación f; —**mark** marca
registrada f, marca de fábrica f; —
agreement acuerdo comercial m; —
balance balanza comercial f; — **barrier**
barrera comercial f; — **name** (of product)
nombre comercial m; (of company) razón
social f; — **school** escuela industrial f; —
union sindicato m; VI/VT (buy and sell)
comerciar, negociar; (exchange) canjear;
(traffic) traficar; **to** — **in** entregar
trader [tréDɚ] N (dealer) comerciante mf; (at
fairs) feriante mf; (of slaves) tratante mf
trading [tréDIŋ] N transacciones f pl, comercio
m; — **partners** socios comerciales m pl
tradition [trədíʃən] N tradición f
traditional [trədíʃənəł] ADJ tradicional
traffic [trǽfɪk] N (of drugs) tráfico m; (of
vehicles) tránsito m, tráfico m; — **accident**
accidente de tránsito m; — **jam** atasco
circulatorio m; — **light** semáforo m; VI
traficar
tragedy [trǽdʒɪdi] N tragedia f
tragic [trǽdʒɪk] ADJ trágico
trail [treł] VI/VT (drag) arrastrar[se]; (follow in a
race) ir detrás [de]; (track) seguir la pista [de],
rastrear; VT (leave a trace) dejar una estela /
un reguero de; VI **to** — **off** desvanecerse,
apagarse; N (trace) rastro m, huella f; (path)
trocha f, sendero m, senda f; (of smoke) estela
f; (of blood) reguero m; — **bike** motocicleta
de trail f
trailer [tréłɚ] N (of a truck) remolque m; (of a
film) sinopsis f, trailer m, avance m; (house)
caravana f
train [tren] N (railroad) tren m; (part of a dress)

cola f; — **of thought** hilo de pensamiento m;
VI/VT (worker) capacitar[se]; (troops, athlete)
adiestrar[se]; Am entrenar[se]; VT (an animal)
amaestrar; (a child) educar, formar; (a
cannon) apuntar; **to** — **on** (a camera, eye)
enfocar
trainee [trení] N aprendiz -iza mf, practicante mf
trainer [trénɚ] N (of animals) amaestrador -ora
mf; (of workers, troops, athletes) entrenador
-ora mf
training [trénIŋ] N (of animals) amaestramiento
m; (of workers) capacitación f; (of troops,
athletes) entrenamiento m, adiestramiento
m; (of children) educación f
trait [tret] N rasgo m, seña f
traitor [tréDɚ] N traidor -ora mf
trajectory [trədʒéktəri] N trayectoria f
tramp [træmp] VT (trample) pisar; VI andar con
pasos pesados; (roam, as a hobo)
vagabundear; N (hobo) vagabundo -da mf;
(promiscuous woman) fam fulana f; Sp pej
golfa f
trample [trǽmpəł] VT pisotear; **to** — **on/over**
pisotear, atropellar; **to** — **out** apagar de un
pisotón
trampoline [træmpəlín] N trampolín m, cama
elástica f
trance [træns] N trance m
tranquil [trǽŋkwıł] ADJ tranquilo
tranquilizer [trǽŋkwılaızɚ] N tranquilizante m
tranquillity [træŋkwílıDi] N tranquilidad f
transact [trænzǽkt] VT llevar a cabo
transaction [trænzǽkʃən] N transacción f,
negocio m; —**s** actas f pl
transatlantic [trænzıtlǽntık] ADJ
transatlántico
transcend [trænsénd] VI/VT trascender
transcendence [trænséndəns] N trascendencia f
transcendental [trænsendéntł] ADJ
trascendental, trascendente
transcribe [trænskráıb] VT transcribir
transcript [trænskrıpt] N transcripción f
transfer [trænsfɚ] VI/VT (on a bus, train)
trasbordar; (a prisoner, worker) trasladar[se];
VT (loyalty, rights, money, data) transferir;
(property) traspasar; N (on a bus, train)
trasbordo m; (of loyalty, rights, money, data)
transferencia f; (of a prisoner, worker)
traslado m; (of property) traspaso m; — **of**
ownership traspaso de propiedad m; —
rate velocidad de transferencia f
transferable [trænsfɚəbəł] ADJ transferible
transfix [trænsfíks] VT (impale) traspasar,
atravesar; (paralyze) paralizar
transform [trænsfɔ́rm] VI/VT transformar[se]
transformation [trænsfɚméʃən] N
transformación f
transformer [trænsfɔ́rmɚ] N transformador m
transfusion [trænsfjúʒən] N transfusión f; **to**

give a— dar una transfusión de sangre, poner sangre

transgress [trænzgrés] VT transgredir; **to**— **against** pecar contra; **to**— **the bounds of** traspasar los límites de

transgression [trænzgréʃən] N transgresión f, pecado m

transient [trǽnziənt] ADJ transeúnte, pasajero; N transeúnte mf, vagabundo -da mf

transistor [trænzístə-] N transistor m

transit [trǽnzɪt] N tránsito m; **in**— en tránsito, de paso

transition [trænzíʃən] N transición f

transitive [trǽnzɪDɪv] ADJ transitivo

transitory [trǽnzɪtɔri] ADJ transitorio, pasajero

translate [trǽnzlet] VI/VT traducir

translation [trænzléʃən] N (rendering in different language) traducción f; (movement) translación f

translator [trǽnzleDə-] N traductor -ora mf

transmission [trænzmíʃən] N transmisión f

transmit [trænzmít] VI/VT transmitir

transmitter [trænzmíDə-] N transmisor m

transnational [trænznǽʃənəł] ADJ transnacional

transom [trǽnsəm] N travesaño m, montante m

transparency [trænzpérənsi] N transparencia f

transparent [trænspérənt] ADJ transparente; **to be**— traslucirse

transpire [trænspáɪr] VI (happen) ocurrir; (become known) descubrirse; VI/VT (perspire) transpirar

transplant¹ [trænsplǽnt] VI/VT trasplantar

transplant² [trǽnsplænt] N trasplante m

transport¹ [trænspórt] VT transportar, acarrear

transport² [trǽnspɔrt] N (moving) transporte m, acarreo m; (airplane) avión de transporte m; (rapture) éxtasis m; (of freight) flete m

transportation [trænspə-téʃən] N transporte m

transpose [trænspóz] VI/VT (letters) transponer; (a song) transportar

transsexual [trænsékʃuəł] ADJ & N transexual mf

transverse [trænsvэ́-s] ADJ transversal; (flute) transverso

transvestite [trænzvéstaɪt] N travestí mf, travesti mf, travestido -da mf

trap [træp] N trampa f; (for hunting) trampa f, cepo m; (under a sink) sifón m; —**door** trampilla f; VI/VT (to capture animals) cazar con trampa, atrapar; VT (to pin) aprisionar

trapeze [træpíz] N trapecio m

trapezoid [trǽpəzɔɪd] N & ADJ trapezoide m

trash [træʃ] N basura f, desechos m pl; (people) pej gentuza f; —**can** cubo de basura m

trashy [trǽʃi] ADJ ordinario

trauma [trómə] N (physical) traumatismo m; (psychological) trauma m

traumatic [trəmǽDɪk] ADJ traumático

travel [trǽvəł] VI/VT viajar [por]; VI (sound waves) propagarse; (in basketball) caminar, hacer pasos; N viaje m; — **agency** agencia de viajes f; — **expenses** gastos de viaje m pl, gastos de desplazamiento m pl; —**s** viajes m pl

traveler [trǽvələ-] N viajero -ra mf; —**'s check** cheque de viajero m

traverse [trəvэ́-s] VI/VT atravesar, cruzar; (skiing) bajar en diagonal; N (crossbar) travesaño m; (crossing) travesía f

travesty [trǽvɪsti] N farsa f

tray [tre] N bandeja f

treacherous [trétʃə-əs] ADJ traicionero, alevoso

treachery [trétʃəri] N traición f, alevosía f

tread [trɛd] VI/VT (trample) pisar, pisotear; VI (walk) andar, caminar; N (step) paso m; (on tire) banda de rodadura/rodaje f; (on shoe) dibujo m; —**mill** cinta rodante f

treason [tr íizən] N traición f

treasure [tréʒə-] N tesoro m; — **hunt** búsqueda del tesoro f; VT atesorar

treasurer [tréʒə-ə-] N tesorero -ra mf

treasury [tréʒəri] N tesorería f, tesoro m; **secretary of the**— ministro -tra de hacienda mf

treat [trit] VI/VT (act toward, discuss in writing, give medical aid) tratar; **I**—**ed myself to ice cream** me di un festín de helado; N (pleasure) placer m; (gift) regalo m; **my**— yo invito

treatable [tríDəbəł] ADJ tratable

treatise [tríDɪs] N tratado m

treatment [trítmənt] N trato m, tratamiento m; (artistic handling) interpretación f

treaty [tríDi] N tratado m

treble [trébəł] ADJ (triple) triple; (of higher clef) de tiple; — **clef** clave de sol f; N tiple m; VI/VT triplicar

tree [tri] N árbol m; — **hugger** ecologista mf; —**top** copa de árbol f; **up a**— en aprietos

treeless [trílɪs] ADJ pelado, sin árboles

trek [trɛk] N expedición f; VI viajar con dificultad

tremble [trémbəł] VI temblar; N temblor m

tremendous [trɪméndəs] ADJ tremendo

tremor [trémə-] N temblor m, sacudida f

tremulous [trémjələs] ADJ trémulo

trench [trɛntʃ] N (military) trinchera f; (for pipes) zanja f; (on sea floor) fosa f; — **coat** trinchera f, gabardina f

trend [trɛnd] N tendencia f

trendy [tréndi] ADJ de moda

trespass [tréspæs] N (illegal entry) entrada ilegal f; (religious) deuda f; VI (enter illegally) entrar ilegalmente; **to**— **against** (violate) violar; (sin) pecar; **no**—**ing** prohibido el paso

triage [triáʒ] N triaje m, clasificación f

trial [tráɪəł] N (testing) ensayo m, prueba f; (attempt) tentativa f; (affliction) aflicción f;

(in a court of law) juicio *m*, proceso *m*; — **balloon** globo sonda *m*; — **by fire** prueba de fuego *f*; — **flight** vuelo de prueba *m*; — **offer** oferta de prueba *f*; — **period** período de prueba *m*; — **run** ensayo *m*, prueba *f*; **by — and error** por ensayo y error

triangle [tráɪæŋgəł] N triángulo *m*

triangular [traɪǽŋgjələ-] ADJ triangular

tribe [traɪb] N tribu *f*

tribulation [trɪbjəléʃən] N tribulación *f*

tribunal [traɪbjúnəł] N tribunal *m*

tributary [tríbjətɛri] ADJ & N tributario *m*, afluente *m*

tribute [tríbjut] N (tax) tributo *m*; (testimonial) homenaje *m*

triceps [tráɪsɛps] N tríceps *m sg*

trick [trɪk] N (ruse) treta *f*, trampa *f*, trapisonda *f*; (magician's) truco *m*; (prank) broma *f*; (in cards) baza *f*; (of a prostitute) *fam* chapa *f*; **to be up to one's old —s** hacer de las suyas; **to play a — on someone** gastarle una broma a alguien; **to turn —s** prostituirse; *slang* hacer chapas; VT hacer trampa, engañar; **to — someone into something** hacer que alguien haga algo por medio de artilugios

trickery [tríkəri] N engaños *m pl*, argucias *f pl*

trickle [tríkəł] VI gotear; **to — in [out]** llegar [irse] de a poco; N goteo *m*

trickster [tríkstə-] N embustero -ra *mf*

tricky [tríki] ADJ (artful) mañoso; (difficult) complicado

tricycle [tráɪsɪkəł] N triciclo *m*

trifle [tráɪfəł] N (worthless thing) fruslería *f*, nadería *f*, bobada *f*; (cheap purchase) bagatela *f*; (small sum) miseria *f*; VI **to — with** jugar con; **to — away** perder

trigger [trígə-] N gatillo *m*; VT desencadenar

trill [trɪł] VI/VT (birds) trinar; (musical instrument) tremolar; (the *r* sound) pronunciar con vibración; N (of birds, etc.) trino *m*; (of the *r* sound) vibración *f*

trillion [tríljən] N billón *m*

trilogy [tríləʤi] N trilogía *f*

trim [trɪm] VT (adorn) adornar, guarnecer; (an edge) bordear; (fingernails, hair, threads) recortar; (hedge) podar; (airplane) equilibrar; (a wick) despabilar; ADJ (neat) cuidado; (slim) delgado; (fit) en buen estado físico; N (embellishment) adorno *m*; (of sails) orientación *f*; (cutting of hair) recorte *m*; (cutting of hedge) poda *f*; (of an airplane) equilibrio *m*

trimming [trímɪŋ] N (act of cutting) recorte *m*; (on a uniform) orla *f*, ribete *m*; —**s** (embellishments) adornos *m pl*; (food) guarniciones *f pl*; (parts cut off) recortes *m pl*

Trinidad and Tobago [trínɪdædəntəbégo] N Trinidad y Tobago *f*

Trinidadian [trɪnɪdǽDiən] ADJ & N trinitense *mf*

trinket [tríŋkɪt] N chuchería *f*, baratija *f*

trio [trío] N trío *m*

trip [trɪp] N (journey, drug-induced condition) viaje *m*; (experience) experiencia *f*; (accidental stumble) tropezón *m*; (making fall) zancadilla *f*; — **planner** planificador de rutas *m*; VT (cause to stumble) hacer una zancadilla a; (trip up) confundir; (release a catch) soltar; (blow a fuse) hacer saltar; VI (stumble) tropezar; (skip) andar con paso ligero; (make a mistake) equivocarse; (hallucinate) viajar; (blow a fuse) saltar

triphthong [trípθɔŋ] N triptongo *m*

triple [trípəł] ADJ & N (also in baseball) triple *m*; VI (in baseball) pegar un triple; VT (multiply by three) triplicar

triplet [tríplɪt] N trillizo *m*

tripod [tráɪpɑd] N trípode *m*

trite [traɪt] ADJ trivial, trillado

triumph [tráɪəmf] N triunfo *m*; VI triunfar

triumphant [traɪʌ́mfənt] ADJ triunfante, triunfador

trivial [tríviəł] ADJ trivial, baladí, fútil

trod [trɑd] *see* tread

trodden [trɑdn̩] *see* tread

trolley [trɑ́li] N (electric bus) trole *m*, trolebús *m*; (on tracks) tranvía *m*

trombone [trɑmbón] N trombón *m*

troop [trup] N (of scouts) tropa *f*; (of soldiers) escuadrón *m*; (of tourists) horda *f*; —**s** tropas *f pl*

trophy [trófi] N trofeo *m*

tropic [trɑ́pɪk] N trópico *m*

tropical [trɑ́pɪkəł] ADJ tropical

trot [trɑt] VI trotar; VT hacer trotar; **to — out** sacar a relucir; N trote *m*; **the —s** *fam* cagalera *f*

trouble [trʌ́bəł] VT (afflict) aquejar; (make turbid) enturbiar; VI/VT (bother) molestar[se]; (disturb) preocupar[se]; **to —shoot** solucionar problemas; N (problem) problema *m*; (difficulty) dificultad *f*, sinsabor *m*; (disturbance) disturbio *m*; (effort) molestia *f*; (ailment) enfermedad *f*, trastorno *m*; (mechanical breakdown) avería *f*, desperfecto *m*; —**maker** agitador -ora *mf*, revoltoso -sa *mf*; —**shooter** solucionador -ora *mf*, localizador -ora de averías *mf*; **to be in —** estar en un aprieto; **it is not worth the —** no vale la pena; **to make —** causar problemas; **to take the —** tomarse la molestia; ADJ —-**free** sin problemas

trough [trɔf] N (for food) pesebre *m*, comedero *m*; (for water) abrevadero *m*, bebedero *m*; (of weather, on ocean floor) depresión *f*

trousers [tráʊzə-z] N pantalones *m pl*

trousseau [trúso] N ajuar *m*

trout [traʊt] N trucha *f*

trowel [tráʊəł] N (for mortar) llana *f*, paleta *f*;

(for digging) desplantador *m*

truant [trúənt] N alumno -na que falta a clase sin permiso *mf*

truce [trus] N tregua *f*

truck [trʌk] N (vehicle) camión *m*; *Mex* troca *f*; (dealings) trato *m*; (vegetables) hortalizas *f pl*; — **driver** camionero -ra *mf*; *Mex* troquero -ra *mf*; VI/VT transportar en camión; *Mex* transportar en troca

trudge [trʌdʒ] VI andar con dificultad

true [tru] ADJ verdadero; (story) verídico; (copy, translation) fiel; (well) a plomo; (wheel) alineado, centrado; —**-blue** leal; —**-false test** prueba de verdadero o falso *f*; **his dream came** — su sueño se hizo realidad

truly [trúli] ADV (surprisingly) verdaderamente; (sincerely) sinceramente; (actually) en realidad, realmente; (accurately) fielmente; **very** — **yours** su seguro servidor, atentamente

trumpet [trʌ́mpɪt] N trompeta *f*; VI/VT (musician) trompetear; (elephant) barritar

trunk [trʌŋk] N (of tree, body) tronco *m*; (receptacle) baúl *m*; (of elephant) trompa *f*; (of a car) maletero *m*, *Mex* cajuela *f*; —**s** traje de baño *m*

trust [trʌst] N (confidence) confianza *f*; (charge) cargo *m*; (firm) trust *m*; (fund) fondo fideicomiso *m*; VI/VT (rely on) confiar en, fiarse de; VT (believe) creer; (hope) esperar

trustee [trʌstí] N (person holding property of another) fideicomisario -ria *mf*; (administrator) administrador -ora *mf*

trusteeship [trʌstíʃɪp] N (position of holding property) fideicomiso *m*; (administrative position) cargo de administrador *m*

trustful [trʌ́stfəł] ADJ confiado

trusting [trʌ́stɪŋ] ADJ confiado

trustworthy [trʌ́stwɝ ði] ADJ fidedigno, digno de confianza

trusty [trʌ́sti] ADJ leal

truth [truθ] N verdad *f*

truthful [trúθfəł] ADJ (account) verídico; (person) veraz

truthfulness [trúθfəłnɪs] N veracidad *f*

try [traɪ] VT (attempt) tratar de, intentar; (test, taste) probar; (strain) poner a prueba; (put on trial) procesar, enjuiciar; **to** — **on** probarse; **to** — **one's luck** probar fortuna; **to** — **and** tratar de; **to** — **out** (test) probar; (for a team) presentarse para; N intento *m*, tentativa *f*; —**out** prueba *f*

trying [tráɪɪŋ] ADJ penoso

tryst [trɪst] N cita romántica *f*

T-shirt [tíʃɝt] N camiseta *f*

tub [tʌb] N (for bathing) bañera *f*; (for butter) envase *m*; (for washing) tina *f*

tuba [túbə] N tuba *f*

tube [tub] N tubo *m* (also electronic); (television)

televisor *m*

tuberculosis [tʊbɝkjəlósɪs] N tuberculosis *f*

tubular [túbjələ-] ADJ tubular

tuck [tʌk] VT (stick in) meter; (make fold) alforzar; **to** — **in one's shirt** meter la camisa dentro del pantalón; **to** — **into bed** arropar; **to** — **something under one's arm** meterse algo bajo el brazo; N alforza *f*

Tuesday [túzde] N martes *m*

tuft [tʌft] N (of feathers) penacho *m*; (of hair) mechón *m*, copete *m*; (of plants) mata *f*

tug [tʌg] VI/VT (pull) tirar, jalar; (drag) arrastrar; **to** — at tironear; N (pull) tirón *m*; (boat) remolcador *m*

tuition [tuíʃən] N matrícula *f*

tulip [túlɪp] N tulipán *m*

tumble [tʌ́mbəł] VI (fall) caer; (collapse) venirse abajo; (do handsprings, etc.) dar volteretas; **to** — **down** rodar; **to** — **dry** secar en la secadora; **to** — **over** tropezarse; N (fall) caída *f*; (gymnastic trick) voltereta *f*

tumbler [tʌ́mblɝ] N (glass) vaso *m*; (person) acróbata *mf*

tummy [tʌ́mi] N barriguita *f*

tumor [túmɝ] N tumor *m*

tumult [túmʌlt] N tumulto *m*

tumultuous [tumʌ́łtʃuəs] ADJ tumultuoso

tuna [túnə] N (fish) atún *m*, bonito *m*; (prickly pear) tuna *f*

tune [tun] N (melody) tonada *f*, aire *m*; (electronic adjustment) sintonía *f*; —**-up** afinación *f*; **to be in** — (in pitch) estar afinado; (adjusted) sintonizado; **to be out of** — estar desafinado; VT (engine) afinar; (musical instrument) afinar, templar; (radio) sintonizar; **to** — **in** sintonizar; **to** — **out** ignorar

tuner [túnɝ] N afinador -ora *mf*; (electronic) sintonizador *m*

tungsten [tʌ́ŋstən] N tungsteno *m*

tunic [túnɪk] N túnica *f*

Tunisia [tuníʒə] N Túnez *m*

Tunisian [tuníʒən] ADJ & N tunesino -na *mf*

tunnel [tʌ́nəł] N túnel *m*; (for traffic) viaducto *m*; — **vision** visión en túnel *f*; VI cavar; VT hacer un túnel

turban [tɝ́bən] N turbante *m*

turbine [tɝ́baɪn] N turbina *f*

turbocharger [tɝ́botʃardʒɝ] N turbocompresor *m*

turbojet [tɝ́bodʒɛt] N turborreactor *m*

turbulence [tɝ́bjələns] N turbulencia *f*

turbulent [tɝ́bjələnt] ADJ turbulento

turd [tɝd] N *vulg* zurullo *m*, mojón *m*

turf [tɝf] N (lawn) césped *m*; (peat) turba *f*; (track for horse races) pista *f*; (territory) territorio *m*; VT cubrir con césped

Turk [tɝk] N turco -ca *mf*

turkey [tɝ́ki] N pavo *m*; — **vulture** buitre

pavo *m*

Turkey [tɔ́ki] N Turquía *f*

Turkish [tɔ́kɪʃ] ADJ turco; — **bath** baño turco *m*

Turkmen [tɔ́kmən] ADJ & N turcomano -na *mf*

Turkmenistan [tɔ́kmɛnɪstǽn] N Turkmenistán *m*

turmoil [tɔ́mɔɪɫ] N confusión *f*, agitación *f*

turn [tɔ̍n] VT (corner) doblar, dar vuelta; (wheel, key) girar, dar vuelta; (page) dar vuelta; (soil) labrar; (stomach) revolver; (ankle) torcer[se]; (a river) desviar; VI (change color) cambiar de color; (become) ponerse; (rotate) girar; (change direction) girar, dar la vuelta; **to** — **against** volverse en contra de; **to** — **around** dar la vuelta, girar; **to** — **away** (face) volver; (eyes) apartar; (person) rechazar; **to** — **back** (return) volver; (a clock) atrasar; **to** — **down** (offer, request) rechazar; (radio) bajar; **to** — **in** (hand in/over) entregar; (go to bed) acostarse; **to** — **inside out** dar vuelta al revés; **to** — **into** convertir[se] en; **to** — **off** (light) apagar; (faucet) cerrar; (a road) salir de; (person in general sense) disgustar; (person in sexual sense) quitarle las ganas a alguien; **to** — **on** (light) encender, prender; (faucet) abrir; (person) excitar; **to** — **out** (light) apagar; (people) expulsar; (product) producir; **to** — **out well** salir bien; **to** — **over** (car) volcar[se]; (engine) arrancar; (thought, idea, etc.) dar vueltas a; (criminal, weapon, etc.) entregar; —**table** plato giratorio *m*; **to** — **to** (have recourse to) acudir a, recurrir a; (become) volver[se]; **to** — **up** aparecer; **to** — **up one's nose** desdeñar; **to** — **up one's sleeves** arremangarse; **to** — **upside down** dar vuelta; N (rotation) vuelta *f*, revolución *f*; (change of direction) giro *m*, vuelta *f*; (change in condition) cambio *m*; (curve) recodo *m*, curva *f*; (opportunity) turno *m*; — **of mind** actitud *f*; —**off** (disgusting thing) asco *m*; (road exit) salida *f*; — **of phrase** giro *m*; —**out** concurrencia *f*; —**over** (of employees) renovación *f*; (of merchandise) volumen *m*; (in football) pérdida de balón *f*; (pastry) empanada *f*, pastelito *m*; (of a ball) pérdida *f*; —**pike** autopista *f*; —**stile** torniquete *m*, molinete *m*; — **signal** intermitente *m*; **at every** — a cada paso; **bad** — mala pasada *f*; **good** — favor *m*; **his bad teeth are a** —**off** sus feos dientes me dan asco / me repugnan; **his foreign accent is a** —**-on** su acento extranjero me excita; **it's my** — me toca a mí; **to take** —**s** turnarse

turnip [tɔ́nɪp] N nabo *m*

turpentine [tɔ́pəntaɪn] N trementina *f*, aguarrás *m*

turquoise [tɔ́kɔɪz] N turquesa *f*

turret [tɔ́ɪt] N (small tower, gun tower) torreta *f*;

(on a ship) torre *f*

turtle [tɔ́dḷ] N tortuga *f*; —**dove** tórtola *f*; —**neck** cuello vuelto *m*

tusk [tʌsk] N colmillo *m*

tutor [túdɚ] N profesor -ora particular *mf*; VI/VT dar clases particulares

tutorial [tutóriəɫ] ADJ de tutoría; N (computer) tutorial *m*; (math, Spanish) cursillo *m*

Tuvalu [túvəlu] N Tuvalu *m*

Tuvaluan [tuvəlúən] ADJ & N tuvaluano -na *mf*

tuxedo [tʌksído] N esmoquin *m*

TV [television] [tíví] N *fam* tele *f*

twang [twæŋ] N (in music) tañido *m*; (of speech) nasalidad *f*; VI (vibrate) vibrar; VT hacer vibrar; VI/VT (speak nasally) ganguear

twangy [twǽŋi] ADJ gangoso

tweak [twik] VT (pinch) pellizcar; (adjust) ajustar; N (pinch) pellizco *m*; (adjustment) ajuste *m*

tweed [twid] N tweed *m*

tweezers [twízɚz] N pinzas *f pl*

twelve [twɛɫv] NUM doce

twentieth [twɛntiɪθ] NUM vigésimo; **it's his** — **birthday** hoy cumple veinte años; **it's the** — **time I've told you** ya te lo dije veinte veces

twenty [twɛ́nti] NUM veinte; —**-five** veinticinco

twerp [twɔ̍p] N idiota *mf*, papanatas *mf sg*

twice [twaɪs] ADV dos veces

twig [twɪg] N ramita *f*

twilight [twáɪlaɪt] N crepúsculo *m*, ocaso *m*; — **zone** zona gris *f*

twin [twɪn] ADJ & N (fraternal) mellizo -za *mf*; (identical) gemelo -la *mf*; — **bed** cama individual *f*

twine [twaɪn] N cuerda *f*; VI/VT (twist) enroscar[se]; (interlace) entrelazar[se]

twinge [twɪndʒ] N (of pain, remorse) punzada *f*

twinkle [twíŋkəɫ] VI (star) titilar, parpadear; (eyes) brillar; N (of stars) titileo *m*, parpadeo *m*; (of eyes) brillo *m*

twirl [twɔ̍ɫ] VI/VT girar, dar vueltas [a]; N giro *m*, vuelta *f*; (of ice cream) espiral *m*

twist [twɪst] VI/VT (wind, coil) torcer[se]; (distort) tergiversar[se]; (writhe) retorcer[se]; (coil) enroscar[se]; N (of an ankle) torcedura *f*; (distortion) tergiversación *f*; (in a road, coil) vuelta *f*; (unforeseen event) vuelta de tuerca *f*

twister [twístɚ] N tornado *m*

twitch [twɪtʃ] VI/VT crispar[se], mover[se]; N (tic) tic *m*; (pang) punzada *f*; (tug) tirón *m*

twitter [twídɚ] VI gorjear; N gorjeo *m*

two [tu] NUM dos; — **hundred** doscientos; —-**point conversion** conversión de dos puntos *f*; **my** — **cents' worth** mi opinión *f*; **to put** — **and** — **together** atar cabos; ADJ —-**bit** de chicha y nabo; —-**edged** de doble filo; —-**faced** (with two faces) de dos caras; (hypocritical) hipócrita, falso; —-**fisted**

pendenciero; —-**way** de dos sentidos
tycoon [taɪkún] N magnate *mf*
type [taɪp] N tipo *m*, índole *f*; —**face** tipo de letra
m; —**script** texto escrito a máquina *m*;
—**writer** máquina de escribir *f*; —**writing**
mecanografía *f*; VI/VT (a letter) escribir a
máquina, mecanografiar, digitar, teclear,
tipiar, tipear; VT (blood) determinar el grupo
sanguíneo; **to** —**set** componer; **to** —**write**
escribir a máquina; ADJ —**written** escrito a
máquina
typhoid [táɪfɔɪd] N tifoidea *f*; — **fever** fiebre
tifoidea *f*, tifus *m*
typhoon [taɪfún] N tifón *m*
typhus [táɪfəs] N tifus *m*
typical [típɪkəł] ADJ típico
typist [táɪpɪst] N mecanógrafo -fa *mf*
typo [táɪpo] N error tipográfico *m*
typographical [taɪpəgrǽfɪkəł] ADJ tipográfico;
— **error** error de imprenta *m*, errata *f*
typology [taɪpáłədʒi] N tipología *f*
tyrannical [tɪrǽnɪkəł] ADJ tiránico
tyranny [tírəni] N tiranía *f*
tyrant [táɪrənt] N tirano -na *mf*

Uu

ubiquitous [jubíkwɪDəs] ADJ ubicuo
U-boat [júbot] N submarino alemán *m*
udder [ÁDɚ] N ubre *f*
UFO [**unidentified flying object**] [júéfó] N
OVNI *m*
Uganda [jugǽndə] N Uganda *f*
Ugandan [jugǽndən] ADJ & N ugandés -esa *mf*
ugliness [Áglinɪs] N fealdad *f*
ugly [Ágli] ADJ feo; (incident) deplorable; (mood)
de perros
uh-huh [ʌhÁ] INTERJ *fam* sí
Ukraine [jukrén] N Ucrania *f*
Ukrainian [jukréniən] ADJ & N ucraniano -na *mf*
ulcer [Áłsɚ] N úlcera *f*
ulcerate [Áłsəret] VI ulcerar
ulcerous [Áłsɚəs] ADJ ulceroso
ulna [Áłnə] N cúbito *m*
ulterior [ʌłtíriɚ] ADJ ulterior; — **motive**
segunda intención *f*
ultimate [Áłtəmɪt] ADJ (destination) último,
final; (authority) final, máximo; (principle)
fundamental; (vacation) perfecto; N
súmmum *m*
ultimately [Áłtəmɪtli] ADV en última instancia
ultimatum [Áłtəmédəm] N ultimátum *m*
ultralight [Áłtrəlaɪt] ADJ & N ultraligero *m*
ultramodern [Áłtrəmádɚn] ADJ ultramoderno
ultrasound [Áłtrəsaʊnd] N ultrasonido *m*; —

imaging imágenes por ultrasonido *f pl*
ultraviolet [Áłtrəváɪəlɪt] ADJ & N ultravioleta *m*
umbilical cord [ʌmbílɪkəłkɔrd] N cordón
umbilical *m*
umbrella [ʌmbrélə] N paraguas *m sg*
umpire [Ámpaɪr] N árbitro *m*; (in tennis) juez
-eza de silla *mf*; VI/VT arbitrar
unable [ʌnébəł] ADJ **to be** — **to** no poder
unabridged [ʌnəbrídʒd] ADJ íntegro
unaccented [ʌnǽksɛntɪd] ADJ sin acento
unacceptable [ʌnɪkséptəbəł] ADJ inaceptable,
inadmisible
unaccustomed [ʌnəkÁstəmd] ADJ (not used to)
no acostumbrado; (uncommon) insólito
unadjusted [ʌnədʒÁstɪd] ADJ no ajustado
unadulterated [ʌnədÁłtəreDɪd] ADJ puro
unaffected [ʌnəféktɪd] ADJ (not affected) no
afectado; (sincere) natural, sincero;
(unpretentious) sin afectación
unaffiliated [ʌnəfílieDɪd] ADJ no afiliado
unanimity [junənímɪDi] N unanimidad *f*
unanimous [junǽnəməs] ADJ unánime
unarmed [ʌnármd] ADJ desarmado
unassuming [ʌnəsúmɪŋ] ADJ modesto, sin
pretensiones
unattached [ʌnətǽtʃt] ADJ (piece of paper)
suelto; (person) soltero
unauthorized [ʌnɔ́θɚraɪzd] ADJ no autorizado
unavailable [ʌnəvéləbəł] ADJ no disponible
unavoidable [ʌnəvɔ́ɪDəbəł] ADJ inevitable,
ineludible
unaware [ʌnəwér] ADJ inconsciente; ADV **to be**
— **of** ignorar; —**s** sin darse cuenta
unbalanced [ʌnbǽlənst] ADJ desequilibrado
unbearable [ʌnbérəbəł] ADJ inaguantable,
insoportable
unbeatable [ʌnbíDəbəł] ADJ imbatible
unbeaten [ʌnbítn̩] ADJ invicto
unbecoming [ʌnbɪkÁmɪŋ] ADJ (behavior)
impropio; (clothes) que no [le] luce
unbelief [ʌnbɪlíf] N incredulidad *f*,
descreimiento *m*
unbelievable [ʌnbɪlívəbəł] ADJ increíble
unbeliever [ʌnbɪlívɚ] N descreído -da *mf*
unbending [ʌnbéndɪŋ] ADJ inflexible
unbiased [ʌnbáɪəst] ADJ imparcial
unbounded [ʌnbáʊndɪd] ADJ ilimitado
unbridled [ʌnbráɪd̩ld] ADJ desenfrenado
unbroken [ʌnbrókən] ADJ (intact) intacto; (not
tamed) indomado; (uninterrupted)
ininterrumpido
unbuckle [ʌnbÁkəł] VT desabrochar
unbutton [ʌnbÁtn̩] VI/VT desabotonar,
desabrochar
uncalled-for [ʌnkɔ́łdfɔr] ADJ injustificado
uncanny [ʌnkǽni] ADJ inexplicable, misterioso
uncertain [ʌnsɝ́tn̩] ADJ incierto
uncertainty [ʌnsɝ́tn̩ti] N incertidumbre *f*
unchanged [ʌntʃéndʒd] ADJ inalterado

uncharitable [ʌntʃǽrɪDəbəł] ADJ duro, poco caritativo

uncivilized [ʌnsívəlaɪzd] ADJ incivilizado

uncle [ʌ́ŋkəł] N tío m; **to say** — darse por vencido

unclean [ʌnklín] ADJ (dirty) sucio; (impure) impuro

uncollectable [ʌnkəléktəbəł] ADJ incobrable

uncomfortable [ʌnkʌ́mfɚDəbəł] ADJ incómodo

uncommon [ʌnkámən] ADJ (unusual) poco común; (extraordinary) extraordinario

uncompromising [ʌnkámprəmaɪzɪŋ] ADJ (intransigent) intransigente; (unfailing) incondicional

unconcerned [ʌnkənsɝ́nd] ADJ indiferente

unconditional [ʌnkəndíʃənəł] ADJ incondicional

unconfirmed [ʌnkənfɝ́md] ADJ no confirmado

unconscious [ʌnkánʃəs] ADJ inconsciente

unconstitutional [ʌnkɑnstɪtúʃənl̩] ADJ inconstitucional

uncontrollable [ʌnkəntróləbəł] ADJ (movement) incontrolable; (urge, laughter) incontenible

unconventional [ʌnkənvénʃənəł] ADJ poco convencional

uncouth [ʌnkúθ] ADJ tosco

uncover [ʌnkʌ́vɚ] VI/VT descubrir[se]; VI (remove bedcovers) destaparse

uncovered [ʌnkʌ́vəd] ADJ descubierto

unctuous [ʌ́ŋktʃuəs] ADJ untuoso, zalamero

uncultivated [ʌnkʌ́łtəveDɪd] ADJ (person) inculto, no cultivado; (land) no cultivado

uncultured [ʌnkʌ́łtʃəd] ADJ inculto

undaunted [ʌndɔ́ntɪd] ADJ impávido, intrépido

undecided [ʌndɪsáɪDɪd] ADJ indeciso

undeclared [ʌndɪklérd] ADJ no declarado

undefined [ʌndɪfáɪnd] ADJ indefinido

undelete utility [ʌndɪlít jutɪlɪDi] N programa para recuperar datos borrados m

undeniable [ʌndɪnáɪəbəł] ADJ innegable, indudable

under [ʌ́ndɚ] PREP (below) bajo, debajo de, abajo de; (in a ranking) por debajo de; (less) menos de; — **the Democrats** durante el mandato de los Demócratas; — **a pseudonym** bajo un pseudónimo; — **cost** a menos del costo/coste, por debajo del costo/coste; — **contract** bajo contrato; — **wraps** oculto; ADV (below) debajo, abajo; (less than) menos; **to be** — estar inconsciente

underage [ʌndə-édʒ] ADJ menor de edad; — **drinking** consumo de alcohol por menores de edad m

underarm [ʌ́ndɚɑrm] N axila f

underbrush [ʌ́ndɚbrʌʃ] N maleza f

undercharge [ʌndɚtʃárdʒ] VI cobrar de menos

underclass [ʌ́ndɚklæs] N subproletariado m

undercover [ʌndɚkʌ́vɚ] ADJ clandestino, secreto

undercut [ʌndɚkʌ́t] VT (undermine) socavar; (sell for less) vender por menos que

underdeveloped [ʌndɚdɪvéləpt] ADJ subdesarrollado

underdog [ʌ́ndɚdɔg] N el de abajo m, la de abajo f

underemployed [ʌndɚɛmplɔ́ɪd] ADJ subempleado

underestimate [ʌndɚéstəmet] VT (person) subestimar; (price) subvaluar

underfed [ʌndɚféd] ADJ desnutrido

underfoot [ʌndɚfút] ADJ (beneath the feet) bajo los pies; (in the way) estorbando

undergird [ʌndɚgɝ́d] VT reforzar

undergo [ʌndɚgó] VT (an operation) someterse a; (a change) experimentar, sufrir

undergraduate [ʌndɚgrǽdʒuɪt] N estudiante de pregrado mf; — **course** clase de pregrado f

underground[1] [ʌndɚgráund] ADV (under the earth) bajo tierra; (secretly) en secreto

underground[2] [ʌndɚgraund] ADJ (under the earth) subterráneo; (secret) clandestino; N resistencia f, grupo clandestino m

underhanded [ʌndɚhǽndɪd] ADJ (secret) secreto, solapado; (illicit) ilícito

underlie [ʌndɚláɪ] VI/VT subyacer [a]

underline [ʌ́ndɚlaɪn] VT subrayar

underlying [ʌndɚláɪɪŋ] ADJ (inflation, racism) subyacente; (problems) de fondo

undermine [ʌndɚmáɪn] VT minar, menoscabar

underneath [ʌndɚníθ] PREP bajo, debajo de, abajo de; ADV debajo, abajo; N la parte inferior

undernourished [ʌndɚnɝ́ɪʃt] ADJ desnutrido

underpants [ʌ́ndɚpænts] N (for men) calzoncillos m pl; (for women) Sp bragas f pl; Mex pantaletas f pl; RP bombacha f

underrated [ʌndɚréDɪd] ADJ infravalorado

underscore [ʌndɚskór] N subrayado m; VT subrayar

undersecretary [ʌndɚsékrətɛri] N subsecretario -ria mf

undersell [ʌndɚséł] VT (to sell at a low price) malbaratar; (to sell cheaper) vender a menos precio

undershirt [ʌ́ndɚʃɝt] N camiseta f

underside [ʌ́ndɚsaɪd] N parte inferior f

undersigned [ʌndɚsáɪnd] N abajo firmante mf, infrascrito -ta mf

underskirt [ʌ́ndɚskɝt] N enaguas f pl

understaffed [ʌndɚstǽft] ADJ falto de personal

understand [ʌndɚstǽnd] VI/VT comprender, entender; **I** — **you're leaving** tengo entendido que te vas; **to** — **about** saber de/ entender de

understandable [ʌndɚstǽndəbəł] ADJ comprensible

understanding [ʌndɚstǽndɪŋ] N

(comprehension) comprensión *f*,
entendimiento *m*; (tolerance) comprensión
mutua *f*; (agreement) acuerdo *m*; ADJ
comprensivo
understate [ʌndəˈstét] VT minimizar
understood [ʌndəˈstúd] ADJ entendido;
(implicit) sobreentendido
understood [ʌndəˈstúd] *see* understand
understudy [ʌ́ndəstʌdi] N suplente *mf*,
sobresaliente *mf*; VI/VT suplir [a], servir de
sobresaliente [para]
undertake [ʌndəˈték] VT emprender, acometer;
to — to comprometerse a
undertaken [ʌndəˈtékən] *see* undertake
undertaker [ʌ́ndəˌtekə] N director -ora de
funeraria / pompas fúnebres *mf*, funerario
-ria *mf*
undertaking [ʌndəˈtékɪŋ] N empresa *f*
under-the-table [ʌ́ndəðətébəl] ADJ ilícito, bajo
cuerda
undertone [ʌ́ndəton] N (low voice) voz baja *f*;
(undercurrent) tónica *f*
undertook [ʌndəˈtúk] *see* undertake
undertow [ʌ́ndəto] N resaca *f*
undervalued [ʌndəˈvæljud] ADJ infravalorado
underwater [ʌ́ndəwɔtə, ʌ́ndəwɔ́tə] ADJ
submarino; ADV por debajo del agua
underwear [ʌ́ndəwɛr] N ropa interior *f*
underweight [ʌ́ndəwet] ADJ de peso
insuficiente
underworld [ʌ́ndəwɜld] N (of criminals)
hampa *f*; (netherworld) el más allá
underwrite [ʌ́ndərait] VI/VT (finance)
financiar; (sign) suscribir; (insure) asegurar
underwriter [ʌ́ndəraidə] N (insurance)
asegurador -ora *mf*; (stock exchange)
suscriptor -ora *mf*
undesirable [ʌndɪzáɪrəbəl] ADJ indeseable
undetermined [ʌndɪtɝ́mɪnd] ADJ
indeterminado
undid [ʌndíd] *see* undo
undisclosed [ʌndɪsklózd] ADJ no divulgado
undisturbed [ʌndɪstɝ́bd] ADJ (unworried,
uninterrupted) tranquilo; (unspoiled) virgen
undivided [ʌndɪváɪdɪd] ADJ indiviso
undo [ʌndú] VT (reverse an action) deshacer,
anular; (unfasten) desabrochar, desabotonar;
(destroy) destruir; (loosen hair) soltar
undocumented [ʌndákjəmɛntɪd] ADJ
indocumentado
undoing [ʌndúɪŋ] N (reversal) deshacer *m*;
(destruction) destrucción *f*, perdición *f*; (of
buttons) desabrochar *m*
undone [ʌndʌ́n] ADJ (unfinished) sin terminar;
(ruined) perdido; (unfastened) desabrochado;
to come — (clothing) desabrocharse;
(person) desquiciarse
undone [ʌndʌ́n] *see* undo
undoubtedly [ʌndáʊDɪdli] ADV

indudablemente, sin duda
undress [ʌndrés] VI/VT desnudar[se],
desvestir[se]
undue [ʌndú] ADJ (inappropriate) indebido;
(excessive) excesivo
undulate [ʌ́ndʒəlet] VI/VT ondular
undying [ʌndáɪɪŋ] ADJ imperecedero, eterno
unearned [ʌnɝ́nd] N inmerecido; — **run**
(baseball) carrera sucia *f*
unearth [ʌnɝ́θ] VT desenterrar
uneasiness [ʌnízɪnɪs] N (feeling) inquietud *f*,
desasosiego *m*, desazón *f*; *Sp* grima *f*; (of
peace) precariedad *f*; (of silence, situation)
incomodidad *f*; (of sleep) agitación *f*
uneasy [ʌnízi] ADJ (feeling) inquieto; (peace)
precario; (silence) incómodo; (situation)
molesto; (sleep) agitado
uneducated [ʌnédʒəkeDɪd] ADJ inculto,
ignorante
unemployable [ʌnɪmplɔ́ɪəbəl] ADJ inempleable
unemployed [ʌnɪmplɔ́ɪd] ADJ (jobless)
desocupado, desempleado, *Sp* parado;
(unused) ocioso
unemployment [ʌnɪmplɔ́ɪmənt] N
desocupación *f*, desempleo *m*, *Sp* paro *m*; —
compensation seguro de paro *m*; *Sp* paro *m*;
— **rate** *Am* tasa de desempleo *f*, *Sp* tasa de
paro *f*
unending [ʌnéndɪŋ] ADJ interminable
unequal [ʌníkwəl] ADJ desigual; **to be — to a
task** no ser capaz de cumplir una tarea
unequivocal [ʌnɪkwívəkəl] ADJ inequívoco,
tajante
unerase [ʌnɪrés] VT recuperar archivos borrados
unethical [ʌnéθɪkəl] ADJ no ético
uneven [ʌnívən] ADJ (rough) irregular,
accidentado; (inequitable) desigual; (not
uniform) desparejo; (odd, of numbers) impar
uneventful [ʌnɪvéntfəl] ADJ sin incidente
unexpected [ʌnɪkspéktɪd] ADJ inesperado
unexpressive [ʌnɪksprésɪv] ADJ inexpresivo
unfailing [ʌnfélɪŋ] ADJ (inexhaustible)
inagotable; (dependable) infalible
unfair [ʌnfér] ADJ (measure, price) injusto;
(competition) injusto, desleal
unfaithful [ʌnféθfəl] ADJ infiel
unfamiliar [ʌnfəmíljə] ADJ (unknown) poco
familiar, desconocido; (unacquainted) poco
familiarizado
unfasten [ʌnfǽsən] VI/VT desabrochar[se],
desprender[se]
unfavorable [ʌnfévəəbəl] ADJ desfavorable
unfeeling [ʌnfílɪŋ] ADJ insensible
unfettered [ʌnféDəd] ADJ (untied) desatado;
(free) libre
unfinished [ʌnfínɪʃt] ADJ (matter) inacabado,
inconcluso; (business) pendiente; (wood) sin
terminar, sin barnizar; (task) inconcluso, sin
terminar

unfit [ʌnfít] ADJ (unsuitable) no apto; (incapable) incapaz

unfold [ʌnfóld] VT (open out) desdoblar, desplegar; VI (happen) desarrollarse; (reveal) revelarse

unforced error [ʌnfɔrst éra‑] N (tennis) error no forzado *m*

unforeseen [ʌnfɔrsín] ADJ imprevisto

unforgettable [ʌnfa‑gédəbəl] ADJ inolvidable

unfortunate [ʌnfɔ́rtʃənɪt] ADJ desgraciado, desafortunado, desventurado

unfortunately [ʌnfɔ́rtʃənətli] ADV desafortunadamente, lamentablemente

unfounded [ʌnfáʊndɪd] ADJ infundado

unfriendly [ʌnfréndli] ADJ (forces) hostil; (person) antipático

unfurl [ʌnfɚ́l] VI/VT desplegar[se]

unfurnished [ʌnfɚ́nɪʃt] ADJ sin amueblar, desamueblado

ungainly [ʌngénli] ADJ (ungraceful) desgarbado, desmadejado; (clumsy) torpe

ungrateful [ʌngrétfəl] ADJ ingrato, desagradecido

unguarded [ʌngárdɪd] ADJ (incautious) descuidado, desprevenido; (unattended) sin vigilancia; (defenseless) indefenso; **an — moment** un momento de descuido

unhappiness [ʌnhǽpinɪs] N infelicidad *f*

unhappy [ʌnhǽpi] ADJ (sad) infeliz, desdichado, desgraciado; (dissatisfied) insatisfecho; (infelicitous) poco afortunado

unharmed [ʌnhármd] ADJ ileso

unhealthy [ʌnhélθi] ADJ (climate, food, lifestyle) malsano, insalubre; (complexion, obsession) enfermizo

unheard-of [ʌnhɚ́Dɑv] ADJ inaudito, desconocido

unhinge [ʌnhíndʒ] VT desquiciar

unholy [ʌnhóli] ADJ (noise) infernal; (alliance) nefasto

unhook [ʌnhúk] VT (disentangle) desenganchar; (undo) desabrochar

unhurt [ʌnhɚ́t] ADJ ileso

uniform [júnəfɔrm] ADJ & N uniforme *m*

uniformity [junəfɔ́rmɪDi] N uniformidad *f*

unify [júnəfaɪ] VI/VT unificar[se]

unilateral [junəlǽDə‑əl] ADJ unilateral

unimportant [ʌnɪmpɔ́rtṇt] ADJ insignificante, sin importancia

uninhabited [ʌnɪnhǽbɪdɪd] ADJ deshabitado

uninhibited [ʌnɪnhíbɪdɪd] ADJ desinhibido, desenfadado

uninspired [ʌnɪnspáɪrd] ADJ poco inspirado

uninstall [ʌnɪnstɑ́l] VT desinstalar

uninsured [ʌnɪnʃúrd] ADJ sin seguro médico

unintelligible [ʌnɪntélɪdʒəbəl] ADJ ininteligible

uninterrupted [ʌnɪntərʌ́ptɪd] ADJ ininterrumpido

union [júnjən] N unión *f*; (labor) sindicato *m*,

gremio *m*; **— dues** cuotas sindicales *f pl*; **— labor** mano de obra sindicalizada/agremiada *f*; **— leader** dirigente sindical *mf*

unionize [júnjənaɪz] VI/VT sindicar[se], agremiar[se]

unique [juník] ADJ único, singular; **that feature is — to the South** ese rasgo es peculiar del sur

unisex [júnəsɛks] ADJ unisex

unison [júnəsən] ADV LOC **in —** al unísono

unit [júnɪt] N (part of a whole) unidad *f*; (part of a machine) módulo *m*

unitarian [junɪtérɪən] ADJ unitario

unitary [júnɪteri] ADJ unitario

unite [junáɪt] VI/VT unir[se]

United Arab Emirates [junáɪDɪdǽrəbémə‑ɪts] N Emiratos Árabes Unidos *m pl*

United Kingdom [junáɪDɪdkíŋdəm] N Reino Unido *m*

United States [junáɪDɪdstéts] N Estados Unidos *m pl*

unity [júnɪDi] N unidad *f*; (concord) unión *f*

universal [junəvɚ́səl] ADJ universal; **— donor** donante universal *mf*; **— joint** acoplamiento universal de cardán *m*

universe [júnəvɚs] N universo *m*

university [junəvɚ́sɪDi] N universidad *f*; **— degree** título universitario *m*

unjust [ʌndʒʌ́st] ADJ injusto

unjustifiable [ʌndʒʌstəfáɪəbəl] ADJ injustificable

unkempt [ʌnkémpt] ADJ (uncombed) desgreñado, despeinado; (messy) desaliñado

unkind [ʌnkáɪnd] ADJ antipático, poco amable

unknown [ʌnnón] ADJ desconocido; **— quantity** incógnita *f*; **it is —** se ignora

unlawful [ʌnlɔ́fəl] ADJ ilegal

unleaded [ʌnlédɪd] ADJ sin plomo

unleash [ʌnlíʃ] VT desatar

unless [ənlés] CONJ a menos que, a no ser que

unlicensed [ʌnláɪsənst] ADJ (without permission) sin permiso, ilícito; (without credentials) no acreditado

unlike [ʌnláɪk] ADJ distinto, diferente; **he is — me** es diferente de mí; PREP a diferencia de; **how — you to forget!** ¡me extraña que te hayas olvidado!

unlikely [ʌnláɪkli] ADJ (improbable) improbable; (not realistic) inverosímil; (exotic) exótico; **I am — to come** es improbable que venga

unlimited [ʌnlímɪDɪd] ADJ ilimitado

unload [ʌnlód] VI/VT (take cargo from) descargar; VI (pour out one's feelings) desahogarse; (sell) liquidar

unlock [ʌnlák] VI/VT abrir con llave

unlucky [ʌnlʌ́ki] ADJ (unfortunate) desafortunado; (ominous) aciago, funesto; **an — number** un número de mala suerte

unmanageable [ʌnmǽnɪdʒəbəl] ADJ (crisis, situation) inmanejable; (person) rebelde
unmanned [ʌnmǽnd] ADJ (deprived of courage) achicado; (with no crew) no tripulado
unmarked [ʌnmárkt] ADJ sin marcar
unmarried [ʌnmǽrid] ADJ soltero
unmask [ʌnmǽsk] VI/VT desenmascarar[se]
unmistakable [ʌnmɪstékəbəl] ADJ inconfundible
unmitigated [ʌnmíɪgeɪd] ADJ absoluto
unmoved [ʌnmúvd] ADJ (unflinching) impasible; (indifferent) indiferente
unnatural [ʌnnǽtʃəɬ] ADJ (contrary to nature) no natural; (unloving) desnaturalizado; (monstrous) monstruoso; (affected) afectado
unnecessary [ʌnnésəsɛri] ADJ innecesario
unnoticed [ʌnnóʊɪst] ADJ inadvertido, desapercibido
unobserved [ʌnəbzɝ́vd] ADJ inadvertido
unobtrusive [ʌnəbtrúsɪv] ADJ discreto
unoccupied [ʌnákjəpaɪd] ADJ (house) desocupado; (territory) no ocupado
unofficial [ʌnəfíʃəl] ADJ extraoficial, no oficial
unoriginal [ʌnərídʒənəl] ADJ poco original
unorthodox [ʌnɔ́rθədaks] ADJ heterodoxo
unpack [ʌnpǽk] VT (a suitcase) deshacer, desempacar; (a carton) desembalar
unpaid [ʌnpéd] ADJ (debt) impagado, por pagar; (work) no remunerado
unplayable [ʌnpléəbəl] ADJ (golf) injugable
unpleasant [ʌnplézənt] ADJ desagradable
unpleasantness [ʌnplézəntnɪs] N (quality or state of being unpleasant) lo desagradable; (unpleasant episode) desavenencia f, disgusto m
unplug [ʌnplʌ́g] VI/VT desenchufar
unpopular [ʌnpápjələ-] ADJ (decision) impopular; she was — in school tenía pocos amigos en la escuela
unprecedented [ʌnprésɪdɛntɪd] ADJ sin precedente, inaudito
unpredictable [ʌnprɪdíktəbəl] ADJ impredecible, imprevisible
unpremeditated [ʌnpriméɪteɪd] ADJ impremeditado; (murder) sin premeditación
unprepared [ʌnprɪpérd] ADJ (surprised) desprevenido; (not ready) no preparado
unpretentious [ʌnprɪténʃəs] ADJ modesto, sin pretenciones
unprincipled [ʌnprínsəpəld] ADJ sin escrúpulos, falto de principios
unprintable [ʌnpríntəbəl] ADJ impublicable
unproductive [ʌnprədʌ́ktɪv] ADJ improductivo
unprofessional [ʌnprəféʃənəl] ADJ poco profesional
unprofitable [ʌnpráfɪɾəbəl] ADJ no rentable
unpublished [ʌnpʌ́blɪʃt] ADJ inédito, sin publicar
unpunished [ʌnpʌ́nɪʃt] ADJ impune

unqualified [ʌnkwáləfaɪd] ADJ (worker) Sp no cualificado; Am no calificado; (support) incondicional; (disaster) absoluto
unquestionable [ʌnkwéstʃənəbəl] ADJ incuestionable, indiscutible
unravel [ʌnrǽvəl] VI/VT (a rope) desenredar[se]; (a sweater) destejer[se]; (cloth) deshilachar[se]; (a plan) deshacer[se]; VT (a mystery) desentrañar
unreal [ʌnríəɬ] ADJ (not real) irreal; (unbelievable) increíble
unreasonable [ʌnrízənəbəl] ADJ (excessive) exagerado; (irrational) irracional, poco razonable
unrecognizable [ʌnrɛkəgnáɪzəbəl] ADJ irreconocible
unrefined [ʌnrɪfáɪnd] ADJ (oil, sugar) no refinado; (behavior) inculto, grosero
unrelated [ʌnriléɪd] ADJ no relacionado
unreliable [ʌnrɪláɪəbəl] ADJ (person) informal; (machine, information) Sp poco fiable; Am poco confiable
unreported [ʌnrɪpɔ́rɪd] ADJ sin declarar
unrest [ʌnrést] N malestar m, agitación f
unrestricted [ʌnrɪstríktɪd] ADJ no restringido
unroll [ʌnróɬ] VI/VT desenrollar[se]
unruly [ʌnrúli] ADJ (student) indisciplinado, revoltoso, díscolo; (country) ingobernable; (hair) rebelde
unsafe [ʌnséf] ADJ (risky) arriesgado; (dangerous) peligroso
unsanitary [ʌnsǽnɪteri] ADJ (behavior) antihigiénico, insalubre; (place, climate) insalubre
unsatisfactory [ʌnsæɪsfǽktəri] ADJ no satisfactorio, insatisfactorio
unscrew [ʌnskrú] VT desatornillar, destornillar
unscrupulous [ʌnskrúpjələs] ADJ sin escrúpulos
unseasonable [ʌnsízənəbəl] ADJ impropio de la estación
unseat [ʌnsít] VT derribar
unsecured [ʌnsɪkjúrd] ADJ sin garantía
unseen [ʌnsín] ADJ invisible, oculto
unselfish [ʌnsélfɪʃ] ADJ desinteresado
unselfishness [ʌnsélfɪʃnɪs] N desinterés m
unsettled [ʌnsédld] ADJ (situation) desordenado; (wilderness) sin colonizar; (case) pendiente; (weather) variable
unsightly [ʌnsáɪtli] ADJ feo, antiestético
unskilled [ʌnskíɬd] ADJ (not trained) inexperto; (not qualified) Sp no cualificado; Am no calificado
unsolicited [ʌnsəlísɪɪd] ADJ no solicitado
unsophisticated [ʌnsəfístɪkeɪd] ADJ sencillo, no sofisticado
unsound [ʌnsáʊnd] ADJ (argument) erróneo, falso; (body) enfermizo; (mind) demente; (foundation) poco sólido; (investment) poco

seguro

unspeakable [ʌnspíkəbəł] ADJ indecible

unspecified [ʌnspésɪfaɪd] ADJ no especificado

unsportsmanlike [ʌnspórtsmənlaɪk] ADJ antideportivo

unstable [ʌnstébəł] ADJ inestable

unsteady [ʌnstéɒi] ADJ (walk) inseguro, inestable; (flame) tembloroso; (pulse) irregular

unsuccessful [ʌnsəksésfəł] ADJ sin éxito, infructuoso

unsuitable [ʌnsúɒəbəł] ADJ (person) no apto; (place) inadecuado, inapropiado

unsuspected [ʌnsəspéktɪd] ADJ insospechado

untenable [ʌnténəbəł] ADJ insostenible

unthinkable [ʌnθíŋkəbəł] ADJ impensable

untidy [ʌntáɪɒi] ADJ (dress) desaliñado, desastrado; (room) desordenado

untie [ʌntáɪ] VI/VT desatar[se], destrabar[se]

until [əntíł] PREP hasta; CONJ hasta que

untimely [ʌntáɪmli] ADJ (ill-timed) inoportuno; (premature) prematuro

untiring [ʌntáɪrɪŋ] ADJ incansable, denodado

untold [ʌntółd] ADJ (riches) incalculable; (suffering) inaudito

untouched [ʌntʌ́tʃt] ADJ (not injured) ileso; (not affected) no afectado; **he left his dessert —** no tocó el postre

untrained [ʌntrénd] ADJ (worker) *Sp* no cualificado; *Am* no calificado; (animal) no amaestrado; (eye) inexperto

untried [ʌntráɪd] ADJ (untested) no probado, no ensayado; (not taken to trial) no juzgado

untrue [ʌntrú] ADJ (incorrect) falso; (unfaithful) infiel; (disloyal) desleal

untutored [ʌntúɒəd] ADJ (unschooled) sin instrucción; (unsophisticated) inculto

untwist [ʌntwíst] VT desenroscar

unused [ʌnjúzd] ADJ (no used) sin usar; (unaccustomed) no habituado

unusual [ʌnjúʒuəł] ADJ (infrequent) desacostumbrado, raro; (highly abnormal) inusitado, insólito

unvarnished [ʌnvárnɪʃt] ADJ (without varnish) sin barnizar; (straightforward) puro

unveil [ʌnvéł] VT (remove a veil) quitar el velo a; (reveal) descubrir

unwarranted [ʌnwɔ́rəntɪd] ADJ injustificado

unwelcome [ʌnwéłkəm] ADJ (untimely) inoportuno; (unpleasant) desagradable; (poorly received) mal recibido

unwholesome [ʌnhółsəm] ADJ malsano

unwieldy [ʌnwíłdi] ADJ poco manejable, difícil de manejar

unwilling [ʌnwílɪŋ] ADJ **to be — to** no estar dispuesto a

unwise [ʌnwáɪz] ADJ imprudente

unwonted [ʌnwɔ́ntɪd] ADJ inusitado, inacostumbrado

unworthy [ʌnwɨ́ði] ADJ indigno

unwrap [ʌnrǽp] VT desenvolver

unwritten [ʌnrítn̩] ADJ no escrito; (agreement) de palabra

unzip [ʌnzíp] VT abrir la cremallera

up [ʌp] ADV (position) arriba; (direction) hacia arriba; **—-front** (paid in advance) inicial; (frank) franco; **— and down** de arriba para abajo; **— against** enfrentado con; **he's — for reelection** se presenta para la reelección; **I'm feeling —** me siento optimista; **I'm — for golf** tengo ganas de jugar al golf; **prices are —** los precios han subido; **that is — to you** queda en tus manos, es cosa tuya; **the children are already —** ya se levantaron los niños; **the moon is —** salió la luna; **the wheat is —** germinó el trigo; **time is —** se terminó el tiempo; **to be — on the news** estar al corriente de las noticias; **to be — to one's old tricks** hacer de las suyas; **what's —?** ¿qué pasa? **he — and went** agarró y se fue; PREP **— the current** contra la corriente; **— the river** río arriba; **— the street** calle arriba; **— to now** hasta ahora; N **—s and downs** altibajos *m pl*; VI; ADJ (assembled) armado; (finished) terminado, concluido; **—-and-coming** prometedor; **—-to-date** actualizado

upbeat [ʌ́pbit] ADJ optimista

upbringing [ʌ́pbrɪŋɪŋ] N crianza *f*

update [ʌpdét] VT actualizar; N actualización *f*

upend [ʌpénd] VI/VT (stand on end) poner[se] de punta; (defeat) derrotar

upgrade [ʌ́pgred] VT (facilities) mejorar; (computer) actualizar; N (facilities) mejora *f*; (computer) actualización *f*

upheaval [ʌphívəł] N trastorno *m*

upheld [ʌphéłd] *see* uphold

uphill[1] [ʌ́phíł] ADV cuesta arriba

uphill[2] [ʌ́phɪ̀ł] ADJ penoso, arduo

uphold [ʌphółd] VT sostener, apoyar; (legal decision) refrendar

upholster [ʌphółstə] VT tapizar

upholstery [ʌphółstəri] N tapicería *f*

upkeep [ʌ́pkip] N mantenimiento *m*

uplift [ʌplíft] VT (physically) elevar; (spiritually) edificar

upload [ʌ́plod] VT cargar, subir; N carga *f*

upon [əpán] PREP sobre, encima de; **— arriving** al llegar; **once — a time** érase una vez

upper [ʌ́pə] ADJ (higher) superior; (high) alto; **to have the — hand** dominar, llevar la ventaja; N (of shoe) pala *f*; (of berth) litera superior *f*; **— class** clase alta *f*; **— crust** flor y nata *f*; **—case** mayúsculo; **—cut** (in boxing) gancho al mentón *m*; **—most** (highest) de más arriba; (most important) mayor; **— respiratory infection** infección respiratoria alta *f*; —**s** dentadura postiza superior *f*

uppity [ʌ́pɪɒi] ADJ presumido

upright [ʌ́praɪt] ADJ (posture) erecto, erguido; (position) vertical; (character) íntegro, recto, cabal; — **piano** piano vertical *m*; N (column) montante *m*; (piano) piano vertical *m*; (post) poste *m*

uprightness [ʌ́praɪtnɪs] N (physical) verticalidad *f*; (moral) rectitud *f*

uprising [ʌ́praɪzɪŋ] N alzamiento *m*, levantamiento *m*

uproar [ʌ́prɔr] N tumulto *m*, alboroto *m*, bulla *f*

uproarious [ʌprɔ́riəs] ADJ (tumultuous) tumultuoso; (funny) graciosísimo

uproot [ʌprút] VT arrancar de raíz, desarraigar

upscale [ʌ́pskeɫ] ADJ de lujo

upset[1] [ʌpsét] VI/VT (overturn) volcar[se], tumbar; (distress) trastornar[se], perturbar[se], alterar[se]; VT (in sports) derrotar al favorito; ADJ (overturned) volcado; (ill) indispuesto; (distressed) disgustado, enojado

upset[2] [ʌ́psɛt] N (overturning) vuelco *m*; (unexpected defeat) derrota inesperada *f*; (emotional state) trastorno *m*, disgusto *m*; (illness) malestar *m*

upshot [ʌ́pʃat] N consecuencia *f*

upside [ʌ́psaɪd] N (upper part) parte superior *f*; (positive prospect) lo bueno; ADJ & ADV — **down** al revés, patas arriba

upstage [ʌpstédʒ] VT eclipsar

upstairs[1] [ʌpstérz] ADV (location) arriba, en el piso de arriba; (movement) [para] arriba

upstairs[2] [ʌ́pstɛrz] ADJ de arriba; N piso de arriba *m*

upstart [ʌ́pstɑrt] N advenedizo -za *mf*

uptake [ʌ́ptek] N **quick on the** — listo; **slow on the** — duro de entendederas

uptight [ʌptáɪt] ADJ (nervous) nervioso; (conventional) estreñido

up-to-the-minute [ʌ́ptəðəmínɪt] ADJ actualizado

upturn [ʌ́ptɚn] N (prices) aumento *m*, subida *f*; (markets) tendencia alcista *f*

upward [ʌ́pwɚd] ADV (toward a higher place) hacia arriba; — **of** más de; ADJ ascendente; — **mobility** ascenso social *m*; — **trend** tendencia al alza *f*

uranium [jʊréniəm] N uranio *m*

urban [ɚ́bən] ADJ urbano; — **blight** tugurización *f*; — **legend** leyenda urbana *f*; — **renewal** renovación urbana *f*; — **sprawl** expansión urbana *f*

urbanism [ɚ́bənɪzəm] N urbanismo *m*

urchin [ɚ́tʃɪn] N pilluelo -la *mf*, guaje -ja *mf*

urethra [jʊríθrə] N uretra *f*

urge [ɚdʒ] VT (exhort) exhortar, urgir; (beg) rogar; (propose) propugnar; **to** — **on** animar;

N impulso *m*, gana *f*

urgency [ɚ́dʒənsi] N urgencia *f*

urgent [ɚ́dʒənt] ADJ urgente

urinal [jʊ́rənɫ] N urinario *m*, mingitorio *m*

urinalysis [jʊrənǽlɪsɪs] N análisis de orina *m*

urinary [jʊ́rəneri] ADJ urinario; — **tract** vías urinarias *f pl*

urinate [jʊ́rɪnet] VI/VT orinar

urine [jʊ́rɪn] N orina *f*

URL [**Uniform Resource Locator**] [jʊárél] N URL *m*

urn [ɚn] N urna *f*

urologist [jʊrálədʒɪst] N urólogo -ga *mf*

Uruguay [jʊ́rəgwaɪ] N Uruguay *m*

Uruguayan [jʊrəgwáɪən] ADJ & N uruguayo -ya *mf*

us [ʌs] PRON nos; **she saw** — nos vio; **he came with** — vino con nosotros; **he gave it to** — nos lo dio [a nosotros]

USA [**United States of America**] [júésé] N EEUU *m sg/pl*

usable [júzəbəɫ] ADJ utilizable, aprovechable

usage [júsɪdʒ] N uso *m*, costumbre *f*

USB [**Universal Serial Bus**] [júésbí] N USB *m*; — **port** puerto USB *m*

use[1] [juz] VT usar, utilizar (also exploit); (consume) gastar; (take advantage of) aprovecharse de; VI **to** — **up** gastar, agotar

use[2] [jus] N (application) uso *m*; (utilization) empleo *m*, utilización *f*, aprovechamiento *m*; (usefulness) utilidad *f*; **it is of no** — es inútil; **out of** — en desuso; **to have no** — **for** no soportar; **to make** — **of** usar, utilizar; **to put to** — utilizar; **what is the** — **of it?** ¿para qué sirve?

used[1] [juzd] ADJ usado

used[2] [just] VI **to be** — **to** estar acostumbrado a; **it** — **to be green** antes era verde

useful [júsfəɫ] ADJ útil

usefulness [júsfəɫnɪs] N utilidad *f*

useless [júslɪs] ADJ inútil, inservible

uselessness [júslɪsnɪs] N inutilidad *f*

user [júzɚ] N usuario -ria *mf*; —**friendly** fácil de utilizar; — **group** grupo de usuarios *m*; —**name** nombre del usuario *m*

usher [ʌ́ʃɚ] N acomodador -ora *mf*; VT conducir, acompañar; **to** — **in** (a person) acompañar; (an era) anunciar, marcar el comienzo de

usual [júʒuəɫ] ADJ (habitual) usual, habitual; (everyday) de todos los días; **as** — como siempre; **she wasn't her** — **self** no era la de siempre; **the** — **thing** lo normal; **more than** — más que de costumbre

usually [júʒuəli] ADV generalmente, normalmente; **he** — **doesn't mind** no suele importarle

usurp [jusɚ́p] VI/VT usurpar

usury [júʒəri] N usura *f*

utensil [juténsəɫ] N utensilio *m*, útil *m*

uterine [júɒə-ɪn] ADJ uterino
uterus [júɒə-əs] N útero *m*
UTI [urinary tract infection] [jútíáɪ] N infección del tracto urinario *f*
utilitarian [jutɪlɪtériən] ADJ utilitario
utility [jutflɪɒi] N (usefulness) utilidad *f*; (public service) empresa de servicio público *f*, empresa de agua o electricidad *f*; — **furniture** muebles prácticos *m pl*; — **program** programa utilitario *m*; — **room** lavadero *m*
utilization [judlɪzéʃən] N utilización *f*
utilize [júdlaɪz] VT utilizar
utmost [ʌtmost] ADJ (extreme) sumo, extremo; (farthest) más distante; N máximo *m*; **he did his** — hizo cuanto pudo; **to the** — al máximo
utopia [jutópiə] N utopía *f*
utter [ʌɒə-] VT (emit) dar, proferir; (say) decir, pronunciar; (make circulate) poner en circulación; ADJ absoluto, completo
utterance [ʌɒə-əns] N (of words) enunciado *m*; (of money) emisión *f*
uvula [júvjələ] N campanilla *f*, úvula *f*
Uzbek [úzbɛk] ADJ & N uzbeko -ka *mf*
Uzbekistan [uzbékɪstæn] N Uzbekistán *m*

Vv

vacancy [vékənsi] N (job) vacante *f*; (room in hotel) habitación libre *f*; **no** — completo
vacant [vékənt] ADJ (position) vacante; (expression) vacío; (seat, room) libre
vacate [véket] VI/VT (a room) desalojar, desocupar; (a contract) anular; (a position) dejar vacante
vacation [vekéʃən] N vacaciones *f pl*; **on** — de vacaciones
vaccinate [væksənet] VI/VT vacunar
vaccination [væksənéʃən] N vacunación *f*
vaccine [væksín] N vacuna *f*
vacillate [væsəlet] VI vacilar
vacuum [vækjum] N vacío *m*; — **cleaner** aspiradora *f*; — **tube** tubo de vacío *m*; ADJ —-**packed** envasado al vacío; VI/VT pasar la aspiradora
vagabond [vægəband] ADJ & N vagabundo -da *mf*
vagina [vədʒáɪnə] N vagina *f*
vaginal [vædʒənl] ADJ vaginal; — **bleeding** hemorragia vaginal *f*; — **discharge** flujo vaginal *m*; — **itching** escozor vaginal *m*
vaginitis [vædʒɪnáɪdɪs] N vaginitis *f*
vagrancy [végrənsi] N vagancia *f*
vagrant [végrənt] ADJ & N vagabundo -da *mf*
vague [veg] ADJ vago, indistinto

vain [ven] ADJ (futile) vano, hueco; (proud of appearance) vanidoso; **in** — en vano
Valencian [vəlénsiən] ADJ & N valenciano -na
valentine [væləntaɪn] N (card) tarjeta del día de San Valentín *f*; (person) querido -da *mf*; —'**s Day** día de San Valentín *m*, día de los enamorados *m*
valet [vælé] N (manservant) criado *m*; (in a hotel) mozo de habitación *m*; (car parker) aparcacoches *m sg*
valiant [væljənt] ADJ valiente
valid [vælɪd] ADJ válido, valedero; **to be/ become** — tener efectividad
validity [vəlídɪti] N validez *f*
valise [vəlíz] N maleta *f*, valija *f*
valley [væli] N valle *m*
valor [vælə-] N valor *m*, valentía *f*
valorize [væləraɪz] VT valorar
valorous [vælə-əs] ADJ valeroso, valiente
valuable [væljəbəl] ADJ valioso, preciado; N —**s** objetos de valor *m pl*
valuation [væljuéʃən] N (value) valoración *f*; (appraisal) tasación *f*, valuación *f*
value [vælju] N valor *m*; VT valorar
valve [vælv] N válvula *f*; (on mollusks) valva *f*
vamp [væmp] N vampiresa *f*; VT seducir
vampire [væmpaɪr] N vampiro *m*
van [væn] N camioneta *f*
vandal [vændl] N vándalo *m*
vane [ven] N (for weather) veleta *f*; (of a fan, windmill) aspa *f*; (of propeller) paleta *f*
vanilla [vənílə] N vainilla *f*
vanish [vænɪʃ] VI desaparecer, esfumarse
vanity [vænɪɒi] N vanidad *f*; — **table** tocador *m*
vanquish [væŋkwɪʃ] VT vencer
vantage point [væntɪdʒpɔɪnt] N mirador *m*
Vanuatu [vɑnuátu] N Vanuatu *m*
Vanuatuan [vɑnuátuən] ADJ & N vanuatuense *mf*
vapor [vépə-] N vapor *m*, humo *m*
vaporize [vépə-aɪz] VI/VT vaporizar[se]
variable [vériəbəl] ADJ & N variable *f*; — **annuity** anualidad variable *f*
variance [vériəns] N discrepancia *f*, desacuerdo *m*; **to be at** — no concordar
variant [vériənt] N variante *f*, modalidad *f*
variation [veriéʃən] N variación *f*
varicose [vérɪkos] ADJ varicoso; — **veins** *Sp* varices *f pl*; *Am* várices *f pl*
varied [vérid] ADJ variado, vario
variegated [vériɪgeDɪd] ADJ variopinto
variety [vəráɪɒi] N variedad *f*
various [vériəs] ADJ vario
varnish [várnɪʃ] N barniz *m*, charol *m*; VT barnizar, charolar
varsity [vársɪɒi] N equipo universitario *m*
vary [véri] VI/VT variar
vascular [væskjələ-] ADJ vascular
vase [ves] N jarrón *m*; (for flowers) florero *m*
vasectomy [vəséktəmi] N vasectomía *f*

Vaseline™ [vǽsəlín] N vaselina f
vast [væst] ADJ vasto, inmenso
vastly [vǽstli] ADV enormemente
vastness [vǽstnɪs] N inmensidad f
vat [væt] N tina f, barrica f
VAT [value-added tax] [viétí] N IVA m
Vatican City [vǽDɪkənsíDi] N Ciudad del
    Vaticano f
vaudeville [vɔ́dvɪł] N vodevil m
vault [vɔłt] N (arched structure) bóveda f; (burial
    chamber) panteón m; (place for valuables)
    cámara acorazada f; (jump) salto m; VT (cover
    with a vault) abovedar; VI/VT (jump) saltar
VCR [videocassette recorder] [vísíár] N Am
    video m; Sp vídeo m
VD [venereal disease] [vídí] N [enfermedad]
    venérea f
veal [vił] N ternera f; — **cutlet** chuleta de
    ternera f
vector [vɛktə-] N vector m
veer [vir] VI/VT virar; N virada f
vegan [vígən] ADJ & N vegan mf
vegetable [véʤtəbəł] N (food) verdura f,
    hortaliza f; (plant, comatose person) vegetal
    m; — **garden** huerto m; (large) huerta f; —
    kingdom reino vegetal m; — **oil** aceite
    vegetal m
vegetarian [veʤɪtériən] ADJ & N vegetariano -na
    mf
vegetate [véʤɪtet] VI vegetar
vegetation [veʤɪtéʃən] N vegetación f
vegetative [véʤɪteDɪv] ADJ vegetativo
vehemence [víəməns] N vehemencia f
vehement [víəmənt] ADJ vehemente
vehicle [víɪkəł] N vehículo m
veil [veł] N velo m; VT velar
vein [ven] N (blood vessel, style) vena f; (small
    deposit of ore) veta f; (large deposit of ore)
    filón m
veined [vend] ADJ (marble) veteado; (leaf)
    nervado
velocity [vəlásɪDi] N velocidad f
velvet [vélvɪt] N terciopelo m; ADJ (of velvet) de
    terciopelo; (like velvet) aterciopelado
velvety [vélvɪDi] ADJ aterciopelado
vendetta [vɛndéDə] N vendetta f
vending machine [véndɪŋməʃin] N expendedor
    automático m, máquina expendedora f
vendor [véndə-] N vendedor -ora mf, proveedor
    -ora mf; (in a stall) puestero -ra mf
veneer [vənír] N (layer of wood) chapa f;
    (outward appearance) barniz m; VT chapar,
    enchapar
venerable [vénə-əbəł] ADJ venerable
venerate [vénəret] VT venerar
veneration [venəréʃən] N veneración f
venereal [vəníriəł] ADJ venéreo; — **disease**
    enfermedad venérea f
venetian blind [vəníʃənbláɪnd] N veneciana f

Venezuela [vɛnɪzwélə] N Venezuela f
Venezuelan [vɛnɪzwélən] ADJ & N venezolano
    -na mf
vengeance [vénʤəns] N venganza f; **with a** —
    (violently) con furia; (energetically) con
    ganas
vengeful [vénʤfəł] ADJ vengativo
venison [vénəsən] N carne de venado f
venom [vénəm] N veneno m
venomous [vénəməs] ADJ venenoso
vent [vɛnt] N (outlet for air) ventilación f;
    (opening of a volcano) chimenea f; **to give** —
    to anger desahogar la ira; VI/VT
    desahogar[se], descargar[se]
ventilate [véntłet] VI/VT ventilar[se]
ventilation [ventłéʃən] N ventilación f
ventilator [véntłeDə-] N ventilador m
ventricle [véntrɪkəł] N ventrículo m
venture [véntʃə-] N (adventure) aventura f;
    (business enterprise) empresa f; — **capital**
    capital de riesgo m; VI/VT aventurar[se],
    arriesgar[se]
venue [vénju] N lugar m
veranda [vərǽndə] N porche m, terraza f
verb [vɝb] N verbo m
verbal [vɝ́bəł] ADJ (linguistic, related to verbs)
    verbal; (not written) oral
verbatim [və-bédəm] ADJ textual; ADV
    textualmente
verbiage [vɝ́biɪʤ] N palabrerío m
verbose [və-bós] ADJ verboso
verdict [vɝ́dɪkt] N veredicto m
verdure [vɝ́ʤə-] N lit verdura f
verge [vɝʤ] ADV LOC **on the** — **of** al borde de, a
    punto de; VI **to** — **on** rayar en, lindar con
verification [vɛrɪfɪkéʃən] N verificación f,
    comprobación f
verify [vérɪfaɪ] VT verificar, constatar,
    comprobar
veritable [vérɪDəbəł] ADJ verdadero
vermillion [və-míljən] ADJ & N bermellón m
vermin [vɝ́mɪn] N bichos m pl
vermouth [və-múθ] N vermú m
vernacular [və-nǽkjələ-] ADJ vernáculo; N (plain
    language) lengua vernácula f
versatile [vɝ́səDł] ADJ versátil
verse [vɝs] N verso m; (stanza) estrofa f; (line of
    poem) verso m; (in Bible) versículo m
versed [vɝst] ADJ versado
version [vɝ́ʒən] N versión f
versus [vɝ́səs] PREP contra; (in sports) versus
vertebra [vɝ́Dəbrə] N vértebra f
vertebrate [vɝ́Dəbrɪt] ADJ vertebrado
vertical [vɝ́Dɪkəł] ADJ vertical
vertigo [vɝ́DɪgO] N vértigo m
very [véri] ADV muy; — **many** muchísimos; —
    much muchísimo; **it is** — **cold today** hace
    mucho frío hoy; ADJ (same) mismo; (mere)
    mero

vessel [vésəł] N (container) vasija f; (duct) vaso m; (ship) nave f

vest [vɛst] N chaleco m; VT conferir; **—ed interests** intereses creados m pl

vestibule [véstɪbjuł] N vestíbulo m, zaguán m

vestige [véstɪʤ] N vestigio m

vet [vɛt] N (veterinarian) veterinario -ria mf; (veteran) veterano -na militar mf; VT evaluar

veteran [védə⋅ən] ADJ & N veterano -na mf

veterinarian [vɛdə⋅ənériən] N veterinario -ria mf

veterinary [védə⋅ənɛri] ADJ veterinario; **— medicine** veterinaria f

veto [víto] N veto m; VT vetar

vex [vɛks] VT molestar, irritar

via [váɪə, víə] PREP (by way of) vía; (by means of) por

viability [vaɪəbílɪDi] N viabilidad f

viable [váɪəbəł] ADJ viable

vial [váɪəł] N ampolla f, frasco m

vibrate [váɪbret] VI/VT vibrar

vibration [vaɪbréʃən] N vibración f

vibrator [váɪbreDə⋅] N vibrador m

vicarious [vaɪkériəs] ADJ indirecto

vice [vaɪs] N vicio m

vice president [váɪspréz̗ɪDənt] N vicepresidente -ta mf

viceroy [váɪsrɔɪ] N virrey m

viceroyalty [vaɪsróɪəłti] ADJ virreinato

vice versa [váɪsəvə́sə] ADV viceversa

vicinity [vɪsínɪDi] N vecindad f, cercanías f pl, alcdaños m pl

vicious [víʃəs] ADJ (violent) violento, sanguinario; (evil) maligno, perverso; (malicious) malicioso; **— circle** círculo vicioso m; **— dog** perro fiero m, perro bravo m

vicissitude [vɪsísɪtud] N vicisitud f, peripecia f

victim [víktɪm] N víctima f

victimize [víktəmaɪz] VT (make victim) victimizar; (dupe) estafar

victor [víktə⋅] N vencedor -ora mf

victorious [vɪktóriəs] ADJ victorioso

victory [víktəri] N victoria f

video [vídio] N Am video m; Sp vídeo m; **—cassette** Am video m; Sp vídeo m; **—cassette recorder** videocasete m; **—conference** videoconferencia f; **— console** videoconsola f; **— game** videojuego m; **— portal** Am portal de videos m; Sp portal de vídeos m; **—tape** Am cinta de video f; Sp cinta de vídeo f; **— clip** videoclip m

vie [vaɪ] VI competir; **to — for power** disputarse el poder

Vietnam [vietnám] N Vietnam m

Vietnamese [viitnəmíz] ADJ & N vietnamita mf

view [vju] N (field of vision) vista f; (opinion) opinión f; (panorama) visión panorámica f; **—point** punto de vista m; **in — of** en vista de; **to be within —** estar a la vista; **with a — to** con el propósito de; VT (see) ver; (consider) enfocar

viewer [vjúə⋅] N telespectador -ora mf, televidente mf

vigil [víʤəł] N vigilia f, vela f; **to keep —** velar

vigilance [víʤələns] N vigilancia f

vigilant [víʤələnt] ADJ vigilante

vigor [vígə⋅] N vigor m, pujanza f, dinamismo m

vigorous [vígə⋅əs] ADJ vigoroso

vile [vaɪł] ADJ (evil) vil, ruin; (foul, bad) pésimo

villa [víłə] N quinta f, casa de campo f

village [vílɪʤ] N aldea f, villa f

villager [vílɪʤə⋅] N aldeano -na mf

villain [vílən] N villano -na mf

villainous [vílənəs] ADJ vil, villano

villainy [víləni] N villanía f, vileza f

vindicate [víndɪket] VT reivindicar, vindicar

vindication [vɪndɪkéʃən] N reivindicación f, vindicación f

vindictive [vɪndíktɪv] ADJ vengativo

vine [vaɪn] N (grapevine) vid f; (decorative) parra f; (stem) sarmiento m; (climbing plant) enredadera f

vinegar [vínɪgə⋅] N vinagre m

vineyard [vínjə⋅d] N viña f, viñedo m

vintage [víntɪʤ] N (act or season of gathering grapes) vendimia f; (harvest of grapes) cosecha f; (year) año m; ADJ (wine) añejo; (classic) excelente; (old) antiguo, de colección; (typical) típico

vinyl [váɪnl] N vinilo m

viola [viółə] N viola f

violate [váɪəlet] VT violar; (a law) violar, quebrantar

violation [vaɪəléʃən] N violación f; (traffic) infracción f

violence [váɪələns] N violencia f

violent [váɪələnt] ADJ violento

violet [váɪəlɪt] N (flower) violeta f; (color) violeta m; ADJ violeta

violin [vaɪəlín] N violín m

violinist [vaɪəlínɪst] N violinista mf

VIP [**very important person**] [víáɪpí] N & ADJ VIP m

viper [váɪpə⋅] N víbora f

viral [váɪrəł] ADJ viral

virgin [və́ʤɪn] ADJ & N virgen f; (uninitiated) no iniciado -da mf; **— Islands** Islas Vírgenes f pl

virginal [və́ʤənl] ADJ virginal

virile [vírəł] ADJ viril

virility [vərílɪDi] N virilidad f

virology [vaɪráləʤi] N virología f

virtual [və́tʃuəł] ADJ virtual; **— community** comunidad virtual f; **— reality** realidad virtual f; **— stores** tiendas virtuales f pl

virtually [və́tʃuəli] ADV (remotely) virtualmente; (almost) prácticamente

virtue [və́tʃu] N virtud f

virtuosity [vɜtʃuásɪDi] N virtuosismo *m*
virtuoso [vɜtʃuóso] ADJ & N virtuoso -sa *mf*
virtuous [vɜtʃuəs] ADJ virtuoso
virulent [vírələnt] ADJ virulento
virus [váɪrəs] N virus *m*; —-**free** libre de virus; — **protection software** programas de protección contra virus *m pl*
visa [vízə] N *Am* visa *f*; *Sp* visado *m*
vis-à-vis [vízəví] PREP con respecto a
visceral [vísɚəł] ADJ visceral
viscous [vískəs] ADJ viscoso
vise [vaɪs] N tornillo de banco *m*
visibility [vɪzɪbílɪDi] N visibilidad *f*
visible [vízəbəł] ADJ visible
Visigoth [vízɪgɔθ] N visigodo -da *mf*
vision [víʒən] N (sense, apparition) visión *f*; (eyesight) vista *f*
visionary [víʒənɛri] ADJ & N visionario -ria *mf*
visit [vízɪt] VT visitar; (afflict) infligir; VI estar de visita; **to** — **with** charlar con; N (stay) visita *f*; (chat) charla *f*
visitation [vɪzɪtéʃən] N (apparition) visitación *f*; (punishment) castigo *m*; (parental right) régimen de visita *m*
visiting [vízɪDɪŋ] ADJ (team) visitante
visitor [vízɪDɚ] N visita *f*, visitante *mf*
visor [váɪzɚ] N visera *f*
vista [vístə] N (visual) vista *f*; (mental) perspectiva *f*
visual [víʒuəł] ADJ visual; — **recognition** reconocimiento visual *m*
visualize [víʒuəlaɪz] VT visualizar, imaginar
vital [váɪdł] ADJ vital; — **signs** signos vitales *m pl*
vitality [vaɪtǽlɪDi] N vitalidad *f*
vitamin [váɪDəmɪn] N vitamina *f*
vituperation [vaɪtupəréʃən] N vituperación *f*, vituperio *m*
vivacious [vaɪvéʃəs] ADJ vivaz, vivaracho
vivacity [vaɪvǽsɪDi] N vivacidad *f*
vivid [vívɪd] ADJ vívido, vivo
vivisection [vívɪsɛkʃən] N vivisección *f*
vocabulary [vokǽbjəlɛri] N vocabulario *m*
vocal [vókəł] ADJ (musical) vocal; (outspoken) vociferante; — **cords** cuerdas vocales *f pl*
vocalic [vokǽlɪk] ADJ vocálico
vocation [vokéʃən] N vocación *f*
vociferous [vosífɚəs] ADJ vociferante
vodka [vádkə] N vodka *m*
vogue [vog] N boga *f*, moda *f*; **in** — en boga, de moda
voice [vɔɪs] N voz *f*; —**mail** correo de voz *m*, contestador automático *m*; — **recognition** reconocimiento de voz *m*; — **synthesis** síntesis de voz *f*; VT expresar
voicing [vóɪsɪŋ] N sonoridad *f*
void [vɔɪd] ADJ (devoid, empty) vacío; (not binding) nulo, inválido; — **of** desprovisto de; N vacío *m*; VT (bowels) evacuar; (a check) anular; —**ed check** cheque anulado *m*

volatile [váləd] ADJ (liquid) volátil; (political situation) explosivo, conflictivo; (stock market) voluble; (temperament) cambiante
volcanic [valkǽnɪk] ADJ volcánico
volcano [vałkéno] N volcán *m*
volition [vəlíʃən] N volición *f*; **of one's own** — por su propia voluntad
volley [váli] N (of firearms) descarga *f*; (of protests, arrows, stones) lluvia *f*; (of a tennis ball) volea *f*; —**ball** voleibol *m*, balonvolea *m*; VI/VT (shoot bullets) descargar; (hit tennis balls) volear
volt [vołt] N voltio *m*
voltage [vółtɪdʒ] N voltaje *m*
volume [váljəm] N volumen *m*, tomo *m*
voluminous [vəlúmɪnəs] ADJ voluminoso
voluntary [váləntɛri] ADJ voluntario
volunteer [valəntír] ADJ & N voluntario -ria *mf*; VI/VT (offer) ofrecer[se], brindar[se]; *RP* comedir[se]; VI (do volunteer work) trabajar de voluntario -ria
voluptuous [vəláptʃuəs] ADJ voluptuoso
vomit [vámɪt] N vómito *m*; VI/VT vomitar
voodoo [vúDu] N vudú *m*
voracious [vɔréʃəs] ADJ voraz
vortex [vórtɛks] N vórtice *m*
vote [vot] N (right, ballot) voto *m*; (act of voting) votación *f*; VI votar; VT (a bill) aprobar; (a political party) votar a/por; **to** — **against** votar en contra; **to** — **in favor** votar a favor; **to** — **to do something** votar por hacer algo
voter [vóDɚ] N votante *mf*
voting [vóDɪŋ] N votación *f*
vouch [vautʃ] VI **to** — **for** dar fe de, salir de fiador a, fiar a; VT **to** — **that** dar fe de que
voucher [váutʃɚ] N (receipt) comprobante *m*; (coupon) vale *m*; (person) fiador -ora *mf*, garante *mf*
vow [vau] N voto *m*; **to take a** — prometer; VT jurar
vowel [váuəł] N vocal *f*
voyage [vɔɪɪdʒ] N (long trip) viaje *m*; (trip by sea) travesía *f*; VI viajar
voyeur [vɔɪɚ] N mirón -ona *mf*
VP [**vice president**] [vípí] N vice presidente -ta *mf*
vulgar [válgɚ] ADJ (rude) ordinario, grosero, soez; (popular, vernacular) vulgar
vulgarity [vałgǽrɪDi] N ordinariez *f*, vulgaridad *f*
vulnerable [válnɚəbəł] ADJ vulnerable
vulture [váłtʃɚ] N buitre *m*
vulva [váłvə] N vulva *f*

Ww

wacky [wǽkl] ADJ (person) chiflado; (idea) descabellado

wad [wɑd] N (for artillery, for filling) taco m; (ball) pelota f, pelotón m; (of money) rollo m, fajo m; (of cotton) bola f; VI/VT (a firearm) atacar; (a piece of paper) hacer una pelota [con]

waddle [wádl] VT anadear, andar como un pato; N anadeo m

wade [wed] VI andar por el agua; **to — through a book** leer con dificultad un libro

wafer [wéfɚ] N (cookie) oblea f; (in Catholic ritual) hostia f; (computer) lámina/oblea de silicio f

waffle [wáfəl] ADJ Sp gofre m; Am wafle m; **— iron** Sp plancha para hacer gofres f; Am waflera f

waft [wæft] VI flotar; VT llevar por el aire; N (of air) ráfaga f; (of odor) ola f

wag [wæg] VI/VT menear[se], mover[se]; **to — the tail** colear; N (movement) meneo m, movimiento m; (joker) bromista mf

wage [wedʒ] N salario m; **— earner** asalariado -da mf; (paid daily) jornalero -ra mf; **—s** salario m; (daily) jornal m; **— scale** escala salarial f; VT (war) hacer; (battle) librar

wager [wédʒɚ] N apuesta f; VI/VT apostar

wagon [wǽgən] N (horsedrawn) carro m; (covered) carreta f; (toy) carrito m; **to fix someone's —** vengarse de alguien; **to be on the —** abstenerse de bebidas alcohólicas

wail [weł] VI lamentar; N lamento m

waist [west] N cintura f; (of garment) talle m; **—band** pretina f; **—coat** chaleco m; **—line** talle m, cintura f

wait [wet] VI/VT esperar; **to — for** esperar; **to — on** servir; **to — tables** trabajar de camarero -ra; N espera f; **to lie in — for** estar en/al acecho de

waiter [wédɚ] N camarero m, mozo m, mesero m

waiting [wéDɪŋ] N espera f; **— list** lista de espera f; **— room** sala de espera f

waitress [wétrɪs] N camarera f, moza f, mesera f

waive [wev] VT (rights) renunciar a; (a rule) hacer una excepción

waiver [wévɚ] N (of rights) renuncia f; (of rules) excepción f

wake [wek] VI/VT despertar[se]; **to — up** despertar[se]; N (at death) velatorio m; (of a ship) estela f, surco m; **—-up call** (in a hotel) llamada del servicio despertador f; (to action) llamada de atención f; **in the — of** después de, detrás de

wakeful [wékfəl] ADJ (awake) despierto; (insomniac) insomne

waken [wékən] VI/VT despertar[se]

Wales [wełz] N Gales m sg

walk [wɔk] VI andar, caminar; (to a place) ir a pie; (go away) marcharse; (in baseball) sacar una base por bolas f; **to — back** volver a pie; **to — down** bajar a pie; **to — in** entrar caminando;

to — out (to go out) salir caminando; (to abandon) dejar; (to strike) declararse en huelga; **to — up** subir a pie; VT (to cause to walk) hacer caminar; (to trace on foot) recorrer; **to — the streets** callejear; **to — someone** (baseball) darle una base por bolas; N (period of walking) paseo m, caminata f; (pace) paso m; (gait) andar m; **— of life** condición f; **—out** huelga f; **to take a —** pasear, dar un paseo

walker [wɔkɚ] N (device to aid walking) andador m; (one who walks) caminante mf; (in sports) marchista mf

walking [wɔkɪŋ] ADJ andante; **— papers** despido m; **— stick** bastón m

wall [wɔl] N (interior) pared f; (garden) muro m, tapia f; (fort) muralla f; (of silence) barrera f; **—paper** papel de empapelar m; **—flower** alhelí m; **—-to-—** de pared a pared; **to have one's back to the —** estar entre la espada y la pared; **to drive someone up the —** sacar a alguien de quicio; **I was climbing the —s** me moría de aburrimiento; **she was a —flower** no la sacaban a bailar; VT **to —paper** empapelar

wallet [wálɪt] N cartera f, billetera f

wallow [wálo] VI (roll) revolcarse; (indulge oneself) regodearse

walnut [wɔłnʌt] N nuez f; **— tree** nogal m

walrus [wɔłrəs] N morsa f

waltz [wɔłts] N vals m; VI valsar

wand [wɑnd] N (rod) vara f; (magic) varita f

wander [wándɚ] VI/VT vagar [por], errar [por]; **to — away** perderse; **my mind —s easily** me distraigo fácilmente

wanderer [wándərɚ] N vagabundo -da mf

wane [wen] VI menguar, flaquear; N **to be on the —** ir menguando

wannabe [wánəbi] N aspirante mf

want [wɑnt] VI/VT (desire) querer; **he —s judgment** le falta juicio; **he's —ed in Texas** se lo busca en Texas; N (desire) deseo m; (lack) falta f; (scarcity) escasez f; **to be in —** estar necesitado; **— ad** [anuncio] clasificado m

wanting [wántɪŋ] ADJ (lacking) falto; (deficient) deficiente

wanton [wántən] ADJ (immoderate) desenfrenado; (immoral) lascivo; (senseless, unprovoked) gratuito

war [wɔr] N guerra f; **— crime** crimen de guerra m; **—fare** guerra f; **— games** juegos de guerra m pl, simulacro de batalla m; **—head** ojiva f; **—ship** acorazado m; VI guerrear, hacer la guerra; **—like** bélico f

warble [wɔrbəl] VI gorjear; N gorjeo m

warbler [wɔrblɚ] N (European) curruca f; (American) arañero m

ward [wɔrd] N (district) distrito m; (of a hospital)

pabellón *m*; (of a tutor) pupilo -la *mf*; VI **to —
off** resguardarse de, conjurar
warden [wɔ́rdn̩] N (of prison) alcaide *m*
wardrobe [wɔ́rdrob] N (room) guardarropa *m*;
(furniture) armario *m*, ropero *m*; (garments)
vestuario *m*, guardarropa *m*
warehouse [wérhaʊs] N almacén *m*, depósito *m*
wares [wɛrz] N mercancías *f pl*
warm [wɔrm] ADJ (bath) caliente; (clothes)
abrigado; (weather) caluroso; (colors,
reception) cálido; —-**blooded** de sangre
caliente; —**hearted** de buen corazón; **it is —
today** hace calor hoy; N —**up**
precalentamiento *m*; VI/VT calentar[se]; **to —
over** recalentar; **to — up** calentar[se],
templar[se]; **it —s my heart** me alegra el
corazón; **she —ed to the idea** se entusiasmó
con la idea
warmth [wɔrmθ] N calor *m*, tibieza *f*
warn [wɔrn] VI/VT (advise of danger) advertir;
(urge to behave) amonestar
warning [wɔ́rnɪŋ] N (of danger) advertencia *f*;
(of punishment) amonestación *f*
warp [wɔrp] N (yarn) urdimbre *f*; (curve) comba
f, alabeo *m*; VI/VT (wood) combar[se],
alabear[se]; (character) deformar[se]; **he has
a —ed personality** tiene una personalidad
retorcida
warrant [wɔ́rənt] N orden *f*; **a — for his arrest**
una orden de arresto contra él; VT garantizar
warranty [wɔ́rənti] N garantía *f*; VT garantizar
warrior [wɔ́riɚ] N guerrero -ra *mf*
wart [wɔrt] N verruga *f*
wary [wéri] ADJ cauteloso, cauto; **to be — of**
desconfiar de
was [waz] *see* be
wash [waʃ] VI/VT lavar[se]; **to — out** (a bottle)
lavar; (a substance) quitar lavando; (a
creekbed) erosionar; **to — up** lavarse; **the
bottle was —ed up on the shore** la botella
fue traída por el mar; **he was —ed away by
the waves** fue arrastrado por las olas; **his
excuse won't —** su excusa no va a colar; N
(act of washing) lavado *m*; (clothes to be
washed) ropa para lavar *f*; (washed clothes)
ropa lavada *f*; —**cloth** toallita para lavarse *f*;
—**out** (erosion) derrubio *m*; (failure) fracaso
m; —**room** lavabo *m*, lavatorio *m*; ADJ —-
and-wear de lava y pon, de no planchar;
—**ed-up** fracasado; —**ed-out** desteñido
washable [wáʃəbəl] ADJ lavable
washer [wáʃɚ] N (washing machine) lavadora *f*,
máquina de lavar *f*; (metal ring) arandela *f*;
—**woman** lavandera *f*
washing [wáʃɪŋ] N lavado *m*; — **machine**
lavadora *f*, máquina de lavar *f*
wasp [wasp] N avispa *f*
WASP [**White Anglo-Saxon Protestant**]
[wasp] N persona blanca, anglosajona y

protestante *f*
waste [west] VI/VT (squander resources)
malgastar, desperdiciar; **to — away**
consumirse; VT (squander time) perder;
(murder) liquidar; N (of resources)
desperdicio *m*, malgasto *m*, derroche *m*; (of
time) pérdida *f*; (refuse) desperdicios *m pl*,
desechos *m pl*; (liquid refuse) vertido *m*;
—**land** tierra yerma *f*, páramo *m*; — **of time**
pérdida de tiempo *f*; —**paper basket**
papelera *f*; — **products** productos de
desecho *m pl*; — **treatment** tratamiento de
residuos *m*; **to go to —** desperdiciarse; **to lay
— to** asolar
wasted [wéstɪd] ADJ (squandered) desperdiciado;
(debilitated) consumido; (drunk) borracho
wasteful [wéstfəl] ADJ (person) despilfarrador,
gastador; (method) antieconómico
watch [watʃ] VI (look) mirar; (be careful)
cuidarse; (be vigilant) vigilar; VT (view)
mirar, ver; (observe) observar; (tend) cuidar;
— **out for the cars!** ¡cuidado con los coches!
to — for estar a la espera de; **to — over**
proteger; N (timepiece) reloj *m*; (period of
wakefulness) vela *f*, vigilia *f*; (vigilant guard)
guardia *mf*; (duty shift) guardia *f*; (lookout)
centinela *m*; —**band** pulsera *f*; —**dog** (type of
dog) perro guardián *m*; (organization)
organismo de control *m*; —**maker** relojero
-ra *mf*; —**making** relojería *f*; —**man**
vigilante *m*, sereno *m*; —**tower** atalaya *f*,
torre de vigilancia *f*; —**word** (password)
contraseña *f*; (motto) consigna *f*, lema *m*; **to
be on the —** estar alerta; **to keep — on/
over** vigilar a
watchful [wátʃfəl] ADJ alerta, atento
water [wɔ́Dɚ] N agua *f*; —**bed** cama de agua *f*;
—**bird** ave acuática *f*; — **buffalo** búfalo de
agua *m*; —**color** acuarela *f*; —**cress** berro *m*;
—**fall** (small) cascada *f*; (large) catarata *f*;
—**front** muelles *m pl*; —**fountain** fuente *f*,
Mex, RP bebedero *m*; —**heater** calentador de
agua *m*; —**lily** nenúfar *m*; —**melon** sandía *f*;
— **pistol** pistola de agua *f*; — **power** energía
hidráulica *f*; —**shed** vertiente *f*; — **ski** esquí
acuático *m*; — **softener** ablandador de agua
m; — **sports** deportes acuáticos *m pl*;
—**spout** (pipe) tubo de desagüe *m*; (tornado)
tromba *f*; — **supply** abastecimiento de agua
m; — **table** capa freática *f*; — **vapor** vapor de
agua *m*; —**way** vía navegable *f*; **my — broke**
se me rompieron las aguas, se me rompió la
fuente; ADJ —**logged** empapado; —**proof**
(fabric) impermeable; (watch) sumergible;
—**tight** hermético; VT (irrigate) regar;
(dilute) aguar; VI/VT (animals) abrevar;
—**ed-down** (with water) aguado; (simplified)
simplificado; (softened) suavizado; **to
—proof** impermeabilizar; **to —-ski** hacer

esquí acuático; **my eyes are —ing** me lloran los ojos; **it makes my mouth** — se me hace agua la boca

watery [wɔ́Dəᵻ] ADJ (watered-down) aguado; (like water) acuoso; (boggy) húmedo

watt [wɑt] N vatio *m*

wattage [wɑ́DIʤ] N vataje *m*

wave [wev] N (radio) onda *f*; (water, heat, fashion) ola *f*; (of disgust, of people) oleada *f*; (with the hand) saludo *m*; **—length** longitud de onda *f*; **on the same —length** en la misma onda, en sintonía; VI (flag) ondear; (hair) ondular[se]; VI (greet) saludar con la mano; **to — good-bye** decir adiós con la mano

waver [wévəᵻ] VI (hesitate) vacilar, titubear; (falter) flaquear

wavy [wévi] ADJ ondeado, ondulado

wax [wæks] N cera *f*; (for seals) lacre *m*; **— paper** papel encerado *m*; VT (cover with wax) encerar; (defeat) derrotar; VI (moon) crecer; **to — poetic** ponerse poético

way [we] N (road) camino *m*; (manner) modo *m*, manera *f*; **—farer** caminante *mf*; **— in** entrada *f*; **— out** salida *f*; **—s** costumbres *f pl*; **—side** borde del camino *m*; **— through** paso *m*, pasaje *m*; **a long — off** muy lejos; **by — of London** por Londres; **by — of comparison** a modo de comparación; **by the —** a propósito; **in no —** de ningún modo; **on the — to** rumbo a; **to get out of the —** apartarse; **to go out of one's — to** desvivirse por; **to look the other —** hacer la vista gorda; **to lead the —** ir a la cabeza; **to be in a bad —** hallarse mal de salud; **to give —** (yield) ceder; (break) quebrarse; **to get one's —** salirse con la suya; **to make — for** abrir paso para; ADJ **—-out** estrafalario; VT **to —lay** (wait in ambush) estar al acecho de; (attack) asaltar; (stop) detener

wayward [wéwəᵻd] ADJ (disobedient) desobediente; (willful) porfiado

we [wi] PRON nosotros -as *mf*

weak [wik] ADJ débil; (deficient) flojo; **— force** fuerza débil *f*; **—-kneed** achicado; **— sister** (coward) cobarde *mf*; **— link** parte más delgada del hilo *f*

weaken [wíkən] VI/VT debilitar[se], quebrantar[se]

weakling [wíklIŋ] N alfeñique *m*

weakness [wíknIs] N debilidad *f*, flaqueza *f*; (deficiency) flojedad *f*

wealth [wɛłθ] N riqueza *f*

wealthy [wɛ́łθi] ADJ rico, adinerado, pudiente

wean [win] VT destetar; **to — oneself of** quitarse el vicio de

weapon [wépən] N arma *f*

wear [wɛr] VT (have on) llevar, tener puesto; (dress in habitually) usar; VI/VT (waste away)

desgastar[se]; **to — away** gastar[se], desgastar[se]; **to — down** (a person) agotar; (a pencil) desgastar; **to — off** perder efecto; **to — on** prolongarse; **to — out** (make unfit) gastar[se], degastar[se], sobar[se]; (expend) agotar; **it —s well** es duradero; N (use) gasto *m*; (clothes) ropa *f*; (durability) durabilidad *f*; (deterioration) desgaste *m*; **— and tear** desgaste *m*

weariness [wírInIs] N cansancio *m*, fatiga *f*

wearing [wérIŋ] ADJ (causing wear) desgastante; (causing fatigue) cansado

wearisome [wírisəm] ADJ fastidioso

weary [wíri] ADJ cansado, fatigado; VI/VT cansar[se], fatigar[se]

weasel [wízəł] N comadreja *f*

weather [wɛ́ðəᵻ] N tiempo *m*; (storm) tempestad *f*; **—-beaten** desgastado/curtido por la intemperie; **— bureau** oficina meteorológica *f*; **— conditions** condiciones atmosféricas *f pl*; **—man** meteorólogo *m*; **— report** parte meteorológico *m*; **—vane** veleta *f*; **it is fine —** hace buen tiempo; **to be under the —** estar enfermo; ADJ **—proof** resistente a la intemperie; VI/VT (a surface) gastar[se]; (skin) curtir; (crisis, storm) capear

weave [wiv] VT (cloth, basket) tejer, entretejer; (to put together) urdir, tramar; **to — together/into** entretejer, entrelazar; **to — one's way** zigzaguear; N tejido *m*

weaver [wívəᵻ] N tejedor -ora *mf*

web [wɛb] N (of a spider) telaraña *f*; (of lies) sarta *f*; (membrane) membrana *f*; (Internet) web *f*; (animal) palmípedo *m*; **— browser** navegador [web] *m*; **—cast** transmisión por la web *f*; **—foot** pata palmada *f*; **— hosting** alojamiento web *m*; **—master** administrador -ora de un sitio web *mf*; **— page** página web *f*; **—site** sitio web *m*; VT; ADJ **—footed** palmípedo; VI/VT **to —cast** transmitir por la web

wed [wɛd] VI/VT casarse [con]; VT casar a

wedding [wédIŋ] N boda *f*, casamiento *m*; **— day** día de boda *m*; **— dress** traje de novia *m*; **— ring** anillo de boda *m*

wedge [wɛʤ] N cuña *f*; **to drive a — between** separar; VT acuñar, meter cuñas entre; **to be —d between** estar apretado entre

Wednesday [wénzde] N miércoles *m*

wee [wi] ADJ chiquito, pequeñito

weed [wid] N mala hierba *f*; (marijuana) hierba *f*; **—killer** herbicida *m*; VT deshierbar, escardar; **to — out** eliminar

week [wik] N semana *f*; **—day** día de semana *m*; **—end** fin de semana *m*; **a — from today** de aquí en una semana

weekly [wíkli] ADJ semanal; ADV semanalmente; N semanario *m*

weep [wip] VI llorar, lagrimear

weeping [wípɪŋ] ADJ lloroso; — **willow** sauce llorón *m*; N llanto *m*

weevil [wívəł] N gorgojo *m*

weigh [we] VI/VT pesar; (consider) ponderar, sopesar, barajar; **to — anchor** levar anclas; **to — down** agobiar, abrumar; **to — on one's conscience** pesar en la conciencia de uno

weight [wet] N (heaviness, importance) peso *m*; (for clocks, scales, barbells) pesa *f*; —**lifting / —training** levantamiento de pesas *m*, halterofilia *f*; —**-watcher** persona a dieta *f*; **to put on** — engordar; **to lose** — adelgazar; VT (add weight) añadir peso; (in statistics) ponderar; **to — someone down** agobiarle a uno

weightless [wétlɪs] ADJ ingrávido

weighty [wéDi] ADJ importante

weird [wírd] ADJ (strange) extraño; (supernatural) misterioso

weirdo [wírDo] N bicho raro *m*, ente *m*

welcome [wéłkəm] N bienvenida *f*; ADJ bienvenido; — **mat** alfombrilla *f*, felpudo *m*; — **rest** descanso agradable *m*; **you are** — no hay de qué, de nada; **you are** — **here** estás en tu casa; **you are** — **to use it** a tus órdenes; VT dar la bienvenida a, acoger

weld [wɛłd] VI/VT soldar[se]; N soldadura *f*

welfare [wéłfɛr] N (good fortune) bienestar *m*; (public assistance) asistencia social *f*; — **state** estado de bienestar *m*

well [wɛł] ADV bien; — **then** pues bien; —**-being** bienestar *m*; —**-nigh** casi, muy cerca de; **he is** — **over fifty** tiene mucho más de cincuenta años; **all is** — todo está bien; INTERJ ¡bueno! ADJ (healthy) bien de salud, sano; N (of water, oil) pozo *m*; (of staircase) caja *f*; —**spring** fuente *f*, manantial *m*; ADJ —**-bred** bien educado; —**-defined** bien definido; —**-done** (steak) bien cocido; (a task) bien hecho; —**-fed** bien alimentado; —**-founded** bien fundamentado; —**-groomed** bien arreglado, aseado; —**-heeled** adinerado; —**-informed** bien informado; —**-known** (of a fact) bien sabido; (of a person) bien conocido, notorio; —**-made** bien hecho; —**-meaning** bien intencionado; —**-off** adinerado, acomodado; —**-read** leído, educado; —**-rounded** completo; —**-spoken** bien hablado; —**-to-do** adinerado; VI **tears** —**ed up in his eyes** se le llenaron los ojos de lágrimas

wellness [wéłnɪs] N (health) salud *f*; (health care) medicina preventiva *f*

welsh [wɛłʃ] VI **to** — **on** (a debt) no pagar; (a promise) no cumplir

Welsh [wɛłʃ] ADJ & N galés -esa *mf*

welt [wɛłt] N verdugón *m*

went [wɛnt] *see* go

wept [wɛpt] *see* weep

were [wɜ˞] *see* be

west [wɛst] N (cardinal point) oeste *m*; (hemisphere) occidente *m*; — **Berlin** Berlín occidental *m*; — **Indies** Antillas *f pl*; ADJ — **wind** viento del oeste *m*; ADV (direction) hacia el oeste; (location) al oeste

western [wéstə-n] ADJ occidental, del oeste; N (movie genre) película del oeste *f*

westerner [wéstə-nə-] N occidental *mf*

westward [wéstwə-d] ADV hacia el oeste; ADJ occidental

wet [wɛt] ADJ (drenched) mojado; (damp, rainy) húmedo; —**back** *offensive* espalda mojada *mf*, mojado -da *mf*; — **blanket** aguafiestas *mf sg*; — **dream** sueño húmedo *m*; —**land** humedal *m*; — **nurse** nodriza *f*; — **paint** pintura fresca *f*; — **suit** traje de buzo *m*; VI/VT (soak) mojar[se]; (dampen) humedecer[se]

wetness [wétnɪs] N humedad *f*

whack [hwæk] VI/VT (hit) golpear, pegar; (assassinate) *fam* liquidar; **to** — **off** (cut) cortar; (masturbate) *vulg* hacer[se] una paja; N (blow) golpazo *m*; *Sp vulg* hostia *f*; **to take a** — **at** hacer un intento de; **out of** — descompuesto, averiado

whale [hweł] N ballena *f*; VI pescar ballenas

wharf [hwɔrf] N muelle *m*, embarcadero *m*

what [hwɑt] INTERR PRON & N qué; — **did you say?** ¿qué dijiste? — **for?** ¿para qué? —**'s the matter?** ¿qué pasa? —**'s the score?** ¿cómo va el marcador? **and** —**not** y demás; REL PRON lo que; **come** — **may** venga lo que venga; **anyplace** —**soever** en cualquier lugar; **so** —**?** y qué? **take** — **you need** toma lo que necesites; ADJ qué; — **books did you want?** ¿qué libros querías? **take** — **books you need** toma los libros que necesites; INTERJ cómo, qué; — **happy children!** ¡qué niños más felices! — **luck!** ¡qué buena suerte!

whatever [hwɑtévə-] PRON lo que; **do it,** — **happens** hazlo, pase lo que pase; — **you may think** piense lo que pienses; — **do you mean?** ¿qué demonios quieres decir? **take** — **you need** toma lo que necesites; ADJ **any person** — una persona cualquiera / cualquier persona; **no money** — nada de dinero; INTERJ (anything) ¡lo que sea! (I give up) ¡lo que tú digas!

wheat [hwit] N trigo *m*; — **germ** germen de trigo *m*

wheel [hwił] N (disc) rueda *f*; (of cheese) horma *f*; (for pottery) torno *m*; (for steering a car) volante *m*; (for steering a ship) timón *m*; —**barrow** carretilla *f*; —**base** batalla *f*, paso *m*; —**chair** silla de ruedas *f*; —**s** (car) *fam* coche *m*; VT (a round object) hacer rodar; (a person, bicycle, wheelchair) empujar; VI **to** — **out** sacar rodando; **to** — **in** entrar rodando;

to — around girar sobre los talones
wheeze [hwiz] N resuello ruidoso *m*; VI resollar
when [hwɛn] ADV & CONJ cuando; INTERJ, ADV, & N cuándo
whenever [hwɛnévɚ] CONJ — **I see him** (each time) cada vez que lo veo; ADV (at a future time) — **I see him** cuando lo vea
where [hwɛr] ADV, N, & INTERR PRON dónde *m*; (direction) adónde; CONJ donde; (direction) adonde
whereabouts [hwérəbaʊts] N paradero *m*; INTERR ADV dónde
whereas [hwɛrǽz] CONJ mientras que; (in preambles) visto que, considerando que
whereby [hwɛrbái] ADV por lo cual
wherefore [hwérfɔr] ADV por lo cual
wherein [hwɛrín] ADV en donde
whereof [hwɛrʌ́v] REL PRON de que; INTERR PRON de qué
whereupon [hwɛrəpán] ADV después de lo cual
wherever [hwɛrévɚ] ADV dondequiera que
wherewithal [hwérwɪðɔ̀ł] N medios *m pl*, fondos *m pl*
whet [hwɛt] VT (stimulate) estimular; (sharpen) afilar; **—stone** piedra de afilar *f*
whether [hwéðɚ] CONJ — **we like it or not** nos guste o no nos guste; **I doubt — we can do it** dudo [de] que lo podamos hacer; **he asked — I was coming** me preguntó si venía
which [hwɪtʃ] INTERR PRON cuál[es]; — **do you want?** ¿cuál[es] quieres? REL PRON que; **the applc, — I just bought** la manzana, que acabo de comprar; **the book of — I spoke** el libro del que / del cual hablé; **that — you don't know can hurt you** lo que no sabes puede hacerte daño; INTERR ADJ qué, cuál[es] de; — **house is it?** ¿qué casa es? ¿cuál de las casas es?
whichever [hwɪtʃévɚ] PRON & ADJ (no matter which) cualquiera [que]; — **you choose, you'll regret it later** elijas el que elijas, te arrepentirás después; (anyone that) el que / la que; **choose — you like** elije el que quieras
whiff [hwɪf] N (waft) soplo *m*; (odors, scandal) bocanada *f*, tufillo *m*; **to take a —** oler
while [hwaɪł] N rato *m*; **a short —** un ratito; **a short — ago** hace poco; CONJ (during) mientras; (whereas) mientras que; (even though) aunque; VT **to — away** pasar
whim [hwɪm] N capricho *m*, antojo *m*
whimper [hwímpɚ] VI/VT lloriquear, gimotear; N lloriqueo *m*, gimoteo *m*
whimsical [hwímzɪkəł] ADJ caprichoso, antojadizo
whine [hwaɪn] VI (whimper) gemir; (complain) quejarse; N (whimper) gemido *m*; (complaint) quejido *m*; **stop whining!** ¡deja de quejarte!
whiner [hwáɪnɚ] N llorón -ona *mf*, quejica *mf*
whiny [hwáɪni] ADJ quejoso, quejica

whip [hwɪp] N azote *m*, látigo *m*, rebenque *m*; VT (hit with a whip) azotar, fustigar; (spank) zurrar, dar una paliza; (beat to a froth) batir; (defeat) vencer; **to — out** sacar; **to — up** (prepare) preparar rápidamente; (incite) incitar
whipping [hwípɪŋ] N zurra *f*, paliza *f*; — **cream** crema para batir *f*
whir [hwɝ] VI zumbar; N zumbido *m*
whirl [hwɝł] VI girar; **to — around** arremolinarse; **my head —s** me da vueltas la cabeza; N (rotation) giro *m*; (of water) remolino *m*; **—pool** remolino *m*; **—pool bath** baño de remolino *m*; **—wind** torbellino *m*, remolino de viento *m*; **—wind tour** gira relámpago *f*; **my head is in a —** me da vueltas la cabeza; **to give it a —** probarlo
whisk [hwɪsk] VT (sweep) barrer; (beat) batir; **to — away** llevarse de prisa; VI **to — by** pasar rápidamente; N (broom) escobilla *f*; (beater) batidor *m*
whisker [hwískɚ] N (hair of beard) pelo de la barba *m*; (sideburn) patilla *f*; (of animals) bigote *m*
whiskey, whisky [hwíski] N whisky *m*
whisper [hwíspɚ] VI/VT (person) cuchichear, secretear; (leaves, water) susurrar; N (people) cuchicheo *m*; (leaves, water) susurro *m*; **to talk in a —** cuchichear
whistle [hwísəł] VI/VT silbar; (loud) chiflar; (in protest) rechiflar; VI (referee, train) pitar; **to — for someone** llamar a uno con un silbido; N (sound) silbido *m*; (loud sound) chiflido *m*; (of a referee) pitido *m*; (instrument) silbato *m*, pito *m*; **—blower** acusador -ora *mf*
white [hwaɪt] ADJ (color, ethnicity) blanco; — **blood cell** glóbulo blanco *m*; — **bread** pan blanco *m*; **—caps** cabrillas *f pl*; **—collar** administrativo, de cuello blanco; — **gold** oro blanco *m*; — **hair** cana *f*; — **lie** mentirilla *f*; — **noise** ruido blanco *m*; — **trash** *offensive* sureño -ña blanco -ca pobre *mf*; **—wash** (paint) lechada *f*; (cover-up) encubrimiento *m*; N blanco *m* (also ethnicity); (of egg) clara *f*; VT **to —wash** (paint) blanquear, enjalbegar; (cover up) encubrir
whiten [hwaɪtn̩] VI/VT blanquear[se], emblanquecer
whiteness [hwáɪtnɪs] N blancura *f*
whitish [hwáɪdɪʃ] ADJ blancuzco, blanquecino
whittle [hwídl̩] VI/VT tallar; **to — away** ir gastando; **to — down expenses** reducir los gastos
whiz [hwɪz] VI zumbar; **to — by** pasar zumbando; VT hacer zumbar; N (sound) zumbido *m*; (ace) as *m*; — **kid** niño -ña prodigio *mf*
who [hu] REL PRON quien[es]; INTERR PRON quién[es]; **he —** el que

WHO [World Health Organization]
[dʌbəljuétʃó] N OMS f
whoa [hwo] INTERJ (to express amazement) ¡jo!
(to stop a horse) ¡so!
whoever [huévɚ] REL PRON (whatever person)
quienquiera que, el/la que; INTERR PRON
(who) quién
whole [hoł] ADJ (complete) completo, íntegro;
(unbroken) entero; (uninjured) ileso; —-
grain integral; **—hearted** sincero;
—heartedly de todo corazón; **— life
insurance** seguro de vida permanente m; —
milk leche entera f; **— note** redonda f;
—sale (in bulk) al por mayor; (massive)
masivo; **—sale slaughter** matanza f; —-
wheat integral; **the — day** todo el día; **to go
— hog** tirar la casa por la ventana; N todo m;
(for amounts) totalidad f; **—sale** venta al por
mayor f, mayoreo m; **—saler** comerciante al
por mayor mf, mayorista mf, almacenista mf;
as a — en su totalidad; **on the —** en general;
ADV **—sale** al por mayor; VI/VT **to —sale**
vender al por mayor
wholesome [hółsəm] ADJ sano
whom [hum] REL PRON a quien[es]; **for/to/
with —** para/a/con quien; INTERR PRON a
quién[es]
whoop [hwup] N (shout) grito m; (gasp)
respiración convulsiva f; VI (person) gritar;
(owl) ulular; **to — it up** armar jaleo
whopper [hwápɚ] N (large thing) cosa enorme f;
(lie) mentira f, trola f
whopping [hwápɪŋ] ADJ enorme
whore [hor] N offensive puta f; **—house** vulg casa
de putas f
whose [huz] REL PRON cuyo; **the man — son is
here** el hombre cuyo hijo está aquí; INTERR
PRON de quién; **— book is this?** ¿de quién es
este libro?
why [hwaɪ] ADV & CONJ por qué; **that's the
reason — he left** es por eso que se fue; N
porqué m; INTERJ **—, of course!** ¡pero claro!
wick [wɪk] N mecha f, pabilo m
wicked [wíkɪd] ADJ malvado, perverso
wickedness [wíkɪdnɪs] N maldad f, perversidad f
wicker [wíkɚ] N mimbre m; **— chair** silla de
mimbre f
wide [waɪd] ADJ (broad) ancho; (of great range)
amplio; (spacious) vasto, extenso; **— apart**
muy apartados; **—-awake** muy despierto,
despabilado; **— body** avión de fuselaje ancho
m; **—-eyed** ojiabierto, con los ojos bien
abiertos; **— of the mark** lejos del blanco; **—-
open** abierto de par en par; **— receiver**
receptor abierto m; **—spread** (over a wide
area) extendido; (among many people)
generalizado; **to open —** (a door) abrir de par
en par; (one's mouth) abrir bien; **two feet —**
dos pies de ancho

widely [wáɪdli] ADV **it is — known that** es bien
sabido que; **he is a — known artist** es un
artista muy conocido; **he is — read** es muy
leído; **— different versions** versiones muy
diferentes
widen [wáɪdn̩] VI/VT ensanchar[se], ampliar[se]
widow [wído] N viuda f
widower [wídoɚ] N viudo m
width [wɪdθ] N ancho m, anchura f
wield [wiłd] VT (power) ejercer; (tool) manejar;
(weapon) blandir, esgrimir
wife [waɪf] N esposa f, señora f, Sp mujer f
wifi [wireless fidelity] [wáɪfaɪ] N wifi f
wig [wɪg] N peluca f
wiggle [wígəł] VI/VT (hips) menear[se]; (toes)
mover[se]; N (of hips) meneo m; (of toes)
movimiento m; **— room** flexibilidad f
wigwam [wígwɑm] N tienda indígena f
wild [waɪłd] ADJ (animal, savage) salvaje, bravío,
bronco; (plant) silvestre; (party)
desenfrenado; (conduct) alocado; (storm,
temperament) violento; (hair) desordenado;
(look) extraviado, desencajado; (enthusiasm)
delirante; **— boar** jabalí m; **— card** comodín
m; **—cat** gato montés m; **—-eyed** de mirada
extraviada, con los ojos desencajados; **—fire**
fuego arrasador m; **—flower** flor silvestre f;
— goose chase búsqueda inútil f; **—life**
fauna f; **I'm just — about Mary** estoy loco
por María; **not in your —est dreams** ni lo
pienses; **to drive someone —** volver loco a
alguien; **to talk —** decir disparates; N **—s**
regiones salvajes f pl
wilderness [wíldɚnɪs] N (near mountains)
monte m; (desert) desierto m; (jungle) jungla f
wile [waɪł] N artimaña f, treta f
will [wɪł] VT (use willpower) conseguir a fuerza
de voluntad; (bequeath) legar, dejar; V AUX **if
you —** si quieres; **she — come** va a venir,
vendrá; **this motorcycle — go 100 mph**
esta motocicleta puede hacer 100 millas por
hora; **in spite of everything, he — not
stop complaining** a pesar de todo, no deja
de quejarse; **she — just sit for hours
doing nothing** se pasa horas sentada sin
hacer nada; **that — do** basta; N (wish)
voluntad f; (testament) testamento m;
—power fuerza de voluntad f; **at —** a
discreción, a voluntad
willful [wíłfəł] ADJ testarudo, porfiado
willies [wíliz] N escalofríos m pl
willing [wílɪŋ] ADJ dispuesto, voluntarioso
willingly [wílɪŋli] ADV de buena gana,
gustosamente
willingness [wílɪŋnɪs] N buena voluntad f,
buena gana f
willow [wílo] N sauce m
wilt [wɪłt] VI/VT (plant) marchitar[se]; VI (person)
languidecer

wily [wáili] ADJ astuto, artero
wimp [wɪmp] N pelele *m*
win [wɪn] VI/VT ganar; VT (support, fame,
affection) ganarse; (victory) alcanzar,
conseguir; **to — out** ganar, triunfar; **to —
over** conquistar; **a —-— situation** una
situación beneficiosa para ambas partes; N
victoria *f*
wince [wɪns] VI hacer una mueca; N mueca *f*
winch [wɪntʃ] N cabrestante *m*, torno *m*, *Am*
guinche *m*
wind[1] [wɪnd] N (air) viento *m*; (gas) gases *m pl*;
—bag charlatán -ana *mf*; **—breaker**™
cazadora *f*; **—fall** ganancia inesperada *f*; **—
instrument** instrumento de viento *m*;
—mill molino de viento *m*; **—pipe** tráquea *f*;
— power energía eólica *f*; **—shield**
parabrisas *m sg*; **—shield wiper**
limpiaparabrisas *m sg*; **—sock** manga de
viento *f*; **—surfing** windsurf *m*; **— tunnel**
túnel aerodinámico *m*; **to get — of** enterarse
de; **to break —** ventosear; **to catch one's —**
recobrar el aliento; ADJ **—ward** de
barlovento; ADV **—ward** hacia/a barlovento
wind[2] [waɪnd] VT enrollar; (watch) dar cuerda a;
VI (take a bending course) serpentear; **to —
around** enrollarse; **to — down** (relax)
tranquilizarse; (come to a conclusion) irse
terminando; **to — up** (string) enrollar; (a
clock) dar cuerda; (a project) completar; (in
jail) acabar; N (turn) vuelta *f*; (bend) recodo
m; **—up** conclusión *f*
winding [wáɪndɪŋ] ADJ sinuoso; **— staircase**
escalera de caracol *f*
window [wíndo] N (in building, on screen)
ventana *f*; (in building, large) ventanal *m*; (in
car, plane) ventanilla *f*; (in a shop) escaparate
m; *Am* vidriera *f*; **—pane** cristal *m*, vidrio *m*;
— shade visillo *m*; **—sill** alféizar *m*
windy [wíndi] ADJ ventoso; **it is —** hace/hay
viento
wine [waɪn] N vino *m*; **— cellar** bodega *f*;
—glass copa *f*; **—grower** viticultor -ora *mf*,
viñatero -ra *mf*; **— industry** industria
vinícola *f*; **—skin** odre *m*; **— tasting** cata de
vinos *f*
winery [wáɪnəri] N bodega *f*
wing [wɪŋ] N (of bird, plane, building, table) ala
f; **— nut** tuerca [de] mariposa/palomilla *f*;
—span/—spread envergadura *f*; **—tip**
extremo del ala *m*; **in the —s** en los
bastidores; **under one's —** al amparo de
alguien; **to take —** levantar vuelo; VI volar;
VT (wound slightly) herir en el ala/brazo; **to
— it** improvisar
winger [wíŋɚ] N (in soccer) ala *mf*, extremo *mf*
wink [wɪŋk] VI/VT guiñar; **to — approval**
guiñar en aprobación; **to — at** hacer la vista
gorda; N guiño *m*, guiñada *f*; **I didn't sleep a**

— no pegué un ojo
winner [wínɚ] N ganador -ora *mf*, triunfador
-ora *mf*
winning [wínɪŋ] ADJ (successful) ganador,
vencedor; (charming) atractivo; **—s**
ganancias *f pl*
wino [wáɪno] N *pej* borracho -cha *mf*
winter [wíntɚ] N invierno *m*; **— weather** clima
invernal *m*; VI invernar
wintry [wíntri] ADJ invernal
wipe [waɪp] VT (sweat, tears) enjugar; (wet
surfaces) secar; (dry surface) limpiar; **to —
away** enjugar; **to — off** limpiar; **to — out**
aniquilar; **to — up** limpiar
wiper [wáɪpɚ] N limpiaparabrisas *m sg*
wire [waɪr] N (filament) alambre *m*; (telegram)
telegrama *m*; **— fence** alambrado *m*; **—tap**
intervención del teléfono *f*, pinchazo *m*; **—
transfer** transferencia electrónica *f*; **by —**
por telégrafo; VT (an appliance) alambrar; (a
house) electrificar; VI/VT (a message)
telegrafiar; (money) girar; **to — together**
atar con alambre; **to —tap** intervenir un
teléfono, pinchar un teléfono
wired [waɪrd] ADJ (installed) alambrado; (tied)
atado con alambre; (electrified) electrificado;
(enthusiastic) sobreexcitado
wireless [wáɪrlɪs] ADJ inalámbrico; **— Internet**
internet inalámbrico *m*
wiring [wáɪrɪŋ] N cableado *m*
wiry [wáɪri] ADJ (skinny) nervudo; (like wire)
crespo
wisdom [wízdəm] N (moral) sabiduría *f*;
(scholarly) saber *m*; **— tooth** muela del
juicio *f*
wise [waɪz] ADJ (discerning) sabio; (prudent)
sensato, prudente; (erudite) erudito; **—ass**
sabihondo -da *mf*; **—crack** broma *f*, chiste *m*;
— guy sabihondo *m*; **the Three — Men** los
Tres Reyes Magos; N **in no —** de ningún
modo; VI **to — up** avisparse
wish [wɪʃ] VT desear; **I — you were here** ojalá
estuvieras aquí; **I — you the best** te deseo lo
mejor; **to — for** pedir; **to — upon a star**
pedir un deseo; N deseo *m*; **to make a —**
pedir un deseo; **best —es** saludos
wishy-washy [wíʃiwɑʃi] ADJ indeciso
wistful [wístfəł] ADJ (pensive) pensativo;
(nostalgic) nostálgico
wit [wɪt] N (intelligence) agudeza *f*, ingenio *m*;
(verbal humor) gracejo *m*, sal *f*, chispa *f*;
(person) persona aguda *f*, persona ingeniosa *f*;
to be at one's —s' end no saber qué más
hacer; **to live by one's —s** vivir de su
ingenio; **to lose one's —s** perder el juicio; **to
use one's —s** valerse de su ingenio
witch [wɪtʃ] N bruja *f*; **—craft** brujería *f*; **—
hunt** cacería de brujas *f*
with [wɪθ, wɪð] PREP con; **rice — chicken** arroz

con pollo *m*; **the man — glasses** el hombre de gafas; **I left my son — Mary** dejé a mi hijo al cuidado de María; **to be — it** está al día; **— me** conmigo; **— you** contigo, con usted

withdraw [wɪðdrɔ́] VI/VT retirar[se]

withdrawal [wɪðdrɔ́əł] N (of troops) retirada *f*; (from public office) alejamiento *m*; (from a bank) *Am* retiro *m*; *Sp* retirada *f*; — **[symptoms]** síndrome de abstinencia *m*

withdrawn [wɪθdrɔ́n] *see* withdraw

withdrew [wɪθdrú] *see* withdraw

wither [wíðɚ] VI/VT (of a plant) marchitar[se]; (of a person) consumir[se]; **she —ed him with a look** lo fulminó con la mirada

withheld [wɪθhéłd] *see* withhold

withhold [wɪθhółd] VT (approval) negar; (funds) retener; (truth) ocultar

withholding tax [wɪθhółdɪŋtæks] N impuesto deducido del salario *m*

within [wɪðín] PREP dentro de; **— five miles** a menos de cinco millas; ADV dentro, adentro

without [wɪðáʊt] PREP sin; **— my seeing him** sin que yo lo vea; ADV fuera, afuera

withstand [wɪθstǽnd] VI/VT resistir

withstood [wɪθstúd] *see* withstand

witness [wítnɪs] N (person) testigo *mf*; (testimony) testimonio *m*; **to bear —** atestiguar; VT (see) presenciar; (sign) firmar como testigo

witticism [wídɪsɪzem] N ocurrencia *f*

witty [wídi] ADJ ocurrente, dicharachero

wizard [wízɚd] N (sorcerer) mago *m*, brujo *m*, hechicero *m*; (computer expert) experto -ta *mf*; (genius) genio *m*

wobble [wábəł] N tambaleo *m*, bamboleo *m*; VI/VT tambalear[se], bambolear[se]

woe [wo] N aflicción *f*; **— is me!** ¡pobre de mí!

woeful [wófəł] ADJ lamentable

wok [wak] N wok *m*

woke [wok] *see* wake

woken [wókən] *see* wake

wolf [wʊłf] N lobo *m*; **— spider** araña lobo *f*

woman [wúmən] N mujer *f*; *fam* tía *f*; **a —'s touch** un toque femenino; **women's lib[eration]** movimiento de liberación femenina *m*; **women's rights** derechos de la mujer *m pl*

womanhood [wúmənhʊd] N (condition) condición de mujer *f*; (all women) las mujeres *f pl*

womanizer [wúmənaɪzɚ] N mujeriego *m*

womankind [wúmənkaɪnd] N las mujeres *f pl*

womanly [wúmənli] ADJ femenino

womb [wum] N (uterus) útero *m*, matriz *f*; (insides of something) vientre *m*; (center) seno *m*

won [wʌn] *see* win

wonder [wándɚ] VI/VT preguntarse; **to — at**

admirarse de, maravillarse de; **I — what time it is** ¿qué hora será? N (marvel) maravilla *f*; (surprise) asombro *m*; (miracle) milagro *m*; **it's a — that** es asombroso que; **it's no — that** no es de extrañar que

wonderful [wándɚfəł] ADJ maravilloso, estupendo

woo [wu] VI/VT cortejar

wood [wʊd] N (material, also golf club) madera *f*; (firewood) leña *f*; **—cutter** leñador -ora *mf*; **—louse** cochinilla *f*; **—pecker** pájaro carpintero *m*; **—s** bosque *m*; **— shaving** viruta *f*; **—shed** leñera *f*; **—sman** leñador *m*; **—winds** maderas *f pl*; **—work** carpintería *f*, maderaje *m*; **to come out of the —work** salir de la nada

wooded [wúdɪd] ADJ arbolado

wooden [wúdn̩] ADJ (of wood) de madera; (lifeless) inexpresivo

woody [wúdi] ADJ (with trees) arbolado; (like wood) leñoso

woof [wʊf] N (of fabric) trama *f*; INTERJ (sound made by a dog) ¡guau!

wool [wʊł] N lana *f*; **— sweater** suéter de lana *m*

woolen [wúlən] ADJ de lana; N **—s** (fabric) tejido de lana *m*; (clothes) ropa de lana *f*

woolly [wúli] ADJ lanudo

word [wɝd] N (lexical unit) vocablo *m*, palabra *f*; (promise) palabra *f*; (news) noticia *f*, aviso *m*; (order) mandato *m*, orden *m*; **— for —** palabra por palabra; **— processing** procesamiento de textos *m*; *Sp* tratamiento de texto[s] *m*; **—s [of a song]** letra [de una canción] *f*; **— spacing** espaciado de palabras *m*; **— wrap** retorno de línea automático *m*; **I found out by — of mouth** me lo dijeron; **may I have a — with you?** ¿podemos hablar? **to eat one's —s** tragarse/comerse las palabras; VT (oral) expresar; (written) formular

wording [wɝdɪŋ] N formulación *f*

wordy [wɝdi] ADJ verboso, prolijo

wore [wɔr] *see* wear

work [wɝk] N (effort) trabajo *m*; (employment) empleo *m*, trabajo *m*; (artistic product, fortification) obra *f*; **—book** cuaderno/libro de trabajo *m*; **—day** día laborable *m*; **— environment** entorno de trabajo *m*; **— flow** flujo de trabajo *m*; **—force** mano de obra *f*; **—load** cantidad/carga de trabajo *f*; **—man** obrero *m*; **— of art** obra de arte *f*; **—out** sesión de ejercicio *f*; **— permit** permiso de trabajo *m*; **—place** lugar de trabajo *m*; **— schedule** horario de trabajo *m*; **—sheet** planilla *f*, hoja de ejercicios *f*; **—shop** taller *m*; **—station** estación de trabajo *f*; **— stoppage** huelga *f*, paro laboral *m*; **—s** fábrica *f*; **the —s** todo; **—week** semana de trabajo *f*; **he's hard at —** está trabajando duro; ADJ —-**related** laboral; VI (labor) trabajar; (function) funcionar; VT (change) efectuar; (metal, land) trabajar; (a crowd) manipular; (a mine) explotar; (employees) hacer trabajar; **to — in[to]** introducir; **to — loose** soltar[se], aflojar[se]; **to — on** (repair) arreglar; (improve) tratar de mejorar; **to — one's way through college** pagarse los estudios trabajando; **to — one's way up** ascender a fuerza de trabajo; **to — out** (a plan) urdir; (a problem) resolver; **he —s out every day** hace ejercicio todos los días; **to — overtime** trabajar horas extras; **it all —ed out** al final todo salió bien; **to be all —ed up** estar sobreexcitado; **to get —ed up** agitarse

workaholic [wɝkəhálɪk] N adicto -ta al trabajo *mf*

worker [wɝkɚ] N trabajador -ora *mf*; (in a factory) obrero -ra *mf*; (in an office) oficinista *mf*

working [wɝkɪŋ] N (act of someone who works, shaping of metals) trabajo *m*; (operation) funcionamiento *m*, operación *f*; (of a problem) cálculo *m*; (of a mine) explotación *f*; ADJ (class) obrero, trabajador; (majority) suficiente; — **class** clase obrera/trabajadora *f*; — **lunch** comida de trabajo *f*; —**man** obrero *m*

workmanship [wɝkmənʃɪp] N (skill) habilidad *f*, destreza *f*; (quality of work) confección *f*

world [wɝld] N mundo *m*; — **Bank** Banco Mundial *m*; — **Cup** Copa del Mundo *f*; —**view** cosmovisión *f*; — **war** guerra mundial *f*; — **Wide Web** web *f*, red [mundial electrónica] *f*; ADJ —-**class** de categoría mundial; —-**famous** de fama mundial; —-**shaking** trascendental; —**wide** mundial

worldly [wɝldli] ADJ (mundane) mundano, temporal; (sophisticated) de mundo, corrido; (material) material

worm [wɝm] N gusano *m*; ADJ —-**eaten** comido por los gusanos, carcomido; VT desparasitar, quitar las lombrices; **to — a secret out of someone** extraerle/sonsacarle un secreto a alguien; **to — oneself into** insinuarse en

worn [wɔrn] ADJ desgastado, usado

worn [wɔrn] *see* wear

worrisome [wɝisəm] ADJ preocupante, inquietante

worry [wɝi] VI/VT preocupar[se], inquietar[se]; VT (harass) hostigar; VI **to — with** juguetear con; N preocupación *f*, inquietud *f*, zozobra *f*; —**wart** preocupón -ona *mf*

worse [wɝs] ADJ & ADV peor; — **and** — cada vez peor; — **than ever** peor que nunca; **from bad to** — de mal en peor; **so much the** — tanto peor; **to be** — **off** estar peor que antes; **to change for the** — empeorar[se]; **to get**

— empeorar[se]

worship [wɝʃɪp] N (act of worshiping) adoración *f*; (ceremony) culto *m*; VT (revere) adorar, venerar; VI (attend services) asistir al culto

worshiper [wɝʃɪpɚ] N (one who worships) adorador -ora *mf*; —**s** fieles *mf pl*

worst [wɝst] ADJ & ADV **the** — one el/la peor; **the** — **thing** lo peor; —-**case scenario** el peor de los casos; VT derrotar

worth [wɝθ] ADJ **to be** — **a dollar** valer un dólar; **to be** — **hearing** ser digno de oírse; **to be** —**while** valer la pena; **it's** — **doing** vale la pena hacerlo; N valor *m*, valía *f*; **ten cents'** — **of** diez centavos de; **to get one's money's** — **out of** aprovechar al máximo

worthless [wɝθlɪs] ADJ (useless) inútil; (despicable) despreciable; — **check** cheque sin fondos *m*

worthy [wɝði] ADJ (meritorious) digno, meritorio; (esteemed) benemérito; — **cause** causa noble *f*; — **of praise** digno de elogio; N persona ilustre *mf*

would [wʊd] V AUX I — **do it if I could** lo haría si pudiera; — **you please open the door?** ¿podrías abrir la puerta por favor? **he said he** — **do it** dijo que lo haría; **as a child, I** — **play all the time** de niño, jugaba todo el tiempo; — **that she were alive!** ¡ojalá estuviera viva!

wound[1] [wund] N herida *f*; VI/VT herir; (with an arrow) flechar

wound[2] [waund] *see* wind

wove [wov] *see* weave

woven [wóvən] *see* weave

wow [waʊ] VT impresionar; INTERJ ¡huy!

wrangle [ræŋgəl] VI/VT (quarrel) discutir; (obtain) agenciarse de; VT (herd) juntar; *Am* rodear; N riña *f*, pendencia *f*

wrangler [ræŋglɚ] N vaquero -ra *mf*

wrap [ræp] VT envolver; **to — up** (a present) envolver; (a baby) arropar; (a task) terminar; (against the cold) abrigar[se]; **to be —ped in** estar envuelto en; **to be —ped up in** estar absorto en; N (coat) abrigo *m*; (shawl) chal *m*; —-**up** (summary) resumen *m*; (end) final *m*; **keep under —s** mantener secreto

wrapper [ræpɚ] N envoltura *f*, envoltorio *m*

wrapping [ræpɪŋ] N envoltura *f*; — **paper** papel para envolver *m*

wrath [ræθ] N ira *f*, cólera *f*

wreak [rik] VT **to — havoc** hacer estragos

wreath [riθ] N corona *f*; — **of smoke** espiral de humo *f*

wreck [rɛk] N (building) ruina *f*; (car, plane) restos *m pl*; (a ship) pecio *m*; (shipwreck) naufragio *m*; (person) desastre *m*, ruina *f*; (accident) accidente *m*; VI tener un accidente; VT (a ship) naufragar; (a car, totally) destrozar; (a car, with minor damage) chocar;

(a building) demoler
wreckage [rékɪʤ] N (of a building) escombros *m pl*; (of a car, plane) restos de un accidente *m pl*; (of a ship) pecio *m*
wrecker [rékɚ] N (tow truck) grúa *f*, camión de remolque *m*; (worker) obrero -ra de demolición *mf*
wrench [rɛntʃ] N (twist) torcedura *f*; (pull) tirón *m*; (tool) llave de tuercas *f*; VT torcer, retorcer; **to — off/out** arrancar de un tirón, arrebatar
wrest [rɛst] VT (pull) arrancar; (take away) arrebatar
wrestle [résəł] VI/VT luchar [con/contra]; N lucha *f*
wrestler [réslɚ] N luchador -ora *mf*
wrestling [réslɪŋ] N lucha libre *f*
wretch [rɛtʃ] N miserable *mf*, infeliz *mf*
wretched [rétʃɪd] ADJ (unfortunate) desdichado, infeliz; (despicable) vil, miserable, arrastrado; (inferior) pésimo
wriggle [rígəł] VI culebrear, serpentear; **to — out of** escabullirse de; VT menear, retorcer
wring [rɪŋ] VT (twist) torcer, retorcer; (extract) arrancar; **to — one's hands** retorcerse las manos; **to — out** escurrir
wrinkle [ríŋkəł] N arruga *f*, surco *m*; (problem) problema *m*; VI/VT arrugar[se]
wrist [rɪst] N muñeca *f*; **—watch** reloj [de] pulsera *m*
writ [rɪt] N auto *m*, mandato *m*
write [raɪt] VI/VT escribir; (transfer data) grabar; **to — back** contestar; **to — down** apuntar; **to — off** cancelar; **to — out** escribir en forma completa; **to —-protect** proteger contra grabación; **to — up** hacer un reportaje sobre; **it's written all over his face** se le ve en la cara; **she —s for a living** es escritora; N **—-up** reportaje *m*; **— protection** protección contra grabación *f*
writer [ráɪDɚ] N escritor -ora *mf*, literato -ta *mf*
writhe [raɪð] VI retorcerse
writing [ráɪDɪŋ] N (act of writing) escritura *f*; (handwriting) letra *f*, escritura *f*; (style) estilo *m*; **— desk** escritorio *m*; **— paper** papel de escribir *m*; **—s** obra *f*; **to put in —** poner por escrito
written [rítn̩] *see* write
wrong [rɔŋ] ADJ (incorrect) incorrecto, equivocado; (improper) inapropiado; **what's — with you?** ¿qué te pasa? **you are — ** estás equivocado; **the — side of a fabric** el revés de una tela; **— side out** con lo de adentro para afuera; **to be on the — side of the road** ir a contramano / en sentido contrario; **that is the — book** ese no es el libro; **it is in the — place** está fuera de lugar; ADV mal; **to go —** salir mal; N (evil) mal *m*; (injustice) injusticia *f*; **to be in the —** (not be right)

estar equivocado; (be to blame) tener la culpa; **to do —** hacer mal; VT perjudicar
wrongful [rɔ́ŋfəł] ADJ injusto, injustificado
wrongly [rɔ́ŋli] ADV (reported) incorrectamente; (accused) injustamente
wrote [rot] *see* write
wrought [rɔt] ADJ forjado; **— iron** hierro forjado *m*
wrung [rʌŋ] *see* wring
wry [raɪ] ADJ (smile) torcido; (remark, humor) irónico; **to make a — face** torcer la cara
WTO [World Trade Organization] [dábəłjutió] N OMT *f*
WWW [World Wide Web] [dábəłjudábəłjudábəłju] N web *f*

Xx

xenophobia [zɛnəfóbiə] N xenofobia *f*
Xerox™ [zíraks] N fotocopia *f*; VI/VT fotocopiar
x-rated [éksreDɪd] ADJ pornográfico
x-ray [éksre] N rayos X *m pl*, radiografía *f*; VI/VT radiografiar
xylophone [záiləfon] N xilofón *m*, xilófono *m*

Yy

yacht [jat] N yate *m*; VI navegar en yate
y'all [jɔ́ł] PRON *Am* ustedes *mf*; *Sp* vosotros -as *mf*
Yankee [jǽŋki] ADJ & N estadounidense del norte del país *mf*
yard [jard] N (measure) yarda [0.9144m] *f*; (spar) verga *f*; (courtyard) patio *m*; (grassy area) jardín *m*; **—stick** (stick) vara de medida [de una yarda] *f*; (criterion) patrón *m*, norma *f*
yarn [jarn] N (material) hilo *m*; (story) cuento *m*
yawn [jɔn] VI bostezar; N bostezo *m*
yeah [jɛ́ə] ADV *fam* sí; *fam* **— right!** ¡de eso, nada! ¡qué va!
year [jir] N año *m*; **—book** anuario *m*; ADJ **—-end** de fin de año; **—-round** de todo el año; **—-to-date** del año hasta la fecha
yearling [jírlɪŋ] N animal de un año *m*; (of cows) añojo -ja *mf*
yearly [jírli] ADJ anual; ADV anualmente
yearn [jɝn] VI anhelar, suspirar por
yearning [jɝnɪŋ] N anhelo *m*
yeast [jist] N levadura *f*
yell [jɛł] VI/VT gritar; N grito *m*
yellow [jélo] ADJ (color) amarillo; (coward) cobarde; **— card** (in soccer) tarjeta amarilla *f*;

— **fever** fiebre amarilla *f*; — **jacket** avispa *f*;
— **pages** páginas amarillas *f pl*; N amarillo *m*;
VI/VT poner[se] amarillo, amarillear
yellowish [jéloɪʃ] ADJ amarillento
yelp [jɛłp] VI gañir, aullar; N gañido *m*, aullido *m*
Yemen [jémən] N Yemen *m*
Yemeni [jéməni] ADJ & N yemení *mf*
yen [jɛn] N (currency of Japan) yen *m*; (desire)
anhelo *m*; VI anhelar
yes [jɛs] ADV sí; **—-no question** pregunta de sí o
no *f*
yesterday [jéstə˞de] ADV & N ayer *m*; **the day
before** — anteayer
yet [jɛt] ADV & CONJ **are they here —?** ¿ya
llegaron? **they aren't here** — todavía no
llegan, aún no han llegado; — **another** otro
más; **ugly** — **charming** feo pero
encantador; **as** — todavía, aún
yield [jiłd] VI/VT (surrender, give in) ceder;
(produce) rendir, redituar; **to** — **5 percent**
dar un cinco por ciento de interés; N
(production) rendimiento *m*, producción *f*;
(of stocks) rédito *m*
yodel [jódḷ] VI cantar a la tirolesa; N canto
tirolés *m*
yoga [jógə] N yoga *m*
yogurt [jógə˞t] N yogur *m*
yoke [jok] N (crossbar) yugo *m*; (pair of animals)
yunta *f*; (on a shirt) canesú *m*; VT uncir
yolk [jok] N yema *f*
yonder [jándə˞] ADJ aquel; ADV (location) allá;
(direction) hacia allá
yore [jɔr] N **in days of** — antaño
you [ju] SUBJ PRON (sg informal) tú; *RP, Central
Am* vos; (sg formal) usted; (pl informal) *Sp*
vosotros; *Am* ustedes; (pl formal) ustedes; **I
see** — (sg informal) te veo; (sg formal) lo veo;
(pl informal) *Sp* os veo; *Am* los veo; (pl
formal) los veo; **I talk to** — (sg informal) te
hablo; (sg formal) le hablo; (pl informal) *Sp* os
hablo; *Am* les hablo; (pl formal) les hablo; **I
went with** — (sg informal) fui contigo; (sg
formal) fui con usted; (pl informal) *Sp* fui con
vosotros; *Am* fui con ustedes; (pl formal) fui
con ustedes; **it's for** — (sg informal) es para
ti; (sg informal) *RP, Central Am* es para vos; (sg
formal) es para usted; (pl informal) *Sp* es para
vosotros; *Am* es para ustedes; (pl formal) es
para ustedes; **this is how** — **make bread**
así se hace el pan
young [jʌŋ] ADJ joven; — **man** joven *m*; —
people gente joven *f*; — **woman** joven *f*; N
(offspring) cría *f*
youngster [jáŋstə˞] N muchacho -cha *mf*,
jovencito -ta *mf*
your [jɔr] POSS ADJ **this is** — **dog** (sg informal)
este es tu perro; (sg formal) este es su perro;
(pl informal) *Sp* este es vuestro perro, *Am* este
es su perro; (pl formal) este es su perro

yours [jɔrz] PRON **this book is** — (sg informal)
este libro es tuyo; (sg formal) este libro es
suyo / de usted; (pl informal) *Sp* este libro es
vuestro; *Am* este libro es suyo / de ustedes; (pl
formal) este libro es suyo / de ustedes; — **is
bigger** (sg informal) el tuyo / la tuya es más
grande; (sg formal) el suyo / el de usted / la
suya / la de usted es más grande; (pl informal)
Sp el vuestro / la vuestra es más grande; *Am* el
suyo / el de ustedes es más grande; (pl formal)
el suyo / el de ustedes es más grande; **a
friend of** — (sg informal) un amigo tuyo; (sg
formal) un amigo suyo / de usted; (pl
informal) *Sp* un amigo vuestro; *Am* un amigo
suyo / de ustedes; — **truly** atentamente
yourself [jɔrsɛłf] PRON **you** — **wrote the
letter** (sg informal) tú mismo escribiste la
carta; (sg formal) usted mismo escribió la
carta; **you yourselves wrote the letter** (pl
informal) *Sp* vosotros mismos escribisteis la
carta; *Am* ustedes mismos escribieron la
carta; (pl formal) ustedes mismos escribieron
la carta; **you are not** — **today** (sg informal)
hoy no eres el mismo de siempre; (sg formal)
hoy no es el mismo de siempre; **you are not
yourselves today** *Sp* hoy no sois los mismos
de siempre; *Am* hoy no son los mismos de
siempre; (pl formal) hoy no son los mismos
de siempre; **you were sitting by** — (sg
informal) tú estabas sentado solo; (sg formal)
usted estaba sentado solo; **you were sitting
by yourselves** (informal) *Sp* vosotros
estabais sentados solos; *Am* ustedes estaban
sentados solos; (pl formal) ustedes estaban
sentados solos; **you look at** — **at the
mirror** (sg informal) tú te miras en el espejo;
(sg formal) usted se mira en el espejo; **you
look at yourselves at the mirror** (pl
informal) *Sp* vosotros os mirais en el espejo;
Am ustedes se miran en el espejo; (pl formal)
ustedes se miran en el espejo; **you bought** —
a house (sg informal) te compraste una casa;
(sg formal) usted se compró una casa; **you
bought yourselves a house** (pl informal)
Sp os comprasteis una casa; *Am* se compraron
una casa; (pl formal) se compraron una casa
youth [juθ] N (person) joven *m*; (young age)
juventud *m*
youthful [júθfəł] ADJ juvenil
yo-yo [jójo] N yo-yo *m*
yuan [juán] N yuan *m*
yucca [jʌ́kə] N yuca *f*
yuck [jʌk] INTERJ puaj, puaf
Yugoslavia [jugosláviə] N Yugoslavia *f*
Yugoslavian [jugoslávian] ADJ & N yugoslavo
-va *mf*
Yuletide [júłtaɪd] N Navidad *f*
yummy [jámi] ADJ delicioso; INTERJ ¡qué rico!
yuppie [jápi] N yuppie *mf*

Zz

Zambia [zǽmbiə] N Zambia *f*
Zambian [zǽmbiən] ADJ & N zambiano -na *mf*
zany [zéni] ADJ loco, chiflado
zap [zæp] VT liquidar
zeal [ził] N celo *m*, fervor *m*
zealot [zélət] N fanático -ca *mf*
zealous [zéləs] ADJ celoso, fervoroso
zebra [zíbrə] N cebra *f*
zenith [zíniθ] N cenit *m*
zephyr [zéfɚ] N céfiro *m*
zeppelin [zépəlɪn] N zepelín *m*, dirigible *m*
zero [ziro] NUM cero *m*; **there's — possibility**
   that he'll come las posibilidades de que
   venga son nulas
zest [zɛst] N entusiasmo *m*
zigzag [zígzæg] N zigzag *m*; ADJ & ADV en zigzag;
   VI zigzaguear, andar en zigzag; VT hacer
   zigzaguear
Zimbabwe [zɪmbábwe] N Zimbabue *m*
Zimbabwean [zɪmbábweən] ADJ & N zimbabuo
   -bua *mf*
zinc [zɪŋk] N cinc *m*, zinc *m*
zip [zɪp] VI/VT cerrar/abrir con cremallera; **to —**
   by pasar volando; **to — over** ir corriendo; N
   cero *m*; **— code** código postal *m*
zipper [zípɚ] N cremallera *f*, cierre [relámpago]
   m
zirconium [zɚkóniəm] N circonio *m*
zodiac [zódiæk] N zodíaco *m*
zombie [zámbi] N zombi *mf*
zone [zon] N zona *f*; **— defense** defensa en zonas
   f; VT dividir en zonas
zoning [zónɪŋ] N zonificación *f*
zoo [zu] N zoológico *m*; *Sp* zoo *m*; **—keeper**
   guardián -ana del zoológico *mf*
zoological [zoəládʒɪkəł] ADJ zoológico
zoology [zoá, lədʒi] N zoología *f*
zoom [zum] VI (make sound) zumbar; **to — in**
   ampliar una imagen; **to — off** salir
   zumbando; **to — out** achicar la imagen; N
   zumbido *m*; **— lens** teleobjetivo *m*, zoom *m*
zucchini [zukíni] N calabacín *m*
zygote [záɪgot] N cigoto *m*, zigoto *m*